MOON HANDBOOKS®

WYOMING

P9-DBY-705

© DON PITCHER

Morning Glory Pool, Yellowstone National Park

CAMERON
Caribou-
Targhee
National
Forest
287

Red Rock
Lakes N.W.R.
MONTANA
IDAHO

191
89
Gardiner
Cooke City
212

Mammoth

Yellowstone

West
Yellowstone
20
Old
Faithful

National

Shoshone
National
Forest

72
310

Bighorn
Canyon
National
Recreation
Area
37
Lovell
14A

Crow
Indian
Res.

296
294
114
Powell
120
14A
295
Cody
32
310
789

14 16 20

14
Shell

Greybull
14

Ashton
20

32
33
33
Rexburg
20
26
Driggs

Snake
31

22
Jackson

Hoback
Junction

189
191
26
Dubois

Yellowstone
Lake

Park
189
191

Grand
Teton
National
Park
Jackson
Lake
189
26

Bridger-Teton
National
Forest
26
287

Wind

River

Shoshone
National
Forest

Yellowstone R.

30
Basin

Meeteetse
16
20
789
Worland

431

120
20
789
Thermopolis

Wind
River
Canyon

Boysen
Reservoir
BOYSEN
STATE PARK
Shoshoni

Moneta

River
River
Indian
Reservation
287
132
134
137
26
Riverton
Ft. Washakie
Lander
135

Wind
River

Palisades
Reservoir
Alpine
26
34

Soda
Springs
30

Montpelier

89
Star Valley
Afton

Bridger-Teton
National
Forest
189
191
Fremont Peak
(13,604 ft.)

189
Pinedale

Marbleton
351
Big Piney

Wind River Mountains

Shoshone
National
Forest

South Pass
City
28
287
789
Atlantic
City

Sweetwater

CONTINENTAL
DIVIDE

Jeffrey
City

30
Logan
89
Wasatch-
Cache
National
Forest

89

IDAHO
UTAH
30

FOSSIL BUTTE
NATIONAL
MONUMENT

Farson
28

191

R e d
D e s e r t

39
16

Kemmerer
Diamondville
30
372

Green River
Rock Springs
80
Wamsutter
789

84
80
Evanston

89
150

Ft.
Bridger
Lyman
Mountain View

Bridger
Valley

WYOMING
UTAH

530

414

Flaming
Gorge
Res.

Flaming
Gorge
National
Recreation
Area
191

430

Baggs

Wasatch-Cache N.F.

0   25 mi
0   25 km

© AVALON TRAVEL PUBLISHING, INC.

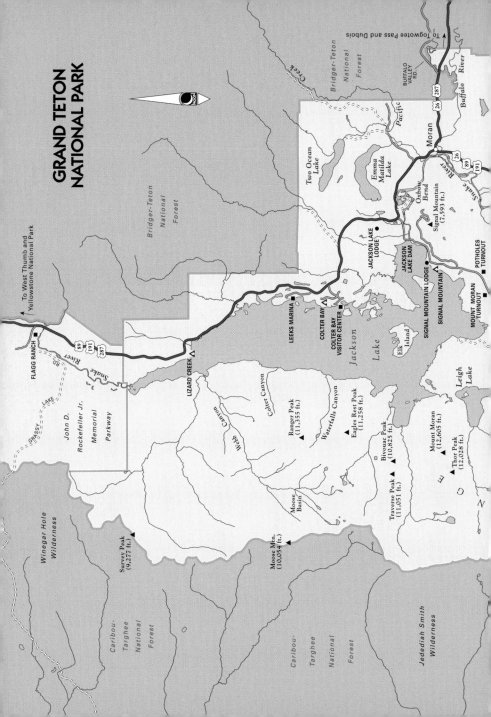

GRAND TETON
NATIONAL PARK

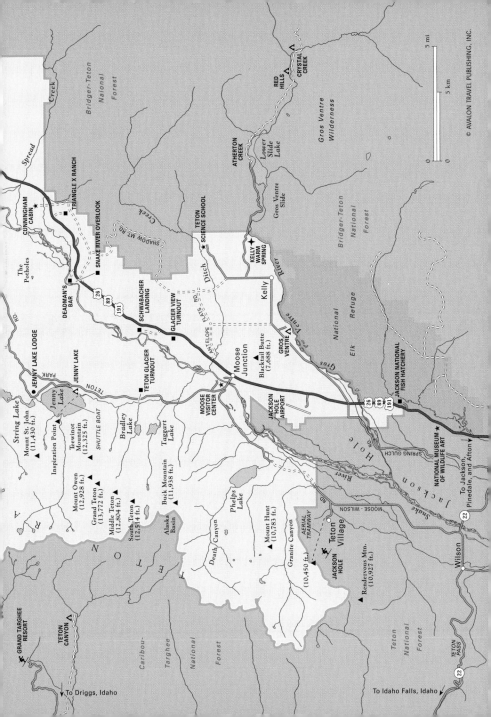

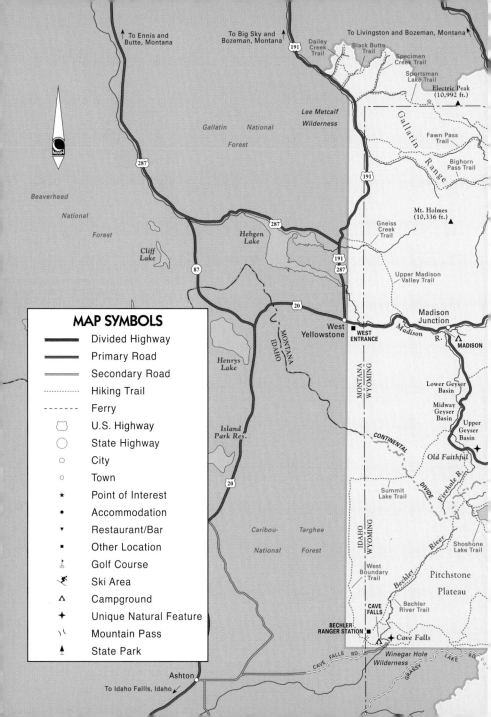

YELLOWSTONE NATIONAL PARK

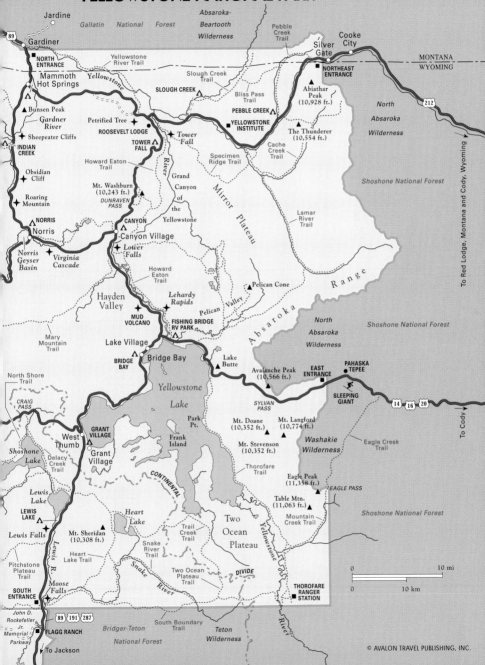

Jardine

Gallatin   National   Forest

Absaroka-
Beartooth
Wilderness

89

Gardiner

Pebble
Creek
Trail

Silver
Gate

Cooke
City

MONTANA
WYOMING

212

NORTH
ENTRANCE

Yellowstone
River Trail

Mammoth
Hot Springs

Yellowstone

Slough Creek
Trail

NORTHEAST
ENTRANCE

Abiathar
Peak
(10,928 ft.)

North
Absaroka
Wilderness

Bunsen Peak

SLOUGH CREEK

Bliss Pass
Trail

Gardner
River

Petrified Tree

PEBBLE CREEK

YELLOWSTONE
INSTITUTE

The Thunderer
(10,554 ft.)

Shoshone National Forest

Sheepeater Cliffs

ROOSEVELT LODGE

INDIAN
CREEK

TOWER
FALL

Tower
Fall

Howard Eaton
Trail

Obsidian
Cliff

River

Grand
Canyon
of
the
Yellowstone

Specimen
Ridge Trail

Cache Creek
Trail

Mt. Washburn
(10,243 ft.)

Mirror Plateau

Lamar
River
Trail

Roaring
Mountain

DUNRAVEN
PASS

NORRIS

Norris

CANYON

Canyon Village

Norris
Geyser
Basin

Lower
Falls

Virginia
Cascade

Howard
Eaton
Trail

Pelican Cone

Range

Hayden
Valley

Lehardy
Rapids

Pelican Valley

North
Absaroka

To Red Lodge, Montana and Cody, Wyoming

MUD
VOLCANO

Mary
Mountain
Trail

Lake Village

FISHING BRIDGE
RV PARK

Absaroka

Wilderness

Shoshone National Forest

North Shore
Trail

BRIDGE
BAY

Bridge Bay

Lake
Butte

Avalanche Peak
(10,566 ft.)

EAST
ENTRANCE

PAHASKA
TEPEE

CRAIG
PASS

Yellowstone
Lake

SYLVAN
PASS

SLEEPING
GIANT

14   16   20

West
Thumb

GRANT
VILLAGE

Park
Pt.

Mt. Doane
(10,352 ft.)

Mt. Langford
(10,774 ft.)

To Cody

Shoshone
Lake

Grant
Village

Frank
Island

Washakie
Wilderness

Eagle Creek
Trail

Delacy
Creek
Trail

Mt. Stevenson
(10,352 ft.)

CONTINENTAL

Thorofare
Trail

Lewis
Lake

Heart
Lake

Eagle Peak
(11,358 ft.)

LEWIS
LAKE

Mt. Sheridan
(10,308 ft.)

Trail
Creek
Trail

Two
Ocean
Plateau

Table Mtn.
(11,063 ft.)

EAGLE PASS

Shoshone National Forest

Lewis Falls

Lewis R.

Heart
Lake Trail

Snake
River
Trail

Mountain
Creek Trail

Pitchstone
Plateau
Trail

Two Ocean
Plateau
Trail

DIVIDE

SOUTH
ENTRANCE

Moose
Falls

Snake River

Yellowstone

THOROFARE
RANGER
STATION

John D.
Rockefeller,
Jr.
Memorial
Parkway

89   191   287

FLAGG RANCH

Bridger-Teton

South Boundary
Trail

Teton
Wilderness

0   10 mi

0   10 km

To Jackson

National   Forest

© AVALON TRAVEL PUBLISHING, INC.

Lusk, Wyoming

MOON HANDBOOKS®

WYOMING

INCLUDING YELLOWSTONE AND
GRAND TETON NATIONAL PARKS

FIFTH EDITION

DON PITCHER

AVALON
TRAVEL

Moon Handbooks Wyoming
Fifth Edition

Don Pitcher

Published by

Avalon Travel Publishing
1400 65th Street, Suite 250
Emeryville, CA 94608 USA

Please send all comments, corrections,
additions, amendments, and critiques to:

Moon Handbooks Wyoming

Avalon Travel Publishing
1400 65th Street, Suite 250
Emeryville, CA 94608, USA
atpfeedback@avalonpub.com
www.moon.com

Printing History
1st edition—1991
5th edition—May 2003
5 4 3 2 1

ISBN: 1-56691-494-9
ISSN: 1542-8869

Editor: Amy Scott
Series Manager: Kevin McLain
Copy Editor: Ginjer L. Clarke
Graphics Coordinator: Melissa Sherowski
Production Coordinator: Justin Marler
Cover Designer: Kari Gim
Interior Designers: Amber Pirker, Alvaro Villanueva, Kelly Pendragon
Map Editor: Naomi Adler Dancis
Cartographers: Kat Kalamaras, Mike Morgenfeld, Chris Folks
Proofreader: Julie Leigh
Indexer: Kevin Millham

Front cover photo: The Grand Tetons, © Don Pitcher

Distributed by Publishers Group West

Printed in the U.S.A by Worzalla

ABOUT THE AUTHOR
Don Pitcher

© DON PITCHER

Perhaps Don Pitcher's love of travel came about because he moved so much as a child; by age 15 he had lived in six states and two dozen East Coast and Midwest towns. Don's family hails from Maine, but being born in Atlanta made him a southerner with New England blood. He moved west for college, receiving a master's degree from the University of California, Berkeley, where his thesis examined wildfires in Sequoia National Park. When his first scientific paper was published, he appeared to be heading into the world of ecological research.

Shortly after graduate school Don landed the coolest job on the planet: being flown around Alaska's massive Wrangell-St. Elias National Park in a helicopter while conducting fire research. Wild places continued to beckon, and over the next 15 years Don built backcountry trails, worked as a wilderness ranger, mapped grizzly habitat, and operated salmon weirs—anything to keep away from an office job. After his first season in Alaska, he spent three months in the South Pacific, and quickly found himself addicted to travel. These explorations eventually took him to all 50 states and 35 countries.

Don started writing *Moon Handbooks Wyoming* after a summer of bear research in the Teton Wilderness and a winter of cleaning condos and skiing at Jackson Hole Ski Resort. Today, the book is in its fifth edition, with more than 100,000 copies in print. Don's other titles include comprehensive Moon guides to Yellowstone & Grand Teton, Alaska, Washington, and the San Juan Islands. He has photographed two books on Wyoming and Alaska, and his images have appeared in a multitude of other publications and advertisements.

Don now works full time as a travel writer and photographer, basing his travels from Homer, Alaska, where he lives with his wife, Karen Shemet, and their children, Aziza and Rio. Find details on his latest projects at www.donpitcher.com.

Contents

INTRODUCTION **1**
Seeing Wyoming; The Sky
THE LAND **3**
Geography; Climate
FLORA AND FAUNA **7**
Vegetation; Wildlife; Bison
HISTORY **14**
Native Americans; Trappers and Explorers; The Oregon Trail; The Pony Express;
The Overland Trail; Connecting the Coasts; Statehood; Cattle Country; Sheep;
Energy Boom and Bust
ECONOMY AND GOVERNMENT **31**
Working for a Living; Politics

SPECIAL TOPICS

Tropical Wyoming *4*	*Pony Expressions* *22*
Lightning Safety *6*	*Bill Nye on Women's Suffrage* *26*
Sagebrush *9*	*Brands* *28*
From Tame Earth to Wild West *14*	*Wyoming Lingo* *34*

ON THE ROAD **38**
OUTDOOR RECREATION **38**
Fishing and Hunting; On the Snow; Riding into History; Getting into the
Wilderness; Backcountry Safety; Safety in Bear Country
ACCOMMODATIONS **50**
Finding Accommodations; Historic Hotels; Chain Hotels and Motels;
Independent Motels; Bed-and-Breakfasts; Dude Ranches
CAMPING **54**
FOOD AND DRINK **54**
EVENTS **55**
Tastes of History; Modern-Day Rendezvous; Other Events; Event Information
RODEO **57**
History; Rodeo Today; The Suicide Sport; Steer Wrestling; Calf Roping; Steer
Roping; Saddle Bronc Riding; Bareback Bronc Riding; Bull Riding and Rodeo
Clowns; Other Events
PRACTICALITIES **61**
Visitors Centers; WWWyoming; Federal and State Offices; On the Radio;
Newspapers; Museums and the Arts; Money and Banking; Post Offices

HEALTH AND SAFETY 66
West Nile Virus; Hantavirus; Ticks
TRANSPORTATION 67
By Air; By Car; Bikes; Long-Distance Buses

SPECIAL TOPICS

Best of Wyoming 40	*Rental Car Contacts* 68
Winter in Wyoming 50	*Airline Contacts* 69
Wyoming Trivia 62	

SOUTHEAST WYOMING 72

CHEYENNE 74
History; Sights; Accommodations; Camping; Food; Entertainment; Frontier
Days; Other Events; Recreation; Shopping; Information; Services; Transportation
CURT GOWDY STATE PARK 97
Accommodations
PINE BLUFFS 98
Information and Archaeological Sights; Other Sights; Accommodations and
Camping; Food; Events and Entertainment; Recreation and Services; North from
Pine Bluffs; LaGrange
CHUGWATER 101
Sights; Practicalities
WHEATLAND 102
History; Sights; Country Drives; Finding Ferrets; Accommodations; Camping;
Food; Recreation; Events; Information and Services; Transportation
GUERNSEY AND VICINITY 107
Guernsey; Hartville Area; Guernsey State Park; Glendo State Park
FORT LARAMIE NATIONAL HISTORIC SITE 111
History; Fort Laramie Today; The Town of Fort Laramie
TORRINGTON 117
History; Homesteaders Museum; Other Sights; Accommodations; Camping; Food;
Recreation; Entertainment and Events; Information and Services; Torrington Area
LUSK 123
History; Stagecoach Museum; Other Sights; Accommodations; Camping; Food;
Recreation and Entertainment; Information and Services; Tours; Events; *Legend of
Rawhide*; Heading North

SPECIAL TOPICS

Southeast Wyoming Sightseeing Highlights . . . 74	*Cheyenne Club* 85
Francis E. Warren 79	*Swan Land and Cattle Company* 101
Cheyenne in the 1860s 80	*Starving to Death on a*
Cheyenne and Black Hills Stage 81	*Government Claim* 119

MEDICINE BOW COUNTRY 128
History; Economy
LARAMIE 131
History; University of Wyoming; Wyoming Territorial Park; Ivinson Mansion;
More Laramie Sights; Accommodations; Camping; Food; Entertainment; Events;
Sports; Recreation; Shopping; Information; Transportation
POLE MOUNTAIN/VEDAUWOO AREA 147
Vedauwoo; Pyramid Power
MEDICINE BOW VICINITY 149
Rock River; Como Bluff; Medicine Bow; Shirley Basin; Hanna; Arlington; Elk
Mountain
MEDICINE BOW MOUNTAINS AND VICINITY 156
Laramie Plains; Albany; Centennial; Snowy Range
NORTH PLATTE VALLEY 163
Saratoga; Encampment and Riverside
SIERRA MADRE AND VICINITY 173
Sights; Aspen Alley; Camping and Cabins; Huston Park Wilderness;
Encampment River Wilderness; Winter Recreation; Little Snake River Valley
RAWLINS 176
History; Frontier Prison; Other Sights; Accommodations; Camping; Food;
Entertainment and Events; Recreation; Information and Services; Transportation
RAWLINS VICINITY 183
Fort Fred Steele; Sinclair; Heading North

SPECIAL TOPICS

Medicine Bow Country	*Black-Footed Ferrets* *153*
Sightseeing Highlights *130*	*Tom Horn* *178*
Bill Nye *135*	*Big Nose George Parrot* *179*
The "Town" of Medicine Bow *150*	

SOUTHWEST WYOMING 186
History
THE RED DESERT 188
Wamsutter; Point of Rocks; Superior; Killpecker Dunes Area
ROCK SPRINGS 191
History; Sights; Accommodations; Camping; Food; Entertainment; Events;
Recreation; Shopping; Information and Services; Transportation
GREEN RIVER 198
History; Trona Mining; Sights; Accommodations; Camping; Food;
Entertainment; Events; Recreation; Information and Services
GREEN RIVER VICINITY 203
Little America; Church Buttes; Granger; Seedskadee National Wildlife Refuge;
Northeast to Farson

FLAMING GORGE NATIONAL RECREATION AREA 205
Access and Sights; Visitors Centers; Exploring Flaming Gorge; Recreation;
Camping; Accommodations and Food
BRIDGER VALLEY 210
Lyman; Mountain View; Piedmont; Fort Bridger
EVANSTON 215
History; The Overthrust Belt; Sights; Accommodations; Camping; Food;
Entertainment; Events; Recreation; Shopping; Information and Services;
Transportation; High Uinta Mountains; North to Kemmerer
KEMMERER 221
History; Sights; Accommodations; Camping; Food; Entertainment; Events;
Recreation; Information and Services
FOSSIL BUTTE NATIONAL MONUMENT 227
Origins; Visitors Center; Hiking
KEMMERER VICINITY 228
Oregon Trail Sights; Cokeville
STAR VALLEY 230
History; Afton; Greys River Loop Road; Thayne; Other Star Valley Towns;
Alpine; Snake River Canyon

SPECIAL TOPICS

Southwest Wyoming Sightseeing Highlights . . 188   *Jim Bridger* 211
The Chinese Massacre 193   *James Cash Penney* 224

CENTRAL WYOMING 240

DOUGLAS 243
History; Sights; Accommodations; Camping; Food; Recreation;
Entertainment; Wyoming State Fair; Other Events; Information and Services;
Transportation
DOUGLAS VICINITY 250
Fort Fetterman; Ayres Natural Bridge Park
THUNDER BASIN NATIONAL GRASSLAND 253
History; Management; Recreation
LARAMIE MOUNTAINS 254
Esterbrook; Camping and a Cabin; Hiking; Winter Recreation
GLENROCK 257
Boom and Bust; Sights; Accommodations; Camping; Food; Entertainment and
Events; Services
CASPER 260
History; Sights; Accommodations; Camping; Food; Entertainment; Events; Sports
and Recreation; Shopping; Information and Services; Transportation and Tours
CASPER VICINITY 276
Casper Mountain; Bessemer Bend

WYOMING'S LAKE DISTRICT 280
   Reclamation; Seminoe Reservoir; Pathfinder Reservoir; Alcova Reservoir
OREGON TRAIL LANDMARKS 284
   Independence Rock; Devil's Gate; Martin's Cove; Split Rock
SALT CREEK 287
   History; Midwest and Edgerton; Tempest in a Teapot
WEST FROM CASPER 289
   Powder River; Hell's Half Acre; Moneta and Lysite; Lost Cabin; Castle Gardens;
   West to Shoshoni

SPECIAL TOPICS

Central Wyoming Sightseeing	*Prairie Dogs* *251*
Highlights *242*	*Discovering Dinosaurs* *258*
Jackalopes *244*	*Arriving at Independence Rock, 1844* *284*

WIND RIVER MOUNTAINS COUNTRY 292
   The Land; Trip Planning
RIVERTON 295
   History; Sights; Accommodations; Camping; Food; Entertainment; Events;
   Shopping; Recreation; Information and Services; Transportation
RIVERTON VICINITY 301
   Shoshoni; Boysen State Park; Gas Hills; Hudson
LANDER 303
   History; Sights; Accommodations; Camping; Food; Recreation; Entertainment;
   Events; Shopping; Information and Services; Transportation and Tours
LANDER VICINITY 312
   East on U.S. Highway 287; Sinks Canyon and the Loop Road
WIND RIVER INDIAN RESERVATION 315
   Shoshone History; Arapaho History; Reservation Life; Indian Powwows;
   Arapahoe and St. Stephens; Ethete; Fort Washakie; West to Dubois
DUBOIS 326
   History; Sights; Accommodations; Camping; Food; Entertainment; Events;
   Summer Recreation; Winter Recreation; Shopping; Information and Services
DUBOIS VICINITY 333
   Horse Creek Area; Union Pass; Over Togwotee Pass
WIND RIVER MOUNTAINS 336
   Wildlife; Access; More Information; Green River Lakes Area; Bridger Wilderness;
   Fitzpatrick Wilderness; Popo Agie Wilderness
SOUTH PASS 347
   South Pass City; Atlantic City
FARSON AND VICINITY 357
   Heading South; Heading West; Heading North

PINEDALE **358**
History; Catching the Drift; Museum of the Mountain Man; Day Trips;
Accommodations; Camping; Food; Entertainment; Events; Recreation;
Shopping; Information and Services; Transportation

PINEDALE VICINITY **366**
Boulder; Daniel; 1840 Rendezvous Site; Big Piney; Marbleton; Lander Cutoff;
To Jackson Hole

SPECIAL TOPICS

Wind River Mountains Country	*The Hard Day's Work of Tie Hacks* *327*
Sightseeing Highlights *294*	*South Pass in 1861* *349*
Chief Washakie *316*	*Calamity Jane* *352*
Powwows *320*	*Mountain Men* *368*
Sacagawea *322*	

JACKSON HOLE **374**

HISTORY **376**
John Colter; Settlers; Jackson Hole Comes of Age

JACKSON **380**
Sights; National Elk Refuge

SHOPPING **387**
Art; Outdoor Gear; Bargains; Books; Kitsch

ACCOMMODATIONS **390**
Under $50; $50–100; $100–150; $150 and Up; Bed-and-Breakfasts;
Condominium Rentals; Cabins; Guest Ranches; Mountain Resorts

CAMPING **403**
Public Campgrounds; RV Parks

FOOD **404**
Breakfast; Lunch; Espresso and Light Meals; American; Pasta and Pizza;
Continental/Nouvelle Cuisine; Mexican and Caribbean; Asian; Breweries; Wine
Shops; Bakeries; Groceries and Natural Foods

ENTERTAINMENT AND THE ARTS **411**
Nightlife; Classical Music; Musicals and Movies; Rodeo; Chuck Wagon Cookouts

EVENTS **413**
Winter; Spring; Summer; Fall

SUMMER RECREATION **415**
River Rafting; Fishing; Boating; Horseback Riding; Day Hikes; Mountain Biking;
Alpine Rides; Swimming and Gyms; Balloon Rides; Golf and Tennis

DOWNHILL SKIING AND SNOWBOARDING **424**
Grand Targhee Ski Resort; Jackson Hole Mountain Resort; Snow King Resort

CROSS-COUNTRY SKIING **430**
Nordic Centers; On Your Own

OTHER WINTER RECREATION **433**
Ice Skating; Snowshoeing; Sleigh Rides; Tubing; Dogsledding; Snowmobiling

INFORMATION AND SERVICES **435**
Information Sources; Jackson Hole on the Web; Trip Planning; Post Offices;
Medical Help; Banking and Currency Exchange; Library; Newspapers; Traveling
with Children; Laundry and Showers; Living in Jackson Hole

TRANSPORTATION **438**
By Air; Airport Shuttles and Taxis; Car Rentals; START Buses; Long-Distance
Buses; Tours and Shuttles

BRIDGER-TETON NATIONAL FOREST **441**
Teton Wilderness; Gros Ventre Wilderness

CARIBOU-TARGHEE NATIONAL FOREST **444**
Jedediah Smith Wilderness

TETON VALLEY, IDAHO **446**
History; Victor; Driggs; Tetonia; Alta, Wyoming

SPECIAL TOPICS

Jackson Hole Sightseeing Highlights *376*	*Jackson Hole Public Campgrounds* *404*
Jackson Hole in 1835 . . . . *377*	*IPSSSDR* *414*
The White Shoshone *378*	*Safety in Avalanche Country* *431*
Saving Jackson Hole *379*	*Lone Highwayman of Yellowstone* *440*

GRAND TETON NATIONAL PARK **453**

GEOLOGY **454**
Building a Mountain Range; Rivers of Ice

WILDLIFE **456**
Bison; Wolves

PARK HISTORY **456**
"Damning" Jackson Lake; Dudes and Development; Rocky to the Rescue;
A National Battleground; Postmortem

EXPLORING THE PARK **459**
Roads; Moose; Menor's Ferry Area; Taggart and Bradley Lakes; Jenny Lake;
Inspiration Point and Cascade Canyon; Signal Mountain Area; Along Jackson
Lake; Colter Bay; Rockefeller Memorial Parkway; Grassy Lake Road; Jackson
Lake to Moran Junction; Moran Junction to Moose; Blacktail Butte and Mormon
Row; Teton Science School; Shadow Mountain Area; Kelly and Vicinity; Gros
Ventre Slide; Gros Ventre River Valley; Moose-Wilson Road

BACKCOUNTRY HIKING **470**
Regulations and Permits; Safety in the Backcountry; Cascade Canyon to
Paintbrush Canyon; Death Canyon Loop; Amphitheater Lake; Rendezvous
Mountain to Death Canyon

MOUNTAIN CLIMBING **472**
First to the Top; Getting There; Climbing Schools; On Your Own

OTHER PARK RECREATION **474**
Day Hikes; Floating the River; Boating; Fishing; Sea Kayaking; Birding;
Bicycling; Trail Rides; Swimming; Winter Recreation

CAMPING 477
Other Camping Options

ACCOMMODATIONS 478
Jackson Lake Lodge; Jenny Lake Lodge; Colter Bay Village; Dornan's; Signal
Mountain Lodge; Flagg Ranch Resort

FOOD 479
Restaurants and Bars; Groceries and Supplies

PRACTICALITIES 480
Getting In; Visitors Centers; Support Organizations; Medical Help; Outdoor
Gear; Other Practicalities; Transportation and Tours

SPECIAL TOPICS

Grand Teton National Park	*The Magic of the Tetons* 459
Sightseeing Highlights 454	*Beaver Dick Leigh* 464

YELLOWSTONE NATIONAL PARK 483
The Setting; A Place of Controversy

GEOLOGY 486
Fire and Ice; Geysers; Other Geothermal Activity

THE GREATER YELLOWSTONE ECOSYSTEM 489
Plants

WILDLIFE 490
Finding Wildlife; Birds; Killing the Predators; Controversy on the Northern
Range; Bears; Bighorn Sheep; Bison; Coyotes; Moose; Pronghorn Antelope;
Wolves

PARK HISTORY 497
Sheepeater Indians; Fur Trappers; Expeditions; Establishing the Park; Roads and
Railroads; The Army Years; The Park Service Takes Over

EXPLORING THE PARK 505
Park Access; South Entrance Road; West Thumb to Upper Geyser Basin; Upper
Geyser Basin; Midway and Lower Geyser Basins; Madison Junction to West
Yellowstone; The Northwest Corner; Madison Junction to Norris; Norris Geyser
Basin; Norris Junction to Canyon; Norris Junction to Mammoth; Mammoth Hot
Springs Vicinity; Mammoth to Tower Junction; Northeast Entrance Road; Tower
Junction to Canyon; Grand Canyon of the Yellowstone; Canyon to Lake
Junction; Yellowstone Lake; East Entrance Road

INTO THE BACKCOUNTRY 534
North Yellowstone Trails; South Yellowstone Trails

OTHER SUMMER RECREATION 541
Fishing; Boating; Bicycling; Trail Rides; Hot Springs

WINTER IN YELLOWSTONE 544
Historical Winter Use; Roads; Accommodations; Services; Snowcoaches; Skiing
and Snowshoeing; Snowmobiles

CAMPING 549
Other Camping Options

HOTELS, LODGES, AND CABINS 550
  Canyon Village; Grant Village; Lake Village; Mammoth Hot Springs; Old
  Faithful; Roosevelt Lodge
FOOD 554
  Restaurants; Cafeterias and Fast Food; Old West Cookout; Groceries and
  Supplies
GETTING AROUND 556
  By Car; Park Tours
OTHER PRACTICALITIES 558
  Vacation Planning; Ranger-Naturalist Programs; Traveling With Children;
  Accessibility; Supporting the Park; Money; Medical Services; Cleaning Up; Other
  Services; Working in Yellowstone
WEST YELLOWSTONE, MONTANA 561
  History; Sights; Accommodations; Camping; Food; Entertainment; Events;
  Summer Recreation; Winter Recreation; Shopping; Information and Services;
  Transportation; Park Tours
GARDINER, MONTANA 571
  Accommodations; Camping; Food; Events and Entertainment; River Rafting;
  Other Recreation; Shopping; Information and Services; Transportation and
  Tours
COOKE CITY AND SILVER GATE, MONTANA 575
  History; Sights; Cooke City Accommodations; Silver Gate Accommodations;
  Camping; Food; Entertainment and Events; Recreation; Information and
  Services

SPECIAL TOPICS

Yellowstone National Park	*Yellowstone's First "Tourist"* 511
Sightseeing Highlights 484	*Grand Prismatic Spring, 1839* 514
The Nez Perce War 498	*Yellowstone National Park Campgrounds* ... 549
Firehole River Area, 1839 499	*Yellowstone Association* 559
The Yellowstone Fires of 1988 502	*Greater Yellowstone Coalition* 560

BIGHORN BASIN 579

SHOSHONE NATIONAL FOREST 580
  History; Recreation; North Absaroka Wilderness; Washakie Wilderness; Sunlight
  Basin; South Fork Area; Beartooth Mountains
WAPITI VALLEY/NORTH FORK 588
  Pahaska Tepee; Skiing and Snowboarding; Down the Road; Camping; Upper
  North Fork Ranches; Lower Wapiti Valley Accommodations; Buffalo Bill State Park
CODY 593
  History; Buffalo Bill Historical Center; Other Sights; Accommodations;
  Camping; Food; Events and Entertainment; Recreation; Shopping; Information
  and Services; Transportation; Tours
CODY VICINITY 613
  Heart Mountain; Heading East from Heart Mountain

MEETEETSE 615
History; Sights and Information; Accommodations; Food and Nightlife; Other
Practicalities; Meeteetse Area

POWELL 617
History; Sights; Accommodations; Camping; Food; Entertainment; Events;
Recreation; Shopping; Information and Services; East to Lovell

LOVELL 621
History; Motels; Guest Ranches; Camping; Food; Recreation and Events;
Information and Services

BIGHORN CANYON NATIONAL RECREATION AREA 623
Sights; Practicalities; Pryor Mountain Wild Horse Range

GREYBULL 629
History; Sights; Shopping; Accommodations; Camping; Food; Entertainment
and Events; Recreation; Information and Services

GREYBULL VICINITY 633
Basin; Shell Valley; Hyattville Area

WORLAND 636
History; Sights; Accommodations; Camping; Food; Events and Entertainment;
Recreation; Information and Services; Transportation

TEN SLEEP 639
Sights; Nearby Sights; Tensleep Canyon; Accommodations and Camping;
Food; Events

THERMOPOLIS 642
Hot Springs State Park; Other Sights; Accommodations; Camping; Food; Events
and Entertainment; Horseback Rides; Other Recreation; Information and Services

WIND RIVER CANYON 650
Floating and Fishing; Geologic History Lesson

SPECIAL TOPICS

Bighorn Basin
   Sightseeing Highlights 580
Wyoming Design 584

Buffalo Bill Cody 596
Caroline Lockhart 627
The Ten Sleep Raid 641

POWDER RIVER COUNTRY 652

BIG HORN MOUNTAINS 654
Cruisin' Through; Camping; Accommodations and Food; Winter Sports; Hikes
and Sights; Medicine Wheel; Cloud Peak Wilderness

SHERIDAN 664
History; Sights; Accommodations; Camping; Food; Entertainment; Events;
Recreation; Shopping; Information and Services; Transportation

NORTHWEST OF SHERIDAN 675
Ranchester; Dayton

EAST OF SHERIDAN 677
Ucross; Clearmont and Leiter Area; Spotted Horse

SOUTH OF SHERIDAN 679
Big Horn; Bradford Brinton Memorial Museum; Story

THE BLOODY BOZEMAN 683
Red Cloud's War; Fort Phil Kearny; Fetterman Fight; Wagon Box Fight; The
Fighting Ends; Exploring the Bozeman Trail; Other Bozeman Trail Sights

BUFFALO 687
History; Sights; Accommodations; Camping; Food; Entertainment; Events;
Recreation; Shopping; Information and Services; Transportation

BUFFALO VICINITY 695
Lake DeSmet; Kaycee; Hole-in-the-Wall Country

GILLETTE 701
History; Sights; Accommodations; Camping; Food; Entertainment; Events;
Recreation; Shopping; Information and Services; Transportation

SOUTH FROM GILLETTE 709
Durham Buffalo Ranch; Wright

SPECIAL TOPICS

Powder River Country
  Sightseeing Highlights *654*
Coalbed Methane *666*
Bill Nye on Rustling *676*
Best Wishes from Spotted Horse *678*

The Johnson County War *690*
The Wild Bunch *698*
Strip Mining *704*
Crow Country Is Just Right *710*

THE BLACK HILLS 711
The Land

NEWCASTLE 713
History; Sights; Accommodations; Camping and Cabins; Food; Entertainment;
Events; Information and Services

NEWCASTLE VICINITY 718
Four Corners Area; Heading South; Upton Area

MOORCROFT AND VICINITY 720
Accommodations and Camping; Other Practicalities; Keyhole State Park

SUNDANCE 721
Sights; Accommodations; Camping; Food; Recreation and Events; Information
and Services

BLACK HILLS NATIONAL FOREST 724
Scenic Drives; Hiking; Camping

THE NORTHERN BLACK HILLS 725
Aladdin and Vicinity; Hulett; Oshoto; Alzada and Colony

DEVILS TOWER NATIONAL MONUMENT 728
Geology; History; Climbing Devils Tower; Hiking Trails; Access and Information;
Camping, Food, and Accommodations

SPECIAL TOPICS

Black Hills Sightseeing Highlights 713
Sundances 722
Just A-Ridin' 725

Kiowa Devils Tower Legend 730
The Moral of the Story 732

RESOURCES 733
SUGGESTED READING 734
INTERNET RESOURCES 746
INDEX 748

Keeping Current

This is the fifth edition of *Moon Handbooks Wyoming,* and readers can play a role in keeping it up to date. I am not always able to check out the multitude of details hidden in this book, but I appreciate any assistance in fixing problems that appear. If a place I mention no longer exists, if certain suggestions are misleading (or flat out wrong), or if you've uncovered anything new, please contact me. I especially appreciate comments from Wyoming residents who have first-hand knowledge. Although I try to reply to all letters and emails, you may need to wait for a response because I'm often on the road or immersed in other projects. To learn more, visit my website, www.donpitcher.com. Happy trails!

Contact me at:
Moon Handbooks Wyoming
Avalon Travel Publishing
1400 65th St., Suite 250
Emeryville, CA 94608, USA
atpfeedback@avalonpub.com

Maps

Wyoming . . . . ii–iii
Grand Teton National Park . . . . iv–v
Yellowstone National Park . . . . vi–vii

INTRODUCTION

Wyoming Geography 3
Wyoming Vegetation 8
Historical Wyoming 15
The Oregon-California-Mormon Trail . . 18
Wyoming Land Status 32–33

ON THE ROAD

Mileage Map of Wyoming 70

SOUTHEAST WYOMING

Southeast Wyoming 73
Cheyenne 76–77
Downtown Cheyenne 78
Wheatland 103
Oregon Trail Country 107
Fort Laramie National Historic Site . . 111
Torrington 118

MEDICINE BOW COUNTRY

Medicine Bow Country 129
Laramie 132
Medicine Bow Mountains 156
Snowy Range Trails 159
Saratoga 164
Rawlins 177

SOUTHWEST WYOMING

Southwest Wyoming 187
Rock Springs 191
Green River 199
Flaming Gorge National
    Recreation Area 206
Evanston 215
Kemmerer Area 222
Star Valley Area 230

CENTRAL WYOMING

Central Wyoming 241

Douglas 243
Laramie Mountains 255
Casper 261
Downtown Casper 262
Casper Vicinity 277
Wyoming's Lake District 280

WIND RIVER MOUNTAINS COUNTRY

Wind River Mountains Country 293
Wind River Mountains
    Wilderness Areas 294
Riverton 296
Lander 304
Dubois Vicinity 334
Pinedale Area Trails 339
Big Sandy Area Trails 344
Sinks Canyon and
    South Pass Area 348
Pinedale 359

JACKSON HOLE

Jackson Hole and the Tetons 375
Jackson 381
Downtown Jackson 382
Jackson Hole 384

GRAND TETON NATIONAL PARK

Teton Hiking Trails 460
Jenny and Leigh Lakes 462

YELLOWSTONE NATIONAL PARK

Yellowstone National Park Mileage . . . 485
Upper Geyser Basin 509
Firehole River Area 516
Mammoth Hot Springs Vicinity 522
Grand Canyon of the Yellowstone . . . 529
Greater Yellowstone Area 536–537

BIGHORN BASIN

Bighorn Basin Area 581
Northern Shoshone National Forest . . 582
Cody 594–595
Downtown Cody 600–601

Powell 618
Bighorn Canyon National
  Recreation Area 624
Worland 637
Thermopolis 643

POWDER RIVER COUNTRY

Powder River Country 653
Medicine Wheel Area 660
Cloud Peak Wilderness Area 662

Downtown Sheridan 664
Sheridan 665
Fort Phil Kearny Area 684
Buffalo 688
Gillette 702–703

THE BLACK HILLS

The Black Hills 712
Newcastle 714
Devils Tower National Monument . . . 728

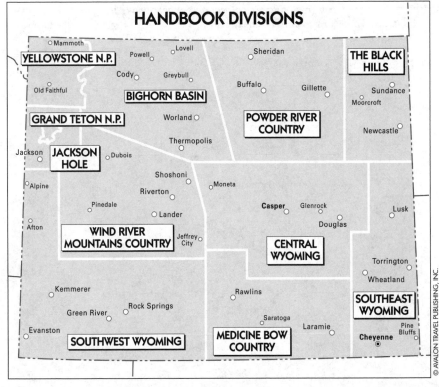

God bless Wyoming and keep it wild.
                last entry in the diary of Helen Mettler,
                who died in the Tetons at the age of 15

Here is your country. Cherish these natural wonders,
cherish the natural resources, cherish the History and
Romance as a sacred heritage, for your children
and your children's children. Do not let selfish men
or greedy interests skin your country of its beauty, its
riches or its romance.
                        Theodore Roosevelt in 1903

Introduction

It's kind of funny how you get used to the country. When I go to town, the noises keep me awake. The coal trains, the sirens going down the road, even if they are a long ways away. People get used to that. We've had people come out here who couldn't sleep because it was so quiet. No noise to lull them to sleep or whatever. My nearest neighbor is five miles away. It takes all kinds of people to make the world go around. If everybody in the world wanted to be a rancher, I probably wouldn't, because there wouldn't be anyplace to live.

Ed Swartz, quoted in Steve Gardiner's
Rumblings From Razor City

The expansively rugged land called Wyoming resonates with the spirit of the American West. For anyone who has spent time in Wyoming, the state evokes vivid images: cattle standing in the lee of snow fences, children riding horses along dusty dirt roads, weather-beaten ranches lit by the slanting light of late afternoon, oil-covered roustabouts struggling with the furious machinery of a drilling rig, the sounds of drumming and singing at a powwow, and cow towns where the area code is larger than the population. Here is the original "Wild West," the real-life inspiration for countless Western novels, movies, and songs.

A frontier spirit pervades both Wyoming's landscape and its people, mixing the past and present so

completely that it sometimes seems as though around the next bend you might see Chief Washakie's men circling a massive herd of bison, or Butch Cassidy and the Sundance Kid shooting it out with lawmen, or a party of fur trappers setting out for the mountains. Officially known as "The Equality State" because it was the first to allow women to vote, Wyoming actually revels in another title, "The Cowboy State." License plates carry the state emblem: a cowboy, hat in hand, atop a furiously bucking bronco. A cowboy hat and boots are acceptable dress anywhere, and the unpolished individuality embodied in the cowboy remains the state's heritage, even for those whose only connection is country-and-western music.

The earliest Anglo explorers described Wyoming in less than flattering terms. The image that stuck was the "Great American Desert," a place where the native peoples flourished along with buffalo, antelope, jackrabbits, and rattlesnakes, but where homesteaders and ranchers struggled to survive. Hundreds of thousands of travelers pushed across Wyoming's basins and mountain ranges in the 19th century, bound for greener pastures and gold. Very few considered staying in such an unforgiving environment. Even today, the vast majority of those who enter Wyoming are en route to someplace else.

SEEING WYOMING

Although Wyoming is divided by three major interstate highways, the best way to see the state is from the smaller asphalt and gravel roads where the pace slows and tumbleweeds pile against fences. From the freeways, the landscape is just a blur, but along the back roads this same land becomes a thing of raw-edged, surreal beauty. Old ranches hunker in the valleys, herds of deer and antelope glance up warily at passing cars, oddly colored rock pinnacles crown the hills, and winding streams become glowing silver ribbons of light. Only the wind, singing birds, and the buzz of insects break the stillness. Writer Gretel Ehrlich in *The Solace of Open Spaces* describes it best:

To live and work in this kind of open country, with its hundred-mile views, is to lose the distinction between background and foreground. When I asked an older ranch hand to describe Wyoming's openness, he said, "It's all a bunch of nothing—wind and rattlesnakes—and so much of it you can't tell where you're going or where you've been and it don't make much difference.

On the back roads you'll find folks lifting a hand to wave as you pass. Small-town cafés serve down-home food, friendly motel owners greet tired travelers, and the pace of living slows measurably. You can almost feel the stress of city life dissipating. People leave their homes, cars, and bikes unlocked; they load up clothes in the laundromat and come back later to move them to the dryer. They pull in at the drive-up liquor store for a six-pack and a to-go cup. Unlike big cities, where waiting in lines becomes a way of life, the bank, grocery store, and post office queues are short or nonexistent. Try on a cowboy hat and boots, look around the local museum, or stop in for a beer at a country bar and joke with the locals. In a short while you'll gain an appreciation for Wyoming and the down-to-earth people who live here.

THE SKY

In the vast open spaces of Wyoming, the sky takes on its own importance, sometimes making the land seem like an afterthought. The land changes slowly with the seasons—first a carpet of winter white, then the mud and first luminescent green buds of spring growth, followed by the verdant summer flowers, and finally the brilliance of fall cottonwood trees along a dry creekbed. But the sky follows the beat of another drummer, changing moment by moment throughout each day. Cotton ball clouds float overhead, sending moving shadows across the landscape and coloring the sun's light. Storm clouds build on a summer afternoon, and in the distance a lightning bolt leaps to earth. Perhaps the most memorable times are the lingering sunsets, when colors seem to bounce back and forth across the sky, finally exiting as a fringe of color on the western horizon. At night, coyotes howl the same way they have for millennia, and an enormous panorama of stars arches above, undimmed by discordant city lights.

The Land

Covering nearly 98,000 square miles, Wyoming is America's ninth-largest state. The states of Connecticut, Delaware, Hawaii, Maryland, Massachusetts, New Hampshire, New Jersey, Rhode Island, Vermont, and West Virginia would all fit within Wyoming's borders—with room to spare. With just 493,782 inhabitants in 2000—the smallest population of any state—Wyoming remains a remarkably undeveloped and unsettled place. Cattle outnumber people by nearly three to one. The population density averages fewer than five people per square mile, and in some counties there is nearly one square mile of land for each person. With an average elevation of 6,700 feet (and a range of 3,125 to 13,804 feet), Wyoming is the third-highest state in the nation. Only Alaska and Colorado are higher.

GEOGRAPHY

On the map, Wyoming is simply a gigantic trapezoidal chunk of earth. Its straight-line border (375 miles from east to west and 276 miles north to south) is an arbitrary human creation that encompasses a surprising diversity

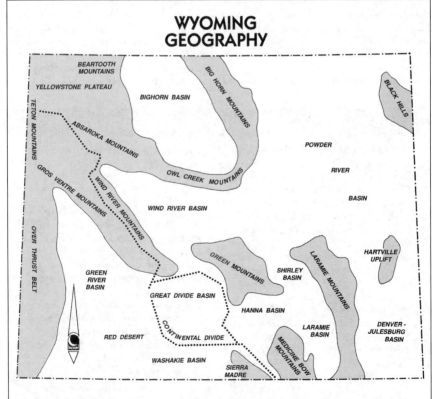

of country. The Continental Divide wanders diagonally across the state's mountains from the northwest corner to south-central Wyoming, forming the barrier that separates waters flowing into the Atlantic and Pacific Oceans. More than 71 percent of Wyoming's lakes, rivers, and streams drain into tributaries of the Missouri River, eventually reaching the Atlantic Ocean; most of the rest flow into tributaries of the Colorado and Columbia Rivers and thence to the Pacific Ocean. Small portions drop into the Great Basin (Salt Lake) or the Great Divide Basin (between Rock Springs and Rawlins), where the water evaporates or percolates into the ground.

Wyoming's mountains generally trend northwest to southeast, but smaller ranges break up this gross overall pattern. Northwest Wyoming is dominated by a complex mélange of mountains: the Absaroka, Teton, Gros Ventre, Wyoming, and Wind River Ranges. North-central Wyoming is divided by the Big Horn Mountains, while the Laramie Range and the Medicine Bow Mountains dominate the south-central region. The far northeast corner holds the Black Hills. In among these ranges, the land spreads out in broad basins, including Bighorn Basin and Powder River Basin in the north, Wind River Basin in the west-central region, and the Green River, Red Desert, and Washakie basins in the southwest. The eastern portion of Wyoming drops gently into the Great Plains.

CLIMATE

Wyoming's climate mirrors its diverse geography, ranging from arid deserts to cool mountain forests. The mountain ranges act as barriers to eastward-moving weather systems. Moist air is forced upward by the mountains, releasing rain or snow along the western slopes. By the time the clouds reach the east side, much of the water has been wrung out, creating a "rain shadow." Because of this, midwinter finds Togwotee Pass smothered under many feet of snow while Dubois, in the lee of the Absaroka Range, may have only a dusting on the ground.

TROPICAL WYOMING

Sometimes I wish that Wyoming had more vegetation and less catarrh, more bloom and summer and fragrance and less Christmas and New Year's through the summer. I like the clear, bracing air of 7,500 feet above the civilized world, but I get weary of putting on and taking off my buffalo overcoat for meals all through dog days. I yearn for a land where a man can take off his ulster and overshoes while he delivers a Fourth of July oration, without flying into the face of Providence and dying of pneumonia. . . . As I write these lines I look out across the wide sweep of brownish gray plains dotted here and there with ranches and defunct buffalo craniums, and I see shutting down over the sides of the abrupt mountains, and

meeting the foothills, a white mist which melts into the gray sky. It is a snow storm in the mountains.

I saw this with wonder and admiration for the first two or three million times. When it became a matter of daily occurrence as a wonder or curiosity, it was below mediocrity. Last July a snow storm gathered one afternoon and fell among the foothills and whitened the whole line to within four or five miles of town, and it certainly was a peculiar freak of nature, but it convinced me that whatever enterprises I might launch into here I would not try to raise oranges and figs until the isothermal lines should meet with a change of heart.

—19th-century humorist Bill Nye

Visitors to Wyoming discover weather typical of the West's high plains and mountains: hot, dry summers punctuated by fierce thunderstorms, and cold winters with a fair amount of snow. Conditions vary greatly throughout the state, however, with cooler summers and heavy winter snows in the mountains. July can sometimes be unbearably hot, with temperatures occasionally topping 100 degrees.

Extremes

Wyoming has a reputation for extreme conditions. Wintertime blizzards periodically lash the land, and strong winds pile the snow into huge drifts. Summertime thunderstorms—particularly in the mountains—can be an almost daily occurrence. Southeast Wyoming has an average of nine hailstorms per year—it's the hail capital of North America. Temperatures have been recorded from –66°F (Yellowstone National Park) to 114°F (the town of Basin). Precipitation shows a similar variation—high mountain ranges of northwest Wyoming see as much as 60 inches (mostly snow) per year, while parched desert areas in Bighorn Basin and Great Divide Basin receive only six.

Wyoming is well known for its wind. Throughout much of the state, the wind never seems to stop blowing, averaging more than 16 miles per hour along the eastern border. Buffalo Bill Cody, a man who symbolizes the West in the American conscience, once defended Wyoming when a friend complained of the wind: "You know where those winds come from? Well, this country up here is so close to paradise you can feel the breezes from heaven. That wind comes from the angels' wings. When they flap their wings the wind comes right down this valley."

Basin Weather

In the expansive basins that cover much of Wyoming, typical midsummer daytime temperatures are in the 80s and 90s, with nights dropping into the 50s and 60s. Low relative humidity makes the heat easier to take. The wettest months are April and May, with lots of sun in the summer. Afternoon thunderheads often build up, temporarily blocking the sun,

Mormon Row, Grand Teton National Park

© DON PITCHER

but generally dropping more lightning than rain. Fall can be a most pleasant time of year, with shirtsleeve days and cool evenings.

When winter arrives in November and December, it can do so with a vengeance, pushing the mercury well below zero. Snowfall is not great, totaling 15 to 60 inches over the winter months, but when combined with winds pushing 50 mph, it can look like a lot more. In places, snow fences extend for many miles beside the highways, attempting to blunt the blowing snow. Ground blizzards sometimes halt traffic along I-80 for days at a time. Locals joke that it only snows a couple of inches in December and then the snow blows back and forth across the state the rest of the winter until it is finally worn out. Actually, winters are not all so bleak, and temperatures occasionally rise into the 50s. You can expect sun 60 percent of the time. *Chinooks* (warm downslope winds) are common in the winters along the eastern slopes of the mountains, particularly around Sheridan, Dubois, and Cody.

Mountain Weather

Many of the favorite sites in Wyoming, includ-

LIGHTNING SAFETY

Lightning is a significant hazard for travelers on foot or horseback in Wyoming, particularly in the high mountains such as the Tetons, Wind River Range, Snowy Range, or the Big Horns. Three people were killed by lightning strikes in 1998 and 1999 in the Snowy Range west of Laramie, and others are struck almost every year around the state. Perhaps the most famous incident came in the 1990s, when acclaimed writer Gretel Ehrlich was struck while riding a horse on her ranch at the foot of the Big Horns. Her long and excruciating recovery is detailed in *A Match to the Heart* (Random House, www.randomhouse.com, 1994).

Creating a Thunderhead

Thunderstorms are created by a combination of convective forces, moisture, and unstable air. On sunny days as the ground warms, heat begins to rise convectively. When the air above is unstable (much cooler at higher altitudes than closer to the ground), the warm air rises rapidly. As it rises, the air cools enough that tiny droplets of moisture precipitate out, forming clouds that may grow into thunderheads if there is enough moisture and atmospheric instability. This rapid development of thunderheads generates enormous amounts of energy that is released as lightning, wind, hail, and rain. During a lightning strike, an electrical charge reaches toward the ground and is met by an opposite charge rising from the earth. They connect in a brilliant flash of light, heat, and noise as 35,000 amperes of charge are released.

Protecting Yourself

Nearly 100 people die each year from lightning strikes in the United States, and hundreds of others are injured. Statistically speaking, golfers are the most likely to get zapped because they are often in open areas carrying metal golf clubs when a storm rolls in. Others at risk include softball and soccer players, mountain climbers, horseback riders, swimmers, and hikers.

Several factors are important in protecting yourself from lightning. One is to pay attention to building storms, even distant ones, and especially those that build quickly. Mountain thunderstorms—created when winds push air masses upslope against a mountain range—are five times more likely to occur than storms over adjacent valleys. The color of thunderheads is another factor to watch; black bases mean significant amounts of moisture and may portend a more violent thunderstorm.

The most dangerous times are—surprisingly—before a thunderstorm comes directly overhead. Strikes can hit up to five miles in front of a fast-moving thunderstorm. In 1999, a Boy Scout was struck in the Tetons while watching a distant thunderstorm; overhead it was mostly blue sky! To determine your distance from an approaching storm, count the number of seconds between a lightning strike and the subsequent thunderclap, then divide by five to get the approximate distance in miles. If thunder arrives within five seconds, the storm is dangerously close, just one mile away.

If you see a storm approaching, get off ridgetops and other high places, move out of open fields, away from single trees or other tall objects, and out of the water. Lightning follows the path of least resistance, which usually means taller objects or those containing metal. Safer places are inside a car or house, or in a stand of even-sized trees. If those options aren't possible, lie down and stay as low as possible—preferably in a *dry* ditch (stay away from wet areas). If you're caught on an open ridge, crouch on an insulated pad or a backpack. Metallic objects attract lightning, so stay away from fence posts, golf clubs, climbing gear, or metal objects in your backpack. Don't stand in a group of people. If you're indoors when a storm hits, move away from windows, doors, appliances, pipes, and telephones.

Lightning strikes are sometimes preceded by a tingling sensation, and your hair may stand on end. If this happens, immediately crouch down (but don't lie down or put your hands on the ground) and cover your ears. If someone near you is struck by lightning, get immediate help and be ready to perform CPR. For additional lightning safety information, contact the **Lightning Protection Institute,** 800/488-6864, www.lightning.org.

ing Yellowstone and Grand Teton National Parks, lie primarily above 7,000 feet. Here, the weather is considerably cooler than in the basins. Summertime temperatures rarely top 80°F, while nights often dip into the 40s. Snow is possible at any time of the year. April and May are generally the wettest months. Spring comes late in the mountains, and drifts often block high passes until mid-July. Summer thunderstorms are common, especially in the northwest mountains, where they gather over the high peaks (and often nearby valleys) most afternoons. Mid-September brings fall conditions as mountain temperatures often drop 20–30 degrees below summer readings, quickly turning the aspen leaves a brilliant orange and sending most folks scurrying for warmer climes.

High-country winters are often severely cold and snowy, with temperatures below zero for days at a time. Snow depths often exceed six feet in the higher mountains. Grand Targhee Ski Resort receives some 42 feet of snow over a typical winter! Fortunately, the relative humidity is quite low, making the temperatures easier to tolerate and creating fluffy powder snow conditions. One surprising winter feature is the presence of temperature inversions in intermountain valleys such as Big Piney and Jackson Hole. These often occur on cold, clear nights when the cold air sinks into the valley floors. Skiers who leave the lodge bundled in down parkas and polypro are often surprised to find temperatures 30 degrees warmer at the top of the mountain.

Flora and Fauna

VEGETATION

Wyoming's topography and climate are reflected in its vegetation, with dense forests in the mountains and dry grasses and shrubs at lower elevations. The vegetation can be classified into six broad categories (see map): mixed-grass prairie, sagebrush steppe, desert shrubland, evergreen forest, deciduous forest, and alpine tundra. Mixed-grass prairies dominate the eastern third of Wyoming and contain such species as grama grass, wheatgrass, junegrass, bluegrass, and sage. The western two-thirds of Wyoming contains vast areas of sagebrush steppe, a threadbare carpet of big sagebrush, wheatgrass, needle-and-thread grass, grama grass, tumbleweed, and other plants. This is the country most folks associate with Wyoming—sagebrush extending to the horizon. (An old cowboy saying goes, "I reckon the Lord done put tumbleweeds here to show which way the wind was a-blowin'.")

Wyoming also contains desert areas, notably the Red Desert and a large part of Bighorn Basin. Dominant plants in the desert shrublands include greasewood, saltbush, shadscale, and various kinds of sagebrush. At higher elevations, where more moisture falls, the land is covered with evergreen forests. Ponderosa pines dominate forested parts of eastern Wyoming, while lodgepole pine, Douglas fir, Engelmann spruce, and subalpine fir exist in mountains to the west. A few areas also have pinyon pine and juniper trees. Deciduous forests are scattered in small patches around Wyoming consisting of cottonwoods along river bottoms, aspens in the middle elevations, and bur oak in the Black Hills. The tree line in much of Wyoming is around 9,500 feet. Above this line, one finds alpine tundra, where the dominant plants are low-growing herbs, grasses, and forbs.

Wyoming's undeveloped character makes it a mecca for those who enjoy watching wild animals.

WILDLIFE

When the first mountain men and explorers wandered into the vast land that became Wyoming, they found an incredible abundance of wildlife: herds of bison stretching to the horizon; antelope, elk, and deer grazing on the broad plains; and grizzly bears, wolves, coyotes, cottontails, and jackrabbits. Although wolves were poisoned to extinction, and only a few hundred bison and

WYOMING VEGETATION

EVERGREEN FORESTS

DECIDUOUS FORESTS

SAGEBRUSH STEPPE

MIXED GRASS PRAIRIE

ALPINE TUNDRA

DESERT SHRUBLAND

0   100 mi

0   100 km

© AVALON TRAVEL PUBLISHING, INC.

grizzlies remain, other animals fared better. Today, the two most common large mammals are mule deer and pronghorn antelope, both of which are found across much of the state. The sagebrush lands also provide cover for sage grouse, a large chickenlike bird (the males perform an elaborate X-rated mating display). In the mountains, one often hears the early-summer drumming of ruffed grouse. Rarest of Wyoming's animals is the endangered black-footed ferret.

Watchable Wildlife

Wyoming's undeveloped character makes it a mecca for those who enjoy watching wild animals. Yellowstone National Park is a favorite place to look for bison, elk, coyotes, moose, mule deer, bighorn sheep, river otters, and trum-

peter swans. Both black and grizzly bears also live here, although they're less commonly seen. Another popular place is the National Elk Refuge in Jackson Hole, the winter home for a herd of more than 7,000 elk. Excellent places to see bighorn sheep are the Whiskey Basin Habitat Area, near Dubois, and the Bighorn National Recreation Area. Wyoming has around 3,500 wild horses; watch for them at Bighorn National Recreation Area near Lovell or in the Red Desert near Rock Springs. Mountain goats live in the Beartooth Mountains along Wyoming's border with Montana. The high mountains of the Tetons and the Wind River Range have such animals as pikas and yellow-bellied marmots, while the sagebrush country abounds with deer, antelope, coyotes, jackrabbits, cottontails, and prairie dogs. Certainly the most distinctive Wyoming critter is the jackalope. For a different sort of watchable wildlife, visit Wyoming in early May when pastures across the state are filled with wobbly baby calves.

The Wyoming Game and Fish Department publishes *Wyoming Wildlife,* an attractive monthly publication, available for just $13 per year. To subscribe, call 307/777-4600 or 800/710-8345. Call 800/548-9453 for a catalog of other wildlife-related products and publications, including videos, T-shirts, caps, mugs, books, posters, and cards. All of these are available on the Game and Fish website: http://gf.state.wy.us.

Rattlesnakes

Everyone's least favorite reptile is the prairie rattlesnake, a heavy-bodied venomous creature with a telltale rattle. Prairie rattlesnakes often reach nearly one yard in length (the longest was 57 inches!) and are found in the plains and foothills of eastern and central Wyoming, generally below 7,000 feet. They're especially common around rock piles and in prairie dog towns. You *won't* find them in mountain country over 7,200 feet, in the Laramie area, in Yellowstone and Grand Teton National Parks, or in the southwestern desert country (with the exception of the lower Green River Valley area). Prairie rattlers feed primarily on ground squirrels, rabbits, chipmunks, prairie dogs, and other small rodents, but they can also kill birds and lizards. They reproduce every other year, and large groups of rattlesnakes gather in dens to spend the winter months in a dormant state.

Prairie rattlesnakes usually offer a warning of their presence—hence the name—but not all the time. At times aggressive, their size and appearance will certainly send your blood pressure up, but the venom is actually less toxic than that of other rattlers and is usually only one-eighth the amount needed to kill a human. Because of this, snakebite fatalities are rare in Wyoming.

A smaller snake, the midget faded rattlesnake, is found in southern Wyoming within the lower Green River Valley around the cities of Green River and Rock Springs, and in Flaming Gorge National Recreation Area. They frequent rocky outcrops and, although smaller in appearance, are 10 to 30 times more poisonous than prairie rattlesnakes. Fortunately, midget faded rattlesnakes are quite timid and pose little threat to humans. They will coil and strike, but only if cornered.

The best defense against rattlers is to always use care when walking in their country and to keep your distance if you spot one. Be especially careful when clambering over rock piles or

SAGEBRUSH

Sagebrush is Wyoming's ubiquitous common denominator, a sweetly pungent bush found from the lowest deserts to 10,000-foot mountains. More sage grows here than anyplace else in North America. The volatile oils make it a last choice for cattle and act as a natural herbicide, preventing competition from other plants. Ranchers consider the plant less than worthless, but native animals such as sage grouse, antelope, and mule deer depend on sage for survival. You won't even find sage grouse where sage doesn't grow.

The terms sagebrush and sage are generally used interchangeably in the West. Note, however, that the spice on your kitchen shelf is not the same as the Wyoming plant *(Artemesia),* and any attempt to cook with sagebrush is likely to leave you gagging. Sage has been in the West for some 25 million years and is well adapted to the poor soils and arid conditions of the desert. Sage survives by using its network of shallow roots to draw moisture from the ground as it percolates down. Wyoming actually has at least seven different species of sage. Some of these exist only on very specific sites: black sagebrush grows on windy ridges between 5,000 and 8,000 feet, where the soil is shallow and stony; alkali sagebrush grows in impermeable soils that are highly alkaline. The predominant species across much of Wyoming is big sagebrush, a bush that grows to three feet in height and often covers extensive areas.

walking through dense grasses and sage. Shake out sleeping bags, boots, and bedding, and wear tall leather boots rather than sneakers.

If a rattlesnake bites someone, immobilize the area of the bite and immediately get him or her to a hospital or medical facility. If the bite is on an arm or leg, keep it below the level of the heart. Time is of the essence. Other treatments are possible for emergency situations when there is no chance of getting to a doctor in time, but the potential for harm is great if you don't know what you are doing. Take a good first-aid class to learn how to handle these situations, or talk with your doctor about where to get and how to use suction pumps. Your best bet is always preventing a bite in the first place. For more on rattlers and other crawly things, see *Amphibians and Reptiles of Wyoming,* by George T. Baxter and Michael D. Stone (Cheyenne: Wyoming Game and Fish Department, 1985).

Pronghorn Antelope

One of the most commonly seen Wyoming animals is the antelope (biologists prefer the name "pronghorn"). More than 400,000 live here, constituting half the world's pronghorn population. Antelope survive on grasses, forbs, and sagebrush—perhaps Wyoming's most abundant plant. They are built for speed: oversized lungs and windpipes give them the ability to run for miles at 30 mph and to accelerate to twice that for short bursts. Despite this speed, pronghorn have an innate inquisitiveness that makes them relatively easy to hunt, an attribute that nearly drove them to extinction by market hunting early in the 20th century. Strict laws and careful management have brought antelope populations back.

Deer

Wyoming has almost as many deer as people. You can see two species along the state's roads: white-tailed deer—common in the Black Hills—and the larger mule deer, found across the state. Be especially careful when driving after dusk during the fall breeding season because the hormone-crazed bucks tend to leap out in front of cars. Nearly everyone who has

© DON PITCHER

Pronghorn antelope are most often seen in the northern part of Yellowstone.

lived in Wyoming has hit a deer under these circumstances, including the author. Slow down at night, especially in areas posted with Deer Crossing signs.

Elk

A majestic member of the deer family, elk (some biologists prefer the term "wapiti") are a favorite with both tourists and hunters. Elk inhabit much of Wyoming, with the largest herds along the western mountains. More than 30,000 elk graze in Yellowstone National Park alone. With bulls averaging 700 pounds and cows averaging 500 pounds, they are some of the largest antlered animals in the Americas.

Elk spend summers high in the mountains, feeding in alpine meadows and along forest edges. Mature bulls graze alone, but the cows and calves—generally born in late May and early June—group in large herds for protection. When the fall rutting season arrives, bulls attempt to herd the cows and calves around, mating with cows when they come into estrus and defending their harems from other bulls. During this time of year the bugling of bull elk is a common sound in the mountains, a challenge to any bull within earshot. When a competitor appears, a dominance display often follows—complete with bugling, stomping, and thrashing of the ground—to show who is the baddest bull around. In a fight, bulls lock their massive antlers and try to push and twist until one finally gives in and retreats. These battles help ensure that the healthiest bulls produce the most offspring. Ironically, other bulls often wait in the wings for battles over harems to occur, then rush in to mate with the cows while the larger bulls are sparring. The snows of late fall push elk to lower-elevation winter ranges, notably at the National Elk Refuge in Jackson Hole. When spring comes, the bulls drop their antlers and immediately begin to grow new ones. The elk head back into the high country, following the melting snowline.

Elk and bison both can be infected with brucellosis, a bacterium causing spontaneous abortions. Brucellosis is transmitted to other animals by contact with the dead fetus or birthing material and can cause undulant fever in humans. Ranchers worry that brucellosis can spread from elk and bison to cattle, particularly around elk feeding grounds in western Wyoming. To lessen the incidence of brucellosis, state employees now routinely vaccinate elk at the feeding grounds, shooting them in the hindquarters with vaccine-loaded pellets.

BISON

The bison is the definitive frontier animal and Wyoming's state mammal—its outline graces the state flag. Weighing up to 2,000 pounds, these are the largest land mammals in the New World. Bison commonly live 12–15 years. The calves weigh 30 to 40 pounds at birth and within minutes are standing and able to nurse. Two races of bison exist: the plains bison, primarily east of the Rockies, and the mountain bison (sometimes called wood bison) in the higher elevations. Tech-

nically, these huge, hairy beasts are bison—the only true buffalo are the water buffalo of Southeast Asia—but the name buffalo is commonly used.

With their massive heads, huge shoulder humps, heavy coats of fur, and small posteriors, buffalo are some of the strangest animals in North America. They look so front-heavy as to seem unstable, ready to topple forward onto their snouts at any time. Despite this impression, buffalo are remarkably well adapted to life on the plains. A bison will use its strong sense of smell to find grass buried in a deep snowdrift and then sweep the snow away with a sideways motion of its head. The animals are also surprisingly fleet-footed, as careless Yellowstone photographers have discovered. In addition, the buffalo is one very tough critter. In 1907, a buffalo was pitted against four of the meanest Mexican bulls at a Juarez, Mexico, bullring. After knocking heads several times with the buffalo, the bulls fled and were saved only when bullfighters opened the chute gates to let them escape.

"Blackening the Plains"

When Europeans first reached the New World, they found massive herds of bison in the Appalachians and even more as they headed west. Daniel Boone hunted them in North Carolina in the 1750s; Pennsylvanians shot hundreds of buffalo that were invading their winter stores of hay. By 1820, settlers had nearly driven the buffalo to extinction in the east, but there were far more living to the west. As explorers, mountain men, and the first tentative settlers reached the "Great American Desert," they were awestruck by the numbers. Travelers told of slowly moving masses of buffalo blackening the plains and watched in astonishment as the herds stopped at rivers and nearly drank them dry. A fair estimate of the original population of buffalo in North America is 60 million. Even in the middle 1860s, travelers through Wyoming's Wind River Valley reported seeing 10,000 bison at one time. A pioneer Kansas settler named William D. Street recalled a trip in which a herd roared past his camp for an entire night. The next morning, he climbed a nearby butte and saw buffalo covering the plains below. According to Street:

> The herd was not less than 20 miles in width—we never saw the other side—at least 60 miles in length, maybe much longer; two counties of buffaloes! There might have been 100,000, or 1,000,000, or 100,000,000. I don't know. In the cowboy days in western Kansas we saw 7,000 head of cattle in one roundup. After gazing at them a few moments our thoughts turned to that buffalo herd. For a comparison, imagine a large pail of water; take from it or add to it a drop, and there you have it. Seven thousand head of cattle was not a drop in the bucket as compared with that herd of buffalo.

Indians and Buffalo

The Plains Indians depended heavily on the buffalo for food and—like the proverbial hot dog, which "contains everything but the moo"—they used every part of the animal. Hooves were carved into spoons, skins became buffalo robes and covers for boats and tepees, rawhide was used for drumheads, calf skins became storage sacks, hair was turned into earrings, and horns were formed into cups and arrow points. Everything that remained—including the muzzle, penis, eyes, and cartilage—was boiled down to use as glue for arrowheads. Their dried testicles and scrotum were used for rattles, and the ubiquitous buffalo chips became a cooking fuel on the treeless prairies.

Hunting techniques varied depending on the terrain. When possible, the Indians drove herds of bison into *arroyos* (dry gulches) with no exits, over cliffs, or into deep sand or snow, making them easier to kill. The arrival of Spanish horses in the 16th century made it far easier to hunt bison. In a surround, mounted hunters attacked from at least two sides, creating chaos in the herd and allowing buffalo to be shot with arrows or guns.

When whites first spread across the plains, they found the bison a plentiful food source but also viewed the massive herds as a hindrance to agriculture and cattle raising. But these were not the only reasons whites wanted to destroy the buffalo.

Killing off the bison would starve the Indians into submission and force them to take a more "civilized" way of life. General Philip Sheridan, commenting in support of white buffalo hunters, said

> Instead of stopping the [white] hunters they ought to give them a hearty, unanimous vote of thanks, and appropriate a sufficient sum of money to strike and present to each one a medal of bronze, with a dead buffalo on one side and a discouraged Indian on the other. They are destroying the Indian's commissary, and it is a well-known fact that an army losing its base of supplies is placed at a great disadvantage. Send them powder and lead, if you will; for the sake of a lasting peace, let them kill, skin and sell until the buffaloes are exterminated.

This reckless slaughter did indeed endanger the Indians, but it also had an unwanted side effect: the Indians went on the warpath. The loss of their primary food source helped convince many Indians that their own extinction was next. The warriors who massacred Custer and his men at Little Big Horn had watched their people pushed to the brink of starvation by the destruction of the buffalo.

The Slaughter

Two factors propelled the slaughter to new heights in the 1870s: new railroads across the plains and a sudden international demand for buffalo robes and hides. Buffalo meat proved to be a readily available food source for railway construction workers, and hunters such as "Buffalo Bill" Cody provided a steady supply, generally taking just the hindquarters and hump and leaving the rest on the plains. Hundreds of thousands were killed. Once the railroads were completed in 1869, a new "sport" appeared—shooting buffalo from the moving railcars and leaving them to rot on the prairie. Wealthy gentry from the East Coast and Europe also discovered the joys of killing. One Irish nobleman had an entourage of 40 servants, with an entire wagon just for firearms; he killed 2,000 buffalo in a three-year carnage.

Conservationists tried to halt the buffalo

© DON PITCHER

was a dead, solitary, putrid desert." Buffalo carcasses dotted the plains in such numbers that in later years bone pickers would collect massive piles of bones for knife handles, combs, and buttons or to be ground up for sugar refining, fertilizer, or glue.

When the buffalo of the central states approached extinction, hunters turned their attention elsewhere, reaching Wyoming, Montana, and the Dakotas in 1880. In 1882, more than 200,000 hides were taken, and another 40,000 the following year. By 1884, only 300 hides were shipped. The slaughter was nearly over; only a few private herds and scattered individual bison remained. The Indians who had once depended so heavily on buffalo for all the necessities of life were reduced to eating muskrats, gophers, and even grass. Some killed their horses, others stole settlers' cattle, and the rest had to beg the government for food. In only a couple of years, an entire culture had been devastated.

But the slaughter ruined the lives not just of the buffalo or the Indians; hide hunters often spiked buffalo carcasses with strychnine, returning later to skin the wolves that had come to feed on the meat. Coyotes, kit foxes, badgers, vultures, eagles, ravens, and anything else that ate the meat were also killed. With both the buffalo and the "vermin" out of the way, Wyoming and the West were safe for domestic sheep and cattle.

slaughter through legislation in 1874, but President Grant's corrupt Secretary of the Interior, Columbus Delano, said, "I would not seriously regret the total disappearance of the buffalo from our western prairies, in its effect upon the Indians. I would regard it rather as a means of hastening their sense of dependence upon the products of the soil and their own labors." The legislation was pocket-vetoed by Grant.

In 1872, thousands of hide hunters spread through Kansas, Nebraska, and Colorado in search of buffalo. Over the next three years, they brought in more than three million buffalo hides, with Indians killing another 400,000 bison for meat and robes. Good hide hunters could bring down 25 to 100 buffalo in a typical day, keeping five skinners busy from sunup to sundown. One hunter, Jim White, killed at least 16,000 buffalo in his career. Only the hides, cured hams, and buffalo tongues (which could be salted and shipped in barrels) were saved. When Gen. Grenville M. Dodge toured Kansas in the fall of 1873, he noted that "the air was foul with a sickening stench, and the vast plain, which only a short twelvemonth before teemed with animal life,

Protection

The first federal legislation protecting buffalo (only in Yellowstone National Park, however) did not pass until 1894. The following year, only 800 buffalo remained in all of North America, a little over one-thousandth of one percent of their original numbers. Despite this dismal picture, the population has rebounded dramatically; today an estimated 65,000 bison roam across America. In Wyoming, small populations can be seen in Hot Springs State Park and Grand Teton National Park, while one of the few large wild populations remains in Yellowstone National Park.

A strong demand for buffalo meat has led some Wyoming ranchers to raise bison. It's a highly specialized ranching endeavor because the animals can flatten most fences, and standard roundup techniques don't work. Durham Buffalo Ranch near Wright has one of the largest private buffalo herds in the country: 3,500 head. Ranchers have discovered that bison are more efficient grazers than cattle, making it possible to produce more meat per acre, and they are less susceptible to disease. Perhaps someday the vast herds of bison may return to Wyoming's rangelands in the form of bison ranches.

History

Although Wyoming is a young state—only reaching the century mark in 1990—it seems to have more history per square inch than just about any other place in America. This history is a mixture of Indians and cowboys, settlers and outlaws, schemers and dreamers, railroad magnates and cattle barons, and plain folks clinging to plots of marginal farmland despite unbelievable odds. Wyoming's 19th-century frontier is a recurring theme in America's imagination, as revealed in countless books, songs, and movies. This rich treasure trove from the past is stored not just in the little-changed landscape, where the ruts from wagon trains are still visible and emigrant names remain carved in rocky buttes, but also in the cattle drives and rodeos and the weather-etched faces of sheepherders and cowboys working the range. It is hard to imagine a place with a richer past. An interesting web source for Wyoming history and historical photos is www.wyomingtalesandtrails.com.

NATIVE AMERICANS

Humans have been in Wyoming for perhaps 25,000 years. The Plains Indians—comprising 27 different tribes—were found from the Mississippi River to the Rockies, and from Texas to central Canada. The lives of these people revolved around the buffalo; they followed the vast herds, migrating where the buffalo led. Because of this nomadic lifestyle, everything they had was pared to the minimum. Pottery, so common in the southwestern deserts, was replaced by woven baskets on the plains. The tepee, an easily portable lodge, offered protection from the elements, and clothing was warm yet not burdensome.

Days of Glory

Although many people view the Plains Indians as existing in a state of balance with their environment, there is ample evidence that things were changing even before whites first pushed their way onto the plains. The arrival of horses and guns in the 17th and 18th centuries created a time of plenty that has rarely been known among nomadic hunting tribes. Horses made it easier to follow and hunt the huge bison herds, and tribes that had been at least partially farmers turned entirely to hunting. Native populations grew rapidly with the abundance of food. The warrior also gained importance with the changing culture as raiding parties stole horses and attacked

FROM TAME EARTH TO WILD WEST

We did not think of the great open plains, the beautiful rolling hills, the winding streams with tangled growth as wild. Only to the white man was nature a wilderness, and only to him was the land infested with wild animals and savage people. To us it was tame. Earth was bountiful, and we were surrounded with the blessings of the Great Mystery. Not until the hairy man from the east came, and with his brutal frenzy, heaped injustices upon us and the families we loved, was it wild to us. When the very animals of the forest began fleeing from his approach; then it was that for us, the 'wild west' began.

—Sioux Chief Standing Bear

other tribes. Villages grew larger as families gathered for mutual protection from their enemies.

The turmoil that resulted led to a constantly changing situation in Wyoming during the 19th century, as the tribes each strove for control. It was this turbulent society that greeted the first Euro-American explorers. Whites were accustomed to well-defined land ownership, with definite boundaries within which one lived; here the territories were in a state of flux, with tribes claiming overlapping areas.

During the 1700s, Indians from the Great Lakes and Canadian plains had moved into what would become Wyoming. By the 1850s, the Sioux were in Powder River Basin, the Crow in Bighorn Basin, and the Cheyenne and Arapaho south of the North Platte River. The Shoshone and the Bannock—originally from the Great Basin—had moved into the Green River and Wind River valleys, while their relatives, the Utes, held the Sierra Madre and desert land to the west. Communication between these diverse tribes was possible in a sophisticated sign language.

Treaties

During the first half of the 19th century, American explorers, fur trappers, traders, and settlers began to push across Wyoming. As emigration westward increased in the 1840s, so did conflicts with Indians. Whites complained of random attacks and stolen horses. Indians complained of trampled grass, polluted water, and wasteful killing of bison. To deal with these problems, a great council was called at Fort Laramie in 1851, attracting 10,000 Indians from many different tribes. Indian agent Thomas Fitzpatrick was eager to gain permission for settlers to use the Oregon Trail across Indian lands in Wyoming. In exchange for gifts from the federal government in the form of annuities, the tribes agreed to stay within specified boundaries and to punish those who violated the accord or attacked white emigrants.

Father Pierre DeSmet drew up the boundaries, with allowances for hunting outside the "home" regions. The unstated long-term goal of the treaty was to transform the Indians from hunters into farmers. By developing a paternalistic

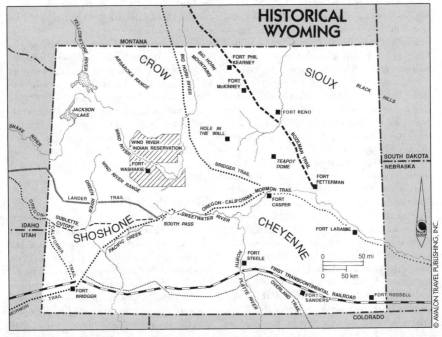

system of dependency on the government, combined with educational programs and settlement, the Indians would—in theory—become like the whites. Violence erupted almost immediately among the tribes and between them and the Anglo emigrants. Soon, whites would be more concerned over how to dispossess the Indians of their land than how to get through it safely.

In 1861, the Fort Wise Treaty abrogated much of the Treaty of 1851, forcing the Arapaho and Cheyenne onto a desolate reservation at Sand Creek, Colorado, to get them away from the suddenly valuable land to the north. Some leaders signed the treaty, but only after the starving individuals saw that they would not receive their annuities without affixing their Xs.

The Battle Begins

Colorado's Sand Creek Massacre of 1865 proved a turning point in the history of Indian–white relations. A small band of Arapaho attacked a family farm, brutally murdering the family. When the mutilated bodies were put on display in Denver, public outrage pushed Col. John M. Chivington—formerly a Methodist minister—to lead one of the most vicious and unwarranted attacks ever perpetrated by the army. Two hundred Cheyenne and Arapaho died in the daybreak attack on Chief Black Kettle's peaceful village.

The Indians—not just the Cheyenne and Arapaho, but also the Sioux—quickly retaliated by striking throughout Colorado and Wyoming, killing some 75 settlers around the Rock Creek Station (northwest of present-day Laramie) and destroying stage stations all along the Oregon Trail. Over the next several years, hundreds died on both sides. The main focus of Indian attacks was the Bozeman Trail through the lush Powder River country of the Sioux. The army responded with an alternating series of military campaigns and peace overtures as the national mood flip-flopped between war and accommodation.

A major cause of these conflicts was the hysteria that gold created. Each new gold rush—California in 1849, Colorado in 1859, Montana in 1864, and finally the Black Hills in 1874—led to new incursions onto Indian lands. When whites found Indians standing in the way of de-

velopment, they attempted to renegotiate the treaties or, failing that, to find some excuse to set them aside. Once gold had been found, the end of Indian culture was almost a given. Sen. John Sherman noted: "If the whole army of the United States stood in the way, the wave of emigration would pass over it to seek the valley where gold was to be found."

Other factors also played critical roles in the destruction of the Indian way of life on the plains. Perhaps the most crucial was the loss of their primary food source, the buffalo. But many tribes were devastated as well by diseases brought by contact with Europeans, especially smallpox, cholera, whooping cough, and venereal diseases.

Cultural Mistrust

Many whites viewed the Indians with deep distrust. Writer James Chisholm reflected a typical frontier attitude, calling them "useless, strutting, ridiculous, pompous humbugs—lying, faithless, stealing, begging, cruel, hungry, howling vagabonds—cowardly, treacherous red devils." In 1869, Gen. Philip Sheridan took matters even further by declaring, "The only good Indian is a dead Indian."

The Indians themselves were not entirely innocent. Attacks on wagon trains were frequent, and many of the trappers, stagecoach drivers, and ranchers who settled in Wyoming were murdered and their bodies mutilated by the Sioux, Cheyenne, or Arapaho. Scalping—a practice introduced by white traders—became commonplace. Whites complained that the federal government was arming and feeding the Indians at the same time it was leading military campaigns against them.

Evicting the Indians

More than one thousand engagements were fought between Indians and whites in the late 19th century, killing at least 2,500 whites and twice as many Indians. On the plains, most of the battles involved the Sioux, Cheyenne, Arapaho, Kiowa, and Comanche tribes. The Shoshone under Chief Washakie always remained peaceful. The final drama came in the 1870s, beginning with the discovery of gold in the Black Hills of

Dakota Territory. A flood of miners overwhelmed attempts by the government to keep them out of Sioux territory, and negotiations to purchase the land bogged down when Red Cloud demanded a $600 million payment.

In 1876, General Sheridan led a three-pronged invasion to forcibly evict the Sioux from the Powder River region. He hadn't counted on two problems: the large numbers of Indians ready to do battle and the rashness of junior officer Col. George A. Custer. At Little Big Horn on June 25, 1876, a combined force of Indians led by Crazy Horse, Sitting Bull, and others wiped out all 225 of Custer's men. This massive Indian victory quickly became the rallying cry for whites anxious to "solve" the Indian problem by forcing them onto reservations. Within five years, the last of the tribes had given up the fight. The uprising that led to the infamous Wounded Knee Massacre of 1890 was a last dying gasp in the attempt to regain land that had once all belonged to Native Americans.

Those who had lived in this land for centuries had been evicted by new peoples from another world. Chief Washakie of the Shoshones described the painfulness of this change (quoted in *Chief Washakie,* by Mae Urbanek):

The white man, who possesses this whole vast country from sea to sea, who roams over it at pleasure, and lives where he likes, cannot know the cramp we feel in this little spot, with the undying remembrance of the fact, which you know as well as we, that every foot of what you proudly call America, not very long ago belonged to the red man. The Great Spirit gave it to us. There was room enough for all his many tribes, and all were happy in their freedom. But the white man had, in ways we know not of, superior tools and terrible weapons, better for war than bows and arrows; and there seemed no end to the hordes of men that followed them from other lands beyond the sea. And so, at last, our fathers were steadily driven out, or killed, and we, their sons, but sorry remnants of tribes once mighty, are cornered in little spots of the
earth all ours of right—cornered like guilty prisoners, and watched by men with guns, who are more than anxious to kill us off.

TRAPPERS AND EXPLORERS

The first Europeans to explore Wyoming were in a party of Frenchmen led by François and Louis-Joseph Verendrye, who crossed northern Wyoming in 1743. Others occasionally passed this way over subsequent decades, and an inscription on a rock northwest of Pinedale had the initials M. A. and the date 1791; it's the oldest dated carving in the state. During the winter of 1807–1808, John Colter—a trapper and former guide for the Lewis and Clark Expedition—explored northwestern Wyoming in an attempt to develop the fur trade with Crow Indians. Other trappers in search of beavers soon followed Colter. It was a hazardous business, with the constant threat of Indian attacks and the many natural hazards such as angry grizzlies, disease, and injuries. Help was hundreds of miles away. The era of the mountain man lasted only until 1840, when demand for the furs plummeted, but the trappers' knowledge of the terrain proved invaluable. Many former trappers became guides for civilian and military expeditions, wealthy hunters, and government explorations of the West. The mountain passes they found (or, more likely, had been shown by Indians) provided a route for the exodus westward in the 1850s.

THE OREGON TRAIL

When God made man,
He seemed to think it best
To make him in the East
And let him travel West.

from an Oregon Trail pioneer's diary

To 19th-century emigrants the Oregon Trail represented perhaps the best example of "Manifest Destiny"—the idea of an American nation reaching from the Atlantic to the Pacific. The Oregon Trail is actually a general term used to describe a whole series of wagon roads that

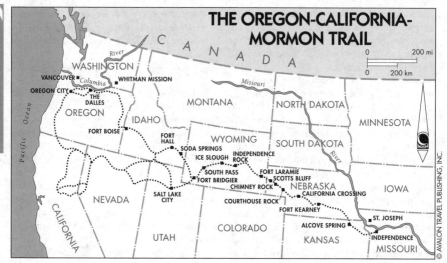

THE OREGON-CALIFORNIA-MORMON TRAIL

© AVALON TRAVEL PUBLISHING, INC.

headed west from Missouri. At different times, and over various paths, this route encompassed the Oregon Trail (to both Oregon and Washington), the California Trail (to the goldfields), the Mormon Trail (to Salt Lake City), and the short-lived Pony Express route. To emigrants it was not a trail but always "The Road."

Wyoming contains the least-changed and longest stretch (487 miles) of the Oregon Trail. From eastern Wyoming, the trail—actually a series of braided paths spreading across the river valleys—followed the North Platte and Sweetwater Rivers upstream to the Continental Divide at South Pass. Travelers chose this route because of abundant forage for stock, good water, and a gentle grade over the divide. As the only route that met all three criteria, the Oregon Trail became a national thoroughfare to the Promised Land of the West.

"Oregon Country" was not simply the area that would become the state of Oregon, but the entire region west of South Pass. Thus the hills just beyond the Continental Divide in Wyoming became the "Oregon Buttes," and emigrants wrote of entering Oregon as they crossed the pass: "Today we entered Oregon. . . . We nooned beyond at a small spring and drank the waters of the Pacific!" (The vast land collectively called Oregon actually

belonged to the British, but this legal nicety was quickly pushed aside by the influx of Americans.) West of South Pass, the route divided at the "Parting of the Ways." California- and Utah-bound travelers turned south to Fort Bridger, while those en route to Oregon and Washington headed due west on the Sublette or Lander Cutoffs.

Origins

Americans emigrated west for several reasons: to escape a severe economic depression in the East and falling crop prices, to get out of the crowded and polluted cities, to find religious freedom in Utah, to search for gold in the mountains of California, or simply to join in a great adventure in a new and undiscovered land. (More than a few also headed west to get away from debts or the law.) The first whites to cross the Continental Divide on what would become the Oregon Trail were a party of fur trappers known as the Astorians. They rode horses over South Pass in 1812, but it was not until a decade later that trappers really moved deeply into this country. The first freight wagons rolled over the pass in 1830, en route to a mountain-man rendezvous on the Green River. By the early 1840s, emigration westward was getting easier and more inviting. Fort Laramie, in eastern

Wyoming, and Fort Bridger, in southwestern Wyoming, provided valuable way stations where travelers could rest up, repair their wagons, trade worn-out stock for fresh animals, and purchase food, whiskey, and supplies.

The turning point in the history of the Oregon Trail came in 1843, when the Applegate Wagon Train left Independence, Missouri, with 875 people, 120 wagons, and 5,000 head of livestock. It was the largest wagon train ever assembled. Under the leadership of Marcus Whitman (later killed in an Indian attack near present-day Walla Walla, Washington) and guided by mountain man Bill Sublette, the party made it all the way to the Columbia and Willamette Rivers by September. It had taken six long months to travel the 2,000 miles, but they had shown that the route was feasible. The gates of history had been cracked open, and they could never be closed again. Soon, the trickle westward turned into a flood tide.

Rolling West

Most travelers tried to depart Independence or St. Joseph, Missouri, in the spring, leaving as soon as the grass would support their stock. Typically, each evening found the emigrant just 15 miles farther down the trail, and it generally took five or six months to travel from Missouri to California or Oregon. They had to be over the mountains before the first snows of winter struck, and those who erred—such as the infamous Donner Party of 1846—paid a high price.

Emigrants were forced to travel as lightly as possible to lessen the burden on oxen. Some traders grew rich on the castoffs from overburdened wagon trains, whereas others profited by operating toll bridges and ferries across the North Platte and Green Rivers. (Toll at the Green River crossing was sometimes an amazing $16 per wagon!) Guidebooks—there were several; this was a big business even in the 19th century—described the crossings and camping places and suggested provisions for the 2,000-mile journey. A wagon, harness, and eight oxen cost travelers around $400.

Because of the scarcity of wood, Oregon Trail travelers used dry grass, sagebrush, or buffalo chips for fuel. Meals were simple but hearty, often consisting of a few staples plus whatever game might be found along the trail. Today, when you drive across the state it is easy to see how trying an experience this must have been for the emigrants—gale-force winds, dust, and lightning combine with the parched ground, the deceptively long distances, and the lack of shade. Wyoming can be a harsh and unforgiving land; it is not a place to wander into unprepared. The words of a 17-year-old emigrant, Eliza Ann McAuley, are typical of the Oregon Trail experience in Wyoming. On July 4, 1852, she wrote:

> *Four miles brought us to the forks of the Salt Lake and California roads. We took the Sublett cut-off, leaving Salt Lake to the south. Made eighteen miles today and camped on Big Sandy. Had to drive the cattle about six miles toward the hills for grass. It had been so windy and dusty today that some times we could scarcely see the length of the team, and it blows so tonight that we cannot set the tent or get any supper, so we take a cold bite and go to bed in the wagons. The wagons are anchored by driving stakes in the ground and fastening the wagon wheels to them with ox chains. . . .*

Perhaps one-tenth of the people who set out on the Oregon Trail never made it to their destination, and fellow travelers noted in their diaries the disturbing presence of graves—sometimes every 80 yards. Many died from diseases such as cholera or from accidents and drownings; others were killed by early winter storms and Indian attacks. Few of the graves are marked.

At the peak of migration in 1850—when California gold fever had struck America—some 55,000 men, women, and children pressed their way across the plains and mountains. One of the lesser-known facts was the two-way nature of the route; in 1851 vast numbers of disillusioned miners headed back east the same way they had come the previous years. The route was also heavily used in both directions by Mormon emigrants to Utah, many of whom returned east for supplies or to guide family members who had been left behind. In addition, stagecoach and freighting operations, along with a limited mail service, were established by 1852, operating in both directions.

It is easy to imagine the impact these wagons had with their thousands of cattle, horses, and mules. The grass quickly became overgrazed under this onslaught, and the already scarce water was badly polluted around popular campsites. Late-summer travelers were forced to range far and wide for better conditions, creating even more paths. The Indians who had lived here were shocked by the magnitude of the migration and began to realize not just what the whites were doing to their buffalo, but also how overwhelmed the native peoples would be by the newcomers. (The entire Plains Indian population probably numbered 40,000 individuals at its peak, and disease and war greatly reduced these numbers.) Indian attacks on Oregon Trail travelers were quite rare, and only 350 emigrants are known to have been killed by Indians. The biggest battles between Indians and Anglos came in 1865, more than a dozen years after the peak of westward travel on the Oregon Trail.

Finale

By 1870, perhaps 350,000 people had traveled across Wyoming by wagon train, stagecoach, horseback, and foot. It was the greatest peacetime migration in history. For most of them, this country seemed a worthless stretch of sagebrush and a barrier to the green lands farther west. It took the railroad to change this perception. Completion of the transcontinental railroad in 1869 turned the Oregon Trail into an anachronism. Suddenly one could cross the nation in relative comfort and in days instead of months. The trail continued to be used by freighters and some pioneers even as late as the turn of the 20th century, but most travelers turned to rail travel. An era had ended.

The Trail Today

It has been well more than 150 years since the first wagon train traveled along the Oregon Trail, but the mystique of the "great migration" continues to draw people from around the world. Much of the trail cuts across publicly owned land, and the tracks are readily visible in many places even after a century and

pulling replicas of Mormon handcarts along the Oregon Trail near Devil's Gate

© DON PITCHER

a half. Explorers still discover artifacts strewn along the way. Visitors to Wyoming will enjoy delving into this rich past at such places as Fort Laramie, Oregon Trail Ruts, Register Cliff, Fort Caspar, Independence Rock, Devil's Gate, South Pass, Names Hill, and Fort Bridger. Hundreds of other lesser sights line the route, from the remains of old trading posts to countless emigrant graves. The recently opened National Historic Trails Center in Casper is a great place to get an in-depth look at the various trails that crossed the West. Portions of the Oregon Trail are described in greater detail in the Southeast, Central, Wind River Mountains, and Southwest chapters of this book. See Outdoor Recreation later in this chapter for descriptions of companies that lead Oregon Trail wagon-train treks.

THE PONY EXPRESS

On April 3, 1860, a lone rider galloped westward from the town of St. Joseph, Missouri. Nearly 2,000 miles away, another rider left the booming city of San Francisco, heading east. One of the most celebrated passages in American history had begun. Although it only lasted 18 months and was a financial disaster, the Pony Express caught the national imagination, proved that rapid mail service was possible even in the winter, and helped keep California in the Union.

The Pony Express was the brainchild of William H. Russell, one of the great wheelers and dealers of the late 19th century and director of the Central Overland California & Pike's Peak Express Company. Russell, along with partners Alexander Majors and William Bradford Waddell, managed the largest freighting company in the West, a business that at one time owned 50,000 oxen for its 3,500 wagons and employed 4,000 workers.

In 1855, the firm of Russell, Majors, & Waddell secured a monopoly to supply all U.S. government military posts west of the Missouri River. Because of Mormon raids on the supply wagons and the failure of the War Department to pay the company for its services, it was soon in financial trouble. To escape, the company

needed the contract for mail service between California and St. Louis, a route then held by the Butterfield Overland Mail Company. Butterfield's route took mail along a circuitous 25-day trek through Texas and Arizona into southern California. With the nation slipping rapidly toward the Civil War—and Texas on the side of the South—there were fears that mail service would be halted and that California might join the Confederacy.

Express Mail

In 1859, the postmaster general signed a contract with Russell, Majors, & Waddell to operate coaches and horses along the central route to California. The Pony Express was born as a flamboyant symbol of the superiority of this route. Experienced young horsemen, some as young as 14 and none weighing more than 120 pounds, would ride the finest horses at a full gallop, carrying telegrams and mail through some of the most desolate land on earth. The trip was to take just 10 days.

Each horse had four mail pouches sewn into a leather *mochilla,* which could be easily transferred between horses. (At $7.50 per half ounce, Pony Express mail was primarily urgent messages and newspapers.) Riders changed horses at relay stations—crude huts with station keepers and stock tenders—every 10 to 15 miles, continuing on for 75–100 miles before passing the precious package to another rider. After a short break, the rider would speed back to his home station with mail headed in the opposite direction. The whole operation required military precision to keep the 119 relay and home stations stocked, make sure the horses were in good condition, and guard against attack. For their work, riders received $120 per month (including room and board).

The Demise

The threat of Indian hostilities became real when Nevada Piutes, angry after decades of abuse and the theft of their land, began attacking white settlements, killing 16 of the men working at the relay stations, taking 150 horses,

PONY EXPRESSIONS

We had had a consuming desire from the beginning, to see a pony-rider, but somehow or other all that passed us and all that met us managed to streak by in the night, and so we heard only a whiz and a hail, and the swift phantom of the desert was gone before we could get our heads out of the windows. But now we were expecting one along every moment, and would see him in broad daylight. Presently the driver exclaims: "HERE HE COMES!"

Every neck is stretched further, and every eye strained wider. Away across the endless dead level of the prairie a black speck appears against the sky, and it is plain that it moves. Well, I should think so! In a second or two it becomes a horse and rider, rising and falling, rising and

falling—sweeping toward us nearer and nearer—growing more and more distinct, more and more sharply defined—nearer and still nearer, and the flutter of the hoofs comes faintly to the ear—another instant a whoop and a hurrah from our upper deck, a wave of the rider's hand, but no reply, and man and horse burst past our excited faces, and go winging away like a belated fragment of a storm!

So sudden is it all, and so like a flash of unreal fancy, that for the flake of white foam left quivering and perishing on a mail-sack after the vision had flashed by and disappeared, we might have doubted whether we had seen any actual horse and man at all, maybe.

—Mark Twain in *Roughing It*

and burning seven stations. A full-scale war was avoided, but it took more than a month to get the Express back into operation, at a cost of $75,000. Already a money loser, this incident helped ensure the collapse of the Pony Express, but it was not just money that brought down the Pony Express. Completion of the first continental telegraph line on October 24, 1861, also contributed; its mission replaced by a much more rapid means of communication, the Pony Express ended just two days later. Riders had delivered 34,753 pieces of mail, losing only one *mochilla* (both horse and rider were killed) in 616 cross-country runs.

The Final Chapter

The story of the Central Overland California & Pike's Peak Express Company does not end here. By late 1860, a year before the Pony Express ceased operations, Russell, Majors, & Waddell's firm already teetered on the verge of bankruptcy (its employees nicknamed it "Clean Out of Cash and Poor Pay"). To stave this off, William Russell

met with a clerk in the U.S. Department of the Interior and received $150,000 in bonds belonging to the Indian Trust Fund. Russell collected more than $870,000 in illegal government funds before being caught.

The whole house of cards came tumbling down when partner Alexander Majors declared bankruptcy and Russell's partner in crime, Godard Bailey, confessed. Russell spent Christmas 1860 in prison, but he somehow managed to escape prosecution, and he never repaid the money. With the start of the Civil War, Congress had greater concerns. In 1861, a joint agreement moved all western mail delivery to the central route, combining the forces of Butterfield's Overland Mail Company with the remnants of the Russell, Majors, & Waddell firm to avoid travel through the Confederate states. Later, Ben Holladay bought the bankrupt firm and transformed it into the Overland Stage Line. Both Russell and Waddell died poor men. Years later, one of the Pony Express riders, "Buffalo Bill" Cody, found Alexander Majors living in a tiny Denver shack. In a gesture typical of him, Cody put Majors on a cash retainer for the rest of his life.

THE OVERLAND TRAIL

Lesser known and shorter lived than the Oregon Trail, the Overland Trail was established by Ben Holladay, owner of the Overland Stage Company. Although the Oregon Trail had served for many years as the primary route west, by the 1860s a need was developing for a new path. Increasing Indian attacks made the Oregon Trail dangerous, and the rapidly growing mining town of Denver was too far away. After Holladay was given the contract to deliver mail to the West, he quickly rerouted travel along a trail originally scouted by Jim Bridger.

The new route proved 60 miles shorter than the Oregon Trail, but it passed directly through the difficult desert country of western Wyoming rather than along the relatively lush North Platte and Sweetwater Rivers. Holladay established stage stations for changing teams every 10–15 miles and built home stations where travelers could stop for meals or lodging every 50 miles. Conditions at these relay stations were primitive at best; one traveler described southwestern Wyoming's Sand Springs station as "roofless and chairless, filthy and squalid, with a smoky fire in one corner, and a table in the center of an impure floor, the walls open to every wind and the interior full of dust." But the stations were better than sitting outside in the blazing hot sun or the bitter winter winds.

The stages covered 100–125 miles in a 24-hour period but were extraordinarily expensive for the time: $500 from Atchison, Kansas, to San Francisco. Still, emigrants began using the new route instead of the Oregon Trail; in a single year (1864), some 17,584 men, women, and children used the Overland Trail, along with 50,000 head of livestock and 4,264 wagons.

Although the new route remained relatively free from attacks for several years, the 1865 Sand Creek Massacre sent Indians on the warpath throughout the plains. Stage stations were destroyed, stagecoaches were attacked, and many died on both sides. The attacks continued sporadically for the next two years. With completion of the transcontinental railroad in 1869, the Overland Stage rapidly faded in importance, and stagecoach service ended. The old Overland Trail continued to be used by wagons until the turn of the 20th century.

CONNECTING THE COASTS

More than any other event, the completion of the transcontinental railroad led to the settlement and development of Wyoming. Most of its major towns and cities originated along the railroad lines. Not only did the railroad bring Wyoming within a couple of days of either coast, but it also led to the opening of coal mines to fuel the engines, hastened development of the logging industry (for railroad ties and mine props), and made it easy to ship cattle to market. Settlers could order almost anything—Sears Roebuck even shipped prefabricated houses that filled two boxcars. It was no coincidence that Wyoming became a territory just as the railroad was being pushed across its southern border. An enduring impact from the railroad is a checkerboard pattern of public and private land ownership along the Union Pacific's route across Wyoming.

Surveying the Route

The Union Pacific's route was planned by Gen. Grenville M. Dodge, a veteran of battles with the Sioux in the Powder River country. The traditional Oregon Trail route ran too close to Sioux country, was too far from the gold-mining city of Denver, and didn't have the rich coal deposits of southwestern Wyoming. The course Dodge chose headed almost straight across southern Wyoming, climbing the Laramie Mountains west of Cheyenne, then cutting through the Laramie Plains and the Red Desert before winding across the mountains of eastern Utah.

Despite Dodge's efforts to avoid direct confrontation with the Indians and the government's diversionary tactic of building the Bozeman Trail through the Powder River country, the Arapaho did not take kindly to the presence of railroad surveying and construction parties in their traditional hunting grounds. They pulled up survey stakes, stole horses, and killed surveyors and loggers, forcing Dodge to request military escorts. Three forts (Russell, Sanders, and Steele) were built in Wyoming to house these troops.

Working on the Railroad

To span the continent, the Union Pacific headed west from Omaha, while the Central Pacific worked east from Sacramento. By July 1867 tracklayers had reached the main division point, which would become Cheyenne, and headed on west to found Laramie, Rawlins, Green River, and Evanston. Most of the Central Pacific's workers were Chinese contract laborers, whereas those on the Union Pacific were a mixture of Americans and emigrants, especially Irishmen. Great competition grew between the two groups, and a record was set as the tracklayers worked across the searing heat of Wyoming's Red Desert: the men laid 7.5 miles of track in a single day. Laborers were paid an extraordinary $2.50 per hour, but the work was equally dangerous; some estimate that the transcontinental railroad was built at the cost of 10 men's lives per one mile of track! Many were buried right in the roadbed. The tracklayers finally pushed their way into Utah and met workers of the Central Pacific at Promontory Point on May 10, 1869.

The railroad brought with it a gang of men who seemed to thrive on corruption, thievery, prostitution, gambling, drunkenness, and murder. As construction moved westward, temporary towns sprang up along the way; many were gone as soon as the tracks were out of sight. The entire procession of construction workers and hangers-on quickly became known as Hell-on-Wheels.

Worst of the temporary frontier towns was Benton, a few miles east of present-day Rawlins. Those who passed through called it "nearer a repetition of Sodom and Gomorrah than any other place in America" and a "congregation of scum and wickedness . . . by day disgusting, by night dangerous." There was no grass, little water, and the alkali dust stood eight inches deep. Murders were a nightly affair at the 25 saloons and five dance halls. The big attraction was gambling, with hundreds of men crowding the big tent each evening, paying for whiskey, dancehall girls, or roulette wheels. Before the short-lived settlement could disappear in the alkali dust—just three months after its founding—more than 100 men lay buried in boot hill.

Newspaper reporter James Chisholm described these men in less than appealing terms:

> *I often speculate on what will finally become of all that rolling scum which the locomotive seems to blow onward as it presses westward. Will they get blown clean off the continent at last into the Pacific Ocean? One is gradually surrounded by the same faces in each successive town, the same gamblers, the same musicians playing the same old tunes to the same old dance, the same females getting always a little more dilapidated. As the excitement dies out of one town, and the railroad leaves it behind in a kind of exhausted repose, these old familiar faces die out to reappear in a new state of existence.*

A rolling newspaper press tagged along with the flotsam and jetsam across Wyoming, printing the weekly *Frontier Index* in each new camp. Its editor, Legh Freeman, angered the primarily northern-born workers by constantly showing his support for the Confederacy; he once labeled Gen. Ulysses Grant "the whiskey bloated, squaw ravishing adulterer, nigger worshipping mogul rejoicing over his election to the presidency." In Bear River City (long gone but near present-day Evanston), Freeman made the mistake of suggesting that several accused murderers then in jail should meet up with Judge Lynch. After a gang of vigilantes followed his suggestion by throwing a necktie party for the three, other ruffians destroyed the *Frontier Index* office and chased its editor out of town.

STATEHOOD

Because of its difficult climate, a paucity of good agricultural lands, and the lack of major deposits of gold, Wyoming was one of the last states to be settled. At various times, portions of

© DON PITCHER

the state capitol in Cheyenne

Ashley introduced a bill to form a "temporary government for the territory of Wyoming." Newspaper editor Legh Freeman has been credited with popularizing the name and having it inserted into the bill that created the Wyoming Territory in 1868.

A triumvirate of politicians—Francis E. Warren, John B. Kendrick, and Joseph M. Carey—governed Wyoming for much of its first half century. Carey, a Republican turned Democrat, was a founder of both the powerful Wyoming Stock Growers Association and the Cheyenne Club. He was a strong proponent of Wyoming statehood and introduced the enabling legislation in the U.S. House. During the debate, he claimed a Wyoming population of more than 110,000 people, an exaggeration that helped sway enough House votes to pass the measure. (The next year, the U.S. census found just 62,555 people in Wyoming.) The act was signed into law by Pres. Benjamin Harrison on July 10, 1890, making Wyoming the 44th state. Interestingly, this was the same year that the director of the U.S. Census Bureau declared that the "frontier of settlement" was no more.

The Equality State

Wyoming's first territorial legislature passed an act granting women the right to vote. The measure was signed into law by Gov. J. A. Campbell on December 10, 1869, making this the first government in the world to grant women the right to vote. (Technically, Wyoming was not the first state to allow women suffrage; New Jersey widows already had limited voting rights.) The name "Equality State" comes from this bold step. It would be another 50 years before the 19th Amendment was finally passed, giving all women in America the right to vote. Not everyone looked upon women's suffrage as such a good step. In 1871, Democrats in the second territorial legislature repealed the measure, then came within one vote of overriding Governor Campbell's veto.

When the territory of Wyoming was seeking admission to the Union in 1890, the issue of giving women the right to vote—a measure included in Wyoming's new constitution—

Wyoming were parts of Indian country, Mexico, Louisiana, Missouri, Texas, Nebraska, Dakota, Idaho, Oregon, and Utah. In 1868, the Wyoming Territory was carved out of the Dakota Territory, a move primarily intended to keep the Democratic voters building the Union Pacific Railroad from overwhelming the Republican power base in distant Yankton. The folks out west were equally happy to gain independence from such a tenuous governmental link. It was not until May 19, 1869, that an organized government was established in the new territory. The first census of Wyoming, in 1870, found just 9,000 people, although the number would have been considerably higher had they counted Indians living in the state.

The word "Wyoming" comes from the Leni Lanape Indians of Pennsylvania; their word "mecheweami-ing" meant "at the Great Plains." The term was first applied to the land that would become Wyoming in 1865, when Ohio's J. M.

BILL NYE ON WOMEN'S SUFFRAGE

There have been many reasons given, first and last, why women should not vote, but I desire to say, in the full light of a ripe experience, that some of them are fallacious. I refer more particularly to the argument that it will degrade women to go to the polls and vote like a little man. While I am not and have never been a howler for female suffrage, I must admit that it is much more of a success than prohibition and speculative science. . . . In Wyoming, where female suffrage has raged for years, you meet quiet, courteous and gallant gentlemen, and fair, quiet, sensible women at the polls, where there isn't a loud or profane word, and where it is an infinitely more proper place to send a young lady unescorted than to the post office in any city in the Union. . . . All these things look hopeful. We can't tell what the Territory would have been without female suffrage, but when they begin to hang men by law instead of by moonlight, the future begins to brighten up. When you have to get up in the night to hang a man every little while and don't get any per diem for it, you feel as though you were a good way from home.

—19th-century humorist Bill Nye

became a hotly contested topic. Alabama's Sen. John T. Morgan led the fight against admitting the new state, with the argument that the other half of the population would be polluted by politicians (such as himself?): "It is the immoral influences of the ballot upon women that I deprecate and would avoid. I do not want to see her drawn in contact with the rude things of this world where the delicacy of her senses and sensitivities would be constantly wounded by the attrition with bad and desperate and foul politicians and men."

Wyoming's status as the home of equal rights took another big step in 1925 after the death of Gov. William B. Ross. His wife, Nellie Tayloe Ross, was nominated to replace him and won the special election on a sympathy vote. She made no effort to get elected, noting, "I shall not make a campaign. My candidacy is in the hands of my friends. I shall not leave the house." She served ably as the nation's first woman governor and achieved considerable national attention. Despite a good record, Ross lost her bid for reelection, primarily because she was a Democrat in a heavily Republican state. In 1933, President Roosevelt appointed her as director of the U.S. Mint, a title she held for the next 20 years. She died in 1967 at the age of 101.

CATTLE COUNTRY

Hardly had the thunder of the Sioux ponies, along the Powder, the thunder of the cavalry died down, when over the southern horizon came a new army. An army of tossing horns, white in the sun; of lithe young men lolling in their saddles; riding at point, on the flanks, on the drag. The Cowboy was coming to Wyoming.

Struthers Burt in Powder River Let 'er Buck

Opening the Range

Once the bison herds had been devastated and the Indians evicted, cattlemen found what seemed like a Garden of Eden in Wyoming: land, grass, and water were essentially free for the taking. The cattle industry began innocently enough. In December 1863, Tom Alsop was returning to Omaha with a train of 50 wagons when a snowstorm pinned them down near present-day Cheyenne. Alsop abandoned the oxen and wagons on the plains and led his men safely home on horseback. The following spring, they rode back to recover the freight and were startled to discover that the cattle they had left to die of exposure had not only survived the winter but were thriving. The discovery soon attracted droves of ranchers.

The first cattle drive through Wyoming came in 1866, when a Montana merchant named Nelson Story decided that what the Virginia City miners needed was fresh beef. Heading south to Kansas with $10,000 sewn in the lining of his clothes, he filled a wagon with supplies, bought 3,000 Texas longhorns, hired 27 cowboys, gave them the finest Remington breech-loading rifles, and headed north for the gold fields. At Fort Kearny (see Sheridan Vicinity in the Powder River Country chapter for more on this notorious fort), Colonel Carrington forbade them from continuing north through Sioux country because they did not have the required 40 armed guards. (Some believe that Carrington actually hoped to requisition the cattle for his men; most of the army's had already been stolen.) In response, an angry Story thumbed his nose at the government, heading north under cover of darkness. Discovering his departure, Carrington was forced to cave in, sending 15 soldiers along to bring Story's force up to the legal minimum. Although one man died, the rest of the men and cattle made it to Virginia City on December 9. Nelson Story had gained himself a place in history.

Millions of cattle headed into or through Wyoming in the 1870s and 1880s. Ranching looked like a can't-lose business; dump a couple thousand head of cows and calves on the range in spring and return a year later to round them up for market. What could be simpler? Investors from Omaha, New York, England, Scotland, and France quickly took note of the potential fortunes to be made.

By 1883, English and Scottish investors had poured some £6 million into Wyoming cattle and had turned Cheyenne into a country club for the European gentry. Some were more gullible than others; stories are still told of an Englishman who watched as the cattle he was buying were driven by to be counted, not noticing that the same cattle had come around the hill a couple of times before. The use of "book counts" also inflated the value of the herds; frequently, nobody bothered to make sure that numbers in the books equaled cattle on the range. The aristocrats were regarded with a mixture of humor and disdain by the hardened cowboys whose every other utterance was a swear word. One British lord rode up to a cowboy in

bull at The Drift, near Pinedale

BRANDS

Branding dates back to the Egyptian pharaohs, who branded not only their cattle, camels, and donkeys, but even their slaves. Slave branding was also practiced in America. The American tradition of cattle branding comes from the Spanish conquistadors and their *vaqueros* but was adapted to the spacious western plains. Because there were no fences, cattle belonging to various ranchers became intermixed, leading to inevitable questions of ownership, which brands helped answer.

Brands appear almost anywhere on an animal, and a given ranch may have a half dozen or more for its cattle, sheep, and horses. An individual animal often bears several different brands or marks. To make them easier to identify on the hoof, cattle are frequently distinctively marked by cutting a notch in the ear, slicing the skin that hangs under the cow's throat (the dewlap), or hacking a flap of hide (a wattle) so that it hangs loose from the neck.

In Wyoming, having a brand is something of a status symbol, and the Wyoming Brand Book lists more than 27,000 currently in use (one for every 18 residents!). Not everyone who has a brand has

stock; some are simply used for mailbox decorations on suburban ranchettes. The more complex ones aren't likely to appear on any cows because they become illegible as the scar heals. Brands that are hard to alter or of historic significance may sell for more than $5,000. Coming up with a design for a new brand can be a problem because the state looks askance on brands that resemble others in the same area or that might be easily altered by rustlers (they still exist). One 19th-century rancher, fed up with having his brand suggestions rejected, wrote the brand department, demanding, "Send me a brand P.D.Q." They complied by giving him the brand PDQ. Reading brands is an art gained by years of experience. They are read from left to right, top to bottom, and outside to inside.

Branding usually takes place in the spring, before cattle and calves are driven into the higher pastures or set loose on the plains. A branding iron is heated to a dull red in a fire and then pressed against the calf as it is held down. Freeze branding is also often used. Most male calves are castrated at the same time.

---

his buggy, asking, "My good man, could you tell me where your master is?" The cowboy glowered back, spat out his tobacco, and proclaimed, "The son-of-a-bitch ain't been born yet!"

During the early years of ranching in Wyoming, cattle were allowed to roam at will and were not sorted out until the annual roundups. Sounds fine in theory, but in practice a few flaws showed up, notably the problem of mavericks. The term "maverick" refers to an unbranded calf or cow of questionable ownership or, as writer Struthers Burt put it: "A calf whose mamma has died and whose father has run off with another lady cow." Unbranded calves were generally divvied up among the ranchers on the basis of which herd they were with, but when herds became mixed together, conflicts were inevitable. In addition, multiple roundups meant that the first cowboys on the scene could pretty much decide for themselves which calves were theirs. Some even went so far as to slit the tongues of calves so they could no longer suckle

and would not follow their mothers, thus becoming instant mavericks.

Cattle Barons and Rustlers

To curb the temptations for such "sooners," the powerful Wyoming Stock Growers Association—an organization dominated by the wealthiest of the cattlemen—gained the authority to dictate when roundups could be held. The organization dominated the political landscape of Wyoming for many years; by the 1880s, one-third of the state legislature belonged to the association. The 1882 Maverick Bill gave the association control over all cattle roundups in the territory, with proceeds from the sales of mavericks going into the association's coffers. It could blacklist cowboys as "rustlers" on the basis of hearsay, and cattle shipped without the association's permission risked being impounded by inspectors in Chicago or Omaha. Even worse, ranchers suspected of rustling (which seemed to include anyone except members) were sometimes ambushed and murdered by enforcers, the most notorious of whom was Tom Horn. Whole regions of Wyoming were terrorized by the practice of dry-gulching, in which suspected rustlers would be shot from behind and left in an out-of-the-way gulch.

Meanwhile, the big cattlemen—commonly called cattle barons—also ran into trouble, especially in the Powder River country. The fierce winter of 1886–1887 devastated their herds; some lost all of their cattle, whereas others had just 20–30 percent of the numbers from the previous year. Big ranching outfits also found themselves hemmed in by homesteading settlers who fenced the land. Fences created a hazard because cattle often moved with the winter winds until they hit the fences and then piled up there to die.

The big cattlemen accused these "nesters" not only of fencing the land but also of taking stray cattle for themselves. Using a "long rope" and a "running iron," they could easily alter the brands and soon have their own herd. The cattle barons decided to put an end to this thievery once and for all with the infamous Johnson County War of 1892, but the campaign proved a complete fiasco. Two men died on each side in pitched battles between the "barons" and the "rustlers." Although the invaders managed to escape prosecution, the small nesters and rustlers had won the day. From that time on, the range would increasingly be fenced in.

SHEEP
History
Cattle arrived in most parts of Wyoming a decade or so before the first sheep munched their way across the grazing lands, but by 1902 the rangeland was crowded with close to six million sheep. Cattlemen considered the public land their own—by right of previous use—although legally it was all open range owned by the government. As competition increased, cattlemen declared "dead lines," across which no sheep would be allowed. Conflicts quickly erupted, and the single herder and his dogs proved no match for a gang of cattlemen on

horseback. Herders were murdered throughout the state, and the violence escalated into the infamous Ten Sleep Raid of 1909, in which three sheepmen were brutally murdered. After this, things quieted down as the land became increasingly settled and government policies divided up the areas. Some cattlemen even turned to raising sheep, but animosity still remains between sheepmen and cattlemen in some areas.

Times have not always been easy for herders. Alfred Mokler in *History of Natrona County* describes one horrific night:

> *During a severe storm the latter part of March 1895, Noel R. Gascho was with a band of sheep on the open range. The band became unmanageable and drifted with the storm. Gascho went with the sheep, which was the only thing to do. The snow came down in blinding sheets, the cold wind swept over the bleak prairie and hundreds of the sheep were frozen. Gascho said it seemed as though the blood in his veins and the marrow in his bones were frozen. He became numb and sleepy and to keep awake he would stick his legs with a knife blade. About midnight he caught one of the sheep, cut its throat and drank the blood. Then he set fire to the wool on the dead sheep and the greasy wool burned readily. Before daylight, he had burned six sheep after he had cut their throats and drank of their blood. This was all that saved his life.*

Sheepherding
Over the years, the number of sheep in Wyoming has steadily dropped; today there are about 660,000 at any given time. Sheep are generally moved up into the mountains each spring to graze in the high meadows and then brought back down in the fall. A long drive along country roads is a sight straight out of the history books. Sheep are sheared in spring, generally just before lambing season. By fall the lambs are big enough to send to market, and the ewes are bred.

Many of the first sheepherders in Wyoming were from Europe's Basque region. Many preferred to take sheep instead of a salary and so gradually gained flocks of their own. The frugal ones eventually became ranch owners in their own right. The herding business has not changed much over the years, however, and herders still spend weeks at a time alone, seeing nobody but the camp mover when he arrives to help move the outfit to new feeding grounds. Today many herders are Mexican immigrants, although some Basque and American herders are still around. The herder's life is a simple and quiet one, with plenty of time for reflection. It takes someone with the right temperament to be a sheepherder.

The sheepherder's wagon—an early version of the RV—was invented by James Candlish, a Rawlins blacksmith, and later improved and marketed by Casper's Schulte Hardware Company. The design proved an efficient one, and herders still use the old wagons, although rubber tires have replaced wagon wheels and the roof is now tin instead of canvas. The layout is simple: a Dutch door opens into a small space filled with a bed at the back with drawers underneath and shelves above. A small woodstove near the entrance is used for both heating and cooking. Almost every Wyoming museum seems to have one of these wagons tucked away in a corner, but quite a few are still in use on the lonely high plains.

ENERGY BOOM AND BUST

Wyoming's economy is heavily linked to the energy industry, with coal, oil, and gas all major employers. The state's first oil well was drilled in 1884, and by 1908—the year of the first oil boom—production approached 18,000 barrels per year. Production continued to climb over the decades, reaching a peak in 1970, when more than 155 million barrels were pumped. Since then, oil production has declined sharply as older fields have become exhausted, and by 2002, production had fallen below 60 million barrels.

The drop in oil production has been offset by dramatic increases in two other energy sources: natural gas and coal. Coal production, particularly in the Powder River Basin, has skyrocketed in the last two decades, topping 370 million tons in 2002. Wyoming is easily the nation's biggest coal-producing state, with nearly all of this being used in power plants. Natural gas is the latest boom, as thousands of wells are being drilled to extract coalbed methane in the Basin.

In the 1970s and '80s, Wyoming rode an economic bucking bronco as oil prices shot up and then suddenly dove, throwing this energy-rich state out of the saddle. The Arab oil embargo of 1973 and subsequent price increases turned Wyoming upside down. Oil-patch towns—particularly Casper, Rock Springs, Evanston, and Green River—became madhouses of pickup trucks, heavily muscled oil workers, honky-tonk bars, strip joints, fast-food outlets, and trailer courts. Drugs, crime, prostitution, and gambling rippled across the state. The population of Rock Springs doubled in two years. In the heady rush of new workers and high-paying oil jobs, many towns embarked on ambitious construction projects such as schools and housing developments, while trailer parks sprouted up across the countryside. (Wyoming still holds top honors as the state with the highest percentage of mobile homes.)

This economic bubble collapsed with the sudden halving of oil prices in 1982, and Wyoming's population actually *dropped* by almost 3 percent during the 1980s. The bust left many towns struggling to survive as unemployment skyrocketed, the state government was forced into consolidation mode, and local residents were saddled with a bloated set of facilities.

The inevitable booms and busts associated with the energy and mining industries will affect Wyoming for the foreseeable future, but growing numbers of tourism and service-sector jobs will help cushion the blows next time around. The money may not approach that of the $24-per-hour coal mining jobs, but at least a sales position at Wal-Mart pays the bills.

Economy and Government

Wyoming's economy grew slowly in the 1990s and has been doing a bit better in the last couple of years. The state's population grew almost 9 percent over the last decade and may finally top 500,000 in this decade. Some parts of the state, especially where agriculture is a mainstay, have not done well of late, and the population has actually declined. Northwest Wyoming, particularly Jackson Hole, continues to prosper from increasing tourism, and Teton County now has the highest per capita income of any county in the nation. The Powder River Basin of northeast Wyoming is another bright spot as coal mining and coalbed methane production bring jobs to the area. In addition, the stable cities of Cheyenne, Casper, and Laramie are all doing fine on a mix of government and private-sector jobs.

Who Owns Wyoming?

Wyoming's economy is affected not only by private developments but also by the government. The federal government owns almost 47 percent of the land, while the state government holds another 10 percent, leaving 43 percent in private hands. The largest public land agency—the Bureau of Land Management (BLM)—owns nearly 18 million acres in Wyoming, but most of this exists in a checkerboard of small parcels with limited public access. The BLM manages only a few patches of wilderness scattered around Wyoming. The U.S. Forest Service has 8.7 million acres within nine national forests that cover the state's largest mountain ranges, and the National Park Service has another 2.3 million acres in five national parks, monuments, and recreation areas. Warren Air Force Base—the most important intercontinental ballistic missile (ICBM) base in North America—is in Cheyenne and represents the state's only major military installation. The military also owns land in other parts of Wyoming today, notably the Camp Guernsey training area north of Wheatland and a Naval Petroleum Reserve at Teapot Dome.

Partly because of all this federal involvement, Wyoming residents are on the receiving end of generous federal monies; the state is second only to Alaska in per capita federal aid. Interestingly, both states are also rich in oil and gas, have most of their land in federal ownership, are small in population, and suffered similar economic doldrums through the 1990s. You'll meet quite a few former Alaskans in Wyoming and an equal number of former Wyomingites in Alaska. Coincidence?

WORKING FOR A LIVING

Oil and Gas

Wyoming's economy putters along on a mixture of oil and gas extraction, coal and trona mining, cattle and sheep ranching, and tourism. Oil production—mainly in the Powder River and Bighorn Basins—has long been the most important source of income, but it is increasingly being eclipsed by coal mining and natural gas production. Despite the recent decrease, some 1,000 Wyoming fields produce 58 million barrels of oil annually, sixth in the nation. Gas production has followed the opposite path in recent years, as production of coalbed methane has come to the fore. Today, Wyoming produces more than 1.3 billion cubic feet of natural gas annually, third in the nation.

Coal

One-quarter of the nation's coal reserves lie beneath Wyoming, and it is easily the largest coal-producing state, far outstripping (pun intended) runners-up West Virginia and Kentucky. Nearly all of the more than 370 million tons extracted each year comes from enormous open-pit mines, primarily in the Powder River Basin. With perhaps one *trillion* tons of coal still below the surface, Wyoming is one of the largest energy storehouses anywhere on the planet. Eight of the nation's ten largest coal mines are in Wyoming, and the low-sulfur coal produced is shipped by train to utility companies in 29 different states.

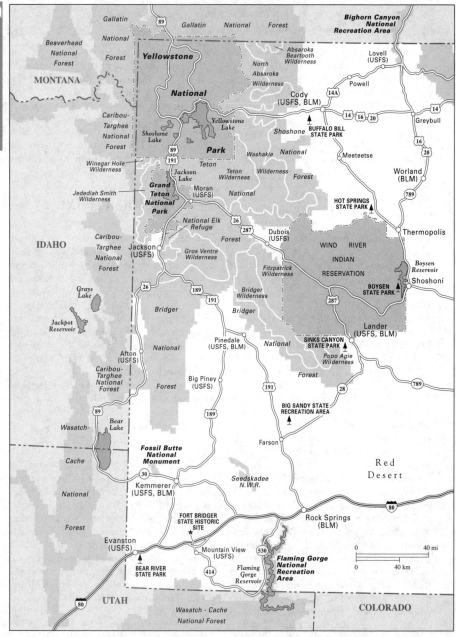

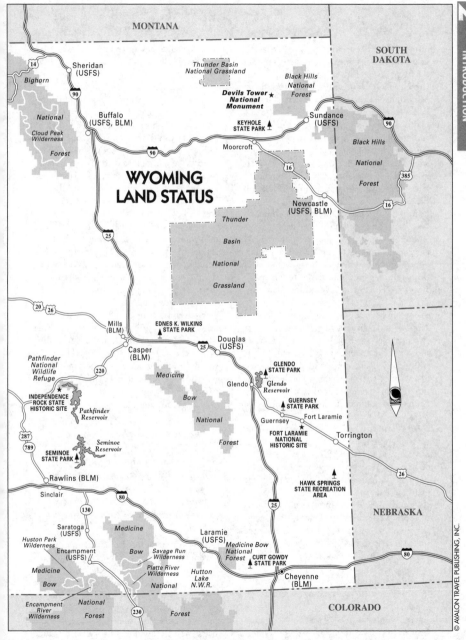

MONTANA

SOUTH
DAKOTA

Sheridan
(USFS)

Bighorn

Thunder Basin
National Grassland

Black Hills
National
Forest

National

Cloud Peak
Wilderness

Forest

Buffalo
(USFS, BLM)

Devils Tower ★
National
Monument

KEYHOLE
STATE PARK

Sundance
(USFS)

Black Hills

National

Forest

Moorcroft

**WYOMING
LAND STATUS**

Newcastle
(USFS, BLM)

Thunder

Basin

National

Grassland

Mills
(BLM)

EDNES K. WILKINS
STATE PARK

Douglas
(USFS)

Casper
(BLM)

Pathfinder
National
Wildlife
Refuge

Medicine

INDEPENDENCE
ROCK STATE
HISTORIC SITE

Pathfinder
Reservoir

Bow

GLENDO
STATE PARK

Glendo

Glendo
Reservoir

National

GUERNSEY
STATE PARK

Seminoe
Reservoir

Forest

Guernsey

Fort Laramie

SEMINOE
STATE PARK

FORT LARAMIE
NATIONAL
HISTORIC SITE

Torrington

Rawlins (BLM)

Sinclair

HAWK SPRINGS
STATE RECREATION
AREA

NEBRASKA

Saratoga
(USFS)

Medicine

Laramie
(USFS)

Huston Park
Wilderness

Encampment
(USFS)

Bow

Savage Run
Wilderness

Medicine Bow
National
Forest

CURT GOWDY
STATE PARK

Medicine

Platte River
Wilderness

Hutton
Lake
N.W.R.

Bow

National

Cheyenne
(BLM)

Encampment
River
Wilderness

National

Forest

COLORADO

WYOMING LINGO

Absaroka—Alternatively pronounced ab-SOR-ka or ab-SOR-aka, the word means "People of the Large-beaked Bird" (hence the name of the Crow Indians, who lived here). The Absaroka Mountains lie east of Yellowstone National Park.

Arapaho—The word is often spelled Arapahoe. An Indian tribe of Algonquin stock originally living on the Canadian plains, the Northern Arapaho now reside on the Wind River Reservation. The name comes from a Crow Indian term meaning "Tattooed People." They call themselves simply "Our People."

bentonite—A special kind of clay that originates from volcanic ash, bentonite absorbs large amounts of water, increasing in volume by 30 percent. Bentonite is used in oil drilling, to line ponds, and even in candy bars. Wyoming is the nation's largest producer of this mineral.

booshway—The boss at a mountain-man rendezvous.

buck-and-rail fence—Consisting of X-shaped supports and connecting poles, this is the classic fence of Jackson Hole, where the soils proved too rocky for ranchers to dig postholes. The abundant lodgepole pines made fine fences. Today, buck-and-rail fences are built more for beauty than function, and they are becoming less and less common in an era of metal fence posts.

calcutta—The auctioning off of various rodeo teams or contestants; it's a popular way to wager on rodeo events. Rules vary.

cattle baron—A cattle owner with extensive holdings; primarily used during the heyday of the giant cattle spreads in the 1880s.

cattle guard—Although immediately obvious to most Westerners, cattle guards are virtually unknown on the East Coast. These wide metal grates are used where fence lines and roads meet; cattle and horses won't cross them but vehicles can do so easily.

chaps—Pronounced SHAPS; protective leather leg coverings, useful when riding horses through brush.

chiselers—Ground squirrels, also called "ground cougars." The lemmings of Wyoming, they seem to delight in waiting until the last minute and then dashing toward car wheels. Lots of them get nailed on dirt roads all across the state.

coup—Pronounced COO; a Plains Indian word that signified an act of great skill and daring, such as striking an enemy in the midst of a battle or performing some other deed of valor. "Counting coups" was similar to gaining today's military medals of honor. Those with many coups wore warbonnets with many feathers.

coyotes—Fans of these ubiquitous critters call them ky-O-tees, whereas those who regard them as "varmints" tend to pronounce the word KY-oats.

creek—Everyone knows what it is, but old-timers in Wyoming pronounce the word CRIK.

dead line—A line established by turn-of-the-20th-century cattlemen who feared competition from sheep. Those herders who brought sheep across the imaginary line risked death and the destruction of their flocks.

dogger—A rodeo term used for steer wrestlers; it originated from Will Pickett, an early wrestler who threw steers to the ground by biting their lips in the manner of a bulldog. The name stuck, even though the lip-biting part didn't.

dogie—A motherless calf. A famous old cowboy poem begins:

As I walked out one morning for pleasure,
I spied a cowpuncher all riding alone;
His hat was throwed back and his spurs
*   was a-jingling,*
As he approached me a-singin' this song,
Whoopee ti yi yo, git along, little dogies,
It's your misfortune, and none of my own.
Whoopee ti yi yo, git along, little dogies,
For you know Wyoming will be your new
*   home . . .*

dog-trot—A type of log cabin common on old Wyoming ranches. Two cabins were connected by a breezeway, making a favorite place for dogs to hang out on hot summer days. This cabin style actually originated in the southern Appalachians.

dude—This term has changed meaning over the years. Writer Nathaniel Burt called the dude "any fancy-pants young man who wore a boutonniere and parted his hair in the middle." Later, the term came to mean a wealthy easterner vacationing on a western ranch, in contradistinction to "tourists," who were viewed as an inferior species. Today, Wyoming's many dude ranches are more proletarian. The wealthy elite generally prefer the term "guest ranches," which are really luxury resorts with a few horses thrown in.

emigrants—The dictionary defines emigrants as people who leave one place to settle elsewhere, in contrast to immigrants, who come into a new place. Guess it all depends on your perspective, but for some reason folks heading west on the Oregon Trail were almost always called emigrants, not immigrants.

hazer—A rodeo term used in steer wrestling. It refers to a cowboy who rides beside the steer to keep it in position for the dogger.

hog ranch—An establishment of ill repute where booze, gambling, and loose women were the primary attractions. The most famous were located near military forts in Wyoming, notably Fort Fetterman and Fort Laramie. The name is generally attributed to the appearance of the women but may also refer to the tiny, squalid rooms where they plied their trade. Author David Lavender called them places offering "the poorest whiskey and women in the west."

hooey—A tie used in calf-roping events at rodeos. Three of the calf's feet are wrapped with a piggin' string and completed with a half hitch.

jackalope—An antlered jackrabbit found most commonly in the vicinity of Douglas, Wyoming, but proliferating throughout the West.

maverick—An unbranded cow or calf of questionable ownership. The term originated from Samuel Maverick, owner of a two-million-acre Texas ranch in the 1840s. Because many of his cattle were never branded, cowboys coming across unbranded cattle on the open range would joke that they were Maverick's. Eventually the term was applied to all unbranded cattle.

piggin' string—A short piece of rope used to tie a hooey around the feet of a roped calf or steer at a rodeo.

rendezvous—French for "appointed place of meeting." Between 1825 and 1840 the annual rendezvous was the big shindig for Rocky Mountain trappers, Indians, and traders. Modern-day versions try to re-create this trading and partying atmosphere.

runnin' iron—An improvised branding iron used by cattle rustlers.

rustler—A cattle thief or someone accused of taking cattle from the cattle barons; during the Johnson County War the term actually became a badge of honor in parts of Wyoming. "Packing a long rope" became the common term applied to folks who rustled.

sage hen—Another name for the sage grouse, a common bird across Wyoming. This was also cowboy slang for women.

scoria—A red rock commonly used on Powder River Basin roads. It was formed when coal beds caught fire and burned underground, baking adjacent shale and sandstone to create a bright red slag. The red comes from iron oxide. *Clinker* is another term commonly used for scoria.

Shoshone—An Indian tribe on Wyoming's Wind River Reservation. The word is also frequently spelled Shoshoni, and it's generally pronounced with a long *e* at the end.

Sioux—The word was derived from a derogatory term meaning "enemy" or "snake" and used by the Chippewa Indians to describe the Indians who lived just to their west. The Sioux actually called themselves Dakota, meaning "alliance of friends."

trona—A mineral (sodium sesquicarbonate) used in glass, detergents, baking soda, and other products. It's mined in huge underground mines west of Green River.

varmint—Any animal you don't like; especially used for prairie dogs, ground squirrels, and coyotes.

wapiti—Pronounced WOP-a-tee. The Indian word for elk, it is occasionally used by biologists who consider it a more precise term.

Other Minerals

Vast deposits of trona (used primarily in glass and chemicals such as baking soda) occur in southwestern Wyoming, where mines produce 90 percent of the nation's supply. The state is also a major supplier of bentonite, helium, and sulfur. Uranium was once an important industry—one-third of America's reserves lie in Wyoming—but since the incident at Three Mile Island, production has dropped to almost nothing.

Tourism

Well more than four million people come to enjoy Wyoming's abundant recreational opportunities each year, and tourism contributes more than $1.3 billion annually to the economy. It is particularly important in northwestern Wyoming, where Yellowstone and Grand Teton National Parks and other attractions are creating a booming Jackson Hole economy (and astronomical land valuations). Lesser levels of growth are taking place in other near-the-mountain towns such as Cody, Sheridan, Buffalo, Laramie, Pinedale, Dubois, Lander, and Saratoga.

Agriculture

The state's most obvious industry—and the one that encompasses 90 percent of its land base—is agriculture. Surprisingly, however, grazing and farming employ just 1.5 percent of the population. Wyoming is third in the nation in terms of sheep and lamb production and has 1.5 million cattle and calves. But it takes 30 acres to support a single cow (versus one acre per cow in parts of Nebraska!), which is why the average Wyoming farm is 3,761 acres—eight times the national average. Only four percent of the state is cultivated; primary crops are sugar beets, barley, alfalfa hay, wheat, oats, and dry beans. These are mainly grown within Bighorn Basin and Wind River Basin and along Wyoming's eastern plains.

Other Economic Mainstays

The state has no truly large manufacturing plants, although every town has its own specialty. The services sector of the economy—from flipping burgers to running copy machines—is the unheralded source of real growth in Wyoming, although the wages are nothing to brag about.

For detailed state economic information (including an annual almanac), visit the Wyoming Department of Administration and Information's website: http://eadiv.state.wy.us.

POLITICS

During the campaign in those days there were always a great many "doubtful voters," and it sometimes required several quarts of liquor and an unlimited number of cigars to convince them.

Alfred J. Mokler, describing the 1898 election campaign for Frank W. Mondell, running for U.S. Senate (he won)

Unlike in many states, where apathy reigns, Wyomingites take their right to vote seriously, with turnout during presidential election years sometimes topping 80 percent of registered voters. Wyoming has 64 elected state representatives (who serve two-year terms) and 30 state senators (elected for four-year terms). The elected statewide officials—governor, secretary of state, auditor, treasurer, and superintendent of public instruction—all stand for office every four years.

Republicans have controlled both houses of the legislature almost since statehood; Wyoming's congressional delegation has long been entirely Republican, and in 1994, for the first time in nearly two decades, Wyoming voted in a Republican governor, creating what is essentially a one-party government. Sierra Club members and other liberals might want to keep a low profile in most parts of Wyoming.

State Symbols

The Great Seal of the State of Wyoming is filled with symbolism. The two dates commemorate establishment of the territorial government (1869) and statehood (1890). The Roman numerals (XLIV) represent Wyoming as the 44th state to be admitted to the Union; the male figures represent the livestock and mining industries, while the central female figure stands for political equality. In early versions the woman was unclothed, but legislators quickly sensed the problems inherent in nudity on Wyoming's official emblem and rejected the design. After a swath of cloth made everything acceptable, the symbol was finally adopted by the state legislature in 1893. The state flag includes both this symbol and the outline of a bison.

Wyoming's best-known symbol is its bucking horse, a figure that has appeared on state license plates since 1936. The silhouette was created by artist Allen True of Denver and was reputedly inspired by the rodeo cowboy Albert "Stub" Farlow. The bucking horse insignia was used earlier by Wyoming soldiers during World War I.

Despite jokes to the contrary, Wyoming's state tree is *not* the telephone pole! Wyoming has all kinds of other official designations: state flower (Indian paintbrush), bird (meadowlark), tree (plains cottonwood), stone (jade), mammal (bison), fossil (a fish called *knightia*), fish (cutthroat trout), and even a state dinosaur (Triceratops). The state nickname seems to suffer from a split personality, being both "Equality State" and "Cowboy State." (To be honest, this really isn't a contest; I'll be the first to tell you that in the hearts and minds of all true Wyomingites, it's the COWBOY STATE.)

On the Road

Outdoor Recreation

Wyoming is famous for its great outdoors, with horizon-to-horizon vistas and an extraordinary variety of activities. The biggest attractions are Yellowstone and Grand Teton National Parks, but other National Park Service, U.S. Forest Service, Bureau of Land Management (BLM), and state park lands offer an array of adventures, from whitewater rafting to horseback riding to skiing.

Note that some popular Forest Service sites in Wyoming and elsewhere now charge a $3 fee for day-use access. Eighty percent of this money goes back to maintaining the area where it is collected, so you can at least be assured that it isn't being wasted on the salaries of Wyoming's congressional delegation. A useful web source for recreation on Wyoming public lands is www.recreation.gov, where you'll find quick links to many federal agencies.

FISHING AND HUNTING

Outstanding fishing opportunities abound throughout Wyoming, and several places—mostly in the Yellowstone area—have attained recognition as some of the finest in America.

Highway 22, near Wilson

© DON PITCHER

Cutthroat, brown, rainbow, brook, and lake trout are favorites of many anglers, but the state's waters also contain mountain whitefish, kokanee, grayling, channel catfish, smallmouth bass, largemouth bass, and others.

The Wyoming Game and Fish Department produces an excellent, free *Wyoming Fishing Guide,* with descriptions of the various river drainages, what fish you can catch in each, state record fish, and basic information on techniques, access, and maps. It's available in visitors centers across the state.

Licenses

Nonresident fishing permits cost $10 for one day or $65 for a season. Resident fishing licenses are $15 for the year. Nonresident youths (ages 14–19) pay $15 for the year ($3 for resident youths). With the exception of the one-day rate, all of these prices include a mandatory $10 conservation stamp in addition to the cost of the permit. Kids younger than 14 don't need a license if they're with an adult who has a valid fishing license. Purchase permits at most sporting-goods stores or from Game and Fish offices. Note that the Wind River Indian Reservation and Yellowstone National Park have their own regulations and permits; see appropriate sections of this book for details. Report fishing violations and illegal fish stocking by calling 800/442-4331. For detailed fishing and hunting information, contact the **Wyoming Game and Fish Department,** 307/777-4600 or 800/548-9453, http://gf.state.wy.us.

An exceptionally helpful online source for fishing information is the private **Wyoming Fishing Network,** www.wyomingfishing.net. Here you'll find details on where to fish, lures, local guides, and up-to-date fishing reports for various rivers and lakes.

Wyoming game laws are enforced with a vengeance, so out-of-state hunters must be sure they know and obey the regulations thoroughly. Access to private land is often available only for a fee, and trespassers are subject to stringent prosecution. For guided hunts, contact the **Wyoming Outfitters and Guides Association,** 307/527-7453, www.wyoga.org.

ON THE SNOW

Downhill Skiing and Snowboarding

Alpine skiing and snowboarding enthusiasts will be pleased to find developed facilities at 11 different Wyoming locations. The finest and largest are in the Jackson area: Jackson Hole, Grand Targhee, and Snow King. Other midsize ski areas include Snowy Range (west of Laramie), Hogadon (near Casper), Sleeping Giant (west of Cody), Big Horn (east of Ten Sleep), and Antelope Butte (east of Greybull). More limited facilities can be found at Pine Creek (east of Cokeville), White Pine (near Pinedale), and Snowshoe Hollow (near Afton). See the appropriate chapters for descriptions of each of these places. During the winter months you can call the Wyoming Division of Tourism at 800/225-5996 for the statewide ski report, or visit its website, www.wyomingtourism.org.

Cross-Country Skiing

Skinny-skiers have an overwhelming choice of places to ski in Wyoming. The only developed Nordic areas are around Jackson Hole, but all of the mountain ranges fill with deep snow and provide inexhaustible opportunities for discovery.

Groomed ski trails are maintained in mountain country all across the state, with notable cross-country ski areas near the following towns: Afton, Buffalo, Casper, Cody, Douglas, Dubois, Encampment, Evanston, Jackson, Lander, Laramie, Pinedale, Saratoga, Sheridan, South Pass, Sundance, and Ten Sleep. In addition, Yellowstone and Grand Teton National Parks have world-class skiing, although the trails are not groomed. See specific chapters for details on all of these cross-country skiing places.

Snowmobiling

Wyoming has one of the most extensive snowmobile trail systems in America, covering more than 2,000 miles. The most popular snowmobile areas lie on national forest lands in the mountains of northwestern Wyoming, in the Medicine Bow Mountains, the Wind River Range, the Big Horn Mountains, and the Laramie Range. Best known is the 365-mile

BEST OF WYOMING

It isn't just the spectacular places in Wyoming—Yellowstone, the Tetons, Devils Tower—that make it wonderful. It's also the absence of such spectacles, the lack of "sights," the lack of people, the lack of civilization. This is a land of rutted dirt roads and a sky that envelops it all. The following places offer a cross section of Wyoming's delights. This highly selective list features just a few of the many places worth exploring; this book is filled with hundreds of others.

The "Biggies" Everyone Should See

Yellowstone National Park
Grand Teton National Park
Jackson Hole
Buffalo Bill Historical Center
Devils Tower National Monument
Fort Laramie
Big Horn Mountains
Hot Springs State Park
Wind River Mountains
Bighorn Canyon National Recreation Area
Snowy Range

Lesser-Known Attractions Well Worth a Look

Ayres Natural Bridge
Black Hills
Casper Mountain
Castle Gardens
Flaming Gorge National Recreation Area
Fort Bridger
Fossil Butte National Monument
Frontier Prison
Guernsey State Park
Hell's Half Acre
Independence Rock
Killpecker Dunes
Little Snake River Museum
Medicine Lodge State Park
Medicine Wheel
Mormon Handcart Visitors Center
National Historic Trails Interpretive Center
National Museum of Wildlife Art
Oregon Trail ruts
Sacagawea Cemetery
St. Stephens Mission
Sierra Madre Range
Snake River Canyon
South Pass City
Sunlight Basin
Trail Town
Vedauwoo Rocks
Wyoming Territorial Park

Interesting Offbeat Attractions

Accidental Oil Company, Newcastle
CallAir Museum, Afton
Charcoal kilns, Piedmont
Crimson Dawn Museum, Casper Mountain
Eagle Bronze Foundry, Lander
Easter Island statue, Rock Springs
Elk antler arch, Afton
Elk antler arches, Jackson
Jackalope statue, Douglas
J. C. Penney house, Kemmerer
Joss house, Evanston
Little America
Midwest-area pumpjacks
Mother Featherlegs monument, Lusk area
Star Valley Cheese factory, Thayne
Torrington Livestock Auction
Windfarm, Arlington
World's "Oldest" Building, Como Bluff
Wright-area coal mines

Great Country Roads

Bitter Creek Rd. between Smoot and Fairview

Grays Loop Rd. (gravel) east of Afton

Little Sandy Rd. (partly gravel) between Farson and Boulder

Pass Creek Rd. (gravel) between Elk Mountain and State Hwy. 130

Piedmont Rd. between Piedmont and Robertson

Red Gulch Scenic Byway between Shell and Hyattville

Sinks Canyon Rd. (partly gravel) between Lander and Atlantic City

State Hwy. 24 between Devils Tower and Aladdin

State Hwy. 70 between Encampment and Baggs

State Hwy. 89 between Cokeville and Alpine

State Hwy. 211 between Chumwater and Cheyenne

State Hwy. 215 between Pine Bluffs and LaGrange

State Hwy. 230 between Laramie and Encampment

State Hwy. 270 between Hartville and Manville

State Hwy. 296 through Sunlight Basin

State Hwy. 414 between Mountain View and Manila

State Hwy. 487 through Shirley Basin

US Hwy. 14/16 between Ucross and Gillette

US Hwy. 14/16/20 between Cody and Yellowstone

US Hwy. 16 between Worland and Buffalo

US Hwy. 18/85 between Newcastle and Lusk

US Hwy. 212 between Cooke City and Red Lodge

US Hwy. 287 between Fort Washakie and Dubois

US Hwy. 26/287 between Dubois and Moran Junction

US Hwys. 14 and 14A over the Big Horn Mountains

Fascinating Small Towns

Aladdin

Atlantic City

Buffalo

Dayton

Dubois

Elk Mountain

Encampment

Esterbrook

Fort Washakie

Jay Em

Kelly

Medicine Bow

Meeteetse

Saratoga

Sundance

Superior

Ten Sleep

Wilson

**Wyoming Ghost Towns
(or Almost Ghost Towns)**

Battle (Medicine Bow)

Cambria (Black Hills)

Carbon (Medicine Bow)

Crosby (Bighorn Basin)

Cumberland (Southwest Wyoming)

Gebo (Bighorn Basin)

Hillsboro (Bighorn Basin)

Jay Em (Southeast Wyoming)

Jeffrey City (Wind River Mountains)

Kirwin (Bighorn Basin)

Old Jelm (Medicine Bow)

Miner's Delight (Wind River Mountains)

Piedmont (Southwest Wyoming)

South Pass (Wind River Mountains)

Sunrise (Southeast Wyoming)

Superior (Southwest Wyoming)

ON THE ROAD

Continental Divide Snowmobile Trail, stretching from Lander around the Wind River Mountains and then north through Grand Teton National Park (this section is quite controversial) to Yellowstone.

Snowmobile trail maps and registration information are available from local visitors centers, or call 307/777-6560 for the nearest place to purchase permits. For trail conditions around the state, call 307/777-7777 or 800/225-5996, and ask for the snowmobile hotline. Snowmobile rentals are available in most mountain towns; see appropriate sections of this book for specifics. Find detailed snowmobile info—and current trail reports—on the web at http://wyotrails.state.wy.us/snow.

RIDING INTO HISTORY

Several businesses attempt to re-create the days of the great westward migration with wagon trips along the historic Oregon Trail and in other historic areas. The trips are all-inclusive, with horses, meals, tents, and other gear provided; you'll need to bring a sleeping bag. They are typically limited to small groups, with a maximum of 12 or so on horseback trips. Wagon trains are larger—as were the original wagon trains—and may have up to 30 people.

Wild Bunch Ride

A unique way to discover the Old West is the **Outlaw Trail Ride** in late July and early August. This six-day, 100-mile trip follows the Outlaw Trail from the Hole-in-the-Wall country of Butch Cassidy and the "Wild Bunch" to Thermopolis. You'll need to bring your own horse (although they can be rented), a bedroll, and personal supplies, but excellent meals are provided, along with nightly entertainment and horse feed. There's a limit of 100 riders. Get additional information on this authentic not-for-profit adventure at 307/864-2287 or 888/362-7433, www.trib.com/~outlaw.

Wagon and Horseback Treks

Several companies offer Conestoga wagon or horseback trips across various parts of Wyoming, including the Oregon Trail. These typically last 5–7 days and include horses, meals, equipment, and tents, but you'll need a sleeping bag (or they'll rent one to you). For details on the many op-

North Fork Meadows, Teton Wilderness

© DON PITCHER

tions, contact: **Great Divide Tours,** 307/332-3123 or 800/458-1915, www.dtoutfitting.com; **Western Encounters,** 307/332-5434 or 800/572-1230, www.horseriders.com; **Historic Trails West,** 307/266-4868 or 800/327-4052, www.historictrailswest.com; or **Wagons A+Cross Wyoming,** 307/859-8629 or 888/818-3581, www.wagonsacrosswyoming.com.

Overnight (or multi-night) wagon-train rides are offered in Jackson Hole by **Wagons West,** 307/543-2418 or 800/447-4711, www.wagonswestwyo.com, and **Double H Bar,** 307/344-6101 or 888/734-6101, www.tetonwagontrain.com. Jackson isn't close to the Oregon Trail, but the scenery is grand.

GETTING INTO THE WILDERNESS

To get a real feel for Wyoming, you need to abandon your car, get away from the towns, and head out into the vast undeveloped public lands. Wyoming's most popular backcountry areas are in the Wind River, Medicine Bow, and Big Horn Mountains, along with the entire northwest corner of the state, including Yellowstone and Grand Teton National Parks. The Yellowstone region contains one of the largest nearly natural ecosystems and some of the most remote country in the Lower 48.

Many campers prefer to use horses for longer trips, but backpacking is very popular on the shorter trails, especially in the Wind River Mountains and in the national parks. Backcountry permits are required only within Yellowstone and Grand Teton. It is, however, a good idea to check in at a local Forest Service ranger station to get a copy of the regulations because each place is different in such specifics as how far your tent must be from lakes and trails and whether wood fires are allowed. Be sure to take insect repellent along on any summertime trip because mosquitoes, deerflies, and horseflies can be quite thick, especially in July and early August.

Trail Information

The **Wyoming State Trails Program,** 307/777-6560, has a useful website (http://wyotrails.state.wy.us/trails) with information on hiking, biking, cross-country skiing, snowmobile, Volksmarch, and other trails around the state.

Several hiking trails, mostly two- or three-day hikes, are described in this book for each of Wyoming's best-known backcountry areas. For more detailed hiking information on Yellowstone, Grand Teton, the Big Horns, or the Wind Rivers, see Suggested Reading at the end of this book. An overall guide is *The Hiker's Guide to Wyoming,* by Bill Hunger (www.falconbooks.com). The National Park Service and the U.S. Forest Service can also provide specific trail information and post much of this information on their websites.

The **Continental Divide National Scenic Trail** stretches for 3,100 miles from Mexico to Canada, including a long section that crosses the Sierra Madre Range and the desolate Great Divide Basin, before traversing the Wind River Mountains, Teton Wilderness, and Yellowstone National Park. Not all sections have been completed, and the route cuts across some desolate and hot places, including the Red Desert. Contact the Park Service, Forest Service, and BLM for maps of the various areas or learn more from the Continental Divide Trail Alliance, 303/838-3760 or 888/909-2382, www.cdtrail.org.

Horses

For many people, the highlight of a Wyoming vacation is the chance to ride horseback into wild country. Although a few folks bring their own steeds, most visitors leave the driving to an expert local outfitter instead. (If you've ever worked around horses in the backcountry, you'll understand why.) Horsepacking is an entirely different experience from backpacking. The trade requires years of experience in learning how to properly load horses and mules with *panniers* (large baskets), which types of knots to use for different loads, how to keep the packstrings under control, which horses to picket and which to hobble, and how to awaken when the horses decide to head down the trail on hobbles at three in the morning. Add to this a knowledge of bear safety, an ability to keep guests entertained with campfire tales and ribald jokes, a complete vocabulary of horse-cussing terms, and a thorough knowledge of tobacco chewing, and you're still only about 10 percent of the way to becoming a packer.

Dozens of outfitters are scattered across Wyoming, but you'll find concentrations in the Jackson Hole, Pinedale, Cody, Dubois, Sheridan, and Saratoga areas. For a listing of permitted outfitters in a given region, contact local Forest Service and Park Service offices. The **Wyoming Outfitters and Guides Association,** 307/527-7453, maintains a statewide listing of their members; find it on the web at www.wyoga.org. The **Wyoming State Board of Outfitters and Professional Guides** 307/777-5323 or 800/264-0981, produces a booklet listing licensed outfitters, or you can get the same information at http://outfitte.state.wy.us.

Although horses are far more common, **llamas** are relatively common in some backcountry areas. You can't ride them, but they're easier to control than horses and do not cause as much damage to trails and backcountry meadows. Llamas are perfect for folks who want to hike while letting a pack llama carry most of the weight. Contact local Forest Service and Park Service offices for permitted llama packers.

Trail Etiquette

Because horses are so commonly used in Wyoming, hikers should follow a few rules of courtesy. Horses and mules are not the brightest critters on this planet, and they can spook at the most inane thing, even a bush blowing in the breeze or a brightly colored hat. Hikers meeting a packstring should move several feet off the trail and not speak loudly or make any sudden moves. If you've ever seen what happens when just one mule in a string decides to act up, you'll appreciate the chaos that can result from sudden noises or movements. Anyone hiking with a dog should keep it well away from the stock and not let it bark. Last of all, never walk close behind a horse, unless you don't mind spending time in a hospital. Their kick is *definitely* worse than their bite.

Backcountry Ethics

Wyoming's wilderness areas represent places to escape the crowds, enjoy the beauty and peace of the countryside, and develop an understanding of nature. Unfortunately, as more and more people head into backcountry areas, these benefits are becoming endangered. To keep wild places wild, always practice "leave no trace" hiking and camping. This means using existing campsites and fire rings, locating your campsite well away from trails and streams, staying on designated trails, not cutting switchbacks, burning only dead and down wood, extinguishing all fires, washing dishes 200 feet from lakes and creeks, digging "catholes" at least 200 feet from lakes or streams, and hanging all food well above the reach of bears. Your tent site should be 100 yards from the food storage and cooking areas to reduce the likelihood of bear problems. Wood fires are not allowed in many areas, so be sure to bring along a portable gas stove. And, of course, haul your garbage out with you. Burning cans and tinfoil in the fire lessens their weight (and the odors that attract bears), but be sure to pick them out of the fire pit before you depart—and make sure the fire is completely out.

For a detailed brochure on minimizing your impact and treating the land with respect, call 800/332-4100. Get the same information on the web at www.lnt.org. (Trivia note: The "leave no trace" concept was spearheaded by a Lander, Wyoming–based organization, the National Outdoors Leadership School.)

Range Etiquette

Wyoming's land ownership pattern includes many areas where private and public lands are intermingled in a complex checkerboard. This arrangement creates all sorts of problems for management of and access to public lands and for private owners. The conflict is most apparent in grazing country, where many ranchers jealously guard their land from trespassers for any reason. There are places where access to public lands is blocked by private landowners who have had problems in the past. A gate left open by a careless visitor or sheep sent running by a barking dog can quickly sour even the most generous rancher. Many of them are living a marginal existence already, so every little problem becomes magnified, especially if created by a city slicker—or even worse, a city slicker with California license plates and a "Save the Planet" bumper sticker.

Private boundaries are not always marked by No Trespassing signs, so it's a good idea to use a detailed and up-to-date map (such as those sold at BLM offices throughout the state) to be sure you are walking on public land. This is a particularly big issue during the fall hunting season, when many ranchers require a hefty "trespass fee" for access. If you *do* hunt despite warning signs, don't expect any help from the state because Game and Fish officers are supportive of private-property rights. Also note that you need to get permission from the landowner—public or private—before collecting anything, including fossils. Because we're talking about ethical issues, here's some more advice: Never ask a rancher how many cattle he has; it's like asking someone how much money he or she earns.

BACKCOUNTRY SAFETY

Beaver Fever

Although Wyoming's lakes and streams may appear clean, you could be risking a debilitating sickness by drinking the water without treating it first. The protozoan *Giardia lamblia* is found throughout the state, spread by both humans and animals (including beaver). The disease is curable with drugs, but it's always best to carry safe drinking water on any trip or to boil any water taken from creeks or lakes. Bringing water to a full boil for one minute is sufficient to kill Giardia and other harmful organisms. Another option is to use water filters available from backpacking stores. Note, however, that these may not filter out other organisms such as *Campylobactor jejuni,* bacteria that are just 0.2 microns in size. Chlorine and iodine are not always reliable, taste foul, and can be unhealthy.

Hypothermia

Anyone who has spent much time in the outdoors will discover the dangers of exposure to cold, wet, and windy conditions. Even at temperatures well above freezing, hypothermia—the reduction of the body's inner core temperature—can prove fatal.

In the early stages, hypothermia causes uncontrollable shivering, followed by a loss of coordination, slurred speech, and then a rapid descent into unconsciousness and death. Always travel prepared for sudden changes in the weather. Wear clothing that insulates well and that holds its heat when wet. Wool and polypro are far better than cotton, and clothes should be worn in layers to provide better trapping of heat and a chance to adjust to conditions more easily. Always carry a wool hat because your head loses more heat than any other part of the body. Bring a waterproof shell to cut the wind. Put on rain gear *before* it starts raining; head back or set up camp when the weather starts to look threatening; eat candy bars, keep active, or snuggle with a friend in a down bag to generate warmth.

If someone in your party begins to show signs of hypothermia, don't take any chances, even if the person denies needing help. Get the victim out of the wind, strip off his clothes, and put him in a dry sleeping bag on an insulating pad. Skin-to-skin contact is the best way to warm a hypothermic person, and that means you'll also need to strip and climb in the sleeping bag. If you weren't friends before, this should heat up the relationship! Do not give the victim alcohol or hot drinks, and do not try to warm the person too quickly because it could lead to heart failure. Once the victim has recovered, get medical help as soon as possible. Actually, you're far better off keeping close tabs on everyone in the group and seeking shelter *before* exhaustion and hypothermia set in.

Frostbite

Frostbite is a less serious but painful problem for the cold-weather hiker. It is caused by direct exposure to the cold or by heat loss from wet socks and boots. Frostbitten areas will look white or gray, and they'll feel hard on the surface and softer underneath. The best way to warm the area is with other skin; put your hand under your arm, your feet on your friend's belly. Don't rub the affected area with snow or warm it near a fire. In cases of severe frostbite, in which the skin is white, hard, and numb, immerse the frozen area in water warmed to 99°F to 104°F until it's thawed. Avoid refreezing the frostbitten area. If you're a long way from medical assistance and the frostbite is extensive, it is better to keep the area frozen and get out of the woods for help; thawing is painful, and it would be impossible to walk on a thawed foot.

Other Safety Tips

Dealing with bears is discussed in the next section of this chapter. The most important part of enjoying—and surviving—the backcountry is to be prepared. Know where you're going; get maps, camping information, and weather and trail conditions from a ranger before setting out. Don't hike alone. Two are better than one, and three are better than two; if one gets hurt, one person can stay with the injured party and one can go for help. Bring more than enough food so hunger won't cause you to continue when weather conditions say stop. Tell someone where you're going and when you'll be back.

Always carry the **10 essentials:** map, compass, water bottle, first-aid kit, flashlight, matches (or lighter) and fire starter, knife, extra clothing (a full set, in case you fall in a stream) including rain gear, extra food, and sunglasses—especially if you're hiking on snow. To this list, you might want to also add a cell phone. Most backcountry areas have no service, but in an emergency you might be able to find a high point where the phone can hit an antenna.

Check your ego at the trailhead; stop for the night when the weather gets bad, even if it's 2 P.M., or head back. And don't press on when you're exhausted; tired hikers are sloppy hikers, and even a small injury can be disastrous in the woods.

SAFETY IN BEAR COUNTRY

Bears seem to bring out conflicting emotions in people. The first is an almost gut reaction of fear and trepidation: What if the bear attacks me? But then comes that other urge: What will my friends say when they see these *incredible* bear photos? Both of these reactions can lead to problems in bear country. "Bearanoia" is a jus-

tifiable fear but can easily be taken to such an extreme that one avoids going outdoors at all for fear of running into a bear. The "I want to get close-up shots of that bear and her cubs" attitude can lead to a bear attack. The middle ground incorporates a knowledge of and respect for bears with a sense of caution that keeps you alert for danger without letting fear rule your wilderness travels. Nothing is ever completely safe in this world, but with care you can avoid most of the common pitfalls that lead to bear encounters.

Brown and Black Bears

Old-timers joke that bears are easy to differentiate: a black bear climbs up the tree after you, whereas a grizzly snaps the tree off at the base. Black bears live in forested areas throughout Wyoming, but grizzlies exist mainly in the northwest corner of the state, primarily within and around Yellowstone National Park. Both grizzlies and black bears pose potential threats to backcountry travelers, although you are considerably more likely to be involved in a car accident while driving to a wilderness area than to be attacked by a bear once you arrive.

Grizzlies once ranged across the entire Northern Hemisphere, from Europe across what is now Russia and through the western half of North America. When Europeans arrived, there were perhaps 50,000–100,000 grizzlies in what would become the Lower 48 states. Unfortunately, as white settlers moved in, they came to view these massive and powerful creatures (average adult males weigh 500 pounds) as a threat to themselves and their livestock. The scientific name, *Ursus arctos horribilis,* says much about human attitudes toward grizzlies.

Grizzlies still have healthy populations in Alaska and western Canada, but elsewhere they were shot, trapped, and poisoned nearly to the brink of extinction. In the Lower 48 states grizzlies survive in only a few of the most remote parts of Montana, Wyoming, Idaho, and Washington. By 1975, when the U.S. Fish & Wildlife Service listed them as threatened, fewer than 1,000 grizzlies survived south of Canada. Since that time the population appears to have recovered somewhat and includes approximately 400–600 grizzlies in Wyoming's Greater Yellowstone Ecosystem.

Avoiding Bear Hugs

Surprise bear encounters are rare but frightening experiences. There were just 23 bear-caused injuries in Yellowstone National Park between 1980 and 1997—one injury for every 2.1 million visitors. Avoid unexpected encounters with bears by letting them know you're there. Most bears hear or smell you long before you realize their presence, and they hightail it away. Surprising a bear, especially a sow with cubs, is the last thing you want to do in the backcountry. Before heading out, check at a local ranger station to see whether there have been recent bear encounters. If you discover an animal carcass, be extremely alert because a bear may be

nearby and may attack anything that appears to threaten its food. Get away from such areas. Do not hike at night or dusk, when bears can be especially active. Safety is also in numbers: the more of you hiking together, the more likely a bear is to sense you and stay away.

Make noise in areas of dense cover or when coming around blind spots on trails. If you're unable to see everything around you for at least 50 yards, warn any hidden animals by talking, singing, clapping your hands, tapping a cup, or rattling a can of pebbles. Some people tie bells to their packs for this purpose, but others regard this as an annoyance to fellow hikers. In general, bells are probably of little value because the sound does not carry far, and they might actually attract bears. If bears can't hear you coming, don't be shy—make a

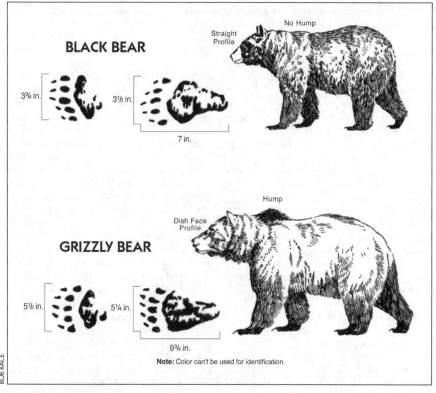

BLACK BEAR

Straight Profile

No Hump

3¾ in.   3½ in.

7 in.

GRIZZLY BEAR

Dish Face Profile

Hump

5½ in.   5¼ in.

9¾ in.

Note: Color can't be used for identification.

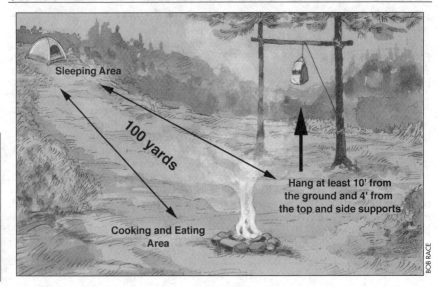

Sleeping Area

100 yards

Cooking and Eating Area

Hang at least 10' from the ground and 4' from the top and side supports

BOB RACE

lot of noise! It might seem a bit foolish, but loud voices may prevent an encounter of the furry kind. Unfortunately, it will probably scare off other animals, so you're not likely to see many critters, and other hikers may not appreciate the noise. Personally, I reserve yelling "Hey Bear!" for situations where I'm walking in brushy bear country with low visibility and have to contend with other noises such as a nearby creek. I wouldn't recommend doing so while walking the paved path around Old Faithful Geyser; you might get carried off in a straitjacket.

Hunters and photographers are the main recipients of bear hugs. Never under any circumstances approach a bear, even if it appears to be asleep. Move away if you see bear cubs, especially if one comes toward you, because mom is almost always close by. Dogs create dangerous situations by barking and exciting bears—leave yours at home (dogs are not allowed in the backcountry in national parks). Never leave food around for bears. Not only is this illegal, but it also trains the bears to associate people with free food. Fed bears become garbage bears, and that almost inevitably means that the bear gets killed. Remember, bears are dangerous wild animals.

This is *their* country, not a zoo. By going in you accept the risk—and thrill—of meeting a bear.

At the Campsite

Before camping, take a look around the area to see if there are recent bear tracks or scat and to make sure you're not on a game trail. Bears are attracted to odors of all sorts, including food, horse feed, soap, toothpaste, perfume, and deodorants. Your cooking, eating, and food storage area should be at least 50 yards away from your tent. Keep your campsite clean and avoid such smelly items as tuna, ham, sausage, and bacon; freeze-dried food is light and relatively odorless (although also relatively tasteless). Store food away from your sleeping area in airtight containers or several layers of plastic bags, and be sure to hang all food and other items that bears may smell at least 12 feet off the ground and four feet from tree trunks. Bring 50 feet of rope for this purpose. Tie two cups or pots to it so you will hear if it's moved. Some Forest Service and Park Service wilderness areas provide food storage poles at campsites. In the Teton and Bridger Wilderness Areas, you can also rent bear-resistant backpacker food tubes or horse panniers from Forest Service offices.

Camping stores in Jackson, Cody, and elsewhere sell similar containers.

Good news: Researchers have reported no evidence that either sexual activity or menstrual odors precipitate bear attacks, despite reports to the contrary. It is, however, wise for menstruating women to use tampons instead of pads and to store soiled tampons in double ziplock bags above the reach of bears.

Encounters of the Furry Kind

If you do happen to suddenly encounter a bear and it sees you, try to stay calm and not make any sudden moves. Do not run because you could not possibly outrun a bear; they can exceed 40 mph for short distances. Bear researchers now suggest that quickly climbing a tree is also not a wise way to escape bears and may actually incite an attack. Instead, make yourself visible by moving into the open so the bear will (hopefully) identify you as a human and not something to eat. Never stare directly at a bear. Sometimes dropping an item such as a hat or jacket will distract the bear, and talking calmly (easier said than done) also seems to have some value in convincing bears that you're a human. If the bear sniffs the air or stands on its hind legs it is probably trying to identify you. When it does, it will usually run away. If a bear woofs and postures, don't imitate—this is a challenge. Keep retreating. Most bear charges are also bluffs; the bear will often stop short and amble off.

If a **grizzly bear** actually attacks, hold your ground and freeze. It may well be a bluff charge, with the bear halting at the last second. If the bear does not stop its attack, curl up facedown on the ground in a fetal position with your hands wrapped behind your neck and your elbows tucked over your face. Your backpack may help protect you somewhat. Remain still even if you are attacked because sudden movements may incite further attacks. It takes an enormous amount of courage to do this, but often a bear will only sniff or nip you and leave. The injury you might sustain would be far less than if you tried to resist. After the attack, prevent further attacks by staying down on the ground until the grizzly has left the area.

Bear authorities now recommend against dropping to the ground if you are attacked by a **black bear** because they tend to be more aggressive in such situations and are more likely to prey on humans. If a black bear attacks, fight back with whatever weapons are at hand; large rocks and branches can be surprisingly effective deterrents, as can yelling and shouting. (This, of course, assumes you can tell black bears from brown bears. If you can't, have someone who knows—such as a park ranger—explain the differences before you head into the backcountry.)

In the rare event of a **nighttime bear attack** in your tent, defend yourself *very* aggressively. Never play dead under such circumstances because the bear probably views you as prey and may give up if you make it a fight. Before going to bed, try to plan escape routes should you be attacked in the night, and be sure to have a flashlight and pepper spray handy. Keeping your sleeping bag partly unzipped also allows the chance to escape should a bear attempt to drag you away. If someone is attacked in a tent near you, yelling and throwing rocks or sticks may drive the bear away.

Protecting Yourself

Cayenne pepper sprays (sold in camping goods stores) have sometimes proven useful in fending off bear attacks. Note, however, that these "bear mace" sprays are only effective at close range (10–30 feet). This is particularly true in open country where winds quickly disperse the mist or may blow it back in your own face. Another problem with bear mace is that you cannot carry it aboard commercial jets because of the obvious dangers if a canister explodes. If you do carry a pepper spray, make sure it is readily available by carrying it in a holster on your belt or across your chest. Also be sure to test-fire it to see how the spray carries. Although they *are* better than nothing, pepper sprays are not a cure-all or a replacement for caution in bear country. It's far better to avoid bear confrontations in the first place. A few clueless individuals have sprayed themselves with the pepper spray thinking it would work like mosquito repellent. Needless to say, this isn't of much help, and there is some evidence it might even attract bears looking for a spicy meal!

ON THE ROAD

Good web sources for up-to-date bear safety information are Yellowstone National Park, www.nps.gov/yell, and the Yellowstone Grizzly Foundation, www.yellowstonegrizzly.com. Two recommended safety books are *Bear Attacks: Their* *Causes and Avoidance* by Stephen Herrero (The Lyons Press, 2002, www.lyonspress.com) and *Bear Aware: Hiking and Camping in Bear Country*, Second Edition, by Bill Schneider (Globe Pequot/Falcon, 2001, www.falconbooks.com).

Accommodations

Lodging in Wyoming covers the complete spectrum, from the finest of luxury accommodations where a king or queen would feel pampered, all the way down to flophouses so tawdry that even the roaches think twice about staying there. In general, visitors will find lodging prices considerably lower than what they might pay in other parts of America. This is especially true in the smaller towns and places where the economy is weak. During the summer, rates at the mom-and-pop motels that line the streets of every Wyoming town start around $35 for one person and $45 for two people. Come wintertime, rates may drop 25 percent or more. In general, visitors will be pleased with Wyoming accommodations. The low rates reflect a less expensive economy, not shoddy conditions. Don't be scared off by a price that seems far too low by New York or Paris standards!

The exception to these low rates is the northwest corner of the state, notably Cody and most egregiously Jackson. During peak summer or winter season in Jackson Hole, you should expect to pay $90–120 for a decent room; even fairly basic rooms with older furnishings fetch $80 per night! Also beware that rates for Cheyenne accommodations skyrocket during Cheyenne Frontier Days (late July). Lodging prices have a way of changing even in a given day. The law of supply and demand holds, and many owners raise prices as the evening progresses and the rooms start to fill up, when a convention comes to town, and on weekends.

The newer (typically chain) motels and hotels often have such room amenities as coffeemakers, irons and ironing boards, Internet access phone lines, and fax services. Parents with young children will appreciate the cribs that are often available at no extra charge; but call ahead to make sure they have one.

FINDING ACCOMMODATIONS

For a complete listing of motels, hotels, bed-and-breakfasts, dude ranches, and places to camp in Wyoming, request a copy of the free ***Wyoming Accommodations Directory*** from the Wyoming Division of Tourism and State Marketing in Cheyenne, 307/777-7777 or 800/225-5996. The booklet lists lodging and campgrounds in every part of the state, or find the same information (and more) on the web at www.wyomingtourism.org.

Throughout this book I typically list two prices for most accommodations: single, or s (one person), and double, or d (two people). Prices listed are the midsummer rates, which are generally the highest of the year. These

WINTER IN WYOMING

Winter looks like a fictional place, an elaborate simplicity, a Nabokovian invention of rarefied detail. Winds howl all night and day, pushing litters of storm fronts from the Beartooth to the Big Horn Mountains. When it lets up, the mountains disappear. The hayfield that runs east from my house ends in a curl of clouds that have fallen like sails luffing from sky to ground. Snow returns across the field to me, and the cows, dusted with white, look like snow-capped continents drifting.

—Gretel Ehrlich in *The Solace of Open Spaces*

prices do not include state and local taxes, which can sometimes be substantial, but are typically 4 to 8 percent. These prices are not set in concrete and will certainly increase over time. If a convention is in town or the motel is nearly full, they may rise; if the economy is marginal or if it's the off-season at a seasonal area, you may pay considerably less. Always ask to see the room before deciding to stay at one of the less-expensive locations—places that I consider more than adequate may be beneath your standards.

If in doubt about where to stay, you may want to choose a place that gets the American Automobile Association (AAA) seal of approval. The annual *AAA TourBook* for Idaho, Montana, and Wyoming (free to AAA members) is a helpful guide to the better hotels and motels, offering current prices and accurate ratings. Members often get discounts on lodging rates and can find the same information on their website, www.aaa.com.

HISTORIC HOTELS

Most of the historic hotels that once offered lodging for weary Wyoming travelers have fallen to the wrecking ball. Only a few of these gems have been restored to their glory; they include Cheyenne's Plains Hotel, Cody's Irma Hotel, Jackson's Wort Hotel, Saratoga's Wolf Hotel, Buffalo's Occidental Hotel, Elk Mountain Hotel in the town of Elk Mountain, and Medicine Bow's Virginian Hotel. Yellowstone National Park offers some of the finest old-time luxury accommodations anywhere in America: Old Faithful Inn, Lake Hotel, and Mammoth Hot Springs Hotel. Of these, Old Faithful Inn is in a category all its own and is perhaps the grandest hotel in any American national park. Don't miss this one!

CHAIN HOTELS AND MOTELS

The various motel chains—Best Western, Days Inn, Comfort Inn, Holiday Inn, Motel 6, and Super 8—all operate across the state, primarily in the larger towns. These cinder block monuments to the bigger-is-better school of lodging stand on the edges of towns, their towering signs glaring eyesores (but visible at 75 mph from the freeway). Each chain publishes a directory listing all of its locations and rates; you can pick up a copy at the chain's location nearest to your home. All of the major chains are also now on the web.

If you're staying with the pricier chains, always be sure to ask about the sometimes substantial discounts, such as AAA-member rates, senior discounts, corporate or government rates, business travel fares, military rates, or web-only specials. Try not to take the first rate quoted at these places, especially if you're calling their 800 number; these "rack rates" are what they charge if they can get away with it. Ask if they have any promotional rates. You may also get better prices sometimes by bargaining with clerks who are more likely to be able to dicker over price than the 800 number operators. Of course, if it's a big convention or festival weekend, you may have no choice. Note that the "free continental breakfast" claimed at some chain motels can be pretty meager—often just a pile of doughnuts and a pot of rotgut coffee.

INDEPENDENT MOTELS

Every town in Wyoming has its locally owned small motels, although they are increasingly being eclipsed by the chain operations. Independent motels vary widely in quality and price but tend to offer the best rates and friendliest service. Actually, some of Wyoming's cheapest motels are owned by immigrants from India or other Asian countries. In a few towns (Rawlins is the most egregious), native-born owners play on racist fears with signs proclaiming "American Owned." In my experience, immigrant-owned places are equal to—and sometimes better than—those who wave the American flag in an attempt to suggest otherwise. Today, many of the AAA-approved Comfort Inns, Best Westerns, Super 8s, and other reputable chain motels are owned by people born in India or Pakistan. If you have any doubts about a budget place, take a look at a room and then decide, but don't avoid a place just because the owner's last name is Patel or Khan!

If you don't smoke and can't stand the stench of tobacco in motel rooms, be sure to request a nonsmoking room; most motels (and nearly all of the newer ones) have them. Older motel units may also suffer from the permanent smell of tobacco smoke. Also take a look around the motel to see if the railroad or a busy highway lies next door. If so, try to get a room on the opposite side of the motel or prepare to put in earplugs. Another thing to watch for is the checkout time; at some places it's as early as 10 A.M.

Wyoming has only one **hostel,** a place called The Bunkhouse in Jackson.

BED-AND-BREAKFASTS

Bed-and-breakfasts are a relatively recent addition to Wyoming's accommodations picture, but more are appearing each year. These range from remote places, where the accommodations are not unlike those at a guest ranch, to historic Victorian homes in the center of town. Some of the best are found in Big Horn, Cheyenne, Cody, Dayton, Douglas, Dubois, Jackson Hole, Lander, Newcastle, Pinedale, Ranchester, Saratoga, and Wheatland. Get a detailed brochure listing many of the state's B&Bs from **Wyoming Homestay & Outdoor Adventures (WHOA),** 307/237-3526. Their website, www.wyomingbnb-ranchrec.com, has descriptions of each of these places, plus web links.

A few of Wyoming's B&Bs don't allow kids, and almost none allow pets or smoking inside. Most guest rooms have private baths, but if they don't, one is probably just a few steps away. Bed-and-breakfasts, favorites of 30- and 40-something professional couples, are a fine way to get acquainted with a new area. They are also a good choice if you're traveling alone because you'll have opportunities to meet fellow travelers in the library, over tea, and at breakfast. Note, however, that the single-person rate often differs little, if at all, from the price for couples.

One problem with B&Bs is that they sometimes get a bit too homey and lack the privacy afforded by motels. I've stayed at places where the owner sits by your table in the morning, feeling it is his duty to hold a conversation. This may be fine sometimes, especially if you want to learn more about the local area, but it's

not so great if you're looking for a romantic place or you just want to read the newspaper in peace. In some places the intense personal attention and strict rules (no hard-soled shoes, no noise after 10 P.M., and so on) get to be a bit much, making you feel less a guest than an intruder. In others, hosts serve breakfast at precisely 8 A.M. and guests who sleep in miss out. Other B&Bs are more flexible, and some even offer separate cottages or suites for honeymooners seeking privacy.

DUDE RANCHES

An old and respected Western tradition is the dude ranch, which began as a sideline to the business of raising cattle. Friends from back east would remember old Jake out there in wild Wyoming, where the buffalo roam and the antelope play, and would decide it was time for a visit. So off they would head, living in the rancher's outbuildings and joining in the chores. The "dudes," as they became known, soon told their friends, and Jake found his ranch inundated. After a couple of years of this, the next step was obvious: get those eastern scoundrels to fork over some cash for the privilege of visiting. Pretty soon the dude ranching business was born. At its peak in the 1920s, dude ranching spread throughout much of Wyoming and the West. Dude ranching saved many cattle ranches from extinction by providing a second source of income and simultaneously brought these magnificent lands to the attention of people who had the money to prevent their development (most notably John D. Rockefeller Jr. in Grand Teton National Park).

At the older ranches, generations of families have returned year after year for a relaxing and rejuvenating vacation in the "Wild West." Many dude ranches now call themselves guest ranches, a term that reflects both the suspicious way people view the word "dude" and the changing nature of the business. Most city folks today lack the desire or skill to actually saddle up their own horses, much less push cattle between pastures. As a result, guest/dude ranches tend to emphasize grand scenery, horseback riding—the centerpiece of nearly every ranch—campfires, hiking, fishing, hearty meals, chuck wagon cookouts, sing-alongs, and evenings around the fireplace. Some folks even camp overnight out there in the fearful wilderness, where the coyotes howl and the mice chew into your stash of potato chips. A few ranches still offer the chance to join in on such activities as cattle drives, branding, pregnancy testing, shot-giving, calving, and roundups. For some folks it's a great chance to learn about the real West; others view it as paying good money (sometimes a lot of good money!) to work as a cowhand.

Practicalities

Wyoming has literally dozens of dude ranches and ranch resorts offering accommodations ranging from spartan to so sumptuous that they bear absolutely no resemblance to ranch life. Not all dude ranches are created equal—some are slick and modern with tennis courts and hot tubs while others are funky and old-fashioned with delightful rough edges. The smaller ones offer more personalized service, but in larger ones you're more likely to find someone your own age (particularly important if there are teens in your entourage). Dudes normally sleep in log cabins. Conditions inside can vary widely, but don't expect TVs or phones in the rooms. The cabins are usually near a central lodge, where meals are served family-style. Many also have large libraries, along with outdoor games such as volleyball and horseshoes. Fishing and photography are other big attractions.

Dude ranch stays generally cost around $2,500 to $3,500 for two people per week, with lower rates for kids and surcharges for those staying by themselves. The price includes all meals, lodging, and horseback rides, but you'll usually pay more for features such as airport shuttles, rafting trips, guided fishing, beer and wine, or back-country pack trips, not to mention local taxes and tips. (A 15 percent gratuity is standard for the dude ranch staff and guides.) The fanciest resort, Lost Creek Ranch in Jackson Hole, will set you back more than $12,000 for two people per week! Many guest ranches offer discounted rates in early

June and late September and for repeat guests. A few also have special adults-only weeks. Most require that you stay a week, or at least three nights, although a few places offer overnight accommodations. To really get into the comfortably slow pace of ranch life, try to set aside at least a week.

Ask plenty of questions before you visit, such as what activities are available, what to bring in the way of clothing, what sort of meals to expect (vegetarians may have a hard time on some ranches), whether there are additional charges, whether they accept credit cards (many don't), what the living accommodations are like, and how many other guests will likely be there at the same time—some house up to 125, others fewer than a dozen. Upon request, the better ranches will provide lists of references from previous clients. Note that it is considered proper to tip the ranch hands, kitchen help, and others who work hard to keep the ranch running; the standard total is 15 percent of your bill. For many of them, this is a way to fund their college education (or buy a winter in Belize).

Finding a Dude Ranch

An outstanding source for detailed information about guest ranches in Wyoming (and elsewhere) is *Gene Kilgore's Ranch Vacations,* by Eugene Kilgore (Avalon Travel Publishing; www.travel-matters.com, 2001). Find Kilgore on the web at www.ranchweb.com.

Established in 1926, the **Dude Ranchers' Association** includes most of the nation's best-known guest ranches. Call 307/587-2339 to request their catalog or visit their website (www.duderanch.org) for links to more than 30 Wyoming ranches. Another useful online source is www.guestranches.com/usa/wy, where you'll find links to 30 Wyoming dude ranches. Also worth a look is www.duderanches.com, which offers ranch descriptions along with employment info for would-be wranglers. Nearly all dude ranches have their own websites, filled with beautiful photos of their ranch, glowing reports from past clients, and details on the packages available and their costs.

Camping

Wyoming has hundreds of public campsites scattered across the state, primarily on Forest Service, BLM, and Park Service lands, and in state parks. Most of these sites have potable running water, garbage pickup, and outhouses, but no showers. The fee is generally $5–10 per night (some are free), and most are open from early June to mid-September. After that, many of the campgrounds remain open (unless inaccessible because of snow) at no charge, but do not have garbage pickup or running water. There is a 14-day limit on camping at any site, so don't plan on moving in permanently. It's also generally legal to camp for free on undeveloped Forest Service or BLM land throughout the state, but check with local offices for any restrictions.

Several Forest Service campgrounds are now on a reservation system; for an extra service charge of $9 you can reserve a site up to one year in advance. Make reservations at 518/885-3639 or 877/444-6777, or www.reserveusa.com. Budget cutbacks have forced the Forest Service and Park Service to contract out the management of many campgrounds. The effect is not especially noticeable to most visitors, but many of these places charge higher fees.

Every town of any size contains at least one private RV park and so-called campground. Most of these are little more than vacant lots with sewer and electrical hookups, showers, and toilet facilities. These private campgrounds generally charge $3–5 for showers if you're not camping there. A better deal in many towns is to use the shower in the local public swimming pool, where you get a free swim thrown in for the entrance charge.

Food and Drink

Wyoming is not known for its haute cuisine. This is cattle country, the land of the free and the home on the range, where juicy steaks and the finest prime rib can be found in every Podunk town in the state. (The two best steak houses may well be in the don't-blink-or-you'll-miss-it town of Hudson.) If you don't like that, try chicken-fried steak, the house specialty at every truck stop and greasy spoon in Wyoming. Wash it down with a beer and then sit back for a big hunk of apple pie. For breakfast, it's pretty much standard all-American fare accompanied by a dark brew that folks in these parts call coffee. Real cowboy coffee, made only over an open smoky fire and not available within 20 miles of any town, is a potent medicine, not advised for children or the weak-kneed. Check local outfitters for a "café au grounds" prescription. Of course, all of the larger Wyoming towns now also have at least one restaurant or drive-through outlet selling lattes and mochas. Unfortunately, you'll also find the standard fast-food outlets that are turning regional differences into a bland mediocrity of frozen burgers and whipped-shortening "milk shakes." No wonder obesity is on the rise—here, and in the rest of the country.

Actually, Wyoming food is not quite as uniformly bland as might be imagined, and travelers will discover several innovative and surprisingly reasonable restaurants in Laramie, Jackson, Cody, Lander, and Sheridan; authentic Chinese food in Cheyenne and Casper; and relatively authentic Mexican restaurants scattered around the state. The most creative (and pricey) food can probably be found in the tourist town of Jackson and the college town of Laramie. One more note about Wyoming restaurants: they can be quite smoky. In many towns there are no regulations mandating nonsmoking sections, so if you don't enjoy a dose of cigarette smoke with your food, you may just be out of luck.

Typical Wyoming breakfasts cost $4–6, with lunches running $5–8. Dinner prices show a greater range, from simple $5 burgers to complete steak, prime rib, chicken, or seafood dinners for $8–20.

On the Town

No man, woman, or child should let a day pass without drinking a good glass of beer. Beer is an article of food and nourishing as bread if it is pure and free from adulteration.

— *1892 ad for the Green River Brewery*

In many Wyoming towns, drinking and carousing hold as much interest as eating, especially on Friday and Saturday nights. Every burg of any size has its resident country-and-western band, and saloon dance floors fill with duded-up cowboys and cowgirls out for a night on the town. Many of these bands also play Eagles-style rock tunes for variety. The larger cities and tourist towns have several nightclubs, some with disc jockeys, others with basic rock-and-roll fare. Don't expect a steep cover charge to get in the door; most places are free.

In the last decade or so, breweries and brewpubs have begun to spread across Wyoming, and you'll find them in Cheyenne, Evanston, Jackson, Laramie, Lander, Pinedale, Rock Springs, Saratoga, and Sheridan.

ON THE ROAD

Events

Although I once saw the changeover to daylight savings time listed as an "event" on a handout from a Wyoming chamber of commerce, the state really *does* have an abundance of notable annual events. During the summer, every town in Wyoming has its own main event, generally centered on a morning parade, an afternoon rodeo, and an evening of country music and dancing. Rodeos are the definitive Wyoming activity, reflecting an enduring nostalgia for cattle and cowboys. Nightly summertime rodeos can be found in Cody and twice-weekly in Jackson. Informal roping events go on all summer long around the state; ask locally for times. See the Rodeo Today section of this chapter for more details.

Laramie's weeklong **Jubilee Days** starts on the Fourth of July and celebrates Wyoming's statehood with rodeos, parades, the biggest fireworks show in Wyoming, live music, barbecues, a pancake breakfast, a carnival, art exhibits, and other activities.

Wyoming's most famous event is **Cheyenne Frontier Days,** a 10-day bash that fills every hotel for a hundred miles and makes Cheyenne streets look like a miniature Los Angeles. It starts the last full week of July each year. The centerpiece of Frontier Days is, of course, the rodeo, which attracts the nation's finest riders, but there are also parades, pancake feeds, art exhibits, and much more. Don't miss this one! The **Cody Stampede** (early July) is another very popular rodeo, parade, and all-round chance to party.

TASTES OF HISTORY

The **Gift of the Waters Pageant** arrives in Thermopolis in early August. It celebrates Chief Washakie's gift of this wonderful hot spring to the federal government to be used by all people. *The Legend of Rawhide,* an outdoor play held each July since 1947, has a cast that seems to include half the town of Lusk. The story is loosely based on the 1849 killing of a Sioux girl by a white gold-seeker and the Indians' retaliatory skinning-alive of the protagonist, hence the name.

Wyoming's largest powwows are the **Plains Indian Powwow** in Cody each June, Fort Washakie's **Eastern Shoshone Indian Days Powwow and Rodeo** in early July, and the **Ethete Powwow** in late June.

MODERN-DAY RENDEZVOUS

In recent years, mountain-man rendezvous have become major summertime attractions in Wyoming. These unusual events attract both tourists and locals to gawk at guys in buckskin pants or breechcloths and women in tanned leather skirts. Unlike the original rendezvous, you won't see many Indians at these get-togethers. The participants are a mixture of Joe Blow Businessman who likes a little diversion, Wendy Waitress who dreams of simpler times, and a lot of folks who find this a great way to live a fantasy life in a semi-legitimate way. You'll see more long hair, beards, braless women, and barefoot kids than you've seen in three decades.

Although the rendezvous offer escapism for both participants and tourists, they also provide a real taste of a far simpler era. Spend an evening at a rendezvous—especially the Fort Bridger Rendezvous on Memorial Day weekend—and you'll soon be in the market for your own buckskins. Lanterns glow inside tepees, musicians play guitars and sing classic songs, and friends sit on folding chairs inside a wall tent, telling jokes and playing cards. True, they didn't have port-a-potties at the original rendezvous, but the sense of history rings true. Participants bake bread over fires, race horses bareback, fire muzzle-loaders, and mug for tourists' clicking cameras. You'll find lots of beef jerky, Indian tacos, and fry bread for sale. This isn't a good place for animal-rights enthusiasts because many of the trade items at the modern rendezvous (as at the original ones) come from wild animals. Many of the people who attend rendezvous have something to offer, such as old beads, leather clothing, tomahawks, knives, moccasins, woven crafts, tanned hides, and lots of fox, coyote, rabbit, ermine, and other furs.

Events at rendezvous include black-powder shooting contests, storytelling, fiddle music, dancing, hide-tanning demonstrations, tomahawk and knife throwing, and footraces for the kids. In the evening, when all the gawkers head back to their air-conditioned motel rooms, the rendezvous really come to life with big campfires, more storytelling, carousing, drinking, and a raucous good time for all. But woe to the visitor who shows up after dark in modern-day civilian clothes!

The biggest and best rendezvous is the **Fort Bridger Rendezvous,** held each Labor Day. Also of note are those in Lander (early June), Riverton (early July), Cheyenne (mid-July), Granger (mid-August), Alpine (late June), and Jackson (mid-July).

OTHER EVENTS

Cutter races—essentially wild chariot races on one-quarter mile of ice—take place in Afton throughout the winter and in Jackson each February.

One of Wyoming's biggest winter events is the **International Pedigree Stage Stop Sled Dog Race** (IPSSSDR), the largest sled dog race in the Lower 48. It begins and ends in Jackson in late January and lasts for eight days, taking mushers on a race across western Wyoming starting from a different town each day. The race boasts a $100,000 purse.

Hundreds of people flood the tiny settlement of Encampment for the **Woodchopper's Jamboree** in late June. Another big attraction is the **Wyoming State Fair,** held in Douglas during mid-August. County fairs take place in each of Wyoming's 23 counties during the summer. Casper's biggest events are the **Central Wyoming Fair and Rodeo** in early August and the **Cowboy State Games** in February.

Jackson Hole has several popular events throughout the year, including the acclaimed **Grand Teton Music Festival** in July and the **Fall Arts Festival,** which attracts entries from all over the world. Jackson's annual **Elk Antler Auction** in late May attracts aphrodisiac (!) buyers from all over the globe. For something completely different, head to Chugwater in late June for the **Chugwater Chili Cook-off.** Bring along a bottle of Maalox.

EVENT INFORMATION

All of the above events—and many more—are described in greater detail in appropriate sections of this book. For a complete calendar of Wyoming events, contact the Wyoming Division of Tourism and State Marketing at 307/777-7777 or 800/225-5996, www.wyomingtourism.org.

Rodeo

Sometimes I think life is just a rodeo,
The trick is to ride and make it to the
bell . . .

                              John Fogerty

It may come as a revelation to many, but rodeo (in Wyoming, always pronounced ROE-dee-oh) is one of the most popular sports in America; more people watch professional rodeos than attend NFL football games! In Wyoming, where even the license plate is graced with a cowboy astride a bucking bronc, it's no surprise that rodeo is king. Every small town in the state has a rodeo of some sort during the summer, and the larger cities have world-class rodeos that attract hundreds of riders and ropers from the Professional Rodeo Cowboys Association (PRCA).

HISTORY

Although rodeo seems to have a few drops of the Spanish bullfight in its blood, and while many of the words—rodeo, bronco, lariat, arena, and honda—have Spanish origins, rodeo's true genesis was in the days of cowboys and cattle in the Wild West. Gradually, groups of cowboys got together to show off their riding and roping skills and to compete with neighboring outfits. Everyone argues over the official origin of rodeo, but credit is generally given to a bucking and roping competition between the Mill Iron and Hash Knife outfits, who met near Deer Trail, Colorado, in 1869.

As the West began to be fenced in, the cowboy events moved into the nearby towns as organized "buckin' shows." Buffalo Bill Cody probably had more to do with popularizing the sport than any other person. For many years his Wild West Show traveled the world, providing a spectacle that included several of the events in present-day rodeos. Lander lays claim to the oldest rodeo in Wyoming; begun in 1893, the Lander Pioneer Days rodeo still comes around each July. By far the most famous Wyoming rodeo, the "Daddy of 'em All," is the Cheyenne Frontier Days, one of the top four rodeos in the world. A good source for rodeo information on the web is www.prorodeohome.com.

RODEO TODAY

Over the years, rodeo has become more professional and less connected to the true cowboy. Many participants today come from cities and have never spent time herding cattle or working on a ranch; a few of the best grew up in Harlem and the Bronx. many other cowboys still come from more traditional farming and ranching backgrounds, although they may work part-time at the local grocery store to fund their travels on the rodeo circuit. When they get enough money, they attend a weeklong rodeo school to pick up pointers from past champions.

> *It may come as a revelation to many, but rodeo is one of the most popular sports in America; more people watch professional rodeos than attend NFL football games!*

Those who make it to the top do so the hard way. Grand Nationals winners are decided on the basis of rodeo earnings, which means that cowboys must compete almost continuously, flying from one rodeo to another and staying in cheap motels or living out of their RVs. Semipros and amateurs compete in the hundreds of smaller rodeos that dot Wyoming and the West, hoping to make it to the professional level. Most don't even come close, losing their stiff entry fees to more experienced competitors and taking home only bruises or broken bones.

The major rodeo events generally fall into two categories: riding and roping. Riding events include saddle bronc riding, bareback bronc riding, and bull riding; roping events include steer wrestling, calf roping, and steer roping. Women's barrel racing, clown bullfighting, and chuck wagon races complete the roundup. In most of the events, luck has much to do with who wins. Much of the scoring is based on the difficulty of the ride; consequently, the toughest broncs or bulls are favorites because they mean higher scores. Times for ropers depend on the speed and behavior of the calf or steer they're trying to tackle.

Many rodeo riders are young, skinny-as-a-rail types, but ropers tend to be bulkier and older. The two groups don't mix much and generally have disparaging words to say about the "skinny cowboys on their rocking horses" or "those fat bulldoggers with no style and no skill." But behind this bluster lies respect—and even more for competitors in a cowboy's own events. Hang around the chutes awhile and you'll discover a surprising generosity among fellow riders and ropers as they warn what to expect from a given bronc, help cinch down the straps, and joke over the new shiner from the horseshoe firmly planted in the bareback rider's face. They party together late into the night, looking for the rodeo queens and girls who like the smell of horse sweat. Small-time winners often spread the loot back among the losers, buying drinks and renting a motel room where everyone can sneak in for a night's rest. In *Rodeo! The Suicide Sport,* writer Fred Schnell tells a story that seems to epitomize rodeo life:

> *Once, when rodeo announcer Mel Lambert explained to the audience that a champion who had just made a good ride neither drank nor smoked and was a college athlete, Jim Shoulders, who has won 16 world titles, turned to a friend behind the chutes and said disgustedly, "Isn't that the worst crap you've ever heard? What the hell is rodeo coming to?"*

One thing newcomers soon notice about rodeo cowboys is the clothes they wear—long-sleeve shirts, cowboy hats, Wrangler jeans (never Levi's—the seam is in the wrong place for riding), and cowboy boots. As writer Mary S. Robertson noted, "In no other sport but rodeo do the players and the spectators dress alike." Interestingly, the

PRCA actually has a rule requiring long-sleeve shirts and cowboy hats; apparently at one time too many riders and ropers were wearing baseball caps and T-shirts, so the more traditional attire was made mandatory. One additional piece of attire is also worn by rodeo cowboys: the plate-sized silver and gold belt buckles. Top winners get these as awards for surviving a season of abuse; others buy them for flash and dash.

THE SUICIDE SPORT

A title occasionally used for rodeo is "the suicide sport." It is, unfortunately, all too true, especially for bull riders. Accidents are common, and rodeos always have an emergency medical technician ready to tend to the inevitable smashed legs, kicked-in ribs, and broken collarbones. Many cowboys are crippled for life, and at least several die each year in the sport, including two at Cheyenne Frontier Days in the 1980s. I recall watching a man in a wheelchair behind the bull chutes at a Jackson rodeo as he encouraged the riders; he had been paralyzed two years earlier in a bull-riding accident at that same rodeo. Even the nation's top riders and ropers can be killed; Lane Frost, a champion bull rider, died at Cheyenne Frontier Days in 1989. Most dangerous of all are the bull rides, but just watching a "dogger" leaping off his horse onto the horns of a speeding steer can give the crowd pause. Rodeos are criticized by animal-rights activists as unnecessarily cruel to animals—steers occasionally die from broken necks and broncs sometimes injure themselves (and their riders) by trying to jump out of the chutes—but the cowboys really do all they can to prevent injury to the animals they ride or rope. Rodeo announcers always point out that the animals spend very little time in the arena; nearly all of their time is in the pasture.

STEER WRESTLING

Steer wrestling, or bulldogging, involves leaping from a quarter horse onto the back of a 700-pound Mexican steer running at 25 miles per hour, grabbing his horns, and wrestling him to

ON THE ROAD

© DON PITCHER

bull rider at Deke Latham Memorial PRCA Rodeo in Kaycee

the ground. If you think that sounds easy, try it some time! Steer wrestling originated in 1903, when Bill Pickett, a black Texas cowboy (many early cowboys were black), jumped on the back of an ornery steer, grabbed its horns, bent over its head, and bit the steer's lower lip like an attacking bulldog. Soon he was repeating the stunt for the 101 Ranch Wild West Show. Others copied this feat, and although the lip-biting part has long since disappeared, the name bulldogging has stuck.

Steer wrestling is a complex endeavor involving two men: a dogger and a hazer. When the steer hurtles into the arena, the two spur their horses in quick pursuit, with the hazer trying to force the steer to run straight ahead while the dogger gets into position to leap onto the steer's horns and wrestle him to the ground with his feet and head facing the same direction. Because they are competing with other doggers on time, every second counts. Good doggers can get a steer down in less than seven seconds.

CALF ROPING

Calf roping originated in the Old West when ropers would pull down a calf and quickly tie it up for branding. Today, this is the most competitive of all rodeo events, and there is often big money for the winners. Calf ropers chase a 300-pound calf on their expertly trained horses, rope it, and then quickly throw it on its side. The piggin' string is wrapped around three ankles and secured with a half hitch ("hooey"), and then the calf is allowed to try to break free. If it can't within six seconds, the time stands and an untie man rides in to free the calf. Time is of the essence in calf roping, and a roper's horse is his most valuable asset. The best horses are in high demand and are often rented to other riders for a cut of any winnings.

STEER ROPING

The most controversial of all rodeo contests is steer roping, an event banned from most rodeos because it is so hard on the animals.

Cheyenne Frontier Days is one place where you can still see it. The procedure is essentially the same as calf roping, but with a much larger animal. When the 700-pound steer is jerked back by the rope and thrown down with a thud, you can almost feel the impact. Fortunately, injuries to the tough old steers are uncommon.

SADDLE BRONC RIDING

When you say the word "rodeo," many people immediately think of saddle bronc riding. The oldest of all rodeo sports, it originated in cowboys' attempts to train wild horses. Rodeo saddle bronc riding is more complex than this, however; it requires a special "association" saddle and dulled spurs and is played by precise rules. It is a judged event, with points taken away for not being in the correct position or in control. The bronc is saddled up in the chute (a fenced-in enclosure along the edge of the arena) and the rider climbs on, grabbing a thick hemp rope in one hand and sinking his boots into the stirrups. When the gate opens the bronc goes wild, trying to throw the rider off. The smooth back-and-forth motion of a good saddle bronc rider makes it appear that he is sitting atop a rocking chair. Rides last only eight seconds (leading to lots of ribald cowboy jokes); when the horn sounds, a pickup man rides alongside the bronc and the rider slides onto the other horse.

BAREBACK BRONC RIDING

Bareback riding is a relatively recent sport, having arrived on the scene in the 1920s. The rules are similar to those for saddle bronc riding, but the cowboy rides with a minimum of equipment—no stirrups and no reins. A small leather rigging held on by a leather strap around the horse is topped with a suitcaselike handle. A second wool-lined strap goes around the flank of the horse to act as an irritant so that he bucks more. The cowboy holds on with one hand and bounces back and forth in a rocking motion, an effort akin to trying to

juggle bowling pins while surfing a big wave. Eight seconds later it's over and a pickup man comes in to rescue the rider—if he hasn't been thrown to the ground.

BULL RIDING AND RODEO CLOWNS

Bull riding is in a class of danger all its own. Unlike broncs, which just want that man off their back, bulls want to get even. When a bull rider is thrown off (and this is most of the time, even with the best riders), the bull immediately goes on the attack, trying to gore or trample him. Many bull riders are seriously injured and some die when hit by this 2,000 pounds of brute force. There are no saddles in bull riding, just a piece of thick rope wrapped around the bull's chest, the free end wrapped tightly around the rider's hand. A cowbell hangs at the bottom of this contraption to annoy the bull even more. When the chute opens, all hell breaks loose as the bull does everything it possibly can to throw his rider off—spinning, kicking, jumping, and running against the fence.

If the rider hangs on for the required eight seconds (style isn't very important), the next battle begins—getting out of the way of one very angry bull. Here the rodeo clowns come in. Dressed in bright red-and-white shirts and baggy pants, they look like human Raggedy Andy dolls. In reality they are moving targets. Clowns use every trick in the book—climbing into padded barrels that the bulls butt against, weaving across the arena, mocking the bulls with matador capes, and simply running for their lives to reach the fence ahead of the bull. Frequently, two clowns work in tandem to create confusion, one acting as the barrel man and the other as a roving target. The rodeo clown also plays another role, that of entertainer between events. A clown's stock of supplies includes rubber chickens, trick mules, pantomime jokes with the announcer, and anything else that might keep folks from getting restless.

In a few of the larger rodeos there are clown "bullfights," in which a clown is pitted against a bull in a specially constructed small arena. He taunts the bull in every possible way, running past and around him, touching him, and maybe even leaping over him—all while trying to stay out of the way of those horns and hooves. These hijinks last only 45 seconds, but that seems like an eternity of danger. No wonder they call this the suicide sport!

OTHER EVENTS

One of the funniest of all rodeo events is the **wild horse race,** a zany event that since 1897 has ended each day at Cheyenne Frontier Days. Twelve teams of three cowboys try to rope, saddle, and then race a collection of the wildest horses imaginable. If they manage to get on the broncs, their next problem is convincing the horses to run around the half-mile track in the right direction. It seems the definition of bedlam, with horses breaking loose and starting off in opposite directions, crashing into mounted riders and other horses. For sheer chaos, wild horse races would even put a Democratic Convention to shame.

Barrel racing—the only female-dominated event—is found at nearly every rodeo and consists of a triangular course around three barrels arranged 100 feet apart. The event requires riding a fast horse in a set pattern around these barrels, trying not to knock any over. The fastest time wins.

Many rodeos also have what is called a **calf scramble**—featuring dozens of children from the stands chasing a calf to get a ribbon off its tail—and a **colt race,** in which young colts are let loose in a race toward their mares. Both events are real crowd pleasers.

Practicalities

VISITORS CENTERS

Chamber of commerce information centers are described for each town in this book. Large **state information centers** are located near Cheyenne, Evanston, Jackson, Laramie, Pine Bluffs, Sheridan, and Sundance.

For a helpful overall guide to Wyoming, along with a listing of events, chamber of commerce offices, and lodging and camping places, request a copy of the free *Wyoming Vacation Directory* from the Wyoming Division of Tourism and State Marketing, 307/777-7777 or 800/225-5996. Both summer and winter versions are available. They also have free **state maps,** or pick them up at any local visitors center. You'll find complete Wyoming travel details—and web links—at www.wyomingtourism.org.

WWWYOMING

Internet addresses are listed in the text for local chamber of commerce offices and a multitude of businesses. Nearly all local libraries have computers with free Internet access, and if you have a free email service such as hotmail or excite, you can check in from almost anywhere. Find a listing of Wyoming libraries and links to their homepages at www.publiclibraries.com/wyoming.htm. In addition, Wyoming's larger towns generally have Internet cafés or businesses with computer terminals for rent by the hour.

The official Wyoming state homepage is www.state.wy.us, and the state's tourism homepage is www.wyomingtourism.org. For something really different, check out www.bootsnall.com, where photojournalist Mike Jamison contributes to the "ultimate resource for the independent traveler." The site covers many places around the world, but Mike is based in Wyoming and has sharply written coverage of Wyoming ghost towns.

FEDERAL AND STATE OFFICES

The U.S. government owns more than 30 million acres within Wyoming, primarily in national forests, national parks, and BLM lands. In addition, the State of Wyoming owns another 3.8 million acres, including more than 118,000 acres of state park lands.

WYOMING TRIVIA

Size: 62,664,960 acres or 97,914 square miles (ninth-largest state)

Lowest point: 3,125 feet, where Belle Fourche River leaves Wyoming

Highest point: 13,804 feet, Gannett Peak in the Wind River Mountains

Number of people in 1970: 332,416
in 1980: 469,557 (+41.3 percent)
in 1990: 453,588 (–3.4 percent)
in 2000: 493,782 (+8.9 percent)

Number of people per square mile: 4.96

Overall crime rate in 2000: 34th in the nation

Abortion rate in 1996: 50th in the nation

Racial mix in the 2000 census:
White: 92.1 percent
Hispanic: 6.4 percent
Native American: 2.3 percent
Black: 0.8 percent
Asian or Pacific Islander: 0.6 percent
Other races: 3.2 percent

Number of cattle in 2000: 1,580,000

Number of sheep in 1900: 3.3 million; in 1999: 660,000

Number of antelope: 400,000

Percentage of people in Wyoming with four or more years of college: 21

Median age of Wyoming residents: 36

Average age of a Wyoming farmer in 1975: 40; in 1997: 54

Number of eligible voters who actually vote: second highest in the U.S.

One-time Wells Fargo agent in Cheyenne and later restaurant critic who had a cake mix named for him in 1949: Duncan Hines

Former president who once worked as a Yellowstone park ranger: Gerald Ford

Vice President and former Wyoming Representative known for his heart attacks and controversial business dealings: Dick Cheney

Consumer activist and presidential candidate who once worked in Yellowstone: Ralph Nader

1960s pop singer who once owned a Cody nightclub: Glen Campbell

Retail-chain founder who named his original Kemmerer shop the Golden Rule Store: J. C. Penney

1976 world champion bareback rider and country musician from Kaycee: Chris LeDoux

Best-known Wyoming attorney: Jerry Spence

Best-known (part-time) Wyoming residents: Dick Cheney and Harrison Ford

Number of Democratic governors: 10

Number of Republican governors: 12

Number of years that Democrats controlled both houses of the Wyoming state legislature between 1890 and 2003: 4; controlled by Republicans: 109

Last time a majority of Wyomingites voted for a Democratic presidential candidate: 1964 (Johnson)

World's largest piece of jade: a 3,366-pound nephrite jade boulder found near Lander in the 1940s

National rank in terms of:
coal production: first
trona production: first
bentonite production: first
average size of farms: first (3,761 acres)
wool production: second
per-capita federal aid: second
sheep and lambs: third

natural gas production: third
oil production: sixth
sugar beets: eighth
dry beans: eighth
barley: eighth
cattle and calves: 22nd
population: 50th
average value of farmland in 1997: 49th ($222/acre)
Estimated Wyoming coal resources: one trillion tons
Years Wyoming's coal would last if it supplied all of the world's coal: 200
Price for a ton of Wyoming coal in 2002: less than $5
Price for a six-pack of Sierra Nevada Ale in 2002: $6.99 (a bit more expensive, but it tastes a lot better)
Number of oil refineries in Wyoming in 1981: 14; in 2002: four
Average daily production for a Wyoming oil well in 2002: 14 barrels
Size of Sweetwater County, Wyoming: 10,495 square miles
Size of Rhode Island, Delaware, and Connecticut combined: 7,859 square miles
Number of Wyoming farms in 1920: 15,800; in 2000: 9,200
Percentage of water behind North Platte River dams in Wyoming used to irrigate Wyoming fields: 20 percent; used for Nebraska fields: 80 percent
Number of acres submerged by the Pathfinder dam: 22,000
Number of acres irrigated in Wyoming by the Pathfinder dam: 4,000

Number of "Peacekeeper" MX missiles in the Cheyenne area: 50
Number in the rest of the nation: 0
Nation's first national park: Yellowstone
Nation's first national monument: Devils Tower
Nation's first national forest: Yellowstone Timber Reserve (now Shoshone National Forest)
Nation's first polo field: north of Sheridan
"Oldest" building on earth: cabin built from dinosaur bones at Como Bluff
Oldest military building in Wyoming: Fort Laramie's "Old Bedlam"
First business west of the Missouri River: a fur trading post called Fort William (it later became Fort Laramie)
First American Legion post in the nation: in Van Tassell, Wyoming
Current population of Van Tassell: 8
First county public library system: Laramie County (Cheyenne) in 1886
First state to grant women full citizenship: Wyoming (in 1868, while still a territory)
First woman governor in America: Wyoming governor Nellie Tayloe Ross (1925)
First football game played under artificial lights in the nation: in Midwest, Wyoming (1925)
First female voter in the nation: Louisa Gardner Swain ("Grandma Swain"), who voted in Laramie on September 6, 1870
World's first female jurors: in Laramie in 1870
World's first female prison chaplain: Mrs. May Slosson at the Laramie Penitentiary in 1899
World's first female fire lookout: Lorraine Lindaley, stationed at Medicine Bow Peak Lookout (west of Laramie) in 1921

National Park Service

The National Park Service manages 2.3 million acres in Wyoming, including:

Grand Teton National Park, 307/739-3399, www.nps.gov/grte

Yellowstone National Park, 307/344-7381, www.nps.gov/yell

Bighorn Canyon National Recreation Area, 307/548-2251, www.nps.gov/bica

Devils Tower National Monument, 307/467-5283, www.nps.gov/deto

Fossil Butte National Monument, 307/877-4455, www.nps.gov/fobu

Fort Laramie National Historic Site, 307/837-2221, www.nps.gov/fola

Forest Service

The U.S. Forest Service manages 8.7 million acres in Wyoming and has ranger district offices in Afton, Big Piney, Buffalo, Cody, Douglas, Dubois, Encampment, Evanston, Greybull, Jackson, Kemmerer, Lander, Laramie, Lovell, Moran, Mountain View, Newcastle, Pinedale, Saratoga, Sheridan, Sundance, and Worland. The following national forests cover portions of the state:

Bighorn National Forest, Sheridan, 307/672-0751, www.fs.fed.us/r2/bighorn

Black Hills National Forest, Sundance, 307/283-1361, www.fs.fed.us/r2/blackhills

Bridger-Teton National Forest, Jackson, 307/739-5500, www.fs.fed.us/btnf

Flaming Gorge National Recreation Area (Ashley National Forest), Manila, Utah, 435/784-3445, www.fs.fed.us/r4/ashley

Medicine Bow-Routt National Forest, Laramie, 307/745-2300 or 800/877-9965, www.fs.fed.us/r2/mbr

Shoshone National Forest, Cody, 307/527-6241, www.fs.fed.us/r2/shoshone

Caribou-Targhee National Forest, Idaho Falls, ID, 208/524-7500, www.fs.fed.us/r4/caribou

Wasatch-Cache National Forest, Evanston, 307/789-3194, www.fs.fed.us/wcnf

Bureau of Land Management

Although not well known by the general public, the BLM is one of the biggest landholders in America. In Wyoming, the agency manages nearly 18 million acres. The **Wyoming State BLM Office** is in Cheyenne, 307/775-6256, www.wy.blm.gov. Local BLM offices are found in Buffalo, Casper, Cheyenne, Cody, Kemmerer, Lander, Newcastle, Pinedale, Rawlins, Rock Springs, and Worland.

Fish & Wildlife Service

The U.S. Fish & Wildlife Service has two staffed refuges in Wyoming: the National Elk Refuge in Jackson, 307/733-9212, http://nationalelkrefuge.fws.gov, and Seedskadee National Wildlife Refuge northwest of Green River, 307/875-2187, http://seedskadee.fws.gov. Wyoming's other two refuges are Hutton Lake National Wildlife Refuge near Laramie and Pathfinder National Wildlife Refuge near Casper.

State Parks

Wyoming's Department of State Parks and Cultural Resources maintains 26 parks, historic sites, recreation areas, and archaeological sites scattered across the state. Most of these charge day-use fees, or you can purchase an annual day-use pass for $4 ($2 for Wyoming residents). For details, contact the **Department of State Parks and Cultural Resources** in Cheyenne, 307/777-6303, http://wyoparks.state.wy.us.

State parks and recreation areas in Wyoming include the following, all of which are described later in this book: **Bear River State Park** near Evanston; **Big Sandy State Recreation Area** near Farson; **Boysen State Park** near Shoshoni; **Buffalo Bill State Park** near Cody; **Connor Battlefield State Historic Site** in Ranchester; **Curt Gowdy State Park** between Cheyenne and Laramie; **Edness K. Wilkins State Park** near Casper; **Fort Bridger State Historic Site** in Fort Bridger; **Fort Fetterman State Historic Site** near Douglas; **Fort Fred Steele State Historic Site** near Rawlins; **Fort Phil Kearny State Historic Site** near Buffalo; **Glendo State Park** near Glendo; **Guernsey State Park** near Guernsey; **Hawk Springs State Recreation Area** south of Torrington; **Hot Springs State Park** near Thermopolis; **Independence Rock State Historic Site** southwest of Casper; **Keyhole State Park** near Moorcroft; **Medicine Lodge State Archaeological Site** near Hyattville, **Seminoe State Park** north of Sinclair; **Sinks Canyon State Park** near Lander; **South Pass City State Historic Site** at South Pass; and **Trail End State Historic Site** in Sheridan.

ON THE RADIO

If you like country-and-western music, you'll love traveling through Wyoming, where the radio dial is packed with country stations playing mournful songs about leaving small towns for greener pastures, hard times, loose women, and truck-driving men. My favorite has to be the one that begins: "You're the first thing that I thought of/when I thought I'd drink you off my mind." Pretty much says it all.

Wyoming Public Radio (http://uwadmn-web.uwyo.edu/wpr) is based in Laramie, with repeaters throughout the state providing in-depth morning and evening news from National Public Radio, along with Wyoming news reports and the "World Cafe" for eclectic music. It's a vast improvement over the Rush Limbaugh broadsides, Top 40 hit stations, and recycled rock pabulum found elsewhere on the radio dial.

NEWSPAPERS

The Wyoming Press Association's website has a complete listing of newspapers in the state, including web links. Find it at www.wyopress.org. The *Casper Star-Tribune,* www.trib.com, is Wyoming's only statewide paper. A great way to check the pulse of Wyoming is to read the letters to the editor. They fill several pages every day and are sometimes quite amusing.

Two daily tabloid-style papers are published in Jackson: the *Jackson Hole News* www.jacksonholenews.com, and the *Jackson Hole Guide* www.jhguide.com. Both of these publish weekly editions with local news, along with freebie versions on weekdays.

Other papers with daily editions include Cheyenne's *Wyoming Tribune-Eagle,* www.wyomingnews.com, the *Laramie Boomerang,* www.laramieboomerang.com, the *Gillette News-Record,* www.gillettenewsrecord.com, *Rawlins Daily Times, Riverton Ranger, Rock Springs Daily Rocket-Miner, Sheridan Press,* www.thesheridanpress.com (not published on Sundays), and Worland's *Northern Wyoming Daily News.* Most other Wyoming towns of any size have their own weekly papers; there's even one for Lingle, population 500.

MUSEUMS AND THE ARTS

The state's finest large museum—Cody's Buffalo Bill Historical Center—should not be missed, but a visit to the smaller and lesser-known museums is also well worth your time. Other notable museums and historical sites are found in Buffalo, Casper, Cheyenne, Douglas, Fort Bridger, Fort Laramie, Grand Teton National Park, Jackson, Lusk, Pinedale, South Pass City, and Thermopolis.

The *Wyoming Cultural Guide* is a free state publication available in visitors centers or on the web at www.wyomingcultural-guide.org. It contains helpful descriptions of museums, theaters, galleries, art studios, and cultural events.

MONEY AND BANKING

Travelers checks (in U.S. dollars) are accepted without charge in most stores and businesses around Wyoming. It's not a good idea to travel with travelers checks in non-U.S. currency; they are accepted only at certain banks and are a time-consuming hassle. If you do arrive with pounds, yen, or Euros, several banks in Jackson, along with the park hotels inside Yellowstone, will exchange foreign currency for greenbacks.

When traveling in Wyoming, I pay for expenses by credit card whenever possible, but also keep an automated teller machine (ATM) card as a backup. You'll find ATMs in all the larger towns and increasingly in even the most remote Wyoming settlements. In this book, I've mentioned ATM locations in the smaller towns, but new ones are added all the time. Note that nearly all Wyoming ATMs now tack on a charge—usually $1.50 per transaction—to your own bank's fees, making this an expensive way to get cash. The charges are posted on the machine. It has become increasingly difficult to avoid these fees, but a few places don't charge. Your best bets are credit union ATMs. Another way to avoid the charge is to buy something at a grocery store that takes ATM cards and simply ask to get cash back over the purchase amount. The state of Wyoming maintains an annual listing of ATMs and their charges online at http://audit.state.wy.us/banking.

The major credit cards, especially Visa and MasterCard, are accepted almost everywhere, including in most larger grocery stores. This is probably the easiest way to travel, especially if you can get airline mileage credit at the same time. The miles can quickly add up if you make all of your purchases this way, but so can your credit card bill!

POST OFFICES

Post offices generally open between 7 A.M. and 9 A.M. and close between 5 P.M. and 6 P.M.; only a few are open on Saturday. After hours, the outer doors usually remain open so you can go in to buy stamps from the machines. Some drug or card stores also operate postal substations where you can buy stamps or mail packages within the United States (you'll have to go to a real post office for mailing to foreign addresses or for other special services). Many grocery store checkout counters also sell books of stamps with no markup.

Health and Safety

A common annoyance for Wyoming travelers will likely be insects, especially mosquitoes and blackflies. These are most prevalent in early summer in the mountains; by late August mosquito populations thin considerably. Use insect repellents containing DEET to help keep them away.

WEST NILE VIRUS

This disease first appeared in New York during 1999 and spread rapidly across the nation in summer 2002. Most people who are infected with West Nile virus show mild (or no) symptoms, but the disease can be fatal. The virus is transmitted through mosquito bites, and it can infect not just humans, but also horses, many species of birds, and other animals—with potentially devastating impacts on wildlife populations. Reduce your chance of infection by applying insect repellents containing DEET. (A higher concentration lasts longer, but there's no benefit in using DEET in concentrations over 50 percent.) You can also spray your clothing with the repellent, wear long-sleeved shirts and long pants, and stay indoors at dusk and dawn when the mosquitoes are their most active. See the Centers for Disease Control and Prevention website, www.cdc.gov, for details on the West Nile virus.

HANTAVIRUS

This potentially fatal respiratory disease is spread by rodents, particularly deer mice. Contact with them or their droppings can lead to such symptoms as fever, muscle aches, coughing, and difficulty breathing caused by fluid buildup in the lungs within 1–5 weeks. Once the symptoms appear, the disease progresses quickly, leading to hospitalization within 24 hours. More than one-third of those who come down with hantavirus die, and over the last decade, it has killed at least three Wyoming residents, including a young woman in 2002. Avoid contact with rodents and their feces or urine to minimize your chances of infection. Campers should never sleep on bare ground and avoid cabins if you find signs of rodents. Fortunately, the disease is not contagious from person to person. For additional information, visit www.cdc.gov.

TICKS

Ticks can be a real bother in parts of Wyoming, particularly lower-elevation brushy and grassy areas in the spring and early summer. They drop onto unsuspecting humans and other animals to suck blood and can spread several potentially devastating diseases, including Rocky Mountain spotted fever, ehrlichiosis, and Lyme disease. All of these diseases have been reported in low numbers throughout Wyoming.

Avoid ticks by tucking pant legs into boots and shirts into pants, using insect repellents containing DEET, and carefully inspecting your clothes while outside. Light-colored clothing and broad hats may also help. Check your body while hiking and immediately after the trip. If possible, remove ticks before they become embedded in your skin. If one does become attached, use tweezers to remove the tick, making sure to get the head. Apply a triple antibiotic ointment such as Neosporin to the area, and monitor the bite area for two weeks.

Lyme disease typically shows up as a large red spot with a lighter bulls-eye center, and it often causes muscle aches, fatigue, headache, and fever. Get medical help immediately if you show these symptoms after a tick bite. Fortunately, the disease can usually be treated with antibiotics. If untreated, it can cause a facial nerve palsy, memory loss, arthritis, heart damage, and other problems. A relatively effective vaccine has been developed for Lyme disease, but it requires a one-year regimen of doses and is expensive; check with your doctor for specifics. In Wyoming, where the disease is relatively uncommon, the vaccine is probably not warranted, and it may give a false sense of security because ticks can still spread other—and more dangerous—diseases. There are no vaccinations available against either Rocky Mountain spotted fever or ehrlichiosis, both of which sometimes kill people. The best action is to prevent tick bites in the first place. For more on tickborne diseases, see the Harvard Medical School's website at www.intelihealth.com.

Transportation

Public transportation is limited in Wyoming, although air service has improved in the last few years. Amtrak no longer offers train service through Wyoming, but the state has reasonably good bus service, even though this is minimal in some areas. Local buses operate in Jackson and Cheyenne.

BY AIR

Commercial airline flights take you to the towns of Casper, Cheyenne, Cody, Gillette, Jackson, Laramie, Riverton, Rock Springs, Sheridan, and Worland. The resort town of Jackson has the best air service in the state—by far—with daily jet flights from several cities. See the Special Topic "Airline Contacts" for details.

If you're flying to Jackson from Seattle, Los Angeles, or San Francisco, you will need to go through either Salt Lake City or Idaho Falls. The latter airport is served by Horizon Air (Alaska Airlines). Many folks opt to fly to either Salt Lake (275 miles away) or Idaho Falls (90 miles away) and pick up a rental car for the drive to Jackson.

The primary air carrier into most Wyoming cities is Cheyenne-based Great Lakes Aviation. They code share with United and Frontier, so you can book flights and get airline miles through either of these airlines. Great Lakes flies commuter planes that seat 19 to 30 passengers. See the Special Topic "Airline Contacts" for specific cities served in Wyoming by this airline, as well as others.

Check airfares to Wyoming and surrounding areas online through Travelocity (www.travelocity.com), Expedia (www.expedia.com), Orbitz (www.orbitz.com), or Hotwire (www.hotwire.com).

BY CAR

Given the expanse and small population of Wyoming, it's no surprise that the automobile—and the pickup truck in rural areas—is the primary means of transportation.

It's a long ways between things in Wyoming. Be sure to gas up in the main towns before heading out, and have a spare tire and a cell phone. If you have little ones onboard, make the kids go to the bathroom before you depart because it's tough to hide behind a sagebrush.

The **Wyoming Department of Transportation** puts out a pamphlet detailing current road projects around the state. You can find it in many visitors centers or get this and much more, including webcams along main roads, on the web at www.wyoroad.info. For a recording with road conditions around the state, call 307/772-0824 or 888/996-7623.

Highway Safety

Wyoming drivers seldom slow down when meeting other vehicles, so flying gravel is a frequent problem on unpaved roads. It's even a problem on paved roads, so make sure your insurance pays for windshield repairs!

Wyoming's official speed limits are 65 mph on most paved state highways (once you get away from the towns) and 75 mph on the interstate highways. Drive at those speeds and you'll find yourself constantly passed by cars going well over the limit. But look out when driving through small towns throughout Wyoming; the cops vigorously enforce local speed limits. When darkness falls on the main interstate highways (I-80, I-15, and I-90), the trucks come out in force, like bats emerging from caves. It can be a bit intimidating if you're driving a compact car.

Travel Maps

Free Wyoming maps can be found at visitors centers across the state, but map aficionados should be certain to purchase ***Wyoming Atlas & Gazetteer*** (www.delorme.com), which has detailed topographic maps of Wyoming. It is indispensable for travelers who are heading off main routes. National forest maps are also helpful for mountain driving in many parts of Wyoming; buy them at local Forest Service offices. The BLM produces a series of 1:100,000 maps for the entire state. These cost $4 each and are sold in many sporting goods stores. They're especially helpful when you're planning to head out into areas with mixed private and public lands.

Thousands of miles of paved and gravel roads cut across the state. Dan Lewis's *8,000 Miles of Dirt: A Backroad Travel Guide to Wyoming* (Casper: Hawks Book Co., 1992) has descriptions of interesting back roads, although I don't find it especially readable.

Car Rentals

You can rent cars in all of the larger towns, and those with airports generally have Hertz, Avis, and other national chains. See the Special Topic "Rental Car Contacts" in this chapter for rental companies serving specific Wyoming cities. You'll

RENTAL CAR CONTACTS

Alamo, 307/733-0671 or 800/327-9633, www.alamo.com

Avis, 307/632-9371 or 800/831-2847, www.avis.com

Budget, 307/733-2206 or 800/527-0700, www.drivebudget.com

Dollar Rent A Car, 307/733-9224 or 800/800-4000, www.dollar.com

Enterprise, 307/632-1907 or 800/325-8007, www.enterprise.com

Hertz, 307/634-2131 or 800/654-3131, www.hertz.com

Thrifty, 307/739-9300 or 800/367-2277, www.thrifty.com

AIRLINE CONTACTS

American, 800/433-7300, www.aa.com: Summer and winter service from Dallas and Chicago to Jackson.

Big Sky Airlines, 406/247-3910 or 800/237-7788, www.bigskyair.com: Daily service connecting Billings with Casper and Gillette.

Continental, 800/523-3273, www.continental.com: Serves Jackson Hole from Newark and Houston in the winter, and usually has service during the summer to the same cities.

Delta/Skywest, 800/221-1212, www.deltaair.com: Year-round service from Salt Lake City to Casper, Cody, and Jackson, with additional winter flights out of Atlanta.

Great Lakes Aviation, 307/432-7000 or 800/554-5111, www.greatlakesav.com: Provides air service most days from Denver to Cheyenne, Laramie, Casper, Sheridan, Gillette, Cody, Riverton, Worland, and Rock Springs. They also fly between Cody and Rock Springs and between Worland and Riverton. In addition, the company has service between Denver and many other cities and towns in the Midwest and Rockies.

Northwest Airlines, 800/225-2525, www.nwa.com: Flies from Minneapolis/St. Paul to Jackson in summer and winter.

United/United Express, 800/241-6522, www.unitedairlines.com: Offers year-round turboprop service from Denver to Jackson.

find 4WD sport utility vehicles available in many locations, including Jackson Hole, but will pay dearly for the privilege.

I've generally found the best car rental rates in the larger cities where there's more competition. If you plan to rent a car for an extended period, it's worth your while to check travel websites such as www.travelocity.com, www.expedia.com, or www.orbitz.com to see which company offers the best rates. Note, however, that these quotes do not include taxes, which can be substantial, especially if you rent at the Denver or Salt Lake

City airports. Even once you've made a reservation it pays to call around again when you arrive at the airport. On one visit I saved hundreds of dollars by getting a last-minute quote for a one-month rental. Cool tip: If you're visiting in the summer, try to get a light-colored car; the dark ones can get incredibly hot in the blazing sun!

Winter Travel

During winter, Wyoming travelers need to take special precautions. Snow tires are a necessity, but you should also have several emergency supplies, including tire chains, a shovel and bag of sand in case you get stuck, a first-aid kit, booster cables, signal flares, a flashlight, lighter and candle, transistor radio, nonperishable foods (granola bars, canned nuts, or dried fruit), a jug of water, an ice scraper, winter clothes, blankets, and a sleeping bag. The most valuable tool may well be a **cell phone** to call for help—assuming you're in an area with reception. If you become stranded in a blizzard, stay in your car. You're more likely to be found, and the vehicle provides shelter from the weather. Run the engine and heater sparingly, occasionally opening a downwind window for ventilation. Don't run the engine if the tailpipe is blocked by snow—you may risk carbon monoxide poisoning. For up-to-date road and travel conditions in Wyoming, call 307/772-0824 or 888/996-7623, or log onto the web at www.wyoroad.info. Get weather information on the web at www.crh.noaa.gov/cys.

BIKES

Because of Wyoming's small population, cyclists will find uncrowded roads in many parts of the state. The long distances between towns, windy conditions, and frequent summer thunderstorms add to the adventure/danger. The Wyoming Department of Transportation publishes a useful *Bicycle Guidance Map*—on waterproof paper—showing the amount of traffic on each paved road, the width of paved shoulders, profiles of the steeper road grades, and general wind patterns. Anyone touring on a bike will find this map immensely valuable. Get a copy by calling the WYDOT Bicycle Coordinator at 307/777-4719.

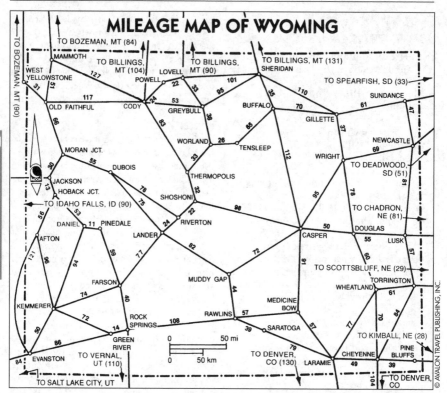

MILEAGE MAP OF WYOMING

© AVALON TRAVEL PUBLISHING, INC.

Many thousands of miles of gravel and dirt roads provide excellent places to explore on mountain bikes; check with local bike shops for nearby routes. Get the BLM's 1:100,000-scale area maps (available at most BLM offices for $4) before heading out. They show land ownership, contour lines, and all roads. On Forest Service lands, purchase equally detailed maps from local district offices. Mountain bikes can be rented in most of the larger Wyoming towns.

LONG-DISTANCE BUSES

Greyhound, 800/231-2222, www.greyhound.com, covers the southern end of Wyoming along the I-80 corridor, stopping in Evanston, Lyman, Fort Bridger, Rock Springs, Wamsutter, Rawlins, Laramie, and

Cheyenne, and connecting onward to other cities throughout the country. They also have service connecting Cheyenne with Denver, and between Salt Lake City and West Yellowstone, Montana (next to Yellowstone National Park).

Based in Gillette, Wyoming, **Powder River Transportation/Coach USA,** 307/682-0960 or 800/442-3682, focuses on the northern and eastern parts of the state. They offer daily service to Basin, Buffalo, Casper, Cheyenne, Cody, Douglas, Gillette, Greybull, Lovell, Moorcroft, Powell, Riverton, Sheridan, Shoshone, Sundance, Thermopolis, Torrington, Wheatland, and Worland. They also serve Colorado (Boulder, Denver, and Ft. Collins), Montana (Billings, Bridger, Hardin, and Laurel), and South Dakota (Rapid City, Spearfish, and Sturgis).

© DON PITCHER

ON THE ROAD

Wyoming stop sign

Alltrans/Jackson Hole Express, 307/733-1719 or 800/652-9510, www.jacksonholealltrans.com, provides daily bus or van connections between Salt Lake City, Idaho Falls, Pocatello, and the resort town of Jackson.

Another option is the nonprofit **Wind River Transportation Authority** (WRTA), 307/856-7118 or 800/439-7118, www.wrtabuslines.com, with trips between Salt Lake City and the towns of Riverton and Lander.

Southeast Wyoming

Southeast Wyoming is farming and ranching country, part of the vast prairie region that drapes America's heartland. In many ways, it is indistinguishable from western Nebraska or eastern Colorado—one long continuum of grass, grain, and grazing. Folks drive big American cars and Ford pickups. Instead of the saddleries and oil companies elsewhere in Wyoming, you'll find farm-equipment dealers and more feed caps than cowboy hats (they hold down better in the wind that seems to never stop blowing).

Buffalo roamed through southeast Wyoming for thousands of years, hunted by nomadic tribes of Plains Indians. Now sheep and cattle follow the same trails, and farmers grow wheat where Cheyenne Indian villages once stood. Alternating bands of wheat and fallow land give some areas a candy-striped appearance, while in others the expansive prairie extends in all directions. Old windmills, white farmhouses, hip-roofed barns, rusting retired farm machinery, and tall silos mark the old homesteads that became permanent farmsteads.

old homestead north of Fort Laramie

© DON PITCHER

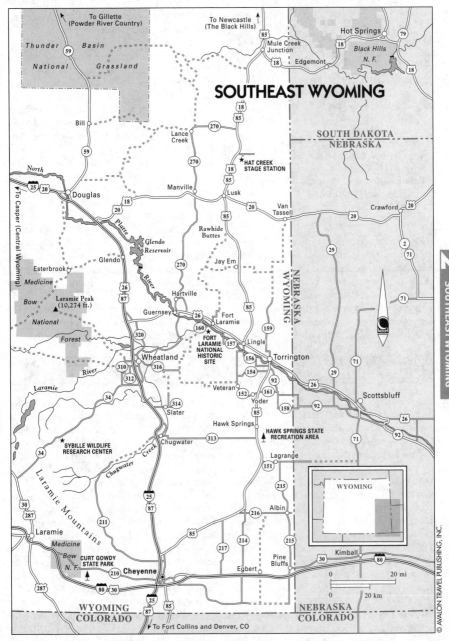

SOUTHEAST WYOMING

To Gillette
(Powder River Country)

To Newcastle
(The Black Hills)

Thunder Basin

National Grassland

Hot Springs

Mule Creek
Junction

Edgemont

*Black Hills
N. F.*

Bill

Lance
Creek

HAT CREEK
STAGE STATION

SOUTH DAKOTA
NEBRASKA

North

Platte River

Douglas

Manville

Lusk

Van
Tassell

Crawford

Rawhide
Buttes

Glendo
Reservoir

Jay Em

Glendo

Esterbrook

Medicine

Laramie Peak
(10,274 ft.)

Bow

Hartville

Guernsey

Fort Laramie

National

Forest

FORT
LARAMIE
NATIONAL
HISTORIC
SITE

Lingle

Torrington

Scottsbluff

To Casper (Central Wyoming)

NEBRASKA
WYOMING

Wheatland

Laramie

River

Veteran

Yoder

Slater

Hawk Springs

SYBILLE WILDLIFE
RESEARCH CENTER

Chugwater Creek

Chugwater

HAWK SPRINGS STATE
RECREATION AREA

Lagrange

Laramie Mountains

Albin

WYOMING

Laramie

Medicine

Bow N. F.

CURT GOWDY
STATE PARK

Cheyenne

Egbert

Pine
Bluffs

Kimball

WYOMING
COLORADO

NEBRASKA
COLORADO

To Fort Collins and Denver, CO

0   20 mi

0   20 km

© AVALON TRAVEL PUBLISHING, INC.

SOUTHEAST WYOMING

SOUTHEAST WYOMING SIGHTSEEING HIGHLIGHTS

State Capitol, Frontier Days Old West Museum, Wyoming State Museum, and Nelson Museum of the West in Cheyenne

Register Cliff and Oregon Trail ruts near Guernsey

Fort Laramie National Historic Site

Torrington Livestock Market

Stagecoach Museum in Lusk

Popular events: Chugwater Chili Cook-off in Chugwater (June), Frontier Days in Cheyenne (July), and *Legend of Rawhide* in Lusk (July)

The gravel roads cut straight across this gently rolling land with sudden right-angled jags around old homestead boundaries. Drive out on these roads and the pace slows to country speed and meadowlarks call from the fence posts. Folks raise a hand to wave as you pass and stop to chat on the crest of a hill. Tune in the radio and you're likely to hear country music, farm market reports, and Paul Harvey commentaries. This is Wyoming's most important agricultural region.

The capital city, Cheyenne, dominates the economy of southeast Wyoming, one of only two real cities in the state (the other is Casper). The other major settlements—Wheatland, Torrington, and Lusk—are small agricultural focal points and governmental centers for their respective counties.

Southeast Wyoming experiences typical high-plains weather. It is hot and windy in the summer, cold and windy in the winter. The wind—averaging more than 13 mph—is a given; this is great country for kites, but not much fun when the gales of winter slice through like a knife. Partly because of this wind, however, Cheyenne has some of the cleanest air in the nation. Explore the back roads and you'll find busy cattle ranches, abandoned mining towns, remnants of many historic trails, archaeological sites, dinosaur bones, and old sod homesteads. Hiking through the gently undulating plains is a delightful experience because vast expanses of this land remain almost unchanged from the time when bison roamed the great grasslands of the West.

Cheyenne

As you drive west toward Cheyenne (pop. 53,000), the Colorado Rockies loom on the southwestern horizon like whitecaps in a sea of barely rolling plains, snow fences, stunted grass, and the highway slashing toward the boundary of sight. You catch quick glimpses of the great mountain ranges that ramble across Wyoming. Gradually they grow larger, and finally you know that the Great Plains will soon be left behind. It's easy to imagine how this must have looked to the railroad passengers who passed this way in the 1860s, watching the mountains loom on the horizon as they rolled into Wyoming. Suddenly you're shaken into the present by the highway sign "Cheyenne Next 4 Exits." Suburban homes crowd over the gentle hillsides, and the state capitol gleams in the setting sun. You have arrived at Wyoming's political and transportation fulcrum.

The city of Cheyenne hunkers down in the southeastern corner of Wyoming, just 10 miles from Colorado and 40 miles from Nebraska. Its wide, tree-draped urban streets and graceful older homes form a gridwork through downtown, while suburbia spreads its tentacles into the surrounding prairie. Cheyenne is remarkably similar to (although smaller than) another state capital—Lincoln, Nebraska. For many visitors, it offers a taste of the West without leaving the Midwest. Folks in Casper or Cody view Cheyenne as the capital of eastern Wyoming and as a city whose ties are really closer to the markets of Denver or Omaha than to the sagebrush, oil, and coal of Wyoming. People in Cheyenne brush aside these criticisms. They know everyone else is just jealous.

As the state capital, the largest city, home to a strategic military base, a center for various governmental agencies, and a major transportation hub, Cheyenne is a big fish in the small pond

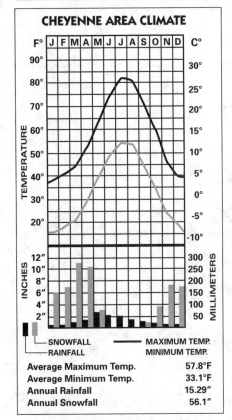

CHEYENNE AREA CLIMATE

	J F M A M J J A S O N D	

SNOWFALL
RAINFALL

MAXIMUM TEMP.
MINIMUM TEMP.

Average Maximum Temp.	57.8°F
Average Minimum Temp.	33.1°F
Annual Rainfall	15.29"
Annual Snowfall	56.1"

Drive out Dell Range Boulevard on the north side of town and you'll run into mile after mile of new developments, with national chains of all stripes moving in: Red Lobster, Burger King, Sam's Club, Kmart, Barnes & Noble, Target, Taco Bell, Applebee's, Chili's, and more. The homogenization of America continues, even in Wyoming.

HISTORY

Like so many other Wyoming cities, Cheyenne is a creation of the railroad. It is the oldest of Wyoming's railroad towns, established as the Union Pacific raced westward in 1867. When Gen. Grenville M. Dodge was planning the new railroad's route, he decided to establish a major rail terminal in the plains just before the long climb over the Laramie Mountains. He named the new settlement Cheyenne, for the Indians who lived in this country. The word is from the Sioux Indian term "Shey an nah," meaning "People of a Strange Tongue." (Some have suggested a less complimentary origin for the word, the French term *chienne,* meaning "bitch.") While Dodge was there, Indians attacked a Mormon grading crew, killing two men. The graveyard was started before the first building was up. By November of that year the new town of Cheyenne had swollen to 4,000 people, earning the nickname "Magic City of the Plains." It was easily the largest town in Wyoming and has remained that way for much of the state's history.

At first, Cheyenne consisted of the usual hell-on-wheels railroad settlement of tents and hastily erected buildings. Railroad workers and army men from nearby Fort D. A. Russell turned the town into a rip-roaring place—every second building was a saloon, and burlesque shows were the rage. At center stage stood a 36-by-100-foot tent housing Headquarters Saloon. Reporter James Chisholm noted:

> *The wildest roughs from all parts of the country are congregated here, as one may see by glancing into the numerous dance houses and gambling halls—men who carry on the trade of robbery openly, and would not scruple to kill a man for ten dollars.*

called Wyoming. The city has one of the most stable and prosperous economies in the state. Its largest employer (nearly 5,000 people) is giant Francis E. Warren Air Force Base, but several thousand other folks work for the federal, state, and local government agencies around town. Railroad tracks of the Union Pacific and Burlington Northern Railroads head to the four points of the compass, and Cheyenne is right at the junction of two of the primary transportation routes across the Plains and the Rockies: I-25 and I-80. Some 800 folks work for Union Pacific, with hundreds more employed in light industry, communications, air transport (Great Lakes Aviation is based here), and shipping firms. As Denver's sprawl heads ever outward, one is even starting to hear Cheyenne being called the northern edge of the Front Range.

SOUTHEAST WYOMING

© AVALON TRAVEL PUBLISHING, INC.

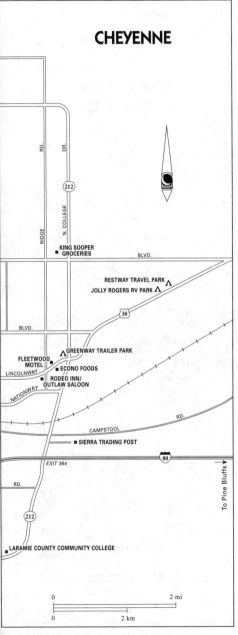

CHEYENNE

RD.

DR.

212

RIDGE

N. COLLEGE

■ KING SOOPER GROCERIES

BLVD.

RESTWAY TRAVEL PARK ▲
JOLLY ROGERS RV PARK ▲

30

BLVD.

▲ GREENWAY TRAILER PARK

FLEETWOOD MOTEL
■ ECONO FOODS

LINCOLNWAY

● RODEO INN/
OUTLAW SALOON

NATIONWAY

RD.

CAMPSTOOL

■ SIERRA TRADING POST

80

EXIT 364

RD.

212

■ LARAMIE COUNTY COMMUNITY COLLEGE

To Pine Bluffs ▶

```
0                    2 mi
|——————————————————|
0          2 km
```

Settling Down

Within a decade, however, Cheyenne had settled into a more urbane stage. The railroad provided access to the East, not only allowing cattle to be shipped but also keeping the town abreast of the latest fashions and furnishings and bringing news of world events. With the discovery of gold in the Black Hills, Cheyenne became the primary shipping center for supplies to the Black Hills and gold bullion from the smelters.

By the 1880s, Cheyenne had grown to a cosmopolitan small city of 14,000 people and was declared the wealthiest city per capita in the world. It was one of the first cities in the West to have electric lights; a power plant charged batteries during the day and then delivered them by wagon in time for the evening's use. In 1882, the elaborate Cheyenne Opera House opened with great fanfare. With seating for up to 1,000 people, luxurious furnishings, and a huge 52-light gas chandelier overhead, it was regarded as the equal of any in New York and attracted such performers as Lily Langtry, Sarah Bernhardt, P. T. Barnum, Buffalo Bill Cody, and the Royal Opera Company.

Despite its peripheral location, Cheyenne was the logical place for Wyoming's territorial capital. The railroad was here, as were Fort D. A. Russell and most of the wealthy cattlemen. In 1869, the first territorial governor, John A. Campbell, made Cheyenne the temporary capital, with the legislature meeting in rented quarters. Five years later it almost lost that title to Laramie in a rump session of the legislature, but after completion of the capitol building in 1888 it became obvious that the governmental seat would remain in Cheyenne.

Rule of the Cattle Barons

Destruction of the once-vast herds of bison and the eviction of Indians who had lived in Wyoming for centuries suddenly opened up nearly all of the territory to cattle grazing. At the time, Laramie County extended all the way to the border with Montana, so it was logical that Cheyenne became the focal point for hundreds of cattlemen who rushed in to make a killing on the booming cattle market. The most famous of these was Alexander Swan, founder of a spread so large that it required a special book to keep track

To Chugwater

MUNICIPAL GOLF COURSE

GOVERNOR'S MANSION (NEW)

DELL RANGE BLVD.

YELLOWSTONE RD.

219

POWDERHOUSE RD.

FRONTIER MALL

C.B. POTTS

KMART

WAL-MART

FAIRFIELD INN

OAK TREE INN

BARNES & NOBLE

KENNEDY

SWIMMING POOL

CAREY

85

CENTRAL AVE.

DOWNTOWN CHEYENNE

25 87

FRONTIER DAYS OLD WEST MUSEUM

Sloans Lake

Frontier Park

Lions Park

BOTANIC GARDENS

8TH AVE.

CHEYENNE MUNICIPAL AIRPORT

F. E. WARREN AIR FORCE BASE

6TH AVE.

HYNDS

CRIBBON

REED

4TH

PIONEER AVE.

CAPITOL

CENTRAL

WARREN

MAIN ENTRANCE

2ND AVE.

BLVD.

85 85

W. PERSHING

E. PERSHING

RANDALL

EXIT 11

3RD ST.

THOMES AVE.

CAREY

LIBRARY

EVANS AVE.

MAXWELL

SEYMOUR

RUSSELL AVE.

ALEXANDER

BRADLEY AVE.

22ND ST.

20TH ST.

19TH AVE.

29TH

HOSPITAL

27TH

SNYDER

BENT

STATE CAPITOL

BARRET STATE OFFICE BUILDING

HISTORIC GOVERNOR'S MANSION

PORCH SWING B&B

Holiday Park

ALT. 30

25TH

POST OFFICE

ST. MARY'S CATHEDRAL

E. LINCOLNWAY

23RD

CIVIC CENTER

ST. MARK'S EPISCOPAL CHURCH

RAINSFORD INN B&B

21ST

FIRST UNITED METHODIST CHURCH

NAGLE-WARREN MANSION B&B

MISSILE DR.

15TH

SANFORD'S

PLAINS HOTEL

UNION PACIFIC RAILROAD YARD

EXIT 10

HAPPY JACK RD.

ALT. 30

W. LINCOLNWAY

17TH

VISITORS BUREAU

CHEYENNE DEPOT MUSEUM

WARREN AVE.

CENTRAL AVE.

To Denver

25 87

WESTLAND RD.

SANDS MOTEL

GUEST RANCH MOTEL

FRONTIER MOTEL

RANGER MOTEL

IKON CENTER

LUXURY DINER

DEMING DR.

9TH ST.

7TH ST.

85

LUXURY INN

BEST WESTERN HITCHING POST INN

STAGE COACH MOTEL

MOTEL 6

180

5TH

SUPER 8 MOTEL

LINCOLN COURT

10TH

3RD ST.

ALT. 30

1ST

BUS STATION

STANFIELD AVE.

PARSLEY BLVD.

LARIAT MOTEL

EXIT 362

80

0   0.5 mi

0   0.5

MOON

FOX FARM RD.

TANK FARM RD.

WALTERSCHEID BLVD.

HOLIDAY INN

85

80

SOUTHEAST WYOMING

of all its cattle brands. Other part-time residents included members of English nobility such as Moreton Frewen (nephew of Sir Winston Churchill) and Sir Oliver H. Wallop, seventh earl of Portsmouth.

Fort D. A. Russell

In 1862, President Lincoln approved creation of a military fort to guard the then-proposed transcontinental railroad against Indian attacks. When the railroad finally arrived five years later, the army established a fort near the new town of Cheyenne. Both the town and fort were officially established on the same day. Originally named for Civil War general David A. Russell, the new fort grew into America's largest cavalry outpost. Troops from the base were sent out to protect railroad survey and construction parties and later served as guards along the route. The **Cheyenne Depot,** commonly called Camp Carlin, was established adjacent to the fort, providing vital equipment for a dozen army posts scattered throughout the Indian frontier. It was abandoned in 1890.

With forced relocation of the Indians to reservations, the role of Fort D. A. Russell changed and it became a training center and strategic garrison for the Rockies. New brick barracks and officers' quarters were completed in 1885, and the

FRANCIS E. WARREN

One of Wyoming's best-known politicians was Francis E. Warren (1844–1929). A lifelong Republican, Warren served as both a territorial and state governor before being elected to the U.S. Senate in 1890. One of the millionaire cattle barons, his ranch once held more than 100,000 sheep. This land later got him in trouble when he was charged with fencing public land for his own gain, but his friendship with Pres. Theodore Roosevelt helped keep him out of prison. While territorial governor in the 1880s, Warren ardently agitated for statehood. His 37 years in the U.S. Senate made him one of its most powerful members, and newspapers labeled him the "Boss of Wyoming." Upon his death, Fort D. A. Russell was renamed in his honor.

dusty parade ground was planted with grass and trees. Wyoming senator Francis E. Warren had long "brought home the bacon" by gaining political plums for his constituents, and one of the biggest was continued support for the fort in Cheyenne. After his death in 1929, the fort was renamed **Francis E. Warren Air Force Base.** The base served as a training center and POW camp in World War II and was transferred to the newly created Air Force in 1947.

The fort's current role began in 1958, when the arrival of Atlas missiles made Warren the nation's first nuclear-missile base. The event was greeted with glee by Cheyenne's then mayor, Worth Story, who exclaimed, "Cheyenne is proud to be the nation's number one target for enemy missiles." Today, the city enjoys a similar privilege as the only place in the nation where the 10-warhead "Peacekeeper" MX nuclear missiles are based. Cheyenne even has a Missile Drive. Warren Air Force Base houses 150 Minuteman III missiles—now rendered unlaunchable in the post–Cold War era—plus all 50 "Peacekeeper" MX missiles in existence, giving it 40 percent of the nation's intercontinental ballistic missiles (ICBMs) and making it one of the most important ICBM centers in America. The missiles are dispersed over a 150-mile radius in Wyoming, Colorado, and western Nebraska, creating an attractive bull's-eye target centered on Cheyenne. Missile silos are manned by two crew members working some 60 feet underground on 24-hour shifts. Each of these "capsules" controls 10 missiles in surrounding areas. The missiles are launched by steam (!) for the first 150 feet before the missile itself ignites, an event one hopes never occurs.

SIGHTS

For a fine introduction to Cheyenne, take one of the **trolley tours** that depart from the old depot at 16th and Capitol daily between mid-May and mid-September. These two-hour tours cost $8 ($4 for kids) and include stops at various historic attractions. Get tickets at the visitors bureau, 309 W. Lincolnway, 307/778-3133 or 800/426-5009.

SOUTHEAST WYOMING

State Capitol

Capitol Avenue—one of the primary streets in Cheyenne—seems to symbolize the city's history. State government buildings line the street, and at the ends are the two main reasons for Cheyenne's existence: the old Union Pacific depot to the south and the State Capitol to the north. The Capitol building is open Monday–Friday 8 A.M.–5 P.M., and free guided tours are available throughout the year. Call 307/777-7220 for more information or group reservations.

Wyoming's capitol falls in the tradition of ostentatious political structures and is modeled after the Capitol in Washington, D.C. The initial building was authorized with a $150,000 appropriation from the territorial legislature in 1886. The cornerstone was laid on May 18, 1887, and the central portion was completed the following year, with the two wings added later. When completed in 1917, the building measured its present 300-foot length. The 146-foot-tall dome has been regilded four times, most

recently in 1986. (Don't bother trying to climb up to steal any; the entire dome is covered with less than an ounce of gold.)

The capitol's central rotunda has a checkered marble floor with cherry wood staircases leading to the second story. Directly overhead is a beautiful blue stained-glass window imported from England. Interesting historical photographs line the second-floor walls. The senate chambers are in the west wing; the house meets in the east wing. You can view the legislature from the third-floor balconies when it is in session. Inside the legislative chambers are four Western murals painted by Allen T. True—designer of Wyoming's bucking-bronco symbol—along with others by Joseph Henry Sharp and Bill Gollings. Look upward in each chamber to see the large Tiffany stained-glass ceilings with the state seal.

From the outside, the capitol dome seems strangely tall; rumor has it that architects once voted it the nation's ugliest state capitol, although Alaska's would give it a run for this dubious honor. Out front stands a bronze statue of **Esther Hobart Morris,** the person credited (incorrectly) with making Wyoming the first state to grant women voting rights. Directly behind the capitol building is the much newer **Herschler Building,** named for the only Wyoming governor to serve three terms, Ed Herschler. It has an attractive interior atrium and houses a cafeteria and various state offices. Between the two buildings is an 18-foot-tall bronze statue by Edward Fraughton, *Spirit of Wyoming,* a bucking horse and rider that seem almost suspended in space. It is perhaps fitting that the two nicknames of Wyoming—"the Equality State" and "the Cowboy State"—are symbolized by statues on either side of the State Capitol. Wander around the flower-garnished grounds and you'll discover a monument to the Spanish-American War, a bronze bison statue, and a replica of the Liberty Bell.

Historic Governors' Mansion

The old governors' mansion, 300 E. 21st St., 307/777-7878, http://wyoparks.state.wy.us/govern.htm, is open year-round Tuesday–Saturday 9 A.M.–5 P.M. Entrance is free. A 10-minute video provides information about the house and its

---

CHEYENNE IN THE 1860S

Astronomical eclipses are of infrequent occurrence, but there is an eclipse taking place on Eddy Street daily and nightly. It is Professor McDaniel's Museum, which eclipses every other place of amusement in Cheyenne. The more money you invest with the Professor the greater equivalent you receive. Call upon him, imbibe one of those Tom and Jerrys, etc., and if not satisfied we pronounce you incorrigible. "Ye Gods!" What nectar the Professor concocts in those little china mugs. Better than the dew on a damsel's lips. Speaking of damsels just step into the museum and you'll see 'em large as life, besides 1,001 other sciences, embracing every known subject. It is an awe-inspiring view.

—ad for McDaniel's Theater and Museum in the 1860s, quoted in *The Magic City of the Plains: Cheyenne 1867–1967*

CHEYENNE AND BLACK HILLS STAGE

With the 1874 discovery of gold in the Black Hills, a stampede of miners headed north in search of riches. A fierce competition quickly developed between Cheyenne, Wyoming, and Sidney, Nebraska, to be the jumping-off point for miners. With support for road construction from the Wyoming Territorial Legislature, a 300-mile stage route was soon laid out, and the first coach headed north on February 3, 1876. The Cheyenne and Black Hills Stage, Mail and Express Line had begun.

The line ran almost straight north from Cheyenne to the vicinity of present-day Lusk before veering into Dakota Territory and ending at Deadwood. Drivers made the trip in three days and three nights, with station stops every 15 miles that usually lasted less than three minutes—just long enough to change horses. It was a strenuous and tiring journey through Sioux Indian territory, over treacherous river crossings, and past hideouts of notorious road agents. On the long trip south from the mines, special armored coaches carried gold bullion in steel strongboxes, protected by four to six armed guards. Often they held up to $100,000 in gold dust and nuggets and sometimes as much as $350,000! Outlaws—

including Frank and Jesse James and Big Nose George Parrot's gang—targeted these coaches, riding off with both the gold and the horses. One of the most infamous attack sites was near the Robber's Roost Stage Station, along the Cheyenne River north of Lusk. Here the stages were frequently attacked, sometimes every day.

The "Deadwood Coaches," such as the one used by Buffalo Bill in his Wild West Show, were actually the famed Concord coaches built by Abbott and Downing of Concord, New Hampshire. They could jam nine passengers inside (first and second class) for $15–20 per head and an equal number on top (third class) at $10 apiece. Riders on top sometimes had to get off and push the stage up hills. (Despite the attention given to stagecoaches, much of the traffic along the goldfields route was in freight wagons pulled by long strings of oxen.) Upon completion of the Chicago and Northwestern Railroad to Rapid City, traffic on the Cheyenne to Deadwood stage dropped, and the last coach ran on February 19, 1887. In just 11 years, the stage line had carved out a big piece of history, and its closing marked the end of one of the most romantic chapters in the history of the West.

inhabitants, including the nation's first woman governor, Nellie Tayloe Ross; she lived here from 1925 to 1927. The home is furnished with pieces from several periods. The 2.5-story brick building was completed in 1905 at a cost of $33,000. It's in the Georgian style, with four Corinthian columns out front.

The current governors' mansion, which was completed in 1976, sits near the intersection of Central Avenue and I-25. Tours of the new mansion are offered only for groups; call 307/777-7398 for appointments.

Wyoming State Museum
Inside the Barrett Building at 2301 Central Avenue, the Wyoming State Museum features a mix of continuing and changing exhibits. Permanent displays showcase coal mining, wildlife, dinosaurs, and Indian artifacts. Visitors will also find a 3-

D model of the state (showing historic sites), an impressive silver service set from the decommissioned battleship USS *Wyoming,* and a fun hands-on history room for kids. Be sure to stop by the museum gift shop for high-quality regional items and Wyoming books. The museum is open Tuesday–Saturday 9 A.M.–4:30 P.M. May–October, and Tuesday–Friday 9 A.M.–4:30 P.M. and Saturday 10 A.M.–2 P.M. the rest of the year. (It's always closed on Sundays, Mondays, and holidays.) Admission is free. Get details at 307/777-7022, http://wyomuseum.state.wy.us.

Frontier Days Old West Museum
Right next to the rodeo grounds in Frontier Park, this is one of the most interesting museums in Wyoming. It's open daily 9 A.M.–6 P.M. from Memorial Day to Labor Day (daily 8 A.M.–8 P.M. during Frontier Days), and Monday–Friday

8 A.M.–5 P.M. and Saturday–Sunday 9 A.M.–5 P.M. the rest of the year. Admission is $5 adults, free for kids under 13. Get details at 307/778-7290 or 800/778-7290, www.oldwestmuseum.org. The museum's focus is on Western heritage, with changing historical and art exhibits, Indian artifacts, early clothing, old films, Frontier Days displays—including a bronc-riding saddle that you can try out—and a special "Hole in the Wall" hands-on kids room. The museum is best known for its extraordinary collection of horse-drawn transportation of all types. More than 40 carriages, including many that appear in the annual Frontier Days parade, are displayed. The stars are a Cheyenne-to-Deadwood stage, a prairie schooner, sleighs, a buckboard (the name came from the lack of springs on the axles), and, of course, a surrey with the fringe on top. Be sure to check out the luxurious landau—sort of an early convertible. The gift shop sells various Frontier Days souvenirs and historical books. Out front is a sculpture of champion bull rider Lane Frost,

who was killed during a 1989 ride at Frontier Days. A big **Western Art Show and Sale** takes place at the museum during Frontier Days, and other exhibits fill the galleries at other times.

Nelson Museum of the West

This surprising private museum is right in the heart of downtown Cheyenne at 1714 Carey Ave., 307/635-7670, www.nelsonmuseum.com. The collection was acquired by Robert L. Nelson, a retired lawyer, big-game hunter, and owner of Manitou Gallery (across the street). It reflects his tastes, with an odd mix of Old West artifacts and memorabilia, along with big-game trophies from around the globe. You'll find a silver and gold saddle valued at $300,000 in the same room as an African lion. Despite its idiosyncrasies, the museum is well worth the price of admission, particularly if you're interested in century-old Indian and cowboy items. The museum covers three floors, so be sure to see it all, including the collection of Western movie posters, furnishings from the homes of Wyoming cattle barons, a painted buffalo robe, Mexican sombreros, cowgirl clothing, and even gruesome photos of dead outlaws. Students of the West will also want to spend time in the research library.

The museum is open Monday–Saturday 8 A.M.–5 P.M. June–August, and Monday–Friday 8 A.M.–noon and 1–5 P.M. the rest of the year. Admission costs $3 adults, $2 seniors, free for kids under 13.

Botanic Gardens

One of Cheyenne's lesser-known gems is the fine Botanic Gardens in Lions Park, 307/637-6458, www.botanic.org. Building hours are Monday–Friday 8 A.M.–4:30 P.M., and Saturday–Sunday 11 A.M.–3:30 P.M.; no charge. Troubled kids, handicapped people, and seniors grow flowers and vegetables here. Visitors find this a pleasant place to relax, especially during the winter, when the warmth and the showy flowers are a welcome break. Inside the passively solar-heated greenhouse (look for the black metal drums filled with water) are three sections containing everything from vegetables to cacti. The central portion is home to tall banana plants, tropical flowers,

© DON PITCHER

missiles at F. E. Warren Air Force Base, Cheyenne

and a pond filled with goldfish and turtles. The angel's trumpet, with its beautiful orange flowers, is the centerpiece. Upstairs is a small library containing gardening magazines and books. Outside are pleasant picnic tables, ponds, a gazebo set among the flower beds, native plants, and shade trees. The grounds are popular for weddings, and a paved path (marked with famous Wyoming cattle brands) connects the gardens to the Old West Museum.

F. E. Warren Air Force Base

The entrance to Warren Air Force Base is flanked by four missiles, but the buildings are surprisingly quaint two- and three-story red-brick structures set back from the tree-lined streets. Some 220 of these immaculate structures are on the National Register of Historic Places. Expansive green lawns give it a country-club feeling. This is essentially a self-supporting city, with child care facilities, schools, stores, a veterinary clinic, and that old neighborhood standby, nuclear warheads. The only aircraft kept here most of the time are UH-60 Blackhawk helicopters, but during Frontier Days jets take off constantly from the airport, screaming overhead in sharp climbs that elicit gasps from the crowd.

Because of heightened security concerns, Wyoming's primary military base is generally accessible only to persons with valid military identification, although the general public can tour the base if you can get 10 or more people together. For specifics, contact public affairs at least two weeks in advance at 307/773-3381, www.warren.af.mil. The general public *is* admitted during Fort D. A. Russell Days in mid-July, when an air show by the U.S. Air Force Thunderbirds, base tours, a living-history camp, and mountain-man rendezvous are the featured events.

If you're able to get a tour, be sure to request time at **Warren ICBM & Heritage Museum,** 307/773-2980, www.pawnee.com/fewmuseum, a free little museum that's open Monday–Friday 8 A.M.–4 P.M. One building has a few artifacts such as sabers, uniforms, and other military memorabilia; more interesting is the annex, which houses missile exhibits. These include photos of the early Atlas rockets and Minuteman I missiles,

© DON PITCHER

SOUTHEAST WYOMING

old Union Pacific depot, Cheyenne

a model of the MX missiles the Air Force euphemistically calls "Peacekeepers," and old launch-control equipment. A staff member here will tell you how the missiles are fired and where they are located—more or less. Grave gazers may want to visit the base cemetery, where soldiers and others have been interred since 1867. An interesting pamphlet available at the museum tells the stories of some who lie here, including German POWs who died on the base during World War II.

Railroad Depot

The railroad business reached its peak in the 1940s, when Cheyenne had the finest equipment and service anywhere in America. The railroad is still an important part of the city's economy, with freight trains rumbling through day and night. Drop by the gorgeous old Union Pacific Railroad depot at the south end of Capitol Avenue to see one of the finest remaining train stations in the West. Built of red and gray sandstone in 1886, the structure was at one time the largest building in the territory and the most elaborate depot between Omaha and San Francisco. (The depot was a political payoff to Gov. Francis E. Warren for restoring order after the 1885 massacre of Chinese workers at the Union Pacific's vital Rock Springs coal mines.) It occupies an entire block, with a clock tower and Romanesque arched openings adding a touch of class.

The depot underwent a major renovation in the last few years, and by 2004 it will house the **Cheyenne Depot Museum** with a focus on railroad history, the **Cheyenne Convention & Visitors Bureau,** and a restaurant. The plaza out front will be used for farmers markets, pancake breakfasts during Frontier Days, and other events. For details, call 307/778-3133 or 800/426-50009. Behind the depot is an enormous Union Pacific roundhouse built in 1931 and still used to maintain locomotives. It is not open to the public.

Holliday Park, along E. 17th St., has a **Big Boy locomotive,** one of only 25 ever made and one of the largest steam locomotives ever built. It was used to haul freight over the mountain tracks between Cheyenne and Ogden, Utah. A couple of blocks east of here is a boxcar from the **French Merci Train,** given as a thank-you for food Americans gave the French after World War II.

Cattle Baron's Row

Cheyenne has many interesting Victorian buildings. Stop by the visitors center for a free walking-tour brochure that leads you through historic downtown. Of particular note are the Victorian homes along 17th Street, "Cattle Baron's Row."

The **Whipple House,** 300 E. 17th St., is a wonderful Victorian built in 1883 by Ithamar C. Whipple, a wealthy merchant, cattleman, mayor, and state legislator. The home was later occupied by attorney and one-time Wyoming Territorial Supreme Court Justice John W. Lacey, who defended both the notorious outlaw Tom Horn and the equally infamous oilman Harry Sinclair. The building is on the National Register of Historic Places.

Right across the street is the **Nagle-Warren Mansion,** another grand place from the same era. Built by businessman Erasmus Nagle in 1888, it later belonged to Francis E. Warren, who served as governor and U.S. senator. War-

ren's friend, Pres. Theodore Roosevelt, slept here several times. Nagle built his home at the same time as the state capitol was being constructed, and he used stones that the capitol masons had rejected. Unfortunately, the masons were proven correct. The stones deteriorated when exposed to the weather and had to be covered with stucco. Today, the Nagle-Warren Mansion is an upscale bed-and-breakfast that has been lovingly restored inside and out. For a taste of gentility, attend the mansion's **English High Tea,** served in Victorian style every Friday and Saturday 3:15–4 P.M. The cost is $10. These gatherings usually fill up, so be sure to make reservations; 307/637-3333 or 800/811-2610, www.naglewarren-mansion.com. Guests are treated to tea, scones, cookies, tea sandwiches, tartlets, and other sweets served in the elegant parlor.

Cathedrals

Cheyenne has several of Wyoming's most ostentatious and interesting churches. **St. Mark's Episcopal Church,** 1908 Central Ave., 307/634-7709, is the oldest, begun in 1886 but not completed until 1893. The exterior is of red lava stones with traditional stained-glass windows, including one by Tiffany. This was the home church for many transplanted British and Scottish cattle barons, so it is fitting that the funeral for gunman Tom Horn, who worked for some of them, was held here in 1903.

Two other impressive churches are **St. Mary's Catholic Cathedral,** 2107 Capitol Ave., 307/635-9261, built in 1907 of native sandstone in the Gothic Revival style, and the **First United Methodist Church,** 18th and Central Aves., 307/632-1410, completed in 1894 and also made from sandstone. The previous Methodist church, on the same site, was where marshal, gunman, and gambler Wild Bill Hickok married a circus performer, Agnes Lake Thatcher, in 1876. The officiating clergyman wrote in the registry, "Don't think they meant it." Five months later, Wild Bill was shot in the back in a Deadwood saloon. Agnes Thatcher is *not* the woman buried next to Hickok in the Deadwood cemetery; instead it's Calamity Jane.

Wyoming Hereford Ranch

In 1883, cattle barons Alexander and Thomas Swan, backed by European investors, formed the Wyoming Hereford Association, placing 400 purebred Hereford bulls and cows on a ranch near Cheyenne. This was the first real attempt to bring quality cattle to the state and was at one time the world's largest herd of thoroughbred cattle. Gradually other ranches followed this lead and the rangy longhorns of Texas were replaced by the more manageable Herefords—now the dominant breed in Wyoming. The 60,000-acre Wyoming Hereford Ranch has survived for more than 120 years and contains many historic structures in immaculate condition. It's the oldest continuously registered livestock operation in America. A small visitors center shows off awards and old photos. Out front you'll find monuments to prize bulls Prince Domino and Lerch, who sired many of the prize whiteface Herefords in America today. Prince Domino's memorial reads, "He lived and died and won a lasting name." How touching. You can wander around the showcase ranch and explore the red barns and other buildings at your leisure. Wyoming Hereford Ranch is five miles east of Cheyenne; take Campstool Rd. (exit 367) off I-80. Call 307/634-1905 for details. Since 1980, the ranch has been owned by a local surgeon, Dr. Sloan Hales, who lives in the enormous Tudor mansion just up the hill.

Other Attractions

The **Cheyenne Gunslingers** put on "gunfights" during June and July at 6 P.M. Monday–Friday, and Saturdays at noon. These events take place at Lincolnway and Carey streets. Get details at 307/635-1028, www.cheyennegunslingers.org. Interested in learning about a real outlaw? Visit the **Tom Horn** historical exhibit on the second floor of the old courthouse on the northwest corner of 19th and Carey streets.

For something a bit more genteel, hop on the horse-drawn carriages that run from the Plains Hotel on summer evenings. Contact **S&V Carriages,** 307/634-0167, for details.

The **Wyoming Department of Game and Fish,** 5400 Bishop Blvd., 307/777-4600, http://gf.state.wy.us, has a small museum/visitors center with wildlife dioramas and photographs, plus an aquarium containing native trout. It's open Monday–Friday 8 A.M.–5 P.M. all year. No charge.

For details on points to the south, see *Moon Handbooks Colorado,* by Stephen Metzger (www.moon.com).

CHEYENNE CLUB

One of the most unusual organizations in frontier Wyoming was the Cheyenne Club, first established in 1880 as an exclusive English-style country club. With membership limited to 200, it included only the wealthiest of the cattlemen, men who quickly became known as cattle barons. Many came from aristocratic social backgrounds, and the club included graduates of the finest universities on the East Coast and Europe. Some were millionaires who summered in Cheyenne and then sailed back to Europe for luxurious winters. With the growing prosperity of the cattle business, the Cheyenne Club claimed the finest French-Canadian chef and steward in the country and was said to be the first club in America to have electricity. Dinner dress was always formal. Despite strict rules on behavior (no card cheating, pipe smoking, or profanity), one member did manage to shoot a hole through a painting of a cow and bull—he claimed it to be an abomination against purebred cattle. Upstairs were elaborate apartments for members and guests, while the lavishly furnished downstairs included a spacious dining room, billiard room, reading room, card room, lounge, and wraparound porch. With the sudden bust that followed the harsh winter of 1886–1887, the cattle barons were brought abruptly back to reality. Many went out of business, and the club quickly followed. The historic Cheyenne Club was razed in 1936.

ACCOMMODATIONS

Cheyenne has more than two dozen different places to stay. The **Cheyenne Convention & Visitors Bureau's** website, www.cheyenne.org/accommodations.asp, has web links and a summary of information for most local accommodations. Check here for a listing of available lodging during Frontier Days; it's updated daily. You can also get the same information by calling the CC&VB at 307/778-3133 or 800/426-5009.

Be certain to take a look around before paying for a room at Cheyenne's cheaper motels, and also check the location. Places near the railroad—and this includes many of the less-expensive places—may suffer from noise as freight trains rumble past at all hours. Bring earplugs or look for a room away from the tracks.

The Frontier Days Shuffle

Finding a room in Cheyenne is usually easy, but when Frontier Days comes to town, motels and campgrounds book up six months in advance, and the rates often double or even triple; some places that cost $40 d in the winter months are $120 d during Frontier Days! Obviously the quality doesn't suddenly improve so drastically. Elsewhere this would be called price gouging, but the motels somehow get away with it. Even towns as far away as Torrington are affected by Frontier Days, so be sure to plan several months ahead for accommodations during the rodeo, especially for the final Saturday night. Most hotels start booking rooms in January. If you're booking a room with one of the chain hotels and folks at the national toll-free number say all of the rooms are gone for Frontier Days, don't just give up. Call the hotel directly and you may still find a place. Also check the hotel website for package deals that may not be listed elsewhere.

Under $50

Don't expect the fanciest furnishings, but **Guest Ranch Motel,** 1100 W. Lincolnway, 307/634-2137, has reasonable prices ($35 s or $40 d), with small fridges and microwaves in the rooms.

Recently remodeled, the **Grand Hotel Plaza,**

1719 Central Ave., 307/637-0100, www.cheyennegrandhotel.com, has a large indoor pool, spacious rooms, an on-site restaurant, and reasonable rates: $40 s or $50–60 d.

Another good economy place is **Fleetwood Motel,** 3800 E. Lincolnway, 307/638-8908 or 800/634-7763, where the clean and quiet rooms are $46–52 s or $55–59 d. A heated outdoor pool is on the premises, and a continental breakfast is included.

Also recommended is **Luxury Inn,** 1805 Westland Rd., 307/638-2550, a friendly motel with rooms for $48 s or $55 d ($100 s or d during Frontier Days), including a continental breakfast. Its off-season rates are an even better bet, starting at just $32 d.

For something different, stay at **Terry Bison Ranch,** 307/634-4171, www.terrybisonranch.com, located eight miles south of Cheyenne along I-25 and just on the Wyoming side of the state line. This 27,500-acre ranch has bunkhouse rooms ($38 d) with a shared bath, and rustic cabins ($79 for up to four) with kitchenettes and private baths.

Cheyenne has several aging family motels strung along Lincolnway on both ends of town. Decent places with rooms for $30–35 s or $40–45 d include: **Firebird Motel,** 1905 E. Lincolnway, 307/632-5505; **Frontier Motel,** 1400 W. Lincolnway, 307/634-7961; **Home Ranch Motel,** 2414 E. Lincolnway, 307/634-3575; **Lariat Motel,** 600 Central Ave., 307/635-8439; **Ranger Motel,** 909 W. Lincolnway, 307/634-7995; **Rodeo Inn,** 3839 E. Lincolnway, 307/634-2171; **Round-Up Motel,** 403 S. Greeley Hwy., 307/634-7741; **Sands Motel,** 1000 W. Lincolnway, 307/634-7771; and **Stage Coach Motel,** 1515 W. Lincolnway, 307/634-4495. You'll probably want to see rooms at any of these places before you pay because they may not be up to your standards.

$50–100

Express Inn, 2512 W. Lincolnway, 307/632-7556, has moderate prices ($40–55 s or $55–72 d), with an indoor pool, hot tub, exercise equipment, and continental breakfasts. **Motel 6,** 1735 Westland Rd., 307/635-6806 or

800/466-8356, www.motel6.com, charges $50 s or $56 d ($6 less Sun.–Thurs. nights), and has an outdoor pool.

Oak Tree Inn, 1625 Stillwater, 307/778-6620, is another chain hotel, with modern rooms for $55–61 s or d, plus a hot tub, exercise room, business center, and free breakfast at the adjacent Penny's Diner. The larger rooms contain fridges and microwaves. **Days Inn,** 2360 W. Lincolnway, 307/778-8877 or 800/329-7466, www.daysinn.com, serves up comfy accommodations for $55–67 s or $59–71 d. Guests will appreciate the hot tub, sauna, and light breakfast. Some rooms have fridges and microwaves.

Super 8 Motel, 1900 W. Lincolnway, 307/635-8741 or 800/800-8000, www.super8.com, charges $55–70 s or $60–80 d ($125–140 s or d during Frontier Days) and has fridges and microwaves in some rooms.

Lincoln Court Motel, 1720 W. Lincolnway, 307/638-3302 or 800/221-0125, has spacious standard rooms for $45–55 s or $60–80 d, including a heated outdoor pool, playground, fitness room, and light breakfast. Guests at Lincoln Court are welcome to use the hot tub and sauna at the adjacent Best Western Hitching Post Inn (same owners).

One of the nicest (and largest) local places is the **Best Western Hitching Post Inn,** 1700 W. Lincolnway, 307/638-3301 or 800/221-0125, www.hitchingpostinn.com. The remodeled rooms follow a cowboy motif, and featured attractions include indoor and outdoor pools, a hot tub, saunas, a large fitness center, plus two fine restaurants, a coffeehouse, and two lounges. Rooms go for $89–129 s or d.

Other dependable midpriced chain hotels include **Comfort Inn,** 2245 Etchepare Dr., 307/638-7202 or 866/257-4900, www.comfortinn.com; **Fairfield Inn (Marriott),** 1415 Stillwater Ave., 307/637-4070 or 800/228-2800, www.fairfieldinn.com; **La Quinta Inn,** 2410 W. Lincolnway, 307/632-7117 or 800/531-5900, www.laquinta.com; and **Quality Inn,** 5401 Walker Rd., 307/632-8901 or 800/876-8901, www.qualityinn.com. All of these have swimming pools and most serve continental breakfasts.

Plains Hotel

Cheyenne is fortunate to have one of Wyoming's few surviving historic lodging places, the five-story **Plains Hotel,** 307/638-3311 or 888/275-2467, www.theplainshotel.com. Built in 1911 for a then-astounding $250,000, this was the political center of Cheyenne for decades, with politicians repairing to the bar to broker issues over beers and stogies. The grand lobby, marble stairway, and the tile mosaic of Chief Little Shield remain, but in 2002 The Plains underwent a multimillion-dollar reconstruction that transformed it into a boutique hotel with 131 luxury rooms and suites, two restaurants, conference rooms, and an exercise facility. Lots of little touches were added too, such as high-speed Internet access, large televisions, original artwork in the rooms, and custom-designed furniture and bed coverings. Standard rooms in the hotel are $89–109 s or d, and suites run $139–199 d.

$100–150

Little America Hotel, 2800 W. Lincolnway, 307/775-8400 or 888/709-8383, www.littleamerica.com, is a large upscale hotel that feels like a resort, with 80 acres of beautifully landscaped grounds, a quiet location, an Olympic-size outdoor pool, an exercise facility, an airport shuttle, and a nine-hole golf course. The spacious rooms go for $86–119 s or $96–129 d. Little America is especially popular with retirees.

Hampton Inn, 307/632-2747 or 800/426-7866, www.hamptoninn.com, is Cheyenne's newest place to stay, with all of the amenities travelers have come to expect, including a fitness center, indoor pool and hot tub, light breakfast, and small fridges. Rates are $100 s or $109 d for standard rooms or $145 s or $155 d for suites or rooms with jetted tubs.

Cheyenne's premier business hotel (it's also popular with vacationers) is the 244-room, **Holiday Inn,** 204 W. Fox Farm Rd., 307/638-4466 or 800/465-4329, www.holiday-inn.com/cheyennewy. Inside you'll find a big lobby with a fireplace, restaurant, and bar, plus an indoor pool, hot tub, sauna, exercise room, airport shuttle, and conference facilities. Guest rooms are large, with modern furnishings and big TVs; $119 s or d for standard rooms or $139 for up to four people in the suites. (Frontier Days rates are $159–200 s or d.)

Bed-and-Breakfasts

Cheyenne has one of the largest and most diverse collections of B&Bs in Wyoming.

Occupying a grand old home built in 1888 and listed on the National Register of Historic Places, the **Nagle-Warren Mansion B&B,** 222 E. 17th St., 307/637-3333 or 800/811-2610, www.naglewarrenmansion.com, provides updated Victorian accommodation near the center of Cheyenne. Owner Jim Osterfoss has transformed this grand old mansion into Cheyenne's premier B&B. Amenities include luxurious rooms with period furnishings and original artwork, a gazebo housing the hot tub, beautiful floral gardens, plus a small exercise room and conference room. Massages are available, along with special honeymoon and romance packages. The gourmet breakfast menu changes every day. The main house and adjacent carriage house contain 11 guest rooms ($108–148 d), plus a luxurious suite ($148 d) that includes a king bed, gas fireplace, and stained-glass skylight. All rooms have private baths, and children are accepted. A formal English High Tea ($10) is served in the parlor on Friday and Saturday afternoons. The mansion is described in the preceding Sights section. Several times a year, Nagle-Warren is the scene for humorous mystery dinners. The mansion is also a favorite spot for wedding receptions and elegant parties.

Another classic place, just a half block away, is **Rainsford Inn B&B,** 219 E. 18th St., 307/638-2337, www.rainsfordinnbedandbreakfast.com. This comfortable 1903 home in the heart of Cheyenne has seven guest rooms (private or shared baths), ceiling fans, and jetted tubs. Room rates are $50–86 s or d, including a full breakfast. Rainsford Inn is on the National Register of Historic Places. Well-behaved children are generally allowed, but only with advance notice. Cheyenne Smokehouse (described in the Food section) is also on the premises.

Also right downtown, **Porch Swing B&B,** 712 E. 20th St., 307/778-7182, www.cruising-america.com/porch.html, is an attractive bungalow built in 1917. Inside is a small room ($50 s or d) with a shared bath and a larger one with private bath ($75 s or d). The back porch, surrounded by flower and herb gardens, is perfect for relaxing on a summer evening. Guest rooms contain antiques, and a full breakfast is served by the helpful hosts. A two-night minimum stay is required.

On the north side of town, **Storyteller Pueblo B&B,** 5201 Ogden Rd., 307/634-7036, www.storyteller-pueblo-bnb.com, is a contemporary home with Native American art, country antiques, fireplaces, and four guest rooms with shared or private baths. It's in a quiet neighborhood and run by dynamic owners. Room rates are $65–100 s or d, including a full breakfast. Children are accepted.

The friendly **Howdy Pardner B&B,** 1920 Tranquility Rd., 307/634-6493, www.howdy-pardner.net, is out in the country just north of Cheyenne; call ahead for directions. The hilltop ranch-style home offers three guest rooms (all with private bath), a fireplace, and great views of the rolling plains. Each morning, the owners produce a delicious country breakfast; bring a big appetite. Rates are $75 s or d, and kids and pets are welcome. For an authentically Wyoming experience, sleep inside the delightful antique sheepherder wagon for $50 d (bath in the house).

Adventurer's Country B&B, 307/632-4087, www.cruising-america.com/country.html, is a modern ranch home in the countryside 15 miles east of Cheyenne. Guests share the grounds with a variety of farm critters, including horses, chickens, geese, turkeys, ducks, cats, and dogs. The four guest rooms ($70–85 s or d) and a suite ($135 for up to four) are arranged around a central courtyard. A four-course breakfast and evening dessert are served, and dinners are available with prior notice. Kids, pets, and horses are welcome.

Double M&N, 773 Latigo Loop, 307/778-7021, has four guest rooms with shared baths in a tri-level home. Rates are $60 s or d, including a full breakfast. Kids okay. This is also perhaps Wyoming's only B&B where smoking is allowed inside.

Halfway between Cheyenne and Laramie on Happy Jack Rd. (State Hwy. 210) lie three excellent B&Bs: A. Drummond's Ranch B&B, 307/634-6042, www.cruising-america.com/drummond.html; Bit-O-Wyo Ranch, 307/638-8340, www.bitowyo.com; and Windy Hills Guest House, 307/632-6423, www.windyhillswyo.com. They are described later in this chapter in the Curt Gowdy State Park section.

CAMPING

Public Campgrounds

Cheyenne's closest public campgrounds are 26 miles west on State Hwy. 210 in **Curt Gowdy State Park,** 307/632-7946; http://wyoparks.state.wy.us, $12 for nonresidents, $6 for residents. Campgrounds ($10) can also be found within the scenic **Pole Mountain** area of Medicine Bow-Routt National Forest, 30 miles west on I-80; www.fs.fed.us/r2/mbr.

Showers are available at the swimming pool in Lions Park or from many of the private RV parks listed as follows.

RV Parks

Note that RV and camping rates are higher during Frontier Days; reserve well ahead to be sure of getting a space at that time. **AB Campground,** 1503 W. College Dr., 307/634-7035, is in a quiet area with plenty of trees. Rates are $14 for tents and $24 for RVs; open Mar.–Oct.

Open year-round, **Restway Travel Park,** 4212 Whitney Rd., 307/634-3811 or 800/443-2751, is one of the nicest RV parks in the area, with an outdoor pool, horseback rides, chuck wagon dinners, mini-golf, volleyball, and horseshoes. Tent sites are $15; RV hookups cost $21.

Terry Bison Ranch, eight miles south of Cheyenne on I-25 (exit 2), 307/634-4171, www.terrybisonranch.com, is a favorite of families, with rodeos, bison tours, trout fishing, horseback and pony rides, and chuck wagon dinners. This is also the only place in Wyoming that has camels! Tent spaces are $14; RV hookups cost $22. Cabins and bunkhouse rooms are also available. Open year-round.

Fifteen miles east of town, **Cheyenne KOA,** 8800 Archer Frontage Rd. (I-80 exit 377), 307/638-8840 or 800/562-1507, www.koa.com,

charges $21–28 for RVs, $19–21 for tents, and $38 d for simple cabins. Amenities include an outdoor pool, mini-golf, and horseshoes. Open Apr.–Oct.

Greenway Trailer Park, on the east edge of Cheyenne at 3829 Greenway St., 307/634-6696, has RV hookups for $16 (no tents); open year-round. On the south side of town, **Hide a Way RV Park,** 218 S. Greeley Hwy., 307/637-7114, charges $14 for tents and $20 for RVs; open year-round.

If you have an RV and don't mind the lack of bathrooms, you may want to stay at **Hyland Park RV Campground,** 2415 Missile Dr., 307/634-0517; $17 for full hookups. No tents. Open May–Sept. **Jolley Rogers RV Park,** 6102 E. Hwy. 30, 307/634-8457 or 800/458-7779, www.jolleyrogers.com, provides east-side tent sites for $8, RV hookups for $15; open mid-April through Sept.

A half dozen miles from downtown Cheyenne is **T-Joe's RV Park,** at I-80 exit 370, 307/635-8750. Open year-round, it has tent spaces for $9 and RV hookups for $22. Fifteen miles east of Cheyenne at exit 377, **WYO Campground,** 307/547-2244, has RV sites close to I-80. Rates are $19 for RVs, $15 for tents; open May–Sept.

FOOD

The city of Cheyenne offers a surprisingly diverse choice of eateries. In addition to all the places listed as follows, the city is jammed with all of the fast-food chains, particularly along East Lincolnway.

Breakfast and Lunch

One of Cheyenne's real treats is **Lexie's,** 216 E. 17th St., 307/638-8712, a comfortable downtown place with good breakfasts that include omelets, eggs Benedict, biscuits and gravy, and even catfish and grits. At noon, Lexie's gets crowded with local office workers savoring burgers (best in town), fajitas, chicken piccata, BLT sandwiches, or other house specialties. Return in the evening for a romantic dinner of pasta, fish, steak, and more, with entrées costing $11–17. But get there early: Lexie's closes Monday at

3 P.M., Tuesday–Thursday at 8 P.M., and Friday–Saturday at 9 P.M. The restaurant is closed Sundays, and service can be uneven.

Part of a small chain, **The Egg & I,** 2300 Carey Ave., 307/632-5577, specializes in—surprise—eggs, with "eggceptional" omelets, frittatas, and other dishes. The atmosphere is bright and friendly, and classical tunes spill from the speakers. They also make commendable croissant sandwiches, soups, and salads for lunch. Early birds will appreciate the 6 A.M. weekday openings.

Driftwood Cafe, 200 E. 18th St., 307/634-5304, is also good for breakfast. The enormous **Little America** coffee shop, 2800 W. Lincolnway, 307/634-2771, is open 5 A.M. until midnight and offers better-than-average truck-stop fare. Little America also has a Sunday buffet brunch and weekday lunch buffet. Another place with a popular Sunday brunch is **Terry Bison Ranch,** eight miles south of Cheyenne off I-25, 307/634-4171, www.terrybisonranch.com.

For a taste of the East Coast, try a Philly steak sandwich or pierogi from **Little Philly,** 1121 W. Lincolnway, 307/632-6824. A downtown lunch and dinner favorite of many locals is **Albany Restaurant,** 1506 Capitol Ave., 307/638-3507.

The cheapest meal in Cheyenne can be found at the state government cafeteria in the **Herschler Building,** directly behind the capitol. Sit in the spacious atrium on rainy days or head outside to brown-bag it with government workers when the sun pops out. Open Mon.–Fri. 6 A.M.–4 P.M., with limited service after 1:30 P.M.

In addition to caffeine jolts, **Zen's Caffeine Cafe,** 2606 E. Lincolnway, 307/635-1889, serves vegetarian and gourmet sandwiches, organic salads, pastries, soups, coffees, and teas. Barnes & Noble Books, 1851 Dell Range Blvd., 307/632-3000, houses a **Starbucks.**

Asian

Wyoming is certainly not known for its Asian food, but Cheyenne has two surprisingly authentic Chinese restaurants worth a visit: **Twin Dragon Restaurant,** 1809 Carey Ave., 307/637-6622, and **San Dong Chinese Restaurant,** 801 W. Pershing Blvd., 307/634-6613. Twin Dragon's lunchtime buffet is an outstanding deal, and the

dinner menu includes such specialties as sesame crispy beef and moo shu pork. Keep your orders small because the portions are not. **Dynasty Cafe,** 1809 Carey Ave., 307/632-4888, has a big menu of reasonably priced Chinese and Vietnamese dishes and vegetarian specialties, along with a lunchtime buffet. Cheyenne is even home to two Korean restaurants: **Korean House Restaurant,** 3219 Snyder Ave., 307/638-7938, and **Seoul Restaurant,** 1907 E. Lincolnway, 307/433-9999.

Mexican

Several places in Cheyenne make very good south-of-the-border food. **La Costa,** 317 E. Lincolnway, 307/638-7372, has perhaps the best Mexican meals, with all the favorites, including fajitas, chiles rellenos, and chalupas. Housed in Cheyenne Plaza Mall, **The Armadillo,** 3617 E. Lincolnway, 307/778-0822, has been in business for more than 30 years, with locally famous margaritas. Also popular is **Estevan's Cafe,** 1820 Ridge Rd., 307/632-6828.

Pizza and Italian

L'Osteria Mondello Italian Cucina & Pizzeria, 1507 Stillwater Ave., 307/778-6068, is *the* place for authentic Southern Italian meals in Cheyenne. Excellent food.

The food isn't anything special, but stuff yourself into obesity at **Avanti Restaurant,** 4620 Grandview Ave. (between Wal-Mart and Office Max), 307/634-3432, where the Italian-American evening buffet is $8.75.

Pete's Pizza, 1801 Warren Ave., 307/632-2267, makes decent pizzas but is better known for its Italian sub sandwiches. For pizza, most folks in Cheyenne seem to prefer **Pizza Hut,** 2215 E. Lincolnway, 307/635-4151.

Dinner

Poor Richard's, 2233 E. Lincolnway, 307/635-5114, has Cheyenne's only Saturday brunch. The seafood and prime rib are excellent and reasonably priced, and the salad bar is one of the biggest around. Enjoy a drink at the fireside lounge. Another favorite steak place is **Cowboy South,** 312 S. Greeley Hwy.,

307/637-3800. For prime rib, fly up to **Cloud 9 Restaurant** at the airport terminal (300 E. 8th Ave.), 307/635-5800.

Housed inside the Best Western Hitching Post Inn at 1700 W. Lincolnway are three restaurants, including a locals' favorite, **Cheyenne Cattle Company,** 307/633-3301. The specialty here is steak, but the menu also offers a variety of other entrées, and a separate patio menu is available. Also at the Hitching Post is **Carriage Court,** 307/638-3301, *the* place to go for fresh fish or oysters, steaks, prime rib, and pasta. The wine list is one of the best in town.

Get away from downtown for a pleasant evening at **Little Bear Inn,** five miles north on I-25, 307/634-3684, where steak, shrimp, rainbow trout, and scallops fill the menu. Entrées are a bit overpriced given the rather pedestrian quality, but the location is relaxing.

Cheyenne Smokehouse BBQ, 219 E. 18th St., 307/638-2337, serves various smoked meats, including pork ribs, beef brisket, and chicken, in sandwiches or by the pound. Open for lunch and dinner.

Pubs

Sanford's Grub & Pub, 115 E. 17th St., 307/634-3381, is Cheyenne's happening place, with a young crowd and live music on weekends. Part of a small chain—others are in Sheridan, Gillette, and Casper, along with Spearfish and Rapid City, South Dakota—Sanford's exudes frat-house chic. Every square millimeter is packed with old photos, sports memorabilia, lawn-sale junk, and TV screens. The chaos ups the volume, although the 55 beers on draught probably help. Sanford's menu is big enough to satisfy almost anyone and includes shrimp jambalaya, barbecued chicken wings, and mushroom monster burgers. On weekend evenings, get there early or be prepared for a wait.

Right across the street from Sanford's is **Catfish Sports Bar &Grill** 112 E. 17th St., 307/637-3262, with soul food (of a sort), and dartboards, pool tables, foosball, and video games.

C. & B. Potts Bighorn Brewery, 1650 Dell Range Blvd., 307/632-8636, is another hopping pub/sports bar with a small brewery on the premises and an eclectic menu that rambles through pasta, burgers, Tex-Mex food, salads, New York–style pizzas, nachos, and buffalo wings. The big-screen TV is great for sports fans.

Groceries

The **Cheyenne Farmers Market** is held Saturday 8 A.M.–1 P.M. during August and September downtown at Depot Plaza. This is the best place to get fresh fruits and vegetables. Cheyenne has several of the regional grocery chains, including Albertson's and Safeway. The largest store in town—with a deli, seafood counter, bakery, and the best produce selection—is the **Safeway,** 307/632-5171, in the Cole Square Shopping Center at 19th and Converse. Get Asian specialties from **International Groceries,** 1505 E. Pershing Blvd., 307/634-4888.

You'll find a big selection of beer and wine at **Town & Country Supermarket Liquors,** 614 S. Greeley Hwy., 307/632-8735, or downtown at **Albany Liquormart,** 1506 Capitol Ave., 307/632-8735.

Bakeries

Mary's Bake Shoppe, 206 W. 16th St., 307/635-6279, is a little place with delicious breads, muffins, cookies, coffee cakes, pastries, and hand-dipped chocolates. Get fresh bagels and coffee at **Mort's Bagels,** 1815 Carey Ave., 307/637-5400. Best pies in town? Try **Pie Lady Bakery & Cafe,** 3515 E. Lincolnway, 307/637-8838.

A Cheyenne favorite, **The Bread Basket,** on the east side at 1819 Maxwell Ave., 307/432-2525, has good deli sandwiches. They also have an outlet downtown in The Plains Hotel.

ENTERTAINMENT

During June and July, visitors gather at Lincolnway and Carey Streets to watch the **Cheyenne Gunslingers** (307/635-1028, www.cheyennegunslingers.org) put on a Hollywood-style shoot-'em-up. Hope I don't give anything away, but the good guys invariably win. It's pretty tacky and bears absolutely no relation to Cheyenne's rather civilized history. The "gunfights" take place at 6 P.M. on weekdays and at "high noon" on

SOUTHEAST WYOMING

Saturdays (more frequently during Frontier Days). Also here at "Gunslinger Square" is a replica of the gallows used to hang Tom Horn (no mock hangings, alas) and a "Soda Saloon." A *soda saloon?* What would a real cowboy say?

During July and early August, tourists fill the historic Atlas Theatre (built in 1887), 211 W. 16th St., to watch comic Western melodramas by the **Little Theatre Players.** The experience includes plenty of audience participation, and popcorn, pizza, and beer are for sale. Details and ticket information at 307/638-6543, www.chyennelittletheatre.org. They also produce eight or so theatrical productions of musicals, comedies, and dramas throughout the year.

The **Cheyenne Symphony Orchestra,** 307/778-8561, performs September–May at the Civic Center, 510 W. 20th St.

Bit-O-Wyo Ranch (see entry in Curt Gowdy State Park Accommodations section) puts on Old-West dinner shows Friday and Saturday nights in the summer; $25 adults, $15 kids.

Nightlife

Cheyenne is a hopping town when it comes to nightlife, especially during Frontier Days, when every country-and-western band this side of the Mississippi finds a place to play. Check the Friday edition of the *Wyoming Tribune-Eagle* (www.wyomingnews.com) for this week's entertainment offerings.

Outlaw Saloon, 307/635-7552, calls itself "Wyoming's #1 country hot spot," with live music Monday–Saturday, plus free dance lessons and nightly drink specials, and weeknight happy hours. Other attractions include dart and pool tournaments. It's located next to the Rodeo Inn at 3839 E. Lincolnway.

For downtown action, head to **Cowboy South,** 312 S. Greeley Hwy., 307/637-3800, another hot country-music bar. They also have happy hour specials. Other places that often have live music include **Hitching Post Inn Lounge,** 1700 W. Lincolnway, 307/638-3301; **Mingles,** 1318 Stillwater, 307/632-9966; and **Little Bear Inn,** three miles north of Cheyenne, 307/634-3684.

Cheyenne Club, 1617 Capitol Ave., 307/635-7777, is a favorite of the Air Force crowd. The big dance floor fills as the DJ spins Top 40 dance tunes nightly. **C. & B. Potts Bighorn Brewery,** 1650 Dell Range Blvd., 307/632-8636, has DJ tunes Thursday–Saturday nights and sports on the big-screen TV other evenings.

Lamp Lounge, 101 W. 6th, 307/635-7557, is a locals' bar with five tables for pool sharks. For something more risqué, head 10 miles south of town to the Wyoming–Colorado border, where **The Clown's Den,** 307/635-0765, is a "gentleman's club" featuring topless performers. Back on the tamer side, you'll find live piano music in the **Western Gold Lounge** at Little America, 2800 W. Lincolnway, 307/775-8400.

Movies

Local film houses are **Frontier Six Theatres,** 307/634-9499 in the Frontier Mall at 1400 Dell Range Blvd.; **Cole Square 3,** 307/635-2923 at 19th and Converse; and **Lincoln Movie Palace,** 307/637-7469, 1615 Central St. The last of these is a classic place that opened in 1926 and today offers second-run and art-house flicks for just $3.

FRONTIER DAYS

Cheyenne Frontier Days—the "Daddy of 'em All"—is Wyoming's largest and most famous annual event, with entertainment covering the spectrum from professional rodeos to parades and free pancake breakfasts. Festivities begin the last full week of July and continue for 10 action-packed days. There's something for everyone at this memorable event, which has been in existence for more than a century, but the rodeo is the main attraction for more than 300,000 visitors from all 50 states and many other nations. The largest number commute in from Denver, while others jam the campgrounds and motels for a hundred miles in all directions.

History

There are several versions of the origin of Cheyenne Frontier Days, the most plausible being that it was inspired when a Union Pacific employee, F. W. Angier, watched a group of cowboys from the Swan Land and Cattle Company trying to load an ornery horse into a railroad car.

© DON PITCHER

Cheyenne Frontier Days Rodeo

The spectacle sparked his imagination, and when he suggested the idea of a Wild West buckin' and ropin' contest, others quickly jumped on the bandwagon. Just one month later (September 1897), the first Cheyenne Frontier Days celebration began. It was a rip-roaring success, with 15,000 people in attendance. In addition to various cowboy contests, Frontier Days included several events that you won't see today—a staged battle between Sioux Indians and the U.S. Cavalry, Pony Express demonstrations, and a mock stage holdup and hanging by vigilantes. Obviously, the production had been influenced by Buffalo Bill's Wild West Show, which was then touring Europe.

Most amusing of all was the dog and hare event, where a rabbit was released to be chased by dogs. Unfortunately, the dogs in the race were quickly joined by many more from the stands, so no winner was declared, although the loser was obvious. Cheyenne Frontier Days has grown over the years to a 10-day celebration (two weekends)

and is regarded as one of the top four rodeos in the world (the others being California's Salinas Rodeo, Canada's Calgary Stampede, and Oregon's Pendleton Round-Up). Local enthusiasts call it the world's largest outdoor rodeo and Western celebration.

Activities

Frontier Days centers on the daily rodeos, with the nation's top rodeo cowboys showing their stuff. The rodeo has all of the standard contests: bareback bronc riding, saddle bronc riding, Brahma bull riding, steer roping, calf roping, team roping, and steer wrestling. Other events include chaotic and amusing wild horse races and a real crowd pleaser, the colt race (where young colts race toward their mares). With a purse of more than $500,000, the largest regular-season payoff in rodeo, Frontier Days attracts more than 1,000 contestants, so many of the timed events must begin at 7 A.M.!

Frontier Park is the center for a range of activities during Frontier Days, including free daily Indian dance performances, along with storytelling, handicrafts, and other popular activities at the **Indian village** on the south end of the parking lot. An Old West town springs to life at **Wild Horse Gulch** with blacksmithing, cowboy cooking, and other demonstrations.

Each evening brings **musical entertainment** by the top stars in country music (along with some rock acts). A large and well-run **carnival** provides stomach-churning rides, sugar and grease in all forms (cotton candy, candy apples, ice cream, corn dogs, burgers, ad nauseam), plus thousands of stuffed animal prizes, velvet paintings, and other necessities. Other entertainment includes comedians, balloon "sculptors," magicians, square dances, a chili cook-off, and a costume contest. After all this debauchery, try attending the **cowboy church services** held nightly at 7 P.M. on the rodeo grounds.

Also in Frontier Park is the Cheyenne Frontier Days Old West Museum (see Sights section), where the annual **Cheyenne Frontier Days Western Art Show and Sale** offers the chance to view or purchase works from more than 50 different Western artists.

Not everything happens in Frontier Park. On Monday, Wednesday, and Friday mornings during Frontier Days, a free downtown **pancake feed** stuffs more than 10,000 folks. The feeding frenzy runs 7–9 A.M. Check out the cement mixer used (in theory at least) to stir up 3,600 pounds of pancake batter and the Boy Scouts trying to catch the furiously flying flapjacks. Visitors sit on bales of hay and are treated to performances by Native American dancers and musicians of all stripes. For many children, the four **parades** (held at 9:30 A.M. on both Saturdays, Tuesday, and Thursday) are a special treat featuring the largest collection of horse-drawn vehicles in the nation. You'll see everything from popcorn wagons to hearses.

The first weekend of Frontier Days is also the time for **Fort D. A. Russell Days** at F. E. Warren Air Force Base (see Sights section for description). Ride the shuttle bus to the base from Frontier Mall. Call 307/773-2980 for details.

Specifics

For information on Frontier Days, including a schedule of events, call 307/778-7222 or 800/227-6336, or visit their website: www.cf-drodeo.com. Some of the night shows sell out well ahead of time, so advance reservations are advised. Rodeo tickets cost $10 for the bleacher seats up to $22 for prime seating over the chutes, and tickets to concerts are $16–27. The best deal is a combination ticket ($30–35) for both the rodeo and a concert. Tickets are available from the ticket office south of the main grandstand or by calling the 800 number. Entrance to the midway is $2 for adults, but persons holding tickets to Frontier Days events are admitted free. Parking costs $5 per vehicle in the huge lot along Carey and 8th Avenues. (Note, however, that overnight camping is not allowed here.) Because of the large number of participants in the calf-roping, steer-roping, and steer-wrestling contests, preliminary events are held each morning 7–10 A.M., with no entrance fee charged. The main rodeo events start promptly at 1:30 P.M. and last three hours. Information wagons are in various locations around the park.

OTHER EVENTS

In addition to Frontier Days, Cheyenne plays host to several popular events. Contact the Cheyenne Convention & Visitors Bureau, 307/778-3133 or 800/426-5009, www.cheyenne.org, for details on upcoming events.

In mid-June, the **Wyoming Brewer's Festival** attracts microbrewers and beer lovers from Wyoming and Colorado for a chance to sample the best local brews. Beer tasting is held at the historic depot, 307/778-3133 or 800/426-5009. For a rather different take on beer, drive 40 miles south to Fort Collins, Colorado, where the enormous Anheuser-Busch Brewery has daily tours in the summer; call 970/490-4691 for details.

Super Day in late June brings rides, games, a carnival, arts and crafts, and entertainment at Lions Park. Another popular event is the **Laramie County Fair,** held the first full week in August at the fairgrounds. It has all the usual county-fair activities, including arts-and-craft contests, rodeos, exhibits, and 4-H competitions. Get details at 307/633-4534, www.laramiecountyfair.com. Regional **horse shows** take place all summer at Laramie Community College; call 307/778-1291 for upcoming shows.

Over Labor Day weekend, the **Cheyenne Cowboy Symposium and Celebration,** 307/635-5788, www.cheyennecowboysymposium.com, features storytelling, cowboy poetry, and music, along with workshops on yodeling, horse whispering, and other topics.

The year winds down with a **Christmas Parade, Craft Show, and Concert** in late November. The nighttime parade includes more than 100 lighted horse-drawn wagons, cars, tractors, and floats, plus a visit from St. Nick. Call 307/638-0151 for more info.

RECREATION

Terry Bison Ranch (see Cheyenne Accommodations section) has wagon tours, horseback and pony rides, chuck wagon dinners (Thurs.–Sat. nights), trout fishing, and even a wine cellar with locally made fruit wines.

Horseback rides are also offered by **Bit-O-Wyo Ranch** (see entry in Curt Gowdy State Park Accommodations section).

The **Cheyenne Greenway** consists of 10 miles of paved walking and biking trails that cross the city. The trails are perfect for a romantic stroll or a morning run. One section follows Crow Creek, and the other parallels Dry Creek. Pick up a map brochure of the trails from the Convention & Visitors Bureau downtown.

Swim or play on the water slide at Lions Park's **indoor municipal pool**, 307/637-6457, or the **Johnson outdoor swimming pool** at 7th St. and House Ave., 307/637-64239. The latter has two fun water slides. **Sloans Lake,** in Lions Park, is a summertime swimming hole and has paddleboat, kayak, and canoe rentals; 307/637-6361. Get swimming information on the web at www.cheyennecity.org/aquatics.htm.

Lions Park also has a botanic garden (described in Sights section), an 18-hole **Airport Golf Course** (307/637-6418), picnic areas, playgrounds, ponds that turn into skating rinks in the winter, and several bison. Cheyenne is home to three other public golf courses: **Little America Golf Course,** 307/775-8400 or 888/709-8383, www.littleamerica.com; **Prairie View,** 307/637-6420; and the 18-hole **Warren Air Force Base Golf Course,** 307/773-3556.

IKON Center, 1530 W. Lincolnway, 307/433-0024, www.ikoncenter.com, is an impressive facility for recreation (including laser tag), concerts, and conventions. In the winter, it houses Wyoming's best ice-skating/hockey rink. Next door is **Wyoming Adventure Miniature Golf,** 307/775-0020, an enjoyable 18-hole course with a distinctive Wyoming theme.

Big Country Speedway, 307/632-2107, www.bigcountryspeedway.com, is the state's only asphalt oval track and has been hosting Saturday night stock car racing since 1948. They're just south of town at 4820 S. Greeley Highway.

SHOPPING

Cheyenne is an automobile town, so most folks shop at the big malls scattered around the edges of the city. **Frontier Mall,** 1400 Dell Range Blvd., is one of the state's largest, with more than 75 stores. Also impressive is **Cole Square Shopping Center** at 19th and Converse. Wal-Mart, Sam's Club, Target, and Kmart add to the town's shop-'til-you-plop allure.

Western Gear

Downtown Cheyenne is home to one of the largest Western clothing stores in the state: **Wrangler** (owned by Corral West), 1518 Capitol Ave., 307/634-3048, www.corralwest.com. This is a great place to pick up a cowboy hat or boots.

Across the street from the Wrangler is **Wyoming Home,** 210 W. 16th St., 307/638-2222, www.wyominghome.com, with unique Western furniture, home accessories, gifts, and artwork. It's the kind of shop you'd expect to find in Jackson (and will). Inside Wyoming Home is a room containing **Far West Trading Co.** 307/638-2396, www.farwestmaps.com, which specializes in 19th-century maps of Wyoming and the American West. They also have some amazing older maps, including a world map from 1673 (and priced at $3,900).

Just Dandy, 212 W. 17th St., 307/635-2565, sells high-end women's Western clothing. Another place for quality Western wear is **Snubbing Post,** 1802 Dell Range Blvd., 307/638-6421. **Mabel the Cowgirl,** 124 W. Lincolnway, 307/772-0300, www.mabelthecowgirl.com, is a fun shop, with hats, t-shirts, saddle purses, games, jewelry, and other cowgirl necessities. Be sure to check out the wall filled with photos and memorabilia from Mabel Strickland and other early-20th-century cowgirls.

Outdoor Supplies

Sierra Trading Post, 307/775-8050, www.sierratradingpost.com, has a large factory outlet store at the Campstool exit off I-80, a few miles east of Cheyenne. Out in Frontier Mall, **Gart Sports,** 1400 Dell Range Blvd., 307/632-0712, www.gartsports.com, is a good-sized sporting-goods shop. Get used outdoor gear from **Play it Again Sports,** in the Cole Shopping Center at 19th and Converse, 307/637-4030, www.playitagainsports.com. **Marv's Place Pawn Shop,** 223 W. Lincolnway,

307/632-7887, is run by a decidedly unique owner. His ads brag of offering the "worst free coffee in town." Give it a taste. For cheap clothes, stop by the large **Salvation Army Thrift Store** at 1401 E. Lincolnway, 307/632-1507, or **Goodwill,** 3301 E. Nationway, 307/634-7751.

Galleries

Cheyenne has several art galleries. The **Wyoming Arts Council Gallery,** 2320 Capitol Ave., 307/777-7742, http://wyoarts.state.wy.us, features changing exhibits throughout the year. **Cheyenne Artist Guild,** 307/632-2263, is the state's oldest art guild (since 1949) and has a nonprofit gallery at 1010 E. 16th St. in Holliday Park. One of the best private collections can be found at **Manitou Gallery,** 1715 Carey Ave., 307/635-0019. Also check out the Western and wildlife art at **Gallery West,** 1601 Capitol Ave., 307/632-1258 or 800/786-2258, www.gallery-westframeplant.com; and the oils, sculpture, glass, and pottery at **Impressions Art Gallery,** 1921 Warren Ave., 307/634-6674.

Books

City News, at 18th and Carey Sts., 307/638-8671, has a decent selection of Wyoming titles, and **Waldenbooks** in Frontier Mall, 307/634-7099, www.waldenbooks.com, is another good-sized shop. The largest bookstore in Cheyenne—in all of Wyoming for that matter—is **Barnes & Noble Books,** 1851 Dell Range Blvd., 307/632-3000, www.bn.com. The store has frequent book talks, signings, and poetry nights. For used books, head to **Book Rack,** 3583 E. Lincolnway, 307/632-2014. **Abundance,** 1809 Warren Ave., 307/632-8237, will fill New Agers' needs for crystals and metaphysical titles.

INFORMATION

You'll find the **Cheyenne Convention & Visitors Bureau** at 309 W. Lincolnway, 307/778-3133 or 800/426-5009, www.cheyenne.org. It's open Monday–Friday 8 A.M.–5 P.M., Saturday 10 A.M.–4 P.M., and Sunday noon–4 P.M. from Memorial Day to Labor Day (daily 8 A.M.–6 P.M. during Frontier Days), and Monday–Friday 8 A.M.–5 P.M. the rest of the year. The Visitors Bureau moves to the historic Union Pacific Railroad depot in 2004.

The state maintains a spacious **Wyoming Travel Information Center** at the College Drive off-ramp (exit 7) along I-25, 307/777-7777 or 800/225-5996. It's so windy at this exposed site that the garbage cans are all set inside concrete pipes to keep them from blowing away! The center is open daily 8 A.M.–5 P.M. all year except Thanksgiving, Christmas, and New Year's days.

The *Wyoming Tribune-Eagle* is Cheyenne's newspaper, and one of the few daily papers in the state. Find them online at www.wyomingnews.com.

SERVICES

Laundromats include **Duds 'n Suds,** 1802 Dell Range Blvd., 307/632-4873; **Sparkling Brites,** 912 E. Lincolnway, 307/635-6881; **Easy Way Laundry,** 900 W. 16th St., 307/638-2177; and **Tip Top Laundry,** 1900 E. 21st St., 307/638-9938.

The expansive **Laramie County Public Library** at 2800 Central Ave., 307/634-3561, www.lclsonline.org, has free Internet access. Also check out the **Wyoming State Library,** 2301 Capitol Ave., 307/777-7281, www.wsl.state.wy.us.

Find the main **post office** at 4800 Converse Ave., 307/772-6580. The **Bureau of Land Management's Wyoming State Office** is north of town at 5353 Yellowstone Rd., 307/775-6256, www.wy.blm.gov.

Laramie County Community College, 1400 E. College Dr., 307/778-5222, www.lccc.cc.wy.us, offers both day and night classes for some 3,500 students. Founded in 1968, the school focuses primarily on technical fields, although there are two-year degrees in everything from accounting to wildlife conservation. The 270-acre campus has 18 buildings, most built in the ugly concrete-box style common to the early 1970s.

TRANSPORTATION

Bus

Cheyenne Transit Program, 307/637-6253, provides bus service around Cheyenne for $1. Buses run Monday–Friday and connect various parts of the city. Door-to-door service is also available for $3.

The bus depot is at 222 Deming Drive on the southeast end of town. **Greyhound,** 307/634-7744 or 800/231-2222, www.greyhound.com, provides connections east and west along I-80. **Powder River Transportation/Coach USA,** 307/635-1327 or 800/442-3682, has daily bus service from Cheyenne to towns in northern and central Wyoming, continuing north all the way to Billings or Rapid City and south to Denver.

Air Travel

Cheyenne Airport is just south of Dell Range Blvd., with the entrance at the east end of 8th Avenue. Cheyenne-based Great Lakes Aviation has daily flights to Denver. See the Special Topic "Airline Contacts" in the On the Road chapter for more information.

Armadillo Express, 307/634-1123 or 888/256-2967, provides daily van service to Denver International Airport for $28 one-way. **Denver Coach,** 308/632-8400 or 800/658-3125, www.windborne.cc, has scheduled service south to Denver International Airport, and north to Torrington.

Cars and Taxis

At the Cheyenne airport you can rent cars from Avis, Enterprise, and Hertz. See the Special Topic "Rental Car Contacts" in the On the Road chapter for more information. **Affordable Rent A Car,** 701 E. Lincolnway, 307/634-5666 or 800/711-1564, has used cars for lower rates. The local Chevy and Honda dealer also rents cars, calling itself **Price King Rent-a-Car,** 2142 W. Lincolnway, 307/638-0688.

There are two Cheyenne taxi companies: **Need-A-Ride Cab Company,** 37/778-0222; **T.L.C. Taxi/Yellow Cab,** 307/635-5555.

Curt Gowdy State Park

The 1,645-acre Curt Gowdy State Park is 26 miles west of Cheyenne along State Hwy. 210 (Happy Jack Rd.), the scenic "back way" to Laramie. The road rises slowly through the grasslands west of Cheyenne. At Curt Gowdy, the Granite Reservoir and Crystal Reservoir offer recreation for anglers, boaters, snowmobilers, and cross-country skiers. The small lakes, constructed between 1904 and 1910, are parts of Cheyenne's water supply, so no swimming is allowed. An elaborate Rube Goldberg scheme completed in 1964 now carries 12 million gallons of water from the west and across the Continental Divide, the Sierra Madre, the Snowy Range, and the Laramie Range to get it to thirsty Cheyenne.

In 1971, the two lakes at the eastern end were set aside as a state park and named for Wyoming native **Curt Gowdy.** Born in the town of Green River in 1919, Gowdy was a basketball player on the University of Wyoming's national championship team in 1943 and the long-time voice of the New York Yankees and Boston Red Sox. He later served as host of television's *The American Sportsman* for two decades and as a broadcaster of professional sporting events of all types, including the World Series, the Olympics, and NFL games. Day use of the park is $4 for non-Wyoming vehicles or $2 for cars with Wyoming plates. No entrance fees are collected in the winter months. Camping costs $12 for nonresidents or $6 for Wyoming residents. There's pleasant hiking in the surrounding pine-covered countryside, but by late summer the lakes tend to get severely drawn down. There are some interesting granitic formations to explore and climb. Also in the park is the historic **Hynds Lodge,** a stone structure completed in 1923 and available for families and groups to rent in the summer. For details, call park headquarters at 307/632-7946, http://wyoparks.state.wy.us. An **ice fishing derby** takes place in mid-February at the park.

ACCOMMODATIONS

The open country surrounding Curt Gowdy State Park boasts three bed-and-breakfasts well worth the drive from either Cheyenne or Laramie. An outstanding lodging option is **A. Drummond's Ranch B&B,** 399 Happy Jack Rd., 307/634-6042, www.cruising-america.com/drummond .html, just 1.5 miles away from the park and offering vistas of the Vedauwoo Rocks. Set on 120 acres, this is a fine place to splurge. The New England–style home includes four guest rooms, one of which contains a fireplace, steam sauna, and private hot tub. A second room also has its own hot tub. Guests will meet the menagerie of pets: llamas, goats, chicken, and sheep, plus a horse, cat, dog, and goose. The Drummonds can serve lunch and dinner (extra fee), and they have an indoor arena for folks who bring their own horses. They will also set up adventure packages to suit your interests, including mountain biking, skiing, hiking, camping, or hiking with a llama. Guest rooms have private or shared baths and cost $70–160 s or d. A delicious full breakfast is served, and kids are welcome.

One mile west of the Drummond's home is **Windy Hills Guest House,** 393 Happy Jack Rd., 307/632-6423 or 877/946-3944, www.windy-hillswyo.com, a modern home with a deck overlooking Granite Lake and the nearby mountains. Eight guest rooms are available: two suites ($75–82

d) in the main house with private entrances; a log home with three guest rooms ($150–180 d for one room; $250 for three rooms and six people), a kitchen, and hot tub; a two-bedroom guest house ($135–150 d for one room; $170 for four people) with a kitchen, fireplace, and hot tub; and a spa house ($200 d). All rooms contain private baths. Mountain bikes are available, and a full breakfast is served. Kids are welcome.

Another impressive and very-Wyoming place is **Bit-O-Wyo Ranch,** 470 Happy Jack Rd., 307/638-8340, www.bitowyo.com, a three-story, 4,800-square-foot log home with picture windows overlooking Table Mountain. Inside you'll find an indoor hot tub and six guest rooms with shared or private baths. On Friday and Saturday nights in the summer, the family puts on memorable dinner shows with Western entertainment; $25 adults, $15 kids. Lodging is available on a nightly basis for $60 s or $70 d, including a full breakfast, or you can opt for a traditional dude ranch stay: $1,500 for two people for six nights, including lodging, meals, horseback rides, and other activities. Guests get the chance to move cattle, explore the backcountry, and enjoy trout fishing, overnight camping, and chuck wagon cookouts. The ranch is open Memorial Day to Labor Day, with B&B accommodations continuing until mid-October, and has space for up to 12 guests.

Pine Bluffs

Pine Bluffs (pop. 1,200) is a small agricultural and transportation center on Wyoming's eastern border. The local economy seems to be spiraling downward, leaving a downtown that is virtually abandoned. But people continue to live in graceful homes beneath spreading shade trees. The surrounding area feels like western Nebraska, with ponderosa pines atop the long ridge just south of town. Wheat fields and irrigated potato fields surround Pine Bluffs, and the countryside is filled with silos, farm equipment, and rifle-racked pickup trucks, while the airwaves feature market reports and hog futures. But Pine Bluffs

is a place where you'll also find racks of tortillas in the grocery store and hear Spanish spoken by migrant workers.

INFORMATION AND ARCHAEOLOGICAL SIGHTS

Stop at the **Tourist Information Center** at the I-80 rest area (exit 401), 307/245-3695, www.pinebluffs.org, for both local and statewide information. It's open daily 8 A.M.–4 P.M. May–October, and until 5 P.M. in midsummer. Just a 10-minute walk from the I-80 rest area is one

© DON PITCHER

Our Lady of Peace, Pine Bluffs

of the most interesting sights in Pine Bluffs, the ongoing archaeological excavation at a major Native American occupation site that dates back more than 10,000 years. Indians pitched their tepees atop the pine-covered bluffs here and headed down to the fertile valley below to hunt game and collect berries. Their tepee rings are still visible. Each summer, a dozen or so University of Wyoming students under the direction of Pine Bluffs native Dr. Charles Reher arrive to slowly dig through the soil in search of a buried treasure trove of prehistory. Discoveries have included arrow and spear points, pottery, scrapers, drills, shell pendants, fire hearths, and thousands of tool-sharpening flakes. The covered site, **Windows of the Past Interpretive Center,** is open daily 9 A.M.–noon and 1–5 P.M. from Memorial Day to Labor Day. Visitors are welcome, and the staff will be happy to answer your questions; call 307/766-5136 for tour information or to see about joining the dig for a day (advance permission re-

quired). A couple of tepees have been erected nearby. Artifacts collected here can be seen in the **High Plains Archaeology Museum and Field Lab** at 2nd and Elm, 307/766-2208, also open daily during the summer.

OTHER SIGHTS

Several **nature trails** with interpretive signs depart from the rest area/information center, looping up the bluff. You can also access the hills by car by following Beech Street south under the freeway and turning right on the dirt road at the crest of the hill. This is an excellent place to watch sunrises and sunsets or to enjoy a picnic lunch amid the pines.

Pine Bluff's most bizarre sight is the five-story-tall **Our Lady of Peace Shrine**—the largest statue of the Virgin Mary in the United States. It faces I-80 and is just a few feet from the Nebraska border. See her 180 tons of glory by heading east from town on U.S. Hwy. 30 to the RV park. Turn south and she'll soon be hard to miss.

A dozen miles southeast of Pine Bluffs are a pair of minor landmarks: the **Tri-State Corner Marker** where Wyoming, Nebraska, and Colorado meet, and a marker at **Panorama Point,** Nebraska's highest spot. The latter is just a small hill that crests at 5,424 feet (versus Wyoming's high point of 13,804 feet). The information center has a map with descriptions and directions for both markers. A buffalo ranch is not far from Panorama Point.

Pine Bluffs lies right along the great **Texas Trail;** at its peak in 1871, more than 600,000 cattle were trailed north from Texas past this point. The town became not just a watering place for the stock, but also a vital shipping point. For several years, more cattle were shipped from the railroad station at Pine Bluffs than anywhere else in the world. A monument to the Texas Trail stands in the adjacent park.

The free **Texas Trail Museum,** at 3rd and Market Sts., 307/245-9347, houses a Conestoga wagon, old photos, and a small collection of homesteading and ranching items. It's open Monday–Saturday 11 A.M.–4 P.M. Memorial Day to Labor Day, or by appointment (stop by

SOUTHEAST WYOMING

the town hall) at other times. Next to the museum are a caboose and several historic buildings—a one-room schoolhouse, an old church, and a railroad boardinghouse.

ACCOMMODATIONS AND CAMPING

Gator's Travelyn Motel, 515 W. 7th, 307/245-3226, has comfortable rooms for $38 s or $48–58 d. **Sunset Motel,** 315 W. 3rd, 307/245-3591, is a run-down place if you're desperate for a spot.

Pine Bluff RV Campground, 307/245-3665 or 800/294-4968, is one-half mile east of town and has year-round tent spaces with no shade but lots of wind for $10. RV sites are $20. A seasonal ice cream shop is also here.

FOOD

Restaurant options are pretty slim in Pine Bluffs. The best bet is **Uncle Fred's Place,** 701 Parsons, 307/245-3443, where you'll find family meals and a salad bar. Locals also eat at the **Wild Horse Restaurant** in the Total station, 600 Parsons, 307/245-9365, but it's a cigarette smoker's heaven and a nonsmoker's hell. The Total station also has an **ATM.**

Subway, 307/245-3405, is housed in the Ampride gas station/mini-mart on Parsons Street. Get groceries at **Texas Trail Market,** 3rd and Elm, 307/245-3302. This is a cooperatively run store, as are the auto-repair shop, local grain elevator, and electric utility. Socialism in a rock-ribbed Republican state!

EVENTS AND ENTERTAINMENT

Pine Bluffs Trail Days comes in early August with rodeos, barbecues, a parade, melodrama, golf, mud volleyball, and dancing.

The popular **Outlaw Saloon Summer Rodeo Series** takes place on Friday nights June–August at the rodeo grounds, with barrel racing, bareback riding, team roping, saddle bronc riding, and bull riding. Call 307/632-3626 for details. You're also likely to see local cowboys and cowgirls practicing roping here several afternoons a week in summer.

RECREATION AND SERVICES

The primary hangout in Pine Bluffs is the local bowling alley, **Pine Bowl,** 3rd and Pine, 307/245-3622. Golfers should check out **Leaning Rock Golf Course,** with nine holes of sand and artificial turf atop the bluff; only $5. Pine Bluffs has an outdoor **swimming pool** at 200 E. 8th, 307/245-3783. Open June–Aug.; $1.

The **library** is at 108 E. 2nd, 307/245-3646. No bus service exists to Pine Bluffs; the nearest Greyhound stops are in Cheyenne (40 miles west) and Kimball, Nebraska (20 miles east).

NORTH FROM PINE BLUFFS

For a delightful break from busy I-80, drive north of Pine Bluffs along State Hwy. 215 through the wheat and grasslands on the Wyoming–Nebraska border. The high plains landscape has a smattering of ponderosa pines capping the rocky bluffs, a handful of ranches, and to-the-horizon vistas. The road rolls past **Albin** (pop. 120) 18 miles north of Pine Bluffs, with a tiny but picturesque catholic church. An old log homestead is worth a look west of here. Head 2.5 miles west on Wyoming 216 and then one mile north on Rd. 159 to the cabin. **Albin Days** takes place the second Saturday in July.

LaGRANGE

The nothing farm village of LaGrange (pop. 330) is 25 miles northwest of Albin. Established in 1889, the town was named for Kale LaGrange, a stagecoach driver on the Cheyenne to Red Cloud route. Just to the north is 66 Mountain, so called because it supposedly has the number hidden in its profile. Stop in LaGrange in early August for the **Mini Fair & Rodeo.**

Bear Mountain Riding Ranch, 307/834-2492, www.wyobearmountain.com, has B&B accommodations in its four-bedroom ranch house, plus thousands of acres of land on the CP Ranch. It's been in the same family for six generations. The cost is $175 d, including lodging, breakfast, and horseback riding.

Chugwater

Chugwater (pop. 240) was once headquarters for the giant Swan Land and Cattle Company, the greatest of Wyoming's cattle spreads during the 1880s. The town itself was founded in 1913 on land sold by the Swan Company. Chugwater has to have one of the strangest origins of any town name in America, coming from the Indian practice of driving buffalo over cliffs. The "chug" sound the buffalo made as they hit bottom led Mandan Indians to call it "Water at the Place Where the Buffalo Chug." The prominent flat-topped mesa over which the bison were driven rises just north of town. When the railroad was built here, thousands of buffalo bones were discovered at the base of these cliffs.

SIGHTS

Chugwater is perhaps best known for **Chugwater Chili,** a mix sold in stores throughout the Rockies or by mail order (307/422-3345 or 800/972-4454), or on the web at www.chugwaterchili.com. Get a free taste at 210 1st Street. The company also sells a full line of Wyoming-made gifts, from skin lotions to salad dressings. The annual **Chugwater Chili Cook-off** is held the third Saturday in June and attracts dozens of chefs and hundreds of fire-breathing chili eaters. Other events include a rodeo and country music. Call 307/422-3493 or 307/422-3201 for cook-off details.

The little **Chugwater Museum** occupies an old bank building on Main Street, 307/422-3227,

SWAN LAND AND CATTLE COMPANY

The most famous of all Wyoming ranching operations was the Swan Land and Cattle Company, Ltd., founded in 1883 by Alexander and Thomas Swan with enormous financial backing from Scottish investors—£600,000 the first year and an additional £1.6 million over the next three years. At its peak in the mid-1880s, the company's holdings reached from its headquarters along Chugwater Creek westward for 120 miles to the North Platte River near Rawlins. More than 110,000 cattle ranged across this vast expanse. The company bought 550,000 acres of Union Pacific Railroad land (and therefore controlled the checkerboard of public land in alternating sections) and purchased government land along major creeks in the area. By doing this, it controlled access to water in this semiarid country, thus keeping others from settling on surrounding public lands. All told, the Swan Land and Cattle Company had its tentacles over nearly one million acres covering more than 30 different ranches. The company had dozens of different brands, but locals knew it as the "Two Bar." Cowboys loved the company because it always provided good working conditions and wages ($20 per month to start) and the best grub around.

In the mid-1880s, though, things began to turn sour, and by 1886 the Scottish investors accused Alexander Swan of fraud and misrepresentation; the 110,000 cattle shown on the books did not all exist on the hoof. A lawsuit eventually led to Swan's firing. Even more devastating was the severe winter of 1886–1887, which killed off thousands of the firm's cows and calves, pushing the company to the brink of bankruptcy. Amazingly, the reorganized company managed to survive for more than 50 years, although it began raising sheep instead of cattle after 1903. It was prosperous during World War I, when wool prices soared, but its fortunes gradually declined with the economy. By 1950, the vast operation had been entirely liquidated. Some folks claim that Steamboat, a wild bronc from the old Two Bar Ranch, was the inspiration for the bucking horse symbol found on Wyoming license plates. Many of the historic ranch's buildings are still intact, and the complex has been designated a National Historic Landmark.

SOUTHEAST WYOMING

and houses an impressive collection of brands, aging farm machinery, and various homestead-era items, along with an early-1900s caboose out front. Open Sat.–Sun. 1–4 P.M. in the summer; if it's closed, stop across the street at the **Chugwater Soda Fountain,** 307/422-3222, for access. In addition to great malts from one of Wyoming's oldest soda fountains, they sell T-shirts, gifts, a few groceries, and liquor.

For an extraordinarily **scenic drive,** take State Hwy. 211 from Chugwater to Cheyenne. It's a mix of gravel and pavement and takes longer than I-25 but is virtually free of traffic. The road passes through a Wyoming landscape of grass and sage-carpeted hills, tree-lined creeks, magnificent old ranches, and herds of deer and antelope. Stop to listen to the meadowlarks on a spring day or to watch the clouds roiling overhead in this peaceful place.

PRACTICALITIES

Get details from the **Town of Chugwater,** 307/422-3493, www.chugwater.com.

On a historic 75,000-acre cattle ranch 15 miles west of Chugwater, **Diamond Guest Ranch,** 307/422-3564 or 800/932-4222, www.diamondgr.com, is popular with families and retirees. The ranch began in 1884 and was for many years a breeding center for Clydesdale and Morgan horses. It has been a guest ranch since 1968 but retains many of the original buildings. Outdoor

recreation opportunities include horseback rides, fishing, hiking, hayrides, mountain biking, and a heated outdoor pool. Also here are a restaurant (open for dinner) and a bar. Campsites cost $15 for tents or $20 for RVs. Lodging is available in the historic ranch house or private cabins (perfect for families). Rates are $55 d, $65 for four people, or $75 for six. Open mid-May to mid-Oct.

Another historic operation, **Grant Ranch,** 307/322-2923, www.grantranchwyoming.com, lies northwest of Chugwater in the picturesque Richeau Hills. Guests take part in everyday ranch activities such as moving cattle, riding, fishing, or just relaxing. A three-day minimum stay is required ($1,050 for two adults, all-inclusive), but most folks opt for a one-week stay ($2,450 for two adults, all-inclusive). Lodging is in the 1890s ranch house, and the meals are hearty.

Back in town, **Super 8 Motel,** 100 Buffalo Dr., 307/422-3248 or 800/800-8000, www.super8.com, has a small outdoor pool and rooms for $47–57 s or $52–68 d (substantially higher during Frontier Days). It's considerably better than most Super 8s.

The building also houses **Buffalo Grill,** a restaurant serving (not surprisingly) buffalo burgers, plus sandwiches, chicken, pasta, pork chops, and more. In addition, lunches and dinners are served inside a rough-hewn restaurant called **The Steak-Out,** 417 1st St., 307/422-3251.

The state has a **rest area** just north of Chugwater on I-25.

Wheatland

Wheatland (pop. 3,500) is a friendly middle-America town with a shady downtown and farming country in all directions. Despite the name, wheat is not the primary crop grown here; sugar beets, dry beans, and barley are. The largest local employer is Laramie River Station, a 1,650-megawatt coal-fired power plant located five miles north of town. It supplies electricity to a grid that feeds an eight-state area. Another substantial employer is a local marble quarry that mines dolomite in the Laramie Mountains and crushes it for use in everything from aquarium

gravel to cattle feed. Don't let on that I told you, but Wheatland also has Minuteman III nuclear missiles out in the country near the power plant. Perhaps for this reason, the town boasts one of the highest number of churches per capita anywhere: 23 different houses of worship crowd the town.

HISTORY

An early settler in this part of Wyoming called it "a desolate looking place, nothing but sagebrush, cactus, rocks, mudhole, rattlesnakes, and coyotes."

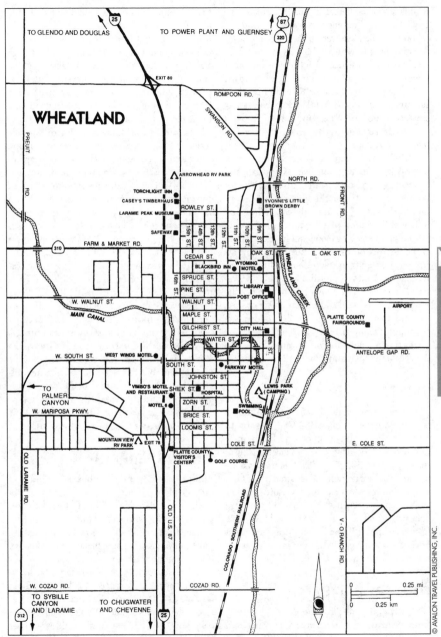

It took water to change all this. Wheatland is a creation of the Wyoming Development Company, founded in 1883 by several individuals, including Senators Joseph M. Carey and Francis E. Warren. In one of the few successful applications of the famous Carey Act in Wyoming, the company built a dam on Big Laramie River and canals to carry the water to some 50,000 acres where homesteaders formed the Wheatland Colony. Today it remains the largest privately owned irrigation system in the nation.

In 1905 the town of Wheatland was incorporated (the name won out over Wheatdale and Wheatridge) and became the hub of activity for the region—and later the Platte County seat. During the late 1970s and early '80s, Wheatland followed the boom pattern common to other Wyoming towns: nearby oil and gas exploration and construction of the giant power plant attracted thousands to town. When things went bust, Wheatland was pulled down, but it has recovered somewhat. Downtown may not be bustling, but it's clean and attractive. Agriculture, that old standby, has increased in importance. Wyoming Premium Farms runs a gigantic hog farm a dozen miles north of Wheatland that produces 100,000 pigs annually. Hold your nose!

SIGHTS

The free **Laramie Peak Museum,** 1601 16th St., is open Monday–Friday 10 A.M.–5 P.M. (until 8 P.M. on Mon., Tues., Thurs., and Fri. in midsummer), and Saturday 10 A.M.–3 P.M. late May to mid-September; 307/322-2764. It houses a variety of homestead-era flotsam and jetsam ranging from early-1900s tricycles to a stuffed vulture. A saddle and cowboy hat here have burn marks from when lightning struck a local cowboy (he lived). The marble-columned **Platte County Court House** at 9th and Walnut is easily the most imposing structure in Wheatland. It was built in 1911.

COUNTRY DRIVES

For a delightful all-day loop drive, head west from Wheatland out **Palmer Canyon Road** through the farm fields and open plains, past the old stone buildings of Muleshoe Ranch, and high into the cool Laramie Range. The first 10 miles are paved. Once in the hills, the dirt road (avoid after rains or in the spring) winds through a rocky ponderosa pine-covered landscape that comes alive with springtime flowers. You can return to Wheatland the same way or do a big loop by turning north onto Cottonwood Park Road and then east again on Fletcher Park Road. Check with the visitors center for the specific route or look over Forest Service or topo maps. They also have a Laramie Peak loop tour pamphlet that describes hiking trails in the area.

A shorter country drive—on a mix of paved and gravel roads—connects Wheatland with Fort Laramie. Head north on State 320 for two miles, turning east onto Grayrocks Road, which leads past the huge **Laramie River Station** power plant. The coal-fired generating station produces 1.65 million kilowatts and is fed by an almost-constant stream of trains filled with coal from mines in the Gillette area. Call 307/322-9601 for free weekday tours, available for groups. Get additional information on the web at www.wmpa.org/laramie_river_station.htm. A few miles up the narrow road is **Grayrocks Reservoir,** which provides cooling water for the power plant and recreation for boaters and anglers. A small store (Cottonwood Canteen) sells gas and groceries. Beyond this you can follow the signs to historic Fort Laramie. It's a scenic and out-of-the-way drive with little traffic.

FINDING FERRETS

Approximately 30 miles southwest of Wheatland on State Hwy. 34 is the Wyoming Department of Game and Fish **Sybille Wildlife Research and Conservation Education Unit** (Sybille is pronounced "suh-BEEL"). The facility houses elk, mule and white-tailed deer, bighorn sheep, moose, buffalo, and the star attraction, black-footed ferrets. The separate black-footed ferret facility is operated by the U.S. Fish & Wildlife Service and is home to 150 of these cute black-masked creatures. The visitors center, 307/322-2571, is open daily 8:30 A.M.–4:30 P.M. April to mid-November (closed the rest of the year) and includes exhibits and videos on the endangered black-footed ferret. To lessen the impact and potential health threats from introduced diseases, tours of the research facility are not available, but one of the live ferrets is kept at the visitors center. Out back is an observation deck and short nature trail along Sybille Creek. Lean more about ferrets at www.black-footedferret.org.

ACCOMMODATIONS

There are several places to stay in Wheatland. Expect to pay substantially higher rates than those listed as follows during Frontier Days, even though it is an hour's drive to Cheyenne.

The friendly **Wyoming Motel,** 1101 9th St., 307/322-5383 or 800/839-5383, www.wyoming-motel.com, has refurbished and clean furnishings, along with in-room fridges and a barbecue. Rates are $32 s or $35–42 d. **Parkway Motel,** 1257 South Rd., 307/322-3080, is similarly priced: $33–44 s or d.

Motel West Winds, 1756 South St., 307/322-2705, charges $37–42 s or $50 d. **Motel 6,** 95 16th St., 307/322-1800 or 800/466-8356, www.motel6.com, has predictable rooms for $41 s or $47 d.

Vimbo's Motel, 203 16th St., 307/322-3842 or 800/577-3842, www.plattenetwork.com/vimbos, has large and well-maintained rooms for $49–69 s or $54–77 d.

Best Western Torchlite Motor Inn, 1809 N. 16th St., 307/322-4070 or 800/662-3968, www.bestwestern.com, charges $75–80 s or $80–85 d and has an outdoor pool and hot tub.

Alternative Accommodations

Blackbird Inn Bed & Breakfast, 1101 11th St., 307/322-4540, www.blackbirdinn.com, is a lovingly restored 1910 Victorian home with a wraparound front porch that makes a fine place to sit on a summer evening. Inside are four guest rooms with shared baths and a two-bedroom suite with a private bath. The home is furnished in antiques. Rates are $65 s or $75 d, or $150 for the four-person suite. A full breakfast is included, and kids are welcome.

Seven miles south of Wheatland, the century-old **Grant Ranch,** offers guided horseback tours and cattle drives in the summer (see Chugwater Accommodations section).

CAMPING

You can camp for free beneath the cottonwoods at 40-acre **Lewis Park** right in town; 307/322-2962. This quiet spot is a perfect place to relax. Showers and RV hookups are available; three-night maximum stay.

Camping is also free at **Grayrocks Reservoir,** northeast of Wheatland beyond the power plant. No RV hookups, but coin-operated showers are available. The nearby **Cottonwood Canteen,** 307/322-2242, sells a few groceries, beer, gas, and bait. Open summers only. In addition, free campsites can be found along **Wheatland Reservoir** and **Rock Lake** a few miles southwest of town, as well as on Forest Service land in the Laramie Mountains west of Wheatland.

RVers may prefer to park at **Mountain View RV Park,** 307/322-4858, 77 20th St. (just west of exit 78). Rates are $17; open May–Sept. On the north end of town, **Arrowhead RV Park,** 2005 N. 16th St., 307/322-3467, has RV hookups for $15 and tent sites for $10. Showers are $3 if you aren't staying here. Open all year.

FOOD

Marie's Goodie Shop, 719 9th St., 307/322-5321, makes good sandwiches for lunch, including cabbage burgers, and serves hot coffee and pastries for a quick breakfast. Pseudo-Mexican food comes to you—in all its microwaved glory—courtesy of the Korean chefs at **El Gringo's,** 705 10th St., 307/322-4402.

Vimbo's Family Restaurant, 203 16th St., 307/322-3725, is a longtime star on the local scene, with dependable homemade food, a big menu, and friendly waitresses. The breakfast and lunch buffets ($7) are especially popular, as is the Friday night seafood buffet ($13). Recommended.

Housed in an attractive log building, **Casey's Timberhaus Family Restaurant,** 1803 16th St., 307/322-4932, is another bring-out-the-gang restaurant, with a so-so salad bar and standard American burgers and steak. Breakfasts are a better bet.

Terra Grano Pizza, 1557 South St., 307/322-4888, is a friendly little place with from-scratch bagels, sandwiches, big salads, homemade soups, espresso, pizzas, and calzones. They even make a tasty "breakfast pizza" with scrambled eggs.

Pizza Hut, 1801 N. 16th St., 307/322-4001, is the only place that's open late most nights. Other chains in Wheatland include Subway and Burger King.

Wheatland's surprise is **Yvonne's Little Brown Derby,** 1707 9th St., 307/322-4257. Occupying a 1950s-era trailer house, it has great food, reasonable prices (including a $2.99 breakfast), and huge portions. They always offer lunch specials, and the burgers and chicken-fried steak are famous. For something different, try the Friday night prime rib specials, but get there early or they may be gone. Even the Burlington Northern freight train stops so the crew can come over for dinner!

Groceries are available at the homey **Huffer's Food Pride,** 702 10th St., 307/322-3343, or the larger **Safeway** on 16th St., 307/322-4530.

RECREATION

There is a fine outdoor **swimming pool** (307/322-9254) in Lewis Park, open in the summer. The nine-hole **Wheatland Golf Course** is at 1253 Cole, 307/322-3675. **Cinema West,** 609 10th St., 307/322-9032, is the local movie house.

EVENTS

Wheatland has a big fireworks show at the fairgrounds on the **Fourth of July.** The **Platte County Summer Festival** takes place in June with live music, dancing, food and craft booths, and a tractor pull in Lewis Park. The **Platte County Fair and Rodeo** occurs in early August and offers a street breakfast, barbecue, parade, rodeo, entertainment, and all the usual fun of a country fair. Most enjoyable of all is the pig wrestling. Call 307/322-2322 for details.

INFORMATION AND SERVICES

The always helpful **Platte County Visitor's Center,** 307/322-2322, www.plattechamber.com, is next to I-25 exit 78. Hours are Monday–Friday 8 A.M.–6 P.M. and Saturday–Sunday 10 A.M.–2 P.M. Memorial Day to Labor Day, and Monday–Friday 8 A.M.–5 P.M. the rest of the year.

Find the **Platte County Library** at 904 9th Street, 307/322-2689, and the **post office** at 852 Walnut Street, 307/332-3287. Wash clothes at **North 16th St. Laundromat,** next to Torchlight Inn on 16th Street. **Wheatland Travel Plaza,** 81 Swanson Rd., 307/322-1884, is a truckstop with showers and laundry facilities. **Platte County Memorial Hospital,** 202 14th St., 307/322-3636, has emergency medical services.

TRANSPORTATION

Powder River/Coach USA, 307/322-2725 or 800/442-3682, has daily bus service from Wheatland to towns in northern and central Wyoming, continuing north to Billings and Rapid City and south to Cheyenne and Denver. Buses stop at the I-25 Conoco.

Rent cars and vans from **Laramie Peak Motors,** 307/322-2355 or 800/564-2355, www.laramiepeakmotors.com.

Guernsey and Vicinity

GUERNSEY

Guernsey (pop. 1,100) is a scenic railroad and ranching town along the once-mighty North Platte River. The river is now just a trickle in late summer, thanks to all the upstream dams. The town is named for Charles A. Guernsey, a prominent local rancher and legislator who came here in the late 19th century. The town is right in the heart of Oregon Trail country, with Fort Laramie just 11 miles east and numerous 19th-century historical markers. The Wyoming Army National Guard maintains Camp Guernsey, a large troop training facility just north of town. Watch your speed here; local cops strictly enforce the 30 mph limit!

Emigrant Trail Sights

The Oregon Trail ran just on the other side of the North Platte River from Guernsey. One mile south of town are some of the deepest and most impressive **Oregon Trail ruts** anywhere along the historic route. Informative plaques describe the site in detail, and a short trail leads uphill to four-foot-deep gouges cut into the soft sandstone. The paths of bullwhackers are visible alongside. The old wagon trail is easy to follow in both directions, and the surrounding landscape has probably changed little since the last wagon train rolled past. Perhaps better than any historic photos or written descriptions, these deep ruts serve as permanent reminders of the great westward migration. Not far away is a white obelisk marking the

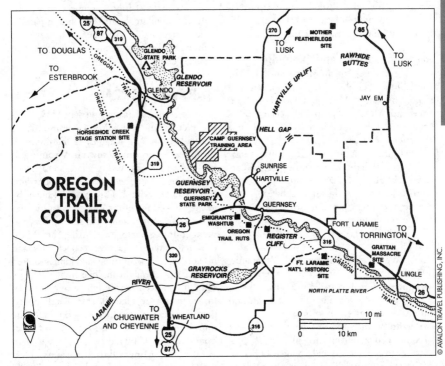

SOUTHEAST WYOMING

© AVALON TRAVEL PUBLISHING, INC.

grave of Lucindy Rollins, one of the thousands who died on the hard road west.

The hundred-foot-tall **Register Cliff** is four miles south of Guernsey. Here the soft limestone made a perfect place for passing emigrants to carve their names, and thousands took the time to do so. The oldest—dating to the 1850s—are now behind a chain-link fence to keep folks from defacing them further. Hundreds of swallows nest on the cliff here. North of Guernsey, ruts of the historic Mormon Trail are visible along **Emigrant Hill,** where Mormon pioneers struggled to hoist their wagons up the steep slope.

Another important nearby site was **Emigrants' Washtub,** a warm springs where weary travelers stopped to bathe and wash clothes. The springs are an enjoyable place to relax even today and are reached via a two-mile walk along a dry creekbed. Access is a bit tricky because you pass through private land along the way and need to watch out for old shells left behind from National Guard training exercises. Get access information from the visitors center.

Accommodations and Camping

No bunkhouse accommodations at the **Bunkhouse Motel,** 307/836-2356, but nice motel rooms are $49–54 s or d. Down the street, **Sagebrush Motel,** 307/836-2331, charges $37 s or $42 d. All the rooms have fridges, and some also offer microwaves.

You'll find pleasant riverside campsites near the Oregon Trail ruts at the town-managed **Larson Park,** 307/836-2255. Camping is $5 for tents or $9 for RVs, including showers. Those who aren't camping here can use the showers for $2. Open Apr. to mid-Oct.

Food

Rob's Riverview Restaurant, 800 W. Laramie, 307/836-2191, is an attractive, modern place with three reasonably priced meals daily. There are specials most nights, including roast prime rib Saturday evenings. Big portions, too.

Burrito Brothers Mexican Food offers decent Mexican food, and **Trail Inn,** 307/836-2573, is the place to go for steaks and a Sunday buffet. **Guernsey Lunch Box,** on the east side of town, has standard American fare in a fast-food setting: burgers, chicken-fried steak, corn dogs, sandwiches, and a salad bar. Get groceries at **B&F Super Foods.**

Other Practicalities

Guernsey's small **visitors center/museum** is at SW Wyoming and W. Sunrise, 307/836-2715. It's open during the summer and situated right in front of the town **swimming pool,** which is also open seasonally. The tiny **Guernsey library** is open Monday–Saturday.

Get fast cash from the **ATM** inside the Phillips 66 station. The nine-hole **Trail Ruts Golf Course,** 307/836-2255, provides a place to putt around, or you can bowl a few games at **Oregon Trail Lanes.** Guernsey's airport is surprisingly large and well equipped, not because of any commercial service—there isn't any—but because of the nearby National Guard training facilities.

Each **Fourth of July,** Guernsey comes to life with the standard small-town fun: a parade, rodeo, street dance, barbecue, and fireworks. **Labor Day** brings a demolition derby and an arts-and-crafts fair.

HARTVILLE AREA

Six miles north of Guernsey on State Hwy. 270 is the picturesque old mining community of Hartville (pop. 80). Established in 1884, it is the **oldest incorporated town in Wyoming.** It was named for Col. Verling Hart, an officer at nearby Fort Laramie and owner of a copper mine here. The Hartville Uplift—as it is known by geologists—is one of the most mineral-rich regions in Wyoming. Indians used its iron as pigment to make war paint. During the 1870s, prospectors found gold, silver, copper, onyx, and iron ore in these scenic pine- and juniper-dotted hills. Copper brought the first miners, but by 1887 it had been mostly mined out and they turned to iron ore. Hartville arose as a shopping, gambling, boozing, and whoring center for the miners; many of the historic stone and false-front buildings still stand.

Of note is **Miners Bar**—the state's oldest drinking establishment, and the only surviving business. The cherry wood back bar was crafted in Germany in 1864 and shipped to Fort Laramie before landing in Hartville in 1881. The bar is only open in the summer and has a horseshoe pit next door. Also in Hartville is an old stone jail.

Sunrise

The mining ghost town of Sunrise (closed to the public) is just one mile east of Hartville. An extraordinarily rich body of iron ore was discovered here in 1887, and a dozen years later the Colorado Fuel and Iron Corp. established an open-pit iron mine, a mine that would eventually reach 650 feet in depth, the largest glory hole in the world. It closed in 1984, and reclamation work has restored the gaping hole to a more natural contour. When the mine first opened, the company hired some 750 predominantly Italian and Greek emigrants to dig the ore, which was shipped to a smelter in Pueblo, Colorado. To house the workers, the well-planned company town of Sunrise sprang up. The mine was closed in 1980 because of a lessened demand for ore, and its brick buildings now stand abandoned. It is a fascinating place to explore but isn't open to the public. You may be able to get access by asking locally for permission. Sunrise claims a minuscule footnote to history: *Ripley's Believe It or Not!* noted that the town had the longest string of car garages in the world. They are still standing, but it is doubtful that just six garages would merit such a rating today.

Spanish Diggings

The Hartville area is part of the so-called Spanish Diggings, an extensive archaeological site that covers hundreds of square miles. Early settlers believed this to be the site of a Spanish gold mine—hence the name—but it is now known to have been used instead by Native Americans gathering flint for arrowheads. They mined quartzite, jasper, moss agate, and chalcedony here for perhaps 10,000 years. Stone flakes and countless old pits up to 15 feet deep and 50 feet wide abound in this region. The material mined was carried all the way to the Missouri River. You'll find hundreds of tepee rings and rock chips here. One of the most important aboriginal places

in Wyoming is in this area: an 11,000-year-old paleo-Indian site called **Hell Gap.**

Heading North

State Hwy. 270 heads north from Hartville over pine-carpeted hills before descending through rolling grassland with a backdrop of rocky buttes and antelope grazing beside old windmills. There are dramatic views of Laramie Peak and Flattop Butte from the hilltops, plus a picturesque smattering of old stone or log houses.

At **Manville** (pop. 100) the road meets U.S. 18/20, which leads to Lusk. There's not much in Manville other than a few old buildings, including one of the smallest post offices in Wyoming, a water tower, a school, and a gas station/café/bar.

GUERNSEY STATE PARK

Two state parks are found along the North Platte River in eastern Wyoming. Seven miles long and covering 6,538 acres, Guernsey is the smaller of the two but is far more interesting than its sister, Glendo State Park. The south entrance to Guernsey State Park is one mile northwest of Guernsey, and the road connects through to the Hartville area. The park surrounds Guernsey Reservoir, which is backed up behind a 105-foot-tall, 560-foot-long earthen dam completed in 1927. Originally, the dam stored 74,000 acre-feet of water, but half that capacity has been lost as a result of siltation. To reduce this problem, authorities now drain the reservoir each summer after the Fourth of July, killing off many of the fish and sometimes creating havoc with boaters because draining can take place with almost no warning. Don't bother bringing your fishing pole. The reservoir generally fills up again by Labor Day weekend.

Guernsey is surrounded by scenic grass-and-sage-covered hills topped with juniper and pine. The drive from Hartville through the park is a surprise after the open sage-and-grass country north of here. Pink-walled sandstone cliffs suddenly appear as the narrow, winding road (not for RVs) enters the canyon, hugs the cliffs as it passes the lake, and then climbs into the pines. There is a pleasant beach five miles west along the southern shore and 19 different **campgrounds,** each costing $12 for nonresidents or $6 for Wyoming residents year-round. The water is warm, making this a popular swimming hole.

Day use at Guernsey State Park costs $4 for nonresident vehicles or $2 for folks with Wyoming plates, but fees generally aren't collected after mid-September. Get additional information at 307/836-2334, http://wyoparks.state.wy.us.

Sights

Other than the scenery, the main attractions in Guernsey State Park are the wonderful stone structures built by the Civilian Conservation Corps (CCC) during the 1930s—some of the best examples of CCC craftsmanship in existence. **Guernsey State Park Museum,** built in 1936, is the finest of all, with an arched stone entrance facing impressive Laramie Peak 35 miles to the west. Inside are enormous hand-hewn timbers, wrought-iron light fixtures, and flagstone floors. This place was built to last! The free museum, 307/836-2900, is open daily 10 A.M.–6 P.M. Memorial Day to Labor Day, closed the rest of the year, and houses 14 displays created by the CCC to illustrate the geology and human use of the surrounding country. Take a look at the historical slide show.

Other park structures built of native materials include roads, overlooks, rock walls, culverts, bridges, and picnic shelters. Most impressive is a massive sandstone picnic shelter known as **The Castle,** which faces the reservoir and Laramie Peak. Take the side road up to **Brimmer Point Overlook** for outstanding sunset vistas. Not far away is the "million-dollar privy," so named because it took so much time and money to build. Guernsey State Park also contains eight miles of hiking trails and a short nature trail near the museum. Pick up a trail guide inside.

GLENDO STATE PARK

Twenty-five miles east of Douglas and 32 miles north of Wheatland, 10,000-acre Glendo State Park surrounds Glendo Reservoir. A 167-foot-high earthen dam backs up water for 14 miles and generates some 24,000 kilowatts of electric-

ity. This is one of the largest reservoirs on the North Platte River, and it has almost 80 miles of shoreline. Note, however, that drought years sometimes reduce the reservoir to little more than a puddle. The surrounding country is treeless and windy, but the towering 10,272-foot summit of Laramie Peak dominates the skyline to the west. The surprisingly warm water at Sandy Beach makes this a play area for families from surrounding towns. Other attractions are the Red Cliffs, where cliff divers agonize over the long drop, and Muddy Bay, where anglers look for walleye (there are some lunkers here), perch, or trout. You can explore dozens of small coves by boat or float down the river below the dam. The wind can really blow, making for good windsurfing conditions but also creating hazards for folks who go out in small boats.

Practicalities

There are seven state park campgrounds ($12 for nonresidents, $6 for Wyoming residents; open year-round) on the eastern end of Glendo Reservoir. Get permits from park headquarters, 307/735-4433, http://wyoparks.state.wy.us, near the dam. Day use costs $4 for nonresident vehicles or $2 for Wyoming vehicles.

Town of Glendo

The desolate town of Glendo (pop. 240) is just two miles from Glendo State Park, near the site of the old **Horseshoe Creek Stage Station.** Built by Mormons in the 1850s, this station was later burned by them to keep it out of government hands. A small **Glendo Historical Museum** next to the town office is open Monday–Friday 8 A.M.–noon and 1–4 P.M. and displays early settlers' gear, dinosaur bones, and rocks.

Cheap lodging (in mobile homes) is available at **Howard's Motel,** 106 A St., 307/735-4252, for $24 s or $30 d. The store here has an ATM. **Lakeview Motel & Trailer Court,** 307/735-4461, is just north of town overlooking the lake, with RV hookups for $15; same price for tent sites. Simple cottages cost $20 s or $30–40 d.

Hall's Glendo Marina, near the dam, 307/735-4216, has rustic motel accommodations overlooking the lake for $48–58 s or d.

Also here are a restaurant and small grocery store, plus RV sites with hookups ($20). Hall's rents fishing boats, pontoon boats, jet skis, and other equipment for water play, and is open May to early October.

Rooster's Old Western Saloon, 307/735-4451, serves the best dinners around, with steak, prime rib, fresh walleye, and Indian fry bread on the menu. Meals are also available at **Diamond A's Lounge and Grill,** 307/735-4265, and **Corner Cafe,** 307/735-4476.

Cribbage players take note: Diamond A's Lounge and Grill, hosts the **Platte Valley Cribbage Tournament** the last weekend of February. It's said to be the oldest consecutive tournament in the United States. **Glendo Days** arrives in mid-June, featuring a hot-air-balloon rally, parade, craft fair, games, food booths, and a street dance. Probably the strangest event is "chicken-poop poker." You probably don't want to know the rules. Call 307/735-4265 for details on Glendo Days. The **Glendo Marina Walleye Tournament,** 307/735-4216, comes around in early June, and a fireworks display takes place on the Fourth of July.

Fort Laramie National Historic Site

One of the most important historic sites in all of Wyoming is old Fort Laramie, located three miles southwest of the town of the same name. The fort played a variety of roles as the West was developed: Indian trading post, emigrant way station, and military center. Fort Laramie stood at the crossroads of history. The budding territory's first school and post office opened here, and nearly every famous citizen of the frontier era—from Jim Bridger to Mark Twain—stopped in. Today Fort Laramie is one of the most popular stopping points for visitors who want a taste of the rich history of this region.

HISTORY

In 1834, trader William Sublette halted along the banks of the Laramie River near its confluence with the North Platte. With him were 35 mountain men, their pack animals weighed down with trade items for the annual rendezvous along the Green River. Sublette had a bold plan to build a permanent trading post here, one that would make it easier to bring supplies west and beaver furs and buffalo robes back east, a place where Indians and whites could parley and profit. He left behind a dozen men to begin work on what would become Fort William (named after its founder) and hurried west to the rendezvous. The men threw up a cottonwood stockade with

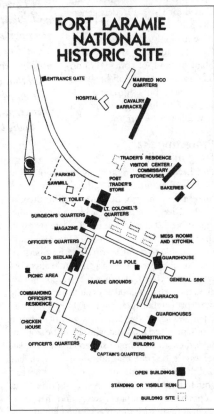

FORT LARAMIE NATIONAL HISTORIC SITE

ENTRANCE GATE
MARRIED NCO QUARTERS
HOSPITAL
CAVALRY BARRACKS
TRADER'S RESIDENCE
VISITOR CENTER / COMMISSARY STOREHOUSES
PARKING
POST TRADER'S STORE
SAWMILL
BAKERIES
PIT TOILET
LT. COLONEL'S QUARTERS
SURGEON'S QUARTERS
MAGAZINE
MESS ROOMS AND KITCHEN.
OFFICER'S QUARTERS
OLD BEDLAM
FLAG POLE
GUARDHOUSE
PICNIC AREA
PARADE GROUNDS
GENERAL SINK
COMMANDING OFFICER'S RESIDENCE
BARRACKS
CHICKEN HOUSE
GUARDHOUSES
OFFICER'S QUARTERS
ADMINISTRATION BUILDING
CAPTAIN'S QUARTERS
OPEN BUILDINGS
STANDING OR VISIBLE RUIN
BUILDING SITE

SOUTHEAST WYOMING

blockhouses on the corners and a tunnel to the outer gate for trading with the Indians.

The post changed hands a couple of times in the next two years. Changing its name to Fort Lucien, it became an important trade center for Pierre Chouteau's American Fur Company. By 1841, competition from another trading post—built just one mile away—forced the company to start again. This time they spent $10,000 building a whitewashed adobe fort near the already rotting old one. Fort John-on-the-Laramie was the official name given to the second fort, but this was quickly shortened to Fort Laramie.

During the next eight years, Fort Laramie emerged as a strategic center for trade with the Indians; more than 10,000 buffalo robes were purchased each year. (Traders generally paid the equivalent of $1 per robe in the form of gunpowder, hatchets, tobacco, coffee, sugar, blankets, and, of course, liquor. The robes were sold in St. Louis for $4 each.) But its time as a trading post gradually gave way to a new role for the fort.

Fort Laramie was not a pleasant place. The food was deplorable, discipline strict, and sanitary conditions so bad that by 1880 it was hard to find an uncontaminated place to dig latrines.

Protecting the Oregon Trail

Fort Laramie stood right along the main trail to Oregon, California, and Salt Lake City. It was one-third of the way from Missouri to the Columbia River mouth and provided a much-anticipated break before the long, desolate trek over the Continental Divide. In 1843, nearly a thousand people passed the fort. The numbers increased each year, reaching a crescendo after gold was discovered in California in 1849. Soon thereafter, more than 50,000 emigrants were trudging into Fort Laramie each summer. They stopped to repair wheels at the carpentry and blacksmith shops, purchase food and whiskey at the store, or trade tired stock for fresh oxen and horses. The latter was the best deal for traders at the fort; all they had to do was put the oxen and horses they had gotten in trade (generally a two-for-one deal) out to pasture for a couple of weeks and then trade them as fresh stock to subsequent emigrants.

This great migration westward had its negative consequences. Indians complained that buffalo were being shot and forced away from their traditional migration routes and that the thousands of stock brought by the emigrants were destroying the grass. The inevitable conflicts began as young warriors halted wagon trains, demanding "tolls" in the form of tobacco, coffee, or sugar. Quickly, this escalated into attacks against the emigrants, and a great hue and cry went up for protection from the "savages." Thus it was that Congress gave Fort Laramie the new role of military garrison mandated to protect the Oregon Trail.

The Army Takes Over

In 1849, the army purchased Fort Laramie for $4,000, establishing the first military post in what would become Wyoming. Some 180 men—both cavalrymen and infantrymen—were assigned to the post. A rapid expansion program was begun; the old adobe fort served as temporary quarters while more elaborate facilities were built. The army's Fort Laramie did not fit the Hollywood stereotype of a frontier fort—it had no log perimeter or blockhouses. The fort was instead laid out around a central parade ground, with clapboard and "lime grout" concrete buildings forming a loose perimeter. In case of attack, the army was prepared to retreat to a single, heavily fortified building. Despite this general lack of protection and the fact that Indians once brazenly drove off the fort's horses, the fort was never attacked by Indians, and most soldiers never engaged in battle with the Indians.

Fort Laramie was essentially a male bastion, although a few officers' wives were present. The only exceptions were laundresses and servant girls. The latter were said to have been hired on the basis of their physical appearance: the less attractive the better, so as to not appeal to the soldiers' prurient interests. After all, if a servant got married, her mistress had to find another one to replace her. A small group of Indians, derisively termed "Laramie Loafers," soon attached themselves to the fort, camping nearby and providing scouts, interpreters, errand boys, and paramours. Fort Laramie—like most 19th-century military posts—was not a pleasant place. The food was deplorable, discipline so strict that even the smallest infraction could land a man in the brig, and sanitary conditions were so bad that by 1880 it was getting hard to find a place to dig latrines that had not already been contaminated. The infrequent paydays turned into drunken brawls. No wonder so many men deserted their post and slipped off for the promising goldfields of California! The inevitable "hog ranches" also grew up near the fort and offered an escape from the day-to-day monotony of the soldiers' lives. In 1877, Lt. John G. Bourke described the "ranches" as

> *tenanted by as hardened and depraved a set of witches as could be found on the face of the globe. Each of these establishments was equipped with a rum-mill of the worst kind and each contained from three to half a dozen Cyprians, virgins whose lamps were always burning brightly in expectance of the coming of the bridegroom, and who lured to destruction the soldiers of the garrison. In all my experience I have never seen a lower, more beastly set of people of both sexes.*

For the next four decades, Fort Laramie served as the nerve center for this part of the plains, providing troops and cavalry to retaliate against Indian attacks and serving as a meeting place for treaty arrangements when the political wind shifted toward negotiation instead of confrontation. The first of these treaties came in 1851, under the forceful leadership of Indian agent Thomas Fitzpatrick, a former mountain man. More than 10,000 Indians attended, representing the Sioux, Cheyenne, Arapaho, Shoshone, Crow, Gros Ventre, and Assiniboin tribes. The treaty consisted essentially of annual bribes (annuities) to be given to the Indians to compensate them for their losses to whites. The various tribes would be assigned to distinct territories but could hunt in other areas. After signing the treaty, a mountain of presents awaited—the first of the $50,000 in

annuities for each of the next 50 years. Shortly thereafter, the federal government reneged on the promise, increasing the annual amount to $70,000 per year but cutting the time to just 10 years. Peace lasted but a short while.

Grattan Massacre

One of the few Indian–white conflicts to occur in the vicinity of Fort Laramie took place in 1854. It began innocently enough when a Mormon emigrant's lame cow wandered off and was butchered by a hungry Miniconjou Indian waiting for the government to dispense annuities. A hotheaded young lieutenant, John Grattan, was sent out to bring in the Indian. Unfortunately, Grattan's interpreter was drunk and began immediately shouting insults at the Sioux in whose village the man was camped. Grattan himself was anxious for a fight, hoping to gain a piece of fame, so when the Sioux refused to give up the man—offering instead to pay for the cow with two horses—Grattan would have nothing of it. His soldiers opened fire and were themselves immediately attacked by a vastly superior force of Sioux. All 29 soldiers died in the massacre that followed, and Fort Laramie stood in danger of being destroyed. But the Indians instead raided local storehouses for the promised annuities and headed out. The army used the Grattan Massacre as proof that the Indians could not be trusted. In reality, the entire incident was an instance of utter stupidity on the part of the army.

More Trouble

One of the least distinguished post commanders at Fort Laramie was the hard-drinking and ill-tempered Col. Thomas Moonlight. In 1865, he publicly hanged two Sioux subchiefs who had brought in two white women captives for reward. Their bodies were left dangling in chains for several days, an act that brought condemnation from the Eastern press. In retaliation, the Sioux killed several soldiers and then managed to drive off most of the horses from Colonel Moonlight's cavalry. A sullen Moonlight led his almost horseless cavalry in the 120-mile hike back to the fort. Although shortly thereafter stripped of his command, Moonlight later served as the politically appointed territorial governor of Wyoming.

With the decline in importance of the Oregon Trail, Fort Laramie became a staging area for military expeditions against the Indians. In the Treaty of 1868, signed at the fort, the Sioux were guaranteed the Powder River country "as long as the grass shall grow and the buffalo shall roam." But the discovery of gold in the Black Hills abruptly changed the picture, and whites now wanted the land itself, not just a road through it. They eventually got it, but not before the massacre of Custer and his men at Little Big Horn in 1876. After this, with the Indians tucked away on reservations, most of the hostilities died down and the fort lost its strategic importance. The railroad had long since supplanted the Oregon Trail as the primary route west, and during the 1880s Fort Laramie served as a way station along the Cheyenne-to-Deadwood stage road. During this time the fort grew more genteel with the planting of trees and completion of numerous substantial homes.

The Army Departs

By 1889, it was clear that Fort Laramie had outlived its usefulness, and it was ordered closed. The following year, the 35,000 acres of military land were opened to homesteaders and the buildings auctioned off. Because of the scarcity of wood in the area, many buildings were stripped and hauled away to become cabins or other structures. Others remained on the site and were used as homes, businesses, or barns. For the next half century the historic fort slowly deteriorated, but in 1937 the state of Wyoming purchased the site and donated it to the federal government. The following year it was declared a national monument, to be managed by the National Park Service. A lengthy and difficult restoration process managed to stabilize the ruins and restore a dozen of the historic structures, but it was not until 1964 that the fort was restored to something approaching the conditions in the 1880s.

FORT LARAMIE TODAY

Each year nearly 90,000 visitors come to historic Fort Laramie for a rewarding traipse back in time. The clear, tree-lined Laramie River still flows close by, and the spacious parade ground engenders a feeling of this fort's importance, while the bleak, windswept setting speaks of its hardships.

Old Bedlam, Fort Laramie National Historic Site

© DON PITCHER

Visiting the Fort

Buildings and grounds of the 830-acre Fort Laramie National Historic Site are open year-round 8 A.M. to sunset. Entrance costs $3 for adults, no charge for kids under 16 or seniors with Golden Age passes. There's no camping at the site, but there is a pleasant picnic area.

For an excellent orientation to Fort Laramie, head to the old commissary building, now the **visitors center/park headquarters,** 307/837-2221, www.nps.gov/fola. Inside are excellent displays and historic photos, including a scale model of the fort, an 1876 Gatling gun, and many photos. Ask about interpretive talks and tours and the dramatic firings of historic weapons. The center is open daily 8 A.M.–7 P.M. mid-May through mid-September and daily 8 A.M.–4:30 P.M. the rest of the year. Informative videos about the fort and the Old West are shown at scheduled times during the summer and by request the rest of the year. The gift shop here offers an extraordinary collection of historic books on the Old West. It also rents out CD audio tours and sells such authentic items as lye soap, brass cavalry spurs, military insignias, bonnets (made by local seniors), wooden tops, old playing cards, and hardtack.

The **Fort Laramie Historical Association,** 307/837-2662 or 800/321-5456, www.fort-laramie.com, manages the bookshop and produces a big publication describing several hundred Western history books available by mail-order.

If you're in the area in early July, be sure to drop by Fort Laramie for an **Old-Fashioned Fourth of July Celebration** with old-time music, locals in period clothing, games, and dancing. In late August comes a **Military Encampment Weekend** with special moonlight programs.

Historical Buildings

By the time it was abandoned in 1890, Fort Laramie was approaching the size of a small town; 60 buildings of all types were scattered around the grounds. The remains of 21 of these are still visible—some simply lime-grout concrete ruins maintained in a state of arrested decay. A dozen have been completely restored and refurbished with authentic period pieces behind Plexiglas doors. The Park Service has an informative *His-toric Buildings Guide* available at the visitors center. Several of the buildings are particularly noteworthy: the cavalry barracks, Old Bedlam, the bakery, and the guardhouse.

Most of the men who soldiered out of Fort Laramie lived under crowded conditions with little privacy. Sometimes this meant living in tents for long periods. The **cavalry barracks** on your left as you enter the fort were an improvement, but quarters were still tight. Walk up to the restored second floor to find row upon row of cots where an entire company of 60 men slept. Then try to imagine all the snoring and the smelly feet after being out on duty for weeks at a time! Baths were taken, in theory, every Saturday night in a half barrel.

The **post trader's store** just right of the entrance provided a break from the army's monotonous food and supplies. Built in 1849, it served not only the military but also the thousands of civilians who poured west along the Oregon Trail and the Indians who traded for various items. The store owner provided everything from essential food supplies to fresh oxen for weary emigrants. He also sold alcohol and benefited from the tons of excess belongings that many overburdened travelers cast aside to lighten their loads.

The officers enjoyed far better living conditions than the cavalry and infantry, including access to a pleasant officers' club and a hired cook. The 1884 **lieutenant colonel's quarters** has been restored to the era when Lt. Col. Andrew Burt and his family lived here (1887–1888). Inside you'll see some of the family's original furnishings. Next door is the **post surgeon's quarters,** completed in 1875. The surgeon had a highly respected rank in the fort and was accorded the responsibility of gathering weather data as well as scientific specimens. The surgeon dealt primarily with such problems as kicks by horses, injuries from brawls, frostbitten fingers and toes, and venereal diseases. War wounds were far less common, but when they did occur many could not be adequately treated and the men often died.

The oldest and most prominent building at Fort Laramie is **Old Bedlam,** an attractive clapboard structure that dominates the west end of the parade grounds. Built in 1849, it was the center of life at the fort. Old Bedlam served a variety of purposes when the military was here; initially the post headquarters, it later became a hotel of sorts for bachelor officers and housing for married officers and their families. The name apparently comes from the bedlam that existed with so many folks jammed together—particularly after payday, when parties raged. Old Bedlam is now refurbished to represent two different periods. The south end represents the post headquarters of the 1864 period and the living quarters of Lt. Colonel William O. Collins, while the north end represents a bachelor officer's quarters of the early 1850s period.

Behind the attractive **Captain's Quarters** on the south end of the parade ground is a model of adobe-walled Fort John, which stood on this spot in 1841. The "bat house" near here was recently built in an attempt to keep bats from roosting in the Captain's Quarters. A footpath leads to the Laramie River. The old stone **guardhouse** on the east side of the fort could house up to 40 prisoners, ranging from soldiers who had violated minor conduct rules to those charged with murder. The basement jail had no furniture, toilet, or light, and no heat even in the dead of winter. Stop by the historic **bakery**—one of four built here at different times—for a taste of bread. One loaf of bread, along with greasy salt pork, beans, rice, and rotgut coffee, was the typical daily allotment for soldiers. Fresh vegetables were often unavailable for months at a time, and scurvy was a constant threat. In the field, the rations were even worse, generally consisting of salt pork, beans, and wormy hardtack.

Oregon Trail Ruts

One of the less-visited sights in the area is **Old Bedlam ruts,** two miles northwest of Fort Laramie. A gravel road leads to the location; get a map from park headquarters. The ruts (marked by posts) climb up into the gentle hills west of the old fort, offering a marvelous panorama of a landscape that has not changed much in the last century. From here, it's easy to imagine emigrants looking back on the fort, their last touch with civilization for hundreds of miles. Laramie Peak is prominent to the west. Nearby is the

Oregon Trail ruts, near Guernsey

© DON PITCHER

grave of Mary Homsley, one of the thousands who died along the difficult trek west. The ruts can be traced all the way to Guernsey, where they grow even deeper. A similar series of ruts extends eastward from the fort. If you're heading to Wheatland from the fort, try the "back way" via **Grayrocks Reservoir**—the source of cooling water for the Laramie River Station Power Plant. The road is rough for the first eight miles or so but is paved beyond that and offers an enjoyable taste of the rugged countryside around the reservoir. Signs point the way to Wheatland.

THE TOWN OF FORT LARAMIE

The town of Fort Laramie (pop. 240) lies three miles northeast of the historic fort and across the North Platte River. Wyoming's oldest post office is here, dating back to the 1880s when the army occupied the fort. One mile south of town is an **iron bridge** built in 1875. Although long superseded by a concrete span just upriver and not much to look at, the bridge bears historical importance. Funded by a $15,000 congressional appropriation, the bridge ensured the establishment of the Cheyenne-Deadwood Stage and Express through here. It remained the major route north for many years thereafter. Note how much longer the old bridge is than the new one. Upstream dams have blocked the river flow, making it barely one-third of the original width. A highway monument east of town along U.S. 26 notes the site of the Grattan Massacre.

Accommodations and Food

A couple of places serve meals in Fort Laramie, but I'd go hungry until I reached a town with a better choice! **Garhart's Pioneer Inn,** is an old frame house across the street from the little log visitors center. Inside are basic rooms for $20–30 d. This one is not to my taste; the last time I visited this place, the drinkers in the basement bar were already pretty sauced at 1 P.M. The Pioneer also serves meals. Basic accommodations are also available at **Fort Laramie Motel,** 307/837-3063; open mid-May through Sept.

Camping

Pitch tents for free at the **Fort Laramie town park** just across the railroad tracks on the south side of town; no showers. **Chuckwagon RV Park,** 307/837-2828, is open mid-April to mid-October, and charges $10 for tents or $16 for RVs. **Bennett Court Campground,** 307/837-2270, charges $12 for RVs, $10 for tents. **Pony Soldier RV Park,** 307/837-3078, five miles east of Fort Laramie and five miles west of Lingle, is open mid-April to mid-October, with tent spaces for $13, RV sites for $19.

The 2,400-acre **Carnahan Ranch,** one-half mile south of Fort Laramie Historic Site, 307/837-2917 or 800/837-6730, www.ravingconcepts.com/carnahanranch, offers both tent sites ($15) and RV sites with hookups ($25 with water and electricity); open mid-Apr. to mid-Oct. Tepees are $25–35. Campers get use of the communal kitchen and the opportunity to explore this peaceful 2,400-acre ranch overlooking the fort. They can also board horses.

Information and Services

A small log-cabin **visitors center** on the main street is staffed daily May to mid-October. Drop by **Fort Laramie Frontier Trading Post,** 307/837-2021, for quality leather crafts, Indian beadwork, and other locally made crafts. Poke around town and you'll find a couple of other places worth a gander.

Torrington

Torrington (pop. 5,800) is a quiet farming and retirement town just eight miles from the Nebraska border. It's the seat of Wyoming's most important agricultural county—Goshen, alias "The Land of Goshen"—and lots of sugar beets, alfalfa, oats, dry beans, corn, and hay are grown here. The tree-lined North Platte River drifts lazily through town.

Torrington's economy is relatively stable; the biggest local employer, a Holly Sugar factory, is on the edge of town, and many productive farms are scattered in the surrounding countryside. Two long waterways—Fort Laramie Canal and the Interstate Canal—provide irrigation water for much of this farmland. Trains filled with coal from Campbell and Weston Counties constant-ly rumble through toward the south and east, a stench from the sugar refinery hangs in the air each fall, and the livestock auction is the big weekly event. A walk along Main Street is a trek through the American heartland; if the cars were older, Torrington could model for a *Saturday Evening Post* cover from the '50s. In recent years the agricultural economy has sputtered a bit, but retirees and wealthy refugees from the Colorado Front Range have moved into the area.

HISTORY

Although several hundred thousand emigrants passed through Goshen County on their way to Oregon, California, or Utah, none bothered to stop. The area was not settled until cattlemen came in the 1880s, followed by homesteaders around the turn of the 20th century including many from Russia and Germany. Many of the "soddies" and wooden shacks these emigrants built still stand in the fields throughout the county. Named for Torrington, Connecticut, the town was incorporated in 1907 as a ranching and farming center. Completion of the Interstate Canal in 1915 and the Fort Laramie Canal in 1924 brought North Platte River water, making it possible to grow a wide variety of crops. The Burlington Railroad arrived from the east in 1900, but it was not until 1926 that the Union Pacific built a

line connecting Torrington with Pine Bluffs to the south. That year proved pivotal because it brought a new train depot and the Holly Sugar plant. The town has grown slowly over the years, and except for a brief flirtation with oil and gas in the 1970s has remained true to its farming and ranching roots.

HOMESTEADERS MUSEUM

Located right at the crossroads of the Oregon Trail, the Cheyenne-to-Deadwood stage route, the Mormon Trail, and the Texas Cattle Trail, the Homesteaders Museum seems to sit atop history.

STARVING TO DEATH ON A GOVERNMENT CLAIM

My name is Frank Taylor, a bachelor I am,
I'm keeping old batch on an elegant plan,
You'll find me out West in the county of Lane
A-starving to death on a Government claim.

Hurrah for Lane County, the land of the free,
The home of the bedbug, grasshopper and flea,
I'll sing of its praises and boast of its fame
A-starving to death on a Government claim.

My clothes they are ragged, my language is rough,
My bread is case-hardened and solid and tough,
But I have a good time and live at my ease
On common sop-sorghum and old bacon grease.

How happy am I when I crawl into bed,
With rattlesnakes rattling just under my head,
And the gay little bedbug, so cheerful and bright,
He keeps me a-going two-thirds of the night.

How happy am I on my Government claim,
I've nothing to lose and I've nothing to gain,
I've nothing to eat and I've nothing to wear,
And nothing from nothing is honest and fair.

Oh, come to Lane County, there's room for you all,
Where the wind never stops and the rains never fall,
Oh, join in the chorus and sing of her fame,
A-starving to death on a Government claim.

Oh, don't be downhearted, you poor hungry men,
We're all just as free as the pigs in the pen,
Just stick to your homestead and fight with your fleas,
And pray to your Maker to send some more breeze.

Now all you poor sinners, I hope you will stay
And chaw on your hardtack till you're toothless and grey,
But as for myself I don't aim to remain
And slave like a dog on no Government claim.

Farewell to Lane County, the pride of the West
I'm going back East to the girl I love best,
I'll stop in Missouri and get me a wife,
And live on corn doggers the rest of my life.

—Anonymous

It is housed in the 1926 brick-and-masonry Union Pacific depot just south of town. The last train stopped at the depot in 1964. The museum, 307/532-5612, is open Monday–Saturday 9:30 A.M.–4 P.M. during summer; closed Saturdays in winter. Although it contains a substantial paleo-Indian collection, the museum focuses on the thousands of early-1900s homesteaders who flocked to eastern Wyoming. The Yoder Ranch collection (artifacts from 1881 on) is particularly noteworthy. Other displays include items from the 4A Ranch and the Bordeau Trading Post near Fort Laramie, a homemade baseball bat from 1920, and a marvelous collection of historic black-and-white photos. Sit down and spend some time looking through these pictures; they will quickly transport you back to a simple era when pioneers scratched out a hardscrabble life on the mixed-grass prairie in wooden or sod shacks. The KKK robe displayed in the museum comes from the 1920s, when a vehemently racist and anti-Catholic spirit dominated much of rural America. Outside are an old homestead cabin, a windmill, and a caboose housing historic railroad photos and memorabilia.

OTHER SIGHTS

More than 120,000 cattle are raised in Goshen County each year—more than in any other Wyoming county—so it is logical that Torrington should also be at the center of the state's livestock trade. Each year nearly a quarter of a million cattle are marketed at the **Torrington Livestock Market,** on U.S. 26 at W. E St., 307/532-3333. Auctions take place every Friday beginning at 10 A.M. and last into the early afternoon, with additional load lot auctions on Wednesday in the fall. All of these auctions are open to the public and are quite interesting, but don't raise your hand or you might just purchase a bull.

Two miles west of town is the University of Wyoming's **College of Agriculture Research and Extension Center,** also open to the public. Tours of nearby cattle ranches are available through the **Goshen Cattlewomen.** Advance arrangements are necessary; call 307/532-4346.

For a walk, saunter along the paved **Grassroots Trail,** built atop an old irrigation canal that slices across the northern edge of town. A small **Botanical Park** occupies the corner of 1st Avenue and S. Main Street. South of Torrington a sign marks the **Cold Springs Campground** used by travelers on the Oregon Trail and later the site of a stage station and a pony express stop. A few miles east of town is a memorial to the party of Astorians who camped nearby in the winter of 1812.

Eastern Wyoming College, 3200 W. C St., 307/532-8200 or 800/658-3195, http://ew-cweb.ewc.cc.wy.us, is one of the oldest junior colleges in the state, first established in 1948 as an extension of the University of Wyoming but now independent. It's located on a small hill on the north end of town and offers a wide range of vocational and academic programs.

ACCOMMODATIONS

Note that noisy freight trains roll through Torrington at all hours of the night, so you may want to choose a place as far as possible from the tracks.

Oregon Trail Lodge, 710 E. Valley Rd., 307/532-2101, has inexpensive lodging: $20–26 s or $30–32 d. The cheaper units are very small, but all rooms include fridges. Also on the low-price end is **Blue Lantern Motel,** 1402 S. Main St., 307/532-8999, where a handful of older units are $24 s or $29–34 d; some with microwaves and fridges.

Maverick Motel, 1.5 miles west of town on U.S. 26/85, 307/532-4064, charges $38–40 s or $42–46 d. **King's Inn,** 1555 S. Main St., 307/532-4011, includes a hot tub and boot-shaped indoor pool, plus fridges in most rooms. Rooms cost $65–70 s or $75–80 d.

Super 8 Motel, 1548 S. Main St., 307/532-7118 or 800/800-8000, www.super8.com, has

rooms for $45–50 s or $50–54 d, including an indoor pool, hot tub, and exercise room.

On the east side of town, **Holiday Inn Express,** 307/532-7600 or 800/465-4329, www.holiday-inn.com, is Torrington's newest, largest, and nicest place to stay, with a breakfast bar, indoor pool, hot tub, and fitness center. Rates are $57–67 s or d in standard rooms. Suites include hot tubs, microwaves, and fridges for $80–112 d.

CAMPING

Camp for free in **Pioneer Park** along the North Platte River on the edge of town. It's open year-round and has electrical hookups, but during the winter you'll need to get water elsewhere. Additional sites are available year-round at the **Goshen County Fairgrounds,** 307/532-2525. RV sites with hookups cost $10, and you can probably pitch a tent for free. In town, but not recommended because of run-down facilities, is **Travelers Court,** 750 S. Main St., 307/532-5517, with riverside tent sites and RV sites with hookups.

FOOD

Torrington has a decent choice of restaurants, but almost none are open on Sundays, and closing time is early—8 or 9 P.M. other nights.

Chuckwagon Cafe, 2113 N. Main St., 307/532-2888, serves breakfast all day long and has tasty all-American stuff-yourself meals. The fare includes inexpensive burgers, steaks, Rocky Mountain oysters, a salad bar, and pies. Sunday all-you-can-eat buffets are especially popular. **Java Jar,** 1940 N. Main St., 307/532-8541, has espresso, soup served in bread bowls, and sandwiches. It's a popular spot for lunch, but it closes at 3 P.M.

Looking for southern fried chicken, burgers, shakes, and fries? Join the flock at **Chicken Hut,** 650 E. Valley Rd., 307/532-4441. It's one of the only places open on Sundays. **Deacons Restaurant,** 1558 S. Main St., 307/532-4766, opens Monday–Saturday at 5 A.M. for dependable meals, plus a substantial salad bar and homemade pies.

Peking Garden, 2126 N. Main St., 307/532-8883, serves up good, authentic Chinese food, and **La Familia Prado,** 1250 S. Main St., 307/534-1975, has Mexican meals and margaritas. Although the owners are Asian-Americans, **Grandpa Chuy's,** 1915 Main St., 307/532-2982, serves Mexican food: tacos, burritos, fajitas, and enchiladas. **Buck's Pizza,** 300 W. Valley Rd., 307/534-4616, has decent pizza.

Ray's Cowboy Restaurant, in the King's Inn at 1555 S. Main St., 307/532-4011, serves breakfast all day, including biscuits and gravy. Steaks, chicken, roast beef, liver and onions, and pork chops are featured at dinnertime. For reasonably priced steaks and seafood in an attractive setting, head to **Little Moon Lake Supper Club,** 307/532-5750, on the state line eight miles east on U.S. 26.

Get groceries from **Kelly's Super Market** on S. Main Street, 307/532-3113, or **Food Pride Grocery Store,** 1542 S. Main St., 307/532-3401.

RECREATION

Torrington has a summertime outdoor **swimming pool** (307/532-7798) in Jirdon Park. Kids will love the 180-foot water slide. There is also an 18-hole municipal **golf course,** 307/532-2418, outside of town. Bowl at **Ten Pin Tropics,** on the east side of Torrington, 307/532-2187.

ENTERTAINMENT AND EVENTS

Watch movies at **Wyoming Theatre,** 126 E. 20th Ave., 307/532-2226. Two local places have live country music on some weekends: **Bronco Bar,** 1924 Main St., 307/532-8660, and **Tote-Away Bar,** 1934 1/2 W. A St., 307/532-5506. Many locals also head over to the **Stateline Oasis,** 307/532-4990, next to the Nebraska line, for the chance to check out the strippers Tuesday–Saturday nights. The Oasis typically has live bands on Saturday nights.

The biggest annual event in Torrington is the **Goshen County Fair,** 307/532-2525, held the first full week in August and presenting everything from a parade to pig wrestling. It's a good place to check out all the 4-H hogs and sheep on display. The indoor arena here is Wyoming's largest.

INFORMATION AND SERVICES

The **Goshen County Chamber of Commerce** office, 350 W. 21st Ave., 307/532-3879 or 800/577-3555, www.go-goshen.com, is open Monday–Friday 9 A.M.–5 P.M.

Find the **public library** at 2001 E. A St., 307/532-3411, and the **post office** at 2145 Main St., 307/532-2213. **Vandel Drugs,** 2041 Main St., 307/532-2214, has a few regional books for sale, and the **Pamida** store on the east end of town has discount items. Wash clothes at **James Laundromat,** 27th Ave and W. C Street.

Denver Coach, 308/632-8400 or 800/658-3125, www.windborne.cc, provides transportation to Cheyenne or Denver International Airport. Rent cars from **Big Sky Ford,** 510 W. Valley Rd., 307/532-2114 or 888/532-2114.

TORRINGTON AREA
South of Torrington

The town symbol for Torrington is the ring-necked pheasant—a fitting logo in this farming country. **Downar Bird Farm,** 17 miles south on U.S. 85, 307/532-3449, raises some 11,000 pheasants each year. It is run by the Wyoming Game and Fish Department, which releases the birds each fall for area hunters. This is basically a release-and-shoot operation because the birds are let go in unfamiliar territory just in time for hunting season. The farm is an interesting place to visit and boasts 27 different pheasant breeds. Incidentally, although the ring-necked pheasant is abundant throughout the Midwest, it is a native of China.

The minuscule town of **Veteran** (pop. 30)—basically a post office and general store located 15 miles southwest of Torrington—was established by Iowa veterans of World War I. A POW camp was established here in World War II. The surrounding landscape is a mixture of grass, wheat, sage, and rocky buttes, with cattle grazing the land and vultures circling above.

Hawk Springs State Recreation Area lies 27 miles south of Torrington off U.S. 85. Get details at 307/836-2334, http://wyoparks.state. wy.us. The small park contains campsites ($12 for nonresidents or $6 for Wyoming residents), picnic tables, and a boat ramp along Hawk Springs Reservoir. Fishing is good for walleye, largemouth bass, yellow perch, black crappie, and channel catfish. Boaters will discover a blue heron rookery on the south end of the reservoir. Park entrance costs $4 for nonresident vehicles or $2 for Wyoming residents.

Seven miles north is the postage-stamp-size town of **Hawk Springs** (pop. 70), home to the **Longbranch Saloon & Steakhouse,** 307/532-4266, open for three meals a day. That's about it here; most of the town is shuttered. Five miles north of Hawk Springs and just off U.S. Hwy. 85 is **Springer/Bump Sullivan Wildlife Management Area,** with more fishing, boating, and camping at Sullivan Reservoir.

Lingle

Ten miles northwest of Torrington is the tidy farming crossroads called Lingle (pop. 500), where trains laden with coal roll through almost continuously. The town has a couple of places to eat but no accommodations. **Lira's,** 307/837-2826, offers authentic Mexican food that attracts folks from miles around. Also here are **Stagecoach Cafe,** 307/837-2614, with Saturday night prime-rib specials, and **The Real McCoy Bake Shop,** 837-2461, with ice cream, malts, and other treats. An **outdoor pool** is open in the summer months.

Five miles west of Lingle (or five miles east of Fort Laramie) is the **Western History Center,** 307/837-3052, www.wyshs.org/mus-westhistc-tr.htm. This small free museum has a variety of displays, including fossils, mammoth bones, and Indian artifacts. The center is open Monday–Saturday 8 A.M.–5 P.M. Noted anthropologist George Zeimens, who manages this private museum, also leads tours to historic and archaeological sites in Wyoming. It's well worth a stop.

Adjacent to the History Center is **Pony Soldier RV Park,** 307/837-3078. Rates are $13 for tents or $19 for RVs; open mid-Apr. to mid-Oct.

Jay Em

North of Lingle on U.S. 85, the irrigated pastures and green fields give way to endless prairies. This is a land of sandy hillocks carpeted with short grasses, similar to the sandhill country of western Nebraska, which lies just a dozen miles eastward. Stop to take in the wind and to listen to squeaking windmills and singing meadowlarks. In summer the dark afternoon sky is accented by slashes of lightning and occasional rainbows.

Halfway between Lingle and Lusk, the road passes the almost ghost town of Jay Em (pop. 15), named for the cattle brand of rancher Jim Moore. Just to the north lies his old Jay Em Ranch. A few people still live in the old wooden houses of Jay Em, and the post office becomes a meeting place each morning, but the town is otherwise deserted. It's a peaceful spot to stop and walk along narrow Rawhide Creek among the cottonwood trees and tall grass. The town is a National Historic District, and the rustic old buildings are a photographer's treat. Tours are available by reservation; call 307/735-4364 or 307/322-2839. Continuing north to Lusk, the country again opens into grassland, windmills, cattle, a few tree-topped hills, and small rocky buttes.

Lusk

Lusk (pop. 1,400) is the seat of Wyoming's least-populated county. Just 2,400 people live in rural Niobrara County—an average of almost 700 acres per person! It's remote grassland country here with long, straight highways heading out in the compass directions. Ranching provides a relatively stable—albeit limited—economic base, but the oil industry that was once so prominent has faded. The town itself has a Midwestern feel, with tree-lined streets and attractive older homes. It's quiet and safe; great for raising a family, but teenagers probably get bored quickly. Downtown businesses are clearly struggling to survive, and more than a few have given up, leaving shuttered doors in their wake. Lusk's main claim to fame is the *Legend of Rawhide*, a July extravaganza.

HISTORY

The first settlers in this part of Wyoming were miners in search of copper, silver, and gold. They built a small settlement around the Silver Cliff Mine but moved one mile east when the Fremont, Elkhorn, and Missouri Valley Railroad arrived in 1886. Lusk was named for Frank Lusk, a local rancher who donated land for the new townsite. In 1917, oil was discovered along Lance Creek 20 miles north of here, and almost overnight Lusk became a boomtown, reaching more than 10,000 residents during the peak years of oil production. Pipelines were built to the 200 producing wells, and a refinery was added in Lusk. By the 1940s, Lance Creek had become Wyoming's largest oil field. More recently, oil production has declined, and the old standby of ranching has regained prominence. In 1984, the town succeeded in getting a women's correctional center built; this is now the second-largest employer in the county (after the local school district).

Mother Featherlegs

Lusk has seen its share of lust over the years. The Yellow Hotel brothel occupied a place of local importance until the late 1970s; rumor has it that the madam, Del Burke, was allowed to keep it open because she owned most of Lusk's water bonds! Mother Featherlegs—so named because she often rode horseback with her red pantaloons blowing in the wind—was a well-known 19th-century madam who was murdered in 1879, apparently for money. Some claim that a fortune in gold she had buried nearby still waits to be claimed. A granite marker southwest of Lusk notes the site of her old place of entertainment along the Cheyenne–Black Hills Stage Line; it's said to be the nation's only historical marker commemorating a prostitute. Get here by heading two miles west of town on U.S. 18 and then turning south at the rest area for another 11 miles. In 1990, Lusk locals swept into a Deadwood saloon and recovered Mother Featherlegs' famous pantaloons, stolen from the historic site in 1964. Today you'll find them on display at the town museum.

STAGECOACH MUSEUM

Lusk has one of the better historic collections in the state at the aptly named Stagecoach Museum, 342 S. Main St., 307/334-3444. The museum is open Monday–Saturday 10–5 P.M. year-round. Admission is $2 for adults, free for kids under 12. Climb up the stairs to find the reason for its name—an old coach built in 1863 by Abbott & Downing of Concord, New Hampshire. Used for many years on the famed Cheyenne and Black Hills Stage and Express Line, the stagecoach is one of only two in existence; its sister resides in the Smithsonian Institution in Washington, D.C. The museum also houses a treasure chest broken open during the Canyon Springs Stage robbery of 1879; it contained gold bullion from the Black Hills destined for Cheyenne. Besides the standard fare—an old buggy, a sulky, a dray wagon, covered wagons, and various Indian artifacts and arrowheads—you'll also find such intriguing odds and ends as a 1950s iron lung, a 30-foot triceratops (made from a mix of real bones and iron), a two-headed calf, an antique bedpan collection and suppository machine, more than 300 salt and pepper shakers, photos of Niobrara County's many one-room schoolhouses, and a 31-star 1876 U.S. flag. Try not to snicker at the kitschy collection of dolls dressed up as the wives of various presidents (including Barbara Bush as a busty Barbie doll). Out back is an old one-room log schoolhouse built in 1886. The famous Mother Featherlegs pantaloons are next to the museum director's desk, where she can make sure they aren't stolen again by folks from Deadwood.

OTHER SIGHTS

The city park at 14th and Linn contains a **homestead cabin** built in the 1880s and originally located at Running Water Stage Station. Another site of historical interest is on the east side of town along the railroad tracks. Here you'll find a **redwood water tower** built in 1886 to supply water for steam engines of the Chicago and Northwestern Railroad. It is one of only six still standing in the nation. Today the water tower

old redwood water tower, near Lusk

© DON PITCHER

is no longer needed, but the railroad is busier than ever, with 115-car coal trains screaming their presence every few minutes.

Just west of downtown is a small hill with fine panoramic views of the area. It's posted, but ask locally for permission to climb to the top. Also of note is the big **Niobrara County building** at E. 5th and S. Elm Streets, with its red brick walls. Etched above the entrances are words that most politicians seem to consider expendable: "A public office is a public trust."

ACCOMMODATIONS

Lusk has several comfortable motels for reasonable rates, but prices may be higher during the *Legend of Rawhide.*

Hospitality House Motor Hotel, 201 S. Main St., 307/334-2120, has rather plain accommodations, some with king-size beds, in upstairs rooms for $26–32 s or d. No phones in the rooms. **Rawhide Motel,** 805 S. Main St., 307/334-2440 or 888/679-2558, www.rawhide-motel.net, charges $34 s or $38 d, and **Town House Motel,** 565 S. Main St., 307/334-2376, www.lusktownhouse.com, has a variety of rooms for $36–42 s or d.

At **Trail Motel,** just west of town on U.S. 18/20 at 305 W. 8th, 307/334-2530 or 800/333-5875, rooms cost $52–67 s or d, and the grounds contain an outdoor pool. **Covered Wagon Motel** (Best Value Inn), 730 S. Main St., 307/334-2836 or 888/315-2378, www.bestvalueinn.com, is the nicest local motel, with an indoor pool, hot tub, sauna, and exercise room. Rooms cost $47–66 s or $75–82 d. Another attractive option is **Best Western Pioneer,** 731 S. Main St., 307/334-2640 or 800/542-9936, www.bestwestern.com, which has an outdoor pool and rooms for $53–75 s or d.

For a totally unique ranch experience, spend a day (or a week) at **Paleo Park,** 307/334-2270, www.paleopark.com, located northwest of Lusk in the heart of the Lance Creek fossil area. Fascinating two-hour tours are offered in the summer, and overnight lodging is generally available (if the rooms aren't taken by dinosaur researchers). Highly recommended. Paleo Park is described more fully under Newcastle in the Black Hills chapter.

CAMPING

BJ's Campground, 902 S. Maple St., 307/334-2314, has unshaded RV sites for $18; open May to mid-Oct. **Prairie View Campground,** two miles west of Lusk on U.S. 18/20, 307/334-3174, is a bit better, with a country location and some shade. RV hookups are $20, and tent sites cost $10. Open year-round.

FOOD

Fireside Inn, 904 S. Main St., 307/334-3477, serves family-style meals. The Sunday brunch is a bargain, and the soup and salad bar offers an inexpensive way to pig out. It opens at 5:30 most mornings. **El Jarro Restaurant,** 625 S. Main St., 307/334-5004, is the local Mexican eatery. Get pizzas at **The Pizza Place,** 218 S. Main St., 307/334-3000, and quick lunches at **Subway,** 601 S. Main St. **BQ Corral Drive-In,** W. 7th and S. Main Sts., 307/334-0128, has carhop service and tasty, fast food.

Outpost, on the south end of town, 307/334-3085, serves most of the standards for ridiculously low prices. When I last stopped in a prime rib dinner was just $6.50!

Get groceries from **Decker's Food Center,** 405 S. Main. St., 307/334-3810.

RECREATION AND ENTERTAINMENT

Swim at the **Lusk Plunge** on the north side of the tracks during the summer; 307/334-3612. The **Lusk Municipal Golf Course,** 307/334-2438, has one of the better nine-hole golf courses in the state. You might catch an occasional live band at the **Cowboy Bar,** 904 S. Main St., 307/334-3634.

INFORMATION AND SERVICES

The **Lusk Visitor Center,** 119 W. 3rd St., is open Monday–Friday 10 A.M.–5 P.M. Contact them at 307/334-2950 or 800/223-5875, www.luskwyoming.com.

The local **Niobrara County Library** is housed in a historic multicolor brick building at 425 S. Main Street, 307/334-3490. Find the **post office** at 116 W. 3rd Street, 307/334-3700, and a laundromat on the north end of town at Main Street and Griffith Boulevard. Get fast cash from the **ATMs** in local gas stations. A state **rest area** is located just west of Lusk on U.S. 18.

True Hatters, 214 S. Main St., 307/334-2746, is an old-time shop (in business since 1908) with custom-made boots, hats, and saddles.

TOURS

Edmond Cook of **E C Ranch and Historical Tour,** 307/334-2134, guides excellent historical tours through the country around Lusk. These start at just $10 per person for a 1.5-hour tour that includes a visit to impressive ruts from the Cheyenne-Deadwood Trail.

Stan Swanson leads tours of his **Silver Sage Bison Ranch,** located 35 miles north and then 15 miles west in the Lance Creek area. These tours include a chance to spend time among a herd of more than 200 buffalo and to do a little dinosaur bone prospecting. Tours require a minimum of five. Call 307/334-3142 for details.

EVENTS

The **Mounted Shooting Sports** takes place in June, and the **Niobrara County Fair** comes to town the first week of August. For rodeo action, check out the **Wyoming Junior Rodeo** in July, the **All Girls Rodeo** in August, and the **Senior Pro Rodeo** on Labor Day. Lusk's featured event is the *Legend of Rawhide.*

LEGEND OF RAWHIDE

In 1946, the people of Lusk were looking for an event to attract visitors—something, say, along the lines of Cheyenne Frontier Days, only different. A local doctor, Walter Reckling, faintly remembered a tale that had been passed down for generations—the legend of Rawhide Buttes. It was one of the enduring yarns of the Old West, one with a thousand variations, claimed by half a dozen states. In the story, an emigrant wagon train headed west to the California goldfields carrying a young man who boasted that he would shoot the first Indian he saw. He killed an innocent Indian girl—a princess, of course—and her tribe retaliated by attacking the wagon train and forcing the young man to surrender. He was skinned alive in revenge. Nobody has ever been able to substantiate the tale, but then again, nobody has proved it *didn't* happen, either.

Dr. Reckling managed to stir up considerable interest for the idea in Lusk and then found a local college student, Eva Lou Bonsell, who was studying theater in Colorado. She wrote a play to be pantomimed as a narrator described the scenes, and the *Legend of Rawhide* was off and running. The first production gained a measure of realism by being staged in the midst of a thunderstorm. The crowd of 10,000 loved it. The *Legend of Rawhide* made the covers of *Life* and *Look* magazines at various times and ran from 1946 to 1966. It was revived in 1986. Today the annual production is still a decidedly local affair, with a cast of 200 folks from the surrounding area. The spectacle has evolved over the years, with the addition of 13 "soiled doves," Father DeSmet, Jim Bridger, some 15 wagons, and several dozen Indians on ponies. The skinning alive of bad guy Clyde Pickett is the gory climax. It's also quite a trick, but I won't give away the secret.

The *Legend of Rawhide* is put on the second weekend in July every year and begins at 8 P.M. on Friday and Saturday nights. Other activities include a parade, art show, square dancing, country music, pancake breakfasts, and a barbecue. Get additional information at 307/334-2950 or 800/223-5875, www.luskwy.com. The *Legend of Rawhide* attracts more than 3,000 visitors, so be sure to book rooms far ahead.

Rawhide Buttes

Whether or not the story is true, the Rawhide Buttes actually do exist; they are 10 miles south of Lusk. Some stories give a less interesting origin of the name Rawhide Buttes, claiming they were the site where raw buffalo hides were prepared for shipment east. A highway marker notes the Cheyenne and Deadwood Stage

station that once stood here. Two miles west of Lusk on U.S. 18/20 is a historical marker along the Cheyenne-Deadwood Trail. The ruts are still visible for a ways here, and George Lathrop, one of the best-known stage drivers, is buried nearby.

HEADING NORTH

U.S. Hwy. 18/85 points due north from Lusk toward Newcastle, passing through mile after mile of rolling and windy grassland with scattered rocky buttes—a few wearing top hats of ponderosa pines. For the first dozen miles the road parallels the historic Cheyenne-Deadwood Stage Route. Bottomland creeks curl through with cottonwoods and willows on both sides. This is gorgeous big-sky country; the land seems almost an afterthought. It's about as remote a place as you'll find, with just a few ranches, windmills, and cattle for company.

Fort Hat Creek

Some 13 miles north of Lusk a sign marks the old **Fort Hat Creek Stage Station,** mistakenly built (in 1876) along Sage Creek, Wyoming, instead of Hat Creek, Nebraska! It's easy to see how the country could start to blend together here. The old stage station, on private land but right next to the road, is two miles east of here on a paved road and then one mile southwest on a gravel road. It is an impressive two-story log structure built in 1887 to replace the original buildings, which had burned. The small fort garrisoned 40 soldiers who would ride out to protect the Cheyenne-Deadwood Stage from attack. Hat Creek was typical of stage stations along the route. One writer of the time, Leander P. Richardson, noted: "At any of these places a traveler can purchase almost anything, from a glass of whiskey to a four-horse team, but the former article is usually the staple of demand."

Lance Creek

Tiny Lance Creek (pop. 50) lies in the middle of Niobrara County and is surrounded by the Lance Creek oil fields. An oil boom peaked here during

World War II; more recently production has declined and the community now ekes out a minimal survival. The Lance Creek area is the site of discoveries of horned dinosaurs (Ceratopsians) and other fossils. Beginning in the 1880s, scientists found an incredible number of fossil plants, dinosaurs, and ancient mammals, including at least 75 different species of vertebrates, many of which were previously unknown. **Paleo Park** (described more fully under Newcastle in the Black Hills chapter.) has tours and lodging; 307/334-2270, http://paleopark.com.

Mule Creek Junction

Halfway between Lusk and Newcastle is Mule Creek Junction (no services since the gas station/motel burned in 1999), where you'll find a state rest area. A couple of miles north of this, U.S. 85 crosses Cheyenne River near the site of the aptly named **Robber's Roost Stage Station.** Here outlaws sometimes attacked the Cheyenne-Deadwood Stage when it slowed to cross the river. In an 1878 robbery attempt an outlaw was killed here by the shotgun messengers, but his partners managed to escape with the mail sacks.

Medicine Bow Country

West from Cheyenne, I-80 climbs a long, gentle ramp into the Laramie Mountains, reaches the highest point on its 3,000-mile trek across America, and then abruptly begins a steep descent onto the expansive Laramie Plains. A distinctly frontier feeling envelops this land: mountains rim the valley, and as you continue west the grass intermixes with more and more sagebrush. You are entering the real West of mountains, sage, and sky.

Medicine Bow Country consists of Albany County—with Laramie and the Laramie Plains at its center and the Laramie and Medicine Bow Mountains on either side—and Carbon County, where Rawlins is the main town and the Sierra Madre mountains dominate the southern horizon. The name "Medicine Bow" has a convoluted origin. The mountains in southern Wyoming were considered a sacred place, and each year Indians gathered nearby to celebrate powwows and build bows from the cedar wood. The Indian term

© DON PITCHER

Grand Encampment Museum, Encampment

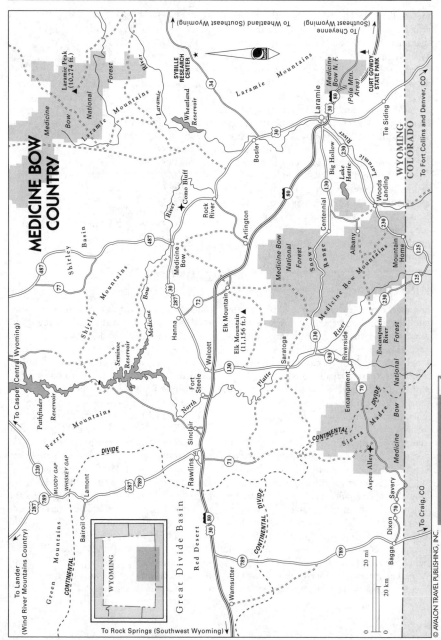

MEDICINE BOW COUNTRY

© AVALON TRAVEL PUBLISHING, INC.

MEDICINE BOW

for "medicine" means something spiritually powerful—symbolized by the mountains, the cedar that made fine bows, and the annual powwows. Whites combined the various tribal activities into "Medicine Bow" and applied the name to a river, a mountain range, a national forest, and a town.

The land is remarkably diverse in terms of both topography and vegetation. Laramie Basin contains the highest short-grass prairie in the world, some 7,200 feet above sea level. Three mountain ranges cross through this region: the Laramie Mountains, the Medicine Bow Mountains (also called the Snowy Range), and the Sierra Madre. Mountain slopes are covered with lodgepole pine, Engelmann spruce, and subalpine fir, while alpine meadows, tundra, and rock dominate the highest elevations. To the north and west of these mountain ranges, the country is a dry landscape of sage and desert.

HISTORY

For many centuries this land was filled with buffalo, elk, and deer, providing a rich home for wandering tribes of Indians. By the time whites arrived in large numbers, the area was claimed and fought over by many tribes, including Oglala Sioux, Northern Arapaho, Eastern Shoshone, Northern Cheyenne, and White River Utes. Although mountain men long trapped in this part of Wyoming, it remained off the beaten path for many years, with emigrants preferring the Oregon Trail through the central part of the state. This began to change in 1862, when the Overland Trail opened across southern Wyoming. Ben Holladay's stage traversed the route, as did many thousands of emigrants who found it shorter and generally safer from Indian attack. As with the rest of southern Wyoming, the coming of the Union Pacific Railroad transformed this area from a place to get through into a place to live. The railroad provided the region's lifeblood for many years. Later, Laramie gained the University of Wyoming and Rawlins the state penitentiary.

> ## MEDICINE BOW COUNTRY SIGHTSEEING HIGHLIGHTS
>
> University of Wyoming Geological Museum, University Art Museum, Ivinson Mansion, and Wyoming Territorial Park in Laramie
> Vedauwoo Rocks
> Sugarloaf Recreation Area in the Snowy Range
> Hobo Pool hot springs in Saratoga
> Grand Encampment Museum in Encampment
> Frontier Prison and Carbon County Museum in Rawlins
> **Popular events:** Woodchopper's Jamboree in Encampment (June), Jubilee Days in Laramie (July), University of Wyoming football games in Laramie (fall)

ECONOMY

The economy of the Medicine Bow region is much like that of the rest of Wyoming—heavily dependent on grazing and energy. More than 170,000 cattle and 75,000 sheep graze this land of sage and grass; mines near Hanna produce large amounts of low-sulfur coal; and wells in Carbon County pump natural gas. Other important pieces of the regional economy are the University of Wyoming, in Laramie, and tourism—particularly in the Snowy Range, Sierra Madre, and Upper North Platte River Valley. Transportation has long been a vital factor in the region. Ben Holladay's stage and the Union Pacific Railroad were followed on this route eventually by I-80, the primary artery across America for truckers and travelers. The remote stretch of I-80 between Laramie and Elk Mountain is still called the "Snow Chi Minh Trail," a joking reference to the ceaseless blowing snow that sometimes shuts down traffic for days at a time during the winter. Gale-force winds have even been known to blow semis over!

Laramie

The countryside around Laramie (pop. 27,000) differs little from that in much of Wyoming—arid plains abruptly broken by rugged mountain ranges—but the town itself offers a real change of pace. True, Laramie does have rodeos, restaurants with names like the Cavalryman, and great country-and-western tunes at the ever-popular Cowboy Saloon, but it also seems to violate one's expectations of a Wyoming town. It's the kind of place where you meet cops drinking mochas while munching bagels instead of hobnobbing with the smokers over cheap coffee and donuts. Bumper stickers demand "Free Leonard Peltier" while others joke "I'm hung like Einstein and smart as a horse."

Take a stroll along downtown's Ivinson Avenue and you'll discover a shop selling fancy chocolates, an upscale children's store, art galleries, a day spa, flower shops, a yoga center, bookstores, and even an organic foods store complete with post-hippie decor. Nearby are vegetarian restaurants, bars that attract reggae and blues bands, and galleries filled with handcrafted items from all over the planet.

Laramie is one of my favorite cities in Wyoming, a place that has a sense of intelligence without being stultified, where culture mixes with fun and games. Tourist brochures call Laramie "Gem City of the Plains." It has the laid-back college-town feel of Chico, California, or Fort Collins, Colorado, but Laramie is considerably less congested. The students add a playful, literary atmosphere—bikes on the streets, rock concerts, heady conversations over beers, and theatrical productions. Laramie has both crowded fast-food outlets and sophisticated restaurants offering more substantial fare. It's probably the only place in the state (other than Jackson) where a restaurant would dare carry wine descriptions on its menu: "A complex, medium-bodied wine with black cherry and wild berry flavors, balanced by toasty-oak nuances."

The Union Pacific Railroad splits Laramie into two distinct parts. The campus, stately older homes, and nearly the entire city lie on the east side; less pretentious quarters lie on "the other side of the tracks." Long and noisy freight trains roll through every few minutes at all hours of the day and night piled high with double-decker containerized freight boxes destined for Chicago, Denver, or Los Angeles.

Located close to the Medicine Bow Mountains (hiking and skiing), Vedauwoo Rocks (rock climbing), Lake Hattie (windsurfing), and the Colorado Rockies (Coors beer), Laramie is a haven for those who love the outdoors. The only problem is the midwinter wind, which makes life in this part of the state difficult. Temperatures may be relatively mild—in the low 20s—but add in a 30-mph wind

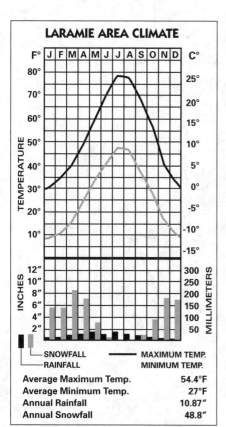

LARAMIE AREA CLIMATE

| | SNOWFALL | MAXIMUM TEMP. |
| | RAINFALL | MINIMUM TEMP. |

Average Maximum Temp.	54.4°F
Average Minimum Temp.	27°F
Annual Rainfall	10.87"
Annual Snowfall	48.8"

LARAMIE

DOWNTOWN LARAMIE

TRAVELODGE
DOWNTOWN MOTEL
COWBOY SALOON
ST. MATTHEW'S CATHEDRAL
JEFFREY'S
WHOLE EARTH GRAINERY
BUCKHORN
EL CONQUISTADOR BISTRO
THE FRONT GALLERY
BAR
GRAND AVE. PIZZA
BRIGHT SIDE GALLERY
ROCKY MTN. SPORTS
WILD WILLIES
PERSONALLY RECOMMENDED BOOKS
THE OVERLAND
PEDAL HOUSE
COAL CREEK COFFEE
ALTITUDE CHOPHOUSE
EARTH, WIND, AND FIRE GALLERY
CROSS-COUNTRY CONNECTION
FIRESIDE

UNIVERSITY OF WYOMING

HALF ACRE GYM
ANTHROPOLOGY MUSEUM
WYOMING UNION
COOPER MANSION
BIOLOGICAL SCIENCES/ PLANETARIUM
AVEN NELSON BUILDING
CONSERVATORY
COE LIBRARY
UNIVERSITY OF WYOMING VISITOR CENTER
OLD MAIN
PRESIDENT'S RESIDENCE
VINSON

JACOBY GOLF COURSE
HOSPITAL
ALBERTSON'S
COMFORT INN
WAL-MART

NATIONAL GUARD ARMORY
ARMORY RD.
AMERICAN HERITAGE CENTER
ART MUSEUM
STUDENT APARTMENTS
SOFTBALL COMPLEX
ARENA-AUDITORIUM
LAW SCHOOL
MEMORIAL STADIUM
THE LIBRARY RESTAURANT & BREWING CO.
UNIVERSITY INN
HIGH SCHOOL (POOL)
WYOMING CHILDREN'S MUSEUM AND NATURE CENTER
Labonte Park
AGRICULTURAL BUILDING
SEE UW DETAIL
GEOLOGICAL MUSEUM
PRAIRIE BREEZE B&B
LARAMIE PLAINS CIVIC CENTER
LARAMIE PLAINS MUSEUM
POST OFFICE
CITY HALL
ALBANY COUNTY LIBRARY
RANGER MOTEL
FIRST INN GOLD
MOTEL 6
EXIT 313
SKYLINE RD.
SOLDIER SPRINGS RD.

GAS LITE MOTEL
GATEWAY PLAZA
KMART
TRAVEL INN
CHAMBER OF COMMERCE
SUNSET INN
VISITOR CENTER (CABOOSE)
HOLIDAY INN
FORT SANDERS
ALBANY COUNTY FAIRGROUNDS

BUD'S BAR
CEDAR ST.
SEE DOWNTOWN DETAIL

West Laramie
SUPER 8 MOTEL
EXIT 310
ECONO LODGE
DAYS INN
LARAMIE KOA
McGUE ST.
River
WYOMING TERRITORIAL PRISON & OLD WEST PARK
EXIT 311
SNOWY RANGE
HOWARD JOHNSON INN
FOREST SERVICE OFFICE
CAMELOT MOTEL
BANNER RD.

To Rawlins
To Rock River and Medicine Bow
To Cheyenne
To Fort Collins and Denver, CO
To Airport and Centennial
To Woods Landing
To Fort Sanders Site
Laramie River

0   0.5 mi
0   0.5 km

MEDICINE BOW

© AVALON TRAVEL PUBLISHING, INC.

and it feels like 20 below zero. Bitter gale-force winds can howl through for days on end in this open country.

HISTORY

The city of Laramie (and several other places in eastern Wyoming) has the name of a French-Canadian trapper who was killed by Indians in the mountains now also named in his honor. Nearly everything about the man is open to question. Jacques LaRamee (or was it Joseph De la Ramie?) was killed in 1820 (or 1821) by Arapahoes (or another tribe), who stuffed his body under the ice in a beaver pond (or left his corpse in his cabin). Be that as it may, he attained a far more lasting legacy through his death than through anything he did while alive.

Fort Sanders

The first permanent settlement in the Laramie area was Fort Sanders, originally known as Fort John Buford, built in 1866. Located approximately two miles south of present-day Laramie, it served to protect emigrants and stagecoaches along the Overland Trail and, later, Union Pacific Railroad construction workers. At its peak, Fort Sanders housed nearly 600 soldiers. As with other posts on the frontier, desertions were rampant; 41 men went AWOL in a single month, taking with them whatever supplies they could grab. As the threat of Indian attacks lessened over the years, so did the value of Fort Sanders. It was abandoned in 1882, and very little remains.

The Union Pacific Arrives

Laramie City (as it was first called) was named and established by Gen. Grenville Dodge, the man in charge of planning the Union Pacific's route westward. The location was chosen because of a major spring that still produces millions of gallons of water, and because railroad ties could be cut in the mountains to the west and brought down the Laramie River. The proximity of Fort Sanders also influenced the location. By the time the first train rolled into Laramie City on May 10, 1868, many "sooners" had already set up business in tents. The first passengers were met with 23 saloons, one hotel, and no churches. Within three months, Laramie had 5,000 people.

Many of the earliest to arrive were the usual end-of-the-track types: hoodlums, gamblers, prostitutes, and others out to make a fast buck. When the tracks headed on westward, the riffraff stayed behind, kept busy by the soldiers. Within a short time, a saloon owner named Asa Moore gained the support of various gambling houses, brothels, and other bars to create a rump town government with himself as mayor. The man they appointed town marshal had recently left Cheyenne after being acquitted on a murder charge, and his assistant was caught stealing mules. Laramie quickly became one of the wildest towns on the frontier, with murders occurring almost daily. Men who were arrested often faced trial in a back room of Asa Moore's saloon, where his men robbed and then killed them, burying their bodies out on the plains. Stories tell of up to 10 men disappearing in a single night.

Seeing that the law was in the hands of criminals, the more respectable citizens decided to put an end to the mayhem. More than 500 men joined a vigilante committee that swept into the saloons, brothels, dance halls, and casinos on the night of October 18, 1868. Three men died in gun battles (including a musician and a vigilante), and dozens of others were wounded. Another three were hanged by vigilantes, including the mayor, Asa Moore. The next day, outlaw Big Steve Young met the same fate, and more than a hundred crooks were piled into railroad cars and sent west. These actions calmed things down rather quickly, and thereafter Laramie City became something of a model town. It is perhaps fitting that four years later Laramie would be awarded the territorial prison.

For many years the main reason for the existence of Laramie was the presence of the railroad and the operations it established, including a roundhouse, an iron foundry, a tie-treating plant, machine shops, and a mill for reprocessing old rails. Gold discoveries in the Snowy Range to the west helped Laramie's economy grow, but the railroad remained the largest employer in Laramie until the 1950s, when it was supplanted by the university.

Women's Suffrage

Laramie was the site of two of the most notable events in the history of women's rights. On September 6, 1870, Louisa Gardner ("Grandma") Swain became the first woman in the nation to vote in an open and public election. A few months before this, a judge in Laramie established the world's first jury with women members. (Reporters noted that the female jurors hid behind heavy veils and held crying babies on their laps.) The women brought about a change in the jury system: breaks for boozing and gambling were ended, and smoking and chewing tobacco in the jury box were also halted. The women also proved more likely to convict men of murder than their male peers, who regarded killing humans a less serious crime than rustling cattle. A stone monument near 1st and Garfield Streets marks the location where the first all-woman jury met.

The University

In 1886, Laramie received a gift from the state legislature that would eventually transform it from a cow town into a college town. Under the leadership of Col. Stephen W. "Father of the University" Downey, the legislature voted to establish the new University of Wyoming. It was part of a deal that carved up Wyoming: Laramie got the university, Cheyenne became the capital, Rawlins landed the prison, and Evanston got the state asylum. The bill was signed into law by Gov. Francis E. Warren in 1886, four years before Wyoming achieved statehood. The school opened the following year with a single building—now called Old Main—built at a cost of $49,000. The new program had five professors and a coed student body of 42, who paid $7.50 each to attend. Over the years, the railroad gradually diminished in importance while the university added more and more to the local economy, until it became the biggest local employer. It remains so today. Because of the university, Laramie has never really experienced the economic booms and busts common to much of Wyoming.

A 1998 crime brought unwelcome notoriety to Laramie when Matthew Shephard, a gay University of Wyoming student, was brutally beaten to death. The two murderers apparently targeted Shephard because of his homosexuality. Anyone who knows Laramie and its people will see this as a frightening anomaly because the town has a reputation for tolerance. Find out more by visiting the Matthew Shephard Foundation online at www.matthewsplace.com.

UNIVERSITY OF WYOMING

Wyoming is the only state to have just one baccalaureate-granting institution. The University of Wyoming campus in Laramie thus gains the state's undivided financial support, much to the chagrin of the two-year colleges. The university lays claim to being the highest university campus in the nation—at 7,200 feet, it makes Denver's mile-high claim to fame look puny. Although not a major research institution, UW has respected programs in atmospheric sciences (ozone-depletion studies), coal production, aquatic toxicology, oil recovery technology, water management, agricultural research, and infrared astronomy. Approximately 11,000 students attend the university under the tutelage of 2,500 faculty and staff members.

The university offers more than 75 different degree programs in seven accredited colleges: agriculture, arts and sciences, business, education, engineering, health sciences, and law. It operates on a semester system, with a summer session open to visiting students. A summertime **Elderhostel** provides classes for folks over 60, and various noncredit classes are also offered throughout the year, covering the spectrum from ballroom dancing to LSAT preparation. For a copy of the school's *General Bulletin,* call the admissions office at 307/766-5160 or 800/342-5996, or find it on the Internet at www.uwyo.edu.

Exploring the Campus

Begin your campus visit at the helpful **University of Wyoming Visitor Information Center,** 1408 Ivinson Ave., 307/766-4075. It's open Monday–Friday 7:30 A.M.–4:30 P.M. in the summer and Monday–Friday 8 A.M.–5 P.M. during the school year. The center can provide maps and complete information on the university,

BILL NYE

Laramie lays claim to one of the most popular humorists of the 19th century, Edgar "Bill" Nye (1850–1896). Born in Maine and raised in Wisconsin, Nye arrived in Laramie in 1876 and soon began writing columns for a local newspaper. His sharp wit and wry sense of humor quickly showed through the news. Local Republicans backed him in publishing his own paper, the *Laramie Boomerang*—named for a flea-bitten gray mule that kept returning no matter how hard Nye tried to get rid of him. The paper first rolled off his "lemon-squeezer" press in 1881. When the news wasn't all that interesting, Nye would embellish it: "[I] write up things that never occurred with a masterly and graphic hand. Then, if they occur, I am grateful; if not, I bow to the inevitable and smother my chagrin."

Even Nye's appointment as Laramie City postmaster (a political plum gained because of his connection with the dominant Republican party) became grist for his humor mill. He wrote the postmaster general, noting, "I look upon the appointment, myself, as a great triumph of eternal truth over error and wrong. It is one of the epoches, I may say, in the Nation's onward march toward political purity and perfection. I do not know when I have noticed any stride in the affairs of state, which so thoroughly impressed me with its wisdom. . . ." Nye only kept the position for a year.

In 1883, an attack of spinal meningitis forced him to leave high-elevation Laramie for a lower climate. By the time he departed, Nye's newspaper was in dire financial condition, but it managed to survive under new, more responsible, management. The *Boomerang* is still published today and is one of the state's few daily papers. The old livery stable where it was originally published is on the corner of 3rd and Garfield; Nye's office was on the second floor.

Bill Nye's witty *Boomerang* columns gained a national following, and by the 1890s he had become the best-paid humorist in America. Nye would eventually write 14 books of humor; *Bill Nye's History of the United States,* published in 1894, sold an incredible 500,000 copies. Unfortunately, the intense stress of life on the road helped shorten his life. Nye died of a stroke when he was just 45 years old.

Much of Nye's humor falls flat today, and its racial stereotypes are certainly dated, but some of the short pieces still have a delightful zing, particularly when he tweaks the noses of famous people such as Oscar Wilde (whom Nye called "Thou bilious pelican from o'er the sea") or a competing newspaper editor ("We have nothing more to say of the editor of the Sweetwater *Gazette*. Aside from the fact that he is a squint-eyed, consumptive liar, with a breath like a buzzard and a record like a convict, we don't know anything against him . . ."). None of his works are currently in print, but you'll find *Bill Nye's Western Humor* in many Wyoming libraries.

The following commentary on Wyoming agriculture and "reclamation" efforts is typical of Nye's tongue-in-cheek writing:

I do not wish to discourage those who might wish to come to this place for the purpose of engaging in agriculture, but frankly I will state that it has its drawbacks. In the first place, the soil is quite course, and the agriculturist, before he can even begin with any prospect of success must run his farm through a stamp-mill in order to make it sufficiently mellow. This, as the reader will see, involves a large expense at the very outset. Hauling the farm to a custom mill would delay the farmer two or three hundred years in getting his crops in, thus giving the agriculturist who had a pulverized farm in Nebraska, Colorado, or Utah, a great advantage over his own, which had not yet been to the reduction works.

MEDICINE BOW

including lectures, films, concerts, dances, and other events open to the public. Also stop here for details on one-hour **campus tours,** offered Monday–Friday at 11 A.M. in the summer, and Monday–Friday at 11 A.M. and 2 P.M. during the school year. At other times, just pick up the walking-tour brochure and head out on your own. Right next door to the visitors center you'll find the historic **Cooper Mansion,** built in 1920 in the Mission Pueblo style and now on the National Register of Historic Places.

An **information desk,** 307/766-3160, www.uwyo.edu/cac, in the Wyoming Union building is open Monday–Saturday 7:30 A.M.–midnight, and Sunday noon–10 P.M. during the school year; Monday–Friday 7 A.M.–4:30 P.M. in the summer. You can check your email or surf the web on free computers near the information desk. Also stop in the union for a listing of campus activities, stamps, cash from the ATM, or snacks. The main campus buildings center around **Prexy's Pasture,** where the school's first president grazed his personal cattle. Today Prexy's is a favorite place to relax on sunny days—and it's still legal to leave your horse here.

A **Campus Shuttle,** 307/766-3344, provides free transport on weekdays during the school year, with stops all around the university.

University Art Museum

This excellent museum, 307/766-6622, www.uwyo.edu/artmuseum, encompasses nine large galleries, including an outdoor sculpture court. It's housed in **Centennial Complex,** which also contains the American Heritage Center (described next). Art exhibits change several times a year, so you aren't likely to see the same thing twice. Some of these are from the university's collection of 6,000 paintings, pieces of sculpture, and other works of art. The permanent collection is mostly by 19th- and 20th-century artists, including paintings and drawings by Thomas Hart Benton, Charles M. Russell, Winslow Homer, Paul Gauguin, Andy Warhol, Thomas Moran, and Pablo Picasso. The museum puts on a variety of special programs, lectures, and other art events throughout the year and has a fine **gift shop** selling distinctive arts and crafts.

The Art Museum is open Monday–Saturday 10 A.M.–5 P.M., all year, plus Sunday noon–5 P.M. from mid-June to Labor Day. Entrance is free.

Another place to view artwork on campus is **Gallery 234,** which exhibits student pieces. It's in the Wyoming Union building and is open Monday–Friday 8 A.M.–5 P.M.

American Heritage Center

This facility serves as both a research center and exhibition space for art and historical pieces. It is not really a tourist destination, but the building also houses the University Art Museum. Designed by famed architect Antoine Predock, this multilevel conical building contains expansive art galleries and thousands of manuscripts, rare books, and artifacts from Wyoming and the West. The building was designed to represent the mountains surrounding Laramie and is oriented so that one small section is lit by the sun during the summer solstice. The building gets a decidedly mixed reaction. To be honest, I found it a big disappointment. The exterior resembles (take your pick) a Darth Vader mask or a stealth jet, and the wonderful central loggia is ruined by a claustrophobic tangle of 32 concrete columns intended—the architect claimed—to resemble a forest.

Nine oil paintings by Alfred Jacob Miller hang on the walls of the loggia, including his best-known work, *The Rendezvous Near Green River—Oregon Territory,* valued at $750,000. Miller was the only artist ever to witness a mountain-man rendezvous; he documented the West during a trip in 1837. Also in the loggia are the saddles of Hollywood cowboys William Boyd ("Hopalong Cassidy") and Duncan Renaldo ("Cisco Kid"). The George Rentschler room on this level contains nine paintings by the Western artist Henry Farney. Also nearby are a room with changing exhibits and another one containing the university's 50,000-volume rare book repository. Wander around a bit more and you will find—surprisingly—Jack Benny's old violin.

Take the elevator to the fourth-floor reading room for access to an outstanding research collection of Western books, documents, and photographs, including the papers of Buffalo Bill Cody, F. E. Warren, Jack Benny, and Irving Wallace. Other pop culture figures have collections here too, including Ozzie and Harriet Nelson, Don Knotts, and Andy Griffith. The fifth floor provides a dramatic view across Laramie to the Snowy Range and historic photos on the walls. There's no charge to walk around the center, which is open Monday–Friday 7:30 A.M.–4:30 P.M. and Saturday 11 A.M.–4:30 P.M. in the summer; Monday–Friday 8 A.M.–5 P.M. and Saturday 11 A.M.–5 P.M. during the school year. Get details at 307/766-4114, http://uwadmnweb.uwyo.edu/ahc.

Geological Museum

Established in 1887, this is Wyoming's oldest museum and one of the most interesting campus sites. A life-size bronze Tyrannosaurus rex greets visitors at the entrance, while dinosaur bones surround the doorway. Inside the museum you'll find fossil and mineral displays from around the state (including fluorescent minerals). An enormous woolly mammoth skull found near Rawlins is one of the most impressive fossils, but the museum's centerpiece is a 75-foot-long skeleton of an *Apatosaurus excelsus,* better known as a brontosaurus. Excavated along Sheep Creek in Albany County, it's one of just five Apatosaurus skeletons on display in the world. Also here, you'll find a cast of the largest Allosaurus skeleton ever found and the largest complete freshwater fossil fish in the world. The Geological Museum is open Monday–Friday 8 A.M.–5 P.M. and Saturday–Sunday 10 A.M.–3 P.M. year-round; no charge. Get details at 307/766-4218, www.uwyo.edu/geomuseum.

Right next door to the Geological Museum is the **Wyoming Geological Survey Building,** which sells interesting maps of all types and guides to the state's geology.

Other University Sights

The first campus building was **Old Main,** completed in 1887 and now housing the administrative offices. The prominent tower that once adorned the building was removed in 1915. Look for Wyoming's territorial seal over the west entrance. Head to the Anthropology Building to view the university's **Anthropology Museum,** representing a small portion of the department's extensive cultural collection. The museum (307/766-5136, http://uwadmnweb.uwyo.edu/anth) is open Monday–Friday 7:30 A.M.–4:30 P.M. and focuses on the Plains Indians. A mammoth skull is here, along with a display on the Vore Site buffalo jump in northeastern Wyoming, where thousands of buffalo were trapped and killed.

On the fourth floor of the Agriculture Building is the **Entomology Museum,** housing thousands of insect specimens. Although primarily for research, it's open to the public; 307/766-2298. Also in the same building is the **Range Herbarium,** considered one of the most complete collections of grasses in the western states. It's open by request; 307/766-5263. At the **Rocky Mountain Herbarium,** on the third floor of the Aven Nelson Building, 307/766-2236, you'll find one of the nation's largest plant collections, but it's open to the general public only by prior arrangement.

The fine **Williams Botany Conservatory** fronts the Aven Nelson Building and is a warm, bright place to escape on a winter day. Inside are dozens of tropical plants, including orchids and bananas. It's open Monday–Thursday 10 A.M.–4 P.M., Friday 10 A.M.–3 P.M., and Saturday 10 A.M.–noon (closed Sat. in summer). Call 307/766-2380 for details.

WYOMING TERRITORIAL PARK

In 1869, the territorial legislature voted to construct a penitentiary at Laramie. (Wyoming prisoners had previously been housed in the Detroit House of Correction at a cost of $1.25 per week.) The imposing three-story stone building in west Laramie off Snowy Range Road was dedicated to "evil doers of all classes and kinds"; fittingly enough, a bottle of bourbon was deposited in the cornerstone. It remained a prison until 1902, when the inmates were transferred to a new facility in Rawlins. After the prisoners were moved out, the building was turned over to the university for use as an experimental livestock farm; the cells became cattle stalls and the prison broom factory a sheep barn. In the 1980s, the university farm

© DON PITCHER

the prison at the **Wyoming Territorial Park, Laramie**

moved to a more modern facility elsewhere, and the historic prison was officially established as Wyoming Territorial Prison & Old West Park. A $5 million facelift transformed the deteriorated buildings into one of the largest western-heritage parks in the Rockies. Some of the stuff here gets a bit cutesified and corny—children can help recapture a "prisoner" attempting an "escape"— but the park does offer a unique and fascinating way to step into Wyoming's frontier past.

Prison

The cornerstone of the historic park is the beautifully restored prison. A wooden stockade surrounds the sandstone building and adjacent broom factory where prisoners were forced to work. Other prisoners made candles, furniture, or musical instruments, or braided leather. Pick up a self-guided tour brochure as you enter the prison or take one of the excellent guided tours, offered hourly. The interior has been reconstructed using the original cells and period fixtures. Excellent displays and short videos describe the prisoners' lives. The convicts who served time here—including inmate number 187, Butch Cassidy—glare down from giant photos on the

walls. Each cell held two prisoners in a tiny six-by-eight-foot arched brick enclosure sealed with an iron door. Inmates slept on straw mattresses. Walk inside one of the cells to get a feeling for the claustrophobic conditions. No wonder Butch Cassidy promised to "never molest the state of Wyoming again" when he was pardoned after 18 months here!

Horse Barn

The old horse barn has been transformed into a museum and theater. Downstairs is the **National U.S. Marshals Museum,** housing everything from frontier-era artifacts, including a bullet-riddled Wells Fargo cash box, to displays on the crack-cocaine busts of today. The Marshals Service is the oldest civilian law-enforcement agency in the world and was responsible for managing the Wyoming Territorial Prison. Visitors will enjoy finding John Wayne, Clint Eastwood, and Ronald Reagan in the film clips that feature Hollywood's version of Old West marshals. Here, too, you'll learn all sorts of lawman trivia and see guns belonging to Bat Masterson and Butch Cassidy. Bet you didn't know that the five-pointed star worn by U.S. Marshals was derived from a pentacle worn by 17th-century soldiers; it was supposed to make them bulletproof.

Upstairs you'll find a **dinner theater** where on summer nights a professional cast puts on musical dinner comedies. It's pretty foolish, but the production and singing are first rate, and the meal is fine. The Horse Barn Dinner Theatre runs summers only, but they also put on occasional productions in the off-season.

Frontier Town and Ranchland

Just west of the prison lies an "end-of-the-tracks town" featuring simple wood and canvas buildings that come alive with living-history characters such as outlaws, marshals, and Calamity Jane—played by her great-great niece. The old warden's house contains a variety of period artisans at work. Frontier Town also houses a blacksmith (in real life the chairman of UW's language department) who creates authentic period items. Other buildings house a printing press that cranks out wanted posters, a saloon, photo studio, general store, and livery stable (but no whorehouse). The Warden's house sells antiques. Stagecoach and buggy rides are available.

The newest addition to Wyoming Territorial Park is a collection of historic buildings called Ranchland. Here you can explore a homesteader's log cabin, a one-room schoolhouse, a chicken house, a barn, and other buildings moved to the site from surrounding ranches and furnished with period pieces. It's a good way to learn about the small ranchers and farmers who lived in Wyoming in the late 19th century. Kids love the petting zoo, complete with a calf, colt, goats, bunnies, chickens, ducks, llamas, and Gus the Wonder Donkey.

The quarter-mile **Laramie River Interpretive Trail** follows the banks of the river near the prison, providing a place to relax and explore.

Practicalities

Wyoming Territorial Park is west of town on Snowy Range Road and has a gift shop that sells souvenirs and books. Combination tickets include guided prison tours (offered on the hour from 10 A.M.–5 P.M.) and entrance to the Marshals Museum and Frontier Town; $12 adults,

free for kids under 12. The prison and Marshals Museum are open daily 9 A.M.–6 P.M. from early May to early October. Frontier Town is open daily 10 A.M.–6 P.M. Memorial Day to Labor Day. Everything is typically closed October–April, but call for off-season hours or group tours.

Horse Barn Theater performances take place Thursday–Saturday evenings June to Labor Day; $30 adults, $20 ages 6–12. The show without dinner costs $16 adults, $11 kids.

The entire park, including the old prison, is fully accessible to those in wheelchairs. Get details at 307/745-6161 or 800/845-2287, www.wyoprisonpark.org. See the Territorial Park Events section for additional park activities.

IVINSON MANSION

Although its official name is the Laramie Plains Museum, this historic site is known to most folks as the Ivinson Mansion. Located at 603 Ivinson, the home is a delightful example of the Queen Anne style of Victorian architecture. The home was built in 1892 for Edward Ivinson, a millionaire merchant turned banker and politician. It's now on the National Register of Historic Places. After his death, the mansion became an Episcopal girls' school. When the school closed, locals managed to raise more than $74,000 to purchase the mansion and turn it into a museum.

The Ivinson Mansion occupies an entire city block, with a carriage house out back and attractive Victorian-style gardens. Few of the original furnishings remain, but much of the interior woodwork, including a freestanding stairway built without nails or screws, is still here. The museum is furnished with antiques, including some elaborate hand-carved furniture built at the Wyoming Penitentiary in 1901, handmade toys (including a doll from the 1840s), a piano that arrived by covered wagon, and several Indian artifacts. More unusual are a quilt that took 60 years to complete (listed in *Ripley's Believe It or Not!*), a seven-headed shower that looks like a medieval torture device, and a square Steinway grand piano. The back carriage house contains a small visitors center, carriages, old bikes, impressive fur coats, and two wonderful antique woodstoves. Also on the grounds is a one-room log schoolhouse built in 1924 and a statue/fountain honoring the events that helped bring equality to women in the West.

The museum, 307/742-4448, www.laramiemuseum.org, is open Tuesday–Saturday 9 A.M.–5 P.M. and Sunday 1–4 P.M. June–August. The rest of the year it is open Tuesday–Saturday 10–2 P.M.; $4.25 adults, $2.25 students and children, $12.50 families. Guided hour-long tours are given throughout the day, with the last one starting one hour before closing time. On one weekend in mid-December, the museum has a special Christmas open house in which local florists decorate the rooms and carolers stroll the halls.

MORE LARAMIE SIGHTS

Downtown

Laramie's downtown buildings—many of them dating from the 19th century—are on the National Register of Historic Places. Along Ivinson Avenue, a major renovation turned what had been a collection of sleazy flophouses and bars into a lively, attractive, and fun section of town. Pick up **walking-tour** brochures describing Laramie's historical and architectural downtown buildings from the chamber of commerce visitors center. **St. Matthew's Cathedral,** at the corner of 3rd and Ivinson, is one of Wyoming's more interesting churches. The limestone structure was built in 1868 and funded by Edward Ivinson.

Laramie has several small art galleries in addition to the larger ones at the university. If you're around early in the month, don't miss the **first Friday gallery walk,** when local shops have art openings, book signings, and hors d'oeuvres. **Earth, Wind and Fire Gallery,** 220 S. 2nd St., 307/745-0227, sells designer jewelry, Indian art, art prints, and fine pottery. **Gem City Clayworks,** 119 E. Grand Ave., 307/721-6233, exhibits distinctive works by other local potters and has studios where you can make and paint your own pottery. It's always a hit with kids. Other places worth a look include **Bright Side Gallery,** 205 E. Grand Ave., 307/745-0222, with all sorts of fun and fanciful art and furniture, and **Artisan's Gallery,** 307/745-3983, with a good selection of Wyoming-made gifts at 215 S. 2nd Street.

The **Wyoming Children's Museum & Nature Center,** 968 N. 9th St. (in La Bonte Park), 307/745-6332, is open Tuesday–Thursday 9 A.M.–5 P.M., Saturday 10 A.M.–4 P.M. This small museum contains fun hands-on exhibits for kids, including an Oregon Trail exhibit with a wagon, trading post, and gold panning. The nature center is home to salamanders, turtles, a great horned owl, and a crawl-through "beaver lodge." Admission costs $2 adults, $3 kids; free for children under three.

On the grounds of the **Laramie Plains Civic Center** at 710 Garfield, you'll find six murals painted in the early 1930s by noted artist Florence E. Ware.

Farther Afield

A granite monument to **Fort Sanders** stands two miles south of town along U.S. 287. Most of the fort site lies under an avalanche of residential and commercial development—the highway bisects the old parade grounds—but a few ruins from the old stone guardhouse and the powder house still stand. One of Fort Sanders' wooden buildings was moved to LaBonte Park, at 9th and Canby Streets in Laramie, where it is used as a recreation center.

Hutton Lake National Wildlife Refuge lies six miles south of Laramie on State Hwy. 230, then three miles south on County Rd. 37. It is a quiet, peaceful place to look for ducks, shorebirds, swallows, and migratory birds.

A warning for motorists, if you're planning to drive U.S. 287 between Laramie and Fort Collins, try to do so in the daytime. The road has a reputation as a deathtrap, with speeding trucks and few passing lanes. It is a popular route for students heading to the bars and party scene in Fort Collins, but it can be treacherous at night or in the winter. The highway's most infamous incident came in 2001, when eight UW athletes were killed in a head-on collision with a truck driven by another student. The driver of the other vehicle, Clinton Haskins, was convicted of drunk driving and is now in prison.

ACCOMMODATIONS

Space is generally not a problem for Laramie's lodging, although you should reserve well ahead during graduation week (mid-May), Jubilee Days (Fourth of July), Cheyenne Frontier Days (mid-July), and on football weekends in the fall. The old rule of supply and demand holds, so rates also rise considerably over those listed at these times.

Long-term housing can be difficult to find in Laramie; if you're moving here, check with Golden Key Realty, 310 University Ave., 307/742-8131, for apartments. Several other property management companies are listed in the yellow pages.

Under $50

For unpretentious accommodations, check out **Ranger Motel**, 453 N. 3rd St., 307/742-6677, where the furnishings are old but clean. Some rooms have fridges and microwaves, and weekly rates are available. Rates are $42 s or $46 d.

Motel 6, 621 Plaza Lane, 307/742-2307 or 800/466-8356, www.motel6.com, has a small outdoor pool and standard rooms with weekend rates of $44 s or $50 d ($6 less Sun.–Thurs.).

$50 and Up

Travel Inn, 262 N. 3rd St., 307/745-4853 or 800/227-5430, charges $40–55 s or $55–65 d, and has an outdoor pool and continental breakfast. **Howard Johnson Inn**, 1561 Jackson St., 307/742-8371 or 800/446-4656, www.hojo.com, features an indoor pool, hot tub, and sundeck. Rates are $50–54 s or $56–60 d.

Sunset Inn, 1104 S. 3rd St., 307/742-3741 or 800/308-3744, has rooms for $52 s or $58 d, some with fridges and microwaves. A heated outdoor pool and hot tub are also on the grounds. **Travelodge Downtown Motel**, 165 N. 3rd St., 307/742-6671 or 800/942-6671, www.vcn.com/~travelodge, charges $55–59 s or $65 d.

For very nice accommodations, stay at **Gas Lite Motel**, 960 N. 3rd, 307/742-6616 or 800/942-6610, where amenities include a continental breakfast and an indoor pool with a retractable roof. Rates are $55–65 d. **Comfort Inn**, 3420 Grand Ave., 307/721-8856 or 800/228-5150, www.comfortinn.com, has an indoor pool, hot tub, fitness room, and continental breakfast. Rates are $50–85 s or $55–90 d.

Super 8 Motel, 1987 Banner Rd., 307/745-8901 or 800/800-8000, www.super8.com, offers rates of $59 s or d, including a continental breakfast. Similar prices ($56 s or $66 d) are available at **Motel 8**, 501 Boswell Dr., 307/745-4856 or 888/745-4800, where some rooms have king beds, microwaves, and fridges.

University Inn, 1720 Grand Ave., 307/721-8855 or 800/869-9466, has accommodations for $60 s or $70 d, with microwaves and fridges in the rooms. **Camelot Motel**, 523 Adams, 307/721-8860 or 866/721-8395, charges $65 for two queens or one king bed.

Days Inn, 1368 McCue St., 307/745-5678, www.daysinn.com, is Laramie's newest place to stay, with standard rooms for $71–94 s or d, and suites for $106 d. Amenities include an indoor pool and continental breakfast. **First Inn Gold**, 421 Boswell, 307/742-3721 or 800/642-4212, www.firstinns.com, offers comfortable rooms for $75–99 s or d, including a large outdoor pool, indoor hot tub, and a light breakfast.

Laramie's **Holiday Inn** is on the south side of town and just off I-80 at 2313 Soldier Springs Rd., 307/742-6611 or 800/465-4329, www.holiday-inn.com. Facilities include an indoor pool, hot tub, restaurant, and sports bar, plus exercise equipment. The rooms have two queens or a king bed, and cost $94 s or d.

Guest Ranch

For an authentic Western experience with a fourth-generation ranching family, spend a night or a week at **Two Bars Seven Ranch**, 27 miles south of Laramie near Tie Siding, 307/742-6072, www.twobarssevenranch.com. The owners raise horses and beefalo (a hybrid cross between domestic cattle and bison) on 7,000 acres of mountains and meadows along the Colorado border. Six-night stays are $2,450 for two people, including lodging, meals, and horseback rides, and an outdoor hot tub. This classic ranch has space for a maximum of 15 guests.

CAMPING

The closest public campgrounds ($10; www.fs.fed.us/r2/mbr) are in the scenic Pole Mountain portion of **Medicine Bow-Routt National Forest,** approximately 10 miles east of Laramie. Other public campsites are 30 miles west in the Snowy Range. Both areas are described later in this chapter. **Curt Gowdy State Park,** 22 miles east of Laramie on State Hwy. 210 (Happy Jack Rd.), has campsites ($12 for nonresidents, $6 for Wyoming residents; open all year). Contact them at 307/632-7946; http://wyoparks.state.wy.us. See the Southeast Wyoming chapter for more on this park.

Laramie KOA, 1171 Baker, 307/742-6553 or 800/562-4153, www.koa.com, charges $12–16 for tents and $21–24 for RVs. Simple "kamping kabins" cost $25–45 d. It also has an outdoor pool and is open April–October.

FOOD

If you like reasonable prices, creative cooking, and a wide selection (who doesn't?), you're bound to appreciate all that Laramie has to offer in the way of dining out. You'll discover some of the best food in Wyoming here, from thick, juicy steaks to nouvelle cuisine. The Laramie Restaurant Guide is an online source for local restaurant reviews; find it at www.laramiewyo.com/restaurants.

American

For earthy and creative breakfasts, lunches, and dinners, visit **The Overland,** 100 Ivinson Ave., 307/721-2800, www.overlandrestaurant.com, but be ready for a wait on weekend mornings. Dinners feature everything from catfish with crayfish cream sauce to teriyaki chicken breast. The wine list includes more than 125 choices.

Get traditional steaks and seafood at **The Cavalryman Supper Club,** 4425 S. 3rd St., 307/745-5551, where the beef is considered the best around. **Cactus Jacks,** 207 S. 3rd St., 307/742-4842, has prime rib specials Tuesday and Saturday nights, along with steaks, pasta, and seafood every evening. **Lovejoy's Bar & Grill,** 101 Grand Ave., 307/745-0141, serves

burgers, steaks, wraps, salads, burritos, nachos, pasta, and microbrews. It's owned by the same folks who bring you Altitude Chophouse and Brewery and has a late-night menu—until midnight on Friday and Saturday nights.

You'll find inexpensive food, pizza, ice cream, and sandwiches at the **University Cafeteria,** in the Wyoming Union building on campus.

Cow-Belle Ranch Cookouts are put on by local ranches several times each summer. Just $8 gets you a tour of a ranch, a barbecued beef dinner, and entertainment. Details at 307/742-6045 or 866/876-1012, www.breedingcattlepage.com/albanycocowbelles.

International

Several places in town offer Mexican food. The best are **El Conquistador,** 110 Ivinson Ave., 307/742-2377; and **Corona Village,** 421 Boswell, 307/721-0167. Stop by the latter on Tuesdays for an all-you-can-eat taco bar. **Chelo's,** 357 University Ave., 307/745-5139, is a tiny greasy spoon that locals rave over but I find just mediocre. Judge for yourself.

Grand Avenue Pizza, 301 Grand Ave., 307/721-2909, bakes some of the best homemade pizzas in Wyoming and cranks out salads and daily soup specials. Get delicious Italian food, Wyoming-style, at **Vitale's Italian Cowboy,** 2127 E. Grand Ave., 307/755-1500. Open only for dinner.

Three places serve Chinese food and lunch buffets: **The Great Wall,** 1501 S. 3rd St., 307/745-7966; **The Mandarin Restaurant,** 1254 N. 3rd St., 307/742-8822; and **Peking Chinese Restaurant,** 1665 N. 3rd St., 307/742-8138. **Teriyaki Bowl,** across from the Albertson's at 3021 Grand, 307/742-0709, has to-go Japanese food.

Eclectic

Jeffrey's Bistro, 123 Ivinson Ave., 307/742-7046, www.jeffreysbistro.com, is a personal favorite. The atmosphere is relaxed and friendly, with a mix of brick, oak, and brass. On the menu are light meals, sandwiches, creative vegetarian specialties, and great homemade bread. Reasonable prices too; the most expensive full meal is $15.

Coal Creek Coffeehouse, 110 Grand Ave.,

307/745-7737, is a great spot to meet friends over espresso in an art-filled setting. On the menu are sandwiches, salads, soups, bagels, and freshly baked sweets. Right across the street is another popular student hangout, **Muddy Waters,** 113 E. Grand Ave., 307/742-6982, with a m|lange of old tables and light breakfasts.

Sweet Melissa Vegetarian Cafe, 213 S. 1st St., 307/742-9607, serves "comfort food for homesick vegetarians." Check the blackboard for the menu (all under $8), which includes sandwiches, soups, salads, stir-fries, chili, quiche, pasta, and unusual desserts.

Brewpubs

Altitude Chophouse and Brewery, 320 S. 2nd St., 307/721-4031, combines good beer (seven or so of their own versions are usually on tap) with a menu that encompasses both standard pub grub (fish and chips, pizzas, bangers and mash, etc.) and more upscale fare, including rack of lamb, ahi tuna, smoked pork chops, and spinach ravioli. In the back are pool and foosball tables.

Right across from campus, **The Library Restaurant and Brewing Co.,** 1622 E. Grand Ave., 307/742-0500, is a favorite of UW students, with fresh-brewed beers, reasonable prices, and ample servings of food.

Groceries and Bakeries

Get groceries from **Albertson's, Safeway,** and **Wal-Mart SuperCenter** stores along the main route through town. **Whole Earth Grainery and Truck Store,** 111 Ivinson Ave., 307/745-4268, is a funky and friendly grocery with all sorts of organic produce, dried foods, teas, spices, and coffees. There are not many places like this in Wyoming!

Head to **Old Town Bagels,** 307 E. Grand Ave., 307/721-8965, for the best bagels in these parts, plus smoothies, ice cream, and espresso. **The Chocolate Cellar,** 115A Ivinson Ave., 307/742-9278, sells imported chocolates.

ENTERTAINMENT

You'll find plenty of night action in this youthful town, where bumper stickers proclaim: "I go

from zero to horny in 2.5 beers." Laramie's oldest saloon—dating to 1890—is the **Buckhorn Bar,** 114 Ivinson Ave., 307/742-3554. Mounted heads of all types—including a two-headed calf—adorn the walls, while students and bikers adorn the pool table and barstools. Notice the bullet hole in the mirror behind the bar—the result of a 1971 incident in which a man opened fire on the bartender (he missed). The Buckhorn is a popular place for TV sports, and when school's in session, the back room thumps to rock or blues most weekends. The bar opens early, attracting the after-school college crowd.

Fireside, 201 Custer St., 307/721-5097, another very popular club, hosts live rock or blues nightly. More rock, pop, or blues tunes are **Ranger Lounge,** 463 N. 3rd Ave., 307/745-9751. **Wild Willies,** 303 S. 3rd St., 307/742-3330, is a good weekend spot, with two dance floors and live rock on one, while a DJ spins tunes on the other. Pool and darts round out the space.

Coal Creek Coffeehouse, 110 Grand Ave., 307/745-7737, has mellower live music or poetry a couple of times a month, plus open mic sessions every Wednesday evening. **Sweet Melissa Vegetarian Cafe,** 213 S. 1st St., 307/742-9607, and **Muddy Waters,** 113 E. Grand Ave., 307/742-6982, also offers up folksy music on occasion.

For hot country-and-western tunes, duded-up cowboys, and fresh-faced cowgirls, saunter on down to **The Cowboy Saloon,** 108 S. 2nd St., 307/721-3165. It's a spacious place with a big dance floor, two bars, and several pool tables. You'll find more country tunes (and free hors d'oeuvres on weeknights) at **Mulligan's,** 1115 S. 3rd, 307/745-9954.

At the popular **Mingles Sports Bar,** 3206 Grand Ave., 307/721-2005, you can sample the 21 beers on tap or shoot pool at any of the 14 tables (free pool daily 3–6 P.M.). It's especially popular for happy hour. **Bud's Bar,** 354 W. University Ave., 307/745-5236, is a favorite with university alumni. Everyone goes there before and after university football or basketball games. Students hang out at "Club UDub"—the **Beergarden** in the basement of the Wyoming Union building—which has live music during the school year. The **Sports Bar & Grill** at the Holiday Inn, 2313 Soldier Springs Rd., 307/742-6611, also has two big-screen TVs, pool tables, and the largest glasses of draft beer you'll ever see.

Local movie houses are the **Fox 4 Theatres,** 505 S. 20th St., 307/742-2842, and the **Wyo Theatre,** 309 S. 5th St., 307/745-4442. The latter features second-run and foreign films for $3.

EVENTS

The **Laramie events hotline,** 307/721-7345, www.laramie-tourism.org, provides information on upcoming activities in the area. **Summer productions** at the university include dance and music festivals and lighthearted plays; call 307/766-6666 for details. **Band concerts** are held at the Washington Park band shell on Wednesday evenings in June and July. The **University of Wyoming Symphony Orchestra,** 307/766-6666, performs concerts at the Fine Arts Center on campus October–May.

Laramie Jubilee Days starts on the Fourth of July and lasts a week, bringing PRCA rodeos, parades, the biggest fireworks show in Wyoming, cowboy poetry, live music, a free pancake breakfast, street dancing, a cattle drive through the center of town, carnival, melodramas, art exhibits, a softball tournament, and other activities to celebrate Wyoming's statehood. It's easily the biggest event in Laramie, and it attracts folks from throughout the region. Get details at 307/745-7339 or 866/876-1012, www.laramiejubileedays.com.

The ever popular **Albany County Fair** is held the first week of August, with 4-H contests, a carnival, and a demolition derby.

Territorial Park Events

There's an event of some sort at the Territorial Park every weekend of the summer; get the complete story at 307/745-6161 or 800/845-2287, www.wyoprisonpark.org. The first week-

The biggest attraction in Laramie comes each fall with the arrival of football season. Half the state seems to turn out at War Memorial Stadium to cheer on the Wyoming Cowboys, better known as "the 'Pokes."

end of June brings a **Model T Show,** with 20 or 30 old jalopies chugging away. The biggest summer event is **Loggers and Lager,** a lumberjack competition with tree felling, sawing races, and other activities on the first weekend of July. Fortunately, they don't have to drink the lager before competing. The **U.S. Marshals Day & Posse Rendezvous** takes place the third weekend of July and attracts marshals from around the country; highlights include an auction and special demonstrations by law-enforcement teams.

Other popular events include a **Horse Expo** in late June, a **Classic Car Show** in August, and **Beerfest** in early September, where you can sample more than 70 brews while listening to live bands. Each Halloween, the Wyoming Territorial Prison opens for spooky nighttime **haunted prison tours,** and the Horse Barn Theater opens for a **Christmas Dinner Theater** and **Children's' Dinner Theater** in March.

SPORTS

The biggest attraction in Laramie comes each fall with the arrival of football season. Half the state seems to turn out to join in the festivities at War Memorial Stadium—tailgate parties, rooting sections, and rock-'em-sock-'em helmeted soldiers battling it out against other citadels of higher learning. Up to 30,000 fans crowd the stadium Saturday afternoons to cheer on the Wyoming Cowboys—better known as "the 'Pokes"—as in "Cowpokes." The football team has a mixed record over the years; a Cody rodeo announcer once joked that Nebraska and Wyoming were uniting so that Nebraska could share Yellowstone and Wyoming could have a real football team! Needless to say, the crowd did not appreciate the humor. The university also competes in several other sports—men's basketball is a primary draw. The athletic facilities are among the finest in the nation and include a modern 15,000-seat arena-auditorium for basketball games, concerts, and other events. Contact the Athletic Ticket Office 307/766-4850 or 800/922-9461, www.wyomingathletics.com.

RECREATION

The paved **Laramie River Greenbelt** currently runs for six miles along the river on the west side of Laramie. It's a fine place for a bike ride, walk, or jog. Supporters hope to see the trail eventually encircle the city, but that is years away.

The public **swimming pool** is in the high school at 11th and Reynolds, 307/721-4426. (University facilities are only for students, faculty, and staff, but a new city rec center should be open by 2005.) Shallow **Lake Hattie,** 20 miles southwest of Laramie on State Hwy. 230, is a good place to swim or to fish for kokanee or rainbow trout in the summer. **West Laramie Fly Store,** 1657 Snowy Range Rd., 307/745-5425 or 888/745-9565, www.flystore.net; and **Four Seasons Anglers,** 334 S. Fillmore, 307/721-4047, www.4seasonsanglers.com, sell fishing gear and offer casting and fly-tying classes and guided fishing. More guided fishing is available through **Westland Guide Service,** 307/742-6224, and **Foxtrot Fishing,** 307/742-8686.

Horseback and wagon rides are offered by **Prairie Rides,** on Sprague Lane west of Laramie, 307/745-5095 or 888/762-5619, www.prairierides.com, and **Two Bars Seven Ranch,** 307/742-6072, www.twobarsseven-ranch.com. Prairie Rides also offers training for riders of all levels, plus mountain trips and sunset dinner rides.

The University's **Jacoby Park Golf Course,** on N. 30th, 307/745-3111, is an 18-hole course open to the public. **Laramie Country Club,** 307/745-8490, is a nine-hole course west of town on U.S. 230 that is also open to the public. For the Lilliputian version, head to **Oasis Mini-Golf,** S. 15th and Skyline Rd., 307/745-7574, which is also home to **Skyline Skate** for roller skating. **Laramie Lanes,** 1270 N. 3rd St., 307/745-3835, is the local bowling alley.

Rent skis, snowboards, snowshoes, and other winter gear from **Cross Country Connection,** 221 S. 2nd St., 307/721-2851; **Rocky Mt. Sports Outlet,** 217 E. Grand Ave., 307/742-3220, which rents and sells all sorts of used gear, including sleeping bags, tents, backpacks, stoves, bikes, rollerblades, skis, and snowshoes; **Westgate Ski & Sports,** 1979 Snowy Range Rd., 307/742-6742 or 800/308-6742; or **Fine Edge Ski Shop,** 1660 N. 4th St., 307/745-4499, www.fineedge.net.

Rent mountain bikes at **Pedal House,** 207 S. 1st St., 307/742-5533. The folks here are knowledgeable about local cycling trails and rent rollerblades and snowboards.

Get a Grip, 821 Skyline Dr., 307/977-3433, is an indoor climbing gym with more than a hundred routes.

SHOPPING

Mountain Woods, 209 S. 2nd St., 307/745-3515, sells a selection of rustic and attractive handcrafted aspen and lodgepole furniture. **Woodscapes,** 1115 Park St., 307/745-9513 or 866/278-9663, features unique inlaid wooden furniture crafted by Dan Ball. Buy hemp garments, imported items, and hippie garb from **Terrapin,** 301 S. 2nd St., 307/745-3027. Art galleries are described under More Laramie Sights.

Bookstores

Laramie is home to several excellent bookstores. The spacious **University Bookstore,** in the Student Union, 307/766-3264, www.uwyobookstore.com, has many regional titles and travel books. **Chickering Bookstore,** 307 S. 2nd, 307/742-8609, is a small and friendly bookshop in downtown Laramie. **Personally Recommended Books,** 105 Ivinson, 307/745-4423, is a relaxing upstairs place to look over local literary favorites, and **The Grand News Stand,** 214 E. Grand Ave., 307/742-5127, has a big magazine selection and lots of Wyoming titles. **Hastings,** 654 N. 3rd St. in Gateway Plaza, 307/745-0312, www.gohastings.com, is a chain store with books, CDs, software, and videos. **Adams and Adams Booksellers,** 216 E. Grand Ave., 307/755-1955, sells used and antiquarian books.

MEDICINE BOW

INFORMATION

The **Laramie Chamber of Commerce,** 800 S. 3rd St., 307/745-7339 or 866/876-1012, www.laramie.org, is open Monday–Friday 8 A.M.–5 P.M. Also look for the chamber visitors center in the **caboose** on the south end of town; open daily 9 A.M.–5 P.M. Memorial Day to Labor Day. If you're planning a trip to the Laramie area, contact the **Albany County Tourism Board,** 307/745-4195 or 800/445-5303, www.laramie-tourism.org for details. The University of Wyoming has its own visitors centers; see the Sights section on the university for location and hours.

If you're heading out to the Medicine Bow Mountains, be sure to stop by the **Medicine Bow-Routt National Forest Supervisor's Office,** 2468 Jackson St., 307/745-2300 or 800/877-9965, www.fs.fed.us/r2/mbr, for maps and up-to-date trail and campground information. The office is open Monday–Friday 8 A.M.–5 P.M. all year, and may also be open Saturday mornings in the summer.

The 100,000-watt **Wyoming Public Radio** station KUWR (91.9 FM, http://uwadmn-web.uwyo.edu/wpr) is based in Laramie, with repeaters throughout Wyoming providing in-depth news and music sans commercials.

Libraries

Albany County Library's Wyoming Room has a big selection of historic books and other documents. It also provides computers with free Internet access. Find it at 310 S. 8th, 307/745-3365, http://acpl.lib.wy.us/info.html. Much more impressive are the eight university libraries (http://www.lib.uwyo.edu) that house more than 1.1 million volumes, including the most complete collection of Wyoming books in existence, plus 150,000 maps and 13,000 periodicals. Most of these publications are in the **William Robertson Coe Library,** 307/766-5312, which also has a map room, an extensive depository of government publications, and the American Heritage Center's outstanding collection of historic books about Wyoming and the West. Also of note are the **Geology Library,** in the Geology Building, 307/766-3374; the **Science and Technology Library,** in the Science Complex, 307/766-5165; and the **Law Library,** in the College of Law, 307/766-2210.

TRANSPORTATION

By Air

Great Lakes Aviation has daily flights between Denver and Laramie Airport, located just west of town on State Hwy. 130. See the Special Topic "Airline Contacts" in the On the Road chapter for more information. **France Flying Service,** 307/324-2361, offers charter and scenic flights.

By Car and Bus

Rent cars at the airport from national agencies Enterprise or Hertz (see the Special Topic "Rental Car Contacts" in the On the Road chapter), or local **McCarthy Rent-A-Car,** 307/745-8921, or **Price King Rent-A-Car,** 307/721-8811.

Greyhound buses, 800/231-2222, www.greyhound.com, stop at the Tumbleweed Express Gas Station on E. Grand at I-80. Buses operate daily in both directions along I-80.

Armadillo Express, 307/634-1123 or 888/256-2967, has daily shuttle vans ($51 one way) to Denver International Airport.

Pole Mountain/Vedauwoo Area

Heading east from Laramie on I-80, the freeway climbs steadily up into the second-growth ponderosa and lodgepole pine forests of the Pole Mountain area. It's a scenic land punctuated by unusual and colorful rock formations. For many years much of the land here belonged to the military and was used as a target and maneuver area for the army's version of off-road vehicles—tanks. Amazingly, the land seems to show little sign of all this abuse today.

Ten miles east of Laramie is the Summit Rest Area, located at the highest point (8,640 feet) along I-80. A 13-foot-tall bronze bust of **Abraham Lincoln** looks over the freeway from atop a granite base. The largest bronze bust in the nation, it was created by Robert I. Russin, former art professor at the university and Wyoming's best-known sculptor. The old road through this pass was known as the Lincoln Highway and was the first transcontinental highway. The sculpture was placed in this area in 1959, on the 150th anniversary of Lincoln's birth. It was moved to the present location when the interstate highway

came through in 1968. The **visitors center** here has information on nearby areas and is open daily 9 A.M.–7 P.M. mid-May through October. Also here is a small theater showing videos.

Choose from four Forest Service campgrounds (most $10; open May–Sept.) in the Pole Mountain/Vedauwoo area, or camp for free on land away from the roads. **Headquarters Trail** extends 4.5 miles from the Summit Rest Area to Headquarters Road. During the winter, Pole Mountain's groomed trails make it a popular cross-country ski area. Many others come to play on the unofficial tubing and tobogganing hill near Happy Jack Trailhead. A $3 day-use fee is charged at trailheads and picnic areas in the Pole Mountain/Vedauwoo area.

East of the summit, I-80 follows a long open plateau and then drops gradually into the shortgrass prairie of southeastern Wyoming via "The Gangplank." The Colorado Rockies form a jagged southern horizon line. This crossing of the Laramie Range was discovered by Gen. Grenville Dodge in 1865. While exploring the

MEDICINE BOW

Vedauwoo Rocks, near Laramie

railroad's new route, an attack by a party of Indians forced his men to flee eastward. In the process they discovered this gentle ramp to the plains of Cheyenne. Unfortunately, today the route is marked for miles by a domino-like line of billboards advertising everything from McDonald's to fireworks. It's too bad the billboards can't topple like dominoes to reveal the expansive grassland beyond!

VEDAUWOO

Just five miles east of the summit you'll find the turnoff to strange rock formations known as Vedauwoo (pronounced "VEE-dah-voo"), a name meaning "earthborn" in Arapaho. In this area, which is considered a sacred place where young Indian men went on vision quests, oddly jumbled rocks form all sorts of shapes: mushrooms, balancing rocks, feminine curves, rounded knolls, lizards, faces, turtles, and anything you might dream up. Imagine it as a Rorschach test. Indians believed that the rocks were created by animal and human spirits. Today, Vedauwoo is considered one of Wyoming's best and most unique places for rock climbing. Climbs go from a difficulty level of 5.0 all the way up to 5.14, with many easy places to practice crack climbs. For more on the area, visit www.vedauwoo.org. Nonclimbers come just to view the rocks, eat a picnic lunch, ride mountain bikes along the dirt roads, hike in the countryside, or scramble up for marvelous vistas of the surrounding land. Vedauwoo Glen Road connects with Happy Jack Road for a nice loop trip. There's a campground right at Vedauwoo. The Forest Service charges a $3 fee for day use.

PYRAMID POWER

Head two miles south from the Vedauwoo exit to one of the strangest monuments in Wyoming: a 60-foot-tall pyramid in the middle of nowhere. The memorial commemorates Oakes and Oliver Ames, two of the most influential figures in building the transcontinental railroad. As a U.S. congressman, Oakes Ames gained passage of a bill that allowed the railroad to sell bonds equal to the amount loaned by the federal government—some $60 million. The company they established to handle this financing was the infamous Credit Mobilier of America. It later came to light that Oakes had bribed fellow congressmen with discounted railroad stock and greatly exaggerated construction costs for his own gain. A congressional investigation labeled Oakes "King of Frauds" and censured him. He died before he could stand trial, and the money was never recovered.

Despite this bit of infamy, nearly $65,000 was spent in 1882 to build this monument to the Ames brothers. It was originally located at the highest elevation of the transcontinental railroad route, near the town of Sherman, a place where trains halted to check their brakes before the long descent on either side. In 1902, the tracks were rerouted a couple of miles to the south, leaving the grandiose pile of rocks by itself. Nothing remains today from the Sherman townsite except a cemetery. The Ames Monument seems to bring out two conflicting emotions: dismay at the obscenity of this monstrosity and amusement at the irony that so much money was wasted on a self-aggrandizing monument soon abandoned even by the railroad the Ames brothers had helped build.

Medicine Bow Vicinity

Two roads head west from Laramie. Most people follow I-80 straight to Rawlins, but U.S. 30/287 (the old Lincoln Hwy.) gets you there in about the same time and provides a strong flavor of the Old West. It doesn't get much traffic and offers grand big-sky country. State Hwy. 34 heads northeast from U.S. 30 near the dot on the map called **Bosler,** climbing over the low mountains to Wheatland 50 miles away. It's a pretty drive with little traffic and is worth a detour to visit **Sybille Wildlife Research and Conservation Education Unit,** 26 miles up the road, where the endangered black-footed ferrets are raised. (The center is described in the Southeast Wyoming chapter.) Two miles east of Sybille is the Johnson Creek Wildlife Habitat Management Area, a popular place for fishing. There are no trails, but hiking is easy in the open country.

ROCK RIVER

This almost ghost town of 180 lonely souls is home to the little **Rock River Museum** at 2nd Street and Avenue C, 307/378-2205; open Wed.–Sat. 10 A.M.–3 P.M. and Sun. noon–3 P.M. from late May to early Sept. Inside you'll find exhibits on dinosaurs, a collection of phosphorescent rocks, and local memorabilia, including a safe blown up by Butch Cassidy. A statue of a Triceratops stands in the town park. The town also has a bar, motel, general store/laundromat, restaurant, and a pretty red-doored church.

Longhorn Lodge Motel and Restaurant 362 N. 4th, 307/378-2555, charges $30–40 s or $37–47 d for log cabin units. A good restaurant is on the premises. **Dodge Creek Ranch,** 307/322-2345, www.dodge-creek-ranch.com, is 35 miles northeast of Rock River and 40 miles southwest of Wheatland on State Hwy. 34. This cattle ranch offers ranch recreation but is probably one of the only Wyoming ranches with no horses.

West of Rock River, the road sails through desolate treeless country, with sagebrush to the horizon and the impressive summit of Elk Mountain rising to the southwest. The Union Pacific Railroad parallels the highway most of the way, and antelope glance up at the passing trains. Anyone coming through in the winter will appreciate the miles of snow fences along the south side of the highway. Still, the snow streams over the roadway almost constantly.

COMO BLUFF

Halfway between the towns of Rock River and Medicine Bow on U.S. 30/287 is a long, low ridge known as Como Bluff. There isn't much to distinguish this from countless other buttes in the West, but paleontologists consider it one of the most important sites ever discovered, a place one author likened to Darwin's *Origin of the Species* in terms of its impact on scientific thought. This was the first large discovery of dinosaurs anywhere, and the first place *Diplodocus* dinosaurs— the largest ever found—were discovered. The mammals discovered here are prized around the world and include all but three of the 250 known Jurassic mammals found in North America. Combined, the dinosaur and mammal fossils from Como Bluff make up a major part of the collections of Yale's Peabody Museum, the Smithsonian Institution, the New York Museum of Natural History, the National Museum in Washington, D.C., and many others around the world.

History

In July 1877, Professor Othniel Charles Marsh of Yale College received a letter from two Wyoming men calling themselves Harlow and Edwards. They told of finding

> *a large number of fossils, supposed to be those of the Megatherium, although there is no one here sufficient of a geologist to state for a certainty. We have excavated one (1) partly, and know where there is several others that we have not, as yet, done any work upon. . . . We are desirous of disposing of what fossils we have, and also, the secret of the others. We are*

working men and are not able to present them as a gift, and if we can sell the secret of the fossil bed, and procure work in excavating others we would like to do so. We have said nothing to any-one as yet. . . . We would be pleased to hear from you, as you are well known as an enthusiastic geologist, and a man of means, both of which we are desirous of finding—more especially the latter.

Marsh was in stiff competition with other paleontologists around the country, and his rival, Professor E. D. Cope from the Philadelphia Academy of Sciences, had just scooped him on a major dinosaur discovery in Colorado. The letter from "Harlow and Edwards" piqued Marsh's curiosity. An assistant sent to investigate wrote that the find was indeed substantive and suggested that Marsh immediately hire the two discoverers—actually two railroad employees, William Reed and William Carlin—to keep them from revealing the secret to others. Reed would later work for many years as a collector for the University of Wyoming and eventually as an instructor in geology and curator of the Geology Museum on the Laramie campus.

Work began almost immediately and continued right through the winter blizzards, but despite efforts to keep the find a secret, Professor Cope soon had his own men working at Como Bluff. The rivalry almost came to blows, and Marsh's men made it a point to smash any bones left behind after their digging was complete and to backfill the quarries with rocks, even if their rivals were working below. Excavations continued until 1889, by which time most of the finest specimens had been unearthed.

Today geology and paleontology classes still visit Como Bluff, but the quarries where the bones were found are now abandoned and can't be seen from the road. Como Bluff itself is visible a little more than one mile north of U.S. 30, and a sign describes the site. Travelers will want to stop to see **"the world's oldest building"** at Como Bluffs, a now-closed museum/gift shop built from dinosaur bones.

MEDICINE BOW

The little town of Medicine Bow (pop. 270) is the sort of place where headlines in the weekly *Medicine Bow Post* complain of dogs getting into garbage or barking at kids. For the most part it's a nondescript town with old boxlike houses and newer boxlike trailers. If Garrison Keillor had been born in Wyoming he'd be positively rhapsodic about this little place that time forgot. Medicine Bow is not unlike hundreds of barely

THE "TOWN" OF MEDICINE BOW

Town, as they called it, pleased me the less, the longer I saw it. But until our language stretches itself and takes in a new word or closer fit, town will have to do for the name of such a place as Medicine Bow. I have seen and slept in many like it since. Scattered wide, they littered the frontier from the Columbia to the Rio Grande, from the Missouri to the Sierras. They lay stark, dotted over a planet of treeless dust, like soiled packs of cards. Each was similar to the next, as one old five-spot of cards resembles another. . . . Yet this wretched husk of squalor spent thought upon appearances; many houses in it wore a false front to seem as if they were two stories high. There they stood, rearing their pitiful masquerade amid a fringe of old tin cans, while at their very doors began a world of crystal light, a land without end, a space across which Noah and Adam might come straight from Genesis. Into that space went wandering a road, over a hill and down out of sight, and up again smaller in the distance, and down once more, and up once more, straining the eyes, and so away.

—from Owen Wister's *The Virginian*

© DON PITCHER

the Virginian Hotel, Medicine Bow

surviving old settlements all over the West, but it was here that novelist Owen Wister had his legendary cowboy hero, the Virginian, face off with Trampas. Over a game of cards, Trampas calls the Virginian a "son-of-a-bitch," leading to the famous encounter in which the Virginian pulls his pistol and says, "When you call me that, smile!" It remains one of the classic lines in American folklore. *The Virginian* became the prototype for the modern Western and was later made into three movies and a TV series.

History

The town of Medicine Bow began in the 1870s as a Union Pacific pumping station along Medicine Bow River and grew into a local supply point and minor army garrison. It has always been a center for the ranchers who run thousands of head of livestock in the surrounding countryside, so it was a logical place for Wister to base his cowboy hero. During the 1930s, Medicine Bow prospered because it lay along the Lincoln Highway (U.S. 30), but following completion of I-80, it lapsed into decay. The coal mines of Hanna (20 miles west) and ura-

nium and oil explorations in Shirley Basin led to temporary energy booms, but the economy has now returned to its ranching base.

Sights

Medicine Bow's main attraction is the boxy, three-story **Virginian Hotel,** built in 1909—seven years after *The Virginian* came out. At the time, it was the largest hotel between Denver and Salt Lake City. It's still a marvelous building, so take a look around, even if you aren't planning on staying here. The Virginian's authentic old-time bar is one of the best in Wyoming. Just down the street is the modern **Diplodocus Bar** (alias "the Dip"), 307/379-2312, containing the largest jade bar in existence, cut from a 4.5-ton jade boulder discovered near Lander. Look down for the only hand-painted dance floor west of the Mississippi. While you're here for a beer, be sure to ask owner Bill Bennett to show you his unusually intricate woodcarvings.

Across from the hotel is the **Medicine Bow Museum,** housed in the old wooden railroad depot (circa 1913). Out front is a cabin built by Owen Wister—it stood in Jackson Hole until being moved here in 1976—and a petrified-wood monument to the novelist. The museum contains the typical things found in small-town museums: various homesteading items, a lamb warmer, a coyote scare made from sawdust and firecrackers, and old fire equipment. It's kind of like wandering through an old attic where you wonder how half the stuff was ever used. There's an old caboose on the side. The museum, 307/379-2383, www.medicinebow.org/museum.htm, is open daily 10 A.M.–5 P.M. Memorial Day to Labor Day, and Monday–Thursday 10 A.M.–3:30 P.M. the rest of the year.

The wind blows almost constantly in Medicine Bow, making it a good place to harness the wind for electricity. Five miles south of the town are 10 **wind turbines,** each of which produces 660 kilowatts. Together they supply enough energy for 1,200 homes in Colorado's fast-growing front-range cities. The turbines are owned by the Platte River Power Authority, www.prpa.org.

Research in the 1970s showed that this area was perfect for windmills because it's one of the windiest spots in the nation. In 1982, the U.S. Department of the Interior built two of the largest wind generators in the world, each reaching 400 feet tall. Unfortunately, the turbines proved unwieldy embarrassments and were abandoned by the government when it discovered that repairs would be prohibitively expensive. One of the $6 million turbines was blasted over with dynamite and sold for $13,000 on the scrap market in 1988. The remaining turbine produced electricity until a 1994 storm destroyed the blades.

Practicalities

Rooms at the historic **Virginian Hotel,** 307/379-2377, are remarkably inexpensive, starting at just $20 s for a tiny room with a twin bed and bath down the hall, or $55 d for a larger room with private bath. Sleep in the two-bedroom suite where Owen Wister stayed for $65 s or d. This is a delightfully old-fashioned place with a grandma's-house feeling, but the rooms lack TVs or phones, and things can get

noisy when downstairs bar patrons shift into high gear. If you miss your TV, try a motel room in the annex for $45 s or d. The downstairs restaurant provides good home cooking, or you can tip a beer in the old-time bar. A few doors away, **Trampas Lodge,** 307/379-2280, has rooms with private baths, fridges, and cable TV for $30 s or $35 d. Pitch your tent or park RVs for free at the town park.

Medicine Bow Days is the annual celebration in town, held at the end of June and including a parade, picnic, bull-chip-throwing contest, live music, and dancing. Learn more about Medicine Bow online at www.medicinebow.org.

SHIRLEY BASIN

State Hwy. 487 heads north from Medicine Bow across vast and remote Shirley Basin, with some of the finest cattle rangeland in Wyoming. The road is smooth with wide shoulders (perfect for bikes), and the vistas are dramatic—colorful badlands, rolling hills covered with sage and grass, and cottonwood-lined creeks. There's lots of wildlife here, too, especially antelope and deer. The basin has large prairie-dog towns, and the endangered black-footed ferrets were released here in the early 1990s. Sylvatic plague later decimated prairie-dog populations, but 18 or so ferrets still survive in Shirley Basin, although it's highly unlikely that you would see them.

Extensive deposits of uranium have been discovered in Shirley Basin—some of the largest and richest in the world—but low prices and an oversupply have all but halted the uranium-mining business. Ask in Medicine Bow for directions to the petrified forest. Nearly every yard in town has a piece out front.

HANNA

The town of Hanna (pop. 900) lies at the center of one of the state's major coal fields. There are lots of mobile homes and company housing in Hanna, but there is nothing particularly interesting about the town, unless you care to check out the miners memorials or the enormous

BLACK-FOOTED FERRETS

On September 25, 1981, near Meeteetse, Wyoming, a dog walked up to its master with a strange creature in his mouth. It was a black-footed ferret, a sleek, black-masked animal last seen in 1972 and feared extinct. Biologists soon discovered that a nearby prairie dog colony housed the only living population of ferrets, the world's rarest mammal. Ferrets eat prairie dogs and were once found in prairie dog colonies from Saskatchewan to Texas. The colonies were huge—one along the Cheyenne River in eastern Wyoming stretched for a hundred miles—but the prairie dogs went the way of many other animals, hunted and poisoned by settlers and their land taken over by plowed fields. Although still present in Wyoming, prairie dog colonies are now far smaller and more isolated. The population of ferrets declined with their shrinking food source.

With the discovery of ferrets living near Meeteetse, national attention focused on saving the population from extinction. A 1985 outbreak of canine distemper threatened to kill all the remaining wild ferrets, so all 18 survivors were captured and taken to the Wyoming Game and Fish Wildlife Research Unit at Sybille. After inoculations, an ambitious captive breeding program was begun. Only five of the animals actually reproduced, but the program proved so successful that the population was split up to reduce the chance that all might be killed in an accident such as a fire or in an outbreak of disease. Ferrets are now raised not only at Sybille but also at breeding facilities and zoos throughout the country.

Reintroducing Ferrets

The captive breeding program has proven highly successful, but the ultimate goal is to reestablish at least 10 healthy ferret populations in the wild. Beginning in 1991, ferrets were released in Shirley Basin (north of the town of Medicine Bow). Unfortunately, sylvatic plague swept through the area, killing both ferrets and their prey, prairie dogs. Fewer than 20 ferrets survive in Shirley Basin.

Most other efforts at reintroduction have also been hampered by plague, but ferrets are doing well in South Dakota, with limited success in Montana, Arizona, Utah, Colorado, and Mexico. A total of 300–350 ferrets now live in the wild at eight different locations. There are plans to eventually release them in Wyoming at Thunder Basin National Grassland if the population of prairie dogs recovers from plague outbreaks and hunting.

Because of their relatively short life span (three years in the wild) and their susceptibility to diseases and predators such as owls and coyotes, ferrets will almost certainly remain endangered for decades to come. The plague, continued destruction of prairie dog colonies by "varmint hunters," and poisoning by ranchers have all made it more and more difficult to find places to release wild ferrets. The habitat is becoming increasingly fragmented into "islands" separated by areas where the prairie dogs have been killed off; less than 10 large and healthy black-tailed prairie dog populations still exist in all of North America! It would indeed be sad if we managed to breed black-footed ferrets in zoos, but they were unable to survive in the wild because of habitat loss.

The **Sybille Wildlife Research and Conservation Education Unit,** on State Hwy. 34 halfway between Bosler and Wheatland, 307/322-2571, is open daily 8:30 A.M.–4:30 P.M. April to mid-November; closed the rest of the year. Inside are exhibits and videos, along with a live black-footed ferret. Ferret out more information at www.blackfootedferret.org.

MEDICINE BOW

Union Pacific snowplow. Mining has been a mainstay of the local economy since coal was discovered here in the late 1800s. Two disastrous explosions in 1903 and 1908 killed 228 miners, and two Hanna monuments commemorate the men who died. The mines remained open until 1954 and were reactivated in the 1970s. The last underground mine closed in 2001. Only the Arch Coal strip mine, 23 miles west, remains open, but high costs associated with the depth of the coal here may force its closure.

The mining ghost town of **Carbon**—established in 1868 as the state's first coal town—once stood a few miles east of Hanna. The coal ran out in 1902, and today only a few ruins and the graveyard remain.

Hanna Basin Museum, on Front St. below the bridge, 307/324-3915, has local memorabilia, including a collection of mine photos and details on the mine disasters. The building once served as a miner's cottage for the old company town and is open Friday–Sunday 1–5 P.M. in summer, and Fridays 1–5 P.M. the rest of the year.

Practicalities

Golden Rule Motel, 307/325-6525, charges $32 s or $34–36 d, for basic prefab rooms. **Home Cafe,** 307/325-6355, and **Sharon's Place,** 307/325-6022, serve meals. Hanna's fine **recreation center** houses a sauna, swimming pool, hot tub, and gym. Groceries are available at **The Super Market.** Other businesses include a hardware store, two liquor stores, a video shop, and a bank, but no ATM.

ARLINGTON

Approximately 30 miles west of Laramie, I-80 drivers are suddenly confronted with a strange apparition: towering **windmills** lining the crest of Foote Creek Rim. Completed in 1998, these 69 turbines crank out 41,000 kilowatt-hours of electricity, enough to power 20,000 homes. One of the windiest spots in America, this hilltop location is perfect for energy generation; the wind farm here is the biggest outside California.

Below the windmills is the freeway off-ramp called Arlington, a tiny place with a surprising amount of history. Park RVs ($17) or pitch tents

abandoned motel near Hanna

($12) at **Arlington Outpost Campground,** 307/378-2350; open mid-May to mid-Oct.

Rock Creek Stage Station

You'll find several buildings from the Rock Creek Stage Station, which stood along the Overland Route, including one of the oldest structures in Wyoming, a log cabin built around 1860. Also in Arlington, on private land south of the freeway, is a combination blacksmith shop/dance hall/gambling palace.

In 1865, Indians attacked a wagon train near the Rock Creek Stage Station and captured two girls, Mary and Lizzie Fletcher. Mary was eventually sold to a white trader, but Lizzie remained with the Arapahoes for the rest of her life. It wasn't until 35 years after their parting that Mary discovered her sister alive and living on the Wind River Reservation. Having grown accustomed to the Arapaho way of life and enjoying a high status in the community, Lizzie chose to stay in her home. She is buried next to her husband, Broken Horn, in the St. Stephen's Mission Cemetery.

ELK MOUNTAIN

The tiny settlement of Elk Mountain (pop. 190) stands just off I-80 halfway between Laramie and Rawlins. Although almost within sight of the freeway, the town seems a world apart. Big cottonwoods line the quiet streets, and the Medicine Bow River, home of blue-ribbon trout fishing, flows right through town. Several buildings are noteworthy: the small New England–style community church, the Elk Mountain Trading Company (with a few groceries), and an enormous log barn are still in perfect condition after more than a century. Directly behind town is the rounded, snow-capped 11,156-foot summit of Elk Mountain, one of the most prominent natural landmarks anywhere along I-80. Unusual clouds frequently hang off its peak, making it a valuable site for the University of Wyoming's atmospheric research program. Ask in town for access information to the mountain; you'll need to get permission from local ranchers.

Accommodations and Food

Built in 1905, the **Elk Mountain Hotel,** 307/348-7774 or 888/348-7774, www.elkmountainho-tel.com, is a grand old hotel that underwent a major renovation in 2002. All rooms now have elegant furnishings and private baths. Rates are $80–100 s or d, including a continental breakfast. The honeymoon suite has a king bed and hot tub, $140 d. The hotel dining room features pressed tin ceilings, a log-burning fireplace, and delicious entrées such as Asian marinated salmon, prime rib, or bison tenderloin; $15–30. Next to the hotel is **Garden Spot Pavilion,** a former dance hall that in the 1930s and '40s attracted the likes of Louis Armstrong, Tommy Dorsey, Glenn Miller, and Lawrence Welk. Renovations were in the works in 2002, and the building may become a spa facility for Elk Mountain Hotel.

Founded in 1866, **Elk Mountain Ranch,** 307/348-7440, www.elkmountain.com, is a working bison ranch that offers fly-fishing vacation packages (starting at $1,250 for four nights) and trophy big game hunts.

Wild Wonder Cafe, 307/348-7478, serves three meals a day and has an adjacent convenience store.

Into the Country

Five miles west of town, a stone monument marks the site of **Fort Halleck,** a short-lived military post built in 1862 to guard the Overland Trail. With the arrival of the transcontinental railroad, it was abandoned in 1866 and its fixtures moved east to Fort Buford (later called Fort Sanders), near present-day Laramie.

Head south from Elk Mountain on Pass Creek Road (Rd. 404) for a wonderful round-the-mountain drive. The gravel road curves south past Elk Mountain, then west along the willow-lined Pass Creek to a junction with State Hwy. 130, where you can continue to Saratoga. This little-traveled road offers open hills with wide vistas of the mountains and plains. While you listen to meadowlarks singing and wind rustling through the grass, you can watch—as the song says—the deer and the antelope play. Not even a line of telephone poles breaks the view, and seldom is heard a discouraging word.

Medicine Bow Mountains and Vicinity

Medicine Bow-Routt National Forest is scattered over four disjunctive areas in Wyoming. The northern portion—the Laramie Mountains—is discussed in the Central Wyoming chapter; the Pole Mountain section is described under Laramie earlier in this chapter. The other two mountainous areas are west of Laramie: the Medicine Bow Mountains, locally called the Snowy Range, and the Sierra Madre. The Forest Service has controlled most of this land since 1902, although the name and boundaries have changed over the years. Mining was the big attraction in the late 1800s, but the major gold and copper deposits were quickly mined out, and logging became the primary use of this mountainous country. Between 1867 and 1940, millions of railroad ties were brought out of the Laramie and Medicine Bow Mountains by tie hacks who logged almost every drivable creek they could find. The area provided ties for not only Wyoming but western Nebraska and Colorado as well. Logging for lumber is

still important in the Medicine Bow-Routt National Forest, but recreation is increasingly becoming the dominant use of the forest as more people discover this scenic country. The supervisor's office for Medicine Bow-Routt National Forest in Wyoming is located in Laramie, 307/745-2300 or 800/877-9965, www.fs.fed.us/r2/mbr, with district offices in Saratoga, Encampment, and Douglas. Pick up a copy of the forest map ($7) at any of these offices before heading out.

LARAMIE PLAINS

Heading west from Laramie on State Hwy. 130, you pass through some of the most desolate country in Wyoming, with flat grassland stretching in all directions, interrupted by mountains to the east, south, and west. An enormous windswept bowl here—**Big Hollow**—was created by howling winds during the last ice age. The only other place like this is

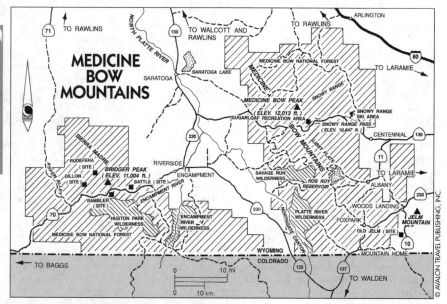

in Russia. Laramie Basin is also unique in having the highest short-grass prairie in the world, some 7,200 feet above sea level. Eleven miles west of Laramie, State Hwy. 130 crosses the historic **Overland Trail,** which carried emigrants, mail, and freight west between 1862 and 1868, when the railroad replaced it. The wagon ruts are still visible, with markers tracing the old route. As you approach the Medicine Bow Mountains, the highway dips down to sample the tree-lined beauty of Little Laramie Creek and then begins the long ascent to Snowy Range Pass.

ALBANY

State Hwy. 11 heads south along Little Laramie Creek to the foothills town of Albany, passing rolling grass and sagebrush country with pine-topped hills. Old ranches are sprinkled around this gorgeous little valley. Rustic cabins with shared bath at the **Albany Lodge,** 307/745-5782, cost $40 for up to four. They also have a four-person cabin with private bath, microwave, and fridge for $85 ($100 in winter), and an eight-person apartment with kitchenette for $100 ($120 in winter). Both of these have a three-night minimum in winter. The nicest option is a large cabin that sleeps 12 and has a full kitchen for $200, or $250 in winter when there's a five-night minimum stay. Albany Lodge is closed mid-April through May.

A dirt road continues south from Albany to Woods Landing, but blowing snows often cause its closure in the winter. Albany is a favorite base for snowmobilers, and the lodge has rentals and gas.

Three miles east of Albany, **Double Mule Shoe Ranch,** 307/742-5629, has two modern cabins with kitchens and private baths. The smaller one sleeps four for $65; the largest is $95 for four people, plus $10 per person for additional guests (seven maximum).

Heaven's Little Wonder B&B, 307/742-2247, www.heavenslittlewonder.com, has four guest rooms with an old-timey decor and private baths. Rates are $50 s or d, including breakfast. Dinners are also available with advance notice.

CENTENNIAL

Thirty-five miles west of Laramie, State Hwy. 130 widens to include the funky old mining town of Centennial (pop. 190). Situated at the foot of the Snowy Range, Centennial was founded in 1875 and gained its name the following year—the centennial of the founding of America. (James Michener claimed not to have known of the town when he wrote his novel of the same name about an early Rocky Mountain town.) Prospectors came here in search of gold. That first year the Centennial Mine produced more than $90,000 worth, but when the vein ran out, only a few people stayed around. Another short boom created by infusions of cash from a Boston financier brought a fish hatchery, hotels, mining explorations, and an exclusive country club to Centennial, but the bubble burst again when the expected gold deposits failed to materialize. Eventually, Centennial became a minor ranching center. Today it's a tourist way station with a devil-may-care mix of old log homes and house trailers.

Sights

The small **Nici Self Museum** (nici is pronounced NEE-chee) in the 1907 railroad depot building contains exhibits on the area's mining, ranching, and logging history. It's open Saturday–Sunday 1–4 P.M. July through Labor Day, and by appointment the rest of the year (307/742-7158). Out front are a Union Pacific caboose and various aging farm implements. Check out the "police car" as you roll through town. Also worth a look is **J-N Mercantile,** 207/745-0001, with an odd amalgamation of hardware, jewelry, coffee, and antiques, including an impressive old back bar.

Accommodations and Food

Old Corral Hotel and Steakhouse, 307/745-5918 or 800/678-2024, www.oldcorral.com, is the biggest place in town, with 35 Western-decor rooms in the lodge for $79 d, including a full breakfast, an outdoor hot tub, and a game room with billiards and darts. Guests can settle into the theater room for movies on the big-screen television; they have 300 flicks to choose from. The restaurant, which is open for three

MEDICINE BOW

meals a day, serves outstanding steaks, chicken, and seafood in a comfortably Old West atmosphere, and the bar has occasional live music on weekends. An ATM is here.

Friendly Motel, 307/742-6033, has eight motel rooms for $48 s or $56 d, and a cabin for $80. The latter sleeps six and requires a two-night minimum. Open year-round. They also operate Spencer Mountain Cafe on the premises. Across the road is **Trading Post Restaurant & Lounge,** 307/721-5074, where you'll find country, blues, or rock most Saturday nights.

Mountain View Historic Hotel, 307/742-5476 or 888/400-9953, www.mtnviewhotel.com, is a classic building from 1907. Most guest rooms ($55–65 s or d) have microwaves and fridges, and three suites ($85–95 s or d) are also available, two with full kitchens. A comfy espresso shop on the premises serves a breakfast and lunch menu.

Built as a bank in 1903, **Centennial Trust B&B** contains two guest rooms furnished in a Victorian style. Open all year, and kids are welcome. Call 307/721-4090 for rates.

East of Centennial, **Vee Bar Guest Ranch,** 307/745-7036 or 800/483-3227, www.vee-bar.com, offers luxury at the foot of the Snowy Range. Stay in comfortable old cabins or in a grand old lodge listed on the National Register of Historic Places. The emphasis is on horseback riding, but the Vee Bar also offers hayrides, trap shooting, trout fishing, and hiking. When the day is done, relax tired muscles in the outdoor hot tub. The 26,000-acre ranch attracts a clientele that includes celebrities and politicians. Accommodations from mid-June to early September cost $2,900 for two people for six nights, all-inclusive. A less expensive option is to stay for Saturday night only; $150 d with breakfast. During the winter, the ranch has nightly B&B lodging for $100 d.

Rainbow Valley Resort, 307/745-0368, www.rainbowvalleyresort.com, is one mile west of Centennial and another mile up Rainbow Valley Road. Accommodations include eight cabins. Rates are $75–95 d, or $135–160 for four-person cabins, and $240 for a three-bedroom rental that sleeps 10 and has a jetted tub.

All of these include full kitchens, and most have fireplaces. Guests have access to a hot tub and private fishing pond.

SNOWY RANGE

Between the Laramie Plains and the valley created by the upper North Platte River lie a portion of the Medicine Bow Mountains that is locally called the Snowy Range. This name is appropriate because it can snow here at any time of the year. Ten-foot drifts are not uncommon in the winter, and snow remains on high passes until late summer. Just southwest of the Snowy Range are the **Savage Run Wilderness** (15,260 acres) and the **Platte River Wilderness** (22,749 acres), both lying close to the Wyoming–Colorado border. Get maps of these from local Forest Service offices. Most visitors simply enjoy the drive over the mountains and the chance to camp beside an alpine lake with a backdrop of 12,000-foot mountains. Numerous short hiking trails and outstanding trout fishing make this a favorite spot for locals.

Information

The Forest Service has detailed maps and helpful brochures at its Laramie office, 2468 Jackson St., 307/745-2300 or 800/877-9965, www.fs.fed.us/r2/mbr. You'll also find Forest Service information centers on both sides of the Snowy Range along State Hwy. 130. The **Centennial Visitor Center,** 307/742-6023, one mile west of Centennial, is open daily 9 A.M.–4 P.M. Memorial Day to Labor Day and Saturday–Sunday 9 A.M.–4 P.M. in winter. **Brush Creek Visitor Center,** 307/326-5562, 20 miles east of Saratoga, is open daily 8 A.M.–5 P.M. Memorial Day through September. Saturday evening interpretive programs, including full-moon walks, are offered at both the Centennial and Brush Creek Visitor Centers during the summer. Other full-moon walks are offered January–October at various sites around the forest; contact the Laramie Ranger District office for details, 307/745-2300 or 800/877-9965, www.fs.fed.us/r2/mbr/rd-laramie.

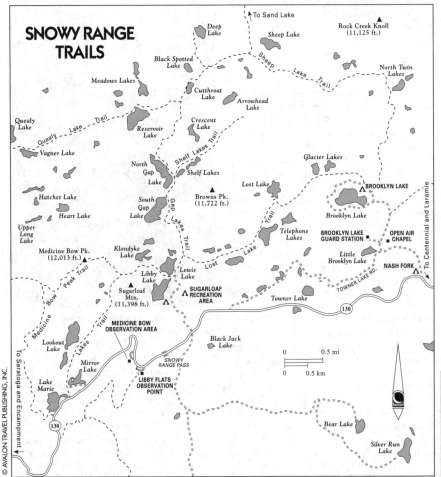

SNOWY RANGE TRAILS

To Sand Lake

Deep Lake

Sheep Lake

Rock Creek Knoll (11,125 ft.)

Black Spotted Lake

Sheep Lake Trail

North Twin Lakes

Meadows Lakes

Cutthroat Lake

Arrowhead Lake

Quealy Lake

Qualy Lake Trail

Reservoir Lake

Crescent Lake

Vagner Lake

Shelf Lakes Trail

North Gap Lake

Shelf Lakes

Glacier Lakes

Lost Lake

BROOKLYN LAKE

Hatchet Lake

South Gap Lake

Gap Lakes Trail

Browns Pk. (11,722 ft.)

Brooklyn Lake

To Centennial and Laramie

Heart Lake

Upper Long Lake

Telephone Lakes

BROOKLYN LAKE GUARD STATION

OPEN AIR CHAPEL

Medicine Bow Pk. (12,013 ft.)

Klondyke Lake

Little Brooklyn Lake

Medicine Bow Peak Trail

Libby Lake

Lewis Lake

Lost Lake Trail

NASH FORK

Sugarloaf Mtn. (11,398 ft.)

SUGARLOAF RECREATION AREA

TOWNER LAKE RD.

MEDICINE BOW OBSERVATION AREA

Towner Lake

130

Medicine Bow Lakes Trail

Lookout Lake

Black Jack Lake

Mirror Lake

SNOWY RANGE PASS

0   0.5 mi

Lake Marie

LIBBY FLATS OBSERVATION POINT

0   0.5 km

130

Bear Lake

Silver Run Lake

© AVALON TRAVEL PUBLISHING, INC.

To Saratoga and Encampment

MOON

MEDICINE BOW

Over the Top

The 40-mile drive on State Hwy. 130 over the Snowy Range is one of the most dramatic in Wyoming and is designated a National Scenic Byway. The pass is closed by snow from late October to Memorial Day but remains open year-round to just beyond the Snowy Range Ski Area on the east side and 20 miles up from the west side. Higher-elevation parts of the road are popular with snowmobilers and cross-country skiers. West of Centennial, the highway climbs sharply through lodgepole and spruce forests to beautiful

Snowy Range Pass at 10,847 feet (second highest in the state). Even taking a short hike is likely to leave you a bit out of breath unless you're acclimated to the altitude. Before heading up the road, pick up a brochure on the scenic byway from one of the local visitors centers or Forest Service offices; it details sights along the way.

Be sure to stop at **Sugarloaf Recreation Area,** just east of the pass. Sharp, glacially carved spires rise above the small lakes, and islands of stunted Engelmann spruce and subalpine fir dot the alpine country. Trails head out to nearby lakes and flower-covered alpine meadows. At the summit, a viewing platform provides panoramic vistas of **Libby Flats,** massive Medicine Bow Peak, and the valleys on both sides. Pull off at the Medicine Bow Peak Observation Point for a three-quarter-mile hike to the picturesque remains of the old **Red Mask Mine.** Just west of here, **Mirror Lake** and **Lake Marie** are two of the most photographed spots in Wyoming, with a spectacular backdrop of steep mountain faces reflected in the dark blue lake waters. Campgrounds and picnic areas are all along here. A wheelchair-accessible path leads along one shore of Lake Marie, and the west parking lot acts as a trailhead for the path up **Medicine Bow Peak.** On the western side of the pass, the highway drops steadily down through the forest, eventually reaching the rolling sage and grass of the Upper North Platte River Valley. A small recreation area at **French Creek** provides an accessible fishing pier and interpretive signs. Stop at the **Brush Creek Visitor Center** on the western end for directions to **Kennaday Peak Lookout,** one of the few fire lookouts still staffed in Wyoming. It's open Friday–Monday 10 A.M.–5 P.M., mid-June through October, and is accessible by high-clearance cars. No RVs.

Mirror Lake is nestled in the Snowy Range, near Laramie.

Route 230

Another route west is State Hwy. 230. While this highway is not as dramatic as the Snowy Pass trek, it's open year-round and is still quite scenic. The road curves around the southern end of the Snowy Range and passes through tiny Woods Landing en route to the Colorado border. This is the only real settlement between Laramie and Encampment—a distance of 87 miles.

Woods Landing Resort comprises most of the town, with a combination country store/lodge/gas station/café/bar, 307/745-9638, www.woodslanding.com. Park RVs for $15, or stay in their rustic cabins for $30–40 d; the larger ones contain kitchenettes, but all use a shared bath facility. Two recently built cabins are much nicer and have decks, queen or king beds, kitchenettes, and private baths; $90 d. RV and tent sites are $15, a tepee is available for $25, and showers cost $5 if you aren't staying here. The

floor of the bar was built atop 24 boxcar springs—courtesy of railroad workers—so the dance floor really starts rocking on Saturday nights when country-and-western bands play. Anglers will find excellent fishing for brown trout in the nearby Big Laramie River.

Several old clapboard buildings from the mining ghost town of **Old Jelm** lie on private property four miles west of Woods Landing. The university's **Jelm Mountain Infrared Observatory** is up a five-mile dirt road from here. Call the university at 307/766-6150 for a tour of the infrared telescope facilities.

Beyond Woods Landing, State Hwy. 230 dips south and passes several mountain lodges including **WyColo Lodge,** 307/755-5160, just two miles north of the state line. Here, you'll find three rustic cabins with a shared bathhouse for $35 s or d. These are mainly used by hunters and hardy snowmobilers who bring their own bedding. Rooms in the house are $55–85 d with private baths. A two-night minimum is required in the winter. WyColo also houses a bar and restaurant and has summertime ATV rentals and wintertime snowmobile rentals. The lodge is open year-round.

South of **Mountain Home,** the road continues into Colorado for nine miles along Colorado Hwy. 127, then back north on Colorado Hwy. 125 for another nine miles before again crossing into Wyoming on State Hwy. 230. Much of this is open rangeland with hills on either side. Only a few abandoned cabins and fences mark the presence of humans on this vast landscape. The huge white hip-roofed barn of the Big Creek Ranch is one of the most beautiful in Wyoming. Turn around for outstanding views of the Colorado Rockies. See Stephen Metzger's *Moon Handbooks Colorado* (www.moon.com) for details on sights to the south.

Camping

Twenty-five different Forest Service campgrounds dot the Medicine Bow Mountains. Most of these are open June–October, but the season varies depending on snow conditions and budget constraints. A few of the campgrounds—those with no water or trash pickup—are free, but most cost $10 per night. Because of heavy use during the summer, you should arrive at the most popular sites early in the day. Four campgrounds along State Hwy. 130 over the Snowy Range—Brooklyn Lake, Libby Creek-Willow, Ryan Park, and Sugarloaf—can be reserved ($9 fee) at 518/885-3639 or 877/444-6777, www.reserveusa.com. In addition to the official campgrounds, dispersed camping is permitted in most areas as long as you're off the main roads, although not along the crest of the Snowy Range. Check with local Forest Service offices for areas closed to dispersed camping. **Campfire talks** are given during the summer; visitors centers have the details.

Cabins

The Forest Service rents out several historic structures in the Medicine Bow mountains, but for all of these you'll need to bring bedding or sleeping bags, plus personal supplies. The **Bow River Ranger Station** is 15 miles south of Elk Mountain on Forest Rd. 101 and sleeps up to eight people for $80 per night. The cabin has two bedrooms and a kitchen, plus electricity and running water. A two-night minimum stay is required, and the cabin is available year-round. Get details at 307/326-525, www.fs.fed.us/r2/mbr/rd-bch.

Built in 1931, **Little Brooklyn Lake Guard Station** sits near the crest of the Snowy Range and can accommodate seven people for $40 per night. It's especially popular with cross-country skiers in the winter but is available year-round. **Spruce Mountain Fire Lookout Tower** is seven miles west of Albany on a gravel road. No longer used for fire detection, the tower can sleep two people and is available mid-June through September for $40 per night. You'll need to bring water. Not far away is the **Keystone Ranger Station,** eight miles west of Albany. The cabin is available mid-November through April, with access primarily by cross-country skis or snowmobile. It can accommodate up to eight people for $120 per night and has electricity, running water, and a full bathroom, plus a large wood-burning stove and complete kitchen. Get details on these last three cabins at 307/745-2300 or 800/877-9965, www.fs.fed.us/r2/mbr/rd-laramie.

Mountain Lodges

At an elevation of 10,000 feet, **Snowy Mountain Lodge,** 307/742-7669 or 866/467-6699, www.snowymountainlodge.com, is just one mile beyond the Snowy Range Ski Area and seven miles west of Centennial. Built as a University of Wyoming science camp in 1927, the 9,000-square-foot lodge was totally refurbished in 2002 but still retains its rustic charm. There's a grand stone fireplace, teak furniture, a pool table made in 1862, a gift shop, and a restaurant that serves three meals a day in the winter. Dinners feature steaks and Alaskan salmon, with entrées costing $15–25. The lodge is a great stop for snowmobilers or cross-country skiers. More than 300 miles of snowmobile trails fan out from here, and snowmobile rentals and tours are available, along with fuel. Snowy Mountain Lodge is open mid-December to mid-April, but there are plans to restore the historic cabins on the grounds, and they may be available in late 2004. If so, the resort will probably be open year-round.

Both Snowy Mountain Lodge and the nearby Old Corral Hotel are owned by The Headrick Companies (www.headricks.com).

Uphill 1.5 miles from Snowy Mountain Lodge is **Mountain Meadow Cabins,** 307/742-6042, with eight cabins. Built in the 1950s, the cabins have been nicely updated with private baths and kitchenettes and are open year-round; you'll need a snowmobile or skis for winter access. The smallest ones sleep two for $50, while four-person cabins are $70, and eight-person units (two bedrooms) cost $90.

Another delightful place is **Brooklyn Lodge B&B,** 307/742-6916, west of Centennial in the Snowy Range at an elevation of 10,200 feet. Built in 1918 and refurbished in the 1990s, the log lodge is on the National Register of Historic Places. Inside, two guest rooms have king-size beds and share a bath. The living room contains a big stone fireplace, and the front porch overlooks a mountain meadow. There's a minimum two-night stay on weekends and a three-night minimum on holidays and in the winter, when access is by skis or snowmobile. The room price of $150 d includes a full breakfast. Brooklyn Lodge fills up far ahead; reserve six months in advance for summer weekends. It is also a favorite spot for summer weddings.

Historic **Medicine Bow Lodge & Guest Ranch,** 307/326-5439 or 800/409-5439, www.medbowlodge.com, is just inside the western national-forest boundary along State Hwy. 130. The main building opened in 1917. Refurbished historic log cabins are $160 d, including three home-cooked meals and access to a workout facility, hot tub, sauna, and cross-country skis in winter. Available for an extra charge are horseback rides, float trips, and mountain biking in summer, along with snowmobile tours in winter. Open all year except November and mid-April to mid-May.

Historic **Ryan Park,** 24 miles east of Saratoga, is home to a pair of lodging places. **B&B Mountain Retreat,** 308/235-3881 or 307/326-8012, www.bbmountain.20m.com, has a four-bedroom log home available by the day or week. Rates are $75 d or $100 for four people, with access to an outdoor hot tub.

Trails

The Medicine Bows are ideal for short one- to five-day hikes; get maps from Forest Service offices or visitors centers. They also have maps showing trails open to **mountain biking,** including many on the west side of the mountains.

The 4.5-mile **Medicine Bow Peak Trail** climbs 1,600 feet to the summit of this 12,013-foot mountain, the highest in southern Wyoming, providing extraordinary vistas. The trail leaves from the west Lake Marie parking area and is in exposed alpine terrain most of the way. You can make a seven-mile loop by following this route to the top and then dropping down the east side to the **Lakes Trail,** which takes you past rock-rimmed Lookout Lake—keep a lookout for marmots—and on to Mirror Lake. Your starting point is just down the road. Medicine Bow Peak can also be climbed via a steeper and shorter trail (four miles round-trip) that leaves from the Lewis Lake Trailhead. The Forest Service charges a $3 day-use fee at the Libby Lake and Lewis Lake Trailheads and picnic areas.

North Gap Lake Trail departs from the Lewis Lake parking lot in the Sugarloaf Recreation Area and follows a gentle grade past Gap Lakes, continuing on to Sheep Lake. Here, you can follow the **Sheep Lake Trail** to Brooklyn Lake, before returning to your starting point via **Lost Lake Trail.** Total distance for this delightful high-mountain loop is 15 miles. This entire area is crisscrossed with other alpine trails, some of which are not shown on topographic maps. Check with the Forest Service for details.

Platte River Trail, a 6.5-mile-long path, parallels the river through a deep and narrow canyon lined with ponderosa pines and Douglas firs. Access is from the south via a trailhead near Sixmile Gap Campground (22 miles south of Encampment). The trail follows the west bank of the river, but by July the river can sometimes be forded, allowing hikers to continue another two miles northward to Pickaroon Campground. Check with the Forest Service for current water levels.

Savage Run Trail crosses the wilderness area of the same name. Nine miles long, it parallels Savage Run Creek, dropping 2,400 feet along the way. Access is too convoluted to describe, but it's not that hard to find if you have a Medicine Bow-Routt National Forest map.

Snowy Range Ski and Recreation Area

In the mountains 32 miles west of Laramie on State Hwy. 130, the Snowy Range Ski and Recreation Area has four lifts and 27 different runs. Outside of Jackson Hole, this is the best place to ski in Wyoming, with a good variety of skiing conditions, uncrowded slopes, and soft powder snow. Snowy Range is open Thanksgiving weekend to early April and charges $32 for adults ($25 per half day), $18 for kids ages 6–12 and seniors ($14 per half day). Children under six are free with a paying adult. The area is open daily 9 A.M.–4 P.M., with ski and snowboard rentals and lessons, along with guided snowmobile trips. The lodge has cafeteria food, beer, and a fireplace. Get more information at 307/745-5750 or 800/462-7669, www.snowyrange.com.

Cross-Country Skiing and Snowmobiling

The Forest Service maintains dozens of miles of groomed Nordic ski trails in the mountains around Snowy Range Ski Area, with a wide variety of loops and longer treks available for those willing to strike out on their own. Get avalanche and trail information on the web at www.xcski-laramie.org,

The Forest Service's historic Little Brooklyn Lake Guard Station is a popular overnight ski-in or snowmobile-in destination. See the preceding Cabins section for details.

Snowmobiling is one of the most popular winter activities in the Snowy Range, and parking lots on all sides of the range fill with vehicles on winter weekends. More than 200 miles of groomed trails follow summertime roads and are maintained by the state of Wyoming. For details on both cross-country skiing and snowmobiling, stop by Forest Service offices in Laramie or Saratoga.

North Platte Valley

SARATOGA

The friendly, laid-back town of Saratoga (pop. 1,700) is one of two towns in Wyoming—the other being Thermopolis—that center around hot springs. The name was borrowed from another well-known spa: Saratoga, New York. Wyoming's version of Saratoga straddles the North Platte River and putters along on a mixed economy. Louisiana Pacific Company has a large lumber mill in town, and many cattle graze in the beautiful river bottom country along the North Platte. Saratoga is also something of a bedroom community for coal miners who work in Hanna but prefer the country around here. Others commute as far as Rawlins to work.

Like many places in Wyoming, Saratoga has long depended on various extractive industries for a livelihood and is only now discovering how attractive the land itself is. With mountains on both sides, "blue ribbon" trout fishing, river float trips, a free hot springs, a rich history, and lots of

wildlife, it's certain that tourism will grow increasingly important. Each year more folks arrive and new businesses sprout up, creating concerns that Saratoga could go the way of other edge-of-the-mountains towns. The town has also become something of a retreat for executives and others in the rich-and-famous crowd who find that locals allow them a measure of privacy and anonymity. Head out to homes bordering Old Baldy Club Golf Course and you just might meet a former president, supreme court justice, or Hollywood star.

History

Indians called Saratoga Hot Springs "Place of the Magic Water"; it was a site of healing where various tribes could mingle without fear of attack. When whites arrived and first bathed here, the Indians noted that the waters boiled more violently than before, indicating an evil spirit. Thereafter most shunned the hot springs, but an 1874 smallpox epidemic forced some to return. Patients were

SARATOGA

To Saratoga Lake and I-80

DEER HAVEN RV PARK

CHATTERTON DR.

North

130

HUGUS AVE.

FARM AVE.

ROCHESTER AVE.

3RD
2ND

PIZZA HUT

FAR OUT WEST BED AND BREAKFAST

KEY BANK

1ST

RIVIERA LODGE

SARATOGA AVE.

8TH
7TH
6TH
5TH
4TH

HOOD HOUSE BED AND BREAKFAST

STUMPY'S EATERY

BUBBA'S BAR-B-QUE RESTAURANT

MAIN AVE.

POST OFFICE

LAZY RIVER CANTINA

BRIDGE ST.

CHAMBER OF COMMERCE

WOLF HOTEL

SPRING AVE.

ST.
ST.
ST.
ST.
ST.

RIVER ST.

ELM AVE.

LIBRARY

SAGE AND SAND MOTEL

HICKORY AVE.

ST.

WALNUT AVE.

MAPLE AVE.

E. FARM AVE.

VETERAN ST.

E. ROCHESTER AVE.

E. SARATOGA AVE.

SILVER MOON MOTEL

E. BRIDGE ST.

STATE ST.

E. RIVER ST.

PIC PIKE COUNTY RD.

SARATOGA INN

VETERAN ISLAND PARK

Platte

GREAT ROCKY MT. OUTFITTERS

HOBO POOL HOT SPRINGS

River

CYPRESS AVE.

VETERANS ST.

MOUNTAIN VIEW AVE.

WILLOW AVE.

CEDAR AVE.

GREENWOOD AVE.

SHIVELY AIRFIELD

MUSEUM

CONSTITUTION AVE.

MEDICAL CENTER

HOLLY AVE.

MOON

130

MYRTLE AVE.

HACIENDA MOTEL

0   0.25 mi

0   0.25 km

VALLEY FOODS

FOREST SERVICE OFFICE

To Riverside and Encampment

soaked in the hot water in an attempt to boil out the disease and then dipped in the cold river water. When all the patients died, the Indians decided that whites had turned the waters from good medicine to bad medicine. The area was littered with the graves of smallpox victims. Thereafter, the Indians moved even farther from the hot springs.

In 1877, William H. Cadwell homesteaded near the springs, built a wooden bathhouse on the site, and offered hot baths, meals, and a place for travelers to stretch out for a night's sleep. People flocked here from all over the region— some even came from England to soak in the waters claimed to cure "rheumatism, eczema, paralysis, stomach trouble, kidney disease, nerves, and all forms of blood and skin disease." The copper-mining boom in the Sierra Madre brought prosperity as miners came to Saratoga to relax and freighters used it as a way station and supply center. A spur route from the Union Pacific line was built south to Saratoga in 1907 to haul ore from the mines, but when they closed shortly thereafter the town was forced to turn to other pursuits, becoming a ranching and logging center.

Indians called Saratoga Hot Springs "Place of the Magic Water;" it was a site of healing where various tribes could mingle without fear of attack.

Sights

The main attraction in Saratoga is **Hobo Pool,** on the east end of Walnut Avenue, where a sandy-bottomed outdoor pool is fed by the odorless 117–128°F water of Saratoga Hot Springs. It's open 24 hours a day and is fully accessible. No charge, no alcohol, and no naked bodies allowed. Heated changing rooms have showers. An adjacent swimming pool— not mineral water—is open daily in the summer. The mineral baths attract both old and young, with more adventurous types sprinting down to the adjacent North Platte River to cool off or to soak in smaller hot springs that feed directly into the river. All this hot water keeps stretches of the river open, and **Odd Fellows Park** at River Street and Main Avenue is a good place to find ducks and geese at all times of the year. You can also use the luxurious spring-fed pool and hot tubs at **Saratoga Inn Resort,** 601 E. Pic Pike Rd., 307/326-5261 or 800/594-0178, www.saratogainn.com. The cost is $10 per person.

Saratoga's wonderful **Wolf Hotel,** 101 E. Bridge St., 307/326-5525, www.wolfhotel.com, was built in 1893 by a German emigrant named Frederick Wolf. Today it's a National Historic Landmark. The old brick building with steeply gabled windows served for many years as a stage stop along the road to the mines of the Sierra Madre. Now restored with antique furnishings, the Wolf offers an enjoyable taste of the past. There are also accommodations and a restaurant and bar on the premises.

Saratoga Museum, 307/326-5511, is housed in the old railroad depot on the south end of town. Inside are items from the region's ranching, logging, and sheepherding past, along with a hands-on archaeology exhibit. The museum is open daily 1–5 P.M. Memorial Day through Labor Day, and by appointment the rest of the year. Outside you'll find an old Union Pacific boxcar and caboose, along with a gazebo. Admission is $2 adults, $1 kids.

The **North Platte River** is one of the only rivers in the United States that flows predominantly north. From the Wyoming–Colorado border to the mouth of Sage Creek, 65 miles north, it is also the only "blue ribbon" trout fishery in southern Wyoming, with outstanding fishing for rainbow and brown trout. Studies have found more than 4,200 catchable wild trout averaging 13–17 inches per mile in the river. See the following River Recreation section for details on floating and fishing the river. You can find Indian petroglyphs along the bluff above the river just north of Saratoga. Fish are raised at the **Saratoga National Fish Hatchery,** five miles north of town, 307/326-5662; open daily 8 A.M.–4 P.M. Constructed in 1915, the hatchery produces fingerling cutthroat, rainbow, and brook trout for Wyoming rivers and lakes.

MEDICINE BOW

River Recreation

The North Platte River forms a major focal point for visitors staying in Saratoga or Encampment. The trout fishing is excellent and the scenery grand; no wonder they call this the "Good Times Valley." Many travelers float downriver either on their own or with guides. Whitewater enthusiasts enjoy **North Gate Canyon,** typically putting in at Routt Access (just inside Colorado) and taking out at Sixmile Campground. Check with local Forest Service offices for river access information and a list of guides.

In Saratoga, **Great Rocky Mountain Outfitters,** 216 E. Walnut, 307/326-8750 or 800/326-5390, www.grmo.com, sells quality Orvis fly-fishing gear and can fill you in on the latest fishing and floating conditions. All-day fishing trips run $375 for two people; overnight camping and fishing trips and boat shuttles are also available. Great Rocky Mountain Outfitters also rents rafts and canoes in summer and cross-country skis in winter.

Hack's Tackle & Outfitters, 307/326-9823, www.hackstackle.com, guides float trips for anglers (and birdwatchers) down the North Platte River and has a tackle shop. They also provide shuttles and tours. Two other outfitters also offers guided fishing trips and can provide lodging: **Nibbles and Bytes,** 307/328-0649, and **Harrison Land Company,** 303/298-0848.

As the North Platte River enters Wyoming from Colorado, it drops into **North Gate Canyon,** a class III and IV stretch of whitewater with several hairy sets of rapids. Beyond Sixmile Gap, the river broadens and becomes a gentler float. If you are a whitewater enthusiast, get here early because the water level drops after June. Check with the aforementioned companies for guided whitewater trips in May and June.

Accommodations

Built in 1893, the historic **Wolf Hotel,** 101 E. Bridge St., 307/326-5525, www.wolfhotel.com. Lodging options here include a range of upstairs rooms, but all now have private baths. Standard rooms are $39–45 s or $47–52 d; these are over the bar and can get noisy when it is hopping. Two-room suites are $69 d, and a top-floor luxury suite includes a wet bar and room; $90 d or $110 for four people. Any of these choices offer a wonderful change from standard motel rooms.

Sage and Sand Motel, 311 S. 1st St., 307/326-

the Wolf Hotel, Saratoga

MEDICINE BOW

© DON PITCHER

8339, charges $39 s or $44 d. Some rooms contain kitchenettes. The rooms are a bit old fashioned, but you'll find clean and cozy accommodations at **Silver Moon Motel**, 412 E. Bridge St., 307/326-5974, where rates are $38 s or $50 d. Full-kitchen units are $40 s or $51 d. The adjacent Louisiana Pacific lumber mill can get noisy at night.

Hacienda Motel, one-half mile south of town, 307/326-5751, has rooms for $54–64 s or $64–74 d, some with kitchenettes. **Riviera Lodge**, 303 N. 1st St., 307/326-5651, offers a riverside location with a variety of recently remodeled rooms. The smallest are $46 s or $55 d. Larger rooms cost $55 s or $65 d, and suites with two beds and a deck over the river are $95 d or $105 for four guests.

Saratoga Inn Resort, 601 E. Pic Pike Rd., 307/326-5261 or 800/594-0178, www.saratogainn.com, underwent a multimillion-dollar remodeling in the late 1990s and is easily the most luxurious place in town. All rooms (some are quite small) follow a Western theme, with rustic lodgepole furniture. The trophy room has a big central fireplace and overstuffed chairs, and the central courtyard contains a large hot-spring-fed pool and five soaking tubs, four of which are covered by tepees. The resort also features a nine-hole golf course, horseback rides (at Brush Creek Guest Ranch), massage and spa treatments, fishing, and other activities. Guest rooms go for $138 d on weekdays or $158 d on weekends; suites cost $198 d weekdays, $218 d weekends.

Bed-and-Breakfasts

Two Saratoga B&Bs offer comfortable in-town accommodations in historic homes. Built in 1920, **Far Out West B&B**, 304 N. 2nd St., 307/326-5869, www.cruising-america.com/farout.html, contains four guest rooms and a cottage, all with private baths and TVs. Two of the rooms are upstairs in the main house, and the other two are out back and have private entries and king beds. Rates are $85 s or $100 d, including a creative home-cooked breakfast. Families will appreciate the spacious three-room cottage ($130 d) with a full kitchen; breakfast not included. There's also a great kid-size playroom and pleasant patio. Deer wander through the yard most summer evenings.

A few blocks away is **Hood House B&B**, 214 N. 3rd, 307/326-8901 or 866/326-8901, www.hoodhousebnb.com, a simple historic home with an enclosed porch and antique furnishings. The four guest rooms contain shared baths, and a full breakfast is served. Rates are $80 s or $90 d. The owner lives next door, and kids are welcome.

Guesthouses

River Cottages, 216 E. Walnut St., 307/326-8750, www.rivercottages.com, consists of three very nice Saratoga places: two houses with full kitchens for $125 d ($25 per person for additional guests) and a suite for $85 d. Hobo Pool hot springs is right next door.

The **Kingfisher House**, 210 W. Saratoga Ave., 307/326-8217, www.kingfisherhouse.com, is a furnished two-bedroom home in a quiet part of town. There's a full kitchen, big back porch, and BBQ grill. Weekend rates are $100 d for one bedroom ($65 Mon.–Thurs. nights) or $140 for the entire house ($90 Mon.–Thurs. nights).

Ten Best Reasons Guest Home, 919/554-8583, www.wyominghuntfishgolf.com, is a renovated and furnished four-bedroom home with a big kitchen and living room, plus a century-old pool table in the rec room. It's available weekends for $300 d (plus $50 per person for additional guests) or by the week for $1,000 d ($100 per person for additional guests).

Harrison Land Company, 303/298-0848, has a three-bedroom, two-bath guest house with a deck facing the North Platte. Rooms rent for $50–75 d.

Guest Ranches

Brush Creek Guest Ranch, 15 miles southeast of Saratoga, 307/327-5241 or 800/726-2499, www.brushcreekranch.com, is a wonderful 6,000-acre cattle ranch that dates back almost a century. Guests stay in the grand 6,500-square-foot main lodge or in comfortable modern cabins. The emphasis is on horseback riding, guided fly-fishing—it's an Orvis-endorsed lodge—hayrides, creekside barbecues, hiking, mountain biking, and wintertime cross-country skiing. Guests can help move cattle between pastures or simply relax on the big front porch overlooking the flower-filled yard.

Weekly rates are $2,550 for two people, all-inclusive; open year-round. Saddle tramps should ask about the annual roundup in late summer.

A-Bar-A Ranch, 307/327-5454, also has guest ranch facilities in the Saratoga area, but it's typically full all summer with a select clientele; call if you qualify.

Camping

Saratoga Lake Campground, 1.5 miles north of town, 307/326-5629, has campsites ($7 without or $10 with electrical hookups) next to the small lake. No trees or showers. It's open year-round. The closest Forest Service campground is 25 miles east, with many more campgrounds ($10) as you continue on State Hwy. 130 over Snowy Range Pass.

Located just north of the Platte River bridge at 706 N. 1st St., **Deer Haven RV Park,** 307/326-8746, has shady RV sites for $20–25 with full hookups (no shower house). Open May–Oct.

Foote Recreation Area is a peaceful little spot along the North Platte River, with a couple of cottonwood-shaded free campsites, singing birds, and an outhouse. It's located five miles north of Saratoga; follow the small sign to the river. Other access points are dotted along the river; get a map showing all of them from the chamber of commerce.

Food and Entertainment

Get savory breakfasts (including eggs Benedict or Belgian waffles) along with espresso and homemade ice cream at **Lollypops,** on E. Bridge St., 307/326-5020.

The historic **Wolf Hotel,** 101 E. Bridge St., 307/326-5525, www.wolfhotel.com, is especially known for its prime rib and steaks, but also delivers more unusual fare such as broiled swordfish or veggie kabobs. There's a salad bar, too. Entrées run $15–20. The Wolf is open Monday–Saturday for lunch and dinner (no breakfast). The bar is the local hangout and offers live country-and-western music periodically.

For inexpensive pizzas, burgers, salads, and sandwiches, you won't go wrong at **Stumpy's Eatery,** 218 N. 1st St., 307/326-8132. **Lazy River Cantina,** 110 E. Bridge Ave., 307/326-8472, has

inexpensive Mexican food, great chicken-fried steaks, and a bar with darts and TV sports. They're also open for breakfast on Sunday mornings and often have live bands on weekends.

Bubba's Bar-B-Que Restaurant, 119 N. River St., 307/326-5427, is another in this small chain of restaurants that started in Jackson. The menu stars hickory-smoked baby back ribs, a turkey plate, pork chops, and other meaty fare served in a convivial atmosphere Bubba's is open for lunch and dinner most of the year and sits right along the river with a deck facing the water. You're likely to see mallards in the yard.

For gourmet meals, head to **Silver Saddle Restaurant and Brewery,** inside the Saratoga Inn. The menu includes prime rib, pasta, and grilled steaks. Breakfast is especially good. A bright and open interior and substantial wine list add to the charm, and dinner entrées run $13–24. The Sierra Madre Brewery here cranks out a variety of brews.

Whistle Pig Saloon, 307/329-7003, is one mile south of town, with big windows facing the Snowy Range, country bands on weekends, and jalapeno popcorn to spice things up. The **Rustic Bar,** 124 E. Bridge St., 307/326-5965, is known for its "fighting" mountain lion mounts and has live music some weekends.

Get groceries at **Valley Foods** on the south end of town, where the deli has baked goods. Or you can hang out with the bald-and-gray-haired set over coffee and doughnuts at **Donut Ranch Bakery** on W. Bridge Street. Actually, the best place to meet locals is the Conoco station, where Saturday mornings find the high school's entire junior and senior classes parked out front. It's obviously the place to be seen.

Events

Start the year dressed in winter clothes for the **Saratoga Lake Ice Fishing Derby** each January. It's considered one of the top fishing derbies in the Lower 48. The following month brings **chariot races,** which offer lots of excitement as two-horse teams race down the straightaway. The **Platte Valley Festival of Birds** attracts flocks of birdwatchers to local wetlands in late May. The three-day **Platte Valley Festival of the Arts** is held around the Fourth of July each year and includes a juried art show, plus a parade, barbecue, live music, and the obligatory fireworks. In early August the **Wyoming Microbrewery Competition** attracts brewers from around the state. At the **Bull Riders Rodeo and Saratoga Chili Cookoff**—held the same weekend—you can watch the amateur rodeo, sample the chili chefs' treats, or two-step to live bands playing for the street dance.

Galleries and Shopping

For such a small town, Saratoga has quite a few places to keep browsers happy. **Blackhawk Gallery,** 100 N. 1st St., 307/326-5063, www.blackhawkgallery.com, sells quality Western artwork, jewelry, and crafts. Next door is **Wyold Aspen Studio,** 307/326-8904, www.wyoldaspenstudio.com, with stone sculptures, landscape paintings, and amazing leatherwork. **Potters Studio,** 128 E. Bridge St., 307/326-5526, sells locally made pottery with a wild-west theme. **The apARTment Gallery,** across from the visitors center on W. Bridge St., 307/326-8418, displays the striking photos of Martin Stupich and watercolors by Judi Morris.

Bill Naylor of **Peg Leg Mountain Furniture,** 413 E. Bridge St., 307/326-5022, makes unique lodgepole items, from walking sticks to bunk beds, and **Whitney's Saddle Shop,** inside the Saratoga Inn, has quality Western gifts and clothing. Also check out **Hat Creek Saddlery & Trading Post,** 107 W. Bridge St., 307/326-5755, with custom saddles, Western memorabilia, jewelry, and handwoven rugs.

Laura M, 114 E. Bridge St., 307/326-8187 or 800/251-3505, www.lauram.com, is a Saratoga-based clothing designer with a line of stylish Western wear for women. Most of the items are sewn on the premises from natural fibers and unique fabrics.

Cover to Cover Books and Things, 112 E. Bridge St., 307/326-8745, sells books, locally made candles, and fabrics for quilters.

Information and Services

The **Saratoga Chamber of Commerce,** 115 W. Bridge St., 307/326-8855, http://spvcc.1wyo.net, is open Monday–Friday 9 A.M.–5 P.M.

The Forest Service's **Saratoga Ranger Station** faces the mountains on the south edge of town, 307/326-5258, and is open weekdays. Find the town **library** at 503 W. Elm St., 307/326-8209, and the **post office** at 105 Main Ave., 307/326-5611. Get cash from **ATMs** at Community First Bank, 302 N. 1st St., or the pretentious Rawlins National Bank at 217 N. 1st Street. Wash clothes at **Carbon County Coin Op,** 105 E. Walnut, 307/326-5384. **Corbett Medical Clinic,** on the south side of town, 307/326-8381, has a doctor on staff.

Transportation

Platte Valley Shuttles & Tours, 307/326-5582, www.plattevalleyshuttles.com, will transport you and your gear to local trailheads and boating spots and provides shuttles to Rawlins, Denver, and other cities. Bike rentals and scenic tours are available.

A real surprise in Saratoga is the airport, with an 8,400-foot runway. No scheduled service, but **Saratoga Aviation,** 307/326-8344, has charter flights. In the summer and fall (especially on the weekend after Labor Day), aircraft executives and other wealthy enthusiasts—alias "the conquistadors"—fly here for a rendezvous at the A-Bar-A Ranch. The tarmac is jammed with corporate jets, turning Shively Field into the third-busiest jetport in Wyoming. There's no bus service to Saratoga.

ENCAMPMENT AND RIVERSIDE

The quaint ranching and tourism town of Encampment (pop. 400) lies in the gorgeous foothills of the Sierra Madre, which were once home to thousands of copper miners. Today the area abounds with ghost towns from that era. Encampment's twin settlement of Riverside (pop. 60) lies just one mile to the east. This area is popular with hunters who come for deer, antelope, and elk, for photographers who enjoy the colorful autumn leaves, and for anglers who cast about for trout. The community is decidedly conservative: Bumper stickers proclaim, "If you're out of work and hungry eat an environmentalist," and each fall finds the back roads crowded with gun-racked pickup trucks and silent, orange-capped hunters scanning the horizon for bucks. Back in town, the smoky bars fill at night with tales of the chase and chubby old men winking at the waitresses over their Budweisers.

History

Encampment takes its name from the Grand Encampment of French-Canadian trappers who rendezvoused along the Encampment River in 1838. Miners had long suspected that the Sierra Madre contained a wealth of minerals, but the first significant gold strike was not made until 1896. Another mineral, however, transformed the region. Encampment itself began in 1897, when British sheepherder Ed Haggerty discovered a rich vein of copper in the Sierra Madre to the west. The mine he developed was named Rudefeha, a word concocted from the letters of the various partners' names—J. M. *Ru*msey, Robert *De*al, George *Fe*rris, and Ed *Ha*ggerty. In the first three months of digging, miners recovered $300,000 worth of copper ore. Haggerty took his 10 percent share and returned to England.

As the wealth of the discovery became known, Chicago promoter and newspaperman Willis George Emerson purchased the mine and built a 16-mile-long aerial tram to haul the ore up over the 10,600-foot Continental Divide and then down to the Boston-Wyoming Smelter at Encampment (elevation 7,200 feet). The tram consisted of 304 wooden towers with buckets supported on thick steel cables. Each bucket held 700 pounds of ore and moved at four miles per hour. The tram could carry almost 1,000 tons of ore per day and was powered by water flowing through a four-foot wooden pipeline. Thousands of men flocked to the mines, creating almost overnight the settlements of Battle, Copperton, Dillon, Elwood, Halfway House, and Rambler. A railroad was completed from the smelter to the main Union Pacific line at Walcott in 1905, and by 1908 more than 23 million pounds of copper had been produced.

The main regional settlement was Encampment, located at the foot of the mountains and numbering 1,500 rough and hardened souls at its peak. By 1900, the town featured three general stores, two lodging houses, two hotels, two restaurants, and three lumber yards, along with nine saloons and two houses of prostitution. Nearby Riverside served as a shipping center for the mines. (Originally known as Dogget, the name was changed to Riverside after folks began calling it Dog Town.) Another 1,500 people lived in the other mining towns. The mining boom came to an abrupt halt after two disastrous fires destroyed the concentrating mill, the smelter, the boiler room, and the powerhouse. Combined with falling copper prices, it forced the company into bankruptcy. Soon, all sorts of illegal actions surfaced, including overcapitalization and fraudulent stock sales.

All but a few diehards left the area, and what had once been the town of Grand Encampment was eventually reduced to simply Encampment. Logging, first for ties and mine supports and later for lumber, became an important part of the economy, but the last mill closed in the 1990s, and many locals now commute to work in the Sinclair refinery or Hanna coal mines. Tourism is becoming increasingly important in the area, and retirees are attracted to the slow pace, moderate prices, and beautiful setting.

Sights

On the south side of Encampment at 6th and Barnett Streets, the excellent **Grand Encampment Museum** includes items from the early-1900s mining camps that filled the Sierra Madre. Displayed here are historic photographs and clothing, Indian artifacts, Forest Service memorabilia, and even a folding bathtub from the 1890s. Teddy the (stuffed) dog greets visitors. Most interesting of all are the 14 historic buildings set up as a frontier town with wooden boardwalks. These include a tie-hack cabin, a bakery, a lookout tower, and a stage station. The transportation barn even houses Noah's Ark, although, alas, it's probably not the original one. Oddest of all is a two-story outhouse modeled after one used in the mining ghost town of Dillon. The lower level was used in summer, with the upper floor reserved for wintertime when the snows drifted many feet deep. The Australian term for privies (long drop) is especially fitting here! Also at the museum are parts of the 16-mile-long aerial tramway that brought ore from the Rudefeha mine.

This free museum is open Monday–Saturday 10 A.M.–5 P.M. and Sunday 1–5 P.M. Memorial Day through Labor Day. The rest of the year, you can see the museum by special appointment only; call 307/327-5558. Retired locals provide informative tours in July and August, and you can even buy bars of homemade soap inside the main building. In mid-July the museum has living-history demonstrations and music.

At the museum, pick up a copy of the local **walking-tour** brochure, which describes some of the town's buildings. Be sure to also see the pretty white **Presbyterian Church** at 9th and Rankin.

A three-quarter-mile trail leads to the **Indian Bathtubs**, natural geologic formations that collect rainwater. Indian hunters used them for bathing. Get there by heading one mile west of Riverside on State Hwy. 230. Turn right onto Blackhall Road and follow it one mile to the trailhead.

Accommodations

Although popular with visitors all year, this area is doubly so during the fall hunting season; book ahead if you're coming through at that time, and bring your bright orange clothes to keep from getting shot. In Encampment, stay at **Vacher's Bighorn Lodge,** 508 McCaffrey, 307/327-5110, where remodeled rooms go for $37 s or $45–52 d, and kitchenettes are $43 s or $51 d. Open all year.

Lazy Acres Campground & Motel in Riverside, 307/327-5968, www.wyomingcarbon-county.com/lazy.htm, has motel units for $29 s or $33–36 d and a cute little cabin (shared bath) for $25 s or d. Open mid-May through Oct. **Bear Trap Cafe & Cabins** in Riverside, 307/327-5277, www.beartrapcafe.com, charges $30 s or $38 d for rustic cabins with shared bath (two also have kitchenettes) or modular motel rooms. Open May–Nov.

More Riverside rusticity can be found at **Riverside Cabins,** 307/327-5361, where most cabins include kitchenettes and private baths but no phones or TVs. Rates start at $28 d for a basic cabin, up to $68 for a two-bedroom unit that sleeps six and has a full kitchen. Open mid-May to Oct. **Cottonwood Cabins,** 307/327-5151, offers three modern cabins with full kitchens, TVs, and picnic tables. Rates are $65–80 d; open June–Oct.

Bed-and-Breakfasts

Twelve miles south of Encampment is **Platt's Rustic Mountain Lodge B&B,** 307/327-5539, www.plattoutfitting.com, an 8,000-acre ranch where a spacious log lodge offers dramatic vistas of the Sierra Madre Range. The lodge also offers horseback trail rides, fishing, pack trips, photo safaris, cross-country skiing, snowmobiling, and incongruously, both hunting and nature retreats! Lodging rates are $45 s or $65 d, including a full breakfast. Also here is a modern "cabin" with a kitchen and two bedrooms for more seclusion. It sleeps four and costs $1,075 for five days. Kids are welcome both in the main lodge and in the cabin but no TV or phones are provided.

Owned by the nationally known artist R. G. Finney, **Spirit West River Lodge B&B,** 307/327-5753 or 888/289-8321, www.spiritwestriverlodge.com, is a massive log riverfront lodge with four guest rooms, all with private baths and access to the deck and hot tub. Many of the furnishings were handcrafted, and a big country breakfast is served each morning. Rates are $75–85 s or d. No kids under 12.

Riverside's **Old Depot B&B,** 307/327-5277 or 877/819-6677, www.oldedepot.com, was built in 1905 and served as a train depot until 1954. Now completely remodeled, it provides three guest rooms for $80 s or d. Each has its own bath, and guests have access to a hot tub on the back deck and a small fitness center. A full breakfast is included at Beartrap Restaurant (same owners). Kids are welcome.

In Encampment, **Grand & Sierra B&B,** 1016 Lomax, 307/327-5200, has its own distinctive features, including animal mounts lining the walls, a pool table, and shag carpet on the floor. This is a hunter's paradise; when I dropped by once, someone was skinning beavers in the garage. The five guest rooms have shared or private baths. Also here is a hot tub. Rates are $65–75 s or d. Kids accepted, and a full breakfast is served.

Camping

The BLM's **Encampment River Campground** ($7; open June–Oct.) is three miles from town. Head west from Encampment and turn south on Rd. 353 (Hog Park Rd.). Ask locally for directions to two free BLM campgrounds: Bennett Peak and Corral Creek.

The nearest Forest Service campsite ($10; open late May–Oct.) is **Bottle Creek Campground,** seven miles southwest of town on State Hwy. 70. Five more campgrounds (free to $10) lie west of here in the Sierra Madre.

Lazy Acres Campground & Motel in Riverside, 307/327-5968, www.wyomingcarbon-county.com/lazy.htm, has pleasant shady tent sites for $15 and RV spaces for $20. Open mid-May through Oct.

Food

Eat in Encampment at **Pine Lodge Saloon,** 518 McCaffrey, 307/327-5203, which also has a pool table. Next door is the seasonal **Split Rail,** with pizzas, steaks, chicken, and Wednesday-night catfish feeds. There's a patio for al fresco dining.

An interesting old two-story brick building at 706 Freeman in Encampment houses both **Kuntzman's Cash Store** and the **Sugar Bowl,** 307/327-5271, with an old-fashioned soda fountain with malts, subs, soups, and banana splits, plus locally made dolls. **Bear Trap Cafe** in Riverside, 307/327-5277, serves standard American food, but be sure to save room for their coconut cream pie. Riverside's **town park** is a great place for picnic lunches amid tall cottonwoods.

Events and Entertainment

On the first full week of February, the **Sierra Madre Winter Carnival** includes a variety of skiing and snowboarding contests, a casino night and melodrama, dances, and lots of other activities. One of the most popular regional events is the **Woodchoppers Jamboree and Rodeo** at Encampment the third full weekend of June. Begun in 1961, this is the state's largest loggers' show, including tree-felling, chainsaw log-bucking, hand-sawing, pole-throwing, and axe-throwing contests. Other activities include a fun amateur rodeo, a parade, a barbecue, and a melodrama featuring "dance hall girls." The town erupts with lots of drunken and rowdy behavior at night, befitting such a festival. (And guess who sponsors the Jamboree? Budweiser.) Call 307/326-8855 for details. In July, the **Sierra Madre Mountain Man Rendezvous** brings mountain men and women to Encampment.

Both **Pine Lodge Saloon** and the **Bear Trap Cafe** have live music during the jamboree.

Information and Services

Get local details at a small **information cabin** next to the rodeo grounds in Encampment; open Mon.–Fri. 9 A.M.–4:30 P.M. in summer. Otherwise, stop by the Grand Encampment Museum or the Forest Service office in Encampment for local information. Encampment's **city hall** is in the historic Opera House, a wooden building with a bell tower that looks like a lighthouse. The **Encampment Library** is on the east end of town at 202 Rankin Ave., 307/327-5775, while the Encampment **post office,** 307/327-5747, sits on the corner of 6th and McCaffrey Streets.

For guided horseback tours into wild country around Encampment, contact **Renegade Wranglers,** 307/327-5996.

Sierra Madre and Vicinity

The historic Sierra Madre—a finger from the Medicine Bow Range that stretches south into Colorado—cover a small section of Wyoming. This is one of the lesser-known parts of the state. Worth a visit are the many mining ghost towns and historic mine sites, and hikers will find many miles of wilderness trails. The highest mountain in the range is 11,004-foot Bridger Peak, named for mountain man Jim Bridger. Before heading out, get maps and camping and hiking information from the Forest Service's **Hayden Ranger Station,** 204 W. 9th in Encampment, 307/327-5481, www.fs.fed.us/r2/mbr. Also ask for their auto-tour brochure.

SIGHTS

The paved **Battle Highway** (State Hwy. 70) crosses the Sierra Madre from Encampment on the east to Baggs on the west, a distance of 57 miles. The smooth, wide-shouldered road (perfect for bikes) is extraordinarily scenic, especially in the fall when the aspens turn golden. Lodgepole pines are the dominant trees at higher elevations. During the winter and spring, generally November to mid-June, State Hwy. 70 is closed at the forest boundary, although snowmobilers and skiers may continue up the road. Approximately 10 miles west of Encampment the road reaches the Continental Divide at 9,916-foot Battle Pass. This is the location of **Battle,** one of many ghost towns capping the Sierra Madre. Battle is named for an 1841 fight between Indians and whites that took place near here.

A 4WD road good for mountain bikes heads north from the east side of the pass to the Bridger Peak summit and then down the western side to the Ferris-Haggerty mine site at the ghost town of **Rudefeha,** where remains of the tramway towers are still visible. One mile to the west you'll find the remains of **Dillon,** estab-

> *The western slopes of the Sierra Madre are carpeted with extensive stands of aspen trees. Aspen Alley, a favorite of photographers, is a half-mile stretch of fabulously flamboyant fall foliage.*

lished after the company town of Rudefeha banned saloons; the saloon owners simply moved a short distance away and started anew, and in no time at all Dillon was the largest town in the Sierra Madre. Many buildings remain here, hidden in the trees.

Two miles west of the Continental Divide on State Hwy. 70 is a turnout overlooking pretty Battle Lake and a monument to **Thomas A. Edison.** While vacationing here in 1878, Edison was pondering over what substance to use as a filament for incandescent lights. One night he threw a broken bamboo fishing pole in the fire and was intrigued by the way the frayed pieces glowed. Carbonized bamboo would make a fine non-conducting filament for his bulbs. This tale has been passed down as fact through the years, but in reality Edison didn't come up with the idea until one year later. Maybe he remembered the old fly rod at that time.

The town of **Rambler** once stood along the lake shore, with the Doane-Rambler copper mine nearby. The mine operated from 1879 to 1902, producing one-half million tons of copper. Another six miles west are a few remains from the settlement of **Copperton.**

ASPEN ALLEY

The western slopes of the Sierra Madre are carpeted with extensive stands of quaking aspen trees that came up after fires swept through this region during the mining era. These reach for many miles along State Hwy. 70. A favorite of photographers is Aspen Alley, a half-mile stretch of fabulously flamboyant fall foliage. Get here by turning north onto Deep Creek Road (Forest Rd. 801). The colors generally peak in late September, but call the Encampment Forest Service office, 307/327-5481, for current conditions.

MEDICINE BOW

Adventurous souls will enjoy the 50-mile drive north from Aspen Alley to Rawlins. Camping is available at the no-longer-maintained Sandstone camping area, approximately four miles up the road.

Once the gravel road emerges from the national forest, the land broadens into sage and grass before once again climbing over the Continental Divide. Stop here on a fall night and listen to the quiet. A few clouds hang on the western horizon, and a few pickups churn clouds of dust up the road—en route to either hunting grounds or a bar. The night lies over the land like a blackened canvas splattered with stars. There aren't many places like this anymore.

CAMPING AND CABINS

The Forest Service has six campgrounds (free to $10; open June–Oct.) in the Sierra Madre, all of which are along State Hwy. 70, the main road across the mountains. These campgrounds are not nearly as crowded as those in the Snowy Range to the east.

Built in 1934, the Forest Service's **Evy Williams Guard Station** is a delightful one-room log cabin in the mountains northwest of Encampment. Facilities are rustic: two sets of bunk beds (bring sleeping bags), wood or propane heat, and propane lights. The cabin costs $40 per night and sleeps four. Nearby is the impressive **Jack Creek Work Center,** a modern five-bedroom facility with space for 15 folks at $150 per night (two-night minimum). Both buildings are located along Forest Rd. 452 approximately 25 miles west of Saratoga. Get additional information on both of these at 307/326-525, www.fs.fed.us/r2/mbr.

HUSTON PARK WILDERNESS

The 30,726-acre Huston Park Wilderness straddles the Continental Divide just south of Battle Pass. It contains spruce, fir, aspen, and lodgepole forests, as well as open alpine country reaching to 10,500 feet. **Continental Divide National Scenic Trail** provides an enjoyable high-elevation trek along the crest of the mountains. The

trail stretches 3,100 miles from Canada to Mexico, and 16 miles of it pass through this wilderness area. The route is marked with rock cairns and blazed trees. Trailheads are located one mile south of the Battle townsite and 2.5 miles west of Hog Park Reservoir.

The nine-mile-long **Baby Lake Trail** is an enjoyable overnight trip through high meadows and along a mountain creek. Take in excellent vistas of the Snake River Valley from the Continental Divide. The trail is accessible from State Hwy. 70 on both ends, but for the easiest hiking, start from a trailhead at the end of a two-mile gravel road just south of Battle Pass. From here, the trail drops 2,600 feet in elevation to a second trailhead off Forest Rd. 811 (near Lost Creek Campground).

North Fork Encampment Trail takes you two miles up North Fork Creek to Green Mountain Falls. Get to the trailhead by driving west from Encampment to Bottle Creek Campground and then south on Forest Rd. 550 for 1.5 miles. This is one of the few waterfalls in the area (but it typically dries up after mid-June).

ENCAMPMENT RIVER WILDERNESS

At just 10,400 acres, Encampment River Wilderness is one of the smallest and least-visited wilderness areas in Wyoming. The centerpiece is the Encampment River, with its narrow canyon, rushing rapids, quiet pools, and fine fishing. Despite the Encampment's current wilderness status, much of this land was logged over at the turn of the 20th century to supply railroad ties and mine timbers for the Union Pacific Railroad. Old cabins and mines offer endless opportunities to explore. The well-maintained **Encampment River Trail** is a 15-mile-long path that follows this scenic river through the heart of the wilderness. Roads provide access from either end, so the trail is easier to hike if you can shuttle a second vehicle to the other end. Start from a trailhead near the BLM's Encampment River Campground, three miles south of Encampment. The trail follows the river upstream, beginning in low-elevation sage-and-grass country and gradually climbing into dense lodgepole and spruce forests. The first five miles are considerably easier hiking than higher up, where the canyon narrows and becomes more rugged. The trail ends at Hog Park, near the Colorado state line.

Another off-the-beaten-path sight near the Encampment River Wilderness is an old abandoned fire tower at **Blackhall Mountain,** approximately 15 miles south of Riverside on Forest Rd. 409. The last several miles are narrow but passable. From the top are long vistas into the mountains of Wyoming and Colorado.

WINTER RECREATION

During winter the Forest Service maintains many groomed miles of **cross-country ski trails** around the Bottle Creek Campground 5.5 miles west of Encampment and along the South Brush Creek (near the visitors center), 20 miles east of Saratoga. Call 307/326-5258 for access details. The Trading Post in Riverside, 307/327-5720, www.wyomingcarboncounty.com/trading.htm, rents cross-country skis and snowshoes. Many forest roads in the Sierra Madre are used extensively by snowmobilers, with 26 miles of groomed trails and an equal amount of ungroomed trails. Contact Forest Service offices in Encampment and Saratoga for details. A major summer home development is in the works for land just east of the Continental Divide along the Wyoming–Colorado border, and it will eventually include a small downhill ski resort open to the public.

LITTLE SNAKE RIVER VALLEY

The Little Snake River Valley is one of the most isolated parts of Wyoming; it lies right along the Colorado border, with the desolate Red Desert to the west and the Sierra Madre to the east. Three little towns—Savery, Dixon (pop. 80), and Baggs (pop. 350)—spread out along the irrigated farmland that follows Savery Creek. Visitors will find a slow pace to life in the valley and a sense of history exemplified by the solid old log cabins that dot the landscape. See Stephen Metzger's *Moon Handbooks Colorado* (www.moon.com) for details on sights south of the Wyoming line.

Savery

Housed in an old grade school, Savery's **Little Snake River Museum,** 307/383-7262 or 307/383-6388, www.lsrvmuseum.homestead .com/homepage.htm, provides a sampling of the area's rich history. The museum, open Wed.–Sat. 11 A.M.–5 P.M. Memorial Day to late Oct., contains the dugout canoe of mountain man Jim Baker, along with many other historical items. Out front is a distinctive two-story log blockhouse built by Baker; he and his wife are buried one mile west of town. Also on the museum grounds are a one-room schoolhouse from the Brown's Hill area and the Strobridge house, a grand two-story log structure that is more than a century old.

The **Savery Store,** 307/383-2711, has groceries, supplies, and a campground. **Stage Stop General Store** also sells supplies. The town's **Russell Community Park** has tent and RV camping with hookups and a rodeo grounds where you'll see **weekly roping events** in the summer.

Not far from town is **Savery Creek Thoroughbred Ranch,** 307/383-7840, www.savery-creek.com, a riding ranch for those who are serious about horses, with training in both English and Western riding. Beautiful country surrounds the ranch, which offers gracious lodging. The three guest rooms have shared or private baths; also available for lodging are two covered wagons. The ranch hosts only six people at a time, allowing for personalized attention. Open May–Sept. Rates are $265–325 daily for two people, with a three-night minimum. This includes lodging, meals, and riding.

Battle Creek Outfitters, 307/383-2418, www.wyoranch.com, has accommodations and activities on the 100,000-acre (!) Ladder Ranch straddling the Wyoming–Colorado border. Lodging and three meals a day costs $120–190 per day for two people, or you can choose an all-inclusive six-day package at $2,100 for two people.

Dixon

Four miles west of Savery and seven miles east of Baggs, the small agricultural settlement of Dixon holds the **Little Snake River Valley Rodeo** each July. It also hosts a **Cutting Horse**

M

MEDICINE BOW

Contest, where cowboys work specially trained horses to move cattle.

Built in 1911, the classic **Dixon Club Bar,** 307/383-7722, is a fun place to explore; its walls are lined with old junk and antiques. Free camping is available at **Dixon Town Park** along Main Street; no hookups or showers.

Baggs

Named for rancher George Baggs and his wife Maggie, Baggs's isolated location and proximity to the state line made it a gathering place for outlaws. In 1900, following a $32,000 bank robbery in Winnemucca, Nevada, Butch Cassidy helped build a cabin here to serve as a refuge for his gang. The cabin, now called the **Gaddis-Matthews House,** still stands in the center of town. Another noteworthy building is the **Bank Club Bar,** listed on the National Historic Register. Built as a bank, it later became a bar. Find it off the main drag on North and Miles.

Stay at **Drifters Inn,** 307/383-2015, for $35 s or $40 d, where the rooms have microwaves and fridges. Accommodations are also available at **Country Inn,** 307/383-6448. Pitch tents or park RVs (no hookups or showers) for free at **Baggs Park** on Hunt Street.

John and Esther Clark of **Wildhorse Country Tours,** 307/383-6865 or 866/753-8501, www.wildhorsetours.com, offer four-wheel-drive tours into the Sand Wash or Horse Shoe Bend area.

Northwest of Baggs is a unique area of badlands known as **Adobe Town.** The colorful terrain is fascinating, but it's easy to get lost in the maze of canyons, basins, ledges, and alcoves. Contact the Rawlins BLM office for access information: 307/328-4200, www.wy.blm.gov.

Rawlins

The small city of Rawlins (pop. 8,500) sits right in the middle of southern Wyoming. To the east and south lie mountain ranges and rich grazing land; to the west is the Great Divide Basin and a vast expanse of desert country. During the late 1970s and early '80s, Rawlins was a hub of development as the "Oil Patch" blossomed and energy companies pumped petrodollars into the economy. But as in so many other Wyoming towns, the inevitable bust that followed was traumatic. Layoffs affected everyone in town, and downtown Rawlins still has many empty storefronts. Not everyone packed up and left, however. Most of the people who lived here before the oil boom stayed around when the bust hit, scraping by on business brought in by freeway travelers, local ranchers, and the energy companies. Many Rawlins workers now commute 40 miles to work in the Hanna coal mines or the Sinclair refinery, while others are employed in the state penitentiary. New businesses have started to spread over the east end of Rawlins, creating the now-standard mix of fast food, discount megamarts, gas stations, and chain motels.

HISTORY

Rawlins is named for Gen. John A. Rawlins, secretary of war under President Grant. In 1867, as the railroad route was being surveyed westward, the crew of Gen. Grenville Dodge met up with soldiers under Rawlins's command. When they discovered a clear, alkali-free spring at the base of a hill, Rawlins remarked, "If anything is ever named after me, I hope it will be a spring of water." Dodge immediately decided to name this Rawlins Spring. When a division point on the Union Pacific was established here in 1868, the town was also named Rawlins Spring. Its name was later shortened to Rawlins.

In 1886, the Wyoming Legislature appropriated $100,000 for a state penitentiary in Rawlins. Two years later, construction began with enormous slabs of sandstone cut and hauled by wagon from a quarry south of town. Because of inadequate funding the new prison was not completed and occupied until December 1901, some 13 years after it was begun. By that time the town had grown, and what had been a relatively remote location was now in central Rawlins. For

RAWLINS

To Casper (Central WY) and Lander (Wind River Mtns. Country)

RAWLINS AIRPORT

To Laramie

HIGLEY BLVD.

MCDONALDS/GREYHOUND STATION

DAYS INN

BRIDGER INN

CITY MARKET

KEY MOTEL

THE LODGE AT RAWLINS

AIRPORT RD.

DALEY ST.

Creek

Sugar

HARSHMAN ST.

RECREATION CENTER

HIGHER EDUCATION CENTER

CARBON CO. FAIRGROUNDS

ROSE'S LARIAT

BROOKS ST.

MURRAY ST.

RODEO ST.

UTAH ST.

WALNUT ST.

MAPLE ST.

SPRUCE ST.

CEDAR ST.

LOCUST ST.

RIP GRIFFIN'S TRUCKSTOP

To State Penitentiary

SLEEP INN

COLORADO ST.

Club Park

WYOMING ST.

1ST ST.

PINE ST.

BUFFALO ST.

FRONT ST.

STATE ST.

DAVIS ST.

FRONTAGE RD.

HEATH ST.

2ND ST.

3RD ST.

LIBRARY

JADE LODGE

CHAMBER OF COMMERCE

OLD DEPOT

JACKSON ST.

LARSEN ST.

KENDRICK ST.

BLM DISTRICT OFFICE

TERRITORIAL PRISON

FERRIS MANSION

ECONOMY INN

5TH ST.

6TH ST.

7TH ST.

8TH ST.

9TH ST.

10TH ST.

POST OFFICE

SAGE CREEK RD.

12TH ST.

SWIMMING POOL

CARBON COUNTY MUSEUM

BEST MOTEL

MAPLE ST.

PINE ST.

SUNSET MOTEL

Washington Park

MOUNTAIN VIEW BLVD.

15TH ST.

IDEAL MOTEL

CLIFF MOTOR LODGE

BUCKING HORSE LODGE

BUDGET INN

LA BELLA MOTEL

ELM ST.

COTTONTREE INN

PRESIDENT'S CAMP RV PARK

HOSPITAL

23RD ST.

EXIT 211

WESTERN HILLS

SUPER 8 MOTEL

RV WORLD

To Rock Springs

To Casper (Central WY) and Lander (Wind River Mtns. Country)

0   0.25 mi

0   0.25 km

EXIT 214

© AVALON TRAVEL PUBLISHING, INC.

MEDICINE BOW

TOM HORN

The story of the murderer Tom Horn will always remain something of a mystery. Over the years, Horn worked as a stage driver, an army scout, a deputy sheriff, a Pinkerton investigator, and a detective for the Wyoming Stock Growers Association. When J. M. Carey (later Wyoming governor and senator) discovered that Tom Horn was out to murder—rather than bring in for trial—accused rustlers, he had Horn fired from the association. Other cattle barons quickly moved to hire him, however, paying $500 for each man killed. Horn is generally blamed for ambushing and assassinating two ranchers (and suspected rustlers) in the Laramie Mountains in 1895, along with two others in Brown's Park, Colorado, five years later.

Wherever Horn went, a trail of dead men was left behind, but nobody was able to pin the blame on him until 1901, when a 14-year-old boy was shot in the back and killed in the Laramie Mountains. It was a case of mistaken identity because the boy had been wearing his father's hat and clothes. The older man was later shot from ambush but survived. Horn was implicated in the boy's slaying by his trademark: a small stone placed under the victim's head.

Horn would probably have escaped even this heinous crime had he not bragged about it. (The confession would never hold up in court today; Deputy U.S. Marshal Joe LeFors had plied Horn with liquor and had a court stenographer listen through a crack in the door as he boasted of the slaying.) Horn had little money himself, but his supporters spent $100,000 in his defense. They hired the finest legal counsel, John W. Lacey, who had never lost any of his 50 previous murder trials (and who, not coincidentally, also represented the Wyoming Stock Growers Association and the Union Pacific Railroad).

Despite this, Horn was adjudged guilty and sentenced to hang. Horn's supporters tried to free him with a dynamite blast, and he later did briefly escape from jail, but on November 20, 1903, Horn was hanged before a large crowd at the corner of Pioneer and 19th Avenues in Cheyenne. Until the last minute, everyone expected a pardon, and many wealthy cattlemen feared what Horn might reveal. His last words were to his friend T. Joe Cahill: "Joe, they tell me you are married now. I hope you're doing well. Treat her right."

Cheyenne's old courthouse building, on the northwest corner of 19th and Carey Streets, houses historical exhibits on Tom Horn and the boy he murdered.

---

the next eight decades this would be Wyoming's only state prison, housing its most hardened criminals. The prison was finally abandoned in 1981, when the inmates were transferred to a new facility south of Rawlins.

FRONTIER PRISON

Rawlins's main attraction is the Frontier Prison at 5th and Walnut Streets, first opened in 1901 and in use until 1981. Actually, it was a state prison for all of its existence, but locals prefer to call it a frontier prison because construction began while Wyoming was still a territory. The imposing turret towers and stonework of the prison's exterior give it the oppressive appearance of a medieval castle. Inside, conditions for the inmates were almost as primitive, bordering on ghastly. There was no plumbing or electricity for the first 15 years, and it wasn't until 1978 that hot water was installed in one block of cells. A special dungeon house was built for uncooperative inmates, and beatings were common in the early years. Ten prisoners were hanged—one by fellow inmates—and another five were executed in the gas chamber in Rawlins, the last in 1965. The gallows were a uniquely gruesome device in which the victim actually hanged himself through an elaborate mechanism by which his weight displaced a water counterbalance, thus releasing a trapdoor and leaving him hanging by a noose. It was built to hang notorious cattle detective and murderer Tom Horn in 1903 and moved into the prison later (Horn was never in this prison). The instrument did not always work;

one man had to be strangled by the "humane" guards when he didn't die fast enough. Science marches onward: Wyoming's death-row inmates now face lethal injection instead.

The old prison was the scene of several escape attempts, including one in which four death-row inmates tunneled out as far as the west wall before being caught. The dirt was secreted away in ceiling panels, where it's still visible. Two other breakouts were successful—one involved 28 men—although nearly all of the escapees were caught or killed in the surrounding community. In later years the penitentiary housed 500 prisoners and employed 100 guards and other workers.

In 1987, the B movie *Prison* was filmed on location here with locals as extras. Parts of the movie set are still visible, and some of the prison floors are still red from the fake blood. If you missed it in the theaters, don't despair;

this is one of those godawful flicks that will eventually make it to the 4 A.M. slot on some obscure cable TV station. Or, you can buy a copy in the Frontier Prison gift shop.

The Lone Bandit

The most famous inmate to spend time here was William Carlisle, the "gentleman train robber." In three Union Pacific train robberies in Wyoming, Carlisle netted barely $1,000. He never robbed female passengers, never shot or injured anyone, and was reported to have bought gifts for children with the loot. After the third robbery, he was caught and sentenced to life in prison. Carlisle was sent to Rawlins in 1916 but escaped in a shirt crate three years later. In another train robbery Carlisle was shot and wounded but still managed to remain free for two weeks before a posse caught up with him. The last conviction landed him another

BIG NOSE GEORGE PARROT

George Manuse, better known as Big Nose George Parrot, was a rustler from the Powder River country who joined up with Dutch Charley Burris and Frank James (of the James Gang) on an 1878 robbery attempt. The trio tried to derail a Union Pacific train by prying up a piece of track and waiting in ambush. Unfortunately for the outlaws, an alert Union Pacific employee discovered the missing rail before the train arrived, and a manhunt ensued. The posse tracked the gang into Rattlesnake Canyon and then stopped in a freshly deserted camp. As a deputy sheriff bent over to check the coals, he commented, "They're hot as hell." Immediately, a voice shouted from behind the bushes, "We'll show you how hot hell is." Two deputies were shot dead, and the three robbers escaped.

After the murders, the trio split up. Dutch Charlie was caught the following year and sent back via train to Carbon, Wyoming, for trial. But the trial never came; a group of masked men pulled him from the train and threw a noose around his neck. When Dutch Charlie was asked if he had any last words, the widow of one of the deputies yelled out, "No, the son-of-a-bitch has nothing to

say!" and booted the barrel from under his feet. The newspaper noted, "the train was delayed only thirteen minutes by the operation."

In 1880, the law finally caught up with Big Nose George in Montana, and he too was hauled back to Rawlins in shackles. When the train pulled into town, 15 armed men forced the sheriff to release the prisoner to them and hauled him off to be hanged. Big Nose George managed to avoid his fate this time by reminding his would-be lynchers that "dead men tell no tales," but he confessed to and was convicted of the murders the following spring and was sentenced to hang. In an escape attempt shortly after the trial, George cracked the skull of a guard with his shackles before finally being subdued. When word of the escape attempt spread through Rawlins, a mob of masked men broke into the jail. Big Nose George was hauled out and lynched in the street, although it took two tries—the rope was too long the first time. The Rawlins jail register notes that Big Nose George Parrot "Went to join the angels via hempen cord on telegraph pole front of Fred Wolf's saloon."

life sentence, but the governor pardoned Carlisle in 1936. He walked out a changed man and eventually became a respected Laramie motel owner and author of a book about his life, *The Lone Bandit.* Carlisle died in 1964.

The Sweet Smell of Sagebrush

A portion of the old prison serves double duty as the **Wyoming Peace Officers Museum,** with memorials, artifacts, and badges. Also here are photos and descriptions of various inmates, along with a souvenir shop selling postcards, books, and other items. One book well worth a look is *The Sweet Smell of Sagebrush.* This is a collection of stories by William Stanley Hudson, a man who served four separate sentences here for such crimes as horse stealing and passing stolen checks. It offers not only a glimpse of early-1900s prison life but also a fascinating account of criminal logic. The title comes from his release from prison after serving his first sentence:

> *i thought little of those things that august day as i walked out from the damp prison air into the glorious sunshine of this enchanted land. i felt only a desire to get away somewhere out of sight. after walking towards the buisness part of town a short way, i turned and went straight out of town untill i reached the high sagebrush. the smell of the sage was that day sweeter to me than a breath from a bed of rarest flowers. for an hour i was content to sit and breathe the pure mountain air and enjoy the warm sunshine.*

Hudson's fate is unknown. After release from his fourth incarceration in 1921, he disappeared. Perhaps he was a reformed man. Or perhaps he learned enough to avoid getting caught again.

Access

The prison motto: "No visitors locked inside since 1981." During summer, the prison is open daily 8:30 A.M.–5:30 P.M., with guided hourly tours at half past the hour. Winter tours are less frequent, but someone is generally here on weekdays. These excellent, hour-long tours cost $5 adults, $4.50 se-

niors or kids (children under six free), and $20 families. Get the full scoop at 307/324-4422, www.wyomingfrontierprison.com. Be sure to bring a sweater or coat with you because the stone prison is chilly even in midsummer. For a scarier visit, ask about the nighttime flashlight tours offered some summer evenings ($6 per person) and on Halloween. Night tours are by reservation only and not recommended for young children.

OTHER SIGHTS

Carbon County Museum

Housed in an old Mormon church at 9th and Walnut Streets, the Carbon County Museum, 307/328-2740, is open Monday–Friday 1–8 P.M. and Saturday 1–5 P.M. June–August, and Monday–Friday 1–5 P.M. the rest of the year. No charge. The museum is a mixed bag, containing Oregon Trail and Indian relics, historic photos, an Essex Motors race car from 1922, a 1920 hook-and-ladder truck, and various stage-station and Civil War artifacts. One case even contains 400-year-old Spanish artifacts discovered in a cave near Hanna. Easily the strangest object in the museum is a pair of two-tone shoes made from the skin of Big Nose George Parrot, a train robber and murderer. These were crafted by Dr. John E. Osborne, who also decided to saw open George's skull to see if the brains of desperadoes differed from those of common men. The skullcap became an ashtray now on exhibit at the Union Pacific Railroad Museum in Omaha, but the bottom of the skull is here, along with Big Nose George's death mask and a photo of the old whiskey barrel in which Osborne decided to store the body. The barrel wasn't discovered until 1950 when a construction crew found it while digging at an old Rawlins drugstore. Incidentally, this same Dr. Osborne went on to serve as Wyoming's governor from 1893 to 1895!

Looking for more criminals? Try **St. Joseph's Cemetery,** where two early train robbers are buried. Ask at the museum for the exact grave locations. Still more crooks? Try the state penitentiary, south of town; you'll meet real live ones there.

The historic Ferris Mansion was built in 1903.

© DON PITCHER

Buildings

Many interesting old sandstone buildings are scattered throughout downtown, built from stone quarried around Rawlins. Pick up a detailed **historic downtown Rawlins walking-tour brochure** of historic buildings from the chamber of commerce at 517 Cedar Street. Notable ones include the Shrine Temple at 5th and Pine (completed in 1909), the Elks Club at 4th and Buffalo (completed in 1909), and the Presbyterian church at 3rd and Cedar (built in 1882). The Union Pacific Railroad depot at 400 W. Front was built in 1901 of granite and brick and is now used as a community meeting room. One of the most attractive buildings in Rawlins is the **Ferris Mansion** at 607 W. Maple, built for the widow of an early mining pioneer, George Ferris. An old **steam locomotive** rests in Tully Park on Elm Street next to the hospital.

"Rockology"

The country around Rawlins is a geologist's and rock hound's paradise; jade, petrified wood, agate, and other minerals are here to be discovered. Of course, oil, gas, and coal are what geologists are most interested in around here. The **Rawlins Uplift** (a thrust-faulted anticline) rises immediately north of town, providing a textbook example of stratigraphy. Plenty of fish and invertebrate fossils are here, too. As a side note, the paint known as "Rawlins Red" originated from iron oxide mined just north of town. The color is still used for barns and buildings in the eastern United States, and this was the color originally chosen by General Rawlins to paint the Brooklyn Bridge (as Secretary of War, he approved the bridge plans).

ACCOMMODATIONS

Given its relatively small size, Rawlins has a surprising number of places to stay. This is partly a legacy of the boom era in the 1970s, when tight housing conditions forced many workers into motels and mobile homes; partly it's attributable to the nightly influx of tired I-80 travelers. If you plan to stay at one of the cheap motels, particularly those not listed, take a look at the rooms first because some may not be up to your standards.

Under $50

Ideal Motel, 1507 W. Spruce, 307/324-3451, is an older place with clean but basic furnishings and some in-room fridges. Rates are a bargain: $32 s or $35 d. Another decent economy place is **Jade Lodge,** 405 W. Spruce, 307/324-2791, where rooms cost $36 s or d, or $39 for kitchenettes.

Quite a few other budget places may be worth investigating if you want cheap rates (starting around $30 s or $40 d) and don't mind aging furnishings. Most of these places have small refrigerators and microwaves in the rooms. Worth-a-look bargain places include **Best Motel,** 905 W. Spruce, 307/324-3456; **Budget Inn,** 1617 W. Spruce, 307/328-1600; **Economy Inn,** 713 W. Spruce, 307/324-4561; **Key Motel,** 1806 E. Cedar, 307/324-2728; **La Bella Motel,** 1819 W. Spruce St., 307/324-2583; and **Sunset Motel,** 1302 W. Spruce, 307/324-3448.

$50 and Up

Stay at **Super 8 Motel,** 2338 Wagon Circle Rd., 307/328-0630 or 800/800-8000,

MEDICINE BOW

www.super8.com, for $50 s or $55 d, including a continental breakfast and exercise room. **Days Inn,** 2222 E. Cedar, 307/324-6615 or 888/324-6615, www.daysinn.com, has an enclosed heated pool and offers a hot breakfast each morning. Rates are $65 s or $75 d.

   The Lodge at Rawlins, 1801 E. Cedar, 307/324-2783 or 877/729-5467, has a heated outdoor pool, and updated rooms—some with king beds, microwaves, and fridges—for $70 s or $75 d. Do a little wildlife watching while here; an active prairie dog town is right behind the hotel. On the south edge of town, **Sleep Inn,** 1400 Higley Blvd., 307/328-1732 or 800/753-3746, www.sleepinn.com, offers modern rooms for $66–72 s or $71–77 d. Amenities include a light breakfast, sauna, and game room.

   Rawlins's premier motel is **Best Western Cotton Tree Inn,** at 23rd and Spruce, 307/324-2737 or 800/662-6886, www.cottontree.net, with an indoor pool, hot tub, and sauna, plus passes to a local health club. Remodeled rooms (some with fridges, microwaves, and king beds) are $79 s or $84 d.

CAMPING

The nearest public campground (free; open June–Oct.) is at **Teton Reservoir,** 17 miles south of Rawlins. More public facilities ($12 for nonresidents, $6 for Wyoming residents; open year-round) are in Seminoe State Park, 28 miles north of Sinclair; 307/320-3013, http://wyoparks.state.wy.us.

   You'll find four parking lot campgrounds in Rawlins. Expect to pay $18 for tents or $20–24 for RVs at **Western Hills Campground,** 2500 Wagon Circle Rd., 307/324-2592 or 888/568-3040, www.trib.com/~whc; **Rawlins KOA,** 205 E. Hwy. 71, 307/328-2021 or 800/562-7559, www.koa.com; **American President's Camp RV Park,** 2346 W. Spruce St., 307/324-3315; or **RV World Campground,** 2401 Wagon Circle Rd., 307/328-1091 or 800/478-9753. All four of these are great places to swelter in the simmering heat of summer as you listen to the freeway traffic. Western Hills and American President's are open all year (but I wouldn't stay at the latter); the

others are typically open April–October. If you aren't camping here, you can take showers at American President's or RV World.

FOOD

Rawlins has several good restaurants. Start the day at **Square Shooter's Eating House,** 311 W. Cedar, 307/324-4380, serving standard American fare amid the ambience of mounted animal heads.

   Locals rave about **Rose's Lariat,** 410 E. Cedar, 307/324-5261, an old favorite with heavy and old-fashioned Mexican meals. Only one small table; everyone else sits at the counter stools, so you'll probably end up waiting to eat. Open Tues.–Sat. until 7 P.M. For Chinese food, head to **China Panda,** 1810 E. Cedar St., 307/324-2198; for pizza, try **Pizza Hut,** 506 Higley Blvd., 307/324-7706, where you'll find lunchtime stuff-yourself specials.

   Occupying a vintage 1881 building, **The Pantry,** 221 W. Cedar St., 307/324-7860, is a fine, family-run place with reasonable prices and American food. Lots of grub for the buck. Another historic home contains **Aspen House Restaurant,** 318 5th St., 307/324-4787. The standout menu includes steaks, seafood, chicken, pasta, and Asian specialties, and the Singaporean owner brings an Eastern touch to the cookery. Open for lunch and dinner only, with $13–35 entrées. Recommended.

   Huckleberry Ice Cream, 509 W. Cedar St., 307/324-5233 or 800/484-5808, has several inside tables and serves espresso, bagels, and ice cream. Get fast service and decent truck-stop grub at **Flying J Truckstop,** two miles west of Rawlins, 307/324-3463, or from **Rip Griffin's Truckstop,** I-80 at Higley Blvd., 307/328-2103. Groceries can be found at **City Market,** 602 Higley Blvd., 307/328-1421, which also has a deli.

ENTERTAINMENT AND EVENTS

Images Lounge at the Day's Inn, has Top 40 DJ tunes most nights and occasional rock bands. Also try **The Keg,** 307 E. Cedar, 307/324-9826, for live music.

   In Rawlins, cowboy poetry enthusiasts will

want to take in the **Carbon County Gathering of Cowboy Poets** in mid-July. The event also includes a Western arts-and-crafts show and country-and-western music and dancing; details at 307/324-2251, www.wyomingcowboypoetry.com. **Crazy Days** occurs at the same time, with a motorcycle rally, outhouse races, barbecue, and street dance.

The biggest local event is **Carbon County Fair and Rodeo,** 307/324-6866, held the first week of August each year. Attractions include livestock and farm exhibits, rodeos, truck pulls, arts-and-crafts displays, parades, a carnival, a street dance, a pancake breakfast, and a demolition derby.

RECREATION

The **Rawlins Family Recreation Center,** 1616 Harshman, 307/324-7529, www.rawlinswyoming.com/recenter.htm, has racquetball, basketball, and volleyball courts, a weight room, an indoor track, and other facilities. Swim at the **high school pool.** Other minor-league attractions are the **Jeffrey Lanes** bowling alley, 1917 W. Spruce St., 307/328-0263, and **mini-golf** courses at RV World Campground and Western Hills Campground. Golfers will find a new nine-hole playground at **Rochelle Ranch Course,** 307/320-7112.

INFORMATION AND SERVICES

The **Rawlins-Carbon County Chamber of Commerce** is next to City Hall at 519 Cedar St., 307/324-4111, www.oldwestfun.com, and is open Monday–Friday 9–noon and 1–5 P.M. year-round. Get regional information and publications from the **Carbon County Visitors Council,** 800/228-3547, www.wyomingcarboncounty.com.

Carbon County Public Library is at 3rd and Buffalo, 307/328-2618, and has computers with Internet access. Find the **post office** at 106 5th St., 307/324-3521.

The **BLM district office** is at 1300 N. 3rd, 307/328-4200, www.wy.blm.gov. **Cedar Chest Gifts,** 416 W. Cedar St., 307/324-7737, is a combination gift shop and gallery with a handful of Wyoming books. The Frontier Prison also sells books on Wyoming. Find **ATMs** at several local banks, grocers, and truck stops, and even in the McDonald's. Wash clothes at **The Washboard,** 504 23rd, 307/324-2434, or **Wash & Dry Laundry,** 515 15th Street.

Carbon County Memorial Hospital, 2221 Elm St., 307/324-2221, has a physician on staff.

TRANSPORTATION

Greyhound, 307/324-5496 or 800/231-2222, www.greyhound.com, has bus service along I-80 in both directions, but there are no direct connections between Rawlins and Casper or other cities in the northern part of Wyoming; the closest routing is via Cheyenne or Rock Springs. Greyhound buses stop at McDonald's, 2225 E. Cedar Street.

Rent cars from **Quality Motors,** 121 W. Cedar St., 307/324-7131. There is no commercial air service to Rawlins.

Rawlins Vicinity

FORT FRED STEELE

Fort Fred Steele—named for Civil War hero Maj. Gen. Frederick Steele—was built in 1868 as one of three Wyoming posts established to protect the transcontinental railroad from Indian attacks. Soldiers from the fort fought against the Utes in northern Colorado during their 1879 uprising against tyrannical Indian agent Nathan C. Meek-er. The troops also helped reestablish peace after the 1885 anti-Chinese riots in Rock Springs.

After the fort was abandoned by the army in 1886, civilians took over the buildings and turned this into a supply base for ranchers and sheepherders. It was headquarters for the Carbon Timber Company, which controlled the enormous railroad tie market for the Union Pacific Railroad in the Rockies and owned nearly 25,000 acres of timberland. Lodgepole pines were felled in the Medicine Bow Mountains and floated down the North Platte River during high flows each spring. At Fort Steele, they were caught by a log boom and loaded onto railway cars or used in the sawmill or box factory. The tie industry remained important well into the 20th century—300,000 ties were sent down the North Platte River in 1938 alone—but when the Union Pacific stopped using hand-hewn ties in 1940, the town of Fort Steele suffered. With the loss of its main industry and the 1939 rerouting of the Lincoln Highway, all but a few people moved away.

Fort Steele Today

Fort Steele, nine miles east of Sinclair on I-80, is now a 137-acre state park. A small visitors center in the old bridge tender's house contains historical photos of the fort and the Carbon Timber Company. The park is open daily 9 A.M.–7 P.M. May to mid-November, but closed to entry the rest of the year. Get additional information at 307/320-3013, http://wyoparks.state.wy.us. Historical plaques are scattered over the grounds, but not much remains of what was a substantial settlement: just a couple of clapboard buildings, some sandstone foundations and chimneys, and the walls of a house once owned by Fenimore Chatterton, Wyoming's governor from 1903 to 1905. Stone walls from the military quartermaster's corral remain just west of the parade grounds, but a disastrous arson fire on New Year's Eve 1976 destroyed two enlisted men's barracks that had stood here for more than a century.

Just up the hill from the fort site is a square **powder magazine** built in 1881 from locally quarried stone, with an adjacent cemetery containing the graves of civilians who died in the area. Only a few headstones remain. The slow-moving North Platte River right next to the fort is a great place for picnics, but there's no camping allowed. Despite the paucity of historical buildings, there's something rather nice about the authenticity of the site. Stop in at dusk on a summer evening and you'll hear the rumble of freight trains while coyotes howl from nearby hills and the North Platte River rolls away from this lonely place.

SINCLAIR

Sinclair (pop. 420) is one of the more distinctive small settlements in Wyoming. In 1923, the Producers Oil and Refining Company (Parco) established a 50,000-barrel-a-day oil refinery here, built a town to house its employees, and named the settlement Parco. When the Sinclair Oil Company bought the refinery in 1934, the name changed, but ownership of all businesses and homes remained in corporate hands for three decades. In 1967, Sinclair finally sold the homes to renters and gave the business buildings to the town government. Today the refinery still lights up the night sky for miles around, and hundreds of giant oil tanks stand behind the facility. I-80 passes right by Sinclair, and most folks don't bother to stop here except to fill up at the Burns Brothers Truckstop one mile east of town. Actually, Sinclair is a pleasant little resting place and a nice spot for a shady picnic lunch.

Parco built the company town, including the large Parco Inn at the center, in Spanish-mission style with red-tile roofs and stucco walls. You'd think you were in Southern California. An elaborate fountain and a nice, small park stand across from the inn, now virtually abandoned but listed on the National Register of Historic Places. A pair of Civil War vintage cannons guard the water fountain from attack by marauding oil executives. They were brought here originally to blow holes in burning oil tanks (if the need ever arose), allowing the oil to drain into the surrounding dikes before the tanks could explode from the heat.

The **Parco/Sinclair Museum** is in the old bank building and contains several local items, including clamp-on ice skates from the 1920s, old photos, and the high point, a newspaper headlined "Nixon Resigns." Open Mon.–Fri. 9–noon and 1–4:30 P.M. Access is through the town hall, next door. The town also has a branch library and recreation center.

Of note in Sinclair is **Su Casa Cafe,** 307/328-1745, which makes genuine Mexican food. There are no motels in town, but the road north of Sinclair leads to popular Seminoe and Pathfinder Reservoirs, where camping is available. (See the Central Wyoming chapter for details on these lakes.) Sinclair is also home to the nine-hole **Sinclair Golf Course,** 307/324-3918; it's located along the North Platte River. The Burns Brothers Truck Stop has an **ATM** and a restaurant serving trucker meals.

HEADING NORTH

U.S. Hwy. 287/State Hwy. 789 points north from Rawlins into Wyoming's heartland, crossing the Continental Divide twice along the way as it dips into the Great Divide Basin and then back out again. Once inside the basin, the highway throws itself straight across this sandy land from point A to point B, with not much in between to deflect it. No need to touch the steering wheel here. Fences collect both tumbleweeds and bits of miscellaneous junk. To the northeast the tilted face of 10,037-foot Ferris Mountain rises, but your sense of distance falters in the featureless desert land where only fence lines and a few gullies halt the relentless horizontal geography. Geologists love this place: long, eroded ridges and scarps in the distance, which appear so parched of water that their barren slopes could be the bleached rib cages of some prehistoric monster. Some amazing badlands formations are here as well.

Lamont and Bairoil

The diminutive settlement of Lamont lies 33 miles north of Rawlins near the Continental Divide. A paved road leads five miles west to another tiny place, Bairoil. The latter is named for Charles Bair, who discovered oil (hence the name) here in 1916. Today the surrounding area is part of Lost Soldier Oil Field, and pumpjacks sprinkle the landscape.

Bairoil lays claim to a slice of air-travel trivia. In 1989, Kevin Christopherson set a world foot-launched hang-gliding record when he took off from Whiskey Peak, caught favorable wind currents, and rode them all the way into North Dakota, 287 miles away.

Campsites and RV hookups can be found in the **Bairoil town park,** 307/324-7653. In Lamont, **Grandma's Cafe & Campground,** 307/324-9870, serves three meals a day (starting at 5 A.M.) and provides RV and tent sites.

Over Whiskey Gap

Forty miles north of Rawlins, the highway climbs through Whiskey Gap, with Green Mountain to the west and the Ferris Mountains to the east. The gap received its name in 1862 when Maj. Jack O'Farrell caught his soldiers drinking from an illegal barrel of whiskey in a trader's wagon. The whiskey was dumped on the ground, but some flowed into a spring that one soldier later called the "sweetest water he had ever tasted."

Another five miles north of Whiskey Gap is the junction of U.S. 287/State Hwy. 789 and State Hwy. 220 at **Muddy Gap,** where you can gas up. The road diverges, with one fork leading northeast to Casper, passing the Oregon Trail landmarks of Devil's Gate and Independence Rock (see Casper Vicinity in the Central Wyoming chapter), and the other heading northwest to Lander, with Split Rock and Jeffrey City along the way (see Lander Vicinity in the Wind River Mountains Country chapter for more on Jeffrey City). In either direction you will find stereotypical Wyoming vistas—sagebrush, grass, cattle, and sky. But no whiskey barrels.

MEDICINE BOW

Southwest Wyoming

Southwest Wyoming is the state's forbidden quarter, a place seen primarily from the windows of cars speeding along I-80. At first glance the land appears stark, barren, and worthless. In 1866, Gen. William T. Sherman wrote, "The Government will have to pay a bounty for people to like it up here." Others said people wouldn't come no matter how many incentives the government might offer. But despite the lack of trees, the broiling hot summers, and the wind-iced winters, people *have* settled here, primarily to extract the area's immense energy and mineral resources. Southwest Wyoming contains both the state's largest county (Sweetwater) and its smallest (Uinta), as well as Lincoln County, seemingly named for its L-shape. The Green River cuts across this part of Wyoming, eventually joining the Colorado River in Utah.

old gas station near Green River

©DON PITCHER

SOUTHWEST WYOMING

To Cody
To Worland
(Bighorn Basin)
120

Shoshone

Grand
Teton

National

Park

River

Moran Jct.

26

189
191

Bridger-Teton

National

National Forest

CONTINENTAL DIVIDE

Jackson

89

Dubois

26

287

Thermopolis

20
789

Boysen
Reservoir

WIND RIVER INDIAN

RESERVATION

Shoshoni

Hoback Jct.

191

189

Forest

Snake R.
Canyon

Alpine
Jct.

Thayne

GREYS RIVER

Bridger-Teton

Gannett Peak
(13,804 ft.)

Bridger-Teton

Ocean
Lake

26

287

Riverton

To Powder River

National

Shoshone

Lander

Snake

IDAHO
WYOMING

To Swan Valley and Idaho Falls, ID

26

To Soda
Springs, ID

34

354

National

Pinedale

National

Forest

Forest

287
789

River

LOOP RD.

Greys River

Forest

Wyoming
Peak
(11,378 ft.)

Marbleton

351

Atlantic
City

South Pass City

Sweetwater

89

350

Big Piney

191

232

Caplet

189

La Barge

28

CONTINENTAL DIVIDE

To Pocatello, ID

Names
Hill

Fontenelle
Reservoir

Farson

Sand Dunes

Sand Dunes

Great Divide
Basin

Border

Cokeville

Lake
Viva-Naughton

Green

Eden

Boars Tusk

30

Seedskadee

National

Fossil Butte
Nat'l Mon.

Wildlife

CONTINENTAL DIVIDE

Red
Desert

Sage

Kemmerer

Refuge

372

White
Mountain

Superior

Point of
Rocks

To Montpelier, ID

Randolf

Elkol

Opal

30

River

Pilot Butte

Rock Springs

To Wamsutter and Rawlins
(Medicine Bow Cntry.)

Diamondville

TRONA
MINES

80

Woodruff

Church
Buttes

Little
America

Green
River

530

412

80

191

89

Almy

Evanston

189

Fort
Bridger

Lyman

Mountain View

Flaming
Gorge
National
Recreation
Area

430

WYOMING
COLORADO

To Ogden, UT

Piedmont

410

414

Lonetree

Burntfork

WYOMING
UTAH

150

Manila

Dutch John

0   20 mi

0   20 km

WYOMING

To Salt Lake City, UT

To High Uintas, UT

To Vernal, UT

© AVALON TRAVEL PUBLISHING, INC.

SOUTHWEST WYOMING

HISTORY

When whites first arrived in southwest Wyoming, they found the Shoshone and Ute Indians hunting buffalo and antelope in this desert country. The first mountain-man rendezvous took place here, and many of the vital emigrant routes passed through, including the Oregon, Mormon, and Overland Trails, as did the Pony Express and the transcontinental telegraph. But the Union Pacific Railroad opened the land to settlement. Completion of the railroad in 1869 brought about the establishment of Rock Springs, Green River, and Evanston, and coal mines were developed in the Rock Springs, Evanston, and Kemmerer areas to fuel these trains. Men of all nationalities came to work the mines, creating a racial diversity that is still visible.

Just as the coal mines began to close in the 1950s, enormous trona deposits were developed in western Sweetwater County, and many miners simply switched employers. Other mines extract phosphates and coal, and the natural-gas fields of Sweetwater and Uinta counties are the most productive in Wyoming. Southwest Wyoming has the world's biggest coal mine, biggest coke-pro-

---

SOUTHWEST WYOMING SIGHTSEEING HIGHLIGHTS

Killpecker Dunes and White Mountain Petroglyphs in the Red Desert

Flaming Gorge National Recreation Area

Fort Bridger

Fossil Butte National Monument and Kemmerer area fossil quarries

Periodic Spring and elk-antler arch in Afton

Greys River Loop Road

Star Valley Cheese factory in Thayne

Snake River Canyon

Popular events: Red Desert Round Up in Rock Springs (July), Oyster Ridge Music Festival in Kemmerer (August), Fort Bridger Rendezvous at Fort Bridger (Labor Day), Cowboy Days in Evanston (Labor Day), and Cutter Races near Afton (winter)

---

ducing plant, biggest trona mine, and biggest helium plant. Put all this together and it's obvious that despite the desert setting and small population, southwest Wyoming is in some ways the most industrialized part of the state.

The Red Desert

The eastern half of Sweetwater County contains a vast treeless area known as the Red Desert, so named because of the brick-red soil that stretches in all directions. It's not a place to be trifled with. Less than nine inches of precipitation falls each year, and summertime temperatures frequently top 100°F in this forbidding, lonely place—the largest stretch of unfenced land in the Lower 48. Some of the largest remaining herds of wild horses roam here, along with desert elk and one of the last wild herds of bison. Antelope are found throughout this country, as are a few cattle and lots of sheep. The signs of humans are few and far between: dirt roads, oil and gas wells, and a few wind-scoured buildings.

I-80 is most folks' sole acquaintance with the Red Desert—two double-wide rivers of as-

phalt cracking open the desiccated land. There aren't many sights to see unless you pull off the main road and slow down. Despite its harshness, the Red Desert has a desolate beauty that grows on you. Pick what may seem the least interesting place, where the ramp ends at a cattle crossing and the road immediately turns to gravel. When you're far enough from the interstate that you can no longer hear the trucks, get out of your car and use all of your senses to grasp this place. Feel the intensity of the sun on a blistering summer day. Look at the way the thin-crusted snow lies in the lee side of the sage in winter, worn out by the incessant wind. Listen to the "scree!" cry of the red-tailed hawk. Taste a couple of the pungent sage leaves. Smell the rusty air as the first drops of a sudden shower pummel the road dust. Watch a herd of antelope bound away and then turn warily back to see who might be stopping in such a place. Or simply let the stillness of this vast land sweep over you, broken by the howl of a distant coyote. This is Wyoming without pretenses.

The Red Desert lies within **Great Divide Basin,** a 90-mile-long region where the little water that falls never makes it to either ocean. Red Lake—a salty playa—fills with water during rare rainy spells, only to have it soak into the sandy soil or evaporate in the summer sun. The Continental Divide splits south of Great Divide Basin and then rejoins on its northern margin, leaving a bowl in the middle. Highway travelers on I-80 thus cross the Continental Divide twice.

WAMSUTTER

As you drive the 108 miles west from Rawlins to Rock Springs, the only town worth noting—and marginally so—is Wamsutter (pop.

Overland Stage trail sign near Point of Rocks

© DON PITCHER

260). Natural-gas wells sprinkle the country to west and south, and the town consists of a trashy collection of old trailer homes, oil field equipment, and smashed-up trucks hauled here from I-80 accidents. This is a good place to read a romance novel and pretend you're somewhere else. Butch Cassidy's Hole-in-the-Wall gang robbed a Union Pacific train near here in 1900, and freight trains still roll by every few minutes, day and night. The surrounding country is a rock hound's paradise, with petrified wood, fossils, and tortilla agate—beautiful when polished—all found on public lands in the area.

Rest your head at the pleasant **Wamsutter Inn,** 307/324-7112, where rooms with microwaves are $40 s or d. **Sagebrush Motel,** 307/328-1584, has rooms in old modular homes. Enjoy good home cooking at **Broadway Cafe,** 307/324-7830, or tip a beer at the **Desert Bar,** 307/324-4949.

POINT OF ROCKS

At Point of Rocks (I-80 exit 130), 25 miles east of Rock Springs, the state has restored an **Overland Stage station** and adjacent stables built in 1862. Constructed from sandstone, the station served as a jumping-off point for a road to South Pass City during the gold-rush years. Get here by following the sign to the historical marker for the Overland Trail and then continuing another one-half mile over the railroad tracks (where freight trains roll through every 10 minutes or so) and south to the stage station. It sits on a hillside overlooking the railroad and freeway, and markers note the old Overland/Cherokee Trail route. The historic stone building is well worth the brief side trip from I-80.

The "town" of Point of Rocks has a gas station/restaurant/store/bar and several dozen trailer homes. Coal is dug from the ground at two enormous strip mines not far from Point of Rocks. The Jim Bridger Mine feeds directly into the equally gargantuan Jim Bridger Power Plant, built in the early 1970s to supply power for the Western United States.

SUPERIOR

For a delightful change of pace from the onward rush of commerce, take I-80 exit 122 (20 miles east of Rock Springs). Follow this winding country road through seven miles of sage and grass to the town of Superior. Movie trivia buffs might recognize the town; parts of the 1992 film *Leaving Normal* were shot here.

Superior was once home to 6,000 people, but most moved away after the coal mines closed in 1963, leaving fewer than 300 today. The only surviving business is Canyon Bar; even the Ghost Town Bar is boarded up! Enjoy a picnic in the shady town park or just check out the many aging structures. Most interesting are the roofless remains of **Union Hall,** a trapezoidal building constructed in 1921. Interpretive signs here detail local history. Additional abandoned structures can be found at Old Superior, just up the road.

One mile north of Superior are the **Natural Corrals,** an area of small corral-like enclosures in the rocks. Caves reach into the volcanic hills and often contain ice even in midsummer. Check with the Rock Springs BLM office, 307/352-0256, www.wy.blm.gov, for directions.

KILLPECKER DUNES AREA

North of Rock Springs, White Mountain rises like a cresting wave over the valley through which U.S. 191 passes. Approximately 11 miles up is the turnoff to Tri-Territory Rd., providing access to the Killpecker Sand Dunes, the largest active dunes in North America. The dunes—some topping 150 feet in height—extend eastward for 55 miles in a band that averages 2–3 miles wide but sometimes reaches 10. The constantly shifting dunes are formed from Eden Valley dirt that blows east on the prevailing winds. Signs point the way to most of the sights in the Killpecker Dunes area. As an aside, the Tri-Territory area received its name as the point at which three major American land acquisitions met: the Louisiana Purchase, the Northwest Territories, and the Mexican Cession.

Petroglyphs and Boars Tusk

Follow gravel Tri-Territory Road 12 miles east from U.S. 191 and head left at the turnoff to **White Mountain Petroglyphs,** following a very rough four-mile track. Avoid this road after rains and early in the year. The road ends at a low sandstone cliff where several hundred petroglyphs were carved into this soft rock by the Indian peoples who lived here in centuries past. Look closely to find elk, bison, horses, feather headdresses, and even a human footprint. Many petroglyphs relate to hunting. Because of the horses pictured here—horses didn't reach this region until the 16th century—it's likely that many of the petroglyphs are of relatively recent origin. The cliff provides a safe location for several large raptor nests. Juniper and sage poke up through the remote desert landscape.

Return to the main gravel road and turn left to reach other interesting sights. Six miles to the east, the road splits. Turn right to reach the off-road vehicle (ORV) area of the dunes or left to visit **Boars Tusk** and dunes where vehicles are not allowed. Follow the latter road 1.5 miles to an unmarked road that leads to the base of Boars Tusk, a 400-foot-high rocky spire—a volcanic plug—that local rock climbers love. The 2.5-mile side road to Boars Tusk may be passable in a high-clearance vehicle, but I'd recommend a 4WD.

The Dunes

The dunes begin 1.5 miles beyond the turnoff to Boars Tusk, 22 miles from U.S. 191. This fascinating area is most beautiful in the early morning or at dusk, when sunlight gleams off the sand. Because it is a wilderness study area, vehicles are not allowed off the roads. Animals are surprisingly common in the Killpecker Dunes, and even a cursory examination will reveal tracks of coyotes, deer, elk, birds, and insects. Small pools of water on the lee side of some dunes are fed by melting snow that gets covered by drifting sand in the winter. This is a great place to hike, but be sure to come prepared for a desert climate: bring food and water, a compass, and a topographic map. The dirt roads are also fine for mountain biking. See the BLM office in Rock Springs for more details on this unusual area.

Rock Springs

As an energy and transportation center, Rock Springs (pop. 19,000) is western Wyoming's largest city. It's also Wyoming's whipping boy and the focus of derisive jokes. Despite recent renovation efforts, the city still doesn't offer much beyond a place to rest up on the way to somewhere else. Pull off the freeway and you'll find the standard grouping of fast-food eateries, chain motels, gas stations, and convenience stores. The rest of Rock Springs consists of a patchwork of dead-end downtown streets, trailer parks, and split-level homes sprawling in various directions, with the train tracks cutting through the middle of it all. The convoluted street system is a legacy of the coal-mining era, when paths taken by miners walking to work gradually evolved into a road network.

Like most other mining and energy towns, Rock Springs has always experienced booms and busts. Most of the underground coal mines are closed, but they still create a hazard as they settle, dropping the buildings above as they go. In the last decade the citizens of Rock Springs have

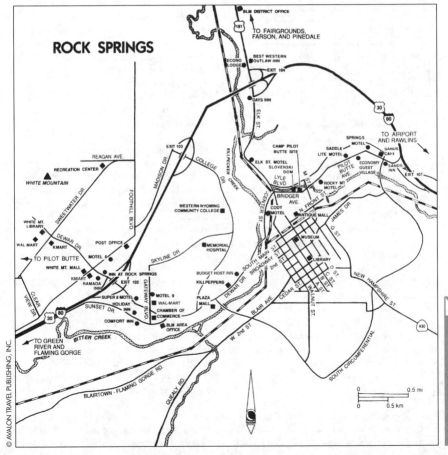

© AVALON TRAVEL PUBLISHING, INC.

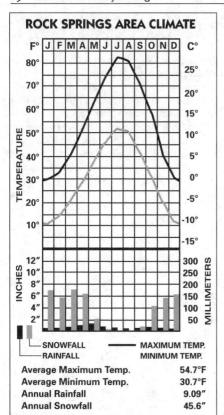

ROCK SPRINGS AREA CLIMATE

| | SNOWFALL | MAXIMUM TEMP. |
| | RAINFALL | MINIMUM TEMP. |

Average Maximum Temp.	54.7°F
Average Minimum Temp.	30.7°F
Annual Rainfall	9.09"
Annual Snowfall	45.6"

Act granted the Union Pacific rights to all coal along the transcontinental route. Although nearly all of Sweetwater County is underlain with coal, in Rock Springs the coal was close to the surface and easily accessible; the mines actually ran beneath the tracks in many places. Eventually the mines spread over a mile in various directions, creating a honeycomb of tunnels under Rock Springs.

Water and Coal

Although Rock Springs is named for flowing water, the lack of water has always been a problem. Rock Spring dried up once coal mining began, and Bitter Creek provided only muddy, bitter water. Killpecker Creek, a sometime stream that flows through Rock Springs, was named by soldiers who noted the alkaline water's rather painful biological effects when they visited the outhouse. Honest. In the early years, Rock Springs was so short on drinking water that it had to be brought by train from Green River. Baths were once-a-week events despite the coal dust that blackened everyone.

Coal mining brought workers from all over the globe; locals call it the 57-variety town, and flags of many nations decorate local streets. Many arrived from Great Britain or Ireland, but others included Chinese, Italians, Scandinavians, Austrians, Hungarians, Yugoslavians, and Czechs. It was an uneasy melting pot. They lived in company housing, riverbank dugouts, or shanties and used Bitter Creek—already notorious because of its undrinkable water—as the local cesspool and garbage dump. Rock Springs continued to expand as more mines were opened by the Union Pacific, and the Chinese Massacre of 1885 (see Special Topic "The Chinese Massacre") had only a minimal impact on production. By 1892, some 943,513 tons of coal were being hauled out by 1,500 miners.

Although various companies mined here, the Union Pacific Coal Co. really owned Rock Springs and its miners. And Union Pacific was to blame for many of the problems: the filth, the poor housing, the lack of water, and the working conditions that spawned racial hatred. After Union Pacific engines switched from coal to diesel in the 1950s, the underground mines were closed and the economy

worked hard to clean up their image. Extensive restoration work on the historic city hall—now a museum—and along Front Street makes downtown a more likable place, and the backfilling of old coal tunnels has lessened subsidence problems. But the town continues to face hard times because coal is cheaper to mine in the Powder River Basin where it is closer to the surface. Declining school populations have led to the closure of grade schools, and downtown Rock Springs seems to be barely hanging on.

HISTORY

Rock Springs began as a stage station along the Overland Trail but grew because of the Union Pacific's need for coal to run its trains. The Railway

THE CHINESE MASSACRE

Rock Springs had the dubious honor of hosting one of the most infamous incidents in Wyoming history—the Chinese Massacre. In 1875, the Union Pacific Railroad tried to step up coal production at its Rock Springs mines, but miners refused when they found their wages simultaneously being cut. To fill the gap, the company brought in Chinese contract laborers who were willing to work for less money. The Chinese immediately became targets of harassment. The railroad hired more and more Chinese while turning whites away, and within a decade more than 500 Chinese miners were in Rock Springs.

Things came to a head on September 2, 1885, when the supervisor of one of the mines began assigning Chinese workers to locations where whites had previously been working. Whites attacked the Chinese, first with picks and shovels, then with rifles. The violence spread, and Chinatown—a ramshackle assemblage of shacks along what is now Ahsay Avenue—was burned to the ground. A mob of 60 men swept after the defenseless Chinese workers, robbing and then murdering them. Twenty-eight Chinese died in the mêlée and many more fled and may have died while trying to cross the desert. The sheriff came down from Green River to protect the whites but did nothing to stop the murders in Chinatown. No one ever faced trial for the attacks.

The riots spawned similar anti-Chinese violence and strikes all over the West and led Gov. Francis E. Warren to call for federal troops to protect the remaining Chinese workers. As a result, Camp Pilot Butte was established to serve as a buffer between the Chinese and the whites. This was the only place in America where an international treaty post was ever established. Some 250 soldiers remained here until the Spanish-American War forced the fort's abandonment in 1899.

The workers—both white and Chinese—gradually filtered back after the riots, and by December the mines had 85 whites and 457 Chinese workers. The massacre led the United States to pay the Chinese government $149,000 in compensation; it was used to fund Chinese student scholarships in America. In the 1920s and '30s, the Union Pacific Coal Co. finally rewarded the few remaining Chinese workers with passage back to their homeland and endowments to pay for their retirement. Only one of the men remained in Rock Springs all of his life. The bones of others who died were shipped home to China.

An unusual legacy of the riots is a still-burning coal mine at Potter Street in Rock Springs. During the mêlée, several miners stole a large amount of Chinese tea and stored it in a mine tunnel, hoping to sell it later. When the authorities came for it, the miners set it on fire, and the burning tea ignited an adjacent coal seam. Smoke still emerges from the ground at what is now called Burning Mountain.

---

began to fade. During another boom in the '70s, Rock Springs' population doubled, and by 1982 high-paying energy and construction jobs had made it the wealthiest city in the nation on a per capita basis. With the crash in oil prices, however, many companies fled town, and the economy went into a tailspin. More recently, the city has rebounded a bit as coal and trona mining, a phosphate fertilizer plant, and gas and oil production bring jobs to Rock Springs. An open-pit mine east of Rock Springs provides coal for the enormous Jim Bridger Power Plant—the largest power plant in Wyoming—while the Black Butte strip mine in the same area feeds power plants elsewhere in the nation. The latter may eventually spread its tentacles over 60 square miles of desert land. There are also two underground coal mines in the vicinity.

SIGHTS

Rock Springs Historical Museum

The Rock Springs Historical Museum, in the old city hall, 201 B St., 307/362-3138, is open in the summer Monday and Wednesday 10 A.M.–8 P.M.; Tuesday, Thursday, and Friday 10 A.M.–5 P.M.; Saturday 11 A.M.–4 P.M. The rest of the year it's open Wednesday–Saturday 10 A.M.–5 P.M. Admission is free. Built in 1894, this attractive sandstone building looks more like

© DON PITCHER

Old City Hall now houses the Rock Springs Historical Museum.

a medieval castle than a city hall. Inside, the local memorabilia—some dating to the 1880s—spreads over two floors and includes exhibits on coal mining and the diverse mix of people who came here for work. The old city jail cells are still in the building; check out the horsehair bedding. Be sure to pick up a copy of the excellent historical downtown walking-tour brochure while here.

Other Downtown Sights

Next to the main library, the **Community Fine Arts Center,** 400 C St., 307/362-6212, is open Monday and Wednesday 10 A.M.–9 P.M., Tuesday and Thursday 10 A.M.–6 P.M., and Friday and Saturday 10 A.M.–5 P.M. Free admission. You'll find some surprising works here, including paintings by Conrad Schwiering, Hans Kleiber, Grandma Moses, and Norman Rockwell. Also here is a 1993 painting of the Chinese Massacre by Taylor Spence.

The building at 432 S. Main Street, now a copy shop, was once a butcher shop. According to some historians, it was while working here and in other local meat shops that Robert LeRoy Parker ("Butch Cassidy") acquired his nickname. (Several other tales purport to explain the origins of his name, but nobody really knows which one is true.) The walking tour details several other Cassidy hangouts, plus the beer garden where Calamity Jane "announced her appearances in town by emptying both of her six shooters and 'shouting verbal oaths well tarnished.'" A monument to Rock Springs coal miners stands next to the old train depot downtown. The second JCPenney store ever opened (it was then called Golden Rule Mercantile) was housed in the building at 531 N. Front Street.

The site of **Camp Pilot Butte** is now occupied by the Saints Cyril and Methodius Catholic Church at 633 Bridger, a major Slovenian center in the community. (Formerly part of Yugoslavia, Slovenia became an independent nation in 1991.) Only one of the original buildings from Camp Pilot Butte remains—a soldiers' barracks now used as a parish school. Chinatown was just north of here.

Slovenski Dom, the old Slovenian community center, is just down the street from Saints Cyril and Methodius Church, at 513 Bridger Street. Built in 1913, this was the home of Slovenian-American fraternal lodges and was a center for dances, skits, raffles, and concerts. A few pieces of the original furniture are still here, including a long back bar in the basement. The building now houses **Local Color Art Gallery,** 307/382-0990, selling quality pottery, crafts, and paintings created by local artisans.

Western Wyoming Community College

On a hilltop overlooking town, Western Wyoming Community College, 2500 College Dr., 307/382-1600, www.wwcc.cc.wy.us, is a two-year college housed in modern brick buildings. Stop here to explore the **art gallery** (open weekdays), to enjoy a light meal in the bright and spacious atrium, or to wander past imposing displays. You'll find several full-size **dinosaurs** (okay, they are actually fiberglass casts of dino bones), including Triceratops and Tyrannosaurus rex. Also here are fish, turtle, and plant fossils and a tall pendulum. The small and free **Natural History Museum** (307/382-1666; open daily 9 A.M.–10 P.M.) houses Indian artifacts, Wyoming minerals, and more fossils.

The most unusual campus sight sits on the lawn out front—a nine-ton replica of an **Easter Island Statue.** The statue is an exact copy of these mysterious stone carvings and was used to test theories on how they were moved across the island. Anthropology professor Charles Love showed that 25 men could drag the piece 135 feet in two minutes by putting it upright on long log rollers. The project was featured in a Nova program about Easter Island.

The community college offers a Western Studies series during the summer, with courses in prehistoric archaeology, flowering plants, backpacking, insects, nature literature, and other topics. Many of these are field classes lasting two or three weeks.

Farther Afield

The **Reliance tipple,** five miles north of town on U.S. 191 and then two miles in on County Rd. 4-42, was used to load coal into railroad cars in the 1930s. Today the impressive structure is open for self-guided walking tours. A paved path leads to interpretive signs describing the facility.

Several miles northwest of Rock Springs is **Pilot Butte,** a prominent spire visible for miles in all directions and a milestone for emigrants along the Overland Trail. Get there via Gookin-White Mountain Road on the west side of town. You'll need a 4WD or a mountain bike unless you want to hoof it. A staircase leads up the rock from the east side. Another interesting rock formation stands across from Plaza Mall on Dewar Drive.

Wild Horses

More than 1,500 wild horses still run free in southwest Wyoming. Although they're often spotted east of Rock Springs along I-80, the best place to view them is along the west side of U.S. Hwy. 191 approximately 28 miles north of Rock Springs and along White Mountain via County Rd. 4-53. The BLM has developed a 23-mile wild horse driving tour that follows these roads between Green River and Rock Springs, with interpretive signs posted along the way. Other Wyoming places to see them are near Lander, Worland, Cody, and Lovell.

The BLM's Rock Springs Field Office is north of town on U.S. 191, 307/352-0256, www.wy. blm.gov, and can supply information on wild horses and the Killpecker Dunes area. Contact them for information on adopting a wild horse from one of the BLM's Red Desert roundups or check out www.adoptahorse.blm.gov.

ACCOMMODATIONS

Rock Springs has several reasonably priced places to stay, but you should take a look inside the rooms at the cheapest motels.

Under $50

You'll find low rates and remodeled rooms at **Economy Guest Village,** 1430 9th St., 307/362-3763; $27 or $36 d. All rooms contain fridges and microwaves. **Rocky Mountain Motel,** 1204 9th St., 307/362-3443, is a basic and older motel with microwaves and fridges in the rooms; $30–41 s or $36–47 d.

At **Sands Inn,** 1556 9th St., 307/362-3739, rooms cost $38 s or $42; some contain microwaves and fridges. **Springs Motel,** 1525 9th St., 307/362-6683, offers comfortable accommodations for $40–45 s or $50–56 d.

Motel 8, 108 Gateway Blvd., 307/362-8200 or 888/362-8200, has standard motel units for $45 s or $51 d. If you're looking for a budget room, also check out **Cody Motel,** 75 Center St., 307/362-6675; and **Elk St. Motel,** 1100 Elk St., 307/362-3705; but see the rooms first.

$50 and Up

Budget Host Inn, 1004 Dewar Dr., 307/362-6673 or 800/282-4678, www.budgethost.com, charges $45 s or $55 d, including a continental breakfast.

With 142 rooms, **Inn at Rock Springs,** 2518 Foothill Blvd., 307/362-9600 or 800/442-9692, is the largest local place to stay. Attractions include an indoor pool, hot tub, and continental breakfast. Rooms cost $42–48 s or $49–55 d; some contain fridges and microwaves.

At **Motel 6,** 2615 Commercial Way, 307/362-1850 or 800/466-8356, www.motel6.com, rooms cost $48 s or $54 d ($6 less Sun.–Thurs.), including access to an outdoor pool. **Days Inn,** 1545 Elk St., 307/362-5646 or 800/329-7466, www.daysinn.com, has an outdoor heated pool and in-room microwaves and fridges. Rates are $59–62 s or d, including a light breakfast.

Econo Lodge, 1635 N. Elk St., 307/382-4217 or 800/548-6621, www.econolodge.com, has reasonable prices ($50–65 s or $60–75 d), plus a heated outdoor pool, hot tub, and continental breakfast. Amenities at the **Comfort Inn,** 1670 Sunset Dr., 307/382-9490 or 800/228-5150, www.comfortinn.com, include an outdoor pool, hot tub, exercise room, and continental breakfast; rates are $70–75 s or $75–80 d.

Holiday Inn, 1675 Sunset Dr., 307/382-9200 or 800/465-4329, www.holiday-inn.com, features an indoor pool, wading pool, and hot tub, plus the star attraction: a rain machine. Rates are $75–85 s or d. One of Rock Springs' finest places to stay, **Best Western Outlaw Inn,** 1630 Elk St., 307/362-6623 or 800/528-1234, www.bestwestern.com/outlawinn, has an indoor pool and atrium, with rooms for $80–90 s or $81–100 d.

CAMPING

The nearest public camping is **Firehole Campground,** 27 miles southwest of Rock Springs in Flaming Gorge National Recreation Area. Camping costs $13; open late May to late Sept. Make reservations ($9 fee) at 518/885-3639 or 877/444-6777, www.reserveusa.com.

The **Rock Springs KOA Kampground,** two miles west of town on North Service Rd., 307/362-3063 or 800/562-8699, www.koa.com, provides great scenic vistas of the oil storage tanks—and you won't need to worry about trees blocking the sun. If you still want to stop, tent sites cost $19, RV sites $22–30. Simple cabins are $37 d, and they have a heated outdoor pool and hot tub. Open Apr. to mid-Oct.

FOOD

Ask folks in Rock Springs where they go for meals and they're likely to say, "Green River." Interestingly, the same question posed to someone from Green River elicits the response, "Rock Springs." Something strange is going on here.

American

Rock Springs has one place you should not miss: **Grub's Drive In,** 415 Paulson, 307/362-6634, where the thick shakes, grease-drenched but exceptional fried chicken, and homemade fries are favorites of both locals and visitors. This old-time family operation features Shamrock burgers, loaded down with all the fixin's. You can almost feel your arteries clogging.

The best place for a down-home breakfast in a greasy-spoon atmosphere is **Renegade Cafe,** 1610 Elk St., 307/362-3052. **Crueljacks Restaurant,** west of Rock Springs, 307/382-9018, has a decent truck-stop menu. **The Candy Basket,** inside Plaza Mall, 307/382-4675, has old-fashioned soda treats and claims Wyoming's largest candy selection.

Bi-Rite Drugs downtown at 410 S. Main St., 307/362-6601, houses a soda fountain where the burgers come with a big pile of sautéed onions. **Broadway Burger Station,** 628 Broadway, 307/363-5858, is where local mechanics (and lots of other folks) go for lunch. The popular '50s-style diner specializes in fountain drinks and enormous burgers.

Bitter Creek Brewing, 604 Broadway St., 307/362-4782, is a downtown favorite with award-winning beers. The menu features tasty pub fare, including pasta, sandwiches, and 18 different burgers for lunch, along with pizzas, steaks, pork medallions, baby back ribs, and chicken at dinner. Dinner entrées are $10–18, and six fresh brews are on tap. Brick walls, high ceilings, big front windows, and oak tables add to the charm.

International

Several places in town serve Chinese-American fare in quantity: **Lew's Family Restaurant,** 1506 9th St., 307/382-9894; **Wonderful House,** 1676 Sunset Dr., 307/382-5462; **China King Buf-**

fet, in the White Mountain Mall, 2441 Foothills Blvd., 307/382-1188; and **Sands Cafe and Bar,** 1549 9th St., 307/362-5633. The Sands has probably the best all-around meal deal in Rock Springs. Try **Santa Fe Trail,** 1635 Elk St., 307/362-5427, for distinctive Mexican and Native American cooking.

Rocky Mountain Noodle, 1679 Sunset Dr., 307/382-7076, has a bistro menu that includes chicken cordon bleu pasta, Italian cowboy pasta, and shrimp portofino. Dinner entrées are very reasonable: $7–10.

Three very good steak-and-seafood places operate off I-80 west of town: **Log Inn Supper Club,** 307/362-7166; **Ted's Supper Club,** 307/362-7323; and **White Mountain Mining Co.,** 307/382-5265. You won't go wrong at White Mountain Mining. All three are closed Sundays.

ENTERTAINMENT

In 1903, some 40 percent of the businesses in Rock Springs were bars; even during Prohibition, many "soft-drink parlors" dispensed Kemmerer moonshine. To produce this booze, 100 train cars of grapes arrived in Rock Springs within a two-month period. Many places still offer nightlife, although many tend toward the sleazy side, particularly those along the railroad tracks. The best spots for live country-and-western music are **White Mountain Mining Co.,** west of Rock Springs, 307/382-5265, and **Saddle Lite Saloon,** 1704 Elk St., 307/362-8704. For exotic dancers, try **Mike's Astro Lounge,** 822 Pilot Butte Ave., 307/382-9876.

Local movie houses are **White Mountain Theatres,** 307/362-8633, next to the White Mountain Mall; **Cinema Theater,** 618 Broadway, 307/362-2101; and **Rock Theater,** 591 Broadway, 307/382-9707.

EVENTS

Start the summer with rhymes and tunes at the **Cowboy Poet & Music Festival** on the second weekend of May at the Sweetwater Events Complex; details at 307/352-6789, www.sweetwaterevents.com. Rock Springs' diverse past is celebrated in **International Day** each June, with ethnic foods and entertainment, music (from polka to bagpipers), rickshaw rides, food and beer booths, and a Chinese dragon parade, all in the center of downtown.

The **Red Desert Roundup,** 800/463-8637, held the last weekend of July, is the second-largest professional rodeo in Wyoming and the primary summertime event. It also features a Saturday-morning pancake breakfast followed by a big parade.

The **Sweetwater County Fair,** 307/352-6789, www.sweetwaterevents.com, takes place in early August right after the Roundup. The biggest county fair in Wyoming, this eight-day festival attracts families to 4-H auctions, a carnival, food, and headline entertainers. Auto-racing enthusiasts will find stock-car racing, motocross, and demolition derbies all summer long at **Sweetwater Speedway,** 3320 Yellowstone Rd., 307/352-6789.

RECREATION

The impressive **Rock Springs Family Recreation Center,** 3900 Sweetwater Dr., 307/352-1440, has an indoor pool and gym, ice-skating rink, racquetball and tennis courts, plus a weight room, sauna, and hot tub. Out front are unique carved-brick sculptures. Additional swimming pools are at **Rock Springs Civic Center,** 410 N St., 307/362-6181; the **YMCA,** 1035 Jackson St., 307/352-6635; and **Western Wyoming Community College.**

The 18-hole **White Mountain Golf Course,** 307/352-1415, lies three miles north of town.

SHOPPING

For books, visit **B. Dalton,** 307/382-4900, in the White Mountain Mall; **Hastings Books, Music, & Video,** 307/382-6610, in the Plaza Mall at 1451 Dewar Drive; or **Western Wyoming Community College Bookstore,** 307/382-1600.

The downtown **Antique Mall,** 411 N. Front St., 307/362-9611, contains a big selection of antiques and collectibles.

INFORMATION AND SERVICES

The **Rock Springs Chamber of Commerce,** 1897 Dewar Dr., 307/362-3771 or 800/463-8637, www.rockspringswyoming.net, is open Monday–Friday 8 A.M.–5 P.M. year-round. If it's closed, you can check the pamphlet rack in the entryway (open 24 hours).

The **Bureau of Land Management's Rock Springs Field Office,** 307/352-0256, www.wy.blm.gov, is just north of town on U.S. 191; open weekdays. Stop here for information on the Red Desert and wild horses.

The **main library** at 400 C St., 307/362-6212, houses a fine collection of Wyoming books. **White Mountain Library,** 2935 Sweetwater Dr., 307/362-2665, is a delightful place to enjoy the view of White Mountain or stroll through a pleasant rock garden. There's a paperback book swap just inside the front door. Find the local **post office** at 2829 Commercial Way, 307/362-9792.

Wash clothes at **Imperial Laundromat,** 1669 Sunset Dr., 307/382-2774; or **9th Street Laundromat,** 1215 9th St., 307/382-6092.

For medical emergencies, visit **Memorial Hospital of Sweetwater County,** 1200 College Dr., 307/362-3711.

TRANSPORTATION

By Air

The Rock Springs airport is eight miles east of town. Great Lakes Aviation has daily service to Denver and Cody. (See the "Airline Contacts" Special Topic in the On the Road chapter.)

By Car and Bus

Rent cars at the airport from Avis, Enterprise, or Hertz. (See the "Rental Cars Contacts" Special Topic in the On the Road chapter.)

Greyhound, 1655 Sunset Dr. (behind the Burger King), 307/362-2931 or 800/231-2222, www.greyhound.com, has I-80 service in both directions.

Green River

Green River (pop. 12,000) straddles the river of the same name and is a prosperous trona-mining and transportation town as well as the seat of Sweetwater County. I-80 cuts a swath just north of town, plunging through tunnels beneath memorable badlands topography. The huge Union Pacific Railroad yard divides Green River. Run-down buildings crowd the railroad tracks, but elsewhere the town appears vibrant. Wander through the older sections to find tidy wooden frame homes, while ranch-style suburbs spread to the south. During the 1970s and '80s, Green River saw an enormous growth surge as the trona mines expanded their operations, as oil and gas explorations attracted thousands of roustabouts, and as a helium facility opened nearby. The population jumped from fewer than 5,000 in 1970 to almost 13,000 in 1980 and has held steady since then.

HISTORY

Green River was established in 1868 as workers constructed the Union Pacific Railroad across southern Wyoming. Three years later, Frederick Dellenbaugh described the town he found in less than flattering terms:

> *This place, when the railway was building, had been for a considerable time the terminus and a town of respectable proportions had grown up, but with the completion of the road through this region, the terminus moved on, and now all that was to be seen of those golden days was a group of adobe walls, roofless and forlorn. The present "City" consisted of about thirteen houses, and some of these were of such complex construction that one hesitates whether to describe them as houses with canvas roofs, or tents with board sides.*

GREEN RIVER

To Lyman and Evanston

EXIT 89

Tollgate Rock

OAK TREE INN

TRONA DR.

HILLCREST WY.

W 4TH N

W 3RD N

Castle Rock

WESTERN MOTEL

N 7TH W

N 5TH W

N 3RD W

W 2ND N

CHAMBER OF COMMERCE

RAILROAD AVE.

N 2ND N

N CENTER ST.

SUPER 8 MOTEL

LIBRARY

E 3RD N

N 2ND E

N 5TH E

HISTORICAL MUSEUM

WALKWAY

COACHMAN INN MOTEL

E 3RD S

E 2ND S

2ND E

4TH

4TH S

Expedition Island

Footbridge

FLAMING GORGE WY.

EXIT 91

30

374

To Rock Springs

UNION PACIFIC RAILROAD

RIVER VIEW DR.

Green River

POST OFFICE

ASTLE AVE.

E TETON BLVD.

Mansface Rock

UINTA DR.

RODEO ARENA

Green River

MONROE ST.

CLEARVIEW LANES

SWEET DREAMS INN

HOSPITAL

FLAMING GORGE VISITOR CENTER

SHOSHONE AVE.

HITCHING POST DR.

W TETON BLVD.

E TETON BLVD.

Greenbelt

530

UPLAND WY.

STRATTON-MYERS PARK

BRIDGER DR.

SMITH'S

PAMIDA

COLORADO DR.

To Flaming Gorge National Recreation Area

RECREATION CENTER

WESTERN WYOMING COMMUNITY COLLEGE

BOTTOM NATURE AREA FMC PARK

0   0.5 mi

0   0.5 km

MOON

N

SOUTHWEST WYOMING

© AVALON TRAVEL PUBLISHING, INC.

In May of 1869, Maj. John Wesley Powell brought fame to the town when his expedition of 10 men climbed off the train at Green River City and began a long float down the Green and Colorado Rivers. According to one observer, while in Green River awaiting orders, Powell and his men "tried to drink all the whiskey there was in town. The result was a failure, as Jake Field persisted in making it faster than we could drink it." They made it all the way through the Grand Canyon in stout wooden boats. Seven men survived; three who decided to hike out rather than face the treacherous rapids were never seen again. Powell returned to Green River in 1871 for a second voyage with a large contingent of scientists, who helped map this region and later directed the U.S. Geological Survey.

Green River claims title to a minor legal footnote. In 1931, Green River passed an antipeddling ordinance that achieved national notoriety and inspired similar ordinances in many other towns and cities. The "Green River Ordinance" declared uninvited peddlers or hawkers to be a nuisance punishable by a fine of $25 and higher. The Fuller Brush Company unsuccessfully fought the ordinance all the way to the U.S. Supreme Court.

TRONA MINING

Wyoming leads the world in the mining of an obscure but important mineral: trona. With processing, trona—sodium sesquicarbonate—becomes soda ash and is used in glass, detergents, pulp and paper, metal refining, and baking soda. There are even plans to use the soda ash in the production of a fuel pellet that could make hydrogen-powered vehicles more economically feasible; see www.powerball.net for details.

Trona is found in a few widely scattered places around the globe, but one-third of the worldwide production comes from a thousand-square-mile area 25 miles west of Green River. Most trona here occurs in a 10-foot-thick bed some 1,500

One-third of the world's production of trona, used in glass, detergents, pulp and paper, metal refining, and baking soda, comes from a thousand-square-mile area 25 miles west of Green River.

feet underground. There's no chance of running out soon because there's enough here to supply the world for 2,000 years. The mineral was deposited 50 million years ago when a saline lake developed, reaching 100 by 60 miles in size and up to 2,000 feet in depth. As the climate fluctuated, the lake periodically dried out, precipitating sodium salts. The trona deposits were first discovered in 1938, when an unsuccessful natural-gas well brought up core samples containing trona. Commercial production began in 1948.

Today the four major trona mines are the region's largest employers, producing more than 18 million tons of trona and 8 million tons of soda ash annually. The world's largest trona mine is run by FMC Corporation and has 2,000 miles of tunnels, more than all the streets of San Francisco. Its tunnels are 14 feet wide and eight feet tall, big enough to use as two-lane roads. Miners get around by driving diesel-powered jeeps or electric golf carts through the maze. Mining methods include a continuous mining machine that grinds out six tons of trona per minute; a long-wall process in which hydraulic rams hold the roof up as it is being mined and then allow the walls to collapse behind after the ore is removed; and solution mining, by which the trona is dissolved underground and pumped to the surface. Once at the surface, trona is processed and sent out on railroad tank cars or in 100-pound bags of soda ash. The production is staggering: at FMC's plant alone the mine extracts more than 900 tons per hour.

SIGHTS

Indoor Attractions

The excellent **Sweetwater County Historical Museum,** in the old post office at 3 E. Flaming Gorge Way, 307/872-6435, www.sweetwater-museum.org, is open Monday–Saturday 10 A.M.–6 P.M. April–December, and Monday–Friday 9 A.M.–5 P.M. the rest of the year. Free admission. The professionally produced displays change each year but typically include exhibits on the Powell expedition, Oregon trail relics, mining and Indian exhibits, items from the Chinese massacre in Rock Springs, and an impressive hadrosaur footprint found in a nearby coal mine. Outlaw enthusiasts will find a rifle from Butch Cassidy's gang and the gun of Big Nose George—with two notches in it. Don't miss the fascinating write-up about the Mormon War and the Mountain Meadows Massacre—without the whitewash so often perpetrated.

Outdoor Attractions

Pick up the *Self-Guided Tour of Historic Green River* from the museum for a detailed walking tour of the town's oldest buildings. Be sure to also walk across the pedestrian overpass that crosses the sprawling **Union Pacific railroad yard.** It's a great place to take in the sounds and sights of freight trains being moved around.

The most distinctive feature of the country around Green River is **Castle Rock,** the stunning rocky pinnacle that rises above the freeway north of town. Other unusual buttes are **Tollgate Rock** on the northwest end of town and **Mansface Rock** behind the post office. The visitors center has a good brochure describing the stories behind these and many other buttes in the area.

Expedition Island—a National Historic Site—is where John Wesley Powell began his expeditions down the Green River. A small plaque memorializes these voyages of discovery. Kayakers enjoy playing in the **whitewater park** near Expedition Island, with a couple of drops with swirling holes and a slalom course.

The **Green River Greenbelt** starts at Expedition Island and continues to **Scott's Bottom Nature Area** on the southeast edge of town. Portions of this route are paved, whereas others are dirt and undeveloped. Pick up a map from the visitors center or just follow the easy path from the Expedition Island footbridge. A fun riverside swing is just below the highway bridge along the trail.

ACCOMMODATIONS

A few other places are available in town, but they're primarily for long-term stays and can be rather decrepit.

At **Coachman Inn Motel,** 470 E. Flaming Gorge, 307/875-3681, rooms are $34–38 s or $40–47 d, and some units contain fridges and microwaves.

Western Motel, 890 W. Flaming Gorge, 307/875-2840, charges $43 for one bed or $48 for two. All rooms have fridges and microwaves in this nicely maintained place.

Super 8 Motel, 280 W. Flaming Gorge, 307/875-9330 or 800/800-8000, www.super8 .com, charges $41–47 s or $49–57 d, including a continental breakfast.

Fill your lodging, food, and entertainment needs at **Sweet Dreams Inn,** 1410 Uinta Dr., 307/875-7554, located next door to the Clearview Lanes bowling alley, Liquid Emotions Lounge (with Friday night karaoke), and Other Place Restaurant. Standard motel rooms are modern and nicely furnished; $53 for one bed or $63 for two beds (and up to four people). Four-person suites with jetted tubs, microwaves, and fridges are $83.

Oak Tree Inn, just off I-80 at exit 89 (1170 W. Flaming Gorge Way), 307/875-3500 or 888/897-9647, is Green River's newest motel. It is also a base for Union Pacific Railroad workers, who occupy the three front buildings. The comfortable motel has inside corridors, along with an indoor hot tub and workout room. Rates are $52 s or $57 d. Out front is a gleaming 24-hour diner (fitting given all the railroad workers who stay here).

CAMPING

The nearest public camping is at **Buckboard Crossing Campground** ($13; open mid-May to mid-Sept.), inside Flaming Gorge National Recreation Area and 25 miles south of Green River on State Hwy. 530. Make reservations ($9 fee) at 518/885-3639 or 877/444-6777, www.reserveusa.com.

Tex's Travel Camp, four miles west on State

Hwy. 374, 307/875-2630, is right along the river and has some shade trees. Tenters camp for $16, RVs for $24; showers cost an exorbitant $7 if you aren't camping here. Open May–Sept. If you're on a bike, ask about pitching a tent next to the visitors center.

FOOD

Some of the most popular local restaurants lie on the way east; see Rock Springs for details.

Breakfast and Lunch

Sage Creek Bagels, 36 E. Flaming Gorge Way, 307/875-4877, is a local hangout. The café features an attractive exposed-brick interior, along with freshly baked breads, bagels, and sweets, and espresso. Stop by for a lunchtime deli sandwich and soup.

Penny's Diner, on the west side of town at 1170 W. Flaming Gorge Way, 307/875-3500, is open 24 hours a day. Built to resemble a 1950s diner, Penny's serves breakfast, burgers, sandwiches, chicken, and salads, along with soda-fountain faves. The shiny silver jukebox plays your dad's tunes. Directly behind the diner are three buildings that house workers from the Union Pacific Railroad.

For stuff-yourself lunch buffets, head to **Pizza Hut,** 615 E. Flaming Gorge Way, 307/875-4562, or **China Gardens,** 190 N. 5th, 307/875-3259.

Dinner

A cozy Alaska-themed restaurant, **Denali Grill & Bakery,** 375 Uinta Dr., 307/875-4654, serves three meals a day, including breakfast omelets and buttermilk pancakes. Prices are reasonable: most dinner entrées are less than $11 and menu headliners include pasta, chicken, ribs, steaks, fish, and Navajo tacos (but surprisingly, no Alaskan halibut or salmon).

Krazy Moose Restaurant, located in the Red Feather Bar at 211 E. Flaming Gorge Way, 307/875-5124, serves creative family fare, including an oriental chicken salad and delicious desserts. **Don Pedro's,** 520 Wilkes Dr., 307/875-7324, has reasonably authentic Mexican food.

Groceries

Get groceries and baked goods from **Smith's,** 905 Bridger Dr., 307/875-6900; it's open until midnight.

ENTERTAINMENT

Given its blue-collar base, it's no surprise that Green River has plenty of bars. You'll find half a dozen along Railroad Avenue, including **The Brewery,** 50 W. Railroad Ave., 307/875-9974, housed in an amusing castle built in 1901. The building was part of Green River Brewery, Wyoming's first. **The Other Place Restaurant,** in the Clearview Lanes Bowling Alley at 1410 Uinta Dr., 307/875-2695, has karaoke Thursday–Saturday nights. **Mast Lounge,** 24 E. Flaming Gorge Way, 307/875-9990, is a biker hangout with rock music, go-go dancers, and striptease artisans. Watch movies at **Star Theatres,** 699 Uinta Dr., 307/875-4702.

EVENTS

The town's **Overland Stage Stampede Rodeo** in mid-June attracts rodeo riders. **Flaming Gorge Days,** 307/875-5711, www.flaminggorge-days.com, the last weekend of June, is the biggest local event, with a parade, bull-riding events, beauty pageant, three-on-three basketball, country and rock concerts, horseshoe contests, kayak races, and tug-of-war. On the **Fourth of July** Green River has rock concerts at the softball complex, along with the obligatory fireworks show.

RECREATION

The big **Green River Recreation Center,** 1775 Hitching Post Dr., 307/872-0511, www.cityof-greenriver.org/parksnrec, houses an Olympic-size L-shaped pool, hot tub, sauna, steam room, gym, weight room, racquetball courts, nursery services, and even miniature golf. During the winter, rent cross-country skis here to explore the nearby Uinta Mountains.

Outfitters of Green River, 100 E. 2nd South, 307/875-8700, sells fly-fishing gear, has up-to-date hatch info, and rents kayaks. **Highland Desert Flies,** 307/875-2358, is a local river guide with float trips down the Green. **Wind River Sporting Goods,** 420 Uinta Dr., 307/875-4075 or 800/568-1551, has a range of outdoor and fishing gear and guides fishing trips.

Roll black balls down the lanes at **Clearview Lanes,** 1410 Uinta Dr., 307/875-2695, or **Rancho Lanes,** 445 Uinta Dr., 307/875-4324.

INFORMATION AND SERVICES

The **Green River Chamber of Commerce,** 541 E. Flaming Gorge Way, 307/875-5711, www.grchamber.com, is open Monday–Friday 8 A.M.–4:30 P.M. Stop by for the latest information or to check out the stuffed outsized lake trout from Flaming Gorge.

The Forest Service operates a **Flaming Gorge National Recreation Area Visitors Center** at 1450 Uinta Dr., 307/875-2871, www.fs.fed.us/r4/ashley. It's open Monday–Friday 8 A.M.–4:30 P.M. and Saturday 8 A.M.–4:30 P.M. Memorial Day to Labor Day; and Monday–Friday 9 A.M.–5 P.M. the rest of the year. Inside is a large relief map of Flaming Gorge, local brochures, and books for sale.

Sweetwater County Library is at 300 N. 1st E, 307/875-3615. Built over an old cemetery, it's said to be haunted. Librarians claim to have seen the ghosts, heard voices from empty rooms, and watched gates open on their own. If you don't mind the ghosts, you can surf the web or check email here.

The local **post office** is at 350 Uinta Dr., 307/875-4920. Wash clothes at **Liberty's Laundry,** 1315 Bridger Dr., 307/875-8134.

Get new and used volumes, along with espresso coffees, from the friendly folks at **Book & Bean,** 55 E. Railroad Ave., 307/875-5445. There's also a small bookstore in the Green River campus of **Western Wyoming Community College** on College Way, 307/875-2278. The school sits atop a hill just south of town, providing a fine view of the surrounding badlands.

Greyhound only stops in Green River by special request, and there are no local taxis.

Castle Rock Medical Center, 1400 Uinta, 307/875-6010 or 800/446-5684, www.crhd.org, has physicians on staff.

Green River Vicinity

LITTLE AMERICA

Find Little America approximately 20 miles west of Green River. From either direction along I-80, billboards announce, "Little America, only 350 (250, 150, 100 . . .) miles ahead!" And then, out in the desolate, windblown landscape, drivers suddenly come to this oasis of consumption where you can cozy up to cable TV or enjoy fresh produce trucked in from California. The repair bays can hold half a dozen tractor-trailers at once and often do. Ten bright red fuel tanks have "Little America" emblazoned on their sides, flanked by two emperor penguins, and a small town's worth of tidy brick buildings occupy the site, including a gift shop, restaurant, grocery mart, and café. It's as if a small suburban town had suddenly been plunked down into the middle of nowhere, with everything open 24 hours a day.

Little America had its origins in the mind of S. M. Covey, a sheepherder who spent a fearful winter near here in the 1890s. Covey resolved to build a way station for travelers, a place to escape the blizzards and wind. Many years later he saw a photo of Admiral Byrd's "Little America" in Antarctica and was inspired in 1932 to create his own Little America, adding over the years a restaurant, a motel, and dozens of gas pumps (65 at current count—OK, one is a propane tank). He died in the 1960s and the operation was bought by Earl Holding. Other Little America stations are flung across the West—Cheyenne, Sun Valley, Flagstaff, Salt Lake City, and even San Diego—but this is the real thing, and the only one that rates a name on the map.

SOUTHWEST WYOMING

Practicalities

Little America Motel, 307/875-2400 or 800/634-2401, www.wyoming.littleamerica.com, has immaculate rooms with big TVs for $63–69 s or $69–75 d. Family rooms and suites are $99 d. The coffee shop is always open and good; you'll find reasonably priced meals both here and in the restaurant. The pastries and pies are favorites, and nearly everyone gets a 35-cent soft ice cream cone to go. But the real reason for Little America's existence is fuel to propel you on down the road. It's fitting that a place with such a patriotic name should be built to worship the internal-combustion engine.

CHURCH BUTTES

West of Little America, I-80 lies across colorful badlands country, passing a temple of a different kind—Church Buttes. Brigham Young and his Mormon pioneers held religious services under these churchlike spires in 1847. Take the Church Buttes exit from I-80 and head 5.5 miles north on a gravel road past several gas wells. The 75-foot-high buttes are at the intersection with Granger Road (County Rd. 233). The historic Mormon Pioneer Trail parallels Granger Road in this area and is marked by concrete posts.

GRANGER

The dinky town of Granger (pop. 150) is five miles north of Little America on U.S. Hwy. 30 and contains the **Granger Stage Station.** The sandstone building was a stopping point on the Overland Trail and housed such visitors as Mark Twain and Horace Greeley.

The **Hams Fork Rendezvous** takes place near Granger in mid-August, with costumed mountain men and women, and traditional contests of daring, including tomahawk throwing, fire-starting contests, rifle shoots, and a horse ride. Located on the site of the 1834 rendezvous, this one really strives for authenticity, with pre-1840s dress required of all the participants. Get details at 307/875-5406.

Church Buttes, near Green River

© DON PITCHER

SEEDSKADEE NATIONAL WILDLIFE REFUGE

The 22,000-acre Seedskadee National Wildlife Refuge is 37 miles northwest of the town of Green River on State Hwy. 372. The word comes from the Shoshone word Seeds-kee-dee, "River of the Prairie Chicken." The refuge stretches 35 miles along the Green River and contains marshes and riparian areas that provide outstanding waterfowl and wildlife habitat. It's one of the finest birding areas in the state; more than 200 species have been sighted. Canada geese are common, along with sandhill cranes, coots, shorebirds, great blue herons, and a variety of ducks. Good fishing can be found here, and canoeists and rafters will see many moose, deer, and antelope along the banks. This is a relatively gentle float trip, although you will need to watch for boulders placed in the channel to improve the fish habitat. Make sure unoccupied boats are tied to the shore because river levels may rise suddenly as a result of releases from Fontenelle Reservoir. The reservoir backs up behind a 139-foot earthen dam a few miles upstream from the refuge.

Practicalities

Refuge headquarters, 307/875-2187, http://seed-skadee.fws.gov, is two miles north from the intersection of State Highways 372 and 28. Be sure to pick up the refuge brochure detailing Seedskadee's surprisingly rich history.

Camping is not allowed within the refuge, but you can camp just upstream at the BLM-run **Weeping Rock, Tailrace,** and **Slate Creek** campgrounds. Weeping Rock and Slate Creek campgrounds are also used as access points to float the river.

NORTHEAST TO FARSON

State Hwy. 28 crosses the Green River at Seedskadee National Wildlife Refuge and continues for 28 little-traveled miles to the tiny settlement of Farson (see Wind River Mountains chapter). It's classic Old West country, with Pilot Butte visible to the south and the Wind River Mountains to the northeast. Amusing wildlife billboards warn of crossing critters along the way, and a roadside marker at **Simpson Hollow** gives a sanitized version of an incident that took place during the short-lived "Mormon War." In 1857, a group of Mormon guerrillas attacked a U.S. Army wagon train filled with supplies in Simpson Hollow. A second wagon train had been destroyed the previous day at the Green River as part of Brigham Young's war against the federal government. In these two incidents 74 wagons were captured and burned by the Mormons.

Flaming Gorge National Recreation Area

Flaming Gorge National Recreation Area covers 94,308 acres of wild country, reaching 91 miles from the town of Green River, Wyoming, into northeastern Utah. The region is named for the impressive canyon that Major John Wesley Powell described in his famous 1869 expedition down the river:

> At a distance of from 1 to 20 miles a brilliant red gorge is seen, the red being surrounded by broad bands of mottled buff and gray at the summit of the cliffs, and curving down to the water's edge on the nearer slope of the mountain. This is where the river enters the mountain range—the head of the first canyon we are to explore, or rather, an introductory canyon to a series made by the river through the range. We name it Flaming Gorge.

Flaming Gorge Reservoir backs up behind a 502-foot-high concrete arch dam, completed in 1964 and located 15 miles south of the Wyoming border. The waters of the Green River back up behind this dam into a 91-mile lake that provides flood control, water storage, and irrigation for Utah farmers down stream, along with recreation for boaters, water-skiers, and anglers. Each of the dam's three enormous generators produces 50,000 kilowatts of power, electricity that powers computers, hair dryers, and factories throughout the West. Many osprey nest on the rocky pinnacles and cliffs around the edges, while below the dam is a renowned trout fishery and river-runner's funhouse. The area attracts nearly one million visitors annually.

ACCESS AND SIGHTS

The landscape surrounding the Wyoming portion of Flaming Gorge is typical high-desert country, but once you cross into Utah, the road climbs into spectacularly rugged mountains covered with forests of juniper and pinyon, lodgepole, and ponderosa pine. This area was a favorite hideout of Butch Cassidy and other outlaws who operated out of nearby Brown's Park. Flaming Gorge Reservoir is encircled by roads—total loop distance 160 miles—providing a pleasant overnight break from the grinding I-80 routine. The main roads don't come particularly close to the dramatic gorge itself except at the dam, but side roads provide access. Day use at Flaming Gorge National Recreation Area is $2 daily, $5 for 16 days, or $20 for an annual pass. Purchase passes from Forest Service offices, visitors centers, or local businesses.

One of the most interesting ways to reach Flaming Gorge is via State Hwy. 414 heading southeast from the town of Mountain View. The road climbs past colorful, eroded badlands topography—as though an enormous skeletal landscape were showing through—before emerging into wide-open spaces carpeted with grass and sage. Then the road dips down along the Henrys Fork, where cottonwoods and willows border lush green pastures. Huge piles of hay crowd the pastures. Keep your eyes open for the many historic log structures. A sign notes the location of the **Henrys Fork mountain-man rendezvous** in July 1825, when 120 trappers and 680 Indians traded furs for supplies from the East. This was the first mountain-man rendezvous in America. Butch Cassidy and other outlaws later frequented Uncle Jack's

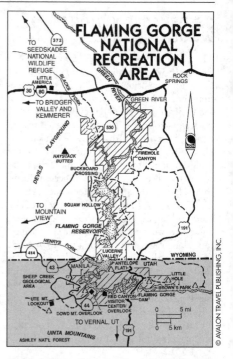

Cabin Saloon, which stood nearby. Today, tiny **Lonetree** is the "smallest town in the world with a parking meter"—it was brought in from Denver—and **McKinnon** has a little store and a post office, but that's about it until you reach Manila, Utah. This is the real West!

VISITORS CENTERS

Flaming Gorge National Recreation Area is administered by the U.S. Forest Service. Get information, maps, and books from Ashley National Forest offices in Manila, Utah, 435/784-3228, or Green River, Wyoming, 307/875-2871. The offices are open Monday–Friday 8 A.M.–4:30 P.M. Find out more on the web at www.fs.fed.us/r4/ashley.

The Bureau of Reclamation and U.S. Forest Service maintain a year-round **Flaming Gorge Dam Visitors Center** atop the dam; open daily 8 A.M.–6 P.M. Memorial Day to Labor Day, and daily 10 A.M.–4 P.M. the rest of the year. **Guided** dam tours are offered daily 9 A.M.–4:30 P.M. April–October; call 435/885-3135 for specifics.

The **Red Canyon Overlook Visitors Center,** 435/889-3713, is open daily 10 A.M.–5 P.M. Memorial Day to Labor Day (closed the rest of the year) and offers breathtaking canyon views. Campfire programs are given on Friday and Saturday evenings in the summer. Get a schedule of activities from the visitors centers.

EXPLORING FLAMING GORGE

U.S. Hwy. 191 heads south from the Rock Springs area over the dry sage-and-juniper landscape. Take the paved turnoff to **Firehole Canyon,** where there are some interesting geological treats, including the two fingerlike projections known as North and South Chimney Rocks. Look for sheepherders tending big flocks nearby. A dirt road continues south along the canyon to the Wyoming border, or you can return to U.S. Hwy. 191 to eventually reach the dam. Utah Hwy. 44 meets U.S. Hwy. 191 near the dam and climbs through the scenic mountain country to the west before dropping down to the town of Manila, where it joins State Hwy. 530 heading north.

Sheep Creek Geological Area is a side loop from the southwestern end of the National Recreation Area and provides views of dramatic geology and land formations. Spectacular rock spires run alongside the Uinta Fault, and frequent roadside signs explain the geological significance of this region. This area is also home to many bighorn sheep. A road leads west from here to **Ute Mountain Fire Tower,** an old wooden lookout with a panoramic view of the Flaming Gorge area and northeastern Uinta Mountains. Built in 1935 by the Civilian Conservation Corps, it was the first one constructed in the state of Utah and the last fire tower still in operation. It is open Thursday–Sunday 10 A.M.–5 P.M. Memorial Day to Labor Day.

Swett Ranch, just south of Flaming Gorge Lodge, is another historic site and a good place to see deer and elk. Open Thurs.–Mon. 10 A.M.–5 P.M. Memorial Day to Labor Day.

Just northeast of Manila and barely in Wyoming

are several unusual Indian petroglyphs; ask at the Forest Service office for directions. As you continue north along the western side of Flaming Gorge along State Hwy. 530, the road passes **Haystack Buttes,** a series of beehive-shaped rocky mounds, followed by the barren, eroded badlands of **Devils Playground,** where sagebrush, sand, and cactus extend as far as you can see.

RECREATION

Hiking

Several trails are noteworthy in Flaming Gorge. **Little Hole National Recreation Trail** follows the north bank of Green River from just below the dam to Little Hole, seven miles away. You may want to set up a car shuttle to save having to hike back the same way. The scenic five-mile **Canyon Rim Trail** connects Greendale Overlook with the Red Canyon Visitors Center. The trail is also accessible from the Skull Creek, Greens Lake, and Canyon Rim Campgrounds and is open to mountain bikes.

The steep **Dowd Mountain-Hideout Canyon Trail** drops five miles from Dowd Mountain Overlook to Hideout Boat Campground; it's open to mountain bikes. The overlook is four miles off the main road. A helpful brochure describing these and other trails is available from Forest Service offices and visitors centers in Manila or Green River.

A cautionary note for hikers in the Flaming Gorge area: Rattlesnakes are common in the desert and can be deadly, although bites are not common. Keep your eyes and ears open at all times.

If you want to explore further, head 30 miles west of Manila to the wonderful **High Uintas Wilderness.** This area is popular with hikers and cross-country skiers from the Evanston and Green River areas and includes Kings Peak, the highest mountain in Utah. Several access roads come in from the north, including Highway 150, a National Scenic Byway. See the Forest Service office in Evanston for details, or stop at the **Bear River Ranger Station,** 435/642-6662, located 30 miles south of Evanston and open June–October. Cabins, boat rentals, and meals are available at **Spirit Lake Lodge,** 435/880-3089; open June–Oct.

Mountain Biking

Excellent opportunities exist for mountain bikers throughout the Flaming Gorge area, particularly on trails in the more rugged southern end. Pick up a brochure describing the most popular routes at Forest Service offices or visitors centers in Manila or Green River. Rent mountain bikes from **Red Canyon Lodge,** nine miles southwest of the dam, 435/889-3759, www.redcanyonlodge.com; or **Flaming Gorge Lodge,** four miles south of the dam, 435/889-3773, www.fglodge.com.

Fishing and Boating

Flaming Gorge Reservoir is famous for its monster fish, including a record 51-pound Mackinaw and a world-record 33-pound brown trout. In addition to these two species, anglers catch lake and rainbow trout, kokanee, and smallmouth and largemouth bass. **Flaming Gorge Fishing Derby** in mid-May is one of the biggest such events in Wyoming. Return on the **Fourth of July** for a popular fireworks display at Cedar Springs Marina.

Three places on the reservoir rent skiffs, ski boats, fishing gear, and ski equipment: **Buckboard Marina,** 307/875-6927 or 800/824-8155, www.buckboardmarina.iboats.com;   **Cedar Springs Marina,** 435/889-3795, www.cedarspringsmarina.com; and **Lucerne Valley Marina,** 435/784-3483 or 888/820-9225, www.flaminggorge.com. Lucerne Valley also rents houseboats. Marinas are open mid-April to mid-October. Most fishing guides operate out of Manila and Dutch John on the Utah side; see visitors centers for a listing.

Below the dam, the Green River is considered the finest fishing in Utah, with up to 16,000 trout per mile. If you have a Wyoming fishing license and plan to fish in the Utah part of Flaming Gorge—or vice versa—you'll need to get a special Flaming Gorge Reservoir Reciprocal Stamp for $10. These can be purchased at local businesses in Manila and Dutch John.

River Rafting

One of the most popular summertime activities is floating on the Green River below Flaming Gorge Dam. An entry station below the dam has safety information. The first several miles of the float are relatively gentle, although there are a half dozen small rapids, and can be run without a guide, but life jackets are mandatory. Float tubes are not recommended.

Most folks put in just below the spillway and take out at Little Hole, seven miles downriver. Plan on three hours for the run. There's no overnight camping allowed along this stretch, but you'll find 18 campsites below Little Hole in the nine-mile stretch before you get to historic Browns Park. Check at the various visitors centers for details and precautions for these longer float trips. For 24-hour information on lake elevation and river flow, call 800/277-7571 or check the web at: www.uc.usbr.gov/wrg/crsp/crsp_40_fgd.txt.

Rent rafts ($60 for a seven-person boat) and inflatable kayaks from **Flaming Gorge Recreation Services** in Dutch John, 435/885-3191; **Flaming Gorge Lodge,** four miles south of the dam, 435/889-3773, www.fglodge.com; or **Green River Outfitters** in Dutch John, 435/885-3338. All of these companies offer guided float fishing trips (around $340 per day for two people) and shuttle services (from Little Hole, $32 for up to eight people). Flaming Gorge Recreation Services and Green River Outfitters also have hot showers. Note that varying releases from the dam may push the river up or down 3–4 feet in a matter of 15–30 minutes. Fortunately, fluctuations are rare and usually occur at night.

Winter Recreation

Snowplows keep the paved highway circling Flaming Gorge National Recreation Area clear throughout the winter, providing access to outstanding places for exploration. (Note, however, that the plows don't operate on weekends in Wyoming!) The Forest Service maintains **cross-country ski trails** at six areas along the Utah side of Flaming Gorge: Death Valley, Elk Park, Dowd Mountain, Canyon Rim, Lake Creek, and Swett Ranch. These vary greatly in length and difficulty; pick up a map from the Ashley National Forest offices in Manila (435/784-3445), Green River (307/875-2871), or the Flaming Gorge Dam Visitors Center

(435/885-3135). Rent snowmobiles from **Flaming Gorge Lodge,** 435/889-3773, www.fglodge.com.

CAMPING

The Forest Service maintains 25 different roadside campgrounds ($6–16) in the Flaming Gorge National Recreation Area, although most of these are managed by concessionaires. Showers are available at the Deer Run, Firehole, and Mustang Ridge campgrounds and cost $3 if you aren't camping. Most campgrounds are on the Utah side of the border, particularly around the dam, and they typically open by mid-May and close in mid-September, although a few remain open year-round. Red Canyon Campground is a favorite, with spectacular canyon vistas. You can make reservations ($9 fee) for approximately half of these campgrounds at 518/885-3639 or 877/444-6777, www.reserveusa.com. You can also camp for free in undeveloped parts of the Flaming Gorge National Recreation Area or in one of several boat-in camps.

Flaming Gorge KOA Campground in Manila, Utah, 435/784-3184 or 800/562-3254, www.koa.com, has tent sites for $18–20, RV sites for $24–26, and basic four-person cabins for $34–36. Open mid-Apr. to mid-Oct. The KOA has an array of facilities, including an outdoor pool and game room. Other places with RV hookups include **Flaming Gorge Recreation Services** in Dutch John, 435/885-3191; **Lucerne Valley Marina,** 435/784-3483 or 888/820-9225, www.flaminggorge.com; or **Buckboard Marina,** 307/875-6927 or 800/824-8155, www.buckboardmarina.iboats.com.

ACCOMMODATIONS AND FOOD

Lodges

Because of the popularity of this area, it's a good idea to reserve a week or two ahead during the summer to be assured of a place to stay—or in July if you need a place on Labor Day weekend. Four miles southwest of the dam, **Flaming Gorge Lodge,** 435/889-3773, www.fglodge.com, has motel rooms for $67 s or $73 d and one-bedroom condos with kitchens for $111 s or $117 d. Also here are a general store, café, and full-service restaurant. The lodge is open year-round.

One of the nicest places in the area is **Red Canyon Lodge,** 435/889-3759, www.redcanyonlodge.com, near Red Canyon Overlook nine miles southwest of the dam. Lodging is available in luxurious duplex log cabins overlooking the lake. These have private baths, kitchenettes, vaulted ceilings, and covered porches; $119 d or $129 for four people. Smaller cabins were under construction in 2002; call for rates. Also offered here are horseback rides, mountain-bike rentals, boat rentals (for East Greens Lake only), a fine restaurant, and a little store with groceries, souvenirs, and fishing tackle. Kids fish for free in a private lake on the grounds. The cabins are available year-round, but the restaurant and store are closed on weekdays late October–April. Recommended.

Manila, Utah

The town of Manila, just three miles south of the Wyoming border on the west side of the reservoir, is home to the Forest Service's **Flaming Gorge National Recreation Area District Office,** 435/784-3445. Manila offers several lodging options. Cheapest is **Steinaker's Motel,** 435/784-3363, where rooms are $41 s or d. Stop by the Chevron station to register. **Vacation Inn,** 435/784-3259, has condos with kitchens for $66 d or $76 for four people. The inn is very clean and nice, and it can also accommodate pets, horses, and boats. Open Mar.–Oct.

On the west end of Manila, **Rainbow Inn,** 435/784-3117, is a modern and comfortable place to stay for $53 s or $60 d. The restaurant here serves three meals a day and specializes in charbroiled steaks. Get groceries, hardware, and pizzas in Manila at the **Flaming Gorge Market,** 435/784-3582, www.flaminggorgemarket.com.

The **Flaming Gorge Area Chamber of Commerce,** 435/784-3154, www.flaminggorgecountry.com, has additional information. For more on points south, see *Moon Handbooks Utah,* by Bill Weir and W. C. McRae (www.moon.com).

Bridger Valley

Bridger Valley is a large splotch of green in the midst of desert country, nourished by numerous irrigation ditches off the Blacks Fork River. This was the first place in Wyoming to be farmed, having been settled by Mormons in 1853. By the way, the various branches of the Green River—Smiths Fork, Blacks Fork, Henrys Fork, La Barge, and Hams Fork—are all named for trappers in Jedediah Smith's party of mountain men, who first spread over this country in 1824. At the time these were considered the richest beaver-trapping waters ever discovered.

LYMAN

Lyman (pop. 2,000) consists of a wide main street and not a whole lot else. Named for a Mormon leader, the town's initial settlers included many members of that religion, and a large Latter-day Saints church sits in the center of town. Lyman's pretentious town complex is the only building of note, more because of its size than for any architectural merit. Upstairs the small **Trona Mining Museum,** 307/787-6738, has exhibits on trona, how it's mined and processed, and its uses. Open Mon.–Fri. 10 A.M.–5 P.M. in summer, and Mon.–Fri. noon–4 P.M. the rest of the year. Downstairs in the town hall is the **Lyman Chamber of Commerce** office, 307/787-6738; open Mon.–Thurs. 8 A.M.–1 P.M.

Practicalities

Stay at **Valley West Motel,** 307/787-3700 or 800/884-7910, where comfortable rooms are $35 s or $40–45 d. Kitchenettes are available. **Rent-A-Flick,** 307/787-3737, has videos on one side and fast food—including thick malts and homemade pizzas—on the other. Meals are also available at **Longhorn Restaurant.** Just north of town, the **KOA Kampground,** 307/786-2762 or 800/562-2762, www.koa.com, has an outdoor pool. The charge is $17–19 for tents or $20–24 for RVs; open late May through Sept. Simple cabins are $31–34 d.

Greyhound, 307/787-6192 or 800/231-2222, www.greyhound.com, stops at Taco Time in Lyman. Wash clothes at **Valley West Laundry,** 307/786-4328. The town also has a public **swimming pool,** 307/787-6333.

Events

Because this is a Mormon town, July 24 has a special meaning; it was on this date in 1847 that pioneers first reached what would become Salt Lake City. Lyman's **Mormon Pioneer Days** offers a week full of activities, including a rodeo, parade, and dance. Call 307/787-6573 for details.

The **International Pedigree Stage Stop Sled Dog Race** (IPSSSDR) stops here. See the Jackson chapter for more info.

MOUNTAIN VIEW

The growing town of Mountain View (pop. 1,200) is appropriately named; to the south, the Uintas form a snow-capped, rough-edged horizon. Mountain View is in the heart of farming and ranching country. There's not much to see in the town itself, but it's obviously a popular place to live, with lots of new developments in the last few years.

You'll find good sub sandwiches, burgers, grilled halibut, soups, salads, and ice cream at **Pony Express,** 307/782-6782, an impressive modern log structure. Other dining-out options include **Mt. View Drive Inn** and **Pizza Hut.** Get groceries from **Benedict's Market,** 307/782-3581. For entertainment, there's always the bowling alley. **Hoedown on the Smiths Fork** comes to Mountain View on Labor Day weekend with polka and country music; call 307/782-3100.

The closest public campground is 22 miles away along the Wyoming–Utah line. Get recreation information from the **Wasatch National Forest District Office** in Mountain View, 307/782-6555, www.fs.fed.us/wcnf. The town also has a public **swimming pool,** 307/782-3525.

JIM BRIDGER

Legendary figures fill the history of the West, but Jim Bridger ranks as the uncrowned king of the mountain men. Like many other 19th-century frontiersmen, Bridger never learned to read or write, but his deep knowledge of the mountains and Indians gained him the name "Old Gabe" because his skills were said to rival those of the angel Gabriel. Jim Bridger has 21 different Wyoming places named for him, more than any other individual.

Bridger was born in 1804 in Virginia and later moved with his family to Missouri. When both his parents died, he was sent off to apprentice with a blacksmith, but the wild country beckoned. When William Ashley advertised for "Enterprising Young Men" to go into the Rockies to trap beaver, Bridger quickly joined up. He was on the first keelboat that headed out in 1822 and wintered that year on the Bear River of southern Idaho. When men began speculating on where the Bear River led, Bridger volunteered to find out, thus becoming the first white man to discover the Great Salt Lake. Bridger took any challenge in stride. When Ashley needed a volunteer to test the possibility of running furs down the Bighorn River, Bridger stepped forward. He nearly died taking his log raft through the wild waters of Bighorn Canyon, but the adventure added to his growing reputation.

Bridger entered the fur-trading business in 1830 when he and four others bought the Rocky Mountain Fur Company from Ashley. They in turn sold the business to William Sublette five years later. Bridger continued to lead trapping parties until the last rendezvous in 1840, after which he turned his attention to the growing tide of emigrants heading west to California and Oregon. Together with partner Louis Vásquez, Bridger built a trading post (Fort Bridger) along the Blacks Fork of the Green River. He later served as a scout for the U.S. Army in the Powder River Basin, although his sage advice was often ignored.

Like many other mountain men, Jim Bridger had several wives. His first was a white Mormon woman, but when Jim refused to join her religion they separated. He later married three different Indian women, none of whom spoke English. The first two died early, but the last one—daughter of the great Shoshone Chief Washakie—returned to Missouri with him.

Bridger's knowledge of sign language was legendary; he once kept an audience of Sioux and Cheyenne Indians in rapt attention for over an hour as he signed a lengthy adventure. In one of his yarns, told to a naive British army captain, Bridger described how the Indians had him trapped in a canyon with his only escape up a 200-foot waterfall. When the captain insisted on discovering how he escaped this predicament, Bridger wryly went on, "Oh bless your soul, Captain, we never did get out. The Indians killed us right there!" Partly because of such yarns, few believed Bridger's true accounts of the geysers and hot springs he had found in Yellowstone or of the stream that split along the Continental Divide, with waters flowing in both directions. Bridger died on his Missouri farm in 1881 at the age of 77.

PIEDMONT

The ghost town of Piedmont is a rarely visited part of Wyoming but worth the seven-mile drive south from I-80. Take the LeRoy Rd. exit (mile 24), head west on County Rd. 128, and follow an old railroad grade south. Continue straight at the intersection and keep your eyes open for the herd of wild buffalo that roams this country. Established as a water and wood refueling station for the Union Pacific, Piedmont was also the scene of an 1869 incident in which 300 railroad workers blocked a train carrying Union Pacific vice president Dr. Thomas Durrant en route to ceremonies at Promontory Point. The workers demanded $200,000 (some reports put the figure at $500,000) in back pay before they finally let Durrant proceed.

Around 1869, Moses Byrne built five **charcoal kilns** near Piedmont, each 30 feet high and 30 feet across and made of stone and mortar. Wood was sealed in the ovens and slowly burned until it turned into charcoal for Utah's Pioneer smelter. Three of these massive kilns still stand, like three oversized breasts emerging

© DON PITCHER

These charcoal kilns in the ghost town of Piedmont once burned charcoal for a Utah smelter.

from the plains. Just up the hill is the old Byrne family graveyard with the graves of many children who died young in this harsh place.

South of the kilns are a dozen buildings from old Piedmont, abandoned when the railroad tracks were moved farther north in 1901. The last store closed in 1940. A local legend claims that Butch Cassidy buried loot from one of his bank holdups near here. Treasure hunters still search for it. The father of Calamity Jane, gunned down in a saloon, lies buried in an unmarked grave in the small Piedmont cemetery.

For a surprising drive, take Piedmont Road east from Piedmont townsite. This narrow gravel road climbs a high and very steep hill to a dramatic viewpoint before dropping down into the conifers at a miniscule place called **Robertson** and then on to Mountain View and Lyman. It's easy to get on the wrong road here and end up heading toward Utah, so make sure you have a good map before heading out.

FORT BRIDGER

The most interesting historic site in Southwest Wyoming is Fort Bridger, located in the town of the same name. The Uinta Mountains form a majestic backdrop to the south, and the Blacks Fork River winds through. The old fort is just three miles off I-80 and provides an easy diversion from the interstate-highway blahs.

History

Fort Bridger was built in 1843 by the famed mountain man Jim Bridger and his Mexican partner, Louis Vásquez. The location—right on the Oregon and Mormon Trails—quickly made this a vital stopping point for emigrants heading west to California, Oregon, or Salt Lake City. In a letter dictated to Vásquez, Bridger remarked

I have established a small store with a blacksmith shop, and a supply of iron in the road of the emigrants, on Black Fork of Green River, which promises fairly. They, in coming out are generally well supplied

with money, but by the time they get there, are in want of all kinds of supplies, horses, provisions, smithwork, etc. They bring ready cash from the states, and should I receive the goods ordered, will have considerable business in that way with them, and establish trade with the Indians in the neighborhood, who have a good number of beaver among them.

The new "fort" consisted of a few crude log huts and a corral surrounded by a log stockade, while the lush riverside country provided pasturage for stock. Conflicts quickly developed between Bridger and the Mormon emigrants, who eyed his prosperous trade with envy and his good relations with the Indians as competition in their own efforts to turn them against the U.S. government. Under the pretext that Bridger was supplying weapons to Ute Indians, Brigham Young ordered Bridger arrested and sent 150 men to do the job. Bridger managed to escape, hiding in a nearby eagle nest while the men searched in vain. He finally fled with his Indian wife to Fort Laramie but lost all of his merchandise, livestock, and buildings to the raiders. The Mormons then built their own base, **Fort Supply,** 12 miles south of Bridger's trading post, and established the first agricultural settlement in Wyoming. Soon Fort Supply had more than 100 log buildings surrounded by a palisade. In 1855, they purchased Fort Bridger from Vásquez—without Bridger's knowledge or consent—and added a variety of structures. When the so-called Mormon War began two years later, the Saints decided to leave nothing for the U.S. Army. They burned both forts and fled to Salt Lake City.

Jim Bridger leased his land to the army in 1858 for $600 per year. The army rebuilt the fort with room for 350 resident troops. A Pony Express station was established in 1860, followed later by an Overland Stage station. The fort was the site of the first newspaper published in Wyoming (1863) and served as a base for Chief Washakie's band of Shoshone Indians until a treaty signed here in 1868 established the Wind River Reservation. Fort Bridger was abandoned by the military in 1890, and many of its buildings were sold at auction. Thirty years later, the state of Wyoming bought the site and has since restored or reconstructed many of the structures.

Access

Fort Bridger, 307/782-3842, http://wyoparks.state .wy.us, is open daily 9 A.M.–5:30 P.M. May–September and Saturday–Sunday 8:30 A.M.–4:30 P.M. in April and October; closed Nov.–Mar. Day use costs $2 for nonresidents, $2 for Wyoming residents; free for youths under 18. Several buildings are open to the public during summer, but only the museum is open the rest of the year. In June, July, and August the staff dresses in 1880s costumes and provides living-history demonstrations and historical information. Various activities take place throughout the year, including a big mountain-man rendezvous (see Fort Bridger Rendezvous in this chapter). In August, take the special moonlight tour ($5 adults, $3 kids), on which you'll meet characters from the past; call several months ahead to book this popular tour.

Sights

The attractive grounds are sprinkled with aspen and cottonwood trees and beautifully restored buildings. First stop is the **museum and visitors center,** housed in the enlisted-men's barracks. Inside you'll gain an excellent glimpse into the past with a model of the old fort, displays of army uniforms and weapons, Indian artifacts—including a bowl made from the hump of a buffalo—a chuck wagon, a papoose board, and even a working telegraph on which to practice your Morse code. Be sure to look for Jim Bridger's old powder horn, vest, and other items, including a photo of a "young" Jim Bridger created by computerized reverse aging. Visitors can watch a slide show on the fort's history.

The **Bridger-Vásquez Trading Co.** stands in one corner of the fort and has a working blacksmith shop in the back. It's open daily 9 A.M.–5 P.M. May–September, but closed October–April. This replica of Bridger's original trading post sells all sorts of interesting items: trade beads, animal furs, coyote and muskrat skulls, "church" dolls, Indian sweetgrass, old-time shirts

tepee at Fort Bridger Rendezvous

and dresses, and even bull-scrotum bags. Ask for demonstrations of the fire steels.

Just south of the museum is a rock wall built by Mormons when they controlled the fort. Other buildings include a small commissary and two guardhouses. On the east side of the fort is the antique-filled **commanding officer's quarters,** built in 1884. Aspen trees line the alleyway connecting this building with the **log officer's quarters,** built in 1858. Look inside for the section from an aspen tree carved by Buffalo Bill Cody. On the south side of the fort is a century-old ranch home—**Goodrick House**—that was moved here and furnished with antiques.

The **post sutler's complex** contains several furnished buildings, including Wyoming's oldest schoolhouse (1860), the post trader's store, and five other structures. Not far away is the fenced-in grave of a local hero: Thornburgh the dog, who once saved a drowning boy and

later warned the post of an Indian attack. A small human cemetery is near the commanding officer's quarters. A display case in the museum houses items found in the dig, including buttons, trade beads, and other items.

Fort Bridger Rendezvous

Each Labor Day weekend the largest modern-day mountain-man rendezvous in Wyoming comes to Fort Bridger. This is one of Wyoming's most enjoyable events, so don't miss it! In addition, there's a big rodeo the same weekend in Evanston, just 30 miles to the west. During the rendezvous, tents and tepees sprawl across the fort grounds, and hundreds of costumed revelers join in the celebration. Trader's row offers 1840s-style crafts and trade items, including beads, furs, and tomahawks. Participants take part in cannon shoots, muzzle-loading contests, Indian dancing, Dutch-oven cooking, tomahawk throwing, and acoustic music. Great cooked-over-the-fire food is offered, too. Be sure to attend performances of *A Ballad of the West,* written by a great-grandnephew of Jim Bridger. The rendezvous attracts 400 buckskinners, squaws, hunters, and pilgrims, along with thousands of spectators.

Other summer events at Fort Bridger include a parade, a rodeo, and a town dance on the **Fourth of July,** and **moonlight tours** of the fort grounds in August; call 307/782-3842 for reservations.

Fort Bridger Town

The town of Fort Bridger contains **Wagon Wheel Motel,** 307/782-6361, where rooms are $35–45 s or d. You can park RVs for $18 or pitch at tent for $10. A restaurant is on the premises, or get limited groceries at **Fort Bridger Cash Store,** 307/782-6744. **Fort Bridger RV Camp,** 307/782-3150 or 800/578-6535, has RV hookups $18. Open Apr.–Sept. **Jim Bridger Trading Post,** 307/782-6115, sells souvenirs, some groceries, and—if you're in the market—washing machines.

Evanston

West of Fort Bridger, I-80 begins a lengthy climb into the hills, leaving the desert behind as it heads toward the Utah border. The attractive, friendly town of Evanston (pop. 12,000) lies just six miles from Utah and only 80 miles from Salt Lake City. Evanston's economy depends on gas and oil wells, tourists, ranching, and a state hospital. On the outskirts of Evanston, fireworks stands crowd the freeway off-ramps, waiting to lure Utahans who create weekend traffic jams in pursuit of booze, bars, betting, cheap gas, and even a busy porn shop (located next to Lotty's Family Restaurant, no less!). Evanston is a blend of the old and new; you'll even find an espresso café next to an old-time cowboy boot and saddle shop.

HISTORY

As the transcontinental railroad's construction crews raced across Wyoming in 1868, the settlement of Evanston was established as the last

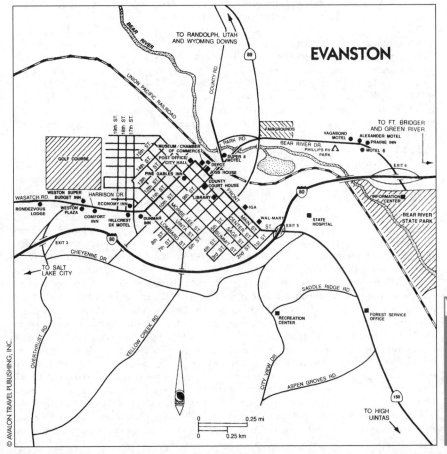

division point before the Wasatch Range. The town received its name from the railroad's surveyor, James A. Evans. In 1886, the territorial legislature offered Uinta County representatives the choice of either a university or an insane asylum. They chose the asylum. By the following year, Evanston had 1,500 people, many of whom worked at the Union Pacific car and machine shops, at an ice plant, or on the tracks. Others logged railroad ties in the mountains or raised sheep and cattle. Rich deposits of coal were discovered four miles north of Evanston, and several mines soon opened, creating the town of **Almy.** In 1869, hundreds of Chinese miners were hired as strikebreakers at the mines, creating tensions that would later erupt into race riots and force the temporary abandonment of Evanston's Chinatown. The Almy mines became notorious for deadly methane-gas explosions. At least 60 whites and uncounted Chinese miners were killed in blasts in 1881, 1886, and 1895. The mines closed in 1906, leaving many of the fires unextinguished; you can still see evidence of the smoldering fires. Many of the old mine buildings still stand at the townsite, but the town has long since been abandoned.

THE OVERTHRUST BELT

Evanston lies at the center of the energy-rich Overthrust Belt, which extends from Canada to Mexico. This 40-mile-wide uplift was formed when two land masses smashed together, thrusting the western portion atop the eastern half and creating folds that trapped oil and gas. It was long believed to contain rich energy deposits, but hundreds of dry holes were drilled before one finally hit home. In 1976, the Yellow Creek Oil Field was discovered, producing both oil and natural gas and unleashing a boomtown atmosphere. Many more oil and gas fields have been discovered since then. Although Uinta County is Wyoming's smallest, it's the largest in terms of natural-gas production; nearly one-third of the state's output comes from here.

SIGHTS
Depot Square

A renovation project in downtown Evanston has created an attractive central area with a fountain and open grassy lawns for relaxing. The focal point is the old **Evanston Depot.** Built in 1900, it was one of the finest along the line and had separate waiting rooms for men and women. A 1944 Union Pacific dining car and caboose stand outside the depot, and the nearby **Beeman-Cashin Implement Depot** is used for dances and community activities. Built around 1886 and restored a century later, this unique wooden structure has no supporting posts.

Located in the old town library (which also houses the visitors center), **Uinta County Museum,** 307/789-2757, is open Monday–Friday 9 A.M.–5 P.M. year-round, plus Saturday–Sunday 10 A.M.–4 P.M. during summer. No charge. Exhibits include historic photos, arrowheads, and a variety of local items. While here, pick up a **walking-tour brochure** of Evanston that details many of the older buildings in town. Outside the museum are several old wagons.

Joss House

Early in this century, Evanston had a prominent Chinatown located along the north side of the tracks. Life centered around the Joss House, a Taoist temple built in 1894 and one of just three in the nation (the others were in San Francisco and New York). Thousands of pilgrims came from hundreds of miles away to worship. After the Chinese workers returned to their homeland, the building was destroyed in a suspicious 1922 fire that leveled much of Chinatown. A replica of the Joss House was completed in 1990 and furnished with historic photos, an 1874 Chinese signboard, decorative panels from the original Joss House, opium pipes, a priceless triangular flag and century-old dragon, a Buddha figure, a gong, lanterns, and more. Check out the pottery, coins, and other artifacts found during **archaeological digs** at the Chinatown site. The digging continues each July; ask here for access details. Be sure to see the video on

© DON PITCHER

Depot Square, Evanston

Mormon Charlie and China Mary, the only Chinese who remained after 1922. The few Chinese-Americans in Evanston today moved here more recently. The Joss House, 307/789-1472, is open daily 7 A.M.–7 P.M. mid-May through September; ask at the museum for access the rest of the year.

Bear River State Park

This 300-acre park surrounds the Bear River Information Center just south of Evanston (I-80 at exit 6). The Bear River, which is just a creek here, flows northward, eventually draining into Great Salt Lake. At 400 miles in length, it's the largest river in the Western Hemisphere that doesn't reach the ocean.

There's no camping, but Bear River State Park has three miles of trails (one mile is paved) for hiking and biking, and it connects with the paved Bear Parkway, which extends westward for 1.5 miles along the river. The park is also home to a small herd of **bison and elk.** In the winter, eight kilometers of groomed cross-country ski trails are maintained within the park, and a

small ice rink is cleared on the ponds. Get additional park information at 307/789-6547, http://wyoparks.state.wy.us.

ACCOMMODATIONS

You'll find several inexpensive places to stay in Evanston. Reserve ahead on summer weekends to be sure of having a place, and on Labor Day you'll need to reserve one month in advance. In winter, the town provides reasonably priced lodging for skiers from Park City, Utah, just 50 miles away.

Under $50

Stay at the comfortable **Vagabond Motel,** 230 Bear River Dr., 307/789-2902 or 800/789-2902, for $30 s or $36 d. Rooms are clean and well-maintained, and some have fridges and microwaves. **Economy Inn,** 1724 Harrison Dr., 307/789-9610, charges $36 s or $41–46 d. **Prairie Inn Motel,** 264 Bear River Dr., 307/789-2920, is a good place with clean rooms (many with fridges and microwaves)

for $38 s or $43 d, including a continental breakfast.

Another place to hitch your wagon for the night is **Weston Plaza (Lamplighter),** 1983 Harrison Dr., 307/789-0783 or 800/255-9840. Rates are $40 s or $45 d, including use of an indoor pool and hot tub. At **Motel 6,** 261 Bear River Dr., 307/789-0791 or 800/466-8356, www.motel6.com, rooms cost $40 s or $46 d, including access to the heated outdoor pool and hot tub.

$50–100

Super 8 Motel, 70 Bear River Dr., 307/789-7510 or 800/800-8000, www.super8.com, charges $45–55 s or $47–57 d. **Hi Country Inn,** 1936 Harrison Dr., 307/789-2810 or 888/621-3220, has rooms for $54 s or $64 d, and an outdoor pool. **Rendezvous Lodge,** 339 Wasatch Rd., 307/789-2220 or 800/357-2220, charges $60 s or $65 d, and has a hot tub and sauna. Kitchenettes cost $10 more, and a luxury suite is $150 d.

A recently opened **Comfort Inn,** 1931 Harrison Dr., 307/789-7799 or 800/228-5150, www.comfortinn.com, offers attractive rooms and such features as an indoor pool, hot tub, fitness center, and light breakfast, plus in-room microwaves and fridges. Rates are $69–89 s or d in standard rooms, or $130 s or d for a suite.

Best Western Dunmar Inn, 1601 Harrison Dr., 307/789-3770 or 800/654-6509, www.bestwestern.com, is one of the nicest places in town, with an outdoor heated pool, hot tub, and exercise room, plus a popular restaurant and lounge. Rates are $79 s or $85–89 d.

Bed-and-Breakfast

Evanston's homiest spot is **Pine Gables Inn B&B,** 1049 Center St., 307/789-2069 or 800/789-2069, www.cruising-america.com/pinegables, built in 1883 and used as a European-style lodging place during the 1920s and '30s. The house was restored in 1981, furnished with antiques, and reopened as a delightful bed-and-breakfast. Six guest rooms are available, all with private baths. Rates are $65–149 d, including a full breakfast. No kids under 12 allowed.

CAMPING

The nearest public campgrounds are in the Uinta Mountains, 30 miles to the south. **Phillips RV Park,** 225 Bear River Dr., 307/789-3805 or 800/349-3805, www.phillipsrvpark.com, charges $15 for tents or $21 for RVs. It's open April to mid-November and has shaded sites.

FOOD

Breakfast and Lunch

Meet Evanston cops over coffee and doughnuts at **Main Street Deli,** 1025 Main St., 307/789-1599. The deli also offers breakfast bargains, along with lunchtime soup, sandwiches, and cornbread.

Main St. Artisans Cafe and Gallery, 927 Main St., 307/789-4991, is an earthy spot with pastries, salads, sandwiches, breakfast burritos, and espresso. The back room contains a fine arts gallery displaying the works of regional artists. It's housed in the historic Blyth & Fargo Building.

Michael's Bar & Grill, 1011 Front St., 307/789-1088, doesn't look that inviting outside, but it's actually a fine lunch and dinner spot that fills with local business folks over the noon hour. Sandwiches, burgers, and healthy salads round out the menu.

Legal Tender Dining Room in the Dunmar Inn, 1601 Harrison Dr., 307/789-3770, is an attractive establishment with lunch specials and reasonably priced steak-house fare.

Dinner

Lotty's Family Restaurant, 1925 Harrison Dr., 307/789-9660, has a big salad bar and buffet with all-you-can-stuff-in prime rib Friday–Sunday nights. Also of note is **Bon Rico's,** 925 Front St., 307/789-1753, with enormous steaks and seafood in an upscale setting. A bit pricey, but worth every penny.

The Old Mill Restaurant, 30 Country Rd., 307/789-4040, is next to Evanston's old Chinatown, where an archaeological dig takes place each July. The historic building is something of a local landmark, and the restaurant serves a varied menu, with karaoke twice a week in the bar.

Best pizza around is at **Pizza Hut,** 134 Yellow Creek Rd., 307/789-1372. Be assured that Evanston also has most of the fast-food chains, including Subway, Little Caesars, Wendy's, Arby's, Domino's, KFC, Taco John's, Burger King, and McD's. **Hamblin Park,** next to the fairgrounds on Bear River Drive, is a pleasant place to enjoy a picnic lunch beneath tall cottonwood trees.

International and Brewpubs

It may seem a bit strange in such a small town, but Evanston has two **Don Pedro's Mexican Restaurants,** the original one at 909 Front St., 307/789-2944, and a larger version at 205 Bear River Dr., 307/789-3322. Good and authentic Mexican fare, and Don Pedro now has restaurants in several other Wyoming and Utah towns.

Bear River Brewing, 1212 Main St., 307/444-6274, combines delicious entrées (pizzas, salads, fettuccini, barbecue ribs, chicken enchiladas, and even Alaskan king crab) with nine of their own microbrews on draught. Tasty appetizers, too. In the front is a **Kathy's Botanicals,** a made-in-Wyoming gift shop.

Located, appropriately enough, across the street from the Joss House is **Hunan Garden,** 933 Front, 307/789-2882, offering Chinese and American cooking. Lunch is a bargain, with $5 specials. Get buffet-style Chinese food at **Dragon Wall,** 140 Front St., 307/789-7788.

Groceries

Get groceries from the **Jubilee Super-Center,** 524 Front St., 307/789-6788, or **Smith's,** 70 Yellow Creek Rd. N, 307/789-0532, or **Wal-Mart SuperCenter,** 120 Beckers Circle, 307/789-0010.

ENTERTAINMENT

Evanston is jam-packed with liquor stores and lounges to quench the parched throats of Utahans who cross the border in droves. **Legal Tender Lounge** at Dunmar Inn, 1601 Harrison Dr., 307/789-3770, has two bars—an upstairs disco with Top 40 tunes and a downstairs saloon where you can dance to live rock

bands on weekends—and draws mainly a young crowd. For rock tunes on summer weekends, drop by **Kelly's Roadhouse Grill,** 240 Bear River Dr., 307/783-7464. It's a favorite of bikers. **Pete's Rock-N-Rye Club,** a long-time bar east of town on U.S. Hwy. 30, 307/789-2135, has occasional live music, and **Bear River Brewing,** 1212 Main St., 307/444-6274, offers live acoustic tunes on Friday and Saturday nights. Or just hang out in the relaxing atmosphere of **Kate's Bar,** 936 Main St., 307/789-7662.

Watch movies at **Evanston Valley Cinema,** 45 Aspen Grove Dr. E, 307/789-0522 or **Strand Theatre,** 1028 Main St., 307/789-2974.

EVENTS

The **International Pedigree Stage Stop Sled Dog Race** (IPSSSDR) stops here. See the Jackson chapter for more info.

One of the most unusual Evanston events is **Chinese New Year,** featuring a parade, Chinese foods, fireworks, rickshaw races, and, of course, the dragon. With so few Chinese-Americans in Evanston today, many of the performers are of other ancestry.

On summer weekends, **Wyoming Downs Racetrack,** 12 miles north of Evanston on State Hwy. 89, 307/789-0511 or 800/842-8722, www.wyomingdowns.com, has horse racing with pari-mutuel betting on Saturdays and Sundays. Wyoming's only live-meet horse track, it is particularly popular with folks from Salt Lake because horse racing is illegal in Utah. At the Western Super Budget Inn, race enthusiasts can also watch and wager off-track bets on races as far away as California.

The **Evanston Rodeo Series** includes amateur rodeo events every other week throughout the summer; call 307/789-5511 for a schedule.

In late June, cyclists compete in the **High Uintas Classic Stage Race,** which traverses the Uinta Mountains in a spectacular 80-mile route; cyclists must climb over a 12,000-foot pass along the way. More cycling in mid-August, when mountain-bikers compete in the **Wolverine Ridge XC Race** on trails south of town.

Mid-July brings the spicy **Evanston Chili Cook-Off,** to the fairgrounds. Ads proclaim "It's a gas!"

Evanston's **Uinta County Fair** the first week of August includes a greased-pig contest, 4-H animal judging, rodeos, carnival rides, concerts, and even pedal-power tractor pulls. The low-key **Bear River Rendezvous** takes place at Bear River State Park on the weekend before Labor Day, attracting mountain men and women who re-create the spirit of the West.

Cowboy Days

Evanston's main event is, predictably, the annual PRCA rodeo, here known as **Cowboy Days.** Labor Day weekend festivities pack all the motels in town as folks come from surrounding states to watch professional cowboys show their stuff at "the biggest little rodeo in the world." The three-day event also includes musical entertainment, dances, an arts-and-crafts fair, a parade, a pancake breakfast, a spaghetti dinner, and clowns. Labor Day is also the weekend for the popular Fort Bridger Rendezvous, just 30 miles east at historic Fort Bridger.

RECREATION

See Bear River State Park for outdoor adventures on the edge of Evanston. The **Evanston Recreation Center,** 275 Saddle Ridge Rd., 307/789-1770, www.evanstonwy.org/parkrec, includes a swimming pool, gyms, racquetball courts, a weight room, and a hot tub.

Purple Sage Golf Course, on Country Club Dr., 307/789-2383, is an 18-hole public course. **Fireside Lanes,** 2631 Hwy. 150 S, 307/789-6716, is the local bowling alley.

Cross-country skiers head to groomed trails at **Deadhorse Ski Trail,** 18 miles south of Evanston, and **Lily Lake Touring Area,** 30 miles south in the Uintas. Lily Lake also has three furnished *yurts* (domed tents) for overnight stays ($25 on weekdays or $50 on weekends for up to eight people); details at 307/789-1770, www.evanstonoutdoors.com.

Snowmobilers will find 40 miles of groomed winter trails starting at the Deadhorse trailhead and continuing all the way to a snowpark on Utah Hwy. 150.

SHOPPING

The old Federal Building (built in 1915), on the corner of 10th and Center Streets, is home to several shops, including an antique store, T-shirt shop, and the **Glass Cat,** 307/783-7901, where you'll find stained-glass pieces with a cat motif. **Quilt Trappings,** 1029 Main St., 307/789-1675, is a good place to find quilts, fabrics, and classes.

Get new and used books, along with magazines and music, from **Bear River Books,** 1008 Main, 307/789-6465 or 888/641-2665, www.bearriverbooks.com. Wash clothes at **Sunfresh Laundro,** 116 Yellow Creek Rd., 307/789-1163. **Rocky Mtn. Lodgepole Furniture Co.,** 1049 Main St., 307/789-9042 or 800/827-9042, creates rustic and functional chairs, benches, beds, and other furnishings.

Sports World, inside the IGA at 524 Front St., 307/789-6788, sells outdoor gear, and its walls are lined with big-game mounts. **Mountain Air Power & Sports,** 50 Jamison Dr., 307/789-7533, rents a bit of everything, including ATVs, motorcycles, jet skis, and canoes.

INFORMATION AND SERVICES

Evanston has two places to go for information. If you're entering the state from the west, stop at **Bear River Information Center,** I-80 exit 6, 307/789-6540. The center has a wealth of statewide information, a pleasant picnic area, and short trails. It's open daily 8 A.M.–5 P.M. year-round. The information center lies within Bear River State Park.

The **Evanston Chamber of Commerce,** 36 10th St., 307/783-0370 or 800/328-9708, www.etownchamber.com, is housed in the county museum and provides more local information. Hours are Monday–Friday 9 A.M.–5 P.M.

Check your email at **Uinta County Library,** 701 Main, 307/789-2770.

TRANSPORTATION

Greyhound, 307/789-2810 or 800/231-2222, www.greyhound.com, runs buses both east and west on I-80 and stops at the High Country Inn, 1936 Harrison Drive.

Rent cars from **Evanston Motor Co.,** 2000 Hwy. 30 W, 307/789-3145. **A-Cab,** 307/677-0059, or **Gypsy Cab,** 307/789-2681, will take you around town, and **Star West Aviation,** 307/789-2256, offers charter service from the Evanston airport.

HIGH UINTA MOUNTAINS

The **Evanston Ranger District,** 1565 Hwy. 150 S, 307/789-3194, www.fs.fed.us/wcnf, has maps of Wasatch National Forest, but only a tiny corner of the forest comes into Wyoming. The **High Uintas Wilderness** is 30 miles south of Evanston via Mirror Lake Highway/Wyoming 150 (a National Scenic Byway). This wilderness area is very popular with hikers and cross-country skiers from the Evanston and Green River areas and includes Kings Peak, the tallest mountain in Utah. Get additional information from the **Bear River Ranger Station,** 435/642-6662, 30 miles south of Evanston inside Utah; open late May–Oct. Recreation access fees are charged in the Mirror Lake area: $3 per day per car, or $25 for an annual pass.

Bear River Lodge, 800/559-1121, www.bearriverlodge.com, has cabins, outdoor hot tubs, a general store, snowmobile rentals in winter, and ATV and watercraft rentals in summer. It's in Utah 32 miles south of Evanston. See *Moon Handbooks Utah* by Bill Weir and W. C. McRae (www.moon.com) for details on the beautiful Mirror Lake Highway.

NORTH TO KEMMERER

North of Evanston, U.S. Hwy. 189 follows a long valley most of the way to Kemmerer. A hogback ridge hems you in to the east. Stop for a look back at the ragged snow-topped Uintas that form a southern horizon line.

Near the junction with State Hwy. 412 (36 miles up) is the small **Cumberland** cemetery, enclosed within a white picket fence. Turn down State Hwy. 412 to see what's left of the ghost town of Cumberland. This was a booming coal-mining town between 1920 and 1935, with four underground mines going at once. Today all that remains are the sandstone Ziller ranch buildings—the old whorehouse and saloon—and the cemetery. The buildings are not open to the public.

Kemmerer

The twin towns of Kemmerer (pop. 2,700) and Diamondville (pop. 700) are at the center of the coal industry in southwestern Wyoming. Drive west of town and you'll even pass coal seams in the road cutbank. Kemmerer is the Lincoln County seat and is located on the Hams Fork River; Diamondville lies just a few yards south. The surrounding country is dotted with mining and energy plants of various types. P&M Coal Mine—the nation's largest strip mine—is several miles south, and a nearby Exxon plant is the world's largest manufacturer of helium and the state's largest consumer of electricity. Another major employer is the FMC coke plant, which provides metallurgical coke for a phosphorous plant in Pocatello, Idaho. It, too, is the largest such operation in the world. Natural gas, oil, and sulfur are also important locally, as are cattle and sheep ranching. Given this setting it should come as no surprise that this is a pickup-truck town. Either that or you better drive a Mustang with growling glaspak mufflers. But watch your speed; local cops are ever vigilant.

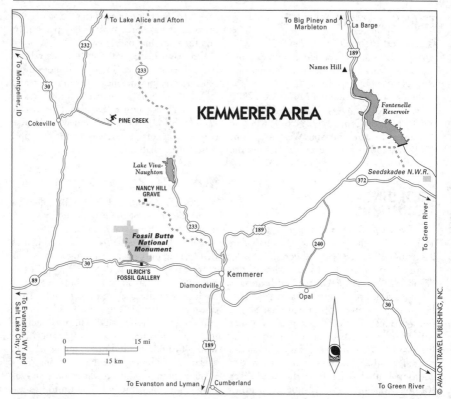

KEMMERER AREA

HISTORY

Coal Mining

Explorer John C. Frémont first chanced upon coal here in 1843, but it wasn't until 1881 that the Union Pacific opened the first underground mine. Things really began to boom when Patrick J. Quealy and his partner Mahlon S. Kemmerer established the Kemmerer Coal Company. Hundreds of men died in mine accidents; the worst was a 1923 explosion that killed 99 miners, mostly emigrants. The operation moved aboveground in 1950, and the Kemmerer mine became the Pittsburg & Midway Coal Company, now a subsidiary of ChevronTexaco. Located six miles south of Kemmerer along U.S. Hwy. 189, P&M is America's largest (physically, but not in terms of production) open-pit coal mine, reaching 800 feet deep and producing nearly five million tons per year. Two-thirds of the coal is used at Pacific Power's adjacent Naughton Plant, which produces 710 megawatts of power. The mine—the longest continuously operating mine in Wyoming—and the power plant are the largest employers in the region. Get details and tour information at 307/828-2200, www.kemmerer.org/pm.html.

Moonshine and Shady Ladies

During the 1920s, Kemmerer became a national center for bootlegging and a major supplier for Chicago. Kemmerer "moon" was a favorite of speakeasies, and winemakers ordered grapes by the trainload. A 1931 bust near Kemmerer found 24,000 gallons of liquor. All this ended when Prohibition was repealed in 1933.

With all the coal miners, the ratio of men to women in Kemmerer was nearly 50 to one, prime pickings for the world's oldest profession. Into these conditions stepped Madam Isabelle Burns, fresh off the train from Salt Lake City with considerable experience in the "sporting" trade. She arrived in 1896 looking for somewhere to invest the $28,500 inheritance from her husband's suicide. With $5,000 in cash she bought a dance hall with enough convenient side rooms to house 50 prostitutes. In a short while, the Green House was a roaring success, allowing Madam Isabelle to build the most elegant house then in town, which is still standing at 301 Ruby Street. Because of the demand for "evening wear," Kemmerer's shoe store reportedly sold more high-heeled satin slippers than any shop west of the Mississippi. A nude painting of one of the Green House ladies with her brother (and lover) is now in the Golden Nugget Bar in Las Vegas. Madam Isabelle quit the business in 1926, left town, and married a New Orleans physician. Her business went on in fresh hands.

Several deaths took place at the Green House, leading to a grand conflagration when a man whose sons had been murdered there burned one of the women to death, igniting the building in the process and leaving it a pile of ashes. After the 1926 fire, it was replaced by the Southern Hotel. A newly elected sheriff finally shut things down in 1967, despite pleas from locals that the loss of all the Utah and Idaho clients would hurt business in town. For more on this tantalizing bit of history, see Ray Essman's *Only Count the Sunny Hours* (Winona, MN: Apollo Books).

SIGHTS

Penney House

The most unusual sights in Kemmerer relate to James Cash Penney, founder of the JCPenney chain. Penney moved to Kemmerer in 1902 from Evanston to open a dry goods store in the booming mining town, and his Golden Rule Store quickly achieved a reputation for quality and honesty. By 1912 there were 34 Golden Rule stores; the following year their name was changed to JCPenney, and the rest is history. The company website (www.jcpenney.com) has more on JCPenney history.

The James Cash Penney House is a little six-room cottage where Penney and his family lived between 1903 and 1909. The nicely restored house is right behind the chamber of commerce office downtown and is open Monday–Saturday 9 A.M.–6 P.M. and Sunday 11 A.M.–4 P.M. in summer. No admission charge. Guides are ready to show you around and put on a video about the company's history, and one room contains family and JCPenney company memorabilia. The house is furnished as it might have been when the Penney family lived here, although the original furnishings—with the exception of a wooden cradle—are long gone. The JCPenney "mother store" is also in Kemmerer, just a few doors up the street (JC Penney Drive, of course). If the home is closed, ask at the store for access.

Museum and Historical Buildings

Kemmerer's **Fossil Country Frontier Museum,** 400 Pine Ave., 307/877-6551, www.hams-fork.net/~museum, is open Monday–Saturday 9 A.M.–5 P.M. in summer and Monday–Saturday 10 A.M.–4 P.M. the rest of the year; no admission charge. It contains a variety of art, mining, and archaeological exhibits, a walk-through underground coal mine exhibit, and dozens of kinds of barbed wire dating from the 19th century. Freak-show enthusiasts will appreciate the lamb with one head and two bodies. The small gift shop sells inexpensive fossil fish, along with Wyoming books and locally made products. The museum puts on evening **campfire chats** most Thursdays at 7 P.M. June–August at Archie Niel Park. This is a great way to learn about the natural and cultural history of the area.

The nicely restored **Lincoln County Courthouse** at Sage and Topaz Streets was built in 1925 and contains a fine collection of fossils. Stop by the post office at Cedar and Sapphire Streets to view the **fossil murals** painted by WPA artists in 1938. For additional historical buildings, head to "downtown" Diamondville, where several classic structures line the old main street.

Fossil Collecting

Although it's illegal to collect fossils within Fossil Butte National Monument, three local

JAMES CASH PENNEY

One of America's best-known retail chains, JCPenney, had its start in Kemmerer, Wyoming, in 1902. The founder was James Cash Penney, a man whose life exemplified the proverbial rags-to-riches story. Born in 1875 to a devout Missouri family, Penney grew up in poverty. His father was a farmer and Baptist minister who, together with his mother—a Southern belle—instilled in the young man a Christian ethical base that emphasized the Golden Rule and self-reliance.

It didn't take long for Penney's resourcefulness to reveal itself. At age eight he needed new shoes and used his meager savings to buy young pigs that he later sold for a profit. After high school he took a job in a local dry goods store where he learned the trade, then he moved to Colorado to open a butcher shop. The shop failed when Penney refused to continue paying bribes (in the form of a bottle of bourbon per week) to his biggest account, a local hotel.

The Golden Rule Stores

J. C. Penney's big break came in 1898 when he began work with a small chain called the Golden Rule Stores. The owners quickly recognized the skills in this ambitious young man and offered Penney a one-third interest in any new stores he would open. With $500 in savings and $1,500 in borrowed money, Penney quickly seized the chance, opening a dry goods store in Kemmerer on April 14, 1902. It wasn't much, just a one-room building away from the center of town and furnished with makeshift fixtures, but Penney was shrewd enough to recognize what people wanted: fair prices that were the same no matter who walked in the store and a cash-only operation; he was opposed to credit because it was often used by unscrupulous merchants to create a class of workers who were never able to pay off their bills. The store proved an immediate hit, and within a year he had opened another store in Rock Springs, followed by a third in Cumberland, Wyoming, in 1904.

Three years later his partners sold the entire operation to Penney, and under his guidance the company took off, quickly making him a millionaire. By the end of 1912 he was the head of a chain of 34 Golden Rule stores, and the following year the name was changed to the J. C. Penney Company. It soon became one of the fastest growing national retail chains. By 1920, the company had 197 stores from coast to coast, and it continued to open stores throughout the next decade at the blistering pace of one new store every three days. By 1929, 1,400 Penney stores were scattered across the country. The bubble burst with the stock market crash of 1929, and Penney's financial empire collapsed around him. It took decades for Penney to recover the wealth he had lost so suddenly.

Later Years

Penney was a devoted family man, but his first two wives died young—the first in 1910 from pneumonia and the second in 1924. He married a third time and remained married until his death in 1971. The loss of his wives led Penney to philanthropy and charitable projects as a way to ease his own pain by helping others. Even today, his charitable foundations continue to fund community renewal, world peace, and environmental efforts. In later years, Penney turned his attention to farming and developed an international reputation for his champion cattle, especially the Guernseys that became the basis for another company he helped found, Foremost Dairies.

Penney remained active far beyond when most people retire. He never forgot a name or face, and even at the age of 85 he kept up a grueling schedule of store visits, conventions, and speaking engagements. He only stopped taking the city bus to work in his nineties, and he was still coming to work within a few months of his death at the age of 95. Today the stores he founded have moved beyond the religious devotion personified in James Cash Penney, but they still bear his name and a reputation for quality merchandise. The town of Kemmerer contains both the JCPenney "mother store" and Penney's old home, now open as a small museum.

areas permit it for a fee. These are only open in summer, and children generally aren't allowed because it is considered dangerous for them. The best-known place—its fossils are exhibited in the Smithsonian—is **Ulrich's Fossil Gallery,** 307/877-6466, located just outside the national monument, 14 miles west of Kemmerer. Out front are enormous dinosaur tracks discovered in a coal mine. Ulrich's has a nearby quarry on state land, where you can dig your own fish fossils for $65 (advance reservations required) in the summer. You're allowed to keep a wooden pallet full of the most common species, although the state gets any rare specimens that turn up. If you don't want to dig, you can buy beautifully prepared fossils at Ulrich's gallery (open year-round).

Warfield Fossil Quarry, 307/883-2445, www.warfieldfossils.com, charges diggers $50 per day. Their remote quarry (no amenities) is a 35-minute drive north of Kemmerer; get their brochure and follow the map closely.

Tynsky's Fossil Fish Shop, just down from the JCPenney store in downtown Kemmerer, 307/877-6885, www.kemmerer.org/tynskys.html, has fossil fish for sale. (The store is closed February–May.) You can also dig at Tynsky's quarry, 12 miles west of town. The cost is $55 for two hours or so, and you can keep up to 10 fossils.

ACCOMMODATIONS

Antler Motel, 419 Coral St. in Kemmerer, 307/877-4461, has older units for $26–34 s or d, along with remodeled rooms for $36–43 s or d. **Fossil Butte Motel,** 1424 Central Ave., 307/877-3996, www.fossilbuttemotel.com, has comfortable rooms with microwaves and fridges; $43 s or $49 d.

Fairview Inn, 501 N. Hwy. 30 in Kemmerer, 307/877-3938 or 800/247-3938, www.wy-biz.com/fairviewmotel, rents standard rooms for $45 d. Larger units containing microwaves and fridges are $60 for up to four people. This is the nicest motel in the area.

Over in Diamondville, **Energy Inn,** 307/877-6901, rents motel rooms for $50 s or $63 d. All of these have fridges, and some include kitchenettes.

CAMPING

Tent camping (no RVs) is available for $6 at **Kemmerer Community Camp,** on State Hwy. 233 north of Kemmerer; open Memorial Day to Sept. Call 307/828-2360 for details. Public camping is also available at **Fontenelle Creek Campground** ($6; open Memorial Day to Sept.), 25 miles northeast of Kemmerer on U.S. Hwy. 189 beside Fontenelle Reservoir. In addition, three free campgrounds are located along the Green River just below the Fontenelle dam, and dozens of free campsites border the lake.

Riverside RV Park, just north of town at 216 Spinel St., 307/877-3416, has RV spaces for $18, but it's a shadeless gravel lot and doesn't have tent sites. Open May–Oct. **Foothills RV Park,** on N. Hwy. 189, 307/877-6634, has grassy RV sites for $19; open year-round. Farther away is **Lake Viva-Naughton Marina,** 15 miles north of Kemmerer, 307/877-9669, with tent spaces ($5), RV hookups ($15), and a few basic cabins for $28. The cabins are available year-round, but camping is allowed only late May–October. They will be closing in July 2004.

FOOD

No standouts for meals in Kemmerer, but several places have solid meals for reasonable prices. Start your day at **Busy Bee Cafe,** 919 Pine Ave., 307/877-6820; open at 5:30 A.M. on weekdays, and also for lunch and dinner. Another place with good breakfasts, plus the best local burgers, is **Polar King Drive In,** on the north side of Kemmerer at 315 U.S. Hwy. 189, 307/877-9448.

Bootlegger's Steakhouse & Grill, downtown at 817 S. Main St., 307/828-3067, has a full menu. **Bon Rico's,** 12 miles south of town, 307/877-4503, is another favorite place to stuff yourself with steak or fish.

Lake Viva-Naughton Marina, 15 miles north of Kemmerer along the reservoir, 307/877-9669, attracts a surprising number of Salt Lake City people with an outstanding seafood and steak menu. Unfortunately, their lease expires in July 2004, so they won't be around after that.

There's a **Pizza Hut** in Diamondville,

307/877-6969, offering lunch deals and predictable pizzas. Local chain outlets include an Arby's, Arctic Circle, Subway, and Taco Time. Located on the north side of Kemmerer, **Jubilee Foods,** 307/877-3698, is the local grocery store.

ENTERTAINMENT

The **Stock Exchange Bar** downtown has a pool table and fills with locals most nights. For live music, try **Bon Rico's,** 12 miles south of town, 307/877-4503, or **Lake Viva-Naughton Marina,** 15 miles north of Kemmerer, 307/877-9669.

EVENTS

The **International Pedigree Stage Stop Sled Dog Race** (IPSSSDR) stops here. See the Jackson chapter for more info.

For five days in late June, Kemmerer celebrates **Fossil Fest** with a parade, melodrama, horse and buggy rides, street dance, fireworks, and food and craft booths. The free **Oyster Ridge Music Festival** is held on the Kemmerer Triangle on the third weekend of August and features an outdoor barbecue, contests, and concerts from guitar, fiddle, banjo, and mandolin musicians. The star attraction is the flatpick guitar contest, but the "band scramble" is particularly fun—musicians must play together without time to rehearse. Get details at 307/877-9761 or 888/300-3413, www.oysterridgemusicfestival.com.

Anglers may want to join in the **Ice Fishing Derby** on the third weekend of February or the **Open Water Fishing Derby** on the last weekend of June. Both of these take place at Lake Viva-Naughton.

RECREATION

Kemmerer Recreation Center, 1776 Dell Rio Dr., 307/828-2365, has an indoor pool, weight room, hot tub, sauna, racquetball courts, and even an indoor climbing wall. The outdoor pool

(307/877-9641) in **Archie Neil Park** is open during the summer. Kemmerer's nine-hole **Municipal Golf Course** is just north of town on Hwy. 189, 307/877-6954. Bowl at **Sage Bowling Lanes,** 918 Sage Ave., 307/877-6642.

Lions Club Park, just north of Kemmerer along scenic Hams Fork River, is a fine place for a picnic. Good fishing is the rule at **Lake Viva-Naughton,** 15 miles north of Kemmerer on State Hwy. 233; the marina, 307/877-9669, rents boats.

INFORMATION AND SERVICES

The **Kemmerer Chamber of Commerce** is housed in a log cabin in Herschler Triangle Park at the center of town, 307/877-9761 or 888/300-3413, www.kemmererchamber.com. (Locals joke that Kemmerer is too small to have a town square, so it has a town triangle instead.) It's open Monday–Saturday 9 A.M.–5 P.M. in summer, and the rest of the year Monday–Friday 9 A.M.–2 P.M., plus additional weekend hours in September and October. Inside are displays of fossils and historical pictures, and you can buy local books and old Wyoming license plates. The office can also provide helpful information on nearby fossil-fish quarries and details on tours of industrial plants in the area. The city's website, www.kemmerer.org, has more local information and links.

The **Rock & Wash**—a combination car wash and rock shop at 502 Coral, 307/877-3220—is a fun place to get petrified wood and other interesting rocks.

Head north on Hwy. 189 to find both the Bridger-Teton National Forest's **Kemmerer Ranger District,** 307/877-4415, www.fs.fed.us/btnf, and the adjacent **BLM's Kemmerer Field Office,** 307/828-4500, www.wy.blm.gov.

Surf the bookshelves or the web at **Lincoln County Library,** 519 Emerald St., 307/877-6961, www.wsl.state.wy.us/lincoln. Get crisp $20 bills from the **ATM** at both Community First Bank and First National Bank in Kemmerer, or the one at Chevron Food Mart in Diamondville.

Fossil Butte National Monument

Established in 1972, Fossil Butte is an 8,198-acre natural area managed by the National Park Service and located 14 miles west of Kemmerer. The dominant feature is an 800-foot-tall escarpment rising above the arid plains. Within this butte are millions of fossil fish, insects, snails, turtles, and plants. This is also one of the few places in the world where fossilized birds and bats have been found. The Green River Formation fossils were first collected by geologist Dr. John Evans in 1865.

ORIGINS

Fossil Butte is not unlike countless other buttes throughout Wyoming: an exposed rocky cliff lit with the red, yellow, and buff colors representing millions of years of deposition and erosion. Despite the arid conditions today, this land once supported a subtropical climate similar to that along the Gulf Coast. During the Eocene Epoch (50 million years ago), palm trees grew along the shore of a lake, now called Fossil Lake, whose waters teemed with fish, crocodiles, turtles, stingrays, and other animals. Over a period of two million years, changing salinity levels and variations in runoff from calcium-rich streams caused calcium carbonate to precipitate out. Dead animals and plants on the deep lake bottom were covered with a blanket of fine sediment. Eventually they were fossilized, and when the lake dried up, the sedimentary deposits were gradually thrust upward by geological forces.

VISITORS CENTER

The free **Fossil Butte Visitors Center,** 307/877-4455, www.nps.gov/fobu, is open daily 8 A.M.–7 P.M. June–August and daily 8 A.M.–4:30 P.M. the rest of the year (closed winter holidays). Located 3.5 miles off U.S. Hwy. 30 (follow the signs), the visitors center houses a fossil preparation lab, along with impressive exhibits on geology, paleontology,

and natural history. You'll find a 13-foot crocodile, the oldest known bat, and more than 75 other fossils on display. Watch videos on local geology, paleontology, or fossil preparation, or stop by the gift shop for natural-history books.

Visitors can assist a Park Service paleontologist in collecting fossils June–August weekends 10 A.M.–3 P.M. You'll hike into the quarry site and actually participate in the collection of fossils and data. Be ready to work! Evening campfire programs are offered at the picnic area periodically in the summer; ask at the visitors center for specific times.

Camping is not allowed at Fossil Butte, and the nearest lodging, campground, and RV parks are in Kemmerer. You can, however, camp on nearby BLM lands; see the bureau's Kemmerer office for details.

HIKING

The 2.5-mile **Historic Quarry Trail** on the south side of the monument provides access to an old fossil quarry site (600 feet up) and has various interpretive signs along the way. It is illegal to remove fossils or other items from the monument; see Fossil Collecting section for nearby areas where it is legal.

Fossil Lake Trail begins near a pleasant picnic area three miles north of the visitors center. It provides an enjoyable 1.5-mile loop hike through open sage country and a grove of aspen trees, with descriptive placards along the way. Many varieties of flowers are blooming throughout the summer. Keep your eyes open for mule deer, coyotes, sage grouse, prairie dogs, and other animals on these paths. Other than these two paths, you're on your own, although the open country makes hiking relatively easy. Topographic maps are sold in the visitors center. Be sure to carry water on any hike in this arid area.

Kemmerer Vicinity

OREGON TRAIL SIGHTS

Ten miles north of Kemmerer on State Hwy. 233 are the still-noticeable ruts of the Oregon Trail's **Sublette Cutoff.** Named for mountain man William Sublette, who first took this route in 1826, the cutoff saved Oregon emigrants more than 50 miles of travel but bypassed the chance to rest and resupply at Fort Bridger. Wagons traversed a rough and waterless desert before finally climbing into the cool and wooded mountains. Thirteen miles west of State Hwy. 233 along the Sublette Cutoff is the grave of a young emigrant, Nancy Hill. An 1852 letter written by her uncle describes how suddenly life could end on the treacherous journey west:

> *July the 6th. Since left off writing we have made slow progress in traveling on account of sickness and lame cattle. On last Friday & Saturday we layby on account of abe. He was very bad but is now in a fair way to get well. This day was called on to consign to the tomb one other of our company N. J. Hill. She was in good health on Sunday evening, taken unwell that knight worse in the morning & a corps at nine o'clock at knight. We had two doctors with her. They pronounced her complaining cholera but I believe it was nothing more than cholera with conjestion connecter.*

Names Hill

Oregon Trail travelers paused to carve their names into the rocks at three well-known places in Wyoming: Register Cliff, Independence Rock, and—westernmost of the three—Names Hill. The last of these is six miles south of the oil and gas town of La Barge, along the Sublette Cutoff at the hazardous Green River crossing. More than 2,000 old names are carved in the sandstone cliff, along with two Indian petroglyphs. The oldest name is dated

1827, when John Danks (probably a trapper) carved his still-visible appellation. Many others are from the 1840s and '50s. A fence surrounds one that reads, "James Bridger 1844 Trapper." Its authenticity is suspect because Bridger could neither read nor write and always signed his name with an X. But Jim Bridger *did* run a ferry at the nearby Green River crossing, so I'll give him the benefit of the doubt; perhaps a companion carved it while he watched. Please do not add your name to this historic rock face; in all too many places modern tourists have incised their inane graffiti next to names more than 150 years old.

Fontenelle Reservoir

Fontenelle Reservoir lies just east and south of Names Hill and provides the area with irrigation water and electricity. The lake backs up behind a 139-foot earthen dam on the Green River, and it's a favorite spot for trout fishing, boating, and free camping. The river below the dam makes for a relatively gentle float trip, and the trout fishing (rainbow, brown, and cutthroat) is excellent. Van Beacham's **Solitary Angler,** 307/877-9459, offers guided fly-fishing on this uncrowded stretch of the river.

La Barge and Opal

As you drive north from Names Hill, red and yellow badlands rise along the east side of the Green River while oil pumpjacks punctuate the land in all directions. Clean and comfortable accommodation is available in La Barge (pop. 430) at **Wyoming Inn,** 307/386-2654, where rooms are $38–48 s or $44–54 d. **Red Cliff Motel,** 307/386-9269, charges $44 s or d, including fridges and microwaves. **Timberline Restaurant,** 307/386-2800, serves three meals per day. The twin towns of Marbleton and Big Piney, 21 miles north of La Barge, are covered in the Wind River Mountains chapter.

U.S. Hwy. 30 heads east from Kemmerer to the little collection of old homes and trailers called Opal (o-PAL; pop. 100). Just north up State Hwy. 240 is the giant Exxon/Mobil Shute Creek Carbon Dioxide Plant. Follow the road to State 372 and turn southeast to reach Seedskadee National Wildlife Refuge (see Vicinity of Green River).

COKEVILLE

Cokeville (pop. 500) lies in a long, fertile valley along the Idaho border south of Star Valley. Directly behind the town is an impressive triangular mountain, **Rocky Point.** The ranching and farming country is punctuated with small white farmhouses, but many locals commute to work at the coal mine and power plant near Kemmerer. Nearly everyone is Mormon here.

The town of Cokeville was founded in 1874 with the arrival of the Oregon Shortline Railroad and is named for the coal that was used to produce coke. By the turn of the 20th century it had become the "sheep capital of the world" and claimed more millionaires per capita than anywhere on earth. Cokeville's proximity to the state line also made it a haven for outlaws—with Utah and Idaho just six miles away, lawbreakers found it easy to leave the posse behind as they fled to a different jurisdiction.

Practicalities

Highway 30 through Cokeville is heavily traveled by trucks and cars heading north to Pocatello, Idaho, or south to I-80; because of this you'll find two gas stations and a large Flying J truck stop in town. Rooms are available ($40–45 d) at **Valley Hi Motel,** 307/279-3251, and **Hideout Motel,** 307/279-3281. The Forest Service's **Hams Fork Campground** ($5, open Memorial Day to Oct.) is the closest public campground; it's 28 miles from Cokeville along the Smiths Fork Road. Get local specifics from the seasonal **Cokeville Visitor Center.**

Pine Creek Ski Area, six miles east of Cokeville, 307/279-3201, consists of a chairlift and rope tow with a 1,200-foot vertical rise. Ski rentals and instruction are available. It's open Tuesday, Saturday, and Sunday January–March. The mountains east of Cokeville also contain many miles of groomed wintertime snowmobile trails.

Lake Alice

Take an enjoyable side trip to Lake Alice, a pristine mountain lake at the end of a 1.5-mile trail in Bridger-Teton National Forest. Three-mile-long Lake Alice was created many centuries ago when a mountain slid across the valley and dammed the creek. Water from the lake flows underground for more than one mile before emerging in springs. Get here by heading northeast from Cokeville on State Hwy. 232 and bearing right at the "Y" 12 miles up where the pavement ends. The gravel road continues to the trailhead 34 miles from Cokeville, where you'll find the very nice **Hobble Creek Campground** ($5; open mid-June to mid-Oct.). There's good fishing both in the creek and at Lake Alice. The road into Lake Alice is generally closed by snow from October to late June. The country around here is some of the only unroaded land left in the Wyoming Range. The route to Lake Alice passes the **Kelly Guard Station,** which you can rent for $30 per night. The cabin sleeps five and is available year-round. Winter access is by snowmobile or cross-country skis, approximately nine miles in. Get details from the Forest Service in Kemmerer, 307/877-4415, www.fs.fed.us/btnf.

Heading North

The drive north from Cokeville to Star Valley follows Salt Creek from the sage-and-grass lowlands into lodgepole pine–covered mountains, eventually reaching Salt River Pass at 7,610 feet. It's a taste of the majestic mountain country that fills the northwest corner of Wyoming. On the north side of the pass, the road begins a long descent into beautiful Star Valley. Accommodation is available at **Canyon Inn Motel,** 307/849-0100, 24 miles north of Cokeville and just inside the Wyoming state line. Rooms go for $30 s or d; open mid-Apr. to mid-Nov.

Star Valley

West of the Wyoming Range, the mountains seem exhausted as they dip into a broad, fertile farming valley that stretches across the Idaho border. This is Star Valley, a place with closer ties to Idaho—in terms of geography, farming, sheep ranching, transportation, and even religion—than to Wyoming. Locals call it the "home of 5,000 people and 20,000 cattle." The valley reaches 10 miles across and 40 miles north to south; an early settler labeled it "The Star of all Valleys." Star Valley is a very pretty place; the Salt River—named for the salt deposits and saline springs along its banks—creates an oasis of greenery, and the mountains make a grand backdrop. Irrigation ditches flow alongside the roads, barbed wire stretches between old lodgepole posts, and dairy cows graze in the velvet green farm fields. Spacious old ranches, built to house large Mormon families, alternate with more modern ranch-style homes. A single main road, U.S. Hwy. 89, heads north the full length of Star Valley, with a network of side roads and scattered pinprick settlements. For details on the land just west of Star Valley, see *Moon Handbooks Idaho* by Don Root (www.moon.com).

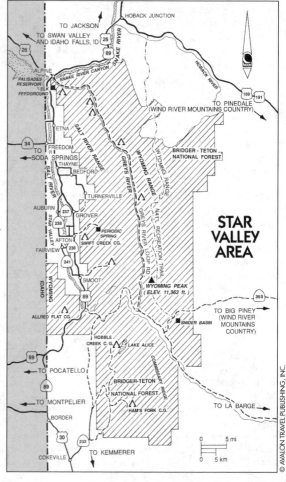

HISTORY

The **Lander Cutoff** of the Oregon Trail angles through the southern half of Star Valley, follows the Salt River as far as the Auburn area, and then cuts northwest along Stump Creek. This 250-mile path—constructed in 1858 under the direction of Frederick W. Lander—was the first federal road built west of the Missouri River. Fur trappers had used the route for 45 years before Lander and his men, funded with a $300,000 appropriation from Congress, upgraded it for wagon travel. The Lander Cutoff saved Oregon-bound travelers more than 100 miles but also entailed climbing over a rugged 9,000-foot pass. You can see parts of the route along the south end of Greys River Road, where concrete posts and emigrant graves mark the way.

The first white settlers came to Star Valley from Idaho in the 1880s, fleeing laws restricting the number of wives a man could have. Polygamy, while outlawed by the federal government in 1882, was winked at by Wyoming authorities for many years. They needed all the settlers they could get, especially the conservative, hardworking Mormons. When Frank W. Mondell was running for Congress in 1894, he came to Star Valley and found that the Afton mayor was a polygamist. Mondell noted,

> We assured our friend we were not disposed to question the propriety of his family affairs and would be glad to accept his hospitality. Thereupon our party partook of a fine supper in the modest home of very pleasant and comely wife No. Three, and thereafter, leaving Miss Reel with her, the remainder of our party was comfortably housed in the larger homes of Wives One and Two.

Polygamy has long since been outlawed, but a large brick Latter-day Saints church still stands in every Podunk town in Star Valley.

AFTON

The primary settlement in Star Valley is Afton (pop. 1,800), a typical small American town and the sort of place where parents complain of kids partying with kegs and making out on back roads. Meanwhile, high-schoolers complain they have nothing to do. Today, tourism has began to kick in as the overflow from Jackson Hole spills into Star Valley. Ranchettes and summer homes are sprouting in what had been farmland, and new real estate offices on the edge of town entice more folks to move in.

Aviat, Inc. manufactures a variety of small aircraft in Afton, including the Pitts Special, considered the finest aerobatics plane in existence; the Eagle homebuilt kit; and the Husky A-1, similar to the famous Super Cub. Also in Afton is a small plant that sews Wyoming Wear garments.

Sights

Afton's best-known attraction is the world's largest **elk antler arch,** an 18-foot-high arch that extends over the main street. Built in 1958, it contains 3,011 antlers. At today's antler

© DON PITCHER

The elk antler arch spans Main Street, Afton.

prices—they're prized as aphrodisiacs in Asia— the arch would be worth more than $300,000!

The **CallAir Museum**, 307/886-9881, is housed in a hangar on the south end of Afton and honors a small aircraft manufacturing company. CallAir began in 1937 and survived until 1962. Many CallAir planes are still in use all over the world, primarily as crop dusters. Founder Reuel Call later made money in the oil business with Maverick Country Stores (headquartered in Afton) and Flying J truck stops, and he invested $2 million to found this free museum. Inside you'll find several CallAir aircraft, historic photos, and a squadron of more than 75 model airplanes. You can watch workers restoring old planes, view educational videos, or purchase flying paraphernalia and books in the gift shop. There's even a kid-size plane for the younger set. Museum hours are daily 9 A.M.–5 P.M. Memorial Day to Labor Day. Staff may be around in the off-season; try knocking on the door. See the Afton Events section for details on the CallAir Fly-In. **Aviat**, 672 Washington, 307/886-3151, does not officially offer tours of its aircraft manufacturing facility, but you may want to drop by on weekdays between 11 A.M. and 3 P.M. just in case.

The small **Pioneer Museum**, next to the fairgrounds, is open seasonally and contains items collected by the Daughters of the Utah Pioneers, including a loom, a spinning wheel, and other memorabilia.

The enormous **Afton Tabernacle**—Latter-day Saints, of course—sits at the corner of Jefferson and 3rd and serves as a community focal point. This impressive sandstone building (architects call this a Middle English design) was begun in 1904 and received further additions in the 1940s.

Periodic Spring

Afton's most unusual sight is Periodic Spring, located in Swift Creek Canyon east of town (take 2nd Avenue). The six-mile drive is quite a contrast to wide-open Star Valley—it parallels a pretty tree-bordered creek and steep rocky slopes. The largest of only three intermittent springs known to exist, Periodic Spring is reached via a three-quarter-mile trail. The crystalline water of this spring emerges from the base of a cliff to feed Swift Creek, the water source for Afton, and is so pure that no chlorination is needed. When the spring is operating it seems as though there were a timer and an on-off switch buried in the mountain. Icy water gushes from a gaping opening in the cliff for approximately 18 minutes, then stops for an equal period.

The Shoshones regarded this as a sacred place of healing and said that a powerful medicine man was able to turn the waters on and off by command. Today, hydrologists believe that a large underground chamber periodically fills with and then empties of water through a natural siphon in the porous limestone rock. The spring loses its intermittence in spring and flows constantly. Best time to see it in action is in late summer or early fall.

Accommodations

The **Corral Motel**, 161 Washington, 307/885-5424, www.silverstar.com/corralmotel, is an American icon, with clean, well-maintained log and plaster cabins from the 1940s. All are non-smoking, and two contain kitchenettes ($10 extra). Rates are $45 s or d, or $65 for four people; open mid-Apr. through Oct. Recommended.

Bar-H Motel, 307/885-2274, rents modern two-bedroom cabins, all with kitchenettes. Rates start at $50 s or d, plus $5 per person for additional guests. No credit cards are accepted, and some rooms lack phones. Right next door is **Colters Lodge**, 355 N. Washington, 307/885-9891, with upstairs rooms for $36 s or $42 d, and suites that sleep six for $60.

Approximately eight miles north of Afton, **Silver Stream Lodge**, 307/883-2440, www.silverstreamlodge.com, charges $50–62 s or d for cabins, one of which has a kitchen. **Lazy B Motel**, 219 Washington, 307/885-3187, charges $55 s or $65 d. The rooms all contain fridges and microwaves, and a heated outdoor pool awaits the kids.

Three-quarters of a mile south of Afton, the modern **Hi-Country Inn**, 307/885-3856 or 866/299-1727, www.hi-countryinn.com, has an outdoor pool and hot tub. Rooms cost $65–75 s or d. A short ways further south is **Mountain Inn**, 307/885-3156 or 800/682-5356, a spotless motel with large rooms and suites, an outdoor pool, sauna, hot tub, and a full breakfast (served at a nearby restaurant). Rates are $55–75 d; $5 per person for additional guests.

The **Rocking P B&B** is in Smoot (nine miles south of Afton), 307/886-0455, and has four guest rooms with private or shared baths; $60 s or $70 d. A big country breakfast is served each morning, and kids are welcome.

Two miles south of Afton is **The Old Mill,** 3497 Dry Creek Rd., 307/886-0520, where you'll find three modern log cabins set on five acres. All are nicely furnished with handcrafted log beds and gas fireplaces. Guests will also enjoy the hot tub in a glass-enclosed gazebo. Two cabins sleep four and cost $89; the third is larger and sleeps up to six for $105. In the winter, you can cross-country ski or snowmobile right from your cabin.

Camping and Cabins

The Forest Service has three campgrounds ($5; open late May to mid-Sept.) in the Star Valley area. Closest is the attractive **Swift Creek Campground,** only 1.5 miles east of Afton (take 2nd Ave.—Periodic Spring is farther up the same road). **Allred Flat Campground** is 20 miles south of Afton, right along U.S. Hwy. 89. **Cottonwood Lake Campground** is a very nice place with lakeside sites and nearby hiking trails. It's seven miles up the Cottonwood Lake Road, south of Smoot.

The Forest Service rents out four guard stations when they are not being used by field crews. These cabins are particularly popular with snowmobilers and skiers in the winter, but running water is only available in summer. The cabins are **Cozier Guard Station, Deer Creek Guard Station, McCain Guard Station,** and **Meadows Guard Station.** Each sleeps six in bunk beds and costs $30 per night. Get details and reservations at 307/886-3166, www.fs.fed.us/btnf.

Food

Colters Lodge, 355 N. Washington, 307/886-9597, is the best place for meals in Afton—filling breakfasts, all-you-can-eat lunch and dinner buffets ($7.50 on Wed. nights; $10.50 on Fri. and Sat. nights), along with pasta, steaks, seafood, burgers, and chicken. The rustic Old West atmosphere and outside patio are added attractions. Get standard American breakfasts at **Golden Spur Cafe,** 486 Washington, 307/886-9890.

Red Baron Drive-In, 838 Washington, 307/886-3745, is the hangout for folks who want burgers and fries. Subway, Taco Time, and Burger King serve quick eats, and the last of these has a big indoor playground for the youngsters. Try the lunchtime pizza buffets at **Gunnar's Pizza,** 845 S. Washington, 307/886-9795, or **Pizza Hut,** 228 Washington, 307/886-9794. Get south-of-the-border fare at **Melina's Mexican Restaurant,** 470 Washington, 307/883-2617.

Homestead Restaurant, just south of town on Hwy. 89, 307/886-3878, offers the area's finest prime rib, along with rich double-fudge desserts.

Get groceries from **Familee Thriftway,** 307/886-5550. Prices are typically a bit lower here than in Jackson, so you may want to stock up before heading north.

Entertainment and Events

For live country-and-western or rock music on Friday and Saturday nights, head to **Colters Lodge,** 355 N. Washington, 307/886-9597. Watch flicks at downtown Afton's **Ford Theatre.**

The **CallAir Fly-In/Star Valley Aviation Days** takes place the last weekend of June and includes a free breakfast, air show, museum tours, and aircraft fly-in.

July kicks off with an **Independence Day** celebration that features a parade, free pancake breakfast, hot-air balloons, various contests, a rodeo, and fireworks. Also in July, the community puts on a two-day **historical pageant** at the high school football field. It typically involves a homespun tale of the Mormon pioneers who settled the valley.

The **Lincoln County Fair** is held in Afton in late July or early August, with all the country fair favorites: musical entertainment, a carnival, a parade, rodeos, 4-H agricultural exhibits, and lots more. Rodeos are also held several other times each summer; see the visitors center for specifics. In late November, Afton's **Parade of Lights** is a small-town event with lighted floats.

Cutter races are held at race grounds one mile northwest of Afton on Saturday throughout the winter; call 800/426-8833 for details.

Recreation

Golfers will find the nine-hole **Valli Vu Municipal Golf Course,** 307/885-3338, www.silverstar.com/~vallivu, one mile south of Afton. Star Valley Ranch Resort in Thayne has two 18-hole courses: **Cedar Creek Golf Course,** 307/883-2230, and **Aspen Hills Golf Course,** 307/883-2899.

During the winter, the town operates **Snowshoe Hollow Ski Area,** 307/885-9831, a small area just east of Afton with a rope tow and snack bar. Stop by the Forest Service office for information on the many miles of groomed **cross-country ski trails** in Star Valley. Closest are trails in Afton at Canyon View Park and one mile to the south at Valli Vu Municipal Golf Course.

The Wyoming Range to the east offer unlimited opportunities for exploration by skiers and snowmobiles, with snow until the Fourth of July some years. Greys River Road is an especially popular snowmobiling area. Rent snowmobiles from **M&J Enterprises** in Grover, 307/886-5299, and **Star Valley Ski-Doo** in Thayne, 307/883-2714. Call 800/225-5996, ext. 4, for current snowmobile-trail conditions.

Shopping

If you're driving north from Afton toward Jackson, be sure to fill up with gas either here or in Thayne; it won't get any cheaper. Besides gas, the best deals in town can be found at the **Wyoming Wear** factory outlet store, 307/886-3851, www.wyomingwear.com, on the north side of Afton. The jackets, hats, socks, vests, pullovers, and other quality outdoor gear sold here are all sewn at factories in Afton and Cokeville, and their prices can't be beat: up to 75 percent off. **Lone Pine Sports,** at Washington and Nield String Rd., 307/886-9581, sells additional outdoor gear and rents cross-country skis in winter.

Two Afton places sell Latter-day Saints and other religious books: **Quiet Place Books,** 460 N. Washington, 307/886-5246, and the **Hastings Store,** inside Ace Hardware on the south end of town, 307/886-3048. For a real dose of Star Valley culture, check out the world map in Hastings showing where local kids have gone as Mormon missionaries.

Information and Services

Afton's tiny **visitors center** at 2nd and Washington is open Tuesday–Saturday 10 A.M.–6 P.M. summers only. For more information, call 307/886-3156 or 800/426-8833, or visit the website: www.starvalleychamber.com.

A fountain outside the visitors center provides a taste of Afton's famous spring water, and next door is a University of Wyoming Research and Extension Center. Directly across the road, the **Bridger-Teton National Forest Greys River District Office,** 307/886-3166, www.fs.fed.us/btnf, dispenses local maps, natural-history books, and information on recreational opportunities.

The **Star Valley Branch Library** at 261 Washington St., 307/886-3158, carries plenty of genealogy titles. You'll find the **post office** at 31 W. 4th Ave., 307/886-3625. Get fast cash from **ATMs** at First Security Bank of Wyoming, 485 N. Washington, or First National Bank, 302 Washington.

Afton's **Star Valley Medical Center,** 307/885-5800, is a modern hospital with physicians on staff and an emergency room.

GREYS RIVER LOOP ROAD

Star Valley is bordered on the east by two parallel mountain ranges: the Salt River and the Wyoming. The Greys River flows between them. Alongside it runs an exceptionally scenic 80-mile-long gravel road used by small numbers of vacationers, hikers, anglers, and hunters. This untrammeled area makes for a great escape from the Jackson Hole mob scene in the summer. The road begins a dozen miles south of Afton and continues north all the way to Alpine. Plan to camp overnight along the way; the narrow and potholed dirt road makes for a torturous day trip. You'll fine excellent fishing for cutthroat, rainbow, brown, and brook trout in the river, and good opportunities to see deer and moose along the way. All this country lies within

© DON PITCHER

The loop road follows the beautiful Greys River for 80 miles.

Bridger-Teton National Forest. Considerable logging takes place in the mountains, and many thousands of sheep and cattle graze the open areas, but much of the land remains wild and beautiful. It is an almost unknown part of Wyoming. If you drive north along the Greys River Road you'll be able to watch the Greys grow from a small creek into a river. Kayakers often paddle the lower stretches of the river; see the Forest Service for specifics.

Snider Basin

Another fascinating drive (great for mountain bikes) is to continue east through Snider Basin to the town of Big Piney on Forest Rd. 10128. The road parallels the still-visible Lander Cutoff of the Oregon Trail for a long distance, and several emigrant graves are noted along the way. Keep your eyes open for elk and deer on the slopes and beaver dams in Piney Creek. The high country is lodgepole-pine forests, passing into open

sage land as you descend toward Big Piney. Note that this route can be confusing (signs are often missing) and sometimes muddy, so be sure to get a Forest Service map and current conditions before heading out from Afton.

Camping and a Cabin

Camping is available at five places along the Greys River Road; nicest are the campgrounds at **Murphy Creek** and **Forest Park,** both of which cost $5 and are open year-round. The road is not plowed in the winter. You can camp off the road for free in most parts of the national forest.

The **La Barge Guard Station** is located approximately 22 miles from the Afton end of the road (26 miles from the La Barge side), and is available year-round. Winter access is by snowmobile or cross-country skis. The cabin sleeps six and costs $30 per night. Get details from the Forest Service in Kemmerer, 307/877-4415, www.fs.fed.us/btnf.

Recreation

More than 450 miles of trails cut across this country, including the 70-mile **Wyoming Range National Recreation Trail,** which climbs through beautiful alpine meadows and over narrow, rocky ridges. Snow covers the trail until July most years.

A side road off the Greys River Road leads to a two-mile trail that climbs 11,363-foot **Wyoming Peak,** tallest in the range. During winter cross-country skiers will find four groomed ski trails and snowmobilers can cruise on 100 miles of groomed routes in the area. See the Forest Service office in Afton for maps and recreation information, including a listing of guides and outfitters.

Accommodations

Box Y Lodge is a grand old ranch with a beautiful setting along Greys River Rd. 30 miles from Alpine. The ranch has a main lodge and eight comfortably rustic log cabins (each sleeps up to six) with propane heat and lights. Activities include fishing, horseback rides, float trips, and mountain biking. All-inclusive summertime rates are $450 for two people per day. Lodging-only rates are $220 d. The ranch is also a busy wintertime resort for snowmobilers; winter rates are

$200 for two people per day, including lodging and three meals a day. The ranch hosts a maximum of 12 people in the summer but can house twice that when the snow flies. Call 307/654-7564 for information, but it may take several days for them to return your call because of the remote location. You will also find them on the web at www.starvalleywy.com/boxy.

THAYNE

Home to 340 people, Thayne is a prosperous and fast-growing settlement best known for its cheese factory. Cutter races started here during the 1920s when dairymen used sleighs to haul milk to the local creamery. To avoid having to wait in line, the farmers often raced each other to get to the creamery first; this sparring eventually grew into a competition that now encompasses seven western states. (The "world finals" are held in Ogden, Utah.) In a cutter race, horses pull wheeled chariots over a snow-covered field at breakneck speeds; the world record stands at 21.64 seconds for the quarter-mile run. Star Valley cutter races now take place at the race grounds north of Afton.

Attractions

If you're heading north to Jackson Hole, fill your gas tank in Thayne; prices only go up from here. Before tanking your car, fill your belly at **Star Valley Cheese,** 307/883-2510, one of the most unusual eating places in Wyoming. The restaurant—an old-fashioned shop straight out of the 1950s—serves reasonably priced burgers, homemade pies, ice cream, malts, shakes, and other fare, and sells fresh cheeses from the coolers. It's open daily all year, and it's almost always filled with locals and tourists. Each day, some 60,000 pounds of mozzarella, provolone, and ricotta cheese are made in the plant right behind the shop. Well worth a stop.

Accommodations

Swiss Mountain Motel, 307/883-2227, www.swissmtmotel.com, is a nine-unit place with nicely maintained rooms—all with fridges—for $35–45. **Snider's Rustic Inn,** 307/883-0222,

www.snidersrusticinn.com, has reasonable rates ($55 s or $60 d), renovated rooms (some with unique log beds), and kitchenettes in all rooms.

Cabin Creek Inn, 307/883-3262, www.cabincreekinn.com, has attractive new log cabins in Thayne. The six-person cabins feature lodgepole beds, homemade quilts, kitchenettes, jetted tubs, and an outdoor pool for $69. Open May–Oct.

Two miles north of Thayne is **Inn at Deer Run B&B,** 307/883-3444, www.silverstar.com/steadman, with modern rooms for $60 d, or $75 for four people. The rooms contain private baths furnished with lodgepole beds and private baths. A TV is available in the central room, where a free breakfast is served each morning.

Camping

Flat Creek RV Park, south of Thayne, 307/883-2231, charges $20 for RVs or $6 per person for tents. Showers cost $4. It's open year-round.

A few miles north of Thayne is **Star Valley Ranch Resort,** 307/883-2670, www.starvalleywy.com, an obscenely elaborate place with more than 600 summer homes, a restaurant, RV park, swimming pools, two golf courses, a sauna, bumper boats, and tennis courts.

Food

JH Ranch Cafe, 307/883-2357, has homemade breads and pastries, plus daily lunch specials. **Dad's Steak House,** 307/883-2300, offers live music on weekends and the finest steaks and prime rib in the area. Inside is a small collection of cutter-racing items (the sport was established by "Dad" Walton). Also in Thayne is a little fruit stand with great summertime deals.

Field of Greens Pizza Pub, at the Star Valley Ranch, 307/883-4653, serves pizza and burgers, along with chicken on Friday and baby back ribs on Saturday. Open summers only. Get groceries at **Valley Market.**

Events

The **Thayne Junior Rodeo** in late July is the big summertime event, with all sorts of kid events, including sheep and calf riding, pig chasing, and barrel racing. For adults, the day also brings the **Salt River Canoe Race,** where canoeists have unusual obstacles: The fire department points fire hoses at passing contestants.

OTHER STAR VALLEY TOWNS

Auburn

The town of Auburn, eight miles north and west of Afton, contains a small area of travertine terraces and hot springs on private land. The nearby countryside is filled with old log homes, cabins, and barns. A historic stone church, built in 1889, sits across from the tiny Auburn post office and is used for summertime melodramas by the **Star Valley Historical Theatre;** call 307/885-3640 for details. Not far away is the Davis Ranch, where Butch Cassidy and his gang holed up one winter.

West of Auburn on County Rd. 134 is **Auburn Fish Hatchery,** where some 50,000 trout are raised annually. It's open daily 8 A.M.–5 P.M. The road to the hatchery parallels the Lander Cutoff of the Oregon Trail for several miles.

Bedford

The tiny farming and sheep-ranching settlement of Bedford lies near the center of Star Valley. On fall days you're likely to meet huge herds of sheep being driven down the main roads as they return from a summer in the mountains.

Freedom

Freedom (pop. 100), Star Valley's oldest settlement, straddles the Idaho–Wyoming border. The town was established by Mormons in 1879 and offered an escape from the Idaho Territory's efforts to ban polygamy. Arthur Clark named the town for his freedom to have multiple wives. Today, Freedom has a small country store just a few feet from the border where you can buy Idaho lottery tickets. **Horse Shoe Cafe** in Etna is a classic small-town eatery, filling with locals every day and deer hunters on cool fall mornings.

Freedom is famous in National Rifle Association circles for a small factory, **Freedom Arms,** 307/883-2468, www.freedomarms.com, which makes handguns, including the massive .454 Casull, the world's most powerful revolver—and

one of the most expensive at $2,000 apiece. No surprise that Clint Eastwood owns one. Don't ever get on the wrong end of this deadly instrument. Visitors can watch a short video and view a gun display here.

Free camping is available three miles west of Freedom, inside Idaho, at the Forest Service's **Tincup Campground.**

Etna

Etna lies near the northern end of Star Valley and has a small country store and an outsized brick Latter-day Saints church that could probably house the entire population of 200. In late summer, the sweet scent of new-mown hay hangs in the air. **Etna Trading Co.,** 307/883-2409, is an old-time general store. Nearby is the historic and nicely restored **Baker Cabin.**

Horse Shoe Motel, 307/883-2281, has remodeled rooms for $40 s or d. Open June–Oct. only. **Salt River B&B,** 307/883-2453, offers cozy in-town accommodations in three guest rooms ($25 s or $50 d). A full breakfast is served, and kids are welcome. The owner is a quilter and sells locally made quilts in the shop next door.

ALPINE

The crossroads settlement called Alpine is an ugly place with a quickly multiplying sprawl of businesses at the intersection of U.S. Highways 26 and 89. You'll find fireworks stands, real estate offices, motels, restaurants, and bars strung out in all directions. During the 1990s, the population grew from 200 to 550, a 175 percent increase. It's a sad sight, and it's all here because of the tourists traveling en route to or from Jackson Hole and as a home for Jackson workers.

The area around Alpine is called Lower Valley and borders on **Palisades Reservoir,** built at the convergence of the Snake, Greys, and Salt Rivers. Water enthusiasts come here for fishing, water skiing, camping, and picnicking.

Approximately 700 elk gather each winter at the **Elk Feedground** one mile south of Alpine on Hwy. 89. You can view the elk from the parking area here: they often approach parked cars rather closely. Best time to visit is in the mornings, when they are fed.

Get cash from the **ATMs** at the Tessoro and Amoco stations. For details on westward destinations, see *Moon Handbooks Idaho,* by Don Root (www.moon.com).

Accommodations

Alpine Junction has several good lodging choices at considerably lower rates than Jackson, where even the Motel 6 is $94 d per night! Reservations are advised during July and August, when everything fills up fast.

Three Rivers Motel, 307/654-7551, www.wybiz.com/3riversmotel, has affordable rooms for $45 s or $50 d, kitchenettes for $10 extra.

Just west of town on U.S. Hwy. 26 is **Alpine Inn,** 307/654-7644, www.starvalleywy.com/alpine inn.htm. Motel rooms in the main building are $60. Separate cabins run $45 for small units with one bed or $70 with a second bedroom and kitchenette. No phones, but most rooms sleep four (or more) people. The inn is set on 10 acres and has picnic tables and tepees. Open year-round.

Alpine's biggest lodge is **Royal Resort,** 307/654-7545 or 800/343-6755, www.royal-resort.com, a chalet-style hotel decorated with Austrian scenes and a hot tub, exercise room, children's carousel, restaurant, and bar. Standard rooms cost $55–70 d; more spacious ones with balconies, queen or king beds, and VCRs are $75–85 d. A special alpine-themed room is $149 d.

For homey and immaculate accommodations, stay at the **Nordic Inn,** 307/654-7556, www.starvalleywy.com/nordic, where the 12 rooms are a reasonable $76–84 s or d. The inn gets lots of repeat visitors, so be sure to reserve ahead for midsummer. Open late May to mid-Oct.

You'll find very attractive rooms ($115–140 for up to four people) and log cottages with a Western theme ($190 for up to three people) at **Best Western Flying Saddle Lodge,** 307/654-7561 or 866/666-2937, www.flyingsaddle.com. Amenities include an outdoor pool and two hot tubs, and many rooms have jetted tubs. The cottages are only open seasonally. Ask staff at the desk about their famous guests over the years, including John Wayne.

Camping

There's plenty of public camping at nearby Forest Service campgrounds; see the Snake River Canyon or Greys River Loop Road sections of this chapter. The closest spot is **Alpine Campground** ($8; open mid-May to mid-Sept.), located two miles west of town along Hwy. 26. Make reservations ($9 fee) at 518/885-3639 or 877/444-6777, www.reserveusa.com. The turnoff to the Forest Service's **McCoy Campground** is three miles south of Alpine on Hwy. 89 and then another five miles along Palisades Reservoir. In addition to these official campgrounds, dispersed camping spots (turnouts off the road) can be found approximately five miles up the Greys River Road, which is just east of Alpine.

Park RVs ($20) at **Royal Resort,** 307/654-7545 or 800/343-6755, www.royal-resort.com, open Apr.–Oct. They also have a few spaces for tents at the same price. Showers for those not staying here are $3.50.

Food and Entertainment

Alpine is home to several cafés and restaurants offering standard American fare. **Royal Ridge Restaurant,** in the Royal Resort, 307/654-7508, has a fine-dining menu, while **Gunnar's Pizza,** 307/654-7778, creates sub sandwiches and pizzas, including whole-wheat and deep-dish versions. They also offer outside dining in the summer.

Kringles Cafe and Bakery, 307/654-7536, serves pasta, meatloaf, country fried steak, and a variety of sweet treats. It's hard to miss their collection of 250 birdhouses, said to be the largest in Wyoming.

The real surprise in town is **Brenthoven's Restaurant,** 307/654-7556, www.starvalleywy.com/brenthov3.htm, where specialties include exquisite soups and entrées such as plumb chicken, cod parmesan, and choice steaks for dinner, along with breakfast crepes. Be sure to save room for their signature bread pudding. The bar has a fine wine selection, and friendly owner Mike Clinger will be happy to discuss opera or tell you about his distinctive Colonial home located behind the Nordic Inn. Chef Brent Johnston is also an accomplished concert pianist, and his Brenthoven quartet performs Sunday evening jazz on the lawn in July and August. The restaurant and inn are open Memorial Day to mid-October. Recommended.

Recreation

Jackson Hole Outfitters (a.k.a. Alpine Riding & Rafts), 307/654-9900, www.jacksonholeoutfitters.com, has all-day horseback rides into the Greys River country for $106 with lunch. They also rent rafts for trips down the Snake River. Float trips can be booked through **Nordic Inn,** 307/654-7556. Many similar rafting operations are run out of Jackson Hole.

Events

The **International Pedigree Stage Stop Sled Dog Race** (IPSSSDR) stops here. See the Jackson chapter for more info.

Alpine Mountain Days, on the third weekend of June, is the big summer celebration, with mountain men, Indian dancing, a black-powder shoot, country music, horseshoe tournament, arts and crafts, a Dutch-oven cook-off, and other activities. Details at www.starvalleywy.com/arda.htm.

SNAKE RIVER CANYON

Northeast of Alpine, the country abruptly changes as U.S. Hwy. 89/26 enters Snake River Canyon, paralleling it all the way to Hoback Junction, 23 miles away. This is a delicious way to enter Jackson Hole, offering numerous pullouts where you can view the roiling, rambunctious rapids of the sinuous Snake River as it slithers through millions of years of rocky cliffs. At sunset, the river glows a silver ribbon of light. A big, powerful river, the Snake eventually feeds into the Columbia in Washington. Riverbanks are lined with ancient cottonwoods, while the higher slopes show lodgepole pines.

The whitewater of Snake River Canyon is a favorite of outdoor enthusiasts, and during the summer you're bound to meet cars with kayaks on their roofs and vans filled with happy rafters heading back to Jackson. See the Jackson Hole section for details on the many river-running options. River access is generally via the West Table Creek and Sheep Gulch boat ramps.

Camping and Hiking

Three Bridger-Teton National Forest campgrounds are located along the canyon at **East Table Creek Campground** ($15; 8.5 miles from Hoback Junction), **Elbow Campground** ($10; six miles from Hoback Junction), and **Cabin Creek Campground;** ($10; five miles from Hoback Junction). All three are open late May–September. No reservations are accepted, and campsites may fill early in the day in midsummer.

A popular hiking trail starts near Cabin Creek Campground and provides a loop into the backcountry. The trailhead is one-half mile up the dirt road from the campground, and **Cabin Creek Trail** follows the creek uphill to an alpine pass filled with late summer wildflowers and fine views of the Snake River drainage. Return the same way, or opt to head downhill along the **Dog Creek Trail,** which ends near the junction of Wilson-Fall Creek Road with U.S. Hwy. 89/26. Either way, it's about six miles of hiking, but if you take Dog Creek Trail you'll need a shuttle back to your car. Get camping and hiking details from the Forest Service at 307/739-5400, www.fs.fed.us/btnf/teton.

Road Conditions

The highway through the Snake River Canyon has been undergoing a $75-million **highway reconstruction** that began in 1998, with completion scheduled for 2004. Get the current status and information about expected delays at 307/733-3665, http://wyoroad.info.

Central Wyoming

The counties of Natrona and Converse enclose definitive Wyoming country: sage-and-grass-carpeted plains, desolate badlands, impressive tree-draped mountainsides, and the big, lazy North Platte River. This is grazing country; each year nearly one-quarter of the sheep raised in Wyoming and 120,000 cattle come from these two counties. The dominant industry, however—and the one that dictates the region's economy—is oil. It means jobs for roughnecks in dozens of oil fields, but it also greases the wheels of city life, creating refinery and transportation jobs, government positions, and a wave of other effects in the local community as the wages pass on to construction workers, shop owners, and schoolteachers. Without oil, Casper—Wyoming's second-largest metropolitan area—would be little more than a cattle town crossroads on the way to Yellowstone.

The Land

Geographically, central Wyoming is quite diverse. The north portion is an open, expansive place. Driving across the long, straight highways that divide this land is like

near the town of Midwest

© DON PITCHER

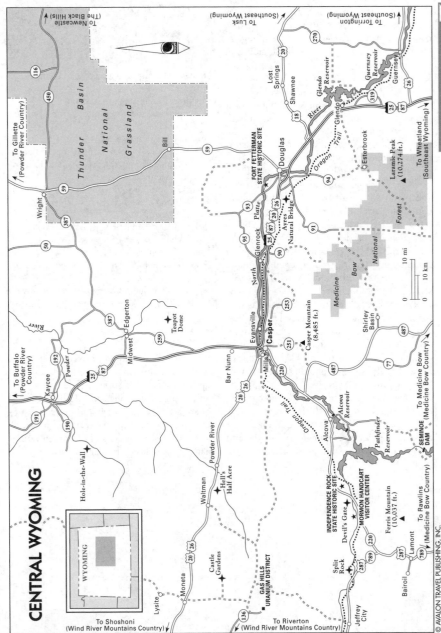

CENTRAL WYOMING

To Newcastle (The Black Hills)
To Lusk (Southeast Wyoming)
To Torrington (Southeast Wyoming)

116
450
To Gillette (Powder River Country)
Thunder Basin National Grassland
Bill
59
Wright
59
387
50
Edgerton
387
River
Teapot Dome
259
Powder
Midwest
To Buffalo (Powder River Country)
192
Kaycee
25
87
191
190
Hole-in-the-Wall
River
Powder River
Waltman
Hall's Half Acre
Bar Nunn
Mills
Evansville
Casper
North Platte
Glenrock
95
93
90
Douglas
FORT FETTERMAN STATE HISTORIC SITE
59
18
20
Lost Springs
Shawnee
270
Glendo Reservoir
Guernsey Reservoir
Guernsey
319
25
87
26
Oesterbrook
Laramie Peak (10,274 ft.)
To Wheatland (Southeast Wyoming)
Medicine Bow National Forest
94
91
487
Shirley Basin
487
77
25
87
20
26
Ayres Natural Bridge
253
Casper Mountain (8,485 ft.)
251
Glendo
River
Oregon Trail

Oregon Trail
220
20
26
Alcova
Alcova Reservoir
Pathfinder Reservoir
Seminoe Reservoir
SEMINOE DAM (Medicine Bow Country)
To Medicine Bow (Medicine Bow Country)
INDEPENDENCE ROCK STATE HISTORIC SITE
Devil's Gate
MORMON HANDCART VISITOR CENTER
Ferris Mountain (10,037 ft.)
To Rawlins (Medicine Bow Country)
Split Rock
789
287
Lamont
789
Bairoil
287
Jeffrey City
Waltman
GAS HILLS URANIUM DISTRICT
136
Castle Gardens
Lysite
Moneta
20
26
To Shoshoni (Wind River Mountains Country)
To Riverton (Wind River Mountains Country)

0   10 mi
0   10 km

WYOMING

© AVALON TRAVEL PUBLISHING, INC.

sailing a boat over an ocean of gentle rollers—the mountains are so far in the distance that they could well be islands. Golden eagles spin giant loops in the sky, and the coal black clouds of distant summertime thunderheads are pierced by brilliant slashes of lightning. The wind blows on, bending the grass as it passes in waves of motion, whirling the old windmills that pump water to sheep, cattle, and deer. This is rolling mixed-grass prairie and sagebrush country, with sharp ridges appearing suddenly, topped by narrow bands of ponderosa pine and juniper.

South of this rangeland lies the North Platte River, carving a slow curve first north, then east, and finally southeast toward Nebraska. Giant dams hold back the water for irrigation and electricity. A green stripe of riparian forests and irrigated fields borders the river. South of the Platte, the land changes again, with the Laramie Mountains rising in a rough-edged jumble of rugged canyons and pine-covered peaks. Elk stand along mountain meadows, bugling in the cool air of late fall. Pickup trucks slow as wild turkeys speed-walk across the gravel roads. Clear mountain brooks cascade down mountain slopes. West of here, central Wyoming becomes drier and more desolate, wrinkled by the badlands of Hell's Half Acre and the barren crests of desert mountain ranges.

Casper dominates the central Wyoming economy with an oil refinery, the primary statewide newspaper, and the state's largest junior college and shopping mall. The towns of Douglas and Glenrock go their own ways, with a mixture of

CENTRAL WYOMING SIGHTSEEING HIGHLIGHTS

Pioneer Museum and Jackalopes in Douglas
Fort Fetterman
Thunder Basin National Grassland
Laramie Peak and Esterbrook in the Laramie Mountains
Ayres Natural Bridge Park
Fort Caspar, Nicolaysen Art Museum, National Historic Trails Interpretive Center in Casper
Casper Mountain
Independence Rock, Devil's Gate, and the Mormon Handcart Visitors Center along the Oregon Trail
Salt Creek oil field near Midwest
Hell's Half Acre west of Powder River
Castle Gardens near Moneta
Popular events: Cowboy State Games in Casper (February), Central Wyoming Fair and Rodeo in Casper (July), Beartrap Summer Festival near Casper (July), Wyoming State Fair in Douglas (August)

ranching, oil, coal, and tourism. Farther north, the tiny settlements of Midwest and Edgerton cap the vast Salt Creek Oil Field. Between these few outposts of civilization lie hundreds of square miles of sagebrush and grass, jackrabbits, and rattlers. Only the scattered roads, oil pumpjacks, windmills, and old ranch houses mark the presence of humans.

Douglas

Douglas (pop. 5,300) epitomizes life in small-town America. It's the sort of place where the big summertime events are the state fair and weekly drag races, where a night on the town means joining a bowling league or doing the two-step at the LaBonte Inn, and where old-timers hang out in the historic College Inn Bar. On both ends of Douglas are more modern slices of Americana, where suburban ranch-style homes cover the hills. It's a friendly, conservative town with pickup trucks, dense American food, and an unusual history.

HISTORY

Douglas came into existence with the arrival of the Fremont, Elkhorn, and Missouri Valley Railroad. Platted in 1886, the town was named for Stephen A. Douglas, the senator from Illinois best known for his debates with Abraham

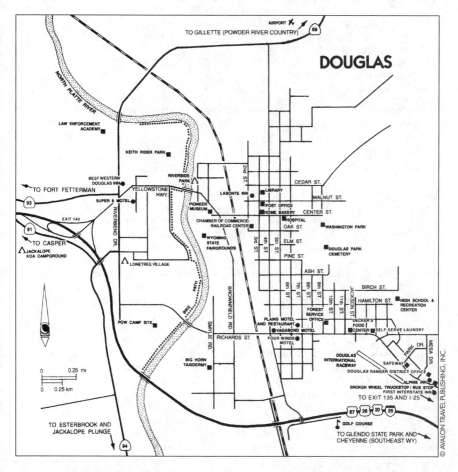

DOUGLAS

AIRPORT
TO GILLETTE (POWDER RIVER COUNTRY)   59

NORTH PLATTE RIVER

LAW ENFORCEMENT ACADEMY

KEITH RIDER PARK

BEST WESTERN DOUGLAS INN
YELLOWSTONE HWY.
TO FORT FETTERMAN
93
SUPER 8 MOTEL
RIVERSIDE PARK
LABONTE INN
CEDAR ST.
LIBRARY
WALNUT ST.
POST OFFICE
HOME BAKERY   CENTER ST.
91
EXIT 140
PIONEER MUSEUM
CHAMBER OF COMMERCE/ RAILROAD CENTER
HOSPITAL
OAK ST.
WASHINGTON PARK
TO CASPER
JACKALOPE KOA CAMPGROUND
WYOMING STATE FAIRGROUNDS
ELM ST.
DOUGLAS PARK CEMETERY
2nd ST.
3rd ST.
4th ST.
5th ST.
PINE ST.
LONETREE VILLAGE
ASH ST.
BIRCH ST.
6th ST.
7th ST.
8th ST.
9th ST.
10th ST.
11th ST.
JACKSON ST.   HAMILTON ST.
HIGH SCHOOL & RECREATION CENTER
POW CAMP SITE
BROWNFIELD RD.
BIKE PATH
SMYLIE RD.
FOREST SERVICE OFFICE
PLAINS MOTEL AND RESTAURANT
VAGABOND MOTEL
DECKER'S FOOD CENTER
SELF-SERVE LAUNDRY
RICHARDS ST.
FOUR WINDS MOTEL
PARK DR.
MESA DR.
BIG HORN TAXIDERMY
DOUGLAS INTERNATIONAL RACEWAY
SAFEWAY
DOUGLAS RANGER DISTRICT OFFICE
ALPINE INN
BROKEN WHEEL TRUCKSTOP / BUS STOP
FIRST INTERSTATE INN
TO EXIT 135 AND I-25
0   0.25 mi
0   0.25 km
87   26   20   25
N
TO ESTERBROOK AND JACKALOPE PLUNGE
94
GOLF COURSE
TO GLENDO STATE PARK AND CHEYENNE (SOUTHEAST WY)

© AVALON TRAVEL PUBLISHING, INC.

JACKALOPES

Jackalopes are unusual mammals that move by bounding. Found originally in Converse County, Wyoming, they are now distributed throughout the western states. The critters have the horns of an antelope, the body of a jackrabbit, and the stealth of both. First observed by trapper Roy Ball in 1829, the jackalope was later noted by cowboys and others after too little sleep, too many days in the saddle, and too much cheap whiskey. Nocturnal animals, jackalopes are never seen during the day. These powerful and vicious animals are reputed to attain speeds approaching 90 mph and often sing and mate during thunderstorms. The hornless does are commonly seen by tourists, while the bucks remain elusive. Westerners, particularly members of the militias, feel that the federal government is hushing up the true story of these dangerous critters to make cowboys look like liars.

Okay, I admit to liking plastic pink flamingos and tacky postcards, but jackalopes are another story. The first time you see a mounted jackalope specimen, it is mildly amusing, but with each tourist junk shop west of the Mississippi offering more jackalopes, the originality quickly fades. The town of Douglas takes credit for this hare-brained idea, although its claim is a bit suspect. In the 1920s, a Douglas resident saw a jackalope mounted in a store in Buffalo, Wyoming. He described the creature to his grandson, Douglas Herrick, who was intrigued by the animal. In 1941, he attached the antlers of a deer to the head of a large jackrabbit he had shot and sold the specimen to the LaBonte Hotel. The rest is history.

In 1960, the State of Wyoming gave the Douglas Chamber of Commerce "jackalope" as a registered trademark. Today you see jackalopes everywhere in Douglas: the town symbol contains one; an eight-foot-tall jackalope statue greets visitors at Jackalope Square; another statue has hopped atop the LaBonte Hotel; and a roadside sign warns "Watch Out For Jackalope." You can buy cans of jackalope milk in the stores, "Rabbit Punch" at a local bar, and jackalope hunting licenses at several spots around town. And, of course, the critters multiply like rabbits on the shelves of local shops.

Lincoln. The town quickly boomed to 1,600 people that first year, boasting three newspapers, several restaurants and hotels, two dance halls, 12 stores, and 21 saloons (easy to see where priorities lay). Once the railroad construction had moved on down the line to Casper, the population dwindled and it became a sleepy little ranching center for the next 70 years. Only the late-summer state fair brought Douglas to life each year.

World War II

One of the strangest pieces of Douglas history is its POW camp, built in 1943 along the North Platte River. The camp contained 180 barracks-style buildings and housed up to 3,000 prisoners of war. The camp was surrounded by an electrified fence, watchtowers, German shepherds, and army guards. One prisoner was shot by a guard and a few others escaped, but they didn't get far in this remote country—2,000 miles from the sea. Although some of the prisoners at Douglas were German Nazi and SS officers, most were Italians, many of whom were happy to be away from the war.

The prisoners worked in local agricultural fields harvesting potatoes and sugar beets for $4 per day or at a variety of art projects in the camp. Most impressive was the work of several Italian artists who painted the interior of the U.S. officers' club with 15 murals of Old West scenes. After the war, the prisoners returned home, although some have returned to visit in later years. The land was sold to Converse County for $1, and the barracks were dismantled or bought by locals, who moved them to other parts of town. Today the POW camp site is an open meadow on the west bank of the North Platte south of Richards Street. Contact the Douglas Chamber of Commerce for access information.

Boom and Bust

Like much of Wyoming, Douglas has watched its fortunes wax and wane over the years. In the 1950s, with the Cold War at fever pitch, prospectors combed Wyoming with Geiger counters, discovering major uranium deposits just north of Douglas. Others found oil, gas, and coal. A giant coal-fired power plant opened in nearby Glenrock, and by the late '70s the region was one of the most prosperous in the state. At the peak of the oil-and-uranium orgy of the early 1980s, the town of Douglas had doubled in size to more than 10,000 people. But then the bust hit, and within a couple of years the population plummeted back to where it had been. Longtime locals had mixed feelings when the balloon suddenly burst; they were happy to see the rabble leave town but were also suddenly burdened with paying for all the new schools, roads, and other facilities ordered up in the heady heyday. Today the economy of Douglas is back to its old mixture of energy and ranching, with some people commuting 60 miles each way to the busy coal mines near Wright while others work for the railroad or at two small uranium mines northwest of town. Most folks are happy to live a simpler life. Of course, the next energy boom could be just around the corner in the form of coal-bed methane gas.

SIGHTS

Pioneer Museum

The people of Douglas point with pride to their large local museum, easily one of the finest in Wyoming. Located just inside the fairgrounds, the spacious and free museum, 307/358-9288, is open Monday–Friday 8 A.M.–5 P.M. and Saturday 1–5 P.M. (closed Sun.) June–September, and Monday–Friday 8 A.M.–5 P.M. the rest of the year.

The main room is filled with old rifles and saddles, including one that belonged to outlaw Tom Horn. Check out the special "running irons" used by rustlers to alter cattle brands. Fittingly enough, the rifle of Nate Champion—a rustler murdered in the Johnson County Wars—is also here. Above one doorway is a pole from the original transcontinental telegraph line; it's one of just six known to survive. Look around the other

rooms and you'll discover the bison-fur mittens worn by Portugee Phillips on his ride to get help for Fort Kearny and an army trumpet and bullets from the Custer battlefield.

The museum also contains hundreds of historic photos, a big doll collection, clothing from the 1890s, and a back room filled with impressive Indian artifacts including baskets, pottery, Sioux and Crow war clubs, a bow from the Custer battleground, and even a tepee used in the movie *Dances with Wolves*. Downstairs are several wonderful old quilts and a collection of homestead items. The stairwell features the 64-inch-waist overalls that belonged to flamboyant C. B. Irwin, one of outlaw Tom Horn's closest friends. Irwin was a stockman, railroad detective, rodeo performer, and manager of Cheyenne Frontier Days. Outside is a schoolhouse constructed in 1886.

Douglas Railroad Interpretive Center

This center consists of seven train cars parked outside the old Chicago Elk Horn Railroad depot (built in 1888 and now home to the chamber of commerce). The collection includes a steam locomotive, dining car, sleeper, baggage car, coach, cattle car, caboose, and a little track inspection car. They represent many different eras—oldest is the 1884 caboose. The train cars are open Monday–Friday 9 A.M.–5 P.M. May–September.

More Sights

Ruts of the **Oregon Trail** are still visible nine miles south of Douglas; ask at the chamber of commerce for directions. The old **officers' club** from the Douglas POW camp is now an Odd Fellows Hall at 115 S. Riverbend Dr., 307/358-2421. Ask to take a look inside at the wall-to-wall murals painted by Italian artists who were prisoners during World War II.

One of Wyoming's oldest churches is the **Christ Episcopal Church,** built in 1896 and now on the National Register of Historic Places. The attractive white structure is at 411 Center, 307/358-5609.

The **Plains Complex,** 628 E. Richards, 307/358-4489, has several historic structures hauled in from all over this part of Wyoming. Included are the old officers' quarters from Fort

© DON PITCHER

Douglas Railroad Interpretive Center

Fetterman and a POW camp building. The ice-cream parlor served at various times as a barn, a boardinghouse, and a maternity center. Check out the doors on the ceiling of the ice-cream shop.

Douglas Park Cemetery, at 9th and Ash Sts., has many interesting old graves from local characters; get a booklet describing them from the chamber of commerce office. One of those buried here is horse thief, cattle-rustler, murderer, and later saloon-keeper "Doc" Middleton. Also here is the grave of the outlaw George W. Pike, whose exploits managed to lead to at least two appearances in court annually for 15 consecutive years, although he was never convicted. His gravestone (found near the center of the cemetery) reads:

> Underneath this stone in eternal rest
> Sleeps the wildest one of the wayward west
> He was gambler and sport and cowboy too
> And he led the pace in an outlaw crew.
> He was sure on the trigger and staid to
>   the end
> But he was never known to quit on a friend
> In the relations of death all mankind is
>   alike
> But in life there was only one George W.
>   Pike.

ACCOMMODATIONS

Seven different motels are available in Douglas, along with two B&Bs and three nearby guest ranches. In July and August you should book reservations up to two months ahead, especially for the weekend drag races and state fair week. Several locals rent out rooms in their homes to visitors while the fair is going on; get a list from the chamber of commerce, 307/358-2950.

Motels

Four Winds Motel, 615 E. Richards, 307/358-2322, charges just $32 s or $36 d, but it's a bit heavy on the Christianity. You'll find more plain rooms at the **Plains Motel,** 628 E. Richards, 307/358-4484, where the rates are $30 s or $40 d, including some with kitchenettes.

Out on the east side of town, **Alpine Inn,** 2310 E. Richards, 307/358-4780, has decent rooms (with microwaves and fridges) for $45–50 s or $55–65 d, including use of a washer and dryer. Opened in 1914, the historic **LaBonte Inn,** 206 Walnut, 307/358-9856, has refurbished rooms with private baths for $45–60 s or d. The bar downstairs can be noisy when bands are playing (Thurs.–Sat. nights).

On the east end of town, **First Interstate Inn,** 2349 E. Richards, 307/358-2833 or 800/462-4667, has accommodations for $36 s or $40 d, with in-room fridges.

Best Western Douglas Inn, 1450 Riverbend Dr., 307/358-9790 or 800/344-2113, www.bestwestern, is the nicest place in town, with a large indoor pool, hot tub, saunas, weight room, and atrium lobby. Rates are $66–83 s or $75–93 d.

Bed-and-Breakfasts

A century-old classic, **Morton Mansion Bed & Breakfast,** 425 E. Center St., 307/358-2129, www.mortonmansion.com, is a stately 1903 Queen Anne with a wraparound porch. Inside are three spacious guest rooms ($65–75 d) and a two-bedroom suite ($110 for four people), all with private baths and a Victorian decor. A continental breakfast is served; no kids under 12 allowed.

Guest Ranches

Deer Forks Ranch, 24 miles south of Douglas, 307/358-2033, www.guestranches.com/deerforks, provides a fine chance to join in horseback riding and other activities on a 5,000-acre working cattle and sheep ranch. It's a long ways out here and the road gets muddy when it rains, but the Laramie Mountain backdrop and friendly down-home owners make this a fun place to stay. Guests stay in two modern houses with kitchens ($100 d without meals) and can ride horses ($40 for a half day) or simply relax in the country. Accommodations are also offered at a second large ranch in the rolling grasslands 25 miles east of Bill. A two-night minimum stay is required.

Two Creek Ranch, 307/358-3467, is a 25,000-acre spread eight miles south of Douglas. The owners run 600 cows with their calves over this land and take on working dudes February–October. Guests ride horseback while helping out in calving, working a 75-mile cattle drive, or assisting with branding, roundups, and other ranch activities. The rates are surprisingly reasonable, starting at $545 per person all-inclusive for five days, up to $1,150 for 11 days on the range. This is the real thing, with guests sleeping in the bunkhouse, travel trailers, or tents.

Located in the Laramie Mountains southwest of Douglas, **LaBonte Canyon Ranch,** 307/358-2447 or 800/894-7262, www.labontecanyonranch.com, has comfortable ranch accommodations in log suites, unlimited horseback rides, home-cooked meals, and very good fly-fishing. Hikes, Jeep tours, and a swimming hole add to the fun. All-inclusive weekly rates are $2,000 for two people.

CAMPING

Pitch tents or park RVs for free at **Riverside Park** along the North Platte River. The free showers have an amusing Western-decor bathroom covered with branded wood. Camping is limited to two nights, and the sprinklers come on at 8 A.M., so get up early! Call 307/358-9750 or 307/358-3311.

See Douglas Vicinity section for details on Forest Service campsites in the nearby Laramie Mountains. In town, the RV crowd heads to **Jackalope KOA,** 307/358-2164 or 800/562-2469, www.koa.com, west of Douglas on State Hwy. 91. Rates are $17–20 for tents, $22–26 for RVs, $30 d for basic cabins; open Apr.–Oct. A heated outdoor pool is on the grounds. **Lonetree Village Mobile Home Park,** 1 Lonetree Dr., 307/358-6669, has RV parking for $15. During the state fair, camping is available on the fairgrounds; call 307/358-2398 for specifics.

FOOD

With a few exceptions, restaurant food in Douglas is pretty standard Wyoming fare. For dependable meals and big portions three times a day, you won't go wrong at **LaBonte Inn,** 206 Walnut St., 307/358-9856. In addition to the expected Wyoming offerings—hamburgers, prime rib, and homemade pies—the restaurant also features Continental-style entrées. (The owner is German.)

Broken Wheel Truckstop, just east of town, 307/358-4446, serves breakfast 24 hours a day. **Trading Post** is a so-so coffee shop at the Plains Complex, 628 E. Richards, 307/358-4489. Open 24 hours, it also houses an old-fashioned ice-cream parlor. For a traditional American version of coffee culture, hang out with the locals at **Bright's Cafe,** 108 N. 3rd St., 307/358-3509. It's a good place for greasy curly fries, burgers, sandwiches, and shakes.

Clementine's Cattle Co., 1199 Mesa Dr., 307/358-9400, serves ribs, steak, prime rib, pizza, pasta, and other all-American favorites, and has a popular lunch buffet and salad bar. There are nightly specials, plus a big-screen TV for sporting events.

Chute's Eatery, in the Best Western, 1450 Riverbend Dr., 307/358-9790, also has a soup and salad buffet, plus an all-you-can-eat Sunday brunch. The quality seems to vary depending on who's cooking that day. **Pizza Hut,** 1830 Richards, 307/358-3657, offers stuff-yourself lunch specials, and **La Costa,** 1213 Teton Way, 307/358-2449, is the place to go for authentic Mexican meals.

Local grocery stores include **Decker's Food Pride,** 1100 E. Richards, 307/358-3645; **Douglas Grocery,** 130 S. 4th St., 307/358-2250; and **Safeway,** 1900 E. Richards St., 307/358-3446. For fresh pastries, head downtown to the classic **Home Bakery,** 119 N. 3rd, 307/358-9251.

RECREATION

A two-mile paved path follows the west bank of the North Platte River through **Riverside Park** and is a great spot for an evening stroll or bike ride. Take along your fishing pole to try for trout, walleye, or channel catfish. If you have your own raft or canoe, the river is a fun place for leisurely float trips; pick up a map of river access points from the chamber of commerce.

The free **Douglas Recreation Center** at the high school, 1701 Hamilton, 307/358-4231, houses an indoor pool, gyms, racquetball courts, a sauna, and weight room. An excellent **outdoor swimming pool** in Washington Park is open in the summer; $2 adults, $1 kids. While there, check out the statue of **Sir Barton,** who in 1919 was the first horse to win the triple crown. He died in Douglas in 1937 at the ripe old age of 21 and is buried near the statue.

An 18-hole **golf course,** 307/358-5099, is southeast of Douglas, but it has no bunkers—the fierce winter winds kept blowing the sands away.

Rent mountain bikes, fishing boats, tent trailers, and other outdoor gear from **Curly's Leisure Sports,** 219 W. Yellowstone Hwy., 307/358-9394.

ENTERTAINMENT

LaBonte Lounge, 206 Walnut, 307/358-5210, is the place for live music Friday and Saturday nights. **Grasslands Restaurant & Saloon,** 2341 E. Richards, 307/358-3575, also feature bands on Friday and Saturday nights, plus karaoke on Wednesdays. **Chutes Saloon** in the Best Western Douglas Inn, 1450 Riverbend Dr., 307/358-9790, has lounge-lizard tunes, a big-screen TV, and free appetizers on weeknights.

The historic **College Inn Bar,** 103 N. 2nd, 307/358-9976, is a favorite place for major-league drinking. Drop by on Wednesday nights for 50-cent draft beers. For movies, head to **Mesa Theatre,** 104 N. 3rd St., 307/358-6209.

WYOMING STATE FAIR

In 1905, the Wyoming Legislature appropriated $10,000 for a Wyoming State Fair in Douglas. With land donated by the Chicago and Northwestern Railroad, the "Show Window of Wyoming" opened that summer, offering a variety of agricultural exhibits, horseback wrestling, Roman races, and concerts. To top it off, two cavalry soldiers added their own drama by putting on an impromptu gunfight. Later, auto polo and motorcycle-riding events were added, but the big hit was Professor Carver's High Diving Girl, who leapt with her horse off a 40-foot platform into a pool of water.

The Wyoming State Fair is held the entire third week of August each year, drawing thousands of visitors from all over the nation. The 113-acre fairgrounds is right next to town and includes a 4,300-seat grandstand, an arts-and-crafts building, a cafeteria, an arena, an open-air pavilion, livestock barns and stalls, and, of course, plenty of carnival rides, cotton candy, and stuffed-animal prizes in the midway. Keep yourself entertained at the market swine evaluation, the 4-H vegetable judging, the demolition derby, or the sheep-to-shawl contest. A free "people shuttle" (tractor-pulled wagon) takes folks around the fairgrounds. Other attractions include evening country-and-western concerts, the Miss Rodeo Wyoming contest, a Saturday morning parade, and the **Douglas Invitational Art Show** (307/358-9288). Because this is Wyoming, the biggest events at the fair are the **PRCA rodeos** held the final three days. Call 307/358-2398 for additional state fair information.

OTHER EVENTS

Both locals and visitors enjoy the **High Plains Old-Time Music Show** in April. Plenty of hot fiddle, guitar, and banjo players provide the entertainment; call 307/358-9006. **Fort Fetterman Days,** 307/358-2864, held the second weekend of June at the old fort, attracts a troop of soldiers and other period-costumed folks for a festival featuring black-powder contests, old-time music, folklore, crafts, living-history demonstrations, Indian dancing, and games.

On the second weekend of June, **Jackalope Days,** 307/358-2950, includes a free pancake breakfast, street dance and beer garden, games, arts and crafts, a motorcycle and classic car show, bed races, and live music.

The **Wyoming High School Rodeo Finals** take place in late June at the fairgrounds, and the first weekend of August brings a popular **Senior Pro Rodeo.**

From May through September, the grandiosely named **Douglas International Raceway** on the southeast edge of town hosts drag races of all types. Located on an old airport runway, it's considered one of the top quarter-mile strips in the nation. The biggest races take place in mid-July; call 307/234-0685 for the rundown. In early August, Douglas plays host to hundreds of motorcycle enthusiasts en route to the Sturgis Rally, with the town providing hospitality tents and other facilities.

Summer ends with a bang as the **Laramie Peak Bluegrass Festival,** 307/358-3909, www.laramiepeakbluegrass.com, brings three days of music to the fairgrounds on the final weekend of August.

INFORMATION AND SERVICES

The **Douglas Area Chamber of Commerce** is inside the old train depot at 121 Brownfield Rd., 307/358-2950, www.jackalope.org. Open Mon.–Fri. 9 A.M.–5 P.M. all year. You can also pick up brochures inside on summer weekends whenever the railroad center is open.

The Forest Service's **Douglas Ranger District Office,** 2250 E. Richards St., 307/358-4690, www.fs.fed.us/r2/mbr/rd-douglas, has maps ($6) and lots of information on Medicine Bow-Routt National Forest and Thunder Basin National Grassland.

The **Converse County Library,** is at 300 Walnut St., 307/358-3644, and the **post office** is at 129 N. 3rd St., 307/358-3106.

Whistle-Stop Mercantile, 206 E. Center, 307/358-3266, has a good selection of Wyoming books and gifts, with a soda fountain/coffee shop in the back. They even sell Krispy Kreme donuts, shipped up from the nearest shop in Denver! Visit the **Meadowlark Gallery** at 300 S. 4th St., 307/358-3808, for local arts and crafts.

Wash your duds at **Sudsy Duds,** 1400 E. Richards St., 307/358-8022, or **Clay St. Laundry,** 2nd and Clay, 307/358-8085.

For medical emergencies, head to **Converse County Memorial Hospital,** 111 S. 5th St., 307/358-2122 or 800/735-8303, where a half-dozen physicians are on staff.

TRANSPORTATION

Powder River Transportation/Coach USA, 307/682-0960 or 800/442-3682, provides daily bus service from Douglas to towns in northern and central Wyoming, continuing north to Billings or Rapid City and south to Cheyenne or Denver. Buses stop at The Plains Motel, 628 E. Richards.

Douglas Vicinity

FORT FETTERMAN

Seven miles northwest of Douglas on State Hwy. 93 is Fort Fetterman State Historic Site. The fort was named for Lt. Col. William J. Fetterman, who was killed by Indians in the Fetterman Massacre of 1866 (see the Powder River Country chapter). Begun in 1867, this was the last fort built in the Rockies. With the signing of the Fort Laramie Treaty of 1868, Forts Casper, Reno, Phil Kearny, and C. F. Smith were all closed, leaving Fort Fetterman the only army base in northern Wyoming. The remote hilltop location afforded commanding views along the infamous Bozeman Trail in both directions, but the location proved inhospitable. A report to headquarters the first winter noted "officers and men were found under canvas exposed on a bleak plain to violent and almost constant gales and very uncomfortable."

Even after the buildings were completed the fort remained a dreaded, windswept, lonely place, and many soldiers deserted as soon as they could get to the nearest railroad. The regimen was strict, with daily parade drills and the prospect of long rides to fight Indians in the surrounding country. Soldiers called the place "Hell Hole," while the Sioux derisively labeled it "Fort Fetterman Reservation." Not far away stood the "Hog Ranch"—sin city on the plains—where gambling, drinking, and women offered a choice of ways to spend the $13 per month the calvarymen received.

Fort Fetterman served as a supply base for the army during the mid-1870s, and both General Crook and Colonel MacKenzie led expeditions from here to attack the Sioux, but the fort itself was never the scene of any conflicts. After the battles had finally died down, the fort was abandoned in 1882. Instead of immediately disappearing, however, "Fetterman City" became the center of ranching and

After Fort Fetterman was abandoned, it was a wide-open town with enough gunfights, hangings, whoring, gambling, and drunkenness to give Fox television stations a run for the money.

trade in the area. For a while, at least, it was a wide-open town with enough gunfights, hangings, whoring, gambling, and drunkenness to give Fox television stations a run for the money. In his novel *The Virginian,* Owen Wister used Fetterman as the basis for his rough-and-tumble town of "Drybone."

Alferd Packer

One of the characters attracted to Fetterman was a prospector who called himself John Swartz. When a waiter was slow in bringing water at a local restaurant, he pulled a gun, saying, "Damn you, ain't you going to bring me that water?" Service quickly improved. The man turned out to be Alferd Packer, wanted for robbing, killing, and then eating his five mining partners in Colorado during the winter of 1875. (Packer called human breast meat the sweetest he'd ever eaten.) After escaping from a Colorado jail, he remained free for the next decade before finally being recognized in Fetterman City. The sheriff captured him at a nearby ranch and spent several nervous nights on the long stage ride to Rock Creek before finally turning Packer over to Colorado authorities. Although convicted of murder, Packer managed to escape from prison again; his body was found in the Rockies in 1903.

The Fort Today

After the railroad arrived in 1886, Douglas became the new center for trade, and Fetterman quickly faded from the scene. Most of the buildings were torn down or moved to Douglas; only two of the original buildings remain: an adobe ordnance warehouse and a log officers' quarters. Inside the officers' quarters is a small state-run **museum** (free), which includes historic displays on the fort, Indian battles, and Fetterman City. The buildings are open daily 9 A.M.–5 P.M. from Memorial Day to Labor

PRAIRIE DOGS

Prairie dogs are cat-sized rodents that live in underground communities and feed on roots and plants. Prairie dog towns sometimes cover thousands of acres with burrow holes spaced every 50 feet or so; a Texas colony was once 100 miles long and 250 miles wide! Two species are found in Wyoming: white-tailed and black-tailed. The latter occur in more than one hundred towns covering some 14,000 acres within Thunder Basin National Grassland, while white-tailed prairie dogs are found in parts of south-central and western Wyoming. Ranchers often complain of lost grazing range resulting from feeding and digging by the "dogs" and injuries to horses and cattle that step into the holes. Research, however, has shown that prairie dogs may actually improve grazing in some situations and that cattle seem to prefer to graze in prairie dog colonies. In addition, prairie dogs provide food for many predators and create habitat used by many other animals.

A Threatened Species

For many decades, ranchers and the Forest Service systematically poisoned prairie dog colonies in the name of "range improvement." These practices proved devastatingly effective and helped create a fragmented population that is susceptible to inbreeding and disease. A century ago, prairie dogs occupied 700 million acres of western grasslands; today they are found on just two million acres. Sightings of the endangered black-footed ferret on Thunder Basin National Grassland helped end most of the poisoning in the 1970s, and prairie dog populations rebounded dramatically. Unfortunately, the animals are highly susceptible to sylvatic plague, an exotic Asian disease that sweeps through the colonies, killing thou-

sands of animals in a short period. In addition, because prairie dogs are still considered varmints in many areas, "sport" hunters don't need a license to shoot them and aren't limited on how many they can kill—at least on private land.

Meanwhile, the U.S. Fish & Wildlife Service is attempting to restore the black-footed ferret—one of the world's rarest mammals—through a captive breeding program and releases into the wild. Prairie dogs are their primary food source, and these varmint hunters may well be endangering the long-term survival of both ferrets and prairie dogs. The U.S. Fish & Wildlife Service now lists black-tailed prairie dogs as a "threatened" species, and the Forest Service has banned prairie dog hunting within Thunder Basin, where ferrets may one day return. Although prairie dogs may be headed for the endangered species list, hunters are still killing them by the thousands on private lands. For more information, see the Fish & Wildlife Service's website at www.r6.fws.gov/btprairiedog.

Seeing Prairie Dogs

If you're interested in viewing prairie dogs, ask at the Douglas Forest Service office for a copy of its prairie dog town map. The largest area is along Horse Creek in the Rochelle Hills, with smaller prairie dog colonies along North Antelope Road. Perhaps the easiest place to view black-tailed prairie dogs is Devils Tower National Monument, where a colony is right along the road. Use caution if you're hiking around prairie dog colonies because the creatures may be infected with the plague bacteria, the cause of Europe's infamous "black death" in the 1300s. Fleas carry the disease, which is potentially deadly but relatively easy to halt with antibiotics.

Day, and by appointment only (307/358-2864; http://wyoparks.state.wy.us) the rest of the year. The grounds are open sunrise to sunset in summer. Entrance is $2 per person for nonresidents or $1 for Wyoming residents; no camping. The surrounding country still exudes a sense of barren loneliness, and it's easy to see how much the soldiers must have hated this

windswept post. Ask the museum staff to point out the faint tracks of the "Bloody Bozeman" Trail to the south.

Fort Fetterman Days, the second weekend of July, brings military demonstrations, Indian dancing, fort tours, firing of artillery pieces, old-time music, crafts, and games. Many of the participants dress in authentic 1870s costume.

AYRES NATURAL BRIDGE PARK

One of the most unusual geological formations in Wyoming lies 14 miles west of Douglas on I-25. Take exit 151 and continue five miles south to tiny 22-acre Ayres Natural Bridge Park, where the main attraction is a 100-foot-long, 50-foot-high rock arch over LaPrele Creek. This natural arch was formed when a meander bend in LaPrele Creek gradually eroded the base of the rock face, leaving the upper part of the cliff unscathed. Eventually the weakened rock gave way, and the creek flowed through the hole that had been created at the bend. The ancient creekbed is 300 feet away from the present creek and 50 feet higher.

History

For the Indians who first lived in this country, the natural bridge was a deadly place. A young brave had been struck by lightning and killed while hunting in the canyon; thus began a legend that an evil spirit lived below the bridge, ready to grab anyone who ventured into his lair. When white settlers realized this, they used the natural bridge as a place to escape from Indian attacks, knowing they would not be pursued across the arch. Early-day mountain men lived in caves here, and Mormon settlers built cabins nearby in the 1850s. It took an expedition by Dr. Ferdinand V. Hayden, director of the U.S. Geological Survey in 1869, to bring the rock arch to national attention. He found it odd "that so great a natural curiosity should have failed to attract the attention it deserves." In 1881, Alva Ayres bought the land and used the lush LaPrele Creek country as headquarters for a freighting business. The natural bridge and surrounding land were donated to Converse County in 1920 by Ayres' heirs.

Visting the Bridge

Today, Ayres Natural Bridge offers a beautiful side trip from I-25. Box elders and cottonwoods line LaPrele Creek, fluorescent green patches against the brilliant red sandstone and the rich blue sky. Along one face of the red-walled amphitheater that circles the park are carved the names of many visitors, some dating from the 1880s. This is a popular weekend picnic and swimming spot and a great place to watch birds. **Free camping** is available on the grounds, with a three-night stay limit. Ayres Natural Bridge Park is open daily 8 A.M.–8 P.M. April–October. A gate blocks the road during the winter, but you can walk in the last half mile. Call 307/358-3532 for more information.

Ayres Natural Bridge spans the waters of LaPrele Creek.

Thunder Basin National Grassland

Thunder Basin National Grassland is an expansive blend of high rolling plateaus, steep rocky escarpments, and gentle plains. It's one of the few places in Wyoming where mountain ranges are not visible, giving the countryside a North Dakota feel. The country seems to reach forever. There's virtually no traffic on some of the main routes across the grassland, especially State Hwy. 450 between Wright and Newcastle. Most of the national grassland is covered with a mixture of western wheatgrass, blue grama grass, and big sagebrush, but some of the ridges have stands of ponderosa pine and juniper, while creek bottoms contain cottonwood trees or greasewood. Naturalists count 170 golden-eagle nests on Thunder Basin—one of the biggest concentrations in Wyoming—along with abundant populations of sandhill cranes, turkeys, antelope, mule deer, elk, and coyotes. Many bald eagles winter here. Look out for the jackalopes, too; lots of the antlerless variety get squashed by cars.

Thunder Basin National Grassland covers 1.8 million acres within Powder River Basin. The land is a mixture of private ranches and property belonging to the Forest Service, the BLM, and the state. The federal government owns 572,000 acres of the total. In the past, a patchwork quilt of land ownership created access and management problems for the grassland. Through a series of land trades, the grassland is now more consolidated and accessible. Get a current ownership map from the Forest Service's **Douglas Ranger District Office,** 2250 E. Richards St., 307/358-4690, www.fs.fed.us/mrnf.

HISTORY

Thunder Basin came about during the glory days of the New Deal and remains today an enclave of pseudosocialism within the rock-ribbed Republican state of Wyoming. Although ranchers had grazed sheep and cattle in the area since the mid-19th century, the arrival of homesteaders caused the land to be divided into smaller parcels. In the arid mixed-grass prairies of eastern Wyoming,

it was nearly impossible for a family to survive because the rains fell too infrequently for farming, and profitable cattle or sheep operations required more than 640 acres of grazing land.

Overgrazing, soil erosion, and five consecutive drought years in the 1930s combined to force many families off the land. Counties risked bankruptcy because of lost tax revenue. The Agricultural Adjustment Administration finally began purchasing homesteads in 1934, giving money to the counties in lieu of taxes. Programs were begun to reestablish grasses to protect the soil and to develop water sources for livestock, while private land ownership was consolidated into larger, more economically manageable units.

MANAGEMENT

Today local ranchers use the grassland in a cooperative grazing scheme that allows 28,000 cattle and 19,000 sheep on the federal land. Improvements such as dams, wells, and fences are cooperatively developed. In addition to livestock grazing, practically every acre of Thunder Basin has been leased for petroleum exploration. Currently, some 327 oil and gas wells pump from 58 oil fields. Vast deposits of subbituminous coal underlie almost the entire area, and there are five gigantic strip mines, including Black Thunder Coal Mine, the largest coal mine in the nation. Revenues from oil and coal development on the grassland reach nearly $5 million annually for the federal and state treasuries, a figure unmatched anywhere else in the Forest Service system. Bentonite—a lubricant and absorptive clay used in everything from oil-drilling muds to candy bars—is also mined on the grassland, and major uranium deposits wait for the public to forget about Three Mile Island and Chernobyl.

RECREATION

A network of more than 1,200 miles of gravel and dirt roads crisscrosses Thunder Basin National Grassland. No developed campgrounds

CENTRAL WYOMING

or trails are available, but you can camp for free anywhere on the public lands. A couple of areas are popular with hunters, birdwatchers, photographers, and others looking for a chance to get out and about.

As with much of Wyoming's rangelands, you should be on guard for prairie rattlesnakes, especially around rock piles and prairie-dog towns. Also, beware of thunderstorms and the lightning that can strike in this open country; this isn't called Thunder Basin for nothing. Because of the lack of drinking-water sources, carry plenty with you in your travels. The Forest Service office in Douglas has additional information on the area, including lists of birds, mammals, and wildflowers.

Rochelle Hills

The Rochelle Hills area, a forested volcanic escarpment near the intersection of Converse, Campbell, and Weston counties, is one of the prettiest parts of the national grassland. A scenic gravel road takes you on a long loop north of the tiny settlement of **Bill** (the name came from four early homesteaders, all of whom had the same first name) and then for 50 miles through the Rochelle Hills before dropping back to State Hwy. 59 eight miles south of Wright. Unfortunately, landslides have destroyed a section of this road, making access difficult in one section.

Upton-Osage Area

The Upton-Osage area also contains miles of ponderosa-pine-topped hills and many small ponds that attract birds. Another fascinating area is in the northern part of the grassland in the Soda Well/Weston area (30 miles north of Gillette on State Hwy. 59). This is a fine place to camp or explore; see the Forest Service for access details throughout the grassland.

Laramie Mountains

The Laramie Peak portion of Medicine Bow-Routt National Forest lies approximately 30 miles south of Douglas, cutting from northwest to southeast along the Laramie Mountains. The mountains are draped with stands of ponderosa, lodgepole, and limber pine, and Engelmann spruce and subalpine fir at higher elevations. Lower elevations are dominated by grass and sagebrush. It's pretty but rugged country, with deep valleys dividing the high granitic ridges and peaks—several exceeding 9,000 feet. Deer, elk, antelope, and wild turkeys are commonly seen in the Laramie Mountains, and rainbow, brook, and brown trout are found in the creeks.

Public and private lands intermingle here, with only a few large tracts of Forest Service property—the biggest being around Laramie Peak. This impressive mountain, clearly visible from Douglas, served as a landmark for travelers along the old Oregon Trail, who called this country the Black Hills. There is some logging around Esterbrook and Albany Peak, especially in insect-killed forests, but Laramie Peak is de facto wilderness.

The Medicine Bow-Routt National Forest **Douglas Ranger District Office,** 2250 E. Richards St., 307/358-4690, www.fs.fed.us/r2/mbr/rd-douglas, has maps ($6) and additional information. A $2 fee is charged for parking at Forest Service trailheads and picnic grounds throughout the Medicine Bow-Routt National Forest, including those in the Laramie Mountains. Annual passes ($20) are also available.

ESTERBROOK

The Esterbrook area, 32 scenic miles south of Douglas on State Hwy. 94, began as a copper-mining town in 1886 but never really had much to show for its effort. Today it provides a delightful escape from the stifling summer heat at lower elevations. Don't attempt to drive on this dirt road after heavy rains or in the spring, when it becomes virtually impassable. Continuing south from Esterbrook, the road cuts through the Laramie Mountains along beautiful Horseshoe Creek Valley, eventually depositing travelers in the town of Rock River.

Along the way are numerous side roads into the mountains, including the access road to the Laramie Peak Trail (further described in the Hiking section).

Esterbrook is famous for its **old log church,** whose rear window frames snowcapped Laramie Peak. It's a favorite place for country weddings and is open May–October, with Sunday Episcopal services at 11 A.M.

Esterbrook Lodge, 307/351-7568, is another classic log building. Stay at small and very rustic cabins or mobile homes for $45 d (plus $15 per person for additional guests)

with a central bathhouse. Also here are tent and RV sites with hookups for $15. The restaurant has a home-cooked lunch and dinner menu that includes such specials as a two-pound (!) Firefighter's All-Day Burger and three-pound steaks. Closed Mondays. The saloon and dance hall attract bands once or twice a month, and they put on all sorts of special events throughout the year.

The **Esterbrook Rendezvous** takes place in early August with a black powder shoot, live music, hayrides, food and craft booths, and a barbecue.

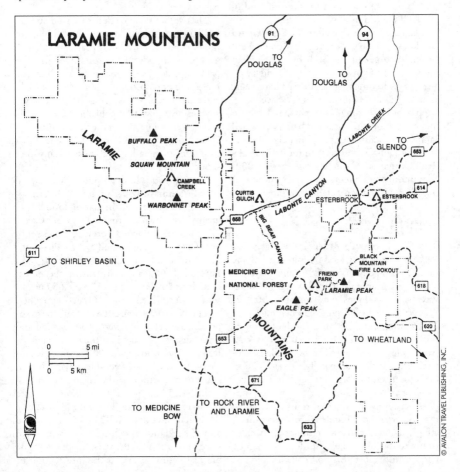

LARAMIE MOUNTAINS

91 TO DOUGLAS
94 TO DOUGLAS
LABONTE CREEK
TO GLENDO 655
BUFFALO PEAK
SQUAW MOUNTAIN
LARAMIE
CAMPBELL CREEK
WARBONNET PEAK
CURTIS GULCH
LABONTE CANYON
ESTERBROOK
614
ESTERBROOK
658
BIG BEAR CANYON
611
TO SHIRLEY BASIN
BLACK MOUNTAIN FIRE LOOKOUT
618
MEDICINE BOW
NATIONAL FOREST
FRIEND PARK
LARAMIE PEAK
EAGLE PEAK
620
0 5 mi
0 5 km
653
MOUNTAINS
TO WHEATLAND
671
TO MEDICINE BOW
TO ROCK RIVER AND LARAMIE
633

© AVALON TRAVEL PUBLISHING, INC.

CAMPING AND A CABIN

Four pleasant Forest Service campgrounds ($5; open mid-May–Oct.) are located in the Laramie Mountains. **Esterbrook Campground**—near the settlement of the same name—is the most accessible, and **Friend Park Campground** is a great base for hikes up Laramie Peak. **Curtis Gulch Campground** is in a scenic area with granite rock formations that are popular with rock climbers. It's located 38 miles south of Douglas. **Campbell Creek Campground** is 40 miles south of Douglas in a remote area on the western end of the Laramie Mountains.

The Forest Service's historic **La Prele Guard Station** is available for rent July to mid-October for $60 per night. Built by the Civilian Conservation Corps between 1937 and 1941, this two-bedroom log structure served for many years as a ranger's home. Inside is space for six people (bring sleeping bags), plus a full kitchen and bath, stone fireplace, and battery-powered lamps. The station is approximately 40 miles south of Douglas and close to the **Twin Peaks Trail,** which takes you 2.5 miles to a 9,000-foot mountain. Get cabin information at 307/358-4690, www.fs.fed.us/r2/mbr.

HIKING

The Forest Service office in Douglas has brochures describing local trails in detail. Some of the finest hiking in central Wyoming is found along the **Laramie Peak Trail,** a five-mile (one-way) path that climbs to the top of the 10,272-foot peak. The trail begins right behind Friend Park Campground, 48 miles south of Douglas (via a gravel road for the last 20 miles). A $2 parking fee is charged. The first mile is relatively easy as the trail parallels Friend Creek, but after this it's a long, arduous climb. Be sure to bring ample water, food, clothing, and supplies because weather conditions can change rapidly. Afternoon thunderstorms occur on an almost-daily basis in the summer. Two miles from the start is a small cascade; water can be hard to find above this point. Periodic forest openings offer dramatic vistas as you continue up the mountain, gaining 2,800 feet along the way. On top find expansive vistas in all directions, including into Nebraska, Colorado, and South Dakota on a clear day. Communication buildings and towers are also here. The trail is generally free of snow by late June. Plan on 4–7 hours for the round-trip hike. Note that a few ATVs also use the trail for access to communications buildings at the top.

A second trailhead, one-quarter mile north of Friend Park Campground, provides access to the four-mile **Friend Park Trail,** which parallels Arapahoe Creek.

The two-mile-long **La Bonte Canyon Trail** offers both pleasant hiking and good fishing for brook trout. The trailhead is at Curtis Gulch Campground, 38 miles south of Douglas. The path drops along a gorgeous steep-walled canyon (keep your eyes open for bighorn sheep and elk) and ends at a big-game refuge. Along the way are meadows, forests of poplar and Douglas fir, and flowers galore. Also near the Curtis Gulch Campground is a 4WD road/hiking trail that climbs for three miles up **Big Bear Canyon** to scenic Devils Pass.

Another good climb is up the 4WD road to **Black Mountain Lookout,** one of the last operating fire towers in the nation. You'll find great views down pristine Ashenfelder Creek. Get there by following Forest Rd. 633 south of Esterbrook Campground for six miles to the Laramie Peak Scout Camp. Turn right onto Forest Rd. 667 and park inside the Forest boundary. Hike up the 4WD road 2.5 miles to the lookout, which is staffed June–September.

The **North Laramie River Trail** starts approximately 20 miles west of Wheatland and descends for 2.5 miles into the North Laramie River Canyon, losing 1,000 feet in elevation along the way. There's good fishing for brown and rainbow trout in the river, and the remains of 15 buildings from a 1920s resort are fun to explore. Get to the trailhead by taking the El Rancho exit from I-25 (between Glendo and Wheatland) and heading west on Fish Creek Road to Fletcher Park Road. Continue on past Camp Grace to the intersection of

Fletcher Park and Cow Camp roads, where signs point the route to the trailhead.

Sunset Ridge Trail is a short 1.6-mile climb to a scenic view over the plains to the east. It originates from the Esterbrook Campground and gains 400 feet along the way before looping back down the hill.

Contact the Forest Service office in Douglas, 307/358-4690, www.fs.fed.us/r2/mbr, for details on these and other trails, including several challenging backcountry routes near Laramie Peak.

WINTER RECREATION

Wintertime snow closes all roads over the Laramie Mountains, transforming the mountains into an excellent place for cross-country skiing, with many miles of scenic country and untracked snow. More than 20 miles of groomed trails surround the Esterbrook area, used primarily by snowmobilers but also by skiers. A warming hut is also here. Pick up a map of snowmobile/ski trails from the Douglas ranger station.

Glenrock

The Podunk cattle-and-coal town of Glenrock (pop. 2,200) lies halfway between Casper and Douglas at the confluence of Deer Creek and the North Platte River. The town's name comes from Rock in the Glen, a large rocky outcrop just to the west. Deer Creek was a favorite camping spot along the Oregon Trail, a place to rest up, do a little fishing, and let the stock graze on the lush creekside grass. Starting in 1847, Mormon emigrants mined the coal visible along the north bank of the river; it was the first coal mined in Wyoming. The first bridge to span the North Platte was built here in 1851 but was washed out in a flood the following year. Deer Creek Station was established in 1857, operating first as a trading post and later as a relay terminal for the Overland Stage and a home station for the short-lived Pony Express. After telegraph wires replaced the Pony Express, Deer Creek became a telegraph relay station. Indians burned the station to the ground in 1866, and it was never rebuilt.

BOOM AND BUST

Around the turn of the 20th century, several underground coal mines opened, transforming the quiet settlement of Glenrock into a raucous mining town. They closed in 1916, just as oil was discovered west of Glenrock. Some 5,000 oil workers flooded the town, along with a raft of less-honorable professionals. Two oil refineries were built, fed by 200 Big Muddy oil wells. One refinery closed in the 1920s and the other in the

'50s. More oil was found in 1949 and again in 1973, leading to temporary booms. The massive coal-fired Dave Johnston Power Plant became one of the largest local employers when it opened in 1958, and the discovery of uranium 25 miles northeast of Glenrock attracted hundreds of people to the area when several large uranium mines opened. Most of them closed in the 1980s, but Rio Algom Mining is still operating a uranium mine 17 miles northeast of Glenrock.

SIGHTS
Museums and Information

The free **Glenrock Paleontological Museum,** 506 W. Birch St., 307/436-2667 or 888/461-5015, www.paleon.org, has original bones and casts from dinosaurs found in the area, including a Triceratops, Hadrosaurs, Nodosaurs, and even Tyrannosaurus rex teeth. It's a surprisingly impressive small collection that also includes the finest Aptosaurus skull ever found and several dinosaur species that have been found nowhere else in the world. During summer, the museum offers special dig-for-a-day programs for $50 per person. It's a great chance to get down and dirty while learning about the creatures that roamed this land more than 65 million years ago. Week-long digs are $1,050 per person, including meals, lodging, and the opportunity to work both in the field and the preparation lab. Museum hours are Tuesday–Saturday 9 A.M.–5 P.M. Casts of dinosaur bones are sold,

DISCOVERING DINOSAURS

Wyoming is prime dinosaur-hunting country, and many important specimens have been discovered, starting with *Diplodocus* dinosaurs (the largest land animal that ever lived) at Como Bluff in 1877. Other significant dinosaur discovery sites are in the Glenrock area, the Lance Creek area southwest of Newcastle, and various places in Bighorn Basin. The **Wyoming Geological Museum,** on the University of Wyoming campus in Laramie, 307/766-2646, www.uwyo.edu/geomuseum, houses a fine collection of dinosaurs, including the 75-foot-long skeleton of an *Apatosaurus.* Listed as follows are other notable places to find dinosaur bones or tracks, or where you can tour dinosaur dig sites. See the appropriate chapters of this book for details on each of these.

The little **Glenrock Paleontological Museum,** 307/436-2667 or 800/996-3466, www.paleon.org, has a surprising collection that includes Triceratops, Hadrosaurs, and Nodosaurs. You can also join ongoing dinosaur digs nearby.

Paleo Park, 307/334-2270, www.paleopark.com, lies in the heart of the Lance Creek fossil area southwest of Newcastle. Daily tours and accommodations are available at this site where several significant dinosaur discoveries have been made, including one of the most complete specimens of Triceratops ever discovered. Also here are the intermingled tracks of both dinosaurs and birds.

Rock River Museum, 307/378-2386, houses

various dinosaur bones. Nearby is world-famous **Como Bluff,** site of the first large discovery of dinosaurs ever found. There's even a little cabin built from dinosaur bones at Como Bluff.

Western Wyoming Community College in Rock Springs, 307/382-1600, www.wwcc.cc.wy.us, exhibits some impressive dinosaur skeleton casts, including ones of Triceratops and Tyrannosaurus rex.

Red Gulch Dinosaur Tracksite, east of Greybull, has hundreds of tracks from *theropods.* Guides are at the site, or you can take a tour from **Geo-Science Adventures,** 307/765-2259 or 866/765-2259, www.geo-sciences.com. The nearby **Greybull Museum,** 307/765-2444, exhibits many fossils, including several dinosaur bones.

The **Wyoming Dinosaur Center** in Thermopolis, 307/864-2997 or 800/455-3466, www.wyodino.org, is Wyoming's premier place to learn about these creatures, with a first-class museum and daily tours to the dig sites in the summer.

Other Fossils
Wyoming is also famous for its other fossilized animals, particularly the treasure trove of Jurassic mammals at Como Bluff and the abundant fish fossils in the Kemmerer area. At **Fossil Butte National Monument,** 307/877-4455, www.nps.gov/fobu, you can learn the full story. Several quarries in the Kemmerer area let you dig your own fish fossils.

and on Tuesdays, Thursdays, and Saturdays you can watch volunteers in the prep lab. The paleo museum doubles as the town visitors center, and the **Glenrock Chamber of Commerce** desk (307/436-5652, www.trib.com/glenrock) is open Monday–Friday 8 A.M.–3 P.M. Brochures are also available when the museum is open.

The free **Glenrock Historical Museum,** 937 W. Birch St., 307/436-2810, occupies an old church building on the west side of town. Inside is a collection of local memorabilia, along with bones from a nearby buffalo jump used by prehistoric hunters. Hours are Friday–Tuesday 10 A.M.–4 P.M., summers only.

Other Sights
Rock in the Glen, one-half mile west of Glenrock, has the carved names of a few of the 19th-century emigrants who passed by on the way to Oregon, California, or Utah. Several **graves** from this era are scattered around Glenrock, sad reminders of the thousands who never made it. One is that of A. H. Unthank, just east of the Dave Johnston Power Plant on Tank Farm Road, who died of cholera just one week after carving his name in Register Cliffs near present-day Guernsey. Four miles west of town is the grave of Ada Magill, a young girl who died of dysentery in 1864 as her par-

ents headed west in a wagon train. Stones were piled on top of the grave to keep wolves from digging up her body.

Glenrock City Park has a granite monument to **Dr. Ferdinand V. Hayden,** a physician who devoted his life to exploration of the West. Hayden helped found the U.S. Geological Survey and led the famed Hayden Yellowstone Expedition of 1870. The Indians considered Hayden a bit wacky, calling him "Man-who-picks-up-stones-running." Hayden used the Deer Creek Station at present-day Glenrock as a base of operations for several of his expeditions around Wyoming, hence the monument—placed here in 1931 by his photographic partner on these trips, William H. Jackson.

A pleasant picnic and fishing spot is **Boxelder Canyon,** approximately 10 miles south of Glenrock on State Hwy. 90. Boxelder Creek is bordered by steep rocky walls.

The country around Glenrock is laced with energy projects of all types. Immediately west of town is the Big Muddy oil field, where nearly three million barrels were pumped out over the last 40 years; production is declining now. The giant **Dave Johnston Power Plant** is six miles east of Glenrock along the North Platte River. It's one of the largest coal-fired power plants in the Rockies, generating 810,000 kilowatts of electricity for the Pacific Northwest. A private railroad feeds the plant with coal from the Glenrock Coal strip mine 16 miles to the north.

Visit the **Central Wyoming Livestock Exchange,** just east of town, 307/436-5391 or 800/967-1467, where cattle, horses, sheep, pigs, and even a few goats are auctioned off on Thursdays year-round, plus Saturdays in the winter. This is an enjoyable way to learn about ranching and to rub shoulders with local ranchers.

ACCOMMODATIONS

All American Inn, 500 W. Aspen, 307/436-2772, has rooms starting at $32 s or $36–42 d, some with fridges and microwaves. **Hotel Higgins,** 416 W. Birch, 307/436-9212 or 800/458-0144, www.hotelhiggins.com, is plain vanilla on the outside—pink shingles on a building built in 1916—but the inside is surprisingly nice. The entire hotel has been lovingly furnished with antique brass beds, wardrobes, lamps, and a ticking old grandfather clock. Rooms cost $60–80 s or $70–90 d, or $90 s or $100 d for a two-bedroom suite, including a full breakfast. No TVs in the rooms. Kids are welcome.

CAMPING

Camping is free at **South Recreation Complex,** three miles south of Glenrock along the river. **Deer Creek RV Park,** on the east end of town, 307/436-8121, has RV sites with hookups for $16; open all year.

FOOD

Located inside Higgins Hotel, **The Paisley Shawl Restaurant,** 307/436-9212 or 800/458-0144, www.hotelhiggins.com, serves bistro cuisine, including lamb chops, grilled chicken pesto pasta, and Cuban pork tenderloin; $12–21 dinner entrées. Open for lunch and dinner, with a back deck for summer evenings.

Four Aces Bar, 307/436-9010, serves three meals a day and has a good steakhouse dinner menu. Get pizza at **Classic Cafe & Pizza,** 201 S. 4th, 307/436-2244. **Fort Diablo Steak House & Saloon,** 307/436-2288, has Friday and Saturday night prime rib, plus buffalo steaks and seafood. Buy groceries from **Williams' Town & Country Food Center,** 218 W. Cedar, 307/436-2344.

ENTERTAINMENT AND EVENTS

At least one of the many local bars (**Four Aces, El Diablo, Knotty Pine, Shoreliner,** or **Deer Creek Lounge**) will have a country-and-western band on most weekends. Knotty Pine has the best Bloody Marys in town, plus their "Humphrey" is not for the fainthearted.

The big annual event is **Deer Creek Days,** with a parade, pancake breakfast, games, craft and food booths, rodeo, street dancing, and lots of drinking. It takes place the first weekend of August.

SERVICES

The **Glenrock Library,** 518 S. 4th, 307/436-2573, exhibits a few dinosaur fossils found in the area and has something a bit newer, Internet access.

A free indoor **swimming pool** is in the middle school at 645 S. 3rd St., and the spacious **Recreation Center,** 125 Mustang Trail, contains weight rooms and basketball courts. Call 307/436-5434 for details. Golfers may want to check out the nine-hole **Glenrock Golf Course,** 307/436-5560.

Casper

Wyoming's second-largest city, Casper (pop. 49,000) is in transition from an oil-dependent economy to a more diversified base. The city sprawls across both sides of the North Platte River and is surrounded by the outlying settlements of **Evansville** (pop. 2,300), **Mills** (pop. 2,600), and **Bar Nunn** (pop. 900), with more suburbs filling the intervening land.

For many years, Casperites trumpeted the city as "Oil Capital of the Rockies." It sits at the center of several large oil fields and is home to a refinery and a large tank farm. In the last decade, however, declining oil production has forced the city into a more diversified base, although the oil industry is still an important economic player. Open up the Casper Yellow Pages and you'll find more than 20 different types of oil-related listings—from oil and gas exploration companies to directional drilling outfits.

With its central location, substantial population, spacious convention facilities, and ties to the state's energy and ranching industries, Casper considers itself the true heart and soul of Wyoming. The only statewide newspaper, the *Casper Star-Tribune,* is based here, along with one of the state's premier medical centers. To Casperites, arch-rival Cheyenne is just a Nebraska city that happened to sneak into Wyoming. The rest of Wyoming, however, views Casper with equal suspicion; in 1904 Casper aspired to become the state capital but failed miserably, coming in third behind Cheyenne and Lander in a statewide vote.

A working-class town, Casper isn't a major tourist destination, but it does have several fine museums, most notably the National Historic Trails Interpretive Center, the Nicolaysen Art Museum, Fort Caspar Museum, and two Casper College museums. You'll discover outstanding

recreational opportunities on nearby Casper Mountain, at local reservoirs, and on the North Platte River, plus many historic sites along the Oregon Trail. In addition, the city is filled with a variety of cultural activities, particularly in winter when symphony concerts, theatrical productions, and art receptions pepper the calendar.

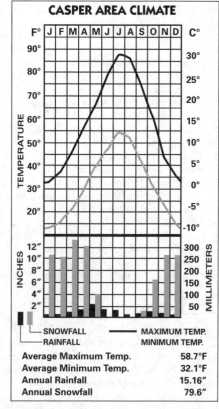

CASPER AREA CLIMATE

SNOWFALL — MAXIMUM TEMP.
RAINFALL — MINIMUM TEMP.

Average Maximum Temp.	58.7°F
Average Minimum Temp.	32.1°F
Annual Rainfall	15.16"
Annual Snowfall	79.6"

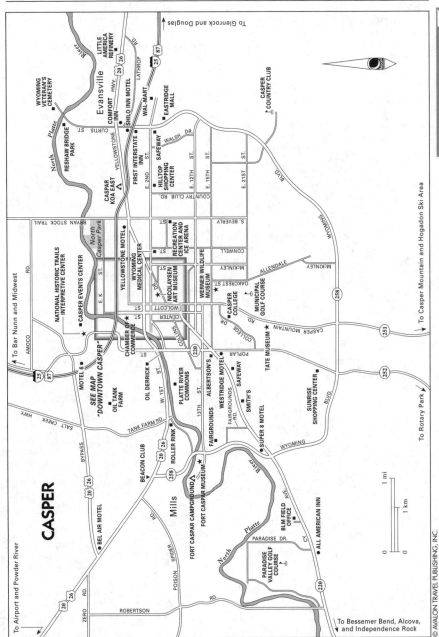

CASPER

To Airport and Powder River

To Bar Nunn and Midwest

To Glenrock and Douglas

To Casper Mountain and Hogadon Ski Area

To Rotary Park

To Bessemer Bend, Alcova, and Independence Rock

LITTLE AMERICA REFINERY

WYOMING VETERAN'S CEMETERY

Evansville

COMFORT INN

SHILO INN MOTEL

WAL-MART

EASTRIDGE MALL

CASPER COUNTRY CLUB

North Platte River

RESHAW BRIDGE PARK

CURTIS ST.

YELLOWSTONE

FIRST INTERSTATE INN

SAFEWAY

WALSH DR.

HILLTOP SHOPPING CENTER

E. 2ND ST.

E. 12TH ST.

E. 15TH ST.

E. 21ST ST.

CASPAR KOA EAST

BRYAN STOCK TRAIL

North Casper Park

COUNTRY CLUB RD.

S. BEVERLY

WYOMING BLVD

NATIONAL HISTORIC TRAILS INTERPRETIVE CENTER

CASPER EVENTS CENTER

YELLOWSTONE MOTEL

E. K. ST.

WYOMING MEDICAL CENTER

RECREATION CENTER AND ICE ARENA

CONWELL

McKINLEY

McKINLEY

ALLENDALE

NICOLAYSEN ART MUSEUM

WERNER WILDLIFE MUSEUM

OAKCREST ST.

CASPER COLLEGE

MUNICIPAL GOLF COURSE

SEE MAP "DOWNTOWN CASPER"

CHAMBER OF COMMERCE

WOLCOTT ST.

CENTER ST.

COLLINS ST.

CASPER MOUNTAIN RD.

COLLEGE DR.

TATE MUSEUM

MOTEL 6

OIL TANK FARM

OIL DERRICK

W. 1ST ST.

PLATTE RIVER COMMONS

220

POPLAR ST.

ALBERTSON'S

WESTRIDGE MOTEL

SAFEWAY

SUNRISE SHOPPING CENTER

WYOMING BLVD

SALT CREEK HWY

BYPASS

TANK FARM RD.

13TH ST.

SMITH'S

BEACON CLUB

ROLLER RINK

258

FAIRGROUNDS

FAIRGROUNDS RD.

SUPER 8 MOTEL

BEL AIR MOTEL

Mills

SPIDER RD.

POISON RD.

ZERO RD.

ROBERTSON RD.

FORT CASPAR CAMPGROUND

FORT CASPAR MUSEUM

North Platte River

BLM FIELD OFFICE

ALL AMERICAN INN

PARADISE DR.

PARADISE VALLEY GOLF COURSE

C.Y. AVE.

220

To Powder River

20 26

20 26

25 87

258

251

252

LATHROP RD.

20 26

25 87

1 mi

1 km

0

0

© AVALON TRAVEL PUBLISHING, INC.

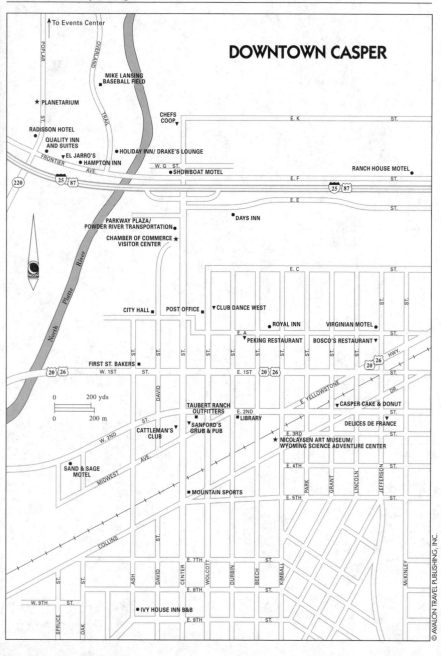

DOWNTOWN CASPER

To Events Center

MIKE LANSING BASEBALL FIELD

★ PLANETARIUM

CHEFS COOP ▼

RADISSON HOTEL
QUALITY INN AND SUITES
▼ EL JARRO'S
● HOLIDAY INN/ DRAKE'S LOUNGE
● HAMPTON INN
● SHOWBOAT MOTEL

RANCH HOUSE MOTEL ●

PARKWAY PLAZA/ POWDER RIVER TRANSPORTATION ●

DAYS INN ●

CHAMBER OF COMMERCE ★ VISITOR CENTER

CITY HALL ■   POST OFFICE ■   ▼ CLUB DANCE WEST

● ROYAL INN   VIRGINIAN MOTEL ●

▼ PEKING RESTAURANT   BOSCO'S RESTAURANT ▼

FIRST ST. BAKERS ■

TAUBERT RANCH OUTFITTERS ■
▼ SANFORD'S GRUB & PUB
■ LIBRARY

CASPER CAKE & DONUT ▼

DELICES DE FRANCE ▼

CATTLEMAN'S CLUB

★ NICOLAYSEN ART MUSEUM/ WYOMING SCIENCE ADVENTURE CENTER

SAND & SAGE MOTEL

■ MOUNTAIN SPORTS

● IVY HOUSE INN B&B

0   200 yds
0   200 m

E. K ST.
W. G ST.
E. F ST.
E. E ST.
E. C ST.
E. A ST.
E. 1ST ST.
E. 2ND ST.
E. 3RD ST.
E. 4TH ST.
E. 5TH ST.
E. 7TH ST.
E. 8TH ST.
E. 9TH ST.
W. 1ST ST.
W. 2ND
W. 9TH ST.

POPLAR ST.
OVERLAND TRAIL
FRONTIER AVE.
DAVID ST.
MIDWEST AVE.
COLLINS
SPRUCE ST.
OAK ST.
ASH ST.
DAVID
CENTER
WOLCOTT
DURBIN ST.
BEECH ST.
KIMBALL
PARK
GRANT
LINCOLN
JEFFERSON ST.
McKINLEY

North Platte River

220
25 87
20 26
20 26

E. YELLOWSTONE HWY.
DR.

HISTORY

The Astorians

Although Casper is identified today with oil, the city began as a way station along the Oregon Trail. Seven of John Jacob Astor's fur traders led by Robert Stuart first traveled through this area in 1812 on their return from Oregon, arriving in late October. Knowing they could not make it back to St. Louis in their emaciated condition, the explorers constructed a rock-walled cabin (the first Anglo building in Wyoming) and covered it with buffalo hides. Game proved amazingly plentiful. They returned from a hunting trip with 47 bison, 28 deer and bighorn sheep, and a bear! But five weeks later, a band of 23 Arapaho warriors appeared on their way to raid the Crow Indians farther north. Intimidated, the Astorians invited them in for a meal. They stayed for a day and a half, promising to return in two weeks. The Astorians quickly decided discretion was the better part of valor and moved to a new camp just across what is now the Nebraska border. They finally reached Missouri the following spring.

Ferries and Bridges

The route pioneered by the Astorians eventually became a virtual highway to the West. The North Platte River was one of the main barriers to this migration, with many emigrants choosing to ford near what is now Casper. In early summer, when the river ran dangerously high, people often died trying to cross it. Others lost their wagons or watched as their oxen and horses were swept downriver. When Brigham Young's party of Mormon emigrants arrived here in 1847, they built a 23-foot-long raft and floated their wagons across. The Mormon ferry became Casper's first business venture, with gentiles charged $1.50 per wagon. Business boomed, and by 1849, several different ferries were competing with the Mormon ferry. Despite this transporation rush, there were still delays of up to one week as California gold-rush travelers waited to cross. (This has to rate as one of Wyoming's only recorded traffic jams.)

In 1852, a French-Canadian trader named John Richard (locally known as Reshaw) built a long wooden toll bridge at present-day Evansville, charging $5 in gold per wagon—less when the river was low and folks would risk fording. To stifle competition, he bought the Mormon ferry for $300 and shut it down. Edwin R. Bird, an 1854 Oregon Trail pioneer, wrote of the toll bridge in his diary:

> *Here we found a good bridge far better than some I have seen at home. There is a store & other buildings connected with it. In the store saw two Frenchmen gambling. The owner of the bridge says he took in seventeen thousand dollars last season. He charges five dollars for a team & five cents a head for loose stock.*

In 1859, another bridge was built six miles upriver by Louis Guinard to compete for the lucrative Oregon Trail traffic. Guinard's bridge must have been one of the most impressive structures along the entire 2,000-mile route. Built at a cost of $40,000, the bridge was 17 feet wide, 1,000 feet long, and supported by 28 log and rock cribs. It soon became the preferred crossing point along the North Platte, and the old Richard bridge was cannibalized for firewood.

Red Cloud's War

Platte Bridge Station served as a trading post for travelers, a Pony Express mail stop, and later a telegraph office. A volunteer force was posted to protect the telegraph and those traveling along the Oregon Trail from Indian and Mormon attacks. After a massacre of Indians at Colorado's Sand Creek in 1865, full-scale war broke out between Indians and whites. One of these battlegrounds that July was at Platte Bridge Station. Expecting a wagon train with vital supplies and ammunition, 20 men under the command of Lt. Caspar Collins left the fort to escort the expected convoy. Once across the bridge, the soldiers found themselves surrounded by Red Cloud and more than a thousand Sioux, Cheyenne, and Arapaho warriors. In their flight back across the bridge, five soldiers died. Collins was killed when he stooped to rescue a fellow soldier and his horse bolted, carrying him into the onrushing warriors. Other soldiers said that when last seen, he had his reins in his teeth and was firing pistols from both hands. His body was found two days later with 24 arrows in it.

A second battle occurred that afternoon—Custard's Wagon Train Fight. When the supply wagons of Sgt. Amos Custard came within sight of the fort, the soldiers tried to warn them with cannon fire. Three men from an advance guard made it to safety within the fort, and the others quickly corralled the three wagons together. Although they put up a fierce fight, within hours Red Cloud's men had killed and mutilated the 22 defenders and burned their wagons. In honor of Caspar Collins, Platte Bridge Station was renamed Fort Caspar. (Fort Collins, Colorado, is named for his father, William Collins.) Because of a never-corrected error by an army telegraph operator—he typed a dot instead of a dot-dash—the town that eventually grew up nearby was misspelled Casper. Two years later, Fort Caspar was abandoned. Much of it was dismantled and the material used in the construction of Fort Fetterman, 40 miles to the east, and a jumping-off point for the Bozeman Trail.

Lawless Days and Nights

In 1888, the Fremont, Elkhorn, and Missouri Valley Railway extended its line up the North Platte River almost to the site of old Fort Caspar. A tent city quickly sprang up, followed by more permanent buildings. For the next 17 years the town of Casper lay at the end of the tracks. It was an exceptionally violent place; employees of the first grocery store surrounded their beds with sacks of flour for protection from stray bullets, and Casper's first public building was a jail. Even the mayor got in on the act, murdering his business partner in an 1890 gun duel on Main Street. The jury let him go free. When the ruffians became too much to tolerate, a street trial was held and those who refused to leave town faced the prospect of being strung up in a "necktie party." Pinned to the shirt of one murderer lynched by a vigilance committee was the fol-

lowing note: "Process of law is a little slow, so this is the road you'll have to go. Murderers and sinners, Beware! People's Verdict."

Oil Changes Everything

In 1851 Jim Bridger, Cy Iba, Kit Carson, and Basil Cimineau Lajeunesse discovered an oil spring just west of Casper at Poison Spider Creek. The oil was mixed with flour and sold as axle grease for wagon trains. By 1889, when the first oil well was drilled near Casper, it was clear that much more oil lay beneath the ground. Land speculators and claim jumpers flocked to Wyoming, and battles quickly broke out over who had staked the first claim; the winner generally had more burly men, guns, and lawyers. Soon the massive Salt Creek oil field, 40 miles north of Casper, was producing; wagons towed by teams of up to 20 horses hauled the oil back to Casper. A small refinery was built in 1895, the first in Wyoming. It was later replaced by more modern facilities, including the now-closed Standard Oil plant, at one time the largest refinery on earth, handling 25,000 barrels of oil per day. Over time, Casper became a center for oil and refining in the northern Rockies.

Boom and Bust

Casper grew into a major industrial town with the development of Salt Creek and other oil fields. So many roustabouts flooded Casper that they had to sleep in shifts in the available tents, motels, garages, basements, or shacks. Dozens of illegal gambling houses and speakeasies helped make a trip to town memorable, and more than 2,000 prostitutes pursued their own boomtimes in the Sandbar district; prostitution was blatant here until the 1950s. Oil production peaked in the 1920s, but the crash of 1929 burst this economic bubble and cut the city's population in half within five years. World War II sent oil prices and Casper's economy soaring. An army air base—home to 4,000 men—opened nearby; it's now the site of Casper's airport. In the late '50s, new technology—injecting water to force the remaining oil to wellheads—helped boost recovery dramatically at

Salt Creek, and there followed another boom for Casper. The discovery of massive uranium deposits in the Pumpkin Buttes, Gas Hills, and Shirley Basin areas further fueled this growth.

The roller-coaster ride continued throughout the last half of the 20th century: down in the late '60s, back up in the '70s. When oil prices soared following the OPEC oil embargo in 1973, Casper experienced such an orgy of growth that planners predicted a population rivaling that of Denver's by the year 2000. After oil prices plummeted in the 1980s, these optimistic—or apocalyptic, depending on your point of view—predictions failed to materialize. Sales tax receipts dropped by half, many of downtown Casper's storefronts were covered with plywood, and the Amoco refinery shut down (the site is now being transformed into a golf course).

The economy has improved dramatically in recent years as Casper diversified its industrial base to include everything from a copper foundry to pepper-spray manufacturing. New stores have invigorated the commercial sector, and the addition of the Nicolaysen Art Museum has added an artistic focal point. Downtown is thriving, the suburbs are once again creeping over the countryside, and Eastridge Mall— Wyoming's largest shopping mall—is packed with chain stores. But you can still find a few fixer-upper homes for less than $50,000 and many houses for less than $90,000, along with a few mansions that top $300,000.

SIGHTS

Fort Caspar

Although the original fort had long since disappeared, in 1936 the WPA reconstructed a half dozen of Fort Caspar's log buildings. Included are a blacksmith shop, an Overland Stage station, a commissary storehouse, a barracks building, and a sutler's store where you can buy various Western items. Many supports from Guinard's long bridge across the North Platte are still visible as mounds of rock. Also here you'll find a replica of the Mormon ferry and a reconstruction of part of the bridge (in poor shape). During summer,

guides dressed as 1860s cavalrymen are on hand to answer your questions.

A brick building at the fort houses an excellent small museum displaying a variety of items, including a reconstructed Mormon handcart and a W. H. Jackson painting of Platte Bridge Station. Be sure to check out the photos and story of the 14-inch-tall Pedro Mountain mummy, a find that seemed to confirm the "little people" stories told by many Indian tribes. The museum, 307/235-8462, www.fortcasparwyoming.com, is open Monday–Saturday 8 A.M.–7 P.M., Sunday noon–7 P.M. May–September, and Monday–Friday 8 A.M.–5 P.M., Sunday 1–4 P.M. the rest of the year. Entrance is $2 adults, $1 ages 6–17. The gift shop has more than 500 Western history book titles available. The fort buildings are open only mid-May to mid-September, but you can wander around the grounds at any time of year. Over in Evansville, the **Town Hall** (open Mon.–Fri. 8 A.M.–5 P.M.) also contains artifacts found along the Oregon Trail.

National Historic Trails Interpretive Center

This $12-million 27,000-square-foot museum opened its doors in 2002, quickly establishing itself as a must-see for Casper visitors and "rut nuts" (as Oregon Trail enthusiasts are known). The Platte River crossing at present-day Casper was a junction for most of the major routes west, including not just the Oregon, California, Mormon, and Pony Express Trails, but also the Bridger and Bozeman Trails. A 16-minute multimedia presentation provides an introduction to the trails and to the people who traversed this land. Exhibits include one on the Indian peoples who migrated through using *travois* (pole-and-net handcarts), as well as the whys, wheres, and ways of 19th-century travel by the traders, explorers, trappers, missionaries, gold-miners, and farmers heading west. Bigger-than-life displays and virtual-reality exhibits present the experience of these migrants through eight exhibit galleries. You'll get to experience the sensation of being on a moving wagon as it crosses the Platte River, step into a cold room to empathize with the tragedies some travelers experienced, and sit on a stagecoach as

© DON PITCHER

downtown Casper

part of the rush to California's goldfields. First-person narratives relate the pioneer and Native American experience, and present-day travelers will learn where they can find the old trails today. A gift shop is also housed within the museum.

Situated atop a hill on the north side of Casper at 1501 N. Poplar St., the center is a joint venture of the BLM, the city of Casper, and the National Historic Trails Interpretive Center Foundation. It is open daily 8 A.M.–7 P.M. April–October, and Tuesday–Saturday 9 A.M.–4 P.M. November–March. Entrance costs $6 adults, $5 seniors, $4 students, $3 ages 6–17, $1 ages 3–5, and free for tots. Get details at 307/261-7700, www.wy.blm.gov/nhtic.

Nicolaysen Art Museum

One surprising aspect of Casper is an emphasis on art and culture as exemplified by the Nicolaysen—"The Nic." Originally a power plant, this beautiful brick building houses six different galleries and is the finest contemporary art exhibition space in Wyoming. Exhibits change every few months, but you're unlikely to see the standard moose-in-the-meadow schlock here. The perma-

nent collection includes more than 4,000 paintings by the late Conrad Schwiering, Wyoming's preeminent artist. His studio and samples from this collection are on display half of the year. Also of note are some 1,900 drawings by German-American illustrator Carl Link, along with a variety of Native American paintings, pottery, and rugs.

Children love the fun **Discovery Center,** where artistic activities and classes take place. Warning: If you have kids, you'll need to drag them out of here! The gift shop sells classy collectibles, and lectures, concerts, and slide shows are offered throughout the year. The Nic is at 400 E. Collins, 307/235-5247, www.thenic.org, and is open Tuesday–Friday 10 A.M.–7 P.M., Saturday 10 A.M.–7 P.M., Sunday noon–4 P.M.; closed Monday.

Upstairs within the Nicolaysen's walls (but a separate operation) is the **Wyoming Science Adventure Center,** 307/261-6130, www.wysac.org, where you can create six-foot-long bubbles, learn how your body works, visit the fish, or even make bowls levitate. Exhibits change regularly, and the Science Center is open Tuesday–Friday noon–5 P.M., and Saturday 1–5 P.M. Entrance costs $2 adults, $1 ages 2–12. No charge for toddlers, and always free for everyone on Saturdays.

More Art

One legacy from Casper's oil-boom times is an abundance of outdoor sculpture, including three pieces by Laramie sculptor Robert Russin. His energetic bronze *Prometheus* livens the library entrance at 307 E. 2nd St., while *Man and Energy* at the chamber of commerce, 500 N. Center, symbolizes Casper's ties to oil and coal. Neither is as controversial as *The Fountainhead,* a red and blue metal sculpture placed in front of the city hall in 1981. Its unorthodox (some say "ugly") appearance and $230,000 price tag raised a few eyebrows—and blood pressures. A statue of Caspar Collins on horseback guards the Casper Events Center; a Pony Express rider welcomes you to the National Historic Trails Center; a monument to sheepherders is in front of the Wyoming Wool Growers Building at 117 Glenn Rd.; and a statue of Chief Washakie stands at 1st and Walcott. One of the largest sculptures in Wyoming is located on State Rd. 220 at Wyoming: a larger-than-life mounted cowboy and steer fleeing from a charging buffalo. It's one of several sculptures that will adorn Casper's entryways. Pick up the *Art for the Streets* brochure at the visitors center for details on local public sculptures.

Other places to see local artwork include **West Wind Gallery,** an artists' co-op at 1040 W. 15th, 307/265-2655, www.casperbusiness.com/artistsguild; **Serendipity Gallery,** 105 E. 2nd St., 307/237-7205, www.mccannjewelers.com/serendipity; **Artist's Choice,** 647 W. Yellowstone Hwy., 307/234-7000; **The Artist's Gallery** in Eastridge Mall, 307/577-1662; and the **student art gallery** at Casper College.

Casper College

Casper College first opened its doors in 1945 and has grown into the state's largest junior college, with more than 6,000 full- and part-time students. The college's brick buildings sprawl up a long hillside. Although many students live in dorms, most commute from around town, making for traffic jams in the parking lots and along adjacent city streets.

Casperites fought for many years to turn their college into a four-year school, but the university at Laramie successfully fended off those moves until 1987. In a joint venture, the University of Wyoming now offers a limited number of bachelor's degree programs at the Casper College campus. A fine 80,000-volume **library** on campus includes a rare-book room with unusual Wyoming titles. An **Elderhostel** program operates at Casper College during the summer, and the excellent **Fitness Center** is open to the public. In the College Center building you'll find a cafeteria, a small bookstore, and other facilities. Contact Casper College at 307/268-2100 or 800/442,2963, www.caspercollege.edu.

Visitors will enjoy stops at two Casper College collections. **Tate Geological Museum,** 307/268-2447, is open Monday–Friday 9 A.M.–5 P.M., Saturday 10 A.M.–4 P.M. all year; free. Inside you'll find one of the largest mineralogical collections in the Rockies, including several meteorites, various types of petrified wood, Indian artifacts, dinosaur fossils, and probably the largest collection of Wyoming jade anywhere. The fossil preparation lab is a highlight, where professionals prepare bones and fossils for display. Polished stones are sold at a small gift shop here.

Werner Wildlife Museum, 405 E. 15th St., 307/268-2676, is open daily 10 A.M.–5 P.M. mid-May to early September, and Monday–Friday 2–5 P.M. the rest of the year; free. The museum houses the usual stuffed critters from Wyoming—dozens of antelope heads, deer mounts, bears, bison, and many birds, along with several African and Alaskan trophies.

Edness Kimball Wilkins State Park

Six miles east of Casper on State Hwy. 256, this 1,420-acre park is perfect for quiet picnics among the cottonwoods, birdwatching (more than 200 species have been observed), and fishing and canoeing in the North Platte River. The park began as a rock quarry but has been transformed into a delightful place to explore. No camping is allowed, but several trails—including a three-mile paved path—provide pleasant day hikes or bike rides, and on hot summer weekends families crowd the sandy beach along the swimming pond. Oregon Trail wagon ruts are visible near the entrance to the park. Day use costs $4 for nonresident vehicles, $2 for cars with Wyoming plates. Get additional information at 307/577-515, http://wyoparks.state.wy.us.

Additional Sights

The paved seven-mile **Platte River Parkway** is a fine place to walk, inline skate, or bike. Get a map from the visitors center or just look for it along the river. It will eventually extend for a dozen miles.

At the intersection of 1st and Poplar Streets, a wooden **oil derrick** stands as a monument to the city's heritage. One of Casper's minor claims to fame is having Wyoming's largest convention and performance center. The **Casper Planetarium,** 904 N. Poplar, 307/577-0310, schedules daily shows at 7 P.M. during the summer; $2.50. **Dr. Spokes Cyclery & Museum,** 240 S. Center St., 307/265-7740, is a unique bike shop with an array of classic bikes and toy pedal cars arranged around the room. Some date back nearly a century.

At **Casper Events Center,** you might run across a mining trade show, rock concert, wrestling tournament, basketball game, graduation ceremony, cat show, or even a monster-truck pull. On a hill overlooking the city, the center is a spacious, modern building with room for more than 10,000 people. Find upcoming events at 307/577-3030 or 800/442-2256, www.cityofcasperwy.com.

The Wyoming Game & Fish Department produces a helpful booklet of wildlife viewing in the area; pick it up at the agency's office (3030 Energy Lane, 307/473-3400) or from the visitors center. Springtime visitors will enjoy a detour from Casper out Hat Six Road (State Hwy. 253) east of town, where **sage grouse** perform spectacular mating displays mid-March to mid-May. Farther out this road is a large **prairie dog town.** The visitors center also has a detailed booklet with self-guided tours of Casper's historic buildings. For a guided taste of Casper's rough history, join one of the candlelight tours offered throughout the summer by **Painted Past,** 307/267-7243, www.cholden.com/PaintedPast.

The **Wyoming Veteran's Memorial Museum,** 307/265-7628, is located at the airport (eight miles northwest of Casper on U.S. Hwy. 20/26), and includes military memorabilia. During World War II, the building was used by men who trained B-17 and B-24 bombing crews, and includes a mural painted by the soldiers. It's open Thursday–Friday noon–5 P.M., Saturday 10 A.M.–5 P.M., and Sunday noon–5 P.M.

ACCOMMODATIONS

Casper accommodations cover the complete quality spectrum, from dumpy little holes-in-the-wall to an elaborate Radisson Hotel. In general you'll find prices in Casper to be quite reasonable. The **Casper Area Convention & Visitors Bureau's** website, www.casper-wyoming.info, has brief descriptions and web links to most local accommodations.

Under $50

Ranch House Motel, 1130 E. F St., 307/266-4044, has some of the cheapest local rates: $25 s or $29 d. The furnishings show considerable wear, so you may want to check out the rooms first. **Red Arrow Motel,** 308 SW Wyoming Blvd., 307/234-5293, is a little 10-room place with budget rooms containing microwaves and fridges for $27 s or $32 d.

A good economy choice is **Royal Inn,** right downtown at 440 E. A St., 307/234-3501 or 877/234-3501. Standard rooms go for $30 s or $38 d, and amenities include an outdoor pool (not heated), fridges, microwaves, and HBO. Kitchenettes are $35–60, with the larger ones sleeping six.

All American Inn, 5755 CY Ave., 307/235-6688, has decent bargain-priced rooms that are popular with smokers: $30 s or $33 d, all with microwaves and small refrigerators. Kitchenettes may also be available. **Sand & Sage Motel,** 901 W. Yellowstone, 307/237-2088, has simple refurbished rooms for $30 s or $50 d; kitchenettes are $40 s or $60 d.

For a few bucks more, stay at the predictable **Motel 6,** 1150 Wilkins Circle, 307/234-3903 or 800/466-8356, www.motel6.com, which also has an outdoor pool. Weekend rates are $42 s or $48 d; Sun.–Thurs. costs $4 less. **First Interstate Inn,** Wyoming Blvd. at I-25, 307/234-9125, www.1stinns.com, charges $45 s or $50 d for older rooms, some with fridges.

Two other good budget places are **Westridge Motel,** 955 CY Ave., 307/234-8911 or 800/356-6268, where rooms are $35–42 s or 39–49 d; and **National 9 Inn Showboat,** 100 W. F St., 307/235-2711 or 866/999-1309, where the cost is $39–46 s or $44–52 d, including a continental breakfast. In addition, the following places are worth a look if you're looking to pinch pennies, although they're mostly used by folks staying by the month: **Bel Air Motel,** 5400 W. Yellowstone, 307/472-1930; **Topper Bob's Motel,** 728 E. A St., 307/266-8407, **Virginian Motel,** 830 E. A St., 307/266-3959; and **Yellowstone Motel,** 1610 E. Yellowstone, 307/234-9174.

$50 and Up

Super 8 Motel, 3838 CY Ave., 307/266-3480 or 888/266-0497, www.super8.com, charges $51 s or $58 d, including a continental breakfast and evening snacks. At **Comfort Inn,** 480 Lathrop Rd., Evansville, 307/235-3038 or 800/228-5150, www.comfortinn.com, you'll find attractive rooms, an indoor pool, hot tub, and light breakfast. Rates are $55–65 s or $60–70 d.

Days Inn, 301 East E St., 307/234-1159 or 888/307-0959, www.daysinn.com, is a well-kept facility with a heated outdoor pool, small exercise room, and a light breakfast. There's even a popcorn machine. Rooms go for $63–68 s or $69–74 d. **Quality Inn & Suites,** 821 N. Poplar, 307/266-2400 or 877/424-6423, www.qualityinn.com, has remodeled rooms for $69–89 s or 75–95 d, including a hot tub, sauna, and light breakfast.

At the large and recently renovated **Holiday Inn,** 300 W. F St., 307/235-2531 or 877/576-8636, www.holiday-inn.com/casperwy, many rooms face the central atrium. The hotel also contains an indoor pool, hot tub, sauna, and fitness center. Rates are $69–109 s or d, including a continental breakfast.

Parkway Plaza Hotel, 123 W. E St., 307/235-

1777 or 800/270-7829, www.parkwayplaza.net, has 287 rooms in a variety of configurations, plus an indoor pool, hot tub, sauna, fitness room, and airport shuttle. Standard rooms are $70 s or $75 d. Two-room suites with microwaves and fridges cost $175–325 d, and a family room with bunk beds and a kitchenette is $125. Also on the grounds is a café, pizzeria, jazz lounge, mini-golf course, video arcade, climbing wall, go-carts, and boat launch. The hotel is right along the Platte River, with a paved path (Platte River Parkway) for evening strolls.

Shilo Inn, 739 Luker Lane, Evansville, 307/237-1335 or 800/222-2244, www.shiloinns .com, features an indoor pool, hot tub, sauna, steam room, hot breakfast buffet, and airport shuttle. Rooms are $70 for one bed or $80 for two beds; fridges and microwaves are also available.

The **Radisson Hotel,** 800 N. Poplar, 307/266-6000 or 800/333-3333, www.radisson.com, is especially popular with business travelers who appreciate the large and modern rooms (many of which open onto the central atrium), big TVs, business desks, meeting rooms, room service, lounge (free appetizers on weekday evenings), restaurants, indoor pool, hot tub, exercise facility, and airport shuttle. Rates are $99 s or d.

Hampton Inn, 400 W. F St., 307/235-6668 or 800/426-7866, www.hamptoninn.com, is another fine place to stay. Rooms cost $94–104 s or $99–109 d, including a continental breakfast and use of a sauna and heated outdoor pool.

Bed-and-Breakfast

The **Ivy House Inn,** 815 S. Ash St., 307/265-0974, www.ivyhouseinn.com, is a 1941 Cape Cod–style home furnished in art deco pieces. Three guest rooms share a bath and rent for $55–75 s or $60–80 d, and two suites with private baths are $105 d. A full breakfast is included, kids are welcome, and a hot tub awaits in the backyard.

CAMPING

The nearest public camping ($5) is in the pines atop Casper Mountain, 10 miles south of Casper and 3,000 feet higher in elevation—

well worth the drive. See Casper Mountain section for details.

The **Fort Caspar Campground,** 307/234-3260 or 888/243-7709, operates year-round on the river just beyond the old fort site and has an outdoor pool. Sites run $14 for tents, $21–23 for RVs.

Casper East KOA, 2800 E. Yellowstone, 307/237-5155 or 800/562-3259, www.koa.com, charges $14–16 for tents. RV sites are $16–22, and basic cabins cost $25–30 d. They're open late February–November and have a heated outdoor pool and indoor hot tub, along with buffalo barbecue dinners in the summer.

Casper North KOA, in Bar Nunn at 1101 W. Prairie Lane, 307/577-1664 or 888/562-4704, www.koa.com, has tent sites for $14–16, RV sites for $16–22, and basic cabins for $25–30 d, including access to an indoor pool and hot tub. Open Apr.–Oct. RVs also park overnight at local shopping mall lots, but you should ask first.

FOOD

Casper has a wide range of dining options that will suit almost any taste, and it shows more diversity every time you visit. All the standard fast-food greasers are here—from Taco Time to Hot Dog on a Stick—but so are some fine-dining establishments.

Breakfast and Lunch

For a home-style, reasonably priced breakfast, visit **TK's Diner,** 5755 CY Ave., 307/266-2027. On the other end of town is the **Red and White Cafe,** 1620 E. Yellowstone, 307/234-6962, a popular greasy spoon. Another local fave for three meals a day is **Johnny J's Diner,** 1705 E. 2nd St., 307/234-4204. It's a modernized nonsmoking version of the classic '50s diner, with gleaming silver sides and a menu that includes 20 kinds of burgers and salads, sandwiches, chicken, and fountain drinks.

During the school year, visitors will find Casper's cheapest lunch eats at the **Casper College cafeteria.** Notable soup, sandwich, and salad places in town are at **Cottage Cafe,** 116 S. Lincoln St., 307/234-1157, and **Cheese Barrel,** 544 S. Center, 307/235-5202 (which also serves good breakfasts).

For the best sub sandwiches, head to **Mountain View Sub Shop,** 239 E. 1st St., 307/237-7999. Create your own sandwiches (and pay by the pound) at the downtown **Sandwich Bar Deli,** 124 E. 2nd St., 307/266-1527. Another downtown eatery with casual meals and a fun setting is **Fajita Cantina,** 208 S. Center St., 307/472-0883, which creates a variety of inspired wraps, plus stuffed potatoes.

A couple of spots serve espresso downtown. **Blue Heron Books & Espresso,** 201 E. 2nd St., 307/265-3774 or 800/585-3774, is a pleasant downtown spot to browse books and enjoy a coffee. Not far away is the classy **Friends & Company,** 2nd at Center Streets, 307/235-5396, with mochas, teas, chai, and smoothies.

Steakhouses

The best local top-carnivore eateries are **Poor Boys Steak House,** in the Parkway Inn at 123 W. E St., 307/235-1777, and **Dorn's Fireside,** 1745 CY Ave., 307/235-6831. In the same vein is **Goose Egg Inn,** nine miles southwest of Casper on State Hwy. 220, 307/473-8838, where prime rib, seafood, and pan-fried chicken are house specialties. Well worth the drive.

Packed with Casperites, **Herbo's,** 4755 W. Yellowstone, 307/266-2293, is one of the local restaurants where big servings win out over quality. **Sedar's Restaurant,** in Sunrise Mall, 4370 S. Poplar, 307/234-6839, serves prime rib, cabbage rolls, lobster, and steak. **Red's Bar-B-Que,** 147 E. 2nd St., 307/261-9908, serves all-you-can-eat BBQ for $10 in a simple setting of checked tablecloths.

Italian and Pizza

Casper has several decent Italian restaurants. The down-home **Bosco's,** 847 E. A St., 307/265-9658, fills with a business crowd on weekday lunches and offers such specialties as veal scallopini, eggplant parmigiana, and chicken piccata.

Botticelli Ristorante Italiano, 129 W. 2nd, 307/266-2700, is one of a small chain of Northern Italian restaurants, with decent food (including paninis, pastas, and pizza) in a pleasantly romantic setting.

If you're looking for good pizza in Casper, try **Barry's Italian Pizzaria** at the Parkway Plaza Hotel, 123 W. E St., 307/237-8523, or one of the chains such as Godfather's, Little Caesars, Papa John's, or Pizza Hut.

Mexican

El Jarro's, 500 W. F St., 307/577-0538, serves up low prices, big margaritas, crispy chips, tangy salsa, and mass quantities of food, but this is Americanized Mexican food. More critical locals call El Jarro's "El Horrible's."

Get more authentic Mexican fare at **La Cocina,** 1040 N. Center St., 307/266-1414. Everything is freshly made, including the hand-rolled tortillas. Also of note is **La Costa,** 1600 E. 2nd St., 307/235-6599, a classy little place with Tex-Mex fare. If you're just looking for a quick and tasty burrito, drop by **Fajita Cantina,** 208 S. Center St., 307/472-0883. For make-it-yourself meals, get south-of-the-border groceries at **Little Mexico,** 138 S. Kimball, 307/268-8580.

Chinese

A real surprise in Casper is the large number of Asian restaurants that dot the town—seven places at last count. The food has suffered a bit from Americanization, but several of these places are quite good. **South Sea Chinese Restaurant,** 2025 E. 2nd, 307/237-4777, offers authentic fare. Also good is **Peking Chinese Restaurant,** 333 E. A, 307/266-2207. **China Buffet,** 4005 CY Ave., 307/237-8911, has a big Asian buffet for lunch and dinner.

Pubs

Located in the heart of town, **The Cattleman's Club,** 256 S. Center St. 307/472-7837, is a big place with a diverse menu of burgers, Rocky Mountain oysters, pasta, sandwiches, and salads, plus Friday and Saturday seafood specials. It's the only entirely nonsmoking bar in Casper. Directly across the street is another bustling beerhouse, **Sanford's Grub & Pub,** 307/234-4555. This cluttered pub is part of a small chain; others are in Sheridan, Gillette, and Cheyenne, along

with Spearfish, South Dakota. On the menu you'll find dozens of sandwiches, all the standard bar appetizers (along with some that aren't so standard such as gizzards and fried pickle spears), burgers, salads, pasta, and more.

Bakeries

First Street Bakers, 260 W. 1st St., 307/472-0255, bakes bagels, breads, and sweets, including enormous cinnamon buns. The shop also sells freshly made pasta. **Casper Cake and Donut,** 604 E. 2nd, 307/234-1180, is another good bakery and has an additional shop in Eastridge Mall. For the authentic Continental variety (the owner is French), head to **Delices de France,** 845 E. 2nd St., 307/237-6614. In addition to fresh croissants, breads, and sweets, the shop offers a lunch menu of quiches, soups, and sandwiches.

Groceries and Produce

Casper has several giant grocery stores scattered across the city, including Albertson's, Safeway, Smith's, and Wal-Mart SuperCenter; all have in-store bakeries and delis. If you're looking for fresh produce, be sure to check out the **farmers market** at the fairgrounds every Saturday morning during the summer. **Alpenglow Natural Foods,** 109 E. 2nd St., 307/234-4156, is a good downtown spot for natural fare.

ENTERTAINMENT
Nightlife

See the *Casper Star-Tribune* for the latest on local nightlife. The biggest and best-known place for live music Tuesday–Saturday is the **Beacon Club,** 4100 W. Yellowstone Hwy., 307/577-1503, with country or rock tunes and a fun, trendy crowd. The **Avalon Club,** 260 E. Yellowstone Hwy., 307/473-7544, has Western dance bands most nights, plus a night of Karaoke for Britney Spears wanna-bes. **Club Dance West,** 225 N. Wolcott, 307/234-8811, delivers country music upstairs and rock or rap downstairs; open Friday and Saturday nights. Find live bands most weekends at **Cowboy Saloon and Dance Hall,** on the west side of town at 1910 Talc Rd., 307/234-7476. One of the newer clubs, **Club X,** 759 CY Ave.,

307/473-1901, attracts rock bands from outside the area. **All that Jazz** offers live jazz inside the Parkway Plaza Hotel, 123 W. E St., 307/235-1777 or 800/270-7829, www.parkwayplaza.net.

The Arts

The state's only professional orchestra, the **Wyoming Symphony Orchestra,** 307/266-1478, www.wyomingsymphony.com, presents eight performances September–May at the high school auditorium, 930 S. Elm Street. During the summer, the **Casper Municipal Band** plays free concerts on Thursday nights at 7 P.M. in Washington Park.

Stage III Community Theatre, 904 N. Center St., 307/234-0946, puts on plays on weekends throughout the year. More actors can be found on stage at Casper College's 465-seat **Gertrude Krampert Theatre,** 307/268-2500, www.caspercollege.edu. In the summer, the theater is home to musicals, dance performances, and comedies. Also on campus are free recitals scheduled by the Casper College Music Department; call 307/268-2606. Contact **Artcore,** 307/265-1564, for tickets to upcoming concerts, literary events, and theatrical productions in Casper.

The **Casper Troopers Drum and Bugle Corps**—one of the finest in the nation—often performs around Wyoming during June before heading out on tour. In existence since 1957, the corps struts their stuff at sporting events and parades around the nation, including the past Tournament of Roses and presidential inaugural parades. Get details at 307/472-2141, www.troopersdrumcorps.org.

Movies

Casper's downtown movie theaters—**Rialto Theatre,** 100 E. 2nd St., 307/237-2416; and **America Theatre,** 119 S. Center, 307/235-5440—have some of the cheapest flick-viewing to be found. The movies are generally a few months old, but it's hard to complain when admission is only $3. For first-run movies, head to **Fox III Movie Palace,** 150 W. 2nd St., 307/235-0900, or the **Iris Stadium 8 Movie Theater,** just west of the Fox at 230

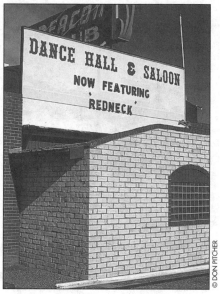

The sign says it all.

W. Yellowstone, 307/472-4747. The Iris features stadium seating. All of these can be found on the web at www.wyomovies.com.

EVENTS

Casper features a multitude of enjoyable events throughout summer, so there's bound to be something going on when you visit. Find a complete listing of upcoming events at www.casper-wyoming.info.

The **Cowboy State Games,** 307/577-1125, www.trib.com/~csg, is an Olympic-style festival that encompasses all sorts of contests, including boxing, basketball, indoor archery, equestrian, snowboarding, volleyball, alpine and Nordic skiing, ice hockey, sport climbing, diving, tennis, and many other events. Events take place over several weekends in February.

On the third weekend of June the **Frontier Festival** brings dozens of costumed mountain men, women, and Indians to old Fort Caspar. See Crimson Dawn Museum in the Casper Mountain section for the year's most unusual event, **Midsummer's Eve** atop Casper Mountain during the summer solstice (June 21).

Casper is home to the **College National Finals Rodeo** in mid-June 2003. This event attracts 350 of the best young cowboys and cowgirls from all over the nation with a full range of events. Details and tickets at 800/442-2256, www.cnfr.com. (It will be held in Gillette during 2004 and 2005, but may return to Casper after that.)

All summer long, you'll find stock car racing and demolition derbies every weekend at **Casper Speedway,** 2201 East Rd., 307/472-7223.

Casperites kick up their heels at the city's biggest annual event, the **Central Wyoming Fair and Rodeo** the second week of July; www.centralwyomingfair.com. The various arts-and-crafts displays, farm animals, rodeos, a demolition derby, and midway attract thousands of locals and visitors. Rodeo festivities include a downtown parade, all the standard rodeo events, and clown "bullfighting."

Up on Casper Mountain the **Beartrap Summer Festival,** 307/235-9325, www.beartrapfestival.com, brings folk, jazz, country, and blues, and even classical music during mid-July. For a glimpse of the city's past, come to Fort Caspar for the **Platte Bridge Encampment** the fourth weekend of July. It includes period fashion shows, living-history demonstrations, and military drills.

In early September, the **Downtown Arts Festival** displays arts and crafts, food, and entertainment. Also in September is **Brewfest,** held on the Platte River Parkway. The Nicolaysen Art Museum has an **Arts and Crafts Festival** on the first weekend of November with more than 75 artisans exhibiting their wares. It's a good place to shop early for Christmas.

SPORTS AND RECREATION

The fine **Casper Recreation Center,** 1801 E. 4th St., 307/235-8383, www.cityofcasperwy.com, provides racquetball and volleyball courts, a weight room, a gym, and a game room. Admission is $2. Next door is **Casper Ice Arena,** 307/235-8484, with skating August–April. Wyoming's largest roller-skating

palace, **Wagon Wheel Roller Skating,** is in Mills at 305 Vanhorn Ave., 307/265-4214.

Biking and Climbing

Mountain bikers will find many miles of roads and trails on the Casper and Muddy Mountains south of town. For maps and info, contact **Backcountry Mountain Works,** 4120 S. Poplar (Sunrise Center), 307/234-5330. Unfortunately, these maps do not show the land ownership status, so you need to make sure you're riding on public land. The BLM's maps show land ownership but don't have trails marked. Rent bikes on Casper Mountain at Elkhorn Canyon Cafe, 307/473-8707.

The Peak, 408 N. Beverly St., 307/472-4084, has a big indoor climbing wall, with climbing shoes and harnesses available for rent.

Horse and Wagon Trips

Looking for a taste of the Old West? **Historic Trails West** leads various Conestoga wagon and horseback rides—from three hours to five days long—along the Oregon Trail. All of these trips include guided tours of Fort Casper and plenty of historical stories. The three-hour trips (with lunch) are $35 adults, $25 kids; overnight rides are $85 adults, $65 kids. A three-day wagon ride costs $595 adults ($695 on horseback) and includes all meals and teepees; bring your own sleeping bag. Five-day rides are $895 adults, or $995 if you ride a horse. These trips are about as authentic as you can get. Get details at 307/266-4868 or 800/327-4052, www.historictrailswest.com.

Water Recreation

If you're looking for a little water activity, check out one of Casper's half dozen **swimming pools.** Five summer-only outdoor pools, 307/235-8403, www.cityofcasperwy.com, are scattered throughout the city. The Paradise Valley pool, 5200 W. Iris, also has a popular corkscrew water slide. Indoor pools can be found at Kelly Walsh High School and the YMCA, 315 E. 15th, 307/234-9187. Trivia note: Casper's high school was the first in the nation to have an indoor swimming pool, built in 1929.

The **North Platte River** flows right through the city of Casper, providing both the city's drinking water and a variety of recreational opportunities. The Platte's slow current and shallow depth—just 2–4 feet in most places—make for a gentle and scenic float trip with plenty of wildlife along the way: beaver, muskrats, ducks, geese, hawks, eagles, mule deer, and antelope. For a map and brochure describing public landings, camping, and parking areas along the 60-mile stretch of the Platte between Alcova Reservoir and Glenrock, contact the Bureau of Land Management, 2987 Prospector Dr., 307/261-7600, www.wy.blm.gov. The **Platte River Trust Whitewater Park,** covers a half-mile stretch of the river in Casper, with boulders and other obstacles for kayakers.

Wyoming River Runners, 307/267-0170, offers guided fishing and float trips, plus canoe and raft rentals. Fishing is excellent for both German brown and rainbow trout; locals call the North Platte one of the West's largest and finest trout fisheries. See the chamber of commerce for a listing of other local fishing guides. Two good fishing shops are **Ugly Bug Fly Shop,** 316 W. Midwest Ave., 307/234-6905, and **Platte River Fly Shop,** 5033 Alcova Hwy., 307/265-6152, www.wyomingflyfishing.com. **Lone Tree Drift Boat Rental,** 307/234-9661, rents drift boats to float the river. They're located 27 miles south of Casper and seven miles from Alcova. See Edness Kimball Wilkins State Park for more on-water recreation.

Casper is one of the nation's windiest cities; winds averaging 13 mph make this a great place for kite flying, hang-gliding, and sailboarding. Pathfinder and Alcova Reservoirs are both popular sailboarding spots.

Golf

Golfers will have fun at the 18-hole **Casper Municipal Golf Course,** 2120 Allendale Blvd., 307/234-2405, www.cityofcasperwy.com. A brand new 18-hole course, the Three Crowns Golf Course (designed by Robert Trent Jones II), opens on the site of the old Amoco refinery in 2004. For the kid-size version, check out **Old Town Mini Golf** at Parkway Plaza Hotel, 123 W. E St.,

307/235-1777 or 800/270-7829, www.parkwayplaza.net. Also here is a go-cart course, climbing wall, and video arcade.

Sporting Events

An affiliate of the Colorado Rockies, the **Casper Rockies,** 307/265-7867, www.casperrockies.com, play minor-league professional ball at the Mike Lansing Baseball Field on the north side of town.

Watch the state's only arena football team, the **Wyoming Cavalry,** 307/577-3030 or 800/442-2256, www.wyomingcavalry.com, play at the Casper Events Center March–June.

SHOPPING

Casper is Wyoming's version of shop-'til-your-car-dies. Sprawling suburbia, fast food, and a half dozen park-anywhere malls combine to make Casper indistinguishable from Modesto, California, or Columbus, Ohio. This is the sort of place where even the Highland Park Community Church is housed in what looks like an old Kmart store. At Wyoming Blvd. and E. 2nd St., **Eastridge Mall** (www.shopeastridge.com) is Wyoming's largest, with 90 stores, including Bon Marché, Sears, JCPenney, and Target. If Norman Rockwell were alive today, he would be painting the high-school girls eyeing the hunks on parade and the over-60, post–heart-attack crowd doing their fast walks around the mall. A Wal-Mart and Sam's Club are right across the street from Eastridge.

Okay, so not all of Casper's stores are in shopping malls. Downtown is the impressive **Lou Taubert Ranch Outfitters,** 125 E. 2nd St., 307/234-2500 or 800/447-9378, a four-floor department store with everything from cowboy boots (10,000 pairs in stock!) to classy gifts. It's a great place to try on a new cowboy hat or shop for fashionable clothing in one of the biggest Western shops anywhere. **Sauders Camera,** 138 S. Kimball, 307/235-6523, is a first-rate camera shop a few blocks away.

Outdoor Supplies

Mountain Sports, 543 S. Center, 307/266-1136 or 800/426-1136, sells quality outdoor gear and rents windsurfers, downhill and cross-country skis, and inline skates. While you're there, take a look at the various rock-climbing maps and books. **Beaver Lodge Rentals,** 2419 Nuclear Dr., 307/234-0644, rents RVs, camping trailers, and canoes. Also check out **The Peak,** 408 N. Beverly St., 307/472-4084, for rock-climbing equipment.

Bookstores

Several places sell new books in Casper. Among them are **Blue Heron Books & Espresso,** 201 E. 2nd St., 307/265-3774 or 800/585-3774; **B. Dalton,** in Eastridge Mall, 307/247-0793, www.barnesandnoble.com; **Waldenbooks,** also in Eastridge Mall, 307/235-2046, www.waldenbooks.com; **Ralph's Books,** at Hilltop Shopping Center, 307/234-0308; and **Westerner Newsstand,** 245 S. Center, 307/235-1022. **Book Exchange,** 323 S. Center St., 307/237-6034, offers Wyoming's largest selection of used books and is a great place to browse.

INFORMATION AND SERVICES

The friendly **Casper Area Chamber of Commerce Visitor Center,** 500 N. Center, 307/234-5311, www.casperwyoming.org, is the place to go for tourist paraphernalia. It's open daily 8 A.M.–6 P.M. in summer, and until 5 P.M. the rest of the year. Contact the **Casper Area Convention & Visitors Bureau,** 307/234-5362 or 800/852-1889, www.casperwyoming.info, for information on Casper before your trip. The **BLM's Casper Field Office** is at 2987 Prospector Dr., 307/261-7600, www.wy.blm.gov.

Check your email or surf the web on computers at the **Natrona County Library,** 307 E. 2nd, 307/237-4935, www.library.natrona.net; open daily. The **post office** is located at 411 N. Forest Dr., 307/266-4000.

Local laundromats include **Clay Street Laundry,** N. 2nd at Clay Streets, 307/358-8085; **Hilltop Laundromat,** 2513 E. 3rd St., 307/234-7331; and **Millview Laundromat** at Millview Shopping Center, 307/472-0117.

The **Wyoming Medical Center,** 1233 E. 2nd St., 307/577-7201 or 800/822-7201,

www.wmcnet.org, is one of the largest hospitals in the state, with strong programs in heart care and cancer treatment. It also has the only hyperbaric oxygen center in Wyoming. For walk-in medical needs, try **Instacare,** 900 CY Ave., 307/237-2273.

The *Casper Star-Tribune* is Wyoming's only statewide paper, and their website, www.trib.com, has regional news stories and classified ads for all the world to see.

TRANSPORTATION AND TOURS

Airlines

Natrona County Airport is eight miles northwest of Casper on U.S. Hwy. 20/26. **Delta/Sky West** has daily service to Salt Lake City, and **Great Lakes Aviation,** has commuter flights to Denver. **Big Sky Airlines,** has daily service between Billings and Casper. See the "Airline Contacts" Special Topic in the On the Road chapter.

Wyoming's largest air charter company, **Bighorn Airways,** 307/235-1212, www.bighornairways.com, provides charter flights throughout the region.

Bus Service and Tours

Powder River Transportation/Coach USA, 123 W. E St. in the Parkway Plaza Hotel, room 1159, 307/266-1904 or 800/442-3682, has daily bus service between Casper and towns in eastern and northern Wyoming, continuing north to Billings, west to Cody, east to Rapid City, and south to Cheyenne and Denver.

Adventure West Tours, 307/577-1226, www.usatouring.com, offers customized historical van tours of the area.

Rental Cars and Taxis

Rent cars locally from **Around Town Rent-A-Car,** 307/265-5667, or **Foss Toyota,** 307/237-3700. National rental car chains include Avis, Budget, Enterprise, or Hertz. See the Special Topic "Rental Car Contacts" in the On the Road chapter.

Call **RC Cab,** 307/235-5203, for local taxi service.

Casper Vicinity

CASPER MOUNTAIN

Scenic mountain country is just a hop, skip, and a drive away from Casper. When the thermometer tops 100°F, Casperites escape to the cool mountains just a 15-minute drive from town. Snow often lingers here until July. Rotary Park, seven miles south of Casper on S. Poplar Street (State Hwy. 252), has several official and unofficial trails that climb the steep canyon cut by Garden Creek. The creek drops 50 feet over **Garden Creek Falls,** one of the few waterfalls in this part of Wyoming. A viewpoint is just a short distance up the trail, or you can cross the bridge and follow a second path (actually a maze of routes) to the top of the falls, one mile up. Other trails head out to a ridge offering views of the surrounding country.

The steep, winding drive up Casper Mountain has turnouts offering panoramas that stretch all the way to the Big Horn Mountains 125 miles north. Casper Mountain's flattened 8,100-foot-summit is carpeted by ponderosa pine trees and pleasant grassy meadows. **Elkhorn Canyon Cafe,** 307/473-8707, serves meals and has mountain-bike rentals near the entrance to Hogadon Ski Area.

Camping

Several county parks—Casper Mountain, Crimson Dawn, Beartrap Meadow, and Ponderosa—are very popular getaways where deer and elk are found. The four **campgrounds** (307/235-9325) on Casper Mountain cost $5 per night; all are open Memorial Day to mid-October. Water is available only at Beartrap Campground (the nicest) and Casper Mountain Campground. Red Valley separates Casper Mountain from its neighbor five miles to the south, **Muddy Mountain.** The gravel road climbs up Muddy Mountain, where the BLM, 307/261-7500, www.wy.blm.gov, maintains **Rim Campground** and **Lodgepole Campground,** both of which cost $5 and are open mid-June to late November. Also atop Muddy Mountain is a self-guided nature trail and other scenic paths. For more information on the various Casper Mountain

Casper Mountain

© DON PITCHER

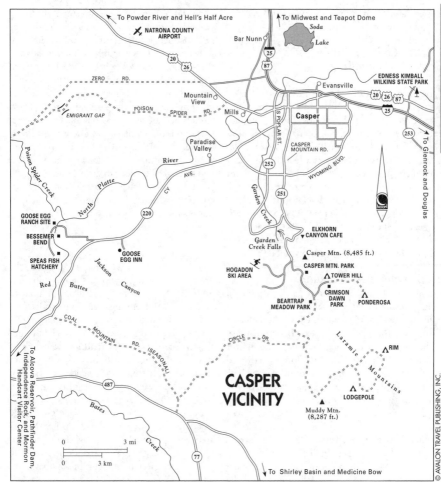

parks, call 307/234-6821. The short **Lee Mc-Cune Braille Trail** has 39 plaques describing the natural world in Braille and English. Nearby is a summer camp for the blind.

Hogadon Ski Area

First opened in 1959, the city-run Hogadon Ski Area is nine miles south of Casper near the top of the mountain. A family area, it includes hills ranging from the easiest bunny slope to black diamonds. Eleven different runs (and a boarders' terrain park) are fed by two chairlifts and a Poma lift, with a vertical rise of 600 feet. Ski and snowboard rentals and lessons are available, and there's a cafeteria. Lift tickets cost $25 adults, $21 ages 12–18, $16 ages 5–11; free for younger kids. Half-day rates are $19 for all age groups, and a Poma-only ticket costs $10. Hogadon is open Wednesday–Sunday 9 A.M.–4 P.M. from Thanksgiving to early April.

Get details and snow conditions at 307/235-8499, www.cityofcasperwy.com.

Cross-Country Skiing and Snowmobiling

Casper Mountain often has surprisingly good powder conditions. **Natrona County Parks,** 307/235-9311, www.caspernordic.com, maintains 15 miles of groomed cross-country ski trails ($5) and a warming hut. Some trails are lit at night. In addition, you'll find extensive undeveloped areas where more adventurous backcountry skiers can practice telemarking. Rent cross-country skis from **Mountain Sports,** 543 S. Center, 307/266-1136; **Backcountry Mountain Works,** 4120 S. Poplar, 307/234-5330; or **Dean's Sporting Goods,** 260 S. Center, 307/234-2788. Casper Mountain also has more than 60 miles of groomed snowmobile trails.

Crimson Dawn Museum

This evocative place lies atop Casper Mountain, 12 miles south of Casper along State Hwy. 251; follow the signs to Crimson Dawn. As the name suggests, this place is best experienced early in the morning or at sunset, when the crimson light brushes across the ochre-colored earth and streams into the dark green forests. Come here alone to really feel the magic that captivated Neal Forsling more than 70 years ago. After growing up in Independence, Missouri—and nearly marrying Harry Truman—she headed west to Casper. There Neal married a lawyer, but a bitter divorce sent her fleeing to then-remote Casper Mountain with her two children, looking to start anew as a homesteader. She quickly fell in love with the country and later fell in love with local rancher Jim Forsling. They were married and settled into a fiercely independent life without electricity or running water and with but a few neighbors. The idyll was broken one bitterly cold winter day when Jim was skiing back from town with a backpack filled with supplies. Caught in a blizzard, he froze to death just a few miles from the cabin. He was 38 years old.

Neal adjusted to the loss by turning inward to grasp the spirit of the land, by painting out her emotions, and by opening outward to her own

and neighboring children with stories. Over the years these grew into a complex series of fairy tales that detailed the good and evil witches, leprechauns, and trolls who inhabit these woods and fields. Midsummers' Eve was a special time when children and adults could enter this magical spirit world through her storytelling. In 1973, Neal Forsling gave her land and cabin to Natrona County for use as a park. She died a few years later and is buried nearby, but her extraordinary love for the earth is revealed in the small cabin, mystical paintings, fairy tales, and the trails that lead through the woods to shrines celebrating the good witches, magical creatures, and witty forest spirits who haunt this land. Neal's philosophy is summed up by a sign in her cabin:

> *What I had, I lost*
> *What I saved, I spent*
> *What I gave, I have.*

Today, her old log home is a small museum, 307/235-1303, open Saturday–Thursday 10 A.M.–7 P.M. from mid-June to mid-October.

Inside the cabin are several of Forsling's somewhat crude paintings, seemingly inspired by both Vincent van Gogh and Grandma Moses, which reveal her mystical sensibilities. A framed letter from Missouri childhood friend Bess Truman hangs on one wall. You may want to purchase a copy of *Crimson Dawn,* a collection of Forsling's tales. And be sure to wander along the nearby woodland trails to enjoy the 20 shrines she created (my personal favorite is Sean the leprechaun). The graves of Jim and Neal Forsling overlook the green mountains. His epithet reads:

> *In this red earth I loved so well*
> *Where I worked and made my home*
> *I am glad my body can rest at last*
> *In this place I loved so well.*
> *But my soul is free to climb*
> *up through the sky's blue arch*
> *free to explore those far away peaks*
> *that once my eyes looked on.*
> *For any land that a man has looked on,*
> *and worked and claimed for his own*
> *Part of that man will always remain*
> *as long as the wind will blow.*

On **Midsummer's Eve** (June 21), be sure to visit Crimson Dawn for a wonderfully mystical celebration of Casper Mountain's witches and spirits. The celebration has gone on every year since 1929. Visitors get to meet the local denizens in person and are invited to throw handfuls of the dark red earth into the bonfire; if it burns, your wish will come true. Hundreds of Casperites will also be there to celebrate, along with a handful of pompous protesters from Sonlight Ministries.

BESSEMER BEND

The bucolic Bessemer Bend area—10 miles southwest of Casper along State Hwy. 220—abounds in history, both real and imagined. A lazy curve in the North Platte River, Bessemer Bend was an important 19th-century crossing point for wagon trains. Rock walls from a shelter built in 1812 by the Astorians are still visible on a knoll overlooking the river. Between 1860 and 1861, the Red Butte Pony Express station stood at the river bend, site of the longest of all Pony Express rides, a 320-mile gallop by Buffalo Bill Cody that lasted a grueling 21 hours and 40 minutes. The nearby Red Buttes were also where Custard's Wagon Train Fight took place (described under History in the Casper section). Bessemer City sprang up along the bend in 1888, calling itself "Queen City of the Plains." It lasted only a couple of years, and when Casper was voted the Natrona County seat, Bessemer City quietly faded away. Many of its buildings were moved to Casper, and today Bessemer City is just a field of alfalfa.

Along the east side of the North Platte River at Bessemer Bend is the site of the famed **Goose Egg Ranch,** once one of Wyoming's largest cattle spreads. In *The Virginian,* Owen Wister used Goose Egg Ranch for a memorable scene in which two drunken cowboys switch blankets on a dozen babies while their parents are dancing, creating havoc when the ranch families drive home with the wrong children. Owned for many years by the Carey family—both father Joseph M. Carey and son Robert Carey served as governor and U.S. senator—it was later renamed the CY Ranch. The southern half of Casper is built on what was once CY land—hence CY Avenue, one of the city's main thoroughfares. Ironically, the old Goose Egg ranch house died partly because of the fame brought to it in *The Virginian.* The abandoned stone buildings gradually deteriorated as tourists chipped away for mementos. Fearing that the buildings might collapse, the owners finally tore down the ranch in 1951. John Wayne's oil-field firefighter movie, *Hellfighters,* was filmed not far away in 1968.

Today folks come to Bessemer Bend to enjoy a steak at Goose Egg Inn or to watch wintering golden and bald eagles in nearby Jackson Canyon—named for famed Yellowstone photographer William H. Jackson. Another five miles down State Hwy. 220 is **Dan Speas Fish Hatchery,** 307/473-8890, Wyoming's largest trout-rearing facility. The hatchery produces more than three million rainbow, brown, and cutthroat trout annually. It's open daily 8 A.M.–5 P.M. year-round.

Wyoming's Lake District

The 655-mile-long North Platte River rises in Colorado, heads north into Wyoming, and then curves a long lazy loop to the east, cutting across western Nebraska and finally joining the South Platte River near the city of North Platte. The entire basin covers 32,000 square miles and in Wyoming is fed by the Sweetwater, Medicine Bow, and Laramie Rivers. The name "Platte" is French for "Broad"; Indians called the river "Nebraska," meaning "flat." Both are appropriate titles along much of the river's path. Cottonwood trees line the banks, and the river offers an essential watering hole for wildlife. (Early settlers in Wyoming called the Platte "a mile wide and an inch deep" and "too thick to drink and too thin to plow.")

Once one of the most impressive rivers in the Plains states—at flood stage it ran 150 yards wide and 10–15 feet deep—the North Platte has been reduced to little more than a creek through much of Wyoming. Near Fort Laramie, where wagon trains in the 1850s found a treacherous crossing, the river today sometimes ceases to flow at all, lying in shallow puddles in the late summer sun. A look at the map makes it obvious what has happened to the water: Agriculture has siphoned it all away.

RECLAMATION

Without irrigation, farming was difficult or impossible in much of the arid West, and the thousands of homesteaders who tried to survive on 640 acres soon saw their hopes and dreams fizzle in the withering summer heat. Irrigation seemed natural for these desert lands. John Wesley Powell's idea of arid lands reclamation through dams and irrigation canals gradually gained favor, and by the 1890s Wyoming's politicians were claiming that irrigation could turn 12–15 million acres of the state into productive farmland. The Carey Act—named for Wyoming's Sen. Joseph M. Carey—tested these claims by having the federal government donate land to the states to be reclaimed by settlers. Wyoming became the first state to try out the new law, but only 10 percent

of the two million acres in the program were finally patented. The costs were simply too high and the return too low; funding for the massive dams and irrigation canals could only come from the federal government. The Reclamation Act of 1902 was designed to do just that.

When Reclamation Act money started flowing, the North Platte was one of the first to be dammed (or damned, depending on one's perspective). It seemed a potential godsend for farmers who had long used waterwheels to lift water from the river into adjacent irrigation ditches. Today, eight giant dams hold back the river and its tributaries in Wyoming: the Seminoe, Kortes, Pathfinder, Alcova, and Gray Reef above the city of Casper, and the

WYOMING'S LAKE DISTRICT

© AVALON TRAVEL PUBLISHING, INC.

Glendo, Guernsey, and Grayrocks farther downstream. Two long irrigation canals—the Interstate Canal and the Fort Laramie Canal—supply water to farms east of Wheatland. Ironically, nearly 80 percent of the water behind Wyoming dams on the North Platte goes to fields in neighboring Nebraska. This is also true at most of the other large reclamation projects in Wyoming: Bighorn Canyon water goes to Montana, Keyhole Reservoir water to South Dakota, Jackson Lake water to Idaho, and Flaming Gorge water to Utah. Meanwhile, more than 100,000 acres of once-valuable farming and grazing land in Wyoming lie under these massive reservoirs. Wyoming, one of the driest states in the nation, has become an exporter of huge quantities of water to surrounding states.

SEMINOE RESERVOIR

The 295-foot-high concrete arch Seminoe Dam was completed in 1939 and is the farthest upstream of the North Platte River dams. It holds back more than one million acre-feet of water, which drives a power plant that produces 45 megawatts of electricity. The reservoir is bounded by 3,821-acre **Seminoe State Park,** 307/320-3013, http://wyoparks.state.wy.us, named for the nearby Seminoe Mountains, which in turn were named after the French trapper Basil Cimineau Lajeunesse—folks apparently had a hard time spelling his middle name. Day use of the park costs $4 for nonresident vehicles, $2 if you're driving a Wyoming vehicle.

The reservoir stretches almost 20 miles south of the dam through desolate, rocky mountains and gigantic dunes of white sand. Sandy beaches along the shoreline attract swimmers in late summer. Juniper and ponderosa pine trees dot the hills, while sagebrush, greasewood, yucca, and salt sage grow on the lower slopes. The steep 500-foot knife-edge of Horseshoe Ridge is visible on the eastern shore. Golden eagles nest along the southern arm of Seminoe Reservoir, and bighorn sheep and elk have been reintroduced. The area also abounds with sage grouse.

Practicalities

Seminoe has two state park **campgrounds** ($12 for nonresidents or $6 for Wyoming residents, open mid-Apr. to mid-Oct.) along its northwest shore. Water, toilets, and boat ramps are available at each. You can also camp for free on Bureau of Reclamation sand dunes along the lake's southern arm. The reservoir is popular for fishing (rainbow, brown, and cutthroat trout, and walleye) and water-skiing. Gas and limited provisions are available at private **Seminoe Boat Club,** 307/320-3043. Access from Rawlins and Sinclair to the western shore of Seminoe is relatively easy via a 34-mile-long paved road, but the 70 miles of mixed pavement and gravel from Casper are a bit harder to take. The eastern shore is even less accessible.

An overlook at the dam site provides views into the steep rocky canyon and the dam that spans the chasm. North of this point, the road drops steeply into the canyon and then climbs up through Morgan Creek Canyon, where big ponderosa pines, willows, and cottonwoods line the creek. A few miles beyond this site, the road descends over a pass and then down through Hamilton Creek Canyon, finally emerging into open sagebrush country near the **Miracle Mile** of the North Platte River. You'll find free camping among the cottonwoods that line the riverbank and excellent trout fishing. More free camping is at Sage Creek Road, one-half mile north of the river crossing. The name Miracle Mile—actually three miles of free-flowing river—refers to this popular "blue ribbon" fishery, maintained by regulated flows from the 244-foot-high **Kortes Dam** power plant just upstream. In reality, the miracle is that any stretch of the North Platte still has anything resembling natural flows.

PATHFINDER RESERVOIR

Pathfinder Reservoir is 30 miles southwest of Casper on State Hwy. 220 and then another 10 miles in along County Rd. 409. In 1905, the federal government provided funds for this dam, the first in eastern Wyoming, to be built near the junction of the Sweetwater and North Platte Rivers. Proponents claimed that the reservoir

© DON PITCHER

The West Platte River runs near Pathfinder Reservoir.

would irrigate more than 700,000 acres, primarily in Wyoming, but instead, only 130,000 acres were irrigated, nearly all in Nebraska.

Completed in 1909, Pathfinder Dam is considered an engineering marvel for its time and is listed on the National Register of Historic Places. The 214-foot-high arched structure is made up of large granite blocks quarried from adjacent hills and held together with cement and steel hauled by wagon teams from Casper, 45 miles away. (The trip sometimes took three weeks.)

Pathfinder is named for explorer John C. Frémont, "Pathfinder of the West." In 1842 he ventured down the river and—against the advice of his guides—decided to run the canyon below the present dam site (now Fremont Canyon). He and his men narrowly escaped alive, as Frémont described:

To go back was impossible; the torrent before us was a sheet of foam; and, shut up in the chasm by the rocks, which in some places seemed to almost meet overhead, the roar of the waters was deafening . . . the boat struck a concealed rock immediately at the foot of the fall, which whirled her over in an instant. . . . For a hundred yards below, the current was covered with floating books and boxes, bales of blankets, and scattered articles of clothing. . . . For a mo-

ment, I felt somewhat disheartened. All our books—almost every record of the journey—our journals and registers of astronomical and barometrical observations—had been lost in a moment.

Practicalities

Pathfinder Reservoir splits into two arms, following the upstream path of the Sweetwater and North Platte Rivers. **Pathfinder National Wildlife Refuge** covers 16,807 acres of land around scattered parts of the reservoir and is home to many mammals and birds. Canada geese nest along the shore, and white pelicans nest on an island here. **Camping** is available at four campgrounds on the east shore of Pathfinder Reservoir ($5; open Memorial Day to mid-Oct.; 307/235-9325), or you can camp for free along much of the lake's hundred-mile shore (except within the refuge). The deep-blue lake is a popular place for anglers in search of cutthroat, brown, and rainbow trout, or walleye. Sailboarders find some of Wyoming's finest sailing conditions. **Pathfinder Marina** has rental boats, fishing gear, gas, and a snack bar.

Not far from the dam is an old stone building that once housed the dam tender but is today used as the **Pathfinder Interpretive Center,** 307/261-5628. Summer hours are Saturday 11 A.M.–5 P.M. and Sunday 10 A.M.–4 P.M.; ask at the adjacent frame house for a peek inside at other times. A pleasant 1.5-mile loop trail crosses the dam, follows Fremont Canyon (lined with hundreds of cliff-swallow nests), and then re-crosses the river over an impressive swinging footbridge before returning to the interpretive center. The interpretive center has a brochure describing sights along the path.

The Lynching of Cattle Kate

Deep beneath the waters of Pathfinder Reservoir lies the site of one of the most infamous Wyoming lynchings. In 1889, James Averell and Ella "Cattle Kate" Watson operated a ranch here. Local cattle barons accused Averell of housing rustlers and operating a saloon and gambling house for them, with Cattle Kate running a sideline business in which cattle were exchanged for "personal favors." The charges were apparently a smoke screen put up by A. J. Bothwell and other large landowners who were angry that Averell and Watson had filed homestead claims on land being grazed by Bothwell's cattle. When Averell had the temerity to call the cattle barons "land sharks" in a letter to the Casper newspaper, they responded by sending a party out to eliminate the two. Averell and Watson were found hanging from a tree along the Sweetwater River. Later, the six men who perpetrated the hanging escaped prosecution when the chief witness suddenly disappeared—apparently murdered by one of the lynching party. Bothwell went on to gain title to Averell and Watson's land, despite national newspaper complaints about "the barbaric lynching of a woman in Wyoming Territory."

ALCOVA RESERVOIR

Although much smaller than Pathfinder or Seminoe Reservoirs, Alcova is a favorite recreation spot for the people of Casper. Sailboarding, sailing, water-skiing, and ice fishing are all popular sports on this windy lake 30 miles southwest of Casper. The upper portion of the reservoir reaches into famed **Fremont Canyon,** a mini-Grand Canyon whose red vertical cliffs rise 500 feet above the river. Access is via dirt roads from both sides. The water makes for exciting river-running if you have a kayak and the necessary skills.

Golden eagles nest here. It's also very popular with rock climbers. You'll find dozens of climbs here, up to a rating of 5.13. For details, stop by Mountain Sports in Casper for a copy of Steve Petro's *Climber's Guide to Fremont Canyon and Dome Rock.* A good place to watch climbers is the Fremont Canyon bridge. Anglers try their luck with the rainbow and cutthroat trout and walleye.

The name Alcova comes from **Alcova Hot Springs** (129°F water), so named because of its location within a series of coves. At the turn of the 20th century, developers tried to turn the hot springs into a spa, but the propensity of Wyomingites to take baths but once a week made the venture a failure. The springs were covered by the reservoir, but an artesian well below the dam pours forth the naturally heated water. Bring your swimsuit!

Practicalities

The 265-foot-high Alcova Dam, part of the depression-era Kendrick Project, was completed in 1938; a 36-megawatt power plant was added in the 1980s. Facilities here include picnic areas, swimming beaches, five summertime campgrounds ($5), and an RV site ($12 with hookups) near the marina; call 307/235-9325 for details. At **Alcova Lake Marina,** 307/472-6666, www.alcovalakesidemarina.com, you can rent boats or personal watercraft, and buy gas or supplies; open mid-Apr. to mid-Sept. Water leaves Alcova Dam and flows into small **Gray Reef Reservoir,** used to control the fluctuating discharges from Alcova and to generate more power. From here some of the water is diverted into the 62-mile Casper Canal to irrigate 24,000 acres of alfalfa, barley, oats, and corn west of Casper. A campground ($5; open Memorial Day to mid-Oct.) below Gray Reef Dam is a favorite place to launch canoes for a leisurely float down the river. Rent canoes, flat-bottom boats, and mountain bikes from **Eagle Creek Recreation Rental,** 307/473-2832, near Alcova Reservoir.

Located 45 miles south of Alcova and seven miles from Pathfinder Reservoir, **Sand Creek Ranch B&B,** 307/234-9597, has B&B accommodations on a 30,000-acre ranch. The remote location—you'll need to drive 20 miles out a dirt road—offers grand Wyoming scenery and accommodation in either a modern log home or private cabins. The rate is $75 s or d. A full breakfast is served, and kids, pets, and horses are welcome. The cabins can sleep six or more, and one offers the ultimate in seclu- sion—a location five miles from the ranch house. Open June–Nov.

North Platte Lodge, 307/237-1182, www.northplattelodge.com, offers fly-fishing packages, starting at $325 per person for two nights and a day of angling, with a fishing guide, lodging, and meals included.

Oregon Trail Landmarks

Three of the most famous landmarks along the entire Oregon Trail lie within Natrona County: Independence Rock, Devil's Gate, and Split Rock. Travelers anticipated these landmarks because they marked the start of a long, gentle approach to the Continental Divide 80 miles west. The route past these landmarks paralleled the Sweet- water River—a ribbon of lush grass in a rugged, desolate landscape. The names applied to adjacent mountains and creeks offer clues to the land's harshness: Rattlesnake Mountains, Poison Spider Creek, Greasewood Creek, Sulfur Creek, and Stinking Creek. Steamboat Lake, just a few miles north of Independence Rock, was a source of bicarbonate of soda used to bake bread. Cattle that drank the lake's putrid water died, while bread made with this baking soda took on a greenish cast. But along the Sweetwater, horses and oxen could find forage, firewood was avail- able, and the clean mountain water offered a re- lief from the alkaline springs to the east. (The name Sweetwater arose when a mule team car- rying sugar lost its load in the river.) Today, State Hwy. 220 crosses the old Oregon Trail several miles east of its junction with U.S. Hwy. 287 at Muddy Gap. The highway parallels the trail for the next 45 miles west.

INDEPENDENCE ROCK

Head southwest from Casper along State Hwy. 220 for 55 miles until the granitic dome of In- dependence Rock rises above the flat surrounding plain. Although not as spectacular or colorful, the setting seems reminiscent of Australia's Ayers Rock. Independence Rock is 1,950 feet long by 850 feet wide; its smoothly rounded top reaches to 136 feet over the surrounding plain. Travelers

---

ARRIVING AT INDEPENDENCE ROCK, 1844

August 16

Moved on up the creek saw the notable rock Independence with the names of its numerious visitors most of which are nearly obliterated by the weather & rav- ages of time amongst which I observed the names of two of my old friends the no- table mountaineers Thos. Fitzpatrick & W. L. Sublette as likewise one of our no- blest politicians Henry Clay coupled in division with that of Martin Van Buren a few miles further up the creek pases

through the south point of ruged & solid looking granite rock by a verry narrow pass after passing which we entered a valy Surounded by low ruged mountains ex- cept to the West whare a defiel Shews it- self the lower vally of this creek is well clothed with short grass the upper with sand & sage the mountains with short scattering pines but in many places noth- ing but the bear rock in large steep Sur- faces made 8 miles & encamped for the night on a good plat of grass

—mountain man James Clyman

© DON PITCHER

Devil's Gate and Sweetwater River

could not resist the chance to note their passing on this gigantic billboard; an estimated 50,000 names were carved, chipped, or painted on Independence Rock during the mid-19th century. Father Jean Pierre DeSmet, a famed Jesuit missionary, labeled it "the Great Register of the Desert." His initials, along with the names of Captain Bonneville, John C. Frémont, and many other explorers, were etched into the rock face.

Independence Rock apparently received its name from explorer and mountain man William Sublette, who arrived here on July 4, 1830, leading the first wagon train across the overland route. Oregon Trail emigrants tried to reach the rock around July 4 to be on schedule for Oregon. When the rock came into view, it was a source of rejoicing because it offered a welcome place to rest alongside the Sweetwater River. During the heyday of migration along the Oregon Trail, dozens of wagon trains would find themselves at the rock on Independence Day, and the celebrations included patriotic flag-waving, the firing of guns, big dinners, and other festivities. Many people did not make it beyond Independence Rock; many unmarked graves surround the rock.

Exploring the Rock

Today the state has a modern rest area next to Independence Rock with signs detailing the area's

rich history. Hundreds of the original names carved into Independence Rock are still visible, although weathering and lichen have obliterated thousands more. Unfortunately, more recent travelers have added their names, sometimes covering up names more than a hundred years old. Independence Rock can be climbed from several points along the perimeter, providing fine views of the surrounding countryside. Some of the oldest and best-preserved names are on top; the oldest known is dated 1824. A path circles the rock, making for an interesting mile-long hike. You can spot names on all sides, and you're bound to see deer and other wildlife along the Sweetwater River. A small footbridge crosses the still-visible Oregon Trail route here. Beware of rattlesnakes around Independence Rock.

DEVIL'S GATE

Visible from Independence Rock and just seven miles to the southwest is another famed Oregon Trail landmark, Devil's Gate. Over the centuries, the Sweetwater River has gradually sliced a giant cleft through the Rattlesnake Mountains, leaving 330-foot cliffs on both sides of a 1,500-foot-long canyon. (An Indian legend offers an alternative origin for Devil's Gate: A gigantic tusked beast had roamed Sweetwater Valley, and when the Indians finally managed to mortally wound the animal, it gouged out the nearby mountains in its death agony.) Devil's Gate was another favorite emigrant campsite. The cut is hard to miss, especially from the east—the direction of most Oregon Trail travelers. Today, the BLM maintains a historic site along State Hwy. 220 with a short loop trail and signboards. At least 20 emigrant graves are nearby.

MARTIN'S COVE
Disaster on the Plains
Just two miles northwest of Devil's Gate, Martin's Cove is the site of the most disastrous experience along the Oregon and Mormon Trails. In 1856, a group of 1,620 British converts to the Mormon religion sailed from Liverpool for America, intent on reaching Salt Lake City before winter. The total cost of the trip to Utah, including ship passage from England and Scandinavia, was just $45 per person.

Instead of the usual wagons, many of these destitute emigrants pushed or pulled small handcarts that held their meager possessions. The converts left Iowa in five groups that summer, but the last two were delayed because their handcarts had not been completed in time. Finally, a company led by James G. Willie left Iowa City on July 15, and a group of 576 people under the direction of Edward Martin departed on July 26. The emigrants knew they were taking a big risk by leaving so late, but they were anxious to reach "Zion" in Salt Lake City.

Trouble started early. The hurriedly built handcarts had been constructed of unseasoned wood that shrank and cracked as the carts rolled over the hot plains of Nebraska. When some broke down, the load was transferred to others, weakening them as well. Then, near present-day Glenrock, the emigrants decided to lighten their carts by discarding extra food, clothing, and blankets—items they would shortly need. Unable to afford the bridge toll at present-day Casper, they waded across the freezing North Platte River on October 19. Soon a blizzard dumped 18 inches of snow on them and the weather turned bitterly cold, with temperatures dropping to −14°F. The

elderly and children died first; eventually even the strongest began to perish. Some bodies were covered with stones to protect them from wolves, but others were simply left on the frozen ground, strewn over 60 miles of trail. When a rescue wagon from Salt Lake City finally arrived on November 1, they found the survivors huddling in Martin's Cove, a protected area near Devil's Gate. Rescuer Daniel W. Jones wrote:

> There were old men pulling and tugging their carts, sometimes loaded with a sick wife or children, women pulling along sick husbands; little children six to eight years old struggling through the mud and snow. . . . The provisions we took amounted to almost nothing among so many people, many of them now on very short rations, some almost starving.

The company of foolhardy emigrants finally reached Salt Lake City in late November, but 145 members had died along the way, and many others lost limbs from frostbite. The handcart company led by James G. Willie suffered a similar fate, losing 67 people to the elements at South Pass. Despite the attention that the handcarts continue to receive, they were really only used by 3,000 out of the 80,000 Mormons who headed to Utah in the great migration.

Mormon Handcart Visitors Center
In 1872 the French-Canadian trapper Thomas De Beau Soleil (Thomas Sun) established a ranch in the Martin's Cove area. Many of the Tom Sun Ranch buildings survive, including Soleil's original cabin (now on the National Register of Historic Places). The buildings were purchased by a private corporation connected with the Mormon church in 1996, and the old ranch house was transformed into the Mormon Handcart Visitors Center, 307/328-2953, www.handcart.com. Stop here to learn more about the handcart companies in this excellent free facility, open daily 8 A.M.–7 P.M. June–Aug., and daily 9 A.M.–4 P.M. the rest of the year. A genealogy center provides a way to search your family history, and an old schoolhouse contains artifacts from the Sun family. Visitors can borrow a hand-

cart replica to walk a 4.5-mile portion of the Oregon/Mormon Trail or to go on an overnight walk to campgrounds located three and six miles from the center. A primitive campground and RV park (running water but no showers) is on the grounds at the Handcart Visitors Center. All of these, and the exhibits, are free—and you don't even need to become a Mormon.

SPLIT ROCK

The final of the three geologic landmarks that lined the Oregon Trail through present-day Natrona County is Split Rock, a bite taken out of a solid granite mountain. The cleft was visible for two days as emigrants trudged along; it seemed to be a gunsight aimed toward the west. In the early 1860s, a Pony Express station, an Overland Stage station, a telegraph station, and a garrison of troops were located nearby. Today, Split Rock is noted at a turnout 10 miles west of Muddy Gap Junction along U.S. Hwy. 287. Tourists sail past in minutes what took the emigrants many long and treacherous days to accomplish. See Lander Vicinity in the Wind River Mountains Country chapter for points west of here on U.S. Hwy. 287, including Jeffrey City and Ice Slough. If you're heading south to Rawlins on U.S. Hwy. 287, see Heading North under Rawlins in the Medicine Bow Country chapter.

Salt Creek

Forty miles north of Casper is the Salt Creek Oil Field, considered the largest light oil field in the world. The 10-mile-long field covers a land of sage, sand, and rock that has produced more than 600 million barrels of oil and 700 million cubic feet of gas. Much more oil has been found nearby. A drive up State Hwy. 259 is a trip through a bizarre alien world of desert land carpeted with giant grasshopper-like electric pumpjacks spaced every couple hundred feet to the horizon. Actually, they look more like the little plastic ostriches sold in tourist shops—the ones that keep tipping down to a bowl of water to "drink." The pumpjacks don't run all the time, allowing the oil to accumulate in the well before pumping resumes. West of the company town of Midwest, things get even stranger, with an incredible grid of pumpjacks, dirt roads, power lines, and storage tanks crisscrossing the harsh land.

HISTORY

This famed oil field occupies a classic anticlinal structure that traps oil—hundred-foot cliffs surround the field. Wyoming's territorial geologist, Samuel Aughey, discovered these unusual structures and brought the first speculators here to file placer claims in 1884. The first well in the area was drilled in 1889 by a Pennsylvania oilman, M. P. Shannon. The oil was hauled by horse-drawn wagon to Casper, 50 miles away. In 1904, Shannon sold his small Casper refinery and 105,000 acres of Salt Creek leases to European speculators for $350,000.

Four years later the real boom came when a Dutch-financed company struck black gold at 1,050 feet in the Salt Creek Field, spouting oil in a massive gusher. When the news hit, battles over land claims quickly escalated to the shouting and shooting stage. The Midwest Oil Company was formed and built the first pipeline to Casper in 1911 to feed the new Midwest refinery there. The Fransco Company added another refinery the following year, and Standard Oil of Indiana built a cracking plant to retrieve more gasoline from the crude.

As World War I steamed over the horizon, the field suddenly gained vital national importance; oil shipped to the Allies from Salt Creek was considered an important factor in the defeat of Kaiser Wilhelm. After the war, Standard Oil (now Amoco) bought out all of Midwest's Salt Creek properties, but the 14 remaining companies competed with each other for the crude, with oil derricks within spitting distance of each other.

Production declined as the companies attempted to pump the oil too fast, trying to get it before it flowed into neighboring wells. Finally, in 1939, Salt Creek became the first oil field in America to run as a unified operation with joint management of the various wells for greater efficiency and conservation. Production in Salt Creek reached a peak in 1923 (when it produced 5 percent of the nation's oil), but the introduction of gas injection in the 1920s and water flooding in the 1950s helped push more oil to the wellheads. Today, more than 100 years after its discovery, workers have recovered just one-third of the oil at Salt Creek. Culling the remaining oil will require more sophisticated techniques, such as flooding with carbon dioxide. Even still, Salt Creek's current yield of 12,000 barrels per day accounts for two-thirds of Natrona County's oil production. It's Wyoming's third-largest producing field.

MIDWEST AND EDGERTON

The twin oil towns of Midwest (pop. 400) and Edgerton (pop. 170) lie near the center of the Salt Creek Field. A paved road north of Midwest leads to the Shannon Pool oil field, where oil was first discovered. Thousands of drill holes surround the towns, laced together by a grid of dirt roads, power lines, and pipes.

Midwest

The company town of Midwest is named for Midwest Oil Company, now a part of BP Amoco. Its four straight streets contain rows of identical wooden houses built in the 1920s and now showing their age. The stench of sulfur from a gas-recovery plant south of town permeates the air. Midwest's golf course is dotted with oil pumps, and folks attending Mass at the Catholic church can hear the quiet, rhythmic "ker-thunk" of a pumpjack just one hundred feet away. Midwest was especially hard hit by the slide in oil prices in the '80s; assessed valuation plummeted from $9.2 million in 1987 to $1.5 million in 1989! More than a decade later, the economy is still marginal, peeling paint decorates the aging wooden box houses, and the town is peppered with boarded-up buildings, aging cars, and a sense of the doldrums.

Worth a look is the small **Salt Creek Museum,** 531 Peak St., 307/437-6513. Inside, you'll find a fun collection of memorabilia and junk, with bedpans, historic photos, farm tools, trophies, old high-school lockers, and even dinosaur eggs. The museum is open Monday–Friday 8 A.M.–5 P.M.; get a key from the Town Hall out front, or call Pauline Schultz at 307/437-6633 for tours. Behind the museum is a new playground for the kids. The **Midwest General Store** sells groceries, booze, and gas, and an adjacent café has the usual fast food. Midwest claims one trivial historical footnote: In 1925 the nation's first nighttime interscholastic football game was played under artificial lights here.

Edgerton

Just six miles east of Midwest, the dumpy little settlement of Edgerton has a bit more to offer, with a grocery, a bank, two bars, a library, a gas station, and an old-time hardware store. For meals, try **Edgerton Cafe.**

The only local accommodation is at **Tea Pot Motor Lodge** in Edgerton, 307/437-6541, where rooms cost $31 s or $36 d.

The big local event—including parades, dancing, food, and a "sand greens" golf tournament—comes in August, when both towns celebrate **Salt Creek Days.** Call 307/437-6513 for details. Points northwest of Midwest and Edgerton are covered in the Powder River chapter.

TEMPEST IN A TEAPOT

Twenty-five miles north of Casper along U.S. Hwy. 87 is a distinctive butte, Teapot Rock. Until a 1962 windstorm knocked down the "spout" that bent away from one side, the rock resembled a teapot. In the first decades of the 20th century, rapid growth in the oil industry sent prospectors and speculators all over the west in search of black gold. To ensure adequate fuel supplies for the navy's ships after World War I, the government set aside three large oil reserves—Elk Hills and Buena Vista in California, and Wyoming's Teapot Dome Oil Field (named for Teapot Rock).

In 1921 and 1922, Secretary of the Interior Albert B. Fall secretly leased Teapot Dome to Edward Doheny and Harry Sinclair, owners of Mammoth Oil Company. Could anyone have ever come up with a more fitting name for a corrupt corporation? Although the action was technically legal, the $100,000 bribe paid by Doheny to President Harding's interior secretary was decidedly not legal, and Fall was forced to resign. The action brought a plethora of charges against the giant oil companies, and political cartoonists had a heyday with Teapot Dome. Interior Secretary Fall was convicted of accepting bribes and spent a year in prison. Harry Sinclair—for whom both the oil company and the Wyoming town are named—hired detectives to spy on a jury investigating Teapot Dome and was sent to jail in 1929 for contempt of court. He also spent three months in jail for refusing to testify before a Senate committee investigating the scandal. Today, the U.S. Navy still owns thousands of acres at Teapot Dome, and there are hundreds of oil wells a few miles east of the highway. A sign points out Naval Petroleum Reserve Number 3, but you won't find any historical signs mentioning this rather sordid piece of Wyoming history. The mailboxes and nearby white buildings of Teapot Dome Ranch mark the site of Teapot Rock.

West from Casper

West of Casper, U.S. Hwy. 20/26 passes through the heart of Wyoming, a dry landscape of sage and grass. For a fascinating diversion, follow the BLM's **Big Horn/Red Wall Byway** in a 100-mile loop over country roads with grand vistas and an outlaw past (Butch Cassidy hid out here). The road starts from the intersection of U.S. Hwy. 20/26 and County Rd. 125, 13 miles northwest of Casper; get a route map from the BLM office in Casper, 307/261-7600, www.wy.blm.gov. The road is rough in places, and high-clearance vehicles are recommended. No services are available along the way, so be sure to carry food, water, and extra clothes. Don't attempt this route in rainy weather when the roads become slick. It's remote and amazingly scenic.

POWDER RIVER

The tiny settlement of Powder River (pop. 50) lies along U.S. Hwy. 20/26 where it crosses this famous river 35 lonely miles west of Casper. Not much is here today; writer James Conaway called the town "little more than a Texaco station and a bunch of pronghorn antelope looking at it." On the third weekend in July, however, several hundred people flock (pun intended) to town for the annual **Sheepherder Fair.** It features sheep dog trials, sheep roping and hooking, a free barbecue, and sheepherding demonstrations of all sorts.

Calcutta wagering goes on for most events, and a band plays country-and-western favorites late into the evening for a happy throng of dancers.

The town has a convenience store and post office, plus the small **Highway 20/26 Motel,** 307/234-7205, where rooms with fridges and microwaves are $40 s or $46 d. Eat at **Tumble Inn,** 307/237-6764, which doubles as a popular strip joint on weekends!

HELL'S HALF ACRE

Forty-five miles west of Casper is one of the freaks of nature, Hell's Half Acre. Actually covering 320 acres, the area includes a strange collection of deeply eroded and colorful badlands surrounded by featureless sage-covered plains. Ancient coal deposits within the badlands caught on fire and burned for many years, and when explorer Captain Bonneville passed by in 1833, he labeled it Devils Kitchen because of these sulfurous fumes. The name Hell's Half Acre was a later title. Indians used these badlands as a buffalo trap, driving herds to their deaths over the canyon walls. In the late 19th century, after whites had slaughtered the bison to the brink of extinction, bone pickers gleaned thousands of these bones from Hell's Half Acre for eastern fertilizer plants. Archaeologists later discovered additional bison bones, along with arrowheads and other artifacts.

Hell's Half Acre was the setting for the 1996 sci-fi movie *Starship Trooper*—a space-station "city" was built on the south half of the badlands. Visitors today enjoy wandering through these colorful badlands. Hell's Half Acre is well worth a stop, but be forewarned that a kitschy souvenir shop, café, motel (307/473-7773), and RV park detract from the view. It's a great place to meet busloads of tottering tourists from hell.

MONETA AND LYSITE

Slow-paced **Lysite** is decidedly off the beaten track, eight miles north of another nowheresville place, **Moneta** (pop. 10). At one time the main route into the Bighorn Basin and Yellowstone lay along the Lysite road, but with completion of a highway through Wind River Canyon in 1927, traffic bypassed this area. Lysite has an old-time country store and is the sort of town where horses are still a means of transportation. The Lysite library is housed in a building slightly larger than a shoebox.

LOST CABIN

Three miles east of Lysite is the flyspeck of a town called **Lost Cabin,** named for a gold mine in the Big Horn Mountains. Miner Allen Hulburt and two partners discovered a stream filled with gold, but Indians killed his partners and partially burned their cabin. The dazed miner scooped up as much gold as he could carry and fled to Casper, where his tale pricked more than a few ears. Despite repeated efforts by Hulburt and others, the Lost Cabin mine was never again found. (This is only one of many such tales about the fabled mine.)

Lost Cabin is centered around the elaborate mansion of John B. Okie. He came to Wyoming as a cowboy with only the clothes on his back, decided sheep were a better bet, and gradually became a millionaire. Okie once ran 30,000 sheep through the surrounding country, gaining the title of "Sheep King." His mansion—called "The Big Tepee" by local Indians—was built in 1900 for $30,000 and contained carved fireplaces, Asian

© DON PITCHER

mansion of John B. Okie, Lost Cabin

chandeliers, imported furniture, stained-glass windows, and Persian prayer rugs. Surrounding it were a greenhouse with flowers tended by Japanese gardeners, a roller rink, a dance hall, and even an aviary housing 140 exotic birds. A power plant was built to supply electricity for Okie's town. In 1930, Okie drowned in a nearby reservoir while hunting ducks. The beautiful old home isn't open to the public but can be viewed from the gate.

CASTLE GARDENS

A remote and little-known archaeological site is Castle Gardens, in desolate country south of Moneta. Head south from Moneta (bear right at the first "Y" in the road, one-half mile south of town) for 16 miles on a gravel road, and then turn east on a dirt road that takes you another six miles to the site. The latter road is quite rutted and not recommended for RVs or after rains, when the road turns into a quagmire. Signs at Moneta and at the turnoff keep you from getting lost. At Castle Gardens are all sorts of odd sandstone formations: Toadstools, spires, and various creatures seem to appear. It's easy to see how this would be a sacred spot for the Indians who came here centuries ago. Small juniper and limber pines grow amid the gray rocks and sand, creating a garden in the castles of Castle Gardens. There's no camping here, but you will find picnic tables and an outhouse.

Dozens of Indian pictographs (presumably Shoshonean in origin) have been sharply incised into the soft rock walls. They include many in the shield motif, believed to represent the round shields of Indian warriors. Although they may be up to 900 years old, these figures are probably more recent than the pecked style of pictographs present in the Dinwoody Creek and Legend Rock areas. Castle Gardens' figures that show horses or tepees are clearly from the period after A.D. 1700. The most elaborate shield found here—the figure of a turtle painted green, yellow, and red—is now in the State Museum in Cheyenne. The remaining pictographs are protected by chainlink fences, but vandals have marred many of these priceless artifacts with graffiti. The site leaves you with mixed emotions: a multitude of questions about what the images represent, a feeling of closeness to the natural world in this remote and fascinating place, and an utter disgust for those who would destroy this cultural heritage.

WEST TO SHOSHONI

The 85 miles of highway (U.S. Hwy. 20/26) that connect Casper with Shoshoni cross an almost featureless plain, a place that seems to define the word "bleak." With no trees in sight, the clouds throw moving shadows across a landscape of sage and grass. This is antelope country. Even the ranches are few and far between out here, and cattle take slow, desultory steps in the summer heat or brace against the bitter winds of winter. For many travelers this is pedal-to-the-metal country, a place to crank up the country tunes and roll on west.

Wind River Mountains Country

The Wind River Mountains—Wyoming's highest and longest range—form a dramatic divide between two of the state's most important rivers. The east side drains into the Wind River, eventually reaching the Atlantic Ocean, and the western slopes drop into the Green River and eventually the Pacific. The name Wind River Mountains originated as a Crow Indian reference to the warm Chinook winds that blow down the Wind River Valley.

THE LAND

This chapter covers Sublette and Fremont Counties, named for two of the state's most famous explorers. Fremont County is a land of sharp contrasts. The eastern end consists of a spacious, arid landscape of sage, grass, and antelope, while to the west you'll find the fluorescent green of irrigated fields along the Wind River and the pastel badlands near

Fort Washakie

© DON PITCHER

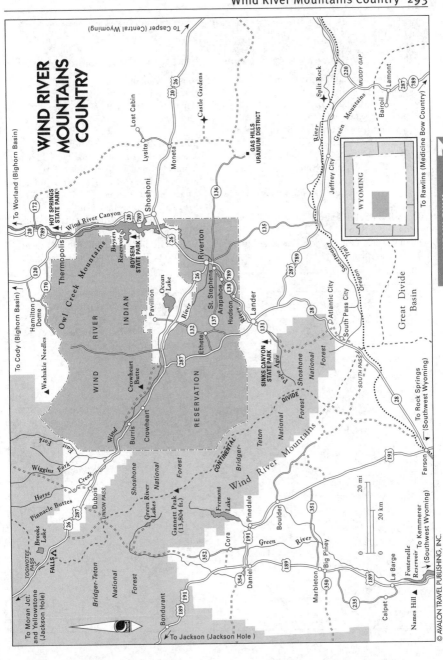

WIND RIVER MOUNTAINS COUNTRY

To Casper (Central Wyoming)

WIND RIVER

WIND RIVER

WIND RIVER MOUNTAINS COUNTRY SIGHTSEEING HIGHLIGHTS

Yellowstone Drug Store in Shoshoni
Eagle Bronze Foundry in Lander
Sinks Canyon and the Loop Road near Lander
Wind River Reservation, including St. Stephens Mission, St. Michael's Mission, Chief Washakie Plunge, Shoshone Tribal Cultural Center, and Sacagawea Cemetery, Crowheart Butte, and Whiskey Basin
Dubois badlands
Togwotee Pass west of Dubois, including Brooks Lake
Green River Lakes and Cirque of the Towers in the Wind River Mountains
South Pass area, including South Pass State Historic Site and Atlantic City

Farson Mercantile
Museum of the Mountain Man in Pinedale
1840 rendezvous site near Daniel
Granite Hot Springs

Popular events: International Pedigree Stage Stop Sled Dog Race (January), Wild West Winter Carnival in Riverton (February), Eastern Shoshone Indian Days Powwow and Rodeo in Fort Washakie (June), Ethete Powwow (June), Mountain Man Rendezvous in Riverton (June), Riverton Rendezvous (July), International Climbers' Festival in Lander (July), Green River Rendezvous in Pinedale (July), The Drift near Pinedale (October)

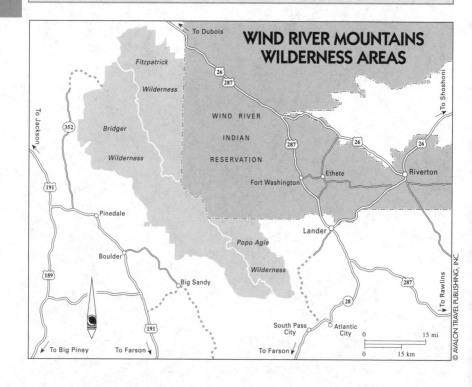

WIND RIVER MOUNTAINS WILDERNESS AREAS

To Dubois

Fitzpatrick

Wilderness

26
287

To Jackson

352

Bridger

Wilderness

WIND RIVER

INDIAN

RESERVATION

287

26

26

To Shoshoni

191

Ethete

Riverton

Fort Washington

Pinedale

Lander

Popo Agie

Boulder

189

Wilderness

Big Sandy

287

To Rawlins

28

191

South Pass City

Atlantic City

0   15 mi

0   15 km

To Big Piney   To Farson

To Farson

© AVALON TRAVEL PUBLISHING, INC.

Dubois. Along the southern and western borders rise the snow-crested Wind River and Absaroka Mountains. At almost six million acres, this is Wyoming's second-largest county after Sweetwater.

The centerpiece of Fremont County is the Wind River Reservation, home to both the Eastern Shoshone and the Northern Arapaho peoples. Within the reservation itself lie the tiny towns of Fort Washakie, Ethete, and Arapahoe, as well as the larger non-Indian settlement of Riverton. Lander borders it on the south; farther south stand the historic mining towns of South Pass and Atlantic City. West of the reservation, the town of Dubois provides an entry point into the Absarokas, the Tetons, and Yellowstone.

The Wind River Valley is farming and ranching country. Some 150,000 acres of alfalfa hay (considered some of the best in America), feed and malt barley, sugar beets, and oats are under irrigation each year. This is Wyoming's second-biggest agricultural county and home to the largest number of horses in the state.

A substantial amount of oil and natural-gas production takes place on the Wind River Reservation, where energy royalties bring in millions of dollars each year. Uranium was discovered in the Gas Hills area east of Riverton during the 1950s and spawned a major industry in the 1960s and '70s before plummeting when the Three-Mile Island accident of 1981 brought the dangers of nuclear power to the forefront.

Sublette County has just 6,000 individuals spread over 10,495 square miles. Cattle exceed people by a 14:1 margin, and you'll find only one town of any size—Pinedale—with a few folks living in the little burgs of Big Piney, Marbleton, Boulder, and Daniel. Not surprisingly, the big industry here is ranching, although the area's scenic beauty draws increasing numbers of tourists. You'll find magnificent vistas of the Wind Mountains all along the western front—far more dramatic than from the eastern side.

TRIP PLANNING

In addition to a very useful website (www.windriver.org), the Riverton-based **Wind River Visitors Council,** 307/856-7566 or 800/645-6233, can provide vacationers with a slew of publications detailing accommodations, tours, events, driving tours, and more for the Wind River Valley. Get online details for the western side of the mountains at www.sublette.com.

Riverton

Near the confluence of the Big Wind River and Little Wind River, aptly named Riverton (pop. 9,000) is the largest settlement in Fremont County and the eighth-largest city in the state. The Wind River Reservation surrounds Riverton on all sides. It's a mid-American suburbia where chain stores and fast-food outlets dominate the outskirts. Even Riverton city hall is housed in a strip mall! Cheap gas and low-priced hotels make visiting easier. Modern Central Wyoming College attracts students from throughout the area.

HISTORY

The Riverton area was the site of two trapping and trading rendezvous, in 1830 and 1838. The land became part of the Wind River Reservation in 1868, but a portion was ceded by the Shoshone and Arapaho tribes in 1904. Almost overnight, the town of Riverton sprang up as would-be farmers drew lots for prime farmland. Canals were dug and fields planted with crops; more than 100,000 acres of irrigated farmland surround Riverton today.

During the 1960s and '70s, enormous uranium deposits were developed in the nearby Gas Hills area. Hundreds of millions of dollars poured into the local economy created rapid growth, but when nuclear power suddenly lost its luster, so did Riverton. After the bust that followed, the town began to diversify and has been slowly rebounding; today businesses include Bonneville Transloaders, a soda-ash hauling company; the Brunton Company, manufacturer of compasses,

WIND RIVER

RIVERTON

To Shoshoni

To Hudson and Lander

789

16TH ST.

WIND RIVER RV PARK

N 12TH ST.

N. 12TH ST.

Wyoming Heritage Trail

WAL-MART

KMART

26

FOREST DR.

N 10TH ST.

Riverton City Park

ROOMERS MOTEL

E PARK AVE.

E JACKSON AVE.

LINCOLN AVE.

E ROOSEVELT AVE.

E PERSHING AVE.

IGA

HOLIDAY INN

FEDERAL BLVD.

SOUTH FEDERAL INN

SUNDOWNER STATION MOTEL

PAINTBRUSH MOTEL

SUPER 8 MOTEL

CITY HALL

SAFEWAY

HI-LO MOTEL

RIVERTON MUSEUM ★

6TH AVE.

5TH ST.

AVE.

AVE.

AVE.

AVE.

AVE.

ST.

ST.

FREMONT COUNTY FAIRGROUNDS

WEBBWOOD RD.

BROADWAY AVE.

2ND

ST.

THUNDERBIRD MOTEL

POST OFFICE

E FREMONT AVE.

TOMAHAWK MOTEL

E WASHINGTON

E ADAMS

E JEFFERSON

E MADISON

E MONROE

SUNSET DR.

PERSHING AVE.

2ND ST. W

W PERSHING AVE.

CHAMBER OF COMMERCE

5TH ST.

6TH ST.

7TH ST.

MT. VIEW MOTEL

N 8TH ST. W

W FREMONT AVE.

MAIN ST.

DRIFTWOOD INN

RIVERVIEW RD.

RAILROAD AVE.

Wyoming Heritage Trail

10TH ST. W

11TH ST. W

DAYS INN

W PARK AVE.

LIBRARY

SMITH'S

ROSE LN.

HOSPITAL

AQUATIC CENTER/ HIGH SCHOOL

PECK AVE.

COLLEGE VIEW DR.

MORFELD DAY DR.

CIRCLE DR.

CENTRAL WYOMING COLLEGE

N HILL ST.

GALLOWAY RD.

Wind River

26

AUGUSTA DR.

RIVERVIEW RD.

RIVERTON COUNTRY CLUB

VILLAGE DR.

Big

River

COUNTRY CLUB

To Airport

To Dubois

AIRPORT RD.

0.5 mi

0.5 km

0

0

© AVALON TRAVEL PUBLISHING, INC.

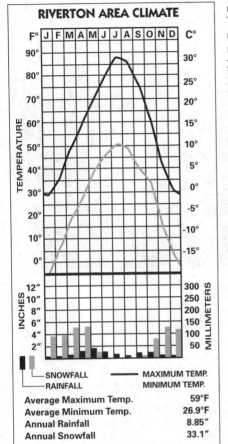

RIVERTON AREA CLIMATE

SNOWFALL — MAXIMUM TEMP.
RAINFALL — MINIMUM TEMP.

Average Maximum Temp.	59°F
Average Minimum Temp.	26.9°F
Annual Rainfall	8.85"
Annual Snowfall	33.1"

binoculars, and pocket transits; and various government agencies. The area is becoming increasingly popular with retirees.

SIGHTS

The **Riverton Museum,** 700 E. Park Ave., 307/856-2665, is open Tuesday–Saturday 10 A.M.–4 P.M. year-round; no charge. Local historical exhibits in this rambling, surprisingly large museum include a tepee containing a buffalo robe and powwow drum, an Indian cradle board with saddle, a model of the Carissa Mine at South Pass, various old farm and mining equip-

ment, and an interesting exhibit on oil drilling. Take a gander at Desert Demon, a stuffed wild mustang that proved untamable—hence his current, more sedate, bullet-tamed condition. While you're here, also check out the photos of Leslie King, the father of former president Gerald R. Ford and a prominent Riverton-area rancher. (President Ford's parents were divorced, and his mother later married a Mr. Ford.) Gerald Ford worked as a Yellowstone National Park ranger after graduating from college in Michigan but is not known to have fallen into any geysers.

Riverton Livestock Auction, on Fairgrounds Rd., 307/856-2209, is Wyoming's second-largest livestock auction barn, after Torrington. Its monthly horse sales are the most enjoyable.

ACCOMMODATIONS

Riverton has more than a dozen different places to bed down for the night, all priced quite reasonably.

Under $50

Several of Riverton's budget places offer bargain rates, but you may want to see the rooms before plunking down your cash. **Jackpine Motel,** 120 S. Federal, 307/856-9251, charges $30 s or $36 d, and has microwaves and fridges in the rooms. **Mountain View Motel,** 720 W. Main, 307/856-2418 or 800/856-2418, has rooms for $30 s or $32–38 d. Some have fridges and microwaves, and a few with kitchenettes are available. **Driftwood Inn,** 611 W. Main, 307/856-4811 or 800/821-2914, charges $36 s or $38–40 d, and also has family rooms.

Another decent older place is **Hi-Lo Motel,** 414 N. Federal, 307/856-9223; $34 for one bed or $40 for two beds, and all rooms contain fridges and microwaves. **Paintbrush Motel,** 1550 N. Federal, 307/856-9238 or 800/204-9238, also has well-kept older units with fridges and microwaves; $36 s or $39–46 d.

Roomers Motel, 319 N. Federal, 307/857-1735 or 888/857-4097, features comfortable and clean rooms for $35 s or $40–45 d, most with fridges and microwaves.

South Federal Inn, 221 S. Federal, 307/856-7455, has 25 recently remodeled rooms for $36

© DON PITCHER

downtown Riverton

with one bed or $40 with two. Another well-maintained place—in a quiet location—is **Thunderbird Motel,** 203 E. Fremont, 307/856-9201 or 888/498-9200, www.t-birdmotel.com, where rooms go for $38–47 s or $40–49 d, most with fridges and microwaves.

$50 and Up

Popular with both business travelers and vacationers, **Sundowner Station Motel,** 1616 N. Federal, 307/856-6503 or 800/874-1116, has attractive rooms (including Lazy-Boy chairs and large TVs), an exercise room, and sauna. Some rooms also include fridges and microwaves. Rates are $50 s or $52 d, or $64 for four guests.

Days Inn, 909 W. Main St., 307/856-9677 or 800/329-7466, www.daysinn.com, charges $55 s or $60 d, including a continental breakfast, microwaves, and fridges. **Tomahawk Motor Lodge,** 208 E. Main, 307/856-9201 or 800/637-7378, is another good midrange place, with comfortable rooms—most with fridges and microwaves—for $55 s or d, or $65 for up to four guests.

Find standard motel units at **Super 8 Motel,** 1040 N. Federal, 307/857-2400 or 800/800-8000, www.super8.com, for $50–65 s or $60–75

d, including a continental breakfast. **Holiday Inn,** 900 E. Sunset, 307/856-8100 or 800/465-4329, www.blairhotels.com, has rooms for $99 s or d. A honeymoon suite—complete with in-room hot tub—is $150. Amenities include an indoor pool and fitness center, an outdoor courtyard, and a restaurant and lounge.

Bed-and-Breakfast

Built in 1907, **Delfelder Inn B&B,** 222 S. Broadway, 307/857-3100, is housed in one of Riverton's oldest residences. Four guest rooms ($90 s or d) are available with shared or private baths and a full breakfast.

CAMPING

The nearest public camping ($12 for nonresidents, or $6 for Wyoming residents; open year-round) is 20 miles north in **Boysen State Park,** 307/876-2796, http://wyoparks.state.wy.us. **Owl Creek Kampground,** five miles northeast of Riverton on U.S. Hwy. 26, 307/856-2869, has shady in-the-trees tent and RV sites for $19; showers for noncampers are $4. Open mid-May to mid-Sept.

Wind River RV Park, 1618 E. Park Ave., 307/857-3000 or 800/528-3913, has riverside tent sites for $16, teepees for $20, and RV sites with hookups for $23–27. Showers run $2 for non-campers; open year-round. **Fort Rendezvous Campground,** 307/856-1144, also has RV sites. It's two miles south of Riverton along the Little Wind River and open year-round.

FOOD
Breakfast and Lunch
One of the best local eateries is, surprisingly, **Airport Cafe,** at the airport, 307/856-2838, where cinnamon rolls and pies are specialties. Fly out here for an inexpensive home-style breakfast. **Country Cove Restaurant,** 301 E. Main, 307/856-9813, makes dependably good home-style breakfasts and lunches.

Get espresso coffees, fruit smoothes, baked goods, and lunchtime sandwiches and bagels from **Split Rock Coffee & Bakery,** 219 E. Main St., 307/856-4334.

American
In business for more than a quarter century, **The Broker Restaurant,** 203 E. Main St., 307/856-0555, is a fine-dining establishment with a romantic atmosphere and a dinner menu ($12–30) that encompasses steaks, halibut, lobster, Caesar salads, lamb chops, and roast duckling. **The Bull Steakhouse,** 1100 W. Main, 307/856-4728, has consistently fine filet mignon, seafood, soup, a salad bar, and daily lunch specials, but save room for dessert. The atmosphere is casual, and the service is punctual.

Claimsteak, inside Sundowner Station at 1616 N. Federal, 307/856-6503, has standard American meals, lots of smokers, and a tasty Sunday breakfast buffet ($5). Head to **Golden Corral,** 400 N. Federal Blvd., 307/856-1152, for stuff-it-in meals from a sprawling salad bar/buffet.

You'll find all the fast-food chains on N. Federal Boulevard or on the west end of Main Street.

International
Housed in the old railroad station, **The Depot,** 1101 S. 1st St., 307/856-2221, is a pleasant lunch and dinner spot with the finest Mexican meals in town. Don't order too much; the enchiladas and chimichangas are big enough for two people. The cozy little bar makes good margaritas.

China Panda, 300 N. Federal Blvd., 307/856-7666, has a popular lunchtime Chinese buffet.

Groceries
Get groceries from **Woodward's IGA,** 619 N. Federal, 307/856-9042; **Safeway,** 708 N. Federal Way, 307/856-6524; **Smith's,** 1200 W. Main, 307/856-4931, or **Wal-Mart SuperCenter,** 1733 N. Federal Blvd., 307/856-3261.

ENTERTAINMENT
The bar at Riverton's bowling alley, **StarLite Lanes,** 837 N. Federal, 307/856-5944, has country music, and **Good Time Charlie's Lounge,** 502 E. Main St., 307/856-4285, generally has rock bands most weekends.

Watch movies at **Acme Theatre,** 312 E. Main, 307/856-3415, or **Gem Theatre,** 119 S. 3rd St. E, 307/856-9589. Central Wyoming College's **Peck Summer Theatre** produces plays; 307/855-2002 or 800/735-8418, www.cwc.cc.wy.us.

EVENTS
Each February, the **Wild West Winter Carnival** includes an ice-sculpture contest, chariot races, winter golf, hockey, tethered balloon rides in Riverton, plus many other events at Boysen Reservoir. Summer kicks off with the **Mountain Man Rendezvous** the last weekend in June on the site of the 1838 rendezvous. Events include shooting matches, basket-making, beading, Indian dancing, a mini-powwow, and other old-time activities.

The **Riverton Rendezvous** covers the second and third weekends of July. The rendezvous features food and craft booths, fireworks, a rodeo, live music, pig wrestling, a demolition derby, stock car races, and a big **Hot Air Balloon Rally** (third weekend), where you're likely to see more than two dozen colorful balloons lifting off at sunrise.

The **Fremont County Fair and Rodeo** comes to the Riverton Fairground the first full week of August, with a carnival, parade, demolition derby,

PRCA rodeo, musical entertainment, and fun for all ages. You can have more Western fun at the **Cowboy Poetry Roundup** in October, where the cowpokes spin tales at the largest cowboy poetry event in Wyoming.

SHOPPING

Wind River Gallery, 312 E. Main St., 307/856-1402, displays pieces by local artists. **Books and Briar,** 313 E. Main, 307/856-1797, is a surprisingly nice shop in downtown Riverton, with many Wyoming and Indian books, along with hundreds of magazine titles. Also worth a visit is **Book Junction,** 321 N. Broadway, 307/856-9270.

RECREATION

The 25-mile **Wyoming Heritage Trail** follows an old railroad grade from Riverton to Shoshoni, providing the chance to hike or mountain-bike. The trail cuts diagonally across Riverton along the route of the old Chicago-Northwestern Railroad. It's paved through town and gravel the rest of the way.

Riverton has a fine indoor **Aquatic Center** at the high school on W. Sunset Dr., 307/856-4230, with a sauna and a whirlpool. The 18-hole **Riverton Country Club** is at 4275 Country Club Dr., 307/856-4779. **Out Sportin',** 412 E. Main, 307/856-1373 or 800/371-1373, sells bikes and supplies.

INFORMATION AND SERVICES

Find the friendly folks at **Riverton Chamber of Commerce,** 213 W. Main, 307/856-4801 or 800/325-2732, www.rivertonchamber.org. The office is open Monday–Friday 8 A.M.–5 P.M. year-round.

The 109-acre campus of **Central Wyoming College,** 307/855-2000 or 800/442-1228, www.cwc.cc.wy.us, is on the west edge of town along U.S. Hwy. 26. Founded in 1966, it offers two-year programs in more than 50 fields for more than 1,000 full-time students. An impressive campus **Arts Center** houses a small gallery with changing exhibits. The college also has a good-sized library.

The modern **Riverton Public Library** is at 1330 W. Park Ave., 307/856-3556, www.fremontcountylibraries.org. For fast cash, you'll find **ATMs** at most local banks. Wash clothes at **American Dry Cleaning & Laundry,** 515 S. Federal Blvd.; **Driftwood Laundry,** 611 W. Main; or **Riverton Laundromat,** 470 E. Pershing Avenue.

Riverton Memorial Hospital, 307/856-4161 or 800/967-1646, www.riverton-hospital.com, is a 70-bed facility at 2100 W. Sunset Drive.

TRANSPORTATION

Riverton Airport is two miles northwest of town. **Great Lakes Aviation** has daily service to Denver and Worland. Rent cars at the airport from **Hertz.** See the "Airline Contacts" and "Rental Car Contacts" Special Topics in the On the Road chapter.

Powder River Transportation/Coach USA, 307/682-0960 or 800/442-3682, has daily bus service from Riverton throughout northern and eastern Wyoming, and onward to Billings, Denver, and Rapid City. The bus stop is at the S. Federal Inn, 221 S. Federal.

The nonprofit **Wind River Transportation Authority** (WRTA), 307/856-7118 or 800/439-7118, www.wrtabuslines.com, has a mix of services, including summertime shuttles ($15 one way) between the Riverton Airport and Lander, trips to the Salt Lake City airport ($75 one way), and a winter schedule connecting Riverton, Lander, and the Wind River Reservation. The Salt Lake trips are especially popular with NOLS students heading to Lander but are open to the general public with a minimum of two people. In addition, WRTA can provide transportation throughout western Wyoming for groups.

Riverton Vicinity

SHOSHONI

During the late 1970s Shoshoni (pop. 630) was a booming oil and uranium town, but the bust of the '80s left abandoned streets with tall grass and peeling paint and plywood windows on much of downtown. Tumbleweeds rolled down Main Street, and locals joked that no one wanted to be the last to turn out the lights because they were afraid of getting stuck with the electric bill! People are now moving back to Shoshoni, and things have begun to turn around in the last few years. You still aren't likely to confuse Shoshoni with Jackson, but at least the town isn't as bleak as Jeffrey City.

Practicalities

Shoshoni's main attraction is the **Yellowstone Drug Store,** 307/876-2539. During summer, legions of tourists stop here for ice-cream floats and ultra-thick malts at the old-time soda fountain. In a typical year the store makes and scoops 15,000 gallons of ice cream for more than 50,000 malts and shakes! In addition to ice cream, the store sells everything from cowboy hats to teddy bears. Trivia tidbit: Former president Ford's grandfather once owned this store.

Also in Shoshoni is the interesting little **CU Rock Shop.** You can still find ancient tepee rings northwest of town, and rock hounds enjoy looking for petrified wood, agate, tourmaline, and other stones in the area. Shoshoni is bordered on the north by Badwater Creek and on the south by Poison Creek. East of Shoshoni is an arid landscape of badlands topography. See Casper Vicinity in the Central Wyoming chapter for points east of Shoshoni, including the minuscule towns of Lysite, Lost Cabin, and Moneta.

Aside from Yellowstone Drug, Shoshoni's primary redeeming qualities are reasonably priced accommodations and gas, although you can also get good breakfasts at **Patti's Biscuits & Gravy Cafe** just north of town. **Desert Inn Motel,** 605 W. 2nd St., 307/876-2273, has standard rooms for $30 s or $37 d, and ones with full kitchens for $51 d. The smaller **Shoshoni Motel,** 503 W. 2nd, 307/876-2216, charges $28 s or $32 d. **Boysen State Park,** 307/876-2796, http://wyoparks.state.wy.us, is just a few miles north of here, with camping facilities costing $12 for nonresidents or $6 for Wyoming residents. Open year-round.

The **Wyoming State Championship Old-Time Fiddle Contest** comes to town in late May. You'll find rodeo action during summer at Shoshoni's rodeo arena, along with the **Flywheelers Antique Engine and Tractor Show** in June.

Powder River Transportation/Coach USA, 307/682-0960 or 800/442-3682, has daily buses from Shoshoni to Riverton and Cody, Billings, Denver, and much of northern and eastern Wyoming.

Yellowstone Drug Store, Shoshoni

WIND RIVER

BOYSEN STATE PARK

Established in 1956, Boysen State Park, 307/876-2796, http://wyoparks.state.wy.us, surrounds a reservoir named for Asmus Boysen, a Danish emigrant who built the first dam here in 1907–1908. When the water from his dam covered tracks of the Burlington Railroad, the railroad sued and had his dam blown up. The dam that now backs up the Wind River is a 230-foot-high earthen structure completed in 1961 and located at the entrance to Wind River Canyon. Boysen Reservoir is a motorboat playground popular with water-skiers and anglers (it's home to the biggest walleye in Wyoming; a 17-pound monster was caught in 1991). Its relatively warm waters attract swimmers to the beach near park headquarters.

Boysen Reservoir lies primarily within the Wind River Indian Reservation and is surrounded by open desert country. A nearly straight highway (U.S. Hwy. 20) rolls north from Shoshoni over the arid hills and rocky buttes, providing a few good vistas across the lake. Southwest of Shoshoni, U.S. Hwy. 26 crosses an arm of the reservoir. **Boysen Lake Marina,** on the north end near the entrance to Wind River Canyon, 307/876-2772, has a restaurant, grocery store, boat rentals, and RV spaces ($10 with electricity). They're open mid-April through September. The reservoir is surrounded by a dozen state park campgrounds ($12 for nonresidents or $6 for Wyoming residents; open year-round). Day use costs $4 for nonresidents or $2 for cars with Wyoming plates.

The **Wild West Winter Carnival** comes to Boysen in early February, with souped-up snowmobile races, ice golf, ATV and motorcycle races, and a carnival, plus additional events in Riverton. In late June, the **Governor's Cup Walleye Tournament** at Boysen hands out a $5,000 grand prize.

GAS HILLS

The paved but almost-untraveled Gas Hills Road (State Hwy. 136) leads east from the Riverton area to several now-closed open-pit uranium mines, including the Lucky McMine, discovered in 1953 by Neil and Maxine McNeice and mined

for many years. Perhaps one-third of the nation's uranium reserves remain in these arid hills. Today signs warn trespassers of the nuclear hazard in the abandoned mines. Dirt roads from the end of the pavement—approximately 45 miles east of Riverton—lead south to Jeffrey City, northwest to tiny Waltman, and east to Casper along Poison Spider Road. This is some of the most remote and desolate country you will ever find, with nary a tree in sight. The antelope love this sage-and-grass landscape. **Castle Gardens** (described in the Central Wyoming chapter) can also be accessed from Gas Hills Road. A sign on the road, which is easy to miss, points out the turnoff.

HUDSON

You could easily drive through Hudson (pop. 400) without paying any attention to this rather run-down little place, but the town really deserves a stop. Although many shops are shuttered, **Blue Heron Gallery,** 307/332-6153, is worth a visit, and the aging Sinclair sign painted on the side of a brick building makes a good photo op. Hudson has a distinct sense of decay, but off the main drag lie quiet, cottonwood-lined streets, simple frame homes, and gardens filled with tall yellow sunflowers. This place overflows with character and characters.

Attractions

Hudson was established in 1905 and became a major coal mining center in the early part of the 20th century. Most of those who settled here were European emigrants, and the town still maintains a strong ethnic flavor; the old fire truck says "Dago Red" on the front. Nowhere is this ethnic heritage as evident as in the two Slavic steak houses that attract folks from all over the state. **Svilar's,** 307/332-4516, is the oldest, and its owners are staunchly Republican. Mama Bessie Svilar founded the restaurant in the 1920s to serve the hungry local miners, but it soon began drawing travelers out of their way to tiny Hudson. Restaurant critic Red Fenwick noted that Svilar's "put Hudson on the map in big red letters that dripped with gravy and honey and meat juices." Mama Svilar died in 1981, but the food is still great, and the bar remains a popular place for drinks.

Just across the road is **Club El Toro,** 307/332-4627, owned by the Vinich family and offering similarly fine steaks and other hearty fare. The homemade ravioli hors d'oeuvres are a specialty. The Vinich family—well-known Wyoming Democrats—also own **Union Bar,** another popular Hudson hangout. Svilar's and El Toro are closed Sundays and on alternating Mondays.

After stuffing yourself with a steak dinner, ask about the badlands country east of Hudson. You'll find some fascinating eroded formations just a few miles out.

Lander

Friendly Lander (pop. 6,900) lies along the banks of the Popo Agie River, with the majestic Wind River Mountains rising just to the west. The town has a state training school for the developmentally disabled, which employs more than 500 people, and there are many jobs in government, ranching, and construction. Smaller and much more homey than nearby Riverton—where Kmart and Wal-Mart reign supreme—Lander seems to epitomize the changing face of Wyoming. It has undergone a rebirth as younger folks move in to raise families, opening shops, restaurants, and small businesses.

Lander is home to several organizations geared to the outdoors, including the National Outdoor Leadership School, a major local employer. The relatively mild winters and lack of wind here make it an attractive place to retire, and Lander's proximity to the Popo Agie Wilderness makes it a jumping-off place for mountain treks into the high country. Lander is also the southeastern starting point for the 365-mile Continental Divide Snowmobile Trail, which reaches around the Wind Rivers and all the way to Yellowstone. I still can't figure out how it does it, but Lander somehow

downtown Lander

© DON PITCHER

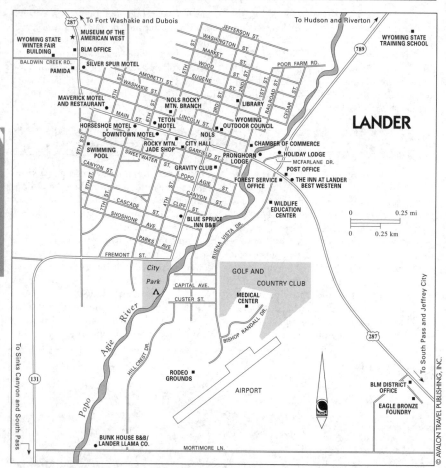

LANDER

To Fort Washakie and Dubois

To Hudson and Riverton

WYOMING STATE WINTER FAIR BUILDING

MUSEUM OF THE AMERICAN WEST

BLM OFFICE

WYOMING STATE TRAINING SCHOOL

BALDWIN CREEK RD.

SILVER SPUR MOTEL

PAMIDA

JEFFERSON ST.

WASHINGTON ST.

MARKET ST.

WOOD ST.

POOR FARM RD.

AMORETTI ST.

EUGENE ST.

WASHAKIE ST.

MAVERICK MOTEL AND RESTAURANT

NOLS ROCKY MTN. BRANCH

LIBRARY

WYOMING OUTDOOR COUNCIL

MAIN ST.

LINCOLN ST.

HORSESHOE MOTEL

TETON MOTEL

DOWNTOWN MOTEL

NOLS

ROCKY MTN. JADE SHOP

CITY HALL

CHAMBER OF COMMERCE

SWIMMING POOL

SWEETWATER

GARFIELD ST.

PRONGHORN LODGE

HOLIDAY LODGE

MCFARLANE DR.

POST OFFICE

CANYON ST.

GRAVITY CLUB

POPO AGIE ST.

FOREST SERVICE OFFICE

THE INN AT LANDER BEST WESTERN

CANYON ST.

CASCADE ST.

CLIFF ST.

WILDLIFE EDUCATION CENTER

SHOSHONE AVE.

BLUE SPRUCE INN B&B

BUENA VISTA DR.

PARKS AVE.

FREMONT ST.

City Park

GOLF AND COUNTRY CLUB

CAPITAL AVE.

CUSTER ST.

MEDICAL CENTER

Popo Agie River

HILL CREST DR.

BISHOP RANDALL DR.

To Sinks Canyon and South Pass

131

RODEO GROUNDS

AIRPORT

MORTIMORE LN.

BUNK HOUSE B&B/ LANDER LLAMA CO.

MOON

BLM DISTRICT OFFICE

EAGLE BRONZE FOUNDRY

To South Pass and Jeffrey City

287

789

0   0.25 mi

0   0.25 km

© AVALON TRAVEL PUBLISHING, INC.

has managed to rope in some of the most affable locals anywhere. It's a delightful town.

HISTORY

Lander began in 1869 when the army established a small military post, Camp Augur (later Camp Brown), to protect Shoshones from attacks by the Sioux and Arapaho. Two years later the post was moved to Fort Washakie. The rich valley along the Popo Agie River proved easy to irrigate and grew ample crops to feed hungry miners in nearby South Pass. Settlers moved here from the dying gold mines of South Pass in the late 1870s, creating the crossroads settlement of Pushroot (named because the vegetables grew so well here). It was later renamed Lander, after Col. Frederick W. Lander, who had surveyed the Oregon Trail's Lander Cutoff. One of the town's early denizens was the outlaw Butch Cassidy, who bought a ranch near Dubois and was often seen at Lander poker tables and dance halls. The town grew more rapidly once the railroad arrived in 1906, but it took local farmers a while to adjust. When the first train rolled into town, people crowded around, and the engineer jokingly yelled from his cab, "Stand back, I'm gonna turn around." The crowd scattered in fear. During the 1960s and '70s, Lander became a mining boomtown as hundreds of workers commuted to the Columbia-Geneva iron mine and mill near Atlantic City. The mine closed in 1983.

SIGHTS

Lander's primary sights aren't in town but just a short drive away in Sinks Canyon; see the Lander Vicinity section for details.

The **Museum of the American West** is located on a 13-acre site at 1445 W. Main St., 307/332-4137, www.amwest.org. A dozen or so historical buildings are on the grounds as of 2003, and the museum building is expected to open in 2004. When open, it will showcase exhibits on the trappers, Indians, and others who settled this region. During the summer, the historical buildings are used for living-history presentations (fee charged), with a blacksmith at work and other activities. Two-hour historical bus tours are available summer evenings.

Located in a strip of shops next to a Foursquare Gospel Church, the small **Lander Children's Museum,** 445 Lincoln St., 307/332-1341, is open Tuesday and Thursday 10 A.M.–4 P.M. in summer, and Saturday 10 A.M.–noon in winter. Entrance is $2 per person, or $1 for seniors.

The **One-Shot Evans-Dahl Memorial Museum,** 545 W. Main St., 307/332-8190, has memorabilia from this bizarre organization for antelope hunters. See the Events section for details on the One-Shot Antelope Hunt each September. You may want to also visit the Department of Game & Fish's **Wildlife Education Center** in its building at 260 Buena Vista Dr. (near the Forest Service office), 307/332-2688. It features wildlife dioramas interactive displays representing Wyoming's ecosystems.

In recent years Lander has gained notoriety for the bronze statues that line Main Street, including a bronze round-up of four larger-than-life steers, horse and cowboy, the "Lander Lil" groundhog, and a giant bull elk at Pronghorn Lodge. These statues are the creations of **Eagle Bronze Foundry,** located in an industrial park at 130 Poppy St., 307/332-5436. It's one of the largest foundries in the western United States. The foundry's pieces can be found in such places as NFL stadiums and outside the headquarters of Cabela's (a sporting-goods company). One piece they completed (now in Dallas) is the largest bronze monument on the planet. The foundry has a fine-art gallery, and interesting tours are offered Monday–Friday at 10 A.M.

Getting Jaded

The Jeffrey City area (60 miles east of Lander) is world-famous for its nephrite jade, a mineral found only in Asia, British Columbia, and Wyoming. The jade comes from Crooks Mountain, and much of it was discovered in the 1930s and '40s by Bert Rhoads, who established **Rhoads' Jewelry,** 423 Main, 307/332-4439. His wife, Verla, discovered the largest piece of jade ever found—a 3,366-pound boulder that required heavy mining equipment to haul out. Wyoming jade varies greatly in value depending on color and rarity. Some of it sells for around $7.50 a pound, but Wyoming emerald jade can sell for several thousand dollars per carat. Warning: Much of the jewelry sold as "Wyoming jade" actually comes from British Columbia. Buy only from reputable dealers.

National Outdoor Leadership School

Established in 1965 by legendary mountaineer Paul Petzoldt, who died in 1999 at the age of 91, the National Outdoor Leadership School (NOLS) is headquartered in an old brick building at 284 Lincoln Street. In the intervening years this nonprofit school has grown to become the nation's leading source for training in wilderness skills and outdoor leadership. Staff members at NOLS have achieved a reputation as the purists in the field, emphasizing low-impact camping, respect for the land, and safety. The school publishes several excellent books on wilderness mountaineering, backcountry first aid, and minimizing your impact. The Wilderness Medicine Institute is also owned by NOLS and based in Lander. Trivia facts: NOLS is the fourth-largest purchaser of U.S. Geological Survey maps in the country and

WIND RIVER

the largest outfitting permittee on federal lands anywhere.

Today NOLS offers classes all over the world lasting from two weeks to three months and covering everything from Alaska sea kayaking to a semester in Australia. These are *not*, however, glorified adventure trips; you'll need to carry your own gear, help with cooking and cleanup, and be willing to work hard. You can rent equipment from NOLS for the classes. The school also owns a grand old hotel in downtown Lander that is used to house students and instructors when they aren't in the backcountry. College credit is available for some courses, as is a limited amount of financial aid. Get all the details and a schedule of classes at 307/332-5300, www.nols.edu.

In addition to the main headquarters at Lincoln and 3rd Streets, Lander is also home to the **NOLS Rocky Mountain Branch,** just up the street at 502 Lincoln St., 307/332-1421. More than 1,100 students come here each year to take part in backpacking, horsepacking, and mountaineering trips to the Wind River Mountains and Absaroka Range. The branch office sells new and used gear of all types and rents tents, backpacks, sleeping bags, clothes, hiking boots, stoves, fishing poles, and other outdoor supplies. Other NOLS regional offices are located in Alaska, Arizona, Idaho, and Washington, and the organization has international bases in Australia, Canada, Chile, Kenya, and Mexico.

Environmental Groups

Partly because of its proximity to the Wind River Mountains, Lander has become a center for the environmental movement in Wyoming. The town is home to the **Wyoming Outdoor Council,** an organization founded in 1967 that emphasizes conservation education and environmental lobbying, especially on such issues as wilderness, wildlife, mining, oil and gas development, growth impacts, and waste management. Tax-deductible memberships start at $25 per year. The council's office is at 262 Lincoln St., 307/332-7031; find them on the web at www.wyomingoutdoorcouncil.org.

The Nature Conservancy has its Wyoming state office at 258 Main St., 307/332-2971,

www.tncwyoming.org. The organization works with landowners to protect important habitats through conservation easements, land donations, and acquisitions. More than 350,000 acres in Wyoming have been protected. Several of these areas are open to the public, including the Tensleep Preserve and Heart Mountain Ranch (both described in the Bighorn Basin chapter), Sweetwater River Project (see Lander Vicinity section of this chapter), and Red Canyon Ranch Preserve (see South Pass Area later in this chapter).

ACCOMMODATIONS

Pets are allowed in most of these establishments.

Under $50

Horseshoe Motel, 685 W. Main St., 307/332-4915, has older rooms for $35 s or $40–45 d, including some with fridges and microwaves. **Teton Motel,** 586 W. Main St., 307/332-3582, charges $36–38 s or d and has an outdoor pool. Kitchenettes are $43–47 d.

Stay at **Silver Spur Motel,** 1240 W. Main St., 307/332-5189 or 800/922-7831, for $37–42 s or $47–52 d, where the amenities include an outdoor pool and a large deck facing the mountains. Kitchenettes and family rooms are also available. Sleep in clean and updated rooms at **Maverick Motel,** 808 W. Main St., 307/332-2300 or 877/622-2300, for $40 s or $45–48 d.

A friendly, easygoing place to stay is **Holiday Lodge (National 9 Inn),** 210 McFarlane Dr., 307/332-2511 or 800/624-1974. Rates are $42 s or $47–52 d. Kitchenettes are $5 extra, and an indoor hot tub is available. Some rooms contain microwaves and fridges, and pets are accepted.

At the **Downtown Motel,** 569 W. Main St., 307/332-3171 or 800/900-3171, rooms cost $44 for one queen bed or $49 for two. Family rooms with two bedrooms and four beds are $79. All rooms contain microwaves and fridges.

$50 and Up

Pronghorn Lodge (Budget Host), 150 E. Main St., 307/332-3940 or 800/283-4678, www.wyoming.com/~thepronghorn, has quality rooms for $56 s or $61–74 d, and four-person suites for $74. Amenities include a hot tub, continental breakfast, and exercise room.

The Inn at Lander (Best Western), 260 Grand View Dr., 307/332-2847 or 800/528-1234, www.bestwestern.com, is a modern place with rooms for $70 s or $80 d, and such features as an outdoor pool, hot tub, a small exercise room, and a light breakfast.

Bed-and-Breakfasts

In a quiet neighborhood a few blocks from downtown, **Blue Spruce Inn B&B,** 677 S. 3rd St., 307/332-8253 or 888/503-3311, www.bluespruceinn.com, is a large brick home built in 1920 and nicely furnished with period pieces. It has four guest rooms with private baths, as well as a rec room housing a dartboard and pool table. Outside are flower gardens, tall spruce trees, and a veranda with a swing. Friendly and helpful owners, too. Rates are $85 s or d, including a full breakfast. Kids older than age 12 are welcome.

Just two miles from downtown, **Bunk House B&B,** 307/332-5624 or 800/582-5262, www.landerllama.com, seems a world away. An old barn has been transformed into a comfortably rustic place to spend the night. Although it isn't spacious and has no phone, this is a perfect spot for families. A branch of the Popo Agie River flows through the property, and llamas are right outside the door. Breakfast is a make-it-yourself affair, but the ingredients—along with a stove and fridge—are provided. The bunkhouse costs $75 per night for up to five people. Owners Scott and Therese Woodruff run **Lander Llama Company,** and the nearby pastures contain llamas used for backcountry trips. Guests, and especially kids, will love the chance to feed and pet them.

Baldwin Creek B&B, 2343 Baldwin Creek Rd., 307/332-7608, www.wyomingbandb.com, is set in the scenic foothills of the Wind River Mountains five miles west of Lander. Here you'll fine a historic log home with two guest rooms ($90 d) and four modern cabins ($95 d; $10 each for extra guests), all with private baths. The cabins contain microwaves, fridges, and small porches facing the Wind River Mountains. A full breakfast is served, and kids are welcome.

Guesthouses and Cabins

For privacy with a view of the Wind River Mountains, stay at **Outlaw Cabins,** five miles northwest of Lander, 307/332-9655, www.outlawcabins.com. Two cabins—one of which dates back more than a century—are available on this working cattle ranch. Both are nicely furnished, with lofts that are perfect for kids, and have decks to relax in the shade. Each also includes a kitchenette and private bath. Rates are $85 d or $95 for four guests. A two-night minimum is required.

Horse lovers will enjoy a night at **High Country Arabians Guest House,** 307/332-2106, www.highcountryarabians.com. This spacious modern home with a bedroom, loft, living room, and full kitchen is three miles west from Lander and sleeps six people. A deck faces the pasture, where you'll see the owner's Arabian horses. The entire house rents for $125 d per night ($10 per person for additional guests), including a continental breakfast.

Ten miles northwest of Lander along the North Fork of the Popo Agie River, **Black Mountain Ranch Country Guest House,** 307/332-6442, www.wyomingmade.com, is a 3,400-square-foot home with four beautifully furnished bedrooms, three baths, a full kitchen, and laundry facilities. It's available for $550 d per week ($750 for up to nine people) or $90 d per night ($130 for up to nine people). There's a two-night minimum. The owners also run an adjacent gift shop with dried flower arrangements and antiques. Black Mountain is a favorite of fly-fishermen, with the river just steps away.

Mountain Rose Cabin, 2986 Sinks Canyon Rd., 307/332-2830, is seven miles from town and near the Popo Agie River. The modern cabin has all of the amenities of home, including a bedroom and sleeping loft, kitchenette, screened porch, phone, and TV. It rents for $100 for up to eight guests and is just one-half mile from Sinks Canyon State Park.

Cottage House of Squaw Creek, 307/332-5003, www.cottagehouseoftails.com, is on Squaw Creek Llama Ranch, five miles west of Lander. The modern log cottage has a view of the mountains. Inside, an upstairs bedroom fills the upper level, and downstairs you will find a kitchen, living room, bath, and laundry. The cottage sleeps six and can be rented as a guesthouse for $65 s or $78 d. Extra persons are $10 each.

Guest Ranches

At an elevation of 9,200 feet on the edge of the Popo Agie Wilderness, **Allen's Diamond Four Ranch,** 307/332-2995, www.diamond4ranch .com, provides a delightful outdoors adventure. The owners are NOLS instructors, and the ranch emphasizes horseback riding, natural-history hikes, wildlife watching, and fishing. Overnight pack trips and cattle roundups are also available. The ranch has basic accommodations with woodstoves and propane lights but no electricity. Guests bring their own sleeping bags and pillows. No swimming pools or golf courses at this ranch! The ranch is open July–September and can accommodate up to 10 guests. All-inclusive weekly rates are $1,800 for two people.

Twin Creek Ranch & Lodge, 307/335-7485, www.twincreekranch.com, is 25 miles southeast of Lander on the edge of the Red Desert. This 20,000-acre ranch covers a mixture of rugged country that includes arid range-land, lush valleys, and crimson red sandstone bluffs. It's a working cattle ranch where the emphasis is on turning grass into beef while preserving the environment. Activity centers on horseback riding, and guests take part in checking or rounding up cattle on the open range, saddling horses, and branding calves. This is a great place to experience a no-frills taste of the West with a maximum of just six people at a time. All-inclusive weekly rates are $1,200 per person when ranch activity is at a peak (May, June, Sept., and Oct.). At other times, guests enjoy mountain biking, birding, hiking, fly-fishing, or just lolling around; $200 d per night with three meals and lodging. Guests stay in a gorgeous log lodge, and every Saturday night it opens for five-course dinners (around $40 per person) that attract folks from Lander and Riverton. Call two days ahead for dining reservations. Twin Creek is open year-round.

CAMPING

Camping costs nothing at **Lander City Park,** 405 Fremont St., right along the banks of the Popo Agie River. Pitch tents on the shady grass here or park RVs in the lot. Local high-schoolers often pull in for a bit of extracurricular activity, so don't expect a quiet night. Camping is available May–September. Take showers at the Lander swimming pool, next to the junior high school, or at local RV parks.

Sinks Canyon State Park, 10 miles southwest of Lander on State Hwy. 131, has two campgrounds ($12 for nonresidents or $6 for Wyoming residents) open May–October. Details at 307/332-6333, http://wyoparks.state.wy.us. For additional information on Sinks Canyon, see Lander Vicinity.

Several private campgrounds operate in the Lander area. Riverside tent sites ($8 per person; no RVs) are available behind (and down a steep hill) from **Holiday Lodge,** 210 McFarlane Dr., 307/332-2511 or 800/624-1974. Tenters can use the motel's hot tub for free. Noncampers can take a shower for $5. Open June–Sept.

Five miles northwest on U.S. Hwy. 287 (inside the Wind River Indian Reservation), **Rocky Acres Campground,** 307/332-6953, is open May–September. Rates are $10 for self-contained RVs (no tent sites); showers are not available.

Ray Lake Campground, nine miles northwest on U.S. Hwy. 287, 307/332-9333, charges $8 for tents, $15 for RVs; open May–Sept. Showers for noncampers run $3. The campground also has a small café.

On a hill out the east end of town, **Sleeping Bear RV Park and Campground,** 715 E. Main, 307/332-5159 or 888/757-2327, www.sleeping-rv-park.com, has tent sites for $16 and RV sites with hookups for $26. Open all year. If you aren't staying here, showers are $5.

Hart Ranch Hideout RV Resort, 10 miles southeast on U.S. Hwy. 287, 307/332-3836 or 800/914-9226, www.hartranchhideout.com, has tent sites for $18 ($10 if you're on a bike), and RV sites with hookups for $23; open May–Oct. Noncampers can use the showers for $2.50. A café is on the premises.

FOOD

Lander is blessed with several excellent restaurants to please almost any taste.

Breakfast and Lunch

For a light start on the day, drop by Lander's standout espresso place, **The Magpie,** 159 N. 2nd, 307/332-5565; closed Sundays. You'll find healthy light breakfasts and creative lunchtime salads. It's a great place to hang out. **Highwayman Cafe,** on the south end of town, 307/332-2566, opens at 5:30 A.M. and is known for its sourdough pancakes. Another favorite morning spot is **The Maverick,** 808 W. Main St., 307/332-2300, where you'll also find good prime rib dinners. On weekends, **The Showboat** at 1st and Main has an all-you-can-eat buffet. Open daily at 6 A.M., it serves breakfast all day. **The Oxbow,** 170 E. Main, 307/332-0233, offers breakfast, lunch, and dinner fare in a casual diner setting.

Get deli sandwiches at **The Breadboard,** 1350 W. Main, 307/332-6090. For ice cream, stop by **Mom's Malt Shop,** 351 W. Main, 307/332-5050, or **Popo Agie One Stop,** 8116 Hwy. 789, 307/332-4402.

Chocolates for Breakfast, next to Wild Iris at 329 W. Main St., 307/332-9273, has juices, espresso, teas, gourmet chocolates, candles, and gifts.

American

The Hitching Rack, one-half mile south on U.S. Hwy. 287, 307/332-4322, has a big salad bar and homemade soups. This is the place locals go for steak and seafood dinners (it's not open for other meals). Actually, two of the most popular night-out places are 10 miles northeast in Hudson: Svilar's and Club El Toro.

Tony's Pizza Shack, 637 W. Main, 307/332-3900, makes good pizzas using homemade dough. Their breadsticks are a local favorite, and the rooftop deck is popular in the summer.

If you have a hankering for barbecue beef, try **Silver Spur BBQ,** 1240 W. Main, 307/332-5189, with nice outdoor seating, or **JB's Wild Wyoming,** 628 W. Main, 307/332-2065 or 888/945-3996, www.wildwyo.com. JB's is known for their baked beans, homemade buffalo bratwursts, and fresh sausage.

Eclectic

Meet the NOLS outdoorsy gang at **Gannett Grill,** 126 W. Main St., 307/332-8228, www.landerbar.com. The café offers pizzas, sandwiches, half-pound burgers, salads, and bar munchies (including crinkle-cut battered fries). The historic **Lander Bar** (connected) pours regional microbrews and has a pool table. Gannett Grill overflows on summer evenings with an informal and noisy crowd, and live music fills the air on weekends. Highly recommended.

Next door, in an 1888 brick building that once housed a Chinese laundry, is **Cowfish,** 148 W. Main St., 307/332-8227. It has the same owners as Gannett Grill and shares a pleasant patio where folks from both places can mingle. Cowfish offers a hip setting and the sort of perfectly prepared meals you'd expect in Jackson. The bistro menu ranges from cow (or fish) burgers and grass-fed beef steaks to salads, grilled halibut, and ginger-soy veggie stir-fry. Dinner entrées run $6–20. The brewery is run by folks from the acclaimed Snake River Brewery.

For more only-in-Lander meals, try the tiny **Hawaii Connection,** an Internet café at 140 N. 7th, 307/332-8015, that boasts the only Hawaiian fare in the Cowboy state. Closed Tuesdays.

International

China Garden, 162 N. 6th St., 307/332-7666, has Chinese lunch specials, reasonable dinners, and vegetarian dishes. Fairly authentic, too.

Big Noi Restaurant, 812 N. Hwy. 789, 307/332-3102, serves authentic Thai food and more standard American fare. This is one of just three Thai restaurants in Wyoming; the others are in Jackson.

Groceries and Bakeries

For groceries, head to **Mr. D's Food Center,** 725 W. Main St., 307/332-2964, or **Safeway,** 485 W. Main St., 307/332-4950. Both have instore delis and bakeries.

Wildflour Bagels and Bread, 545 W. Main, 307/332-9728, is the best local bakery, specializing in hand-rolled bagels and delicious fresh breads. Lunch specials include homemade soup in a bread bowl, or try a smoothie from the juice bar.

RECREATION
Rock Climbing

When most folks think of recreation in Lander, they think of the wonderful mountain country just a few miles away. **Wild Iris Mountain Sports,** 333 Main St., 307/332-4541 or 888/284-5968, www.wildirisclimbing.com, sells books detailing local climbing areas, including the **Wild Iris Climbing Area,** 29 miles south of Lander on Limestone Mountain. This area has around 150 different climbs, with pitches from 5.7 to 5.14. Fifteen miles west of Lander is the BLM's **Baldwin Creek Rock Climbing Area,** another challenging area with climbs ranging in difficulty from 5.11 to 5.14. Get a map and access details (high-clearance vehicles are recommended) from the BLM office at 1335 Main St., 307/332-8400, www.wy.blm.gov. Climbers will want to talk with folks at Wild Iris about other rock faces in Sinks Canyon and at Fossil Hill.

Horseback and Wagon Treks

Western Encounters, 307/332-5434 or 800/572-1230, www.horseriders.com, offers horseback or wagon rides along the Oregon Trail and other historic paths. Most treks last a week, and the company provides horses, food, tents, and equipment; you bring the sleeping bag. Trips include the Oregon Trail, Pony Express rides, Butch Cassidy's Hole-in-the-Wall country, rides across the Great Divide Basin, and horse and cattle drives. All-inclusive costs are $1,530–1,800 per person.

Other Recreation

Rent cross-country and downhill skis, snowboards, or snowshoes from **Freewheel Ski & Cycle,** 258 W. Main St., 307/332-6616, www.freewheelski.com.

Lander's Olympic-size **swimming pool,** 450 S. 9th, 307/332-2272, is open year-round. You'll also find a weight room and hydrotherapy pool here. The 18-hole **Lander Golf Club** is on Capi-

tol Hill, 307/332-4653. During the winter, skate for free at City Park, where you'll also find a warming hut and skate rentals.

ENTERTAINMENT

Gannett Grill/Lander Bar, 126 W. Main St., 307/332-8228, www.landerbar.com, brings in live bands—from bluegrass and country to hardcore rock—Friday (and some Saturday) nights. Other places to check for music are **One Shot Lounge,** 695 W. Main St., 307/332-2692, and **The Hitching Rack,** one-half mile south on U.S. Hwy. 287, 307/332-4322.

Watch flicks at **Grand Theatre,** 250 W. Main St., 307/332-3300.

EVENTS

The **International Pedigree Stage Stop Sled Dog Race** (IPSSSDR) stops here. See the Jackson chapter for more info.

Lander plays host to the **Wyoming State Winter Fair** the first weekend in March, with livestock exhibits, dog weight-pulling contests, horse shows, entertainment, and dancing.

Lander Valley Powwow occurs in early May, with Indian dancing, a princess contest, food, and crafts. From early July to mid-August, Wednesday evening **Native American Cultural Programs** are offered at Jaycee Park (1st and Main).

On the second weekend of June the **Popo Agie Rendezvous** commemorates the 1829 rendezvous held near here. Activities include a mountain-man encampment, parade, art auction, buffalo barbecue, pack race, and all sorts of historical demonstrations and games.

Pioneer Days, a three-day party around the Fourth of July, is Lander's big event. It features a big parade with dozens of floats, marching bands, vintage autos, and performers, along with a buffalo barbecue, Indian dancing, street dances, and evening fireworks. The primary event is the nightly **rodeo,** the oldest paid rodeo on earth, first established in 1893. Call the Chamber of Commerce for details.

An **International Climbers' Festival** attracts rock climbers to Lander the second weekend of

July with clinics, slide shows and films, a trade fair, and more. Details at 307/332-4541 or 888/284-5968, www.climbersfestival.org.

The **Lander Jazz Festival,** held every Labor Day weekend, brings Dixieland to Wyoming for three days of shows, rambles, gospel performances, and the finale meltdown. Details at 800/433-0662, www.landerjazz.com. The **Chokecherry Festival** in mid-August brings live music and booths to Jaycee Park.

The **One-Shot Antelope Hunt** attracts hunters in mid-September; teams of three head out to see how quickly they can bring down an antelope with just one shot. The governors of Wyoming and Colorado are "team captains," and celebrities sometimes participate. All sorts of convoluted rules and ridiculous ceremonies make this akin to a fraternity initiation rite. Old men find strange ways to amuse themselves, including cross-dressing!

SHOPPING

Lander is a town of book readers and supports three good bookshops. **Main Street Books,** 381 W. Main St., 307/332-7661 or 877/332-7661, www.mainstreetbooks.com, is the largest, with a fine choice of books, plus espresso and Internet access. **The Book Basket,** 325 W. Main, 307/335-7997, has used books, and **Cabin Fever Books,** 163 S. 5th, 307/332-9580 or 800/836-9580, offers both new and used titles.

Stop by **Wild Iris Mountain Sports,** 333 W. Main St., 307/332-4541 or 888/284-5968, www.wildirisclimbing.com, for outdoor gear and climbing books, including guidebooks to climbing areas in Fremont Canyon, Dome Rock, Sinks Canyon, Baldwin Creek, and Wild Iris. Owner Todd Skinner is a world-renowned rock climber; in 1999 he and six others were the first to free-climb a 3,800-foot cliff in Greenland, the tallest in the world. Check the shop's bulletin board for climbing partners or used gear.

INFORMATION AND SERVICES

The **Lander Chamber of Commerce** is in the old railroad depot at 160 N. 1st Street, 307/332-

3892 or 800/433-0662, www.landerchamber.org; open Mon.–Fri. 9 A.M.–5 P.M. all year; limited Sat. hours June–Aug. The chamber rents taped audio tours of the Loop Road, describing sights along the way, for $6 plus a refundable deposit.

The **BLM's Lander Field Office** is at 1335 W. Main Street, 307/332-5460, www.wy.blm.gov, and the Shoshone National Forest's **Washakie Ranger District Office** is at 333 E. Main Street, 307/332-5460, www.fs.fed.us/r2/shoshone. Stop at the Forest Service office for Shoshone National Forest maps and hiking information, plus lobby exhibits on the forest. The staff can also provide a list of permitted horsepackers, llama outfitters, and even a local company that provides pack goats for use in the backcountry.

Lander's **post office** stands at the junction of U.S. Hwy. 287 and State Hwy. 789, 307/332-2126. Unfortunately, it rests atop what was previously Wyoming's only in-town prairie-dog town. The **Lander Library** at 2nd and Amoretti, 307/332-5194, www.fremontcountylibraries.org, has computers where you can surf the web or check email.

Wash clothes at **American Dry Cleaning & Laundry,** 175 N 5th St. or 550 Lincoln Street.

The **Lander Valley Medical Center,** 1320 Vishop Randall Dr., 307/332-4420, www.landerhospital.com, has 24-hour emergency services.

TRANSPORTATION AND TOURS

The nearest airport with scheduled flights is in Riverton, 25 miles from Lander. **Winds Aloft Aviation,** 307/332-9233, provides flightseeing and charter trips over the Wind River Mountains out of the small Lander airport.

Rent cars from **Fremont Motors,** 555 E. Main St., 307/332-4355 or 800/788-9496, or **Rent-A-Wreck,** 323 N. 2nd St., 307/332-9965 or 888/332-9965.

The nonprofit **Wind River Transportation Authority** (WRTA), 307/856-7118 or 800/439-7118, www.wrtabuslines.com, has a mix of services, including summertime shuttles ($15 one way) to Riverton Airport, trips to the Salt Lake City airport ($75 one way), and a winter schedule connecting Riverton,

WIND RIVER

Lander, and the Wind River Reservation. The Salt Lake trips are especially popular with NOLS students but are open to the general public with a minimum of two people. In addition, WRTA can provide transportation throughout western Wyoming for groups.

Lander Vicinity

EAST ON U.S. HIGHWAY 287

A few miles east of Lander on U.S. Hwy. 287, the highway passes an impressive vermilion sandstone butte. Near here is a beautiful, century-old red-rock barn that once stabled horses used on the stage route through here. In 1884, Wyoming's first oil well was drilled not far away. The site—now called the Dallas Dome oil field—was known to Indians and described in Washington Irving's *Adventures of Captain Bonneville* as the "Great Tar Springs." Nineteenth-century emigrants used the oil to grease wagon axles, in lamps, and as a balm for their aches. Mountain man Osborne Russell described coming across the spring in 1837:

> *This spring produces about one gallon per hour of pure oil of Coal or rather Coal Tar the scent of which is often carried on the wind 5 or 6 mls. The Oil issues from the ground within 30 feet of the stream and runs off slowly into the water Camp stopped here eight days We set fire to the spring when there was 2 or 3 Bbls. of oil on the ground about it, it burnt very quick and clear but produced a dense column of thick black smoke the oil above ground being consumed the fire soon went out.*

As you continue eastward, the Wind River Mountains gradually diminish in magnitude. Stop to look up at them for a while. It is easy to see how the pioneers from the east—where a mountain is anything over 1,000 feet—would watch these mountains grow closer with each day's travel and wonder at their rugged crowns. It's also easy to see why they would choose to go around the southern end of this range—at South Pass—instead of crossing over the top.

Sweetwater Preserve

One mile west of the junction of U.S. Hwy. 287 and State Hwy. 135 is the Nature Conservancy's **Sweetwater River Project,** www.tncwyoming.org, a 3,000-acre natural area that preserves six miles of riparian habitat along the Oregon Trail. The preserve is open only to Nature Conservancy members, but camping and rustic cabins are available. For access information, call the Conservancy in Lander at 307/332-2971.

Ice Slough

Forty miles east of Lander, the highway passes a marker describing Ice Slough, one of many landmarks along this portion of the Oregon Trail. Dense grasses in a small marsh kept ice all through the summer, a real treat for emigrants on a hot summer day. The trail is visible just to the right of the historical sign that describes Ice Slough; it's just north of the wire gate. In *Roughing It,* Mark Twain described Ice Slough as follows:

> *In the night we sailed by a most notable curiosity, and one we had been hearing a good deal about for a day or two, and were suffering to see. This was what might be called a natural ice-house. It was August, now, and sweltering weather in the daytime, yet at one of the stations the men could scrape the soil on the hill-side under the lee of a range of boulders, and at a depth of six inches cut out pure blocks of ice—hard, compactly frozen, and clear as crystal.*

Jeffrey City

The bleak, almost ghost town of Jeffrey City is a casualty of the bust that followed the uranium-mining boom of the 1970s. First called Home on the Range, the town was renamed for a

Rawlins philanthropist, Dr. Charles W. Jeffrey. The town was built on the nuclear industry, and as a company town its survival was tied to the fortunes of Western Nuclear Company. By 1980, the population had swollen to 4,000. Today you'd be lucky to find 50 folks around here, and weeds grow through the concrete sidewalks around empty bunkhouses with plywood-covered windows. The gas station and modern grade school survived for awhile, but they too closed a few years back. Open still are **Split Rock Bar & Cafe** and **J.C. Motel,** 307/544-9317, where rooms run $25 s or $28 d. Ranching, oil, and gas keep Jeffrey City from drying up and blowing away, and a uranium mine in the desert south of town is ready to reopen if prices ever rise. Rock hounds should ask for directions to the famed jade deposits around the city, but make sure you're on public land or have permission from landowners.

East of Jeffrey City lies definitive Wyoming country with rolling sage and grassland, a few weathered old homesteads, and distant mountains on all sides. A sign notes the turnoff to **Cottonwood Campground** ($6; open June–Oct.), a BLM facility six miles east of Jeffrey City and then 11 miles south on Green Mountain Loop Road. Campsites are set in a surprisingly pleasant aspen forest. You aren't likely to meet many folks here, but you may come across some wild horses (look for their long manes and tails), particularly near a picnic area at the aptly named Wild Horse Point, eight miles from the campground. Free campsites can be found at county-run **Green Mountain Park,** on the road to Cottonwood Campground.

For a glimpse of the **Oregon Trail,** head eight miles east of Jeffrey City on U.S. 287, and turn north up Agate Flat Road. In less than one mile you'll see the trail ruts and a concrete post marking them.

See the Central Wyoming chapter for more on the country east and north of Jeffrey City, including the Oregon Trail sites of Independence Rock, Devil's Gate, and Split Rock, and the Indian pictographs at Castle Gardens.

SINKS CANYON AND THE LOOP ROAD

State Hwy. 131 climbs south from Lander through fascinating Sinks Canyon and then over the mountains to Atlantic City. A popular loop trip is to follow this road to Atlantic City, returning to Lander via State Hwy. 28, a total distance of 56 miles. Plan to spend at least one full day if you want to savor the many sights along the way. Locally known as the Loop Road, it is very popular with both visitors and residents. **Bighorn sheep** were transplanted into Sinks Canyon in 1987 and a dozen or so survive; look for them along the road. Rock climbers practice their skills on the steep cliffs of the canyon. Of interest to climbers and geologists are the three different types of rock in a five-mile stretch: sandstone, limestone, and granite. You'll find several campgrounds here, lots of lakes, trails, and big mountain country. Get to State Hwy. 131 by heading south on Lander's 5th Street. Sinks Canyon begins seven miles away.

The Sinks

The Popo Agie River (usually pronounced "po-PO-zha," but you'll hear lots of other versions) begins in the snowfields of the Wind River Mountains and drops northeast to its junction with the Wind River near Riverton. **Sinks Canyon State Park** contains one of Wyoming's geological wonders. Here the Middle Fork of the Popo Agie plunges into a cave (the "Sinks"), only to emerge again one-half mile down in a gigantic spring (the "Rise"). The river's name—Popo Agie—is a Crow Indian word meaning "Beginning of the Waters." Apparently, the stream originally flowed aboveground—it still does during high spring runoff—but over time a cave formed in the water-soluble Madison Limestone that underlies this region, allowing the water to disappear into enormous underground caverns or convoluted passages from which it slowly drains. In 1983, researchers put dye in the Sinks. The dye did reappear at the rise, but not until two hours later! The water was also a few degrees warmer, and more water appeared

WIND RIVER

than entered the cavern. Lots of fat rainbow and brown trout congregate in the pool at the Rise, waiting for visitors to toss them bits of food. A vending machine sells fish food (fish do not live by bread alone). No fishing is allowed. Also keep your eyes open for the muskrat that lives in the spring here.

Sinks Visitor Center, 307/332-3077, http://wyoparks.state.wy.us, houses displays of fish and animals, along with geological exhibits. Open daily 8 A.M.–7 P.M. during summer only. The windows face down this steep-walled canyon, offering dramatic vistas. The cave into which the stream disappears is directly behind the visitors center. This area is a fine place to watch birds. Look for dippers—the odd birds that walk underwater—on the rocks above the Sinks.

Three nearby campgrounds operate April–October: state-run **Sawmill Campground** and **Popo Agie Campground** ($12 for nonresidents or $6 for Wyoming residents; http://wyoparks.state.wy.us), plus just up the road, the Forest Service's **Sinks Canyon Campground** ($8). Get brochures at the visitors center for the mile-long **nature trail** near Popo Agie Campground. More interesting is the **Popo Agie Falls Trail,** which takes off from Bruce's Parking Area one mile above Popo Agie Campground. This fairly easy 1.5-mile trail climbs 600 feet in elevation to a series of attractive waterfalls, the largest being 60 feet. Horses and mountain bikes are allowed on the trail, which is passable for some wheelchairs. During winter, skiers enjoy groomed cross-country trails in the canyon at Sinks Canyon Campground.

Into the Mountains

Several miles above the state park, the road turns to gravel and switchbacks steeply up the canyon's south face. The Owl Creek Mountains—50 miles to the north—are visible from the overlook. The road is usually open mid-June to mid-October and gets washboarded in sections, so be ready for a buckin'-bronc ride and lots of traffic on summer weekends. The rough ride is made worthwhile by excellent vistas and several attractive lakes (enlarged by dams). This is pri-

marily lodgepole and limber pine country, but around Louis Lake you'll discover some huge old Engelmann spruce and subalpine fir trees. (There is talk of paving Loop Road, but many locals want to keep it unpaved.)

The Forest Service maintains five delightful campgrounds along the Loop Road: **Fiddler's Lake** ($8; open July to mid-Sept.), **Louis Lake** ($8; open mid-June to mid-Sept.), **Popo Agie** (free; open July to mid-Sept.), **Sinks Canyon** ($8; open May–Oct.), and **Worthen Meadows** ($8; open mid-June to mid-Sept.). Fiddler's Lake has fully accessible facilities and, at 9,400 feet, is the highest. Louis Lake is easily the most popular, made more scenic by a sharp granite cliff that rises directly behind the lake. There's good fishing for brown and Mackinaw trout, and moose are commonly seen around Louis Lake's margins. Other folks car-camp for free around Frye Lake or off the road. Hiking trails head west from Loop Road to the lake-dotted Popo Agie Wilderness (see the Wind River Mountains section).

The Resort at Louis Lake, 307/332-5549 or 888/422-2246, www.louislake.com, rents rustic four-person cabins (built in 1937) with oil lanterns, handmade furnishings, and a shared bathhouse for $65. Newer cabins (these sleep up to eight) contain kitchens and private baths and cost $135. Also available are horse and llama pack trips, drop-pack trips, and rentals of fishing boats and canoes in the summer, or snowshoes and cross-country skis when the snow flies. This is a classic Wyoming lodge with a peaceful mountain setting and friendly owners. Book well ahead, though, because it's full all summer long! The cabins are available all year and make a favorite winter base for cross-country skiing and snowmobiling.

South from Louis Lake the road opens into a high plateau with limber pine trees and wide vistas south to the Oregon Buttes. Antelope are common in the sagebrush country, and moose are seen in the aspen stands along the road and in the marshes around Fiddler's Lake. The Loop Road meets State Hwy. 28 beside the now-abandoned U.S. Steel iron-ore mine. From here you can continue back to Lander on the highway or visit historic South Pass (see South Pass Area later in this chapter).

Wind River Indian Reservation

At more than 2.2 million acres, the Wind River is one of America's largest Indian reservations. Home to both the Northern Arapaho and the Eastern Shoshone tribes, it reaches some 70 miles from north to south and 55 miles east to west. You'll find some of the most unforgettable vistas in Wyoming here: fabulous badlands on the western edge; the beautiful Wind River, where the cottonwoods glow a brilliant yellow in the cool fall air; deep green irrigated pastures where horses, sheep, and cattle graze; and desolate, wide-open spaces where only cactus, sagebrush, jackrabbits, and rattlesnakes grow. Bright yellow sunflowers add color to the roadsides in late summer, and horses seem to be everywhere. All this is backdropped by the enormous, snowcapped Wind River Mountains. The eminent guide Jim Bridger reportedly attempted to convince Brigham Young that this basin would be a far better home for the Mormons than the deserts around Salt Lake. Young refused to listen. It is just as well because this was—and still is—Indian country.

The Wind River Reservation was the scene for the classic Zane Grey Western *War Paint,* a film that featured Tim McCoy and hundreds of Arapaho and Shoshone Indians. Today, hundreds of people, both Indian and nonnative, come to watch a different form of entertainment—the many powwows that occur throughout the summer months on the reservation. The annual sun-dance ceremonies are more intense, spiritual events at which outsiders are only tolerated. The Shoshone and Arapaho peoples maintain separate sundances and powwows; absolutely no cameras or tape recorders are allowed during the sundances.

Despite the proximity of the reservation to Lander and Riverton, there isn't really a lot of mixing between Indians and nonnatives, except in business situations. After more than 125 years, the various cultures—Arapaho, Shoshone, and Anglo—are still like oil and water. Some whites continue to view the Indians as disorganized, drunken, and lazy, while some Indians regard whites as pushy, materialistic, selfish, and disrespectful. Even between the Shoshones and Arapaho, relations are still somewhat strained.

Public Access

Although you can drive through with no problems, access to many parts of the reservation is controlled by Indian authorities, and trespassers may be fined. If you want to explore the reservation, pick up a copy of the fishing regulations from sporting-goods stores in Lander, Riverton, and Dubois, or from the **Tribal Fish and Game Office** in Fort Washakie, 307/332-7207. These regulations detail not only fishing, but also hiking, boating, camping, and other recreation options on the reservation. For most of these activities you'll need a $5 recreation stamp, and anyone planning to fish will also need to purchase a fishing permit (nonresidents $20 for one day or $60 for a week). Restrictions apply, and several areas, including the entire northern end of the reservation near the Owl Creek Mountains, are closed to the non-Indian public. Hunting by outsiders on the reservation is strictly verboten. The map that comes with the permit lists public camping areas on the reservation.

SHOSHONE HISTORY

Originally peoples of the Great Basin, the Shoshones first entered southwestern Wyoming in the 16th century, then gradually pushed northward until they controlled most of the land now known as Wyoming, as well as territory all the way into Canada. As they moved onto the plains, and with the acquisition of the horse, Shoshone life changed drastically from a simple Stone Age culture of grubbing for roots and eating whatever they could catch by hand to a sophisticated buffalo-centered livelihood. Because Shoshone culture extended far to the south, they came into contact with Spanish traders and were some of the first Indians to have horses. The Shoshone introduced horses to the northern plains region around 1700, forever transforming Plains Indian culture. To the trappers and traders

WIND RIVER

CHIEF WASHAKIE

The history of Wyoming in the 19th century is one that resonates with battles between Indians and the invading white settlers. Only one tribe—the Shoshone—provided an exception to this rule. The reason for this stems from Chief Washakie (pronounced WASH-a-key), a man whose life spanned the entire tumultuous century. Washakie was born in 1798 of Shoshone and Flathead parents. His birth name was Pina Quanah, but later in life he gained the name Washakie—literally, "The Rattler"—a reference to a rattle made from the dried scrotum of a buffalo that he used to scare Sioux ponies during his daring raids. Because the Blackfeet tribe killed his father, Washakie lived something of an orphan's existence, growing up among both the Lemhi and Bannock peoples. He eventually joined the Eastern Shoshones and quickly proved himself a fearless and extraordinary warrior.

In the 1830s, Washakie, who was fluent in sign language, met and became a close friend of famed mountain man Jim Bridger, and one of his daughters became Bridger's third wife. From Bridger and other trappers, Washakie learned English, along with a realization that a union with whites against his enemies was wiser than trying to fight the countless hordes coming across the plains from the east. Around 1843, after the death of the previous chief, Washakie gained control over a band of Shoshones based in the Upper Green River. As their lifelong chief, he was recognized as an extraordinarily charismatic and forceful leader and a skilled orator. Because of his skills, white settlers sought Washakie out whenever trouble appeared with other tribes.

Washakie's people had been devastated over the years by smallpox, cholera, and other diseases, and they were no match for the Sioux, Cheyenne, and Arapaho. Because of this, Washakie viewed an allegiance with whites as a way to push back other tribes. When some of his young warriors began to complain that the old man was losing his warrior abilities and becoming a lackey, Washakie disappeared for a few weeks and returned with seven enemy scalps. The grumbling ended. Those Shoshones who attacked whites became instant outcasts.

In 1876, Washakie's Shoshones joined with General Crook against the Sioux and Cheyenne in the Battle of the Rosebud. The battle was a stand-off, but Washakie's sage advice almost certainly prevented Crook's troops from facing what befell General Custer one week later. When Pres. Chester Arthur visited Wyoming in 1883, he asked Chief Washakie to meet him at a reception in Fort Washakie. The proud chief demurred, instead insisting that the president come to him. They met in Washakie's tepee.

Chief Washakie died on the Wind River Reservation on February 22, 1900, and was buried with a full military funeral, the only Indian chief ever to be so honored. The procession, which was escorted by the U.S. cavalry, stretched nearly two miles. He was 102 years old and had led his people for more than 60 years. With Washakie died the tradition of having one man as chief of the Shoshones. Although his name is not nearly as well known today as that of Red Cloud or Crazy Horse, Washakie deserves a place as one of the great warriors and peacemakers of American history. A dozen different Wyoming places are named in his honor, including the Washakie Wilderness and Mt. Washakie.

who first encountered them, the Shoshone were known as "the Snakes" because of the serpentine hand signals they used to signify their tribal name. The word *Shoshone* refers to the simple willow-and-sagebrush lodges in which they lived before the great flowering of their culture in the 18th and 19th centuries. The Eastern Shoshone occupied western Wyoming, while their cousins the Western Shoshone lived in Idaho.

In the late 18th century, the expanding Shoshone culture was halted when their enemies—the Sioux, Crow, and Arapaho—forced the Shoshone west of the Laramie Mountains. The Wind River and Fort Bridger vicinities became wintering areas. After a spring sundance and buffalo hunt, the various tribal members would move into the mountains of northern Utah to hunt, fish, and gather berries and roots.

Each fall the entire tribe would gather in the Great Divide Basin and head across the Continental Divide for the fall buffalo hunt in the Wind River and Bighorn basins. Led by Chief Washakie, the Eastern Shoshone—unlike most other Plains Indians—maintained an unbroken friendship with the invading whites.

Onto the Reservation

The Shoshones were not recognized in the great Fort Laramie Treaty of 1851, and the Wind River Basin and Bighorn Basin where they had long lived were assigned to the Crows. The Fort Bridger Treaty of 1863 gave the Shoshones and Bannocks a reservation covering parts of Colorado, Utah, Wyoming, and Idaho. In 1868, this enormous, 45-million-acre spread was whittled down to just the 2.2-million acre Wind River region, and the Bannocks were given a separate Idaho reservation.

Several years later, the government lopped off 600,000 acres around the rich gold region of South Pass City, paying Chief Washakie $500 a year and $5,000 worth of cattle for five years—around four cents per acre. More land—Thermopolis Hot Springs—was ceded to the government in 1897 for $60,000, and in 1905 1.4 million acres were opened to homesteaders north of the Wind River. In exchange for the latter, the Shoshones and Arapaho received per capita payments, schools, payment for water rights, and an irrigation system on what remained of their reservation. The reservation and adjacent lands are now some of the state's most important agricultural regions.

In 1878, Wyoming's territorial governor asked Chief Washakie if the destitute Arapaho—archenemies of the Shoshone—could be allowed to stay temporarily on the Wind River Reservation. Washakie's sympathetic heart finally gave in:

It is plain they can go no further now. Take them down to where Popo Agie walks into Wind River and let them stay until the grass comes again. But when the grass comes again take them off my reservation. I want my words written down on paper with the white man's ink. I want all you to sign as

witnesses to what I have said. And I want a copy of that paper. I have spoken.

Despite this agreement, the "temporary" arrangement became permanent, and urgent pleas by Washakie went unheeded. Once again the government had abused its most loyal friend.

Many years after Chief Washakie's death, the Shoshones sued over this gross injustice. In 1937, the tribe was awarded $6.4 million for the land given to the Arapaho, minus the expenses for every building ever built by the government on the reservation and any services rendered. The cheapskate federal government even deducted $125 for a silver saddle given by President Grant to Chief Washakie as a token of appreciation! What was left amounted to a grand total of $2,350 per capita, distributed almost entirely in various Bureau of Indian Affairs (BIA)-run programs.

ARAPAHO HISTORY

The Arapaho (a Blackfeet Indian term meaning "Tattooed People") always called themselves simply "Our People." They originally lived a farming life in what is now northern Minnesota, but the arrival of whites on the East Coast created a domino effect among eastern Indians, pushing tribes westward on top of each other. Because of this pressure, the Arapaho, along with the Sioux and Crow, migrated onto the Great Plains in the late 18th century. They quickly adopted the nomadic life associated with Plains Indian culture, a life centered on the buffalo and made possible by the horse. Pressure from the Sioux, who numbered perhaps 25,000 individuals versus 3,000 Arapaho, forced the Arapaho to join with the Cheyenne and move south to the Arkansas and Platte River regions.

Around 1830, the Arapaho split into northern and southern divisions, partly because of the establishment of Fort Laramie on the Laramie River in Wyoming and Bent's Fort on the Arkansas River in Colorado. For many years, the Northern Arapaho wintered in northern Colorado, scattering along the North Platte River with the coming of spring and then gathering again in late summer to hunt buffalo and prepare for winter. In the 1851 Fort Laramie Treaty, the

Arapaho and Cheyenne tribes were assigned the area east of the Rockies between the Arkansas and North Platte Rivers, but as gold was discovered in the Rockies, whites began to push the Arapaho off this land.

After Cheyenne and Arapaho warriors began raiding white ranches in Colorado during the early 1860s, the governor demanded action. In the Sand Creek Massacre of 1864, a peaceful Cheyenne and Arapaho village was viciously attacked by U.S. cavalry soldiers under Colonel John M. Chivington. The action sparked a massive retaliation—Arapaho, Sioux, and Cheyenne warriors sacked Julesburg, Colorado, tore down miles of telegraph wire, stampeded cattle herds, and burned ranches and stage stations throughout the Rockies.

After this event, the Arapaho shifted their living patterns and began spending winters along Wyoming's Powder River and summers in the Medicine Bow country to the south. They continued to attack Shoshones on the Wind River Reservation, emigrant trains along the Overland Trail, and miners around South Pass until the early 1870s, but gradually lessened their raids as the futility of their condition became more apparent.

The end came in the Bates Battle of 1874, when the Shoshones and the U.S. Army attacked the Arapaho, leaving them demoralized and without horses or supplies. In the late 1870s, many Arapaho served as army scouts, and some even joined an Arapaho unit of the army during the 1880s. Best-known of the Arapaho scouts was Friday, an orphan Arapaho boy adopted by mountain man and Indian agent Thomas Fitzpatrick and taught in eastern schools. He returned to his tribe and became their most important translator and a force for peace. Friday's friendship with Chief Washakie probably led Washakie to finally tolerate Arapaho on his reservation.

Onto the Reservation

With the buffalo gone and their way of life under constant pressure from white settlers and the deadly diseases they brought, the Arapaho were in desperate straits, shuttling from one temporary home to another. The government refused to set aside a separate reservation, insisting that they live with the Cheyenne in Oklahoma or the Sioux in South Dakota, far from their Wyoming home.

In 1878, the Northern Arapaho were shoehorned onto the Wind River Reservation with their hated enemies in what was to be a "temporary" stay. Only 913 Arapaho, mostly women and children, remained from the tribe that had once been so powerful. (Interestingly, the Arapaho now outnumber the Shoshones on the reservation.) The two bands of Arapaho that settled on the Wind River Reservation were led by Chief Black Coal, whose people settled in present-day Arapahoe, and Chief Sharp Nose, whose people settled around present-day Ethete. Chief Sharp Nose served with the U.S. Army and later lobbied in Washington for the General Allotment Act of 1887, which issued parcels of land (160 acres to the head of a house, 80 acres to single persons over 18, and 40 acres to those under 18) to everyone on the reservation. Sharp Nose even named one of his sons after General Crook, whom he fought alongside during the Sioux wars of the 1870s.

The two tribes continue to jointly occupy the Wind River Reservation, with the Arapaho holding the eastern half (the towns of Ethete and Arapahoe) and the Shoshones the west (the towns of Fort Washakie, Burris, and Crowheart). In 1891, the Arapaho were given equal rights on the reservation, despite Shoshone Chief Washakie's continued attempts to have them removed. Although Chief Washakie's son married an Arapaho woman, there is still very little intermarriage between the tribes and little blending of the two cultures, even after more than a century.

RESERVATION LIFE

In the early reservation years every effort was made to break the spirit of the "savages" and make them into red-skinned Europeans (today's derogatory term is "Apples"—red on the outside, white on the inside). Even that most basic attribute—one's name—was taken away in the 1890s by the Commissioner of Indian Affairs. Thus Yellow Calf became George Caldwell and Night Horse became Henry Lee Tyler. Even William Shakespeare and Cornelius Vanderbilt suddenly became tribal members! The effort was not entirely successful: William Shakespeare was credited with bringing Peyotism—an important Native American religion today—to the Wind River Reservation. Other measures helped weaken the culture, including the repression of sundances and other native religious practices, indoctrination by Christian missionaries, prohibition of face painting, and the forced cutting of young boys' long black hair. Today the nation is paying the price for these all-too-successful attempts to destroy Native American culture.

Most of the 5,100 Arapaho and 2,500 Shoshones live in housing built by the tribal council or in the hundreds of mobile homes that dot the reservation. From a non-Indian point of view, they are decidedly untidy, with junk of all sorts piled outside, but the folks who live here really don't care what outsiders think. You'll find older log cabins all over the back roads, their sod roofs collapsing and their log walls slowly returning to the earth. Several missions are scattered throughout this area, marked by attractive log or stucco churches.

Oil and gas revenues from major fields on the reservation provide millions of dollars each year in the form of monthly dividend payments. These royalties—along with various BIA assistance programs, ranching, farming, and tribal-owned businesses and leases—are the main source of income. An elected Business Council serves as the manager of tribal income. For a good overview of government on the reservation, see *Tribal Government: Wind River Reservation* by Janet Flynn (Lander, WY: Mortimore Publishing).

Despair and Hope

Unemployment is high on the reservation, and more than half of all Indian residents of the Wind River Reservation have incomes below federal poverty guidelines. Pawnshops in Lander and Riverton often acquire valuable cultural items from desperate individuals when the money runs out before the month does. For many on the reservation, sports are the way out. Every kid, it seems, plays basketball; hoops hang outside all of the trailer homes and government-built houses. For older folks, bingo is a major source of en-

tertainment; there are games almost every night of the year. The reservation also has serious problems with drugs and alcohol, as evidenced by high rates of fetal alcohol syndrome, alcohol-related car accidents or fights, and suicide.

Despite all the problems, the Arapaho and Shoshone peoples take pride in their cultural history. To attack the problems of alcoholism and the loss of cultural identity, young people learn their native tongue in special classes and take part in powwows, sundances, and personal vision quests. The warrior tradition is expressed in a high enlistment in the nation's armed forces. For many on the reservation, sports are the way out. Every kid, it seems, plays basketball; hoops hang outside all the trailer homes and government-built houses. For older folks, bingo is a major source of entertainment—there are games almost every night of the year.

The reservation is a center for fine beaded clothing and moccasins much prized by collectors. Arapaho patterns are geometric in nature, with rectangles and triangles appearing frequently. Arapaho women generally use red, black, blue, yellow, orange, and white as the main colors, with mountains, tepees, and butterflies as common motifs. Eastern Shoshone patterns tend to be more circular, with the rose a popular theme.

INDIAN POWWOWS

Powwows fill the calendar on the Wind River Reservation, with events nearly every summer weekend; for details, contact the Wind River Visitors Council, 307/856-7566 or 800/645-6233, www.wind-river.org. Shoshone Indian Days and the Ethete Powwow are the biggest of these, and other powwows occur in Lander and Riverton.

The **Arapahoe Community Powwow** takes place the second weekend of June in the town of Arapahoe. On the fourth weekend of June, Fort Washakie is home to the **Treaty Day Celebration,** which includes Indian games, dancing, and a feast. It is immediately followed by the **Eastern Shoshone Indian Days Powwow and Rodeo,** with participants from across the west. In existence for more than 40 years, this all-Indian rodeo features bull riding, saddle

WIND RIVER

POWWOWS

The Indian "powwow" (an Algonquian term meaning "medicine man") is a colorful celebration of Native American culture that cuts across tribal boundaries. Nobody knows the exact origin of powwows, but they may have developed from the Grass Dance of the Omaha and Pawnee tribes, who passed the dance on to various Plains tribes. The dance was used as a way of communicating with the Great Spirit, and the rhythmic beat of the drum helped send prayers skyward. Buffalo Bill Cody first introduced Indian dancers to audiences all over America and Europe, and in 1887 the Ponca Tribe began the first Indian fair and powwow. Other tribes joined in, and powwows became increasingly popular with the coming of the 20th century. The creation of "fancy dancing" allowed more personalized costumes and dances. Women were allowed to dance, and by the 1940s, Indians began traveling long distances to join other tribal powwows.

Dancers perform to a beat set up by different groups of drummers, who sing a repetitious song as they pound out the rhythm. The chant evokes images of somber ceremonies far out on the plains and of a lost culture. The dances originated from different tribes but have been adapted using the more colorful synthetic fabrics and beads of today. Professional dancers travel a circuit throughout the western states, and even non-Indians take part in powwows. Contestants wear numbers similar to those at track meets or rodeos and compete for cash awards (up to $5,000 at the biggest national powwows).

Traditional and Fancy Dancing

Two main styles of powwow dance exist. In **traditional dancing,** the movements are slow and graceful, and dancers adhere to more authentic costumes and traditional dance steps. Male dancers wear bustles of eagle feathers, representing the birds of prey that once gathered over battlefields to feed on dead warriors. They also wear head roaches made from porcupine guard hairs. **Fancy dancing** is more casual—sort of an anything-goes dance in which the steps are chosen by the individual dancers. It generally involves lots of spins, bows, and head movements. Men's costumes are equally freeform, with all sorts of gaudy additions, particularly colorful bustles added to the shoulders and arms. Women's costumes for both traditional and fancy dancing are not as showy as men's, although they do include bells, elk teeth (or plastic copies), and shell decorations on the dresses, along with shawls and necklaces of hairpipe (originally small hollow bones, now often plastic).

Powwow Activities

The Wind River Reservation has a half dozen powwows throughout the year, most of which are held outdoors in arbor arenas. Tepees are set up, and the event becomes a joyful celebration of life and culture. Most of these are three-day-weekend events involving not just singing and dancing, but also traditional games, parades, and a "giveaway ceremony." Activities last all day and late into the evening. Things generally begin with a festive parade that includes a military honor guard and a powwow queen seated atop a car hood. Visitors are welcome at powwows, and photos are not usually a problem, although this is less true at Arapaho powwows. Be sure to stand when the eagle staff is brought in during the grand entry, and those wearing hats should remove them. If an eagle feather drops to the ground, all action must stop until it has been properly returned.

For information on powwows and other events on the reservation, contact the Shoshone Tribal Cultural Center at 307/332-9106 or the Wind River Visitors Council, 307/856-7566 or 800/645-6233, www.wind-river.org.

© DON PITCHER

St. Stephens Church

bronc and bareback riding, calf roping, team roping, and the favorite—Indian relay horse racing, in which bareback riders rocket around the track in a chaos of flying dirt and colliding horses. In August, Fort Washakie hosts the **Shoshoni Tribal Fair.**

Ethete is home to the **Wyoming Indian High School Powwow** in May, and the **Ethete Powwow** in late June. The latter is one of the biggest in the area. The **Northern Arapaho Powwow** (oldest on the reservation) is held in Arapahoe the first weekend of August.

In addition to the powwows, **sundances** take place in July and August at Ethete and Shoshone, but these are not really open to the public.

ARAPAHOE AND ST. STEPHENS

The town of Arapahoe (known locally as Lower Arapaho) is a small village on the southeastern edge of the reservation. It arose from animosity between the tribes, as a subagency through which annuities could be distributed to the Arapaho without their having to face the taunts of "beggar" or "dog eater" from the Shoshones at Fort Washakie. The town's prominent white water tower is visible for miles.

St. Stephens Mission

In 1884, the St. Stephens Mission was established by Father John Jutz, a Jesuit missionary. Chief Black Coal consented to allow a mission to be built and later proved an ardent supporter of the school for Arapaho children. Until 1939, the Catholic Church operated a boarding school here. It was replaced by a day school that ran until the 1970s, when it became increasingly difficult to find priests and nuns to run the mission.

Visitors entering St. Stephens Mission pass a modern grade school built in 1983 and run by a secular corporation with an entirely Indian leadership. The most interesting sight at the mission is **St. Stephens Church,** built in 1928. Its white stucco exterior is covered with brilliant Arapaho geometric symbols. If the doors are unlocked, take a look at the colorful interior painted by local high-school students. Mass takes place on Sunday at 8 A.M., 10 A.M., and 5 P.M.

The **St. Stephens Mission Heritage Center,** 307/856-4330, contains a small museum and gift shop. Some of the most interesting items for sale are locally made beadwork and collector dolls dressed in Arapaho costumes. The center is open Monday–Wednesday and Friday 9 A.M.–noon and 1–3:30 P.M. year-round. While here, pick up a copy of the quarterly magazine *Wind River Rendezvous,* published by the mission; subscriptions are just $10 per year. Although this is a religious organization, the magazine deals with a range of historical and social issues. Call 307/856-6797 for subscriptions.

A cemetery near the mission contains the graves of Chief Lone Bear, Francis Setting Eagle, and John Broken Horn, along with that of his wife, Sarah Broken Horn—a white woman (born Lizzie Fletcher) who had been captured as a child and raised as an Indian. (See Arlington in the Medicine Bow Country chapter for more on this story.) The outlaw Butch Cassidy was a frequent visitor to Chief Lone Bear's camp.

SACAGAWEA

Fictional books about Sacagawea (pronounced sak-uh-juh-WEE-uh) describe her as a beautiful Indian maiden, a guide, a peacemaker, a heroine, and a mother—sort of the original Superwoman. Historian James Truslow Adams declared her one of the six most important women in American history. The reality is a bit less romantic but still fascinating. Sacagawea—her name meant "Bird Woman" in Shoshone—was born around 1784 in what is now eastern Idaho. As a child, she was captured by the Minnetaree tribe and later sold to a French-Canadian trapper and interpreter named Toussaint Charbonneau. He eventually made her one of his many wives.

The Lewis and Clark Expedition

In 1803, Pres. Thomas Jefferson negotiated the Louisiana Purchase from the French. For the fire-sale price of $16 million he suddenly doubled the size of the young United States of America. Captains Meriwether Lewis and William Clark were selected to lead a secret exploration of this vast land. They left St. Louis in late 1804 and camped that first winter in North Dakota, where they met Sacagawea and her husband Charbonneau. Lewis and Clark didn't think much of the ill-tempered and untrustworthy Charbonneau, but they realized the value of having with the expedition a Shoshone woman who was fluent in English and French. Charbonneau was hired, with the stipulation that his wife come along.

Over the winter, Sacagawea gave birth to a baby boy (Baptiste), and when the troupe headed out two months later, the child was on her back in a cradle board. Contrary to the romanticized novels, her role was not so much that of guide as interpreter, as one who knew the edible plants along the way, and as a symbol of the expedition's friendly intentions. When the expedition reached the Continental Divide, they happened upon Sacagawea's sister and brother, whom she had not seen since being kidnapped six years before. The Shoshones agreed to provide guides and horses to cross the Rockies.

After an arduous journey, the exploration party reached the Pacific Ocean that fall and established winter quarters near the mouth of the Columbia River. They returned across the mountains the following summer, and Sacagawea, Charbonneau, and their son returned to their old existence in Mandan country. The rest of the expedition party reached St. Louis on September 23, 1806, long after everyone but President Jefferson had given them up for dead. The trip proved a vital step in bringing the Northwest under the U.S. flag.

ETHETE

Ethete (pronounced "EEE-thuh-tee") is the primary Arapaho settlement on the reservation. People live in trailer homes scattered on small plots around town or in ticky-tacky box houses built by the BIA. (The prefabricated houses are known as the "Easter Egg Village" because of the bright colors.) Tepee poles lean against the barns, and the bright tribal colors and geometric patterns dominate the laundromat/video store. "Downtown" Ethete consists of a stoplight—the only one on the reservation—surrounded by a grocery store, a gas station, a community hall, a high school, and the laundromat. All of this is entirely forgettable, but not nearby St. Michael's Mission.

The **Wind River Transportation Authority,** 307/856-7118 or 800/439-7118, www.wrtabuslines.com, has a winter schedule connecting Riverton, Lander, and the Wind River Reservation.

St. Michael's Mission

Established in 1887 by Rev. John Roberts of the Episcopal Church, this mission is the town's reason for existence. When Chief Sharp Nose was asked for his approval to build here, the response was *Ethete,* meaning "Good." Constructed between 1910 and 1917, the buildings are arranged in a circle around a grassy lawn. Most are fabri-

Later Years

From here, Sacagawea's story becomes murkier. Some researchers claim that she died in 1812 of "putrid fever" at Fort Mandan in North Dakota. Dakota folks generally tell this version. Wyoming partisans prefer another story: that the woman who died so young was one of Charbonneau's other wives, and that Sacagawea continued to live for many years. After leaving her abusive husband, she wandered all over the West—gaining the name Wad-ze-Wipe (Lost Woman)—before finally ending up on the Wind River Reservation with her fellow Shoshones. She served a crucial role as translator for Chief Washakie in negotiations to establish the reservation and was often seen wearing one of the peace medals given out by Lewis and Clark. Sacagawea (or at least the Wyoming version) died on April 9, 1884, and was buried near Fort Washakie in a cemetery overlooking the Wind River. Although the Shoshones had heard her tell of the expedition many times, it wasn't until 25 years later that Anglo historians began to realize who the "Lost Woman" really was. The 13,569-foot Mt. Sacagawea in the Wind River Mountains is named for the remarkable woman who remained unrecognized much of her life. An image representing Sacagawea also appears on America's one-dollar coins.

© DON PITCHER

cated from cobblestones, with Arapaho designs on the doors, but the **Church of Our Father's House** is made of log. Inside this fascinating building built in the shape of a cross are rustic handmade wooden benches and a central Arapaho drum. Altar seats are made of elk antlers, and the back window faces the great Wind River Mountains. Sunday communion starts at 11 A.M.

Across the circle is the **Arapaho Cultural Museum,** housing a small but remarkable collection of artifacts that encompasses beaded garments, medicine pouches, peace pipes, photographs, and warbonnets, including that of Yellow Calf, last chief of the Arapahos. No charge. The museum is open only by appointment, and you should call two or three days ahead to visit: 307/332-2660 or 307/332-6836.

FORT WASHAKIE

Fort Washakie is the center of activity on the Wind River Reservation. The BIA compound is here (locals insist the initials stand for Boss Indians Around) and so is the tribal council headquarters. Fort Washakie was the home of Chief Washakie, the longtime leader of the Shoshones. Behind Chief Washakie's town are a series of dramatic escarpments and canyons, and through a gap in the hills you can peer into the mighty Wind River Mountains.

In 1869, the U.S. Army established a fort, Camp Augur (later Camp Brown), along the Popo Agie River to protect the Shoshones from attacks by Arapaho and Sioux warriors. The fort was later moved a dozen miles west and renamed Fort Washakie, making this the only fort ever named for an Indian chief. It remained open until 1909, when the threat of conflict between the Shoshones and Arapaho had diminished. A few buildings still stand, including a **stone guardhouse.** They are now used by the BIA.

Sights

Despite its minuscule size, Fort Washakie has an array of interesting sights. The **Shoshone Tribal Cultural Center,** 307/332-9106, moved in 2003 to a new building that also contains a library and learning center. Museum displays include Chief Washakie's leather shirt, pipe, and pipe bag, along with other historical items. His gorgeous eagle-feather headdress may also be on display, and out front is a dramatic statue of the chief; it's identical to one in the state capital building. The cultural center is open Monday–Friday 8 A.M.–4:45 P.M. year-round; donation requested.

Built in 1913, Fort Washakie's historic **White House** is another interesting building. South Fork Road west from Fort Washakie passes the **Washakie Graveyard,** where a substantial granite memorial notes that Washakie was "Always loyal to the government and his white brothers. A wise ruler." Washakie was buried here with full military honors, the only chief of his time to be so recognized by the U.S. government. Directly across the road from the cemetery is the **R.V. Greeves Art Gallery,** 307/332-3557, open by appointment only. Greeves is one of the state's most famous sculptors; his *The Unknown* is in the Buffalo Bill Historical Center.

Continue another mile along this road (stay left at the "Y" and turn left again at the Full Gospel Revival Center's log church) to the **Sacagawea Cemetery,** perhaps the most beautiful cemetery in Wyoming. The remote setting offers views of the Wind River Mountains. When I last visited, the sun was playing behind darkly rumbling thunderheads atop the Wind Rivers while horses whinnied in the fields below. Sacagawea's gravesite (the Wyoming version) is marked by an impressive granite headstone, and one of her sons, John Baptiste, is buried alongside. A granddaughter and other descendants are up the hill. The graveyard also contains an old log church and several old bed frames over graves, a burial practice that was common for many years on the reservation.

The historic **Shoshone Episcopal Mission** is on Trout Creek Rd., 1.5 miles southwest of Fort Washakie (turn east just beyond the Hines General Store), and was founded in 1883 by Rev. John Roberts, a Welsh missionary known as "White Robe." A boarding school for Indian girls was built in 1891. The two-story brick-and-stone building still stands, although the school closed in 1945. A simple log mission chapel is nearby.

Hot Springs

Three miles east of Fort Washakie on the way to Ethete is **Chief Washakie Plunge,** 307/332-4530, where 110°F sulfur-rich water flows from a hot springs into an outdoor swimming pool complete with a water slide, diving board, and hot tub. The springs were a favorite place of Chief Washakie. Maybe these mineral waters are what helped him live for 102 years! Private indoor tub baths are also available, and the facilities are handicapped accessible. Open Wed.–Sun. 8 A.M.–9:30 P.M. in the summer, and Wed.–Sun. 9:30 A.M.–7:30 P.M. the rest of the year. The pool costs $5 adults, $2.50 seniors and kids, free for anyone under seven.

Arts and Crafts

Wind River Trading Co., 307/332-3267, next to Hines General Store, has tacky mass-produced beadwork, moccasins, blankets, and baskets. Fortunately, the store also houses **Gallery of the Wind,** 307/332-4321, containing moccasins, beaded garments, and jewelry from the Wind River Reservation. The Shoshone Tribal Cultural Center, described previously, also has locally made pieces, or visit the nursing home, Morning Star Manor. The **Shoshone Tribal service station** has a deli and sells locally made crafts and beadwork.

Practicalities

Situated along the Wind River between Crow-heart and Dubois, **Early Ranch B&B,** 307/455-4055 or 800/532-4055, www.earlyranch.com, has ranch accommodations on deeded land inside the reservation. It also offers log cabin lodging and breakfast for $85 d or $100 for four people. The ranch is open mid-May through August. There are no other lodging options on the reservation, although many places are available in the surrounding towns of Lander, Riverton, and Dubois.

Camping is available at Ray Lake, Red Rocks, and along the Little Wind River just north of Wind River Agency. You'll need a $5 recreation stamp from the Tribal Fish and Game Office; call 307/332-7207 for details.

Ray Lake Campground, at the intersection of U.S. Hwy. 287 and State Hwy. 132, 307/332-9333, charges $8 for tents, $15 for RVs, and the café has meals. It's run by friendly folks, and the remote country setting provides classic Wyoming scenery. Open May–Sept.

WEST TO DUBOIS

As you head northwest along U.S. Hwy. 26/287, the Wind River Mountains and Absarokas grow ever closer, and the Wind River Valley begins to narrow. Crowheart Butte dominates the skyline to the north for many miles, and then you drop over a rise to discover a stunning landscape of red-rock badlands accented by the green of cottonwoods along the Wind River. For the next 20 miles, travelers are treated to a constantly changing panorama of gloriously colorful badlands topography, with 11,635-foot Ramshorn Peak rising in the distance. It's a geologist's dreamworld. Several reservoirs provide irrigation and recreation on the Wind River Reservation. Largest is **Bull Lake,** along the western margin. The Shoshones say that it is haunted by a supernatural water buffalo. The aquamarine waters of **Ocean Lake** are well-known for bass and crappie fishing. Other people come to swim, water-ski, windsurf, hunt, or birdwatch. Seven free camping areas are scattered around the lakeshore.

Pavillion

This Lilliputian farming settlement of 165 folks lies north of the Wind River approximately 25 miles from Riverton. If you're in the area around dinner time and are craving a hearty Wyoming steak, drop by **The Roost,** 307/857-6019. This Old West saloon with a jukebox and pool table fills up on weekends; reservations recommended.

Crowheart Butte

The tiny settlement of **Crowheart** consists of an old-fashioned country store and gas station surrounded by irrigated fields and grazing cattle. A couple miles northeast of the store—and visible for many miles in any direction—is a regal summit, Crowheart Butte, looking like a pyramid whose top got caught in a giant lawn mower.

The name comes from an 1866 battle in the Wind River Valley. The Shoshones and Bannocks fought the Crows over hunting rights. The Crows had been "given" the valley in the Fort Laramie Treaty of 1851, while the Shoshones and Bannocks were "given" the same land in the 1863 Fort Bridger Treaty. Four days of intense fighting led to a standoff, and to prevent further bloodshed the chiefs declared a winner-takes-all fight near this butte. Charging each other on horseback with lances drawn, both were thrown in the collision, and the fight turned into a hand-to-hand struggle. In the battle, Shoshone Chief Washakie killed Crow Chief Big Robber and then carried his heart around on a lance, a gesture of admiration for a brave fighter. Hence the name, Crowheart Butte. When Chief Washakie was later asked about the story, he replied, "When a man is in battle and his blood runs hot, he sometimes does things that he is sorry for afterwards. I cannot remember everything that happened so long ago." Washakie later took one of the captured Crow girls as one of his wives.

Crowheart Butte is regarded as something of a sacred place by local Indians and is used as a place of spiritual renewal for young men on a vision quest. A small rock shelter stands on the top for this purpose. Non-Indians are legally forbidden to climb Crowheart Butte, and legends claim that those who do so may disappear.

WIND RIVER

M

WIND RIVER

Whiskey Basin

The highway continues its slow and scenic climb to Dubois, crossing the cottonwood-lined Wind River three times en route. Approximately 25 miles west of Crowheart (five miles east of Dubois), a sign points the way to Whiskey Basin. Follow the gravel road two miles to the **Dubois State Fish Hatchery,** where rainbow, cutthroat, golden, brook, and brown trout as well as grayling are raised. Open daily 8 A.M.–5 P.M. The bucolic setting is hard to beat: a tree-lined creek surrounded by sage, mountains, and badlands.

A short distance up the road is a wildlife-viewing kiosk for the **Whiskey Basin Wildlife Habitat Area.** During winter the valley is home to the largest population of **Rocky Mountain bighorn sheep** anywhere on earth. Some 900 sheep congregate here because of the mild winters and the shallow snow. Although you're likely to find sheep all winter, the best time to photograph them is in the breeding season, from late November–December. During this period you'll see rams charging head-first into each other over the chance to mate. It's enough to give you a headache. The lambs are born in late May and early June high up on rocky slopes. Bighorn sheep are also sometimes seen in the meadows along the highway or in the hills just above Dubois. The National Bighorn Sheep Interpretive Center in Dubois leads wildlife tours of Whiskey Basin.

Beyond the wildlife-viewing kiosk, the road follows Torrey Creek up past a string of three small bodies of water: Torrey, Ring, and Trail Lakes. These were created by retreating glaciers centuries ago, but small dams have enlarged them. State Game and Fish **campsites** (free) are located along Ring and Trail Lakes. **Ring Lake Ranch,** 307/455-2663, www.ringlake.org, houses an ecumenical religious facility used for a variety of retreats, seminars, and other activities.

A very popular trailhead at the end of the road up Whiskey Basin (12 miles from the turnoff) provides access to the primary route up to Dinwoody Glacier and 13,804-foot Gannett Peak (Wyoming's highest). Keep your eyes open for the osprey nest at mile five. The Audubon Society has a field camp at mile eight.

You'll discover quite a few **Indian pictographs** on large boulders in the Trail Lake vicinity; look for them along the hillside between Trail and Ring Lakes. These figures—some four feet tall—are elaborate otherworldly creations with horns and headdresses, and they are believed to represent shamans performing ceremonies under altered states of consciousness. While their age is unknown, they are probably at least 2,000 years old and of Athapaskan (a Canadian tribe) rather than Shoshonean origin. This is some of the oldest rock art in Wyoming.

Dubois

Approaching Dubois (pop. 1,000) from either direction, you drive through the extraordinary red, yellow, and gray badlands that set this country apart. The luxuriant Wind River winds its way down a narrow valley where horses graze in the irrigated pastures and old barns and newer log homes stand against the hills, while the tree-covered Absaroka and Wind River Mountains ring distant views. The town of Dubois consists of a long main street that makes an abrupt elbow turn and then points due west toward the mountains. The many log buildings and snatches of wooden sidewalks give the place an authentic frontier

feel. Locals live in cabins, trailer homes, and simple frame houses. Dubois weather is famously mild; warm Chinook winds often melt any snow that falls. Grand scenery reigns in all directions. Snowmobilers, hunters, and anglers have discovered that Dubois provides a good place to relax in Wyoming's "banana belt" while remaining close to the more temperamental mountains. The area basks in an average of 300 days of sunshine each year. By the way, Dubois is pronounced "DU-boys"; other pronunciations will reveal your tenderfoot status. Locals sometimes jokingly call it "Dubious."

HISTORY

Dubois began in the 1880s when pioneer ranchers and more than a few rustlers, including Butch Cassidy, settled in the area, followed by Scandinavian hand-loggers who cut lodgepole for railroad ties. The town that grew up along the juncture of Horse Creek and the Wind River was first known as Never Sweat, but when citizens applied for a post office the Postal Service refused to allow the name and suggested Dubois instead—the name of an Idaho senator who just happened to be on the Senate committee that provided funding for the post office.

Like many edge-of-the-mountain towns, Dubois is in transition. For most of its existence, it served as a logging and ranching center. In 1987, the Louisiana Pacific sawmill shut down, throwing many loggers and millworkers onto the unemployment rolls. Loggers blamed environmentalists and the Forest Service for sharply reducing the timber available; environmentalists countered that the company was simply using the reductions as an excuse to close an aging mill. After everyone ran out of mud to sling, they decided to look at what Dubois had to offer and discovered that, lo and behold, they just happened to be sitting in an almost-undiscovered recreational and retirement gold mine. In the 1990s the town leapt full force into the tourism business. The transformation of Dubois to a visitor-oriented economy certainly has its downside—elaborate "trophy" log summer homes are beginning to overrun the lush pastures on both ends of town—but so far this pretty little place has been spared the onslaught of "industrial tourism." Stay tuned.

SIGHTS

National Bighorn Sheep Center

The National Bighorn Sheep Interpretive Center, 907 W. Ramshorn, 307/455-3429 or 888/209-2795, www.bighorn.org, houses displays on desert bighorn, Rocky Mountain bighorn, stone sheep, and Dall sheep. The museum details how the population was brought back from the brink of extinction, and it includes hands-on exhibits and interactive displays on how bighorns live. Also here is a diorama of a Sheepeater Indian

THE HARD DAY'S WORK OF TIE HACKS

Many of the trees cut in Wyoming's forests between 1870 and 1940 went to supply railroad ties for an ever-expanding network of rails throughout the Rockies. The men who cut these ties—tie hacks—spent long, hard months in the mountains, working through the winter. Many of the woodsmen were emigrants from Sweden, Norway, Finland, Austria, and Italy. Tie hacks first felled a suitable lodgepole pine using a bucksaw, then limbed the tree and used a broadax to hew the tie into shape, finally peeling the remaining bark from the sides and cutting it to length. Hundreds of thousands of ties—each eight feet long and at least five inches on each side—were produced annually by tie hacks. Horses dragged the ties down to a creek bank or flume to await high spring flows, when thousands of ties could be sent downriver at once. The enormous log jams that resulted sometimes required dynamite to loosen. Downstream booms caught the logs, where they could be hauled up and loaded onto railway cars.

Tie hacks found work in many parts of Wyoming, but especially in the Medicine Bow Mountains, Laramie Mountains, Sierra Madre, Big Horn Mountains, and Wind River Mountains, where major streams provided a way for the ties to reach the railheads. In the upper Wind River country, the industry spanned three decades, from 1914 to 1946. During this time, more than 10 million ties were cut and floated downstream to Riverton, where the Chicago and Northwestern Railroad used them. A stone monument to the tie hacks stands along U.S. Hwy. 26/287 approximately 18 miles west of Dubois. The visitors center in Dubois has a handout that provides a self-guided tour of historical sights associated with the tie hacks.

trap and mounted specimens around a 16-foot-high central "mountain." A theater shows videos on bighorn sheep and other topics, and a gift shop sells books and other items. The center is open daily 9 A.M.–8 P.M. Memorial Day to Labor Day, and daily 9 A.M.–5 P.M. the rest of the year. Entrance costs $2 adults, 75 cents kids under 12, or $5 families.

The center offers **wildlife tours** of the Whiskey Basin Habitat Area just west of town. These four-hour van-and-hiking trips cost $25 for adults or $10 for kids and include binoculars and spotting scopes to view the animals. During winter the focus is on bighorn sheep, while summertime visitors take nature hikes and look for birds. Reservations are required; call the center for details, or visit their website. The center also has brochures describing self-guided tours of Whiskey Basin and the **Spence/Moriarity Wildlife Habitat Management Area** east of Dubois.

Dubois Museum

The Dubois Museum, 909 W. Ramshorn (next door to the Bighorn Sheep Center), 307/455-2284, www.windriverhistory.org, is open daily 9 A.M.–5 P.M. Memorial Day to mid-September, and Tuesday–Saturday 10 A.M.–4 P.M. the rest of the year. Entrance is $1 adults or 50 cents kids under 12. The small museum houses a handful of exhibits on the Sheepeater Indians, with other displays on ranch life, geology, and wildlife. Be sure to check out the hilarious photo of 1930s movie star Tim McCoy teaching golf to a rather skeptical group of Shoshone Indians! Out front are seven historic log cabins and an old gas station, all containing interesting displays.

Other Attractions

Just west of Dubois is a signed turnoff to a **scenic overlook.** The gravel road climbs sharply (no RVs) for approximately one mile to the viewpoint, where displays note the surrounding peaks. Enjoy marvelous views of 11,635-foot Ramshorn Peak from here. **Rocky Mountain bighorn sheep** crowd the Dubois area in the winter. Many are visible on the hills just south of

town, with hundreds more gathered in the Whiskey Basin Habitat Area, five miles east and described earlier.

The magnificent badlands on both sides of Dubois, but especially to the east, are well worth exploring. The BLM maintains a fascinating **Badlands Interpretive Trail** up Mason Draw, 2.4 miles northeast of town. Pick up a booklet describing the trail at the visitors center. Depending on your route, the hike should take an hour or two to complete.

Rock hounds will find all sorts of petrified wood, agates, and other colorful rocks up the Wiggins Fork and Horse Creek drainages; ask at the chamber of commerce for directions.

One thing you certainly would not expect to find in Dubois is a training center for lawyers, but famed Wyoming attorney Gerry Spence has one on his Thunderbird Ranch east of town. His nonprofit (!) **Trial Lawyers College** puts some 50 lawyers through an intense four-week session each summer, with mock trials and professional actors; 307/455-2389, www.triallawyerscollege.com. Watch your step with all these lawyers around Dubois!

badlands near Dubois

© DON PITCHER

ACCOMMODATIONS

Dubois makes an excellent stopping point on the way to Yellowstone and Grand Teton National Parks, with lodging prices well below those in Jackson Hole. All places are open year-round unless noted otherwise.

Under $50

If you're looking for quietude, head three miles east of town to **Riverside Inn & Campground,** 307/455-2337 or 877/489-2337, www.dteworld.com/riversideinn, where the motel rooms (some with microwaves and fridges) are $30–35 s or $40–49 d. Guests have fishing access to a private stretch of the river. Riverside is open May–November.

Right on the river, **Wind River Motel,** 519 W. Ramshorn, 307/455-2611 or 877/455-2621, www.wyoming.com/~dtewindriver, has a mix of rustic cabins, motel rooms, and suites for $30–75 s or d. Some rooms contain kitchenettes.

$50 and Up

Branding Iron Inn, 401 Ramshorn, 307/455-2893 or 800/341-8000, www.brandingironinn.com, has cozy and well-maintained duplex log cabins that were built in the 1940s. Rates are $35–80 s or d; kitchenettes cost $10 extra. Out back are corrals for folks traveling with horses.

One-half mile east of Dubois, **Chinook Winds Mountain Lodge,** 307/455-2987 or 800/863-0354, has a variety of rooms. Riverside motel units are $40–65 s or d and contain small fridges. Cabins with full kitchens cost $65–85 d. The Wind River is right out the back door. They're open mid-May to mid-October.

Trail's End Motel, 511 Ramshorn, 307/455-2540 or 888/455-6660, www.trailsendmotel.com, has recently remodeled rooms starting for $48 s or $52 d. The nicer rooms ($72–138 d) have decks facing the Wind River and include in-room fridges and microwaves. An exercise room is also available.

A fine riverside place is **Black Bear Country Inn,** 505 W. Ramshorn, 307/455-2344 or 800/873-2327, www.blackbearcountryinn.com, where rooms cost $40–60 s or d, including fridges and microwaves. A kitchenette apartment sleeps up to seven people for $95. The motel is open mid-May through October.

Find attractive accommodations at the largest motel in town, **Stagecoach Motor Inn,** 103 Ramshorn, 307/455-2303 or 800/455-5090, www.dteworld.com/stagecoach. Rates are $52 s or $62–68 d, including use of an outdoor pool; kitchenettes cost $80–98 and sleep four to six. King suites are $80 d. Families will appreciate the outdoor pool, hot tub, and shady backyard play area.

For historic rooms, stay at **Twin Pines Lodge & Cabins,** 218 Ramshorn, 307/455-2600 or 800/550-6332, www.dteworld.com/twinpines. Built in 1934 and listed on the National Register of Historic Places, the lodge has modern and rustic cabins for $55 s or $60–65 d, with fridges and VCRs in all, plus microwaves in some units.

Two miles west of town is **Bald Mountain Inn,** 307/455-2844 or 800/682-9323, www.baldmountaininn.com, where spacious motel rooms cost $64–74 s or d; add $7 for kitchenette units. Bring your fishing pole; the Wind River is just out back. Closed Apr. to mid-May.

Bed-and-Breakfasts

Jakey's Fork Homestead, 307/455-2769, www.frontierlodging.com, has B&B accommodations in a delightful century-old homestead four miles east of town. It's close to the bighorn sheep refuge in Whiskey Basin and offers extraordinary views of both the Wind River Mountains and nearby badlands. Birdwatchers will find a host of feathered friends in the trees and marsh. Be sure to ask owner Irene Bridges about Butch Cassidy's encounter with Indians nearby. Guests can stay in the modern home or a rustic sod-covered cabin. A sauna and hot tub bathtub are available, and the rooms have shared baths. A full breakfast is served, and children will enjoy the toy-filled playroom. Rates are $70–85 d in the house or $105–125 d ($20 extra for four people) in the cabin.

Just two blocks from downtown Dubois is **The Stone House B&B,** 207 S. 1st St., 307/455-2555, www.duboisbnb.com. Inside this stately home are two guest rooms ($50 s or $55 d) with shared baths, along with a basement suite ($70 d) that has a private bath. Adjacent is a three-room cottage for $80 d or $100 for four people. A full breakfast is served each morning, and the sitting room faces Whiskey Mountain, a good place to watch for bighorn sheep. Open May–Oct.

Dude Ranches

Quite a few dude ranches/mountain lodges are found in the Dubois area. Five are described as follows, and another five places are described in the Over Togwotee Pass section of this chapter.

Ten miles out East Fork Rd., **Lazy L&B Ranch,** 307/455-2839 or 800/453-9488, www.lazylb.com, is a century-old ranch offering creekside log cabins, horseback riding, overnight pack trips, cowboy poetry and songs, a swimming pool, hot tub, stocked fishing ponds, kids' programs, volleyball and pool, fly-fishing, and a rifle range. The ranch's horseback-riding program is excellent, and guests can choose trips through the badlands or high into the mountains. Lazy L&B is open June–September, with all-inclusive weekly rates of $2,300 for two people. The ranch also operates **Bear Basin Wilderness Camp,** www.bearbasincamp.com, a great base from which to explore the Washakie Wilderness. A maximum of eight guests stay in wall tents.

Sixteen miles north of Dubois in gorgeous Dunoir Valley, **Absaroka Ranch,** 307/455-2275, www.dteworld.com/absaroka, has all of the typical guest ranch offerings: horseback riding, guided fly-fishing, hiking, and cookouts. The ranch accommodates just 18 guests and emphasizes the personal touch. It is surrounded by national forest land and has a comfortable main lodge (built in 1910), attractively restored log cabins, and a redwood sauna. The ranch is open mid-June to mid-September. All-inclusive weekly rates are $2,600 for two people.

Bitterroot Ranch, 307/455-2778 or 800/545-0019, www.ridingtours.com/wyoming.htm, emphasizes horseback riding for experienced riders; each guest gets to ride several different horses. The owners breed Arabian horses and offer cross-country jumping courses, pack trips, cattle drives, fly-fishing, and kids' programs. Both French and

German are spoken here, attracting an international clientele. The ranch is open June–September and has space for 32 guests in a dozen cabins. All-inclusive weekly rates are $3,100 for two people. The owners also run Equitors, www.equitours.com, a travel agency that sets up horseback rides all over the globe.

South of Dubois in beautiful Jakeys Fork Canyon, **CM Ranch,** 307/455-2331 or 800/455-0721, www.cmranch.com, is one of Wyoming's oldest dude ranches; it's been here since 1927. The ranch offers dramatic badlands topography and a variety of fossils, making it a favorite of geologists (and amateur rock hounds). Trails lead into the adjacent Fitzpatrick Wilderness, a destination for horseback trips. Fishing is another popular activity, and a fishing guide is available. The immaculate lodge buildings have space for 60 guests, and kids love the big outdoor pool. All-inclusive weekly rates at this delightful old-time ranch are $2,200–2,400 for two people. The ranch is owned by the Kemmerer family, whose ancestors founded the town of Kemmerer, Wyoming. The Kemmerers also own Jackson Hole Mountain Resort.

Operating as a dude ranch since 1920, **T-Cross Ranch,** 307/455-2206, www.ranch-web.com/tcross, is 15 miles north of Dubois near Horse Creek, and is open mid-June through September. Surrounded by the Shoshone National Forest, this remote ranch has weekly accommodations at $2,400 for two people, including horseback riding, all meals, activities for kids, trout fishing, and a hot tub. Backcountry pack trips and other activities are also available. Lodging is in eight comfortable log cabins, and the main lodge has a massive stone fireplace and spacious front porch.

CAMPING

The closest public camping spot is **Horse Creek Campground** ($5; open late May–Sept.), 12 miles north of Dubois on Horse Creek Road.

Circle-Up Camper Court, 225 W. Welty, 307/455-2238, charges $17 for tents (some shade), $26 for RVs, and $25 for basic cabins. Kids love the tepees for $20. Folks not camping here pay $4 for showers. Open year-round, this is one of Wyoming's better private campgrounds. You can also park RVs ($18–20) or pitch tents ($15) at **Riverside Inn & Campground,** three miles east of town, 307/455-2337 or 877/489-2337, www.dteworld.com/riversideinn. Open May–Nov.

FOOD

Breakfast and Lunch

Popular with both locals and tourists, **Cowboy Cafe,** 115 E. Ramshorn, 307/455-2595, has good home-style breakfasts with big helpings of biscuits and gravy. For a real artery-clogger, try the steak and eggs.

Ramshorn Bagel and Deli, 202 E. Ramshorn, 307/455-2400, serves bagels, sandwiches, and espresso for breakfast and lunch. **Village Cafe/Daylight Donuts,** 515 W. Ramshorn, 307/455-2122, offers doughnuts and coffee in the morning and pizza and fried chicken dinners when evening rolls around.

Fine Dining

Cafe Wyoming, 106 E. Ramshorn, 307/455-3828, sits back from the street along Horse Creek. The food is distinctive and creative, with a lunch and dinner menu that changes every week. They always have pastas, chicken, seafood, sandwiches, and vegetarian specials, along with a couple of house favorites: broiled ribeye with bleu cheese sauce, and Cajun broiled catfish. There's a diverse wine list, and dinner entrées run $13–21. Reservations are highly recommended. The café is closed Sundays and Mondays, during April, and mid-October to mid-November. Housemade sauces are available in the café or online at www.howlingwolfsauce.com.

Line Shack Lodge, 307/455-3232 or 888/266-4695, www.lineshack.com, serves three meals a day with daily specials but is best known for Friday night prime rib dinners. They're located at the top of Union Pass, 13 scenic miles west of Dubois. The saloon here has live bands in the winter, when this is a very popular snowmobile destination.

American

Bernie's Cafe, next to the Super 8 at 1408 Warm Springs Dr., 307/455-2115, opens at 6 A.M. each morning, and it doesn't close until 10 P.M. You'll find down-home cooking, fast service, and all-American meals for reasonable prices. It's a favorite of families.

Rustic Pine Steakhouse, 119 E. Ramshorn, 307/455-2772, is a carnivore's delight, with prime rib on Friday and Saturday nights; open for dinner only.

Get malts and sundaes from the old-time soda fountain inside the **Dubois Drugstore,** 126 E. Ramshorn, 307/455-2300.

The Really Wild Bunch Grill & Bar, 112 E. Ramshorn, 307/433-3670, www.pinnaclebuttes.com, is a downtown place with a covered front porch for streetside dining.

Groceries and Bakeries

Get groceries at **Ramshorn Food Farm,** 610 W. Ramshorn, 307/455-2402. For pastries, breads, and tasty hardtack made from an old Swedish recipe, stop by **Circle-Up Camper Court,** 225 W. Welty, 307/455-2238.

ENTERTAINMENT

Dubois is a hopping place during the summer, especially on weekends. Find country-and-western bands at **Rustic Pine Tavern,** 119 E. Ramshorn, 307/455-2430, and **Outlaw Saloon,** 204 W. Ramshorn, 307/455-2387. The Rustic Pine is a classic Western bar with elk and moose heads, plenty of old wood, and a pool table. Check out the ashtrays, which note, "God spends his vacation here." The famous Tuesday night **square dances** bring in dudes from local ranches in July and August. You may want to avoid this night if you don't want to be overwhelmed with fellow visitors.

EVENTS

The **International Pedigree Stage Stop Sled Dog Race** (IPSSSDR) stops here. See the Jackson chapter for more info.

The Dubois **Spur Spangled Celebration**

on Fourth of July weekend is the biggest local event, with an ice-cream social, parade, rodeo, Western barbecue, fireworks, and rubber-ducky races down the river. In mid-July, **Dubois Museum Day** is a folk art festival with Indian dancing, frontier crafts demonstrations, and lectures. Another mid-July event is the **Badlands Classic Mountain Bike Race,** with 12- and 16-mile bike courses.

A **National Art Show** comes to town on the last week of July, attracting both professionals and amateurs. Also don't miss the always popular Dubois firefighter's **Buffalo Barbecue,** held the second Saturday of August. Get specifics on these and other events from the Dubois Chamber of Commerce, 307/455-2556.

Budding musicians should check out the **Greater Yellowstone Music Camp** in late June, with nationally known instructors, concerts, and jam sessions in acoustic blues and swing for guitar, fiddle, and bass players. Get details at 307/455-3748, www.greateryellowstonemusic-camp.com.

SUMMER RECREATION

Dubois sits at the confluence of the Wind River and Horse Creek, and both streams provide good trout fishing right in town. Hot springs keep the Wind River flowing all year. See the visitors center for descriptions of local fishing holes and for brochures from local outfitters who offer pack trips and horseback rides.

The nine-hole **Antelope Hills Golf Course,** 307/455-2888, is on the western end of Dubois. Rent mountain bikes from **Bob's Bike Corral,** 124 E. Ramshorn St., 307/455-3193.

WINTER RECREATION

The Absarokas and Wind River Mountains around Dubois are crowded with **snowmobilers** during winter, and several places rent "sleds" in town and nearby. Don't expect peace and quiet with all of these machines roaring through the backcountry! More than 300 miles of trails head out in all directions, with the Union Pass area a particular focus.

For something quieter, **cross-country skiers** will find trails near Falls Campground and Brooks Lake (both 23 miles west of town) and Cowboy Village Resort at Togwotee (40 miles west) and in backcountry wilderness areas off-limits to snowmobiles. **Dogsled** trips are popular winter diversions and are detailed in the Over Togwotee Pass section.

SHOPPING

Teddy Bear Shoppe, inside the Black Bear Country Inn, 505 W. Ramshorn, 307/455-2344 or 800/873-2327, www.blackbearcountryinn.com, has more then 500 different teddy bears on display and for sale. It's touted as the largest selection of teddy bears in the West. Don't let your three-year-old know about this place!

Trapline Gallery, 120 E. Ramshorn, 307/455-2800, sells Indian-crafted beadwork, jewelry, and artwork, as well as furs. **Tukadeka Traders/Horse Creek Gallery,** 104 E. Ramshorn, 307/455-3345, has an impressive collection of antique trade beads for sale, along with tacky antler carvings and Indian trinkets. A few doors down is a nice bookshop, **Two Ocean Books,** 128 E. Ramshorn, 307/455-3554. **Water Wheel Gift Shop,** 113 E. Ramshorn, 307/455-2112, also carries a selection of Wyoming titles.

Purchase stylish Western wear inside the historic **Welty's General Store,** 113 W. Ramshorn, 307/455-2377. The hours are haphazard. Be sure to ask them about Butch Cassidy's priceless old pistol, although you won't be able to see it because it's locked away.

For fishing supplies, head to **Wind River Fly Shop,** 116 E. Ramshorn, 307/455-2140, or **Whiskey Mountain Tackle,** 1418 Warm Springs Dr., 307/455-2587.

INFORMATION AND SERVICES

The **Dubois Chamber of Commerce,** 616 W. Ramshorn, 307/455-2556, www.duboiswyoming .org, is open Monday–Saturday 9 A.M.–7 P.M., Sunday noon–5 P.M. Memorial Day to Labor Day, and Monday–Friday 9 A.M.–5 P.M. the rest of the year. Ask for a self-guided tour map of old logging flumes, tie-hack cabins, and other historic structures.

Stop by the Shoshone National Forest **Wind River Ranger District** office at 1403 W. Ramshorn (one mile west of town), 307/455-2466, www.fs.fed.us/r2/shoshone, for maps of Shoshone and Bridger-Teton National Forests and information on local trails. They also have a listing of local horsepacking outfitters. See the chapter on Bighorn Basin for more on the Washakie Wilderness. The Fitzpatrick Wilderness is described in the Wind River Mountains section.

Dubois does not have a hospital, but the **Dubois Medical Center,** 706 Meckem, 307/455-2516, has nurse practitioners. Wash clothes at the **Laundromat** at 410 W. Ramshorn (across from Branding Iron Motel).

Check your email or surf the web for free at the new **Dubois Library,** 201 1st St., 307/455-2032, www.fremontcountylibrar ies.org; or for a fee at **Cyber Cafe,** 116 E. Ramshorn, 307/455-4011.

Trail's End Motel, 307/455-2540 or 888/455-6660, www.trailsendmotel.com, provides shuttle van service to the airports in Jackson or Riverton.

Dubois Vicinity

Anyone who loves the outdoors will discover an abundance of pleasures around Dubois. There's good fishing for rainbow, cutthroat, brown, and brook trout in Wind River and for rainbow, brook, and Mackinaw trout in the many alpine lakes. You'll also see lots of deer, elk, and bighorn sheep. Hikers and horse-packers will find hundreds of miles of Forest Service trails in the area. Photographers love the brilliantly colored badlands that frame Dubois on both the east and west sides. Each winter, hundreds of snowmobilers climb on their "sleds" and cross-country skiers strap on their boards to enter the world of deep powder in the Absarokas.

HORSE CREEK AREA

Horse Creek Road heads north from Dubois, with scenic views of the Absarokas and nearby badland country. Several dude ranches are in the area. **Horse Creek Campground** ($5; open late May–Sept.) is 12 miles north. Forest Road 504 continues another five miles, providing access to the Washakie Wilderness via Horse Creek Trail. Forest Road 508 splits off near Horse Creek Campground and leads another 17 miles to **Double Cabin Campground** ($5; open late May–Sept.). Several trails head into the wilderness from here; the most popular are Frontier Creek Trail and the Wiggins Fork Trail. You'll find remnants of a petrified forest six miles up the Frontier

Creek Trail, but they have been rather picked over by illegal collectors. (It's unlawful to remove petrified wood from a wilderness area. Please leave pieces where you find them.) For other Washakie Wilderness trails info, ask at the Dubois Ranger Station.

UNION PASS

The first road across the Absarokas headed through Union Pass southwest of Dubois. The pass forms a divide between the waters of the Columbia, Colorado, and Mississippi Rivers and marks the boundary of the Absaroka, Wind River, and Gros Ventre Mountain Ranges. Near the pass are an interpretive sign and a nature trail through a flower-filled meadow. Union Pass Road (gravel) leaves U.S. Hwy. 26/287 eight miles northwest of Dubois and climbs across to connect with State Hwy. 352 north of Pinedale. A major reconstruction project has dramatically improved the road in recent years, and the road is kept open year-round, providing a beautiful over-the-mountains connection between Pinedale and Dubois.

A scenic 20-mile side road begins a few miles up Union Pass Road, heads along Warm Springs Creek, and eventually reconnects with U.S. Hwy. 26/287. Find fantastic views of the Absaroka and Wind River Ranges along this route. The remains of an old tie-hack logging flume are visible, and a warm spring (85°F) flows into the creek.

Accommodations and Food

The Union Pass area is popular with mountain-bikers, cross-country skiers, and hordes of wintertime snowmobilers. The center of all this frenzy is **Line Shack Lodge,** located five miles up the road near the 8,600-foot summit, 307/455-3232 or 888/266-4695, www.lineshack.com. The modern 15,000-square-foot lodge has a wonderful setting, with an inviting interior, windows facing the mountains, and a deck that's especially popular for summertime weddings. Guests stay in 18 suites, all with two queen beds, hot tubs, fridges, microwaves, and VCRs. Most of these cost $75 d in summer or $120 d in winter, but two larger suites also have a queen futon, private deck, and stone fireplace for $100 d in summer or $150 d in winter. Extra guests are $30 per person (free for kids), but various package deals are offered if you want to add in meals, snowmobile rentals in winter, or ATV rentals and horseback rides in the summer. Peak season is January and February, when you'll need to book a room one year in advance! The Line Shack has a full-service restaurant that gets packed with folks from Dubois for their Friday night prime rib and salad bar ($11). The saloon has live music December–February, and there's a snowmobile shop on the grounds.

One-quarter mile downhill from Line Shack is **The Sawmill,** 307/455-2171 or 866/472-9645, www.thesawmill.org, with condo-style rooms ($75 d) and two-level suites ($110 d). A separate bunkhouse (popular with snowmobilers on a budget) has nine beds that go for $35 per person, including access to a large hot tub. A restaurant and bar are on the premises, and snowmobile rentals are available.

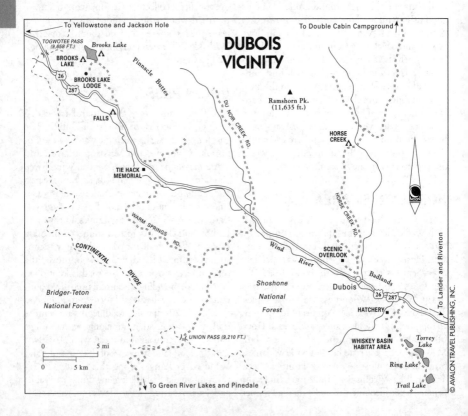

OVER TOGWOTEE PASS

The enjoyable drive west from Dubois first cuts through the colorful badlands, playing tag with the Wind River as it begins a long ascent to 9,658-foot Togwotee Pass (pronounced "TOE-go-tee"). The pass is named for a subchief under Chief Washakie. Togwotee was one of the last independent Sheepeater Indians—a branch of the Shoshones—and the man who led a U.S. government exploratory expedition over this pass in 1873. He even guided Pres. Chester Arthur on his month-long visit to Yellowstone in 1883.

Togwotee Pass is one of the most scenic drives imaginable, with Ramshorn Peak peeking down from the north for several miles until the road plunges into dense lodgepole forests (Shoshone National Forest) with lingering glimpses of the Pinnacle Buttes. At the crest it emerges into grass-, willow-, and flower-bedecked meadows with Blackrock Creek winding through. Whitebark pine and Engelmann spruce trees cover the nearby slopes. As the highway drops down the western side into the Bridger-Teton National Forest, another marvelous mountain range—the Tetons—dominates the horizon in dramatic fashion. Snow lies along the roadsides until early July; notice the high posts along the road used by snowplows. Togwotee Pass is a complete shock after all the miles of sagebrush and grassland that control the heartland of Wyoming. It's like entering another world—one of cool, forested mountains and lofty peaks instead of the arid land with horizonwide vistas.

Pinnacle Buttes and Brooks Lake

Dominating the view along U.S. Hwy. 26/287 for perhaps 15 miles are the castlelike Pinnacle Buttes. Twenty-three miles west of Dubois, you'll come to the turnoff to Brooks Lake, elevation 9,100 feet. Take it, even if you don't plan on camping here. A five-mile gravel road leads to the cliff-rimmed lake, and a clear creek flows east and south from here. The Forest Service's excellent **Pinnacles** and **Brooks Lake** Campgrounds are along the lakeshore and cost $10 per night; open mid-June to mid-Sept. Facing the lake is historic Brooks Lake Lodge (described in more detail in the Accommodations section of the Jackson Hole chapter).

Back on the main highway, you'll want to stop at **Falls Campground** (also $6; open June to mid-Sept.). Here, Brooks Creek tumbles into a deep canyon. Catch impressive views of **Brooks Creek Falls** along the short trail beginning from the parking lot. In winter, cross-country skiers will find an easy but ungroomed ski trail that heads out two miles from here. **Wind River Lake** is another five miles up the hill, just below the pass. It's a gorgeous place for picnics and fishing, with deep blue water and the sharp cliffs of Pinnacle Buttes behind. There's even a wheelchair-accessible float for anglers.

Mountain Lodges and Dude Ranches

Sixteen miles west of Dubois is **Mackenzie Highland Ranch**, 307/455-3415, where accommodations are offered in a variety of cabins and other rustic buildings. The simplest cabins share a bathhouse and cost $45–90 for up to four people. Nicer cabins with kitchens and private baths are $135–215 for four guests, and the finest is a modern four-bedroom home (it sleeps eight) with two baths and a full kitchen for $245. There's a three-night minimum stay. This isn't an all-inclusive dude ranch, but trail rides, meals, ATV rentals, and guided fishing trips are offered in the summer, and the ranch is a base for snowmobilers, skiers, dog mushers, and hunters at other times of the year. A portion of Mackenzie Highland Ranch is used for lepidopterology research each summer, with graduate-level classes offered through Sam Houston State University. This unique program is run by professor Karölis Bagdonas, a specialist in moths and butterflies; he discovered the vital importance of moths in the diet of Yellowstone grizzlies.

Crooked Creek Ranch, 307/455-3035 or 888/238-2647, www.crookedcreek-gr.com, is 16 miles from Dubois along Union Pass Road. In summer, the ranch has horseback rides, ATV rentals, hiking, and fishing. In winter it's the haunt of snowmobilers; the Continental Divide Snowmobile Trail is very close. The ranch rents snowmobiles, sells gas, and has a restaurant,

WIND RIVER

lounge, and convenience store. Guests stay in modern log cabins for $75 s or $150 d.

In the mountains 18 miles west of Dubois, **Triangle C Dude Ranch,** 307/455-2225 or 800/661-4928, www.trianglec.com, was established as the first tie-hack camp in the region and now operates as a summertime guest ranch and wintertime snowmobiling and cross-country skiing center. In summer, the main emphasis is horseback riding, but guests will also enjoy fishing, hiking, children's activities, wagon rides, and evening entertainment. Weekly rates are $3,400 for two people. The ranch is open Memorial Day to Labor Day for summer fun, plus mid-December through March for snowmobiling.

Twenty miles west of Dubois is **Pinnacle Buttes Lodge and Campground,** 307/455-2506 or 800/934-3569, www.pinnaclebuttes.com, where motel rooms are $65 s or $70 d, and cabins with kitchenettes (but no TVs) go for $75–160. The cabins and motel rooms sleep four people each. You'll also find a restaurant with home-cooked meals, an outdoor pool, hot tub, and camping spaces ($10 for tents, $19 for RVs). Open year-round, with snowmobile rentals in the winter.

See the Jackson Hole chapter for information on **Brooks Lake Lodge**—on the lake of the same name—and **Cowboy Village Resort at Togwotee**—a few miles west of Togwotee Pass.

Dogsledding

Washakie Outfitting, 307/733-3602 or 800/249-0662, www.dogsledwashakie.com, leads trips from Brooks Lake Lodge. On these trips, Iditarod veteran Billy Snodgrass offers half-day ($140 adults, $90 kids), all-day ($210 adults, $115 kids), overnight ($450 adults, $280 kids), and trips that combine time behind the dogs with time on a snowmobile.

Continental Divide Dogsled Adventures, 307/739-0165 or 800/531-6874, www.dogsled adventures.com, also leads dogsled tours in the Brooks Lake area, starting with a half-day trip that costs $175 for adults or $80 for kids. A variety of longer trips are available, including a three-night adventure where you stay overnight in a surprisingly comfortable yurt; $1,920 per person, with meals. All trips include round-trip transportation from Jackson.

Wind River Mountains

The Wind River Mountains begin near South Pass and continue 100 miles northwest to Union Pass, forming part of America's Continental Divide backbone. The range is visible for more than one hundred miles across the sagebrush country of central and southwestern Wyoming, its rugged snowcapped peaks gleaming in the light. The Shoshones traversed this range each spring and fall, and Sheepeater Indians hunted in the high country, but to most of the white pioneers whose wagon trains rolled across South Pass the peaks represented a forbidding, mysterious place. In 1868, writer James Chisholm offered a description of the range that still rings true today:

I think the best inspired painter that ever drew would fail in attempting to describe these mighty mountains. He may convey correctly enough an impression of their

shape, their vast extent and sublime beauty. But there is something always left out which escapes all his colors and all his skill. Their aspects shift and vary continually. Their very shapes seem to undergo a perpetual transformation like the clouds above them. There is a mystery like the mystery of the sea—a silence not of death but of eternity.

Today, the Wind River Mountains are considered Wyoming's premier backpacking area, offering perhaps 700 miles of trails. Much of the country is well above timberline, featuring glacially carved mountains and countless small lakes. Mountain climbers enjoy practicing moves on thousands of granitic precipices representing all degrees of difficulty. The Wind River Mountains contain Gannett Peak—at 13,804 feet the tallest in Wyoming—and all but one of the state's 15 other highest peaks. The 150 extant glaciers in the mountains all formed during the Little Ice Age, between A.D. 1400 and 1850. The glaciers that actually carved these mountains were far larger—so massive, in fact, that they covered the mountaintops to great depths and spilled over to create the hanging valleys, cirques, alpine lakes, U-shaped valleys, and steep cliffs of today.

Three different Forest Service wilderness areas cap these mountains; the largest is Bridger Wilderness, on the western side of the Continental Divide (in Bridger-Teton National Forest); the other two are Popo Agie and Fitzpatrick Wilderness Areas east of the crest (in Shoshone National Forest). Add in the BLM's Scab Creek Wilderness Study Area for a total of more than 735,000 roadless acres. The lower elevations of the Wind Rivers are also U.S. Forest Service lands but are managed for other purposes—primarily timber harvesting and grazing. On the northeast border is the Wind River Reservation, which includes some of the high mountain country, but access is restricted. Contact the Tribal Fish and Game Office in Fort Washakie,

307/332-7207, to purchase a limited hiking, fishing, and camping permit and recreation stamp ($25 per day or $65 per week for nonresidents).

WILDLIFE

Most of the streams and larger lakes in the Wind Rivers have been planted with rainbow, cutthroat, California golden, brook, German brown, or Mackinaw trout and grayling and mountain whitefish. Although grizzlies are only infrequently sighted, black bears are still in these mountains—mainly below tree line—and have caused considerable problems in recent years. Always hang food out of their reach; check with local Forest Service offices for current conditions and precautions. Other creatures, such as mosquitoes and biting flies, are more common annoyances in the mountains. Be sure to bring insect repellent during July and August, when they are at their worst. Other critters you're likely to see include bighorn sheep, moose, elk, mule deer, and coyotes. Pikas and yellow-bellied marmots are common in the high-country boulder fields.

Wind River Mountains west of Pinedale

ACCESS

Three highways circle the Wind River Range: U.S. Hwy. 26/287 on the northeast, U.S. Hwy. 191 on the southwest, and State Hwy. 28 on the southeast. The mountains are traversed by only one road, gravel Union Pass Road. Most people cross the relatively gentle southern slopes at South Pass or over Togwotee Pass to the northeast. You can gain access to the three wilderness areas from either side, but the high passes and long distances keep many hikers on one side or the other. See descriptions of the three different wilderness areas later in this chapter for specific access points.

Most trails in the Wind Rivers are relatively free of snow by early July and remain so until mid-September, but the high passes may not open until late July. Because of the open country in the alpine, off-trail travel is relatively easy here but is advised only for experienced hikers who know how to read topographic maps and can take care of themselves in an emergency. Be prepared for the thunderstorms that often roll in during the afternoon; lightning is a real problem above timberline. It can snow at any time in this mountain country, and night temperatures can drop below freezing even in midsummer. You won't find a lot of wood in many parts of the range, so be sure to bring a gas stove to cook on. In addition, wood fires are prohibited at many of the most heavily used sites.

Unlike the mountain country farther north, most of the people who head into the Winds do so on foot rather than atop a horse. Horses are used by one-quarter of the people, and "spot-packing," in which horses carry supplies for base camps but everyone hikes in on foot, is a popular way to get into the backcountry without carrying everything on your back. Many outfitters offer these services; stop by local Forest Service offices for a list of outfitters. Most backcountry users do not need permits, but visitor permits (free) are required for groups using stock animals and organized groups like the Boy Scouts and schools.

MORE INFORMATION

Three Forest Service offices have details on backcountry areas in the Winds. The Southern Shoshone National Forest, www.fs.fed.us/r2/shoshone, has a district office in Lander, 307/332-5460, that covers the Popo Agie and Southern Fitzpatrick Wilderness areas, and another one in Dubois, 307/455-2466, for the Northern Fitzpatrick Wilderness. The Bridger-Teton National Forest's Pinedale district office, 307/367-4326, www.fs.fed.us/btnf, covers the Bridger Wilderness. All of these offices sell maps of the wilderness areas and can provide copies of backcountry use regulations and lists of approved outfitters for pack trips.

You'll find brief descriptions of the most popular hikes in this chapter, but with literally hundreds of treks available in the Winds, don't think these are your only options. In fact, to avoid the crowds you should probably pick up a few topo maps and discover your own trails. The late Finis Mitchell's *Wind River Trails* (www.upress.utah.edu) is a folksy, inexpensive guide by a man who hiked this country from 1909 nearly until his death in the 1990s. Mitchell personally planted trout in dozens of high-country lakes during the 1930s and even had a mountain named for him. Pick up this guide if you plan to do any fishing. *Climbing and Hiking in the Wind River Mountains* by Joe Kelsey (www.falconbooks.com) has accurate information on most of the hiking trails and describes hundreds of technical climbs. For a guide directed to hiking and fishing—not climbing—see *Walking the Winds: A Hiking & Fishing Guide to Wyoming's Wind River Range,* by Rebecca Woods (www.alpenbooks.com). Topographic maps are available from sporting-goods stores in the surrounding towns.

GREEN RIVER LAKES AREA

The long drive to Green River Lakes is one of the most popular getaways in the Wind River Mountains. The road parallels the Green River as it first drifts northward then makes a U-turn to

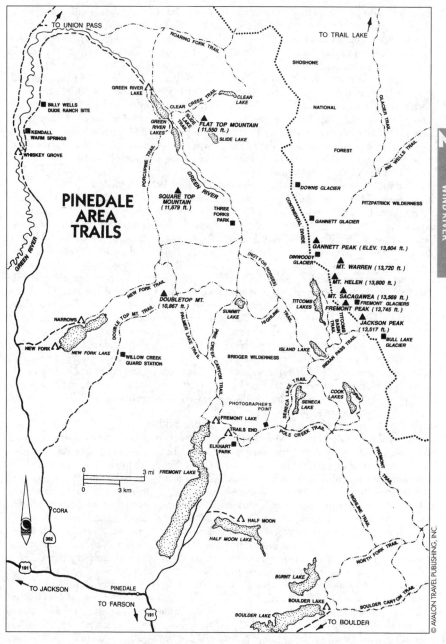

WIND RIVER

meander across southwestern Wyoming, eventually joining the Colorado River in Utah. Willows line the riverbanks in this open valley, while sagebrush and aspen cover the hills. Cattle and horses graze on the lush grasses.

Get to Green River Lakes by driving seven miles west of Pinedale on U.S. Hwy. 191, and then north up State Hwy. 352. The first 26 miles of the road to Green River Lakes are paved and kept plowed all winter. Approximately 15 miles up, a sign points the way to **New Fork Lake,** four miles away on a gravel road. Camp here at either **New Fork Lake Campground** ($5; open June to mid-Sept.) or the popular **Narrows Campground** ($10; open June to mid-Sept.). Make reservations ($9 fee) for Narrows Campground at 518/885-3639 or 877/444-6777, www.reserveusa.com. **New Fork Trail** takes off from the Narrows Campground, providing one of many routes into the Winds.

At the Forest Service border, state maintenance ends and the road becomes gravel and gets rougher and more washboarded as you go the remaining 18 miles (a total of 51 miles from Pinedale). Watch the weather because this upper portion can become a quagmire after heavy rains. It's especially a problem if you're towing a trailer. Fantastic scenery makes the trip worthwhile despite the road conditions. Look for some enormous "erratic" boulders a couple of miles up the road from here, evidence of the glaciers that once scoured this valley and carried the boulders along with them.

Just inside the Forest Service border, a signboard describes the tie drives that sent several hundred thousand railroad ties down the Green River between 1869 and 1871. They made it all the way to Green River City (130 miles away), where a boom caught them and they were loaded on railcars. The crew boss, Charles Deloney, later became first superintendent of the Yellowstone Preserve and opened the first store in Jackson. The Green River Lumber and Tie Company came here in the 1890s, employing at least 50 men who lived in the town of Kendall. The company only lasted until 1904, but you can still find the tall stumps in the second-growth forests nearby.

Approximately three miles beyond the Bridger-Teton National Forest border, a rough gravel

road splits off and heads over **Union Pass** to Dubois. Although this route was used by Indians and mountain men, today it probably sees more use by snowmobiles in the winter than cars in summertime. Although very rough in spots and muddy each spring, the road is passable in midsummer, even for two-wheel-drive cars. Union Pass Road is especially popular with elk hunters in the fall. The Forest Service's **Whiskey Grove Campground** ($10; open mid-June to mid-Sept.) is just west across the bridge at the site of the old logging town of Kendall.

Kendall Warm Springs

Back on Green River Lakes Road, you pass Kendall Warm Springs 1.5 miles above the turnoff to the campground, its 85°F waters issuing from a few hundred feet up the hill. This is the only place in the world where you can find **Kendall dace.** Fully grown, these tiny fish are just two inches long, or, as the Forest Service notes, shorter than their scientific name, *Rhinichthys osculus thermalis.* The water drops over a 12-foot-high travertine terrace into Green River. The terrace was built up over thousands of years; at the same time the river was cutting into its banks, thus separating these fish and allowing them to survive away from larger predators. To protect them, wading is not allowed in the waters of Kendall Warm Springs.

More Sights

Another two miles up the road are the log and red-sandstone remains of **Gros Ventre Lodge,** one of Wyoming's first dude ranches. Billy Wells built a hunting lodge here in 1897 and operated it until 1906, when stricter enforcement of game laws made it more difficult to attract clients. The lodge drew wealthy big-game hunters from England and the East Coast, who enjoyed the chance to slaughter wildlife. (Bannock Indians who hunted out of season in nearby Jackson Hole were shot at, while rich white "sportsmen" could take whatever they wanted for trophies.)

The road ends at the popular **Green River Lakes Campground** ($10; open mid-June to mid-Sept.). Weekends and the Fourth of July holiday may fill the campground to overflowing.

© DON PITCHER

Square Top Mountain, Shoshone National Forest

Several unofficial campsites are just off the road below the lake. **Square Top Mountain** stares back across the lake and is especially beautiful at sunrise, when the water is calm and the first light catches its cliff faces. When winter comes, ice drapes the front of Square Top, creating the longest single-pitch ice route in the nation. It has never been climbed. Trails in the Green River Lakes area are described later.

BRIDGER WILDERNESS

The 428,169-acre Bridger Wilderness reaches 90 miles along the western side of the Wind River Mountains, encompassing 27 active glaciers, 2,300 alpine lakes, and 600 miles of trails. It's named for famed mountain man and guide Jim Bridger and was first designated a primitive area in 1931, gaining wilderness status with the original Wilderness Act of 1964. Despite this status, a considerable amount of sheep grazing still takes place in the Bridger Wilderness; it was "grandfathered" in with the wilderness legislation. Sheep are allowed to graze on the southern end of the wilderness (south of Raid Lake), while cattle graze north of there. The Forest Service office in Pinedale is now trying to control sheep grazing more and reduce the conflicts between backcountry hikers and the herds.

Regulations and Access

Before heading out, be sure to pick up a copy of Bridger Wilderness regulations from the Pinedale Forest Service office, 307/367-4326, www.fs.fed.us/btnf. Call ahead for the latest on trail conditions and snow depths in the high country and for recommendations on avoiding crowded areas. The office also loans out **bear-resistant food storage containers.** These are available on a first-come, first-served basis, or you can buy your own at The Outdoor Shop in Pinedale. Habituated black bears are becoming a problem in many backcountry camps, and some have even learned how to obtain properly hung food.

To keep from polluting the water, pitch your tent at least 200 feet from lakes or trails in the wilderness and 100 feet from streams. Campfires are allowed only below timberline and only then with dead and down wood; gas stoves are recommended. Organized groups such as scouts or school groups, and groups traveling with horses, mules, llamas, and pack goats must all get a free visitor permit from the Pinedale District office. If you're using an outfitter to pack in your supplies, make sure the Forest Service permits them to operate within the wilderness.

Access to the Bridger Wilderness comes from nine different entrances along the western side of the range. The three most popular points of entry are described as follows, as are several favorite trails. If you're looking for solitude, you may want to avoid these popular paths. Note that the open alpine country means that anyone with topographic maps and a good sense of orientation can strike off in interesting directions and quickly escape the crowds. If you plan to do any fishing, be sure to pick up the Forest Service's guide to fishing lakes in the Bridger Wilderness, with details on which species are where.

Green River Lakes Trails

Easily the most scenic entry into the Winds is from Green River Lakes, located on the end of a paved-then-dirt road that leads north from Cora. The road ends at a campground ($10; open mid-June to mid-Sept.) facing onto Lower Green River Lake, where the unforgettable 11,679-foot summit of Square Top Mountain dominates the view.

For an easy five-mile day hike, follow the trails that circle Lower Green River Lake (Highline Trail on the east and Lakeside Trail on the west). You'll have excellent views of Flat Top Mountain (not to be confused with Square Top Mountain) from the Lakeside Trail and of the Clear Creek Falls along the Highline Trail. Keep your eyes open for moose and osprey. An interesting side trip is the short hike to Upper Green River Lake, where Square Top proves even more startling. Another side trip heads up **Clear Creek Trail;** it takes off from the southeastern end of Lower Green River Lake, climbs two miles to a natural bridge, then continues an equal distance to Clear Lake. Some of this country was burned in a 1988 fire. Flat Top is relatively easy to climb; see one of the trail guides for specifics.

Those interested in longer hikes will find several trails in the Green River Lakes area. **Roaring Fork Trail** climbs up to Faler Lake, 14 miles away and 2,200 feet higher. The **Highline Trail** follows the northeast shore of Lower Green River Lake and then continues south to the uppermost headwaters of the Green River. From there, the trail stays in the alpine much of the way to its destination at the Big Sandy Trailhead on the southern end of the Bridger Wilderness. The total distance is 72 miles, but few people actually follow it that far, preferring to branch off to other sights. Another popular trek is up **Porcupine Trail** to Porcupine Pass and then down **New Fork Trail** to New Fork Lake (a total of approximately 17 miles). Porcupine Trail begins at the upper end of Lower Green River Lake, splitting off from Lakeside Trail.

Elkhart Park Trails

Skyline Drive is a paved road that heads northeast from Pinedale along the eastern side of Fremont Lake, ending 17 miles later at Elkhart Park Trailhead (elevation 9,100 feet). The Forest Service generally has someone around to answer questions at the big parking area that fills with cars in July and August. An overlook along the way provides vistas across Fremont Lake and Bridger Wilderness. The **Trails End Campground** at Elkhart Park ($10) is open from late June to mid-September. For a pleasant day hike that ends with a bang-up vista of Fremont Peak and the Wind River Range, hike four miles out the Pole Creek Trail to **Photographer's Point.**

Backcountry trails head out from Elkhart in two directions. **Pine Creek Canyon Trail** leads north, providing a relatively direct connection with Summit Lake (13 miles) and then down into Green River Lakes (30 miles total). Because of its steepness, it is not recommended for stock use. The main drawback to this trail is that it loses 2,000 feet by dropping into Pine Creek Canyon—elevation that you must regain to reach Summit Lake. You can make a nice loop by heading east from Summit Lake along the Highline Trail to Elbow Lake and Seneca Lake, where you follow the Seneca Lake and Pole Creek Trails back to Elkhart Park. This loop takes you through some of the more scenic areas in the wilderness and covers approximately 31 miles.

The most popular destination from Elkhart is **Titcomb Basin.** Access from Elkhart Park is via a series of connected trails: the Pole Creek, Seneca Lake, Indian Pass, and Titcomb Basin Trails. Many hikers and climbers overnight at Island Lake, making for crowded conditions much of the summer. It is 15 miles from Elkhart Park to Upper Titcomb Lake, a mountain cirque with abundant wildflowers. A side hike goes up through gorgeous Indian Basin to Indian Pass (three miles). Mountaineers can then descend to the Knife Point and Bull Lake glaciers within the Fitzpatrick Wilderness.

The valley above Titcomb Basin is open, giving climbers access to the west side of a whole row of peaks, including Mt. Helen (13,600 feet), Mt. Sacagawea (13,569 feet), Jackson Peak (13,517 feet), and **Fremont Peak** (13,745 feet). Climbers can tackle the last two without technical expertise, although Fremont does require some rough scrambling in places. It is most easily climbed from the southwest side; see a topographic map to find the route. Those with greater expertise will find many outstanding opportunities to test their skills on the cliff faces here. Warning: Some folks have died climbing Fremont Peak; use extreme caution when rock scrambling, and never push beyond your skills or ability.

Fremont Peak is named for **John C. Frémont,** the son-in-law of Sen. Thomas Hart Benton, promoter of the Manifest Destiny that would lead Americans all the way to the Pacific. Because of this familial association, Frémont was given the task of exploring and mapping the western territories, work that brought him the nickname the "Great Pathfinder." Some of his ventures—such as floating through the wild waters of Fremont Canyon on the North Platte River or crossing the Rockies in the dead of winter—were downright stupid, and his guides tried to stop him. Frémont's best asset was his wife, who painted his adventures in such a heroic light that his presidential ambitions were nearly realized.

In 1842, Frémont and his men climbed what appeared to be the highest mountain in the Wind River range, a summit they called Snow Peak (now Fremont Peak). From the west, it is obvious why Frémont and his men would mistake this for the highest: Gannett Peak (59 feet taller) is barely visible from a distance, hidden behind other summits. It was not until years later that the mistake was discovered. Frémont was led on his wilderness treks by men with far more experience, including Kit Carson and Tom Fitzpatrick, and his real role was to transfer their innate knowledge of the land onto maps. (Although most people believe Frémont did climb the peak bearing his name, others say he climbed another peak instead, or none at all. One of his scouts, Basil Lajeunesse, stated bluntly, "Frémont never ascended the peak." Perhaps that would account for the discrepancies between what Frémont described and what is actually there.)

Big Sandy Trails

One of the most popular entry points into the Bridger Wilderness is from Big Sandy Trailhead. Access is from several different directions, but all require traversing long stretches of gravel road.

Easiest access is from the north. From the town of Boulder, take State Hwy. 353 where it turns west off U.S. Hwy. 191 and follow it until it turns to gravel (16 miles). Bear left at the intersection one-half mile up and go another nine miles to another junction (signed), where you again turn left and go seven more miles to the turnoff (left) to the Forest Service's Dutch Joe Guard Station and then on to Big Sandy Opening. The road ends at **Big Sandy Campground** ($5; open mid-June to mid-Sept.), where the trails begin. The Forest Service generally has someone stationed here in the summer. Note that the rough road into Big Sandy becomes slick and hazardous when it rains, so watch the weather reports closely. This is especially a problem if you're towing a trailer.

Big Sandy Lodge is just to the north near the end of Big Sandy Road (44 miles from Boulder) and provides guided trail rides and a historic 1929 lodge containing a trophy-head-filled lounge and two stone fireplaces. Ten rustic log cabins lack electricity or running water; $55 s or d, or $70 for four people. Three meals per day are available for guests; others can eat here by reservation. Spot-pack trips and guided pack trips are also available, or you can stay by the week with everything included ($1,330 for two people for six days). There are no phones here, but you can leave messages at 307/382-6513, or find them on the web at www.bigsandylodge.com. Open June–Oct. Recommended.

A maze of trails departs from Big Sandy Opening. The **Highline Trail** heads north, extending across the Bridger Wilderness to Green River Lakes, and continues from there to Union Pass, 100 miles away. The trail connects with numerous others, including **Shadow Lake Trail,** a 2.5-mile route to this alpine lake. More adventurous types can continue up over Texas Pass and down to Lonesome Lake in the Cirque of the Towers, a distance of 15 miles. (The very popular Cirque of the Towers area is described under Popo Agie Wilderness.)

Another side route off the Highline Trail is the **Washakie Trail,** a path used by this famous Shoshone chief during his people's biannual migration between the Wind River Valley and the Green River country. This trail goes into the

BIG SANDY AREA TRAILS

Washakie Lakes area of the Popo Agie Wilderness, where you can connect with the Bears Ears Trail.

The most popular trail out of Big Sandy Opening is **Big Sandy Trail,** a 5.5-mile trek to crowded Big Sandy Lake, where it meets a spider web of trails and cairn-marked paths to other high-country lakes. Beyond the lake, **Big Sandy Pass Trail** climbs steeply up North Creek and over Big Sandy Pass (shown as Jackass Pass on some maps) before dropping into Lonesome Lake and Cirque of the Towers (total distance 8.5 miles). Big Sandy Pass Trail is a long—but beautiful—slog. A strenuous loop trip consists of the Big Sandy Trail–Big Sandy Pass Trail route combined with the Texas Pass–Shadow Lake Trail–Highline Trail route described previously. Total distance is 24 miles.

FITZPATRICK WILDERNESS

The 198,838-acre Fitzpatrick Wilderness occupies the northeast side of the Wind River Mountains, sandwiched between the Bridger Wilderness just over the Continental Divide and the Wind River Indian Reservation to the east. The wilderness is a rugged landscape of rock and ice, with dozens of mountain lakes and cascading mountain brooks. Wyoming's highest mountain, Gannett Peak, forms part of the western border, and 44 active glaciers crowd against the summits; the largest covers 1,220 acres. The Fitzpatrick is a favorite of folks with considerable backpacking or mountaineering experience.

Although long maintained as a primitive area, the Fitzpatrick Wilderness was officially established by Congress in 1976 and is named for Tom Fitzpatrick, a respected mountain man, guide, head of the Rocky Mountain Fur Company, army scout, and Indian agent. To the Indians, he was "Broken Hand," a name received after he lost three fingers in a rifle accident while being pursued by Blackfeet Indians; despite this loss, he still managed to kill two of his attackers. As an Indian agent, Tom Fitzpatrick pushed for several important treaties, including the 1851 Fort Laramie Treaty. His untimely death from pneumonia in 1854 was a blow to the peace process, and few of the agents who followed could match Fitzpatrick's diplomatic skills or knowledge of the West. Fitzpatrick's adopted Arapaho son, Friday (named for the day of the week on which Fitzpatrick found him), later became a respected chief and translator for his people.

Access

The primary entrance point into the Fitzpatrick Wilderness is from **Trail Lake.** Head five miles southeast from Dubois on U.S. Hwy. 26/287 and turn right (south) onto a gravel road. The road leads into Whiskey Basin, with a rutted dirt road continuing to the left past a string of small lakes, the last being Trail Lake. The trails begin here, 12 miles off the highway. Note that access to the Cold Springs/Burris Trailhead requires that you cross Wind River Reservation land. You'll need to hire an Indian outfitter to drive you to the trailhead, and you'll have to obtain a reservation fishing/hiking permit and recreation stamp (nonresidents of Wyoming pay $25 per day or $65 per person for a week). Contact the Tribal Fish and Game Office in Fort Washakie, 307/332-7207, for details.

Forest Service regulations in the Fitzpatrick prohibit camping within 100 feet of trails or lakes. In addition, no campfires or overnight horse use is allowed above the confluence of Dinwoody and Knoll Lake Creeks. For details, contact the Forest Service's **Wind River Ranger District** office in Dubois, 307/455-2466.

Trails

Three major trails lead from Trail Lake into the high country. The **Whiskey Mountain Trail** climbs over the peak of the same name and then on to heavily used Simpson Lake, a dozen miles away. From here it's possible for experienced hikers to continue over a pass above Sandra Lake (another 3.5 miles) and then down into the Roaring Fork drainage of the Bridger Wilderness. The **Bomber Basin Trail** leads from Trail Lake Trailhead to Bomber Lake, eight miles away and 2,600 feet higher, crossing the deep canyon created by Torrey Creek on a high bridge. The basin is named for a B-17 bomber that crashed here during World War II when its crew was practicing a strafing run on either a bear or a bighorn sheep. The plane wreckage is still visible. The upper portion of this trail (above Bomber Falls) is not maintained but passable.

A very popular moderately long hike is up **Glacier Trail** all the way to Dinwoody Glacier. It is a sweaty and difficult 23 miles but passes lots of lakes and ruggedly beautiful alpine country. Bighorn sheep are often seen along the way. The first several miles are without water, so be sure to bring plenty with you. The trail ends at the glacier, providing access for mountaineers who want to scale 13,804-foot **Gannett Peak,** the highest in Wyoming. (The peak is named for Henry Gannett, chief topographer for the Hayden Survey of the 1870s, and it was first climbed in 1922 by Arthur Tate and Floyd Stahlnaker.) Because it is nearly surrounded by glaciers, most routes require roping up, particularly the popular one across Gooseneck Glacier.

Many mountaineers come up this trail to climb Gannett and the cluster of peaks over 13,000 feet just to the south, including Mt. Woodrow Wilson, the Sphinx, Mt. Warren, Doublet Peak, and Turret Peak. See Joe Kelsey's *Climbing and Hiking in the Wind River Mountains* for details. If you want to go with the pros, two first-rate mountaineering operations based in Jackson Hole lead climbs up Gannett Peak: **Exum Mountain Guides,** 307/733-2297, www.exumguides.com, and **Jackson Hole Mountain Guides,** 307/733-4979 or 800/239-7642, www.jhmg.com. These guides aren't cheap; expect to pay $1,200 per person for a six-day trip with three clients.

POPO AGIE WILDERNESS

The Popo Agie Wilderness is a 101,991-acre parcel of magnificent mountain real estate with jagged peaks, deep valleys, and more than 240 lakes. At least 20 peaks rise above 13,000 feet; Wind River Peak is the tallest at 13,225 feet. Popo Agie was first established as a primitive area in 1932 and enlarged and reclassified as wilderness in 1984. The Popo Agie is bounded to the west by the Bridger Wilderness and to the north by the Wind River Indian Reservation. Access to the Popo Agie Wilderness is generally from the east side, in the Lander vicinity, although it is possible to cross the Continental Divide from the Bridger Wilderness via several different passes. Camping is not allowed within 200 feet of trails, lakes, or streams. Anyone bringing in horses, mules, llamas, or pack goats will need to get a free livestock-use permit from the Forest Service. Get this and other Popo Agie Wilderness information from the **Washakie Ranger District Office** in Lander, 307/332-5460, www.fs.fed.us/r2/shoshone.

Dickinson Park Access

The primary jumping-off point into the Popo Agie Wilderness is the Dickinson Park area, northwest of Lander at an elevation of 9,300 feet. Get here by turning west on Moccasin Lake Road (paved) just south of Fort Washakie at the Hines Store. Stay right where the road turns to dirt and continue to Moccasin Lake/Dickinson Park junction, a total of 19 very rough and rutted miles. Turn left here and head another four miles to **Dickinson Creek Campground** (free; open July to mid-Sept.; no water), passing the Dickinson Park Work Center along the way. Note that you'll pass a "No Trespassing without Proper Tribal Travel Permit" sign on Moccasin Lake Road; it's okay to ignore this if you're en route to Dickinson Park.

Allen's Diamond Four Ranch, 307/332-2995, www.diamond4ranch.com, is near the Dickinson Park Campground and offers rustic dude-ranch accommodations with three meals a day, horseback riding, fishing, and nature hikes. They also have guided horsepacking trips and spot-pack trips, popular with those who want to hike while still enjoying the pleasures of a horse-packed base camp. The ranch is open July–September and can accommodate a maximum of 10 guests. All-inclusive weekly rates are $1,800 for two people.

The **Bears Ears Trail** takes off from the end of a half-mile dirt road that turns west at the Dickinson Park Work Center and climbs quickly into the alpine before going over Adams Pass. It passes Bears Ears Mountain (look for the "ears") and follows through the alpine before dropping into the lake-filled headwaters of the South Fork of the Little Wind River, 14 miles away. Along the way are all sorts of connections to other trails, including a variety of loops.

From the North Fork/Smith Lake trailhead near Dickinson Creek Campground, the popular **Smith Lake Trail** heads south and then west to Smith and then Cathedral Lakes (eight miles). The **North Fork Trail** splits off the Smith Lake Trail approximately one-quarter mile up. This trail will eventually (15 miles) take you straight to Lonesome Lake at the base of the soaring Cirque of the Towers. Unfortunately, the hike requires four different fordings of the North Fork of the Popo Agie River, a dangerous feat for your feet when the water is high. It's best to wait until late summer to attempt this one.

Loop Road Access

The Loop Road (State Hwy. 131) cuts south from Lander through Sinks Canyon and then over the mountains to South Pass, providing several entry points into the Popo Agie Wilderness. **Middle Fork Trail** begins at **Bruce Picnic Ground,** 13 miles south of Lander on the Loop Road, and follows the Middle Fork of the Popo Agie River upstream to Sweetwater Gap (16 miles), where you enter the Bridger Wilderness. Many people use this trail to reach the Cirque of the Towers area via the Pinto Park and North Fork Trails (total one-way distance approximately 23 miles). The **Tayo Creek Trail** splits off from the Middle Fork Trail approximately 13 miles up and continues another four miles to Tayo and Coon lakes. **Sheep Bridge Trail** begins at **Worthen Reservoir,** 20 miles south of Lander on the Loop Road, and heads west for three miles to its junction with the Middle Fork Trail. Many people use this trail to cut distance and elevation off their trek into the Tayo Lake or Cirque of the Towers areas. (It starts 1,200 feet higher than the Middle Fork Trail.)

Cirque of the Towers

This is one of the best-known and most-visited places in the Wind River Mountains, an incredible semicircle of pinnacles at the headwaters of the North Fork of the Popo Agie River. **Lonesome Lake** is in the center, backdropped by peaks with such names as Warbonnet, Pingora, Sharks Nose, Camels Hump, Lizard Head, and Watch Tower. All of these peaks are well-known in the climbing community and attract folks from around the globe. Lonesome Lake is not so lonesome these days; on a typical day in early August you're likely to find a minitown of tents in the vicinity. To help protect the area, the Forest Service prohibits camping within one-quarter mile of the lake, and no campfires are allowed.

The most popular way to reach Cirque of the Towers is from the Big Sandy Opening Trailhead (see Bridger Wilderness), but the longer North Fork Trail (described earlier) is also commonly used and does not require traversing any passes. The other popularly used route is the Sheep Bridge Trail (described earlier). Campers often choose to base themselves at Big Sandy

© DON PITCHER

Warbonnet and Warrior peaks, Cirque of the Towers

Lake and then day hike into Cirque of the Towers. It makes for a long day, but at least you won't need to carry a heavy pack over challenging Big Sandy Pass.

South Pass

At the southern end of the Wind River Mountains, a broad, relatively gentle pass provides a corridor across the Continental Divide. This part of Wyoming is packed with history, particularly around South Pass, which is now traversed by State Hwy. 28.

Red Canyon

Approximately 15 miles southwest of Lander, State Hwy. 28 climbs to an overlook above Red Canyon, where maroon sandstone rocks rise like a backbone out of the sage and grass rangeland. A separate route, Red Canyon Road follows Red Canyon Creek for a close-up view of

this colorful valley. The 35,000-acre **Red Canyon Ranch Preserve** is a working cattle ranch maintained by the Nature Conservancy. It's a center for research on the ecological effects of different grazing techniques. Get details on classes and guided walks at 307/332-5990, www.tncwyoming.org.

Over the Pass

West of Red Canyon, the highway passes just north of the almost ghost towns of Atlantic City and South Pass before starting the long descent into the Green River Basin and the junction town of Farson. Winters on the pass are long,

WIND RIVER

cold, and windy; the snow fences stretch for miles along the highway.

Gold was first mined here during the 1860s, and a long series of booms and busts followed. For a brief time in 1867–1868, the **Sweetwater Mines** attracted national attention, and thousands of men (and a few women) flocked to the area. The land was officially part of the Wind River Reservation at the time, but legalities didn't matter much when gold could be found. South Pass was ceded by the Shoshones in 1878. Prospectors still head out each spring in search of the elusive mother lode, and various schemes to reopen the old mines surface periodically. Today the area is enjoyed by thousands of tourists and others attracted by the rich historical and recreational opportunities.

> *We traveled up a long, gradual slope, or plain, free of rocks, trees, or gullies, and came at half past eleven o'clock to the summit of the South Pass of the Rocky Mountains. . . . The ascent was so smooth and gentle, and the level ground at the summit so much like a prairie region, that it was not easy to tell when we had reached the exact line of the divide.*
>
> from the diary entry of Oregon Trail emigrant
> Margaret A. Frink, June 24, 1850

History

South Pass was first discovered by the game animals who traversed this country and the Indian hunters who followed them. The first whites to traipse through were the Astorians, fur traders led by Robert Stuart in 1812. The first wagon wheels rolled over South Pass in 1824, and between 1841 and 1866 more than 350,000 emigrants followed what had become the primary route west. Of all the sights along the Oregon Trail, South Pass was one of the most anticipated. West of here the waters flow to the Pacific Ocean, and the entire country became known as the Oregon Territory (hence the **Oregon Buttes** south of South Pass). Travelers took great pleasure in stopping at Pacific Springs, happy in the knowledge that its waters eventually reached the Pacific. An important stage and Pony Express

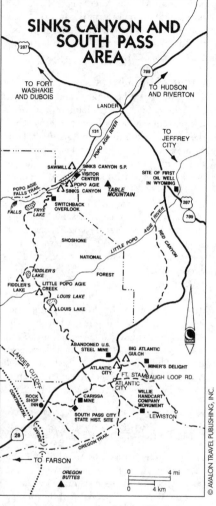

SINKS CANYON AND SOUTH PASS AREA

© AVALON TRAVEL PUBLISHING, INC.

station stood here; some of the buildings from a later ranch are still standing.

Today, State Hwy. 28 traces a similar route across South Pass. Signboards denote various historic sites along the way. At the signboard that describes the Oregon Trail, a rough dirt road leads one mile back to the clear waters of Pacific Creek, where posts mark the historic route. Don't believe everything you read on the signs, however: the **Parting of the Ways** mon-

SOUTH PASS IN 1861

In 1861, Mark Twain rumbled west through Wyoming on a stagecoach, a trip later made famous in his book *Roughing It*. At South Pass, Twain found that the pre-mining-days settlement was not exactly a hubbub of activity:

Toward dawn we got under way again, and presently as we sat with raised curtains enjoying our early-morning smoke and contemplating the first splendor of the rising sun as it swept down the long array of mountain peaks, flushing and gilding crag after crag and summit after summit, as if the invisible Creator reviewed his gray veterans and they saluted with a smile, we hove in sight of South Pass City. The hotelkeeper, the postmaster, the blacksmith, the mayor, the constable, the city marshal and the principal citizen and property holder, all came out and greeted us cheerily, and we gave him good day. . . . South Pass City consisted of four log cabins, one of which was unfinished, and the gentleman with all those offices and titles was the chiefest of the ten citizens of the place. Think of hotelkeeper, postmaster, blacksmith, mayor, constable, city marshal and principal citizen all condensed into one person and crammed into one skin. Bemis said he was "a perfect Allen's revolver of dignities." And he said that if he were to die as postmaster, or as blacksmith, or as postmaster and blacksmith both, the people might stand it; but if he were to die all over, it would be a frightful loss to the community.

WIND RIVER

ument actually marks the South Pass City–Green River stage road where it intersects the Oregon Trail rather than the famous point where the Sublette Cutoff took Oregon- and California-bound travelers west while Mormon voyagers (and others in need of supplies) diverged southwest to Fort Bridger. The true Parting of the Ways lies 10 miles southwest of this marker. The highway west to Farson rolls up and down the sage-carpeted hills, cutting straight as a carpenter's plumb line. The Wind River Mountains dominate the northern horizon, while to the south the distant Killpecker Sand Dunes slide into view.

SOUTH PASS CITY

At 7,800 feet above sea level, South Pass City is one of Wyoming's highest settlements. Tall snow fences line the roads here in an attempt to halt the snow that blows all winter long. Although commonly called a ghost town, South Pass City never really died out. The town is now a State Historic Site, providing one of the most interesting and authentic historical settings in Wyoming.

Gold in the Hills

During the days of 1849, many thousands of would-be miners streamed through South Pass on their way to California, little knowing that gold lay beneath their feet. Gold was first found in 1842, but its discoverer was killed by Indians; other miners faced similar fates. First to file a claim was Henry Reedal, who discovered what became known as the Carissa Lode in 1867. Shortly thereafter, the Miner's Delight Lode was discovered. The finds attracted an onslaught of miners, and by that fall the town of South Pass City had mushroomed into Wyoming's largest settlement, with nearly 3,000 residents.

The discovery of gold at South Pass helped propel the effort to make Wyoming a territory separate from Dakota, a move that took place the following year. At its rip-roaring peak, there was even an effort to make South Pass the Wyoming territorial capital. The town included six general stores, three butcher shops, several restaurants, two breweries, seven blacksmith shops, five hotels, and dozens of saloons and "sporting houses." In 1868, writer James Chisholm described his return to the town after an absence: "Late at night we arrived at Miner's Delight where everything was just as we had left it. The card table in the corner was in full blast. The parties whom we had left on a drunk were now sobering off and those we had left sober were getting on a drunk."

The Carissa Mine's shafts would eventually reach 400 feet down, and the mill would produce gold worth more than $6 million. But this was primarily hard-rock mining, requiring large capital investments and long hours. The lack of water in this arid country meant that placer mining was possible only in the spring, while summers were spent toiling in the hard-rock mines for $5 per day. The Sweetwater mines were a short-lived bubble that burst almost as quickly as it grew. Instead of the hoped-for mother lode, miners found only small pockets of gold. Within five years most of the miners gave up and moved away. By 1875, fewer than one hundred people remained, but South Pass City refused to die. There were more booms (followed by busts) in the 1880s, 1890s, 1930s, and 1960s. Miners still come to these hills in search of gold.

Women's Suffrage

Given the rough mining crowd that jammed the streets of South Pass City, it seems odd to find the town at the center of the effort to gain equal rights for women. In late 1869, the first territorial representative from South Pass City, William Bright, introduced a women's-suffrage bill before the first territorial legislature. It was a measure supported by his wife and other South Pass women but probably opposed by many of the local men. The measure surprised almost everyone by being passed and signed into law by Gov. John Campbell. In anger, the local judge resigned his post as justice of the peace for South Pass City, only to be replaced by a woman, Esther Hobart Morris. She was the first woman judge in America. In her 8.5 months of service, Morris tried 26 cases and gained recognition for her fairness, along with considerable national exposure.

The more exalted claim that Morris was the "Mother of Women's Suffrage" is suspect. In 1869, she is supposed to have held a tea party in which the South Pass City women extracted a promise from then-candidate William Bright to introduce legislation to grant women the right to vote. The tea party tale somehow made it into the history books, even though her son—a newspaper editor—concocted it after her death. A statue of Morris in front of the state capitol credits her with the bill. Morris never claimed any such thing, and in fact was not an active suffragist. According to Bright, the reason he introduced the legislation was not because of lobbying by local women but because "If Negroes had the right to vote, women like [his] wife and mother should also."

South Pass State Historic Site

In 1965, South Pass City's buildings risked being carted off to Southern California's Knott's Berry Farm theme park. With the help of Alice "Flaming Mame" Messick, a committee of Wyoming folks outbid the Californians for the buildings and managed to keep them. The following year, the state purchased the site and began the process of restoration. South Pass State Historic Site contains some 25 old buildings and 30,000 authentic artifacts, 90 percent of which actually came from the area. The buildings are open daily 9 A.M.–6 P.M. May 15 through September; $2 for nonresident adults, $1 for Wyoming residents, and free for kids under age 18. Get details at 307/332-3684, http://wyoparks.state.wy.us. The rest of the year, visitors can wander the streets, but many items are in storage and the windows are covered with plywood.

On summertime weekends the old town comes alive with gold-panning and blacksmithing demonstrations by costumed old-timers. Be sure to drop by the Morris cabin for fresh-baked cookies. The **Old-Fashioned Fourth of July** celebration at South Pass is great fun, with country dancing, a barbecue, a pie-baking contest, horseshoe pitching, old-time music, exhibits, and lots of folks in old-time costumes.

Entrance fees are collected at the **visitors center** in what was once an 1890 dance hall. Inside are interpretive displays and a book and gift shop. The small theater shows a 28-minute video on the area's rich history. Pick up a brochure here describing the buildings. A short

© DON PITCHER

WIND RIVER

South Pass State Historic Site

way up the street is the **Smith Sherlock Co. Store,** where you can check out the old items or buy boulder-size jaw breakers, English marbles, homemade soap, gold pans, bonnets, distinctive candies and jellies, plus historical books. Barb and Dan Jackson run the store (which is also an official post office) and will be happy to tell tales of local ghosts and magical properties in the area. They also often provide lodging and a hot bath at their home (donation appreciated) for hikers coming through. Ask about their 125-pound Great Pyrenees.

Just up from the Smith Sherlock Co. Store is a small museum with historical photos. Other interesting buildings that have been restored and furnished with original items include a blacksmith shop, a restaurant, a butcher shop, a hotel, a miner's cabin, a saloon, a newspaper office, a bank, a school, and a dugout cave used to keep perishables cool. A gold-mining exhibit on the hill behind town has a huge stamp mill, carts, and railroad track, along with other mining equipment. Gold panning demonstrations are given periodically throughout the summer. **Sweetwater County Jail,** built in 1870, is the oldest nonmilitary government

building in Wyoming, and the **"pest house"** was a place where patients with contagious diseases were left in isolation. Built in 1869, this is the state's oldest hospital, although the level of treatment wasn't always the finest.

The reconstructed **Esther Morris cabin** stands at the eastern end of the row of buildings. Out front is a granite marker from 1939 that credits her with originating women's suffrage. Next to it is a more recent disclaimer. Adding more insult to injury is the fact that the reconstructed cabin is now believed to be in the wrong place; the actual Morris cabin site is not far away, and this was the location of a print shop instead.

Just east of the Morris cabin is a half-mile **nature trail** along Willow Creek offering the chance to explore the Carie Shields Mine (it produced $35,000 worth of gold) and other mines, cabins, and mill sights. Be careful where you walk around these old structures. Along the creek you're likely to see all sorts of animals, from beavers and bighorn sheep to mule deer and moose. Pick up a trail map at the Smith-Sherlock Store. The state also has a 10-km **Volksmarch trail** that is popular with the RV crowd.

CALAMITY JANE

Calamity Jane—born Martha Jane Canary in 1852—is surely one of the most unusual characters to come out of the 19th-century West. In an era when the few women who found their way west almost invariably fell into one of three categories—housewife, washerwoman, or prostitute—Calamity Jane was all three, plus a lot more. At age 12, Martha Canary's family trekked west from Missouri to Montana. The trip took five months, and by the time they reached Virginia City, she noted: "I was considered a remarkable good shot and a fearless rider for a girl of my age." Her mother died shortly after they arrived, and the family had a hard time surviving the harsh winter; Martha and her sisters were forced to beg on the streets. Her father died the following spring, and from that time on, Martha Canary was on her own. She landed in Miners Delight (near South Pass City) in 1870–1871; here some claim she "entertained" men at Hyde's Hall Saloon. She certainly occasionally worked in "the sporting profession."

A Man's World

It was around this time that Calamity Jane gained her nickname. She claimed in a brief autobiography to have signed on as a scout for General Custer in Fort Russell, Wyoming, and to have soon thereafter "donned the uniform of a soldier. It was a bit awkward at first but I soon got to be perfectly at home in men's clothes." At other times she even masqueraded as a man and could by all accounts work, shoot, drink, and cuss as hard as the rough-edged men around her. While employed as a scout for General Crook's campaign near Sheridan she supposedly rescued the post commander, Captain Egan, from an Indian raid, helping him to safety. Egan then named her "Calamity Jane, the heroine of the plains." The name stuck for life.

Whether the story is true or not, Calamity Jane *did* live up to the sobriquet many times in later years. She was often found nursing men down with smallpox—she was immune to the disease—buying meals for the destitute, or assisting ill "soiled doves," even if it meant rolling a man for his money to pay the bills. She saved many lives at a time when life was short and cheap. This is not to suggest that Calamity Jane was the Mother Teresa of the Plains; the same woman who could care so much for others could also be loud and obnoxious when drunk, which was often. Her binges were legendary and landed her behind bars on numerous occasions, including a monthlong stint in the Rawlins jail for a drunken brawl with one of her many husbands and an eight-day trip to the Laramie jail for drunkenness. Beer would never do: "Give me a shot of booze and slop her over the brim" was always the bartender's order. As a friend (Deadwood madam Dora DuFran) noted:

Her many friends—she had no enemies—would buy her drinks until she reached the howling stage. Then someone would steer her to the next saloon. Her time was limited in each one when that howling began. She would finally wind up by howling up and down Main Street. Even the law was paralyzed. Nothing could quell the howling completely, so some friend would escort her home with a quart of whiskey hugged to her breast to act as a night cap and put her to sleep. In the morning she would awaken with a hangover and start all over again. The only way to sober her up was to tell her someone was sick and needed her services. Not another drink would she take. Next day she would be ready for business.

In her autobiography, Calamity Jane said she married Clinton Burk in El Paso and went on to give birth to a girl "the very image of its father . . . but who has the temper of its mother." Nobody knows what became of the girl in later life, but Calamity went on to marry several other men. DuFran noted that "Jane had a very affectionate nature. There were very few preachers around to bother her, so whenever she got tired of one man she soon selected a new one." Calamity also alludes in her autobiography to an affair with famed gambler and gunfighter Wild Bill Hickok, and after her death a woman professed to be their illegitimate child raised by a wealthy East Coast family. Most folks put little stock in Calamity's relationship with Wild Bill, although the two did end up in Deadwood in 1876. A desperado shot Wild Bill in the back while he was seated at a gambling table; Calamity claimed to have helped capture the murderer.

Workin' and Boozin'

In later years, Calamity Jane seemed to spin her way across the West, stopping long enough to make money as a prospector, stagecoach driver, laundress, or some less seemly trade before getting the urge (or urging) to move on. Given the regimented code of behavior under which women lived in her era, it's easy to see how her appearance caused such a stir. Newspapers trumpeted her arrival in town, and saloons attracted crowds as her exploits grew with each telling. Someone was always willing to buy a round of drinks for the chance to hear Calamity's tales. As a young woman she was certainly attractive, but the years of hard drinking and rough living were not especially kind. As author Ellen Mueller put it, however, "perhaps the men standing in a saloon dead broke and hankering for a drink would have found the woman beautiful who would get drinks 'on the house' for everybody."

Alhough she spent a brief period with Buffalo Bill's Wild West Show, Calamity Jane's biggest moment of glory came in an 1895 return to Deadwood after a 17-year absence. A masquerade ball was held in her honor, and the local newspaper noted that

> *she was in great demand by the Dancers, many who were anxious to spend 25¢ to dance with her, just to have it to say they had danced with "Calamity Jane." She had a fair sized jag on board, and this, together with a vile cigar which she smoked, made her look anything but the beautiful woman which novelists and story writer have said so much about.*

Calamity died in 1904, just 52 years old. Her deathbed plea was to be buried next to Wild Bill Hickok, who she said was the only man she had ever loved. Her funeral was one of the largest ever for Deadwood. Today, they lie next to each other at the Mt. Moriah Cemetery overlooking town. The testimony of fellow tough-living Dora DuFran again sums up Calamity's life best:

> *It is easy for a woman to be good who has been brought up with every protection from the evils of the world and with good associates. Calamity was a product of the wild and woolly west. She was not immoral; but unmoral. She took more on her shoulders than most women could. She performed many hundreds of deeds of kindness and received very little pay for her work. With her upbringing, how could she be anything but unmoral.*

Practicalities

Outside the State Historic Site is a cluster of old log cabins owned by a handful of locals. Stop by the seasonally open **South Pass Trading Company,** www.south-pass.com, 307/332-6810, for a selection of gifts, books, snacks, and T-shirts.

The **Continental Divide Snowmobile Trail** traverses this area, and the **South Pass Cross-Country Ski Trails** take off from the pass, with seven kilometers of trails, although they aren't always groomed.

Gold Rush Days, held the last full weekend of July, feature a vintage baseball game with old rules and costumes, living-history demonstrations, old-time music, hard-rock drilling contests, gold panning, billiards, fresh lemonade and cookies, plus a variety of vendors. Call 307/332-2684 for details.

Oregon Trail Trips

Several companies offer wagon-train or horseback trips across various parts of Wyoming, including the Oregon Trail. These typically last 5–7 days and include horses, meals, equipment, and tents, but you'll need to bring a sleeping bag (they can rent you a bag). For details on the various options, contact **Great Divide Tours,** 307/332-3123 or 800/458-1915, www.dtoutfitting.com; **Western Encounters,** 307/332-5434 or 800/572-1230, www.horseriders.com; or **Historic Trails West,** 307/266-4868 or 800/327-4052, www.historictrailswest.com. **Wagons A+Cross Wyoming,** 307/859-8629 or 888/818-3581, www.wagonsacrosswyoming.com, uses historic iron-wheeled wagons pulled by draft horses along the Lander Cutoff of the Oregon Trail.

ATLANTIC CITY

The funky, friendly little town of Atlantic City has dirt streets, old log-and-stone buildings, and a delightfully infectious country atmosphere. It's the sort of town where old-timers plunk themselves atop the Merc's barstools to talk cattle, football, and the old days; where many homes (and the church, too) still have outhouses; and where the big event is the volunteer fire department picnic (late August). Residents pile up huge stacks of firewood to make it through the long, cold winters. The snow can get deep here near the top of the Continental Divide (elevation 7,660 feet). One winter, the drifts topped 27 feet and the snowplows didn't get in for several weeks! Most residents like the quiet beauty that winter brings to Atlantic City and depend on snowmobiles and skis to get around. This is one of the few places left in Wyoming where the past seems so immediately present.

History

Atlantic City was formed in 1868 when gold mines had attracted thousands of miners to the Sweetwater Mining District. As miners arrived in South Pass, they spread out over the surrounding country in search of other gold deposits, founding the settlements of Atlantic City, Miner's Delight, and Lewiston at promising locations. As with most frontier towns, saloons vastly outnumbered churches in early Atlantic City. The first county sheriff owned a local brothel! **Fort Stambaugh** was established a few miles to the east in 1870 to protect miners from Sioux and Arapaho raids. It lasted only until 1878, and the buildings were auctioned off four years later.

In the 1880s, another miniboom hit as French capitalist Emile Granier built a 25-mile-long ditch from the Wind River Mountains to Atlantic City for hydraulic mining. The effort failed when the money ran out before gold could be found. Another boom hit in the late 1920s and '30s when a dredge worked its way down Rock Creek (leaving behind enormous piles of gravel). By the early 1960s, Atlantic City's population had been reduced to a handful of folks. Development of a U.S. Steel iron-ore (taconite) strip mine nearby brought prosperity after 1962, but the mine closed in 1983 and left behind a gaping pit now filled with water. Today Atlantic City depends on tourism and summer homes. But as a local brochure notes, "The wind of this old gold town always whispers of another boom on its way."

The Merc

Atlantic City's main attractions are its mining-era buildings, many dating from the turn of the 20th century. The centerpiece is **Atlantic City Mercantile,** built in 1893 from adobe brick. Its false front is covered with old metal siding, and the interior is stuffed with stuffed heads, historic photos, mining artifacts, a big woodstove (usually in use), and a rich sense of the past. Pick up a brochure at the kiosk describing the town's many other historic buildings.

The "Merc," 307/332-5143, rents A-frame cabins for $55 s or d ($5 per person for additional guests) during the summer. The bar often has live music on Saturday nights in the summer, along with a piano where you can display your own musical talents at other times. Maybe someone decided to shoot the piano player and missed because the mirror behind the bar has a bullet hole. The Merc's dinners are well-known throughout this part of Wyoming. In the front, you can munch on inexpensive but very good burgers and sandwiches all week. Back-room guests, on the other hand, are treated to an old-timey setting of oil lanterns and pine walls and a menu (entrées $15–30) that includes aspen-grilled meats and seafood Thursday–Sunday in the summer or Friday–Saturday in winter. Come here on the third Wednesday of the month for a seven-course Basque dinner ($22). Reservations are advised.

Other Services

Adjacent to the Merc is **The Dredge,** 332-8120, with a breakfast and lunch menu, homemade bread for the sub sandwiches, and delicious thick steaks, plus a few groceries and local crafts for sale. Bar patrons hang out at the pool table or in front of the big-screen TV.

The stone structure one block to the east of the Merc housed the **McAuley Store,** later Hyde's Hall. Calamity Jane once provided the entertainment in the saloon here. Up the hill is **St. Andrews Episcopal Church,** a rustic old log church built in 1913 and still used today. Sunday services start at 10 A.M. The **Gratrix Cabin,** one block east of the church, was built in the late 1860s and was home to Judge Buck Gratrix, a man who noted that he lived in three different counties, two territories, and one state while living in one place!

One of the most attractive buildings in Atlantic City is the mint-condition **Miner's Delight B&B,** 307/332-0248 or 888/292-0248. Originally known as the Carpenter Hotel, it was constructed in 1895 and run as a boardinghouse for miners and others until 1961. Today it's a cozy B&B with two Victorian-style rooms with private baths in the main building ($75 s or d), a small room with twin beds and a shared bath ($60 s or d), plus four rustic hand-chinked log cabins ($60 d) with shared bath facilities. A full country breakfast is included, and Miner's Delight is open all year.

Rolls-Kenardley Tours, 307/332-8155, guides one-hour tours of Atlantic City at $70 for two people. They also have a room for rent with a shower and toilet; $50 s or $55 d. Be sure to check out their distinctive Chinese knots, tied by Mei Zhen Jie.

Nearby Sights

Rock Creek flows through Atlantic City, and on the west end of town the banks are lined with huge piles of boulders left behind by the gold-dredging operations of the '30s. Fort Stambaugh Road heads east from Atlantic City and follows a 12-mile loop past the site of Fort Stambaugh (not marked) and the ghost town of Miner's Delight. A side road leads to **Lewiston,** another abandoned gold-mining town. The loop road is a scenic drive through open grassland and scattered patches of young aspen and lodgepole. (Miners wiped out previous stands.) Antelope are sure to be seen along the way. The settlement called **Miner's Delight** consists of a dozen log buildings in various states of decay. A small beaver pond and graveyard are also in Miner's Delight, with other old mining buildings visible just west of here.

The road west from Atlantic City to South Pass City passes more old gold mines, notably the **Duncan Mine** (two miles out) and the famous **Carissa Mine,** just before dropping down to South Pass City. Most of the mines and buildings are on private land, and many contain hazardous structures and shafts without covers. Watch your step!

A little more than seven miles south of Atlantic City is a monument to the **Willie Handcart Company.** In 1856, a large group of

© DON PITCHER

Miner's Delight B&B, Atlantic City

Mormon emigrants led by James G. Willie was caught in a series of early winter storms and camped here awaiting help and provisions from Salt Lake City. Sixty-seven of them died before they could reach the promised land. This and the Mormon handcart monuments at Rocky Ridge and Rock Creek are described in a pamphlet available at South Pass State Historic Site. (See the Central Wyoming chapter for details on another Mormon handcart disaster at Martin's Cove.)

Practicalities

Groceries are not available in either Atlantic City or South Pass, so stock up elsewhere. Atlantic City Mercantile and Miner's Delight B&B both have rooms, as described previously. Meals are available at the Merc and The Dredge.

The BLM maintains two attractive campgrounds ($6; open June–Oct.) in young aspen stands—brilliantly yellow in the fall—along the Fort Stambaugh Loop Road: **Atlantic City Campground** and **Big Atlantic Gulch Campground.**

Farson and Vicinity

Farson (pop. 240) stands at the busy highway junction where State Hwy. 28 and U.S. Hwy. 191 greet each other. Locals live in trailer homes—the modern versions of log cabins—and work at a couple of local businesses. All around are long straight roads, flat sagebrush desert, a few irrigated pastures, and antelope. It's a long way to anywhere else, so almost everyone stops for a road break at this oasis of sorts. In the simmering summer sun, **Farson Mercantile,** 307/273-9511, is crowded with people buying ice-cream cones to eat in the shade of the olive trees out front. Join the crowd; these are *huge* cones—"one scoop" is actually two or three scoops. In addition to the ice cream shop, the old brick building houses a classic country market. Also worth a look is the historic and picturesque log church in Farson.

Mitch's Cafe, 307/273-9606, serves standard road grub and features burlwood seats at the counter. **Sitzman's Motel,** 307/273-9246, charges $40–48 s or d, but is often full in mid-summer and during the fall hunting season. Check in at Mitch's.

Park RVs behind Farson Mercantile at **Oregon Trail Campground,** 307/273-5586; $5 for tents or $12 for RVs. It's open late May–September.

HEADING SOUTH

Four miles south of Farson is tiny **Eden,** where irrigated green fields bring the arid landscape alive. Of note here is the old **Oregon Trail Baptist Church,** with its brown log walls, quaint bell tower, and back window facing the Wind River Mountains. The view probably makes it hard to concentrate on the service. Kitty-corner across the road is the Eden Saloon, where the view may not be as great, but after a few beers it really doesn't matter. Bicentennial Park makes a shady place to enjoy a picnic. South of Eden, U.S. Hwy. 191 cruises into the bleak Bad Lands Hills country on its way to Rock Springs. Killpecker Dunes rise on the eastern horizon.

WIND RIVER

© DON PITCHER

Farson Mercantile, Farson

HEADING WEST

West of Farson, State Hwy. 28 takes you west from Farson through a little-traveled landscape of dry sage and grass. Pilot Butte is visible to the South, and funny wildlife billboards are the main attraction. The road crosses the Green River at Seedskadee National Wildlife Refuge, where it meets State Hwy. 372 south to Green River.

HEADING NORTH

Immediately north of Farson, the highway crosses the Big Sandy River, which is little more than a creek much of the year, with Big Sandy Reservoir (free camping here) holding back much of its water for irrigation. Flat irrigated fields of hay surround Farson. As you continue north to Pinedale (58 miles), the jagged snow-topped crowns of the Wind River Mountains loom ever larger and the sagebrush grows more abundant on the arid landscape rolling away to the mountains. The highway crosses both the **Sublette Cutoff,** one of the original routes to Oregon Country, and the 1858 **Lander Cutoff,** the first federal road west of the Mississippi. Tune in to KQSW (96.5 FM) for country tunes to speed you on your way.

A gravel road that begins two miles east of Farson and heads north along Little Sandy Creek and then northwest to Boulder is even more dramatic, passing along the foothills of the Winds. It's used for access to the Big Sandy Trailhead into the Bridger Wilderness. This is one of my favorite drives in Wyoming. Clouds often drape the distant mountains, but when they part—like curtains at a Broadway premier—they reveal the 13,000-foot crest of the Wind River Mountains in all its majesty. This is truly one of the classic Western vistas, and the interplay of land, light, and sky creates an unforgettable scene.

The land knocks you out: Mountains climb above the distant plain, crowning the eastern horizon with slanting patches of enormous rock faces and snow-mantled slopes, reflecting back the light from a westering sun. Antelope glance up as you drive past; a rough-legged hawk hunches down on a fence post; several horses paw the ground. Periodically a narrow set of pickup-truck tracks angles over the horizon to some remote ranch. In places like this, it is hard not to love the wildly beautiful state of Wyoming.

Pinedale

Located in the upper Green River Valley, with the Wind River Mountains creating a dramatic backdrop, Pinedale (pop. 1,400) is surrounded by hay-filled meadows, grazing horses, and modern ranchettes. In addition to the economic mainstays of ranching and tourism, Pinedale is also a minor governmental center with BLM, Forest Service, Game and Fish, and Sublette County offices.

Pinedale is similar in many ways to its neighbor across the mountains, Dubois. Both towns long depended on ranching and logging but are now starting to appreciate the visitors who come simply to enjoy the country. Pinedale has a solid core of downtown businesses, new log houses sprouting on the outskirts, and a couple of national chains (Best Western and Super 8 motels). Residents fear that it could become "another Jackson," but the town has kept its Old West flavor without falling (yet) under the complete domination of the almighty tourist dollar. Wealthy people from all over the world have bought up old ranches around Pinedale, turning them into summer homes; their small jets sprinkled across the tarmac—if it can be called that—at the local airport. Most of these folks are corporate bigwigs, such as the head of Pepsi-Co, but others include John Barlow (former lyricist for the Grateful Dead) and James Baker III (former secretary of state).

HISTORY

The first inhabitants of the Upper Green River Valley were the Shoshone, Gros Ventre, Sheep-eater, and Crow Indians, who hunted buffalo,

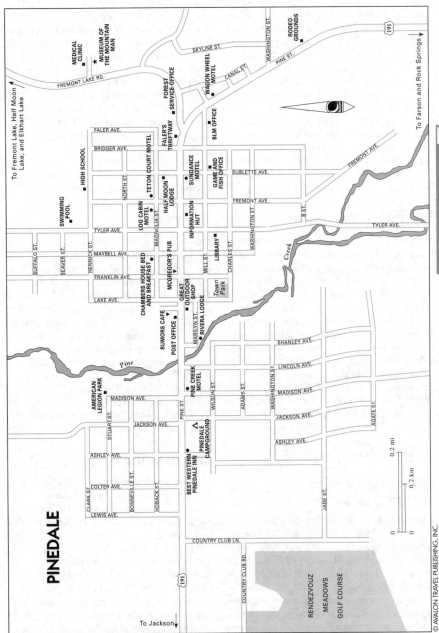

PINEDALE

To Fremont Lake, Half Moon Lake, and Elkhart Lake

To Farson and Rock Springs

To Jackson

MEDICAL CLINIC

MUSEUM OF THE MOUNTAIN MAN

SKYLINE ST.

WASHINGTON ST.

RODEO GROUNDS

191

PINE ST.

FREMONT LAKE RD.

CANAL ST.

WAGON WHEEL MOTEL

FOREST SERVICE OFFICE

FALER'S THRIFTWAY

BLM OFFICE

FALER AVE.

BRIDGER AVE.

HIGH SCHOOL

TETON COURT MOTEL

SUNDANCE MOTEL

GAME AND FISH OFFICE

SUBLETTE AVE.

FREMONT AVE.

SWIMMING POOL

NORTH ST.

LOG CABIN MOTEL

HALF MOON LODGE

MAGNOLIA ST.

INFORMATION HUT

FREMONT AVE.

B ST.

TYLER AVE.

TYLER AVE.

MCGREGOR'S PUB

MAYBELL AVE.

HENNICK ST.

BEAVER ST.

BUFFALO ST.

CHAMBERS HOUSE BED AND BREAKFAST

MILL ST.

LIBRARY

CHARLES ST.

WASHINGTON ST.

Creek

FRANKLIN AVE.

LAKE AVE.

GREAT OUTDOOR SHOP

Town Park

RUMORS CAFE

POST OFFICE

MARILYN ST.

RIVERA LODGE

Pine

AMERICAN LEGION PARK

MADISON AVE.

STUART ST.

JACKSON AVE.

PINE CREEK MOTEL

PINE ST.

WILSON ST.

ADAMS ST.

WASHINGTON ST.

SHANLEY AVE.

LINCOLN AVE.

MADISON AVE.

JACKSON AVE.

ASHLEY AVE.

AGATE ST.

ASHLEY AVE.

COLTER AVE.

CLARK ST.

BONNEVILLE ST.

HOBACK ST.

LEWIS AVE.

BEST WESTERN PINEDALE INN

PINEDALE CAMPGROUND

JADE ST.

COUNTRY CLUB LN.

COUNTRY CLUB RD.

RENDEZVOUS MEADOWS GOLF COURSE

0.2 mi

0.2 km

0

0

© AVALON TRAVEL PUBLISHING, INC.

elk, and antelope in this rich country. Whites first came as explorers and fur trappers in the early 1800s, and by the 1830s this was the "capital" of the fur trade in the Rockies. Six different rendezvous were held along the Upper Green River. The first white settler arrived with his cattle in 1878, and within a few years a small trading center sprang up alongside Pine Creek. The town prospered with development of the tie-hack industry in the late 19th century. Pinedale was platted in 1904, and within a year the town consisted of a general store, newspaper, blacksmith shop, saloon, photography studio, and other businesses. It later became the Sublette County seat.

CATCHING THE DRIFT

The Upper Green River is still important cattle country; in fact, it's the largest range allotment in the entire national forest system, home to 7,500 cattle. Get here in June to watch cowboys (locals more commonly use the term "riders") pushing the cattle into the mountains. Some are driven as far as 90 miles from the winter range in the desert. Cattle graze in the mountains all summer, watched over by a handful of riders who stay in cabins or trailers. Each fall, the cattle drift back down from their summer home in the mountains when cool mid-October weather hits the high country. Six miles west of Pinedale at the junction of U.S. Hwy. 191 and State Hwy. 352 (the Cora "Y"), cowboys from 20 local ranches sort out the 300–700 cattle that pile up against fences in the "Green River Drift."

MUSEUM OF THE MOUNTAIN MAN

Pinedale's Museum of the Mountain Man, 700 E. Hennick St., 307/367-4101 or 877/686-6266, www.museumofthemountainman.com, is open daily 10 A.M.–5 P.M. May–September, and by appointment the rest of the year. Entrance costs $4 adults, $3 seniors, $2 ages 6–12; free children under age six. Located on a hill overlooking town, this modern, spacious museum contains displays, artifacts, and memorabilia from the fur-trapping era. One of Jim Bridger's rifles (he probably owned

several) is here, along with a covered wagon and a fascinating educational video about the fur trade. You'll learn about the daily lives of trappers, how they trapped beaver and processed furs, and how the market for hats helped open the American West. Be sure to check out the inscribed section from an Aspen tree cut along the old Lander Cutoff of the Oregon Trail. Downstairs are changing displays on the history of Sublette County, and a small gift shop sells historical books. The museum puts on special programs, living-history demonstrations, and evening lectures on the history of the West during the Green River Rendezvous and throughout the year.

DAY TRIPS

Pinedale is a perfect base for explorations of the Wind River Mountains, with a multitude of day trips and overnight—or longer—adventures in all directions. Of particular note is **Skyline Drive,** a paved road that follows the eastern side of Fremont Lake (a destination in its own right), ending 17 miles later at a campground on the edge of the Bridger Wilderness. Hiking trails fan out from here, including a four-mile path to the aptly named **Photographer's Point.** Also high on my list of scenic attractions is **Green River Lakes** 51 miles up a paved and then gravel road—and worth every rut along the way. Both of these roads are described earlier in this chapter.

ACCOMMODATIONS

Pinedale has several attractive places offering friendly and clean rooms in pleasant settings. Because of this, more and more folks are choosing to spend time in Pinedale on their way to Yellowstone, thus avoiding the crowds and higher rates in Jackson. It's a good idea to book one month ahead for July and August to be sure of space, particularly during the Wind River Blue Grass Festival in June. Some local motels close in the off-season, so call ahead if you're coming during the winter. Go to www.pinedaleonline.com for web links to most local motels and other accommodations.

Motels

Wagon Wheel Motel, 407 S. U.S. Hwy. 191, 307/367-2871, has a range of room types, but all are in good condition and spacious. Prices run $60–105 d. Open all year. **Teton Court Motel,** 123 E. Magnolia, 307/367-4317 or 877/841-0499, has 18 renovated rooms—all with fridges—for $69–79 s or d. Kitchenettes cost $85 for up to four guests. Open year-round.

Half Moon Lodge Motel, 46 N. Sublette, 307/367-2851, has attractive rooms for $65–80 d. It's open May–October. **Pine Creek Inn,** 650 W. Pine, 307/367-2191 or 888/839-7446, charges $62–67 d for nicely appointed standard rooms, or $72 d for kitchenettes. A continental breakfast is available in the morning, and guests will appreciate the outdoor hot tub.

Sun Dance Motel, 148 E. Pine, 307/367-4336 or 800/833-9178, www.98.net/sundance, has clean and quiet rooms for $65–75 s or $70–80 d. Other options include a suite that sleeps six for $95, or a four-person cabin with kitchenette for $95. Open year-round.

Rivera Lodge, 442 W. Marilyn, 307/367-2424 or 888/819-1053, www.pinedaleonline.com, is right in town, but it's off the main street and quiet. The cozy and well-maintained cabins ($70–100 d) sit along Pine Creek and are open May–September. Most have kitchenettes. The friendly owners put on a free creekside breakfast every Sunday morning.

The appropriately named **Log Cabin Motel,** 49 E. Magnolia, 307/367-4579, www.thelogcabinmotel.com, features 10 attractive and beautifully maintained cabins. Built in 1929, they are now on the National Register of Historic Places. The smallest cabins go for $90 s or d. Larger two-bedroom units sleep five, have kitchenettes, and cost $120. The cabins are open June–September. In the off-season, call 956/772-9805 for reservations.

Pinedale's newest lodging choice is **Super 8 Motel,** 1054 W. Pine St., 307/367-8800 or 800/800-8000, www.super8.com. Amenities include an indoor pool and hot tub, light breakfast, and business center with a computer to check your email. Rates are $95 for one bed or $105 for two beds.

The largest local motel (60 rooms) is the **Best Western Pinedale Inn,** 850 W. Pine St., 307/367-6869 or 800/528-1234, www.bestwestern.com. Rooms are $106 for up to four guests, and amenities include an indoor pool, hot tub, fitness center, and continental breakfast.

Bed-and-Breakfasts

Right in town you'll find **Chambers House B&B,** 111 W. Magnolia St., 307/367-2168 or 800/567-2168, www.chambershouse.com, an elegant two-story log home that is a local landmark. Inside are five guest rooms (private or shared baths) and two sitting rooms. One room is handicapped accessible. Built in 1933, the home was recently renovated. Rates are $52–108 s or $75–118 d, including a full breakfast. Children are welcome.

Pole Creek Ranch B&B, three miles southeast of Pinedale, 307/367-4433, www.bbonline.com/wy/polecreek, is a modern log home in the country with an outdoor hot tub, a barn, and corrals. Two guest rooms share a bath and a third has its own; horse riding and buggy rides are available by arrangement. The view of the Wind River Mountains is impressive, and the friendly owners will be happy to share their Christianity. Rates are very reasonable: $50 s or $55 d ("married couples"), including a full breakfast. Kids and pets welcome.

Guest Ranches and Resorts

Half Moon Lake Resort, 307/367-6373, www.halfmoonlake.com, is a full-service facility overlooking the lake for which it is named. It's 10 miles northeast of Pinedale. Stay in modern log cabins with fridges and microwaves ($105–170; the largest sleeps six or more comfortably), and enjoy meals in a pleasant restaurant with a redwood deck along the shore. Fishing boats, pontoon boats, and canoes are available for rent, or you can head out on a horseback ride for two hours or all day. The lodge is closed in November and April.

Five miles northeast of Pinedale on the south end of Fremont Lake is **Lakeside Lodge Resort & Marina,** 307/367-2221 or 877/755-5253, www.lakesidelodge.com. Accommodations include rustic log cabins ($60 s or $65 d) with a shared bathhouse, along with a dozen deluxe shorefront log cabins with fireplaces and private baths for $120 s or $129 d. RV hookups are $20, and you can rent kayaks, canoes, pontoon boats, and fishing boats. The lodge is open early May to mid-October and has a restaurant and lounge with a great deck along the lake.

Overlooking the Green River 30 miles north of Pinedale, **Elk Ridge Lodge,** 307/367-2553, www.elkridgelodge.com, has guest ranch accommodations in modern log buildings on the edge of the national forest. Mid-summer rates are $2,000 for two people, including lodging, meals, horseback rides, fishing, and float trips. In June and September, shorter stays are available; $360 d for two nights, including breakfast and dinner. The lodge is also a winter destination for snowmobilers.

Fort William Guest Ranch, eight miles east of town, 307/367-4670, www.fort-william.com, is a rustic lodge with nightly accommodations ($80 d including breakfast), a hot tub, restaurant, lounge, and dance floor, plus an abundance of nearby outdoor activities: horseback riding, guided pack trips, spot-packing, and fly-fishing. Open May–Oct.

Twenty-nine miles north of Pinedale, the secluded and historic **DC Bar Guest Ranch,** 307/367-2268 or 888/803-7316, www.bwo.com, nestles within the Upper Green River Valley at an elevation of 8,200 feet. The ranch is surrounded by national forest land, and has room for up to 50 guests in seven cabins and a new luxury lodge. Horseback riding, fishing, kids' activities, archery, and other fun fill the agenda. A two-night minimum stay is required, $150 d per night for lodging and three meals. All-inclusive rates are $2,000 for two people for a six-night stay. The ranch is open year-round and is popular for wintertime snowmobiling and fall hunting trips.

Flying A Ranch, 307/367-2385 (summers), 307/336-3339 (winters), or 800/678-6543, www.flyinga.com, has space for just a dozen adults (no kids) in a casual Western atmosphere. Horseback rides are the featured attraction, but guests also enjoy wildlife watching, hiking, fishing, mountain biking, or simply relaxing with a book or luxuriating in the hot tub. The ranch

was built in 1929, and both the main lodge and cabins have been lovingly restored. Each cabin features handmade furniture, a private bath, kitchenette, and fireplace or woodstove. Some provide extraordinary views of the Wind River Mountains. Six-night rates at Flying A are $2,200–2,600 for two people, all-inclusive.

Lozier's Box R Ranch, near Cora, 307/367-2291 or 800/822-8466, www.boxr.com, is a working cattle ranch with accommodations for 20 guests. The emphasis is on horseback riding, with the opportunity to help move cattle and otherwise pretend to be a cowboy. Optional excursions take you to gorgeous mountain country on horseback, and Box R also has spring cattle drives and fall cattle roundups. It's open late May to mid-September, with all-inclusive weekly rates of $2,400–2,800 for two people.

See also **Boulder Lake Lodge,** described under Boulder, and **Triple Peak Lodge** under Big Piney in the Pinedale Vicinity section.

CAMPING

The closest public camping is **Fremont Lake Campground** ($10; open late May to mid-Sept.), seven miles northeast of Pinedale along the lake. Even if you aren't staying here or planning any wilderness hikes from the trailheads, *do* take the 15-mile (paved) drive from Pinedale to road's end, where you'll find the free Upper Fremont Lake Campground. The road is narrow but delivers gorgeous views of several lakes and the rugged crest of the Wind River Mountains, and has a good turnaround space for RVs and horse trailers at the upper end.

Half Moon Lake Campground ($5; open June to mid-Sept.) is on the northwest shore of Half Moon Lake, 10 miles northeast of Pinedale. A dozen other Forest Service and BLM campgrounds are dotted all along the western side of the Wind River Mountains. See Pinedale Vicinity for additional BLM campsites northwest of Pinedale.

The private **Pinedale Campground,** 204 S. Jackson Ave, 307/367-4555, charges $12 for tents, $20 for RVs; open May–Oct. Showers for noncampers are $4. This is ye olde parking lot masquerading as a "campground."

Lakeside Lodge Resort & Marina at Fremont Lake, five miles northeast of town, 307/367-2221 or 877/755-5253, www.lakesidelodge.com, charges $20 for RVs with full hookups. Open early May to mid-Oct.

FOOD

Pinedale has a good selection of eating and drinking establishments, but prices are somewhat higher than in most other parts of the state.

Breakfast and Lunch

In existence for more than three decades, **Patio Grill,** 35 W. Pine, 307/367-4611, serves dependably good family breakfasts, along with lunch and dinners. **Rumors Cafe,** 423 W. Pine (behind the post office), 307/367-2150, has excellent deli sandwiches, soups, salads, and daily lunch specials. For a filling lunchtime pizza buffet, head to **Wind River Rendezvous Pizza,** 4 Country Club Lane, 307/367-6760.

Sweetwaters Soda Shoppe, 307/367-7632, is a delightful old-time fountain (130 snowcone flavors), candy store, pizzeria, and burger joint. It's right across N. Franklin Avenue from McGregor's.

Dinner

A favorite of travelers, **McGregor's Pub,** 25 N. Franklin Ave., 307/367-4443, serves prime rib, steak, pasta, and even seafood. There's an outside deck in the summer. **Bottoms Up Brewery & Grill,** 402 W. Pine St., 307/367-2337, provides several fresh-brewed beers and a light menu that includes bratwurst, fajitas, fish and chips, and grilled (!) pizzas. It's a fine place to relax with the locals over a brew.

Calamity Jane's, in the Corral Bar at 30 W. Pine, 307/367-2469, is the place to go for burgers and fries, grinders, Mexican food, and pizzas. But it's a bar, so the atmosphere might not suit everyone. **Stockman's Steak Pub,** 117 W. Pine, 307/367-4563, has the finest steaks in Pinedale, plus a salad bar, veal, seafood, and chicken.

Eight miles east of town on Fall Creek Road is **Fort William Guest Ranch,** 307/367-4670, www.fort-william.com, where the specialties include thick steaks, beans, and other hearty fare served Thursday–Monday in the summer. Open May–Oct.

For a meal and drink with a view, drive five miles northeast of Pinedale along Fremont Lake to **Lakeside Lodge Resort and Marina,** 307/367-2221 or 877/755-5253, www.lakesidelodge.com. Enjoy steaks, chicken, pasta, and nightly specials while taking in the view from the big patio that fronts Fremont Lake and the Wind River Mountains. The upstairs lounge houses a big screen TV and has occasional bands.

Also of note is **Half Moon Lake Resort,** 307/367-6373, www.halfmoonlake.com, 10 miles northeast of Pinedale, with fine dining and drinks on the lakeside deck.

Groceries

Get groceries at **Faler's Thriftway,** 341 E. Pine, 307/367-2131. Inside is a deli, plus one of the largest collections of critter heads anywhere. Pack a picnic lunch and head to the **Town Park** at Franklin and Tyler, with a kid's fishing pond and playground and a paved path along Pine Creek. **American Legion Park** on the north side of Pine Creek also has picnic tables, plus a gazebo and a pretty streamside view.

ENTERTAINMENT

Both **Cowboy Bar,** 104 W. Pine, 307/367-4520, and **Stockman's Bar,** 16 N. Maybell Ave., 307/367-4562, have live country-and-western tunes some summer weekends. Stockman's attracts a younger crowd. **Fort William Guest Ranch,** eight miles east of Pinedale, 307/367-4670, www.fort-william.com, is a popular place to unwind in a cozy atmosphere; open May–Oct. only. **Lakeside Lodge Resort & Marina,** 307/367-2221 or 877/755-5253, www.lakesidelodge.com, has occasional live music in the summer, along with impressive mountain-and-lake vistas.

The modern **Pinedale Entertainment Center,** 153 S. Entertainment Lane, 307/367-6688, has two stadium-seating movie theaters, a bowling alley, an arcade room, and a billiards room.

WIND RIVER

EVENTS

The **International Pedigree Stage Stop Sled Dog Race** (IPSSSDR) stops here. See the Jackson chapter for more info.

Another popular winter event is **Green River Winter Carnival** in late February and early March, with a kid's Olympics, various adult contests of strength, a dance, and even a drag queen contest. The **Pinedale Blues Festival** in June is another fun event.

Pinedale's acclaimed **Green River Rendezvous** was established in 1936 and had its last full-scale run in 2002, but a lesser event of the same name still takes place on the second weekend in July. It commemorates the raucous rendezvous activities of the 1830s on nearby Horse Creek. Today's version includes four days of educational events at the Museum of the Mountain Man, with a variety of programs and guest speakers over four days. A mini-pageant may still be offered, but it won't be anything like those of the past. Get details at 307/367-4101 or 877/686-6266, www.museumofthe-mountainman.com.

RECREATION

Summer Recreation

Swim year-round at the high school's **indoor pool,** 307/367-2832. Golfers will enjoy Pinedale's nine-hole **Rendezvous Meadows Golf Course,** 307/367-4252.

Horseback rides are available from Fort William Guest Ranch, 307/367-4670; Half Moon Lake Resort, 307/367-6373, www.half-moonlake.com; Boulder Lake Lodge, 307/537-5400 or 800/788-5401, www.boulderlake.com; and Pole Creek Ranch B&B, 307/367-4433.

Stop by the Bridger-Teton National Forest **Pinedale Ranger District** office at 29 E. Fremont Lake Rd., 307/367-4326, www.fs.fed.us/btnf, for maps and hiking information on trails in the nearby Bridger Wilderness. The office can also provide a listing of fishing guides and wilderness outfitters.

The **Great Outdoor Shop,** 332 W. Pine, 307/367-2440, www.greatoutdoorshop.com, sells quality outdoor gear of all types, along with topo maps. Ask about equipment rentals in the summer, including tents, sleeping bags, climbing

© DON PITCHER

Green River Rendezvous

equipment, and fishing gear. They also operate a shuttle service with rides to Wind River Mountain trailheads. Faler's Thriftway has additional outdoor supplies.

The Adventure Cycling Association's **Great Divide Mountain Bike Route** (www.adv-cycling.org) passes through Pinedale, and the town serves as a restocking point before heading south into very remote county between South Pass and Rawlins.

The **Wilderness Adventure Center,** 888/419-9992, www.wyomingoutdoors.com, provides outdoor education for ages 9–18 at a camp on Burnt Lake east of Pinedale. Established in 1956 by the Skinner family, this was the first youth-oriented wilderness program of its kind in the nation. The family tradition continues, and Todd Skinner—one of the nation's best mountaineers—teaches some courses. Kids learn mountaineering, rock climbing, horseback riding, and other skills during two-week summer sessions.

On the Water

The eastern slope of the Wind River Mountains contains several large lakes created when glaciers retreated after the last major ice age some 10,000 years ago. The terminal moraines they left behind acted as dams, although some have been enlarged with human-created dams in recent years. The lakes are very popular with anglers. **Fremont Lake** is Wyoming's second-largest natural lake, reaching 11 miles in length, one-half mile across, and up to 600 feet deep. There's even a nice sandy beach. It's just three miles northeast of Pinedale and is famous for Mackinaw that approach 40 pounds. Fremont has three Forest Service campgrounds along its shore (free to $10; one accessible only by boat). Rent a fishing boat, canoe, kayak, or pontoon boat from **Lakeside Lodge Resort & Marina,** 307/367-2221, www.lakesidelodge.com, open May to mid-Oct. Comfortable cabins and a restaurant are also here.

Other lakes of note are **Half Moon Lake, Willow Lake,** and **Boulder Lake.** (See Wind River Mountains earlier in this chapter for information on the Green River and New Fork Lakes.) All of these lakes have Forest Service campgrounds (free to $10) and trails that lead into the Bridger Wilderness. In addition, the BLM maintains free camping areas on the west end of Boulder Lake and at Scab Creek (southeast of Boulder Lake). **Half Moon Lake Resort,** 307/367-6373, www.halfmoonlake.com, rents canoes, pontoon boats, and canoes.

The lakes and streams near Pinedale offer outstanding fishing for cutthroat, rainbow, brook, Mackinaw, golden, and brown trout, plus grayling and whitefish. Several local outfitters offer float-fishing trips down the Green River; see the chamber of commerce for a listing. **Two Rivers Emporium,** 307/367-4131 or 800/329-4353, www.2rivers.net, is a good place to find fly-fishing supplies and conditions or to book a drift trip. Canoeists or kayakers will also enjoy floating stretches of the Green River. The Forest Service office has details.

Swim at Pinedale's Olympic-sized **indoor pool,** 307/367-2832, at the high school on the corner of Hennick Street and Tyler Avenue.

Winter Recreation

Located 10 miles northeast of Pinedale near Fremont Lake, **White Pine Ski Area,** 307/367-6606, www.whitepineski.com, has two triple chairlifts and 25 ski trails. All-day lift tickets cost $24. The modern day lodge houses ski and snowboard rentals, a restaurant, and a lounge. In addition, 15 km of groomed cross-country ski trails are accessible from the base lodge parking lot.

Cross-country skiers should pick up a copy of the **Skyline Drive Nordic Touring Trails** map from the Forest Service office in Pinedale. Maps are available on the web at www.pinedale-online.com/x-countryskiing.htm. The 60 km of trails are marked but not always groomed. More adventurous skiers will find all sorts of places to explore in the Bridger Wilderness just a few miles east of Pinedale. Rent cross-country skis from the **Great Outdoor Shop,** 332 W. Pine, 307/367-2440, www.greatoutdoorshop.com.

The lower elevations of the Wind River Mountains are also extremely popular with snowmobilers; trails head out right from town. See the chamber of commerce for a list of local companies offering snowmobile rentals and tours. The 365-mile **Continental Divide Snowmobile Trail** passes through Pinedale, continuing north to Yellowstone and around the Wind River Mountains to Lander. **Green River Outfitters,** 307/367-2416, www.greenriveroutfitters.com, leads snowmobile tours into the mountains around Pinedale, including overnight trips to a mountain cabin.

SHOPPING

In business since 1947, the **Cowboy Shop,** 137 W. Pine, 307/367-4300, www.cowboyshop.com, has an outstanding selection of Western clothes, boots, and other necessities of life. Recommended. **Moosely Books,** 7 W. Pine St., 307/367-6622, www.pinedaleonline.com/mooselybooks, sells volumes on Wyoming and the West.

Rock Rabbit Art Gallery, 36 W. Pine St., 307/367-2485 or 888/303-5082, www.rockrabbit.com, is a good place to find contemporary Western oil paintings, fine art photography, metal sculptures, watercolors, and carvings from regional and national artists.

INFORMATION AND SERVICES

An **information hut,** on Pine St. near Fremont Ave., 307/367-2242 or 888/285-7282, is open daily 9 A.M.–5 P.M. April–October, and Monday–Friday 10 A.M.–2 P.M. the rest of the year.

For Pinedale information on the web—and links to local businesses—visit www.pinedale-online.com.

The Forest Service's **Pinedale Ranger District Office** is at 29 E. Fremont Lake Rd., 307/367-4326, www.fs.fed.us/btnf. Find the **BLM's Pinedale Field Office** at 432 E. Mill St., 307/367-5300, www.wy.blm.gov.

Check your email on computers at the beautiful new **Sublette County Library** at 155 S. Tyler St., 307/367-4114. Wash clothes at **Highlander Center Laundromat** on Pine Street, and get (unlaundered) cash from the **ATMs** at 1st National Bank of Pinedale, Faler's General Store, the Sinclair gas station, and Stockman's Restaurant.

TRANSPORTATION

Drivers en route to Jackson should fill up in Pinedale; gas prices only get higher from here north. There is no commercial bus service to Pinedale, and the nearest commercial airports are in Jackson and Rock Springs. Shuttle services are available through **Pinedale Cab,** 307/367-7668. The **Great Outdoor Transportation Company,** 307/367-2440, www.greatoutdoorshop.com, provides shuttle rides to Wind River Mountain trailheads from Pinedale, Jackson, or Rock Springs, and can also move your vehicle for you.

Pinedale Vicinity

Although Pinedale is the largest town in Sublette County, several other burgs provide services and a taste of history. A fine online source for information on the various communities is www.sublette.com.

BOULDER

A dozen miles south of Pinedale is Boulder, and on the drive down (about halfway between the two towns) you'll pass two roadside telephone poles topped by active osprey nests. Boulder (pop. 30) holds a handful of businesses, including the century-old **Boulder Store.** Next door is **Basecamp Restaurant,** serving three meals a

day, including deli sandwiches for lunch and prime rib at dinner. The modern **Boulder Inn,** 307/537-5480, has nine guest rooms, all with hand-hewn lodgepole-pine furnishings, including two rooms with king beds. Rates are $65 s or $85 d; closed Sundays.

The BLM's free **Stokes Crossing Campground** is two miles east on State Hwy. 353, then eight miles north on a gravel road. Located along Boulder Creek, this is a relaxing place for anglers. One mile north of Boulder is the private **Wind River View Campground,** 307/537-5453 or 800/352-9146, open mid-May to mid-Sept. There's no shade on this exposed site, but the views are noteworthy.

Twelve miles up State Hwy. 353, **Boulder Lake Lodge,** 307/537-5400 or 800/788-5401, www.boulderlake.com, is a modern ranch with guest rooms for $65 d with a two-night minimum. In addition to lodging, they serve family-style meals and offer horseback rides, along with pack trips and spot-packing. Also available are all-inclusive one-week stays for $2,770 for two people. The ranch is open Memorial Day to September.

Sunset Ranch, 307/367-6224 or 307/382-2325, www.sunsetranchstables.com, has trail rides, overnight lodging, meals, and multiday ranch packages. The ranch is located in the foothills of the southern Wind River Mountains, approximately 45 miles east of Boulder.

DANIEL

Head 11 miles west of Pinedale and then another mile south on U.S. Hwy. 189 to tiny Daniel, where the Green River Bar makes some of the best Bloody Marys in Wyoming. The community is within spittin' distance from the original Green River rendezvous grounds and is home to a historic little red **schoolhouse,** built in 1920 and used until 1939.

A roadside marker north of Daniel notes the site of **Fort Bonneville,** constructed in 1832 to serve as a fur-trade center run by Capt. Benjamin Bonneville. It lasted only a year but gained the nickname "Fort Nonsense" because of the severely cold and snowy winters that made life difficult for Bonneville's men. The fort consisted of two blockhouses guarding a perimeter of tall log posts and was used as a storage site for men and their supplies. Although nothing remains of the fort today, it was significant as one of the earliest "forts" in Wyoming.

Practicalities

Located in the foothills west of Daniel, the **David Ranch,** 307/859-8228, www.david ranch.com, provides a chance to sample the cowboy life in spades. Guests stay in comfortable log cabins and enjoy ranch-style meals in the main house. Days are spent on horseback

rides, herding cattle, mending fences, roping, or participating in cattle drives. The ranch is open mid-May to mid-September, with a maximum of 10 guests. Weekly rates are $2,800 for two adults; no kids under 15. Their popular cattle drive home takes place on the nearby Barney Ranch in October; $2,400 per person for two weeks, all inclusive. During the winter, the ranch reopens for snowmobiling adventures.

The BLM's **Warren Bridge Campground** ($6; open all year) sits beside the Green River nine miles north of Daniel on U.S. Hwy. 191/189. Another dozen rustic campsites (free) are spread out along 10 miles of the gravel road that parallels the river upstream. These grassy sites are popular with anglers; ask the attendant at Warren Bridge Campground which ones are available.

Daniel hosts several community events, including the **Aniel Daniel Chili Cookoff** in April, and an **Old Timer's Picnic** in July.

1840 RENDEZVOUS SITE

Two miles south and then 2.5 miles east of Daniel is the site of the 1840 rendezvous, the last grand gathering of mountain men and Indians. The dirt access road cuts through barren sage and grass country, but the vista changes abruptly as you reach the site. Below you, the Green River twists its way through a lush landscape of grass, cattle, and cottonwoods. It's pretty easy to see why the rendezvous was held in this area! Get here for a summer sunrise, when you can imagine a multitude of Indians and mountain men spread out below for the annual festivities. The meadow contains a memorial to missionaries Narcissa Whitman and Eliza Spalding, who in 1836 became the first white women to venture by land across the American continent.

A tiny shrine overlooks the meadow, marking Wyoming's first Mass, performed by Belgian Jesuit missionary **Father Pierre Jean DeSmet** during the 1840 rendezvous. DeSmet's description of the event is as follows:

> *On Sunday, the 5th of July, I had the con-solation of celebrating the holy sacrifice of*

MOUNTAIN MEN

The era of the fur trapper is one of the most colorful slices of American history, a time when a rough and hardy breed of men took to the Rockies in search of furs and adventure. Romanticized in such films as *Jeremiah Johnson*, the trappers actually played but a brief role in history and numbered fewer than 1,000 individuals. Their real importance lay in acting as the opening wedge for the West, a vanguard for the settlers and gold miners who would follow their paths—often led by these same mountain men.

The Fur Business

Fashion sent men into the Rockies in the first place, since the waterproof underfur of a beaver could be used to create the beaver hat, which was all the rage in the early part of the 19th century. (It cost a month's wages for a man in England to buy a fine beaver hat in the 1820s!) Beavers in the eastern United States were soon trapped out, forcing trappers to head farther and farther west. Several companies competed for the lucrative fur market, but John Jacob Astor's American Fur Company proved the most successful. In 1811, Astor sent a party of men across the Rockies to the mouth of the Columbia to build a trading post and then set up a chain of posts across the West. The men—known as the Astorians—were probably the first whites to follow the route that would later become the Oregon Trail.

John Jacob Astor's trappers went head to head against the Rocky Mountain Fur Company, which was owned at various times by some of the most famous mountain men—Jedediah Smith, David Jackson, William and Milton Sublette, Jim Bridger, Thomas Fitzpatrick, and others. Competition for furs became so intense that Astor's men began following Jim Bridger and Tom Fitzpatrick to discover their trapping grounds. After trying unsuccessfully to shake the men tailing them, Bridger and Fitzpatrick deliberately headed into the heart of Blackfeet country, where Indians killed the

leader of Astor's party and managed to leave Bridger with an arrowhead in his shoulder that was not removed until three years later.

A large number of Indians (particularly from the Flathead and Nez Perce tribes) were also involved in the fur trade, and a standard Indian trade value was 240 beaver pelts for a riding horse. In the mountains, anything from the world back east had considerable value: guns sold for $100 each, blankets for $40 apiece, tobacco for $3 per pound, and alcohol (often diluted) for up to $64 per gallon. After just two years of such trading, William Ashley retired with an $80,000 profit. Control of the fur market continued to change hands as the Rocky Mountain Fur Company and the American Fur Company competed with each other and with a mysterious company headed by Capt. Benjamin Bonneville, which some believe was a front for the U.S. Army to explore the West.

Most of the men who trapped in the Rockies were hired and outfitted by the fur companies, but others worked under contract and traded furs for overpriced supplies. Many men found themselves in debt to the company at the end of a season. At the top of the heap were the free trappers, men who worked either alone or with others but who sold their furs to whoever offered the highest prices. Some men, primarily those who brought trade goods to the rendezvous, became rich in the process. Others, such as John Colter, Jim Bridger, James Beckwourth, Jedediah Smith, Thomas Fitzpatrick, and Kit Carson, would achieve fame for their rich knowledge of the land and their ability to survive against insurmountable odds. Many trappers married Indian women, learned sign language and various Indian tongues, and lived in tepees.

Trappers worked through the winter months when the beaver pelts were their finest; most summers were spent hunting and fishing, or hanging out with fellow trappers or friendly Indians. In his *Journal of a Trapper 1834-1843*,

Osborne Russell described a campfire scene among fellow mountain men:

A large fire was soon blazing encircled with sides of Elk ribs and meat cut in slices supported on sticks down which the grease ran in torrents The repast being over the jovial tale goes round the circle the peals of loud laughter break upon the stillness of the night which after being mimicked in the echo from rock to rock it dies away in the solitary. Every tale puts an auditor in mind of something similar to it but under different circumstances which being told the "laughing part" gives rise to increasing merriment and furnishes more subjects for good jokes and witty sayings such as Swift never dreamed of Thus the evening passed with eating drinking and stories enlivened with witty humor until near Midnight all being wrapped in their blankets lying around the fire gradually falling to sleep one by one until the last tale is "encored" by the snoring of the drowsy audience The Speaker takes the hint breaks off the subject and wrapping his blanket more closely about him soon joins the snoring party—The light of the fire being supersed by that of the Moon just rising from behind the Eastern Mountains a sullen gloom is cast over the remaining fragments of the feast and all is silent except the occasional howling of the solitary wolf on the neighboring mountain whose senses are attracted by the flavors of roasted meat but fearing to approach nearer he sits upon a rock and bewails his calamities in piteous moans which are re-echoed among the Mountains.

A good trapper could take in more than 150 beaver in a year, worth $4–6 apiece. It was an arduous job, and the constant threat of attacks by the Blackfeet Indians made it even more difficult. The great letting-go came with the summer rendezvous, an event anticipated for months ahead of time.

The Rendezvous

William H. Ashley, founder of the Rocky Mountain Fur Company, was one of the most important figures in the fur trade. In 1822, he ran an ad in a St. Louis paper that read:

To Enterprising Young Men. The subscriber wishes to engage ONE HUNDRED MEN, to ascend the river Missouri to its source, there to be employed for one, two or three years.—For particulars enquire of Major Andrew Henry, near the Lead Mines, in the County of Washington, (who will ascend with, and command the party) or to the subscriber at St. Louis.

—Wm. H. Ashley.

Ashley's company of men—along with $10,000 in supplies—made it up into the Yellowstone River country, where he left them the following year, promising to resupply them in 1825 on the Henrys Fork near its confluence with the Green River, along the present-day Wyoming–Utah border. Thus began the first rendezvous. They would take place every summer until 1840. Ashley failed to bring booze that first summer, and the rendezvous lasted only two days. In future years, however, the whiskey flowed freely, and the festivities lasted for weeks.

The rendezvous—a French word meaning "appointed place of meeting"—was a time when both white and Indian trappers could sell their furs,

continued on next page

WIND RIVER

MOUNTAIN MEN (cont'd)

trade for needed supplies and Indian squaws (the women had little say in the matter but most took considerable pleasure in the arrangement), meet with old friends, get rip-roaring drunk, and engage in storytelling, gambling, gun duels, and contests of all sorts. Horse racing, wrestling bouts, and shooting contests were favorites—Kit Carson killed Shunar, a big French bully, in a duel during one of the Green River rendezvous. Debauchery reigned supreme in these three-week-long affairs, and by the time they were over, many of the trappers had lost their entire year's earnings.

During the heyday of the fur trade, a common saying was "all trails lead to the Seedskeedee [Green River]." Six rendezvous were held here in the 1830s, others were held in the Wind River/Popo Agie River area, on Ham's Fork of the Green River, and in Idaho and Utah. Sites were chosen where there was space for up to 500 mountain men and 3,000 Indians, plenty of game, ample grazing for the thousands of horses, and good water. Not coincidentally, all were held in Shoshone country rather than farther east or north, where the hostile Sioux, Blackfeet, and Crow held sway. Despite such precautions, more than half of Ashley's men were scalped by Indians.

Changing Times

The end of the rendezvous system—and most of the Rocky Mountain fur trapping—came about for a variety of reasons: overtrapping, the financial panic of 1837, and the growing use of other materials, particularly the South American nutria and Chinese silk, for hats. In addition, permanent trading posts such as Fort Laramie drew Indians away from the mountains to trade for buffalo robes instead of beaver furs. By 1840, when the last rendezvous was held on the banks of the Green River near present-day Pinedale, it was obvious there would be no more. One of the longtime trappers, Robert Newell, said to his partner, Joseph Meek:

> We are done with this life in the mountains—done with wading in beaver dams, and freezing or starving alternately—done with Indian trading and Indian fighting. The fur trade is dead in the Rocky Mountains, and it is no place for us now, if ever it was. We are young yet, and have life before us. We cannot waste it here; we cannot or will not return to the States. Let us go down to the Wallamet and take farms.

Mass **sub dio** *[under the open sky]. The altar was placed on an elevation and surrounded with boughs and garlands of flowers; I addressed the congregation in French and English, and spoke also by an interpreter to the Flatheads and Snake Indians. It was a spectacle truly moving for the heart of a missionary, to behold an assembly composed of so many different nations, who all assisted at our holy mysteries with great satisfaction. The Canadians sang hymns in French and Latin, and the Indians in their native tongue.*

An idealist of the first order, DeSmet spent more than three decades working with Indians in an attempt to protect them from being subsumed by America's territorial ambitions. His goal was to create communities where Indi-

ans could preserve their culture while adopting some of the technological advantages of Western civilization. Although the mission failed miserably, DeSmet was one of the few 19th-century men who maintained lifelong friendships with the Indians. "Blackrobe," as he was known, always traveled unarmed throughout the West and served as a peacemaker during treaty negotiations. The shrine on the site of DeSmet's 1840 service is used during a commemorative mass on the second Sunday of each July.

Pinckney Sublette, one of four brothers from the famous family of fur trappers, is buried not far from the DeSmet monument. Just up the dirt road are the red log barn and white log home of the historic Quarter Circle 5 Ranch, a definitive Wyoming spread.

BIG PINEY

An oil boomtown in the late 1970s, Big Piney (pop. 400) faced hard post-boom times and now putters along with a handful of little businesses. The settlement doesn't have a lot to offer, but you may want to look around the **Green River Valley Museum,** 307/276-5343, www.grvm.com, for a sampling of the area's ranching, homesteading, and oil and gas history. Open Tues.–Sat. noon–4 P.M. June–Oct. Get local information here or from the town office.

Practicalities

The BLM maintains a handful of free riverside sites at **New Fork River Campground,** 12 miles east of Marbleton on State Hwy. 351. Stay in basic rooms at **Big Piney Motel,** 307/276-3352, for $36 for one bed or $46 for two. No standouts on the food scene here, but **Happy Trails Cafe,** 307/276-5776, is open for lunch and dinner, with pizza, chicken baskets, sandwiches, and ice cream.

The main annual event is the **Big Piney Chuckwagon Days** on the Fourth of July. Festivities include a rodeo, a parade, fireworks, and a free barbecue. Big Piney is also home to the **Sublette County Fair** held the first weekend of August each year. One of the attractions here is the **Little Buckaroo Rodeo** for children. Other rodeos take place throughout the summer at the fairgrounds.

The town has a library, and a public **swimming pool** is at the high school on the west side of town.

Bridger-Teton National Forest's **Big Piney Ranger District Office,** 307/276-3375, www.fs.fed.us/btnf, has details about the route west into the Wyoming Range. Three of their classic old cabins are available for rent throughout the year: the **Snyder Guard Station,** 23 miles west of Big Piney; the **Scaler Guard Station,** 18 miles from the LaBarge Trailhead; and the **Hoback Guard Station,** 65 miles northwest of Big Piney. All three cost $30 per night and can sleep four. Contact the Forest Service for details.

Triple Peak Lodge, 307/276-3408 or 866/302-7753, www.triplepeak.com, is 20 miles west of Big Piney on South Cottonwood Creek near the Wyoming Range. This lodge is open

year-round and looks like an Old West hotel. They offer eight guest rooms with or without meals, along with outfitting and guide services, chuck-wagon dinners, a cow camp each fall, special historical sessions in July, and wintertime snowmobiling. Lodging is $65 s or $70 d; add $25 per person for three meals daily.

High Wide and Lonesome offers real cowboy adventures, including cattle drives, trips along the Pony Express Trail, and other Old West horse trips. All-inclusive six-night trips cost $1,600 per person. Contact them at 307/276-3208 or 877/276-3485, www.hwl.net.

Get additional local information from the **Big Piney-Marbleton Chamber of Commerce** website, www.bigpiney.com.

MARBLETON

Marbleton (pop. 700) is just a couple hundred yards up U.S. Hwy. 189 from Big Piney. There's not much to do here, but you can watch flicks at **The Flick Theatre,** 307/276-5404.

Country Chalet Inn, 307/276-3391, is a comfortable place to stay, with rooms for $38 s or $44 d. For a few bucks more ($40 s or $46 d), **Marbleton Inn,** 307/276-5231, offers the best accommodations in the area and serves all-American meals at its **Three Pines Restaurant and Lounge,** 307/276-3523. Across the street is **Rio Verde Grill,** 307/276-5353, serving Southwestern-style food.

Camp at **Harper's RV Park,** 307/276-3611; $20 for RVs, $12 for tents. Open year-round. Backpackers and campers can wash off road grime in hot showers at the **Laundry Basket Laundromat.**

The **Waterhole,** 307/276-9977, is the center of nightlife in the area and puts on a popular cowboy open golf tournament each summer.

LANDER CUTOFF

North of Marbleton, the enormous Wind River Mountains become more conspicuous and the highway crosses the Lander Cutoff, its ruts still discernible across the sagebrush. Built in 1858 by Col. Frederick W. Lander and his soldiers, it served as both a shorter route to California and Oregon and a way to bypass the Mormon communities in Utah. The route offered good grazing and water as well as abundant game, and it quickly became the preferred route to California and Oregon. It was also the only portion of the Oregon Trail funded with government money.

Many miles of the old Lander Cutoff can still be driven and are denoted with Oregon trail markers. These roads are readily visible and used today by locals for hunting access, ranching, and recreation. You'll need a high-clearance, four-wheel-drive rig to do it, and expect to poke along at five miles per hour, but it's a very interesting trip. Sections that go into private land are gated off, and roads bypass those places and take you to the more improved roads. The Lander Cutoff is also good for explorations by mountain bikers, but be sure to bring plenty of water. Contact the BLM in Pinedale for details.

TO JACKSON HOLE

U.S. Hwy. 189/191 provides a scenic route to Hoback Junction and Jackson Hole, crossing the Green River and then slowly climbing into the hills. Aspens begin to appear on the hilltops, and willows line the creeks. The 11,000-foot-tall Gros Ventre Mountains are visible to the northwest. Gradually, lodgepole pine and aspen begin to replace the sagebrush. At **the Rim,** the road enters Bridger-Teton National Forest. West of here, the land drains into the Hoback River, which joins the Snake River at Hoback Junction 40 miles away. The road curves gradually down through this mountainous country, crossing the Hoback River repeatedly. (The crossroads settlement of Hoback Junction is covered in the Jackson Hole and the Tetons chapter.)

Bondurant

The spread-out town of Bondurant (pop. 160) straggles along the road through a gorgeous mountain valley, its pastures dotted with piles of hay, creekside willows, and grazing horses. The Gros Ventre Mountains form a dramatic backdrop, but the developments consist of just a few scattered log homes. Bondurant is named

for Sarah Ellen and Benjamin Franklin Bondurant, the first settlers here. Between 1907 and 1927, they ran a popular dude ranch and had as pets all sorts of wild animals: antelope, elk, and even young bears.

On the west end of "town," **Elkhorn Bar and Trading Post,** 307/733-8358, consists of a friendly general store, gas station, café, country watering hole, and laundromat. Six small cabins ($65 d) contain fridges and microwaves; open year-round. The bar has a menu that includes pizzas, burritos, and sandwiches on weekdays, with steaks on Friday and Saturday nights.

The **Bondurant Barbecue** takes place at the end of June and includes a big barbecue feast at the Church of St. Hubert the Hunter, a classic log structure.

Located near Bondurant, the Forest Service's **Hoback Guard Station** is available for rent year-round and sleeps four for $30. It includes two rooms with a seasonal bathroom and running water. Access is by skis or snowmobile in the winter. Get details at 307/276-3375, www.fs.fed.us/btnf.

Hoback Canyon

A few miles west of Bondurant, the road clings to the walls of Hoback Canyon as it passes the high face of Battle Mountain, site of one of the few conflicts between Indians and whites in this part of Wyoming. It was here in 1895 that whites from Jackson Hole attacked Bannock Indians who had been hunting "out of season" along the Hoback River. Just before you reach Hoback Junction, a signpost describes John Hoback, the trapper and guide who led the Astorian trappers of Wilson Price Hunt through here in 1811.

The canyon is occasionally blocked by avalanches in the winter but is a great place to see deer, moose, and bighorn sheep.

Granite Hot Springs

Just west of Battle Mountain on U.S. Hwy. 189/191 is the turnoff to Granite Hot Springs, 307/734-7400. *Do* take this very scenic side trip! A well-maintained gravel road follows Granite Creek for 10 miles, affording impressive views of the Gros Ventre Range and the 50-foot drop of

Granite Falls. The road ends at a parking lot just a short walk from the hot springs. The deep pool was built in 1933 by the CCC and recently improved with a deck and changing rooms. The pool stays around 93°F in the summer but rises to 112°F in winter when the water flow is slower. The springs are open 10 A.M. until dusk (around 8 P.M.) in the summer, and 11 A.M.–5 P.M. in winter; closed in the fall and spring. No showers or running water are available at the pool, but vault toilets are nearby. The cost is $5.50 adults, $3.50 ages 3–12, and free for infants. Suits and towels ($2.50) can be rented, and they sell a few snacks. Granite Canyon Road is not plowed in winter but is groomed for use by both snowmobilers and cross-country skiers. A nearby campground ($15) is open late June–September. The campground almost never fills up and is managed by folks from the hot springs. Dispersed camping is allowed on the road to Granite Hot Springs, except along the final 1.3 miles before the springs.

During the winter, you can ride a dog sled to the hot springs. Iditarod musher Frank Teasley's **Jackson Hole Iditarod Sled Dog Tours** offers half-day trips for $135 per person including lunch, and all-day trips for $225 per person including a big dinner. Get details at 307/733-7388 or 800/554-7388, www.jhsleddog.com.

WIND RIVER

Jackson Hole

Jackson Hole is one of the most-visited slices of wild country in North America, attracting well more than three million travelers each year. They come here for a multitude of reasons: to camp under the stars in Grand Teton National Park, to play and shop in the New West town of Jackson, to hike flower-bedecked trails up forested valleys, to ride sleighs among thousands of elk, to raft down the Snake River, to ski or snowboard at one of the local resorts, or to simply stand in wonderment as the sun colors the sky behind the mountains. Many continue on north to Yellow-stone National Park, another place on everyone's must-see list. Drive north from Jackson toward Yellowstone and you'll quickly discover the biggest reason so many people are attracted to this place—its beauty. The Tetons act as a magnet, drawing your eyes away from the road and forcing you to stop and absorb some of their majesty. Welcome to one of the world's great wonderlands.

In the lingo of the mountain men, a "hole" was a large valley ringed by mountain ranges, and each was named for the trapper who based himself there. Jackson Hole, on Wyoming's far western border, is justifiably the most famous of all these intermountain valleys. Although Jackson Hole reaches an impressive 48 miles north to

Conestoga Wagons, Jackson

© DON PITCHER

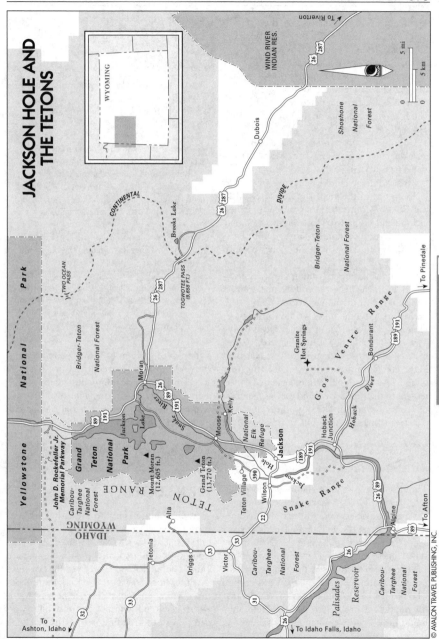

JACKSON HOLE AND THE TETONS

WYOMING

JACKSON HOLE

To Riverton

WIND RIVER INDIAN RES.

Shoshone National Forest

Dubois

CONTINENTAL

DIVIDE

Brooks Lake

TWO OCEAN PASS

TOGWOTEE PASS (9,658 FT.)

Bridger-Teton National Forest

Granite Hot Springs

Gros Ventre Range

Bondurant

To Pinedale

National Park

Yellowstone

John D. Rockefeller Jr. Memorial Parkway

Caribou-Targhee National Forest

Grand Teton National Park

Moran

Jackson Lake

Snake River

Mount Moran (12,605 ft.)

Grand Teton (13,770 ft.)

TETON RANGE

Moose

Kelly

National Elk Refuge

Jackson

Hoback Junction

Hoback River

Jackson

Snake Range

Teton Village

Wilson

Jackson Hole

Hoback

IDAHO
WYOMING

Alta

Tetonia

Driggs

Victor

Caribou-Targhee National Forest

To Afton

Alpine

Caribou-Targhee National Forest

Palisades Reservoir

To Ashton, Idaho

To Idaho Falls, Idaho

N

5 mi

5 km

south and up to 16 miles across, the magnificent range of mountains to the west is what defines this valley. Shoshone Indians who wandered through this country called the peaks Teewinot (Many Pinnacles); later explorers would use such labels as Shark's Teeth or Pilot Knobs. But lonely French-Canadian trappers arriving in the early 1800s provided the name that stuck: les Trois Tetons (literally, the Three Tits).

Contrary to what you may have been told, Jackson Hole is *not* named for Michael Jackson. The valley, originally called Jackson's Hole, was instead named for likable trapper David E. Jackson, one of the men who helped establish the Rocky Mountain Fur Company. When Jackson and his partners sold out in 1830, they realized a profit of more than $50,000. Jackson's presence remains in the names of both Jackson Hole and Jackson Lake. Eventually, more polite folks began calling the valley Jackson Hole, in an attempt to end the ribald stories associated with the name Jackson's Hole. (It's easy to imagine the jokes with both Jackson's Hole and the Tetons in the same place.) By the way, in 1991, a group calling itself the Committee to Restore Decency to Our National Parks created quite a stir by suggesting that Grand Teton National Park be renamed. A letter sent to the Park Service and various members of Congress noted: "Though a great many Americans may be oblivious to this vulgarity,

JACKSON HOLE SIGHTSEEING HIGHLIGHTS

Town Square, art galleries, restaurants, and shoot-out in downtown Jackson
National Museum of Wildlife Art
National Elk Refuge
Snake River whitewater rafting and trout fishing
Horseback rides and chuck wagon cookouts
Jackson Hole Mountain Resort, Snow King Resort, and Grand Targhee Ski Resort for winter skiing and summertime lift rides
Grand Teton National Park for spectacular mountain vistas and hikes

Popular events: International Pedigree Stage Stop Sled Dog Race (January), Pole-Peddle-Paddle Race (April), Elk Antler Auction (May), Old West Days (Memorial Day), Grand Teton Music Festival (all summer), Jackson Hole Rodeo (all summer), Jackson Shoot-out (all summer), and Jackson Hole Fall Arts Festival (September)

hundreds of millions of French people around the world are not! How embarrassing that these spectacular, majestic mountains are reduced to a dirty joke overseas." After a flurry of letters in response, the hoax was revealed; it was a prank by staff members of *Spy* magazine.

History

The first people to cross the mountain passes into Jackson Hole probably arrived while the last massive glaciers were still retreating. Clovis stone arrowheads—a style used 12,000 years ago—have been found along the edges of the valley. These early peoples were replaced in the 16th and 17th centuries by the Shoshone, Bannock, Blackfeet, Crow, and Gros Ventre tribes, who hunted bison from horses. When the first fur trappers tramped into Jackson Hole, they found Indian paths throughout the valley.

JOHN COLTER

Transport yourself back to the early 19th century, a time when people from the new nation called America saw the world west of the Mississippi River as just a blank spot on the map. In 1803, Thomas Jefferson purchased the Louisiana Territory from France, and to learn more about this gigantic piece of real estate he sent Meriwether Lewis and William Clark on a military expedition to the Pacific coast, a trip that took nearly 2.5 years. Although the expedition skirted around Wyoming—heading across Montana instead—it proved the opening wedge for the settlement of the West, and indirectly, the discovery of Jackson Hole. On the return trip, the party met two fur trappers en route to the upper Missouri River. One of Lewis and Clark's respected scouts, John Colter, was allowed to join the trappers, "provided no one of the party would ask or expect a Similar permission."

After a winter of trapping with his partners, Colter headed alone down the Platte River, but before he could get back to civilization he met up with a company of trappers led by Manuel Lisa. They were on their way to the Rockies, determined to cash in on the huge demand for beaver furs by trapping the rich beaver streams that Lewis and Clark had described. Wealth beckoned, and John Colter gladly turned around again, guiding Lisa's men up to the mouth of

JACKSON HOLE IN 1835

This Valley is called "Jackson Hole" it is generally from 5 to 15 mls wide: the southern part where the river enters the mountain is hilly and uneven but the Northern portion is wide smooth and comparatively even the whole being covered with wild sage and Surrounded by high and rugged mountains upon whose summits the snow remains during the hottest months in Summer. The alluvial bottoms along the river and streams inter sect it thro. the valley produce a luxuriant groth of vegetation among which wild flax and a species of onion are abundant. The great altitude of this place however connected with the cold descending from the mountains at night I think would be a serious obstruction to growth of most Kinds of cultivated grains. This valley like all other parts of the country abounds with game.

—From *Journal of a Trapper 1834–1843*, by Osborne Russell

the Big Horn River, where they built a small fort. From there Colter was sent on a mission: contact Indians throughout the region, trading beads and other items for beaver furs.

His wanderings in the winter of 1807–1808 were the first white exploration of this region. A map produced by William Clark in 1814 and based on Colter's recollections shows an incredible midwinter journey around Yellowstone and Jackson Lakes, across the Tetons twice, and up through Jackson Hole. He did not get back to the fort until the following spring, telling tales of huge mountain ranges and a spectacular geothermal area that others quickly laughed off as "Colter's Hell."

Colter went on to become one of the most famous of all mountain men, and his later harrowing escape from the Blackfeet in Montana has become the stuff of legend. After being captured and stripped naked, he was forced to literally run for his life. Somehow he managed to outdistance his pursuers for six miles before hiding in a pile of logs until dark. He walked barefoot the 300 miles back to Manuel Lisa's fort, surviving on roots and tree bark. Shortly thereafter, Colter was reported to have thrown his hat on the ground, declaring, "I'll be damned if I ever come into [this country] again." He returned to St. Louis, married, and established a farm near that of fellow explorer Daniel Boone. Colter lived long enough to give William Clark a description of the country he had visited, but he died from jaundice just three years later, in 1813.

Because of the abundance of beavers along tributaries of the Snake River, Jackson Hole became an important crossroads for the Rocky Mountain fur trade. Although no rendezvous was ever held in the valley, many of the most famous mountain men spent time here. They first trapped beavers in Jackson Hole in 1811, but it was not until the 1820s that fur trapping really came into its own as mountain men fanned throughout the wilderness in search of the "soft gold." This quest continued for the next two decades, finally dying out when overtrapping made beavers harder to find and silk hats replaced fur hats. After the last rendezvous in 1840, most of the old trappers headed on to new adventures, the best becoming guides for those en route to Oregon and California. Because Jackson Hole was not near the Oregon Trail or other routes west, the area remained virtually deserted until the late 19th century.

SETTLERS

The first Jackson Hole homesteaders arrived in 1884, followed quickly by a handful of others fleeing the law. The settlers survived by grazing cattle, harvesting hay, and acting as guides for rich hunters from Europe and eastern states. Gradually they filled the richest parts of the valley with homesteads. Conflicts soon arose between the Bannock Indians, who had been hunting in Jackson Hole for more than a hundred years, and the new settlers who made money guiding wealthy sportsmen.

By 1895, Wyoming had enacted game laws prohibiting hunting during 10 months of the year. Claiming that the Indians were taking elk out of season, Constable William Manning and 26 settlers arrested a group of 28 Indians (mostly women and children) who had been hunting in Hoback Canyon. When the Bannocks attempted to flee, an elderly Indian was shot four times in the back and died. Most of the others escaped. Settlers in Jackson Hole feared revenge and called in the cavalry, but the Indians who had been hunting in the area all returned peaceably to their Idaho reservation. Astoundingly, *The New York Times* headlined its report of the incident, "Settlers Massacred—Indians Kill Every One at Jackson's Hole—Courier Brings the News—Red Men Apply the Torch to All the Houses in the Valley." Absolutely none of this was true, but the attack by whites succeeded in forcing the Indians off their traditional hunting grounds, an action eventually upheld in a landmark U.S. Supreme Court case.

JACKSON HOLE COMES OF AGE

By the turn of the 20th century, the Jackson Hole settlements of Jackson, Wilson, Kelly, and Moran had all been established. The towns grew slowly; people survived by ranching, guiding, and engaging in the strange new business of tending to wealthy "dudes" from back east. Eventually,

THE WHITE SHOSHONE

The little Jackson Hole town of Wilson is named for one of Wyoming's most fascinating characters, "Uncle Nick" Wilson. Born in 1842, Wilson grew up in Utah, where he made friends with a fellow sheepherder, an Indian boy, and learned to speak his language. Then, suddenly, Nick's life took a strange twist. The mother of Chief Washakie (from Wyoming's Wind River Reservation) had recently lost a son, and in a dream she was told that a white boy would come to take his place. Unable to convince her otherwise, Washakie sent his men out to find the new son. They came across Nick and offered him a pinto pony and the chance to fish, hunt, and ride horses all he wanted. It didn't take much persuading, and for the next two years he lived as a Shoshone, learning to hunt buffalo, to use a bow and arrow, and to answer to his new name, Yagaiki. He became a favorite of Chief Washakie, but when word came (falsely) that Nick's father was threatening to attack the Shoshones with an army of men to retrieve his son, the chief reluctantly helped Nick return home.

At age 18, Nick Wilson became one of the first Pony Express riders, a job that nearly killed him when he was struck in the head during a Paiute Indian attack. A doctor managed to remove the arrow point, but Wilson remained in a coma for nearly two weeks. Thereafter, Wilson always wore a hat to cover the scar, even inside buildings. He went on to become an army scout and a driver for the Overland Stage before returning to a more sedate life as a farmer. Many years later, in 1889, Nick Wilson led a party of five Mormon families over steep Teton Pass and down to the rich grazing lands in Jackson Hole. The town that grew up around him became Wilson. In later years, "Uncle Nick" recounted his adventures in *The White Indian Boy*.

SAVING JACKSON HOLE

The Jackson Hole economy has been stuck in permanent high gear for the last few decades as Jackson has grown from a sleepy burg to a national focal point for outdoor fun. From 1990 to 2000, the population nearly doubled, and today the area is home to almost 9,000 people. Expensive homes now spread across old ranch lands, retailers such as Kmart have moved in, and development reaches for miles south from Jackson itself. Surrounding towns such as Alpine and Driggs have become bedroom communities for those willing to endure the long commute to Jackson, and their growth spreads the problems outward from Jackson.

Although 97 percent of the land in Teton County is in the public domain, the 70,000 acres of private land that remain are rapidly being developed, and Jackson Hole is in grave danger of losing the wild beauty that has attracted visitors for more than a century. This dilemma is immediately obvious to anyone arriving in Jackson. Instead of the wide-open spaces that remain protected by public land ownership, the edges of Jackson are falling under a proliferation of trophy homes, real-estate offices, chain motels, fast-food outlets, megamarts, gas stations, and elaborate banks, all competing beneath a thicket of signs. Summertime traffic jams are becoming all too common in this once-quiet place, where more than 35,000 visitors can be found on a summer afternoon.

In 1994, Jackson voters got fed up with the pace of development and voted to scrap the town's 2 percent lodging tax, which had provided more than $1 million per year in funding to promote Jackson Hole around the world. Despite this lack of promotional effort, growth shows no signs of slowing down. A large new Albertson's store went up in 1999, followed by an equally impressive Smiths in 2002, located next to the sprawling new high school. Housing costs continue to spiral upward, pushed by a wealthy clientele willing to drop $1 million or more for a Jackson Hole home. Anti-growth sentiment remains strong, however. In 2002, Jackson voters overturned the town council's efforts to annex the 822-acre Jackson Hole Hereford Ranch just south of town by a two-to-one margin.

The **Jackson Hole Conservation Alliance,** 307/733-9417, www.jhalliance.com, is a 1,600-member environmental group that works to preserve the remaining natural areas of Jackson Hole. Membership starts at $25 per year and includes a bimonthly newsletter and a chance to help control the many developments that threaten this still-beautiful valley.

Another influential local group is the **Jackson Hole Land Trust,** 307/733-4707, www.jh-landtrust.org. Established in 1980, this nonprofit organization obtains conservation easements to maintain ranches and other land threatened by development. The group has protected more than 10,000 acres in the valley this way, including the 1,740-acre Walton Ranch, visible along the highway between Jackson and Wilson.

tourism would vastly eclipse raising cattle in importance, but even today Teton County has nearly as many cattle as people.

Jackson, Jackson Hole's primary settlement, was named by Maggie Simpson, who opened a post office here in 1894. Three years later Grace Miller—wife of a local banker known derisively as "Old Twelve Percent"—bought a large plot of land and planned a townsite, but the town wasn't officially incorporated until 1914. In an event that should come as no surprise in "The Equality State," Jackson later became the first town in America to be entirely governed by women. The year was 1920, and not only was the

mayor a woman (Grace Miller), but so were all four council members, the city clerk, the treasurer, and even the town marshal. They remained in office until 1923.

Over the years Jackson has grown, spurred on by the creation of Grand Teton National Park and the development of Jackson Hole Mountain Resort. In the last 25 years, Jackson Hole has seen almost continuous growth; tourists have flooded the region to play, investors have built golf courses and ostentatious hotels, and wealthy families have snatched up their own parcels of paradise. Today, Teton County has the highest per capita income of any county in America (around

$70,000), and locals quip that the billionaires are buying land so fast that they're driving the millionaires out of Jackson Hole.

Although much of the area is public land and will remain undeveloped, rapid growth on private land is transforming Jackson Hole into the Wyoming version of Vail or Santa Fe. Even the formerly quiet town of Wilson failed to fight off the development onslaught, with a massive new grade school and a collection of modest new homes that locals call Whoville (after those in the Dr. Seuss book). As a former resident of Wilson, I

can appreciate the joke going the rounds: How many Wilsonites does it take to change a light bulb? Seven. One to screw it in, and the other six to talk about how good the old one used to be.

Growth in Jackson Hole has forced land values sky-high, and affordable housing has become an oxymoron. Despite all of the problems brought on by growth, the area is still remarkably beautiful, and the surrounding public lands will remain wild. Locals like to point out that this is more than a place to visit; for them it is a place to live surrounded by the best of the old (and new) West.

Jackson

The town of Jackson (pop. 9,000) lies near the southern end of Jackson Hole, hemmed in on three sides by Snow King Mountain, the Gros Ventre Range, and East Gros Ventre Butte. At 6,200 feet in elevation, Jackson experiences cold snowy winters, wet springs, delightfully warm and sunny summers, and crisp but color-filled falls. Jackson is unlike any other place in Wyoming; on a typical summer day more than 35,000 tourists flood the town. Sit on a bench in Town Square on a summer day and you're likely to see cars from every state in the Union. Tourists dart in and out of the many gift shops, art galleries, fine restaurants, Western-style saloons, and trendy boutiques. The cowboy hats all look as if the price tags just came off. This sure isn't Rock Springs!

In other parts of Wyoming, Jackson is viewed with a mixture of awe and disdain—awe over its booming economy, but disdain that Jackson is not a "real" town, just a false front put up to sell things to outsiders. Yes, Jackson is almost wholly dependent on the almighty tourist dollar, but as a result it enjoys a cultural richness lacking in other parts of the state. Besides, if you don't like all the commercial foolishness, it's easy to escape to a campsite or remote trail in the wonderful countryside of nearby Grand Teton National Park or Bridger-Teton National Forest.

Keep your eyes open around Jackson and you're likely to see well-known residents such as Hollywood stars Harrison Ford, Danny DeVito and his wife Rhea Perlman, Connie Stevens, and Sandra

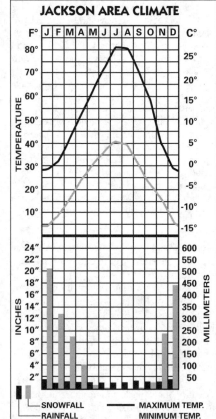

JACKSON AREA CLIMATE

SNOWFALL — MAXIMUM TEMP.
RAINFALL — MINIMUM TEMP.

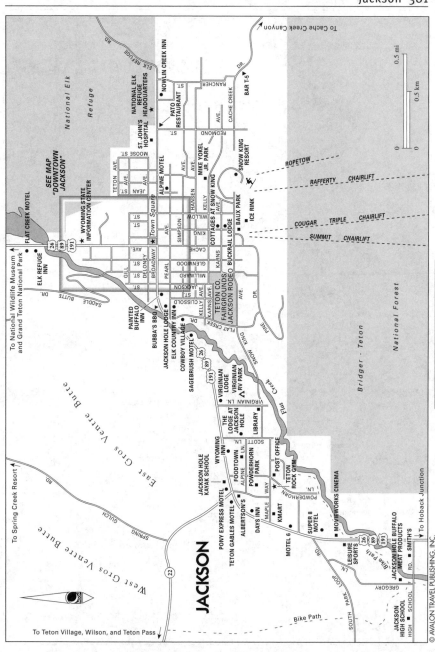

JACKSON HOLE

To National Museum of Wildlife Art,
Grand Teton and Yellowstone National Parks

DOWNTOWN JACKSON

26 89 191

National

Elk

Refuge

WAGON WHEEL RV PARK

WYOMING STATE INFORMATION CENTER

WAGON WHEEL VILLAGE

DAVY JACKSON INN

PERRY ST.

WYOMING GAME AND FISH

MOON

CACHE CREEK MOTEL

ROSECRANZ

WILD FLOUR BAKERY

SNAKE RIVER KAYAK AND CANOE SCHOOL

BRIDGER-TETON NATIONAL FOREST OFFICE

JACKSON HOLE HISTORICAL CENTER

INN ON THE CREEK

MERCILL

AVE.

KUDAR'S MOTEL

WOLF MOON INN

ALPINE HOUSE COUNTRY INN

NANI'S PASTA HOUSE

TRAPPER INN

PUBLIC PARKING

ANGLERS INN

NIKAI

JACKSON RECREATION CENTER

EL RANCH MOTEL

PUBLIC RESTROOMS

TETON INN

GILL

RUSTY PARROT LODGE

ANVIL MOTEL AND BUNKHOUSE

AVE.

TETON MOUNTAINEERING

IMAGES OF NATURE GALLERY

TETON CYCLERY

Miller

MERRY PIGLETS

JACKSON HOLE MOUNTAIN GUIDES

PROSPECTOR INN

Park

RIPLEY'S BELIEVE IT OR NOT

THE BUNNERY

ROBERT DEAN GALLERY

BLUE LION RESTAURANT

BROWSE 'N BUY

MEYER GALLERY

PARKWAY INN

FOUR WINDS MOTEL

WILD BY NATURE GALLERY

TETON THEATRE

SKINNY SKIS

VALLEY BOOKS

LIGHT REFLECTIONS GALLERY

PUBLIC PARKING

PUBLIC RESTROOMS

TRAILSIDE GALLERIES

DELONEY

JACKSON HOLE PLAYHOUSE

JACKSON HOLE MUSEUM

CADILLAC GRILLE/ BILLY'S BURGERS

AVE.

CENTER ST. GALLERY

HUFF HOUSE INN B&B

PUBLIC PARKING

SUNDANCE INN

SILVER DOLLAR BAR AND WORT HOTEL

Town Square

JEDEDIAH'S

CASWELL GALLERY

GOLDEN EAGLE MOTEL

NEW YORK SUB SHOP

MOUNTUNES

COWBOY BAR

HARVEST NATURAL FOODS

W. BROADWAY

E. BROADWAY

BROADWAY BOTTLE CO.

26 89 191

RANCHER BAR

JACK DENNIS'

TETON KIDS

HOBACK SPORTS

MT. HIGH PIZZA PIE

MAINSTAGE THEATRE

SNAKE RIVER GRILL

BETTY ROCK CAFE

JACKSON HOLE CINEMA

TETON BOOKSHOP

ANTHONY'S ITALIAN RESTAURANT

PUBLIC RESTROOMS

SHADES CAFE

RAWSON GALLERIES

RAWHIDE MOTEL

PEARL ST. BAGELS

THAI ME UP

SWEETWATER RESTAURANT

TETON STEAKHOUSE

LE JAY'S CAFE

RANCH INN

ST.

PEARL

ART ASSOCIATION

POST OFFICE

PONY EXPRESS MOTEL

49ER INN

ANTLER INN

CITY HALL

JACKSON

MILLWARD

GLENWOOD

CACHE

KING

0   100 yds

0   100 m

SIMPSON

AVE.

SIMPSON

AVE.

SNAKE RIVER BREWING COMPANY & RESTAURANT

© AVALON TRAVEL PUBLISHING, INC.

Bullock, along with former Secretary of the Interior James Watt (who resigned in disgrace in 1983), attorney Gerald Spence (of Karen Silkwood and Imelda Marcos notoriety), Yvon Chouinard (mountaineer and founder of Patagonia), industrial heir Charles DuPont, and members of the extended Rockefeller family. Vice President Dick Cheney also has a luxury home in Jackson Hole and is a frequent visitor, which explains all of the Blackhawk helicopters, Secret Service agents, and Suburbans with dark-tinted windows.

SIGHTS

Town Square

In 1932, the local Rotary Club planted trees in the center of Jackson, adding four picturesque arches made from hundreds of elk antlers in the 1950s and '60s. Today the trees offer summertime shade, and at any time of day or night you'll find visitors admiring or posing for photos in front of the arches that mark the corners of Town Square. During winter, the snow-covered arches and trees are draped with lights, giving the square a festive atmosphere. Surrounded by dozens of board-walk-fronted galleries, bars, restaurants, factory outlets, and gift shops, the square is the focal point of tourist activity in Jackson.

During summer, stagecoaches wait to transport you on a leisurely ride around town, and each evening "cowboys" put on a free **shoot-out** for throngs of camera-happy tourists. The shoot-out starts every summer night (except Sun.) at 6:15 P.M. They've been killing each other like this since 1957. With stereotypical players and questionable acting, the "mountain law" system seems in dire need of reform. Most folks love the sham; Kodak and Fuji love it even more. Warning: The sound of blanks is surprisingly loud and can be frightening for small children.

National Museum of Wildlife Art

Jackson is home to the magnificent National Museum of Wildlife Art, which lies two miles north of town along U.S. Hwy. 26/89, directly across from the National Elk Refuge. Built from brown Arizona sandstone, the exterior blends in with nearby rock outcroppings. Step inside the doors of this 51,000-square-foot museum to discover a marvelous interior space. As visitors enter

© DON PITCHER

National Museum of Wildlife Art

the main gallery, a larger-than-life bronze mountain lion crouches above, ready to pounce. Kids will have fun in the hands-on Children's Gallery. Adults will appreciate the artwork spread throughout a dozen galleries, along with the video theater, Rising Sage Cafe (delicious lunches), 200-seat auditorium, and gift shop.

The museum collection features pieces by Carl Rungius, George Catlin, Albert Bierstadt, Karl Bodmer, Alfred Jacob Miller, N. C. Wyeth, Conrad Schwiering, John Clymer, Charles Russell, Robert Bateman, and many others. Of particular interest are the reconstructed studio of John Clymer and the spacious Carl Rungius Gallery, where you'll find the most complete collection of his paintings in the nation. Also of note is the exhibit on the American bison, which documents these once vastly abundant animals and their slaughter. Six galleries contain changing exhibitions of photography, painting, and other art. Spotting scopes in the lobby and the cozy members' lounge (open to the public) are useful for watching residents of the adjacent National Elk Refuge.

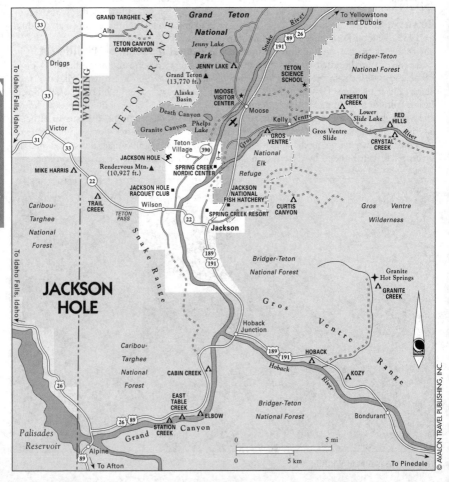

Admission to the museum costs $8 adults, $7 seniors and students, $16 families; kids under six get in free. It's open daily 9 A.M.–5 P.M. year-round, with the exception of April, May, and November, when the hours are Sunday 1–5 P.M. and Monday–Saturday 9 A.M.–5 P.M. Free museum tours are sometimes offered; ask at the front desk is a docent is available. Call 307/733-5771 for details on the museum, or visit their website, www.wildlifeart.org.

Wildlife films, slide lectures, talks, concerts, kids' programs, and other activities take place throughout the year in the auditorium and galleries; pick up a schedule of upcoming events at the entrance desk. One of the most popular events is the **Miniature Show and Sale** in mid-September; it attracts more than a hundred of the country's leading artists.

During winter, come to the museum to purchase tickets for sleigh rides on the refuge. A combination museum entrance and Elk Refuge sleigh ride costs $15 adults, $11 ages 6–12, free for kids under six.

Historical Museums

The small **Jackson Hole Museum,** 105 N. Glenwood, 307/733-2414, www.jacksonhole-history.org, has a surprising homespun charm. Inside are displays and collections illustrating the days when Indians, trappers, cattlemen, and dude ranchers called this magnificent valley home. Check out the Paul Bunyan–size bear trap, the old postcards, and a replica of the "Colter stone." Admission costs $3 adults, $2 seniors, $1 students, and $6 families. Hours are Monday–Saturday 9:30 A.M.–6 P.M. and Sunday 10 A.M.–5 P.M. from Memorial Day to early October; closed the rest of the year. The museum sponsors hour-long **historical walking tours** of Jackson's downtown on Tuesday, Thursday, Friday, and Saturday at 10 A.M. Memorial Day to Labor Day. These cost $2 adults, $1 seniors and students, or $5 families.

Also managed by the local historical society, the **Jackson Hole Historical Center,** 105 Mercill Ave., 307/733-9605, is a small research facility housing photo archives, a library of old books from the area, and rotating exhibits

throughout the year. Hours are Monday–Friday 8 A.M.–5 P.M. year-round; free admission.

Information Center

Anyone new to Jackson Hole should be sure to visit the spacious **Wyoming State Information Center** on the north end of town at 532 N. Cache Dr., 307/733-3316, www.jacksonholechamber.com. Hours are daily 8 A.M.–7 P.M. between Memorial Day and Labor Day, and daily 8 A.M.–5 P.M. the rest of the year. (The phone is answered only on weekdays, but on weekends you can leave a message and they'll mail you an information packet.)

The information center is a two-level, sod-roofed wooden building (jokingly called the "little prairie on the house") with natural-history displays, a blizzard of free leaflets extolling the merits of local businesses, a gift shop selling books and maps, and an upstairs rear deck overlooking the National Elk Refuge. Ducks and trumpeter swans are visible on the marsh in the summer, and elk can be seen in the winter. The information center is staffed by the Jackson Hole Chamber of Commerce, along with Fish & Wildlife Service and Forest Service personnel in the summer. Free naturalist talks are generally given daily at 10 A.M. and 2 P.M. in the summer.

NATIONAL ELK REFUGE

Immediately north of Jackson is the National Elk Refuge, winter home for thousands of these majestic animals. During summer, the elk range up to 65 miles away to feed on grasses, shrubs, and forbs in alpine meadows. But as the snows descend each fall, the elk move downslope, wintering in Jackson Hole and the surrounding country. The chance to view elk up close from a horse-drawn sleigh makes a trip to the National Elk Refuge one of the most popular wintertime activities for Jackson Hole visitors.

History

When the first ranchers arrived in Jackson Hole in the late 19th century, they moved onto land that had long been an elk migration route and

National Elk Refuge

wintering ground. The ranchers soon found elk raiding their haystacks and competing with cattle for forage, particularly during severe winters. The conflicts peaked early in the 20th century when three consecutive severe winters killed thousands of elk, leading one settler to claim that he had "walked for a mile on dead elk lying from one to four deep."

Fortunately, local rancher and hunting guide Stephen N. Leek had been given a camera by one of the sportsmen he had guided, George Eastman (founder of Kodak). Leek's disturbing photos of starving and dead elk found a national audience and helped pressure the state of Wyoming to appropriate $5,000 to buy hay in 1909. Two years later the federal government began purchasing land for a permanent winter elk refuge that would eventually cover nearly 25,000 acres. Today it's administered by the U.S. Fish & Wildlife Service. Famed biologist, illustrator, and conservationist Olaus Murie came to Jackson Hole in 1927 to begin his studies of the elk, remaining here until his death in 1963. Murie and his wife, Margaret "Mardy" Murie, chronicled their adventures in *Wapiti Wilderness*. Conservationist Mardie Murie—now older than 100—still lives in Moose, holding near-sainthood status among conservationists.

Today more than 7,000 elk (two-thirds of the local population) spend November–May on the refuge. Because development has reduced elk habitat in the valley to one-quarter of its original size, refuge managers try to improve the remaining land through seeding, irrigation, and prescribed burning. In addition, during the most difficult foraging period, the elk are fed alfalfa pellets paid for in part by sales of elk antlers collected on the refuge. During this time, each elk eats more than seven pounds of supplemental alfalfa per day, or 30 tons per day for the entire herd. Elk head back into the mountains with the melting of snow each April and May; during summer you'll see few (if any) on the refuge.

Visiting the Refuge

The National Elk Refuge, 307/733-9212, http://nationalelkrefuge.fws.gov, is primarily a winter attraction, although it's also an excellent place to watch birds and other wildlife in summer. Trumpeter swans nest and winter here. The refuge has staff members on duty year-round in the Wyoming State Information Center. Find them on the web at www.jacksonholechamber.com.

The main winter attraction here is the chance to see thousands of elk up close from one of the **horse-drawn sleighs** that take visitors through the refuge. The elk are accustomed to these sleighs and pay little heed, but people on foot would scare them. A tour of the National Elk Refuge is always a highlight for wintertime visitors to Jackson Hole. In December and January the bulls have impressive antlers that they start to shed by the end of February. The months of January and February are good times to see sparring matches. You might also catch a glimpse of a wolf or two because a pack now resides in the area year-round and hunts elk in winter. Morning is the best time to look for wolves.

Begin your wintertime visit to the refuge at the National Museum of Wildlife Art (see previous description). Purchase your sleigh ride tickets here; $12 adults, $8 ages 6–12, free for kids under age six. A better deal is the combination ticket that includes museum entrance and an Elk Refuge sleigh ride for $15 adults, $11 ages 6–12, and free for younger kids. For reservations, contact Bar-T-Five (they run the sleighs) at 307/733-5386 or 800/772-5386, www.bart5.com. The museum shows an interpretive slide show about the refuge while you're waiting for a shuttle bus to take you downhill to the sleighs. The sleighs run daily 10 A.M.–4 P.M. mid-December through March (closed Christmas), heading out as soon as enough folks show up for a ride—generally just long enough for the early-comers to finish watching the slide show. The rides last 45–60 minutes. Be sure to wear warm clothes or bring extra layers because the wind can get bitterly cold.

Four miles north of town and next to the elk refuge is the **Jackson National Fish Hatchery,** 307/733-2510, which rears a half million cutthroat and lake trout annually. It's open daily 8 A.M.–4 P.M. year-round.

Shopping

If you have the money (or a credit card), Jackson is a great place to buy everything from artwork to mountain bikes. Even if you just hitchhiked in and have no cash to spare, it's always fun to wander through the shops and galleries surrounding Town Square.

ART

Artists have long been attracted by the beauty of Jackson Hole and the Tetons. Mount Moran, the 12,605-foot summit behind Jackson Lake, is named for Thomas Moran, whose watercolors helped persuade Congress to set aside Yellowstone as the first national park. The late Conrad Schwiering's paintings of the Tetons have attained international fame; one was even used on the Postal Service's Wyoming Centennial stamp in 1990. Ansel Adams's photograph of the Tetons remains etched in the American consciousness as one of the archetypal wilderness images. A copy of the image was included in the payload of the *Voyager II* spacecraft currently en route out of our solar system. Today many artists live or work in Jackson Hole, and locals proclaim it "Art Center of the Rockies," ranking it with New York, San Francisco, Santa Fe, and Scottsdale.

More than 30 galleries crowd the center of Jackson, their collections covering the spectrum from Indian art of questionable authenticity to impressive photographic exhibits and shows by nationally acclaimed painters. Unfortunately, many of these galleries offer recycled ideas now manufactured in mass quantity with every possible cliché thrown in. Particularly egregious examples are the Southwestern-style pastel pottery, the campy cowboy sculptures, and the prints of sexy Indian maidens with windblown hair and strategically torn garments. See the local free newspapers for a complete rundown of current exhibitions and displays, along with maps showing gallery locations, but don't believe everything the galleries say about themselves in their ads. For descriptions of local artists and galleries, visit

JACKSON HOLE

the **Jackson Hole Gallery Association's** website, www.jacksonholearts.com.

Art Galleries

Several Jackson galleries are worth a visit, most notably the outstanding National Museum of Wildlife Art. For physical sustenance with your visual nourishment, don't miss the weekly **Gallery Walks** that take place every Thursday 5–8 P.M. in the summer. Many downtown galleries serve appetizers and wine for these fun and low-key events.

The nonprofit **Art Association,** 260 W. Pearl, 307/733-6379, www.artassociation.org, offers art classes of all types throughout the year and displays changing exhibitions by local and national artists in its **ArtWest Gallery,** open Mon.–Fri. 9 A.M.–5 P.M.

Just off Town Square at the corner of Center and Deloney, **Trailside Galleries,** 307/733-3186, www.trailsidegalleries.com, focuses on Western works, but you'll also find everything from impressionism to wildlife art in this big gallery. Two other Western-themed galleries worth a visit are **Mountain Trails Gallery,** 150 N. Center St., 307/733-8150, www.mtntrails.net; and **Legacy Gallery,** 75 N. Cache, 307/733-2353, www.legacygallery.com. More unusual is **Center Street Gallery,** 30 Center St., 307/733-1115 or 888/733-1115, www.centerstreetgallery.com, where the emphasis is on vivid contemporary art and jewelry.

Also downtown, the **Caswell Gallery & Sculpture Garden,** 145 E. Broadway, 307/734-2660, www.caswellgallery.com, is home to Jackson's only outdoor sculpture garden, with wildlife bronzes by Rip Caswell. These are not my cup of tea (or espresso for that matter), but you may appreciate the innovative sculptures from other artisans displayed in this gallery.

Jack Dennis' Wyoming Gallery, 50 E. Broadway, 307/733-7548, www.jackdennis.com, specializes in wildlife and traditional landscape paintings and photography. **Rawson Galleries** features traditional watercolors, displayed in a crowded space at 50 King St., 307/733-7306. They're open July–October. **Meyer Gallery,** 155 N. Center St., 307/733-0905 or 877/681-8900, www.meyergallery.com, presents beautifully passionate oil paintings and bronzes by respected Western artists at 155 Center Street. These artworks are well worth seeing, but they're priced for serious art patrons only. **Robert Dean Gallery,** 172 Center St., 307/733-9290, is known for its quality Indian artwork, with pottery, silver and gold jewelry, leather belts, and more.

The **Hennes Studio & Gallery,** 5850 N. Larkspur Dr. (off Spring Gulch Rd. near the Jackson Hole Golf and Tennis Club), 307/733-2593, features oil and watercolor paintings of the Tetons by Joanne Hennes. Two of her commissioned works hang in the Moose Visitor Center and Jenny Lake Lodge.

One of Jackson's largest private exhibition spaces is **Wilcox Gallery,** one mile north of town on U.S. Hwy. 26/89, 307/733-6450, www.wilcoxgallery.com. Inside are traditional oil paintings by Jim Wilcox, along with works by other prominent Western painters and sculptors.

Photo Galleries

Many nationally known photographers live or work in Jackson Hole and exhibit their prints in Jackson galleries. Tom Mangelsen displays his outstanding wildlife and landscape photos at **Images of Nature Gallery,** 170 N. Cache Dr., 307/733-9752 or 888/238-0177, www.mangelsen.com, and has galleries at 14 other locations around the country.

Inside **Light Reflections,** 35 E. Deloney, 307/733-4016 or 800/346-5223, www.lightreflections.com, are many of Fred Joy's large-format visions of the American West. Also well worth a visit is **Wild by Nature Gallery,** 95 W. Deloney, 307/733-8877 or 888/494-5329, www.wildbynature.com, where photographer Henry H. Holdsworth shows prints of his strikingly beautiful wildlife and nature imagery.

Located in Gaslight Alley at 125 N. Cache **Brookover-Muench Fine Art Photography,** 307/733-3988, www.davidbrookoverphotos.com, exhibits beautiful (and big) landscapes by photographers David Brookover and David Muench. **Wild Exposures Gallery,** 60 E. Broadway Ave. (upstairs next to Snake River Grill), 307/739-1777, www.wildexposuresgallery.com, shows works from a half-dozen local photographers.

OUTDOOR GEAR

Outdoor enthusiasts will discover several excellent shops in Jackson. Climbers, backpackers, and cross-country skiers head to America's oldest climbing shop, **Teton Mountaineering,** 170 N. Cache Dr., 307/733-3595 or 800/850-3595, www.tetonmtn.com, for quality equipment, maps, and travel guides. They also rent tents, sleeping bags, backpacks, cookstoves, climbing shoes, ice axes, cross-country skis, and even climbing and skiing videos. Check the bulletin board for used items.

Jack Dennis' Outdoor Shop, 50 E. Broadway, 307/733-3270 or 800/570-3270, www.jackdennis.com, is a large upscale store with fly-fishing and camping gear in summer and skis and warm clothes during winter. They also rent almost anything: tents, stoves, lanterns, cookware, sleeping bags, fishing poles, fly rods, waders, float tubes, backpacks, skis, snowshoes, and more.

Skinny Skis, 65 W. Deloney Ave., 307/733-6094 or 888/733-7205, www.skinnyskis.com, has more in the way of high-quality clothing and supplies, especially cross-country ski gear. Rent sleeping bags, tents, climbing shoes, ice axes, inline skates, baby carriers, and backpacks here. Another place to rent outdoor gear of all types—including volleyball sets, fishing gear, float tubes, tents, sleeping bags, backpacks, campstoves, and lanterns—is **Leisure Sports,** 1075 South U.S. Hwy. 89, 307/733-3040, www.leisuresportsadventure.com.

Moosely Seconds Mountaineering, in Moose, 307/739-1801, sells climbing and outdoor gear and rents trekking poles, ice axes, crampons, rock shoes, approach shoes, plastic boots, day packs, and snowshoes. It's open summers only.

Purchase used outdoor gear of all types from **Gear Revival,** 854 W. Broadway, 307/739-8699. The least expensive place to buy rugged outdoor wear, cowboy boots, and cowboy hats is **Corral West,** 840 W. Broadway, 307/733-0247.

BARGAINS

Buy used clothing and other items at **Browse 'N Buy Thrift Shop,** 139 N. Cache Dr., 307/733-7524, or the more chaotic **Orville's,** 285 W. Pearl, 307/733-3165. Hint: Browse 'N Buy puts out new items on Wednesday, attracting a queue of discount shoppers for their 1 P.M. opening. Get there early for the real deals! Orville's sometimes sells old Wyoming license plates, which are a big hit with European tourists.

BOOKS

Unlike many Wyoming towns where the book selection consists of a few bodice-buster romance novels in the local pharmacy, Jackson is blessed with several fine bookstores. **Valley Bookstore,** 125 N. Cache Dr., 307/733-4533, www.valleybook.com, is the largest local bookshop, with a great choice of regional titles. The store has occasional author signings and readings. **Teton Bookshop,** 25 S. Glenwood, 307/733-9220, is a small downtown shop with a knowledgeable owner. **Main Event,** in the Powderhorn Mall at 980 W. Broadway, 307/733-7112, sells new books and CDs and rents a wide choice of videos. A few doors away in the mall is **Jackson Hole Book Trader,** 307/734-6001 or 800/722-2710, www.wybiz.com/jacksonholebook, where you'll find a surprising choice of used and rare books.

KITSCH

If you're a fan of the *National Enquirer,* check out the weird and wacky collection at **Ripley's Believe It or Not,** 140 N. Cache, 307/734-0000, www.ripleys.com/jac.htm. Here you'll discover a shrunken head, six-legged buffalo calf, six-foot-long cigar, antique bedpan collection, and even art created from dryer lint. Who says art is only for the elite? Entrance costs a steep $8 adults, $5 ages 5–12; free for kids under five. The family rate is $28, a bargain price for families of 10 from Salt Lake City. Ripley's is open daily 9 A.M.–10 P.M. in summer and daily 10 A.M.–6 P.M. the rest of the year.

For more foolishness, have the kids drag you to the **Teton Maze,** across from the Snow King chairlift, 307/734-0455. As the ads proclaim, it's a-Maze-ing.

Accommodations

As one of the premier centers for tourism in Wyoming, Jackson Hole is jam-packed with more than 70 different motels, hotels, and B&Bs, plus many more condominiums and guest ranches. Other lodging can be found just to the north within or near Grand Teton National Park; these are detailed in the Grand Teton National Park chapter. See my *Moon Handbooks Yellowstone & Grand Teton* for comprehensive coverage of local lodging options. The Jackson Hole Chamber of Commerce's website (www.jacksonholechamber.com) has brief descriptions and web links for most local accommodations.

Because of the town's popularity, Jackson accommodations command premium prices—a marked contrast to rates in other parts of Wyoming. With a few exceptions, you'll pay at least $90 s or d during the peak visitor seasons of July–August and late December to early January. Rates can drop more than 50 percent in the off-season, so if you can visit March–May or late September to mid-December, you'll save a lot of cash. (The same Super 8 Motel rooms that go for $100 in July cost just $46 in April!) In the town of Jackson, the highest rates are usually in July and August, while at Teton Village, skiers and snowboarders send room rates to their peak between mid-December and early January.

Reservations are highly recommended. For midsummer, make reservations at least two months ahead, or longer if you really want to be certain of a place. During the Christmas-to-New Year's period you should probably reserve six months in advance to ensure a spot. Summer weekends tend to be the most crowded, with many families driving up from Salt Lake City for a cooling break in the mountains.

UNDER $50

Jackson's least-expensive option, the **Bunkhouse,** 307/733-3668 or 800/234-4507, www.anvilmotel.com, is in the basement of the Anvil Motel at 215 N. Cache Drive. Right in town, the hostel almost always has space. It costs $21 per person and includes a TV room and a kitchen with a refrigerator and microwave (but no stove or dishes). The big sleeping room contains 27 bunk beds with linen and adjacent storage lockers; bring your own lock. Although men's and women's showers and restrooms are separate, the sleeping space is coed. Alcohol is not allowed. Folks who aren't staying here can take showers for $5.

Despite the name, **Hostel X,** 307/733-3415, www.hostelx.com, really isn't a hostel, but it does provide budget rates in a scenic location. Private rooms cost $50 s or d, or $63 for up to four people. The very small plain-vanilla rooms lack TV or phones, but there's a central lounge for camaraderie. The lounge includes a TV, pay phones, a pool table, table tennis, a children's play area, a fireplace, a microwave, games, Internet access, and a ski-waxing room. Because of its Teton Village location at the foot of Jackson Hole Mountain Resort, Hostel X is very popular with skiers on a budget; reserve three months ahead for mid-winter rooms.

$50–100

Alpine Motel, 70 S. Jean St., 307/739-3200, is in a quiet part of town but just a few blocks from Town Square. The furnishings may not be the newest in town, but the rooms are clean and start at $64 s or d or $72 for four people. Kitchenettes with two queen beds sleep up to four for $90. A small outdoor pool (heated but seasonal) is also on the premises.

Despite its name, **The Cottages at Snow King,** 470 King St., 307/733-3480, doesn't have cottages, but it does rent modest but comfortable motel rooms in a residential part of town. These range from rooms with one queen bed for $68 s or d, up to full-kitchen units that sleep four for $106. All rooms have microwaves and fridges, and a continental breakfast is served in the lobby each morning. Winter rates provide skiers with some of the best deals in Jackson: $175 d for a week! The motel is entirely nonsmoking.

A recommended place is **Anvil Motel,** 215 N. Cache Dr., 307/733-3668 or 800/234-4507, www.anvilmotel.com, where the modern rooms are $94 d or $119 for two beds (four people). All rooms here have microwaves and small fridges, plus access to the outdoor hot tub.

One of the nicer reasonably priced Jackson motels is **Wolf Moon Inn,** 285 N. Cache Dr., 307/733-2287 or 800/964-2387, www.jakbiz.com/wolfmooninn. Clean and spacious rooms feature log furnishings, fridges, microwaves, and ceiling fans (but no air-conditioning). Rates are $85–89 d in standard rooms (some with hot tubs); $159 for six people in two-room suites.

Ranch Inn, 45 E. Pearl St., 307/733-6363 or 800/348-5599, www.ranchinn.com, offers a wide variety of accommodations just one block from Town Square, all with fridges and microwaves. These include newly remodeled standard rooms ($98 d), tower rooms with balconies facing Snow King, fridges, and microwaves ($155 d), and suites with king beds, wood-burning fireplaces, balconies, and hot tubs ($175–185 d). Extra guests are $5 per person. Other amenities include indoor and outdoor hot tubs and a continental breakfast. Some of the tower rooms are wheelchair accessible.

One of Jackson's better deals for standard motel rooms is—not surprisingly—**Motel 6,** 1370 W. Broadway, 307/733-1620 or 800/466-8356, www.motel6.com, but even here the summertime rates are $88 s or $94 d. You'll find humdrum rooms and an outdoor pool, but reserve six months in advance for July and August. The off-season rates ($36 s or $42 d) are a much better bargain.

Twelve miles south of Jackson in Hoback Junction, **Hoback River Resort,** 307/733-5129, www.hobackriverresort.com, has large motel rooms and cabins for up to six people on attractive grounds facing the Hoback River. The rooms are very clean and well maintained, but the location—away from busy downtown Jackson—is the real draw here. Rates are $75–85 s or d in motel rooms with decks, or $110–145 d in rustic cabins with full kitchens (but no maid service). Modern cottages (also

with full kitchens) are $135–155 for up to four guests. A three-night minimum stay is required in the cabins and cottages.

Other good places with rooms less than $100 include **El Rancho Motel,** 240 N. Glenwood, 307/733-3668 or 800/234-4507, www.anvilmotel.com; **Kudar's Motel,** 260 N. Cache Dr., 307/733-2823; **Pony Express Motel,** 1075 W. Broadway, 307/733-3835 or 800/526-2658, www.ponyexpresswest.com; **Teton Gables Motel,** 1140 W. Broadway, 307/733-3723, www.tetongables.com; **Teton Inn,** 165 W. Gill St., 307/733-3883 or 800/429-8873, www.jacksonlodging.com; and **Sagebrush Motel,** 550 W. Broadway, 307/733-0336 or 888/219-0900.

$100–150

Many Jackson accommodations fall in the $100–150 range, with pricing factors being location, type of room, quality of furnishings, and presence of amenities such as pools and hot tubs. Several comfortable midrange options are described as follows. These are not the corporate lodging giants, but they offer good value and down-home friendliness.

Downtown Accommodations

Elk Country Inn, 480 W. Pearl, 307/733-2364 or 800/483-8667, www.townsquareinns.com, is popular with families and small groups of travelers. The spacious motel rooms (a bit old-fashioned but nicely maintained) all have three beds and cost $102 d. Also available are loft units that sleep six for $126; add $6 for a kitchenette unit. Modern log cabins with kitchenettes and lodgepole furnishings go for $144 d or $152 for four.

The rooms are a bit small, but guests appreciate the friendly service and extra touches at **Sundance Inn,** 135 W. Broadway, 307/733-3444 or 888/478-6326, www.sundanceinnjackson.com. The motel is close to Town Square and serves a light homemade breakfast plus evening cookies and lemonade. Guests can also use the outdoor hot tub (with alleyway ambience, alas). Standard rooms cost $104 s or $114 d, while two-room suites are $154 for four people. The hotel does not have air-conditioning.

Antler Inn, 50 W. Pearl Ave., 307/733-2535 or 800/522-2406, www.townsquareinns.com, is a large property with 110 rooms just one block off Town Square. Most contain two queen beds and cost $104 for up to four, but also available are a dozen large family rooms/suites ($130) with three beds and space for six people. Some of these contain wood-burning fireplaces or jetted tubs. Rounding out the options here are some attractive (but small) log-walled rooms for $92 d. All guests have access to an exercise room, sauna, and a big indoor hot tub.

Anglers Inn, 265 N. Millward St., 307/733-3682 or 800/867-4667, www.anglersinn.net, has attractive rooms with Western-style fixtures, lodgepole beds and chairs, and small baths. This cozy motel is right on Flat Creek but just a couple of blocks from Town Square. Rates are $105–115 s or d, and all rooms contain fridges and microwaves.

Jackson Hole Lodge, 420 W. Broadway, 307/733-2992 or 800/604-9404, www.jacksonholelodge.com, has a diverse mixture of rooms, but the featured attractions are a large indoor swimming pool, wading pool, hot tub, sauna, and game room on attractive grounds. Standard motel rooms are a bit dated but clean and in good condition for $109–134 d. Condo-type units are much nicer, with an upscale decor that includes log furniture; $184 for a studio unit, $219 for a one-bedroom unit (sleeps four) with a living room, fireplace, and full kitchen. Two-bedroom units cost $394 for up to eight people.

Another very comfortable option is **Trapper Inn,** 235 N. Cache Dr., 307/733-2648 or 800/341-8000, www.trapperinn.com, where the spacious standard rooms are $103–137 s or d. Family rooms are $169 for four people, and some have hot tubs and king-size beds. Also available are two-bedroom units that sleep four guests for $231. The motel features indoor and outdoor hot tubs, along with fridges and microwaves in many rooms.

On the quiet north side of town, **Cache Creek Motel,** 390 N. Glenwood, 307/733-7781 or 800/843-4788, www.cachecreekmotel.com, is a good moderately priced lodging choice. All rooms include full kitchens, and an outdoor hot tub is available. Standard rooms are $110 d or $130

for four people. One-bedroom suites cost $175, and two-bedroom suites are $190; the suites sleep up to six for the same price.

Rawhide Motel, 75 S. Millward, 307/733-1216 or 800/835-2999, www.rawhidemotel.com, is a fine place with large rooms containing handmade lodgepole furniture. Rates are $113 s or $117 d; $127 for four.

Golden Eagle Inn, 325 E. Broadway, 307/733-2042 or 888/748-6937, www.goldeneagleinn.com, is a quiet family motel with standard rooms for $95–123 d, and larger rooms for $141–175 d. All include microwaves and small refrigerators, plus access to the heated seasonal pool. Adjacent is a two-bedroom house with a full kitchen for $267 d.

Other midrange downtown places worth investigating include **Buckrail Lodge,** 110 E. Karns Ave., 307/733-2079, www.buckraillodge.com; **Four Winds Motel,** 150 N. Millward St., 307/733-2474 or 800/228-6461, www.jacksonholefourwinds.com; **49'er Inn & Suites (Quality Inn),** 330 W. Pearl, 307/733-7550 or 800/483-8667, www.townsquareinns.com; and **Prospector Inn,** 155 N. Jackson, 307/733-4858 or 800/429-8835, www.jacksonlodging.com.

Nearby Accommodations

Two midpriced motels are adjacent to each other and one mile north of Jackson on U.S. 89. Both face the Elk Refuge (and the busy highway). **Elk Refuge Inn,** 307/733-3582 or 800/544-3582, www.elkrefugeinn.com, is the smaller and more homey of the two, with a mixture of rooms and friendly management, plus corrals where horses can be boarded at no additional charge. Rates are $105 s or d ($10 per person for extra guests), and all rooms contain fridges, microwaves, and a small deck. A family room ($125 for six) and kitchenettes ($115 d) are also available. All rooms have drive-up access, but no air-conditioning. **Flat Creek Inn,** 307/733-5276 or 800/438-9338, www.flatcreekinn.com, is a large two-level motel just a few hundred feet north of Elk Refuge Inn. The rooms are functionally furnished, and all include microwaves and small fridges. Standard rooms cost $95–114 for up to four guests, and spacious kitchenettes are $140 for up to five.

Motel amenities include a hot tub, sauna, and ski-waxing room.

In the heart of Teton Village action, and right next to the tram, **Village Center Inn,** 307/733-3990 or 800/443-8613, www.jhresortlodging.com, charges $110–125 s or d for studio or loft units and $165 for two-bedroom units that sleep six. All units include full kitchens. Peak season winter rates rise to $175 d for a one-bedroom unit, up to $230 for two bedrooms. The decor is fairly utilitarian, but other than Hostel X, this is the cheapest Teton Village accommodation.

Other midrange edge-of-town places worth investigating include **Virginian Lodge,** 750 W. Broadway, 307/733-2792 or 800/262-4999, www.virginianlodge.com; and **Super 8 Motel,** 750 South U.S. Hwy. 89, 307/733-6833 or 800/800-8000, www.super8.com. Farther away (39 miles northeast of Jackson in Buffalo Valley) is **Hatchet Resort**, 307/543-2413 or 877/543-2413, www.hatchetresort.com, another good midrange choice.

Log Cabin Motels

Several local motels offer log cabin accommodations for a step back to the Old West while keeping such newer amenities as televisions and private baths. Set amid tall cottonwood trees, **Wagon Wheel Village,** 435 N. Cache Dr., 307/733-2357 or 800/323-9279, www.wagonwheelvillage.com, has well-maintained and cozy log cabins and log motel units. These go for $100–170 d, depending on the amenities. The most luxurious are modern log cabin–style suites ($170 for up to six people), each with a fireplace, fridge, microwave, and small deck facing Flat Creek. All guests have access to two outside hot tubs at this friendly, family-run place.

Near a busy Jackson intersection, **Cowboy Village Resort,** 120 Flat Creek Dr., 307/733-3121 or 800/962-4988, www.townsquareinn.com, has 82 modern, but jammed-together cabins with kitchenettes. The cabins start at $135 d ($145 for four) in a cabin with two queen bunkbeds, up to $169 d ($179 for four) with one queen bed and a sleeper sofa. Guests have access to two enclosed hot tubs.

Other places with log units are described above: Elk Country Inn Sagebrush Motel, Hoback River Resort, Kudar's Motel, and Hatchet Resort.

$150 AND UP

It should come as no surprise that tony Jackson Hole has several elaborate, pricey, and sumptuous places to stay, with rooms starting around $150 and hitting the stratosphere at more than $1,000 per night.

Downtown Accommodations

Close to Town Square, the **Wort Hotel,** 50 N. Glenwood St., 307/733-2190 or 800/322-2727, www.worthotel.com, has been a Jackson favorite since 1941 and is the only downtown hotel earning a four-diamond rating from AAA. A disastrous 1980 fire—started by a bird that built a nest too close to a neon sign—destroyed the roof and upper floor. The hotel was completely restored within a year, and today it's better than ever, with such modern amenities as a fitness center and two hot tubs. The Wort's spacious rooms are attractively decorated with a New West motif that includes lodgepole-pine beds, creative fixtures, and barbed-wire-patterned wallpaper. Rates are $235 d for standard rooms (with two queens or one king bed), or $260 d for larger and more luxurious rooms. Spacious junior suites with king beds and wet bars cost $325, while the three-bedroom luxury suite will set you back $485 d.

An outstanding in-town choice is **Parkway Inn,** 125 N. Jackson St., 307/733-3143 or 800/247-8390, www.parkwayinn.com. This midsize lodge has a delightful Victorian ambience with antique furniture and quilts in every room. The rooms are immaculate, and guests will also enjoy a small indoor lap pool, two hot tubs, two saunas, and a gym in the basement. A light breakfast is served in the lobby each morning. Rates are $169 d for standard rooms with two queen beds or a king bed, $199 for larger suites, or $209 d for two-room suites; $12 each for additional guests (maximum of four in a room).

An excellent nine-room lodge just a few blocks from Town Square, **Inn on the Creek,** 295 N. Millwood, 307/739-1565 or 800/669-9534, www.innonthecreek.com, has a peaceful location beside Flat Creek. Standard rooms ($179–199 s or d) feature designer furnishings, down comforters, and VCRs. The deluxe rooms ($209–229 s or d) also include balconies, fireplaces, and in-room hot tubs, while a gorgeous suite ($379) sleeps four and has a full kitchen, hot tub bath, and private patio. A light breakfast is served in the lounge, and all guests have access to the outdoor hot tub facing the creek.

A very attractive downtown lodging option is **Davy Jackson Inn,** 85 Perry Ave., 307/739-2294 or 800/584-0532, www.davyjackson.com, where modern rooms ($199 d) come in a variety of styles, including some with old-fashioned clawfoot tubs. A full breakfast is delivered to your room each morning, and guests can relax in the outdoor hot tub. The two honeymoon suites ($249 d) include steam showers, gas fireplaces, and king-size canopy beds.

Rusty Parrot Lodge and Spa, 175 N. Jackson, 307/733-2000 or 800/458-2004, www.rustyparrot.com, offers outstanding accommodation just two blocks from Town Square. The 31 rooms feature handcrafted furniture, original artwork, oversize tubs, and goose-down comforters; some also contain fireplaces and hot tubs. A gourmet breakfast (it's never the same) is served each morning in the luxurious dining room, and guests can relax in the hot tub on a deck overlooking Jackson, borrow a book from the library, or enjoy a massage, aromatherapy session, or facial from Body Sage Day Spa (extra charge). Rates are $284–329 s or d for standard rooms, or $500 d for the luxurious suite. No children under age 12 are allowed. The lodge also serves gourmet dinners each evening to its guests (and others).

Snow King Resort

Located at the base of Jackson's in-town ski hill and just a few blocks from downtown, Snow King Resort, 400 E. Snow King, 307/733-5200 or 800/522-5464, www.snowking.com, includes more than 200 hotel rooms and 58 condos, plus such amenities as a year-round heated outdoor pool and two hot tubs, a sauna, an exercise facil-

ity, restaurants, a bar, a concierge, a business center, a game room, and a spa. A free shuttle provides connections to the airport and Teton Village (winters), and guests receive discounted passes for Snow King Ski Area. Hotel rooms at Snow King cost $200–210 d, and two-room suites are $200–400 d. Condos start at $200 d, up to an ultra-luxurious four-bedroom unit that will set you back $600 per night.

Spring Creek Ranch

Some of the most dramatic vistas of the Tetons are from the luxurious Spring Creek Ranch, 307/733-8833 or 800/443-6139, www.springcreekranch.com. Located on a thousand-acre estate, the resort sits high atop Gros Ventre Butte four miles west of Jackson and includes a wide range of lodging options. Hotel rooms are $250 d, and suites cost $310 for four people. Studio units run $275; one- to three-bedroom condos are $375–695 and sleep four to six. Also available are executive four-bedroom homes that sleep eight and cost a mere $2,200 per night. All rooms at Spring Creek Ranch contain fireplaces and lodgepole furnishings, and the condos and studios have full kitchens. Other amenities include a private pond, tennis courts, an outdoor pool, a hot tub, a fitness center, and a day spa with massage and other offerings.

Teton Pines Resort

Located four miles south of Teton Village, Teton Pines Resort & Country Club, 307/733-1005 or 800/238-2223, www.tetonpines.com, features the amenities you'd expect in a year-round resort, including an 18-hole golf course, tennis center, and classy restaurant. The accommodations are varied, but all include a continental breakfast, access to the outdoor pool and hot tub, athletic-club privileges, concierge service, and an airport shuttle. One-bedroom units (with separate his and hers baths) are $395 d, while two-bedroom and living-room suites cost $750 d ($40 per person extra for additional guests). The resort also has two furnished three-bedroom townhouses, each with a kitchen, two decks, a fireplace, washer and dryer, and garage. These sleep up to eight for $950 per night.

Amangani

Atop Gros Ventre Butte near Spring Creek Ranch is stunning **Amangani,** 307/734-7333 or 877/734-7333, www.amanresorts.com, the only representative of Amanresorts in America. (Most of the company's other lavish resorts are in Southeast Asia.) Aman groupies and business travelers know to expect the utmost in luxury, and they will certainly not be disappointed here, starting with a knowledgeable staff and spare-no-expenses construction. The three-story sandstone-faced hotel contains 40 suites, each with a patined-metal fireplace, mountain-facing balcony, king-size bed, deep soaking tub (with a window view), minibar, and terrazzo dining table. Amangani's central lobby is particularly impressive, blending sandstone columns, redwood accents, custom furnishings, and soaring two-story windows. Outside, those soaking in a whirlpool and heated 35-meter pool enjoy a remarkable view of the Tetons. Among other amenities are a complete health center (exercise facility, gym, steam rooms, yoga and meditation classes, and massage), a gourmet restaurant (The Grill) that specializes in steaks, chops, and seafood, and a lounge. Amangani's accommodations include suites ($700 d), six deluxe suites ($825 d), four large luxury suites with two baths and spacious balconies ($900 d), and the premier Sena suite ($1,100) for the utmost in luxury.

Teton Village Lodges

If you're looking for beautifully appointed accommodations in Teton Village instead of downtown Jackson, you can't go wrong at **Snake River Lodge & Spa,** 307/733-3657 or 800/445-4655, www.snakeriverlodge.com. The lodge features a New West–style lobby with stone fireplaces and whimsically carved bears, plus rooms that continue the theme with rustic lamps, pine furniture, and colorful prints. A gorgeous free-form indoor/outdoor heated pool has a cascading waterfall, and other attractions include indoor and outdoor hot tubs, a sauna, ski lockers, a ski-in concierge service, and a five-story spa and health club with exercise equipment, facials, manicures, hydrotherapy, massages, soaking tubs, and steam

baths. Rates are $200–500 d in the guest rooms or $350–1,500 d in the condominiums.

Also in Teton Village, **Alpenhof Lodge,** 307/733-3242 or 800/732-3244, www.jackson-hole.com/alpenhof, exudes a European ambience, and its owners come from Switzerland and Germany. Some of the recently remodeled rooms follow through with Bavarian furnishings, and all guests have access to the heated year-round outdoor pool, hot tub, and sauna. Summertime rates start at $134 d for the simplest rooms, up to $418 for four people in their nicest suite. Winter ski-season rates are $193–538 d.

Jackson Hole's newest upmarket lodging option, **Teton Mountain Lodge,** 307/734-7111 or 800/801-6615, www.tetonlodge.com, sits at the base of the mountain in Teton Village. The lodge offers an array of amenities and services, including indoor and outdoor heated pools, hot tubs, a fitness center/spa, and underground parking. Guests can choose rooms or studios for $275–375 d, or one-, two-, or three-bedroom suites for $350–800.

Another Teton Village option is **The Inn at Jackson Hole (Best Western),** 307/733-2311 or 800/842-7666, www.innatjh.com, where standard rooms (recently renovated with log furniture) cost $189–209 d. Family-friendly loft suites with kitchenettes are $249 d (plus $10 per person for additional guests). The hotel also has an outdoor heated pool, three outdoor hot tubs, a sauna, and ski lockers.

Four Seasons Resort, 307/734-5040 or 800/819-5053, www.fourseasons.com/jackson-hole, opens in time for the 2003–2004 ski season and includes a 124-room luxury hotel with ski-in access, 57 condos (most with fractional ownership), a fine-dining restaurant and après ski bar, and an outdoor heated pool and hot tub, health club, and spa. They're all under one roof in Wyoming's third-largest building.

BED-AND-BREAKFASTS

Jackson hosts many fine B&Bs, where those who can afford it can relax in comfort at the homes of locals. Be sure to reserve space far ahead during the peak summer season, although you might get lucky at the last minute if someone cancels. The **Jackson Hole Bed & Breakfast Association's** website, www.jacksonholebnb.com, has links to a half-dozen local B&Bs, all of which are described as follows.

Teton View

On the way to Teton Village, Teton View B&B, 2136 Coyote Loop, 307/733-7954 or 866/504-7954, www.tetonview.com, features two guest rooms that share a bath ($115 d) and one with its own bath ($150 d). Guests enjoy a full breakfast and a dramatic view of the Tetons from the indoor hot tub. A five-night minimum stay is required in winter and two nights in summer. The owners also rent out a comfortable cabin with space for six, a kitchen, and private yard; $175 d plus $20 per person for additional guests. Breakfast is not included, and the cabin is available only in the summer.

Alpine House Country Inn

You'll find outdoorsy owners at Alpine House Country Inn, 285 N. Glenwood, 307/739-1570 or 800/753-1421, www.alpinehouse.com; both Hans and Nancy Johnstone were skiers for U.S. Olympic teams. The modern timber-frame lodge is just two blocks from Jackson's Town Square and has 21 guest rooms in two connected buildings. Both are bright and modern, accented by Swedish-style stenciling on the walls. All rooms have private baths and balconies, plus access to the outdoor hot tub. A healthy full breakfast is served, along with evening wine and cheese. Rates are $155 d in the original rooms, and $170–215 d in the new building, which also features TVs and air-conditioning, along with gas fireplaces and hot tubs in most rooms. Suites cost $265 for up to four guests. Children are welcome for $25 extra.

Huff House Inn

For quiet close-to-downtown accommodations, another fine option is The Huff House Inn, 240 E. Deloney Ave., 307/733-4164, www.jacksonwyomingbnb.com. Built in 1916, this was for many years the home of one of Jackson's first doctors, Charles Huff. Today it

is a gracious place with a feminine sense of style. The three guest rooms ($139 d) are attractive, and all have private baths. Also available are four modern cottages with cathedral ceilings, king-size beds, sleeper-sofas, VCRs, and hot tubs. These go for $215 d. An outdoor hot tub is on the premises, and a creative full breakfast is served family-style each morning. Kids are welcome in the cottages. A three-night minimum is generally required, but shorter stays may be available.

The Painted Porch

On the road to Teton Village, The Painted Porch, 3755 N. Moose-Wilson Rd., 307/733-1981, www.jacksonholebedandbreakfast.com, was built in 1901 in Idaho and moved here many years later. Located on three acres and surrounded by a white picket fence and tall aspen trees, this rambling red farmhouse has a guest room ($160 d) with a king bed, and a two-room suite ($225 d) with space for the kids. Each has a microwave, fridge, TV/VCR, private bath with jetted tub, and access to the game room that includes a pool table. For more privacy, stay in the adjacent cottage for $180 d. The fridge has juice and fruit, or you can join breakfast in the house for an extra $20. An outdoor hot tub and game room with pool table are available for guests, and children are welcome ($25 extra) in the suite and cabin. A two-night minimum stay is required; closed Nov. to late Dec. and Apr. to mid-June.

Teton Treehouse

A personal favorite—it gets high marks from all who visit—is Teton Treehouse B&B, 307/733-3233, www.cruising-america.com/tetontreehouse, a gorgeous four-story hillside home in Wilson. This spacious open-beam B&B sits up 95 steps (needless to say, it's not accessible for disabled people) and contains six guest rooms with private baths. It really does offer the feeling of living in a treehouse, and it's a great place for birdwatchers. Decks provide impressive views across the valley below, and you can soak in the outdoor hot tub each evening and enjoy a healthy full breakfast each morning. Rooms cost $165–200 d. No young children, but ages 10 and older are welcome. There's a three-night minimum stay in July and August.

Sassy Moose Inn

Near the Aspens along the road to Teton Village, The Sassy Moose Inn, 307/733-1277 or 800/356-1277, www.sassymoose.com, is a modest log house with five guest rooms, each with private bath, TV, and VCR. A full breakfast is served each morning, along with complimentary wine and fruit in the evening. An indoor hot tub is also available. Rates are $129–189 d. Family rooms provide space for kids, and pets are welcome (a rarity for B&Bs).

Wildflower Inn

A recommended place is Wildflower Inn, 307/733-4710, www.jacksonholewildflower.com. This spacious log house sits on three acres of country land along Teton Village Road and contains five bright guest rooms. Four rooms have their own private decks, and all contain private baths and handcrafted lodgepole beds. One of the rooms is actually a suite with a separate sitting room, hot tub, and gas fireplace. Wildflower's hot tub occupies a plant-filled solarium. The owner/builders are an Exum climbing guide and a former ski instructor. Rates are $220–260 d ($340 d in the suite) including an earthy breakfast served family-style. Children are welcome.

Bentwood

One of the most impressive local lodging options is Bentwood B&B, just north of the junction on the road to Teton Village, 307/739-1411, www.bentwoodinn.com. This 6,000-square-foot log home sits amid tall cottonwood trees and is a favorite place for weddings and receptions. The grand living room is centered on a three-story stone fireplace, and each of the five luxurious guest rooms has its own fireplace, TV, deck or balcony, and jetted tub. The loft room is perfect for families. The interior is filled with Western styling and English antiques, not to mention gracious hosts and the enormous chocolate Lab. Drinks and hors d'oeuvres are served each evening, and morning brings a creative breakfast. Rates are $255–325 d. Children are welcome in this very special place. A three-night minimum stay is sometimes required in the summer.

Don't Fence Me Inn

This 5,000-square-foot custom log home sits on six acres along Teton Village Road, 307/733-7979, www.dontfencemeinn.com. The home is set back from the road, with a pond in the back and an active osprey nest nearby. Four large bedrooms ($199 d) and a suite ($259 for up to four guests) are available, all with private baths. Relax in the large common area with its crackling fire or soak in the outdoor hot tub. A gourmet breakfast is served each morning, and children are welcome.

CONDOMINIUM RENTALS

Condominiums provide a popular option for families and groups visiting Jackson Hole. These privately owned places are maintained by several local property-management companies and range from small studio apartments to spacious five-bedroom houses. All are completely furnished (including dishes) and have fireplaces, cable TV, phones, and midstay maid service. The nicest also include access to pools and hot tubs and have balconies overlooking the spectacular Tetons. Many of the condominiums are in Teton Village (adjacent to the ski area) or just to the south in Teton Pines or the Aspens; others are scattered around Jackson Hole.

Condo prices vary widely, but during the winter holiday season (Christmas to early January), expect to pay $160–185 per night for studios (one or two people). Two-bedroom units (up to four people) cost $275–425 per night, and full four-bedroom condos (these sleep eight and also have a private hot tub and stone fireplace) are $720–800. The most sumptuous places, such as those at the base of the tram, will set you back $1,500 per night in the peak winter season! Summer and off-peak winter rates are typically 35–45 percent lower, with spring and fall rates 50–75 percent less than peak-season prices. In fall or spring, condos offer a real bargain for traveling families looking to stay several nights in the area. Minimum stays of 2–7 nights are required throughout the year, with the longest minimum stays required in the peak winter season. Midstay maid service is generally offered if you stay more than five nights.

If you have the luxury of time, do a little comparison shopping before renting a condo. Things to ask include whether you have access to a pool and hot tub, how close you are to the ski slopes, how frequent the maid service is, and whether the units include such amenities as VCRs and washing machines. Also be sure to find out what beds are in the rooms because couples might not enjoy sleeping in twin bunk beds.

Condo Companies

For condo rental information, including prices and available dates, you can go to www.jackson-holenet.com and click on lodging for connections to most of the larger condo companies. You can also contact the following companies directly:

Black Diamond Vacation Rentals, 307/733-6170 or 800/325-8605, www.blackdiamond-vrre.com

Ely & Associates, 307/733-8604 or 800/735-8310, www.jackson-hole-vacations.com

Jackson Hole Lodge, 307/733-2992 or 800/604-9404, www.jacksonholelodge.com

Jackson Hole Resort Lodging, 307/733-3990 or 800/443-8613, www.jhresortlodging.com

Jackson Home Management, 307/739-3000 or 800/739-3009, www.wy-biz.com/jacksonhome

Mountain Property Management, 307/733-1684 or 800/992-9948, www.mpmjh.com

MTA Resorts of Jackson Hole, 307/733-0613 or 800/272-8824, www.mtaresorts.com

Rendezvous Mountain Rentals, 307/739-9050 or 888/739-2565, www.rmrentals.com

Snow King Resort Condominiums, 307/733-5200 or 800/522-5464, www.snowking.com

Spring Creek Ranch, 307/733-8833 or 800/443-6139, www.springcreekranch.com

Teton Pines Resort & Country Club, 307/733-1005 or 800/238-2223, www.tetonpines.com

The largest of these companies—and a good place to begin your search—is Jackson Hole Resort Lodging. Owned by Jackson Hole Mountain Resort, it manages more than 260 units, more than all of the other companies combined.

Among the largest of the other management companies on the list are Black Diamond Vacation Rentals, Jackson Hole Lodge, and Snow King Resort Condominiums.

CABINS

Several Jackson Hole places offer log cabin accommodations for a taste of old-time living. These small places are generally rented for several days or a week at a time and are favorites of families and groups. They may or may not have TVs and phones, and maid service may not be on a daily basis. In addition to these places, several log cabin motels were described previously, with others available in Grand Teton National Park and at Teton Village KOA.

North of Jackson

Out in the quiet town of Kelly (12 miles northeast of Jackson), **Anne Kent Cabins,** 307/733-4773, www.annekentcabins.com, offers rustic accommodations with an unbeatable Teton view. These cabins are perfect for those who want a real taste of Wyoming from a family with a long local history. Two rental options are available. Your best bet is to request the very comfortable log house, which has bedrooms in the loft and basement, two baths, a complete kitchen, washer, and dryer. The home could sleep 12 people in a pinch and goes for $200 per night (plus $25 per person for more than four guests). Next door are two cabins that rent together and sleep four guests for $150. The front one (built in 1939) includes a bedroom and kitchen, while the back cabin contains a second bedroom plus bath. The Anne Kent Cabins feature handmade lodgepole furniture created by co-owner Ron Davler, who crafts them at the adjacent Jackson Hole Log & Rawhide Furniture. Kids under 12 are free.

Moulton Ranch on Historic Mormon Row, 307/733-3749, www.moultonranchcabins.com, offers several cabins in one of Jackson Hole's most majestic locations. This is the only private property on Mormon Row inside Grand Teton National Park, and the much-photographed Moulton Barn—one of the prototypical Wyoming images—is just a few hundred feet away. The four

© DON PITCHER

Anne Kent Cabins

cabins are cozy but not at all elaborate. Nevertheless, where else might you awake to a spectacular Teton vista with bison grazing outside your window? Rates start at $85 for a two-person cabin with a separate bathhouse, up to $135 for four people in the bunkhouse. The latter is especially poplar and features a kitchenette, deck, and picture window facing the Tetons.

Budges' Slide Lake Cabins, 307/733-9061, www.jacksonholecabins.com, are four secluded but modern cabins along Slide Lake, six miles east of Kelly. Each has a woodstove, full kitchen, VCRs, and phone. Rates are $215 d, plus $10 each for each additional guest (maximum of eight). Weekly rates are $1,300 d. Open year-round.

Split Creek Ranch, 307/733-7522, www.splitcreekranch.com, is seven miles north of Jackson and right along the Snake River. The ranch covers 25 acres of land and is a good place to see elk, moose, and other animals. Nine rooms are available. Eight of these are attractive log motel–type units ($95–110 d; plus $10 per person for additional guests) with either kitchenettes or microwaves and fridges. A separate honeymoon cabin ($250 d) includes a fireplace, full kitchen, and private hot tub. Evening campfires are a favorite of guests, and other amenities include a stocked fishing pond and continental breakfasts. There's a two-night minimum stay, and Split Creek is open mid-May through September.

Buffalo Valley

Buffalo Valley Ranch, 307/543-2026 or 888/543-2477, www.heartsix.com, has six cabins with fine views across Buffalo Valley to the Tetons. Three of these cabins are basic older units that share a bathhouse and cost a very reasonable $60 d. A separate triplex log building houses a one-bedroom unit ($100 d), along with a pair of two-bedroom units ($150 for up to four guests), all with kitchenettes and private baths. They're next to Heart Six Ranch in Buffalo Valley, 45 miles northeast of Jackson.

You'll discover spectacular views of the Tetons from **Luton's Teton Cabins,** 36 miles northeast of Jackson (five miles east of Moran Junction), 307/543-2489, www.tetoncabins.com. The modern duplex cabins have full kitchens, private baths, and front porches facing the mountains. One-bedroom units cost $162 d, and two-bedroom units are $250–285 for up to six people. They're open May–November and have horse boarding facilities.

South of Jackson

Camp Creek Inn, 16 miles south of Jackson in quiet Hoback Canyon, 307/733-3099 or 877/338-4868, www.camp-creek-inn.com, has nine A-frame cabins costing $89 for up to four people, or $134 for a unit with three double beds. No TVs or phones in the rooms, but a bar and restaurant are on the grounds. Camp Creek also offers horseback rides, pack trips, fishing trips, and wintertime snowmobiling.

GUEST RANCHES

Several of Wyoming's best-known and most luxurious dude ranches are in Jackson Hole, providing wonderful places for families who are looking to rough-it in style. In addition to the local places listed alphabetically, many more guest ranches are just over Togwotee Pass in the Dubois area and to the south in the Pinedale area; get details on these ranches in the Wind River Mountains Country chapter.

Flat Creek Ranch

Located at the base of Sheep Mountain, Flat Creek Ranch, 307/733-0603 or 866/522-3344, www.flatcreekranch.com, is packed with history. The land was originally homesteaded by cowboy, hunting guide, and rustler Cal Carrington, but he sold it to his close friend, "Countess" Cissy Patterson in 1923. Previously married to a Polish count, Cissy came from a wealthy Chicago newspaper family, but her love of the West and horses matched Cal's. For two decades Cissy and Cal were grist for the gossip mill, mostly during her trips to Wyoming, but also when she took him along on a grand tour of Europe. Cissy died in 1948, and her relatives now own the ranch. After a long hiatus and extensive improvements in 2001, this historic ranch in a gorgeous setting is once again open for guests. The emphasis is on fly-fishing in legendary Flat Creek; the ranch owns

1.5 miles along the stream. Other activities include horseback rides and hikes into the Gros Ventre Wilderness, boating, and a wood-fired sauna for chilly evenings. There's a three-night minimum stay in the summer; $420 for two people per night, all-inclusive. There are separate family periods and times when kids aren't allowed. The ranch is 15 miles up a bumpy dirt road, but the ranch provides transportation if you don't have a four-wheel-drive with high clearance.

Goosewing Ranch

Looking for a peaceful place to relax? Twenty miles up a dirt road in undeveloped Gros Ventre Valley (30 miles northeast of Jackson), Goosewing Ranch, 307/733-5251 or 888/733-5251, www.goosewingranch.com, is one of the most remote guest ranches in Jackson Hole. The well-appointed modern log cabins have fireplaces, private baths, and decks. Guests can use the outdoor hot tub all year and the outdoor heated pool in the summer. Popular summertime activities include horseback excursions, riding instruction, fishing, and hiking. All-inclusive weekly summertime rates are $3,260 for two people. There's a three-night minimum stay. When winter arrives, the ranch becomes a favorite destination for snowmobiling, with a variety of packages available.

Gros Ventre River Ranch

This small ranch has accommodations for up to 34 guests in modern log cabins and a homestead house and is known for its delicious meals. The ranch sits up undiscovered Gros Ventre River Valley, 18 miles northeast of Jackson near Slide Lake. The main activities are horseback riding, world-class fly-fishing, cookouts, canoeing, and mountain biking. The lodge has a pool table, table tennis, and a large-screen television. A one-week minimum stay is required May–October, and summertime weekly all-inclusive rates are $2,720 for two people. Contact Gros Ventre River Ranch at 307/733-4138, www.grosventreriverranch.com.

Heart Six Ranch

This classic family dude ranch is in the heart of Buffalo Valley, 12 miles east of Moran Junction and 43 miles northeast of Jackson. Horseback rides are a star attraction, along with kids' programs, day trips to Yellowstone National Park and the Jackson Hole rodeo, and a range of evening activities including cookouts, nature programs, and country music. All-inclusive weekly rates are $2,900 for two people. The ranch takes in up to 50 guests at a time and is open year-round. Only weekly stays are available June–August, but at other times of the year the ranch offers nightly lodging. This is a favorite base for snowmobilers mid-December through March. Contact Heart Six Ranch at 307/543-2477 or 888/543-2477, www.heartsix.com.

Lost Creek Ranch

Wyoming's most elaborate—and expensive—guest ranch, Lost Creek Ranch, 307/733-3435, www.lostcreek.com, is 21 miles north of Jackson. This showplace resort emphasizes fitness, with a spa facility that includes exercise classes, a weight room, steam room, sauna, and hot tub, along with massage and facials (extra charge). Guests stay in modern duplex log cabins and enjoy gourmet meals in the main lodge's patio overlooking the Tetons. Amenities include such nontraditional items as a heated swimming pool, tennis courts, and a skeet range, in addition to more standard horseback riding, kids' programs, float trips, hiking, Yellowstone tours, and fly-fishing. It's all a bit too Disneyesque for my tastes, and the prices are too Madison Avenue. Weekly all-inclusive rates run $5,400 for two people in a duplex cabin or an astounding $12,425 for four people (even if two of these are children!) in a luxurious two-bedroom, two-bath cabin with a living room and fireplace. Some consider this a small price to pay for such pampering. The ranch hosts up to 60 guests at a time and is open late May to mid-October. A one-week minimum stay is required except after Labor Day, when it drops to a three-night minimum.

R Lazy S Ranch

Another historic dude ranch is R Lazy S Ranch, 13 miles northeast of Jackson, 307/733-2655, www.rlazys.com. The ranch has space for 45 guests, who enjoy horseback rides, fishing, and other Western adventures. Tykes under age seven are not allowed, but teenagers can take advantage of a special program just for them. A one-week minimum stay is required. All-inclusive rates are $2,225–3,110 for two people per week, and the ranch is open early June through September.

Red Rock Ranch

Located along the rolling Gros Ventre River, Red Rock Ranch, 307/733-6288, www.theredrockranch.com, faces spectacular orange-red badlands. The ranch is 32 miles northeast of Jackson, and the quiet location and drop-dead-gorgeous scenery are reason enough to stay here. Guests settle into comfortable log cabins with woodstoves, and they can take part in horseback riding, cattle drives, cookouts, and other activities. The ranch also features kids' programs, stocked fishing ponds, a swimming pool, and a hot tub. There's space for a maximum of 30 guests, and a six-night minimum stay is required. Open June to early Sept. All-inclusive weekly rates are $3,170 for two adults.

Spotted Horse Ranch

Located on the banks of the Hoback River, 16 miles south of Jackson, this ranch exudes a comfortable rusticity. The main lodge and cabins contain lodgepole furniture, and guests stay in log cabins with modern conveniences. Activities include horseback riding (some Appaloosas), fly-fishing, and cookouts, and you can unwind in the hot tub or sauna. All-inclusive weekly rates are $3,800 for two adults. A three-night minimum stay is required. Contact Spotted Horse Ranch at 307/733-2097 or 800/528-2084, www.spottedhorseranch.com.

Triangle X Ranch

Located within Grand Teton National Park, 25 miles north of Jackson, Triangle X Ranch, 307/733-2183 or 888/860-0005, www.trianglex.com, is a classic family-oriented ranch with unmatched Teton views. The ranch has been in the Turner family for more than six decades, and the acclaimed author Barry Lopez once worked as a wrangler here. Horseback riding is the main focus, but they also offer

JACKSON HOLE

kids' programs and nightly events such as Dutch-oven cookouts, naturalist presentations, square dancing, and campfire sing-alongs. All-inclusive weekly rates are $2,600 for two adults. The ranch is open May–October and January–March. In winter Triangle X goes upscale, with fewer guests (maximum of 35 versus 80 in the summer), a hot tub, and three gourmet meals a day. The nightly winter rate is $200 d, including lodging, meals, and use of cross-country skis and snowshoes. There's a two-night minimum stay in winter and a one-week minimum stay in summer.

Turpin Meadow Ranch

A longtime favorite—it began taking guests in the 1920s—is Turpin Meadow Ranch, 307/543-2496 or 800/743-2496, www.turpin-meadowranch.com. The ranch's Buffalo Valley location provides impressive Teton vistas, along with all of the traditional ranch activities: horseback riding, cookouts, fishing, and pack trips, plus weekly nature programs by Forest Service naturalists. Guests stay in modern cabins and have access to an indoor hot tub. Summertime all-inclusive rates are $175 per day for two adults, with a three-night minimum stay. The ranch is open year-round and is a favorite snowmobile spot in winter.

MOUNTAIN RESORTS

Two noteworthy mountain resorts are east of Moran Junction off U.S. Hwy. 26/287. At Togwotee Pass (9,658 feet) the highway tops the Continental Divide and then slides eastward towards Dubois and the Wind River Valley. The Togwotee Pass area is famous for luxuriously deep snow all winter and is a destination for snowmobilers, cross-country skiers, and dogsledding enthusiasts. Just north of the pass is Teton Wilderness, a place to discover what solitude means. Facing west from the pass, the Teton Range offers a jagged horizon line. This entire area provides a delicious escape from hectic Jackson and is home to two attractive high-elevation resorts: Cowboy Village Resort at Togwotee and Brooks Lake Lodge.

Cowboy Village Resort at Togwotee

Forty-eight miles northeast of Jackson and just a few miles west of Togwotee Pass is Cowboy Village Resort at Togwotee, 307/733-8800 or 800/543-2847, www.cowboyvillage.com, a pleasantly rustic place to spend a night or a week. The resort is a busy place, offering horseback rides, mountain-bike tours, fly-fishing, a ranger-naturalist program, and backcountry pack trips in summer, along with snowmobiling (the primary winter activity), dogsledding, and cross-country skiing when the snow flies. Togwotee has a variety of accommodations, and guests will enjoy the sauna and four large hot tubs. Summer rates are $109 d for rooms in the lodge, $129 d for mini-suites, and $159 d for cabins. The mini-suites and cabins sleep up to six people ($10 per person for more than two). In winter, the resort has package deals that include lodging, breakfast and dinner, snowmobile use, a guide, and free airport shuttle. There's a four-night minimum stay in winter. The resort also houses a steak house, bar, gas station, and convenience store. Togwotee is closed from early April to mid-May, and from mid-October to late November.

Brooks Lake Lodge

This lodge may have the finest location of any Wyoming resort, with a placid lake in front and the cliffs of Pinnacle Buttes nearby. Built in 1922, it has long served travelers en route to Yellowstone, and its enormous great hall contains big-game trophies from all over the world. The lodge was completely restored in the late 1980s and is now on the National Register of Historic Places. Six guest rooms are available in the main lodge, and six private cabins are hidden in the trees; all are furnished with handmade lodgepole furniture. In addition, three luxurious suites are available, along with a recently added spa that features a workout room, sauna, and a large outdoor hot tub; massages are extra. Guests can ease into the hot tub or pull on hiking or cowboy boots to explore the magnificent country nearby.

The turnoff for Brooks Lake Lodge is 65 miles northeast of Jackson (34 miles east of Moran Junction) and another five miles off the highway via Brooks Lake Road. The lodge is open late June to mid-September and late December to early March. There's a three-night minimum stay, and the two-person rates are $500 per day in the lodge, $560 per day in the cabins, or $600 in the luxury suites. Weekly rates are also available, but be sure to reserve far ahead. These rates include gourmet meals, horseback riding, canoeing, and fishing in summer, or meals, cross-country skis, and snowshoes in winter. Snowmobile rentals are also available for guests, and dogsled tours are offered. Contact Brooks Lake Lodge at 307/455-2121, www.brookslake.com.

Camping

PUBLIC CAMPGROUNDS

Both the National Park Service and the U.S. Forest Service maintain campgrounds around Jackson Hole. The Jackson Hole/Grand Teton Public Campgrounds chart shows two-dozen public campgrounds within 50 miles of Jackson. For more specifics on public sites, contact Bridger-Teton National Forest in Jackson at 340 N. Cache Dr., 307/739-5500, www.fs.fed.us/btnf, or Grand Teton National Park in Moose, 307/739-3603, www.nps.gov/grte. In addition to these sites, many people camp for free on dispersed sites on Forest Service lands; see the Forest Service for locations and restrictions.

RV PARKS

Jackson has several RV parks scattered around town and in surrounding areas, but the rates are shockingly high in midsummer. Additional privately run campgrounds are located at Colter Bay and Flagg Ranch Resort inside Grand Teton National Park.

None of the private RV parks in the town of Jackson is really noteworthy; "parking lots" would be a better term. They can also be surprisingly expensive: Some places charge more for a tent space than it would cost to stay in a motel room in many Wyoming towns! Even more expensive is a ticket for parking RVs overnight on Jackson city streets. It's illegal to do so, and local police strictly enforce the ordinance.

Virginian RV Park, 750 W. Broadway, 307/733-7189 or 800/321-6982 (summer) or 800/262-4999 (winter), www.virginianlodge.com, is the biggest RV parking lot in the area, with more than 100 sites (including many pull-through sites) on the south end of town. Full hookups cost $40–50; no tents. Guests at the RV park can use the Virginian Lodge's outdoor pool and hot tub. The park is open May to mid-October.

Wagon Wheel RV Park & Campground, 525 N. Cache, 307/733-4588, www.wagonwheelvillage.com, is along Flat Creek on the north end of town. Located behind the motel of the same name, it has both RV hookups ($42 d) and grassy tent spaces ($24 d) and is open May–September.

Teton Village KOA, 307/733-5354 or 800/562-9043, www.koa.com, is five miles south of Teton Village and six miles from Jackson. The location is out of the way and quiet, with trees providing shade (lacking in other local RV parks). Full RV hookups cost $40 d, tent sites are $30 d, and basic camping cabins run $50–57 d. Also here are a game room and playground. It's open May to mid-October.

Grand Teton Park RV Resort is 37 miles northeast of Jackson (six miles east of Moran Junction) along Hwy. 26/287, 307/733-1980 or 800/563-6469, www.yellowstonerv.com. There are fine views of the Tetons, and facilities include a heated seasonal pool and hot tub, recreation room, and grocery store. The cost is $42 d for RVs with hookups, $30 d for tents. Simple camping cabins go for $52–58 d, and tepees run $39–43. Open year-round.

Two private campgrounds are in the Hoback Junction area, 12 miles south of Jackson. **Lazy J Corral,** 307/733-1554, is right on the highway at Hoback Junction, but the rates are low: RV sites

JACKSON HOLE

JACKSON HOLE PUBLIC CAMPGROUNDS

The following public campgrounds are available on a first-come, first-served basis with no reservations. They are listed by distance and direction from Jackson. Get details for each from Bridger-Teton National Forest (BTNF; 307/739-5400; www.fs.fed.us/btnf/teton), Grand Teton National Park (GTNP; 307/739-3603; www.nps.gov/grte), or Caribou-Targhee National Forest (CTNF; 208/354-2312; www.fs.fed.us/r4/caribou). See the text for private RV campgrounds in the area.

Campgrounds North of Jackson

Curtis Canyon Campground; seven miles northeast of Jackson; open late May–Sept.; $12; BTNF; six miles of gravel road with a fine view of the Tetons

Gros Ventre Campground; 10 miles northeast of Jackson; open May to mid-Oct.; $12; GTNP; along Gros Ventre River; dump station; campground often fills by evening in midsummer

Atherton Creek Campground; 18 miles northeast of Jackson; open Memorial Day to Sept.; 12; BTNF; six miles up Gros Ventre Rd. near Gros Ventre River

Jenny Lake Campground; 20 miles north of Jackson; open mid-May to late Sept.; $12; GTNP; tents only (no RVs); campground fills by 8 A.M. in midsummer

Red Hills Campground; 22 miles northeast of Jackson; open late May–Sept.; $10; BTNF; 12 miles up Gros Ventre Rd. (partly dirt) along Gros Ventre River

Crystal Creek Campground; 23 miles northeast of Jackson; open late May–Sept.; $10; BTNF; five miles up Gros Ventre Rd. (gravel) along Gros Ventre River

Signal Mountain Campground; 32 miles north of Jackson; open mid-May to mid-Oct.; $12; GTNP; on Jackson Lake; dump station; no vehicles over 30 feet; campground fills by 10 A.M. in midsummer

Colter Bay Campground; 40 miles north of Jackson; open mid-May to mid-Sept.; $12; GTNP; on Jackson Lake; coin-operated showers and laundry nearby, dump station; campground fills by noon in midsummer

Hatchet Campground; 40 miles northeast of Jackson; open June–Sept.; $10; BTNF; in Buffalo Valley eight miles east of Moran Junction

Box Creek Campground; 46 miles northeast of Jackson; open mid-June through Sept.; $10; BTNF; on Buffalo Valley Rd., no potable water

Pacific Creek Campground; 46 miles north of

---

with full hookups for $22. They do not have tent spaces and are open May–October. **Snake River Park KOA,** 307/733-7078 or 800/562-1878, www.koa.com, is one mile north of Hoback Junction and has RV spaces for $40 d, tent sites for $30 d, and simple "kamping kabins" for $52–62 d. Open Apr. to mid-Oct. The KOA has a little riverside beach and a game room.

Food

Jackson stands out from the rest of Wyoming on the culinary scene: chicken-fried steak may be available, but it certainly isn't the house specialty! You won't need to look far to find good food; in fact, the town seems to overflow with memorable (and even more memorably priced) eateries. If you stood in Town Square and walked in any direction for a block you would find at least one restaurant that would be a standout in any other Wyoming town. More than 70 local restaurants do business here—in a town that contains just 9,000 people.

To get an idea of what to expect at local restaurants, pick up a copy of the free *Jackson Hole Dining Guide* at the visitors center or local restaurants. You'll find the same information online at www.focusproductions.com/jhdining. The guide includes sample menus and brief descriptions of many local establishments. If you don't find a place to your liking among those

Jackson; open mid-June through Sept.; $5; BTNF; nine miles up Pacific Creek Rd. (enter through Grand Teton National Park)

Lizard Creek Campground; 48 miles north of Jackson; open early June to early Sept.; $12; GTNP; on Jackson Lake; no vehicles over 30 feet; campground fills by 2 P.M. in midsummer

Turpin Campground; 48 miles northeast of Jackson; open June–Sept.; $10; BTNF; in Buffalo Valley 10 miles east of Moran Junction

Angles Campground; 49 miles north of Jackson; open mid-June through Sept.; $10; BTNF; small site one-half mile northeast of Cowboy Village Resort on U.S. 287

Sheffield Creek Campground; 55 miles north of Jackson; open mid-June through Sept.; $5; BTNF; small campground off Hwy. 89/191/287 near Flagg Ranch Resort; poor road access until late summer

Campgrounds South of Jackson

Cabin Creek Campground; 19 miles south of Jackson; open late May–Sept.; $10; BTNF; along Snake River Canyon five miles from Hoback Junction

Elbow Campground; 22 miles south of Jackson; open late May–Sept.; $10; BTNF; along Snake River Canyon six miles from Hoback Junction

Hoback Campground; 22 miles southeast of Jackson; open late May–Sept.; $12; BTNF; along Hoback River seven miles east of Hoback Junction

East Table Creek Campground; 24 miles south of Jackson; open late May–Sept.; $15; BTNF; along Snake River 8.5 miles southwest of Hoback Junction

Kozy Campground; 19 miles southeast of Jackson; open late May–Sept.; $12; BTNF; along Hoback River seven miles southeast of Hoback Junction

Granite Campground; 35 miles southeast of Jackson; open late May–Sept.; $15; BTNF; near Granite Hot Springs, nine miles up Granite Creek Rd. (gravel)

Campgrounds West of Jackson

Trail Creek Campground; 20 miles west of Jackson; open mid-May to mid-Sept.; $8; CTNF; on the west side of Teton Pass. Reservations ($9 extra charge) at 518/885-3639 or 877/444-6777

Mike Harris Campground; 21 miles west of Jackson; open mid-May to mid-Sept.; $8; CTNF; on the west side of Teton Pass

JACKSON HOLE

listed here or in the dining guide, be assured that all of the major fast-food outlets line Jackson's streets, ready to grease your digestive tract.

BREAKFAST

The best breakfast place in Jackson isn't in Jackson, but in Wilson, where **Nora's Fish Creek Inn,** 307/733-8288, www.jacksonholenet.com/noras, attracts a full house each morning. The food is great, the setting is authentically rustic, and the waitresses are friendly and fast. Nora's also serves tried-and-true lunches and dinners at very good prices, from tuna fish sandwiches for $4.50 to 16-ounce steaks for $19. Highly recommended, but you may have to contend with a smoky atmosphere at the counter in the morning.

Very popular for breakfast and lunch is **Jede-** **diah's House of Sourdough,** 135 E. Broadway, 307/733-5671, www.wy-biz.com/jedediah sourdough, where, as the name implies, sourdough pancakes are the morning specialty. Housed in a 1910 log cabin, the restaurant gets noisy and crowded in the morning, making it perfect for families with young kids. The lunch menu stars burgers, sandwiches, and salads, while the summer-only dinners include steaks, chicken, trout, and burgers. A half-dozen tables are on the deck, shaded by tall cottonwoods.

Another longtime breakfast and lunch standout is **The Bunnery,** 130 N. Cache Dr., 307/733-5474, with good omelets and delicious lunch sandwiches on freshly baked breads, along with fresh salads and homemade soups.

The old-time crowd heads to **LeJay's Sportsman's Cafe,** 72 S. Glenwood St.,

307/733-3110, a greasy spoon that's open 24 hours a day. This is the place to go when no other restaurant is open and your stomach is demanding all-American grub. But be ready for clouds of cigarette smoke.

LUNCH

One of the most popular noontime spots in Jackson is **Sweetwater Restaurant,** 85 King St., 307/733-3553, where the lunch menu includes dependably good salads, homemade soups, and a variety of earthy sandwiches. For dinner, try Moroccan lamb over couscous or the roasted eggplant and leek lasagna. Dinner entrées are $13–28. Recommended.

Get delicious sub sandwiches on tangy homemade bread at **New York City Sub Shop,** 20 N. Jackson St., 307/733-4414. It's a little pricey ($6 for a half hoagie or more than $10 for a whole), but the service is fast, and the hot sandwiches are always vastly better than Subway. Definitely recommended.

Pearl Street Bagels, 145 Pearl St., 307/739-1218, serves home-baked bagels (they're on the small side, however) along with good espresso and juices. Open daily until 6 P.M. in summer. They have a second shop in Wilson, 307/739-1261. The latter is *the* groovy place to be seen in Wilson (OK, so are Nora's and the 'Coach).

If you're in search of a substantial vegetarian breakfast or lunch, try the café at **Harvest Natural Foods,** 130 W. Broadway, 307/733-5418. The salad-and-soup bar in the back is a favorite lunch break for locals. Great sandwiches, fruit smoothies, and baked goods are offered, too. You won't go wrong here.

Much to the chagrin of locals (and visitors), Jackson's famous corner drug store closed in 2001, and the historic stone building is now occupied by a rug gallery. Fortunately, **Jackson's Original Soda Fountain,** 307/733-5260, has opened a half-block away at 85 Cache Street, with the same old backbar and a similar menu that includes sandwiches, homemade ice cream, shakes, banana splits, floats, sundaes, inexpensive sandwiches, and chili.

ESPRESSO AND LIGHT MEALS

The hip crowd heads for breakfast and lunch to two excellent local cafés: Betty Rock and Shades. **Betty Rock Cafe and Coffeehouse,** 325 W. Pearl, 307/733-0747, is a great and noisy place for lunch, with delectable homemade breads, paninis, wraps, salads, soups, and espresso. Highly recommended. You'll find similar food and service at the oft-crowded **Shades Cafe,** 82 S. King St., 307/733-2015. This tiny log cabin has a shady summer-only patio on the side. Breakfasts feature waffles, egg dishes, fruit, and yogurt, plus lattes, mochas, and other coffee drinks. At lunch, the standouts are salads, quiches, burritos, and paninis. Shades is a relaxing place to hang out with the latte habitués, although it does close early in the fall, winter, and spring.

Out in Teton Village across from the tram, **Village Cafe,** 307/733-2233, serves very good breakfasts, baked goods, sandwiches, wraps, pizza by the slice, espresso, and microbrewed beer. Open summers and winters only.

AMERICAN

Jackson's most popular family eatery is **Bubba's Bar-B-Que Restaurant,** 515 W. Broadway, 307/733-2288. Each evening the parking lot out front is jammed with folks waiting patiently for a chance to gnaw on barbecued spare ribs, savor the spicy chicken wings, or fill up at the salad bar. Get there before 6:30 for shorter lines. Lunch is a real bargain, with specials for less than $6. Drinks come in recycled Mason jars, but they don't serve alcohol, so BYOB (no corkage fee). Cheap breakfasts are served, too. Although based in Jackson, Bubba's now has restaurants in five other locations around Wyoming, Colorado, and Idaho.

Get great all-American burgers at the '50s-style **Billy's Burgers,** 55 N. Cache Dr., 307/733-3279, adjacent to the more upscale Cadillac Grille. The Billy burger is a half-pound monster. It's not on the menu, but recommended if you aren't absolutely famished is the one-third-pound Betty burger. Ask for it.

Next door to Billy's and in the basement of the bar of the same name, the **Million Dollar Cowboy Steakhouse**, 307/733-4790, www.milliondollarcowboybar.com, offers "casual Western elegance" and great steaks, from porterhouse to filet mignon. In addition, the menu includes salads, rack of lamb, seafood, pasta, ribs, and vegetarian specials. The bar features a dozen different single-malt scotches. Not for kids, and not cheap: entrées are $20–32. Reservations are advised.

Also popular is **Gun Barrel Steakhouse**, 862 W. Broadway, 307/733-3287, www.gunbarrel.com, where the mesquite-grilled steaks, elk, and buffalo are served in a hunting-lodge atmosphere with trophy game mounts; they came from a wildlife museum that previously occupied the site. You'll find lots of historic guns and other Old West paraphernalia around the Gun Barrel too, making this an interesting place to explore even if you aren't hungry. It's a bit on the pricey side, with dinner entrées for $16–26. The bar has a wide choice of beers on tap.

The classic Wort Hotel at 50 N. Glenwood St., 307/733-2190, www.worthotel.com, is home to **Silver Dollar Bar & Grill,** with chop house fare, including buffalo prime rib, elk chops, fresh mahi-mahi, and seafood linguini in a white-linen setting. Very good Caesar salads are served, too. The bar next door is a fun place for an after-dinner drink, and the Plug Nickel Cafe features home-style family dining.

A very popular place with both locals and ski bums is the **Mangy Moose** in Teton Village, 307/733-4913, where you'll find a big salad bar and fair prices on steak, prime rib, pasta, chicken, and fresh fish (dinner entrées $12–36). It's a fun and lively place. Downstairs is The Rocky Mountain Oyster (don't ask), offering killer breakfasts and inexpensive burgers, pizza, and sandwiches for lunch.

Get chicken atchaflaya, seafood gumbo, and other Cajun specialties at **The Acadian House**, 180 N. Millward, 307/739-1269. The menu has broadened lately and now includes a diversity of other entrées, including ginseng tea–basted duck, grilled tuna, and Thai curry vegetable sauté. Don't miss the Louisiana bread pudding for dessert.

The menu and setting at **Teton Steakhouse,** 40 W. Pearl St., 307/733-2639, www.tetonsteakhouse.com, reflect this restaurant's previous incarnation as a Sizzler, but that doesn't faze anyone. The central location (one block off Town Square), inexpensive stuff-yourself meals, and noisy, kid-friendly setting bring a crowd every day. Line up to put in your order for steaks, ribs, or chicken, or just sidle up to the big salad, soup, and dessert bar to fill your plate. Steaks are $10–20, and they also have a cheap breakfast buffet. No booze is sold here, but bring your own beer or wine and they'll provide the glasses (no corkage fee).

See **Chuck Wagon Cookouts** section for outfits that combine cowboy cookery with Old West entertainment.

PASTA AND PIZZA

One of the tried-and-true local eateries is **Anthony's Italian Restaurant**, 62 S. Glenwood St., 307/733-3717. In business since 1977, Anthony's has built a reputation for simple food (a bit heavy for some tastes) and attentive, efficient service. Vegetarians will find several good menu items. Meals come with homemade soup, salad, and fresh-baked garlic bread—guaranteed to fill you up and then some. Open for dinner only.

Hidden away on the north end of town, **Nani's Genuine Pasta House,** 242 N. Glenwood, 307/733-3888, www.nanis.com, is Jackson's gourmet Italian restaurant. Meals are served in a charming little home with an old-country ambience and friendly service. Prices are surprisingly reasonable, with most entrées for $10–20. Many vegetarian and vegan dishes are available, and be sure to ask about the nightly specials. Nani's is open for dinner year-round, plus lunch in the summer.

Several pizza places stand out in Jackson. You'll find **Calico Italian Restaurant & Bar,** 307/733-2460, www.calicorestaurant.com, in a garish red-and-white building three-quarters of a mile north on Teton Village Road. The menu has gone a bit upscale, but prices are still reasonable: $11–19 entrees. Thursday means tapas night. During the summer, be sure to get a side salad, fresh from the big house garden. The bar at Calico is a very popular locals' watering hole. Kids love the 2.5-acre lawn/playground.

Mountain High Pizza Pie, 120 W. Broadway, 307/733-3646, www.mountainhighpizza.com, is a favorite downtown place offering free delivery in Jackson. In the winter Mountain High also serves pizza by the slice.

For other notable pizza places, see Yellowstone Garage and Grand Teton Brewing Company.

CONTINENTAL/NOUVELLE CUISINE

If you want fine continental dining and aren't deterred by entrées costing $20 or more, Jackson has much to offer you.

Just off Town Square, **Snake River Grill,** upstairs at 84 E. Broadway, 307/733-0557, www.snakerivergrill.com, is one of Jackson's finest gourmet restaurants—with prices to match (most entrées $18–35). The meals are exquisite, and the seasonal menu typically contains a variety of seafood, free-range beef, and organic vegetables that are artfully presented. The wine list is equally impressive, and a few outside tables face the square. Reservations are a must; reserve one week in advance for prime-time seatings in the summer. Try the fallen chocolate soufflé for dessert. Snake River Grill is a good place to watch for Jackson's best-known resident, Harrison Ford. Closed Nov. and Apr.

For views so spectacular they make it difficult to concentrate on your meal, don't miss **The Granary,** 307/733-8833 or 800/443-6139, www.springcreekranch.com, located atop East Gros Ventre Butte west of Jackson. This is also a very popular place for evening cocktails. Dinner entrées run $22–32 and include rack of lamb, fresh seafood, and a very popular elk tenderloin.

Jackson's most popular nouvelle cuisine restaurant is **Cadillac Grille,** 55 N. Cache (on the square), 307/733-3279. The food is artfully prepared and includes a changing menu of seafood, grilled meats, and game. The art deco decor of the Cadillac helps make it one of the most crowded tourist hangouts in town. The restaurant includes

a bar and rear patio for summertime dining under the stars. Dinner entrées run $14–30.

Old Yellowstone Garage, 115 Center St., 307/734-6161, serves exceptional Italian meals that can be matched with their Italian wines. There's outside dining in the summer, and most entrees cost $16–36. The restaurant was formerly located in an old garage in Dubois, hence the name. Yellowstone Garage is famous for their all-you-can-eat Sunday pizza fest. Servers come around as each pie emerges from the oven, offering slices to diners. Don't come here expecting to eat and run because the pizzas are served at a leisurely pace that can be annoying to some folks. The owners say this is in keeping with the Italian ambience, but it also means you'll probably be ordering drinks and salads while you wait. The restaurant is open for dinners only and closed Mondays.

Inside the ultra-luxurious Amangani Resort atop Gros Ventre Butte, **Amangani Grill,** 307/734-7333 or 877/734-7333, www.amanre-

© DON PITCHER

The luxurious Amangani Resort houses the popular Amangani Grill.

sorts.com, is open to the public for three meals a day, with a menu that includes seared ahi tuna, grilled filet of beef, venison loin, and a wonderful Caesar salad. Great breakfasts are served, too; try the smoked trout eggs Benedict. Reservations are advised, and this is decidedly *not* a place for T-shirts or shorts. Dinner entrées run $27–32.

Out in the Aspens on Teton Village Road, **Stiegler's,** 307/733-1071, has a menu with names big enough to eat—you could start with leberknödel suppe, before a main course of veal sweetbreads forestiere, followed by a topfen palatschinken. The dense Austrian cuisine is outstanding, and the service is exceptional. If you're around in the fall, make reservations for their popular Oktoberfest, a celebration of Austrian food and beer.

Alpenhof, 307/733-3462, is another fine Teton Village dining experience, with a changing menu that often features rack of lamb, tenderloin of venison, Barbarie duck, and some wonderful appetizers, not to mention an award-winning wine list. The **Alpenhof Bistro** upstairs has a more casual setting and a less-expensive dinner menu. People come to the bistro for balcony dining with a close-up view of Teton Village.

MEXICAN AND CARIBBEAN

For the fastest Mexican food in town (with the possible exception of Taco Bell), drop by **Pica's Mexican Taqueria,** 307/734-4457. You'll find tasty tacos, burritos, quesadillas, enchiladas, and tortas in a hip setting. The shop is in the Buffalo Junction strip mall at 1160 Alpine Lane (near the Albertson's store).

In business since 1969, **The Merry Piglets,** 160 N. Cache Dr., 307/733-2966, serves very good Mexican meals, including their specialty, the cheese crisp. Excellent margaritas, pitchers of beer, and an open front section add to the appeal.

Pato Restaurant, 680 E. Broadway, 307/739-9191, is an out-of-the-way place with eclectic offerings inspired by Central American and Caribbean cookery. I suppose you could think of it as World Beat food. On the menu are such items as shrimp Cubano, spice-rubbed ribeye, achiote chicken, fish tacos, and even Vietnamese

spring rolls. They use locally grown organic vegetables when possible and have a great Sunday brunch.

ASIAN
Chinese
Chinatown Restaurant, 850 W. Broadway, 307/733-8856, makes good Chinese dishes—particularly the mu shu vegetables, lemon chicken, and pot stickers—and offers $5.50 weekday lunch specials.

Looking for a fast and filling Chinese meal? **Hong Kong Buffet,** in Grand Teton Plaza at 826 W. Broadway, 307/734-8988, is popular and cheap.

Japanese
Nikai, 225 N. Cache, 307/734-6490, is open for dinner only, and reservations are advised. Creatively prepared sushi is the main attraction, but the restaurant also has a menu of Asian fusion items from the open kitchen, including tuna ume, miso-crusted pork, and wakame seaweed salad. The atmosphere is contemporary and stylish. Most items cost $10–19.

Get freshly rolled sushi, including a variety of vegetarian rolls, at **Masa Sushi,** 307/733-2311, located inside The Inn at Jackson Hole in Teton Village.

Thai
In the previous edition of this book I bemoaned the lack of Thai restaurants in Jackson. Fortunately, two local places have stepped up for those of us who love food from Thailand. **Thai Me Up,** 75 E. Pearl St., 307/733-0005, has a gimmicky name and chefs born in the United States, but the food is spicy and delicious. They're open for dinners only seven days a week and have a few sidewalk tables. The location is a bit quieter than places on the Square, but the entrées aren't cheap: $10–18. The restaurant is closed in April and May. Recommended.

For the downscale version, check out **Teton Thai Restaurant,** across the street from Teton Theater at 135 N. Cache Drive, 307/733-0022, with a handful of plastic tables and seats under a

JACKSON HOLE

covered deck. The food is simple and authentic, with lunch specials such as chicken satae or tom yum koong for $7–8.

BREWERIES

Grand Teton Brewing Company, 208/787-4000, www.grandtetonbrewing.com, now brews just over Teton Pass in Victor, Idaho, where you can sample Teton Ale, Old Faithful Ale, Moose Juice Stout, Teton Golden Ale, Teton Huckleberry Wheat, and Sweetgrass IPA. You'll find them on tap at many Jackson-area bars and restaurants and for sale in six-pack bottles.

An old downtown warehouse has been beautifully transformed into **Snake River Brewing Co. & Restaurant,** 265 S. Millward, 307/739-2337, www.snakeriverbrewing.com. The bright and spacious setting fills with a convivial crowd of young outdoors enthusiasts most evenings, and the bar generally has seven of their award-winning beers on tap. Particularly notable—they've all won gold medals at various brew festivals—are Zonker Stout, Snake River Lager, and Snake River Pale Ale. The lunch and dinner café menu includes delicious thin-crust pizzas and calzones baked in their cherrywood-fired oven, flavorful appetizers, daily pasta specials, sandwiches, and salads. It's great food in a lively atmosphere, and one of *the* places to be seen in Jackson. Most dinner entrées run $9–11, but they have a variety of $6 lunch specials.

WINE SHOPS

The most complete local wine and beer shops are **Westside Wine & Spirits,** in the Aspens along Teton Village Rd., 307/733-5038; **The Liquor Store,** next to Albertson's on W. Broadway, 307/733-4466, www.wineliquorbeer.com; and **Dornan's Wine Shoppe** in Moose, 307/733-2415, ext. 202, www.dornans.com. The Liquor Store features an impressive upstairs wine department and a wine bar with free wine tastings Friday and Saturday evenings. You can even use their computer to check your email. **Jackson Hole Wine Company,** 200 W. Broadway, 307/739-9463, also has a fine selection and offers

free Friday evening wine tastings all summer long, with a different choice of wines each week. It's a great way to learn about various vintages from wine experts. You'll generally find the lowest wine prices from **Jackson's Original Discount Liquor Store at Sidewinders,** on West Broadway, 307/734-5766.

BAKERIES

The Bunnery, 130 N. Cache Dr., 307/733-5474, bakes a big variety of treats and sweets, but it's best known for its hearty-flavored OSM (oat, sunflower, and millet) bread—on the pricey side at around $4.50 a loaf. Another place for fresh-baked—and organic—goods is **Harvest Natural Foods,** 130 W. Broadway, 307/733-5418.

The location is a bit out of the way, but a visit to **Wildflour Bakery,** 345 N. Glenwood, 307/734-2455, is a must if you're in search of French baguettes and other breads (different choice every day). Tasty pastries, cookies, and muffins are served, too. You can also find the company's goods in several local grocers, and they bake the house bread for several of Jackson's gourmet restaurants.

GROCERIES AND NATURAL FOODS

Get groceries from the large **Albertson's,** on the south end of town at the corner of Buffalo Way and Broadway, 307/733-5950. Inside you'll find a bakery, pharmacy, deli, one-hour photo lab, bank branch, and coffee bar. A few blocks farther south (right in front of the high school) is the new **Smith's,** 1425 South U.S. Hwy. 89, 307/733-8908, www.smithsfoodanddrug.com, with the same features as Albertson's.

Meet the locals at the less ostentatious (and generally cheaper) **Food Town,** in the Powderhorn Mall at 970 W. Broadway, 307/733-0450. The best spot for fresh vegetables and fruit is the little **market stand** next to the Maverik gas station on the south end of town. It's open Thursday–Saturday only in the summer, and it has better prices and higher quality than local grocers. In business since 1947, **Jackson Hole Buf-**

falo Meat, 1655 Berger Lane, 307/733-8343 or 800/543-6328, www.buybuffalomeat.com, sells smoked buffalo salami, jerky, sausage, steaks, and burgers, along with buffalo meat gift packs and New Zealand elk steaks.

For health foods, head downtown to **Harvest Natural Foods,** 130 W. Broadway, 307/733-5418, or to the smaller **Here & Now Natural Foods,** 1925 Moose-Wilson Rd., 307/733-2742.

Jackson's popular **Farmers Market** comes to Town Square Saturdays 8–11 A.M. in the summer. Shop for fresh veggies, fruits, and other farm products, including flowers. Live music and cooking demonstrations add to the attraction.

Entertainment and the Arts

NIGHTLIFE

Barflies will keep buzzing in Jackson, especially during midsummer and midwinter, when visitors pack local saloons every night of the week. At least one nightclub always seems to have live tunes; check Jackson's free newspapers to see what's where. Cover charges are generally $3–5 on the weekends, and most other times you'll get in free.

The famous **Million Dollar Cowboy Bar,** on the west side of Town Square, 307/733-2207, www.milliondollarcowboybar.com, is a favorite of real cowboys and their wannabe cousins. Inside the Cowboy you'll discover burled lodgepole pine beams, four pool tables (nearly always in use), display cases with stuffed dead bears and other cuddly critters, bars inlaid with old silver dollars, and barstools made from old saddles. Until the 1950s, the Cowboy was Jackson's center for illegal gambling. Bartenders kept a close eye on Teton Pass, where messengers used mirrors to deliver warnings of coming federal revenuers, giving folks at the bar time to hide the gaming tables in a back room. Today the dance floor fills with honky-tonking couples as the bands croon lonesome cowboy tunes six nights a week. Looking to learn swing and two-step dancing? Every Thursday you can join an excellent free beginners' class at 7:30 P.M., then dance up a storm when the band comes on at 9.

Just across the square and up the stairs is **Rancher Spirits & Billiards,** 307/733-3886, where the room is filled with a half dozen tables for billiards aficionados.

Silver Dollar Bar & Grill, in the Wort Hotel at 50 N. Glenwood St., 307/733-2190, offers a setting that might seem more fitting in Las Vegas: gaudy pink neon lights curve around a bar inlaid with 2,032 (count 'em!) silver dollars. It tends to attract an older crowd (best martinis in Jackson), and the music is generally of the piano or acoustic variety.

Right next to the tram in Teton Village is **Mangy Moose Saloon,** 307/733-4913, Jackson Hole's jumpingest pickup spot and *the* place to rock out. The Moose attracts a hip skier/outdoorsy crowd with rock, blues, or World Beat bands Wednesday–Saturday both summer and winter. This is also where you'll hear nationally known acts.

Sidewinders Tavern & Sports Grill, on West Broadway, 307/734-5766, is filled with big-screen TVs for sports enthusiasts. Smokers head to the cigar bar, but there's also a big smoke-free section.

The **Shady Lady Saloon** at Snow King Resort, 400 E. Snow King Ave., 307/733-5200, typically serves up live music most Wednesday nights, along with a Tuesday DJ and open mike Fridays. More popular is the Monday night **Jackson Hole Hootenanny,** held in the lodge room of the Snow King Center throughout the summer, or at the nearby ice rink in spring and fall. Local and visiting musicians get together to jam in an all-acoustic set, and anyone can join the onstage fun if they have musical talent—or can pretend.

Over in Wilson, **The Stagecoach Bar,** 307/733-4407, is *the* place to be on Sunday nights 6–10 P.M. (Wyoming bars close their doors at 10 P.M. on Sunday.) In the early '70s, when hippies risked getting their heads shaved by rednecks at Jackson's Cowboy Bar, they found the 'Coach a more tolerant place. Today tobacco-chewing cowpokes show their partners slick moves on the tiny dance floor as the Stagecoach

Band (jokingly known as the "worst country-western band in the U.S.") runs through the country tunes one more time; the band has performed here every Sunday since February 16, 1969! Outside you'll find picnic tables and a volleyball court for pickup games in the summer, or pick up a cue stick and show off you billiard skills indoors. The bar food is notable, especially the buffalo burgers.

CLASSICAL MUSIC

In existence since 1962, the **Grand Teton Music Festival** takes place at Walk Festival Hall in Teton Village, with performances of classical and modern works by a cast of 200 world-renowned symphony musicians. Concerts take place evenings late June to mid-August each year, with chamber music on Tuesday and Wednesday, small ensembles on Thursday, and festival orchestra concerts on Friday and Saturday. They also perform a free outdoor "Music in the Hole" concert on the Fourth of July, plus special young people's concerts in July and August. The three-hour-long Friday morning rehearsals are just $10. Call 307/733-3050 for a schedule of events and ticket prices, or get details on the web at www.gtmf.org.

MUSICALS AND MOVIES

In addition to the bar scene, summers bring several lighthearted acting ventures to Jackson. For family musicals such as *Paint Your Wagon, The Unsinkable Molly Brown,* or *Oklahoma,* head to **Jackson Hole Playhouse,** 145 W. Deloney, 307/733-6994, www.jhplayhouse.com. Shows take place Monday–Saturday evenings in a campy 1890s-style setting. A family saloon (no alcohol) and restaurant are next door.

Productions of Broadway and Western musical comedies play throughout the summer at **Mainstage Theatre,** in Pink Garter Plaza at 50 W. Broadway, 307/733-3670, www.jacksonholetheatre.com. The rest of the year, the Mainstage puts on more serious plays from the Performing Arts Company of Jackson Hole and attracts national touring productions. Both Mainstage and Jackson Hole Playhouse are very popular with families, and reservations are strongly recommended.

Watch flicks at **Teton Theatre,** 120 N. Cache Dr., **The Cinema,** 295 W. Pearl St., or **MovieWorks Cinema Four-plex,** 860 South U.S. Hwy. 89. All three of these have the same ownership, phone number, and website: 307/733-4939, www.jhmovies.com.

RODEO

On Wednesday and Saturday nights in summer you can watch bucking broncs, bull riders, barrel racers, rodeo clowns, and hard-riding cowboys at the **Jackson Hole Rodeo** on the Teton County Fair Grounds. Kids get to join in the amusing calf scramble. The rodeo starts at 8 P.M. and costs $10 adults, $8 ages 4–12, free for kids under four, or $30 for the whole family. Rodeos take place Memorial Day to Labor Day, with Saturday night rodeos all summer and Wednesday night rodeos starting in mid-June. Get details at 307/733-2805, www.jhrodeo.com.

CHUCK WAGON COOKOUTS

Jackson Hole is home to several chuck wagon affairs offering all-you-can-eat barbecue cookouts and Western musical performances in the summer. Each has its own advantages, but reservations are highly recommended at all of these.

Bar-T-Five

Run by the Thomas family since 1973, Bar-T-Five, 790 Cache Creek Rd., 307/733-5386 or 800/772-5386, www.bart5.com, is one of the best chuck wagon feeds. Horse-drawn Conestoga-style wagons depart just east of Snow King, carrying visitors along Cache Creek past costumed mountain men, cowboys, and Indians. At the in-the-trees cookout site, cowboys serenade your meal, tell stories, and crack corny jokes that aren't entirely politically correct. It's great fun for families and busloads of Japanese tourists. Rates are $30 adults, $23 ages 6–12, and free for kids under six. Open mid-May through September, with departures at 5:30 and 6:30 P.M. Monday–Saturday. Recommended.

A/OK Corral

Located 10 miles south of Jackson near Hoback Junction, A/OK Corral, 307/733-6556, www.horsecreekranch.com, has 45-minute horseback or wagon rides that end at an outdoor cookout. Big ranch breakfasts and steak suppers are on the menu. Breakfasts cost $33 adults, $12 kids; dinners are $51 adults with the horseback ride, $38 with a covered-wagon ride. For kids, a covered-wagon ride and dinner are $16. Western musical entertainment is provided with the evening meals.

Bar J

Along the Teton Village Road near Teton Pines, the Bar J, 307/733-3370 or 800/905-2275, www.barjchuckwagon.com, does a land office business throughout the summer, with seating for up to 750 people in a cavernous building, including busloads of gray-haired Gray Liners. In existence for more than 25 years, Bar J is famous for its first-rate musicians who fiddle (one is a two-time national fiddle champion), sing, yodel, and regale the audience with cornball jokes and dollops of cowboy poetry. Before the show everyone queues up for heaping servings of barbecued beef, roast chicken, or ribeye steak served with baked potatoes, beans, biscuits, applesauce, spice cake, and lemonade (no alcohol). Amazingly, they manage to feed the entire crowd in a half hour. The picnic-table seating is cramped, but after dinner you're treated to 90 minutes of rollicking entertainment. The cost is $16–24 for adults (depending on your meal), $6 for kids under eight, or free for tots. Bar J is open Memorial Day to late September, with dinner at 7:30 P.M.; many folks arrive earlier to get front-row seats for the show. It's a good idea to make reservations at least one week ahead. The Bar J does not offer wagon or horseback rides.

Castagno Outfitters

Located in beautiful Buffalo Valley, 45 miles northeast of Jackson, Castagno Outfitters Covered Wagon Cookouts start with a 30-minute ride in covered wagons. The wagons stop at an isolated aspen grove, where guests enjoy a dinner of steak, beans, baked potato, salad, and dessert. Dinners cost $25 adults, $20 kids, and run mid-June to late August. They also have breakfast rides for $15 adults, $12 kids. Get details at 307/543-2407, www.castagnooutfitters.com.

JACKSON HOLE

Events

Jackson Hole is packed with entertaining events almost every day of the year. Some of these are homegrown affairs such as the county fair, whereas others attract people from near and far. Of particular note are the International Pedigree Stage Stop Sled Dog Race (IPSSSDR), the Pole-Peddle-Paddle Race, the Elk Antler Auction, the Grand Teton Music Festival, and the Jackson Hole Fall Arts Festival. (In addition to the events listed, see Grand Targhee Ski Resort later in this chapter for a year-round calendar of events on the other side of the Tetons.)

WINTER

December is a particularly beautiful time in downtown Jackson. Lights decorate the elk antler arches, and a variety of events take place. Buy arts and crafts during the **Christmas Bazaar** early in the month, or take the kids to visit Saint Nick and his elves on Town Square starting in mid-December; they're there daily 5–7 P.M.

Kick the year off by watching (or participating in) the annual **torchlight ski parades** at all three local ski areas. They take place on Christmas evening and New Year's Eve at both Jackson Hole Mountain Resort and Grand Targhee Ski Resort, and on New Year's Eve at Snow King.

Each February, local Shriners hold horse-drawn **cutter races**—essentially a wild chariot race on one-quarter mile of ice—at Melody Ranch, six miles south of Jackson. Call 307/733-1938 for more info.

In February, the **Cowboy Ski Challenge** provides a different kind of race, with skiers pulled behind a horse and rider at speeds of up to 40

IPSSSDR

In existence since 1996, the **International Pedigree Stage Stop Sled Dog Race** (IPSSSDR; pronounced IPS-der) is the largest sled dog race in the lower 48 states and a qualifying event for the Iditarod. Unlike the Iditarod and most other mushing events, this one is run in short 30- to 60-mile legs, with teams operating from a different town each day. As with the Tour de France, it's the total time that counts in this stage race. IPSSSDR starts in Jackson and goes on to Dubois, Lander, Evanston, Kemmerer, Alpine, and Pinedale, before a final day out of Teton Village. The race boasts a $100,000 purse and has attracted some of the top names in dog mushing, including Iditarod winners Jeff King, Rick Swenson, and Susan Butcher. It's held over eight days in late January. Get the complete story at 307/734-1163, www.wyomingstagestop.org.

miles per hour. The race takes place at the base of Jackson Hole Mountain Resort.

Ski and snowboard races take place all winter long, ranging from elegant "Powder Eight" Championships in early March to blazingly fast downhill races. (Volunteer to work one of the gates at a downhill race and you get to ski free the rest of the day.)

The ski season ends the first weekend of April with the **Pole-Pedal-Paddle Race,** combining alpine skiing, cross-country skiing, cycling, and canoeing in a wild, tough competition. It's the largest such event in the West and great fun for spectators and contestants, many of whom dress up in goofy costumes. Get the full story at 307/733-6433, www.polepedalpaddle.com.

SPRING

Spring in Jackson Hole is the least favorite time of the year for many locals. The snow is going, leaving behind brown grass and trees; biking and hiking trails aren't yet passable; and the river is too cold to enjoy. For many folks, this is the time to load up the car and head to Utah for a desert hike in Canyonlands. Despite these conditions, April and May can be a good time to visit, especially if you want to avoid the crowds, need to save money on lodging, or are planning to stay for the summer and need a job and a place to live. (Housing gets progressively more difficult to find after April.)

On the third Saturday in May, the world's only public **elk antler auction** takes place at Town Square, attracting hundreds of buyers from all over the globe. Local Boy Scouts collect five tons of antlers from the nearby National Elk Refuge each spring, with 80 percent of the proceeds helping to fund feeding of the elk. This may sound like an odd event, but the take is more than $100,000! Prices average $10 per pound, and the bidding gets highly competitive; perfectly matched pairs can go for more than $2,000. The antlers are used in taxidermy, belt buckles, furniture, and most important, to satisfy the high demand for antlers in the insatiable (pun intended) South Korean and Chinese aphrodisiac markets. There's more than a touch of irony in the Boy Scouts making money from the sale of sexual stimulants! Call 307/733-5935 for more info.

SUMMER

Memorial Day weekend brings **Old West Days,** complete with a parade, street dance, barbecue dinner, cowboy poetry, bed races, pony rides, children's rodeo and games, and **mountain-man rendezvous.** Call 307/733-3316 for details. The **Fourth of July** is another big event in Jackson, with a parade, rodeo, and an impressive fireworks show from Snow King Mountain. Another very popular Fourth of July event is the free **Music in the Hole** outdoor classical concert by the Grand Teton Music Festival orchestra; details at 307/733-1128, www.gtmf.org.

The **Jackson Hole Rodeo** (307/733-2805; www.jhrodeo.com) brings spills and thrills to town, with Saturday night rodeos all summer and Wednesday night rodeos starting in mid-June. Another ongoing event is the **Grand Teton Music Festival,** www.gtmf.org, providing summertime classical music at Teton Village. These latter two activities are detailed in the preceding Entertainment and the Arts section.

The **Mountain Artists' Rendezvous Art Fair** is a great late July event, with more than 100 artisans displaying their works at Miller Park. Contact the Art Association for details, 307/733-8792, www.artassociation.org.

The last week of July brings an always fun **Teton County Fair,** 307/733-5289, www.teton-wyo.org/fai, with 4-H exhibits (from lambs to photography), pig wrestling in the mud, a horse show, free pony rides and a petting zoo, watermelon- and pie-eating contests, live music and comedy acts, a carnival, rodeos, monster trucks, and everyone's favorite: a bang-up demolition derby ($10) on the final Sunday night.

FALL

Jackson Hole is at its most glorious in the fall, as aspens and cottonwoods turn into a fire of yellow and orange against the Teton backdrop. Most tourists have fled back home, leaving locals and hardier visitors to savor the cool autumn nights.

The peak time for **fall colors** is generally the first week of October—considerably later than most people expect.

The primary autumn event is the **Jackson Hole Fall Arts Festival,** featuring exhibits at the National Museum of Wildlife Art and local galleries, a juried art fair, a miniature art show, art and cooking demonstrations, silent auctions, cowboy poetry and old-time cowboy music, and other events over a 10-day period from mid- to late September. Also fun is a "quickdraw" in which artists paint, draw, and sculpt while you watch; the pieces are then auctioned off. For more information and a schedule of the many events, call 307/733-3316, or head to www.jacksonholechamber.com on the web. The festival's **Arts for the Parks National Art Competition** attracts thousands of paintings representing scenes from America's national parks. This isn't for amateurs; the top prize is $50,000. The banquet and silent auction seats fill by mid-August; call 307/733-2787 or 800/553-2787 for reservations (required), or get additional details at www.artsfortheparks.com.

Summer Recreation

RIVER RAFTING

Jackson Hole's most popular summertime recreational activity is running Wyoming's largest river, the Snake. Each year more than 150,000 people climb aboard rafts, canoes, and kayaks to float down placid reaches of the Snake or to blast through the boiling rapids of Snake River Canyon. (As an aside, the name "Snake" comes from the Shoshone Indians, who used serpentine hand movements as sign language for their tribal name—a motion trappers misinterpreted as a snake and applied to the river flowing through Shoshone land.)

Almost 20 different rafting companies offer dozens of raft trips each day of the summer. Although you may be able to walk up and get a raft trip the same day, it's a good idea to reserve ahead for any river trip in July and August. In general, try to book a trip three or four days in advance if possible and at least one week ahead if you need a specific time, prefer an overnight float trip, or are traveling with a larger group. One or two people are more likely to get onboard at the last minute.

You may want to ask around to determine the advantages of each company. Some are cheaper but require you to drive a good distance from town; others offer more experienced crews; still others provide various perks such as fancy meals, U-paddle trips, overnight camps along the river, interpretive trips, or boats with fewer (or more) people. Several operators also lead seven-hour combination trips that include a lazy float followed by a meal break and a wild whitewater run.

The rafting companies generally operate from mid-May to late September, and river conditions change throughout the season. Highest flows—and the wildest rides—are generally in May and June. Get a complete listing of floating and boating outfits, along with descriptive brochures, from the Wyoming State Information Center in Jackson.

Float Trips

The gentlest way to see the Snake is by taking one of the many commercial float trips. Along the way, you'll be treated to stunning views of the Tetons and glimpses of eagles, ospreys, beavers, and perhaps moose or other wildlife along the riverbanks. Several companies—Fort Jackson, Barker-Ewing, Grand Teton Lodge Co., Heart Six, Signal Mountain, Solitude, and Triangle X—offer five- or 10-mile scenic float trips along the quiet stretch within Grand Teton National Park, putting in at Deadman's Bar (10 miles) or Schwabacher Landing (five miles) and taking out in Moose. Flagg Ranch Resort has float and whitewater rafting on the Snake River above Jackson Lake.

Several other rafting operations offer 13-mile South Park float trips *outside the park* (these typically include a lunch), putting in at the bridge near Wilson and taking out above Hoback Junction. Companies offering this trip include Barker-Ewing, Dave Hansen, Flagg Ranch, Lewis & Clark, Sands, Snake River Kayak & Canoe School, and Teton Expeditions. The in-the-park trips are considerably more scenic, so know what you are getting before you sign up because the differences are not usually emphasized by the rafting companies (at least not by those who don't operate inside the park).

Float trip prices on the longer 13-mile runs outside the park typically cost $35–40 for adults and $25–35 for children. Expect to pay around $40 ($25 kids) for the 10-mile trips inside the park, or $25 (18 for kids) for the five-mile in-the-park floats. Age limits vary, but kids must generally be at least eight to float the river. Raft companies usually have folks meet up in either Jackson or Moose, but Heart Six departs from their ranch in Buffalo Valley, 45 miles northeast of Jackson. A wide variety of special voyages are also available from the various companies, including overnight camping and fish-and-float trips.

Call one of the following rafting outfits for details or pick up their slick brochures at the visitors center or from their offices scattered around town: **Barker-Ewing Float Trips,** 307/733-1000 or 800/448-4202, www.barker-ewing.com; **Dave Hansen Whitewater,** 307/733-6295 or 800/732-6295, www.dave-hansenwhitewater.com; **Fort Jackson Scenic Snake River Float Trips,** 307/733-2583 or 800/735-8430, www.scenicfloats.com; **Grand Teton Lodge Float Trips,** 307/543-2811 or 800/628-9988, www.gtlc.com; **Heart Six Ranch,** 307/543-2477 or 888/543-2477, www.heartsix.com; **Lewis & Clark Expeditions,** 307/733-4022 or 800/824-5375, www.lewisandclarkexpeds.com; **Sands Wild Water,** 307/733-4410 or 800/358-8184, www.sandswhitewater.com; **Signal Mountain Lodge & Marina,** 307/733-5470 or 307/543-2831, www.signalmountainlodge.com; **Mad River Boat Trips,** (a.k.a. Snake River Expeditions), 307/733-6203 or 800/458-7238, www.mad-river.com; **Snake River Kayak & Canoe School,** 307/733-9999 or 800/529-2501, www.snakeriverkayak.com; **Solitude Scenic Float Trips,** 307/733-2871 or 888/704-2800, www.solitudefloattrips.com; **Teton Expeditions** (a.k.a. Jackson Hole Whitewater), 307/733-1007 or 888/700-7238, www.tetonexpeditions.com; and **Triangle X Float Trips** (a.k.a. National Park Float Trips), 307/733-5500 or 888/860-0005, www.trianglex.com.

Flagg Ranch Rafting, 307/543-2861 or 800/443-2311, www.flaggranch.com, leads 10-mile float trips down the upper Snake River ($40 adults; $27 kids), starting at Flagg Ranch Resort and heading downriver to Jackson Lake.

You can also float the river with any of the local fishing outfitters and combine angling with drifting downriver. One good company—they give a really personalized tour—is **Wooden Boat River Tours,** 307/732-2628, www.woodboattours.com, which has classic wooden dories.

Note that a few of the raft operators are regarded as "training grounds" for other companies; recommended outfits with good records include Barker-Ewing, Solitude, Grand Teton Lodge Co., and Triangle X.

Whitewater Trips

Below Jackson, the Snake enters the wild Snake River Canyon, a stretch early explorers labeled "the accursed mad river." The usual put-in point for whitewater "rapid-transit" trips is West Table Creek Campground, 26 miles south of Jackson. The take-out point is Sheep Gulch, eight miles downstream. In between, the river rocks and rolls through the narrow canyon, pumping past waterfalls and eagle nests and then over the two biggest rapids, Big Kahuna and Lunch Counter, followed by the smaller Rope and Champagne Rapids. For a look at the action from the highway, stop at the paved turnout at milepost 124, where a trail leads down to Lunch Counter. The river changes greatly throughout the season, with the highest water and wildest rides in June. By August the water has warmed enough for a quick dip. Be sure to ask your river guide about the Jeep that sits in 60 feet of water below Lunch Counter!

Whitewater trips last around 3.5 hours (including transportation from Jackson) and cost around $40 adults, $31 children (age limits vary). Seven-hour combination trips that include a float trip, meal, and whitewater run are around $69 adults, $53 kids. You'll find discounted rates early or late in the summer and with operators who use Titanic-size 16-person rafts. The U-paddle versions are more fun than letting the guide do all the work in an oar raft, and the smaller eight-person rafts provide the most challenging (and wettest) runs. Most companies include round-trip transportation from Jackson.

Expect to get wet, so wear lightweight clothes and bring a jacket for the return ride. Most rafting companies provide wetsuits and booties. Note that this is not exactly a wilderness experience, especially in mid-July, when stretches of the river look like a Los Angeles freeway with traffic jams of rafts, kayaks, inner tubes, and other flotsam and jetsam. The river isn't as crowded on weekdays and early in the morning; take an 8 A.M. run for the fewest people.

Don't take your own camera along unless it's waterproof; bankside float-tographers are positioned along the biggest rapids to shoot both commercial and private rafters. Stop by **Float-O-Graphs,** 130 W. Broadway, 307/733-6453 or 888/478-7427, www.floatographs.com, for a photo from your run. Another company with a similar service is **Whitewater Photos & Video,** 140 N. Cache Dr., 307/733-7015 or 800/948-3426, www.snakeriverphotos.com. Both companies also post photos online.

© DON PITCHER

rafters on the Snake River

For details on whitewater raft trips, contact one of the following companies: **Barker-Ewing Whitewater,** 307/733-1000 or 800/448-4202, www.barker-ewing.com; **Dave Hansen Whitewater,** 307/733-6295 or 800/732-6295, www.davehansenwhitewater.com; **Jackson Hole Whitewater,** 307/733-1007 or 800/700-7238, www.jhww.com; **Lewis & Clark Expeditions,** 307/733-4022 or 800/824-5375, www.lewisandclarkexpeds.com; **Mad River Boat Trips,** 307/733-6203 or 800/458-7238, www.mad-river.com; **Sands Wild Water,** 307/733-4410 or 800/358-8184, www.sandswhitewater.com; **Snake River Kayak & Canoe School,** 307/733-9999 or 800/529-2501, www.snakeriverkayak.com; or **Snake River Park Whitewater,** 307/733-7078 or 800/562-1878, www.srpkoa.com. In addition to these, **Flagg Ranch Rafting,** 307/543-2861 or 800/443-2311, www.flaggranch.com, guides three-hour scenic floats down the upper Snake River (above Jackson Lake) for $40 adults, $27 kids.

Recommended companies with good safety records and well-trained staff include Barker-Ewing, Dave Hansen, and Sands. The largest local rafting company, Mad River, has a reputation as a proving ground for novice guides. It's your choice, but I personally would not raft with Snake River Park Whitewater.

Float It Yourself

Grand Teton National Park in Moose, 307/739-3602, www.nps.gov/grte, has useful information on running the park portions of the river; ask for a copy of *Floating the Snake River*. Note that life jackets, boat permits ($5 for a seven-day permit), and registration are required to run the river through the park, and that inner tubes and air mattresses are prohibited. Floating the gentler parts (from Jackson Lake Dam to just above Pacific Creek) is generally easy for even novice boaters and canoeists, but below that point things get dicier. The water averages two or three feet deep, but it sometimes exceeds 10 feet and flow rates are often more than 8,000 cubic feet per second, creating logjams, braided channels, strong currents, and dangerous sweepers. Peak flows are

between mid-June and early July. Inexperienced rafters or anglers die nearly every year in the river. Flowrate signs are posted at most river landings, the Moose Visitor Center, and the Buffalo Ranger Station in Moran. If you're planning to raft or kayak on the whitewater parts of the Snake River, be sure to contact the Bridger-Teton National Forest office in Jackson, 307/739-5500, for additional information, including their *Snake River Floater's Guide*.

Excellent waterproof maps of the Grand Canyon of the Snake River are sold at the Wyoming State Information Center, 532 N. Cache. In addition to showing the rapids, these maps describe local geology and other features.

Rent rafts from **Leisure Sports** in Jackson at 1075 South U.S. Hwy. 89, 307/733-3040, www.leisuresportsadventure.com; **Riding & Rafts** in Alpine (35 miles southwest of Jackson), 307/654-9900, www.jacksonholeoutfitters.com; **Rent-A-Raft** in Hoback Junction (12 miles south of Jackson), 307/733-2728 or 800/321-7328; or **Snake River Kayak & Canoe School,** 307/733-9999 or 800/529-2501, www.snakeriverkayak.com. Rent whitewater kayaks from Leisure Sports, Snake River Kayak & Canoe School, and **Jackson Hole Kayak School,** 307/733-2471 or 800/733-2471, www.jhkayakschool.com. Both **Alltrans,** 307/733-4325 or 800/443-6133, www.jacksonholealltrans.com, and **Teton Taxi & Backcountry Shuttle,** 307/733-1506, www.tetontaxi.com, offers a shuttle service; around $18 to transport your car from the put-in point to your take-out spot.

FISHING

Jackson Hole has some of the finest angling in Wyoming, with native Snake River cutthroat (a distinct subspecies) and brook trout in the river, along with Mackinaw (lake trout), cutthroat, and brown trout in the lakes. The Snake is a particular favorite of beginning fly-fishing enthusiasts; popular shoreside fishing spots are just below Jackson Lake Dam and near the Wilson Bridge. Jackson Lake may provide higher odds for catching a fish, but you'll need to rent a boat from one of the marinas. This is the place parents take kids. Another very popular fishing hole is just below the dam on Jackson Lake. Flat Creek on the National Elk Refuge is an acclaimed spot for fly-fishing. Note that Wyoming fishing licenses are valid within Grand Teton National Park but not in Yellowstone, where you'll need a separate permit.

Fishing Guides

Many local companies offer guided fly-fishing float trips down the Snake River and other area waterways. Two people (same price for one person) should expect to pay $350 per day for a guide, rods and reels, lunch, and boat. Your fishing license and flies are extra. The visitors center has a listing of local fishing guides and outfitters, and its racks are filled with their brochures.

On Your Own

If you'd rather do it yourself, pick up a copy of the fat and free *Western Fishing Newsletter,* which offers descriptions of regional fishing areas and advice on which lures to try. Find it at **Jack Dennis' Outdoor Shop,** 50 E. Broadway, 307/733-3270 or 800/570-3270, www.jackdennis.com. While there, you may want to buy a regional guide to fishing such as *Flyfisher's Guide to Wyoming* by Ken Retallic (Wilderness Adventures Press; www.wildav. com) or *Fishing Wyoming* by Kenneth Lee Graham (Globe Pequot Press; www.falconbooks.com).

Jackson has several excellent fly-fishing shops, including the aforementioned Jack Dennis' Outdoor Shop. **Westbank Anglers,** 3670 Teton Village Rd., 307/733-6483 or 800/922-3474, www.westbank.com, is a nationally known fly-fishing dealer with a slick mail-order catalog, excellent fishing clinics, and float trips. Both **High Country Flies,** 185 N. Center St., 307/733-7210, www.highcountryflies.com, and **Orvis Jackson Hole,** 485 W. Broadway, 307/733-5407, offer fly-fishing classes and sell quality gear. Rent fishing rods, fly rods, float tubes, and waders from Jack Dennis, High Country Flies, or **Leisure Sports,** 1075 South U.S. Hwy. 89, 307/733-3040, www.leisuresportsadventure.com.

BOATING

Kayaking and Canoeing

In business for more than 25 years, **Snake River Kayak & Canoe School,** 365 N. Cache, 307/733-9999 or 800/529-2501, www.snakeriverkayak.com, offers a wide variety of river kayaking and canoeing classes for all levels of ability, plus fishing trips and raft trips. Full-day private lessons—including transportation, boats, paddles, wetsuit, rubber booties, and lifejackets—cost $330 for two students. Beginners may want to start out with one of the three-hour "rubber duckie" inflatable kayak river trips for $49. In addition, the school has sea kayak tours of all lengths in Yellowstone National Park. They rent practically anything that floats: canoes, sea kayaks, whitewater kayaks, inflatable kayaks, driftboats, and rafts, all with paddles and roof racks included. Also available are dry bags and life jackets.

The folks at **Rendezvous River Sports/Jackson Hole Kayak School,** 945 W. Broadway, 307/733-2471 or 800/733-2471, www.jhkayakschool.com, teach a wide range of kayaking courses from the absolute beginner level to advanced "hairboating" for experts. Classes include kayak roll clinics ($80), river rescue ($135), and special women's and kids' classes. Two-day introductory classes cost $245; four days of instruction is $475. Private lessons are available, and the company rents sea kayaks and whitewater kayaks, plus inflatable kayaks.

Leisure Sports, 1075 South U.S. Hwy. 89, 307/733-3040, www.leisuresportsadventure.com, rents rafts, canoes, inflatable kayaks, water skis, wet suits, dry bags, life jackets, and all sorts of other outdoor equipment (including jet skis). **Adventure Sports** in Moose, 307/733-3307, also rents canoes and kayaks.

HORSEBACK RIDING

Trail Rides

Think of the Wild West and one animal always comes to mind—the horse. A ride on Old Paint gives city slickers a chance to saunter back in time to a simpler era and to simultaneously learn how ornery and opinionated horses can be. If it rains, you'll also learn why cowboys are so enthralled with cowboy hats. In Jackson Hole you can choose from brief half-day trail rides in Grand Teton National Park all the way up to weeklong pack trips into the rugged Teton Wilderness. The visitors center has a brochure listing more than a dozen local outfitters and stables that provide trail rides and pack trips.

For rides by the hour or day (approximately $25 for a one-hour ride or $60–65 for a half-day), try **Scott's Jackson Hole Trail Rides** in Teton Village, 307/733-6992; **Snow King Stables,** behind Snow King Resort, 307/733-5781, www.snowking.com; **Spring Creek Ranch,** atop Gros Ventre Butte off Spring Gulch Rd., 307/733-8833 or 800/443-6139, www.spring creekranch.com; **A/OK Corral,** in Hoback Junction, 307/733-6556, www.horsecreekranch.com; **Mill Iron Ranch,** 10 miles south of Jackson, 307/733-6390 or 888/808-6390, www.mill ironranch.net; or **Goosewing Ranch,** 25 miles east of Kelly near the Gros Ventre Wilderness, 307/733-5251 or 888/733-5251, www.goosewing ranch.com. Of these, Scott's Jackson Hole Trail Rides, Spring Creek Ranch, and Mill Iron Ranch are the most popular, but you probably won't go wrong with any of these companies. Spring Creek Ranch and A/OK Corral also offer rides that include breakfast or dinner cookouts. Farther afield are several companies offering trail rides, including four that operate out of Buffalo Valley (45 miles northeast of Jackson): **Buffalo Valley Ranch,** 307/543-2026 or 888/543-2477; **Castagno Outfitters,** 307/543-2407, www.castagnooutfitters.com; **Two Ocean Pass Ranch & Outfitting,** 307/543-2309 or 800/726-2409; and **Yellowstone Outfitters/Wagons West,** 307/543-2418 or 800/447-4711, www.yellowstoneoutfitters.com. More trail rides are offered at **Cowboy Village Resort at Togwotee,** 307/733-8800 or 800/543-2847, www.cowboyvillage.com, 48 miles northeast of Jackson on the way to Togwotee Pass. The minimum age for horseback riding is typically five or six; these young children typically ride while the horse is being led around by a parent.

Rides of all sorts are available in Grand Teton National Park at **Jackson Lake Lodge** and **Colter Bay Corral;** get specifics at 307/543-2811 or 800/628-9988, www.gtlc.com. In Alpine (35 miles southwest of Jackson), **Riding & Rafts,** 307/654-9900, www.jacksonholeoutfitters.com, offers unguided horse rentals for $15 for the first hour and $12 for subsequent hours; it's the only place for do-it-yourselfers in the area.

Jackson Hole Llamas, 307/739-9582 or 800/830-7316, www.jhllamas.com, offers backcountry treks with these fascinating and gentle animals.

Chuck wagon cookouts are a very popular family option in Jackson Hole during the summer. Guests travel in horse-drawn wagons (or by horseback) and are treated to a delicious all-you-can-eat meal and entertainment. See Chuck Wagon Cookouts (in Entertainment and the Arts) for details.

Wagon Trains

Two local companies lead overnight wagon-train rides (in wagons with rubber tires) into the country around Jackson Hole. Guests split their time between riding in the wagons and riding on horseback. **Wagons West,** 307/543-2418 or 800/447-4711, www.wagonswestwyo.com, heads up into the Mt. Leidy Highlands for 2–6 days. The shortest trips (two days and one night) are $340 adults, $300 kids under 14. Four-day, three-night trips are $650 adults, $575 kids; and six-day, five-night trips run $875 adults, $775 kids. **Double H Bar,** 307/734-6101 or 888/734-6101, www.tetonwagontrain.com, charges $745 adults ($695 ages 9–14, and $645 for younger kids) for a three-night package that includes horseback and wagon riding, meals, and camping gear.

DAY HIKES

The country around Jackson abounds with hundreds of miles of hiking trails, providing recreation opportunities for all levels of ability. Many of the most popular local trails are within nearby **Grand Teton National Park.**. Notable in-the-park hikes are found in the Taggart Lake and Jenny Lake areas, at Colter Bay, and off the Moose-Wilson Road. The Information Center in Jackson has a brochure detailing these hikes.

For a fast trip to the alpine, take the **tram at Jackson Hole Ski Resort** to the summit Rendezvous Mountain ($15), where trails fan out in various directions and the bird's-eye view is hard to beat. See the section Alpine Rides in this chapter for specifics.

A local outdoors shop, Skinny Skis, 65 W. Deloney Ave., 307/733-6094 or 888/733-7205, www.skinnyskis.com, produces an excellent free summertime guide to hiking in the area called *Trailhead.* Another good free source (for Forest Service trails) is *Top Ten Trails,* available from the Bridger-Teton National Forest office at 340 N. Cache Dr. 307/739-5500, www.fs.fed.us/btnf/teton.

Guided Hikes

The **Teton County Parks and Recreation Department,** inside the Recreation Center at 155 E. Gill St., 307/739-9025, www.teton-wyo.org/parks, sponsors a wide range of outdoor activities throughout the summer. Adult hikes ($7–10) take place every Tuesday from May–October, plus on Thursdays from June–August. Longer hikes (including an overnighter) take place several times a summer, and free senior walks are offered on Monday mornings during May and June. For a break from the younguns, take them to the kids outings on Wednesdays (for age five and up; $10–12 for half-day) or Fridays (ages eight and up with more strenuous activities; $26 for all day). You don't need to be a local resident to take part in any of these activities, but reserve ahead because some fill up. The Parks and Rec office also rents out volleyballs, horseshoes, and croquet sets.

Educational nature walks into the mountains around Jackson are offered by **The Hole Hiking Experience,** 307/690-4453 or 866/733-4453, www.holehike.com. Rates start at $55 ($45 for kids) for a four-hour hike. For a free version, Grand Teton National Park offers guided walks and nature talks throughout the year.

Get a geologist's perspective from **Earth Tours,** 307/733-4261, www.earth-tours.com. These outstanding day hikes are led by Dr. Keith Watts and include a ride on the Jackson Hole Resort tram. He also guides full-day trips into Yellowstone.

For a different sort of guided hike, check out the excellent **historical walking tours** offered by the Jackson Hole Museum; they're described under Sights.

MOUNTAIN BIKING

Jackson Hole offers all sorts of adventures for cyclists, particularly those with mountain bikes. Most local bike shops provide maps of local mountain-bike routes, or you can purchase a waterproof Jackson Hole mountain-biking map. Note that mountain bikes are not allowed on hiking trails in Grand Teton National Park or in Forest Service wilderness areas. If you visit Jackson early in the season, check out the Jenny Lake road inside the park; in April it's plowed but closed to cars. It's great for an easy and scenic ride.

Bike Paths

The easiest local places to ride are the **Jackson Hole Community Pathways,** an expanding series of paved paths that may eventually continue for 50 miles. There are ongoing efforts to put a bike path over Teton Pass via the Old Pass Road, thus allowing riders to go all the way to Driggs, Idaho. Get details from the Teton County, 307/733-4609, www.tetonwyo.org/pathways, or from the Friends of Pathways website, www.jh-pathways.com.

Currently a seven-mile path connects Wilson with Teton Village, and a second seven-mile paved trail heads south of town, paralleling the highway to the Snake River bridge. It provides a connection to the very popular Game Creek Trail, which meets the Cache Creek Trail, circling back to Jackson behind Snow King. In addition, the trails at Snow King are open to mountain bikers, and you can either peddle uphill or ride the chairlift with your bike ($8). Jackson Hole Mountain Resort has seven miles of bike trails on the lower sections of the mountain for all levels of ability, although you can't ride the road to the summit or take a bike on the tram.

A four-mile path starts behind the main post office on Maple Way, crosses U.S. Hwy. 89, and continues past the high school before turning north to meet the road to Wilson (State 22). This road has wide shoulders but gets lots of traffic.

Bike Rentals and Tours

Rent mountain bikes from **Teton Cycle Works,** 175 N. Glenwood St., 307/733-4386, www.tetoncycleworks.com; **Hoback Sports,** 40 S. Millward St., 307/733-5335, www.hobacksports.com; **The Edge Sports,** 490 W. Broadway, 307/734-3916; **Wilson Backcountry Sports,** in Teton Village, 307/733-5228; and **Adventure Sports** in Moose, 307/733-3307. All of these places rent bikes and helmets for around $30–40 per day, $20–25 per half day, and several also rent bike trailers, car racks, and kid bikes. Most also sell and repair bikes.

Half-day mountain-bike tours are available for $40–55 per day from **Fat Tire Tours/Hoback Sports,** 307/733-5335, www.hobacksports.com; one of the tours includes a chairlift ride to the top of Snow King. **Teton Mountain Bike Tours,** 307/733-0712 or 800/733-0788, www.tetonmtbike.com, offers scenic half- or all-day bike trips through Grand Teton and Yellowstone National Parks as well as Bridger-Teton National Forest and the National Elk Refuge. These trips are for all levels of ability, with prices starting at $45 for a four-hour ride.

ALPINE RIDES

Jackson Hole Resort

Take a fast and scenic ride to the top of Rendezvous Mountain (10,450 feet) aboard the **aerial tram** at Teton Village. The tram ride takes 10 minutes, gains more than 4,000 feet in elevation, and costs $15 adults, $13 seniors, $5 ages 6–12, and free for kids under six. Details at 307/733-2292 or 888/333-7766, www.jacksonhole.com. Open daily late May to late September, this is a sensational way to reach the alpine. Dogs and bikes aren't allowed on the tram.

On top is a small snack shop, but you should bring a lunch because the choices are limited and pricey. Several trails provide enjoyable hikes from the summit, and naturalists lead free two-hour walks twice daily. Be sure to pack drinking water and a warm jacket.

Rendezvous Mountain is a favorite place for paragliders to launch. Tandem paragliding flights ($200) are available from **Jackson Hole**

Paragliding, 307/739-2626, www.jhparagliding.com. No experience is needed for these half-hour flights.

Snow King

At Snow King Mountain right on the edge of Jackson, the resort's main **chairlift** operates during summer, taking folks for a 20-minute ride to the summit of the 7,751-foot mountain for $8 round-trip. The chairlift runs daily 9 A.M.–8 P.M. in midsummer. On top you'll find a short nature trail and panoramic views of the Tetons.

Also at Snow King is the 2,500-foot-long **Alpine Slide,** a favorite of kids. For anyone older than six, the cost is $8 for one ride or $22 for three rides. For children under six (riding with an adult) it's just $1 per ride. Get details on both the chairlift and slide at 307/733-7680 or 800/522-5464, www.snowking.com.

Grand Targhee

On the other side of the Tetons at **Grand Targhee Ski Resort,** 307/353-2300 or 800/827-4433, www.grandtarghee.com, you can ride the chairlift for $8 ($5 for kids) to the 10,200-foot summit of Fred's Mountain, where Grand Teton stands just seven miles away. The lift operates daily July to mid-August, plus Wednesdays, Saturdays, and Sundays in June, and from mid-August to Labor Day.

SWIMMING AND GYMS

Jackson is home to the marvelous **Teton County/Jackson Recreation Center,** 155 E. Gill St., 307/739-9025, www.tetonwyo.org/parks, which includes an indoor aquatics complex with a lap pool, 185-foot corkscrew water slide, and hot tub, plus a wading pool featuring a waterfall, slide, and water geyser. Basketball and volleyball courts are also inside the Rec Center, and after your workout, relax in the sauna and steam room. Nonresident prices are a steep (but worth it!) $6 adults, $4.75 ages 13–17, $3.50 seniors and ages 3–12, and $16 families; free for tots under three. The rec center also offers a variety of courses and activities, including yoga, toddler swimming, basketball, volleyball, and aerobics. It's open Monday–Friday 6 A.M.–9 P.M., Saturday noon–9 P.M., and Sunday noon–7 P.M.

Out of the way is the wonderful hot mineral pool (93°F in summer and 112°F in winter) at **Granite Hot Springs**, 307/733-6318. Head south 12 miles to Hoback Junction and then 12 miles east on U.S. Hwy. 189 to the turnoff for Granite. The pool is another 10 miles out a well-maintained gravel road—a total of 35 miles from Jackson. Entrance is $5.50 adults, $3.50 ages 3–12, free for infants. Towel and swimsuit rentals are available. The springs are open 10 A.M. until dusk (around 8 P.M.) in summer, and 11 A.M.–5 P.M. in winter; closed fall and spring. No showers or running water at the pool, but vault toilets are nearby.

Teton Rock Gym, 1116 Maple Way, 307/733-0707, www.jacksonholenet.com/tetonrockgym, has large indoor climbing walls, a weight room, and gear rentals. An **outdoor climbing wall** is located in the heart of Teton Village next to the pond. See the Grand Teton National Park chapter for mountain-climbing options.

BALLOON RIDES

Two local companies offer hot air balloon rides in the summer. **Wyoming Balloon Co.,** 307/739-0900, www.wyomingballoon.com, takes off from the Jackson Hole side of the mountains. An hour-long flight is $195 adults, $125 kids (six and older). **Grand Teton Balloon Flights,** 307/733-0470 or 800/378-0470, www.hometown.aol.com/tetonballooning, picks people up in Jackson and transports them over the mountains to Teton Valley, Idaho, for a one-hour flight; $189 per person.

GOLF AND TENNIS

Jackson Hole Golf & Tennis Club, one mile north of town, 307/733-3111, www.gtlc.com, has an 18-hole golf course designed by Robert Trent Jones, Jr. and rated one of the 10 best in America. Also here are a private swimming pool, tennis courts, and The Strutting Grouse Restaurant and Lounge, a perfect place for patio dining in the summer.

JACKSON HOLE

© DON PITCHER

Granite Hot Springs, open in both winter and summer, is nestled in the Bridger-Teton National Forest south of Jackson.

Teton Pines Country Club, on Teton Village Rd., 307/733-1773 or 800/238-2223, www.tetonpines.com, is Jackson Hole's other golf spot. Its Arnold Palmer–designed 18-hole championship course is very challenging; 14 of the holes require over-water shots. The club also features a grand clubhouse, tennis courts, a large (and private) outdoor pool, and fine dining at The Pines restaurant. Both Teton Pines and Jackson Hole Golf & Tennis Club have rentals and lessons for golfers and tennis aficionados. **Public tennis courts** are located on the east end of the rodeo grounds along Snow King Drive, and within Miller Park at Deloney and Gill streets.

For the truly serious professional golfer, **Alpine Miniature Golf,** 307/733-5200 or 800/522-5464, www.snowking.com, has a Lilliputian 18-hole hillside course next to the Alpine Slide at Snow King Resort.

Downhill Skiing and Snowboarding

Jackson Hole has an international reputation as a winter destination. As access has become easier and the facilities more developed, many people have discovered the wonders of a Jackson Hole winter, especially one centered on a week of skiing or snowboarding. Three very different ski resorts attract the crowds: Grand Targhee for downhome, powder-to-the-butt conditions; Snow King for steep, inexpensive, edge-of-town slopes; and Jackson Hole for flashy, world-class skiing. All three places have rental equipment, ski schools, and special programs for kids. Snowboarders and telemarkers are welcome on the slopes. These resorts combine with an incredible abundance of developed and wild places to ski cross-country to make Jackson Hole one of the premier ski and snowboard destinations in America.

See your travel agent for package trips to any of the Jackson-area resorts. For daily ski reports, including information on both downhill and Nordic areas and the backcountry, listen to KMTN (FM 96.9) in the morning.

Ski Club

If you plan to spend more than a couple of days in the area, it is probably worth your while to join the **Jackson Hole Ski Club,** 307/733-6433, www.jhskiclub.com. In return for a $30 annual membership, you receive an impressive number of premiums, including reduced rates for lift tickets and season passes at all three local ski areas, plus discounted lodging, meals, drinks, snowmobile trips, and shopping at dozens of local stores. Join up at any local ski shop.

Ski and Snowboard Rentals

Rent or buy downhill skis and snowboards from **Hoback Sports,** 40 S. Millward St., 307/733-5335, www.hobacksports.com; **Gart Sports,** 485 W. Broadway, 307/733-4449, www.gartsports.com; **Jack Dennis' Outdoor Shop,** 50 E. Broadway, 307/733-3270 or 800/570-3270, www.jackdennis.com, and in Teton Village, 307/733-6838; **Pepi Stiegler Sports** in Teton Village, 307/733-4505; **Wildernest Sports,** Teton Village, 307/733-4297; or **Teton Village Sports,** 307/733-2181 or 800/874-4224, www.skitvs.com. Rentals are also available at all three ski areas.

Snowboarders will find the latest gear at **Boardroom of Jackson Hole,** 245 W. Pearl, 307/733-8327; **Hole in the Wall Snowboard Shop,** 307/739-2689; **Low Rider Board Shop** at Pepi Stiegler Sports in Teton Village, 307/733-4505; and **Village Board Shop,** at Teton Village Sports, 307/733-2181 or 800/874-4224, www.skitvs.com. At Grand Targhee Ski Resort, rent or buy boards from **Phat Fred's,** 307/353-2300 or 800/827-4433, www.grandtarghee.com.

GRAND TARGHEE SKI RESORT

On the west side of the Tetons 42 miles from Jackson, Grand Targhee Ski Resort offers the friendliness of a small resort with the amenities and snow you'd expect at a major one. To get here you'll need to drive into Idaho and turn east at Driggs. The resort sits at the end of a beautiful road (recently rebuilt) 12 miles east of

© DON PITCHER

Driggs and just six miles inside Wyoming. Their motto says it all: "Snow from heaven, not from hoses." With an annual snowfall topping 500 inches (42 feet!)—most of which is champagne powder—Targhee became the spot where powderhounds got all they could ever want. Ski magazines consistently rank it as having North America's best (or second-best) snow. In fact, the resort guarantees its snow: If you find conditions not to your liking, you can turn in your ticket within an hour of purchase and get a "snow check" good for another day of skiing. By the way, the official name is Grand Targhee Ski and Summer Resort, but most folks call it Grand Targhee, or simply Targhee.

Now owned by George Gillett—he previously owned Vail Resort—Grand Targhee has seen some changes in the last few years, including a quad chairlift that opened 500 acres of intermediate skiing terrain on adjacent Peaked Mountain. A second quad chairlift is expected to open for the 2003–2004 winter season, and additional hotel rooms are on the drawing boards. The resort is negotiating a land swap with the Forest Service to gain ownership of the public land on which the resort sits. If this happens (and it is controversial), it could lead to several major developments at Targhee. But some things won't change: the beautifully groomed slopes, the uncrowded and relaxed setting, the dramatic Teton backdrop, and the friendly staff, including at least one cowboy-hatted potato farmer who doubles as a lift operator.

The biggest drawback to Grand Targhee Ski Resort is the same thing that makes it so great—the weather. Lots of snow means lots of clouds and storms, and because it snows so much there are many days when the name cynics apply—"Grand Foghee"—seems more appropriate. Many folks who have returned to Targhee year after year have still not seen the magnificent Grand Teton backdrop behind the ski area! Be sure to bring your goggles. The quad lift up Peaked Mountain provides intermediate skiing on slopes that are more protected and suffer less wind and fog.

Skiing and Snowboarding

Get details for Grand Targhee at 307/353-2300 or 800/827-4433, www.grandtarghee.com. The resort has two quads, one double chairlift, and a surface lift on Fred's Mountain, plus a quad on adjacent Peaked Mountain. The top elevation is 10,230 feet, with the longest run dropping 2,822 feet over almost three miles. Some 750 acres are groomed, but you'll always find track-free skiing on the remaining 2,250 acres of ungroomed powder, so bring your snorkel. In addition, snowcat skiing ($299 per day including lunch and guide) is offered on a 1,000-acre section of Peaked Mountain reserved for powderhounds.

Lift tickets at Grand Targhee cost $49 per day ($36 half day) for adults and $31 per day for children ages 6–14 and seniors (free under age six). Substantial discounts are offered for multi-day lift tickets or lodging-and-ski packages.

Fully 70 percent of Targhee's groomed runs are intermediate to advanced-intermediate, but advanced skiers will find an extraordinary number of deep-powder faces to explore. Snowboarders can play at the half-pipe. The ski school offers lessons for all abilities, and children's programs make it possible for parents to leave their kids behind. Cross-country skiers enjoy the Nordic center (described later), and ski and snowboard rentals are available at the base of the mountain. The ski area usually opens in mid-November and closes in late April, although some years you may be able to ski even into July. Lifts operate 9:30 A.M.–4 P.M. daily.

Other Winter Activities

Moon Mountain Ranch (www.sharplink.com/dogsled) leads **dogsled tours** from the lodge in winter, starting with a half-day trip for $115 per adult for single riders or $200 for two riders. Lunch trips and moonlight rides are also available. Guided **snowshoe wildlife tours** ($16) will appeal to amateur naturalists, and on the **sleigh ride dinner** ($32 adults, $15 kids), you'll ride in a horse-drawn sleigh to a yurt where a Western-style meal is served. Targhee's **tubing park** ($8 per hour; opens at 5 P.M.) is a fun place for kids to slide down a snowy hill, and the resort also has an outdoor **skating pond** and skate rentals ($5). A **Kid's Club** at Targhee provides supervised child care.

Summer Activities

Not far from Grand Targhee are several popular summertime hiking trails within the Jedediah Smith Wilderness. The resort is a popular place to relax in the summer and offers many activities. The quad chairlift ($8 adults, $5 ages 6–14) takes you up the 10,200-foot summit of Fred's Mountain for strikingly close views of the Tetons. The lift operates daily July to mid-August, plus Wednesdays, Saturdays, and Sundays in June, and from mid-August to Labor Day. A Forest Service naturalist leads **guided walks** on weekends, or by request Wednesday–Friday.

Horseback rides and lessons are a favorite Targhee summertime activity; one-hour rides are $24. The area is also a fun mountain-biking destination, with bike rentals and guided tours; you can also take them up the ski lift. The climbing wall ($6) is open to all abilities and is a good place to learn some basic—or advanced—moves. Even more challenging is the adventure ropes course, for those who have always wanted to walk the high wire. There's a special Science Explorers program for older kids, and a Camp Targhee for ones under six, both with tons of fun activities. Other summer activities and facilities at Targhee include a zip line, basketball courts, an outdoor swimming pool and hot tubs, a fitness center, horseshoes, teatherball, tennis, and volleyball. The nine-hole **Targhee Village Golf Course** is just down the road. After all this excitement, you'll probably want to relax with a massage, aromatherapy, facial, or steam bath from the on-site spa.

Based at the resort, the nonprofit **Targhee Institute,** 307/353-2233, directs four-day science programs for ages 6–13 in summer, including a range of fun classes. The institute also offers weeklong Elderhostel programs, covering everything from snowshoeing to photography.

Targhee Accommodations

Call Targhee at 307/353-2300 or 800/827-4433 for details on lodging options at or near the resort, or visit their website: www.grandtarghee.com. The three lodges at the base of the mountain—Targhee Lodge, Teewinot Lodge, and Sioux Lodge—offer ski-in, ski-out access, a large heated outdoor pool, a hot tub, and a workout room. Rates quoted are for the winter holiday season; they're approximately 40 percent lower in summertime. Most lodging places are closed from early September to mid-November, and from mid-April to mid-June.

Get standard motel accommodations at **Targhee Lodge** with holiday winter rates of $181 d. Deluxe hotel rooms with lodgepole furnishings and access to an indoor hot tub are $231 d at **Teewinot Lodge.** The lobby here is a fine place to relax in front of the fire on winter evenings. **Sioux Lodge** continues the Western theme with lodgepole furnishings, but also has kitchenettes, adobe-style fireplaces, and small balconies. Studio units are $331 for up to four people, loft units $436 for four people, and two-bedroom units run $610 for up to eight.

Summer packages are good bargains, including two nights of lodging with breakfast, a scenic chairlift ride, and a one-hour horseback ride; $215 d in the high season. A wide variety of wintertime package deals are also available for stays longer than three nights. One that provides seven nights of lodging and six days of skiing costs $1,700 for two people during the holiday season at Targhee Lodge; rates are considerably higher at Teewinot or Sioux Lodge. You can cut these rates substantially if you ski in the "value" season before mid-December and after late March, with a complete seven-night package for just $1,000 d.

The resort also has off-site condo lodging available approximately 10 miles down the hill at **Teton Creek Resort** and **Powder Valley Condominiums.** Choose from one-, two-, and three-bedroom condominiums, each with a fireplace, kitchen, private patio, and VCR. Outdoor hot tubs are also available. Nightly holiday-season rates start at $210 d for the one-bedroom units, up to $536 for eight people in a three-bedroom unit. Most people rent these condos on a weekly basis; four people can stay in a two-bedroom unit for $3,300 per week during the peak winter holiday season. Rates are, of course, lower if you can come at other times.

In addition to the places at the base of the resort, lodging is available just down the hill in Alta, Wyoming, and in the nearby Idaho towns of Driggs, Victor, and Tetonia. These are described in the Teton Valley, Idaho section of this chapter.

Food and Entertainment

At the base of Grand Targhee is a compact cluster of shops and places to stay. You won't have to walk far to find a cafeteria, pizza place, and burger joint. The nicest place is **Parghee's Steakhouse,** serving hearty breakfasts and lunches, along with cozy dinners. Grand Targhee's social center is the **Trap Bar,** with live music on winter weekends and pub grub on the menu all the time. Guests at Targhee can also take a **horse-drawn sleigh** on a 15-minute ride to a Mongolian-style yurt for a home-cooked steak or chicken dinner. The price is $32 ($15 for kids ages 7–12), and reservations are required. Other shops here sell groceries, ski and snowboard gear, clothing, and gifts. **Lost Horizon Dinner Club,** 307/353-8226, five miles below the resort in the town of Alta, is highly recommended for a relaxing formal dinner with an Asian flair.

Getting There

Grand Targhee is 42 miles northwest of Jackson on the western side of the Tetons in Alta, Wyoming. Get there by driving over Teton Pass (occasionally closed by winter storms), north through Victor and Driggs, Idaho, and then east back into Wyoming.

The **Targhee Express/Alltrans** bus makes daily wintertime trips (90 minutes each way) to Grand Targhee from Jackson Hole. Buses pick up skiers from Jackson and Teton Village hotels shortly after 7 A.M., returning from Targhee at 4:30 P.M. for a round-trip fare of $61, including a full-day lift ticket. Round-trip bus fare without a lift ticket costs $20. Reservations are required; make them before 9 P.M. on the night before by calling 307/733-4325 or 800/443-6133, or on the web at www.jacksonholealltrans.com. Van service is also available year-round to airports in Jackson or Idaho Falls, Idaho.

Events

End the year—and start a new one—with **Torch Light Parades** at Grand Targhee on the evenings of December 25 and 31. Also on New Year's Eve is a fireworks display over the mountain. Each March, the resort celebrates telemark skiing with **Nordic Fest.** Ski races of all sorts take place, and Targhee rocks to great music, an outdoor barbecue, and fun events.

The resort pulls out the stops for the always popular **Targhee Bluegrass Festival** in mid-August, with nationally known acts. Bring your dancin' shoes! The music attracts hundreds of people, so call the resort well ahead of time for camping or lodging reservations. Other big summertime events at Targhee include the **Grand Teton Summer Festival** around Fourth of July and the **WYDAHO Mountain Bike Race,** at the same time.

JACKSON HOLE MOUNTAIN RESORT

Just 12 miles northwest of Jackson is Jackson Hole Mountain Resort, the largest and best-known Wyoming ski area. A true skiers' and snowboarders' mountain, Jackson Hole is considered the most varied and challenging of any American ski area. The powder is usually deep (average snowfall is 38 feet), lift lines are short, the slopes are relatively uncrowded, and the vistas are unbelievable. First opened in 1965, Jackson Hole Mountain Resort has become one of the nation's favorite ski areas. The resort has invested many millions of dollars over the last decade or so, upgrading facilities, adding lifts, expanding snowmaking, completing a spacious children's center, and building an ice rink and snowboarding half-pipe. These improvements have helped expand the resort's reputation as an expert's paradise to also include facilities that are more friendly to families and intermediate skiers.

The mountain has one unusual feature that occurs in midwinter: A temperature inversion frequently develops over the valley, meaning that when it's bitterly cold at the base of the mountain, the top is 15–20°F warmer. Skiers often remain on the upper slopes all day to enjoy these warmer temperatures.

Contact Jackson Hole Mountain Resort at 307/733-2292 or 888/333-7766, www.jackson-hole.com. It is owned by the Kemmerer family, whose ancestors founded the town of Kemmerer, Wyoming, and is one of the few major American ski resorts that is still independently owned.

Superlatives

With an unsurpassed 4,139-foot vertical drop (longest in the United States), 2,500 acres of terrain spread over two adjacent mountains, runs that exceed four miles in length, and 24 miles of groomed trails, Jackson Hole Mountain Resort is truly a place of superlatives. Half of the resort's 60 runs are in the advanced category—including several of the notorious double-diamonds—but it is so large that even rank beginners will find plenty of bunny slopes on which to practice. (As a trivial aside, Montana's Big Sky Resort also claims the longest vertical drop of any American mountain—4,300 feet—but this involves taking three lifts and ending your run below where you start.)

The only way to the summit of 10,450-foot **Rendezvous Mountain** is aboard one of the 63-passenger aerial tram cars. Powered by 500-horsepower engines, they climb nearly 2.5 miles in 10 minutes, offering jaw-dropping views across Jackson Hole. Rendezvous Mountain is where experts strut their stuff on these steep and fast slopes, and if you're not at least close to the expert status you'll find your blood pressure rising as the tram heads up the mountain. More than a few skiers and boarders have taken the tram back down after seeing what lies below. Yes, those death-defying cliff-jumping shots are real; from the tram, check out infamous **Corbet's Couloir,** a rocky gully that requires a leap of faith and suicidal urges.

Fortunately, intermediate skiers and boarders are not given short shrift at Jackson Hole Mountain Resort, particularly on the friendlier slopes of 8,481-foot **Apres Vous Mountain.** Intermediate (and advanced) downhillers could spend all day playing on these slopes, and a high-speed quad here means that riders can blast to the summit of Apres Vous in just five minutes. Because of the speed of this and other lifts, the wait at the base is now usually just a few minutes.

In addition to these lifts, you can ride a gondola, three other quad chairs, a triple chair, double chair, and poma lift. Snowboarders will appreciate the half-pipe and boarders' terrain trail. The resort's Kids Ranch provides supervised day care, including a spacious play area. Not far away is a special "magic carpet" (a conveyer belt of sorts) for children learning to ski or snowboard.

Rates and Services

Get to Teton Village from the town of Jackson by hopping on the START bus ($3 each way; 307/733-4521, www.startbus.com). This is the only inexpensive part of a visit to Jackson Hole Resort because prices for lift tickets approach the stratosphere. Single-day tickets for all lifts (including the tram) are $61 adults ($45 per half day), $48 ages 15–21 ($34 per half day), and $31 kids under 14 and seniors older than 65 ($23 per half day). Multiday all-lift tickets—the most common kind bought—are $280 per week (five days of skiing) for adults, $210 for ages 15–21, and $140 for younger kids under 14 and seniors. Lifts are open 9 A.M.–4 P.M. daily (last tram departs at 3:30 P.M.) from Thanksgiving until early April.

Skis and snowboards can be rented at shops in Jackson or Teton Village. The ski school offers a special Kinderschule program for children, and beginning snowboarders can learn from the pros. Jackson Hole Resort even has special steep snowboarding and skiing camps, where you learn from extreme downhill fanatics. Tommy Moe—gold and silver medalist at the 1994 Winter Olympics—teaches a "Steep and Deep" ski camp and is a ski ambassador for the resort. Jackson Hole's director of skiing (he headed the ski school here for 30 years) is Pepi Stiegler, the Austrian winner of a silver medal in the 1960 Olympics and a gold medal in the 1964 Olympics. You can ski with Pepi on weekdays at 1 P.M.; meet him at the Bridger Gondola.

Ski hosts are scattered around the mountain, ready to provide information and free hourly tours of the slopes from the top of Rendezvous Mountain. Racers and spectators will enjoy NASTAR events each Tuesday, Friday, Saturday, and Sunday, along with various other competitions throughout the winter. (The acronym NASTAR is derived from National Standard Race. In NASTAR, ski racers of all ages and abilities compete against each other, using a handicap system that helps you gauge your progress through the season. See www.nastar.com for complete details.)

For more information on Jackson Hole Mountain Resort, call 307/733-2292 or 888/333-7766. Get recorded snow conditions by calling 307/733-2291; the messages are changed each morning before 5 A.M. Their website, www.jacksonhole.com, is packed with additional details, including the current weather and snow conditions.

Teton Village

At the base of the mountain is the Swiss-style Teton Village—alias "the Vill." Everything skiers and boarders need is crowded together here: lodges, condominiums, espresso stands, restaurants, après-ski bars, gift shops, groceries, ski, snowboard, and snowshoe rentals and lessons, storage lockers, car rentals, a skating pond, child

care, personal trainers, dogsled tours, and even a travel agency for escapes to Hawaii.

On-the-mountain facilities include Casper Restaurant at the bottom of Casper Bowl and snack bars at the top of the tram, the base of Thunder chairlift, and the top of Apres Vous chairlift. Casper Restaurant serves a barbecue picnic most days and is a popular place to join friends for lunch.

SNOW KING RESORT

Snow King Resort has three things that other local ski areas lack: location, location, and location. The resort sits directly behind town and just seven blocks from Town Square. This is the locals' place, Jackson's "town hill," but it also offers surprisingly challenging runs. It may not be the largest or fanciest place around, but the King's ski runs make up in difficulty what they lack in size. From below, the mountain (7,808 feet at the summit) looks impossibly steep and narrow. High atop the big chairlift, the vista provides a panoramic tour of Jackson Hole and the Tetons.

Snow King was the first ski area in Wyoming—it opened in 1939—and one of the first in North America. The original chapter of the National Ski Patrol was established here in 1941. The mountain has a 1,571-foot vertical drop. You'll find more than 400 acres of skiable terrain at Snow King, with the longest run stretching nearly a mile. A triple chair, two double chairs, and a Poma lift climb the mountainside. Other features include snowmaking, a tubing park, and a very popular 300-foot half-pipe and terrain park for snowboarders. It's the only local resort with lights for nighttime skiing.

Rates and Services

Prices for lift tickets at Snow King are well below those at other Jackson Hole resorts: $32 per day ($20 per half day) for adults and $22 per day ($14 per half day) for kids under 15 and seniors. Hours of operation are 9:30 A.M.–4:30 P.M., with **night skiing** (Mon.–Sat. 4:30–8:30 P.M.) available on the lower sections of Snow King for an additional $15 adults or $10 kids and seniors. In addition, the King has special two-hour rates for lift tickets ($15 adults, $10 kids and seniors); these are perfect for skiers and boarders who arrive late in the afternoon and want to hit the slopes for a bit. With some of the best snowmaking in Wyoming, the resort usually opens by Thanksgiving and remains in operation through March.

At the base of Snow King you'll discover a lodge with reasonable ski-and-stay packages, starting at $199 for three nights of lodging, plus breakfasts and two days of skiing. Also at Snow King are two restaurants, the Shady Lady Saloon, ski and snowboard rentals and lessons, plus a variety of other facilities, including an indoor ice rink and mountaintop snack shack. A plethora of lodging options are scattered around the adjacent town of Jackson. Jackson's START buses (307/733-4521, www.startbus.com) offer frequent service to town (free) or Teton Village ($3). For more information on Snow King Resort, call 307/733-5200 or 800/522-5464, or find them on the web at www.snowking.com.

Cross-Country Skiing

For many Jackson Hole residents the word "skiing" means heading across frozen Jenny Lake or telemarking down the bowls of Teton Pass rather than sliding down the slopes of the local resorts. Jackson Hole has become a center for cross-country enthusiasts and offers an impressive range of conditions—from flat-tracking along summertime golf courses where a gourmet restaurant awaits to remote wilderness settings where a complete knowledge of snowpack structure, avalanche hazards, and winter survival techniques is essential. Beginners will probably want to start out at a Nordic center, progressing to local paths and the more gentle lift-serviced ski runs with experience. More advanced skiers will quickly discover incredible snow in the surrounding mountains.

Ski Rentals

Rent or buy cross-country skis from **Skinny Skis,** 65 W. Deloney Ave., 307/733-6094 or 888/733-7205, www.skinnyskis.com; **Teton Mountaineering,** 170 N. Cache Dr., 307/733-3595 or 800/850-3595, www.tetonmtn.com; **Wilson Backcountry Sports,** Wilson, 307/733-5228; or **Leisure Sports,** 1075 South U.S. Hwy. 89, 307/733-3040, www.leisuresportsadventures.com. All of the local Nordic centers also rent equipment. Most places rent both classical cross-country skis and skate skis (much faster and a better workout), along with telemarking and randonnée (alpine touring) skis.

NORDIC CENTERS

Jackson Hole Nordic Center

Nordic skiing enthusiasts will find three different developed facilities near Jackson and others at Grand Targhee and near Togwotee Pass. The largest is Jackson Hole Nordic Center, 307/739-2629, www.jacksonhole.com/skiing, with 17 km of groomed trails—both set track and skating lanes—that cover a wide range of conditions. Call 307/733-2291 for the snow report. Located in Teton Village, this is the best place to learn cross-country skiing. Daily trail passes are $8 per day for adults or $4 per day for children and seniors. Traditional cross-country skis, skate skis, and telemarking equipment are available for rent, and the center offers a wide spectrum of lessons and tours. Hours are daily 8:30 A.M.–4:30 P.M. You can exchange your alpine lift ticket at Jackson Hole Mountain Resort for one at the Nordic center (but, hey, it better be for no extra charge since you've already dropped $61!).

Teton Pines Cross-Country Ski Center

Located along Teton Village Road, Teton Pines, 307/733-1005 or 800/238-2223, www.tetonpines.com, features 14 km of groomed track (both classical and skating) on a summertime golf course. Daily trail passes cost $10 adults or $5 children, and ski rentals and lessons are available. Hours are daily 9 A.M.–5 P.M. The clubhouse here has a restaurant for gourmet après-ski lunches and dinners.

SAFETY IN AVALANCHE COUNTRY

Backcountry skiing is becoming increasingly popular in the mountains surrounding Jackson Hole. Unfortunately, many skiers fail to take the necessary precautions. Given the enormous snowfalls that occur, the steep slopes the snow piles up on, and the high winds that accompany many storms, it should come as no surprise that avalanches are a real danger.

Nearly all avalanches are triggered by the victims. If you really want to avoid avalanches, ski only on groomed ski trails or "bombproof" slopes that, because of aspect, shape, and slope angle, never seem to slide. Unfortunately, this isn't always possible, so an understanding of the conditions that lead to avalanches is imperative for backcountry skiers. The Forest Service produces a useful booklet called *Basic Guidelines for Winter Recreation,* available in many of its offices around Wyoming.

The best way to learn about backcountry safety is through an avalanche class. These are offered in the Jackson Hole area by **American Avalanche Institute,** 307/733-3315, www.avalanchecourse.com; **Exum Mountain Guides,** 307/733-2297, www.exumguides.com; **Jackson Hole Mountain Guides,** 307/733-4979 or 800/239-7642, www.jhmg.com; and **Yöstmark Backcountry Tours,** 208/354-2828, www.yostmark.com. Failing that, you can help protect yourself by following these precautions when you head into the backcountry:

• Before leaving, get up-to-date avalanche information. On the web, you can visit www.avalanche.org for links to avalanche forecasting sites throughout the western states. For the Jackson Hole area, call the Forest Service's 24-hour **Backcountry Avalanche Hazard & Weather Forecast** line at 307/733-2664, or find the forecasts on the web at www.jhavalanche.org. For areas around Yellowstone—including West Yellowstone and Cooke City on the margins and the Washburn Range inside the park—contact the **Avalanche Advisory Hotline** in Bozeman, 406/587-6981, www.mtavalanche.com. If the message says avalanche danger is high, ski on the flats instead. **Jackson Hole Snow Observations,** www.jhsnowobs.org, provides an online forum

where backcountry users share observations on snowpack conditions and avalanche activity.

• Be sure to carry extra warm clothes, water, high-energy snacks, a dual-frequency avalanche transceiver (make sure it's turned on and that you know how to use it!), a lightweight snow shovel (for digging snow pits or excavating avalanche victims), an emergency snow shelter, first-aid supplies, a Swiss Army or Leatherman knife, a topographic map, an extra plastic ski tip, a flashlight, matches, and a compass. Many skiers also carry that cure-all, duct tape, wrapped around a ski pole. Let a responsible person know exactly where you are going and when you expect to return. It's also a good idea to carry special ski poles that extend into probes in case of an avalanche. Check with local ski shops or talk to Forest Service or Park Service folks for details on specific areas.

• Check the angle of an area before you ski through it. Slopes of 30–45 degrees are the most dangerous; lesser slopes do not slide as frequently.

• Watch the weather; winds over 15 mph can pile snow much more deeply on lee slopes, causing dangerous loading on the snowpack. Especially avoid skiing on or below cornices.

• Avoid the leeward side of ridges, where snow loading can be greatest.

• Be aware of gullies and bowls; they're more likely to slip than flat open slopes or ridgetops. Stay out of gullies at the bottom of wide bowls; these are natural avalanche chutes.

• Look out for cracks in the snow, and listen for hollow snow underfoot. These are strong signs of dangerous conditions.

• Look at the trees. Smaller trees may indicate that avalanches rip through an area frequently, knocking over the larger ones. Avalanches can, however, also run through forested areas.

• Know how much new snow has fallen recently. Heavy new snow over older weak snow layers is a sure sign of extreme danger on potential avalanche slopes. Most avalanches slip during or immediately after a storm.

• Learn how to dig a snow pit and how to read the various snow layers. Particularly important are the very weak layers of depth hoar or surface hoar that have been buried under heavy new snow.

JACKSON HOLE

Spring Creek Ranch Nordic Center

Three miles north of State Hwy. 22 on Spring Gulch Road, Spring Creek Ranch, 307/733-1004 or 800/443-6139, www.springcreekranch.com, is open 9:30 A.M.–4:30 P.M. daily. If you're staying in town, you can catch the free shuttle bus at the Wort Hotel; call the Nordic center for specifics. Guests of Spring Creek Ranch ski free here. The center has 15 km of gentle groomed trails with skating lanes, making this perfect for beginners. Trail passes are $10 per day for adults or $7 per day for seniors or kids. Ski rentals and lessons are available.

Grand Targhee Nordic Center

On the west side of the Tetons 42 miles out of Jackson, Grand Targhee Nordic Center, 307/353-2300 or 800/827-4433, www.grandtarghee.com, has 15 km of groomed cross-country ski trails covering rolling terrain. Trail passes are $10 adults and $5 seniors and kids. Lessons and ski rentals are also available. Hours are daily 9:30 A.M.–4 P.M. Guests with Targhee lodging packages can ski free on the cross-country tracks.

ON YOUR OWN

Nordic skiers who would rather explore Jackson Hole and the mountains that surround it on their own will discover an extraordinary range of options, from beginner-level treks along old roads to places where only the most advanced skiers dare venture. Because Jackson has so many cross-country fanatics (and visiting enthusiasts), tracks are quickly broken along the more popular routes, making it easier for those who follow. For complete coverage of all these options, pick up a copy of the helpful free winter outdoors guide *Trailhead* at Skinny Skis, 65 W. Deloney Ave., 307/733-6094 or 888/733-7205, www.skinnyskis.com. The store also rents cross-country, skating, and telemark skis, and snowshoes. If you're heading out on your own, be prepared for deep snow (four feet in the valley) and temperatures that often plummet below zero at night.

The **Teton County Parks and Recreation Department,** 155 E. Gill, 307/739-9025, www.tetonwyo.org/parks, leads a variety of all-day cross-country ski outings most Tuesdays from mid-December to mid-March for $7 per person. Bring your own skis and a lunch; they provide the guide and transportation. The department also offers a full-moon ski tour once each winter.

Ski Tours

Jackson Hole Mountain Guides, 307/733-4979 or 800/239-7642, www.jhmg.com, runs winter ascents of Grand Teton, plus safety and avalanche courses and ski mountaineering trips. Longer winter trips, including a six-day Teton Crest tour, are also available.

Over on the western slopes of the Tetons, **Rendezvous Ski Tours,** 208/787-2906 or 877/754-4887, www.skithetetons.com, maintains three Mongolian-style yurts in the Jedediah Smith Wilderness, each located several hours of skiing (or hiking) from the next. The huts can sleep up to eight and have kitchens, bunks, sleeping bags, and woodstoves. Rates are $180 per night, but you need to be experienced in backcountry skiing and have the necessary safety equipment and avalanche training. If you don't quite measure up, they can provide guided backcountry ski tours to the huts. These start at $340 per person for a two-day and one-night tour.

Both Spring Creek Ranch Nordic Center and Jackson Hole Nordic Center offer guided ski tours into Grand Teton National Park; $45 for a half-day.

Other Winter Recreation

ICE SKATING

Each winter, the town of Wilson floods a hockey-rink-sized part of the town park for skating, hockey, and broomball. A warming hut stands next to the rink. Jackson maintains a smaller ice rink at 155 E. Gill Avenue, plus a rink in Snow King Ballpark which is used for hockey and broomball. All three of these rinks are free to the public and are lighted 6–10 P.M. Call 307/733-5056 for details.

All three local ski resorts have ice skating and skate rentals. You'll find skating ponds in Teton Village at the base of **Jackson Hole Mountain Resort** and over in Alta at **Grand Targhee Ski Resort.** For the out-of-the-elements version, skate over to **Snow King Resort,** where the indoor ice-skating rink is open in the winter and offers skate rentals and lessons.

SNOWSHOEING

Snowshoeing began as a way to get around in the winter, but the old-fashioned wood-and-rawhide snowshoes were bulky and heavy. In recent years snowshoeing has become a popular form of recreation, as new technology created lightweight and easily maneuverable snowshoes. Snowshoeing requires no real training: Just strap them on, grab a pair of poles, and start walking. But be careful where you walk; see the Special Topic "Safety in Avalanche Country" for tips.

Rent snowshoes from **Skinny Skis,** 65 W. Deloney Ave., 307/733-6094 or 888/733-7205, www.skinnyskis.com; **Teton Mountaineering,** 170 N. Cache Dr., 307/733-3595 or 800/850-3595, www.tetonmtn.com; **Gart Sports,** 485 W. Broadway, 307/733-4449, www.gart-sports.com; **Wilson Backcountry Sports,** Wilson, 307/733-5228; **Leisure Sports,** 1075 South U.S. Hwy. 89, 307/733-3040, www.leisure-sportsadventure.com; **Jackson Hole Mountain Resort,** 307/733-2292 or 888/333-7766, www.jacksonhole.com; and **Grand Targhee Ski Resort** in Alta, 307/353-2300 or 800/827-4433.

Guided Trips

Grand Teton National Park has excellent naturalist-led **snowshoe hikes** several times each week during winter. Snowshoes are provided at no charge, and no experience is necessary. These trips generally depart at 2 P.M. from the visitors center in Moose, but for specifics call 307/739-3399. Reservations are required; no kids under eight are permitted. Free naturalist-led snowshoe tours are offered at **Grand Targhee Ski Resort'** details at 307/353-2300 or 800/827-4433, www.grandtarghee.com.

Snowshoe walks into the mountains around Jackson are also offered by **The Hole Hiking Experience,** 307/690-4453 or 866/733-4453, www.holehike.com, the only company permitted to guide snowshoeing trips in nearby national forests. Their most popular trips go to Shadow Mountain north of Kelly. Rates start at $60 ($45 for kids) for a four-hour snowshoe trek.

The Saddlehorn Activity Center at **Jackson Hole Mountain Resort** has snowshoe rentals ($12 per day), along with guided snowshoe tours within Grand Teton National Park: $80 for a half-day or $160 for a full-day tour with lunch. In addition, a snowshoe trail ($5) parallels the ski tracks at the Nordic Center at the resort, and Forest Service naturalists lead occasional snowshoe hikes in the area. Get details at 307/733-2292 or 888/333-7766, www.jacksonhole.com. Snowshoe trails and tours are also available at **Spring Creek Ranch Nordic Center,** three miles north of State 22 on Spring Gulch Rd., 307/733-1004 or 800/443-6139, www.springcreekranch.com.

SLEIGH RIDES

Several companies offer romantic dinner horse-drawn sleigh rides in the Jackson Hole area mid-December through March. Make reservations well in advance for these popular trips. If you don't have the cash for one of these, take a daytime sleigh ride at the National Elk Refuge (described earlier in this chapter).

Jackson Hole Mountain Resort picks up

Teton Village guests for a romantic 30-minute ride to a rustic log cabin where they are served a four-course roast prime-rib or broiled salmon dinner (vegetarian options available) with nightly entertainment. Prices are $57 adults, $35 children under 11, and $16 infants. There are two seatings each night, and reservations are required; call 307/739-2603. Additional details are on the web at www.jacksonhole.com.

Spring Creek Ranch, 307/733-8833 or 800/443-6139, www.springcreekranch.com, has 45-minute afternoon sleigh rides at the top of Gros Ventre Butte for $15 per person. They also have packages that combine a sleigh ride with a meal at the Granary Restaurant. This is one of Jackson's finer restaurants, so bring dress clothes.

Mill Iron Ranch, 307/733-6390 or 888/808-6390, www.millironranch.net, is a friendly family-run operation with evening sleigh rides in a down-home setting 10 miles south of Jackson. Guests get a 30-minute ride that takes you past an elk herd to the lodge for a big T-bone steak dinner; $57 adults, $48 kids. This is the most authentic of the local sleigh rides, but access may require a 4WD vehicle, so call ahead for road conditions.

Dinner sleigh rides are also offered at **Grand Targhee Ski Resort,** 307/353-2300 or 800/827-4433, www.grandtarghee.com, where a horse-drawn sleigh transports you to a remote yurt for a Western-style meal; $32 adults, $15 kids.

TUBING

Two local ski areas have sliding parks with customized inner tubes and rope tows. At Snow King Resort it's called **King Tubes,** 307/734-8823 or 800/522-5464, www.snowking.com, and is available on weekday evenings and weekends after noon. Rates are $10 per hour for adults, $7 per hour for kids. The **Grand Targhee tube park** is open for après-ski fun only (after 5 P.M.) and costs $8 per hour; 307/353-2300 or 800/827-4433, www.grandtarghee.com.

DOGSLEDDING

Founded by Iditarod musher Frank Teasley, **Jackson Hole Iditarod Sled Dog Tours,** 307/733-7388 or 800/554-7388, www.jh-sleddog.com, offers half-day trips ($135 per person including lunch) and all-day trips ($225 per person including a big dinner). The main destination is wonderful Granite Hot Springs, but when snow conditions are right, the teams also run in the Grays River, Shadow Mountain, and Gros Ventre areas. All trips include round-trip transportation from Jackson. Overnight trips to remote lodges are also available for $450–600 per person, depending on the lodge.

Washakie Outfitting, 307/733-3602 or 800/249-0662, www.dogsledwashakie.com, leads a variety of dogsled tours in the Jackson Hole area, using Alaskan husky racing dogs. Rides out of Teton Village are $120 ($80 for kids) and take 1.5 hours. For a more remote experience, join their trips from Cowboy Village Resort at Togwotee (48 miles north of Jackson) or Brooks Lake Lodge (65 miles northeast of Jackson). On these trips, Iditarod veteran Billy Snodgrass offers half-day ($140 adults, $90 kids), full-day ($210 adults, $115 kids), overnight ($450 adults, $280 kids), and trips that combine time behind the dogs with time on a snowmobile.

Continental Divide Dogsled Adventures, 307/739-0165 or 800/531-6874, www.dogsledadventures.com, also leads dogsled tours of the Brooks Lake area, starting with a half-day trip for $175 adults or $80 kids. A variety of longer trips are available, including a three-night adventure with lodging in a surprisingly comfortable yurt; $1,920 per person, with meals. All trips include round-trip transportation from Jackson.

Grand Targhee Ski Resort, 307/353-2300 or 800/827-4433, www.sharplink.com/dogsled, has dogsled trips on the west side of the Tetons. Half-day rates are $115 for one person or $200 for two riders on a sled.

SNOWMOBILING

One of Jackson Hole's most popular—and controversial—wintertime activities is snowmobiling. Hundreds of miles of packed and groomed snowmobile trails head into Bridger-Teton National Forest as well as Yellowstone and Grand Teton National Parks. Some of the most popular places include the Togwotee Pass area 48 miles north of Jackson, Cache Creek Road east of town, and Granite Hot Springs Road 25 miles southeast. More than a dozen different Jackson companies offer guided all-day snowmobile trips into Yellowstone and elsewhere. Yellowstone tours (including breakfast and lunch) typically cost $190–205 for one rider or $250–300 for two riders. Tours to other areas are usually less expensive, and some motels offer package deals.

You can also rent machines for self-guided trips for around $120 per day for one person or $170 for two riders. The visitors center has a complete listing of local snowmobile-rental companies and maps of snowmobile trails.

The 365-mile-long **Continental Divide Snowmobile Trail** passes through the heart of Grand Teton National Park, connecting the Yellowstone road network with snowmobile trails that reach all the way to Atlantic City at the southern end of the Wind River Mountains. Unfortunately, this means that snowmobiles now roar into two of America's great national parks. Don't be a part of this desecration; instead, enjoy these parks in quieter, less hurried ways such as on snowshoes or cross-country skis. If you must use a snowmobile, make sure it is one of the new less-polluting four-stroke versions.

Information and Services

INFORMATION SOURCES

Jackson's big **Wyoming State Information Center** is detailed earlier in this chapter. Find it on the north end of town at 532 N. Cache Dr., 307/733-3316, www.jacksonholechamber.com. It's open daily all year. Immediately south of the Information Center is an impressive building housing the **Wyoming Game & Fish** offices, 307/733-2321.

The **Bridger-Teton National Forest** supervisor's office is at 340 N. Cache Drive, 307/739-5500, www.fs.fed.us/btnf, and is open Monday–Friday 8 A.M.–4:30 P.M. Get information and Forest Service maps from the Wyoming State Information Center.

JACKSON HOLE ON THE WEB

A great place to begin your web tour is the chamber of commerce site: www.jacksonholechamber.com. Also very useful are www.jacksonholetraveler.com, from Circumerro Publishing; and www.jacksonholenet.com, sponsored by *Jackson Hole Magazine*. All three

of these sites contain links to dozens of local businesses of all types.

Internet Access

To keep in touch with folks via email, use the free terminals in the library. Another option is **Mountunes,** 265 W. Broadway, 307/733-4514 or 800/982-2241, www.mountunes.com. In addition to a big and diverse collection of CDs for sale, they have an Internet café where computer time costs $5 per half-hour.

TRIP PLANNING

Several local travel agencies offer reservation services for those who prefer to leave the planning to others. They can set up airline tickets, rental cars, lodging, horseback riding, fishing trips, whitewater rafting, ski vacations, and other packages. The biggest is **Jackson Hole Central Reservations**, 307/733-4005 or 800/443-6931, www.jhsnow.com. Central Reservations will also send out big glossy brochures describing local ski areas and lodging. **Do Jackson,** 307/739-1500 or 866/500-3654, www.dojacksonhole.com, has an office next to the Albertson's store with lots of visitor information. Also helpful for trip planning are **Jackson Hole Reservations,** 307/733-6331 or 800/329-9205, www.jacksonholeres.com, and **Llama Lou's Reservations,** 307/733-1617 or 800/709-1617, www.jhsummerfun.com.

POST OFFICES

Jackson's main post office is at 1070 Maple Way, near Powderhorn Lane, 307/733-3650; open Mon.–Fri. 8:30 A.M.–5 P.M., Sat. 10 A.M.–1 P.M. Other post offices are downtown at 220 W. Pearl Ave., 307/739-1740; in Teton Village, 307/733-3575; in Wilson, 307/733-3335; and in Kelly, 307/733-8884.

MEDICAL HELP

Because of the abundance of ski and snowboard accidents, orthopedic specialists are in high demand in Jackson and are some of the best around. The specialists at Orthopaedics of Jackson Hole are official physicians for the U.S. and French national ski teams! Head to **St. John's Hospital,** 625 E. Broadway, 307/733-3636, www.tetonhospital.org, for emergency medical attention.

Medical service by appointment or on a walk-in basis is available at **Gooder Family Care,** 545 W. Broadway, 307/733-7003; **Emerg-A-Care,** 975 W. Broadway (Powderhorn Mall), 307/733-8002; and **Jackson Hole Medical Clinic,** 988 South U.S. Hwy. 89, 307/739-8999. Unfortunately, none of these facilities will bill your insurance company; you'll have to fork out the cash and hope for a refund later.

BANKING AND CURRENCY EXCHANGE

Get fast cash from **ATMs** at many locations around town, including banks, Albertson's, downtown in front of Sirk Shirts, at the airport, and in Teton Village and the Aspens.

International travelers will appreciate the **currency exchange** where you can swap those Euros or colorful Canadian bills at all three Jackson State Bank locations: 112 Center Street, 50 Buffalo Way, and in the Aspens on Teton Village Road. Call 307/733-3737 for details.

LIBRARY

The spacious **Teton County Library,** 125 Virginian Lane, 307/733-2164, http://will.state.wy.us/teton/home, is the kind of library every town should have. Inside this modern building is a large collection of books about Wyoming and the West, plus a great kids' section (complete with a fenced-in children's garden with a tepee). Computers provide free **Internet access** and are available by reservation or on a walk-up-and-wait basis. In the summer the queue can get long if you don't have a reservation. They take reservations up to one week in advance. Library hours are Monday–Thursday 10 A.M.–9 P.M., Friday 10 A.M.–5:30 P.M., Saturday 10 A.M.–5 P.M., and Sunday 1–5 P.M. If you plan to be in the Jackson area for a week or more, it may be worth your while to get a visitor's library card. For a one-time fee of $5 you can check out up to four books at a time.

NEWSPAPERS

Jackson has not just one but two thick local newspapers, each produced in tabloid format. The *Jackson Hole News* (307/733-2047; www.jacksonholenews.com) and the *Jackson Hole Guide* (307/733-2430; www.jhguide.com) both publish weekly editions with local news for 50 cents, as well as weekday freebies found in local shops. The *Guide* typically represents more traditional Wyoming views (i.e., it's basically Republican) while the *News* has more liberal leanings. Despite any leanings, both are excellent sources of information and strive for balanced news coverage.

TRAVELING WITH CHILDREN

Those traveling with children will find an abundance of kid-friendly options in Jackson Hole. A few noteworthy examples include:

* the hands-on Children's Gallery at the National Museum of Wildlife Art
* playgrounds at Mike Yokel Jr. Park (Kelly and Hall streets) and Miller Park (Powderhorn Lane and Maple Way)
* the excellent swimming pool and corkscrew water slide at the Teton County Recreation Center
* the fine children's section of the library
* chuck wagon dinners at Bar-T-Five or Bar J
* pizzas at the Calico (where the lawn is great for kids)
* comedies and melodramas at Jackson Hole Playhouse or Mainstage Theatre
* the Alpine Slide at Snow King Resort
* the aerial tram up Rendezvous Mountain at Jackson Hole Resort
* the evening shoot-outs at Town Square
* horseback or wagon rides
* a trip to the fish hatchery
* a night at the rodeo (including the kids-only calf chase)
* a boat ride and hike at Jenny Lake inside Grand Teton National Park.

During summer, older kids will also enjoy hiking, mountain-biking, Snake River float and whitewater trips, and the putting course at Alpine Miniature Golf. In winter, snowboarding and skiing are favorites of older kids, but sleigh rides, dogsledding, ice skating, and snowshoeing are also fun.

For those traveling with tots, **Baby's Away**, 307/733-0387 or 888/616-8495, rents all sorts of baby supplies, including car seats, cribs, gates, backpacks, swings, and high chairs. You'll find more stroller and backpack rentals—along with kids' clothing—at **Teton Kids**, 130 E. Broadway, 307/739-2176. Just down the street is a large toy shop, **Broadway Toys and Togs**, 48 E. Broadway, 307/733-3918. But don't come here looking for Wal-Mart prices; the last time I visited, they were selling a toddler's overalls (with cute rodeo decorations) for $80! **Second Helpings**, 141 E. Pearl Ave., 307/733-9466, has an excellent selection of quality used baby and children's clothes. For child care, contact **Babysitting by the Tetons**, 307/733-0754, www.babysittingbythetetons.com, or

Jackson Hole Babysitting, 307/733-7720, www.jacksonholebabysitting.com.

LAUNDRY AND SHOWERS

Wash clothes at **Soap Opera Laundry**, 850 W. Broadway, 307/733-5584, or **Ryan Cleaners**, 545 N. Cache Dr., 307/733-2938. You'll find public lockers at Jackson Hole Mountain Resort during winter. **Showers** ($5 with towel) are available in the Bunkhouse portion of Anvil Motel, 215 N. Cache Dr., 307/733-3668 or 800/234-4507, www.anvilmotel.com.

LIVING IN JACKSON HOLE

Jackson Hole is an increasingly popular place to live and work—a fact that angers many longtime residents who came here to escape crowds elsewhere. The surrounding country is grand, with many things to do and places to explore, the weather is delightful, and you're likely to meet others with similar interests, not to mention the great-looking babes and snowboard studs. Jobs such as waiting tables, operating ski lifts, driving tour buses, cleaning hotels and condos, and doing construction work are plentiful. The unemployment rate generally hovers around 2 percent, and housing is so scarce—and jobs so plentiful—that the local rescue mission kicks folks out after a week if they don't find work. Wages are not high but have improved with the rising demand for workers. Get to Jackson in mid-May and you'll find the papers filled with half a dozen pages of employment ads and Help Wanted signs at virtually every shop. Even in midsummer, many places are looking for workers.

Finding Work

The best jobs are those that either offer such perks as housing or free ski passes or give you lots of free time to explore the area. To get an idea of available jobs, check local classified ads or stop by the Wyoming Job Service Center, 155 W. Gill, 307/733-4091. You can also search for jobs on the state's Job Bank homepage: http://wyjobs.state.wy.us. Other good web sources are www.jacksonholejobs.com, www.jacksonholenews.com, and www.jhguide.com.

Navigating the Housing Maze

Because of Jackson Hole's popularity, finding a place to live is extremely difficult, especially during the peak summer and winter tourist seasons. As the moneyed class has moved in, those who work in service jobs find it tougher and tougher to obtain affordable housing. Many Jackson workers now suffer long commutes from Victor or Driggs in Idaho, or the Wyoming towns of Alpine, Afton, or Pinedale. Land prices (and consequently housing costs) have been rising an average of 15 percent per year over the past decade or so, and because of this, the median home price is now twice what the median household income will buy! Two-bedroom apartments rent for $900–1,100 per month. The median single-family home in Jackson costs $400,000, and the average home in the area sells for a cool $1 million. More prestigious local homes sell for $2–3 million, and the very finest log mansions ("log cabins on steroids") can fetch more

than $6 million. The inflation of real estate has attracted the major players: both Christie's and Sotheby's (the auction folks) have offices in Jackson. As a side note, Teton County is the wealthiest county in America, with the highest average taxable income anywhere in the nation. (These figures are, of course, skewed by a relatively small number of ultra-rich individuals; you'll find many folks working at $8-an-hour jobs.)

Because of the extreme difficulty in finding rental housing, many Jackson-area businesses include this perk as a way to lure workers. Those workers who are not so lucky are often forced to jam into too-small apartments or to join the commuters from Driggs. The best times to look for a place to live are in April and October. Check the local newspapers (or their online versions if you haven't yet arrived in the area) as well as local laundromat and grocery-store bulletin boards for apartments or cabins. The *Trash and Treasure* morning program on radio station KMTN (96.9 FM; www.jacksonholeradio.com/kmtn.htm) is another place to try.

Transportation

Access to Jackson Hole has become easier in recent years, with several airlines and daily buses now serving the valley. Most summer visitors arrive by car, although a few more adventurous souls pedal in on bikes. If you're looking for or offering a ride, KMTN (96.9 FM), 307/733-4500, www.jacksonholeradio.com/kmtn.htm, has daily ride-finder announcements during its Trash and Treasure radio program. Tune in weekdays 9:30–9:50 A.M.

Road Work

The highway through the Snake River Canyon has been undergoing a $75-million highway reconstruction that began in 1998, with completion scheduled for 2004. Get the current status and information about expected delays at 307/733-3665, http://wyoroad.info.

BY AIR

Jackson Hole Airport is eight miles north of Jackson inside Grand Teton National Park. It's the only commercial airport within any national park. The airport is small and cozy but offers daily jet service to several U.S. cities. The tarmac is often crowded with Lear and Gulfstream jets and other noisy transportation symbols of the elite. See the "Airline Contacts" Special Topic in the On the Road chapter for information on all major airlines.

Delta/Skywest, has year-round service from Salt Lake City, with additional winter flights out of Atlanta. Some of the Salt Lake flights are in smaller turboprops, others in jets; all of the Atlanta flights are in 757s. **American,** has summer and winter service from Dallas and Chicago.

Northwest Airlines, flies from Minneapolis/St. Paul in summer and winter. United/United Express, offers year-round turboprop service from Denver. Continental, serves Jackson Hole from Newark and Houston in the winter and usually has service during summer to the same cities.

If you're flying in from Seattle, Los Angeles, or San Francisco, you will need to go through either Salt Lake City or Idaho Falls. The latter airport is served by Horizon Air (Alaska Airlines). Many folks opt to fly to either Salt Lake (275 miles away) or Idaho Falls (90 miles away) and pick up a rental car for the drive to Jackson.

Jackson Hole Aviation, 307/733-4767 or 800/437-5387, www.jhaviation.com, offers scenic flights over the valley as well as charter air service.

AIRPORT SHUTTLES AND TAXIS

Alltrans/Gray Line of Jackson Hole, 307/733-4325 or 800/443-6133, www.jacksonholealltrans.com, provides airport shuttle service to and from motels in Jackson ($13 one-way or $23 round-trip per person) and Teton Village ($20 one-way or $35 round-trip per person). The shuttles meet nearly all commercial airline flights in winter and most summertime flights, but you should make advance reservations to be sure of an airport pickup. Make outgoing reservations for a motel pickup 24 hours in advance.

Local taxis also provide direct service from the airport to Jackson; $12 for one or two people. To Teton Village you're best off getting a roundt-rip ticket for $35 per person. The taxi companies are A Snake River Taxi, 307/732-2221; Airport Taxi/Alltrans, 307/733-1700 or 800/443-6133, www.jacksonholealltrans.com; Airport Shuttle Service, 307/730-3900; All Star Taxi, 307/733-2888; Buckboard Transportation, 307/733-1112 or 877/791-0211, www.buckboardtrans.com; Bullseye Taxi, 307/730-5000; Cowboy Cab, 307/734-8188; Elks Country Cab, 307/733-8181; and Teton Taxi & Backcountry Shuttle, 307/733-1506, www.tetontaxi.com.

CAR RENTALS

Most of the national and regional chains offer rental cars in town or at the airport. See the "Rental Car Contacts" Special Topic in the On the Road chapter for national companies. Local companies include Eagle Rent-A-Car, 307/739-9999 or 800/582-2128, www.jacksonholenet.com/eagle, and Leisure Sports, 307/733-3040, www.leisure-sportsadventure.com. Of the national chains, Alamo, Avis, Budget, and Hertz all have counters at the airport, while the others provide a free shuttle bus to town. You may be better off getting a car in town, where you don't have to pay the additional taxes imposed at the airport. Most of these companies also rent 4WD cars and minivans.

START BUSES

Local buses are operated by Southern Teton Area Rapid Transit (START) and serve Jackson and Teton Village all year. START fares are free within town and $3 to Teton Village (cheaper for seniors and children). Discount coupons are available for multiple rides. Hours of operation are generally 6 A.M.–10 P.M. During summer, buses run seven days a week, with in-town service every 15 minutes from noon to 6:45 P.M. Service to Teton Village is eight times a day in summer and more often in winter. Reduced bus service is available in fall and spring. Get bus schedules and route maps in the visitors center. Buses stop near most Jackson hotels and motels and are equipped to carry skis (in winter) and bikes (in summer) on outside racks. Wintertime service is also offered to the National Museum of Wildlife Art and National Elk Refuge. Unfortunately, START buses do not run to the airport, Kelly, or Moose, but winter service is available to Wilson. Call 307/733-4521 for more information, or find them on the web at www.startbus.com.

As this book was being written, the Park Service was developing a new transportation plan for Grand Teton National Park that may include scheduled bus service from Jackson. Get the latest information at 307/739-3399, www.nps.gov/grte.

LONG-DISTANCE BUSES

Greyhound buses don't come even close to Jackson; the nearest stopping places are Evanston, West Yellowstone, Idaho Falls, and the regional hub at Salt Lake City. **Alltrans/Jackson Hole Express,** 307/733-1719 or 800/652-9510, www.jacksonholealltrans.com, provides daily bus or van connections between Salt Lake City ($54 one-way), Idaho Falls ($31 one-way), Pocatello ($42 one-way), and Jackson.

TOURS AND SHUTTLES

Grand Teton Lodge Company, 307/543-2811 or 800/628-9988, www.gtlc.com, has five-times-daily summer shuttle buses between Jackson and Jackson Lake Lodge for $20 one-way (plus a $10 park entrance fee), and on to Colter Bay Village for an additional $4 one-way. Transportation to the airport is $30 from the airport to Jackson Lake Lodge or $20 in the other direction. Reservations are required for all of these. and N. Cache Drive. The company also offers three-hour bus tours of Grand Teton National Park and eight-hour tours of Yellowstone National Park.

Park Tours

Summertime bus tours of Grand Teton and Yellowstone National Parks are available several times a week from **Alltrans/Gray Line of Jackson Hole,** 307/733-4325 or 800/443-6133, www.jacksonholealltrans.com. Jackson taxi companies also offer shuttle services within the park and guided tours.

Operated by Teton Science School, **Wildlife Expeditions,** 307/733-2623 or 888/945-3567, www.tetonscience.org/wildlife, leads a variety of wildlife-viewing safaris throughout the region. Multiday wildlife tours into Yellowstone are also available. Other companies with guided van tours of the area include **Callowishus Park Touring Company,** 307/733-9521,

LONE HIGHWAYMAN OF YELLOWSTONE

Because of its remote location, Teton Valley became a rendezvous place for rustlers and outlaws in the 1880s. Horses stolen from the soldiers at Fort Hall, along with cattle "liberated" from Wyoming and Montana ranches made their way through Pierre's Hole to the railroads. Hiram C. Lapham was the first to try his hand at ranching in the valley, but his cattle quickly disappeared. With the help of a posse from Rexburg, Lapham tracked down the culprits, one of whom was killed in the ensuing gunfight. The others surrendered but escaped from jail when the wife of bandit Ed Harrington smuggled a gun to her husband in clothing worn by his baby. Harrington and partner Lum Nickerson were eventually tracked down and sent to jail.

Although Harrington was sentenced to 25 years, the governor pardoned him after just three. Harrington went on to become Teton Valley's first postman, but his criminal activity continued. Using the alias Ed Trafton, Harrington went on to rob stores throughout Teton Valley and eventually spent another two years behind bars. After getting out, he turned his attention to the tourism business in Yellowstone, but not in the standard way. Although it was never proven, he was suspected of being behind a string of stagecoach robberies in 1908 where cash and jewelry were taken from tourists at gunpoint. Harrington's most brazen feat came on July 29, 1914, when he single-handedly robbed 15 stages, earning the nickname "the lone highwayman of Yellowstone." The tourists were particularly impressed with his gentlemanly manner as he asked them to "please" hand over all their cash and jewelry. Harrington made off with $915.35 in cash and $130 in jewelry, but he made the mistake of posing for photos in the process. He was caught the following year and spent five years in Leavenworth Prison.

When Harrington died, a letter in his pocket claimed that he had been Owen Wister's model for the Virginian in the famous novel of the same name. Others suspected that he was more likely to have been Wister's model for the villain, Trampas.

www.callowishus.com; **Jackson's Hole Adventure,** 307/654-7849 or 800/392-3165, www.jacksonholeadventure.com; and **Up-** **stream Anglers and Outdoor Adventures,** 307/739-9443 or 800/642-8979, www.upstreamanglers.com.

Bridger-Teton National Forest

One of the largest national forests in the Lower 48, Bridger-Teton ("the B-T") National Forest stretches southward for 135 miles from the Yellowstone border and covers 3.4 million acres. Portions of the forest are described elsewhere (see Bridger Wilderness in the Wind River Mountains Country chapter and Greys River Area in the Southwest chapter). In Jackson Hole, the two areas of most interest for recreation are the Teton Wilderness and the Gros Ventre Wilderness. Much of the remaining nonwilderness land managed by the Forest Service is multiple-use, meaning a mix of recreation, logging, cattle grazing, and oil and gas leasing.

The Bridger-Teton National Forest **supervisor's office** is at 340 N. Cache Drive in Jackson, 307/739-5500, www.fs.fed.us/ btnf. The Wyoming State Information Center, a couple of blocks north on Cache, usually has a Forest Service worker on duty who can provide recreation information. The center also sells Bridger-Teton maps and has a good choice of outdoor books. Local ranger stations are the **Jackson Ranger District,** also at 340 N. Cache Dr., 307/739-5400, and the **Blackrock Ranger Station,** nine miles east of Moran Junction, 307/543-2386.

Short Hikes

Forest Service lands around Jackson provide an amazing array of hiking and mountain-biking options. Pick up a copy of *Top Ten Trails* from the Forest Service office in town for descriptions of the most popular trails, or find the same information on their website. Some of these hikes are detailed in the Day Hikes section under Summer Recreation.

TETON WILDERNESS

The Teton Wilderness covers 585,468 acres of mountain country, bordered to the north by Yellowstone National Park, to the west by Grand Teton National Park, and to the east by the Washakie Wilderness. Established as a primitive area in 1934, it was declared one of the nation's first wilderness areas upon passage of the 1964 Wilderness Act. The Teton Wilderness offers a diverse mixture of rolling lands carpeted with lodgepole pine, spacious grassy meadows, roaring rivers, and dramatic mountains. Elevations range from 7,500 feet to the 12,165-foot summit of Younts Peak. The Continental Divide slices across the wilderness, with headwaters of the Yellowstone River draining the eastern half and headwaters of the Buffalo and Snake Rivers flowing down the western side. Teton Wilderness has a considerable amount of bear activity, so make sure you know how to avoid bear encounters and bring pepper spray.

The 585,468 acres of the Teton Wilderness offer a diverse mixture of rolling lands carpeted with lodgepole pine, spacious grassy meadows, roaring rivers, and dramatic mountains.

One of the most unusual places within Teton Wilderness is **Two Ocean Creek,** where a creek abruptly splits at a rock and the two branches never rejoin. One branch becomes Atlantic Creek, and its waters eventually reach the Atlantic Ocean, while the other becomes Pacific Creek and its waters flow to the Snake River, the Columbia River, and thence into the Pacific Ocean! Mountain man Osborne Russell described this phenomenon in 1835:

> *On the South side about midway of the prairie stands a high snowy peak from whence issues a Stream of water which after entering the plain it divides equally one*

half running West and other East thus bidding adieu to each other one bound for the Pacific and the other for the Atlantic ocean. Here a trout of 12 inches in length may cross the mountains in safety. Poets have sung of the "meeting of the waters" and fish climbing cataracts but the "parting of the waters and fish crossing mountains" I believe remains unsung yet by all except the solitary Trapper who sits under the shade of a spreading pine whistling blank-verse and beating time to the tune with a whip on his trap sack whilst musing on the parting advice of these waters.

Two natural events have had a major effect on the Teton Wilderness. On July 21, 1987, a world-record high-elevation tornado created a 10,000-acre blowdown of trees around the Enos Lake area, and it took years to rebuild the trails. In 1988, extreme drought conditions led to a series of major fires in Yellowstone and surrounding areas. Within the Teton Wilderness, the Huck and Mink Creek Fires burned (in varying degrees of severity) approximately 200,000 acres. More than half of the wilderness remained untouched. Don't let these incidents dissuade you from visiting; this is still a marvelous and little-used area. Herds of elk graze in alpine areas, and many consider the Thorofare country abutting Yellowstone National Park the most remote place in the Lower 48. This is prime grizzly habitat, so be very cautious at all times. Poles for hanging food have been placed at most campsites, as have bear-resistant boxes or barrels. Local Forest Service offices have brochures showing the locations of these poles. You can rent bear-resistant backpacker food tubes or horse panniers from the Blackrock Ranger District, 307/543-2386, but it's a good idea to make reservations for these items before your trip.

Access

Three primary trailheads provide access to the Teton Wilderness: Pacific Creek on the southwestern end, Turpin Meadow on the Buffalo Fork River, and Brooks Lake just east of the Continental Divide. Campgrounds are located at each of these trailheads. Teton Wilderness is a favorite of Wyomingites, particularly those with horses, and in the fall elk hunters from across the nation come here. Distances are so great and some of the stream crossings so intimidating that few backpackers head into this wilderness area. No permits are needed, but it's a good idea to stop in at the **Blackrock Ranger District,** 307/543-2386, nine miles east of Moran Junction on U.S. Hwy. 26/287, for topographic maps and information on current trail conditions, bear problems, regulations, and a list of permitted outfitters offering horse or llama trips.

For a shorter trip, you could take a guided horseback ride with one of two companies based at the Turpin Meadow Trailhead: **Two Ocean Pass Outfitting,** 307/543-2309 or 800/726-2409, www.twooceanpass.com; **Yellowstone Outfitters,** 307/543-2418 or 800/447-4711, www.yellowstoneoutfitters.com. Additional rides are available from nearby **Turpin Meadow Ranch,** 307/543-2496 or 800/743-2496, www.turpinmeadow.com, **Buffalo Valley Ranch,** 307/543-2026 or 888/543-2477. All four of these have horses available for hourly or all-day rides into the Teton Wilderness. **Teton Horseback Adventures,** 307/856-3628 or 307/739-7176, www.horsebackadv.com, has horseback rides and wilderness trips out of the Pacific Creek Trailhead.

Unfortunately, the U.S. Geological Survey maps don't show the many Teton Wilderness trails built and maintained (or not maintained) by private outfitters and hunters. These can make hiking confusing. A few of the many possible hikes are described as follows.

Whetstone Creek

Whetstone Creek Trail begins at the Pacific Creek Trailhead, on the southwest side of Teton Wilderness. An enjoyable 20-mile round-trip hike leaves the trailhead and follows Pacific Creek for 1.5 miles before splitting left to follow Whetstone Creek. Bear left when the trail splits again another three miles upstream and continue through a series of small meadows to the junction with Pilgrim Creek Trail. Turn right here and follow this trail two more miles to Coulter Creek Trail, climbing up Coulter Creek to scenic Coulter Basin and then dropping down along the East Fork of Whetstone Creek. This rejoins the Whetstone Creek Trail and returns you to the trailhead, passing many attractive small meadows along the way. The upper half of this loop hike was burned in 1988; some areas were heavily scorched, while others are patchy. Flowers are abundant in the burned areas, and this is important elk habitat.

South Fork to Soda Fork

A fine loop hike leaves Turpin Meadow and follows South Buffalo Fork River to South Fork Falls. Just above this point, a trail splits off and climbs to Nowlin Meadow (excellent views of Smokehouse Mountain) and then down to Soda Fork River, where it joins the Soda Fork Trail. Follow this trail back downstream to huge Soda Fork Meadow (a good place to see moose and occasionally grizzlies) and then back to Turpin Meadow, a distance of approximately 23 miles round-trip. For a fascinating side trip from this route, head up the Soda Fork into the alpine at Crater Lake, a six-mile hike above the Nowlin Meadow–Soda Fork Trail junction. The outlet stream at Crater Lake disappears into a gaping hole, emerging as a large creek two miles below at Big Springs. It's an incredible sight.

Cub Creek Area

The Brooks Lake area just east of Togwotee Pass is a popular summertime camping and fishing place with magnificent views. Brooks Lake Trail follows the western shore of Brooks Lake and continues past Upper Brooks Lakes to Bear Cub Pass. From here, the trail drops down to Cub Creek, where you'll find several good campsites. You can make a long and scenic loop by following the trail up Cub Creek into the alpine country and then back down along the South Buffalo Fork River to Lower Pendergraft Meadow. From here, take the Cub Creek Trail back up along Cub Creek to Bear Cub Pass and back out to Brooks Lake. Get a topographic map before heading into this remote country. Total distance is approximately 33 miles round-trip.

GROS VENTRE WILDERNESS

The 287,000-acre Gros Ventre Wilderness was established in 1984 and covers the mountain country just east of Jackson Hole. This range trends mainly in a northwest-southeast direction and is probably best known for Sleeping Indian Mountain (maps now call it Sheep Mountain, but locals never use that appellation), the distinctive rocky summit visible from Jackson Hole. Although there are densely forested areas at lower elevations, the central portion of the wilderness lies above timberline, and many peaks top 10,000 feet. The tallest is Doubletop Peak at 11,682 feet. The Tetons are visible from almost any high point in the Gros Ventre, and meadows line the lower-elevation streams. Elk, mule deer, bighorn sheep, moose, and black bears are found here, and a few grizzlies have been reported. The Forest Service office in Jackson has more information on the wilderness, including brief trail descriptions and maps.

Access and Trails

Several roads provide good access to the Gros Ventre Wilderness: Gros Ventre River Rd. on the northern border; Curtis Canyon Rd. on the western margin; and Granite Creek Rd. to the south. Flat Creek is rough and only accessible in a 4WD vehicle. Hikes beginning or ending in the Granite Creek area have the added advantage of nearby Granite Hot Springs, a great place to soak tired muscles.

For a beautiful hike, follow **Highline Trail** from the Granite Creek area across to Cache Creek, a distance of 16 miles. This route passes just below a row of high and rugged mountains, but because it isn't a loop route, you'll need to hitchhike or set up a shuttle back. Plan on three days for this hike. The area is crisscrossed with game and cattle trails, making it easy to get lost, especially on the headwaters of Little Granite Creek. Talk with Forest Service folks before heading out, and make sure that you know how to read a map and compass.

A third hike begins at the **Goosewing Ranger Station,** 12 miles east of Slide Lake on Gros Ventre River Road. Take the trail from here to Two Echo Park (a fine camping spot) and then continue up to Six Lakes. You can return via the same trail or take the Crystal Creek Trail back to Red Rock Ranch and hitch back to Goosewing. The trail distance is approximately 23 miles round-trip.

Caribou-Targhee National Forest

Covering nearly three million acres, Caribou-Targhee National Forest extends from Montana to Utah. Most of the forest lies within Idaho, but it also includes the western edge of Wyoming along the Tetons. Much of the forest is heavily logged, but two wilderness areas protect most of the Wyoming portion. Cattle and sheep graze many backcountry areas; contact the Forest Service office in Driggs, Idaho, 208/354-2312, www.fs.fed.us/r4/caribou, for areas where you can avoid running into livestock.

JEDEDIAH SMITH WILDERNESS

The 123,451-acre Jedediah Smith Wilderness lies on the west side of the Teton Range, facing Idaho but lying entirely within Wyoming. Access is primarily from the Idaho side, although trails breach the mountain passes at various points, making it possible to enter from Grand Teton National Park. This area was not declared a wilderness until 1984. A second wilderness area, the 10,820-acre **Winegar Hole Wilderness** (pronounced "WINE-a-gur"), lies along the southern border of Yellowstone National Park. Grizzlies love this country, but hikers will find it uninteresting and without trails. In contrast, the Jedediah Smith Wilderness contains nearly 300 miles of paths and some incredible high-mountain scenery.

Several mostly gravel roads lead up from the Driggs and Victor areas into the Tetons. Get a map ($7) showing wilderness trails and access points from the Caribou-Targhee National Forest ranger station in Driggs, Idaho, 208/354-2312, or from the Forest Service offices in Jackson. Be sure to camp at least 200 feet from lakes and 100 feet from streams. Group size limits are also in place; check with the Forest Service for specifics on these and other backcountry regulations. In addition, anyone planning to cross into Grand Teton National Park from the west side will need to get a park camping permit in advance. Wilderness permits are not required for the Jedediah Smith Wilderness. Both grizzly and black bears are present throughout the Tetons, so all food must be either hung out of reach or stored in bear-resistant containers.

Hidden Corral Basin

At the northern end of the wilderness, Hidden Corral Basin provides a fine loop hike. Locals (primarily those on horseback) crowd this area on late-summer weekends. Get to the trailhead by driving north from Tetonia on Idaho 32 to Lamont, then turn north on a gravel road. Follow it one mile and then turn right (east) onto Coyote Meadows Road. The trailhead is approximately 10 miles up, where the road dead-ends. An eight-mile trail parallels South Bitch Creek (the name Bitch Creek comes from the French word for a female deer, *biche*) to Hidden Corral, where you may see moose. Be sure to bring a fishing pole to try for the cutthroats.

Above Hidden Corral you can make a pleasant loop back by turning north onto the trail to Nord Pass and then dropping down along the Carrot Ridge and Conant Basin Trails to Bitch Creek Trail and then on to Coyote Meadows, a distance of 21 miles round-trip. Note that this is grizzly and black bear country, and bear-resistant containers are required. By the way, Hidden Corral received its name in the outlaw days, when rustlers would steal horses in Idaho, change the brands, and hold the horses in this natural corral until the branding wounds healed. The horses were then sold to Wyoming ranchers. Owen Wister's *The Virginian* describes a pursuit of horse thieves through Bitch Creek country.

Alaska Basin

The most popular hiking trail in the Jedediah Smith begins near the **Teton Canyon Campground** ($8; open late May to mid-Sept.; reservations at 518/885-3639 or 877/444-6777, www.reserveusa.com) and leads through flower-bedecked meadows to mountain-rimmed Alaska Basin. It's great country, but don't expect a true wilderness experience because many others will also be hiking and camping here. Get to the campground by following the Grand Targhee Ski Resort signs east from Driggs, Idaho. A gravel road splits off to the right approximately three miles beyond the little settlement of Alta. Follow it to the campground. (If you miss the turn, you'll end up at the ski area.) For an enjoyable loop, follow Alaska Basin Trail up the canyon to Basin Lakes and then head southwest along the Teton Crest Trail to the Teton Shelf Trail. Follow this trail back to its junction with the Alaska Basin Trail, dropping down the Devils Stairs—a series of very steep switchbacks. You can then take the Alaska Basin Trail back to Teton Campground, a round-trip distance of approximately 19 miles. You could also use these trails to access the high peaks of the Tetons or to cross the mountains into Death Canyon within Grand Teton National Park (camping permit required). Campfires and horse camping are not allowed in Alaska Basin.

Moose Meadows

For a somewhat less crowded hiking experience, check out the Moose Meadows area on the southern end of the Jedediah Smith Wilderness. Get to the trailhead by going three miles southeast of Victor on Idaho State Hwy. 33. Turn north (left) on Moose Creek Road and follow it to the trailhead. The trail parallels Moose Creek to Moose

© DON PITCHER

Alaska Basin

JACKSON HOLE

Meadows, a good place to camp. You'll need to ford the creek twice, so this trail is best hiked in late summer. At the meadows, the trail dead-ends into Teton Crest Trail, providing access to Grand Teton National Park through some gorgeous alpine country. A nice loop can be made by heading south along this trail to flower-covered Coal Creek Meadows. A trail leads from here past 10,068-foot Taylor Mountain (an easy side trip with magnificent views), down to Taylor Basin, through lodgepole forests, and then back to your starting point. This loop hike will take you 15 miles round-trip.

Teton Valley, Idaho

The west side of the Tetons differs dramatically from nearby Jackson Hole. As the road descends from Teton Pass into Teton Valley, Idaho (a.k.a. Pierre's Hole), the lush farming country spreads out before you, reaching 30 miles long and 15 miles across. This, the "quiet side" of the Tetons, offers a slower pace than bustling Jackson, but the Teton Range vistas are equally dramatic.

In recent years the growth in Jackson Hole has spilled across the mountains. The potato farms, horse pastures, and country towns are now undergoing the same transformation that first hit Jackson in the 1970s. As land prices soar and affordable housing becomes more difficult to find in Jackson, more people have opted to move over the pass and commute from the Idaho side. Glossy ads now fill *Teton Valley Magazine,* offering ranchland with a view, luxurious log homes, cozy second homes, balloon flights, espresso coffee, mountain-bike rentals, and handmade lodgepole furniture. Despite these changes, Teton Valley remains a laid-back place, and spud farming is still a part of the local economy. The primary town here—it's the county seat—is Driggs, with tiny Victor nine miles south and even more insignificant Tetonia eight miles north.

See Don Root's *Moon Handbooks Idaho* (www.moon.com) for excellent coverage of eastern Idaho, including the Swan Valley to the south and the Island Park area to the north.

HISTORY

The area now known as Teton Valley was used for centuries by various Indian tribes, including the Bannock, Blackfeet, Crow, Gros Ventre, Shoshone, and Nez Perce. John Colter—a member of the Lewis and Clark expedition—was the first white man to reach this area, wandering through in the winter of 1807–1808. In 1931, an Idaho farmer claimed to have plowed up a stone carved into the shape of a human face, with "John Colter 1808" etched into the sides. The rock later turned out to be a hoax created by a man anxious to obtain a horse concession with Grand Teton National Park. He got the concession after donating the rock to the park museum.

Vieux Pierre, an Iroquois fur trapper for the Hudson's Bay Company, made this area his base in the 1820s, but was later killed by Blackfeet Indians in Montana. Many people still call the valley Pierre's Hole. Two fur trapper rendezvous took place in Pierre's Hole, but the 1832 event proved pivotal. Some 1,000 Indians, trappers, and traders gathered for an annual orgy of trading, imbibing, and general partying. When a column of men on horseback appeared, two white trappers headed out for a meeting. The column turned out to be a group of Gros Ventre Indians, and the meeting quickly turned sour. One trapper shot the Gros Ventre chief point-blank, killing him. A battle quickly ensued that left 38 people dead on both sides and forced rendezvous participants to scatter. Later rendezvous were held in valleys where the animosities were not as high. For the next 50 years, virtually the only whites in Pierre's Hole were horse thieves and outlaws. Hiram C. Lapham was the first to try his hand at ranching in the valley, but his cattle were rustled by three outlaws, including Ed Harrington, alias Ed Trafton.

In 1888, a lawyer from Salt Lake City, B. W. Driggs, came to the valley and liked what he found. With his encouragement, a flood of Mormon settlers arrived over the next few years, establishing farms along the entire length of Teton Valley. By the 1940s the valley was home to a cheese factory, sawmills, a railroad line, and numerous sprawling ranches. Teton Valley's population plummeted in the 1960s, but in 1969 development began at Grand Targhee Ski Resort, and the economy started to turn around. Recent years have seen the area come into its own as tourism-related businesses began to eclipse farming and ranching. In the last decade the valley was positively booming, and Teton County, Idaho, has been one of the fastest-growing counties (on a percentage basis) in the nation.

VICTOR

Twenty-four miles west of Jackson, the town of Victor, Idaho, is little more than the proverbial wide spot in the road. It does, however, have several places that make it worth visiting.

Pierre's Playhouse, on Main St. in Victor, 208/787-2249, www.pierresplayhouse.com, puts on old-fashioned melodramas twice weekly from mid-June to early September. A Dutch-oven chicken dinner is served before the show. You know you're in for a serious production when the villain is named Gustavo Scumsuckler.

Accommodations

Built in the 1940s, **Timberline Inn,** 38 W. Center St., 208/787-2772 or 800/711-4667, has an attractive log-cabin exterior, with standard motel rooms for $60–65 s or d. Open June–Sept. **Trails End Motel,** 208/787-2973, rents four-person log cabin units for $49. Open May–Oct.

Four miles southeast of Victor at the foot of Teton Pass, **Moose Creek Ranch,** 208/787-2784 or 800/676-0075, www.moosecreekranch.com, has guest ranch accommodations on a weekly basis; $2,300 for two people. This rate includes lodging, meals, horseback lessons and rides, children's programs, whitewater float trips, chuck wagon dinners, and other ranch activities. Accommodations are cozy cabins with private baths, and the ranch also has an outdoor pool and hot tub.

Camping

The Forest Service's pleasant **Trail Creek Campground** ($8; open mid-May to mid-Sept.) is six miles southeast of Victor and just across the Wyoming state line. Make reservations ($9 fee) at 518/885-3639 or 877/444-6777, www.reserveusa.com. **Teton Valley Campground,** one mile west of Victor on Idaho Hwy. 31, 208/787-2647, www.tetonvalleycampground.com, has RV hookups ($32–34), tent sites ($22), basic cabins ($42), and a small outdoor pool. The campground also rents canoes, mountain bikes, and fishing gear.

Food

For the finest meals in Teton Valley, make dinner reservations at **The Old Dewey House Restaurant,** 37 S. Main St., 208/787-2092, www.odh.com. Everything is made from scratch by the owners, and the entrées ($13–30) are accompanied by freshly baked breads, salads with homemade dressings, fresh vegetables, and spicy appetizers. The menu changes frequently at this eight-table restaurant, but house favorites include blackened chicken and jalapeño pistachio sauce, and charbroiled rack of lamb. Delectable desserts are offered, too. No young children are permitted to dine here in the evening, and the menu warns: "Undisciplined children will be impounded and sent to the local taxidermist or fed to the Yellowstone wolves!" Closed Tuesday. The same characters also run tiny Grumpy's Goat Shack next door, with wines, beers, and appetizers, including wonderful roasted garlic with homemade goat cheese from their own goats.

Victor Emporium, 208/787-2221, houses an old-fashioned soda fountain with good fish tacos and famous shakes, especially their huckleberry shakes in season. They've been in business for more than 50 years and also sell fishing supplies and Idaho souvenirs.

Also in Victor is **Knotty Pine Restaurant,** 208/787-2866, considered one of the better local places for ribs and steaks, but be ready for clouds of cigarette smoke with your meal. It's an old-fashioned place with low ceilings and log walls, plus a large deck for outside dining. Live bands crank out the dance tunes most summer weekends.

Brewery

Grand Teton Brewing Company, 208/787-4000, www.grandtetonbrewing.com, is on the east side of Victor at 430 Old Jackson Highway. Drop by weekdays for a free tour or to sample Teton Ale, Old Faithful Ale, Moose Juice Stout, Teton Huckleberry Wheat, or Sweetgrass IPA. The gift shop sells T-shirts, glasses, and beer to go.

DRIGGS

Driggs (pop. 1,000) is an odd conglomeration, mixing an old-time farming settlement and new-fangled recreation mecca. It's also fast becoming a bedroom community for commuters to Jackson Hole. A major development on the south end of town will bring many more homes and businesses. There isn't much to downtown Driggs, so it's pretty easy to find your way around. But don't expect things to stay small for long because the area has been discovered; in 2002, *Men's Journal* put Driggs at the top of their list for best small towns in America.

Sights

Driggs is perhaps best known as home to the delightfully amusing **Spud Drive-In,** here since 1953. You can't miss the big truck out front with a flatbed-sized "potato" on the back. The drive-in even attracts folks from Jackson, who cross the pass for an evening of fun beneath the stars. Call 208/354-2727 or 800/799-7783 for upcoming flicks. The drive-in is locally famous for Gladys burgers and Spud buds—served by carhops.

The spacious **Teton Valley Museum** opened in 2003 and houses historical displays from the valley's past. It's located on the north side of town just beyond the Super 8 Motel. Call 208/354-2200 or 208/456-2652 for details.

Located at the airport just north of town, **Warbirds Museum** is an interesting collection of nicely restored historic planes in a hanger at the Teton Aviation Center, 208/354-3100 or 800/472-6382, www.tetonaviation.com. No charge, and they're open daily 7 A.M.–7 P.M. in summer and daily 8 A.M.–5 P.M. the rest of the year. They have several unusual fighter aircraft—including a T-28 Trojan and a Mig-15—but only five or six are displayed at any given time. Warbirds Cafe is adjacent.

Accommodations

For a town this small, Driggs offers a surprising number of places to stay. In addition to those listed, you'll find others just east in Alta, Wyoming. **The Pines Motel Guest Haus,** 105 S. Main St., 208/354-2774 or 800/354-2778, is a delightful European-style guest house built in 1900. Run by the Nielson family, the home has

Spud Drive-In, Driggs, Idaho

© DON PITCHER

seven rooms, each different but all nicely appointed with tasteful touches such as handmade quilts. A hot tub is available outside. Rates are very reasonable: $40 s or $50 d, and children are welcome. Breakfasts cost $10 per person.

Super 8 Motel, on the north side of Driggs at 133 Hwy. 33, 208/354-8888 or 800/800-8000, www.super8.com, has standard rooms for $78 d, including an indoor pool, sauna, hot tub, and continental breakfast.

Intermountain Lodge, 34 Ski Hill Rd. (one mile east of Driggs), 208/354-8153, offers modern log cabin lodging with an outdoor hot tub. All rooms include kitchenettes. Rates are $69 s or d, plus $5 per person for additional guests.

Best Western Teton West, 476 N. Main St., 208/354-2363 or 800/252-2363, www.best-western.com, features a continental breakfast, indoor pool, and hot tub. Rates are $80–90 d in standard rooms. Closed Oct. to mid-Dec. and Apr. to mid-May.

Bed-and-Breakfasts

Teton Sunrise Inn, 208/456-2777 or 888/456-2777, www.tetonsunriseinn.com, is a recently built B&B halfway between Driggs and Tetonia (three miles in either direction). The lodge-style home contains five large guest rooms, each with a private bath. An enclosed hot tub faces the Tetons, and a full breakfast is served, along with evening snacks. Rates are $80 s or d, and children are welcome.

Willowpine B&B, 136 E. Little Ave., 208/354-2735, has two guest rooms that share a bath in a refurbished 1940s home. It's right in town. Rates are $65 s or d, including a full breakfast. No kids under 12 are allowed, and the B&B is only open on weekends and holidays.

Camping

The nearest public campsites are at **Teton Canyon Campground** ($8; open mid-May to mid-Sept.), 11 miles east of Driggs in the Tetons. This is a delightful camping spot, and the trailhead into beautiful (and very popular) Alaska Basin is nearby. Make reservations ($9 fee) at 518/885-3639 or 877/444-6777, www.reserveusa.com.

Food

One benefit of Teton Valley's rapid growth is a dramatic improvement in the local restaurant scene. Driggs now has several good dining places. (The best local meals, however, are Dewey's in Victor and Lost Horizon in Alta.)

Auntie M's Sweet Shoppe & Coffee, 189 N. Main St., 208/354-2010, is not a place for fast food or young children. The owner makes virtually everything from scratch, and the menu exists only in Auntie's head. Just ask her for today's sandwich, soup, and dessert specials, or get an espresso and check out her collection of homemade jams, jellies, and fruit butters for sale. It's a friendly and classy little spot.

Miso Hungry Cafe, 165 N. Main St., 208/354-8015, is a hip spot with several covered tables on the front porch and a small art gallery in the back room. The food is flavorful, with an ethnic twist, and they bake their own breads and pastries. Check the chalkboard for today's specials.

Warbirds Cafe, 208/354-2550, www.teton-aviation.com, is an aviation-themed restaurant located—appropriately enough—at the airport just north of town. The à la carte menu includes such treats as buffalo burgers, blackened catfish, vegetable fettuccini alfredo, or beef stew served over garlic mashed potatoes. Their wonderful Sunday brunch is $14—and worth it.

Tony's Pizza & Pasta, 364 N. Main St., 208/354-8829, serves hand-tossed New York–style pizzas, plus focaccia, calzone, and Italian meals. Choose from a big choice of microbrewed beers, with many on draught. Tony's flavorful "Avalanche" pizza comes with ricotta, mozzarella, and garlic—but no tomato sauce. No smoking allowed here.

Get malts, shakes, and hot fudge sundaes at the old soda fountain inside **Corner Drug,** 10 S. Main St., 208/354-2334. Lime freezes are their claim to fame. Where can you find the best local espresso? Try **Java the Hut,** next to the bike shop on Main Street.

Latino's Delights, 190 N. Main St., 208/354-2718, is the real thing, with tamales, enchiladas, guaraches, gorditos, flautas, and Mexican pastries, along with a TV blaring Spanish-language broadcasts. It's a good place to bone-up on your Spanish skills.

The main place for groceries is **Broulim's,** 52 S. Main St., 208/354-2350. Right next door is tiny **Barrels and Bins,** 208/354-2307, selling health foods and freeze-dried backcountry meals.

Teton Valley Events

The main summer event comes on Fourth of July weekend, the **Grand Teton Summer Festival.** Highlights include hot air balloon launches (more than 20 balloons) and tethered rides for the kids at the airport, a parade and crafts fair in Victor, a rodeo in Tetonia, arts exhibits, a pig roast, live music, evening fireworks in Driggs, and barbecue lunches at Grand Targhee Resort. That same weekend, the resort puts on the **WYDAHO Mountain Bike Race,** a cross-country event that attracts everyone from beginners to pros.

Grand Targhee Ski Resort pulls out the stops for the always popular **Targhee Bluegrass Festival** in mid-August, with nationally known acts. The music attracts a throng, so make camping or lodging reservations well ahead of time. Get details at 307/353-2300 or 800/827-4433, www.grandtarghee.com.

Heritage Days in late July celebrates the area's Mormon settlers; featured attractions are a parade through the center of Driggs, art shows, and a theatrical production.

In mid-August, the **Teton County Fair** brings down-home fun with livestock judging, arts and crafts, quilts, pies, jams, and other fare on display. Call 208/354-2961 for details.

Teton Valley Recreation

Outdoor enthusiasts will discover an array of activities at all times of the year in the Driggs area. The Teton River runs the entire length of Teton Valley and is renowned among fly-fishing enthusiasts. A plethora of hikes can be found both to the east in the Tetons and to the west in the Big Hole Mountains.

A paved **bike path** parallels Hwy. 33 between Victor and Driggs, providing a pleasant running, cycling, or in-line skating opportunity. A new section of the path continues east from Driggs to the Wyoming border at Alta, and the path may eventually continue over Teton Pass to Wilson. Get details at 208/353-2252, www.tetonvalley-chamber.com/pathways.html. Kids and their parents will appreciate the **Driggs Town Park,** with an attractive playground and sprinklers that make for impromptu summer fun. It's located on Ashley Street.

Peaked Sports, 70 E. Little Ave., 208/354-2354 or 800/705-2354, rents mountain bikes, bike trailers, and in-line skates, but **Big Hole Mountain Sports,** 65 S. Main St., 208/354-2209 or 877/574-3377, is for the real biking enthusiast. The store rents high-quality mountain bikes in the summer, along with skis and snowboards in winter. You can join locals for a ride out local trails most afternoons, but this is for advanced riders only—unless you want to get left in the dust.

High Peaks Health & Fitness Center, on Little Ave., 208/354-3128, has guest passes for $10 per day. **The Links at Teton Peaks,** 208/456-2374, is a Scottish-style nine-hole golf course at 127 N. 400 West.

For horseback rides, contact **Dry Ridge Outfitters,** 208/354-2284, www.dryridge.com, or **Bar H Ranch,** 888/216-6025, www.tetontrail-rides.com, Trail rides are also available at Grand Targhee Ski Resort.

Bagley's Teton Mountain Ranch, 265 W. 800 South, 208/787-9005 or 866/787-9005, www.elkadventures.com, raises 130 elk as breeding stock and for their antlers. They offer summertime wagon rides and wintertime sleigh rides among the elk for $8 ($5 for ages 4–9), plus horseback rides (starting at $35 for a one-hour ride).

Teton Aviation Center, 208/354-3100 or 800/472-6382, www.tetonaviation.com, is best known for their scenic glider flights past the Tetons, but they also offer airplane rides and have an impressive collection of vintage military aircraft. **Rainbow Balloon Flights,** 307/733-0470 or 800/378-0470, www.hometown.aol.com/rain-bowballoons, offers one-hour hot air balloon flights over Teton Valley for $189 per person.

Shopping

For a unique shopping experience at "the cultural hub of the universe," drop by **Moun-**

taineering Outfitters, 62 N. Main St., 208/354-2222 or 800/359-2410. Inside the jam-packed aisles are hiking boots, sleeping bags, Patagonia clothing (good prices), army-surplus wool pants, and maps. Owner Fred Mugler opened his shop in 1971 and has been cramming it with supplies ever since. Stop for a chat and a laugh.

Considerably more organized is **Yöstmark Mountain Equipment,** 12 E. Little Ave., 208/354-2828, www.yostmark.com, which sells a wide range of outdoor equipment. They also rent fishing gear, drift boats, backpacks, tents, sleeping bags, boots, inflatable kayaks, rafts, and all sorts of other summer gear, along with snowshoes, cross-country skis, skate skis, snowboards, and telemark and alpine touring skis in winter. Open daily 8 A.M.–7 P.M. Ask them about guided backcountry ski tours.

Browse the eclectic selection of regional books at the friendly **Dark Horse Books,** 76 N. Main St., 208/354-8882 or 888/434-8882, www.darkhorsebooks.com.

Bergmeyer Manufacturing Co., 229 N. Hwy. 33, 208/354-8611 or 800/348-3356, www.bergmeyermfg.com, creates quality log furniture in traditional and modern styles.

Information and Services

The **Teton Valley Chamber of Commerce,** 208/354-2500, www.tetonvalleychamber.com, is in downtown Driggs at 81 N. Main Street. Their hours are officially Monday–Friday 10 A.M.–3 P.M., but call first to make sure someone is there.

Get Caribou-Targhee National Forest information from the **Teton Basin Ranger District Office,** just south of town at 525 S. Main St., 208/354-2312, www.fs.fed.us/r4/caribou. Wash clothes at the appropriately named **Coin Laundry** next to Latino's Delight, 190 N. Main Street.

Teton Valley Hospital is at 283 N. 1st East, 208/354-2383. Also here is **Teton Valley Medical Center,** 208/354-2302, for nonemergency care.

TETONIA

Tiny Tetonia is eight miles north of Driggs. The town is surrounded by farming country and grand old barns; it's a good place to see kids riding horse-back. The crest of the tourist wave is just starting to lap at the shores of Tetonia, and at last check no local place sold espresso, focaccia, or cell phones.

Practicalities

Teton Mountain View Lodge, 208/456-2741 or 800/625-2232, www.tetonmountainlodge.com, has large and modern rooms with rustic furnishings; some also have fireplaces. Other amenities include a continental breakfast and an enclosed hot tub. Rates are $60–100 s or d.

Locanda di Fiori (The Inn of Flowers), 208/456-0909, www.rpgwebs.com/locanda, is a modern log cabin with masses of wildflowers (hence the name) and stunning views of the Tetons to the east. Two comfortable guest rooms are available, both with private baths and entrances, plus access to an outdoor hot tub. A full breakfast is served each morning, along with wine and cheese in the afternoon. Rates are $95 d. The inn is open June–mid-October; no kids under age 15 are allowed.

Trail's End Cafe, 208/456-2202, attracts local farmers and ranchers from all around for home-cooked meals of turkey, gravy, mashed Idaho potatoes, burgers, and other hearty fare. The homemade pies are worth the visit. This is where you'll meet the hardworking good ol' boys. Open at 6 A.M. daily.

ALTA, WYOMING

The little place called Alta sits right along the Wyoming border and just six miles northeast of Driggs, Idaho. There are no stores in Alta, but the settlement does have a stellar restaurant and several places to stay. East from Alta, the road climbs through heavily timbered country, with periodic views of the Big Hole Mountains to the west and up-close looks at the Teton Range. Also in Alta is the nine-hole **Targhee Village Golf Course,** 208/354-8577 or 307/353-8577.

Grand Targhee Ski Resort, 307/353-2300 or 800/827-4433, www.grandtarghee.com—just five miles above Alta—is the main attraction for the entire Teton Valley area. The resort offers excellent skiing and snowboarding in winter, along with a wide range of summer activities. Get the complete scoop, including details for on-mountain lodging and meals, in the Downhill Skiing and Snowboarding section.

Accommodations

Alta Lodge B&B, 307/353-2582, www.pdt.net/altalodge, is a large modern home with tall picture windows framing the Tetons. Four guest rooms are here (two with private baths), and a hot tub is available. Rates are $65–85 d, including a full breakfast. No kids are allowed.

Teton Teepee Lodge, 470 W. Alta Rd., 307/353-8176 or 800/353-8176, www.teton-teepee.com, is a winter-only place with a spacious common area at the center of a tepee-shaped building. Twenty-one guest rooms (no TV or phones in rooms) surround it, and two large dorm rooms—primarily used by kids—occupy a lower level. The lodge is a favorite of skiers and snowboarders, with a large central stone fireplace, dining area, pool table, game room, TV room, and outdoor hot tub. The rooms are rented on a package basis only: $864 for three days for two people, including private room, breakfast, dinner, drinks, transportation to Grand Targhee, and lift tickets. In other words, everything but your lunch and skis. For five days, the all-inclusive rate is $1,340 for two people. The packages are also available in dorm rooms: $384 per person for a complete three-day stay

($296 for ages 15–18; $156 for ages 6–14). The lodge is only open during ski season, mid-November through April.

Also in Alta is **Wilson Creekside Inn B&B,** 130 Alta North Rd., 307/353-2409, where you'll find a century-old home on a 200-acre sheep farm. Four guest rooms are available and all contain family heirlooms. One costs $90 d and includes a king-size bed and private bath; the others share a bath and run $80 d. Guests are served an ample country breakfast. Kids are welcome, but no credit cards are accepted. The owner's son raises some 150 ewes on the ranch.

Food

Lost Horizon Dinner Club, 307/353-8226, is one of two standout places in the Teton Valley area (the other being the Dewey Restaurant in Victor). The restaurant/home has space for just a dozen guests, who sit down to a memorable 10-course Japanese and Chinese meal ($40 plus wine) prepared by co-owner and chef Shigako Irwin. This isn't for vegetarians or for those in a hurry; expect to be here for three leisurely hours. Dinners are served Friday and Saturday nights at 7 P.M., and reservations are required. No credit cards are accepted. Formal dress isn't necessary, but don't come in shorts, sandals, or T-shirts. Recommended.

Grand Teton National Park

Note: Please see color map **Grand Teton National Park.**

Grand Teton National Park remains one of the preeminent symbols of American wilderness. The Tetons rise abruptly from the valley floor, their bare triangular ridges looking like broken shards of glass from some cosmic accident of creation. With six different summits topping 12,000 feet, plus some of the finest climbing and hiking in Wyoming, the Tetons are a paradise for lovers of the outdoors. They have long been a favorite of photographers and sightseers and once even appeared in an ad promoting Colorado tourism! The Tetons change character with the seasons. In summer the sagebrush flats are a garden of flowers set against the mountain backdrop. When autumn arrives, the cottonwoods and aspens become swaths of yellow and orange. Winter turns everything a glorious, sparkling white, set against the fluorescent blue sky.

© DON PITCHER

the majestic Tetons

Geology

BUILDING A MOUNTAIN RANGE

The precipitous Teton Range contains perhaps the most complex geologic history in North America. Although the Tetons are ancient by any human scale, they are the youngest mountains in the Rockies, less than 10 million years old (versus 60 million years for the nearby Wind River Mountains). The Tetons are a fault-block range, formed when the earth's crust cracked along an angled fault. Forces within the earth have pushed the western side (the Tetons) up, while the eastern portion (Jackson Hole) dropped down like a trapdoor. Geologists believe the fault could slip up to 10 feet at a time, producing a violent earthquake. All this shifting has created one of the most dramatic and asymmetric mountain faces on earth.

Unlike typical mountain ranges, the highest parts are not at the center of the range but along the eastern edge, where uplifting continues. The western slope, which drops gently into Idaho, is much less dramatic, although the views are still impressive. This tilting-and-subsidence process is still going on today, pushed by the movement of a plume of magma beneath Yellowstone as the continental plate slides over the top. Because

of this subsidence, the town of Wilson in Jackson Hole now lies 10 feet below the level of the nearby Snake River; only riverside dikes protect the town from flooding.

As the mountains rose along this fault, millennia of overlying deposits were stripped away by erosion, leaving three-million-year-old Precambrian rock jutting into the air above the more recent sedimentary deposits in the valley. Because of this shifting and erosion, sandstone deposits atop Mt. Moran match those 24,000 feet below Jackson Hole. Although the most recent major earthquake on the Teton Fault was at least 2,000 years ago, geologists are convinced that Jackson Hole could experience a major temblor at any time.

RIVERS OF ICE

In counterpoint to the uplifting actions that created the general outline of the Tetons, erosional forces have been wearing them down again. Glaciers, which are created when more snow falls than melts off, have proven to be one of the most important of these erosional processes. After a period of several years and under the weight of additional snow, the accumulated snow crystals change into ice. Gravity pulls this ice slowly downhill, creating essentially a frozen river that grinds against whatever lies in the way, plucking loose rocks and soil and polishing hard bedrock. This debris moves slowly down the glacier as if on a conveyer belt, eventually reaching the glacier's terminus.

When a glacier remains the same size for a long period, large piles of glacial debris accumulate at its end, creating what glaciologists call a terminal moraine. One of these created Jackson Lake, when a huge glacier dumped tons of rock at its snout. After the glacier melted back, this terminal moraine became a natural dam for the waters of the Snake River. Similar mounds of glacial debris dammed the creeks that formed Jenny, Leigh, Bradley, Taggart, and Phelps Lakes within Grand Teton National Park.

GRAND TETON NATIONAL PARK SIGHTSEEING HIGHLIGHTS

Menors Ferry/Chapel of the Transfiguration
Jenny Lake
Signal Mountain
Jackson Lake Lodge
Colter Bay Indian Arts Museum
Mormon Row
Gros Ventre River Valley
Schwabacher Landing
Snake River Overlook
Moose-Wilson Road
Cascade Canyon

© DON PITCHER

Mount Moran, Grand Teton National Park

The earth has experienced cyclical periods of glaciation for hundreds of thousands of years, probably due to changes in the earth's orbit around the sun. During the colder portions of these cycles, glaciers appear and advance. The entire Yellowstone region has undergone a series of massive glaciations, the last of which is called the Pinedale Glaciation. It began around 70,000 years ago and had essentially disappeared by 15,000 years ago. At its peak, the Pinedale Glaciation covered all of Yellowstone and reached well into Jackson Hole.

Streams flowed from the ends of these glaciers, carrying along gravel, sand, silt, and clay. The cobbles and sands from these streams were dropped on the flat valley below, while the finer silts and clays continued downstream, leaving behind soils too rocky and nutrient-poor to support trees. Only sagebrush grows on this plain today, while the surrounding hills and moun-tain slopes (which were spared this rocky depo-sition) are covered with lodgepole and subalpine fir forests. Trees can also be found covering the silty terminal moraines that ring the lakes.

Other reminders of the glacial past are the "potholes" (more accurately termed "kettles") that dot the plain south of Signal Mountain. These depressions were created when large blocks of ice were buried under glacial out-wash. When the ice melted, it left a kettle-shaped pond surrounded by glacial debris. Only a dozen or so small glaciers remain in the Tetons; the largest is the 3,500-foot-long Teton Glacier, visible on the northeastern face of Grand Teton. For a far more detailed picture of Teton geology, read *Interpreting the Landscape: Recent and Ongoing Geology of Grand Teton & Yellowstone National Parks,* by John Good and Kenneth Pierce (Moose, WY: Grand Teton Natural History Association, 1996).

GRAND TETON

Wildlife

Grand Teton National Park is an excellent place to look for wildlife. Moose are often seen in the willow meadows along Jackson Lake, south of the settlement of Moose, and along the Snake River. The best times to see animals are in the early morning or at dusk. Herds of pronghorn antelope are common on the sagebrush flats near Kelly. Elk are frequent sights in fall as they migrate down from the high country to the elk refuge near Jackson, but smaller numbers are in the park during summer. (Grand Teton is the only national park outside of Alaska that allows hunting. The rules are pretty strange, however, requiring elk hunters to become temporarily deputized park rangers before they head out!) Grizzlies are currently found only on the park's northern margins, but black bears are present in wooded canyons and riverbeds, so be careful when hiking or camping in the park. Moose are often seen along the Snake River, at Oxbow Bend, and at Willow Flats. Other animals to look for are bald eagles and ospreys along the Snake River and trumpeter swans and Canada geese in ponds and lakes. Look for mule deer in meadow areas and at forest edges, such as those near Colter Bay.

BISON

Herds of bison (buffalo) are commonly seen in the Moran Junction area and in the Mormon Row area. They were present historically (hence the name Buffalo River) but had been extinct for perhaps a century when eight bison were released into Grand Teton National Park in 1969. The population grew slowly for the first decade until they discovered the free alfalfa handout at the elk refuge north of Jackson. Partly because of this winter feeding, the population has grown to almost 600 animals—much to the chagrin of the elk-refuge managers. A few bison are hunted outside the park to control their numbers.

WOLVES

Wolves were reintroduced to Yellowstone National Park starting in 1995, and they continue to spread into new territory. By the winter of 1998–1999, they had moved into Grand Teton National Park and are now denning in the park. They're most easily seen in winter, particularly on the adjacent National Elk Refuge where they prey on elk, but they may sometimes be seen during summer inside the park.

Park History

Once the wonders of Yellowstone came to widespread public attention, it took only a few months for Congress to declare that area a national park. But the magnificent mountain range to the south proved an entirely different story. Early on, there were suggestions that Yellowstone be expanded to include the Tetons, but it would take decades of wrangling before Jackson Hole would finally be preserved.

"DAMNING" JACKSON LAKE

Jackson Lake represents one of the sadder chapters in the history of northwestern Wyoming. Jackson Lake Dam was built in the winter of 1910–1911 to supply water for Idaho potato and beet farmers. The town of Moran was built to house construction workers for Jackson Lake Dam and at one time included more than a hundred ramshackle structures. Virtually nothing remains of the town. The 70-foot-tall dam increased the size of the natural lake, flooding out more than 7,200 acres of trees and creating a tangle of floating and submerged trunks and stumps. To some, the dam seemed like the serpent in the Garden of Eden, a symbol of the development that would destroy the valley if not stopped. The trees remained in Jackson Lake for many years, creating an eyesore until the Park Service and the CCC finally launched a massive cleanup project in the 1930s. The dam was completely rebuilt in 1988–1989, and while the lake now looks attractive, it remains yet another example of how Wyoming provides water for farmers in surrounding states. Late in the fall, especially in dry years, the lake can drop to a large puddle with long stretches of exposed bottom at the upper end. Fortunately, Idaho irrigators did not succeed in their planned dams on Jenny, Leigh, and Taggart Lakes in what is now Grand Teton National Park.

DUDES AND DEVELOPMENT

Because of the rocky soils and long winters, Jackson Hole has always been a marginal place for cattle ranching, and only in the southern end of the valley are the soils rich enough to support a decent crop of hay. This poor soil and harsh climate saved Jackson Hole from early development and forced the ranchers to bring in dudes to supplement their income. (One old-timer noted, "Dudes winter better than cattle.")

Louis Joy established the first Jackson Hole dude ranch, the JY, in 1908 along Phelps Lake. It was followed a few years later by the Bar BC Ranch of Struthers Burt, an acclaimed East Coast author who had come west as a dude but learned enough to go into the business for himself. The dude ranchers were some of the first to realize the value of Jackson Hole and to support its preservation. Burt proposed that the valley and mountains be saved not as a traditional park but as a "museum on the hoof," where ranching and tourism would join hands to stave off commercial developments. The roads would remain unpaved, all homes would be log, and Jackson would stay a frontier town. Needless to say, that didn't happen.

The movement to save Jackson Hole coalesced in a 1923 meeting at the cabin of Maude Noble. Horace Albright, superintendent of Yellowstone National Park, was there, along with local dude ranchers, businessmen, and cattlemen who were eager to save the remote valley from exploitation. To accomplish this goal, they proposed finding a wealthy philanthropist who might be willing to invest the $2 million that would be needed to buy the land. Fortunately, one of Struthers Burt's friends happened to be Kenneth Chorley, an assistant to John D. Rockefeller, Jr. Burt used this contact to get Rockefeller interested in the project.

ROCKY TO THE RESCUE

In 1926, Rockefeller traveled west for a 12-day trip to Yellowstone. Horace Albright used the chance to take him on a side trip into Jackson Hole and to proselytize for protection of the valley. What they saw portended badly for the future: the Jenny Lake dance hall, roadside tourist camps and hot dog stands, rusting abandoned cars, and a place that billboards proclaimed "Home of the Hollywood Cowboy." Rockefeller was angered by the prospect of crass commercial developments blanketing Jackson Hole and quickly signed on to the idea of purchasing the land and giving it to the Park Service.

To cover his tracks as he bought the land, Rockefeller formed the Snake River Land Company; if ranchers had known that the Rockefeller clan was behind the scheme, they would have either refused to sell or jacked up the price. Only a few residents—mostly supporters—knew of the plan. The local banker, Robert Miller, served as land-purchasing agent, although even he opposed letting the Park Service gain control of the valley. Miller used his position to buy out ranches with delinquent mortgages at his Jackson State Bank and then resigned, claiming the whole thing was part of a sinister plot to run the ranchers out and halt "progress." In 1929, Congress voted to establish a small Grand Teton National Park that would encompass the mountains themselves, which stood little chance of development, but not much else. Conservationists knew that without preservation of the valley below, the wonderful vistas would be lost.

A NATIONAL BATTLEGROUND

Rockefeller and Albright finally went public with their land-purchasing scheme in 1930, releasing a tidal wave of outrage. Antipark forces led by Sen. Milward Simpson (father of recently retired Sen.

Alan Simpson) spent the next decade fighting the park tooth and nail, charging that it would destroy the economy of Jackson Hole and that ranchers would lose their livelihood. Rockefeller's agents were falsely accused of trying to intimidate holdouts with strong-arm tactics. Congress refused to accept Rockefeller's gift, and local opposition blocked the bill for more than a decade.

Finally, in 1943, President Roosevelt made an end run around the antipark forces; he accepted the 32,000 acres purchased by Rockefeller, added 130,000 acres of Forest Service land, and declared it the Jackson Hole National Monument. The move outraged those in the valley, prompting more hearings and bills to abolish the new national monument. Wyoming's politicians attacked Roosevelt's actions. A bill overturning the decision was pocket-vetoed by the president, but for the next several years, the Wyoming delegation kept reintroducing the measure.

Things came to a head when Wallace Beery—a Reaganesque Hollywood actor—threatened to "shoot to kill" park officials. Beery, who had to use a stepladder to climb on his horse, organized a cattle drive across the monument. Unable to find anyone to fire on in the new monument, his cadres sat on a creek bank and drank a case of beer, cussing out the damn bureaucrats. So much for the Wild West.

By 1947, the tide had turned as increasing postwar tourism revitalized the local economy. Finally, in 1950, a compromise was reached granting ranchers lifetime grazing rights and the right to trail their cattle across the park en route to summer grazing lands. The new-and-improved Grand Teton National Park had finally come to fruition.

POSTMORTEM

Some of the early fears that Rockefeller would use the new park for his own gain seem at least partly justified. His descendants still own the old JY Ranch and use Phelps Lake as something of a semiprivate playground, while most of the other dude ranches have long since been taken over by the Park Service. Rockefeller also built the enormous Grand Teton Lodge along Jackson Lake and facilities at Colter Bay Village and Jenny Lake, leading some to accuse the family of attempting to monopolize services within the park. The company, Grand Teton Lodge Company, is now owned by Vail Resorts, which manages Jackson Lake Lodge, Jenny Lake Lodge, and Colter Bay Village, along with Jackson Hole Golf & Tennis Club (near Jackson).

Looking back on the controversial creation of Grand Teton National Park, it's easy to see how wrong park opponents were. Teton County has Wyoming's most vibrant economy, and millions of people arrive each year to enjoy the beauty of the undeveloped Tetons. As writer Nathaniel Burt noted, "The old enemies of the park are riding the profitable bandwagon of unlimited tourism with high hearts and open palms." Park opponents' claims that the Park Service would "lock up" the land ring as hollow as similar antiwilderness claims today by descendants of the same politicians who opposed Grand Teton National Park half a century ago. Without inclusion of the land purchased by Rockefeller, it is easy to imagine the valley covered with all sorts of summer-home developments, RV campgrounds, souvenir shops, motels, billboards, and neon signs. Take a look at the town of Jackson to see what might have been.

Exploring the Park

Grand Teton National Park has fewer "attractions" than Yellowstone—its big sister to the north—and an easy day's drive takes you past the road-accessible portions of the park. The real attractions are the mountains and the incomparable views one gets of them from Jackson Hole. This is one backdrop you will never tire of seeing.

ROADS

Grand Teton National Park is bisected by the main north-south highway (U.S. Hwy. 26/89/191) and by the road heading east over Togwotee Pass (U.S. Hwy. 26/287). Both of these routes are kept open year-round, although wintertime plowing ends at Flagg Ranch Resort, just south of the Yellowstone boundary. In addition, a paved park road cuts south from Jackson Lake Dam to Jenny Lake and Moose. Only the southern end of this road is plowed in winter; the remainder becomes a snowmobile and cross-country ski route. South of Moose, a narrow, winding road (the Moose-Wilson Road) connects the park to Teton Village, nine miles away. It is rough dirt in places—no trailers or RVs—and is closed in winter.

As this book was being written, the Park Service was developing a new transportation plan for Grand Teton National Park that may include the closure of some roads to motorized vehicles and the addition of a scheduled bus service from Jackson to the park.

MOOSE

The following tour takes you past points of interest along the main roads. The route follows a general clockwise direction beginning at the **Moose Visitor Center,** 307/739-3399, www.nps.gov/grte. Before heading out, step inside the center (open daily year-round) for a fine introduction to the park and a look at the natural-history videos, books, and oil paintings. A large three-dimensional map here reveals the lay of the land.

The commercial center at Moose is across the Snake River bridge and just east of the visitors center. Here you'll find a plethora of operations run by **Dornan's,** 307/733-2415, www.dornans.com: a general store, gift shop, lodging, restaurant and bar, wine shop, bike shop, canoe and kayak rentals, and a chuck wagon eatery. Also here is a sporting-goods store (Moosely Seconds, 307/739-1801) and fishing shop (Snake River Anglers, 307/733-3699). Moose has pretty much everything you might need for a day in the park.

THE MAGIC OF THE TETONS

Somewhere at the eastern base of the Tetons did those hoofprints disappear into a mountain sanctuary where many crooked paths have led. He that took another man's possession, or he that took another man's life, could always run here if the law or popular justice were too hot at his heels. Steep ranges and forests walled him in from the world on all four sides, almost without a break; and every entrance lay through intricate solitudes. Snake River came into the place through canyons and mournful pines and marshes, to the north, and went out at the south between formidable chasms. Every tributary to this stream rose among high peaks and ridges, and descended into the valley by well-nigh impenetrable courses. . . . Down in the bottom was a spread of level land, broad, and beautiful, with the blue and silver Tetons rising from its chain of lakes to the west and other heights residing over its other sides.

—from Owen Wister's *The Virginian*

GRAND TETON

TETON HIKING TRAILS

Jackson Lake

Cirque Lake

Mt. Moran

Caribou-Targhee N.F.

Leigh Canyon

Leigh Lake

GRAND TARGHEE RESORT

Freds Mtn.

Paintbrush Divide

Paintbrush

Canyon

Trail

Lake Solitude

Rockchuck Pk.

To Jackson Lake Dam

TETON CANYON

Range

Mt. St. John

JENNY LAKE LODGE

Cascade Canyon Trail

Inspiration Point

Jenny Lake

JENNY LAKE

Jedediah Smith

Table Mtn.

Hidden Falls

SHUTTLE BOAT

Mt. Owen

Teewinot Mtn.

Grand Teton

Wilderness

HURRICANE PASS

Grand Teton

LUPINE MEADOWS

National Park

TETON PARK RD.

Middle Teton

Ampitheater L.

DEVIL'S STAIRS

Alaska Basin

Alaska Basin Trail

South Teton

Bradley L.

To Moran

Snowdrift Lake

Taggart L.

CLIMBERS RANCH

Darby Canyon

Teton

Crest

Static Peak Trail

Valley Trail

0   2 mi

0   2 km

Death

Canyon Trail

DEATH CANYON PATROL CABIN

WHITE GRASS RANGER STATION

MENOR'S FERRY

Trail

Phelps

MOOSE VISITOR CENTER

DORNAN'S

Fox

Creek

FOX CREEK PASS

Mt. Hunt

Canyon Trail

Lake

J Y RANCH

Blacktail Butte

Jackson Hole

Open

Granite Canyon Trail

AIRPORT

GROS VENTRE

Snake River

JACKSON HOLE SKI AREA

AERIAL TRAMWAY

Teton Village

MOOSE-WILSON RD.

Lake Creek

Gros Ventre River

Rondervous Mtn.

Teton

National

Forest

National Elk

Refuge

26

89

191

COAL CREEK

TETON PASS

Fish Creek

390

To Jackson

GRAND TETON

© AVALON TRAVEL PUBLISHING, INC.

MENOR'S FERRY AREA

Just inside the South Entrance to Grand Teton National Park, a side road leads to **Chapel of the Transfiguration** and Menor's Ferry. The rustic log church (built in 1925) is most notable for its dramatic setting. Episcopal services are held on summer Sundays, with Eucharist at 8 and 10 A.M.

The back window faces directly toward the Tetons, providing ample distractions for worshippers. The bell out front was cast in 1842. Nearby **Menor's Ferry** is named for William D. Menor, who first homesteaded here in 1894 and later built a cable ferry to make it easier to cross the river. His old whitewashed store still stands. You can cross the river in a reconstructed version of the old ferry when the water level is low enough; check out the ingenious propulsion mechanism that uses the current to pull it across. For many years, Menor's ferry served as the primary means of crossing the river in the central part of Jackson Hole. Wagons were charged 50 cents, while those on horseback paid 25 cents. (William Menor's brother, Holiday, lived on the opposite side of the river, but the two often feuded, yelling insults across the water at each other and refusing to acknowledge one another for years at a time.)

Also here is the half-mile **Menor's Ferry Trail;** a brochure describes historic points of interest along the path. Bill Menor's cabin houses a small country store that sells the old-fashioned supplies he stocked at the turn of the 20th century. It is open daily 9 A.M.–4:30 P.M. from late May to late September; closed the rest of the year.

Menor sold out to Maude Noble in 1918, and she ran the ferry until 1927, when a bridge was built near the present one in Moose. Her cabin now houses an excellent collection of historical photos from Jackson Hole. Maude Noble gained a measure of fame in 1923 when she hosted the gathering of residents to save Jackson Hole from development (see Park History).

TAGGART AND BRADLEY LAKES

Heading northwest beyond the Menor's Ferry area, the main road climbs up an old river bench, created by flooding from the rapid melting of the glaciers, and passes the trailhead to the turquoise waters of Taggart Lake. The land around here was burned in the 1,028-acre Beaver Creek lightning fire of 1985, and summers find a riot of wildflowers. A very popular day hike leads from the parking lot at the trailhead to Taggart Lake and then back via the Beaver Creek Trail, a distance of 4.4 miles round-trip. A side loop to Bradley Lake adds about two miles to this journey. These trails provide a fine way to explore the dam-like glacial moraines that created these lakes. You can also continue beyond Bradley Lake on a trail that climbs to beautiful Amphitheater Lake, the primary access point for climbs up Grand Teton. (Climbers generally begin from Jenny Lake, however.)

JENNY LAKE

The most loved of all Grand Teton lakes is Jenny Lake, nestled at the foot of Cascade Canyon and surrounded by a luxuriant forest of Engelmann spruce, subalpine fir, and lodgepole pine. Jenny Lake is named for Jenny Leigh, the Shoshone wife of Beaver Dick Leigh. A

© DON PITCHER

Jenny Lake, at the foot of Cascade Canyon

JENNY AND LEIGH LAKES

To N. Jenny Lake Jct., Jackson Lake, and Yellowstone

TETON PARK RD.

TWOWAY

ONE-WAY

JENNY LAKE LODGE

LEIGH LAKE

STRING LAKE/
PICNIC AREA

String Lake

Leigh Lake

Bearpaw Lake

Mystic Isle

Boulder Island

Trapper Lake

Jenny Lake

SHUTTLE BOAT

JENNY LAKE
VISITOR CENTER,
RANGER STATION, AND
STORE

Jenny Lake Jct.

S. Jenny Lake Jct.
To Moose Junction
and Jackson

To Moose Junction
and Jackson

WEST SHORE
BOAT DOCK

EAST SHORE
BOAT DOCK

Inspiration Pt.

Hidden
Falls

Moose Ponds

To Lupine
Meadows Trailhead

Grand Teton

National Park

Paintbrush Canyon Trail

Rockchuck Pk.
(11,144 ft.) ▲

Mt. St. John
(11,430 ft.) ▲

Lake of the
Craggs

Rock of Ages
(10,895 ft.) ▲

Falling Ice
Glacier

Mt. Woodring
(11,590 ft.) ▲

The Jaw
(11,400 ft.) ▲

Teewinot Mtn.
(12,325 ft.) ▲

Cascade Canyon Trail

Cirque
Lake

Leigh Canyon

Grizzly
Bear Lake

Holly
Lake

(11,012 ft.) ▲

Mt. Owen
(12,928 ft.) ▲

Valhalla Canyon

Cleaver Pk.
(11,055 ft.) ▲

Maidenform Pk.
(11,137 ft.) ▲

Mink Lake

Lake
Solitude

Mica Lake

Petersen Glacier

(10,855 ft.) ▲

The
Wigwams

Teton Crest Trail

Teton   Range

Little Pk.
(10,712 ft.) ▲

Caribou-
Targhee
National
Forest

Table Mtn.
(11,106 ft.) ▲

0   0.5 mi

0   0.5 km

© AVALON TRAVEL PUBLISHING, INC.

one-way loop road leads south past Jenny and String Lakes, providing excellent views of the **Cathedral Group:** Teewinot, Grand Teton, and Mt. Owen. This is the most popular part of the park, and day-hikers will find a plethora of trails to sample, along with crowds of fellow hikers. Paths lead around both Jenny and String Lakes, while another nearly level trail follows the east shore of **Leigh Lake** to several pleasant sandy beaches. **String Lake** is narrow but very pretty and makes a fine place for canoeing or swimming. Get supplies from the small store at Jenny Lake and information or guidebooks from the **Jenny Lake Visitor Center** (open June to early Labor Day). Coin-operated storage lockers are next to the store.

Beautiful **Jenny Lake Lodge** sits on the northeast end of the lake and provides the finest lodging in the park. The gourmet meals are legendary, but reservations are necessary; call 307/733-4647.

INSPIRATION POINT AND CASCADE CANYON

One of the most popular attractions in the area is Inspiration Point, on the west side of Jenny Lake. It's 2.4 miles by trail from the Jenny Lake Ranger Station on the east side, or you can ride one of the summertime shuttle boats that cross the lake every 20 minutes or so for $7 round-trip ($5 for ages 7–12, free for younger kids). In midsummer, the shuttle boat lines lengthen around 11 A.M., so get here early in the morning to avoid the crush and to better your odds at finding a parking spot. Afternoon thunderstorms frequently build up over the Tetons, which is another good reason to start your hike early. Boat tickets are not available in advance. Scenic boat cruises and fishing-boat rentals are also available at Jenny Lake; call 307/734-9227. Boats operate early June to early September.

From the boat dock on the west side, the trail climbs one-half mile to picturesque **Hidden Falls,** then continues steeply another one-half mile to Inspiration Point, which overlooks Jackson Hole from 400 feet above Jenny Lake. Avoid the crowds on the way down from Inspiration Point by following a second trail back to Jenny Lake. If you

miss the last boat at 6 P.M., it's a 2.4-mile hike around the lake to the parking area.

Many day-hikers continue at least part of the way up Cascade Canyon from Inspiration Point. The trail climbs gradually, gaining 640 feet in the next 3.6 miles, and provides a good chance to fish for trout or watch for moose and other animals along Cascade Creek. Those with strong legs can make a *very* long day hike all the way up to Lake Solitude (18.4 miles round-trip) or even Hurricane Pass (23.2 miles round-trip and gaining almost 3,600 feet on the way up). If you're into hiking that far, it probably makes more sense to reserve a backcountry campsite and take things a bit more leisurely. See Backcountry Hiking for details.

SIGNAL MOUNTAIN AREA

As the road approaches Jackson Lake, a paved but narrow side road (no RVs or trailers) turns east and leads to the summit of Signal Mountain, 800 feet above Jackson Hole. On top are panoramic views of the Tetons, Jackson Lake, the Snake River, and the long valley below. To the south lies **The Potholes,** a hummocky area created when retreating glaciers left behind huge blocks of ice. The melting ice created depressions, some of which are still filled with water. Signal Mountain was burned by a massive 1879 fire and offers a good opportunity to see how Yellowstone may look in a century.

Hugging the southeast shore of Jackson Lake, **Signal Mountain Lodge,** 307/733-5470 or 307/543-2831, www.signalmountainlodge.com, includes cabins and campsites, plus a gift shop, convenience store, gas station, marina with boat rentals, restaurant, and bar. Just east of the lodge is **Chapel of the Sacred Heart,** a small Roman Catholic church that has summer services on Saturdays at 5:30 P.M. and Sundays at 10 A.M. The road then crosses **Jackson Lake Dam,** which raises the water level by 39 feet, alters the river's natural flow, and inundates a large area upstream. Many conservationists fought to have Jackson Lake excluded from the park, concerned that it would establish a bad precedent for allowing reservoirs in other parks. Nevertheless, once you get away from the dam, the lake appears relatively natural today.

BEAVER DICK LEIGH

Around 1863, Richard "Beaver Dick" Leigh became the first white man to attempt a permanent life in Jackson Hole. An Englishman by birth, Beaver Dick lived in a log cabin with his Shoshone wife, Jenny, and their four children, scraping out the barest existence by hunting, trapping, and guiding. As guide for the 1872 Hayden Survey of the Jackson Hole area, Beaver Dick gained the respect of the surveyors, who named Leigh Lake for him and Jenny Lake for his wife. Today a local bar denigrates this remarkable man by calling itself Beaver Dick's and using a cartoonish image of him in its ads. The real man was nothing like this, and reading his diaries and letters is a lesson in how difficult life was for early Wyoming settlers. On one terrible Christmas in 1876, Beaver Dick watched his entire family—Jenny, their newborn baby, and the four other children—all slowly die from smallpox. Their deaths left him badly shaken, as he related in a letter to a friend:

i got Dick in the house and to bed and Tom went over to get Mr. Anes. Wile Tom and Anes was sounding the ice to see if a horse could cross my wife was struck with Death. she rased up and looked me streaght in the face and then she got excited . . . and she sade she was going to die and all our chidron wold die and maby i wold die . . . she was laying very quiet now for about 2 hours when she asked for a drink of water. i was laying downe with one of my daughters on eatch arme keeping them quiet because of the fevor. i told Anes what she wanted

ALONG JACKSON LAKE

A turnout near Jackson Lake Junction provides views over **Willow Flats,** where moose are frequently seen, especially in the morning. Topping a bluff overlooking the flats is **Jackson Lake Lodge,** built in the 1950s with the $5 million financial backing of John D. Rockefeller, Jr. Architects are not thrilled about the design (one author termed it "the ugliest building in Western Wyoming"), but the 60-foot-tall back windows frame an unbelievable view of the Tetons and Jackson Lake. Immediately across from the lodge is a trail leading to **Emma Matilda** and **Two Ocean** Lakes. It is 14 miles round-trip around both lakes, with lots of wildlife along the way, including moose, trumpeter swans, pelicans, and ducks. You may have to contend with large groups on horseback.

COLTER BAY

Colter Bay Village is one of the most developed parts of Grand Teton National Park, with a full marina, stores, a gas station, cabins, a campground, restaurants, and acres of parking. The main attraction here is the visitors center, which houses the **Colter Bay Indian Arts Museum,** 307/739-3594. It's open daily 8 A.M.–5 P.M. mid-May to Memorial Day and Labor Day to September; daily 8 A.M.–8 P.M. from early June to Labor Day. The museum is closed the rest of the year. Admission is free. Inside you will find the extraordinary David T. Vernon collection of Indian arts, the finest of its kind in any national park and one of the best in Wyoming. The collection spreads through several rooms on two floors and includes exquisitely beaded buckskin dresses, moccasins, masks, ceremonial pipes, war clubs, shields, bows, baskets, headdresses, and other decorated items. Stop to chat with Native artisans as they work on paintings, beaded items, wood carvings, pottery, and weaving. They're at the museum daily Memorial Day to Labor Day. This museum should not be missed! Step out back to join the shoreside fun or to rent a canoe or boat from the nearby marina.

A mostly level trail leads from the marina out to **Hermitage Point** before looping back again, a distance of nine miles round-trip. Along the way you pass beaver ponds and willow patches where trumpeter swans, moose, and ducks are com-

and he gave hur a drink and 10 minuts more she was ded . . . i can not wright one hundreth part that pased thrue my mind at this time as i thaught deth was on me. i sade Jinny i will sone be with you and fell asleep. Tom sade i ad beene a sleep a half hour when i woke up everything was wet with presperation i was very weak. i lade for 10 or 15 minuts and saw William and Anne Jane had to be taken up to ease themselves every 5 minuts and Dick Juner very restlas . . . Anne Jane died about 8 o clock about the time every year i used to give them a candy puling and thay menchond about the candy puling many times wile sick . . . William died on the 25 about 9 or 10 o clock in the evening . . . on the 26th Dick Juner died . . . Elizabeth was over all danger but this, and she caught cold and sweled up agane and died on the 28 of Dec about 2 o clock in the morning. this was the hardist blow of all . . . i shall improve the place and live and die near my famley but i shall not be able to do enything for a few months for my mind is disturbed at the sights that i see around me and [the] work that my famley as done wile thay were liveing.

But the human spirit is remarkably resilient. Beaver Dick later married a Bannock girl, raised another family, and guided for others, even meeting Theodore Roosevelt on one of his hunting trips. Beaver Dick Leigh died in 1899 and was buried on a ridge overlooking Idaho's Teton Basin.

monly seen. Get a map of Colter Bay trails from the visitors center. Shorter loop paths include the two-mile **Lakeshore Trail** and the three-mile **Swan Lake-Heron Pond Trail**.

ROCKEFELLER MEMORIAL PARKWAY

North of Colter Bay, the highway cruises along the shore of Jackson Lake for the next nine miles, providing some fine vantage points of the Tetons. The burned area on the opposite shore was ignited by lightning in the 1974 Waterfalls Canyon Fire, which consumed 3,700 acres. By late fall each year, Idaho spud farmers have drawn down water in the lake, leaving a long, barren shoreline at the upper end.

Shortly after the road leaves the upper end of Jackson Lake, a signboard announces your entrance into **John D. Rockefeller Jr. Memorial Parkway**. This 24,000-acre parcel of land was transferred to the National Park Service in 1972 in commemoration of Rockefeller's unstinting work in establishing Grand Teton National Park. The land forms a connection between Grand Teton and Yellowstone and is managed by Grand Teton National Park. Much of this area was severely burned by the 1988 Huck Fire, which began when strong winds blew a tree into power lines. Despite immediate efforts to control the blaze, it consumed 4,000 acres in the first two hours and later grew to cover nearly 200,000 acres, primarily within the Forest Service's Teton Wilderness. Dense young lodgepole pines now carpet much of the land.

On the northern end of Rockefeller Parkway is **Flagg Ranch Resort**, 307/543-2861 or 800/443-2311, www.flaggranch.com, where the modern facilities include a gas station, convenience store, gift shop, cabins, restaurant, and campground with RV hookups. The park service operates the **Flagg Ranch Information Station** here from early June to Labor Day. During the winter, Flagg Ranch is the jumping-off point for snowcoach and snowmobile trips into Yellowstone, and snowmobiles are available for rent.

Two nearby trails provide easy day hikes. The nearly level **Polecat Creek Loop Trail** is 2.3 miles round-trip and follows a ridge overlooking a marsh and through conifer forests. **Flagg Canyon Trail** is five miles round-trip and provides views of a rocky canyon cut through by the Snake River.

GRASSY LAKE ROAD

Grassy Lake Road takes off just north of Flagg Ranch Resort and continues 52 miles to Ashton, Idaho. It's a scenic drive, but don't attempt this narrow and rough dirt road with a trailer or an RV. This route provides a shortcut to the Bechler River area of Yellowstone and is a popular wintertime snowmobile route. Huckleberry Hot Springs, a short hike north from the Grassy Lake Road bridge over the Snake River, was the site of a public swimming pool until 1983, when the facility was razed by the Park Service. The hot springs are accessible via an unmaintained trail, but you'll need to wade Polecat Creek to reach them. Although they remain popular with hikers and cross-country skiers, it's worth noting that the springs may pose a risk from dangerously high radiation levels.

A few miles east of the Idaho–Wyoming border on Grassy Lake Road is **Squirrel Meadows,** where Caribou-Targhee National Forest has a two-room guard station with three sets of bunkbeds, a hand pump for water, and an outhouse. The cabin sleeps six and costs $35; details at 208/652-7442, www.fs.fed.us/r4/caribou. During the winter, access is via snowmobile or skis for the last 12 miles to the cabin from the Idaho side. Lodging is also available just across the Idaho border at **Squirrel Creek Guest Ranch,** 208/652-3972, www.idahoranch.com.

JACKSON LAKE TO MORAN JUNCTION

Heading east and south from Jackson Lake, the road immediately passes **Oxbow Bend,** where the turnout is almost always filled with folks looking for geese, ducks, moose, and other animals. The oxbow was formed when the meandering river cut off an old loop. The calm water here is a delightful place for canoes, although the mosquitoes can be a major annoyance in midsummer. Come fall, photographers line the shoulder of the road for classic shots of flaming aspen trees with Grand Teton and **Mt. Moran** in the background. Mt. Moran is the massive peak with a flattened summit, a skillet-shaped glacier across its

front, and a distinctive black vertical diabase dike that looks like a scar from some ancient battle. It rises 12,605 feet above sea level and is named for Thomas Moran, whose beautiful paintings of Yellowstone helped persuade Congress to set aside that area as the world's first national park.

At **Moran Junction** you pass the park's Buffalo Entrance Station and meet the road to Togwotee Pass and Dubois. A post office and school are the only developments remaining here. The epic Western *The Big Trail* was filmed nearby in 1930, starring an actor named John Wayne in his first speaking role. (Wayne had never ridden a horse before this.) An interesting side trip is to head east from Moran on U.S. Hwy. 26/287 for three miles to **Buffalo Valley Road.** This narrow and scenic road leads to Turpin Meadow, a major entryway into the Teton Wilderness (see the Jackson Hole chapter). It is very pretty, especially in early summer when flowers carpet the fields. Buck-and-rail fences line the road, and the pastures are filled with horses and cattle. Beyond Turpin Meadow, the road turns to gravel and climbs sharply uphill, rejoining the main highway a couple of miles below Cowboy Village Resort at Togwotee. The Blackrock Ranger Station of Bridger-Teton National Forest is eight miles east of Moran Junction on U.S. Hwy. 26/287. Nearby is historic **Rosie's Cabin,** built early in the 20th century by Rudolph Rosencrans, an Austrian emigrant who was the first forest ranger in this part of the Tetons.

MORAN JUNCTION TO MOOSE

Heading south from Moran, U.S. Hwy. 26/89/191 immediately crosses the Buffalo River (a.k.a. Buffalo Fork of the Snake River), where bison were once abundant. With a little help from humans, bison have been reestablished and are now often seen just south of here along the road. The turnoff to the **Cunningham Cabin** is six miles south of Moran Junction. The structure actually consists of two sod-roofed log cabins connected by a covered walkway called a "dogtrot." Built around 1890, it served first as living quarters and later as a barn and smithy. A park brochure describes the locations of other structures on the property.

Pierce Cunningham came here as a homesteader and, with his wife Margaret, settled to raise cattle. Although this was some of the better land in this part of the valley, the soil was still so rocky that they had a hard time digging fencepost holes. Instead, they opted to build the buck-and-rail fences that have become a hallmark of Jackson Hole ranches. Cunningham Ranch gained notoriety in 1893 when a posse surrounded two suspected horse thieves who were wintering at Cunningham's place while he was away. Vigilantes shot and killed George Spencer and Mike Burnett in an example of "mountain justice." Later, however, suspicions arose that hired killers working for wealthy cattle barons had led the posse and that the murdered men may have been innocent. **Spread Creek** is just north of the Cunningham cabin; it gained its name by having two mouths, separated by a distance of three miles.

The highway next rolls past **Triangle X Ranch,** one of the most famous dude ranches in Jackson Hole. Although it's on park land, the Turner family has managed Triangle X for more than 60 years. (One of the owners, John Turner, was director of the U.S. Fish & Wildlife Service under the first President Bush.) Stop by just after sunup to watch wranglers driving 120 head of horses to the corrals. It's a scene straight out of an old Marlboro ad.

Southwest from Triangle X, the road climbs along an ancient river terrace and passes **Hedrick Pond,** where the 1963 Henry Fonda movie *Spencer's Mountain* was filmed. Although the book on which the movie was based was set in Virginia, the producers found the Tetons a considerably more impressive location. Trumpeter swans are often seen on the pond. Hedrick Pond isn't really visible from the road and there are no signs pointing it out, but you can get there by parking near the S-curve road sign 1.4 miles south of Triangle X. The pond is a good example of a kettle pond, created when retreating glaciers left behind a block of ice covered with gravel and other deposits. The ice melted, leaving behind a depression that filled to become Hedrick Pond.

Several turnouts provide popular photo-opportunity spots, the most famous being **Snake River Overlook.** Ansel Adams's famous shot of the Tetons was taken here and has been repeated with less success by generations of photographers. Throughout the summer, a progression of different flowers blooms in the open sagebrush flats along the road, adding brilliant slashes of color. They're prettiest in late June; in the high country, the peak comes a month or more later than elsewhere.

Just north of Snake River Overlook is the turnoff to **Deadman's Bar.** A steep partially dirt road (not for RVs) drops down to one of the primary river-access points used by river rafters. The river bar received its name from an incident in 1886. Four German prospectors entered the area, but only one—John Tonnar—emerged. Bodies of the other three were found along the Snake River, and Tonnar was charged with murder. The jury in Evanston believed his claim of self-defense, and he was set free, an act that so angered locals that they vowed to take care of future Jackson Hole criminals with a shotgun. A skull from one of the victims is on display in the Jackson Hole Museum.

Another popular put-in for river runners is **Schwabacher Landing,** at the end of a one-mile gravel road that splits off just north of the Glacier View Turnout. This is a pleasant place for riverside picnics. Some of the most famous Teton Range photos—the ones you see in local galleries—were taken just a few hundred yards upstream from the parking area.

BLACKTAIL BUTTE AND MORMON ROW

One mile north of the turnoff to Moose, Antelope Flats Road heads east along Ditch Creek. Just south of here lies Blacktail Butte, a timbered knoll rising over the surrounding sagebrush plains. It's a favorite of rock climbers and has a hiking trail up the back (east) side. You will want to stop at the much-photographed old farm buildings known as Mormon Row. The farmland here was homesteaded by predominantly Mormon settlers in the early 1900s but was later purchased by Rockefeller's Snake River Land Company and transferred to the Park Service. Only one set of buildings—an acre of the Moulton Ranch—is still in private hands. The other buildings were allowed to decay until the 1990s when the Park Service recognized their value and stepped in to preserve the structures. Herds of bison often wander past the old farmsteads in summer, providing one of the best places to view them. Also keep your eyes open for small groups of pronghorn antelope in the vicinity.

TETON SCIENCE SCHOOL

Hidden away in a valley along upper Ditch Creek is Teton Science School (TSS), a fine hands-on school for both young and old. Founded in 1967 as a summer field-biology program for high-school kids, it has grown into a year-round program with classes that run the gamut from elementary-school level all the way up to intensive college courses and a residency program. Summertime visitors will enjoy their one- to four-day adult seminars on such diverse subjects as entomology for fly-fishers, birdwatching, the biology of bugs, wildflower identification, river channels, and grizzly bear biology. These classes are limited to 12 students and fill up fast, so make reservations in the spring to be sure of a spot. The school's excellent month-long wilderness emergency medical technician (EMT) course in early winter ($2,400 per person) is one of the few programs of its kind in the nation. TSS also offers a fine **winter speaker series** at the National Museum of Wildlife Art covering a spectrum of scientific, environmental, and social issues. In addition, the school operates **Wildlife Expeditions,** 307/733-2623 or 888/945-3567, www.tetonscience.org/wildlife, with wildlife-viewing safaris throughout the Grand Teton and Yellowstone area.

Based at the old Elbo dude ranch (started in 1932), TSS includes two dormitories, a central kitchen, a dining area, and other log structures. Visitors to the school should visit the **Murie Natural History Museum,** which displays thousands of specimens of birds, mammals, and plants. Included are casts of animal tracks used by famed wildlife biologist Olaus Murie in producing his *Peterson's Guide to Animal Tracks.* It's open to the public, but call ahead to arrange an appointment. Get a copy of the course catalog by contacting TSS at 307/733-4765, www.tetonscience.org.

SHADOW MOUNTAIN AREA

North from the TSS turnoff, the paved road splits. Turn left (west) on Antelope Flats Road to head back to Mormon Row and the main highway, or continue straight ahead to climb up Shadow Mountain (8,252 feet). The name comes from the shadows of the Tetons that fall across the mountain's face each evening. The road is paved for the first mile or so, but turns to gravel as it snakes rather steeply up the mountain. The road is definitely not recommended for RVs or trailers, or for any vehicles after rains when some sections turn to slippery mud. The views from the top of Shadow Mountain are truly amazing, with the Tetons in all their glory. Several dispersed campsites can be found along this route on Forest Service land.

KELLY AND VICINITY

The small settlement of Kelly borders on the southeastern end of Grand Teton National Park and has log homes and a cluster of Mongolian-style yurts—certainly the most unusual dwellings in Wyoming. Folks living in the yurts share a common bathhouse and rent the land. The town has a shoebox-size post office and a couple of rental cabins. The Park Service's **Gros Ventre Campground** is three miles west of here.

Gros Ventre Road leads east from the Kelly area, passing **Kelly Warm Spring** on the right. Its shallow and warm waters are a favorite place for local kayakers to practice their rolls or for families to swim on a summer afternoon. A short distance up the road and off to the north (left) are the collapsing remains of the *Shane* **cabin,** where a scene from the classic 1951 Western was filmed. Beyond this point, the road enters Bridger-Teton National Forest and the Slide Lake area, where there is a Forest Service campground.

GROS VENTRE SLIDE

One of the most extraordinary geologic events in recent Wyoming history took place in the Gros Ventre (pronounced "GROW-vont"—"Big Belly" in French trapper lingo) Canyon, named for the Gros

Kelly Warm Spring

Ventre Indians of this area. Sheep Mountain, on the south side of the canyon, consists of sandstone underlain by a layer of shale that becomes slippery when wet. Melting snow and heavy rains in the spring of 1925 lubricated this layer of shale, and on June 23 the entire north end of the mountain—a section 2,000 feet wide and one mile long—suddenly slid 1.5 miles downslope, instantly damming the river below and creating Slide Lake. A rancher in the valley, Guil Huff, watched in amazement as the mountain began to move, but he managed to gallop his horse out of the way as the slide roared within 30 feet. Huff's ranch floated away on the new lake several days later.

For two years folks kept a wary eye on the makeshift dam of rock and mud. Then, on May 18, 1927, the dam suddenly gave way, pushing an enormous wall of water through the downstream town of Kelly. Six people perished in the flood, and when the water reached Snake River Canyon nine hours later it filled the canyon to the rim with boiling water, trees, houses, and debris. Today a smaller Slide Lake still exists, and the massive landslide that created it more than 75 years ago remains an exposed gouge visible for miles around. Geologists say that, under the right conditions, more of Sheep Mountain could slide. Dead trees still stand in the upper end of Slide Lake. The Forest Service has a **Gros Ventre Geological Trail** 10 miles up Gros Ventre Road. This quarter-mile path leads to an incredible viewpoint overlooking the slide and is marked with interpretive signs.

GROS VENTRE RIVER VALLEY

Above Slide Lake (six miles up), the road turns to gravel, becoming quite rutted in places. Surprising scenery makes the sometimes bone-jarring route easier to take. The landscape here is far different from that of the Tetons, with brilliant red-orange badland hills rising sharply above the Gros Ventre River. Two more Forest Service campgrounds (Red Hills and Crystal Creek) are four miles above Slide Lake, or you can camp in dispersed sites off the road. **Grizzly Lake Trail** starts at the Red Hills Campground and continues for 3.5 miles to this small mountain lake. There are wonderful vistas of the Red Hills and Gros Ventre River valley below.

The road continues another 15 beautiful miles along the river above the lake, getting rougher at the upper end. Several remote guest ranches are up here. Beyond Cow Creek Trailhead (29 miles from Kelly) the route is virtually impassable unless you have a high-clearance 4WD and are ready to get stuck. Hard-core mountain-bikers sometimes continue up this road/trail and then drop down into the Green River watershed north of Pinedale. Cow Creek Trail and other paths lead into the Gros Ventre Wilderness, which borders the south side of the road. On the drive back down the Gros Ventre River valley you will discover some fine views across to the Tetons.

MOOSE-WILSON ROAD

This narrow and winding road heads south from park headquarters in Moose, continuing nine miles to Teton Village. It is paved most of the way, but a sometimes bone-jarring middle section is dirt. Keep your speed down to reduce the amount of dust in the air. No trailers or RVs are allowed, and the road is not plowed in the winter. It is especially pretty in the fall when the aspens are turning. This is also a good place to watch for moose and other animals in summer or for easy cross-country ski adventures on a sunny winter day. Note: As this book was being written, the Park Service was considering closing the Moose-Wilson Road to most vehicles. If this happens, it will still be open to bicycles and foot traffic.

Two backcountry trailheads—Death Canyon Trailhead and Granite Canyon Trailhead—are accessed from the Moose-Wilson Road. A long loop hike up Death Canyon is described as an overnight hike later. For something less challenging, start from Death Canyon Trailhead (three miles south of Moose) and hike about one mile to **Phelps Lake Overlook,** where you get a view across this beautiful mountain lake 600 feet below. The historic JY Ranch (built in 1908) sits back from Phelps Lake and still belongs to the Rockefeller family; any motorboats you see are probably theirs. This is one of the only remaining private inholdings within Grand Teton National Park. From Phelps Lake Overlook you can hike steeply down for a lakeside picnic on the sandy beach (four miles round-trip from the trailhead). An alternative day-hiking option is to continue from the overlook to **Death Canyon Patrol Cabin.** Getting to the cabin requires losing 400 feet in elevation and then climbing 1,000 feet higher. The small log cabin was built by the Civilian Conservation Corps in the 1930s and is still used by trail maintenance crews. Continue one-half mile beyond the cabin up the trail to Fox Creek Pass for a dramatic vista into Death Canyon. It's a bit more than eight miles round-trip between this viewpoint and Death Canyon Trailhead.

Backcountry Hiking

The precipitous Tetons that look so dramatic from the roads are even more impressive up close and personal. Grand Teton National Park is laced with 200 miles of trails, and hikers can choose anything from simple day treks to weeklong trips along the crest of the range. Unlike nearby Yellowstone, where most of the country is forested, the Tetons contain extensive Alpine scenery. This means, however, that many of the high passes won't be free of snow until late July and may require ice axes before then. Check at the visitors centers or Jenny Lake Ranger Station for current trail conditions. In addition, this high country can be dangerous when frequent thunderstorms roll through in summer. Several people have been killed by lightning strikes in the Tetons.

The most popular hiking area centers on the crest of the Tetons and the lakes that lie at its feet, most notably Jenny Lake. **Teton Crest Trail** stretches from Teton Pass north all the way to Cascade Canyon, with numerous connecting paths from both sides of the range. Three relatively short (two- to three-day) loop hikes are described later. For more complete descriptions of park trails, see *Jackson Hole Hikes* by Rebecca Woods (Jackson: White Willow Publishing) or *Teton Trails* by Katy Duffy and Darwin Wile (Grand Teton Natural History Association, www.grandtetonpark.org). Get topographic maps at the Moose Visitor Center or Teton Mountaineering in Jackson. Best is the waterproof version produced by Trails Illustrated.

REGULATIONS AND PERMITS

The hiking trails of Grand Teton National Park are some of the most heavily used paths in Wyoming, and strict regulations are enforced. Backcountry-use permits are required of all overnight hikers, and you'll need to specify a particular camping zone or site for each night of your trip. Get permits and detailed backcountry brochures from the visitors centers in Moose or Colter Bay or the Jenny Lake Ranger Station. Get there early in the morning during summer for permits to popular trails. A limited number of backcountry permits can be reserved in advance from January 1 to May 15 by writing the Permits Office, Grand Teton National Park, P.O. Drawer 170, Moose, WY 83012. For faster service, send a fax to 307/739-3438. You'll need to pick the permit up in person and pay a $15 service fee for reservations. There's no charge for permits if you get them the day of your trip. Get more information on permits and reservations by calling 307/739-3309 or 307/739-3397. Be sure to also request their Backcountry Camping publication, with details on regulations, snow conditions, minimizing impacts, and bear safety issues. On the back is a trail map that shows camping zones and access. The same information is available on the web at www.nps.gov/grte.

SAFETY IN THE BACKCOUNTRY

Grizzlies are primarily found in the northern end of Grand Teton National Park, but you still need to hang all food because black bears roam throughout the park, particularly in the forested areas along the lakes. Special boxes are provided for food storage at some backcountry campsites. Campfires are not allowed at higher elevations, so be sure to bring a cooking stove. Bikes are not permitted on trails anywhere in the park.

Backcountry hikers (and day-hikers for that matter) need to be aware of the dangers from summertime thunderstorms in the Tetons. A common weather pattern is for clear mornings to build to blustery thunderstorms in late afternoon, followed by gradual clearing as evening arrives. Lightning is a major threat in the park's exposed alpine country, and rain showers can be surprisingly heavy at times. Make sure all of your gear is wrapped in plastic (garbage bags work well), and carry a rain poncho or other rainwear. Many hikers carry cell phones for emergencies, but coverage is spotty in the mountains. Unfortunately, the phones can also create a

false sense of security for those who are not familiar with backcountry travel. Don't head unprepared into the mountains thinking you can always call for a rescue if you sprain your ankle.

CASCADE CANYON TO PAINTBRUSH CANYON

One of the most popular hikes in Grand Teton National Park is this 19-mile loop trip up Cascade Canyon, over Paintbrush Divide, and down Paintbrush Canyon (or vice versa). The trip offers a little of everything: dense forests, alpine lakes, flower-covered meadows, and magnificent views of the Tetons. This trip is best done in late summer because a cornice of snow typically blocks Paintbrush Divide until the latter part of July. Most folks do it as an overnight trip, but it's possible to do the entire loop in a single very long day if you're in good shape and have a masochistic streak. Be sure to bring plenty of water along.

Begin at the String Lake Trailhead and head south around Jenny Lake, stopping to enjoy the views (and crowds) at Inspiration Point before heading up along Cascade Creek. The trail splits at the upper end of this canyon; turning left takes you to Hurricane Pass and the Teton Crest Trail, where you'll discover wonderful views of the back side of Grand Teton. Instead, turn right (north) and head up to beautiful Lake Solitude. Behind you, Teewinot, Mt. Owen, and Grand Teton are framed by the glacially carved valley walls. Above Lake Solitude, the trail climbs sharply to Paintbrush Divide and then switchbacks even more quickly down into Paintbrush Canyon. The trail eventually leads back to String Lake. Be sure to stop at beautiful Holly Lake on the way down.

DEATH CANYON LOOP

Another fine loop trip departs from the Death Canyon Trailhead, approximately three miles south of park headquarters on the Moose-Wilson Road. Many hiking options are available here, with trails leading to Phelps Lake, up Open Canyon, or into Death Canyon. (The name came about when a survey party was in the area in 1899 and one of the men disappeared. He was never seen again.) Despite the name, Death Canyon provides a wonderful 26-mile loop hike that takes you over three high passes and into spectacular alpine country. From the trailhead, hike to Phelps Lake Overlook before dropping down to a junction, where you turn right to hike up Death Canyon. Bear left at a patrol cabin built in the 1930s, and continue climbing all the way to Fox Creek Pass (9,520 feet). After this the going is fairly easy for the next three miles along Death Canyon Shelf to Mt. Meek Pass, where you drop into famous **Alaska Basin** (described in the Jackson Hole chapter). Return to your starting point by climbing east from Alaska Basin over Static Peak Divide (10,800 feet) and then switchbacking downhill to the CCC cabin and the trailhead. This is a late-season trek because snow often blocks the passes until July; get snow conditions at the Jenny Lake Ranger Station.

AMPHITHEATER LAKE

A relatively short but very steep hike begins at the Lupine Meadows Trailhead just south of Jenny Lake. Amphitheater Lake is only five miles up the trail but is 3,000 feet higher, making this the quickest climb to the Teton treeline. Many folks day hike this trail to savor the wonderful vistas across Jackson Hole along the way. Camping is available at Surprise Lake, one-half mile below Amphitheater Lake. More adventurous folks may want to climb **Disappointment Peak,** the 11,618-foot summit directly in front of Grand Teton. (It was named by climbers who mistakenly thought they were on the east face of Grand Teton.) If you plan to do so, first talk to the climbing rangers at Jenny Lake—and only attempt it if you're able to handle a few areas of Class 3 moves.

RENDEZVOUS MOUNTAIN TO DEATH CANYON

This 23-mile-long loop hike is different in that much of the way is downhill. Begin at the Jackson Hole tram in Teton Village, where a $15 ticket takes you to the top of Rendezvous Mountain. From the summit, the trail leads down to a saddle, across the South Fork of Granite Creek, and up to Teton Crest Trail. Head north on this trail to Marion Lake—a popular camping site—and then over Fox Creek Pass. The trail splits, and the right fork drops sharply down into scenic Death Canyon. At the lower end of Death Canyon, cliffs rise nearly 3,000 feet on both sides. The trail forks at Phelps Lake, and from here you can either hike back to Teton Village via the Valley Trail or head to the trailhead at White Grass Ranger Station, 1.5 miles northeast of Phelps Lake. Note: If you reverse the direction of this hike you can save your money because there is no charge for riding the tram down to Teton Village.

Mountain Climbing

The Tetons are considered some of the premier mountaineering country in the nation, with solid rock, good access, and a wide range of climbing conditions. Hundreds of climbing routes have been described for the main peaks, but the goal of many climbers is Grand Teton, better known as "the Grand." At 13,772 feet, this is Wyoming's second-highest summit, exceeded only by 13,804-foot Gannett Peak in the Wind River Mountains.

FIRST TO THE TOP

In the climbing trade, first ascents always rate highly, but the identity of the first climbers to have scaled Grand Teton has long been a matter of debate. The official record belongs to the party of William Owen (as in nearby Mt. Owen), Bishop Spalding (as in nearby Spalding Peak), John Shive, and Frank Petersen, who reached the summit in 1898. Today, however, it appears that they were preceded by two members of the 1872 Hayden Expedition: Nathaniel P. Langford (first superintendent of Yellowstone National Park) and John Stevenson. In addition, another party apparently made it to the top in 1893. Owen made a big deal out of his climb and spent 30 years trying to work himself into the record books by claiming the Langford party never reached the top. The whole thing got quite nasty, with Owen even accusing Langford of bribing the author of a history book to gain top honors. In 1929, Owen convinced the Wyoming Legislature to declare his group the first on top. Few people believe it today, and the whole thing looks pretty foolish because even seven-year-old kids have made it up the Grand.

Several thousand people climb the mountain each summer, many with no previous climbing experience (but with excellent guides and a couple days of training). The record time is an unbelievable three hours, six minutes, and 25 seconds for Bryce Thatcher in 1983. This time includes starting—and returning—to the parking lot at the foot of the mountain! And just to prove that it could be done, in 1971 one fanatic actually skied the Grand (he's the ski-school director at Snow King Resort), followed in 1989 by a snowboarder. Both lived to tell the tale.

GETTING THERE

Most climbing takes place after the snow has melted back (mid-July) and before conditions again deteriorate (late September). Overnight mountain climbing or off-trail hiking requires a special permit available from the **Jenny Lake Ranger Station,** staffed daily June to mid-September. There's no need to register if you're climbing or doing off-trail hiking for the day only, just for overnight trips. (Still, it's a good idea to leave a detailed trip itinerary with a responsible person in case of an emergency.) Winter climbers should register at the Moose Visitor Center. The climbing rangers—one of the most prestigious and hazardous jobs in the park—are all highly experienced mountaineers and can provide specific route information for the various summits. Call 307/739-3604 for recorded climbing info, or talk to folks at the Jenny Lake Ranger Station, 307/739-3343, for weather conditions, route information, and permits.

Many climbers who scale Grand Teton follow the Amphitheater Lake Trail from Lupine Meadows to its junction with the Garnet Canyon Trail. This leads to the **Lower Saddle,** which separates Grand Teton and Middle Teton. Exum and the Park Service have base-camp huts and steel storage boxes here, along with an outhouse. (The park is experimenting with high-tech carry-out bags for human waste—complete with a system that breaks down feces. They have been optional but may become mandatory for climbers.) Other folks pitch tents behind boulders in this extraordinarily windy mountain gap. See Park Service handouts for camping restrictions and recommendations in this fragile alpine area where heavy use by 4,000 climbers each year has caused considerable damage. The final assault on the summit of Grand Teton requires technical equipment and expertise. No motorized drills are allowed for placing climbing bolts.

Mountaineers who have registered to climb the Grand can stay at **Climbers' Ranch,** near Taggart Lake, for $8 per night. Lodging is in small log cabins with four to eight bunks; hot showers and a cooking shelter are close by, but you'll need to bring your own sleeping bag and food. The ranch is open mid-June to mid-September. Call 307/733-7271 after June 1 for reservations, or visit the American Alpine Club's website, www.americanalpineclub.org, for details.

CLIMBING SCHOOLS

Jackson Hole is blessed with two of the finest climbing schools in North America: **Jackson Hole Mountain Guides,** 165 N. Glenwood, 307/733-4979 or 800/239-7642, www.jhmg.com; and **Exum Mountain Guides,** 307/733-2297, www.exumguides.com, with a summertime office at the south end of Jenny Lake near the boat dock. Both are authorized concessions of the National Park Service and the U.S. Forest Service and offer a wide range of classes, snow training, and climbs in the Tetons and elsewhere—even as far away as Alaska and the Himalayas. Exum has been around since 1931, when Glenn Exum pioneered the first solo climb of what has become the most popular route to the top of the Grand, the Exum Route. It's the only company permitted to guide all Teton peaks and routes throughout the year. Exum's base camp is in the busy Lower Saddle area, while Jackson Hole Mountain Guides' base camp is 450 feet lower in elevation in a more secluded location (it takes an extra hour of climbing on the day of your ascent). Exum has some of the most experienced guides in the world, but they take up to four clients in a group, while Jackson Hole limits its Grand Teton ascent parties to three clients.

During midsummer, you'll pay around $600–900 (depending on the number of people in the group) for an ascent of Grand Teton; this includes two days of basic and intermediate training followed by a two-day climb up the Grand and back. Food, gear, and shelter are also included. If you're planning to climb the Grand during the peak summer season, be sure to make reservations several months in advance to be assured of a spot. For July and August, make Grand Teton climbing reservations before the end of March.

Reservations generally are not needed for the companies' one-day basic ($95) and intermediate ($120) climbing schools. Also available are climbs of other faces, such as Baxter's Pinnacle, Symmetry Spire, and Cube Point, along with more advanced classes and climbs in the Wind River Mountains and up Devils Tower and other precipices throughout the western states. In addition, both companies offer many winter classes, such as avalanche safety and ski or snowboard mountaineering.

ON YOUR OWN

If you already have the experience and want to do your own climbing, the most accessible local spot is **Blacktail Butte,** just north of Moose near Ditch Creek. The parking lot here fills on warm summer afternoons as hang-dogging enthusiasts try their moves on the rock face. Get climbing supplies at **Moosely Seconds Mountaineering** in Moose, 307/739-1801, or in Jackson at **Teton Mountaineering,** 170 N. Cache Dr., 307/733-3595 or 800/850-3595, www.tetonmtn.com. Both stores rent climbing shoes and other gear. **Teton Rock Gym,** 1116 Maple Way, 307/733-0707, has challenging indoor climbing walls where you can practice your moves. They also rent climbing gear and have special kid's climbing classes in the summer.

For complete details on local climbing, see Reynold Jackson's *A Complete Guide to the Teton Range* (The Mountaineers Books, www.mountaineerbooks.org, or the smaller but well-written *Teton Classics,* by Richard Rossiter (Chockstone Press). Online, check out **Way Wired Mountaineer,** www.way-wired.com for details on climbing and skiing in the Tetons.

Other Park Recreation

DAY HIKES

Short hikes are detailed in the Exploring the Park section of this chapter. Notable ones are found in the Taggart Lake and Jenny Lake areas (particularly the hike to Inspiration Point), at Colter Bay, and off the Moose-Wilson Road (Granite Canyon). All are described previously, or get the day hikes pamphlet from park visitors centers. In addition, the tram at Jackson Hole Ski Resort provides instant gratification for folks looking to get into the alpine; it's described under Backcountry Hiking. Start your hike early in the day or you may well find all of the trailhead parking spaces filled, especially on warm summer weekends. Besides, afternoon thunderstorms often build over the mountains.

For the guided version, get a schedule of free **ranger walks and hikes** (including special ones for kids) from visitors centers or in the park newspaper. These are offered daily throughout the summer.

FLOATING THE RIVER

Several rafting companies lead scenic half-day float trips down the Snake River inside the park, generally putting in at Deadman's Bar or Schwabacher Landing and taking out in Moose. Expect to pay around $40 for the 10-mile trips from Deadman's Bar, or $25 for the five-mile floats from Schwabacher Landing. See the Jackson Hole chapter for details.

BOATING

Canoeists will discover several excellent places to paddle within Grand Teton, particularly the Snake River Oxbow Bend, String Lake, and Leigh Lake. Canoes are available for rent both in the park at Colter Bay Marina and Signal Mountain Lodge, and in Jackson.

Boaters within Grand Teton will need to purchase a permit; seven-day permits cost $10 for motorboats, $5 for nonmotorized craft. Motorboats are only allowed on Jackson Lake, Jenny Lake (10-horsepower max), and Phelps Lake. Sailboarding, water-skiing, and sailing are permitted on Jackson Lake, but no personal watercraft are allowed anywhere in the park. Get the park boating brochure for details.

Jackson Lake has three marinas, all of which are generally open from sometime in May to late September. At **Signal Mountain Lodge Marina,** 307/733-5470 or 307/543-2831, www.signalmountainlodge.com, can rent water-ski boats and skis, life jackets, deck cruisers, fishing boats, pontoon boats, and canoes. **Colter Bay Marina,** 307/543-2811 or 800/628-9988, www.gtlc.com, is near a Park Service campground, cabins, and the Colter Bay Indian Arts Museum. It's an exceptionally busy place in the summer, with motorboat, rowboat, and canoe rentals, along with guides to take you to the hot fishing spots. Scenic **Jackson Lake cruises** ($15 adults, $7.50 kids under 12) are also available from Colter Bay Marina, as are breakfast or evening cruise-and-dine trips ($28 for breakfast; $46 for dinner).

A short distance north of Colter Bay is **Leek's Marina,** 307/543-2494, a simple place with a couple of docks, a pizza restaurant, and gas pumps.

FISHING

Grand Teton National Park rivers and lakes contain cutthroat, lake, and brown trout, along with whitefish. Park anglers must have a valid Wyoming state fishing license, available for $10 for one day if you aren't a resident. Pick up a handout describing fishing regulations from park visitors centers. Fishing licenses and supplies are available at park marinas and stores.

© DON PITCHER

the Snake River's Oxbow Bend

For more on fishing in the park, see the Jackson Hole chapter.

SEA KAYAKING

O.A.R.S., 209/736-4677 or 800/346-6277, www.oars.com, offers one- to four-day sea kayaking trips around Jackson Lake—perfect for beginning kayakers and families. You don't need any paddling experience for these trips, which are supported by a motorized skiff. One-night overnight trips cost $216 adults or $175 youths; four-day kayak trips will set you back $637 adults or $546 kids. O.A.R.S. also has combination trips that include kayaking on the lake and rafting down the Snake River. Their two-day combo trips cost $366 adults or $304 youths; five-day trips run $817 adults or $700 kids. They supply kayaks, a guide, and dry bags, and have tents and sleeping bags available for rent. Reserve well ahead for these popular trips.

BIRDING

The diversity of habitat types within Grand Teton National Park means that birdwatchers can find everything from trumpeter swans to calliope

GRAND TETON

hummingbirds. The park produces a free *Bird-Finding Guide* with descriptions of birding hot spots. A couple of the best places are Willow Flats and Blacktail Ponds. A checklist of park birds is also available from visitors centers.

BICYCLING

The main roads through Grand Teton get heavy traffic, and the shoulder width varies (although it is wide from Moose to Jenny Lake). Pick up the park's bicycling pamphlet for details on cycling options. Bikes are not allowed on any trails within Grand Teton National Park, but you *can* ride mountain bikes on several wonderful dirt roads, including Two-Ocean Lake Road (three miles), Grassy Lake Road (52 miles from Flagg Ranch to Ashton, Idaho), and the River Road (15 surprisingly remote miles in the heart of the park). In addition, the paved secondary roads in the Antelope Flats–Mormon Row–Kelly area see less traffic and provide the opportunity to see bison and spectacular mountain vistas. Shadow Mountain Road is an off-the-beaten-path dirt road that takes off from the Antelope Flats area and climbs through Forest Service land to splendid vistas.

TRAIL RIDES

Horseback and wagon rides, including popular breakfast and dinner rides, take place at **Jackson Lake Lodge Corral** and **Colter Bay Village Corral.** Trail rides start at $25 for 1.5 hours, with dinner wagon rides for $32. Get details on both of these activities from Grand Teton Lodge Company, 307/543-2811 or 800/628-9988, www.gtlc.com. In the Rockefeller Parkway between Grand Teton and Yellowstone, **Flagg Ranch Resort,** 307/543-2861 or 800/443-2311, www.flaggranch.com, offers hour-long horseback trail rides in the summer for $25.

SWIMMING

Swimming is allowed in all park lakes, but they can be quite cold. Jenny, String, and Leigh lakes all have delightful spots for swimming on the east side, including some sandy or gravelly beaches. The Snake River is dangerous and swimming isn't recommended. Jackson Lake Lodge has a large outdoor pool, but it's only open for guests at the lodge or nearby Colter Bay Village. In addition, the town of Jackson has a wonderful recreation center with pools, and the pond at Kelly Warm Spring is a fun spot to splash around.

WINTER RECREATION

The snow-covered landscape of Grand Teton National Park draws cross-country skiers, snowshoers, and snowmobilers throughout the winter.

Skiing

Cross-country skiing is possible on several trails within the lower reaches of the park, but the high country is dangerous because of extreme avalanche hazards. Park ski trails are not machine-groomed but are generally well packed by other skiers. After a new snowfall you'll need to break trail as you follow the orange markers. See Cross-Country Skiing in the Jackson Hole chapter for information on Nordic skiing in the park, or pick up a brochure describing ski trails from the Moose Visitor Center. If you're planning to camp overnight in the park, you'll need to get a free permit here as well. Skiers and snowshoers are not allowed on the Continental Divide Snowmobile Trail for safety reasons. Unfortunately, snowmobilers ride on Teton Park Road, so your peace and solitude may be broken by the roar of distant machines.

Snowshoeing

Park naturalists lead two-hour **snowshoe hikes** from late December through March and provide snowshoes at no charge. No experience is necessary. The hikes generally depart from the Moose Visitor Center at 2 P.M. several times a week. Reservations are required; no kids under age eight. Call 307/739-3399 for details on these and other winter activities in the park.

Snowmobiling

The controversial 365-mile-long **Continental Divide Snowmobile Trail** cuts through 33 miles of Grand Teton National Park, providing a link between the Wind River Mountains and Yellowstone National Park. Within Grand Teton the trail is generally open from early January to mid-March and essentially parallels U.S. Hwy. 26/287 from the east park boundary to Moran Junction and then along U.S. Hwy. 89 north to Yellowstone. A spur trail connects the trail with other snowmobile routes along the Teton Park Road and up Signal Mountain. Snowmobiles are allowed only on designated routes, and specific regulations are enforced within the park. Get a copy of the park snowmobiling handout from the Moose Visitor Center, or call 307/739-3612 for recorded information on the Continental Divide Snowmobile Trail.

Winter Access

During winter, **Alltrans/Gray Line of Jackson Hole,** 307/733-4325 or 800/443-6133, www.jacksonholealltrans.com, has daily bus runs between Jackson and Flagg Ranch Resort for $40 one-way or $60 round-trip, arriving in time to meet the snowcoach departures for Yellowstone. Reservations are required. Taxi companies in Jackson can also provide shuttles to Flagg Ranch in the winter, including **Buckboard Transportation,** 307/733-1112 or 877/791-0211, www.buckboardtrans.com, and **All Star Taxi,** 307/733-2888.

Camping

Grand Teton National Park has five campgrounds, with sites at all of these costing $12. These are available on a first-come, first-served basis with no reservations, and by midafternoon in the peak summer season all park campgrounds may be full. The maximum stay is seven days at Jenny Lake or 14 days at other campgrounds. Camping (or overnight parking) is not allowed along roadsides, overlooks, or parking areas within the park. Off-the-road camping is restricted to specific sites and requires a special permit; see Backcountry Hiking for specifics.

The largest park campground—and last to fill—is Gros Ventre Campground near the town of Kelly. The most scenic location—and quickest to fill—is Jenny Lake Campground. Showers and a laundromat are available at Colter Bay Village. Several special hiker/biker sites are at Jenny Lake and Colter Bay for $5. Group sites can be found at Colter Bay and Gros Ventre campgrounds, but advance reservations are required. All Grand Teton National Park campgrounds are closed in winter, but limited tent camping and RV parking ($5; restrooms and water but no hookups) are available near the Colter Bay Visitor Center.

For details on Park Service and nearby Forest Service campgrounds, see the **Jackson Hole Public Campgrounds** chart in the Jackson Hole chapter.

Grand Teton rangers lead popular evening campfire programs at all five campgrounds throughout the summer. All campgrounds have running water but no utility hookups. Get park campground information at 307/739-3603, or on the web at www.nps.gov/grte.

OTHER CAMPING OPTIONS

In addition to the five NPS campgrounds, park concessioners maintain two seasonal RV parks with full hookups, showers, washers, and driers. **Flagg Ranch Resort** on Rockefeller Parkway, 307/543-2861 or 800/443-2311, www.flaggranch.com, has 100 pull-through RV sites with full hookups for $38 and 75 tent sites for $22. The resort is open early to mid-May until early October, but reservations are highly recommended.

On the south shore of Jackson Lake, **Colter Bay RV Park,** 307/543-3100 or 800/628-9988, www.gtlc.com, charges $38 for RV hookups and is open late May to mid-September. No tent spaces are available here. Evening nature programs are offered in summer.

Not far from the park is **Grand Teton Park RV Resort** six miles east of Moran Junction along Hwy. 26/287, 307/733-1980 or 800/563-6469, www.yellowstonerv.com. Facilities include a heated seasonal pool and hot tub, recreation room, and grocery store; $42 per day for RVs with hookups, $30 per day for tents. Simple camping cabins go for $52–58 per day, and tepees run $39–43. Open year-round.

The Forest Service has quite a few campgrounds in the surrounding country, and several private RV parks are available in Jackson.

Accommodations

Several places provide concessioner lodging inside Grand Teton National Park. As in all national parks, none of the lodge rooms contains TVs or radios. Reserve at least nine months ahead to be sure of getting a room in the peak summer season. Dozens of additional accommodations are south of the park in Jackson, and the pleasant **Hatchet Resort,** 307/543-2413 or 877/543-2413, www.hatchetresort.com, has cozy and moderately priced rooms in the heart of Buffalo Valley.

JACKSON LAKE LODGE

Built on a grand scale, the 385-room Jackson Lake Lodge, 307/543-2811 or 800/628-9988, www.gtlc.com occupies a bluff above Willow Flats on the southeast side of Jackson Lake. Sixty-foot-high windows look across to the Tetons, and fireplaces flank the spacious central hall. Outside is a large swimming pool and kiddie pool (major attractions for families), and inside you'll find restaurants, a lounge, a gift shop, a newsstand, a clothing shop, and an ATM. All rooms contain two double beds and phones; some also have small fridges. Rooms in the lodge without a view (unless you count the parking lot) are $124 d, while those with big windows fronting the Tetons are $225 d. Cottages cost $154 d ($164 d with a patio), or $220 d for ones with mountain vistas. Luxury suites in the lodge are $394–564 d. Extra guests (beyond two) in any of these rooms are $9.50 per person. The lodge is open mid-May to mid-October.

JENNY LAKE LODGE

For four-star accommodations a stone's throw from the Tetons, stay at Jenny Lake Lodge, 307/733-4647 or 800/628-9988, www.gtlc.com, where 37 comfortably appointed cabins surround a cozy Old West main lodge. This is a marvelous

honeymoon or big-splurge place, and the $348 s or $429 d price includes horseback rides, bikes, breakfast, and a marvelous six-course dinner. (Note, however, that the meals are only served at specific times, so you'll need to adjust your schedule accordingly.) For the ultimate in extravagance, choose the lodge's luxurious suites; $579–619 d. Jenny Lake Lodge is open June to early October.

COLTER BAY VILLAGE

Family-oriented Colter Bay Village, 307/543-2811 ext. 1080 or 800/628-9988, www.gtlc.com, has 166 rustic cabins of varying sizes and types, some of which sleep six people. There are no phones or cooking facilities in any of these cabins. The most basic are canvas-and-log structures with outdoor grills and picnic tables, indoor woodstoves, and bring-your-own-linen bunk beds. Restrooms are nearby, and the showers are coin-operated. These tent cabins cost just $34 d ($4.50 for each additional person up to six). Sleeping bags and other camping supplies are available for rent. The tent cabins are open early June to early September.

A bit nicer are little one-room cabins that share a bath for $34 d. Cabins with a private bath start at $69 d for ones with a double bed, up to $104 d for those with two double beds and a twin bed. Two-room cabins with a bath are $109 d or $129 for up to four. Additional guests are $4.50 each in all of these, and the cabins are open late May to late September. Guests at Colter Bay Village can use the big swimming pool at nearby Jackson Lake Lodge.

DORNAN'S

Near park headquarters in Moose, Dornan's Spur Ranch Cabins, 307/733-2522, www.dornans.com, has a dozen modern log cabins filled with handcrafted lodgepole pine furniture. One-bedroom cabins are $140 s or d or $170 for up to four people, and two-bedroom cabins cost $210 for up to six people. There's a three-night minimum stay in the summer. All cabins include full kitchens and are open year-round.

SIGNAL MOUNTAIN LODGE

On the south shore of Jackson Lake, Signal Mountain Lodge, 307/733-5470 or 307/543-2831, www.signalmountainlodge.com, offers a variety of lodging options. Simple and rustic log cabins start at $95 d, up to $135 for a room that sleeps six. Motel-style rooms with fridges and microwaves are $114 for up to four people or $163 for a nicer room with a fireplace and king bed. The lodge's finest options include suites for $182, cozy bungalows with

kitchens and private decks for $137–195 d, and a three-room cabin with fireplace in the living room, full kitchen, and laundry for $225. Signal Mountain Lodge is open early May to mid-October.

FLAGG RANCH RESORT

In Rockefeller Parkway just three miles south of Yellowstone, Flagg Ranch Resort, 307/543-2861 or 800/443-2311, www.flaggranch.com, has modern four-plex log cabins with patios and two queen beds or a king bed. Rates are $139–145 d in summer or $110 d in winter, and kids stay free. Additional adults are $10 each. Flagg Ranch is open late May–September and mid-December to mid-March. The main lodge houses a convenience store, restaurant, deli, gift shop, and central area with couches and a large fireplace.

Food

RESTAURANTS AND BARS

Several dining options exist at **Jackson Lake Lodge,** including the Mural Room with its 60-foot windows fronting the Tetons. The restaurant serves three meals a day, while the nearby Blue Heron Lounge offers up equally impressive views and musicians provide accompaniment for your cocktails. Dinner reservations are required in summer; call 307/543-2811 ext. 1911. Casual meals are available at Pioneer Grill, also inside Jackson Lake Lodge, or the very popular Pool Grill and BBQ, next to the big outdoor swimming pool. The latter is an all-you-can-eat buffet with steaks, barbecue chicken and ribs, and other Western grub; it's open daily in July and August, and costs $15 adults or $8 kids.

Marvelous old **Jenny Lake Lodge** has impeccable service, windows that face the mountains, and a cozy setting. Six-course dinners are the featured attractions, and the wine list is extensive. Lunch is à la carte, but breakfast and dinner are fixed price (and pricey: $48 for dinner, $16 for breakfast). Jenny Lake Lodge is open June to early October, and reservations

are required; call 307/733-4647. This is a dress-up place, so a jacket is recommended for dinner. For details on Jackson Lake Lodge and Jenny Lake Lodge, visit the Grand Teton Lodge Company's website, www.gtlc.com.

Colter Bay Village has two dining choices: the Chuckwagon for steaks and pasta and the John Colter Cafe Court for chicken, pizza, deli sandwiches, salads, and snacks.

An old favorite with an egalitarian setting (look for the tepees) is **Dornan's Chuck Wagon Restaurant,** 307/733-2415, www.dornans.com, offering reasonable meals every summer since 1948. The all-you-can-eat breakfasts include pancakes, ham, bacon, and eggs. Sandwiches are the main lunch attraction, and dinners include grilled-to-order barbecue ribs, chicken, steaks, salmon, or trout, plus a big outdoor salad bar. The Chuck Wagon is open mid-June through Labor Day.

Across the street—and open all year—is Dornan's **Spur Bar/Moose Pizza & Pasta Co.,** 307/733-2415, offering a wide range of superb homemade pizzas ($13–15), sandwiches, calzones, and pastas. Dining is available on two outside decks with can't-beat-the-view Teton vistas, and folk musicians perform once or twice a month. The bar puts on monthly wine tastings ($5) on the first Sunday of the month, October–May. Check out the club on the wall. In 1944, local resident Farney Cole used it to defend himself from a bear attack. He survived, as did the bear.

Signal Mountain Lodge, 307/733-5470 or 307/543-2831, www.signalmountainlodge.com, houses both Trapper Grill with casual fare and a popular deck for al fresco dining, along with Peaks Restaurant with an upscale menu and spectacular vistas of the Tetons. Deadman's Bar at Signal Mountain is famous for blackberry margaritas and also serves a pub menu.

Leek's Marina 307/543-2494, is home to a very popular pizzeria that also serves calzones, sandwiches, salads, and beer on tap. Musicians drop by every other Wednesday evening for an open mic session.

The main lodge at **Flagg Ranch Resort,** 307/543-2861 or 800/443-2311, www.flaggranch.com, houses Bear's Den Restaurant, serving three meals a day. Also here is a deli, saloon, and grocery store.

GROCERIES AND SUPPLIES

The best in-the-park store is **Dornan's Trading Post,** 307/733-2415, located near park headquarters in Moose. The store is open all year and stocked with groceries, tasty deli sandwiches, fresh baked goods, and camping supplies. The cart out front has espresso, and next door is **Dornan's Wine Shoppe** with the biggest selection of fine wine and beer in Jackson Hole, including more than 1,700 different wines. Other nearby Dornan's operations include Moose Pizza & Pasta Co. and the Chuck Wagon (both described previously), and a gift shop. In winter, the gift shop rents cross-country skis, snowshoes, and pull-behind sleds.

Colter Bay General Store, 307/543-2811, has a good choice of groceries and supplies, and convenience stores operate at Signal Mountain, Flagg Ranch Resort, and Jenny Lake. The store at Flagg Ranch Resort is open in both summer and winter seasons (mid-May to mid-Oct., and mid-Dec. to mid-Mar.). All of the others are only open for summer.

Practicalities

GETTING IN

Entrance to Grand Teton National Park is $20 per vehicle or $10 for individuals entering by bicycle, foot, or as a bus passenger. Motorcycles and snowmobiles are $15. *The pass covers entrance to both Yellowstone and Grand Teton National Parks and is good for seven days.* If you're planning to be here longer or to make additional visits, get an annual pass covering both parks for $40, or the National Park Pass—good for all national parks—for $50 per year. A Golden Age Passport for all national parks is available to anyone over 62 for a one-time fee of $10, and people with disabilities can get a free Golden Access Passport. Both of these also give the holders 50 percent reductions in most camping fees. Call 307/739-3600 for additional park information, or visit the park on the web at www.nps.gov/grte.

At the entrance stations, park visitors receive a copy of *Teewinot,* the park newspaper. It lists park facilities and services, along with interpretive programs, nature walks, and other activities. Family favorites for generations are the evening **campfire programs** held at campground amphitheaters throughout the summer. The park also produces a helpful **Easy Access** brochure with details on wheelchair-accessible visitors centers, trails, sights, picnic areas, activities, campsites, and accommodations.

VISITORS CENTERS

Grand Teton National Park headquarters is in the settlement of Moose near the southern end of the park. **Moose Visitor Center,** 307/739-3399, is open daily 8 A.M.–7 P.M. from early June to early September, and daily (except Christmas) 8 A.M.–5 P.M. the rest of the year. **Jenny Lake Visitor Center** is open daily 8 A.M.–7 P.M. from early June to early September; closed the remainder of the year.

On the east side of Jackson Lake, **Colter Bay Visitor Center,** 307/739-3594, is open daily 8 A.M.–8 P.M. from early June to early September, and daily 8 A.M.–5 P.M. from mid-May to early June and for most of September; closed the rest of the year.

Just north of Grand Teton inside John D. Rockefeller Jr. Memorial Parkway is **Flagg Ranch Information Station,** open daily 9 A.M.–5:30 P.M. between early June and early September, and with varying hours from mid-December to mid-March.

SUPPORT ORGANIZATIONS

The **Grand Teton Natural History Association** operates bookstores in park visitors centers and the store at Menor's Ferry. They also have a mail-order service for books about the park. For a catalog, call 307/739-3403, or find everything on the web at www.grandtetonpark.org.

The nonprofit **Grand Teton National Park Foundation,** 307/739-0629, www.gtnpf.org, provides support for park projects that would not otherwise be funded, and all contributions are tax-deductible. Their big project is to help fund the much-needed construction of a new visitors center at Moose.

MEDICAL HELP

Get emergency medical assistance at the **Grand Teton Medical Clinic,** 307/543-2514, near the Chevron station at Jackson Lake Lodge. It's open daily 10 A.M.–6 P.M. mid-May to mid-October. The nearest hospital is in Jackson.

OUTDOOR GEAR

The little settlement of Moose has several businesses in addition to the Dornan's shops and eateries described previously. **Adventure Sports,** 307/733-3307, www.dornans.com, rents mountain bikes, recumbents, canoes, and kayaks. Next door is **Moosely Seconds,** 307/739-1801, with good deals on outdoor clothing and climbing gear; open mid-May through September. They

also rent ice axes, crampons, rock shoes, trekking poles, approach shoes, plastic boots, day packs, and snowshoes. **Snake River Anglers,** 307/733-3699, sells and rents fishing supplies and camping equipment.

OTHER PRACTICALITIES

Gas is available year-round at Dornan's in Moose and Flagg Ranch Resort, and summers only at Colter Bay Village, Signal Mountain Lodge, and Jackson Lake Lodge. You'll find gift shops at Signal Mountain, Flagg Ranch Resort, Jackson Lake Lodge, Moose, and Colter Bay. Year-round **post offices** are located in Moran, Moose, and Kelly. Get cash from **ATMs** located at Dornan's in Moose, Jackson Lake Lodge, Colter Bay Village, Flagg Ranch Resort, and Signal Mountain Lodge.

TRANSPORTATION AND TOURS

As this book was being written, the Park Service was developing a new **transportation plan** for Grand Teton, and it could have a major impact on access to certain areas. Some of the options being considered were to provide transit bus service between Jackson and the park and to close some roads to most motorized vehicles, including the Moose-Wilson Road. Contact the park for the latest at 307/739-3399, www.nps.gov/grte.

Grand Teton Lodge Company, 307/543-2811 or 800/628-9988, www.gtlc.com, has five-times-daily summer shuttle buses connecting Jackson with Jackson Lake Lodge for $20 one-way, and on to Colter Bay Village for an additional $4 one-way. Transportation is $30 from the airport to Jackson Lake Lodge or $20 in the other direction. Reservations are required for all of these shuttles. The company also offers three-hour bus tours of Grand Teton National Park on Mondays, Wednesdays, and Fridays for $30 ($15 for kids under 12) and eight-hour tours of Yellowstone National Park on Tuesdays, Thursdays, and Saturdays for $50 ($30 for kids).

Summertime bus tours of Grand Teton and Yellowstone National Parks are available several times a week from **Alltrans/Gray Line of Jackson Hole,** 307/733-4325 or 800/443-6133, www.jacksonholealltrans.com. Yellowstone tours last 11 hours and cost $80 plus park entrance fees. Eight-hour Grand Teton tours are $69 plus the park entrance. Gray Line's four-day tours of the Yellowstone and Grand Teton areas start at $900 for one person or $1,200 for two, including lodging (but only one meal).

Operated by the respected Teton Science School, the nonprofit **Wildlife Expeditions,** 307/733-2623 or 888/945-3567, www.teton-science.org/wildlife, leads wildlife-viewing safaris throughout the region. Half-day Grand Teton trips are $85, and all-day jaunts cost $145. Multiday wildlife tours into Yellowstone are also offered. Other companies offering guided van tours of the park include **Callowishus Park Touring Company,** 307/733-9521, www.callowishus.com; Jackson's Hole Adventure, 307/654-7849 or 800/392-3165, www.jacksonholeadventure.com; and Upstream Anglers and Outdoor Adventures, 307/739-9443 or 800/642-8979, www.upstreamanglers.com.

Yellowstone National Park

Note: Please see color map
Yellowstone National Park.

The words "national park" seem to stimulate an almost Pavlovian response: Yellowstone. The geysers, canyons, and bears of Yellowstone National Park are so intertwined in our collective consciousness that even 1960s American cartoons used the park as a model—Jellystone Park, where Yogi Bear and Boo Boo were constantly out to thwart the rangers. One source estimated that nearly one-third of the U.S. population has visited the park, and each year three million people roll through its gates.

Yellowstone has always been a place of wonder. There is considerable evidence that the Indians who first lived in this area viewed it as a place of great spiritual power and treated it with reverence. Yellowstone was to later become the birthplace for the national-park movement, and Americans today still love the park, although they don't always treat it with reverence.

There is something about Yellowstone National Park that calls people back again and again, something more than simply the chance to see the curiosities of the natural world.

Morning Glory pool, Yellowstone National Park

© DON PITCHER

Generations of parents have brought their children to see the place that they recall from their own childhood visits. Other cultures have the Ganges River, Rome, or Mecca as places with deep spiritual meaning. In America, our national parks have become places for similar renewal, and as the nation's first national park, Yellowstone remains one of our most valued treasures.

So, into the park we come in our cars with our crying babies in the back—babies who suddenly quiet down at the sight of a bison or elk. I recall bringing relatives to Yellowstone after I had worked in the vicinity all summer and had become a bit jaded. Their emotional reaction surprised me, and more than a decade later they still tell stories of the bison calves, the astounding geysers, the rush of the waterfalls, and the night they spent at Old Faithful Inn. Yellowstone is a collective religious experience that sends us back to our roots in the natural world.

YELLOWSTONE NATIONAL PARK SIGHTSEEING HIGHLIGHTS

Upper Geyser Basin, including Old Faithful, Old Faithful Inn, Morning Glory Pool, Giant Geyser, and Riverside Geyser
Grand Prismatic Spring in Midway Geyser Basin
Great Fountain Geyser
Fountain Paint Pot
Norris Geyser Basin, including Echinus Geyser
Mammoth Hot Springs and the Albright Visitor Center
Lamar Valley
Roosevelt Lodge
Tower Fall
Mount Washburn
Grand Canyon of the Yellowstone, including Brink of the Lower Falls, Uncle Tom's Trail, Artist Point, and Inspiration Point
Hayden Valley
Mud Volcano
Yellowstone Lake, Fishing Bridge, and Lake Yellowstone Hotel
Wildlife viewing, particularly bison, elk, wolves, grizzlies, and moose

The smell of wood smoke from a campfire, the picnic lunch on the shore of Yellowstone Lake, the backcountry horseback ride, the hike down to the lip of Lower Falls, the quick strike of a trout on the line, the gasp of the crowd as the first spurt of Old Faithful jets upward, the herds of bison wading Firehole River, the evening piano tunes drifting through the air at Lake Hotel, the howl of a distant wolf, and even the cheesy Yellowstone trinkets—all of these things combine to leave an indelible mark on visitors to Yellowstone National Park.

THE SETTING

On a map, Yellowstone appears as a gigantic box wedged so tightly against the northwest corner of Wyoming that it squeezes over into Montana and Idaho. The park measures 63 by 54 miles and covers 2.2 million acres, making it one of the largest national parks in the Lower 48 (although it is dwarfed by Alaska's Wrangell-St. Elias National Park and Preserve, which covers almost six times as much land). The United Nations has declared Yellowstone both a World Biosphere Reserve and a World Heritage Site.

The park is accessible from all four sides, and a loop road provides easy access to all of the best-known sights. Because of its popularity as a destination, tourist towns surround Yellowstone: Jackson to the south, Cody to the east, Gardiner and Cooke City on the northern margin, and West Yellowstone on its western border. Also because so many people visit the park, there is a well-developed network of facilities inside the park, including visitors centers, campgrounds, hotels, restaurants, a hospital, gift shops, ATMs, one-hour photo shops, espresso stands, and other supposed necessities of modern life. Although less than 2 percent of the park is developed, Yellowstone contains more than 2,000 buildings of various types. In some spots (most egregiously around Old Faithful), these developments have grown to the point that the natural world seems simply a backdrop for the human world that pulls visitors in to buy T-shirts or to watch park slide shows on wildlife or geysers while missing the real thing just outside the door.

More than any other national park, Yellowstone seems to provide the oddities of nature, creating, as historian Aubrey L. Haines noted, "a false impression that the park is only a colossal, steam-operated freak show." Yellowstone is a mix of the real and the unreal, a place where our fantasies of what nature should be blend with the reality of crowds of fellow travelers and the impact we have on the place we love so much. In midsummer, a trip into Yellowstone can be something less than a natural experience. Long lines of cars back up behind RVs creeping up the narrow roads, and throngs of visitors crowd the benches around Old Faithful Geyser waiting for an eruption, while dozens of others cluster around bewildered elk to get photos to email their friends. Despite this crowding—or perhaps because most folks prefer to stay on paved paths—many parts of the park remain virtually uninhabited. In the Yellowstone backcountry, one can still walk for days without seeing more than a handful of other hardy hikers.

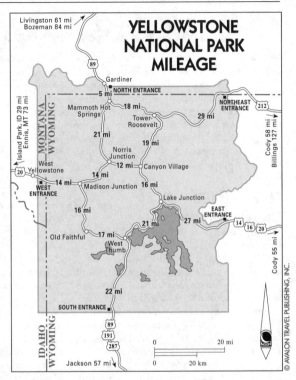

A PLACE OF CONTROVERSY

Yellowstone National Park evokes a torrent of emotions in anyone with a knowledge of and concern for the natural world. Perhaps more than any other wild place in America, the park seems to be in a perpetual state of controversy, be it over fire policies, bison and wolf management, snowmobile use, or some other issue; there's always something getting folks stirred up. Perhaps it is because so many Americans have visited the park that we feel a vested interest in what it means to us. Writer Paul Schullery in his wonderful book *Searching for Yellowstone* put it best when he noted, "Caring for Yellowstone National Park brings to mind all the metaphors of growth and change; it is a process more organic than political; a crucible of ideas, ambitions, dreams, and belief systems; a cultural, intellectual, and spiritual crossroads at which we are forever debating which way to turn." As visitation has risen in recent decades, more and more folks have begun to suggest some sort of limits on numbers to preserve the experience and protect the park. Don't-tread-on-me Westerners consider the idea of limits an example of environmental extremism for the elite, but as visitation increases, conflicts and controversies are a natural outcome.

Geology

Yellowstone is, without a doubt, the most geologically fascinating place on this planet. Here the forces that elsewhere lie deep within the earth seem close enough to touch. They're palpable not only in the geysers and hot springs but also in the lake that fills part of an enormous caldera, the earthquakes that shake this land, the evidence of massive glaciations, and the deeply eroded Grand Canyon of the Yellowstone.

FIRE AND ICE
The Yellowstone Hotspot
When geologists began to study the Yellowstone area in depth, they found a surprising pattern. Extending far to the southwest was a chain of volcanic fields, the most ancient of which—16 million years old—lay in northern Nevada. In addition, geologic fault lines created a hundred-mile-wide semicircle around the Yellowstone area, as if some deep-seated force were pushing the land outward and upward the way a ripple moves across a pond.

Both the volcanic activity and the wavelike pattern of faults are caused by the same source: a plume of superheated material moving up from the core of the planet through a narrow tube, creating a hotspot beneath the earth's crust. As the North American continent has slid to the southwest over the eons, this plume has traced a line of volcanoes across the West, and as the land continues to move, the plume causes massive deformations in the crust that show up as mountain ranges, fault lines, and earthquakes. It's a little like somebody tugging a piece of cloth across a candle. Approximately 40 such hotspots are known to exist around the globe, but most are beneath the seas. Other than Yellowstone, the best-known example is the chain of Hawaiian Islands. The earth has been moving over the Yellowstone hotspot at the rate of 15 miles per million years for the last 10 million years, and on the present track, the spot might eventually end up in Hudson Bay in 100 million years or so. Don't hold your breath.

Tambora on Steroids
The volcanic activity revealed by Yellowstone's geysers, hot springs, and fumaroles is not always benign. Within the last two million years there have been three stupendous volcanic eruptions in the area, the most recent taking place 650,000 years ago. The largest of these eruptions took place two million years ago and created an event beyond the realm of imagination: 600 cubic miles of ash were blasted into the atmosphere! This eruption—probably one of the largest to ever occur on earth—ejected 17 times more material than the massive Tambora eruption of 1815, an explosion that was heard 1,600 miles away. Compared to an explosion that is better known to Americans, the 1980 eruption of Mt. St. Helens, the first Yellowstone event was 2,400 times as large. Ash from this first Yellowstone eruption carried east to Iowa, north to Saskatchewan, south to the Gulf of Mexico, and west to California. This titanic infusion of ash into the atmosphere undoubtedly affected the global climate for years to follow.

The process that creates these explosions starts when molten rock pushes up from the center of the earth, bulging the land upward into an enormous dome. Eventually the pressure becomes too great and fractures develop around the dome's margins, sending hot gases, ash, and rock blasting into the atmosphere. After the most recent eruption (650,000 years ago), the magma chamber collapsed into a gigantic, smoldering pit reaching 28 by 47 miles in surface area and perhaps several thousand feet deep. Over time, additional molten rock pushed up from underneath and flowed as thick lava over the land. The most recent of these lava flows was 70,000 years ago.

Two resurgent domes—one near Old Faithful and the other just north of Yellowstone Lake near LeHardy Rapids—have been discovered by geologists. Measurements at LeHardy Rapids showed that the land rose almost three feet from 1923 to 1985, although it has since been subsiding. This upsurge raised the outlet of Yellowstone Lake, causing the water level to increase and flooding trees along the lake's margins. Obviously, Yellowstone's volcanism is far from dead, and scientists believe another eruption is possible or even likely, although nobody knows when it might occur.

Glaciation

Not everything in Yellowstone is the result of volcanic activity. The entire Yellowstone region has undergone a series of at least eight major glaciations over the last million years, the last of which—the Pinedale Glaciation—began around 70,000 years ago. At its peak, the Pinedale Glaciation covered almost all of Yellowstone and reached southward into Jackson Hole and north much of the way to Livingston, Montana. Over Yellowstone Lake the icefield was 4,000 feet thick and covered 10,000-foot mountains. This period of glaciation ended about 15,000 years ago, but trees did not appear in the Yellowstone area until 11,500 years ago, and it wasn't until around 5,000 years ago that the landscape began to appear as it does today.

GEYSERS

Yellowstone is famous for geysers, and geyser-gazers will not be disappointed. At least 60 percent of the world's geysers are in the park, making this easily the largest and most diverse collection in existence. Yellowstone's more than 300 geysers are spread over nine different basins, with half of these in Upper Geyser Basin, the home of Old Faithful.

Geysers need three essentials to exist: water, heat, and fractured rock. The water comes from snow and rain falling on this high plateau, while the heat comes from molten rock close to the earth's surface. Massive pressures from below have created a ring of fractures around the edge of Yellowstone's caldera. This is one of the hottest places on the planet, with heat flows more than 60 times the global average.

How They Work

Geysers operate because cold water is dense and sinks, while hot water is less dense and rises. The periodic eruption of geysers is caused by constrictions in the underground channels that prevent an adequate heat exchange with the surface. Precipitation slowly moves into the earth, even-

CONSTRICTION
BOILING
CONSTRICTION
BOILING
CONSTRICTION
BOILIING
SUPERHEATED WATER AND STEAM
BOB RACE

tually contacting the molten rock. Because of high pressures at these depths, water can reach extreme temperatures without vaporizing (as in a pressure cooker). As this superheated water rises back toward the surface, it emerges in hot springs, fumaroles, mud pots, and geysers. The most spectacular of these phenomena are geysers. Two general types of geysers exist in Yellowstone. Fountain geysers (such as Great Fountain Geyser) explode from pools of water and tend to spray water more widely, whereas cone-type geysers (such as Old Faithful) jet out of nozzlelike formations.

In a geyser, steam bubbles upward from the superheated source of water and expands as it rises. These bubbles block the plumbing system, keeping hot water from reaching the surface. Eventually, however, pressure from the bubbles begins to force the cooler water above out of the vent. This initial release triggers a more violent reaction as the sudden lessening of pressure allows the entire column to begin boiling, explosively expelling steam and water to produce a geyser. Once the eruption has emptied the plumbing

YELLOWSTONE

system, water gradually seeps back into the chambers to begin the process anew. Some of Yellowstone's geysers have enormous underground caverns that fill with water; in its rare eruptions, massive Steamboat Geyser can blast a million gallons of water into the air!

As an aside, the term "geyser" is one of the few Icelandic terms in the English language; it means to "gush forth." There are probably 30 active geysers in Iceland, many more on Russia's Kamchatka Peninsula, and a few in New Zealand, where geothermal development has greatly lessened geyser activity. A fine online source with details about Yellowstone's geysers—and others around the globe—is maintained by the nonprofit **Geyser Observation and Study Association,** www.geyserstudy.org.

Protecting the Geysers

Unfortunately, some of Yellowstone's geysers have been lost because of human stupidity or vandalism. At one time, it was considered great sport to stuff logs, rocks, and even chairs into the geysers for a little added show. Others poured chemicals into them to make them play. As a result of such actions, some geysers have been severely damaged or destroyed, and some hot springs have become collection points for coins, rocks, sticks, and trash. It shouldn't be necessary to point out that such actions ruin these thermal areas for everyone and destroy something that may have been going on for hundreds of years.

OTHER GEOTHERMAL ACTIVITY

Although geysers are Yellowstone's best-known features, they make up only a tiny fraction of perhaps 10,000 thermal features in the park. **Hot springs** appear where water can reach the ground surface relatively easily, allowing the heat that builds up in the chambers of geysers to dissipate. When less groundwater is present, you may find **fumaroles,** vents that shoot steam, carbon dioxide, and even hydrogen sulfide gas. **Mud pots** (also called paint pots) are essentially wet fumaroles. Hydrogen sulfide gas combines with water to produce hydrosulfuric acid. This acid breaks down surrounding rocks to form clay, and the clay combines with water to create mud. As gas passes through the mud, it creates the bubbling mud pots. Probably the best examples of these different forms are at Fountain Paint Pot in Lower Geyser Basin, where geysers and hot springs are found in the wetter areas below, while mud pots and fumaroles sit atop a small hill.

The colors in Yellowstone's hot springs come from a variety of sources, including algae and bacteria as well as various minerals, particularly sulfur, iron oxides, and arsenic sulfide. The algae and bacteria are highly temperature-specific and help create the distinct bands of colors around many hot springs. Interestingly, many of these algal species are found only in hot springs, although they exist around the world. The bacteria have proven of considerable interest to science because of their ability to survive such high temperatures. One such organism, *Thermus aquaticus,* was discovered in a Yellowstone hot springs in 1967, and scientists extracted an enzyme that was later used to develop the increasingly important technique of DNA fingerprinting. Above 190°F, even these hot-water bacteria and algae cannot survive, so the hottest springs may appear a deep blue because of the water's ability to absorb all wavelengths of light except blue, which is reflected back into our eyes.

More Terminology

A couple of other terms are worth learning before heading out to see the sights of Yellowstone. **Sinter** (also called "geyserite") is a deposit composed primarily of silica. The silica is dissolved by hot water deep underground and brought to the surface in geysers or hot springs. At the surface the water evaporates, leaving behind the light gray sinter, which can create large mounds (up to 30 feet high) around the older geysers. The rate of accumulation is very slow, and some of the park's geysers have obviously been active for many thousands of years. The other precipitate that is sometimes deposited around Yellowstone's hot springs and geysers is **travertine,** consisting of calcium carbonate that has been dissolved underground. (See Mammoth Hot Springs for more on this process.)

A Note of Warning

The surface around many of the hot springs and geysers is surprisingly thin, and people have been killed or seriously injured by falling through into the boiling water. Stay on the boardwalks in developed areas, and use extreme caution around backcountry thermal features. If in doubt, stay away!

The Greater Yellowstone Ecosystem

One of the largest intact temperate-zone ecosystems on the planet, Yellowstone was for decades viewed as an island of nature surrounded by a world of human development. Unfortunately, this attitude has led to a host of problems. Despite its size, Yellowstone alone is not large enough to support a viable population of all the animals that once existed within its borders, and developments outside the park pose threats within. In recent years, there have been increasing calls to treat the park as part of the larger Greater Yellowstone Ecosystem—18 million acres of land at the juncture of Wyoming, Montana, and Idaho covering both public and private lands. With each year that passes it has become more obvious that Yellowstone can never be simply an island. Most of the issues that have made headlines in the last decade or so—from fisheries problems to snowmobile use—have spread beyond the artificial park boundaries.

Within surrounding lands, conflicts between development and preservation are even more obvious than within the park itself. Logging is one of the most apparent of these problems, and along the park's western border aerial photos reveal a perfectly straight line, with lodgepole pines on the park side and old clearcuts on the Forest Service side. One of these clearcuts was the largest timber sale ever made outside of Alaska! Near the park boundaries, housing developments, the massive growth of the tourism industry, oil and gas drilling, mining, a grizzly bear and wolf theme park, and other activities all create potential problems within the park and for the Yellowstone ecosystem as a whole.

The way everything is tied together is perhaps best exemplified by two seemingly un-related issues that have been on the front burner in recent years: bison and snowmobiles. I talk more about both later, but basically environmentalists think there are far too many snowmobiles heading into the park, and Montana ranchers think there are far too many bison coming out of the park about the same time of year. As a result, bison are being sent to slaughter, sometimes in large numbers. But these two problems are partially linked; some bison exit the park on roads kept smooth for the snowmobiles. If the roads were not groomed, it is possible that more of the bison would remain inside the park in heavy snow years. The point here is not that we should immediately ban all snowmobiles in Yellowstone (although I wish that would happen), but that our actions can have unforeseen ramifications both outside and inside the park.

PLANTS

Yellowstone National Park is primarily a series of high plateaus ranging from 7,500 to 8,500 feet in elevation. Surrounding this gently rolling expanse are the Absaroka Mountains along the east and north sides and the Gallatin Range in the northwestern corner. Elevations are lowest along the northern end of the park, where the Yellowstone River and other rivers cut through, and highest on the eastern and northwestern margins. The plants that carpet Yellowstone are predominantly determined by the amount of precipitation and the type of soils in which they grow: areas underlain by Absaroka volcanic bedrock have more nutrient-rich soils than areas with Yellowstone rhyolites. Vegetation types within the park include sagebrush-steppe, lodgepole pine forests, spruce-fir forests, and subalpine areas.

YELLOWSTONE

Wildlife

Yellowstone is world-famous for its wildlife and provides a marvelous natural setting in which to view bison, elk, moose, wolves, coyotes, pronghorn antelope, bighorn sheep, and other critters. One of the easiest ways to find wildlife is simply by watching for the brake lights, the cars pulled half off the road, and the cameras all pointed in one direction. Inevitably, you'll find an elk or a bison placidly munching away, trying to remain oblivious to the chaos that surrounds it. Be sure to bring binoculars for your trip to Yellowstone. A spotting scope is also helpful in searching for distant bears and wolves.

FINDING WILDLIFE

The Park Service has a free brochure showing where you're most likely to see wildlife in Yellowstone. Pick one up at any visitors center. During summer, the best wildlife-viewing hours are early in the morning and in the late afternoon to early evening.

The park contains some 60 species of resident mammals, ranging from shrews and bats to bison and grizzlies. In addition, 309 species of birds have been recorded, along with 18 species of fish (five of which are nonnative), four amphibians, and six reptiles. The only poisonous animal is the prairie rattlesnake, found at low elevations in the northern end of Yellowstone. Oh yes, countless insect species live here, too. Some Yellowstone critters are more friendly than others, most notably the mosquitoes that show up in large numbers early in the summer. By mid-August they're much less of a hassle, and winter visitors will have no problems at all.

Safety

Because of the constant parade of visitors and the lack of hunting, many of Yellowstone's animals appear to almost ignore the presence of people, and it isn't uncommon to see visitors approach an animal without respecting its need for space. Although they may appear tame, Yellowstone's animals really are wild, and attacks are not

uncommon. Those quiet bison can suddenly erupt with an enormous ferocity if provoked by photographers who come too close. Between 1983 and 1994, four people were killed by bison in Yellowstone and Grand Teton National Parks. **Stay at least 25 yards away from bison and elk and at least 100 yards away from bears.** Do not under any circumstances feed the park's animals. This creates an unnatural dependency, is unhealthy for the animal, and may even lead to its death.

Wildlife Tours

Several nonprofits, companies, and individuals guide wildlife tours in the park. Of particular note is the nonprofit **Yellowstone Association Institute,** 307/344-2294, www.yellowstoneassociation.org, whose naturalists lead two- to five-day programs that blend education, recreation, and lodging. They also can act as private guides. Tours from **Wildlife Expeditions,** 307/733-2623 or 888/945-3567, www.tetonscience.org/wildlife, are run by guides from the Teton Science School, another highly respected nonprofit.

Tory and Meredith Taylor, 307/455-2161, provide personalized wildlife package tours and have a good reputation. Other wildlife guiding companies include **Callowishus Park Touring Company,** 307/733-9521, www.callowishus.com; **Jackson's Hole Adventure,** 307/654-7849 or 800/392-3165, www.jacksonholeadventure.com; **Upstream Anglers and Outdoor Adventures,** 307/739-9443 or 800/642-8979, www.upstreamanglers.com; and **Yellowstone Country Adventures,** 406/994-0422, www.yellowstonecountry-adventures.com. Get a complete list of licensed tour operators from the Park Service at 307/344-7381, www.nps.gov/yell.

BIRDS

Trumpeter swans—beautiful white birds with seven-foot wingspans—are a fairly common sight in Yellowstone, particularly on the Madison and Yellowstone Rivers and on Yellowstone Lake.

Many trumpeter swans winter in hot spring areas. These are some of the largest birds in America, weighing 20–30 pounds. Another large white bird here is the ungainly looking and bulbous-billed **white pelican**, a common sight on Yellowstone Lake and near Fishing Bridge. More than 350 pairs of pelicans nest on the Molly Islands in Yellowstone Lake; this is one of the largest white-pelican breeding colonies in the Rockies. **Bald eagles**—America's national bird—and **ospreys** have managed comebacks in recent years and are frequently seen along the Yellowstone River and above Yellowstone Lake. Look for **golden eagles** flying over the open grasslands of Lamar Valley or Hayden Valley.

KILLING THE PREDATORS

Wildlife has always been one of the big drawing cards at Yellowstone, and early on there were constant charges of mass slaughter by poachers and market hunters. It was not until 1894 that Congress passed the Lacey Act, finally making it illegal to hunt within the park. Unfortunately, predators such as wolves, coyotes, mountain lions, and wolverines were regarded as despoilers of the elk, deer, and moose and became fair targets for poisoning and shooting by early park managers. (This happened throughout the West, not just in the park.) The campaign proved all too successful, devastating the wolf and mountain lion populations. In recent years, wolves have returned in a spectacular way, although mountain lion numbers remain low.

CONTROVERSY ON THE NORTHERN RANGE

A recurring area of strife in Yellowstone has been the suggestion that elk and bison are overgrazing and destroying the Lamar and Yellowstone River basins, an area known as the northern range. The issue periodically flares up, fed in part by the efforts of Montana ranchers and others who suffer from bison and elk that migrate out of Yellowstone onto their land each winter. They—and some researchers—believe that the Park Service has allowed too many animals to survive and that overgrazing is damaging the land. Most research, however, points in the opposite direction—that the land is not overgrazed, and that ecological processes are working fine in a system termed "natural regulation." The populations of elk and bison fluctuate over time; some years numbers are up, and other years they drop because of harsh winters, predation, hunting outside the park, or other factors.

Safety in grizzly country is always a concern, but statistically you are considerably more likely to be hurt in a traffic accident than to be mauled by a bear.

BEARS

During Yellowstone's early years, bears were commonly viewed as either pets or nuisances. Cubs were tethered to poles in front of the hotels, and other bears fed on the garbage piles that grew up around the camps and hotels. Older folks still recall the bear-feeding grounds at the garbage dumps, where visitors might see 50 bears pawing through the refuse. The feeding shows continued until 1941, but it wasn't until 1970 that the park's open-pit dumps were finally sealed off and the garbage cans bear-proofed. Closure of the dumps helped create confrontations between "garbage bears" and humans; the bears nearly always lost. Between 1970 and 1972, dozens of grizzlies died in showdowns with humans in the park or surrounding areas. Fortunately, careful management in the intervening years has helped the population rebound. Today there are believed to be at least 400 grizzlies in the Greater Yellowstone Ecosystem, and their numbers have been increasing fairly steadily since the 1980s. (Some scientists believe there are more than 600 grizzlies.)

One unusual aspect of the Yellowstone grizzlies was just discovered in recent years: the importance of moths as a food source in the grizzly diet. Millions of army cutworm moths congregate on Yellowstone's high alpine slopes during summer, where they feed on nectar from the abundant flowers. Bears are attracted to this food source because of the insect's abundance and high fat content. Researchers have sometimes seen two dozen bears feeding on a single slope!

Bear Viewing

Both black and grizzly bears are found throughout Yellowstone, but the days of bear jams along the park roads are long past because rangers actively work to prevent bears from becoming habituated to people. Most bears have returned to their more natural ways of living, although problems still crop up with individuals wandering through campgrounds in search of food. You're more likely to encounter a bear in the backcountry areas, and some places are closed to hiking for extended periods each year for this reason. The best places to watch for grizzlies along the road system are in the Hayden and Lamar Valleys, near Mt. Washburn, and in the Antelope Creek drainage (just south of Tower Fall).

Safety in grizzly country is always a concern, but statistically you are considerably more likely to be hurt in a traffic accident than to be mauled by a bear. There were just 22 bear-caused injuries in the park between 1980 and 1997—one injury for every 2.1 million visitors! Most of these injuries took place in backcountry areas and involved female bears with cubs or yearlings, and nearly all attacks took place following a surprise encounter with a bear. Three people were killed by Yellowstone bears in the last three decades of the 20th century, the most recent being a 1986 fatality caused when a photographer approached an adult female grizzly too closely. For details on staying safe around bears, see the Safety in Bear Country section in the On the Road chapter.

Protecting the Bears

The **Yellowstone Grizzly Foundation,** 307/734-8643, www.yellowstonegrizzly.com, is an excellent nonprofit organization dedicated to conserving grizzlies within the Greater Yellowstone Ecosystem. Established by Steve and Marilynn French—who have been studying grizzly bears since 1983—the foundation emphasizes nonintrusive observations. One of their groundbreaking projects involved collecting hair samples as

bears crawled under barbed wire. DNA analysis of these hairs led to a new understanding of how grizzly bears in Yellowstone are related to other bears. It turns out that more than 90 percent of Yellowstone grizzlies originated from the same maternal lineage, a fact that may have important ramifications for management. The research also showed that the grizzlies of Yellowstone differ markedly from Alaskan grizzlies such as those found at the wildlife park in West Yellowstone.

The **Sierra Club** is also deeply involved in the politics of grizzly bear management around the park. For their take on the issues, see www.grizzly.sierraclub.org.

BIGHORN SHEEP

These stocky mountain dwellers are named for the massive curling horns of the males (rams) and can be seen in several parts of Yellowstone. They have a tan-colored coat with a white rump patch. Bighorns were once abundant throughout the western United States, and early trappers in the mountains east of Yellowstone reported finding thousands of sheep in and around the present-day park. They were also an important source of food for the Sheepeater Indians who lived in Yellowstone before the arrival of whites. Bighorn sheep were virtually wiped out by hunters in the late 19th century, and domestic sheep overran their lands and brought deadly diseases. Within a few decades, the millions of sheep that had roamed the West were reduced to a few hundred survivors.

Both the rams and ewes (females) have horns that remain for life, but only the rams get the massive curl for which bighorn sheep are known. Rams are 125–275 pounds in size, with ewes 75–150 pounds. During the mating season in November and December you're likely to see the original head-bangers in action as rams clash to establish dominance. The clashes can be surprisingly violent, and to protect the brain, bighorns have a double cranium that absorbs much of the shock. Those with the larger horns are typically the dominant bighorns and the primary breeders. The young lambs are born in May and June. In

Yellowstone is home to one of the largest free-ranging herds of bison anywhere.

summer the sexes separate, with the ewes and lambs remaining lower while the bachelor herds climb higher into the mountains. Bighorns use their ability to climb steep and rocky terrain as protection from predators such as coyotes, wolves, and mountain lions. Winter often finds bighorns in mixed herds at lower elevations. Around 250 bighorns live within Yellowstone National Park, with much larger populations in the surrounding national forests.

Finding Bighorns

Look for bighorn sheep on cliffs in the Gardner River Canyon between Mammoth Hot Springs and the town of Gardiner. Ewes and lambs are also frequently seen just off the road on Dunraven Pass north of Canyon, and day-hikers commonly encounter rams up-close on the slopes of Mt. Washburn. Another place where bighorns may be seen is along Specimen Ridge.

BISON

Before their virtual annihilation in the 19th century, around 60 million bison were spread across America. When Yellowstone was estab-

lished in 1872, hundreds of mountain bison (also called wood bison) still ranged across this high plateau. Sport and meat hunting—legal until 1894—and later poaching reduced the population so that by 1902 perhaps fewer than 25 remained. That year, 21 plains bison were brought in from private ranches in Montana and Texas to help restore the Yellowstone herd, and today there are approximately 2,500 in the park, making this the largest free-ranging herd of bison anywhere on earth. Unfortunately, interbreeding between the mountain and plains bison means that the animals in Yellowstone today are genetically different from the original inhabitants.

Bison are typically found in open country throughout the park, including Hayden, Lamar, and Pelican Valleys, along with the Firehole River Basin (including Old Faithful). A favorite time to see bison in Yellowstone is late May, just after the new calves have been born. The calves' antics are always good for laughs. Be sure to use caution around bison; many people have been gored when they've come too close. Always stay at least 25 yards away, preferably farther.

YELLOWSTONE

Cattle Versus Bison

Bison are carriers of brucellosis, a disease that causes cows to abort calves and is the source of undulant fever in humans. Brucellosis can be spread when other animals lick a contaminated fetus or birthing material, a situation that is unlikely given the timing of bison movements. In 1985, Yellowstone's bison began wandering north into the Gardiner area for the winter. Montana and Wyoming are certified as "brucellosis-free" states, and although there is absolutely no evidence that wild bison have ever transmitted the disease to cattle, ranchers feared that the bison might threaten Montana's brucellosis-free status. If cattle become infected with brucellosis, ranchers might be prohibited from shipping livestock out of state.

A highly controversial "hunt" during the late 1980s let hunters shoot bison when they wandered outside the park. After a public outcry, the job was turned over to the Montana state Division of Livestock (DOL), an agency accustomed to dealing with cattle, not wildlife. Things came to a head in the heavy-snow winter of 1996–1997 when nearly 1,100 Yellowstone bison were sent to slaughter, cutting the park bison herd by one-third. It was one of the largest killings of bison anywhere since their destruction on the Great Plains in the 1880s. Smaller numbers of bison have been killed in recent winters, although it topped 200 in 2002 (out of a population now numbering 4,000).

Today, the Park Service, Montana DOL, and U.S. Forest Service operate under a controversial bison management plan that attempts to simultaneously maintain a free-ranging bison population while reducing the risk of transmission of brucellosis to cattle. Under this plan, some bison are tolerated on outside lands when cattle aren't present, and if the population continues to be high, others can be captured in pens and slaughtered when they wander outside the park, even if they haven't been tested for brucellosis. It's not a pleasant situation, especially for a national park that was established in part to help protect wild bison. Even a Yellowstone publication admits, "Many park visitors are confused about why the National Park Service is a partner in a plan that can result in killing bison, a natural resource the National Park Service goes to great lengths to protect within the boundaries of the park and an animal so representative of the agency's successful protection of wildlife that it is prominently featured on the National Park Service's familiar 'arrowhead' logo." You can find much more about this issue on the Yellowstone National Park website, www.nps.gov/yell.

Ironically, Yellowstone's far more numerous elk also carry brucellosis, and during 2002, elk infected an Idaho cattle herd with the disease, leading to their destruction. Although elk migrate each fall out from Yellowstone, you won't hear Montana authorities talking about slaughtering all of the elk that wander across the park's borders! The state of Wyoming has managed to keep its brucellosis-free status despite the presence of cattle, bison, and elk in Jackson Hole. There, most ranchers vaccinate their cattle and work with the Park Service to keep bison and elk separate from livestock. Why won't it work in Montana? The answer probably has far more to do with Montana politics than biology.

Buffalo Field Campaign is a nonprofit environmental group that has been at loggerheads with the Park Service and DOL over bison management for years. You may meet their outspoken activists handing out literature at Old Faithful. Get their take on the issue at www.wildrockies.org/buffalo.

COYOTES

Although wolves get the media attention, visitors to Yellowstone are probably more likely to see another native of the dog family: the coyote. Keep your eyes open for coyotes anywhere in Yellowstone but especially in open grassy areas where they are more easily spotted. During summer, they're often seen in small packs or alone as they hunt small mammals such as mice, voles, and pocket gophers. At other times of the year they prey on larger animals, including the calves of elk and pronghorn antelope, and scavenge carrion.

Differentiating coyotes from wolves can be a bit tricky, especially from a distance without binoculars. Coyotes are considerably smaller animals;

adult male coyotes weigh around 30 pounds, whereas wolves are far more massive, with many weighing 100 pounds or more. The wolf has a large head, short and rounded ears, and a broad and blocky muzzle, whereas the coyote has a small head, large and pointy ears, and a narrow, pointy nose. From a distance coyotes are more delicate in appearance, with smaller feet and thin legs.

The coyotes within Yellowstone generally live in packs containing six or seven animals led by a dominant pair called the alpha male and female. Most packs have a long family lineage and a well-defined territory; some coyote packs have been using the same denning areas for at least 50 years! The average coyote lives around six years. The alphas mate in early February, and pups are born in early April. Other members of the pack guard the den from wolves and other predators and regurgitate food to feed the pups.

Top Dog No More

Before the reintroduction of wolves, coyotes were the big dogs (so to speak) in northern Yellowstone, and the primary predators of elk calves, killing about 1,200 each year. Wolves occupy a similar ecological niche to coyotes, and their return has led to a 50 percent reduction in coyote numbers in northern Yellowstone. Some of this decrease comes from outright killing of coyotes by the far larger wolves, particularly alpha coyotes. The ever-resourceful coyotes have responded by banding together in larger packs, denning in rocky areas, becoming more wary, and staying on the margins of wolf territories. Despite competition, coyotes remain common and are certainly in no danger of being displaced from Yellowstone; after all, both species were here for thousands of years before the extermination of wolves in the 20th century. Good places to look for coyotes are in the Blacktail Plateau area and Lamar Valley, along with the Upper and Lower Geyser Basins near Old Faithful.

Deer

Mule deer (also known as black-tailed deer) are common in many parts of Yellowstone during summer, but most migrate to lower elevations when winter comes. They are typically found in open areas containing sagebrush or grass. Mule deer are named for their long mulelike ears. They also have black-tipped tails and a peculiar way of pogoing away when frightened. Adult males (bucks) grow antlers each summer, and mating season arrives in November and December. Fawns are born in May or June.

The smaller **white-tailed deer** are occasionally seen within Yellowstone but are far less common. You are most likely to find them along rivers or in brushy areas at low elevations, such as around Mammoth Hot Springs or in Lamar Valley. Other places to watch for them are along Yellowstone Lake and in the Upper Geyser Basin.

Elk

One animal virtually every visitor to Yellowstone sees is elk. About 30,000 of these regal animals summer in the park, and approximately 15,000 remain through the winter, primarily on the north end of Yellowstone. In summer, look for elk in Mammoth Hot Springs, Elk Park, and Gibbon Meadows, but you're certain to also see them elsewhere in Yellowstone. Bull elk can top 700 pounds, whereas the cows (females) weigh around 500–525 pounds, making elk the second-largest members of the deer family after moose. Each summer, adult bulls grow massive antlers that can weigh 30 pounds or more, which prove useful in the fall mating season as bulls spar with each other. Dominant bulls herd females into harems during the rut and may sometimes control 25 or so cows, mating with those that come into estrus and battling with rivals intent on taking over their harems. The bugling of bull elk is a common autumn sound in Yellowstone, as anyone who visits Mammoth Hot Springs at that time of year can attest. It's a strange sound that starts out low, followed by a trumpetlike call and then a series of odd grunts. Approximately 90 percent of the elk cows become pregnant each year.

The mating season ends by mid- to late November, and winter snows push the elk to lower elevations on the north side of Yellowstone or out of the park into surrounding areas. With the arrival of spring, bulls lose their antlers, and elk start moving back toward the high country. Calves are born in late May or early June (sometimes during the migration) and weigh 25–40 pounds at birth. Elk—particularly young calves—are an important food source for predators in Yellowstone; almost one-third of the calves are killed each year by wolves, grizzly and black bears, coyotes, and golden eagles.

MOOSE

The largest members of the deer family, moose are typically seen eating willow bushes in riparian areas inside Yellowstone National Park. During winter, these moose migrate into high-elevation forests where the snow isn't as deep (tree branches hold the snow) or as crusty as in the open. In these forests they browse on subalpine fir and Douglas fir. The fires of 1988 burned through many of these forests, and the loss of cover has hurt the Yellowstone moose population. The best places to look for moose are Hayden Valley, around Yellowstone Lake, the Willow Park area north of Norris, the southwestern corner along the Bechler and Falls Rivers, and along the Gallatin, Lamar, and Lewis River drainages.

PRONGHORN ANTELOPE

These speedy and colorful ungulates (hoofed mammals) are common sights on the plains of Wyoming, but most of Yellowstone doesn't provide adequate habitat for them. Pronghorn antelope are only found in sagebrush and grassy areas on the northern end of the park from Lamar Valley to the Gardiner area. Their populations declined sharply in the 1990s within the park, and as of 2000 pronghorn numbered around 200. Coyotes and other predators take many newborn fawns each spring and may be a significant factor in the decline, combined with several other factors such as inbreeding caused by the small population; changes in vegetation; loss of habitat to development in their Paradise Valley wintering area north of the park; increasing numbers of fences across their range; and hunting.

WOLVES

The wolves are back! One of the most exciting developments for visitors to Yellowstone has been the reintroduction of wolves to the park, making this one of the few places in the Lower 48 where they can be viewed in the wild. Wolves once ranged across nearly all of North America, but white settlers regarded them—along with mountain lions, grizzly bears, and coyotes—as threats to livestock and unwanted predators on game animals. Even in Yellowstone, wolves were hunted and poisoned by both the army and the Park Service. By 1940, the wolf was probably gone from the park, although a few lone animals turned up briefly again in the early 1970s.

In the United States, until 1995 wolves could only be found in Alaska, in northern Minnesota, and in Isle Royale and Glacier National Parks. With the more enlightened public attitude evident in recent years, ecologists and conservationists began pushing for the reintroduction of wolves to Yellowstone, considered one of the few remaining areas in the Lower 48 that could support a viable wolf population.

The proposal to return wolves to Yellowstone set off a firestorm from ranchers (with ardent support from Wyoming's Republican senators), who feared that the wolves would wander outside the park to destroy sheep and cattle. Opponents said hundreds of livestock would be killed each year around the park and that the reintroduction cost might reach $1.8 million per wolf, a figure that proved grossly inflated. Despite these dire predictions, the U.S. Fish & Wildlife Service began reintroducing wolves to Yellowstone in 1995, initially releasing 14 gray wolves that had been captured in British Columbia. Additional wolves were set free the following spring. During subsequent years things have gone far better than anyone had predicted. By 2002, biologists estimated that 24 groups of wolves totaling 216 individuals inhabited the Greater Yellowstone Ecosystem from north of Yellowstone to the Pinedale area on the south and eastward into Shoshone National Forest. Because of the successful reintroduction, it's only a matter of time until wolves are removed from the endangered species list (which will inevitably create still more controversy and lawsuits).

Finding Wolves

The return of the wolf to Yellowstone has created a buzz of excitement as visitors gather to watch for them in the distance. The best place to look is the open terrain of Lamar Valley, where the **Druid Peak Pack** has taken up residence and are visible at many times of the year. Visit early in the morning or near dusk to increase your odds of seeing them. You may well hear their plaintive cry from your campground late at night, particularly at Slough Creek or Pebble Creek campgrounds. Binoculars or spotting scopes are helpful for roadside wolf watching. Do not follow the wolves around because this may disturb them and affect their survival. Denning activity typically takes place early April to early May, with active denning areas closed to humans; check with the Park Service for currently closed areas.

Wolves are the largest members of the canids (dog family), with males averaging 70–120 pounds and stretching up to six feet long from head to tail. They are much more massive than coyotes, although the two are sometimes confused. Wolves live in packs of two to eight, led by an alpha male and female, and establish territories to exclude other wolf packs. Most pack members are from an extended family, but they may include outside members. The alphas are the only ones that generally mate, and a litter of six or so pups is born in early spring. Once they are weaned, the pack feeds pups regurgitated meat until they are large enough to join the hunt. Wolves hunt primarily in the evening and morning hours when their prey—elk, deer, moose, bison, and pronghorn—are feeding.

The park website, www.nps.gov/yell, has additional details on wolves, or visit www.wolftracker.com (not affiliated with the Park Service).

Park History

Yellowstone National Park has a rich and fascinating history that reaches back through thousands of years of settlement. The most thorough source for history is *The Yellowstone Story* (University Press of Colorado, www.upcolorado.com), an excellent two-volume set by former park historian Aubrey L. Haines. For an engaging and personal journey through the past, read *Searching for Yellowstone* by Paul Schullery (Houghton Mifflin, www.hmco.com).

SHEEPEATER INDIANS

The last major glaciation ended around 15,000 years ago, and the first peoples may have reached Yellowstone while the ice was still retreating. There is good evidence that the country was occupied for at least 10,000 years, although the tribes apparently changed over time. By the mid-19th century, the country was surrounded by Blackfeet to the north, Crow to the east, and Shoshone and Bannock to the south and west.

These tribes all traveled through and hunted in Yellowstone, building temporary shelters, called *wickiups,* made of aspen poles covered with pine boughs; a few of these still exist in the park. The primary inhabitants of this high plateau were the Sheepeater Indians, who may have been here for more than 2,000 years. Of Shoshone stock, the Sheepeaters hunted bighorn sheep (hence the name) and made bows from the sheep horns, but their diet also included other animals, fish, roots, and berries. Because they did not have horses, the Sheepeaters used dog-pulled travois to carry their few possessions from camp to camp. Summers were spent in high alpine meadows and along passes, where they hunted migrating game animals or gathered roots and berries. They wintered in protected canyons.

The Sheepeaters were smaller than other Indians and have achieved an aura of mystery because so little is known of their way of living. Yellowstone was at the heart of their territory, but with the arrival of whites came devastating diseases,

YELLOWSTONE

THE NEZ PERCE WAR

One of the saddest episodes in the history of Yellowstone took place in 1877 and involved the Nez Perce Indians of Oregon's Wallowa Valley. When the government tried to force the people of Chief White Bird and Chief Joseph onto an Idaho reservation so that white ranchers could have their lands, the Indians stubbornly refused. A few drunken young Indians killed four whites, and subsequent raids led to the deaths of at least 14 more. The army retaliated but was turned back by the Nez Perce. Rather than face government reinforcements, more than 1,000 Nez Perce began an 1,800-mile flight in a desperate bid to reach Canada. A series of running battles followed as the Indians managed to confound the inept army using their geographic knowledge and battle skills. The Nez Perce entered Yellowstone from the west, and a few hotheads immediately attacked vacationing tourists and prospectors. Two whites were killed in the park, others were kidnapped, and another man nearly died from his wounds.

The Nez Perce exited Yellowstone two weeks after they arrived, narrowly missing an encounter with their implacable foe, Gen. William T. Sherman, who just happened to be vacationing in Yellowstone at the time. East of the park, the Indians plotted a masterful escape from two columns of army forces, feinting a move down the Shoshone River and then heading north along a route that left their pursuers gasping in amazement—straight up the narrow Clarks Fork Canyon, "where rocks on each side came so near together that two horses abreast could hardly pass." Finally, less than 40 miles from the international border with Canada, the army caught up with the Nez Perce, and after a fierce battle the tribe was forced to surrender (although 300 did make good their escape).

Chief Joseph's haunting words still echo through the years: "Hear me, my chiefs, I am tired; my heart is sick and sad. From where the sun now stands, I will fight no more forever." Despite promises that they would be allowed to return home, the Nez Perce were hustled onto reservations in Oklahoma and Washington while whites remained on their ancestral lands. Chief Joseph spent the rest of his life on Washington's Colville Reservation and died in 1904, reportedly of a broken heart. Yellowstone's Nez Perce Creek, which feeds the Firehole River, is named for this desperate bid for freedom.

---

particularly smallpox. The survivors joined their Shoshone brothers on the Wind River Reservation or the Bannock Reservation in Idaho. The last of the tribe left Yellowstone in the 1870s.

FUR TRAPPERS

The word "Yellowstone" appears to have come from the Minnetaree Indians, who called the river "Mi tse a-da-zi," a word French-Canadian trappers translated into "Rive des Roche Jaunes"—literally, "Yellow Rock River." The Indians apparently called it this because of the yellowish bluffs along the river near Billings, Montana (not because of the colorful Grand Canyon of the Yellowstone). The term "Yellow Stone" was first used on a map made in 1797. When the Lewis and Clark Expedition traveled through the country north of Yellowstone in 1805–1806, the Indians told them tales of this mysterious place: "There is frequently heard a loud noise like thunder, which makes the earth tremble, they state that they seldom go there because children Cannot sleep—and Conceive it possessed of spirits, who were adverse that men Should be near them." (This certainly was not the attitude of all the native peoples, for the park had long been inhabited.) The first white man to come through Yellowstone is believed to be John Colter, a former member of the Lewis and Clark Expedition who wandered through the region in the winter of 1807–1808. A map based on Colter's recollections shows Yellowstone Lake ("Eustis Lake"), along with an area of "Hot Spring Brimstone."

As fur trappers spread through the Rockies in the 1820s and '30s, many discovered the geysers and hot springs of Yellowstone, and stories quickly spread around the rendezvous fires. The word of the trappers was passed on to later settlers and explorers but not entirely believed. After all, mountain man Jim Bridger described not just petrified trees, but petrified birds singing petrified songs! His tales of a river that "ran so fast that it became hot on the bottom" could well have referred to the Firehole River. When Bridger tried to lead a party of military explorers into Yellowstone, they were stymied by deep snows. Still, word gradually got out that something very strange could be found in this part of the mountains. Little remains today from the mountain-man era, although in 1880 the letters "J.O.R. Aug. 19, 1819" were found carved in a tree near the Upper Falls of the Yellowstone, and later a cache of iron beaver traps similar to those used by the Hudson's Bay Company was discovered near Obsidian Cliff.

EXPEDITIONS

National attention finally came to Yellowstone with a series of three expeditions to check out the wild claims of local prospectors. In 1869, David E. Folsom, Charles W. Cook, and William Peterson headed south from Bozeman, finding the Grand Canyon, Yellowstone Lake, and the geyser basins. When a friend pressured them to submit a description of their travels for publication, the *New York Tribune* refused to publish it, noting that the paper "had a reputation that they could not risk with such unreliable material."

The adventures of this first expedition led another group of explorers into Yellowstone the following year, but this time money was the motive. Jay Cooke's Northern Pacific Railroad needed investors for a planned route across Montana. A good public-relations campaign was the first step, and it happened to coincide with the visit of a former Montana tax collector named Nathaniel P. Langford, who had heard of the discoveries of Folsom, Cook, and Peterson. The party of 19 soldiers and civilians, including Langford, headed out in August of 1870 under Gen. Henry D. Washburn. They were thrilled by what they discovered and proceeded to give the geysers names—Old Faithful, Castle, Giant, Grotto, Gi-

FIREHOLE RIVER AREA, 1839

*At this place there is also large numbers of hot Springs some of which have formed cones of limestone 20 feet high of a Snowy whiteness which make a splendid appearance standing among the ever green pines Some of the lower peaks are very serviceable to the hunter in preparing his dinner when hungry for here his kettle is always ready and boiling his meat being suspended in the water by a string is soon prepared for his meal without further trouble. . . .
Standing upon an eminence and superficially viewing these natural monuments one is half inclined to believe himself in the neighborhood of the ruins of some ancients City whose temples had been constructed of the whitest marble.*

—mountain man Osborne Russell

antess—which became permanently attached to the features. The joy of the trip was marred when one man—Truman Everts—became separated from the others and then lost his horse. He was not found until 37 days later, by which time he weighed just 50 pounds. His rescuer did not even recognize him as human. Amazingly, Everts survived and recovered.

With the return of the Washburn Expedition, national newspapers and magazines finally began to pay attention to Yellowstone, and Langford began lecturing in the East on what they had found. One of those listening was Dr. Ferdinand V. Hayden, director of the U.S. Geological Survey. Hayden asked Congress to fund an official investigation. With the help of Representatives James G. Blaine (coincidentally a supporter of the Northern Pacific Railroad) and conservationist Henry M. Dawes, Congress appropriated $40,000 for an exploration of "the sources of the Missouri and Yellowstone Rivers." Thus began the most famous and influential trip into Yellowstone—the 1871 Hayden Expedition. The troop included 34 men, an escort of cavalry, painter Thomas Moran, and photographer William H. Jackson.

ESTABLISHING THE PARK

When Hayden returned to Washington to prepare his report, he found a letter from railroad promoter Jay Cooke. In the letter, Cooke proposed that "Congress pass a bill reserving the Great Geyser Basin as a public park forever—just as it has reserved that far inferior wonder the Yosemite valley and big trees." (Abraham Lincoln had established Yosemite earlier as a state park.) In an amazingly short time, a bill was introduced to set aside the land, and Hayden rushed to arrange a display in the Capitol rotunda of geological specimens, sketches by Moran, and photos by Jackson. The bill easily passed both houses of Congress and was signed into law on March 1, 1872, by Pres. Ulysses S. Grant. The first national park had come into existence, a culmination not just of the discoveries in Yellowstone but also of a growing appreciation for preserving the wonders of the natural world.

Congress saw no need to set aside money for this new creation because it seemed to be doing fine already. Besides, it was thought that Jay Cooke's new railroad would soon arrive, making it easy for thousands of vacationers to explore Yellowstone. In turn, concessioners would build roads and hotels and pay the government franchise fees. The park was placed under the control of the Secretary of the Interior, with Nathaniel P. Langford as its unpaid superintendent. Meanwhile, the planned railroad fizzled when Jay Cooke & Co. declared bankruptcy, precipitating the panic of 1873.

ROADS AND RAILROADS

Because of the difficult access, fewer than 500 people visited in each of Yellowstone's first few years as a park, most to soak in tubs at Mammoth Hot Springs. Not a few decided to take home souvenirs, bringing pickaxes and shovels for that purpose. Meanwhile, hunters—including some working for the Mammoth Hotel—began

shooting the park's abundant game. Two brothers who had a ranch just north of the park killed 2,000 elk in a single year. Superintendent Langford did little to stop the slaughter and only bothered to visit the park twice. Finally, in 1877, the Secretary of the Interior fired him, putting Philetus W. Norris in charge instead. Norris proved a good choice, despite a knack for applying his name to everything in sight. (Most of his attempts at immortality have been replaced by other titles, but Norris Geyser Basin, Norris Road, and even the town of Norris, Michigan, remain.)

Norris oversaw construction of the first major road in Yellowstone, a rough 60-mile route built in just 30 days to connect Upper Geyser Basin with Mammoth and the western entrance. All of this was precipitated by the raids of the Nez Perce Indians earlier that summer and threats that the Bannock Indians would strike next. In addition, Norris began, but never completed, the Queen's Laundry, a bathhouse that is considered the first government building built for the public in any national park. The log walls are still visible in a meadow near Lower Geyser Basin.

By 1882, Norris had managed to alienate the company that helped found the park, the Northern Pacific Railroad. The company announced plans to build a railroad line to the geysers and construct a large hotel, "being assured by the Government of a monopoly therein." Norris's opposition led to his being fired and replaced by railroad man Patrick H. Conger. Soon, however, the scheme began to unravel. The Yellowstone Park Improvement Company—whose vice-president happened to be construction superintendent for the Northern Pacific's branch line into Gardiner—had planned not just a lodging monopoly but also a monopoly on all transportation, timber rights, and ranching privileges in the park. Later it was discovered that the company had contracted for 20,000 pounds of venison (killed in the park) to feed the construction crews. As one newspaper writer commented, "It is a 'Park Improvement Company' doing this, and I suppose they consider it an improvement to rid the park, as far as possible, of game."

Finally, in 1884 Congress acted by limiting the land that could be leased—thus effectively ending the railroad's plans—and adding funding to hire 10 assistants to patrol Yellowstone. Unfortunately, they neglected to include any penalties for the poachers and despoilers other than expulsion, so even the few assistants who did decent work found the culprits quickly returning. The problems were myriad. Cooke City miners were fishing with spears, seine nets, and even dynamite. Guides were throwing rocks into the geysers, squatters had ensconced themselves on prime land in Lamar Valley, and visitors were leaving fires unattended and breaking off specimens from the geysers.

Superintendent Conger was later replaced by Robert E. Carpenter, a man about whom historian Hiram Chittenden noted, "In his opinion, the Park was created to be an instrument of profit to those who were shrewd enough to grasp the opportunity." Carpenter lobbied Congress to remove lands from the park so that the Northern Pacific could construct a railroad along the Yellowstone and Lamar Rivers to Cooke City. In return, friends promised to locate claims in his name along the route so that he too might profit from the venture. The landgrab fell apart when the Senate vetoed the move, and Carpenter was summarily removed from office. Not long thereafter, Congress flatly refused to fund the civilian administration of Yellowstone, and the Secretary of the Interior was forced to request the aid of the military in 1886. It proved a fortuitous step.

THE ARMY YEARS

The U.S. Army finally brought a semblance of order to Yellowstone, eliminating the political appointees who viewed the park as a place to get rich. That first year, a temporary fort—Camp Sheridan—was thrown up and a troop of soldiers arrived, but it wasn't until 1891 that work began on a permanent Fort Yellowstone at Mammoth. By 1904, the fort consisted of some 26 buildings housing 120 men. The soldiers had clear objectives—protecting wildlife (or at least bison and elk) from poachers, fighting fires, stopping vandalism, and generally achieving order out of chaos. These goals were accomplished with a fervor that gained widespread respect, and

in a way that would later influence the organization of the National Park Service. One of the major accomplishments of the soldiers was completion of the Grand Loop Road, which passes most of Yellowstone's attractions. The basic pattern was completed by 1905.

Fort Yellowstone was a favorite station for soldiers, and it was considered something of an honor to be sent to such a setting. The life of the soldiers was not always easy, however, and some died in the bitter winters or in accidents. A series of 16 soldier stations—actually little more than large cabins—was established around the park, and each was manned year-round, usually by four soldiers.

Before the arrival of cars, many visitors to Yellowstone were wealthy people from the East Coast or Europe intent on doing the grand tour of the West. The railroads (Northern Pacific to the north, Union Pacific to the west, and the Burlington to the east) deposited them near park borders, where they were met by carriages, Tallyhos (26-passenger stagecoaches), and surreys. In 1915, some 3,000 horses were in use within the park! Most "dudes" paid approximately $50 for a six-day tour that included transportation, meals, and lodging at the hotels. They paid another $2.50 for the privilege of sailing across Yellowstone Lake on the steamship *Zillah*. By contrast, another group, the "sagebrushers," came to Yellowstone in smaller numbers, arriving in their own wagons or hiring a coach to transport them between the "Wylie Way" campgrounds. These seasonal tent camps were scattered around the park, providing an inexpensive way to see the sights—just $35 for a seven-day tour. Even as early as 1908, Yellowstone was being seen by 18,000 visitors per year.

The Northern Pacific was still intent on carving Yellowstone into a moneymaking resort, even going so far as to propose an electric railroad, to be powered by a dam at the falls of the Yellowstone River. Fortunately, equally powerful forces—notably Gen. Philip Sheridan and naturalist Joseph Bird Grinnell—saw through their designs and thwarted each attempt to bring railroads into Yellowstone. Still, the Northern Pacific's interests were represented by

THE YELLOWSTONE FIRES OF 1988

Many will long remember the summer of 1988 as the year that fires seared Yellowstone National Park. TV reporters flocked to the park, pronouncing the destruction of America's most famous national wonder as they stood before trees turned into towering torches and 27,000-foot-high clouds of black smoke. Newspaper headlines screamed, "Park Sizzles," "Winds Whip Fiery Frenzy Out of Control," and "Firestorms Blacken Yellowstone." Residents of nearby towns complained of lost tourism dollars, choking smoke, and intentionally lit backfires that threatened their homes and businesses; Wyoming politicians berated the Park Service's "Let Burn" policy; President Reagan expressed astonishment that fires were ever allowed to burn in the national parks, although the policy had been in place for 16 years. Perhaps the most enduring image is from a forest that had been blown down by tornado-force winds in 1984 and then burned by the wind-whipped fires of 1988. The media ate it up, with one headline reading, "Total Destruction: Intense Heat and Flames from the Fires in Yellowstone Left Nothing but Powdered Ash and Charcoal Near Norris Junction." Unfortunately, the real story behind the fires of '88 was lost in this media feeding frenzy.

A Century of Change

In reality, these fires were not unprecedented; we were just fortunate enough to witness a spectacle of nature that may not occur for another 300 years. When Yellowstone National Park was established in 1872, most of the land was carpeted with a mixture of variously aged stands of lodgepole pine established following a series of large fires. Fewer large fires, partly because of a fire-suppression policy in effect until 1972, meant that by the 1980s one-third of the park's lodgepole stands were more than 200 years old. Yellowstone was ripe to burn.

Since the early 1950s, Smokey the Bear had drummed an incessant message: "Only You Can Prevent Forest Fires." Forest fires were viewed as dangerous, destructive forces that had to be stopped to protect our valuable public lands. Unfortunately, this immensely effective and generally valid ad campaign convinced the public that *all* fires were

bad. Ecological research has shown not only that this is wrong, but also that putting out all fires can sometimes create conditions far more dangerous than if fires had been allowed to burn in the first place. Fire, like the other processes that have affected Yellowstone—cataclysmic volcanic explosions, geothermal activity, and massive glaciation—is neither good nor evil. It is simply a part of the natural world that national parks are attempting to preserve. Unfortunately, national parks are no longer surrounded by similarly undeveloped land, so when fires burned in Yellowstone and on adjacent Forest Service lands, they also affected nearby towns and the people who made a living from tourism or logging.

Fire in Lodgepole Forests

Fire has played an important role in lodgepole pine forests for thousands if not millions of years, and as a result the trees have evolved an unusual adaptation. Some of the cones are sealed with a resin that melts in a fire, thus releasing the seeds. The parent trees are killed, but a new generation is guaranteed by the thousands of pine seeds released to the bare, nutrient-rich soil underneath the blackened overstory. Within five years the landscape is dotted with thousands of young pines, competing with a verdant cover of grasses and flowers.

Although some animals are killed in the wildfires (including, in 1988, at least 269 of Yellowstone's 30,000 elk), and others, weakened by the lack of food available immediately after the fire, succumb to the rigors of the next succeeding winter, the early decades following major fires create conditions that are unusually rich for many animals. Wildlife diversity in lodgepole forests reaches a peak within the first 25 years after a fire as woodpeckers, mountain bluebirds, and other birds feed on insects in the dead trees, and elk and bears graze on the lush grasses.

As the forest ages, a dense thicket of trees develops, keeping light from reaching the forest floor and making it difficult for understory plants to survive. These trees are eventually thinned by disease and windthrow, creating openings in the forest, but after 200–300 years without fire, lodgepole forests become a tangle of fallen trees that are difficult to walk through, are of lesser value to many animals, and burn easily. They also become susceptible to attacks by bark beetles, such as those that killed thousands of acres of trees in Yellowstone starting in the 1960s and continuing through the 1980s. These beetle-killed trees added to the fuel available to burn once a fire started.

Yellowstone in 1988

Yellowstone's 1988 fires were caused by not just the heavy fuel loading from aging forests but also by weather conditions that were the driest and windiest on record. The winter of 1987–1988 had been a mild one, and by spring there was a moderate-to-severe drought in the park, lessened only by above-normal rainfall in April and May. Since 1972, when Yellowstone Park officials first began allowing certain lightning fires to burn in backcountry areas, the acreage burned had totaled less than 2 percent

new lodgepole pines from 1988 fire near Norris, Yellowstone National Park

© DON PITCHER

of the park. (Mistakenly called a "Let Burn" policy, the natural fire program actually involved close monitoring of these lightning-ignited fires to determine when and if a fire should be suppressed. All human-caused fires were immediately suppressed, as were any that threatened property or life.)

When the first lightning fires of the 1988 season began in late May, those in the backcountry areas were allowed to burn, as fire management officials anticipated normal summer weather conditions. Many fires went out on their own, but when June and July came and the rains failed to materialize, the fires began to spread rapidly. Alarmed park offi-

cials declared them wildfires and sent crews to put them out. (Ironically, the largest fire, the North Fork/Wolf Lake Complex, was started by a logger outside the park who tossed a lit cigarette to the ground. Although firefighters immediately attacked the blaze, it consumed more than 500,000 acres.) As the summer progressed, more and more firefighters were called in, eventually totaling more than 25,000 personnel, at a cost exceeding $120 million. Firefighters managed to protect most park buildings but had little effect on the forest fires themselves. Experts say that conditions in summer 1988 were so severe that even if firefighters had immediately responded to all of the natural fires, it would likely have made little difference. Yellowstone has experienced these massive fires in the past and will again in the future, no matter what humans do.

Out of Control

August brought worsening conditions with each passing day. Winds blew steadily at 20–40 miles per hour, and gusts up to 70 mph threw firebrands two miles in beyond the firefront, across fire lines, roads, and even over the Lewis River Canyon. The amount of moisture in the large logs was less than that in kiln-dried wood. By mid-August, more than 25 fires were burning simultaneously across the park and in surrounding national forests, with many joining together to create massive complexes, such as the Clover-Mist Fire, the Snake River Complex, and the North Fork/Wolf Lake Complex. On a single day—September 7—more

continued on next page

YELLOWSTONE

THE YELLOWSTONE FIRES OF 1988 (cont'd)

than 100,000 acres burned. Also torched that day were 20 cabins and outbuildings in the vicinity of Old Faithful (out of the more than 400 structures there). Fortunately, all of the major historical buildings were spared. The fires seemed poised to consume the remainder of Yellowstone, but four days later the season's first snow carpeted the park. Within a few days firefighters had the upper hand.

A Transformed Landscape

The fires had burned nearly 800,000 acres—more than one-third of the park—plus another 600,000 acres on adjacent Forest Service lands. Of the park total, 41 percent was consumed in canopy fires in which all of the trees were killed, and another 35 percent burned in a mixture of ground fires and canopy fires. The remaining acreage suffered lighter burns. Less than one-tenth of 1 percent of the land was burned hot enough to sterilize the soil. The fires killed countless small mammals, along with at least 269 elk, nine bison, six black bears, four deer, and two moose. The drought of 1988 followed by the severe winter of 1988–1989 led to a large die-off of elk and bison, but their carcasses provided food for predators. Since then, wildlife populations have rebounded and may even exceed prefire levels.

It's been more than 15 years since the massive fires were put out, and much has changed, including the park's natural-fire program. It was replaced by a

somewhat more conservative version that requires managers to provide daily certifications that fires are controllable and that they will remain "in prescription" for another 24 hours. Visitors to Yellowstone today will find dense thickets of young lodgepole pines in many areas that burned, and the first seedlings of other evergreen species are starting to emerge. In other places, grasses, colorful wildflowers, forbs, and other plants dominate. Not everything burned, of course, so you'll also see many green older forests next to burned stands, creating a complex mosaic of habitats that supports a high diversity of animal life. Once you grow accustomed to the burned areas and understand that they are a part of the natural process, they actually add interest to the park and help you appreciate Yellowstone as a functioning ecosystem rather than a static collection of plants and animals.

Take a hike through one of the burned areas to discover the wealth of new life within Yellowstone. Vistas that were long blocked by forests are now more open and will gradually become more so; by the end of this decade most of the standing dead trees will have fallen. The Park Service has placed informative signboards at sites around Yellowstone describing the fires of 1988 and the changes they brought about. The Grant Village Visitor Center offers an informative exhibit and film about the fires.

its indirect control of many of Yellowstone's hotels, stagecoaches, wagons, and other vehicles used to transport tourists.

All of this changed when the first car was allowed through the gate on August 1, 1915. (Entrance fees were a surprisingly stiff $5 for single-seat vehicles and $7.50 for five-passenger cars.) Almost immediately, it became clear that horses and cars could not mix, and motor buses replaced the old coaches. From then on, the park would be increasingly a place for "autoists." Interestingly, within a year the park would come under the jurisdiction of the newly created National Park Service.

THE PARK SERVICE TAKES OVER

After years of army control, supporters of a separate National Park Service finally had their way in 1916. The congressional act created a dual role for the new park system: to "conserve the scenery" and to "provide for the enjoyment of the same," a contradictory mandate that would later lead to all sorts of conflicts. The first couple of years were tenuous, as management flip-flopped between the army and civilians; the final changeover came in 1918 and ended three decades of military supervision. The management of Yellowstone fell on the shoulders of two men, Horace M. Albright and his mentor, Stephen Mather, both of whom had been heavily involved in lobbying to create the new agency. Mather became the Park Service's first director, while Albright served as superintendent at Yellowstone and later stepped into Mather's shoes to head the agency.

Albright quickly upgraded facilities to meet the influx of motorists who demanded more camping facilities but also cabins, lodges, cafeterias, and bathhouses. Forty-six camps of one sort or another were constructed (only 12 survive today), fulfilling Albright's dream of "a motorist's paradise." The focus of the new Park Service was clearly visitation rather than preservation. Albright assembled a first-rate force of park rangers and instituted the environmental-education programs that have been the agency's hallmark ever since.

As the automobile took over Yellowstone, the railroads gradually lost their sway, and the final passenger train to the park's gateway towns stopped in 1960. In the 1950s, the Park Service initiated "Mission 66," a decade-long project to upgrade facilities and add more lodging. By the late '60s, a growing appreciation for the natural world was shifting public opinion away from such developments, and the 1973 master plan scaled back proposed developments. From day one, Yellowstone National Park had been set up for what Edward Abbey called "industrial tourism." The park had come into existence in part because of a railroad promoter who hoped to gain from its development, and it grew to maturity on a diet of roads, hotels, and curio shops. In recent years, Americans have taken a second look at this heritage and have begun to wonder which matters more: providing a public playground or preserving an area that is unique on this planet. The inherent conflict between the need for public facilities and services in Yellowstone and the survival of a functioning ecosystem will continue to create a tug-of-war between various factions.

Certainly the most famous recent event was the series of massive fires that swept across nearly half of Yellowstone in 1988. The land has recovered surprisingly well since then, and in recent years other issues came to the fore: wolf reintroduction, bison being killed on the park boundaries, snowmobile and other winter use, and problems caused by exotic species and fish disease. There's always something stewing in the mud pots of Yellowstone! Some things have been improving in recent years, including efforts to repair aging roads and to replace outdated buildings in the park. Despite any problems and controversies, the park is just as fascinating as ever. The geysers never cease to amaze visitors, the scenery remains majestic, the Grand Canyon of the Yellowstone is still just as stunning, and the superb wildlife viewing continues to make this the Serengeti of America.

Exploring the Park

Yellowstone is perhaps the most accessible large national park in America. Nearly all of the famous sights are within a couple hundred feet of the Grand Loop Road, a 142-mile figure-eight through the middle of the park. The speed limit on all park roads is a vigilantly enforced 45 mph (or less); exceed the limit and you're likely to get a ticket! (Be especially cautious on the south side of the park where rangers seem to await most evenings and the relatively straight road makes it easy to speed.) Whatever you do, *don't* see Yellowstone at 45 miles per hour; that's like seeing the Louvre from a passing train.

For all too many visitors, Yellowstone becomes a checklist of places to visit, geysers to watch, and animals to see. This tends to inspire an attitude that treats this great national treasure as a drive-through theme park, where the animals come out to perform and the geyser eruptions are predicted so everyone can be there on time. If you're one of this crowd, give yourself a giant kick in the rear and take a walk, even if it is just around Upper Geyser Basin where you see something beyond Old Faithful.

The following loop tour of Yellowstone begins in the south and traces a clockwise path around the Grand Loop with several side trips. Although it is possible to follow this sequence

YELLOWSTONE

(or some variation) the entire distance, a far better way to learn about Yellowstone is to stop for a while in the places that are the most interesting to you and really explore them, rather than trying to see everything in a cursory way. If you have the time, the entire park is well worth visiting, but if you only have a day or two, pick a couple of spots and see them right. Don't just check out the views everyone else sees; find a nearby trail and do a little exploring on your own. If you are planning a trip to the area, try to set aside a bare minimum of three days in Yellowstone.

PARK ACCESS

Entrance to Yellowstone costs **$20 per vehicle,** or $10 for individuals entering by bicycle, foot, or as a bus passenger. Motorcycles and snowmobiles are $15. The pass covers both Yellowstone and Grand Teton National Parks and is good for seven days. If you're planning to be here longer or to make additional visits, get an annual pass covering both parks for $40, or the National Park Pass—good for all national parks—for $50 per year. A Golden Age Passport for all national parks is available to anyone older than 62 for a one-time fee of $10, and people with disabilities can get a free Golden Access Passport. Both of these passes also give you 50 percent reductions in most camping fees.

Upon entering the park, you'll receive a Yellowstone map and a copy of *Yellowstone Today,* a quarterly newspaper that describes facilities and services and provides camping, fishing, and backcountry information. This is the best source for up-to-date park information. It's also packed with enough warnings to scare off a platoon of Marines. Examples include cautions against falling trees, bathing in thermal pools (infections and/or amoebic meningitis), unpredictable wildlife, improper food storage, health problems from the altitude, narrow roads, theft, spotlighting elk, and scalding water. And, oh yes, "swim at your own risk." Pets are prohibited on trails or boardwalks anywhere in Yellowstone. Kennel facilities are not available in the park but can be found in Jackson and Cody.

Visitors Centers

The Park Service maintains visitors centers at Mammoth Hot Springs, Norris Geyser Basin, Old Faithful, Canyon Village, Fishing Bridge, and Grant Village. All of these sell maps and natural-history books covering the park and surrounding areas. In addition, you'll find smaller information stations at Madison and West Thumb. Hours, seasons, and phone numbers for all of these are listed in this chapter. Get complete Yellowstone National Park information on the web at www.nps.gov/yell, or call 307/344-7381 for additional details and publications.

Seasonal Road Closures

Most roads in Yellowstone close with the first heavy snows of early November and usually open again by mid-May. The roads connecting Mammoth to West Yellowstone open first, while Dunraven Pass is plowed last. Only the road between Mammoth and Cooke City is kept open all year. If you're planning a trip early or late in the season, call the park for current road conditions; 307/344-7381.

SOUTH ENTRANCE ROAD

The South Entrance Station consists of several log structures right along the Snake River. Just 1.5 miles beyond the entrance is an easily missed turnout where you can walk down to 30-foot-high **Moose Falls.** Beyond this point, the road climbs up a long, gentle ramp to Pitchstone Plateau, passing green forests of lodgepole pine. Stop at a turnout to look back at the majestic Tetons. Abruptly, this gentle country is broken by the edge of **Lewis River Canyon,** with rhyolite walls that rise up to 600 feet. The fires of 1988 burned hot throughout much of this area, and dead trees line both sides of the canyon in all directions, although young trees are now carpeting many areas.

The road parallels the river for the next seven miles. Nearly everyone stops for a look at 29-foot-high **Lewis Falls.** Camping is available at the south end of **Lewis Lake,** which—like the lake, falls, river, and canyon—was named for the Lewis and Clark expedition's Meriwether

Lewis. Lewis Lake is the park's third-largest body of water (after Yellowstone Lake and Shoshone Lake) and is popular with canoeists, kayakers, and anglers. The clear waters contain brown trout and Mackinaw (lake trout). Approximately four miles north of Lewis Lake, the highway tops the Continental Divide, 7,988 feet above sea level. This is one of three such crossings that roads make within Yellowstone.

Day Hikes in the Lewis Lake Area

Two trailheads one mile north of Lewis Lake provide access west to Shoshone Lake and east to Heart Lake. At the Dogshead Trailhead you can choose between two trails to Shoshone Lake, both of which cross land burned in the 1988 fires. The four-mile-long **Dogshead Trail** is more direct, while the seven-mile **Lewis Channel Trail** takes a much more scenic trek via the channel that connects Shoshone and Lewis Lakes. This slow-flowing channel is popular with anglers who come to fish for brown and cutthroat trout during the fall spawning season, and it's also used by canoeists and kayakers heading into Shoshone Lake. Once you reach Shoshone Lake, follow Delacy Creek Trail northward along the shore for fine vistas. The area gets considerable overnight use, and campsites are scattered around the lake.

Heart Lake Trailhead is on the opposite side of the road and south a few hundred feet from Dogshead Trailhead. Heart Lake is a scenic and interesting area that gets considerable day-use, but it's probably best visited on a backpacking trip of several days or longer because it's an eight-mile (one-way) hike to the lake. Be sure to bring water with you. Hard-core hikers may want to attempt a day trip all the way to the summit of Mt. Sheridan, but this is 22 miles round-trip, and you gain (and lose) 2,700 feet in elevation along the way. The Heart Lake area is closed to access before July because of grizzly activity. For details on longer hikes in the Heart Lake and Shoshone Lake areas, see Into the Backcountry later in this chapter.

Grant Village

This odd scattering of buildings is named for Pres. Ulysses S. Grant, who signed the act establishing Yellowstone, and whose terms in office were marked by massive corruption scandals. Grant Village was built in the 1980s to replace facilities at Fishing Bridge, an area of important grizzly habitat. Unfortunately, instead of one bad development, Yellowstone now has two because some of the buildings at Fishing Bridge still stand. Unlike some of the more historic places in Yellowstone where a natural rusticity prevailed, Grant Village has less charm than most Wal-Marts. An ugly steakhouse restaurant and waterside cafeteria face Yellowstone Lake, but the marina that was once here is closed. Also sprawled around Grant Village are a campground, rows of chintzy condos, a Yellowstone General Store, a gas station, and post offices. Much of the area around here was consumed in the 1988 Snake River Fire; unfortunately, the fire missed this scar on the Yellowstone landscape.

Grant Village Visitor Center, 307/242-2650, houses an informative exhibit and film on the fires of 1988. These provide a good background to help understand the changes taking place as the burned areas recover. The visitors center is open daily 8 A.M.–7 P.M. Memorial Day to Labor Day, and daily 9 A.M.–6 P.M. for the rest of September. It's closed the rest of the year. The visitors center at Grant is scheduled for a major revamping, but it probably won't be completed until 2005.

West Thumb

If you look at a map of Yellowstone Lake, it's possible to imagine the lake as a giant hand with three mangled fingers heading south and a gnarled thumb hitching west. Hence the name West Thumb. This portion of Yellowstone Lake is the deepest (to 390 feet) and is actually a caldera that filled with water after erupting 150,000 years ago. There is still considerable heat just below the surface, as revealed by **West Thumb Geyser Basin.** Get a Park Service booklet (50 cents) from the box for details on the area's geothermal origins and attractions.

A short loop trail leads past steaming hot springs and pools at West Thumb. Right on the shore is **Fishing Cone,** where tourists once caught fish and then plopped them in the cone to be cooked; after several clowning tourists were injured, the Park Service put a stop to this stunt. The

West Thumb Information Station is open daily 8 A.M.–7 P.M. from Memorial Day to Labor Day, and daily 8 A.M.–7 P.M. for the rest of September. A small bookstore is housed here, and in winter the station is used as a warming hut.

A fine day hike takes off across the road from the entrance to West Thumb Geyser Basin and climbs for one mile to **Yellowstone Lake Overlook.** The two-mile loop trail gains 400 feet in elevation, enough for a commanding vista across the lake, with the Absaroka Mountains behind.

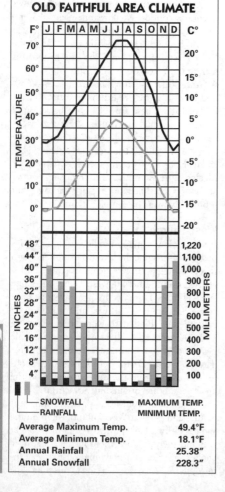

OLD FAITHFUL AREA CLIMATE

SNOWFALL		MAXIMUM TEMP.
RAINFALL		MINIMUM TEMP.

Average Maximum Temp.	49.4°F
Average Minimum Temp.	18.1°F
Annual Rainfall	25.38″
Annual Snowfall	228.3″

WEST THUMB TO UPPER GEYSER BASIN

Heading west from West Thumb, the highway climbs over the Continental Divide twice. Most of these forests escaped the 1988 fires. A few miles beyond the eastern crossing of the divide is a turnout at **Shoshone Point,** where you catch glimpses of Shoshone Lake and the Tetons.

DeLacy Creek Trail provides access to Shoshone Lake—Yellowstone's largest backcountry lake—and begins at the picnic area between the two passes. It's three miles to the lake, which is circled by more trails. Keep your eyes open for moose and other animals in the meadows along the way. The western crossing of the Continental Divide is at **Craig Pass,** where a tiny pond (Isa Lake) empties into both the Atlantic and Pacific Oceans through its two outlet streams.

Approximately 14 miles beyond West Thumb, pull off to see the Firehole River as it drops over **Kepler Cascades.** Just to the east, a wide and partly paved trail (actually an old road) leads five miles round-trip to **Lone Star Geyser.** This is a popular route for bicyclists in the summer and skiers in the winter. Bikes are not allowed beyond the geyser. Lone Star Geyser erupts every three hours from a distinctive nine-foot-high cone, with eruptions generally reaching 45 feet and lasting for 30 minutes. Hikers can also get to Lone Star via the Howard Eaton Trail out of Old Faithful. For a longer hike, you can continue south from Lone Star on **Shoshone Lake Trail** to Shoshone Lake, eight fairly easy miles from the main road. (See Into the Backcountry later in this chapter for other Shoshone Lake hikes.)

UPPER GEYSER BASIN

As you approach Old Faithful from either direction, the two-lane road suddenly widens into four, and a cloverleaf exit takes you to Yellowstone's most fabulous sight. Welcome to Upper Geyser Basin, home of Old Faithful, some 400 buildings of all sizes, and a small town's worth of people. For many folks, this is the heart of Yellowstone, and a visit to the park without seeing Old Faithful is like a baseball game without the

UPPER GEYSER BASIN

To Madison Junction

Biscuit Basin

Mustard Spring
Avoca Spring
Sapphire Pool
Shell Geyser
Jewel Geyser

To Mystic Falls

Little Firehole River

Mirror Pool

Firehole

Gem Pool

Atomizer Geyser
Artemisia Geyser

River

Morning Glory Pool

Far, Mortar, and Spiteful Geysers

Riverside Geyser

Grotto Geyser

Comet Geyser
Daisy Geyser

Splendid Geyser

Giant Geyser

Punch Bowl Spring

Round Spring

Chromatic Spring
Beauty Pool

Black Sand Pool

Grand Geyser

Firehole

River

Solitary Geyser

OBSERVATION POINT

Crested Pool

Castle Geyser

Lion Geyser

Geyser Hill

Giantess Geyser

Sunset Lake
Rainbow Pool
Cliff Geyser
Opalescent Pool

Black Sand Basin

Emerald Pool

Iron Spring Creek

Beehive Geyser
Chinese Spring

Old Faithful

SERVICE STATION
STORE
YELLOWSTONE GENERAL STORE

VISITOR CENTER

RANGER STATION/CLINIC

SNOW LODGE

OLD FAITHFUL LODGE

STORE
SERVICE STATION

POST OFFICE

To Fern Cascades

To Lone Star Geyser

To West Thumb

	PAVED TRAIL
	UNPAVED TRAIL
	BOARDWALK

0   0.5 mi
0   0.5 km

YELLOWSTONE

© DON PITCHER

Old Faithful, Yellowstone's most famous geyser, erupts about once every 90 minutes.

national anthem. If you came to Yellowstone to see the wonders of nature, you're going to see more than your share here, but you'll probably have to share your share with hundreds of other folks. On busy summer days more than 25,000 visitors come through the Old Faithful area! Fortunately, the Upper Geyser Basin contains the largest concentration of geysers in the world, and the adventurous will even discover places almost nobody ever visits. But be very careful: The crust can be dangerously thin around some of the hot springs and geysers, and people have been badly scalded and even killed by missteps. Stay on the boardwalks and trails.

Old Faithful

The one sight seen by virtually everyone who comes to Yellowstone is Old Faithful Geyser, easily the most visited geyser in the world. Old Faithful is neither the tallest nor the most frequently erupting geyser in Yellowstone, but it always provides a great show and is both highly accessible and fairly predictable. Contrary to the rumors, Old Faithful never erupted "every hour on the hour," but for many years its period was a little more than an hour. It has slowed in recent years and is now averaging around 92 minutes per cycle, but varies from 45 to 120 minutes. In general, the longer the length of the eruption, the longer the interval until the next eruption. Check at the visitors center for the latest prognostications on this and other geysers in the basin.

An almost level paved path circles Old Faithful, providing many different angles from which to view the eruptions, although none of these is particularly close to the geyser because of the danger from hot water. Along the north side is **Chinese Spring,** named in 1885 for a short-lived laundry operation. Apparently, the washman had filled the spring with clothes and soap, not knowing that soap can cause geysers to erupt. One newspaper correspondent claimed—although the tale obviously suffered from embellishment and racism—that,

The soap awakened the imprisoned giant; with a roar that made the earth tremble, and a shriek of a steam whistle, a cloud of steam and a column of boiling water shot up into the air a hundred feet, carrying soap, raiment, tent and Chinaman along with the rush, and dropping them at various intervals along the way.

Old Faithful provides a textbook example of geyser activity. The first signs of life are when water begins to splash out of the vent in what is called preplay. This splashing can last up to 20 minutes, but it's generally only a few minutes before the real thing. The water quickly spears into the sky, reaching 100–180 feet for 2–5 minutes before rapidly dropping down. During a typical eruption, between 3,700 and 8,400 gallons of water are sent skyward.

On any given summer day, the scene at Old Faithful is almost comical. Just before the predicted eruption time, the benches encircling the south and east sides are jammed with hundreds of people waiting expectantly for the geyser to erupt, and with each tentative spray the camera shut-

YELLOWSTONE

YELLOWSTONE'S FIRST "TOURIST"

From the surface of a rocky plain or table, burst forth columns of water of various dimensions, projected high in the air, accompanied by loud explosions, and sulphurous vapors, which were highly disagreeable to the smell. . . . The largest of these wonderful fountains, projects a column of boiling water several feet in diameter, to the height of more than one hundred and fifty feet. . . . After having witnessed three of them, I ventured near enough to put my hand into the water of its basin, but withdrew it instantly, for the heat of the water in this immense couldron, was altogether to great for comfort, and the agitation of the water, disagreeable effluvium continually exuding, and the hollow unearthly rumbling under the rock on which I stood, so ill accorded with my notions of personal safety, that I retreated back precipitately to a respectful distance.

—Angus Ferris, in 1833

ters begin to click. Listen closely and you'll hear half the languages of Europe and Asia. Once the action is over, there's a mad rush back into the visitors center, the stores, and Old Faithful Inn, and within a few minutes the benches are virtually empty. A tale is told of two concessioner employees who once decided to have fun at Old Faithful by placing a large crank atop a box and putting the contraption near the geyser. When they knew it was ready to erupt, they ran out and turned the crank just as Old Faithful shot into the air. Their employer failed to find humor in the prank, and both were fired, or so the story claims.

Geyser Hill Area

Upper Geyser Basin is laced with paved trails that lead to dozens of nearby geysers and hot springs. The easiest path loops around Geyser Hill, just across the Firehole River from Old Faithful. Here are more than 40 different geysers. Check at the visitors center to get an idea of current activity and predicted eruptions, and while you're there pick up the excellent Upper Geyser Basin map (50 cents), which describes some of them. Several geysers are particularly noteworthy. When it plays, **Beehive Geyser** (it has a tall, beehive-shaped cone) vents water as high as 180 feet into the air. These spectacular eruptions vary in frequency; one time you visit they may be 10 days apart, while the next time you come they may be happening twice daily. **Lion Geyser Group** consists of four different interconnected geysers with varying periods of activity and eruptions up to 50 feet. Listen for the roar when Lion is ready to erupt. **Giantess Geyser** may not be active for years at a time—or may erupt several times a year—but the eruptions are sensationally powerful, sending water 100–200 feet skyward. **Doublet Pool** is a beautiful deep-blue pool that is a favorite of photographers. Not far away is **Sponge Geyser,** which rockets water an astounding 2.29 billion angstroms into the air (that's nine inches for the nonscientific crowd). It's considered the smallest named geyser in Yellowstone and gets its title by sending up a spurt of water big enough to be mopped up with a sponge.

Observation Point Loop Trail splits off shortly after you cross the bridge on the way to Geyser Hill and climbs to an excellent overlook where you can watch eruptions of Old Faithful. This is also a good place to view the effects of, and recovery from, the 1988 North Fork Fire. It's two miles round-trip to Observation Point from the visitors center. Another easy trail splits off from this path to **Solitary Geyser,** which is actually just a pool that periodically burps four-foot splashes of hot water. This is not a natural geyser. In 1915, the hot spring here was tapped to provide water for Old Faithful Geyser Bath, a concession that lasted until 1948. The lowering of the water level in the pool completely changed the plumbing system of the hot springs and turned it into a geyser that at one time shot 25 feet in the air. The system still hasn't recovered, although water levels have been restored for many decades.

More Geyser Gazing

Another easy, paved path follows the Firehole River downstream from Old Faithful, looping back along the other side for a total distance of three miles. Other trails head off from this loop to the Fairy Falls Trailhead, Biscuit Basin, and Black Sand Basin. The loop is a very popular wintertime ski path, and portions are open to bikes in the summer. Twelve-foot-high **Castle Geyser** does indeed resemble a ruined old castle. Because of its size and the slow accretion of sinter (silica) to form this cone, it is believed to be somewhere between 5,000 and 50,000 years old. Castle sends up a column of water and steam 90 feet into the air and usually erupts every 10–12 hours. Check at the visitors center for a guess at the next eruption.

Daisy Geyser is farther down the path and off to the left. It is usually one of the most predictable of the geysers, erupting to 75 feet approximately every 90–125 minutes. The water shoots out at a sharp angle and is visible all over the basin, making this a real crowd pleaser.

Just east of Daisy is **Radiator Geyser,** which isn't much to look at—eruptions to two feet—but was named when this area was a parking lot and the sudden eruption under a car led people to think its radiator was overheating. A personal favorite, **Grotto Geyser** is certainly the weirdest of all the geysers, having formed around a tangle of long-petrified tree stumps. It is in eruption one-third of the time, but most eruptions only reach 10 feet.

Look for **Riverside Geyser** across the Firehole from the path and not far downstream from Grotto. This picturesque geyser arches spray 75 feet over the river and is one of the most predictable, with 20-minute-long eruptions approximately every six hours. The paved trail crosses the river and ends at famous **Morning Glory Pool.** For many years, the main road passed this colorful pool, which became something of a wishing well for not just coins but also trash, rocks, logs, and other debris. Because of this junk, the pool began to cool, and the beautiful blue color is now tinged by brown and green algae, despite efforts to remove the debris.

Turning back at Morning Glory, recross the bridge and head left where the path splits at Grotto Geyser. **Giant Geyser** is on the left along the river. Years may pass between eruptions of Giant (or it might erupt every week or so), but when it does go, the name rings true because the water can reach 250 feet. Cross the river again and pass **Beauty Pool** and **Chromatic Pool,** which are connected below the ground so that one declines as the other rises. Very pretty.

Grand Geyser is a wonderful sight. The water column erupts in a towering burst every 7–15 hours, with a series of bursts lasting 10 minutes or so and sometimes reaching 200 feet. It's the tallest predictable geyser on the planet; see the visitors center for the next eruption. When Grand isn't playing, watch for smaller eruptions from nearby **Turban Geyser.** Two little fun geysers are a short distance to the south: **Sawmill** and **Tardy Geysers.** The latter is just 10 feet or so from the trail, providing an up-close look at a small but active geyser. Cross the river again just beyond these two geysers and pass **Crested Pool** on your way back to Castle Geyser. The pool contains deep-blue water that is constantly boiling, preventing the survival of algae.

Black Sand Basin

Just one mile west of Old Faithful is Black Sand Basin, a small cluster of geysers and hot springs. Most enjoyable is unpredictable **Cliff Geyser,** which often sends a spray of hot water 25–30 feet over Iron Spring Creek. Three colorful pools are quite interesting in the basin: **Emerald Pool, Rainbow Pool,** and **Sunset Lake. Handkerchief Pool** is now just a small spouter but was famous for many years as a place where visitors could drop a handkerchief in one end and recover it later at another vent. In 1929, vandals jammed logs into the pool, destroying this little game. The pool was covered with gravel in subsequent eruptions of Rainbow Pool.

Biscuit Basin and Mystic Falls

Three miles north of Old Faithful, this basin is named for biscuitlike formations that were found in one of the pools; they were destroyed in an eruption following the 1959 Hebgen Lake earthquake. From the parking lot, the trail leads across the Firehole River to pretty **Sapphire Pool** and then past **Jewel Geyser,** which typically erupts every 7–10 minutes to a height of 15–20 feet. The boardwalk follows a short loop through the other sights of Biscuit Basin.

From the west end of the boardwalk, a one-mile trail leads to where the Little Firehole River cascades 100 feet over **Mystic Falls.** You can switchback farther up the trail to the top of the falls and then connect with another trail for the loop back to Biscuit Basin (three miles round-trip). This is a very nice short hike and can be lengthened into a trip to **Little Firehole Meadows** (10 miles round-trip), where bison are often seen in the summer.

Old Faithful Inn

Matching one of the great sights of the natural world is one of America's most majestic hotels, Old Faithful Inn. The largest log structure of its kind in existence, the inn has delighted generations of visitors and continues to enthrall all who enter. The building was designed by Robert Reamer and built in the winter of 1903–1904. Its steeply angled roofline reaches seven stories high, with gables jutting out from the sides and flags flying from the roof. Surprisingly, the hotel does not face the geyser. Instead, it was built facing sideways to allow newly arriving visitors the opportunity to view the geyser as they stepped from carriages. As you open the rustic split-log front doors with their hand-wrought hardware, you enter a world of the past. The central lobby towers more than 75 feet overhead and is dominated by a massive four-sided stone fireplace that required 500 tons of stone from a nearby quarry. Four overhanging balconies extend above, each bordered by posts made from gnarled lodgepole burls found within the park. Above the fireplace is an enormous clock designed by Reamer and built on the site by a blacksmith. Reamer also designed the two wings that were added in 1913 and 1928.

On warm summer evenings, visitors stand out on the porch, where they can watch Old Faithful erupting, or sit inside at the handcrafted tables to write letters as music spills from the grand piano. It's enough to warm the heart of even the most cynical curmudgeon. A good restaurant is on the premises, along with a rustic but comfortable bar, a gift shop, fast-food eatery, ice cream shop, and ATM. Free 45-minute **tours** of Old Faithful Inn are given daily at 9:30 A.M., 11 A.M., 2 P.M., and 3:30 P.M. from mid-May to late September. Meet at the fireplace in the lobby. Old Faithful Inn closes during the winter; it would be hard to imagine trying to heat such a cavern when it's 30° below zero outside!

Another nearby building of interest is **Old Faithful Lodge.** Built in 1928, this is the large stone-and-log building just south of the geyser of the same name. The giant fireplace inside is a joy on frosty evenings, and cafeteria windows face the geyser—unlike those at the Inn.

Much newer, but an instant classic, is the award-winning **Old Faithful Snow Lodge,** which opened in 1999. This large building offers a sense of rustic elegance, with heavy timbers, a window-lined main entrance, a large stone fireplace, overstuffed couches, and handmade wrought-iron light fixtures and accents. It is one of just two places (the other being Mammoth Hot Springs Hotel) open in winter.

Old Faithful Services

The Park Service's **Old Faithful Visitor Center,** 307/545-2750, is generally open mid-April to early November and mid-December to mid-March. It's open daily 8 A.M.–7 P.M. from Memorial Day to Labor Day, daily 8 A.M.–6 P.M. the rest of September. During the fall, winter, and spring when park gates are open, the visitors center operates daily 9 A.M.–5 P.M. Among the films about Yellowstone shown throughout the day here is a fascinating production (narrated by Walter Cronkite) on the lifeforms that survive in Yellowstone's hot springs. The center has a big selection of books, maps, and other Yellowstone publications. In summer, be sure to check the board for the predicted eruptions of six major geysers in the area: Old Faithful, Grand, Daisy, Riverside, Great Fountain, and Castle. The rangers can provide you with all sorts of other info, from where to see bighorn sheep to where to find the restrooms. A much-needed new visitors center is in the planning stages for Old Faithful, but don't expect to see it until at least 2005 because the Park Service needs to raise $15 million for its construction.

Backcountry permits are available from the ranger station, while food, supplies, and postcards can be purchased at either of the two Yellowstone General Stores. Old Faithful Inn has a gift shop, restaurant, snack bar, ice cream parlor, lounge, and ATM. Cafeteria meals, espresso, and baked goods are available at Old Faithful Lodge, and Old Faithful Snow Lodge houses a restaurant and snack bar. Both of these also have gift shops. In addition, the Old Faithful area has two gas stations, a post office, photo shop, and medical clinic. See the Camping and Hotels, Lodges, and Cabins sections later in this chapter for lodging details. Note that camping is *not* available in the Old Faithful area, and it's illegal to stay overnight in the parking lots. The closest campgrounds are in Madison (16 miles north) and Grant Village (19 miles southeast).

MIDWAY AND LOWER GEYSER BASINS

Heading north from Upper Geyser Basin, the road follows the Firehole River past Midway and Lower Geyser Basins, both of which are quite interesting. This stretch of the river is popular with fly-fishing enthusiasts, and several side roads provide access to a variety of hot springs and other sights.

Fairy Falls

Just south of Midway Geyser Basin (or 4.5 miles north of the Old Faithful Interchange) is a turnoff that leads to the southern end of Fountain Freight Road. This four-mile-long trail is closed to cars, but it's a great place for mountain bikers and those out for a relatively level walk. A steel bridge crosses the Firehole River at the trailhead, and the road soon passes the west side of Grand Prismatic Spring; rough trails lead up the hillside for a better view. One mile up from the trailhead you'll come to **Fairy Falls Trail** on your left. It's an easy 1.5-mile walk to the falls, a 200-foot ribbon of water that cascades into a large pool. The hike to Fairy Falls can be combined with longer treks to Little Firehole Meadow and

GRAND PRISMATIC SPRING, 1839

At length we came to a boiling Lake about 300 ft in diameter forming nearly a complete circle as we approached on the south side The steam which arose from it was of three distinct Colors from the west side for one third of the diameter it was white, in the middle it was pale red, and the remaining third on the east light sky blue Whether it was something peculiar in the state of the atmosphere the day being cloudy or whether it was some Chemical properties contained in the water which produced this phenomenon I am unable to say and shall leave the explanation to some scientific tourist who may have the Curiosity to visit this place at some future period—The water was of deep indigo blue boiling like an imense caldron running over the white rock which had formed the edges to the height of 4 or 5 feet from the surface of the earth sloping gradually for 60 or 70 feet. What a field of speculation this presents for chemist and geologist.

—mountain man Osborne Russell

Mystic Falls (both described earlier) or to a pair of small peaks called Twin Buttes. One-half mile beyond Fairy Falls is **Imperial Geyser,** which was active in the 1920s and from 1966–1984, but is now just a boiling pool. Nearby **Spray Geyser** erupts frequently, sending water six feet in the air. For a longer version of the hike to Fairy Falls (10 miles round-trip), start from the north end, where Fountain Flat Drive ends.

Midway Geyser Basin

Midway is a large and readily accessible geyser basin with a loop path leading to most of the sights. **Excelsior Geyser** is actually an enormous hot spring that pours 4,000 gallons per minute of steaming water into the Firehole River. The water is a deep turquoise. During the 1880s, this geyser was truly stupendous, with explosions that reached 380 feet in the air and almost as wide. These violent eruptions apparently damaged the plumbing system that fed them, and the geyser was dormant for nearly a century until smaller eruptions took place in 1985. At 370 feet across, **Grand Prismatic Spring** is Yellowstone's largest hot spring. The brilliant reds and yellows around the edges of the blue pool are from algae and bacteria that can tolerate temperatures of 170°F. It's difficult to get a good perspective on this spring from the ground; see aerial photos to really appreciate its pulchritude.

Firehole Lake Drive

This road (one-way heading north) goes three miles through Lower Geyser Basin, the park's most extensive geyser basin. **Great Fountain Geyser** is truly one of the most spectacular geysers in Yellowstone. Charles Cook, of the 1869 Cook-Folsom-Peterson Expedition, recalled his impression of the geyser: "We could not contain our enthusiasm; with one accord we all took off our hats and yelled with all our might." Modern-day visitors would not be faulted for reacting similarly.

Great Fountain erupts every 8–12 hours (although it can be irregular) and usually reaches 100 feet, but has been known to blast more than 200 feet. Eruptions begin an hour or so after water starts to overflow from the crater and last for 45–60 minutes in a series of decreasingly active eruptive cycles; but don't leave too early or you may miss the real show! Eruption predictions are posted at the geyser and in the Old Faithful Visitor Center. While you're waiting, watch the periodic eruptions of **White Dome Geyser** just a hundred yards down the road. Because of its massive 30-foot cone, this is believed to be one of the oldest geysers in the park. Eruptions occur every 10 minutes to three hours and spray 30 feet into the air.

Another mile ahead, the road literally cuts into the mound of **Pink Cone Geyser,** which now erupts every 6–20 hours and reaches a height of 30 feet. The pink color comes from manganese oxide. Just up from here at the bend in the road is **Firehole Lake,** which discharges 3,500 gallons of water per minute into Tangled Creek, which in turn drains across the road into **Hot Lake. Steady Geyser** is unusual in that it forms both sinter (silica) and travertine (calcium carbonate) deposits. The geyser is along the edge of Hot Lake and, true to its name, erupts almost continuously, although the height is only five feet. Firehole Lake Drive continues another mile to its junction with the main road right across from the parking area for Fountain Paint Pot. In the winter, Firehole Lake Drive is popular with skiers but is closed to snowmobiles.

Fountain Paint Pot

Always a favorite of visitors, Fountain Paint Pot seems to have a playfulness about it that belies the immense power just below the surface. Pick up a trail guide (50 cents) as you head up the walkway for the full story. **Silex Spring,** off to the right as you walk up the small hill, is colored by different kinds of algae and bacteria. The spring has been known to erupt as a geyser (to 20 feet) but is currently dormant. The famous **Fountain Paint Pot** is a few steps up the boardwalk and consists of colorful mud that changes in consistency throughout the season depending on soil moisture. The pressure from steam and gases under the Paint Pot can throw gobs of mud up to 20 feet into the air. Just north of here are fumaroles that spray steam, carbon dioxide, and hydrogen sulfide into the air. Continuing down the boardwalk, you come upon an impressive overlook above a multitude of geysers that change constantly in activity, including **Morning Geyser,** which has been known to erupt more than 200 feet. The most active is **Clepsydra Geyser,** which is in eruption much of the time. **Fountain Geyser** explodes in a stunning display that can last 30 minutes and reach up to 50 feet. Eruptions are unpredictable but impressive, particularly at sunset. The rest of the loop trail passes dead lodgepole pines that are being petrified as the silica is absorbed, creating a bobby-socks appearance.

Fountain Flat

Fountain Flat Drive provides access to meadows along the Firehole River and is a good place to see bison and elk. The paved road ends after one mile at a parking area, but hikers and cyclists (or

YELLOWSTONE

FIREHOLE RIVER AREA

To Norris

Mount Jackson

Madison Junction

Gibbon Falls

Madison   River

Gibbon   River

To West Yellowstone, MT

MADISON

Howard Eaton Trail

Mount Hayes

National Park Mountain

FIREHOLE CANYON DR.

Firehole Falls

Firehole

River

Mary Mountain Trail

Lower Geyser Basin

FOUNTAIN FLAT DR.

FIREHOLE LAKE DR.

Fountain Paint Pot

Imperial and Spray Geysers

Goose Lake

Great Fountain Geyser

Midway

Fairy Falls

Geyser

Grand Prismatic Spring

Fairy Creek Trail

Basin

Mallard Creek Trail

Mystic Falls

Upper

SEE MAP "UPPER GEYSER BASIN"

Geyser

Mallard Lake

Basin

Summit Lake Trail

Kepler Cascades

CRAIG PASS

To West Thumb

Howard Eaton Trail

Summit Lake

0   2 mi

0   2 km

Lone Star Geyser

MOON

skiers in winter) can continue another four miles on Old Fountain Freight Road to its junction with the main road again near Midway Geyser Basin. The road ends in a parking area near **Ojo Caliente**—a small hot springs with a big odor— right along the river. Several more hot springs are upstream from here, and the **Fairy Falls Trail** starts three miles south of the parking area. See Midway Geyser Basin for details on this scenic and popular day hike.

Firehole Canyon Drive

This one-way road (south only) curves for two miles through Firehole Canyon, where dark rhyolite cliffs rise hundreds of feet above the river. The road begins just south of Madison Junction and was intensely burned in the 1988 North Fork Fire, giving the canyon's name a dual meaning. **Firehole Falls**, a 40-foot drop, is worth stopping to see, as is **Firehole Cascades** a bit farther up. Kids of all ages enjoy the popular hot-springs-warmed swimming hole a short distance up the road. It's one of the few places along the Yellowstone road system where swimming is openly allowed (albeit not encouraged). No lifeguard is provided, of course.

MADISON JUNCTION TO WEST YELLOWSTONE

At Madison Junction, the Gibbon and Firehole Rivers join to form the Madison River, a major tributary of the Missouri River. The 14-mile drive from Madison Junction to the West Entrance closely parallels this scenic river, in which geese, ducks, and trumpeter swans are commonly seen. Bison and elk are other critters to watch for in the open meadows. The 406,359-acre North Fork Fire of 1988 ripped through most of the Madison River country, so be ready for many blackened trees, but also expect to see many flowers in midsummer. The river is open only to fly-fishing and is considered one of the finest places in the nation to catch trout (although they can be a real challenge to fool). On warm summer evenings, you're likely to see dozens of anglers casting for wily rainbow and brown trout and mountain whitefish. **West Entrance** is the busiest of all the park

entry stations, handling more than one-third of the more than 3 million people who enter Yellowstone each year. The tourist town of West Yellowstone, Montana, is right outside the boundary.

Madison Canyon is flanked by mountains named for two photographers who had a marked influence on Yellowstone. To the north is 8,257-foot **Mt. Jackson** (as in William H. Jackson, whose photos helped bring the area to national attention), and to the south is distinctive, 8,235-foot **Mt. Haynes,** named for the man who held the park photo concession for nearly four decades. These mountains and the surrounding slopes were created by rhyolite lava flows.

THE NORTHWEST CORNER

Highway 191 heads north from West Yellowstone, Montana, to Bozeman, passing through a small corner of Yellowstone National Park en route. There are no entrance stations or developed facilities here, but the area provides backcountry access for hikers and horsepackers from several trailheads. The drive itself is scenic, and the road is wide and smooth. The road enters the park approximately 10 miles north of West Yellowstone and gradually climbs through stretches that were burned in the fires of 1988 before emerging into unburned alpine meadows near tiny Divide Lake. North of here, U.S. Hwy. 191 follows the growing Gallatin River downhill through a pretty mix of meadows, sagebrush, rocky outcrops, and forested hillsides with grassy carpets beneath. Approximately 31 miles north of West Yellowstone, the road exits Yellowstone and enters Gallatin National Forest. It's another 17 miles from here to the turnoff for Big Sky Resort or 60 miles from the park boundary to Bozeman.

Bighorn Peak Hike

If you're up for a long and challenging day hike, climb Bighorn Peak on the northern boundary of Yellowstone. Start from the Black Butte Creek Trailhead just south of milepost 29 on U.S. Hwy. 191. The hike is steep, rising 3,100 feet in just seven miles and providing spectacular views. Look for pieces of petrified wood along the way, but leave them in place; it's illegal to take them from the park. As an added bonus, this country was untouched by the 1988 fires. Be sure to bring plenty of water because it is nonexistent on the upper portion of this hike. It is possible to do an overnight loop trip (21 miles round-trip) by continuing north from Bighorn Peak along the beautiful **Sky Rim Trail** and dropping back down Dailey Creek Trail to Black Butte Cutoff Trail. (A backcountry permit is required for this, however.) This connects to Black Butte Trail and your starting point. See one of the Yellowstone hiking guides for details on this hike.

MADISON JUNCTION TO NORRIS

The **Madison Information Station,** near Madison Junction, is open daily 8 A.M.–7 P.M. Memorial Day to Labor Day and daily 9 A.M.–5 P.M. from early September to early October. Closed the rest of the year. A small bookstore is also here. Directly behind Madison Campground is 7,500-foot **National Park Mountain,** named in honor of a fabled incident in 1870. Three explorers were gathered around the campfire, discussing the wonders that they had found in this area, when one suggested that rather than letting all of these wonders pass into private hands, they should be set aside as a national park. Thus was born the concept that led to the world's first national park. The tale was passed on as the gospel truth for so long that the mountain was named in honor of this evening. Unfortunately, the story was a complete fabrication. Cynics may read something into the fact that National Park Mountain was torched by the fires of 1988.

North of Madison Junction, the road (in very poor condition in 2002) follows the Gibbon River nearly all of the 14 miles to Norris. It crosses the river five times and hangs right on the edge through Gibbon Canyon. The pretty, 84-foot-high **Gibbon Falls** is approximately five miles up the road and situated right at the edge of the enormous caldera that fills the center of Yellowstone. The 1988 fires consumed most of the trees around the falls. Another five miles beyond this point, the road emerges from the canyon into grassy **Gibbon Meadows,** where elk and bison are com-

monly seen. The prominent peak visible to the north is 10,336-foot Mt. Holmes. On the west end of Gibbon Meadows is a barren area that contains **Sylvan Springs Geyser Basin.** No maintained trail leads to this small collection of pools and springs, but hikers sometimes head across the north end of the meadows at the Gibbon River Picnic Area. The path is wet most of the summer.

An easy half-mile trail leads to **Artist Paint Pots,** filled with colorful plopping and steaming mud pots and hot springs. Although it's a short hike, the paint pots see far fewer visitors than roadside sites, making it a nice place to escape the crowds. The forest was burned in the North Fork Fire, so it's also a good place to see how the lodgepole pines are regenerating. Just south of the parking area for Artist Paint Pots is a trail to **Monument Geyser Basin,** where there isn't much activity, but the tall sinter cones form all sorts of bizarre shapes, including Thermos Bottle Geyser. The mile-long hike climbs 500 feet and provides views of the surrounding country. Another attraction is **Chocolate Pots,** found along the highway just north of Gibbon Meadows. The reddish-brown color comes from iron, aluminum, and manganese oxides. Just before you reach Norris, the road crosses through the appropriately named **Elk Park.**

NORRIS GEYSER BASIN

Although Old Faithful and the Upper Geyser Basin are more famous, many visitors to Yellowstone find Norris Geyser Basin equally interesting. Norris sits atop the junction of several major fault lines, providing conduits for heat from the molten lava below. Because of this, it is apparently the hottest geyser basin in North America, if not the world; a scientific team found temperatures of 459°F at 1,087 feet underground and was forced to quit drilling when the pressure threatened to destroy the drilling rig! Because of considerable sulfur (and hence sulfuric acid) in the springs and geysers, the water at Norris is acidic; most of the world's acid geysers are here. The acidic water kills lodgepole trees in the basin, creating an open, nearly barren place. Norris Basin has been around at least 115,000 years, making it the oldest of any of Yellowstone's active geyser basins. It is a constantly changing place, with small geysers seeming to come and go on an almost daily basis.

The paved trail from the often crowded parking area leads to **Norris Museum,** 307/344-2812, built of stone in 1929–1930. The small museum houses exhibit panels on hot springs and geothermal activity and is open daily 10 A.M.–5 P.M. from Memorial Day to early October. Closed the rest of the year. Be sure to pick up the detailed brochure (50 cents) describing the various features at Norris. Ranger-led walks are given several times a day in the summer, and there's usually one in the area ready to answer your questions. A little bookstore is housed in a nearby building. From the museum, the Norris Basin spreads both north and south, with two rather different trails to hike. Take the time to walk along both. The Norris Campground is only one-quarter mile from the geyser basin.

Porcelain Basin

Just behind the museum is an overlook that provides an impressive view across the always changing Porcelain Basin. The path descends into the basin, passing hissing steam vents, bubbling hot pools, and small geysers, including **Constant Geyser,** with frequent and sudden bursts to 20 feet or more. **Big Whirligig Geyser** is another one that is often active, spraying a noisy fan of water. (Watch your glasses and camera lenses in the steam; silica deposits can be difficult to remove.) For an enjoyable short walk, follow the boardwalk around the mile-long loop through Porcelain Basin. Stop to admire the bright colors in the steaming water, indicators of iron, arsenic, and other elements, along with algae and cyanobacteria.

Back Basin

A mile-long loop trail takes you to the sights within the Back Basin south of the museum. Before heading out, check at the museum for the latest on geyser activity. Most people follow the path in a clockwise direction, coming first to **Emerald Spring,** a gorgeous green pool with acidic water just below boiling. A little ways farther down the path is **Steamboat Geyser.** Wait a

few minutes and you're likely to see one of its minor eruptions, which may reach 40 feet. On rare occasions, Steamboat erupts with a fury that is hard to believe, blasting more than 300 feet into the air—more than twice the height of Old Faithful—making this the world's tallest geyser. Eruptions can last up to 20 minutes or more, enough time to pour out a million gallons of water, and the explosions have been heard up to 14 miles away. Steamboat's unforgettable eruptions cannot be predicted; a 50-year span once passed between eruptions, while several eruptions may occur in one year. If you ever see this one erupt, consider yourself incredibly lucky!

The path splits just below Steamboat; on the right is **Cistern Spring,** whose deep blue waters are constantly building deposits of sinter and have flooded the nearby lodgepole-pine forests, killing the trees. If you turn left where the trail splits, you come to **Echinus Geyser,** a personal favorite. (It's pronounced e-KI-nus.) The name—Greek for "spiny"—comes from the pebbles that lie around the geyser; resembling sea urchins, they are a result of sinter accumulation. The eruptions of Echinus have varied in recent years. Sometimes it settles into a regular pattern, with eruptions every hour or two, but at other times you may wait four hours for an eruption. Whatever the case, it's certainly worth the wait. When Echinus does erupt, the geyser sends explosions of acidic steam and water (pH 3.5) 40–60 feet. These generally last 3–5 minutes but sometimes continue for much longer. Unlike Old Faithful, this is one geyser where you can get up close and personal. Bench-sitters may get splashed, although the water is not hot enough to burn.

Continue along this trail beyond Echinus to see many more hot springs and steam vents. **Porkchop Geyser** was in continuous eruption for several years, but in 1989 it self-destructed in an explosion that threw rocks more than 200 feet, leaving behind a bubbling hot spring.

NORRIS JUNCTION TO CANYON

From Norris Geyser Basin to Canyon, the road cuts across the center of the park on the high Solfatara Plateau. This dozen-mile stretch of road is best known for what looks like a scene from an atomic blast, with the blackened remains of a forest seemingly blown down by the ferocity of the 1988 North Fork Fire. This is the place the news media focused on after the fires, making it appear as if it were typical of the park as a whole. In reality, the lodgepole pines were all uprooted in a wild 1984 windstorm that flattened many miles of forest both here and farther south in the Teton Wilderness. The dead trees dried out over the next four years, and when the wind-whipped fires arrived, the trees went up in a holocaust. In 50 years, this may well be a meadow. **Virginia Cascades Road** is a 2.5-mile-long, one-way road that circles around this blow-down area and provides a view of the 60-foot-tall Virginia Cascade of the Gibbon River. Back on the main highway heading east, keep your eyes open for elk and bison as the road approaches Canyon. Also note the thick young forest of lodgepole pines that was established after a fire burned through in 1955.

NORRIS JUNCTION TO MAMMOTH

The park road between Norris and Mammoth Hot Springs provides some interesting sights, although much of this country burned in the 1988 North Fork Fire. Just beyond the highway junction is the **Norris Soldier Station.** Built by the army in 1897 and modified in 1908, it is one of just three stations still standing in the park. The attractive log building now houses the small **Museum of the National Park Ranger,** 307/344-7353, with displays and a video on the history of park rangers. It is open daily 9 A.M.–6 P.M. from Memorial Day to Labor Day, and daily 9 A.M.–5 P.M. the rest of September. Closed the rest of the year.

Just up the road is **Frying Pan Spring** (named for its shape), where the water is actually not that hot. The bubbles are from pungent-smelling hydrogen-sulfide gas. **Roaring Mountain** is a bleak, steaming mountainside four miles north of Norris. In 1902, the mountain erupted into activity with fumaroles that made a roar audible at great distances. It is far less active today and is best seen in winter, when the temperature difference results in much more steam.

Obsidian Cliff

Stop at Obsidian Cliff to see the black glassy rocks formed when lava cooled rapidly. One mountain man (not, as many sources claim, Jim Bridger) told tall tales of "Glass Mountain," where his shots at an elk kept missing. When he got closer, he found he had actually been firing at a clear mountain of glass. The elk was 25 miles away, but the mountain was acting as a telescope to make the animal appear close. Obsidian Cliff was an important source of rock for Indians in making fine arrowheads and other tools. The obsidian from here was of such value that Indians traded it extensively; obsidian points made from this rock have even been found in Ohio and Ontario. (It is illegal to remove obsidian; leave it for future generations to enjoy.) North of here the countryside opens up along Obsidian Creek at **Willow Park,** one of the best places to see moose, especially in the fall.

Sheepeater Cliff and Golden Gate

Approximately 13 miles north of Norris, the road passes Indian Creek Campground (one of the quietest in the park) and the basalt columns of Sheepeater Cliff, named for the Indian inhabitants of these mountains. North of this point, the country opens into Swan Lake Flats, where you get a fine gander at 10,992-foot Electric Peak nine miles to the northwest.

At Golden Gate the road suddenly enters a narrow defile, through which flows Glen Creek. Stop to look over the edge of **Rustic Falls** and to note how the road is cantilevered over the cliff edge. Acrophobics should *not* stop here. Instead, have someone else drive, close your eyes, and say three Hail Marys.

Bunsen Peak

Just south of Mammoth is Bunsen Peak, an 8,564-foot inactive volcanic cone. Any chemistry student will recognize the name because Robert Wilhelm Eberhard von Bunsen not only first explained the action of geysers but also invented the Bunsen burner. Parts of Bunsen Peak look like a chemistry experiment run amok. The North Fork Fire of 1988 swept through this area in a patchy mosaic, leaving long strips of unburned trees next to those that are now just blackened telephone poles.

Bunsen Peak Road is a dirt track open to hikers and mountain bikers but closed to cars. Starting approximately five miles south of Mammoth and just beyond the Golden Gate, it circles the east side of the mountain, connecting with the main road six miles later. Approximately four miles in on the road is a side trail to **Osprey Falls.** This steep trail drops 800 feet in less than a mile to the base of a stunning 150-foot waterfall, but you'll need to climb back out the same way, so don't get too late of a start. Trails also lead to the summit of Bunsen Peak from both the east and west sides. Most folks choose the west trail (four miles round-trip with an elevation difference of 1,300 feet), which begins a short way up the road from the Golden Gate entrance. From the mountaintop you can drop down the east side and hike back along the road, making a total of nine miles round-trip.

The Hoodoos

North of Golden Gate, the main road soon passes the Hoodoos, a fascinating jumble of travertine boulders leaning in all directions. The rocks were created by hot springs thousands of years ago and toppled from the east face of Terrace Mountain. Just before Mammoth, turn left onto Upper Terrace Drive, a half-mile loop road providing access to the upper end of Mammoth Hot Springs. (No trailers or large RVs.)

MAMMOTH HOT SPRINGS VICINITY

Mammoth Hot Springs lies at an elevation of 6,239 feet near the northern border of Yellowstone, just five miles from the town of Gardiner, Montana. Here you'll find park headquarters, a variety of other facilities, and delightfully colorful hot springs. The Mammoth area is an important wintering spot for elk, pronghorn antelope, deer, and bison. During the fall, at least one bull elk and his harem can be seen wandering across the green lawns, while lesser males bugle challenges from behind the buildings or over the hill. The bugling may even keep you awake at night if you're staying in the Mammoth Hotel.

© DON PITCHER

elk at Mammoth Hot Springs terraces

YELLOWSTONE

YELLOWSTONE

MAMMOTH HOT SPRINGS VICINITY

To Roosevelt and Tower

BLACKTAIL PLATEAU DR.

BLACKTAIL

LOOP RD.

GRAND

Blacktail Deer Plateau

2 mi

2 km

0

0

Black Canyon of the Yellowstone

Gallatin National Forest

Park Boundary

Blacktail Creek Trail

Knowles Falls

Yellowstone River Trail

Yellowstone River

Rescue Creek

Trail

Lupine Creek

Wraith Falls

Undine Falls

Lava Creek Trail

Lava Creek

▲ Mt. Everts (7,841 ft.)

Gardner Canyon

To Livingston and Bozeman, MT

Gardiner

NORTH ENTRANCE ■

89

ONE-WAY

Beaver Ponds

MAMMOTH ▲

Mammoth Hot Springs

MAMMOTH HOT SPRINGS

MAMMOTH TERRACE DR.

SNOW PASS

HORSE CORRALS ■

Gardner River

Osprey Falls

Cliffs

Sheepeater

Trail

Bunsen Peak Trail

Bunsen Pk. (8,564 ft.) ▲

Bunsen

Rustic Falls

Hole

Yellowstone National Park

THE HOODOOS

GOLDEN GATE

Glen Creek Trail

Gardners

Swan Lake

SHEEPEATER CLIFFS

89

To Norris

INDIAN CREEK △

MONTANA

WYOMING

Electric Peak (10,992 ft.) ▲

Sepulcher Mtn. (9,652 ft.) ▲

Cache Lake

Sportsman Lake Trail

Gardner River

Fawn Pass Trail

Pass

Panther Creek

Bighorn Pass Trail

© AVALON TRAVEL PUBLISHING, INC.

Origins

Mammoth Hot Springs consists of a series of multihued terraces down which hot, mineral-laden water trickles. This water originates as snow and rain that falls on the surrounding country, although some is believed to come from the Norris area, 20 miles to the south. As it passes through the earth, the water comes into contact with volcanic magma containing massive amounts of carbon dioxide, creating carbonic acid. The now-acidic water passes through and dissolves the region's sedimentary limestone, and the calcium carbonate remains in solution until it reaches the surface at Mammoth. Once at the surface, the carbon dioxide begins to escape into the atmosphere, reducing the acidity and causing the lime to precipitate out, forming the travertine terraces that are so prominent here. As the water flows over small obstructions, more carbon dioxide is released, causing accumulations that eventually grow into the lips that surround the terrace pools. The rate of accumulation of travertine (calcium carbonate) is astounding: more than two tons a day at Mammoth Hot Springs. Some terraces grow by eight inches per year. The first explorers were fascinated by these terraces; mountain man Jim Bridger noted that they made for delightful baths. A later operation—long since ended—coated knickknacks by dipping them in the hot springs!

The springs are constantly changing as underground passages are blocked by limestone deposits, forcing the water in new directions. As a result, old dried-out terraces stand on all sides, while new ones grow each day. Areas that were active just a few years ago may now be simply gray masses of crumbling travertine rock, and new areas may appear and spread in a matter of days. Mammoth is guaranteed to be different every time you visit. One of the most interesting aspects of the hot springs here is the variety of colors, results of the many different species of algae and bacteria that live in the water. Various factors, including temperature and acidity, affect the survival of different species; bright yellow algae live in the hottest areas, whereas cooler waters are colored orange and brown by other algae.

Visiting the Springs

Mammoth Hot Springs covers a steep hillside and consists of a series of colorful springs in various stages of accretion or decay. The area is accessible by road from below or above (Upper Terrace Dr.), and a boardwalk staircase connects the two. At the bottom of Mammoth Hot Springs and off to the right is a 37-foot-tall mass of travertine known as **Liberty Cap** for its faint similarity to the caps worn in the French Revolution. The spring that created this formation no longer flows. (You may well find the Liberty Cap shows a striking similarity to something else.)

The springs at Mammoth change continuously, and every visit brings something new. For details on currently active areas, pick up the Park Service's informative brochure (50 cents) from the box at the parking area. When I last visited, the most interesting areas were **Angel Terrace** along Upper Terrace Drive, along with **Palate Spring** near the base, and **New Blue Spring** and **Canary Spring** in the vicinity of the overlook.

All of the water flowing out of Mammoth terraces quickly disappears into underground caverns. In front of the Mammoth Hotel are two sinkholes from which steam often rises. Caverns above the terraces were once open to the public but later were closed when it became apparent that they contained poisonous gases. Dead birds are sometimes found around one of the small pools in this area appropriately named Poison Spring.

Albright Visitor Center

The Albright Visitor Center, 307/344-2263, is named for Horace Albright, the first National Park Service superintendent at Yellowstone. The center is housed in the army's old bachelor officers' quarters and is open daily 8 A.M.–7 P.M. from Memorial Day to Labor Day, daily 9 A.M.–5 P.M. the rest of the year. Spread over the two floors are exhibits on park wildlife and history, but the real treats are the works of two artists who helped bring Yellowstone's magnificent scenery to public attention. Twenty-three of painter Thomas Moran's famous Yellowstone watercolors line the walls, and his studio has been re-created in one corner. Equally impressive are 26 classic photographs—including one of

Thomas Moran at Mammoth Hot Springs—taken by William H. Jackson during the 1871 Hayden Survey. The paintings and photos are must-sees for anyone with an artistic bent. The center also has an information desk, racks of books, and films about the park and Moran. Check at the information desk for schedules of wildlife talks and frequent ranger-led walks to surrounding sights in the summer.

Other Buildings

Mammoth contains several other historic structures built during the army's tenure at **Fort Yellowstone.** The most distinctive are the six buildings (all in a row) constructed between 1891 and 1909 as quarters for the officers and captains. Most of the grunt soldiers lived just behind here in barracks, one of which is now the park administration building. The U.S. Engineers Department was housed in an odd stone building with obvious Asian influences; it's right across from the visitors center. The visitors center has an informative pamphlet (50 cents) that describes the Fort Yellowstone Historic District in detail. Displays around the grounds provide additional details.

Although one wing survives from a hotel built in 1911, most of the **Mammoth Hot Springs Hotel** was constructed in 1937. Step inside to view the large map of the United States built from 15 different types of wood. Mammoth also features a Yellowstone General Store, post office, gas station, restaurant, fast-food eatery, and medical clinic. Mammoth Campground is just down the road. Just up the hill—less than one mile from the hotel—is the Mammoth corral, where horseback rides are offered. Also here is a small **cemetery** populated mostly by infants and a few civilians who died here in the early 1900s.

North to Montana

The main road north from Mammoth Hot Springs follows the Gardner River, dropping nearly 1,000 feet in elevation before reaching the town of Gardiner, Montana. (Both the river and the misspelled town are named for Johnson Gardner, a ruthless trapper from the 1820s.) The river is a favorite of fly-fishing enthusiasts. A turnout near the Wyoming–Montana border notes the "boiling river" section of the Gardner River; it's well worth a stop. Sometimes during the winter you can spot bighorn sheep on the mountain slopes just north of the river as you head down to Gardiner.

The "back way" to Gardiner is the Old Gardiner Road, a five-mile gravel road (great for mountain bikes, but not for RVs or trailers) that starts behind Mammoth Hot Springs Hotel. Traffic is downhill only, so you'll need to take the main road for your return into the park; mountain bikes can go in both directions. This is one of the best places to spot pronghorn antelope in the park, and it also provides a fine escape from the crowds at Mammoth.

Day Hikes

For a relatively easy loop hike, try the five-mile (round-trip) **Beaver Ponds Trail,** which begins between Liberty Cap and the stone house. It gains 500 feet in elevation, passing through spruce and fir forests along the way and ending at several small beaver ponds. The path then drops down to join Old Gardiner Road, which you can follow back to Mammoth. This trail provides a good opportunity to see mule deer, elk, pronghorn antelope, and moose, but is best hiked in the spring or fall when temperatures are cooler. Black bears are sometimes seen along the way, so be sure to make noise while you walk.

A longer (12 miles round-trip) hike is the **Sepulcher Mountain Trail,** which climbs to the top of this 9,652-foot peak just northwest of Mammoth. There are several possible routes to the top, and any of them can be combined into a nice loop hike. One begins at the same place as the Beaver Ponds Trail. You'll find many flowers in the expansive meadows on the south side of Sepulcher Mountain (named for several strange rocks at its summit). From Mammoth, it is a 3,400-foot elevation gain, so be ready to sweat. Before heading out, check at the visitors centers to see if there are any major bear problems in the area and to get a topographic map and hiking tips.

MAMMOTH TO TOWER JUNCTION

The 18-mile drive from Mammoth to Tower Junction takes visitors through some of the driest and most open country in Yellowstone. Two waterfalls provide stopping places along the way. Beautiful **Undine Falls** is a 60-foot-high double falls immediately north of the road. Just up the road is a gentle half-mile path to the base of **Wraith Falls,** where Lupine Creek cascades 90 feet. Look for ducks and trumpeter swans in **Blacktail Pond,** a couple of miles farther east.

Blacktail Plateau Drive, approximately nine miles east of Mammoth, turns off from the main road. The rough seven-mile dirt road is a one-way route that loosely follows the Bannock Trail, a path used by the Bannock tribe on their way to buffalo-hunting grounds east of here. Their travois trails are still visible. The Bannocks used this route from 1838 to 1878, but it was probably used for hundreds or thousands of years by various tribes crossing the high plateau. Much of Blacktail Plateau Drive is through open sagebrush, grass, and aspen country, where you're likely to see deer and pronghorn antelope. The trees are very pretty in the fall. On the east end, the road drops back into a forest burned by a severe crown fire in 1988 but now containing young aspen and lodgepole trees and abundant summertime flowers.

The Park Service has developed a two-thirds-mile boardwalk **Forces of the Northern Range Self-Guiding Trail** approximately six miles east of Mammoth Hot Springs. Trailside exhibits describe the natural world. One-half mile beyond where Blacktail Plateau Drive rejoins the main road is the turnoff to the **petrified tree.** The 20-foot-tall stump of an ancient redwood tree (50 million years old) stands behind iron bars; a second petrified tree that used to stand nearby was stolen piece by piece over the years by thoughtless tourists. The **Tower Ranger Station,** originally occupied by the U.S. Army, is located just before Tower Junction where the road splits, leading to either Northeast Entrance Road or Canyon.

NORTHEAST ENTRANCE ROAD

Of the five primary entryways into Yellowstone, Northeast Entrance is the least traveled, making this a great place to escape the hordes in midsummer. It is also one of the best places to see tall mountains in Yellowstone. The road heads east from Tower Junction and immediately enters **Lamar Valley,** an area of grass and sage along the sinuous Lamar River. Osborne Russell, who trapped this country in the 1830s, described it with affection:

We descended the stream about 15 mls thro. the dense forest and at length came to a beautiful valley about 8 Mls. long and 3 or 4 wide surrounded by dark and lofty mountains. The stream after running thro. the center in a NW direction rushed down a tremendous canyon of basaltic rock apparently just wide enough to admit its waters. The banks of the stream in the valley were low and skirted in many places with beautiful Cotton wood groves. Here we found a few Snake indians comprising 6 men 7 women and 8 or 10 children who were the only Inhabitants of this lonely and secluded spot. They were all neatly clothed in dressed deer and Sheep skins of the best quality and seemed to be perfectly contented and happy. . . . We stopped at this place and for my own part I almost wished I could spend the remainder of my days in a place like this where happiness and contentment seemed to rein in wild romantic splendor surrounded by majestic battlements which seemed to support the heavens and shut out all hostile intruders. . . . There is something in the wild romantic scenery of this valley which I cannot . . . describe; but the impressions made upon my mind while gazing from a high eminence on the surrounding landscape one evening as the sun was gently gliding behind the western mountain and casting its gigantic shadows across the vale were such as time can never efface from my memory.

This is still one of the best places in Yellowstone to view bison, with a gorgeous backdrop of open country and wooded mountains. Elk and mule deer are also commonly seen, and the reintroduction of wolves has added another dimension to wildlife viewing. The valley contains several small ponds created when the retreating glaciers left large blocks of ice that formed "kettles." Erratic glacial boulders are scattered along the way. There are campgrounds at Slough Creek and Pebble Creek and very good fishing in Slough Creek, too. But look out for one other critter: the ubiquitous ground squirrels that dart into the road, playing chicken with your tires.

Yellowstone River Picnic Area

Picnic areas don't generally merit a mention, but this one—1.5 miles east of Tower Junction on the Northeast Entrance Road—is an exception because of its proximity to a grand view. A two-mile trail takes off from here for Grand Canyon of the Yellowstone River. The hike is easy and provides a good chance to see bighorn sheep, but be careful to stay away from the canyon rim. For a loop hike (four miles round-trip), continue to the Specimen Ridge Trail, where you turn left and follow it back to your starting point.

Slough Creek Area

Slough Creek Campground is a favorite of fly-fishers who come here to try for the area's acclaimed cutthroat trout. The **Slough Creek Trail** starts at the campground and is one of the more distinctive in the park. The trail—actually a wagon road—makes for a delightful and gentle day hike through Douglas fir forests and open meadows. It continues all the way to the park boundary, 11 miles north of the campground, and is used for access to Silver Tip Ranch. This is the only way into the ranch, and because no motor vehicles are allowed you may meet folks on a horse-drawn wagon during your hike. Day hikers often go up the road as far as the first meadow, a distance of eight miles round-trip.

Yellowstone Association Institute

The nonprofit Yellowstone Association Institute teaches many classes out of Lamar Valley's historic Buffalo Ranch, approximately 10 miles east of Tower Junction. To augment the park's small wild herd, bison were brought here in 1902 from private ranches. The bison stayed in pens at night and were herded during the day. After 1915, they were allowed to roam freely in summer, although all of the park's bison were rounded up and driven here for winter. After 1938, the roundups ended, but the bison were fed hay every winter in Lamar Valley. Finally in 1952, even this practice was halted and the bison were allowed to roam throughout the park. The historic buildings are worth a look, or better still, take one of the institute's excellent classes. Get details at 307/344-2294, www.yellowstone association.org.

Specimen Ridge

Just east of the historic Buffalo Ranch is a turnout across from Specimen Ridge, where explorers discovered the standing trunks of petrified trees that had been buried in volcanic ash and mudflows some 50 million years ago. Over the centuries, the trunks literally turned to stone as silica entered the wood. The process was repeated over the centuries as new forests gradually developed atop the volcanic deposits, only to be buried by later flows. Scientists have found 27 different forests on top of each other, containing walnut, magnolia, oak, redwood, and maple—evidence that the climate was once more like that of today's Midwestern states. Erosion eventually revealed the trees, many of which are still standing. This is one of the largest areas of petrified trees known to exist.

There is no trail to the petrified forest, but during summer rangers lead hikes into the area. Check at the Mammoth Visitor Center for upcoming treks. Mark Marschall's *Yellowstone Trails* provides a description of the 1.5-mile route if you want to try it on your own. A lesser-known petrified forest in the northwest corner of Yellowstone is accessible via U.S. Hwy. 191.

Wolf Watching

Between the Slough Creek and Pebble Creek Campgrounds, wolf aficionados fill roadside turnouts each morning and evening, waiting patiently for members of the Druid Peak Pack to appear. Bring your binoculars and spotting scope! During the wolf denning season, the Park Service prohibits parking or walking along certain stretches of the road, but two turnouts are available.

Northeast Entrance

At the east end of Lamar Valley, the road continues northeast up Soda Butte Creek and between the steep rocky cliffs of **Barronette Peak** (10,404 feet) and **Abiathar Peak** (10,928 feet). Stop at **Soda Butte,** where you'll find a substantial travertine mound similar to those at Mammoth. Although the springs are no longer very active, the air still reeks of hydrogen sulfide, the "rotten egg" gas. South of Soda Butte and several miles up a backcountry trail is **Wahb Springs,** found within Death Gulch. Here poisonous gases are emitted from the ground, killing animals in the vicinity. Early explorers reported finding dead bears that had been overcome by the fumes. Less than one mile north of Soda Butte is a pullout where a half-mile trail leads to pretty **Trout Lake.** It's a nice afternoon break from the crowds elsewhere in Yellowstone.

North of Pebble Creek Campground, the road squeezes through beautiful **Icebox Canyon,** past Barronette Peak, and into the (unburned) lodgepole pine forests. It follows the creek all the way to the edge of the park, crossing into Montana two miles before the park border. The **Northeast Entrance Station** is a classic log building built in 1935 and now designated a National Historic Landmark. The twin towns of Silver Gate and Cooke City (see Gateway Towns later in this chapter) are just up the road.

A fine day hike starts from the Warm Creek Picnic Area, 1.5 miles west of the entrance station. The trail climbs 1,100 feet in 1.5 miles before dropping into flower-filled mountain meadows along Pebble Creek. If you continue more than two miles you'll need to ford the creek, which can be deep before late summer. Backpackers use this trail for longer trips into the area; see Into the Backcountry for details.

TOWER JUNCTION TO CANYON

Roosevelt Lodge

Lying at the junction of the roads to Canyon, Mammoth, and Lamar Valley, Roosevelt Lodge was built in 1920 and named for Pres. Theodore Roosevelt, who camped a few miles to the south during his 1903 visit. A lifelong supporter of Yellowstone, Roosevelt helped push through legislation that clamped down on the rampant destruction of park wildlife early in the 20th century.

The Roosevelt area is a favorite of families, wolf-watchers, and anglers, many of whom return year after year. The main building has the rough-edged flavor of a hunting lodge and a peacefulness that you won't find at Old Faithful, Canyon, or Mammoth. Inside are two large stone fireplaces, and the porch out front has comfortable rocking chairs that fill each evening. Folks plop their feet on the rail, nurse a beer, and watch the evening roll in. Heavenly. Rustic cabins—most built in the 1920s—provide simple accommodations, and Roosevelt has a restaurant and little gift shop/general store, along with horseback rides. It's also the only place in Yellowstone to offer wagon rides and Old West cookouts; call well ahead for reservations.

Lost Lake Trail starts behind Roosevelt Lodge and climbs through forested hills to the lake, where you can either return back via the Roosevelt Horse Trail or contour along the hillside to the Petrified Tree parking area, where another path loops back to the lodge, a distance of four miles.

Stop at the overlook to **Calcite Springs,** two miles southeast of the junction, where a walkway provides dramatic views into the canyon of the Yellowstone River, with steaming geothermal activity far below. The cliff faces contain a wide strip of columnar basalt, some of which overhangs the highway just to the south.

Tower Fall

On summer afternoons the parking lot at Tower Fall fills with cars as folks stop to see Tower Creek plummeting 132 feet before joining the Yellowstone River. The towerlike black rocks of the area are made of volcanic basalt. Nearby are a

Tower Fall

the highest point along any park road, even higher than the three other places where the road crosses the Continental Divide! Look for whitebark pines near the road, and be sure to stop just south of here for a view across to the distant Grand Canyon of the Yellowstone.

For an outstanding day hike, climb **Mt. Washburn,** a 10,243-foot peak with commanding vistas in all directions. The two trails up the mountain both gain about the same elevation (1,400 feet) and are around six miles round-trip. The most popular route begins from the often full parking lot at Dunraven Pass and heads up from the south side. A few miles north of the pass, the old Chittenden Road turns off and leads to another access point; drive the first mile up this road to a large parking area and then hike—or mountain-bike—to the summit of Washburn from the north side. Many wildflowers bloom in midsummer, and bighorn sheep may be seen right along the trail. Bring warm clothes and rain gear because conditions on top may be much cooler and windier than below.

campground and a Yellowstone General Store. Tower Fall overlook is just a couple hundred paved feet from the parking area, or you can follow the path one-half mile down the switchbacks to the canyon bottom, where the vista is far more impressive and a rainbow is sometimes visible. Be prepared to get wet in the spray! A ford of the Yellowstone River—used by Bannock Indians in the 19th century—is just one-quarter mile away. For more than a hundred years, a huge boulder stood atop Tower Fall; the water and gravity finally won in 1986.

Dunraven Pass and Mt. Washburn

Continuing southward, the road climbs along Antelope Creek and eventually switchbacks up the aptly named Mae West Curve. The North Fork Fire swept through this country in 1988, but the area is now verdant with new trees, grasses, and flowers. **Dunraven Pass** (8,859 feet) is named for the Earl of Dunraven, who visited the park in 1874 and whose widely read book *The Great Divide* brought Yellowstone to the attention of wealthy European travelers. This is

GRAND CANYON OF THE YELLOWSTONE

Yellowstone is best known for its geysers and animals, but for many visitors the Grand Canyon is the park's most memorable feature. This 20-mile-long canyon ranges from 1,500 to 4,000 feet across and has colorful yellow, pink, orange, and buff cliffs that drop as much as 1,200 feet on either side. The river itself tumbles abruptly over two massive waterfalls, sending up a roar that's audible for miles along the rims. Grand Canyon is accessible by road from both the north and south sides, with equally amazing views. The lodgepole pine forests around here escaped the fires of 1988.

Carving a Canyon

After the massive volcanic eruptions some 650,000 years ago, rhyolite lava flows came through what is now the Grand Canyon. The flows eventually cooled, but geothermal activity within the rhyolite weakened the rock with hot steam and gasses, making it susceptible to erosion. Over the centuries, a series of glaciers blocked water upstream, each time creating a lake. As each glacier retreated it undammed the stream, allowing the water in the lake to empty suddenly. The weakened rhyolite was easily eroded by these periodic floods of water and glacial debris, thus revealing pastel yellow and red canyon walls colored by the thermal activities. The **Lower Falls** are at the edge of the thermal basin, above rock that was not weakened by geothermal activity. The **Upper Falls** are at a contact point between hard rhyolite that does not erode easily and a band of rhyolite that contains more easily eroded volcanic glass. Today the canyon is eroding more slowly, having increased in depth just 50 feet over the last 10,000 years.

Canyon Village

Canyon Village on the north rim is a forgettable shopping mall in the wilderness, complete with a visitors center, various stores and eating places, a post office, a gas station, cabins, lodges, and a campground. It's a good place to come on a rainy summer afternoon when the kids are starting to scream for ice cream. Horseback rides are available less than one mile south of here. Step into **Canyon Visitor Center,** 307/242-2550, for park information or to see the natural-history exhibits. Hours are daily 8 A.M.–7 P.M. Memorial Day through September, and daily 9 A.M.–6 P.M. until mid-October. It's closed in winter. A revamped and larger visitors center here should be completed in 2004.

North Rim Vistas

A one-way road takes visitors to a series of extremely popular overlooks along the north rim of Grand Canyon of the Yellowstone. Farthest east is **Inspiration Point,** where the views of the canyon and Lower Falls are, well, inspirational. **North Rim Trail** leads along the rim from Inspiration Point up to Chittenden Bridge, three miles away. Some sections of this scenic and nearly level path are paved. Just a couple hundred feet up from Inspiration Point, be sure to look for a 500-ton boulder deposited by a glacier

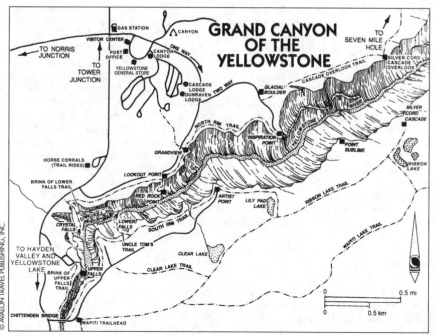

during the glaciation that ended 15,000 years ago. It originated in the Beartooth Mountains at least 30 miles north of here and was carried south atop a moving river of ice.

The five-mile-long **Seven Mile Hole Trail** takes off near this boulder, providing fantastic views for the first mile or so, minus the crowds at Inspiration Point. Look for **Silver Cord Cascade,** a thin ribbon of water dropping over the opposite wall of the canyon, but be careful not to go too close to the very loose edge. It's a very long way down! The trail switchbacks steeply to the Yellowstone River, passing odoriferous thermal areas en route. Many anglers come to Seven Mile Hole (it's seven miles downriver from Lower Falls) while other folks come to relax along the river. Save your energy for the strenuous 1,400-foot climb back up. Three campsites are available near the base of the trail for those who want to make this an overnight hike (permit required).

The one-way road continues westward to overlooks at **Grandview** and **Lookout Point.** From Lookout Point, a half-mile trail drops several hundred feet to **Red Rock Point** for a closer view of Lower Falls. Farthest west along the one-way North Rim Road is the trail to the **Brink of the Lower Falls.** The trail is one-half-mile long and paved, descending 600 feet to a viewing area where you can peer over the edge as the water plummets in a thunderous roar over the 308-foot precipice (twice the height of Niagara Falls). This is probably the most breathtaking sight in Yellowstone, but if you suffer from vertigo don't even think about looking over the brink! Just south of where the one-way road rejoins the main highway is a turnoff to **Brink of the Upper Falls,** where a short walk takes you to a less dramatic but still beautiful view of the 109-foot-high Upper Falls.

A party of prospectors wandered north into this country in 1867, following the Yellowstone River downstream without suspecting the canyon below. A. Bart Henderson wrote in his diary of strolling down the river and being

> *very much surprised to see the water disappear from my sight. I walked out on a rock & made two steps at the same time, one forward, the other backward, for I had un-*

> *awares as it were, looked down into the depth or bowels of the earth, into which the Yellow plunged as if to cool the infernal region that lay under all this wonderful country of lava and boiling springs.*

South Rim Vistas

The south rim is lined with additional dramatic views into Grand Canyon. Cross the Chittenden Bridge over the Yellowstone River (otters are sometimes seen playing in the river below) and continue one-half mile to Uncle Tom's parking area, where a short trail leads to views of the Upper Falls and Crystal Falls. More unusual is **Uncle Tom's Trail,** which descends 500 feet to Lower Falls. The trail is partly paved, but it's steep and includes 328 metal steps before you get to the bottom—good exercise if you're in shape. It was named for "Uncle" Tom Richardson who, with the help of wooden ladders and ropes, led paying tourists to the base of the falls around the turn of the 20th century. Because there was no bridge, Uncle Tom also rowed his guests across the river near the present Chittenden Bridge. After his permit was revoked in 1903, visitors had to make do on their own.

One mile beyond Uncle Tom's parking area, the road ends at the parking area for **Artist Point,** the most famous—and crowded—of all Grand Canyon viewpoints. A short paved path leads to an astoundingly beautiful spot where one can look upriver to the Lower Falls or down the opposite direction into the canyon. Look for thermal activity far below. The point is apparently where artist Thomas Moran painted some of his famous watercolors. Avoid the crowds and afternoon thunderstorms by getting here early in the morning; it's almost always deserted at sunrise.

South Rim Trail begins at the Chittenden Bridge and continues for two miles along the rim to Artist Point, providing more viewpoints en route. The least-traveled part of this trail continues eastward from Artist Point, providing an amazingly quick escape from the mob scene at Artist Point, as well as a chance to see the kaleidoscopically colored canyon, hear the roar of the river from far below, and watch for squirrels and birds. But be careful to stay away from the edge where the rocks are loose. It's doubtful that anyone could survive such a fall, and I once came dangerously close to testing that postulate. The trail continues to Lilly Pad Lake, where you can follow the **Ribbon Lake Trail** to a pair of lakes. From here, a spur path leads to a hill that provides a wonderful view of the canyon and Silver Cord Cascade. With a drop of 1,200 feet, Silver Cord is the highest falls in Yellowstone. Also nearby are two campsites for those wanting to spend a night on the rim of the canyon; see Into the Backcountry for camping details. From the Artist Point parking area to Ribbon Lake, it's four miles round-trip. A variety of other trails on the South Rim provide alternate starting points and possible loop hikes to the Ribbon Lake area. (As an aside, the old trail to Point Sublime has been closed because of unsafe conditions along the canyon rim.)

CANYON TO LAKE JUNCTION

Hayden Valley

Just a few miles south of Canyon, the country abruptly opens into beautiful Hayden Valley, named for Ferdinand V. Hayden, leader of the 1871 expedition into Yellowstone. Reaching eight miles across, this relatively level part of the park was once occupied by an arm of Yellowstone Lake. The sediments left behind by the lake, along with glacial till, do not hold sufficient water to support trees. As a result, the area is occupied primarily by grasses, forbs, and sage. This is one of the best areas in the park to see wildlife, especially bison and elk. The Yellowstone River wanders across Hayden Valley, and streams enter from various sides. The waterways are excellent places to look for Canada geese, trumpeter swans, pelicans, and many kinds of ducks. Although they are less common, grizzly bears sometimes can be found feeding in the eastern end of the valley. Because of the bears, hikers need to be especially cautious when tramping through the grasses and shrubs, where it is easy to surprise a bear or to be likewise surprised. On the north end of Hayden Valley, the road crosses **Alum Creek,** named for its highly alkaline water, which could make anything shrink. In the horse-and-buggy days, Yellowstone wags claimed that a man had forded

the creek with a team of horses and a wagon but came out the other side with four Shetland ponies pulling a basket!

Mud Volcano Area

Shortly after the road climbs south out of Hayden Valley, it passes one of the most interesting of Yellowstone's many thermal basins. On the east side of the road, a turnout overlooks **Sulphur Caldron,** where a highly acidic pool is filled with sulfur-tinted waters and the air is filled with the odor of hydrogen-sulfide gas. Directly across the road is the Mud Volcano area, where a two-thirds-mile loop trail provides what could be a tour through a bad case of heartburn. Pick up a Park Service brochure (50 cents) from the box for descriptions of all the bizarre features here. The area is in a constant state of flux as springs dry up or begin overflowing, killing trees in their path. **Churning Caldron** is a frothing pool where periodic jets send superheated water into the air. Just up the trail is one of the most interesting features, **Black Dragons Caldron,** where an explosive spring blasts constantly through a mass of boiling black mud. The wildest place at Mud Volcano is **Dragon's Mouth,** which the Park Service notes is named for "the rhythmic belching of steam and water shooting from the cavernous opening." It's easy to imagine the fires of hell not far below this spring. The waters are 180°F. During winter (and often in summer), the Mud Volcano area is a good place to see elk or bison.

Along the Yellowstone

South of Mud Volcano, the road parallels the Yellowstone River. At **LeHardy Rapids** a boardwalk provides an overlook where early summer visitors see blush-red spawning cutthroats. In late summer, this part of the Yellowstone River is a very popular fly-fishing spot—some call it the finest stream cutthroat fishing in the world—and a good place to view ducks and swans. Earlier in the year, it's open only to the bears that gorge on the cutthroats. By the way, the Yellowstone River, which begins at Yellowstone Lake, is the longest free-flowing (undammed) river in the Lower 48.

YELLOWSTONE LAKE

When first-time visitors see Yellowstone Lake, they are stunned by its magnitude. The statistics are impressive: 110 miles of shoreline, 20 miles north to south and 14 miles east to west, with an average depth of 139 feet and a maximum depth of 390 feet. Yellowstone Lake can seem like a sheet of glass laid to the horizon at one moment and just a half hour later be a roiling ocean of whitecaps and wind-whipped waves. These changeable waters can be dangerous to those in canoes or small boats; several people have drowned, including experienced park rangers. The water is covered by ice at least half of the year, and breakup does not come until late May or early June. Even in summer, water temperatures are often only in the 40s. David Folsom, who was part of an exploration party traveling through the area in 1869, described Yellowstone Lake as an

inland sea, its crystal waves dancing and sparkling in the sunlight as if laughing with joy for their wild freedom. It is a scene of transcendent beauty which has been viewed by few white men, and we felt glad to have looked upon it before its primeval solitude should be broken by the crowds of pleasure seekers which at no distant day will throng its shores.

Fishing Bridge

The area around famous Fishing Bridge (built in 1937) was for many years a favorite place to catch cutthroat trout. Unfortunately, these same fish are a major food source for grizzlies, and this area is considered some of the most important bear habitat in Yellowstone. Conflicts between bears and humans led to the death of 16 grizzlies here. To help restore trout populations and to provide food for the grizzlies, the Park Service banned fishing from Fishing Bridge in 1973 and tried to move the developments to the Grant Village area. Lobbying by folks from Cody (worried lest they lose some of the tourist traffic) kept some of the facilities at Fishing Bridge from closing. Remaining facilities include an RV park, Yellowstone General Store, and gas station. **Fishing Bridge Visitor Center,** 307/242-2450, houses exhibits of birds, animals, and geology. It's open daily 8 A.M.–7 P.M. Memorial Day to early September, and daily 9 A.M.–6 P.M. for the rest of September.

Yellowstone Lake near Bridge Bay

© DON PITCHER

YELLOWSTONE

It's closed the remainder of the year. The bridge itself is still a popular stopping point and a good place to see large cutthroat trout in the shallows. For a nice loop hike, take **Elephant Back Mountain Trail,** which begins one mile south of Fishing Bridge Junction. This three-mile (round-trip) trail climbs 800 feet in elevation through dense lodgepole forests to panoramic views across Yellowstone Lake and into Pelican Valley.

Lake Yellowstone Hotel

Lake Yellowstone Hotel, the oldest extant park hostelry, was built in 1889–1891 by the Northern Pacific Railroad and originally consisted of a simple boxlike structure facing Yellowstone Lake. The hotel was sold to Harry Child in 1901, and two years later Robert Reamer—the architect who designed Old Faithful Inn—was given free rein to transform this into a more attractive place. Hard to believe that the same architect could create a grand log masterpiece and a sprawling Southern colonial mansion with distinctive ionic columns in the same park! Lake Yellowstone Hotel is the second-largest wood-framed building in North America and requires 500 gallons of paint each year to keep it in shape. During the 1960s and '70s the hotel fell into disrepair under the management of General Host Corporation, and in disgust, the Park Service bought out the concession and leased it to another company. Major renovations in the 1980s transformed the dowdy old structure into a luxurious grand hotel with much of the charm it had when Pres. Calvin Coolidge stayed here in the 1920s.

Today, Lake Yellowstone Hotel is one of the nicest places to stay in the park, with fine vistas out over the lake and comfortable quarters. Relax with a drink in the sunlit **Sun Room** while a pianist or a string quartet provides the atmosphere. Free 45-minute historic **tours of Lake Yellowstone Hotel** are given Monday–Friday at 5:30 P.M. from early June to late September. The hotel also houses a restaurant, gift shop, and snack bar.

Be sure to take a walk along the lakeshore out in front of the hotel, where the Absaroka Range forms a backdrop far to the east. The highest mountain is Avalanche Peak (10,566 feet). Almost due south is the 10,308-foot summit of Mt. Sheridan, named for Gen. Philip Sheridan, a longtime supporter of expanding the park to include the Tetons. Watch for the big white pelicans catching fish on the lake.

Just east of Lake Yellowstone Hotel is the **Lake Ranger Station,** built in 1922–1923 and now on the National Register of Historic Places. Inside the octagonal main room you will find a massive central fireplace, exposed log rafters, and rustic light fixtures. A short walk away is **Lake Lodge,** another rustic log structure that houses a reasonably priced cafeteria with grand windows fronting the lake. A Yellowstone General Store stands nearby, and dozens of plain cabins are behind it.

To West Thumb

The highway south from Lake Junction to West Thumb follows the lakeshore nearly the entire distance. A campground and boat harbor are at **Bridge Bay,** along with a ranger station, marina, and store. Stop here for hour-long boat tours of Yellowstone Lake, offered several times a day throughout the summer, or for guided fishing trips and boat rentals.

For an enjoyable day hike, visit **Natural Bridge,** a 51-foot-high span of rock that was carved by the waters of Bridge Creek. The three-mile (round-trip) trail starts from the marina parking lot. The last part of the way into Natural Bridge is along a paved road that was open to cars until recently. Cyclists can ride bikes to Natural Bridge on a separate trail that starts south of the marina.

Back on the main road, keep your eyes open for Canada geese and trumpeter swans as you drive south. **Gull Point Drive,** a two-mile-long side road, offers views of **Stevenson Island** just offshore; farther south, **Frank Island** and tiny **Dot Island** become visible. The small **Potts Hot Springs Basin,** just north of West Thumb, is named for fur trapper Daniel T. Potts, one of the first white men to explore the Yellowstone country. His travels here in 1826 were described the following year in a Philadelphia newspaper article. It was perhaps the first published mention of Yellowstone Lake and the hot springs.

EAST ENTRANCE ROAD

Heading east from Fishing Bridge, the road follows the shore of Yellowstone Lake past country that escaped the fires of 1988. Three miles east of the bridge are Indian Pond—popular with birders—and the trailhead for **Storm Point Trail.** This pleasant three-mile (round-trip) loop trail is essentially level and goes past a large colony of yellow-bellied marmots before reaching Storm Point, where waves often pound against the rocks. The trail is often closed in spring and early summer because of grizzlies, and mosquitoes may make a June or July trip less enjoyable. North of here, Pelican Valley is considered important grizzly habitat and is closed to all overnight camping year-round. Even daytime use is not allowed until July 4, and then only between 9 A.M. and 7 P.M. Before venturing out on the Storm Point Trail or into Pelican Valley, check at the Lake Ranger Station for current bear information. The half-mile-long **Pelican Creek Nature Trail** starts one mile east of Fishing Bridge and provides an easy hike to a beach along Yellowstone Lake. Much of the way is on boardwalk over a marshy area.

At **Steamboat Point** the road swings out along the shore, providing excellent views across the lake and of a noisy fumarole. For an even better view (don't miss this one!), take the **Lake Butte Overlook** road, which continues one mile to a small parking area 1,000 feet above the lake.

This is a fine place to watch sunsets and to get a feeling for the enormity of Yellowstone Lake. Back on the main highway and heading east, Yellowstone Lake is soon behind you and visible in only a few spots as the road climbs gradually, passing scenic **Sylvan Lake,** a nice place for picnics. Just up the road is tiny Eleanor Lake (little more than a puddle) and the trail to 10,566-foot **Avalanche Peak.** This two-mile-long unmarked trail begins across the road on the east side of the creek and climbs steeply. It emerges from the forest halfway up, with the top gained via a scree slope. At the summit, you can see most of the peaks in the Absarokas and in the Tetons 70 miles away, but snow is present on top until mid-July.

Immediately east of Eleanor Lake, the main road climbs to 8,530-foot **Sylvan Pass,** flanked by Hoyt Peak on the north and Top Notch Peak to the south. Steep scree slopes drop down both sides. East of Sylvan Pass, the road descends quickly along Middle Creek (a tributary of the Shoshone River), providing good views to the south of Mt. Langford and Mt. Doane. **East Entrance Ranger Station** was built by the army in 1904. For many years, the road leading up to Sylvan Pass from the east took drivers across Corkscrew Bridge, a bridge that literally looped over itself as the road climbed steeply up the narrow valley. The road continues eastward to Cody through beautiful Wapiti Valley; see the Bighorn Basin chapter for details.

Into the Backcountry

Most Yellowstone visitors act as though they were chained to their cars with a hundred-yard tether—as if by getting away from their vehicles they might miss some other sight down the road. For the 2 percent or so who *do* abandon their cars, Yellowstone has much to offer beyond the spectacular geysers and canyons for which it is famous. Although many parts of the Yellowstone backcountry are heavily visited, regulations keep the sense of wildness intact by separating campsites and limiting the number of hikers. If you head out early or late in the season, you'll discover solitude just a few miles from the traffic jams.

Much of Yellowstone consists of rolling lodgepole (or burned lodgepole) forests. With a few exceptions, anyone looking for dramatic alpine scenery would probably be better off heading to Grand Teton National Park, the Beartooth Mountains, or the Wind River Mountains. The Yellowstone backcountry is still enjoyable to walk through, however, and many trails lead past waterfalls, geysers, and hot springs. Besides, this is one of the finest places in America to view wildlife—including bison, elk, grizzlies, and wolves—in a setting other than a zoo.

Before August, when they start to die down, you should also be ready for the ubiquitous mosquitoes. Ticks are a nuisance from mid-March to mid-July in lower elevation parts of Yellowstone. The fires of 1988 created some problems for backcountry hikers, but trails have all been cleared, and hikers will get a good chance to see how the land is recovering.

Day Hikes

This section covers multiday backcountry hikes, but many hikers just head out on day outings, many of which are described in the Exploring the Park section of this chapter. Every part of the park has something different to offer day-hikers, but notable ones include the Dogshead and Lewis Channel trails to Shoshone Lake, Yellowstone Lake Overlook Trail near West Thumb, Lone Star Geyser Trail, various trails (some paved) in the Old Faithful area, Mystic Falls Trail (accessed from Biscuit Basin), the Fairy Falls Trail in Midway Geyser Basin, trails to Bunsen Peak and Osprey Falls (south of Mammoth), Beaver Ponds and Sepulcher Mountain Trails (from Mammoth), Yellowstone River Picnic Area Trail (near Tower Junction), Slough Creek Trail (from Slough Creek Campground), Lost Lake Trail (from Roosevelt Lodge), Mt. Washburn trails, North Rim, Seven Mile Hole, and South Rim, and Ribbon Lake trails in the Canyon area, Elephant Back Mountain Trail near Fishing Bridge, Natural Bridge Trail near Bridge Bay, and the Storm Point Trail on Lake Yellowstone. All of these are described in previous sections, or you can pick up day-hike pamphlets and detailed hiking books from park visitors centers.

Rules and Regulations

The Park Service maintains more than 300 campsites in the Yellowstone backcountry, most of which have pit toilets and fire rings, along with storage poles to keep food from bears.

Most Yellowstone visitors act as though they were chained to their cars, but the 2 percent or so of visitors who abandon their cars find that Yellowstone has much to offer beyond the spectacular geysers and canyons for which it is famous.

Hikers may stay only at designated campsites. Wood fires are not allowed in many areas and are discouraged elsewhere, so be sure to have a gas stove for cooking. Bear-management areas have special regulations; they may be for day-use only, include seasonal restrictions, or specify minimum group sizes. Pets are not allowed on the trails within Yellowstone, and special rules apply for those coming in with horses, mules, burros, and llamas. Because of wet conditions and the lack of forage, no stock animals are permitted before July.

A free **backcountry-use permit** is required of each overnight party and is available in person from various Yellowstone ranger stations and visitors centers within 48 hours of your hike. Because of the popularity of backcountry trips, you should make reservations before your arrival in the park. Unfortunately, the Park Service has taken a lesson from the IRS and makes the process as complex as bureaucratically possible. Try to follow me here. Reservations cost $20 per trip, and the reservation forms are available from the Backcountry Office, P.O. Box 168, Yellowstone National Park, WY 82190, 307/344-2160. Campsite reservation requests must be mailed in, using these forms; reservations are not accepted by phone, fax, or over the web (but they have a printable version on the park website, www.nps.gov/yell). You'll receive a confirmation notice by return mail and will exchange the notice for a permit when you get there; the permit must be obtained in person at a ranger station within 48 hours of your first camping date. Before receiving your permit, you will be given a lengthy rundown on what to expect and what precautions to take, and you'll be shown a bear-safety video. The ranger stations are open seven days a week June–August, generally from 8 A.M. to 4:30 P.M.

For backcountry rules, bear safety tips, and suggestions for hiking and horse-packing, pick up

GREATER YELLOWSTONE AREA

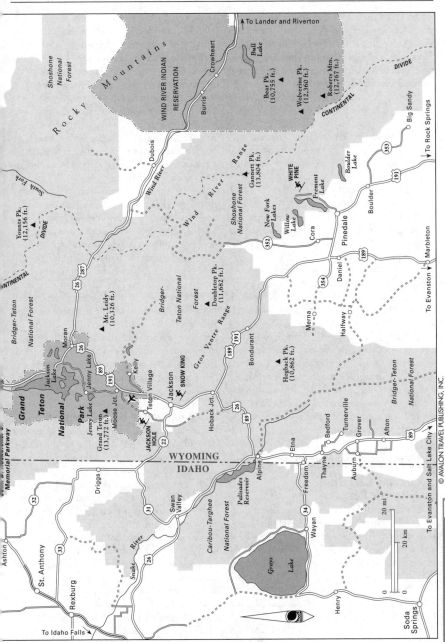

YELLOWSTONE

(or find it on the web) Yellowstone's **Backcountry Trip Planner**, which shows locations of campsites throughout the park and provides detailed information on wilderness access and precautions. You may want to also pick up or request the free park pamphlet *Beyond Road's End.*

Those interested in horsepacking or llama trips should contact the park at 307/344-7381, www.nps.gov/yell, for a list of outfitters authorized to operate in Yellowstone. The outfitters offer everything from day trips to weeklong adventures deep into the backcountry.

More Information

Following is a description of a few two- to four-day backcountry hikes covering various parts of Yellowstone. The park has more than 1,000 miles of trails, so this is obviously a tiny sampling of the various hiking options.

Before you head out you will probably want to look over your hiking options. Two excellent source books are *Yellowstone Trails,* by Mark Marschall (Yellowstone Association, www.yellowstoneassociation.org), and *Hiking Yellowstone National Park,* by Bill Schneider (Globe Pequot Press, www.falconbooks.com). Get them from park gift shops or visitors centers, which also sell topographic park maps. The best maps are those produced by Trails Illustrated; these feature all of the major trails and show the severity of burn from the 1988 fires—a considerable help when planning hiking trips.

NORTH YELLOWSTONE TRAILS

Sportsman Lake Trail and Electric Peak

The land west of Mammoth is some of the most rugged in Yellowstone, with several peaks topping 10,000 feet. Several trails cut westward across this country, one of the most interesting being the 24-mile-long Sportsman Lake Trail. The route begins at Glen Creek Trailhead five miles south of Mammoth and follows Glen Creek (a good place to see elk in autumn) for four miles before crossing into the Gardner River drainage. Along the way, a short spur trail leads to pretty Cache Lake. Considerably more

challenging is a second side trip, the climb up 10,992-foot **Electric Peak,** the tallest mountain in this corner of Yellowstone. Many folks camp near Electric Peak and spend a day climbing. It's eight miles round-trip and you gain 3,000 feet on the way up, but the trail becomes harder to follow the higher you climb. See a park trail guidebook for details and precautions on this hike. It is possible to day-hike to the top of Electric Peak from the Glen Creek Trailhead, but it's not recommended unless you have a masochistic streak, have done a lot of hiking, and are in great shape.

Beyond the side trail to Electric Peak, Sportsman Lake Trail crosses the Gardner River twice, and there are no bridges. The water can be dangerously deep early in the summer, so this hike is generally done in August or September. After you ford the river, the trail climbs to Electric Divide (watch for bighorn sheep) and then drops steeply to Sportsman Lake and down along pretty Fan Creek to the Fawn Pass Trailhead on U.S. Hwy. 191. Because this is a one-way hike you will need to set up some sort of vehicle shuttle. Another problem is bears. This country overflows with grizzly activity, and a party size of four or more is recommended for travel here. Off-trail travel is prohibited in some areas; see the Park Service for details.

Black Canyon of the Yellowstone

For an early-summer backpacking trip, it's hard to beat this 19-mile trek along the northern edge of Yellowstone. Start at the Hellroaring Trailhead, 3.5 miles west of Tower, and follow the Yellowstone River Trail in a steep descent to the river, 600 feet below. A suspension bridge crosses the river, and from here on you remain on the north side all the way to Gardiner. One ford at Hellroaring Creek can be dangerous before August, but it can be avoided if you hike a mile or so upstream to a stock bridge crossing. After this point, the hike alternates between high ridges overlooking Black Canyon of the Yellowstone and quieter stretches where the trail drops down along the edge of the water. Dramatic Knowles Falls is a highlight. The trail is in good condition, but you may find it hot and dry in midsummer.

Pebble Creek and Bliss Pass Trails

Pebble Creek Trail cuts through a section of Yellowstone that is far away from the geysers and canyons for which the park is famous. The crowds don't come here, but the country is some of the nicest mountain scenery to be found. The trail connects with the Northeast Entrance road at both ends, making access easy. You can start from either end, but if you begin at Warm Creek Picnic Area (1.5 miles west of the entrance station), you get to the high meadows quicker. From the picnic area the trail climbs 1,100 feet in the first 1.5 miles, but beyond this it's all downhill. The best time to hike this trail is in late summer, when the water levels are lower (there are four fords) and the mosquitoes have abated. Hikers are treated to abundant alpine flowers and grand mountain scenery along the way, with the chance to see moose or elk in the meadows.

For a longer alternative hike, follow Pebble Creek Trail 5.5 miles from the picnic area and then turn west onto **Bliss Pass Trail.** The path crosses Pebble Creek (quite deep until late summer) before climbing 1,400 feet over Bliss Pass and then dropping down 2,700 feet to Slough Creek Trail. From here it is an easy walk to Slough Creek Campground. Total distance from the Warm Creek Picnic Area to Slough Creek Campground is 20 miles. The easy Slough Creek Trail is described as a day hike in the Northeast Entrance Road section.

SOUTH YELLOWSTONE TRAILS

Shoshone Lake

The largest lake in the Lower 48 without direct road access, Shoshone Lake is probably the most visited part of Yellowstone's backcountry. Its shoreline is dotted with more than two dozen campsites, but most of these fill on midsummer nights with hikers, canoeists, and kayakers. Because of the lake's popularity, reserve well ahead for a summertime campsite. On-water access is via Lewis Lake and the Lewis River Channel. Anglers come to fish in the channel or lakes; Shoshone Lake has good numbers of brown, lake, and brook trout, all of which were planted here. Hikers access Shoshone Lake primarily from the DeLacy Creek Trailhead on the north side between West Thumb and Old Faithful, or from the east side via Dogshead Trailhead. A 22-mile trail circles Shoshone Lake, although it is away from the shoreline much of the distance. You may see moose or elk and are certain to meet clouds of mosquitoes before August. The finest lake vistas come from the east side, where the trail follows the lakeshore for four miles. On the west end of the lake, hikers will find **Shoshone Geyser Basin,** an area filled with small geysers, beautiful pools, and bubbling mud pots. Most of the lake escaped the 1988 fires, but trails from the east side (via Dogshead Trailhead) traverse burned stands of lodgepole.

Heart Lake

The Heart Lake area is another extremely popular backcountry and day-hiking area, offering easy access, a pretty lake, hot springs, and impressive mountain vistas. **Heart Lake Trail** begins just north of Lewis Lake (six miles south of Grant Village). The trail is fairly easy, climbing slowly through unburned forests for the first five miles and then following Witch Creek down past burned forests to Heart Lake, eight miles from the trailhead. Witch Creek is fed almost entirely by the hot springs and geysers scattered along it.

Near the Heart Lake patrol cabin the trail splits. Continue straight ahead another 26 miles to eventually reach the isolated and challenging Thorofare Trail on the southeast end of Yellowstone Lake; getting there requires fording the Yellowstone River, which may be waist deep even in late summer. For something a bit less remote, turn right and hike one-half mile to the **Mt. Sheridan Trail,** which heads west and climbs 2,800 vertical feet in three miles. Reaching the 10,308-foot summit will certainly leave you winded. A fire lookout at the top provides views across Yellowstone Lake and south to the Tetons.

At the base of Mt. Sheridan and just to the north is a small thermal area that contains **Rustic Geyser** (eruptions to 50 feet, but irregular) and **Columbia Pool,** among other attractions. Be very careful when walking here because of the overhanging rim at the pool edge.

Although many people simply hike to Heart Lake for an overnight trip, one could take many longer hikes out of here, including into the remote Thorofare (described later). A complete loop around the lake is approximately 34 miles round-trip but requires two Snake River fords that are at least to your knees in late July; check with the rangers for flow levels. The Heart Lake area is prime grizzly habitat and is closed until the first of July. Do not take chances in this country!

Bechler River

The southwest portion of Yellowstone is known as Cascade Corner, a reference to its many tall waterfalls; more than half of the park's falls are here. This scenic and wild country escaped the fires of 1988 and is popular with anglers. Primary access is from either the Bechler Ranger Station (pronounced "BECK-ler") or the Cave Falls Trailhead, both of which are well off the beaten path and must be reached via Cave Falls Road from the Idaho side. It's 22 miles in from Ashton, Idaho, the last 10 on a gravel road. As an alternative, **Grassy Lake Road** provides a narrow and rough gravel connection to Cave Falls Road. Grassy Lake Road begins at Flagg Ranch Resort near Yellowstone's South Entrance; see a good map for the exact route.

All hikers must register at the Bechler Ranger Station, even if they are heading out from Cave Falls Trailhead, three miles farther down the road. Cave Falls is a wide but not particularly tall drop along the Falls River. It's named for a cave on the west end of the waterfall. The Forest Service's **Cave Falls Campground** ($10) is open mid-May through August.

A spiderweb of trails cuts across the Bechler country, leading to many waterfalls and past several hot springs. One popular hike goes from Bechler Ranger Station to the Old Faithful area, a distance of 30 miles; its downhill much of the way if you do this in reverse by starting at Old Faithful. From Bechler Ranger Station the trail cuts across expansive Bechler Meadows and then up narrow Bechler Canyon, passing Colonnade, Ouzel, and Iris Falls along the way. Many people stop overnight at Three River Junction to enjoy the hot springs–warmed water. Beyond this

point, the trail punches over the Continental Divide and then runs west of Shoshone Lake to Lone Star Geyser and the trailhead at Kepler Cascades. It's best to hike this route in August or September after the Bechler River drops enough to be more safely forded. This also allows time for the meadows to dry out a bit (watch out for leeches) and for the mosquitoes to quiet to a dull roar. For the long trek between Bechler Ranger Station and Old Faithful you will need to set up some sort of vehicle shuttle, but shorter in-and-out loop trips could be created by reading the various Yellowstone hiking guides and studying topographic maps.

The Thorofare

If any part of Yellowstone deserves the title untamed wilderness, it has to be the Thorofare. Situated along Two Ocean Plateau and cut through by the upper Yellowstone River, this broad expanse of unroaded country reaches from Yellowstone Lake into the Teton Wilderness south of the park. This is *the* most remote country anywhere in the Lower 48; at its heart you'd need to hike 30 miles in any direction to reach a road. Because of the distances involved, many people choose to traverse the Thorofare via horseback. There is considerable grizzly activity in this area, so various restrictions are in place. In addition, some major river crossings are impassable until late summer. Access to the Thorofare is via Heart Lake Trail (described previously), the Thorofare Trail, or through Teton Wilderness within Bridger-Teton National Forest.

The **Thorofare Trail** begins at Nine Mile Trailhead on the East Entrance Road and hugs the shore of Yellowstone Lake for the first 17 miles. This stretch was spared from the fires of 1988 and provides some incredible opportunities to watch sunsets over the lake, particularly from campsites near Park Point. The trail continues along Southeast Arm and then follows the broad Thorofare Valley upstream beside the Yellowstone River (great fishing). There are several difficult creek and river crossings before you reach the Thorofare Ranger Station at mile 32, but this is not even the halfway point! Civilization is another 36 miles away. To get there, the often muddy South Boundary Trail heads west over the Continental Divide, through four difficult creek or river fords, through forests burned in the 1988 fires, and past Snake Hot Springs before finally ending at the South Entrance Station.

Needless to say, trips into the Thorofare are only for those with a lot of stamina and extensive backcountry experience. Shorter variations are possible, of course, but most involve hiking in and out the same way. Check at the Lake Ranger Station for conditions in the Thoro-

fare and study Yellowstone hiking guides before even considering a big trip here. It's spectacular and remote country, but that means you're on your own much of the time.

One way to cut nine miles off your hike into the Thorofare is by a boat ride across Yellowstone Lake. The folks at Bridge Bay Marina, 307/344-5217, can drop you off at a few campsites on the east side, but this is a pricey option. Contact the Park Service's Backcountry Office at 307/344-2160 to find out which campsites are accessible by motorboat. These sites tend to fill up fast, so you'll need to reserve well ahead.

Other Summer Recreation

FISHING

In the early years of the park, fish from Yellowstone Lake were a specialty at the various hotels, and because there was no limit on the take, up to 7,500 pounds of fish were caught each year. After commercial fishing was halted, park policy shifted to planting nonnative species. But by the 1970s, Yellowstone Lake had been devastated by overfishing, and new regulations were needed. Beginning in 1973, bait fishing was banned, Fishing Bridge was closed to anglers, and catch-and-release rules were put into place. Increased fish populations have been a boon for wildlife, especially grizzlies, bald eagles, and osprey. Because of these regulations, Yellowstone National Park has achieved an almost mythical status when it comes to fishing. Each year some 75,000 visitors spend time fishing in the park. The most commonly caught fish in Yellowstone are cutthroat, rainbow, brown, lake, and brook trout, along with mountain whitefish. Montana grayling are found at only a few small lakes within the park, most notably Grebe Lake. All native species in the park—including Montana grayling, cutthroat trout, and mountain whitefish—are now catch-and-release only. Fishing regulations are complex and are described in a booklet available at park visitors centers or on the web at www.nps.gov/yell.

The Yellowstone River is still considered one of the best places in the world to catch cutthroat trout, and the Madison River is a justifiably famous fly-fishing river with a wide range of conditions. Yellowstone Lake is where the lure anglers go to catch cutthroats and lake trout. Beginners may have luck in the Gallatin River, but they're less likely to do well in the Firehole River, where the fish are smart and wary. Peaceful Slough Creek in the northeast corner of Yellowstone is filled with fat rainbows and cutthroats, attracting fly-fishers from around the globe.

Trouble in Paradise

The last decade was not at all kind to aquatic ecosystems in Yellowstone as a series of diseases and nonnative threats appeared. Perhaps the greatest threat comes from lake trout (Mackinaw), a species that had been illegally planted either accidentally or intentionally in the 1980s or earlier. Lake trout were first discovered in Yellowstone Lake in 1994, and studies have since revealed that many thousands of them now inhabit the lake. A highly aggressive and long-lived species, lake trout feed on and compete with the prized native cutthroat, threatening to devastate the population. (The average lake trout eats 80–90 cutthroat trout per year in Yellowstone.) Cutthroat spawn in the shallow waters of the lake's tributary streams, where they are caught by grizzly bears, bald eagles, and other animals. Lake trout spawn in deeper waters that are inaccessible to predators, so fewer cutthroat and more lake trout could have an impact on grizzlies and eagles. Eradication of the lake trout is virtually impossible, but the Park Service has used gill nets to catch thousands of them. There are no size or possession limits on lake trout caught in Yellowstone Lake or Heart Lake, but any lake trout you catch in these lakes must be kept and shown to rangers to help determine the population size.

Another problem is threatening trout, especially rainbow trout, throughout the Rockies. **Whirling disease,** a devastating parasite-caused disease, has seriously hurt populations of rainbow trout in parts of the Madison River outside Yellowstone. The disease was discovered in Yellowstone Lake cutthroats in 1998, and there are fears that it could spread to other lakes and rivers in the park. It is spread in part when mud or water is brought in from contaminated areas on waders, boats, and boots. Be sure to clean up thoroughly with a bleach solution before entering or leaving an area. Get details on whirling disease at www.whirlingdisease.org.

As if the other problems weren't enough, **New Zealand mud snails** were discovered in park waters in 1995. These miniscule snails (natives of New Zealand) are now in the Firehole, Gibbon, Madison, and Snake Rivers, where they can form dense colonies on aquatic plants and streambed rocks, crowding out native aquatic insects that are a food source for fish.

Fishing Regulations

In most parts of Yellowstone, the fishing season extends from Memorial Day weekend to the first Sunday of November, but check the regulations for specifics. Hayden Valley and some other areas are entirely closed to fishing, and only artificial lures and flies are allowed in the park. Lead cannot be used. All native species in the park—Montana grayling, cutthroat trout, and mountain whitefish—are catch-and-release only. Barbless hooks are preferable for catch-and-release fishing because they cause less damage and are easier to remove. Some rivers, including the Madison River, the Firehole River,

and the Gibbon River (downstream from Gibbon Falls) are open only to fly-fishing.

Anglers don't need a state fishing license but must obtain a special Yellowstone National Park permit, available from visitors centers, ranger stations, and Yellowstone General Stores, plus fishing shops in surrounding towns. The adult **fishing fee** is $10 for a 10-day permit or $20 for a season permit. Kids ages 12–15 get permits for free, and younger children do not need a permit. Park visitors centers and ranger stations have copies of current fishing regulations.

BOATING

Bridge Bay Marina runs hour-long scenic **boat tours** of Yellowstone Lake ($9.25 adults, $5 ages 2–11) several times a day in the summer, providing a fine introduction to the area. Also available at the marina are **guided fishing trips** ($55–72 an hour for up to six people) and **boat rentals** ($7.50 per hour for a 16-foot rowboat; $30 per hour for a 18-foot motorboat with a 40-horsepower outboard).

The best Yellowstone Lake fishing is from boats rather than from the shoreline. If you're bringing your own boat or canoe to Yellowstone, pick up a park boat permit at the Lake Ranger Station or Grant Village Visitor Center. Boat slips are available at Bridge Bay Marina for $12–18 per night. All streams are closed to watercraft, with the exception of the Lewis River Channel between Shoshone and Lewis Lakes. Motorboats are allowed only on Lewis Lake and parts of Yellowstone Lake.

Sea Kayaking

Several companies offer guided sea kayak trips in the park. **Snake River Kayak & Canoe School,** 307/733-9999 or 800/529-2501, www.snakeriverkayak.com, leads a variety of trips on Yellowstone Lake, starting with three-hour sunset tours ($75 per person) and half-day paddles in the West Thumb area ($165 per person), all the way up to eight-day paddling trips that leave the crowds behind as you explore the lake; these cost $1,095 per person, all-inclusive. They also guide sea kayaking tours of Lewis and Shoshone Lakes, and have a full range of kayaking classes (taught in Jackson and Grand Teton National Park).

Jackson Hole Kayak School, 307/733-2471 or 800/733-2471, www.jhkayakschool.com, has day tours of Yellowstone Lake or Lewis Lake for $150 per person. They also offer three-day tours of Yellowstone Lake for $680 per person, and three-day tours of Lewis and Shoshone Lakes for $600 per person. The overnight trip prices include transportation from Jackson, kayaking and camping gear, supplies, and all meals.

O.A.R.S., 209/736-4677 or 800/346-6277, www.oars.com, offers half-day sea kayak trips from Grant Village for $60 adults or $40 kids. In addition, they guide multiday trips to the quiet south and southeast arms of Lake Yellowstone. Adult rates are $525 for three days or $637 for four days. Tents and sleeping bags are available for rent, or bring your own.

BICYCLING

Cycling provides a unique way to see Yellowstone up close. Unfortunately, park roads tend to be narrow shoulders and traffic is heavy, making for dangerous conditions. These problems are exacerbated early in the year by high snowbanks, so bikes are not allowed on certain roads. Call 307/344-7381 for current road conditions.

If you're planning a cycling trip through Yellowstone, be sure to wear a helmet and high-visibility clothing. A bike mirror also helps. If you want to avoid some of the hassles and don't mind spring conditions, visit the park between late March and the third Friday in April, when motorized vehicles are usually prohibited from entering the park (except for park administrative vehicles). During this period, cyclists are allowed to ride only on the stretch between West Entrance and Mammoth Hot Springs; other roads are closed to cycling because they're being plowed. Fall is also a good time to ride because traffic is much lighter than in summer. The best times to ride in summer are in the morning before traffic thickens or late in the afternoon before the light begins to fade and you become less visible to motorists.

Where to Ride

The best main park roads to ride (less traffic or better visibility and shoulders) are the following sections: Mammoth to Tower, Tower to Cooke City, Canyon to Lake, and Lake to Grant Village. Bikes are not allowed on backcountry trails or boardwalks inside Yellowstone. Several relatively short but fun mountain-bike rides are available around the park, including the paved trail from Old Faithful to Morning Glory Pool (two miles), the partly paved trail to Lone Star Geyser in the Old Faithful area (two miles), Fountain Flat Drive (six miles) to the vicinity of Midway Geyser Basin, the old Chittenden Road up Mt. Washburn (three miles each way, but gaining 1,400 feet on the way up), Bunsen Peak Road near Mammoth (six miles and steep in places), the Old Gardiner Road from Mammoth to Gardiner (five miles), and Blacktail Plateau Drive (seven miles) east of Mammoth. Of these routes, cars are allowed only on the Old Gardiner Road and Blacktail Plateau Drive, but traffic is light on these two.

Bike Rentals and Tours

Unfortunately, there are no bike rentals inside Yellowstone or Gardiner, although they are available in the surrounding towns of West Yellowstone, Jackson, and Cody. **Backroads,** 800/462-2848, www.backroads.com, has six-day multisport trips into Yellowstone and Grand Teton that include biking, hiking, rafting, and kayaking. These are offered as either camping trips ($1,200 per person including meals) or trips where you stay at local inns ($2,200 per person including meals). Contact the Park Service for a list of other permitted bicycle-tour operators.

TRAIL RIDES

Summertime **horseback rides** are available from the corrals at Mammoth Hot Springs, Canyon Village, and Roosevelt Lodge. These cost $25 for one hour or $37 for a two-hour ride. Kids must be at least eight years old and 48 inches tall, and there is a 250-pound weight limit, much to the relief of the horses. Roosevelt also has **stagecoach rides** ($7 adults, $6 ages 2–11) several times a

YELLOWSTONE

day in the summer. In addition, **Old West dinner cookouts** at Roosevelt combine a horseback or wagon ride with a filling steak dinner.

For details on trail rides, contact Xanterra Parks & Resorts, 307/344-7311, www.travelyellowstone.com. Several outfitters provide backcountry pack trips inside Yellowstone; get a list from Park Service visitors centers or at 307/344-7381, www.nps.gov/yell.

HOT SPRINGS

Many people are disappointed to discover that there are no places in Yellowstone where you can soak in the hot springs. Not only is it illegal, but it can also be dangerous because temperatures often approach boiling and bathers can cause severe damage to these surprisingly fragile natural wonders. Legal bathing pools are found in cold-water streams that have hot springs feeding into them. You're not allowed to enter the source pool or stream itself. Families often stop for a swim in the Firehole River along Firehole Canyon Drive near Madison. The Park Service doesn't encourage this, and there are no lifeguards, so parents need to watch children closely.

Thirty miles north of Yellowstone in the little burg of Pray, Montana, is **Chico Hot Springs.** If you're staying in the Mammoth Hot Springs area of Yellowstone, a side trip to Chico may be worthwhile. The large outdoor pool is a great place to relax, the gourmet restaurant serves some of the best dinners anywhere around, and the classic old hotel is a favorite. Details at 406/333-4933 or 800/468-9232, www.chicohotsprings.com.

Winter in Yellowstone

Winter transforms Yellowstone into an extraordinarily beautiful place where the fires and brimstone of hell meet the bitter cold and snow of winter. The snow often averages four feet in depth but can exceed 10 feet on mountain passes. The snow is usually quite dry, although late in the season conditions deteriorate as temperatures rise. Early in the winter or after major storms, backcountry skiing can be difficult because of the deep powder. Temperatures are generally in the 10–25°F range during the day, while nights frequently dip below zero. (The record is –66°F, recorded on February 9, 1933.) Winds can make these temperatures feel even colder, so visitors should come prepared for extreme conditions.

The thermal basins are a real wintertime treat. Hot springs that are simply colorful pools in summer send up billows of steam in the winter, coating nearby trees with thick layers of ice and turning them into "ghost trees." The geysers put on astounding displays as boiling water meets frigid air; steam from Old Faithful can tower 1,000 feet into the air! Bison and elk gather around the hot springs, soaking up the heat and searching for dried grasses, and bald eagles are often seen flying over the heated waters of Firehole River. The bison are perhaps the most interesting to watch as they swing their enormous heads from side to side to shovel snow off the grass. Grand Canyon of the Yellowstone is another place transformed by the snow and cold. Although the water still flows, the falls are surrounded by tall cones of ice, and the canyon walls lie under deep snow. A good resource on winter access to Yellowstone is *Yellowstone Winter Guide* by Jeff Henry (www.roberts-rinehart.com).

HISTORICAL WINTER USE

During Yellowstone's first 75 years as a park, winter visitation was almost unknown. The only people in the park were caretakers who spent months at a time with no contact with the world outside. This began to change in 1949, when snow-plane tours were first offered from the West Entrance. The planes skimmed over the surface and could only hold two people—the driver and a passenger—so visitation barely topped 30 people that winter. In 1955, snowcoaches were permitted to come into Yellowstone, and more than 500 people visited, although few stayed overnight.

Snowmobiling Changes Everything

The first snowmobilers arrived in 1963, when the machines were still a novelty. As snowmobiling became increasingly more popular, communities around Yellowstone benefited economically and began promoting the park as a winter wonderland. In the winter of 1971–1972 the Park Service began encouraging snowmobile use by grooming the roads and opening Old Faithful Snow Lodge (it has since been replaced by a much nicer building of the same name). By the end of that winter, more than 25,000 people had visited. Since then, winter use has rocketed; today, more than 140,000 people visit Yellowstone each winter, and the park admits more snowmobiles than all other national parks combined. Prior to 2003, as many as 1,600 snowmobiles flooded into Yellowstone on busy days, spewing choking blue smoke that created localized pollution and sometimes sickened park employees working at entrance stations. While these numbers pale in comparison to summer visitation, environmentalists worry that snowmobilers and skiers could adversely affect the park's wildlife at a time when the animals are already under great stress.

In the heavy snow winter of 1996–1997 large numbers of bison moved out of Yellowstone, some of them along the groomed snowmobile road out the west side of the park. Nearly 1,100 bison were killed that year as part of Montana's effort to protect cattle from brucellosis. The slaughter precipitated a lawsuit by the Fund for Animals that forced the Park Service to rethink its winter-use policies. To address the effects of snowmobiles and other uses, the Park Service under President Clinton attempted to ban snowmobiles from the park. Industry groups and others successfully fought the closure, with support from the snowmobile-friendly Bush administration. New rules are now in place, allowing a maximum of 1,100 snowmobiles daily, and mandating that cleaner and quieter machines with four-stroke engines be used for rentals. (Private owners of snowmobiles won't be required to have four-stroke machines until 2004–2005.) The regulations also require that 80 percent of snowmobilers must be led by commercial guides.

ROADS

Most of Yellowstone's roads officially close to cars on the Monday after the first Sunday in November and remain shut down all over except for the 56 miles between Mammoth and Cooke City. Roads don't open for cars again until sometime between mid-May and early June. The roads are groomed for snowmobiles and snowcoaches from mid-December to mid-March. The rest of the winter you'll only find skiers and park personnel on the roads. During winter, the most popular (and crowded) times to visit Yellowstone are around Christmas and New Year's and over the Presidents' Day weekend in February. If you plan to arrive at these times, make lodging reservations six months to a year in advance. The rest of the winter, you should probably reserve at least three months ahead.

ACCOMMODATIONS

During winter only two places offer lodging inside the park. **Mammoth Hot Springs Hotel,** on the north end of the park, is the only accommodation accessible by road and has ski and snowshoe trails nearby, while the recently built **Old Faithful Snow Lodge and Cabins** puts you close to the geysers and many miles of ski trails. Each has a restaurant, lounge, gift shop, and rentals of skis and snowshoes. Mammoth has a couple of advantages over Old Faithful: far fewer snowmobiles so it's much quieter, and road access to the Lamar Valley where wolves, bison, and elk are major attractions. You might even see a pack of wolves take down an elk. Lodging prices and seasons are described in Yellowstone Accommodations.

A wide variety of package trips are offered in winter, from two-night specials to a version that encompasses three nights at Old Faithful, three nights at Mammoth, breakfasts and lunches, skis and snowshoes, hot tub use, ice skating, and snowcoach tours. Mammoth also offers Sunday breakfast buffets and special dinners, along with ice skate and hourly hot tub rentals. Get details on winter lodging options in the park from Xanterra Parks & Resorts, 307/344-7311, www.travelyellowstone.com.

Just south of Yellowstone in the Rockefeller Parkway is **Flagg Ranch Resort,** 307/543-2861 or 800/443-2311, www.flaggranch.com, where you'll find modern cabins that are open in winter. See the Grand Teton National Park chapter for specifics on Flagg Ranch. It's another 55 miles from Flagg Ranch to Jackson, a wintertime base for many Yellowstone visitors. On the east side of Yellowstone, lodging is available just outside the park at Pahaska Teepee and other lodges in the Wapiti Valley area; see the Bighorn Basin chapter for details. Other accommodations (described in the Yellowstone Gateway Town sections) can be found just outside the park in the towns of West Yellowstone, Gardiner, Cooke City, and Silver Gate.

The only wintertime camping place is Mammoth Campground, where temperatures are milder and the snow lighter.

SERVICES

Only the Mammoth and Old Faithful visitors centers are open during winter. Free ranger-led activities include evening programs at Mammoth and Old Faithful. Check the winter edition of *Yellowstone Today* for details, or find it on the web at www.nps.gov/yell.

Xanterra Parks & Resorts, 307/344-7311, www.travelyellowstone.com, offers a variety of guided ski and snowmobile tours and provides wildlife bus or van tours; call for details. In addition, the Yellowstone Association Institute, 307/344-2294, www.yellowstoneassociation.org, has outstanding winter classes.

The Mammoth Clinic, 307/344-7965, is open weekdays (except Wednesday afternoons) in the winter for medical emergencies.

Supplies and Warming Huts

The Yellowstone General Store at Mammoth is open for groceries and supplies year-round, but only meals and gas are available at Old Faithful. Warming huts are located at Old Faithful, Madison Junction, Canyon, West Thumb, Fishing Bridge, and Indian Creek (south of Mammoth Hot Springs). All contain restrooms and snack machines (except Indian Creek and West Thumb), and all are open 24 hours (except for Old Faithful, where other facilities are available). The huts at Madison and Canyon also have snack bars selling hot chili or soup. Park rangers are often at the warming huts during the middle of the day.

SNOWCOACHES

The easiest and most enjoyable way to get into Yellowstone in the winter is on the ungainly snowcoaches—machines that look like something the Norwegian Army might have used during World War II. Most were actually built by a Canadian company, Bombidier. They can be noisy, and the windows fog up (hence the spray bottles of antifreeze). But despite their ancient condition and spartan interiors, these beasts still work well and can carry 10 passengers, gear (two suitcases per person), and skis. You will also see (or ride in) several other oversnow vehicles, including vans on tracks.

Snowcoach Tours

A variety of snowcoach tours are provided by Xanterra Parks & Resorts, 307/344-7311, www.travelyellowstone.com. All snowcoach tours and transportation are half-price for kids ages 2–11 and free for toddlers. Adult per-person rates to Old Faithful are $102 round-trip from Flagg Ranch (where the plowing ends just south of Yellowstone), $92 round-trip from West Yellowstone, and $97 round-trip from Mammoth. They also provide tours most days from Mammoth to Canyon for $92 round-trip, and Old Faithful to Canyon for $97 round-trip.

Shorter snowcoach tours depart two or three times a week from Old Faithful for the Firehole River/Fountain Flats area (three hours; $24 round-trip) and West Thumb Geyser Basin (three hours; $24). Three-hour winter wildlife bus tours to the Lamar Valley ($21) depart from Mammoth on Wednesdays, providing a good opportunity to see wolves. Also available from Mammoth is a daybreak bus tour (3.5 hours; $21 with a continental breakfast). Children under 12 are half-price, and kids under two are free on all snowcoach trips. See following description for combination snowcoach and cross-country skiing trips. For any of these trips, be sure to make reservations well in advance.

During the winter, Alltrans/Gray Line, 307/733-4325 or 800/443-6133, www.jacksonholealltrans.com, has daily bus runs from Jackson to Flagg Ranch for $40 one-way, arriving in time to meet the snowcoach departures for Yellowstone. Reservations are required.

Yellowstone Alpen Guides, 406/646-9591 or 800/858-3502, www.yellowstoneguides.com, leads snowcoach tours from West Yellowstone. All-day trips are $97 ($89 seniors, $77 kids) to Grand Canyon of the Yellowstone, or $87 ($79 seniors, $66 kids under 12) to the Old Faithful area. Guests on the latter run have an option of getting dropped at Biscuit Basin, where they can ski to Old Faithful and meet the rest of the group for the return trip. Special snowcoach-and-guided-ski tours are $109 per person. Also available is a three-night package trip that includes two nights in West Yellowstone, a night at Old Faithful Snow Lodge, and two days of wildlife snowcoach tours for $395 per person.

Buffalo Bus Touring Co., 406/646-9564 or 800/426-7669, www.yellowstonevacations.com, also operates snowcoach vans from West Yellowstone, with tours to Old Faithful for $84 adults or $64 kids.

For a truly unique experience, book a trip with another West Yellowstone–based company, **Yellowstone Expeditions,** 406/646-9333 or 800/728-9333, www.yellowstoneexpeditions.com. They run converted vans jacked up above tracks and skis and have a remote base camp near Canyon that is perfect for those who want to really explore Yellowstone in winter. Guests stay in eight heated tent cabins, with two yurts providing a central kitchen and dining/social area. These overnight trips start at $1,400 for two people for three nights and four days, up to $2,280 for two people for seven nights and eight days. The price includes lodging, food, bedding, round-trip transportation from West Yellowstone to the base camp near Canyon, and backcountry ski guides. Ski and snowshoe rentals are extra. Days are spent skiing or snowshoeing in the Canyon area or along trails around Hayden Valley, Norris, or Mt. Washburn. The camp sauna is perfect after a long day in the backcountry. This is the only overnight accommodation at the Canyon area during the winter. Recommended.

SKIING AND SNOWSHOEING

Cross-country skis and snowshoes provide the finest ways to see Yellowstone in the winter. Rent them from Old Faithful Snow Lodge or Mammoth Hot Springs Hotel. Both places also provide lessons and guided tours for groups or individuals. The towns surrounding Yellowstone also have shops that rent skis and snowshoes. The Old Faithful area is the center for skiing within Yellowstone, with trails circling the Upper Geyser Basin and leading to nearby sights. You'll find similar ski trails (marked but not groomed) in the Tower Fall, Canyon, Northeast, and Mammoth areas. Get free ski-trail maps at the visitors centers. Old Faithful Snow Lodge is open in winter, providing an excellent base for day trips into nearby areas or for a snowcoach tour of the park.

Skiers and snowshoers sometimes assume that they can't possibly cause problems for Yellowstone's wildlife, but studies show that elk and bison often move away from skiers, which forces the animals to expend energy they need to survive through the bitterly cold winters. It's best to stay on the trails and to keep from skiing into areas where elk or bison may be disturbed by your presence. For more on skiing and winter visitation in the park, see Jeff Henry's *Yellowstone Winter Guide* (www.robertsrinehart.com), or *Winter Tales and Trails: Skiing, Snowshoeing and Snowboarding in Idaho, the*

Grand Tetons and Yellowstone National Park by Ron Watters (Great Rift Press).

Shuttles and Tours

Xanterra Parks & Resorts, 307/344-7311, www.travelyellowstone.com, operates **skier shuttles** ($12.50 round-trip) from Mammoth eastward by van to Blacktail Plateau and Tower Junction, or southward by snowcoach to Golden Gate and Indian Creek. From these last two many folks choose to ski back to Mammoth because it's mostly downhill. A similar snowcoach shuttle is available from Old Faithful to Fairy Falls Trailhead or the Continental Divide area for $11. In these last two trips you ski back to the Snow Lodge on your own; the Continental Divide run is eight miles long and primarily downhill.

Skiers will also appreciate the van service offered between Mammoth and Cooke City ($59 round-trip), where you're given all day to ski into the beautiful Absaroka Mountains. In addition, Xanterra has all-day Grand Canyon snowcoach-and-guided-ski tours ($99 round-trip) twice a week from Old Faithful and once weekly from Mammoth. **Afternoon ski-daddles** are guided five-hour ski tours from Old Faithful to Fairy Falls or DeLacey Creek. They're offered twice a week and cost $35.

Guided snowshoe tours ($27 with snowshoes provided) are offered from Old Faithful twice weekly and Mammoth once a week. They last three hours and are a great way to explore the country. Besides these concessioner-run tours, park naturalists sometimes lead ski trips from Old Faithful to nearby sights. Stop by the visitors center for details.

Safety on Skis

Yellowstone's roads are heavily traveled by snowmobiles and snowcoaches, making for all sorts of potential conflicts. Be sure to keep to the right while skiing. Most trails are identified by orange metal markers on the trees. If you're planning a backcountry trip, pick up a use permit from one of the ranger stations. A thorough understanding of winter camping and survival is imperative before you head out on

any overnight trip, and avalanche safety classes are a wise investment of your time.

Before heading into backcountry areas, get avalanche-safety information from the **Avalanche Advisory Hotline** in Bozeman, 406/587-6981, www.gomontana.com/avalanche. The recording does not cover the entire park, but it does include the Washburn Range and areas near Cooke City and West Yellowstone. It's updated daily in the winter.

SNOWMOBILES

Nearly three-quarters of all winter visitors to Yellowstone enter the park on snowmobiles, and it isn't uncommon to meet long lines of machines ripping down the roads at any time of the day, disrupting Yellowstone's pristine winter silence. Despite the fact that the five national forests surrounding Yellowstone have many hundreds of miles of groomed trails and thousands of square miles of terrain open to the machines, Yellowstone's 180 miles of roads have become the focus of this mechanized winter onslaught.

Practicalities

If you really *must* come into Yellowstone by snowmobile, please show a few courtesies and precautions. In particular, stay on the roads and stay well away from the bison and elk commonly found along or on the roads. This is a highly stressful time of the year for them already, without being harassed by a steady stream of machines. If they stop in the middle of the road, wait for them to move, don't try to make them move. Also, if skiers are on the road, slow down and give them a wide berth as you pass. The speed limit (45 mph) is enforced, and one of the most bizarre Yellowstone sights is a park ranger waiting in a speed trap with his radar gun, ready to catch speeding sleds. Park regulations now require that all rental snowmobiles must be the cleaner and quieter four-stroke machines, but private owners have until the winter of 2004–2005 to get four-stroke machines. The new regulations also require that 80 percent of snowmobilers must be led by commercial guides.

Snowmobiles are available for rent from all

four sides of the park, with most snowmobilers coming in from West Yellowstone, where prices are usually a bit lower and access is quicker. Expect to pay $100–150 per day, including clothing and helmet, for a machine or $140–190 for a guided tour. The machines can also be rented at Mammoth and Old Faithful inside the park.

You'll need a valid driver's license to drive snowmobiles into Yellowstone. Contact chamber of commerce offices in West Yellowstone, Jackson, or Cody for a listing of snowmobile rental companies. You can purchase gas inside the park at Mammoth Hot Springs, Canyon, Fishing Bridge, and Old Faithful.

Camping

Tent camping in Yellowstone's early days left a bit to be desired. One 1884 tourist noted that during the height of summer, "the principle upon which the beds are populated is said to be the addition of visitors so long as they may arrive, or until the occupants 'go for their guns.' The plan is simple, and relieves the authorities of responsibility." It's still crowded in the park, but at least guns are prohibited today!

Camping is available at a dozen sites scattered along the Yellowstone road network; see the "Yellowstone National Park Campgrounds" chart for specifics. Most of these campsites are open from at least Memorial Day to mid-September, but only Mammoth Campground remains open throughout the year. Generators are allowed in more than half of the campgrounds but can only be used between 8 A.M. and 8 P.M. Roadside or parking-lot camping is prohibited, and rangers vigorously enforce this rule.

Reservations are available—and advised—for five concessioner-managed campgrounds: Bridge Bay Campground, Canyon Campground, Grant Village Campground, Madison Campground, and Fishing Bridge RV Park. Contact Xanterra Parks & Resorts for reservations (no extra charge) at 307/344-7311, www.travelyellowstone.com. The other seven

YELLOWSTONE NATIONAL PARK CAMPGROUNDS

Bridge Bay Campground; $15; fills early, flush toilets, dump station, generators permitted, open late May to mid-Sept.; reservations at 307/344-7311, www.travelyellowstone.com

Canyon Campground; $15; fills early, laundry facilities, showers for $3 per person, flush toilets, dump station, generators permitted, open early June to early Sept.; reservations at 307/344-7311, www.travelyellowstone.com

Fishing Bridge RV Park; $27 fills early, hard-sided RVs only, full hookups, laundry facilities, showers $3 per person, flush toilets, sewer system, generators permitted, open mid-May through Sept.; reservations at 307/344-7311, www.travelyellowstone.com

Grant Village Campground; $15; fills early, showers nearby for $3 per person, flush toilets, dump station, generators permitted, open late June–Sept., reservations at 307/344-7311, www.travelyellowstone.com

Indian Creek Campground; $10; vault toilets, open early June to mid-Sept.

Lewis Lake Campground; $10; vault toilets, fills early, open late June to early Nov.

Madison Campground; $15; fills early; flush toilets, dump station, generators permitted, open May to late Oct.; reservations at 307/344-7311, www.travelyellowstone.com

Mammoth Campground; $12; near a residential area and along the park road, flush toilets, generators permitted, open year-round

Norris Campground; $12; fills early, flush toilets, generators permitted, open early May–Sept.

Pebble Creek Campground; $10; vault toilets, open June–Sept.

Slough Creek Campground; $10; vault toilets, open late May–Oct.

Tower Fall Campground; $10; fills early, vault toilets, open mid-May through Sept.

(Park Service-managed) campgrounds inside Yellowstone are available on a first-come, first-camped basis with no reservations. You can pay with cash, check, or credit card.

During July and August, virtually all campsites in Yellowstone fill *before noon,* so get there early or reserve a space in advance! The busiest weekends are—not surprisingly—around Fourth of July and Labor Day, but Yellowstone's most popular campgrounds fill up even in late fall and early summer. Call the Park Service at 307/344-2114 for a recording noting which campgrounds are currently full.

OTHER CAMPING OPTIONS

When everything else is packed, folks head to campgrounds on surrounding Forest Service and Grand Teton National Park lands or to private campgrounds and lodging in the gateway towns. All are described elsewhere in this book. The farther you get from Yellowstone, the more likely you are to find space. If you reach Nebraska, you should have no trouble at all. Campers can take showers ($3 per person) at Old Faithful Lodge, Grant Village, Fishing Bridge RV Park, and Canyon Village Campground.

Hotels, Lodges, and Cabins

Yellowstone accommodations range from extremely basic cabins with four thin walls starting at $40, up to luxury suites that will set you back $400. Following a fine old Park Service tradition, the rooms do not have TVs, and most lack phones. What they do offer is the chance to relax in comfortable accommodations and explore the magical world outside. Most are open early June to mid-September, with additional winter lodging at Mammoth Hot Springs Hotel and the Old Faithful Snow Lodge. Several hundred more motels and other places to stay operate outside park boundaries in the towns of Jackson, Cody, West Yellowstone, Gardiner, and Cooke City.

Xanterra Parks & Resorts is Yellowstone's lodging concessioner. For reservations, call 307/344-7311, or visit them online at www.travelyellowstone.com. **Make Yellowstone lodging reservations six months ahead** for the park's prime hotels, or you may find that the only rooms available are in Grant Village, the laughing stock of park lodges. Those traveling with small children should also request cribs when making reservations. Special wheelchair-accessible (ADA-compliant) rooms are available at most of the park's cabins and hotels. (As an aside, several web-based companies purport to make reservations for hotels and lodges inside Yellowstone, but all of these charge a service fee. Save yourself money and hassles by just going direct to Xanterra.)

At the turn of the 20th century, most visitors to Yellowstone stayed in park hotels rather than roughing it on the ground. Three of these wonderful old lodging places remain: Old Faithful Inn, Lake Yellowstone Hotel, and Mammoth Hot Springs Hotel. Standard motel rooms can be found at Grant Village. In addition, three nicer places opened in the 1990s: the Old Faithful Snow Lodge and two small lodges at Canyon Village. All told, more than 2,200 rooms and cabins provide overnight accommodations in Yellowstone.

Not all lodging options inside the park are nearly as pleasant, however. Hundreds of simple boxes are clustered in the Lake, Mammoth, Old Faithful, and Roosevelt areas. Most of these cabins offer a roof over your head, simple furnishings, and communal showers, but the more expensive cabins are considerably nicer, and two of them even include private hot tubs. Fortunately, prices are fairly reasonable for all of the cabins.

Lodging rates are listed for two people; children under age 12 stay free. Add $10 per person for additional older kids or adults in the hotel rooms or cabins. Prices may be lower in May when snow still covers much of the park. Also available are a variety of winter and summer package deals that include lodging, tours, hikes, and more. Especially noteworthy are the two- to five-day **Lodging and Learning** packages that combine tours, educational activities, and hikes led by naturalist-guides from the Yellowstone Association Institute, with accommodations in park hotels, plus breakfasts and lunches. Get details at 307/344-2294, www.yellowstoneassociation.org.

Rates listed are without tax, which is 6 percent on the south half of the park (inside Teton County—including Old Faithful, Grant Village, and Lake Village) and 8 percent on the north half (inside Park County—including Roosevelt, Mammoth Hot Springs, and Canyon Village).

CANYON VILLAGE

The centrally located **Canyon Lodge** is just one-half mile from Grand Canyon of the Yellowstone, one of the park's premier attractions. The main lodge is part of a late-1950s complex of ugly structures built around a large parking lot. The area has all the charm of an aging shopping mall from an era when bigger meant better. The lodge itself covers the space of a football field and houses a dining room, cafeteria, lounge, and snack shop, but no guest rooms.

Cabins

Behind the lodge in the trees (at least the setting is peaceful), the road circles past three sprawling clusters of cabins, all with private baths. You'll find 540 cabins here. The most basic "pioneer" units start at $56 d and aren't much to look at outside but are actually fairly roomy and comfortable inside. Two newer types of cabins are available at Canyon: the "frontier" units for $79 d and the "western" cabins for $112 d.

Lodges

Providing far better accommodations are two 1990s additions: **Dunraven Lodge** and **Cascade Lodge.** Rooms at both of these attractive log- and rock-trimmed structures are furnished with rustic lodgepole pieces and have two double beds and private baths. Rooms in the lodges cost $123 d. The cabins and lodges at Canyon are open June to mid-September.

GRANT VILLAGE

The southernmost lodging in Yellowstone, Grant Village offers accommodations in condo-type units from the 1980s, with exceptional parking-lot views from the rooms. These buildings would be completely out of place in *any* national park, especially Yellowstone. Six hideously ugly lodge buildings contain proletarian motel-type units for $90 s or d, and slightly nicer rooms for $101 s or d. All of these have two double beds and private baths, and several wheelchair-accessible rooms are available. A park visitors center and campground are in the area, along with a variety of concessioner facilities, including a restaurant, waterside café, general store, lounge, snack shop, and gift shop. Grant Village is open from late May–September and has 300 units.

LAKE VILLAGE

The Lake Village area has a full range of lodging options for travelers.

Lake Yellowstone Hotel

This fascinating Southern Colonial-style building delivers a magnificent view across Yellowstone Lake. Begun in 1889, the building expanded and changed over the decades to yield its current configuration of 158 guest rooms. The hotel has been lovingly restored and exudes a grandeur and charm rarely found today. It's the sort of place where Fred Astaire and Ginger Rogers would feel comfortable dancing—if they were still alive.

The Lake's inviting hotel rooms all contain updated furnishings, private baths, and in-room phones. Standard units cost $157 d on the backside or $167 d facing the lake, and a delightfully spacious two-bedroom suite is the most elaborate (and most expensive) accommodation in the park at $392 for four people. For the best vistas, ask for a third-floor room on the lake side when making your reservations.

Downstairs is a good restaurant (reservations required for dinner), along with a fast-food eatery; the cafeteria at Lake Lodge is only a short walk away. The real treat at Lake Yellowstone Hotel is the **Sun Room,** where rows of windows front the lake. The room's ambience is further enhanced by period wicker furnishings and evening chamber music or classical piano. It's a great place to sip a martini or write a postcard. The hotel is open mid-May to early October.

Annex and Cabins

Out back is the **Lake Yellowstone Hotel Annex,** where the recently refurbished rooms cost $107 d. No view, but each room has two double beds, phones, a bath, and pleasant furnishings.

Also behind Lake Yellowstone Hotel are more than a hundred rather dingy old boxes from the 1950s, each with two double beds. These have been jammed together in row after identical row to create the **Lake Yellowstone Hotel Cabins.** Fortunately, they're fairly reasonable ($83 d), and cabin guests can pretend they're traveling on a more ample budget by spending time in the hotel dining room and the Sun Room. Lake Yellowstone Hotel Cabins all contain two double beds and private baths, and they're open mid-May to early October.

Lake Lodge Cabins

A short distance east of Lake Yellowstone Hotel is **Lake Lodge.** Built in the 1920s, this archetypal log building has a gracious lobby containing two stone fireplaces, rustic furnishings, an open ceiling where the supporting log trusses and beams are visible, and a delightful front porch. One end of the building houses a large and reasonably priced cafeteria with picture windows framing Lake Yellowstone, and the other end contains a recreation hall for employees. Lodging options at Lake Lodge are not nearly as gracious, consisting of plain-vanilla "pioneer" cabins from the 1920s and '30s, each with a double bed and private bath for $51 d, and a bit more comfortable "western" cabins built in the 1950s and '60s that include two double beds and private baths with showers for $112 d. The 186 cabins at Lake Lodge are open mid-June to late September. Guests here often walk over to the nearby Lake Yellowstone Hotel for fine dining and the chance to relax in the Sun Room.

MAMMOTH HOT SPRINGS

The rambling **Mammoth Hot Springs Hotel** sits in the northwest corner of Yellowstone near park headquarters in the settlement of Mammoth. Built in 1937 (one wing was constructed in 1911 and the original hotel was built even earlier), the hotel has 222 rooms in a variety of configurations. Elk are a common sight on the grounds, and in the fall the bulls' bugling may wake you in the morning. There's live piano music downstairs in the map room most summer evenings as a counterpoint to the elk songs. (The room is named for a distinctive map of the United States crafted from 16 types of wood; it's on the northern wall.) Also just off the lobby is a gift shop. Just steps away are Park Service headquarters, the fine Albright Visitor Center and other historical buildings, along with places to eat and buy groceries, gas, and trinkets.

Hotel rooms are comfortable but modest at Mammoth. Several rooms on each floor provide low-cost accommodations ($65 d) with communal baths down the hall, but most have two beds and private baths ($90 d); ask for a corner room with windows if available. The hotel also houses two luxury suites ($261 d). The hotel is open early May to early October and late December to early March. Rates are the same in summer and winter, but early-season discounts are available. In the winter, "getaway packages" are a better bet, including one that provides two nights' lodging, two breakfasts, hot tub access, ice skates, skis, and a skier drop-off starting at $232 for two people. Hot tubs are available on an hourly basis during winter, offering a great way to relax after a day of cross-country skiing. Mammoth Hotel and Old Faithful Snow Lodge offer the only wintertime hotels inside the park.

Cabins

Behind the hotel are 116 cabins, including budget units ($54 d) with a shared bathhouse, and delightful "frontier" cottages (from $86 d) with small porches and private baths. Most of these accommodations were built in 1938, and all contain two double beds. Some are duplex units that can be joined for families or friends traveling together. Dozens of ground squirrels populate the grounds, providing endless entertainment for the kids. Two units also have private outdoor hot tubs and are the nicest cabins in Yellowstone ($135 d). The cabins are open from early May to early October.

OLD FAITHFUL

The Old Faithful area contains a plethora of lodging options, including two large hotels—Old Faithful Inn and Old Faithful Snow Lodge—and several dozen cabins.

Old Faithful Inn

Built in 1903–1904, the timeless Old Faithful Inn (described in the Exploring the Park section of this chapter) is easily the most delightful place to stay inside Yellowstone—if not in all of America. I wouldn't trade it for a thousand Hiltons. If you're able to get a room here during your visit to the park, do so; you certainly won't regret it! The hotel contains 327 guest rooms to suit all budgets. Even those staying in the simplest rooms here will enjoy the five-star lobby with its towering stone fireplace, the old-fashioned writing tables, cushy overstuffed chairs, a classy bar and restaurant, and evening piano music.

Most rooms in the original section of the hotel are cramped spaces with a brass double bed, dresser, in-room sink, bare-bulb lighting, older carpets, log walls, and communal baths down the hall; these go for $69 d. Of the cheap rooms, the best ones (these are often reserved a year ahead) are the dormer rooms on the second floor—particularly room 229—but those who stay there must walk past folks in the lobby to take a shower! Many other types of rooms are available throughout this sprawling hotel. The attractively appointed midrange rooms ($92 d) are comfortable and contain two double beds, phones, and tub baths with colorful tiles. Premium rooms vary in price from $113 to $164 d depending in part on whether they face the geyser, but personally I don't think they are much better than the midrange units. If you have the money, rent a suite for $334 d. When booking, ask for a room or suite in the East Wing facing the geyser if possible. Good choices include numbers 2002, 2010, 2012, 2014, and 2016; all have notable views of Old Faithful Geyser. Old Faithful Inn is open early May to mid-October, but a major preservation project starting in 2003 may shorten the season somewhat in the fall.

Old Faithful Lodge Cabins

Although it is an attractively rustic building that would be a major focal point almost anywhere else, Old Faithful Lodge is overshadowed by its grand neighbor, Old Faithful Inn. The lodge does not contain guest rooms but houses a large cafeteria (open for lunch and dinner only), recreation hall, gift shop, bake shop, ice cream stand, espresso cart, and showers. Unlike the inn, the lodge has enormous windows that face the geyser, providing those eating in the cafeteria with dramatic views of the eruptions. The lodge's massive fir logs and stone pillars add to a feeling of permanence. Behind and beside Old Faithful Lodge are approximately 130 moderately priced but cramped cabins. These contain older (but functional) furnishings, and most have two beds. The simplest budget units share communal bathhouses and cost just $40 d; they're the cheapest rooms in Yellowstone and just a few steps from Old Faithful. Slightly nicer (but still small) cabins have one or two beds and private baths, and cost $65 d. There is even a pair of handicapped-accessible cabins here. The cabins at Old Faithful Lodge are open mid-May to mid-September.

Old Faithful Snow Lodge

Completed in 1999, the 100-room Old Faithful Snow Lodge provides accommodations in both summer and winter (Mammoth Hot Springs Hotel is Yellowstone's only other wintertime hotel). Both inside and out, Snow Lodge evokes the spirit of "parkitecture" from the early 1900s. The building blends the past and present, with timbers (recycled from old buildings), hardwood floors, a central stone fireplace, custom-designed overstuffed couches, and wrought-iron accents, along with all the modern conveniences you expect from a fine hotel—unless you're expecting TVs, which no park hotels contain. Rooms are beautifully appointed and comfortable, and all have private baths. The hotel also houses a restaurant, snack shop, lounge, and gift shop, along with a ski shop and snowmobile rentals in winter. Rates are $134 d.

In addition to the hotel, 34 four-plex Snow Lodge Cabins are available behind the building, costing $112 d. Built in 1989, these **Western**

Cabins have standard motel furnishings, with two double beds and a full bath. In addition, duplex **Frontier Cabins** provide simple accommodations with bath for $68 d. The Snow Lodge and Cabins are open early May through October and mid-December to early March. Rates are the same in summer and winter, but early-season discounts are available. During winter, "getaway packages" are a better bet, including one that provides two nights' lodging, two breakfasts, skis, a round-trip snowcoach ride to Old Faithful, and a skier drop-off starting at $470 for two people.

ROOSEVELT LODGE

Located at the junction of the roads to Canyon, Mammoth, and Lamar Valley, this is *the* place to escape the crowds and return to a quieter and simpler era. Roosevelt Lodge is decidedly off the beaten path to the major Yellowstone sights, and that suits folks who stay here just fine. Named for Pres. Theodore Roosevelt—perhaps the most conservation-minded president ever—the lodge has the well-worn feeling of an old dude ranch, and many families treat it as such. More than a few folks book cabins for several weeks at a stretch, enjoying the wolf-watching, fly-fishing, horseback and wagon rides, and barbecue cookout dinners. (Cookouts book up six months ahead, so reserve your space when you make a Roosevelt Lodge reservation.)

The main lodge features two large stone fireplaces, a family-style restaurant with notable meals, a lounge, a gift shop, a little general store, and a big front porch with old-fashioned rocking chairs. Surrounding it are 82 utilitarian cabins, most of which were built in the 1920s. Most basic—and just a step up from camping—are the "Roughrider" cabins, with one, two, or three beds, a writing table, and a woodstove (the only ones in any Yellowstone lodging). These cabins share a communal bathhouse, cost $48 for up to six guests, and fill up quickly. Call far ahead to reserve one of these classics! The same price will also get you larger cabins without the woodstove (but still no private bath). Nicer "frontier" cabins with hardwood floors, one or two double beds, and private baths go for $86 d. All of these cabins can get stuffy in midsummer, and the windows lack screens. Two of the Roosevelt cabins are wheelchair-accessible. The Roosevelt Lodge and cabins are open early June to early September.

Food

RESTAURANTS

You'll find good restaurants at Mammoth Hot Springs, Lake Yellowstone Hotel, Old Faithful Inn, Old Faithful Snow Lodge, Grant Village, Roosevelt Lodge, and Canyon Lodge. All of these are open for three meals a day throughout the summer, and the Snow Lodge also opens for the winter season (mid-December to early March).

The enormous **Old Faithful Inn Dining Room** is easily the nicest of these eating options, with impressive all-you-can-eat breakfast and lunch buffets, plus a dinner menu that stars prime rib, halibut, chicken, steaks, and pork chops ($15–20 entrées). The cozy lounge serves single-malt scotches, tequilas, and cognacs, with a backdrop of etched-glass windows.

Another excellent choice is the **Lake Yellowstone Hotel Dining Room,** with breakfast buffets, a lunch that features blackened salmon wrap and good salads, plus dinner selections such as shrimp cocktails, beef tenderloin, or rack of lamb.

Meals in other restaurants throughout the park are also reasonably priced and quite good. Typical menus include steaks, burgers, seafood, pasta, chicken, and vegetarian dishes. The filling breakfasts and chocolate pecan pie at **Mammoth Hot Springs Dining Room** are noteworthy, and **Roosevelt Lodge Dining Room** emphasizes down-home carnivore fare such as barbecue ribs, country fried steaks, sandwiches, chili, and fried chicken. The dinner menu at **Grant Village Dining Room** includes huckleberry chicken, ribeye steak, polenta lasagna, prime rib, and trout. They also have a substantial breakfast buffet. The building is one of the newer ones in the park, with a bland exterior but big windows facing the lake (although trees obscure the view). **Obsidian Dining Room** at the Snow Lodge has a fun Western flair. In addition to an extensive breakfast menu, the restaurant serves specialty burgers, steaks, and seafood.

Dinner reservations are *required* in the summer at Old Faithful Inn Dining Room (307/545-4999), Lake Yellowstone Hotel Dining Room (307/242-3899), and Grant Village Dining Room (307/242-3499), and they should be made before your arrival. For a dinner table at Old Faithful Inn, reserve a week ahead if you want a choice of seating times.

CAFETERIAS AND FAST FOOD

Yellowstone has always catered to families, and several park cafeterias provide dependably good food for decent prices. Your kids' noise will almost certainly be drowned out by racket from the rest of the hoi polloi (I'm speaking from experience here). Of particular note are **Lake Lodge Cafeteria** and **Old Faithful Lodge Cafeteria,** both of which are housed in grand stone-and-timber buildings with tall windows. Lake Lodge faces Lake Yellowstone, and Old Faithful Lodge faces the geyser. Less distinguished are **Canyon Lodge Cafeteria**—with a 1960s design that hasn't aged well—and the **Grant Village Lake House.** At the latter, big windows open onto Yellowstone Lake (great for sunsets), and you can graze a pasta and salad bar in the evenings or order a pizza. In addition to these options, you'll find snack shops or delis selling burgers, vegieburgers, sandwiches, espresso, and ice cream in Mammoth, Old Faithful, Lake, and Canyon.

Many of the park's **Yellowstone General Stores** have food services of the burger, fries, and milkshake variety, and can put together box lunches for a to-go meal.

OLD WEST COOKOUT

The Old West wagon cookouts at Roosevelt Lodge's are a longtime family favorite and so popular that you'll need to make reservations at least six months in advance of your visit. These events take place every evening from early June to early September, and you either hop onboard the horse-drawn wagons or astride a horse for a saunter into history. Cookouts take place in Pleasant Valley, three miles from the lodge, and include cowboy music, a campfire, and a big buffet dinner of steak, baked beans, coleslaw, potato salad, corn, corn muffins, watermelon, apple cobbler, and beverages. Top it off with a cup of cowboy coffee. No discounts are given for vegetarians, but they can make substitutions if you notify them in advance. Covered seating is available in case of rain.

Wagon rides last 1.5 hours round-trip, and cost $32 adults, $20 ages 5–11, or free for younger kids. Horseback riders can choose either a one-hour trail ride and meal at $43 adults, $33 ages 8–11, or a two-hour trail ride that costs $53 adults or $43 kids. Make reservations at 307/344-7311, www.travelyellowstone.com. If you're in the area and don't have a reservation, ask to get on the waiting list. You might get lucky and have someone cancel at the last minute.

GROCERIES AND SUPPLIES

The park's 11 Yellowstone General Stores are located at Mammoth, Canyon, Old Faithful, Fishing Bridge, Grant Village, Lake, and Roosevelt. Each outlet has its own personality, and several of these—most notably the Lower Basin store at Old Faithful and the ones at Lake and Fishing Bridge—are grand old log structures. The Mammoth general store is another historic structure, here for nearly a century.

In addition to groceries, beer, and liquor, these stores sell a variety of merchandise, clothing, souvenirs, film and photo supplies, T-shirts, and accessories. Featured items include locally made arts and crafts, and they even offer interpretive programs. The larger ones also have popular soda fountains with burgers, shakes, and other fast food. General stores at Canyon and Old Faithful deliver the best selection, and the Mammoth store is open year-round. The others are generally open mid-May through September. The stores are managed by Delaware North Park Services, www.yellowstonegeneralstores.com.

Getting Around

BY CAR

Yellowstone's roads were long a source of irritation to travelers. Much of the roadbed was built at the turn of the 20th century, when horses and carriages were the primary means of travel. Increasing traffic and larger vehicles contributed to deterioration of park roads, as did stretched-thin park maintenance budgets. By the early 1990s many miles of park roads were pockmarked with bone-jarring potholes. Yellowstone is now at the tail end of a massive road reconstruction program, and each summer you'll find a different section undergoing rebuilding, so be ready for delays somewhere during your journey. In 2003 and 2004, most of the attention will be on the roads between Canyon and Roosevelt and between Madison and Norris. This may mean delays of up to 30 minutes at times. Fortunately, all this work means that the roads are vastly better than they were just a few years ago. Check with the park for the latest on the road situation and this year's construction delays, or see the free park newspaper.

The **speed limit** on all park roads is a strictly enforced 45 mph, although during summer you're not likely to approach this speed because long lines of traffic form behind monstrous RVs. **Gas stations** are located at Old Faithful, Canyon Village, Mammoth Hot Springs, Fishing Bridge, Grant Village, and Tower Junction, while repair services are available at all of these except Mammoth Hot Springs and Tower Junction. Additional service stations can be found in the surrounding towns.

Seasonal Access

Most roads in Yellowstone close on the Monday after the first Sunday in November and usually open again by mid-May. Plowing begins in early March, and the roads reopen in sections. The roads connecting Mammoth to West Yellowstone open first, and Dunraven Pass is plowed last. Note that spring storms may cause closures or restrictions on some park roads; get the latest from entrance stations or visitors centers. Only the road between Mammoth and Cooke City is kept plowed all winter long. The roads are groomed for snowmobiles (snow conditions permitting) by mid-December. If you're planning a trip early or late in the season, contact the park for current road conditions; 307/344-7381, www.nps.gov/yell.

PARK TOURS

During summer, most people come into Yellowstone in private cars or RVs, but there *are* other ways of getting around. For many people, an interpretive bus tour provides a quick overview of the park while leaving the driving to an expert. This is especially true for RVers who can park at Fishing Bridge RV Park or Bridge Bay Campground and don't need to worry about driving on narrow park roads.

In-Park Tours

From mid-May to late September, **Xanterra Parks & Resorts,** 307/344-7311, www.travelyellowstone.com, offers full-day bus tours from Canyon Lodge, Lake Hotel, Old Faithful Inn, Fishing Bridge RV Park, Bridge Bay Campground, and Grant Village. Tours of either the upper or lower loops are $38 adults or $17 ages 12–16 (free for younger kids). A longer Grand Loop tour (not recommended unless you're into sensory overload and more than 10 hours of riding around) costs $42 adults or $20 teens. The Grand Loop tour is only available from Mammoth or Gardiner.

Xanterra also offers **Lamar Valley wildlife excursions** that originate from Canyon Lodge, Bridge Bay, Lake Yellowstone Hotel, or Fishing Bridge RV Park and cost $30 adults or $13 teens. These last three or four hours and provide an opportunity to catch a glimpse of wolves. In addition, amateur photographers may want to join a professionally taught **Photo Safari** provided several times a week out of Old Faithful Inn and Lake Yellowstone Hotel; $40 adults for four hours, or $23 for teens. All-day trips to **Mt.**

Washburn from Bridge Bay Campground, Lake Yellowstone Hotel, Fishing Bridge RV Park, or Canyon Lodge are $34 adults, $16 teens.

Also available are three-hour **Firehole Basin** tours ($19 adults, $9 teens), and two-hour **Hayden Valley twilight tours** (a top time to find bears) for $14 adults or $8 teens. One of the most distinctive tour offerings is to ride a classic canvas-topped **1937 Yellowstone bus** on sunset tours around Lake Yellowstone. The vehicle gets almost as much attention as the scenery during these fun trips back in time. They cost $17 adults or $8.50 teens.

Other Bus Tours

Upper or lower loop tours are available out of West Yellowstone from **Buffalo Bus Touring Co.,** 406/646-9564 or 800/426-7669, www.yellowstonevacations.com, and **Gray Line,** 406/646-9374 or 800/523-3102, www.graylineyellowstone.com. The latter is a couple of bucks cheaper at $38 adults or $25 kids.

Additional Yellowstone tours leave out of Cody ($60) aboard **Powder River Transportation/Coach USA,** 307/527-6316 or 800/527-6316, and from Jackson ($80) aboard **Alltrans/Gray Line,** 307/733-4325 or 800/443-6133, www.jacksonholealltrans.com. Those without vehicles can use Gray Line tours for access to the parks; the bus can pick you up at many places along the road system, but you'll need to schedule this in advance. This is not a separate service from the Gray Line tours; instead the regular tour bus stops, meaning that you get a portion of the tour at the same time.

4x4 Stage, 406/848-2224 or 800/517-8243, offers by-request connections around the park and to surrounding communities. Call 24 hours ahead for reservations. **Karst Stage,** 406/388-2293 or 800/287-4759, www.karststage.com, has wintertime transportation between the Bozeman airport and Mammoth Hot Springs.

Specialized Tours

In addition to traditional classes, the Yellowstone Association Institute, 307/344-2294, www.yellowstoneassociation.org, also offers a popular series of **Lodging and Learning** packages. These two- to five-day programs blend education, recreation, and comfortable lodging. Naturalist-guides from the Association lead excursions, and participants are provided with accommodations in park hotels, plus breakfasts and lunches. The programs include special ones for families, winter ski treks, winter wildlife, and one that emphasizes hiking. For the private touch, the Institute has **Educational Adventures,** tours in which a wildlife biologist travels with you in your own vehicle. It's sort of like having your own personal trainer for Yellowstone wildlife.

For a listing of licensed tour operators offering wildlife, natural history, and photography tours in the park, contact the Park Service at 307/344-738, www.nps.gov/yell. Operated by the highly respected Teton Science School, **Wildlife Expeditions,** 307/733-2623 or 888/945-3567, www.tetonscience.org/wildlife, leads a variety of wildlife viewing safaris throughout the region, including multiday wildlife tours into Yellowstone. Other good companies and individuals offering guided tours of the area include **Callowishus Park Touring Company,** 307/733-9521, www.callowishus.com; **Jackson's Hole Adventure,** 307/654-7849 or 800/392-3165, www.jacksonholeadventure.com; **Tory and Meredith Taylor,** 307/455-2161; **Upstream Anglers and Outdoor Adventures,** 307/739-9443 or 800/642-8979, www.upstreamanglers.com; and **Yellowstone Country Adventures,** 406/994-0422, www.yellowstonecountry-adventures.com.

YELLOWSTONE

Other Practicalities

Complete details on park entrance fees, visitors centers, and sights are provided in the Exploring the Park section of this chapter.

VACATION PLANNING

If you're planning a trip to Yellowstone, call the park at 307/344-7381 to request a copy of their *Yellowstone Guide.* It provides detailed up-to-date information on hiking and camping, fishing, services, road construction, safety issues, park highlights, and lots more. The same information (and much more) is available online at www.nps.gov/yell. Also check out the web-only **Yellowstone Traveler,** www.yellowstoneparktraveler.com, maintained by Circumerro Publishing.

RANGER-NATURALIST PROGRAMS

Park naturalists lead slide shows, films, guided walks, kids' programs, campfire talks, and other activities at the campgrounds and visitors centers. These are always favorites of visitors, and on summer days you can choose from more than two dozen different Yellowstone activities, all of which are free. Get a complete listing in the *Yellowstone Today* paper you receive upon entering the park, or online at www.nps.gov/yell. Evening slide programs are also offered in winter at Mammoth and Old Faithful. For a more in-depth look at the park, take a class through the Yellowstone Association Institute, www.yellowstoneassociation.org, or join one of their popular **Lodging and Learning Packages.**

TRAVELING WITH CHILDREN

Yellowstone is a major family destination in summer, and visiting the park has become something of a rite of passage for middle-class American families (along with thousands of European and Japanese families). Families will especially appreciate the woodsy campgrounds, the inexpensive but simple cabins, and the rea-

sonable cafeteria meals that are available around the park. Most lodges and hotels have cribs for those traveling with infants. Of special interest to kids ages 5–12 is the **Junior Ranger Program** ($3), in which children attend a nature program, hike a trail, and complete other activities. They're rewarded with an official Junior Ranger patch and are sworn in. It's always a big hit, but your kids may later try to arrest you if you get too close to an elk.

ACCESSIBILITY

Disabled visitors to Yellowstone will find that the park is making a concerted effort to provide accessible facilities, although they have a long way to go. Most of the major tourist areas, including Old Faithful, have at least some paths that are paved, and accessible accommodations can be found at Canyon, Grant Village, Old Faithful, and Lake. Accessible campsites are also available throughout the park. For details, call 307/344-2018 to request a copy of the *Visitor Guide to Accessible Features in Yellowstone National Park,* or find the same information on the web at www.nps.gov/yell.

SUPPORTING THE PARK

The **Yellowstone Association,** 307/344-2289, www.yellowstoneassociation.org, is a nonprofit organization that assists with education, research, publishing, and book sales inside the park. The organization also teaches classes through the Yellowstone Association Institute.

The **Yellowstone Park Foundation** is another nonprofit group that works with the National Park Service by providing funds for projects and programs that would not be otherwise supported. Their biggest project is to help raise the $15 million needed for a new visitors center at Old Faithful. All funding comes from individuals and corporations, not from the government. Contact the foundation at 406/586-6303, www.ypf.org, for more details.

YELLOWSTONE ASSOCIATION

Founded in 1933, the nonprofit Yellowstone Association assists in educational, historical, and scientific programs. The organization publishes several natural-history publications and provides funds to produce trail leaflets and park newspapers, along with the excellent *Yellowstone Science* magazine. In addition, the association manages book sales at visitors centers, funds park exhibits and research, and otherwise assists the park in educating the public. The group is probably best known for the **Yellowstone Association Institute,** operating out of the historic Buffalo Ranch in Lamar Valley.

Instructors at the institute lead more than 100 different natural-history and humanities classes in the summer, along with several others in winter. Most of these last 2–5 days and typically cost around $60 per day—a real bargain. Courses cover the spectrum from wolf ecology to horsepacking and provide a great way to learn about this wonderful wild place. Class size is small; most classes contain 10–15 students. Participants typically stay at the Buffalo Ranch in comfortable log cabins ($22 per person per night) and cook meals in the shared kitchen.

In addition to these classes, the Yellowstone Association Institute also offers a **Lodging and Learning Program,** two- to five-day packages that blend education, recreation, and lodging. Naturalist-guides from the Association lead small-group excursions (13 people max), and participants are provided with accommodations in park hotels, plus breakfasts and lunches. Their *Yellowstone for Families* program is especially popular, with a mix of activities for both kids and parents over four days: animal tracking, wildlife watching, photography, painting, hiking, and more.

For folks who really want the personalized touch (and can afford it), the Institute has **Educational Adventures,** private tours in which a wildlife biologist travels with you in your vehicle for 6–8 hours, providing an introduction to park wildlife and ecology.

Membership in the Yellowstone Association starts at $30 per year and is tax-deductible. Members get discounts on classes taught by the Yellowstone Association Institute and can sign up early. They also receive quarterly newsletters and discounts for purchases of items sold by the Association. For details and a listing of classes and books on the park, contact the Yellowstone Association Institute at 307/344-2294, www.yellowstoneassociation.org.

MONEY

You'll discover **ATMs** at most of the settled areas, including Old Faithful Inn, Old Faithful Snow Lodge, Fishing Bridge, Lake Yellowstone Hotel, Mammoth Hot Springs Hotel, Mammoth General Store, Canyon General Store, Canyon Lodge, and Grant Village. Park lodges and hotels are able to provide a limited **currency exchange** for international travelers Monday–Friday 8 A.M.–5 P.M.

MEDICAL SERVICES

For medical emergencies 24 hours a day, the park manages **Lake Hospital,** 307/242-7241, an acute-care facility with 10 beds. It's open late May to mid-September; also here are a clinic and pharmacy. Outpatient services are available both here and at the **Old Faithful Clinic,** 307/545-7325, open mid-May to mid-Oct. Open weekdays year-round, the **Mammoth Hot Springs Clinic,** 307/344-7965, has a physician available. Call 911 for emergencies.

CLEANING UP

In summer, find coin-operated **washers and dryers** at Fishing Bridge RV Park, Canyon Village Campground, and Grant Village Campground. **Public showers** ($3) are at Fishing Bridge RV Park, Lake Lodge, Old Faithful Lodge, Grant Village, and Canyon Village Campground.

OTHER SERVICES

For a complete directory of the many other Yellowstone visitor services, see *Yellowstone Today,* which you receive upon entering the park. You can also download a copy off the web from the Yellowstone site, www.nps.gov/yell.

A year-round **post office** is located in a 1930s-era stone building at Mammoth Hot Springs, and seasonal post offices can be found at Old Faithful, Lake Village, Canyon Village, and Grant Village.

Check the visitors centers for a schedule of **church services.** Process film (prints only) in **one-hour film labs** at Old Faithful, Canyon, and Fishing Bridge. **Cell phone** users will find spotty service in many parts of Yellowstone, but your phone will probably work in the country around Old Faithful, Lake, and Mammoth (and possibly elsewhere).

WORKING IN YELLOWSTONE

During summer, both the National Park Service and private concessioners provide several thousand jobs in Yellowstone. These positions rarely last more than six months. You can find much more about Yellowstone jobs—both public and private—by heading to www.nps.gov/yell/technical/jobs on the web.

Park Service Jobs

Yellowstone National Park hires more than 300 seasonal employees each year, but many more people apply, so the competition is stiff for new hires. Most seasonals start out as a park ranger (leading naturalist walks, working in entrance stations, etc.) or laborer (building trails, cleaning campgrounds and restrooms, etc.), but more specialized positions are available in the fields of natural resources or law enforcement. Seasonals typically make $10–12 per hour, with housing taken out of this pay. You must be a U.S. citizen to be employed by the Park Service. Although there is a national register for seasonal rangers, specific vacancy announcements come out when jobs are available, and you will need to apply within the specified time frame and meet all qualifications. For details on seasonal park service jobs, call Yellowstone's human resources office at 307/344-2052, or visit www.usajobs.opm.gov for a listing of park jobs. The Department of

---

Interior's site, www.doi.gov/hrm/jobs.html, has additional job info.

Volunteer Positions

Unpaid volunteers do many jobs in Yellowstone and other national parks, and it isn't necessary to be a U.S. citizen to do volunteer work. The Park Service operates a **Volunteers in Parks** (VIP) program at Yellowstone that includes more than 300 people each year. To join the ranks of the employed but unpaid, call the park's VIP coordinator at 307/344-2039, or visit the volunteer website: www.nps.gov/volunteer.

A national nonprofit organization, the New Hampshire–based **Student Conservation Association** (SCA), 603/543-1700, www.sca-inc.org, provides workers for Yellowstone who do a wide range of activities, from trail maintenance to answering visitors' questions. Volunteers get most expenses paid. Contact SCA for details.

Concessioner Jobs

The park has two primary concessioners, Xanterra Parks & Resorts and Delaware North Parks Service, plus the smaller Yellowstone Park Service Stations. Most employees of these companies are college students (who live in dorm-style accommodations), retired folks (who live in their RVs), or young people from other countries (including many from Poland, Czech Republic, Russia, Finland, and other European nations). Don't expect high pay; entry-level positions start at around $6 per hour, with meals and lodging deducted from this paltry sum.

Contact Xanterra Parks & Resorts at 307/344-5324, www.ynpjobs.com, Delaware North Park Services at 406/586-7593, www.yellowstonegeneralstores.com, and Yellowstone Park Service Stations at 406/848-7333, www.ypss.com. A good overall website for concessioner jobs inside Yellowstone is www.coolworks.com/yell.htm.

West Yellowstone, Montana

Yellowstone National Park is most commonly entered via one of several Wyoming or Montana towns. West Yellowstone is the definitive Western tourist town. With a year-round population of only 1,000 (three times that in the summer) but more than 50 places to stay, it's pretty easy to see what makes the West Yellowstone cash registers ring. The West Entrance gate—most popular of all Yellowstone entrances—lies just a couple hundred feet away. "West," as the town is known locally, isn't particularly attractive, and in the 1990s a major development added several corporate hotels and other ugly additions to an already crowded mix of restaurants, motels, T-shirt stores, and gift shops.

West Yellowstone may be decidedly middle-brow, but the surrounding land is anything but, with Gallatin (GAL-a-tin) National Forest lying north and west, Caribou-Targhee National Forest just a few miles to the south, and Yellowstone National Park just a few feet to the east. It's just a couple of miles east from West Yellowstone to the Wyoming border, and the Idaho border lies only nine miles west.

HISTORY
In 1907, the Union Pacific Railroad completed laying tracks for its Oregon Short Line to the western border of Yellowstone. The following summer, Yellowstone Special trains began rolling in from Salt Lake City, dropping tourists for their stagecoach tours of the park. A small town—West Yellowstone—quickly developed on the margins of the park, providing lodging, meals, and tourist trinkets.

After World War II, interest in rail travel declined and more people came to Yellowstone by automobile. Although the last passengers stepped off the train in 1960, the Union Pacific's historic stone depot and neighboring buildings still stand; they now house a museum, library, police station, jail, medical clinic, and other offices.

The West Yellowstone area was rocked by a devastating magnitude-7.5 earthquake on August 17, 1959. One of the most powerful temblors ever recorded in the Lower 48 states, the quake cracked Hebgen Dam and caused a massive landslide (estimated at more than 80 million tons of debris!) that generated a 20-foot-high tsunami and created Earthquake Lake. Twenty-eight people died, and the geysers and hot springs of Yellowstone were dramatically affected for years.

SIGHTS
Museum of the Yellowstone
The **Museum of the Yellowstone,** 124 Yellowstone Ave., 406/646-1100, www.yellowstone-historiccenter.org, is a stone-and-log structure from the railroad days that served for decades as the town's train depot. Entrance is $6 adults, $4 students and kids, and $15 families; free for kids under three. The museum is open daily 8:30 A.M.–7 P.M. (until 10 P.M. in the summer) from mid-May to mid-October; closed the rest of the year. Inside are exhibits on the history of park transportation (including railroads and stagecoaches), the 1959 Hebgen Lake earthquake, the fires of 1988, and wildlife displays, including "Old Snaggletooth" the grizzly and

an enormous cave bear skull. Videos and movies about Yellowstone are shown in the theater, and the museum offers 45-minute free walking tours at noon and 4 P.M. daily in the summer, along with afternoon nature or history talks most days. Also here is a good collection of regional books for sale. Out front is a grand old park bus that was last used in 1959.

Right next door is another wonderful stone structure (built in 1925) that served until the late 1950s as an elegant Union Pacific Dining Lodge. The building has a spacious dining hall containing an enormous fireplace, a 45-foot-tall vaulted ceiling, and handmade light fixtures. Also worth a look-see is an **Oregon Short Line Railroad car** housed at the Holiday Inn Sunspree Resort, 315 Yellowstone Avenue. Built in 1903, the railroad car has been beautifully restored with antiques.

Grizzly and Wolf Discovery Center

In the early 1990s, a massive $50 million project covering 67 acres transformed (some might prefer the term decimated) the town of West Yellowstone. Included are a grizzly and wolf theme park, an IMAX theater, three major hotels, cabins, a restaurant, fast-food joints, an RV park, and a post office. The centerpiece is the **Grizzly and Wolf Discovery Center,** 201 S. Canyon St., home to 10 Alaskan and Canadian grizzlies and seven captive-born gray wolves. Not all of the bears are visible at any given time, but visitors are bound to see at least one in the pseudo-natural habitat. The center is open daily all year 8 A.M. to dusk. Entrance costs $8.50 adults, $8 seniors, $4 ages 5–12, free for kids under five. This center attracts throngs of visitors and photographers who might otherwise never see a grizzly or wolf, and there's always a staff member out to answer any questions. The center remains controversial, however. Scientists note that the bears here are genetically distinct from those in Yellowstone, and anyone who has spent time around grizzlies in the wild will be dismayed to see them in captivity, even in a facility less oppressive than traditional zoos. The folks at Grizzly and Wolf Discovery Center counter

that all these bears were either raised in captivity or were "problem" bears that would almost certainly have been killed had they not been moved here. In addition to the bears and wolves, the center has wildlife exhibits (including a walk-in bear den), bear safety tips (I recommend not entering bear dens), a 40-minute video on bears, plus the obligatory gift shop. Get details at 406/646-7001 or 800/257-2570, www.grizzlydiscoveryctr.com.

Yellowstone IMAX Theatre

Directly in front of the Grizzly and Wolf Discovery Center is the **Yellowstone IMAX Theatre,** 406/646-4100 or 888/854-5862, where you can watch the big-budget production of *Yellowstone* on the 60- by 80-foot screen; other movies typically are on wolves, bears, or some other nature or Old West topic. The theater is open daily 9 A.M.–9 P.M. May to mid-October, with reduced hours the rest of the year. Admission costs $8 adults, $6 ages 3–11; free for younger children. The featured attraction is a 35-minute movie that presents Yellowstone history and geology complete with stirring music and a cast of dozens. If you haven't seen IMAX flicks before, hold onto your seat—lots of jaw-dropping scenes here. The movie packs in the crowds on summer days, but the film seems like a Disneylandish version of reality, ignoring many of the things you're likely to see in the park—such as burned forests and crowds of visitors—and putting history into a pretty little box. Reality wasn't—and isn't—quite like this. Even more disconcerting is that this glorification of the park stands right next to the park. To me it symbolizes the make-a-buck attitude that holds Yellowstone up as an attraction while developing a massive complex on its very margin.

Other Sights

Family-run **Eagle's Store,** on the corner of Canyon and Yellowstone, 406/646-9300, is definitely worth a stop. Built in the 1920s, this historic log building contains all of the standard tourist knickknacks, along with quality Western clothing, jewelry, fishing tackle, and a delightful old-fashioned soda fountain open in summer.

Evidence of the powerful 1959 earthquake is still visible north of West Yellowstone along Hebgen Lake. The Forest Service has an **Earthquake Visitor Center;** get there by heading eight miles north on U.S. Hwy. 191 and turning left on U.S. Hwy. 287. Continue another 17 miles west to the center; open daily 8:30 A.M.–6 P.M. from Memorial Day to late September only.

ACCOMMODATIONS

The proximity to Yellowstone makes the town of West Yellowstone an extremely popular stopping place for vacationers in both summer and winter. More than 2,000 rooms are available. It is also a pricey place to stay; only a few places have rooms for less than $65 during the peak seasons. The streets are lined with more than three dozen motels, so I won't try to describe all of them, although you'll find general information and links at the West Yellowstone Chamber website, www.westyellowstone chamber.com. For the printed version, call them at 406/646-7701.

Be aware that during summer everything in West Yellowstone fills up by early afternoon, so get there early or make advance bookings. Motels can even be full on weekends in late September. Reserve a room in March or April for the peak summer season.

Hostel

Budget travelers will be happy to discover the West Yellowstone International Hostel (not affiliated with AYH) in the historic **Madison Hotel,** 139 Yellowstone Ave., 406/646-7745 or 800/838-7745, www.wyellowstone.com/madisonhotel. Now on the National Register of Historic Places, the hotel has friendly owners and a delightfully rustic lobby crowded with deer and moose heads. Presidents Harding and Hoover stayed here (though it wasn't a hostel at the time, of course). Travelers stay in clean and comfortable bedrooms (three or four beds in each, with bedding provided) that have been furnished with handmade lodgepole furniture. The classic hotel rooms are a delightful mix of old and new,

providing the ambience of a place that has been here since 1912. No televisions or phones are provided in the rooms, but they do have a small fridge and microwave for hostelers in the back, plus a TV in the lobby. A computer is available to check your email ($5 per hour). Lodging costs $20 per person in three-bed dorm rooms. Make hostel reservations a few days ahead in midsummer or get here before evening to be sure of a space in the dorms.

In addition to hostel rooms, the hotel has a range of other economical options, starting with a basic room with a bath down the hall and no TV for $26 s or $36 d; or $52 for a room with space for four and a private bath. Behind the hotel is a separate building with standard motel accommodations (private baths and TVs) for $49 d or $75 for a room with three double beds. The Madison Hotel is open late May to early October only.

$50–100

A good budget choice is **Lazy G Motel,** 123 Hayden, 406/646-7586, www.wyellowstone.com/clients/lazyg, where the clean and cozy rooms cost $48–59 s or d. All contain fridges and phones; kitchenettes are $10 extra. Closed in April.

Al's Westward Ho Motel, 16 Boundary St., 406/646-7331 or 888/646-7331, www.wyellowstone.com/alswestwardho, charges $52–66 s or d, and some rooms contain kitchenettes. Open May–Oct., no in-room phones. **Alpine Motel,** 120 Madison Ave., 406/646-7544, is similar: $55 for one bed, $65–67 for two beds, six-person units with kitchens for $95; $5 extra for fridges and microwaves. The Alpine also has a family suite that sleeps six with a full kitchen for $100. No phones or air conditioning. It is open mid-May through October.

Pony Express Motel, 4 Firehole Ave., 406/646-7644 or 800/323-9708, www.yellowstonevacations.com, has a quiet location but no phones; $49 for one bed or $64 for two beds. A kitchenette is $75 for up to four people. A little nicer, but still reasonably priced is another property with the same owners, **City Center Motel,** 408/646-7337 or 800/742-0665, www.yellowstonevacations.com, where rooms are $69 for one queen bed or $89 for two. A community kitchen and indoor hot tub are available for guests.

Wagon Wheel Cabins and Campground, 408 Gibbon, 406/646-7872, www.wyellow-stone.com/wagonwheel, has a collection of 10 attractive cabins, most containing full kitchens. The cabins are on large lots surrounded by trees, and each has a barbecue grill and picnic table. Basic "camping cabins" cost $45 d, and a one-bedroom unit starts at $75 d. The largest unit has three bedrooms and a fireplace, and sleeps six for $175. There's a three-night summertime minimum on the larger cabins and a five-night minimum in winter (if they are open). The cabins at Wagon Wheel fill early, so book well ahead. They may be closed in the winter.

Golden West Motel, 429 Madison Ave., 406/646-7778, www.wyellowstone.com/gold-enwest, is a small motel with a dozen well-maintained rooms costing $52–62 s or d; $8 extra for kitchenettes. Closed Nov. and Apr.

Three Bear Lodge, 217 Yellowstone Ave., 406/646-7353 or 800/646-7353, www.three-bear-lodge.com, is probably best known for its popular restaurant of the same name. The 74-room motel features contemporary rooms, plus four indoor hot tubs and an outdoor pool. A wide variety of rooms are available, starting at $75 for standard rooms, up to $110 for ones that include a jetted tub. Two-room family units are $85–148; the largest sleeps six. Open year-round.

You'll find very good accommodations at **Brandin' Iron Inn,** 201 Canyon St., 406/646-9411 or 800/217-4613 www.yellowstoneva-cations.com. Rooms cost $89 for one bed or $99 for two, including fridges, a light breakfast, and two indoor hot tubs.

$100 and Up

One of the nicer places in West Yellowstone is **Stage Coach Inn,** filling an entire block at 209 Madison Ave., 406/646-7381 or 800/842-2882, www.yellowstoneinn.com. Rooms go for $99–129 s or d, and include access to a sauna and two hot tubs. The hotel features an impressive Western-style lobby with fireplace, plus a restaurant and heated underground parking.

At **Hibernation Station,** 212 Gray Wolf Ave., 406/646-4200 or 800/580-3557, www.hiber-nationstation.com, you'll find 40 modern cabins—each a bit different inside—with handmade log furniture and down comforters. Some also contain kitchenettes. Rates start at $99 d for a cabin with a queen bed, or $159 for one that sleeps four and contains a queen-size bunk bed, fireplace, and kitchenette. Families (not on a budget) will appreciate the large condo unit with room for eight, a full kitchen and dining area, fireplace, and jetted tubs for $269. A big indoor hot tub is available for all guests.

The motel chains have moved into West Yellowstone in a big way. One of the nicest of these is **Comfort Inn,** 638 Madison Ave., 406/646-4212 or 888/264-2466, www.w-yellowstone.com/com-fortinn. The featured attraction here is the biggest indoor pool in town, but the motel also has a small exercise room, hot tub, and continental breakfast. Rates are $129 s or d in standard rooms, or $189 for six-person suites.

The large **Gray Wolf Inn & Suites,** 250 S. Canyon, 406/646-0000 or 800/852-8602, www.graywolf-inn.com, features a hot tub, sauna, and a small indoor pool, plus a breakfast buffet. An added attraction, especially in the winter, is the heated underground parking garage. Rates are $109 s or d in standard rooms, $199–239 for one- and two-bedroom suites that come with full kitchens.

The most elaborate place in town is the ludicrously named **West Yellowstone Conference Hotel Holiday Inn Sunspree Resort,** 315 Yellowstone Ave., 406/646-7365 or 888/633-1724, www.yellowstoneholidayinn.com, with spacious rooms, an indoor pool, an exercise room, a sauna, and a hot tub. Standard rooms cost $139 d, two-room family suites are $191 and sleep six, and luxurious executive suites (king bed, jetted tub, and wet bar) run $175–200.

CAMPING
Public Campgrounds

The nearest Park Service camping place is inside Yellowstone at **Madison Campground,** 14 miles east of West Yellowstone. The cost is

$15, and it's open May to late October. Make reservations (advised) at 307/344-7311, www.travelyellowstone.com.

Gallatin National Forest has several campgrounds in the West Yellowstone area. The closest camping spot is **Baker's Hole Campground** ($12; open May–Sept.), just three miles north of West Yellowstone. It's open for RVs and other hard-sided vehicles only because of bear problems. Tent campers will need to go north of town to **Hebgen Lake,** where five different tenting areas are strung westward along the lake; closest is the **Lonesomehurst Campground** ($12; open May–Sept.), 12 miles from West Yellowstone. No reservations are taken at these Forest Service sites.

The Forest Service maintains four public-use cabins ($30 a night for four people) in the country around West Yellowstone. Three of these are open year-round. The closest is **Basin Station Cabin,** eight miles west of town. Get details on Forest Service camping and cabins at 406/823-6961, www.fs.fed.us/r1/gallatin/recreation.

RV Parks

West Yellowstone has six private campgrounds right in town, and several more are west or north of town. Most of the in-town places are just RV parking lots. Far nicer are two places with shady trees and quiet sites: **Rustic Wagon Campground,** 634 U.S. Hwy. 20, 406/646-7387, www.rusticwagonrv.com, ($25 for tents or $34–36 for RVs); and **Wagon Wheel Cabins and Campground,** 408 Gibbon Ave., 406/646-7872, www.wyellowstone.com/wagonwheel, ($24 for tents or $32 for RVs). Non-campers can shower at either of these for $5. Rustic is open mid-April through October, and Wagon Wheel is open Memorial Day to September.

The other in-town RV parks are **Pony Express RV Park,** 4 Firehole Ave., 406/646-7644 or 800/323-9708, www.yellowstonevacations.com; **Hideaway RV Campground,** 310 Electric St., 406/646-9049, www.hideawayrv.com; **Yellowstone Cabins & RV Park,** 504 U.S. Hwy. 20 West, 406/646-9350; and **Yellowstone Grizzly RV Park,** 210 S. Electric, 406/646-4466, www.grizzlyrv.com. Two

places are west of town on U.S. Hwy. 20: **Yellowstone Park KOA,** 406/646-7606 or 800/562-7591, www.koa.com; and **Lionshead Resort/Super 8 Motel,** 406/646-9584 or 800/800-8000, www.wyellowstone.com/lionshead. The KOA has an outdoor pool. **Yellowstone Holiday Resort,** 406/646-4242 or 800/643-4227, www.yellowstoneholiday.com, is an RV campground along Hebgen Lake north of West Yellowstone.

FOOD

West Yellowstone has many restaurants, but prices are generally higher than in Wyoming towns and the menu is plebeian, with burgers and fries as the dominant food group. Expect to pay $12–20 for dinner entrées.

Breakfast and Lunch

For omelets, buckwheat pancakes, and other good breakfast items, run on over to **Running Bear Pancake House,** 538 Madison Ave., 406/646-7703, but be ready for a long wait in midsummer. Tasty lunches too; open 7 A.M.–2 P.M. only.

Ernie's Deli & Bakery, 406 U.S. Hwy. 20 West, 406/646-9467, is the local doughnut shop in the morning, and it makes unbeatable sandwiches for lunch. They'll put together a big box lunch for $7.25 if you're heading into the park and want to leave the sandwiches to the experts.

Stop by **Mocha Mammas** (inside Free Heel and Wheel), 40 Yellowstone Ave., 406/646-7744, www.wyellowstone.com/freeheelwheel, for espresso and bagels. Another good espresso destination is **The Book Peddler,** 106 Canyon St., 406/646-9358, www.thebookpeddler.com, where you'll find several tables in the back for bagels and coffee. It's a good place to hang out on a cold winter day. They're open until 10 P.M. in the summer.

American

If you're searching for a down-home greasy spoon serving three meals a day, your hunt will end at **Old Town Cafe,** 18 Madison, 406/646-9633. Chicken-fried steaks, biscuits and gravy, buffalo burgers, and hot open-faced sandwiches grace the menu, and pine paneling decorates the walls.

Fans of '50s diners will appreciate the simple and filling meals here.

Beartooth BBQ, 118 Madison Ave., 406/646-4252, is a busy walk-up stand with two picnic tables out front and a menu of beef brisket sandwiches, hot dogs, and Friday–Sunday pork spare ribs. Open seasonally. Just up the street is the local high-schoolers' hangout, the **Dairy Queen.**

Pig out cheaply at tiny **Mountain Mike's Cafe,** 38 Canyon, 406/646-9462, which serves all-American faves: burgers, sandwiches, steak, and chicken, plus freshly baked pies for dessert. A couple of picnic tables sit outback. Justifiably popular for both lunch and dinner, **Bullwinkles Saloon & Eatery,** 19 Madison Ave. W, 406/646-7974, cranks out steaks, burgers, pork chops, salads, and homemade pastries. Big portions too.

Three Bear Restaurant, 205 Yellowstone Ave., 406/646-7811, is a friendly place with an upmarket dinner menu of shrimp, halibut, trout, chicken, and steaks. They have a good salad-and-soup bar, a children's menu, and apple brown Betty à la mode for dessert. Open three meals a day and entirely nonsmoking. Dinner entrées are $12–20.

International

Wild West Pizza, 20 Madison Ave. (next to Strozzi's Bar), 406/646-4400, makes the best local pizzas and calzones. I'm not sure how they came up with the pizza names, but somehow the "Sacajawea" has fresh spinach, feta, kalamata olives, and artichoke hearts!

Chinatown, 100 Madison Ave., 406/646-7088, serves surprisingly authentic Chinese meals, and has $5 lunchtime specials.

Texas Rose Restaurant, 335 U.S. Hwy. 20 West, 406/646-0095, www.texasrosewestyellowstone.com, serves authentic Tex-Mex mealsm including vegetarian items and homemade salsa. They're open until 1 A.M. daily in summer. Drop by on Tuesday nights when the tacos are just 79 cents.

Steaks and More

Coachman Restaurant, downstairs in the Stage Coach Inn, 209 Madison Ave., 406/646-7381 or 800/842-2882, www.yellowstoneinn.com, serves three meals a day, including big traditional breakfasts (great omelets), along with steak, seafood, and pasta for dinner. They also feature a salad bar and a substantial wine list.

The most unusual local eatery is rustic **Eino's Bar,** 406/646-9344, nine miles north of town on U.S. Hwy. 191. It's a cook-your-own steak, burger, and chicken place with a big indoor grill and a motley, hard-drinking crowd. The bar is famous for its bloody Marys and is popular with snowmobilers. Open for lunch and dinner year-round. The patio features a view across Hebgen Lake, and the bar has a big-screen TV and pool tables.

Brewpub

Wolf Pack Brewing Co., 139 N. Canyon St., 406/646-7225, www.wolfpackbrewing.com, generally has four German-style beers on draught, including Wapiti Wheat, Old Snaggletooth Scwartzbier, Jim Bridger Marzen, and Lone Mountain Amber. The menu includes pub fare such as bratwursts, sandwiches, and Polish sausages.

Groceries

Market Place, 22 Madison Ave., 406/646-9600, and **Food Roundup Supermarket,** on the corner of Madison and Dunraven, 406/646-7501, are the local grocery stores. Market Place also contains a deli and bakery. For sweet treats, head to **Arrowleaf Ice Cream Parlor,** 29 Canyon St., 406/646-9776. In addition to homemade ice cream, shakes, banana splits, and waffle cones, Arrowleaf serves burgers, chili dogs, and surprisingly good soups.

ENTERTAINMENT

During summer, you can attend lighthearted comedies and musicals for the whole family at **Playmill Theatre,** 124 Madison Ave., 406/646-7757, www.playmill.com. They've been in operation for more than four decades.

Watch flicks at **Bears Den Cinema,** 15 Electric St., 406/646-7777. In addition to the IMAX films described earlier, **Yellowstone IMAX Theatre,** 406/646-4100 or 888/854-5862, shows Hollywood's latest efforts most evenings.

The bar at **Stage Coach Inn,** 209 Madison Ave., 406/646-7381, has live bands Tuesday–Saturday nights, or try **Iron Horse Saloon,** inside the West Yellowstone Conference Hotel at 315 Yellowstone Ave., 406/646-7365. **Lionshead Super 8 Lodge,** seven miles west of town, 406/646-9584, www.wyellowstone.com /lionshead, has square dancing in the summer.

EVENTS

On the second weekend of March, the **Rendezvous Marathon Ski Race,** a nationally known Nordic ski race, attracts hundreds of participants; 406/646-9222, www.rendezvousski-trails.com. The following weekend brings a very different event, the **World Snowmobile Expo,** 406/646-7001, www.snowmobileexpo.com, with races, demos, and other activities.

A fun parade, live music, and fireworks highlight the town's **Fourth of July** festivities, and the **Yellowstone Rod Run** takes place on the first full weekend of August, bringing vintage cars of all types to the oldest such event in the Pacific Northwest. The **Wild West Yellowstone Rodeo** features bareback riding, team roping, saddle bronc riding, bull riding, and more to the rodeo arena on two weekends in July and August. The **Burnt Hole Mountain Man Rendezvous** on the third weekend of August includes arts and crafts, traditional games, tall-tale competitions, and other old-time events.

At the **Yellowstone Film Festival,** 406/646-1100, www.yellowstonefilmfestival.org, in late September more than 60 films are screened, and you can attend workshops, a tradeshow, and other events.

SUMMER RECREATION

Horses and Bikes

Horseback trail rides and Western cookouts are available from **Parade Rest Guest Ranch,** seven

miles north of town, 406/646-7217 or 800/753-5934, www.paraderestranch.com, and **Diamond P Ranch,** seven miles to the west, 406/646-7246. Several other ranches farther afield also offer horseback rides; contact the chamber of commerce for details.

The 30-km Rendezvous Trail System becomes mountain-bike central when summer rolls around. It starts from the southern edge of town; get a map at the visitors center. Rent mountain bikes from **Yellowstone Bicycles,** 132 Madison Ave., 406/646-7815, or **Free Heel and Wheel,** 40 Yellowstone Ave., 406/646-7744, www.wyellowstone.com/free-heelwheel. Free Heel also rents bike trailers, bike racks, and baby joggers; ask about their free daily bike rides.

Fishing

You'll find five different **fly-fishing shops** in town, a reflection of the sport's importance in the Yellowstone area. In business for more than 45 years, **Bud Lilly's Trout Shop,** 39 Madison Ave., 406/646-7801 or 800/854-9559, www.budlillys.com, is the best-known local place, with fishing tackle, clothing, guides, and even a gallery. Also well worth a look are **Arrick's Fishing Flies,** 125 Madison Ave., 406/646-7290, www.arricks.com; **Eagle's Tackle Shop,** 3 Canyon St., 406/646-7521; **Jacklin's Fly Shop,** 105 Yellowstone Ave., 406/646-7336, www.jacklinsflyshop.com, and **Madison River Outfitters,** 117 Canyon St., 406/646-9644, www.flyfishingyellowstone.com. All of these offer guided fishing and equipment.

River Rafting

Three rafting companies run all-day and half-day whitewater trips down the Gallatin River approximately 50 miles north of West Yellowstone (near Big Sky): **Geyser Whitewater Expeditions,** 406/995-4989 or 800/914-9031, www.raftmontana.com; **Montana Whitewater,** 307/763-4465 or 800/799-4465, www.montanawhitewater.com; and **Yellowstone Raft Company,** 406/995-4613 or 800/348-4376, www.yellowstoneraft.com.

WINTER RECREATION

Cross-Country Skiing

West Yellowstone is infamous for its bitterly cold winters, when the thermometer can drop to −50°F. Fortunately, it doesn't always stay there, and by March the days have often warmed to a balmy 20°F. In November, West Yellowstone becomes a national center for cross-country skiers, with the U.S. Nordic and biathlon ski teams training here.

Two trail systems provide a wide variety of Nordic skiing conditions. The 30-km **Rendezvous Trail** system (www.rendezvousski-trails.com) takes off from the southern edge of town and is groomed with both classical and skating tracks from early November through April. The nine-km **Riverside Trail** begins on the east side of town and leads to the Madison River within Yellowstone National Park. This trail is partially groomed and provides a good opportunity to see bison, elk, and possibly moose; it's closed to skate skiing. You can also ski the snowpacked streets in winter. Find many more places for flat tracking or telemarking in adjacent Yellowstone National Park and the Gallatin and Caribou-Targhee National Forests. Before heading out, get recorded avalanche-safety information from the **Avalanche Advisory Hotline,** 406/587-6981, www.gomontana.com/avalanche. It's updated daily in the winter.

Rent skinny skis from **Bud Lilly's Trout Shop,** 39 Madison Ave., 406/646-7801 or 800/854-9559, www.budlillys.com; or **Free Heel and Wheel,** 40 Yellowstone Ave., 406/646-7744, www.wyellowstone.com/free-heelwheel. Freeheel also rents snowshoes, as does **Yellowstone Rental & Sports,** eight miles west of town on U.S. Hwy. 20, 406/646-9377 or 888/646-9377.

Dogsledding

For a delightfully different way to explore the Gallatin National Forest backcountry, take a sled dog tour from **Klondike Dreams,** 406/646-5988, www.klondikedreams.com. Half-day tours are $100 per person ($85 kids), and all day is $165 per person ($150 kids), including lunch. Owner Roger Vincent can also shuttle skiers into backcountry cabins by dog sled.

Snowcoach Trips

Yellowstone Alpen Guides, 406/646-9591 or 800/858-3502, www.yellowstoneguides.com, leads snowcoach tours from West Yellowstone. All-day trips are $97 ($89 seniors, $77 kids) to Grand Canyon of the Yellowstone, or $87 ($79 seniors, $66 kids under 12) to the Old Faithful area. Guests on the latter run have an option of getting dropped at Biscuit Basin, where they can ski to Old Faithful and meet up with others. Special snowcoach-and-guided-ski tours are $109 per person. Also available is a three-night package trip that includes two nights in West Yellowstone, a night at Old Faithful Snow Lodge, and two days of wildlife snowcoach tours for $395 per person.

For a truly unique experience, book a winter trip with another West Yellowstone–based company, **Yellowstone Expeditions,** 406/646-9333 or 800/728-9333, www.yellowstoneexpeditions.com. The company has homey tent-cabins at the Canyon area during the winter, with a variety of multinight adventures for skiers.

Snowmobiles

The chamber of commerce trumpets West as the "snowmobile capital of the world," and each day between November and late March hundreds (and sometimes thousands) of snowmobilers show up to roar through Yellowstone's West Entrance or across thousands of acres of adjacent Forest Service lands. On busy days long lines of snowmobiles belch blue smoke into the air while waiting to enter the park.

At least 15 different snowmobile tour and rental companies operate out of West Yellowstone. Rentals run $100–175 per day depending on the type of machine; guided Yellowstone tours are more expensive. Hundreds more folks bring in their own "crotch rockets" to ride on park roads or national forest lands, and many local motels offer snowmobile/lodging packages. The West Yellowstone Chamber of Commerce, 406/646-7701, can provide current snow and trail conditions, a detailed map of local trails, and a listing of companies that rent snowmobiles.

A quieter option is to take a snowcoach tour of Yellowstone from **Yellowstone Alpen Guides,** 555 Yellowstone Ave., 406/646-9591 or 800/858-3502, www.yellowstoneguides.com; or **Yellowstone Expeditions,** 406/646-9333 or 800/728-9333. Tours cost $87–97 per day, and both companies also have multinight trips.

SHOPPING

Many West Yellowstone shops sell the obligatory Yellowstone souvenirs, corny T-shirts, and other items with mass appeal. You'll probably get bored after one or two of these gift shops, but many more await your exploration. Fortunately, the town does have several more distinctive places, including **Seldom Seen Knives,** 406/646-4116, www.seldomseenknives.com, at 115 Yellowstone Ave., and **Homeroom,** 121 Madison St., 406/646-4338, www.yellowstoneshop.com.

The Book Peddler, 106 Canyon St., 406/646-9358, www.thebookpeddler.com, is a large and attractive bookstore with an abundance of regional titles. A pleasant café sells espresso, bagels, and pastries in the back. This is a great place to hang with the locals. **Bookworm Books,** 14 Canyon St., 406/646-9736, is another good shop with both new and used titles, including many first editions; it's open nightly until midnight all summer! Check out their collection of vintage Yellowstone tourist antiques, particularly the collectable spoons, plates, and stereo views. The small local **library** is housed in the railroad's old stone dining lodge at 200 Yellowstone Ave., 406/646-9017.

Yellowstone Rental & Sports, 406/646-9377 or 888/646-9377, www.wyellowstone.com/yellowstonerentals, rents a variety of outdoor gear, including tents, sleeping bags, cookstoves, fishing boats, canoes, mountain bikes, baby strollers and car seats, snowshoes, and even backhoes for those who want to dig things up a bit. It's eight miles west of West Yellowstone along U.S. Hwy. 20.

INFORMATION AND SERVICES

The **West Yellowstone Chamber of Commerce,** 30 Yellowstone Ave., 406/646-7701, www.westyellowstonechamber.com, is open daily 8 A.M.–8 P.M. Memorial Day to Labor Day; daily 8 A.M.–5 P.M. in May and Labor Day to October; and Mon.–Fri. 8 A.M.–5 P.M. the rest of the year. The office is also staffed by Park Service employees (406/646-4403) whenever Yellowstone is open. Daily ranger talks are a feature in July and August.

In addition to the Chamber's website, you'll find useful information at www.westyellowstonetraveler.com, maintained by Circumerro Publishing, and Yellowstone Park Net's www.westyellowstonenet.com. Check your email or surf the web at **West Yellowstone Web Works,** 27 Geyser St., 406/646-7006, www.wyellowstone.com, or inside the **Madison Hotel,** 139 Yellowstone Ave., 406/646-7745 or 800/838-7745, www.wyellowstone.com/madisonhotel.

The **Hebgen Lake Ranger District Office** is just north of town on U.S. Hwy. 191/287, 406/646-7369, www.fs.fed.us/r1/gallatin, Pick up maps of Gallatin National Forest, along with an interesting brochure on the Madison River Canyon Earthquake Area.

West Yellowstone's **post office** is at 209 Grizzly Ave., 406/646-7704. You'll find **ATMs** in several local banks, hotels, and other businesses.

Wash clothes at **Canyon Street Laundromat,** 312 Canyon St., 406/646-9733, where you'll also find showers. Other laundry options are **Econo-Mart Laundromat,** 307 Firehole Ave., 406/646-7887, or **Swan Cleaners & Laundromat,** 520 Madison Ave., 406/646-7892.

The Clinic at West Yellowstone, 236 Yellowstone Ave., 406/646-7668, takes walk-in patients. It generally has a doctor and physicians assistant on duty and is open Monday–Saturday.

TRANSPORTATION
By Air
Sky West/Delta, 406/646-7351 or 800/453-9417, www.delta.com, has three flights a day to West Yellowstone airport (just north of town)

from Salt Lake City June–September. The rest of the year, the closest air service is in Bozeman, Idaho Falls, or Jackson Hole.

By Bus and Taxi

Greyhound, 800/231-2222, www.greyhound.com, has daily summer-only runs between Bozeman and Salt Lake City, with a stop in front of West Yellowstone Office Services at 132 Electric Street.

Community Bus Service, 406/646-7600, provides bus service ($10) between West Yellowstone and Bozeman on Thursdays in summer and Tuesdays and Thursdays in winter. Two companies offer winter shuttles between the Bozeman airport and West Yellowstone: **4x4 Stage,** 406/848-2224 or 800/517-8243, and **Karst Stage,** 406/388-2293 or 800/287-4759, www.karststage.com. The cost is $65 per person round-trip. In summer, both companies have custom shuttles throughout the Yellowstone region, but call 24 hours ahead for reservations.

Yellowstone Taxi, 406/646-1111, provides local transport and private transport to other towns in the region, including Jackson ($115 per person).

By Car

West Yellowstone has some of the highest gas prices in the region; fill up before you get here! Rental cars are available through **Budget** (at the airport), 406/646-7882 or 800/527-0700, www.budget.com; or **Big Sky Car Rentals,** 406/646-9564 or 800/426-7669, www.yellowstonevacations.com. Rates start around $45 per day for a compact.

PARK TOURS

Several companies offer all-day tours of Yellowstone June–September. **Gray Line,** 633 Madison Ave., 406/646-9374 or 800/523-3102, www.graylineyellowstone.com, offers lower loop park tours daily and upper loop tours three times a week for $40 ($36 seniors, $30 kids) plus park entrance fees. They also lead Grand Teton National park tours for $50 from West Yellowstone, along with a wildlife tour that goes through Lamar Valley for $40.

Buffalo Bus Touring Co., 429 Yellowstone, 406/646-9564 or 800/426-7669, www.yellowstonevacations.com, has narrated loop tours of Yellowstone for $38 per person or $25 for kids under 16 (plus the park entrance fee). They do the lower park loop daily and the upper loop on Mondays, Wednesdays, and Fridays. In the winter, they operate snowcoach vans, with tours to Old Faithful for $84 adults, $64 kids.

Yellowstone Tours & Travel, 406/646-9310 or 800/221-1151, www.yellowstone-travel.com, takes smaller groups (maximum 12) on van tours of the park for a bit more: $50 for either loop of the park, $60 for Grand Teton/Jackson Hole.

Yellowstone Alpen Guides, 555 Yellowstone Ave., 406/646-9591 or 800/858-3502, www.yellowstoneguides.com, leads more personalized tours, from day trips to multiday excursions. The company provides the naturalist-guide, and you travel around the park in the company van or your own car.

Gardiner, Montana

The little tourist town of Gardiner, Montana (pop. 800), lies barely outside the northwest entrance to Yellowstone, just three miles from the Wyoming line. The Yellowstone River slices right through town. Park headquarters at Mammoth Hot Springs is just five miles away, and the large warehouses of park concessioner Xanterra Parks & Resorts dominate the vicinity. Gardiner is the only year-round entrance to Yellowstone, and the Absaroka-Beartooth Wilderness lies just north of here. The town sits at an elevation of 5,300 feet—some 900 feet lower than Mammoth—and has warm, dry summers and relatively mild winters.

Gardiner was founded in 1880, and three years later the Northern Pacific Railroad extended a line to the edge of Yellowstone, making the town the first major entryway into the park. A reporter of that era described Gardiner as having "200 hardy souls, with 6 restaurants, 1 billiard hall, 2 dance halls, 4 houses of ill-fame, 1 milk man and 21 saloons." Today, the most distinctive structure in town is the monumental stone park entryway—similar to France's Arc de Triomphe—which was the primary entry point into Yellowstone for many years. Built in 1903, **Roosevelt Arch** was dedicated by Pres. Theodore Roosevelt, a man regarded by many as Yellowstone's patron saint. A tablet above the keystone is inscribed, "For the Benefit and Enjoyment of the People." (The arch was actually built to offset the park visitors' initial disappointment at finding the rather ordinary country in this part of Yellowstone!)

ACCOMMODATIONS

Gardiner has many places to stay, but be sure to reserve ahead in the summer; rooms may be hard to find even in mid-September. Rates plummet after (and before) the gold rush of seasonal tourists; $75 summertime rooms suddenly go for $35!

Under $100

Yellowstone River Motel, 406/848-7303 or 888/797-4837, www.yellowstonerivermotel.com, is open May–October. Economy rooms in the older building are $55 s or $59 d, while rooms in the new addition run $75 s or d. A garden patio overlooks the river, and a family unit with kitchenette is also available. **Jim Bridger Motor Court,** 406/848-7371 or 888/858-7508, is a classic Western place with clean and well-kept log cabins built in 1937. Rates are $60 d to $70 for four people; open mid-May to mid-Oct. The three-story **Motel 6,** 406/848-7520 or 800/466-8356, www.motel6.com, has predictable rooms and a view of the parking lot. Summer rates are $70 s or $76 d.

Originally built in the 1950s but updated with newer furnishings, **Hillcrest Cottages,** 200 Scott St., 406/848-7353 or 800/970-7353, www.hillcrestcottages.com, has cozy 15 units, all with kitchenettes and picnic tables. Most have showers, but a few contain tubs.

Roosevelt Arch in Gardiner, Montana, marks the northwest entrance to Yellowstone.

© DON PITCHER

No phones. Rates are $76 d, plus $6 per person for up to six. Open May–Sept. **Riverside Cottages,** 406/848-7719 or 877/774-2836, www.riversidecottages.com, is a little place with motel units ($69–79 s or d), cottages ($89–109 d) with full kitchens, and suites (119–129 for up to six). Rooms are updated, and guests will appreciate the gazebo out back that contains a hot tub overlooking the Yellowstone River.

Located on the north end of town next to the rodeo grounds, **Yellowstone Village Inn,** 406/848-7417 or 800/228-8158, www.yellowstonevillageinn.com, has modern rooms for $75–86 s or d, and kitchenette suites for $135–165; the larger suites sleep six. Amenities include an indoor pool, sauna, and light breakfast. The modern **Best Western by Mammoth Hot Springs,** 406/848-7311 or 800/829-9080, www.bestwestern.com/mammothhotsprings, has an indoor pool, saunas, and a hot tub. Rooms are $95–115 s or d, and suites cost $185.

$100 and Up

Absaroka Lodge, 406/848-7414 or 800/755-7414, www.yellowstonemotel.com, is a modern motel with immaculate rooms for $90 s or d, and suites with kitchenettes that cost $100 s or d, or $110 for four people. All rooms have balconies overlooking the Yellowstone River.

Out in the country five miles northwest of Gardiner, **Maiden Basin Inn,** 406/848-7080 or 800/624-3364, www.maidenbasininn.com, is a recently built eight-room lodge with a variety of accommodations. The inn exudes country charm, and rooms start at $100. A two-bedroom townhouse with a full kitchen, living room, and loft rents for $175. The latter sleeps seven people. All rooms have private decks where you can sit on a rocking chair with a view of Electric Peak inside Yellowstone. An outdoor hot tub is available, and a continental breakfast is served in the lobby. The inn is open mid-May to mid-October.

Comfort Inn, 406/848-7536 or 800/228-5150, www.yellowstonecomfortinn.com, charges $99 s or d for contemporary rooms with log furnishings; suites and hot tub rooms are $150. A

light breakfast is available in the lobby, and the motel has three indoor hot tubs.

Bed-and-Breakfasts

One of the nicest local places to stay is **Yellowstone Inn B&B,** 406/848-7000 or 800/704-5685, www.yellowstoneinnbandb.com, consisting of a beautifully restored stone house (built in 1903) that has been furnished in a New West style. The three guest rooms cost $85–95 d and have shared or private baths. Out back is a private, two-level cottage with kitchenette for $115 d. A full breakfast is served, and guests will enjoy the outdoor hot tub. Well-behaved kids are welcome.

Also of note is **Yellowstone Suites B&B,** 506 4th St., 406/848-7937 or 800/948-7937, www.wolftracker.com/ys, another stone house that's nearly a century old. Features include Victorian antique furnishings, hardwood floors, a veranda, a hot tub, and full breakfasts. The four guest rooms have shared or private baths and cost $85–108 s or d; one contains a kitchenette. Kids are welcome.

North Yellowstone B&B, 406/848-7651, www.northyellowstone.com, is a delightful country place, with two modern log cabins located two miles up Jardine Road. The cabins are $85 s or d; $5 per person for additional guests up to six. A full breakfast is served at the main house. No phones and only a tiny TV are provided, but the cabins have private baths, small fridges, and barbecue grills. Outside, weeping willow trees provide shade, and gorgeous sagebrush country heads out in all directions.

Headwaters of the Yellowstone B&B, 406/848-707 or 888/848-7220, www.headwatersbandb.com, is a large and recently built house on five acres of land along the Yellowstone River. It's located one mile north of the Gardiner airport and has four guest rooms and a suite (all $125 s or d), along with two modern cabins with full kitchens ($150 for up to six). All of these rooms have private baths, and the rate includes a full breakfast. Many Yellowstone visitors stay by the week in the cabins; $125 without breakfast.

Guesthouses

Arch House, 406/848-2205, is a historic rock

home located just two blocks from the arch entryway into Yellowstone. The two-bedroom guesthouse sleeps up to six and includes a full kitchen, bath, living room with stone fireplace, and dining room. It rents for $125 d, plus $10 each for additional guests up to a maximum of six. The owners run Electric Peak Espresso next door, a good place to start your morning with a jolt of caffeine, and serve a continental breakfast.

Above the Rest Lodge, 406/848-7747 or 800/406-7748, www.abovetherestlodge.com, has five modern and well-appointed cabins less than two miles north of Gardiner up Jardine Road. Smallest is a one-bedroom unit with a spiral staircase and full kitchen; $125 for four people. Largest is a spacious three-bedroom home that sleeps 10 people for $260 per night. All of these have full kitchens and decks facing Yellowstone. Open year-round.

CAMPING

Yellowstone National Park's **Mammoth Campground** is five miles up the hill at Mammoth Hot Springs and costs $12. The campground is open year-round but sits close to a busy road. No reservations are taken.

Closer—and more peaceful—is the small **Eagle Creek Campground** ($7; open year-round), less than two miles northeast of Gardiner up the gravel road on the way to Jardine. This Gallatin National Forest campground (www.fs.fed.us/r1/gallatin/recreation) is approximately 500 feet higher than Gardiner, and you will need to bring water from town or treat water from the creek here. Two other Forest Service campgrounds (free; open mid-June through Oct.) are a few miles up Jardine Road.

Park RVs at **Rocky Mountain Campground,** 406/848-7251, www.rockymountaincampground.com, for $26 ($15 for tents); open mid-May to mid-Oct. Showers for noncampers cost $4, and a public laundromat is on the site. Campsites are also available in crowded, along-the-river

sites at **Yellowstone RV Park,** 406/848-7496, open May–Oct. on the northwest end of town. Rates are $31 for RVs, $22 for tents.

FOOD

K Bar Club, 406/848-9995, doesn't look like much either outside or inside, but the from-scratch pizzas are very good in this locals' hangout; kids and families are welcome. Also popular with families is **Outlaw's Pizza,** in the Outpost Mall on the northwest end of town, 406/848-7733, for standard pizzas, pasta, and calzones, and a small salad bar.

Town Cafe, 406/848-7322, has sandwiches and burgers. Better food, including a big salad bar, is upstairs in the Town Loft (summer only), where you can enjoy the vistas while you eat. Also downtown is **Sawtooth Deli,** 406/848-7600, with cold and hot subs, grilled sandwiches, soups, salads, and espresso for lunch, or pasta, steaks, chicken, and more for dinner. The covered deck is a favorite hangout. Closed Sun. and Nov.–Apr.

At **Corral Drive Inn,** 406/848-7627, Helen and her sons serve up the biggest, juiciest, and messiest (grab a handful of napkins) hamburgers anywhere around.

Park Street Grill & Café, 406/848-7989, seems out of place in down-home Gardiner. Most of the menu isn't your standard Old West fare, although they do serve steaks and prime rib. Instead, it's Italian food with flare, including such delights as shrimp fra diavolo (large shrimp sautéed with garlic, peppers, and tomatoes served over linguine) or Crazy Mt. Alfredo with chicken breast, soppressata, Italian sausage, and hot peppers. Meals come with a big house salad, and the atmosphere is rustic elegance. Park Street Grill is open for dinners only ($12–21 entrées) and is closed in the off-season.

Shop for groceries, fresh baked goods, and deli items at **Food Farm,** 406/848-7524, across the river on the northwest end of town. For a sweet treat, step into **Electric Peak Espresso and Ice Cream,** 406/848-2205; it's close to the arch on Park Street.

YELLOWSTONE

EVENTS AND ENTERTAINMENT

The big annual event in town is the **Gardiner Ranch Rodeo,** which comes around the third weekend of June. Other **NRA rodeos** come to Gardiner two or three times a month in May, June, and July. End summer with a blast at **Buffalo Days,** held the Friday before Labor Day and featuring live music, dancing, and plenty of barbecued buffalo, beef, and pork. Look for live bands on some weekends at the **Two-Bit Saloon,** 406/848-7743.

RIVER RAFTING

During summer, three rafting companies offer whitewater trips from Gardiner down the Yellowstone River. **Yellowstone Raft Company,** 406/848-7777 or 800/858-7781, www.yellowstoneraft.com, has been running trips since 1978. Other good companies are **Montana Whitewater,** 307/763-4465 or 800/799-4465, www.montanawhitewater.com; and **Wild West Rafting,** 406/848-2252 or 800/862-0557, www.wildwestrafting.com.

The rapids in this stretch of the Yellowstone River are relatively gentle, in the Class II–III range, and the featured attractions are half-day eight-mile trips or all-day 17-mile trips. Expect to pay around $31 adults, $21 kids for three-hour trips, or $66 adults, $46 kids for a full-day voyage.

OTHER RECREATION

There are two fly-fishing shops in Gardiner: **Park's Fly Shop,** 406/848-7314, and **Big Sky's Flies and Guides,** 107 S. 2nd St., 406/848-9998 or 888/315-3789, www.bigskyflies.com. During the winter, Park's also rents cross-country skis.

For horseback rides and backcountry pack trips, contact **Wilderness Connection,** 406/848-7287, www.wilderness-connection.com, or **Rendezvous Outfitters,** 406/848-7697 or 800/565-7110.

Mountain Biking

No local companies rent mountain bikes, but if you bring your own there are a pair of fine biking options. The Old Gardiner Road to Mammoth gains 900 feet in a distance of five miles and makes for a fun ride back down. Also worth a ride is the old road to Livingston, a gravel road that follows the west side of the Yellowstone River out of Gardiner. It starts near the arch and passes an interesting old cemetery with century-old graves a few miles up.

SHOPPING

Silvertip Bookstore, 501 Scott St., 406/848-2225, sells new and used titles and serves espresso and smoothies. You'll also find a choice of Western books, along with espresso coffee, downtown on Park Street at **High Country Trading,** 406/848-7707.

Yellowstone Gallery & Frameworks, 406/848-7306, www.yellowstonegallery.com, is an excellent place for quality pottery, jewelry, paintings, and photography. Also worth a look downtown is **Off the Wall Gallery,** 406/848-7775.

Flying Pig Camp Store, 406/848-7510, www.flyingpigcampstore.com, sells quality outdoor gear, and has rental computers to check your email.

INFORMATION AND SERVICES

The **Gardiner Chamber of Commerce,** 222 Park St., 406/848-7971, www.gardinerchamber.com, has local information and is open Monday–Friday 9 A.M.–4 P.M., and Saturday–Sunday 10 A.M.–2 P.M. May–September, and Tuesday–Thursday 10 A.M.–4 P.M. the rest of the year. If the office is closed, check the information kiosk on the north end of town for maps, brochures, and events.

The **Gardiner District Office** of Gallatin National Forest, 406/848-7375, www.fs.fed.us/r1/gallatin, has maps and information on the 930,584-acre **Absaroka-Beartooth Wilderness.** The portion around Gardiner is lower in elevation and covered with forests, while farther east are the alpine peaks of the Beartooth Mountains.

The **post office** is on the north end of town along U.S. Hwy. 89, 406/848-7579. Get fast cash at the ATM inside the Exxon station just north of the river or from the First Interstate Bank on the northwest end of town. Wash clothes at **Arch Laundrette,** next to High Country Trading on Park Street. Both Yellowstone Village Inn and Rocky Mountain Campground also have washers and driers available to the public.

TRANSPORTATION AND TOURS

Based in Bozeman, **4x4 Stage,** 406/848-2224 or 800/517-8243, offers taxi service through-

out the Yellowstone area, including into Gardiner. Call 24 hours ahead for reservations. Livingston-based **V.I.P. Taxi,** 406/222-0200 is also available.

From mid-May through September, **Xanterra Parks & Resorts,** 307/344-7311, www.travelyellowstone.com, operates full-day bus tours of Yellowstone out of Gardiner. Rates are $42 adults, $20 ages 12–16, and free for kids under 12; park entrance fees are extra. These tours are a bit grueling because you leave at 8:30 A.M. and don't get back until 6:15 P.M.

Cooke City and Silver Gate, Montana

Shortly after you exit Yellowstone's northeast corner along U.S. Hwy. 212, the road widens slightly as it passes through two settlements: Silver Gate and the larger Cooke City, Montana. The towns are just three miles apart and almost within spitting distance of the Wyoming line. The area code—406—is larger than the combined population of both settlements! Although they depend on tourism, these quiet, homespun places lack the hustle and bustle of West Yellowstone and have a more authentic feel. No leash laws exist here, so you're likely to see dogs sleeping on the sidewalks or wandering lazily down the middle of the road. Most establishments are built of log, befitting the mining heritage of this area. Silver Gate even has a building code that requires all structures to be of log or rustic architecture—it's the only municipality in the country with such a code. Pilot and Index Peaks are the prominent rocky spires visible along the highway east of Cooke City. Dramatic Amphitheater Peak juts out just south of Silver Gate.

During winter, the road is plowed all the way from Gardiner, through the northern part of Yellowstone, and into Cooke City, making this a popular staging area for snowmobilers and skiers heading into the Beartooth Mountains. East of Cooke City, the Beartooth Highway across 10,947-foot Beartooth Pass is closed by the first of November (often earlier) and doesn't open again until late May.

HISTORY

The town of Cooke City was first called Shoo-Fly, but the name was changed in honor of Jay Cooke Jr., a promoter of the Northern Pacific Railroad. The promised railroad never materialized, but the name stuck. Cooke City had its start in 1882 when the boundaries of the Crow Reservation were shifted to the east, opening this area to mining. A small gold rush ensued, and by the following summer, Cooke City had grown to hold several hundred miners, along with two smelters, two sawmills, and a cluster of businesses. At its peak, the town was also home to 13 saloons. As with many 19th-century mining towns, the population of Cooke City had wild swings, with up to 1,000 people at one time, but just 20 souls a few years later. The isolation, modest gold and silver strikes, and high transportation costs (no railroad was ever built into the settlement) kept mining from ever really booming. Today fewer than a hundred people live in Cooke City year-round, but the population triples with the arrival of summer residents.

The town of Silver Gate has a briefer history. The land here was first homesteaded in the 1890s, but the town didn't appear until 1932 when John Taylor and J. J. White founded it as a haven for summer residents looking for a home close to Yellowstone. Only a handful of folks live here in the winter, but that swells to 100 or so when the long days of summer return.

The country around Silver Gate and Cooke City was torched in the Storm Creek Fire of 1988, leaving charred hills just a couple hundred feet to the north and prompting alterations in the road signs to read "Cooked City." Today, tourism is the ticket to ride for both Cooke City and Silver Gate. In summer the towns are crowded with folks en route to (or from) Yellowstone. Both Soda Butte Lodge and Miners Saloon in Cooke City have one-armed bandits with slot-machine poker and keno gambling. In the fall, hunters head into the surrounding mountains, and when the snow flies, the snowmobiles come out of hibernation.

Reminders of the mining era abound in the surrounding country, but not all of it is benign. Reclamation ponds catch toxic runoff from some of these old mines.

SIGHTS

It's hard to miss the red **Cooke City General Store,** 406/838-2234, one of the oldest buildings in the area. Built in 1886, this classic country market sells groceries, quality T-shirts, and gifts that include Indian jewelry and imported items from all over the globe. They also have Yellowstone and Wyoming fishing licenses. Open summers only. Across the street is another summertime place that is well worth a look, **Blain Gallery,** 406/939-2474, features original watercolors by Mary Blain, along with pottery, baskets, and photographs.

COOKE CITY ACCOMMODATIONS

Cooke City and Silver Gate have quite a few old-fashioned motels and cabins that provide a delightful Old West feeling. As with other towns surrounding Yellowstone, advance reservations are always a good idea in midsummer or midwinter.

Cabins

Three miles east of Cooke City, **Big Moose Resort,** 406/838-2393, www.cookecitybigmoose.com, has rustic cabins, a small store, and gas pumps, all open June–October, and December–March. The seven cabins contain older furnishings and private baths; two include kitchenettes. Rates start at $55 d, up to $65 for a four-person cabin with kitchenette.

Right across the road, **Big Bear Lodge,** 406/838-2267, www.sandersbigbearlodge.com, is primarily a fishing lodge but offers nightly accommodations throughout the year. Guests stay in six older but well-kept log cabins, each of which has two double beds. Rates are $55–65 d, and breakfasts are available in the main lodge for an extra $6.50 per person. The lodge is a popular destination for fly-fishing enthusiasts, who come here on three- to six-night package trips that include lodging, meals, and guided horseback rides and fishing. Anglers head into backcountry areas inside Yellowstone, returning each evening to the lodge. In winter, Big Bear is a popular overnight rest stop for skiers and snowmobilers.

Antler's Lodge, 406/838-2432, www.yellowstonelodges.com, charges $50–70 for a range of cabins, some that include kitchens and lofts. It's open late May–September. **Absaroka Cabins,** 406/838-2018, rents out three modern cabins with kitchenettes. These cost $73 d, or $83 for four people, and are open year-round.

Beartooth Plateau Lodge, 406/445-2293 or 800/253-8545, www.beartoothoutfitters.com, is a comfortable log home with space for six people. It has a full kitchen and bath with clawfoot tub; open June–Sept. The house rents for $85 d, plus $10 for each additional person. The owners also run Beartooth Plateau Outfitters, next door.

Located 4.5 miles north of Cooke City up a jeep/hiking trail, the Forest Service's **Round Lake Cabin** sleeps four, and costs just $25. It's open July to mid-September and mid-December through March. For details, call 406/848-7375, or visit www.fs.fed.us/r1/gallatin/recreation.

Motels

You'll find spacious, clean, and comfortable rooms and cabins at **High Country Motel,** 406/838-2272. Rates are $55–78, including some units with kitchenettes. Open all year, and recommended. **Hoosier's Motel,** 406/838-2241, has good rooms for $65 s or d; open mid-May to mid-October. **Alpine Motel,** 406/838-2262 or 888/838-1190, www.ccalpinemotel.com, is also open all year and has rooms for $58–68 s or d. They have two apartment-style units with two bedrooms and a full kitchen for $85 d, plus $10 per person (maximum of six).

With 32 guest rooms on two floors, **Soda Butte Lodge,** 406/838-2251 or 800/527-6462, www.cookecity.com, is the largest lodging place in the area. The hotel contains one of the best restaurants in these parts (Prospector), and guests are welcome to use the small indoor pool and hot tub. Rooms with king beds cost $75, those with two queens are $80, and family suites are $130 for up to six guests. Open year-round.

Elk Horn Lodge, 406/838-2332, www.beartooths.com/elkhorn, has attractive and spotless motel rooms ($52 s or $57 d) and two cabins ($67 d or $77 for four guests). Open year-round.

SILVER GATE ACCOMMODATIONS

Range Riders Lodge, 406/838-2359, is a classic two-story log building with a bar downstairs and rooms above. Rates are reasonable—$35–50 d—but no phones or TVs are provided, and the bath is a few steps down the hall. The original 1930s furniture is still here. Range Riders is open Memorial Day to Labor Day.

Silver Gate Cabins, www.silver-gate-cabins.com, features eight attractive log cabins from the 1930s that contain kitchenettes and cost $57–75 s or d. Also here are five motel units for $42–68 s or d. Outside, you'll find barbecue grills, volleyball and horseshoes, and a playground for kids. It's open June–September; call 406/838-2371 in the summer, or 307/733-3774 in winter.

Grizzly Lodge, 406/838-2219, www.yellowstonelodges.com, is a century-old log building right on the river and close to the Yellowstone border. Guests stay in a variety of rooms (including kitchenettes, two-bedroom units, and rooms with lofts) inside the lodge for $50–75. Also here are a sauna and hot tub. Open Memorial Day to Oct.

CAMPING

Heading east from Cooke City, you'll find four forest service campgrounds ($8; open mid-July to mid-Sept.) within 10 miles of town. Closest is **Soda Butte Campground,** just one-half mile from town; another mile to the east is **Colter Campground.** Get details at 406/848-7375, www.fs.fed.us/r1/gallatin/recreation.

Park RVs ($20) in Cooke City at **Big Moose Resort,** 406/838-2393, www.cookecitybigmoose.com; open only in the summer. Showers are available from Soda Butte Lodge (Cooke City) for $5.

FOOD

Inside Cooke City's Soda Butte Lodge, **Prospector Restaurant,** 406/838-2251, is well known for prime rib cooked to perfection, but it's also open for breakfast and lunch. Also here is the **Ore House Saloon,** with sports on the TV and video poker and keno machines to take your money. Everything at Soda Butte Lodge is open year-round.

Cooke City Bike Shack, 406/838-2412, cranks out espresso coffees and is a great place to meet locals. **Bistro Cafe,** in Cooke City, 406/838-2160, serves standard American fare for lunch, but dinner is when this authentically French bistro shines, with quality steaks, veal, lamb, and fish. Entrées are $13–21.

Beartooth Cafe, in Cooke City, 406/838-2475, has good sandwiches for lunch, dinners that star free-range Angus beef steaks, and more than 100 kinds of beer. They serve breakfast on weekends and are open summers only. Also in Cooke City, **The Grizzly Pad,** 406/838-2161, has reasonable prices, three meals a day, and locally famous milkshakes, burgers, and fries.

In peaceful Silver Gate, **Log Cabin Cafe,** 406/838-2367, is a consistent favorite, with well-prepared trout, pasta, barbecued beef, steaks, and homemade soups. Open in the summer and fall only. Cooke City's **Miner's Saloon,** 406/838-2214, is a classic Old West bar where the stools are filled with locals and tourists. Pull the handles on the one-armed bandits, or try a game of pool, foosball, or air hockey. The menu includes surprisingly good pizzas and burgers.

For groceries and supplies, head to Cooke City General Store (described under Sights) or **Summit Provisions** in Silver Gate, 406/838-2248.

ENTERTAINMENT AND EVENTS

Drinking is the most popular recreational activity in these parts, but **Range Riders Lodge** in Silver Gate, 406/838-2359, also has live country music on weekends all summer. The twin towns have a fun **Fireman's Picnic and 4th of July fireworks,** and Silver Gate is home to **Shakespeare in the Parks** in late August. Summer wraps up with a **Chili Cookoff and Open Container Golf Tournament** over Labor Day weekend. Sounds dangerous.

RECREATION

Yellowstone is less than four miles away, and it's the obvious site for recreation in the Cooke City–Silver Gate area during the summer. The **Absaroka-Beartooth Wilderness** is accessible from Cooke City and various points to the east along the gorgeous Beartooth Highway. One of the more unusual sights is **Grasshopper Glacier,** eight miles north of Cooke City and 4,000 feet higher. The glacier contains the remains of a swarm of locusts that was apparently caught in a snowstorm while flying over the mountains.

Summertime horseback rides, pack trips into the Absaroka-Beartooth Wilderness, and guided fly-fishing expeditions are provided by several local outfitters: **Beartooth Plateau Outfitters,** 406/445-2328 or 800/253-8545, www.beartoothoutfitters.com; **Castle Creek Outfitters,** 406/838-2301; **Skyline Guide Service,** 406/838-2380 or 877/238-8885, www.flyfishyellowstone.com; and **Stillwater Outfitters,** 406/855-0016, www.stillwateroutfitters.com.

Bikes and Skis

Cooke City Bike Shack, 406/838-2412, www.cookecitybikeshack.com, is a hub for the outdoor adventure crowd. The friendly owner

Bill Blackford is a jack of all trades, running the espresso machine one minute and fixing a bike or selling outdoor gear the next. In the winter he rents snowshoes, backcountry skis, avalanche transceivers, and other supplies, and guides tele-marking and cross-country ski trips; $95 per person for an all-day trek. Backcountry skiers and snowboarders who want to head out on their own can catch a five-mile snowmobile ride ($15 per person) into the high country at Daisy Pass, gaining 2,100 feet of elevation along the way. This makes for a great day of skiing and a fun downhill run back to town.

Snowmobiling

Cooke City has become a hub for winter sports. Pick up a map of groomed cross-country ski trails and snowmobile routes from local businesses. The area consistently ranks among the top snowmobiling destinations in America. Snowmobile rentals (and summertime ATV rentals) are available from **Cooke City Exxon,** 406/838-2244, and **Yamaha Shop,** 406/838-2231 or 800/527-6462. The local snowmobile club grooms approximately 60 miles of trails in the surrounding mountains; call 406/838-2272 for information. Be sure to also call the **Avalanche Advisory Hotline** at 406/838-2341 for the latest on backcountry conditions before heading out, or check the website: www.mtavalanche.com.

INFORMATION AND SERVICES

The **Cooke City-Silver Gate Chamber of Commerce,** 406/838-2495, has a small summertime visitors center in Cooke City. It's generally open daily 11 A.M.–5 P.M. June to mid-September. When it's closed, drop by High Country Motel or Elk Horn Lodge for local information. Put away your cell phone in Cooke City and Silver Gate; there's no service here. If you're heading here from other areas, fill your tank because gas prices here are some of the highest in the region.

Despite its remoteness, you'll discover three (count 'em) **ATMs** in Cooke City. The town also has a laundromat.

Bighorn Basin

Bighorn Basin is an enormous intermountain desertscape reaching almost 100 miles north to south and 50 miles east to west. Mountain ranges rim the basin—the Absarokas (pronounced ab-SOR-kas) rise as a western border, the Owl Creek Mountains line the southern horizon, and the snowcapped Big Horns gleam in the east. The basin's rolling desert hills are topped with oil pumpjacks, and the wind blows incessantly. Cactus and sagebrush struggle up through a hardened surface of small rocks, and rugged badlands buttes rise above dry creekbeds. The countryside looks like southern Nevada.

Much of the basin gets less than 10 inches of precipitation per year; in some places just half that, and even in midwinter there isn't much snow on the ground. Three lazy rivers—Big Horn, Greybull, and Shoshone—create long green corridors through this desolation, offering an oasis in the dry desert country. Because of the lack of water, this was one of the last parts of Wyoming to be settled, and most of the towns did not spring up until the 1890s, when passage of the Carey Act brought a flood of irrigation speculators, investors, and farmers. The Carey Act, named for Wyoming Senator Joseph M. Carey, allowed the federal government to donate land to the states for reclamation by settlers. Canals have created wide swatches of irrigated green around the towns and along the rivers. Much of this water comes from the Buffalo Bill Reservoir just west of Cody and a series of canals supplying water to sugar beet and barley farms along the Big Horn and Greybull Rivers.

near the town of Shell

In the early part of the 20th century, boom-times came to the basin with discoveries of oil and natural gas at Grass Creek and Byron. Along with cattle and sheep ranching (important since the 1880s), these industries still dominate the economy of Bighorn Basin. To most tourists, the basin (with the exception of Cody) is a place to get through on the way to Yellowstone or the Black Hills. Locals, however, call it a retirement haven and offer as proof the dry, sunny climate (more than 300 days of sun per year), relatively mild winters, cheap housing, low crime rate, and proximity to the recreational wonderlands of Yellowstone and the Absaroka and Big Horn Mountains. (In case you're confused, the word "Bighorn" is used for the national forest, canyon, river, lake, and basin, while "Big Horn" is the correct spelling for the mountain range, town, and county. Even Wyoming state maps get these spellings wrong!)

Shoshone National Forest

Shoshone National Forest encompasses more than 2.4 million acres and extends along a 180-mile strip from the Montana border to the Wind River Mountains. Sagebrush dominates at the lowest elevations, but as you climb, lodgepole, Douglas fir, Engelmann spruce, and subalpine fir cover the slopes. Above 10,000 feet, the land opens into alpine vegetation and barren rocky peaks. The **Shoshone National Forest Supervisor's Office** is in Cody at 808 Meadow Lane, 307/527-6241, www.fs.fed.us/r2/shoshone. Get information and forest maps there or from ranger stations in Cody, Dubois, and Lander.

BIGHORN BASIN SIGHTSEEING HIGHLIGHTS

Wapiti Valley, Sunlight Basin, and Beartooth Pass within Shoshone National Forest

Buffalo Bill Historical Center and Trail Town in Cody

Homesteader Museum in Powell

Devil Canyon in Bighorn Canyon National Recreation Area

Aerial Firefighting Museum in Greybull

Red Gulch Dinosaur Tracksite near Shell

Medicine Lodge State Park near Hyattville

Washakie Museum and Cultural Center in Worland

Hot Springs State Park, Hot Springs Historical Museum, and Wyoming Dinosaur Center in Thermopolis

Legend Rock Petroglyph Site between Thermopolis and Meeteetse

Wind River Canyon

Popular events: Cody Stampede (early July), Cody Nite Rodeo (all summer), Cody Gunslingers Shootout (all summer), and Gift of the Waters Pageant in Thermopolis (August)

HISTORY

Shoshone is America's oldest national forest. On March 30, 1891, Pres. Benjamin Harrison signed a proclamation creating Yellowstone Park Timberland Reserve adjacent to Yellowstone National Park. At first this title meant very little, but in 1902 Pres. Theodore Roosevelt appointed rancher and artist A. A. Anderson to control grazing and logging and catch poachers. His strong management almost got him lynched. Three years later under Gifford Pinchot, the forest reserves were transferred to the Department of Agriculture and renamed national forests. The land was renamed Shoshone National Forest in 1908.

RECREATION

More than half of Shoshone National Forest lies inside wilderness boundaries; the Absaroka-Beartooth, North Absaroka, and Washakie Wilderness Areas cover much of the country east of Yellowstone National Park, while the Wind River Mountains contain the Fitzpatrick and Popo Agie Wildernesses (see the Wind River

Mountains Country chapter for more on these areas). Part of the credit for the surprising expanse of wilderness areas on the national forest goes to Buffalo Bill. By bringing people into the area to hunt, fish, and explore, he helped create what one author called a "dude's forest." In addition, the Buffalo Bill Dam (which he vociferously supported) prevented logs from being sent down the North Fork of the Shoshone River and thus made logging less important.

More than 1,500 miles of trails offer hiking and horseback access to much of this country.

Shoshone has more than 50 campgrounds, most costing $5–10 per night during summer. Once the water has been shut off for winter (generally Oct.–Apr.), you can camp for free but will have to haul out your own trash. Space is generally available even at the busiest times of year. In addition, free dispersed camping is possible at undeveloped sites throughout the forest, with the exception of heavily traveled U.S. Hwy. 14/16/20, where you must be one-half mile off the road.

Although they are uncommon, black bears roam throughout the forest, and grizzlies are

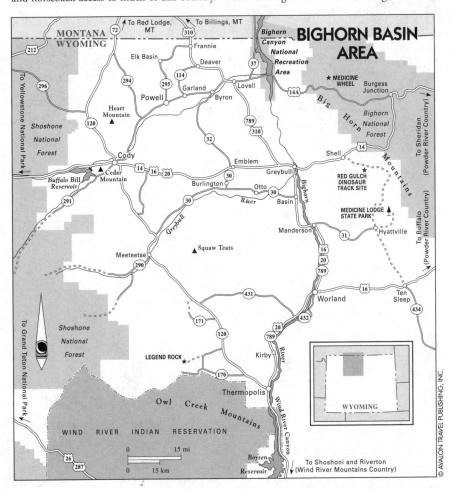

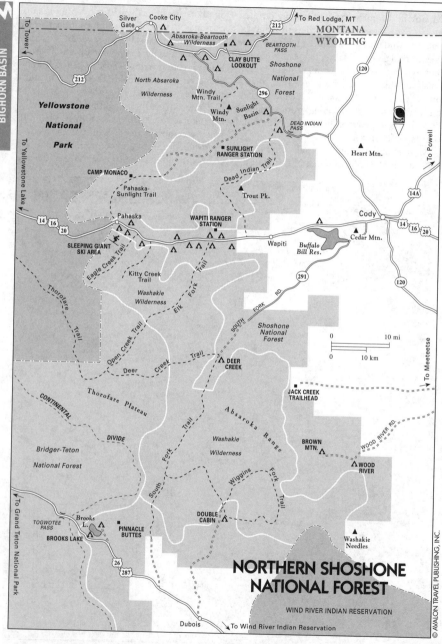

NORTHERN SHOSHONE
NATIONAL FOREST

found within the northern portions, including the North Absaroka and Washakie Wilderness Areas. Be sure to take the necessary bear precautions anywhere in the backcountry. Bears also sometimes wander into campgrounds along U.S. Hwy. 14/16/20 near Yellowstone National Park. Actually, you are more likely to encounter mosquitoes, deer flies, and horse flies in midsummer, so be sure to bring insect repellent.

NORTH ABSAROKA WILDERNESS

The 350,488-acre North Absaroka Wilderness is one of the lesser-known wild places in Wyoming. It abuts Yellowstone National Park to the west and is bordered by the Sunlight Basin and Beartooth Highways to the north and U.S. Hwy. 14/16/20 to the south. North Absaroka Wilderness is primarily used by hunters who arrive on horseback. The few hikers here tend to be quite experienced with backcountry travel and willing to tolerate the lack of trail signs and the steep and frequently washed-out paths. Much of the wilderness is relatively inaccessible, and snow may be present on passes until mid-July. Ask at the ranger stations for current trail conditions, and be sure to get topographic maps before heading out. Large populations of grizzly and black bears, bighorn sheep, moose, and elk are found in the Absaroka Mountains, and golden eagles are a common sight. The tough landscape is of volcanic origin, and the topsoil erodes easily, turning mountain creeks into churning rivers of mud after heavy summer rainstorms.

Hikes

The enormous 1988 Clover-Mist Fire that began in Yellowstone burned through a large portion of the North Absaroka Wilderness, but the land is recovering as young trees and other plants become established. Some areas were also replanted following the fire. Many hikers begin from trailheads near the Crandall Ranger Station along the Chief Joseph Scenic Highway. The **North Crandall Trail** is the most popular, a 16-mile hike up the North Fork of Crandall Creek. It is primarily

used by horsepackers and offers great views of Hurricane Mesa along the way. Another popular wilderness path is **Pahaska-Sunlight Trail**, an 18-mile trek that begins at Pahaska Campground on U.S. Hwy. 14/16/20 and heads north through historic Camp Monaco to Sunlight Basin.

WASHAKIE WILDERNESS

Covering 704,529 acres, Washakie Wilderness is one of the largest chunks of wild land in Wyoming. Named for Shoshone Chief Washakie, it lies between U.S. Hwy. 14/16/20 (the road connecting Yellowstone and Cody) and U.S. Hwy. 26/287 (Dubois area). To the west are Yellowstone National Park and Teton Wilderness. The Washakie is a land of deep narrow valleys, mountains of highly erodible volcanic material, and steplike buttes. The mountains—a few top 13,000 feet—are part of the Absaroka Range. About half of the land is forested. One of the unique features of Washakie Wilderness is a petrified forest, a reminder of the region's volcanic past.

Hikes

There are numerous trails through the Washakie Wilderness, but most require that you either return the same way or end at a location far from your starting point. Several trails stretch into Yellowstone National Park and are popular with extended horsepacking trips. The most popular Washakie Wilderness hikes are from U.S. Hwy. 14/16/20 in Wapiti Valley. Most folks use them for short day hikes or horseback rides rather than attempting longer backcountry treks.

Kitty Creek Trail leaves from the Kitty Creek summer home area, nine miles east of Yellowstone. Low-clearance vehicles will need to park along the highway. The trail follows the creek past two large scenic meadows to Flora Lake, 6.5 miles and 2,500 feet higher. This is the shortest hike in the area and one of the most popular.

The 21-mile-long **Elk Fork Trail** starts at Elk Fork Campground and crosses Elk Creek several times en route to remote Rampart Pass at nearly 11,000 feet. It is steep and rocky in the higher elevations. West of the Continental Divide you enter the Teton Wilderness. For the really ambitious, the Open Creek and Thorofare Trails continue on into Yellowstone National Park.

Deer Creek Trail departs from the free Deer Creek Campground, 42 miles southwest of Cody on State Hwy. 291 (South Fork Rd.). The trail switchbacks very steeply uphill at first and after two miles reaches an attractive waterfall. Continue another eight miles from here to the Continental Divide and the Thorofare portion of the Teton Wilderness. This is probably the quickest route into this remote country and is popular with both horsepackers and hikers.

South Fork Trail takes off from the South Fork Guard Station across the creek from Deer Creek Campground. (Take a signed spur road to get there.) It climbs up along South Fork Creek to Shoshone Pass on the Continental Divide (9,858 feet). From here you can continue on several trails to the south, rambling over three more passes to eventually reach Double Cabin Campground, 27 miles north of Dubois. Another long hike into Washakie Wilderness leaves from this campground and follows the **Wiggins Fork Trail** up into a connecting series of paths: Absaroka, Nine Mile, East Fork, and Bug Creek Trails. It ends back at Double Cabin Campground. Total length is 60 miles. Along the way you're likely to see hundreds of elk in the high country as well as bighorn sheep. You won't see many other hikers.

SUNLIGHT BASIN

The **Chief Joseph Scenic Highway** (State Hwy. 296) is a 46-mile route through a magnificent Wyoming landscape. Popularly known as Sunlight Basin Road, it is paved and most of it remains open year-round, providing access for backcountry skiers and snowmobilers to the beautiful Beartooth Pass area. (An eight-mile portion between Cooke City, Montana, and Pilot Creek, Wyoming, is not plowed in the winter. It typically opens by early May.) Chief Joseph Highway begins 17 miles north of Cody off State Hwy. 120, with Heart Mountain prominent to the southeast, and climbs sharply up from the dry east side, passing a brilliant red butte en route

WYOMING DESIGN

Wyoming seems to be the doing of a mad architect—tumbled and twisted, ribboned with faded, deathbed colors, thrust up and pulled down as if the place had been startled out of a deep sleep and thrown into a pure light.

—Gretel Ehrlich in *The Solace of Open Spaces*

to **Dead Indian Pass,** named for an incident during an 1878 fight between Bannocks and the U.S. Army. After the battle, Crow scouts found a wounded old Bannock warrior here. They killed and scalped him, burying the body under a pile of rocks. Other tales claim that the name came from the body of an Indian propped up as a ruse to trick the army during Chief Joseph's attempted escape to Canada in 1877. Chief Joseph *did* lead the Nez Perce through this country, avoiding the cavalry by heading up Clarks Fork Canyon, a route the army had considered impassable. An overlook on top of Dead Indian Pass provides a panoramic vista of the rugged mountains and valleys below. The river forms a boundary between the volcanic Absarokas to the south and the granitic Beartooth Mountains to the north.

Indians weren't the only ones killed in this era. In 1870, two miners, Marvin Crandall and T. Dougherty, headed into the Upper Clarks Fork following reports of gold in the area. When they failed to meet up with other miners, a search party was sent out. The searchers were themselves attacked by Indians, but they later found the bodies of Crandall and Dougherty—scalped and decapitated, with their heads atop mining picks. In a perverse bit of humor, tin cups sat in front of each skull and the right hand of each man held a spoon. The men had apparently been killed while eating and the bodies were left as a warning against further white exploration of the area.

West of the overlook, the road switchbacks down hairpin turns into remote and beautiful Sunlight Basin. The name came about in the 1840s. Fur trappers worked this area for beaver and discovered a place flooded with light, but it was so remote that "the only thing that can get into this valley most of the year is sunlight." Today it is considerably more accessible but still just as beautiful. A gravel side road leads seven miles up the valley to **Sunlight Ranger Station,** built in 1936 by the CCC. It's open summers only. This is some of the finest elk winter range anywhere and the home of several scenic old guest ranches (described later).

Back on the main road, a bridge—highest in Wyoming at 300 feet above Sunlight Creek—spans deep, cliff-walled **Sunlight Gorge.** Sorry, no bungee jumping allowed. The highway then continues northwest past Cathedral Cliffs and through a scenic ranching and timbering valley, offering views into the deep gorge that belongs to the Clarks Fork of the Yellowstone River. In some sections, sheer cliffs tower 1,200 feet above the water. Part of the area burned by the 1988 Clover-Mist Fire is visible near **Crandall Ranger Station.** This area also contains the only large herd of mountain goats in Wyoming. Eventually you reach the junction with U.S. Hwy. 212, the Beartooth Highway (see Beartooth Mountains section for a description of this beautiful route).

Camping and Hiking

The Forest Service's Lake Creek, Hunter Peak, and Dead Indian Campgrounds ($5–10; open mid-May through Sept.) are found along Chief Joseph Scenic Highway. **Dead Indian Trail** (just uphill from Dead Indian Campground) goes two miles to a fine overlook into Clarks Fork Canyon. Also of interest is **Windy Mountain Trail** which climbs 10,262-foot Windy Mountain. It starts from a trailhead four miles east of the Crandall Ranger Station (interesting old log buildings here), is approximately seven miles one-way, and gains 3,700 feet in elevation. Windy Mountain can also be climbed from the other side near the Sunlight Ranger Station. Trailheads into the North Absaroka Wilderness are at the Crandall Ranger Station and beyond the Little Sunlight Campground (free; open year-round) on Forest Rd. 101.

River Running

Clarks Fork of the Yellowstone River (named for William Clark, of the Lewis and Clark ex-pedition) is Wyoming's only designated Wild and Scenic River. Experienced kayakers will find a couple of great stretches of class IV–V white-water in the upper Clarks Fork; however, use considerable caution because there are several big drops. Be sure to pull out before dangerous Box Canyon, which is considered unrunnable. Find more class IV waters farther down the river. Check with the Forest Service for specifics. Below the rapids are quieter stretches. Based in Cody, **Red Canyon River Trips,** 1374 Sheridan Ave., 307/587-6988 or 800/293-0148, www.imt.net/~rodeo/raft.html, leads gentle float trips down a scenic 12-mile section of the Clarks Fork. The half-day trip costs $50 per person and is offered from late May to early August.

Accommodations

In the heart of beautiful Sunlight Basin, **Seven D Ranch,** 307/587-9885, www.7dranch.com, is a family-oriented guest ranch offering horseback rides, cookouts, fly-fishing, hiking, and pack trips, and something parents will really appreciate: free child care for tots during riding periods, along with a special program for older kids. The setting is spectacular—it's where some of the Marlboro ads were shot—and the cabins are comfortable and cozy. Weekly all-inclusive rates are $3,020 for two people. The ranch has space for a maximum of 32 guests. Open early June to mid-Sept.; adults only in Sept.

K Bar Z Guest Ranch, 307/587-4410, www.agonline.com/kbarz, is off the Chief Joseph Scenic Highway in the Crandall Creek area. Nightly log cabin accommodations are available for $85 d, or two people can stay for six nights for $1,700, all-inclusive (horseback rides, Yellowstone sightseeing, backcountry pack trips, and guided fishing trips). A hot tub and sauna are waiting at the end of a long day. The ranch is open year-round, and features fall hunting and winter snowmobile adventures. A maximum of 30 guests can stay here.

Hunter Peak Ranch, 4027 Crandall Rd., 307/587-3711, www.nezperce.com/ranchhp.html, is on the banks of the upper Clarks Fork River and offers lodging in rustic log cabins or motel-style rooms. Unlike most dude ranches, this one operates on an à la carte basis. Lodging is $90–100 d per night or $560 d per week, with extra charges for meals, horseback rides, and pack trips. The main lodge was built from hand-hewn logs in 1917. Open year-round.

Also in Sunlight Basin, **Elk Creek Ranch,** 307/587-3902 (summers) or 207/384-5361 (winters), www.elkcreekranch.com, provides a unique co-ed opportunity for teenagers to gain a wide range of ranching and wilderness skills. Ranch stays ($2,900 per person all-inclusive for a four-week session) include lots of time on horseback and the opportunity to train horses, build cabins, cut hay, and learn other ranch work. The back-packing adventures ($2,800 per person all-inclusive for a four-week session) give kids plenty of time in the backcountry, where they learn a range of outdoor and mountain-climbing skills. Two month-long sessions are offered each summer with a maximum of 30 kids at a time.

Bluebird Condos, 307/527-6589, www.tct west.net/~jim, is near the Clark Fork bridge, 24 miles from Yellowstone and 42 miles from U.S. 120. One large unit is available with six beds and a full kitchen. It rents for $90 s or d, plus $20 for each additional guest.

Other Services

The little settlement called **Painter** is 21 miles southeast of Cooke City on Chief Joseph Hwy. and right along the Clarks Fork River. Here you'll find a general store and gas pumps, along with year-round RV hookups ($15) at **Painter Estates RV Resort,** 307/527-5248. Open May–Nov. Not far away is the seasonal **Cary Inn Restaurant,** 307/527-5510, serving three meals a day.

SOUTH FORK AREA

South Fork Road heads southwest from Cody and follows the South Fork of the Shoshone River for 42 miles to the edge of the Washakie Wilderness (described later). It's a beautiful drive through definitive Western country with tree-covered mountains and the rich valley below. During winter, the South Fork area has one of the largest collections of frozen waterfalls in the Lower 48, with more than 200 world-class mul-

tipitch climbs. Ice climbers are here all winter, and the **Water Fall Ice Roundup** takes place each February. Get details at www.southforkice.com.

Accommodations

The **Double Diamond X Ranch,** 307/527-6276 or 800/833-7262, www.ddxranch.com, is an excellent family-oriented dude ranch near the South Fork River, 34 miles southwest of Cody. The ranch covers only 200 acres, but it is surrounded by Shoshone National Forest land. Guests take part in horseback rides, trout fishing, hiking, cookouts, and day trips to Cody. The kid's program is one of the best around, with entertaining and educational activities every day, and the ranch brings in professional entertainers several times a week. There's space for up to 36 guests. Facilities include remodeled log cabins—some dating to 1914—and lodge accommodations, plus an indoor pool and hot tub. Meals are noteworthy. All-inclusive rates are $3,700 for two people for six nights; open mid-Apr.–Oct.

Bison Willy's Bunkhouse, 307/587-0629, www.bisonwillys.com, is open from mid-October through mid-April, and is primarily used by ice climbers. The hostel has two co-ed sleeping rooms with bunk space for 12 people at $22 each, plus a kitchenette and showers. You'll need to bring your own sleeping bag. It is located on Double Diamond X Ranch and houses dude ranch workers in summer. The cabin is part of the American Alpine Club's national hut system, and members get a discount. Guided ice climbs may be available.

Rustler's Roost Guest House, 307/587-8171 or 800/667-6352, www.rustlersroost.home-stead.com/guesthouse.html, is a small furnished house with a deck overlooking the South Fork, plus a full kitchen and outdoor hot tub. It sleeps four for $100.

BEARTOOTH MOUNTAINS

Spectacular Beartooth Highway (U.S. Hwy. 212) connects Cooke City and Yellowstone National Park with the historic mining town of Red Lodge, Montana. Along the way, it passes through the Beartooth Mountains on a road built by the

CCC in the 1930s. Some have called this the most scenic route in America. If you like alpine country, towering rocky spires, and a landscaped dotted with small lakes and scraggly trees, you're going to love this drive. A small corner (23,750 acres out of a total of 945,334 acres) of the **Absaroka-Beartooth Wilderness** lies in Wyoming just north of the highway—the rest is right across the Montana border.

Over the Top

A national scenic byway, Beartooth Highway sails across a high plateau and then over the twin summits of **Beartooth Pass**—the east summit is 10,936 feet, and a short distance farther is the west summit at 10,947 feet. A scenic overlook at west summit provides views of the Absarokas to the south and west, the Beartooths to the north, and Bighorn Basin to the east. Majestic rock faces rise in all directions, the most obvious being Beartooth Mountain (its sharp point resembles the tooth of a bear), Pilot Peak, and Index Peak. This is the highest highway pass in Wyoming and one of the highest in North America.

As the road enters Montana, it passes Beartooth Mountain and begins a rapid elevator ride down folded ribbon curves into the resort town of Red Lodge. On top, keep your eyes open for moose, mule deer, mountain goats, bighorn sheep, marmots, and pikas. Be ready for strange weather at this elevation, including snow at any time of year. The highway is closed with the first heavy snowfall (generally in September) and doesn't open until June. The flowers don't really get going until mid-July.

Twin Lakes Ski Area sits near the Wyoming–Montana border and provides Olympic ski training for teens in June and July. South of the summit is the appropriately named Top of the World Store (see description in Camping and Supplies), and another mile or so farther south is the turnoff to an old fire lookout tower at **Clay Butte**, where you'll discover horizon-to-horizon views of the surrounding countryside. A narrow gravel road climbs three miles to the tower, perched at an elevation of 9,811 feet. The small visitors center here is staffed July to mid-September.

Camping and Supplies

There are four developed campgrounds (all $8–10; open July to Labor Day) along this stretch of U.S. Hwy. 212, and more once you drop into Montana. **Beartooth Lake** and **Island Lake** Campgrounds border alpine lakes. In addition, dispersed camping is allowed for free once you get off the main roads. Grizzlies inhabit this country, so be sure to store your food safely.

Top of the World Store, 307/899-2482, sits along the highway between the two Forest Service campgrounds. It's a popular stopping point for cyclists and other travelers over the pass. The general store has a limited selection of food and gifts, plus gas pumps, three motel rooms ($30 d), and a handful of RV spaces ($14) with hookups. The store and motel generally open in late May and close in mid-October. They reopen for winter weekends January–March when the area is a snowmobile destination (but no lodging in winter).

Hiking

The open country at this elevation is dotted with whitebark pines and Engelmann spruce, and it delivers marvelous cross-country hiking opportunities. Anglers should bring a fishing pole to take a few casts for the brook, cutthroat, and rainbow trout in the alpine lakes. Two major trail systems are found in the High Lakes area.

The **Beartooth High Lakes Trail**—actually a series of trails—connects Island Lake, Beartooth Lake, Beauty Lake, and many smaller alpine ponds and puddles. A good place to start is from the boat ramp at Island Lake; see topographic maps for specific routes. This is a very popular late-summer area for day hiking or for access to the Beartooth Wilderness. Be sure to bring a compass, topo map, and warm clothes before heading out on a day hike; the weather can close in very quickly at this elevation, and afternoon thunderstorms are frequent. Always be aware of lightning activity when hiking in this exposed country.

Beartooth Loop National Recreation Trail is just two miles east of Beartooth Pass. This 15-mile loop traverses alpine tundra and passes several lakes and a century-old log stockade of unknown origins.

Wapiti Valley/North Fork

Wapiti Valley provides one of the most popular and scenic routes into or out of Yellowstone National Park, connecting Cody with the park's East Entrance. Pres. Theodore Roosevelt came here often and called it "the most scenic 50 miles in the U.S." The valley is bisected by the North Fork of the Shoshone River, which U.S. Hwy. 14/16/20 parallels for the entire 50 miles from Yellowstone to Cody. Heading east out of Yellowstone, the highway drops through high forests and past an array of volcanic pinnacles and cliffs as the country becomes drier and more open. Cottonwoods line the gradually widening river, and Douglas firs intermix with sage, grass, and rock at lower elevations. Trailheads provide access to two backcountry areas that border the highway: North Absaroka Wilderness and Washakie Wilderness. After a major reconstruction in the late 1990s, the road is in excellent condition the entire distance from Cody to Yellowstone.

Wapiti Valley (the tourism promoters have recently started promoting it as **"East Yellowstone Valley"**) is dotted with lodges, dude ranches, and resorts, many of which offer family-style meals, barbecue cookouts, horseback rides, pack trips, fishing, hiking, river rafting, and other outdoor recreation. If you aren't staying on an all-inclusive plan, most of these perks will cost extra, and some—such as meals or horseback rides (around $20 for one hour or $45 for a half-day)—are often available to both guests and the general public. The lodges generally do not have TVs or phones in the rooms, but most will provide transportation from Cody on request. Those Wapiti lodges and guest ranches that are open in winter are favorite bases for snowmobiling and cross-country skiing. Get additional information on Wapiti Valley at 307/587-9595, www.yellowstone-lodging.com.

On the western end of the valley are Shoshone National Forest campgrounds and hiking trails. The fishing is great in the river, and at Buffalo Bill Reservoir on the eastern end of Wapiti Valley.

PAHASKA TEPEE

Less than three miles from Yellowstone's East Entrance (48 miles west of Cody), Pahaska Tepee was built in 1904 to house Buffalo Bill's guests and others on their way to the park. Pahaska (pronounced "pa-HAZ-ka") was Buffalo Bill's nickname, a Crow Indian word meaning "Long Hair."

The original Pahaska Tepee is a two-story log building that contains a few of Buffalo Bill's original items, including an old buffalo skull over the stone fireplace and several flags that were given to him. Although it is no longer used and in need of major repairs, the main lodge is open for fascinating free tours on weekdays during the summer. The bar inside Pahaska Tepee is small but contains a stunning Thomas Molesworth chandelier crafted in 1938; it's said to be worth $2 million. Look around for other furnishings from Molesworth and a beautiful stained-glass window.

On one of Buffalo Bill's many hunting treks with European royalty, he led the Prince of Monaco into the North Fork country. **Camp Monaco,** 15 miles up the Pahaska-Sunlight Trail from Pahaska Tepee, was named in his honor. Unfortunately, the old spruce tree inscribed with the words "Camp Monaco" was killed when the Clover-Mist Fire burned through here in 1988.

Pahaska Tepee Resort has a mix of old and new cabins and small A-frame motel rooms; summer rates start at $90 d in a small housekeeping cabin up to $450 for a two-bedroom condo (two-night minimum for this one). Wintertime guests can use the outdoor hot tub. Also here are a restaurant, gift shop, gas pumps, and

Wapiti Valley provides one of the most popular and scenic routes into or out of Yellowstone National Park, connecting Cody with the park's East Entrance. Pres. Theodore Roosevelt called it "the most scenic 50 miles in the U.S."

© DON PITCHER

Pahaska Tepee

limited supplies. Pahaska is open year-round. In winter the road is not plowed beyond Pahaska, and the lodge becomes a popular place to rent snowmobiles and cross-country skis for trips into Yellowstone. Contact Pahaska at 307/527-7701 or 800/628-7791, www.pahaska.com.

SKIING AND SNOWBOARDING

Just four miles from Yellowstone's East Gate, **Sleeping Giant Ski Area** is a small family skiing and snowboarding hill with a chairlift and T-bar providing a 500-foot vertical rise. Lifts operate mid-December to early April, and tickets cost $20 adults, $10 kids under 12. Nordic skis, alpine skis, and snowboards are available for rent. For details, contact them at 307/587-4044 (Shoshone Lodge), www.skisleepinggiant.com, or get the ski report at 307/587-7669 (24 hours).

Also based here is **North Fork Nordic Trails,** with more than 50 km of groomed cross-country ski trails for both classical and skate skiing. No charge, and the grooming is generally completed in time for the weekend rush of skiers. Trails cover a widely varied terrain along the river and right to the edge of Yellowstone National Park. Call Shoshone Lodge at 307/527-4044 for specifics.

DOWN THE ROAD

Below Sleeping Giant Ski Area the road passes a whole series of delightfully weird volcanic rock formations. Signs point out several of the most obvious. Stop at the **Firefighters' Memorial,** which honors 15 firefighters who were killed nearby in the Blackwater Fire of 1937. The picnic area here has a special pond for anglers with disabilities.

Eight miles farther east is the historic **Wapiti Ranger Station.** Built in 1903, it was the nation's first Forest Service ranger station. Just a few hundred feet away and right along the highway is **Wapiti Wayside Visitor Center,** 307/587-3925, open Mon.–Fri. 8 A.M.–8 P.M. and Sat.–Sun. 8:30 A.M.–5 P.M. between Memorial Day and Labor Day; closed the rest of the year. Pull in for details on local camping and recreation opportunities, and watch the informative video on safety in bear country. Check the board for recent bear sightings. A few miles to the west (not marked and on an old section of the highway) is Mummy Cave, where a 10,000-year-old mummified body was discovered in 1957.

Next up is a parking area at **Holy City,** an impressive group of dark red volcanic rocks with the North Fork of the Shoshone River cutting away at their base. Try to pick out Anvil Rock, Goose Rock, and Slipper Rock here. The highway leaves Shoshone National Forest and then passes the scattered settlement called **Wapiti**—an Indian word meaning "elk"—20 miles east of Cody. As you might guess, a large elk herd winters in this valley. An unusual volcanic rock ridge near here is locally called Chinese Wall. The eastern half of the road between Cody and Yellowstone passes through this broad and fertile valley; it's quite a change from the rock-lined route to the west. On the east end, the road borders Buffalo Bill Reservoir (see Buffalo Bill State Park) before plunging through three tunnels on the descent into Cody.

CAMPING

Nine different Shoshone National Forest campgrounds provide rustic accommodations along the North Fork of the Shoshone River. Most of these are open mid-May through September (some remain open through October) and cost $5–10 per site; no reservations are taken. All sites have picnic tables, fire rings, potable water, and outhouses. In areas where bears are a problem, the campgrounds also contain bearproof food-storage boxes. All of these Forest Service campgrounds are on the west half of the 50-mile stretch of highway between Cody and Yellowstone. Of these, **Big Game Campground** is closest to Cody at 25 miles to the west, and **Three Mile Campground** is closest to the park, just three miles from Yellowstone's East Gate. Get details on public campgrounds from the Forest Service's Wapiti Wayside Visitor Center (described previously). Dispersed camping outside designated campsites is not allowed anywhere between Cody and Yellowstone along U.S. Hwy. 14/16/20.

Two campgrounds are within Buffalo Bill State Park, described later. Also mentioned are two Wapiti Valley lodges that have RV campgrounds: Green River Inn and Yellowstone Valley Inn.

UPPER NORTH FORK RANCHES

More than 20 lodges, motels, and guest ranches line the road between Yellowstone and Cody. Lodging places west of the midpoint between Cody and Yellowstone are in the more secluded and wooded canyon country of the upper North Fork of the Shoshone River. These places are listed as follows, arranged by their distance from downtown Cody on U.S. Hwy. 14/16/20, starting with those nearest the East Entrance to Yellowstone. Places east of the midpoint between Cody and Yellowstone are situated in the broad and beautiful Wapiti Valley and are typically visible from the highway. Pahaska Tepee—the closest lodge to Yellowstone—is described previously.

Shoshone Lodge

Located 46 miles west of Cody (four miles east of Yellowstone), Shoshone Lodge, 307/587-4044, www.shoshonelodge.com, is a classic mountain lodge with rustic log cabins and home-cooked meals served in the main lodge. The cabins have been updated with Western furnishings, and they range in size from one to three rooms; some contain kitchens. Nightly lodging rates start at $100 d or $110 for four guests, although the nicest cabins are considerably more expensive (up to $260 for a three-bedroom cabin that sleeps six). Horseback rides are available, and Shoshone Lodge is open mid-May to October. The owners also run Sleeping Giant Ski Area, directly across the road.

Crossed Sabres Ranch

Established in 1898, Crossed Sabres Ranch, 307/587-3750, www.crossedsabres.com, 42 miles west of Cody (eight miles east of Yellowstone), has a beautiful historic lodge, plus space for 40 guests in modernized two-bedroom cabins with log furniture and Western décor. After a day of horseback riding, hiking, river rafting, square dancing, or exploring Yellowstone, guests can relax with an evening cookout or soak in the hot tub. All-inclusive weekly packages are $1,990 for two people; open June to mid-Sept.

Goff Creek Lodge

Stay in deluxe log cabins at Goff Creek Lodge, 307/587-3753 or 800/859-3985, www.goffcreek.com, 40 miles west of Cody (10 miles east of Yellowstone). Cabins are offered on either a nightly basis ($95 d) with activities and meals extra, or by the week ($1,880 for two people) on an all-inclusive basis. Goff Creek is open May to mid-October. A variety of outdoor adventures fill the bill here, including horseback rides, pack trips, fly-fishing, and chuck wagon cookouts. All of these options, including meals at the restaurant, are also open to the general public.

Elephant Head Lodge

Forty miles west of Cody (10 miles east of Yellowstone), Elephant Head Lodge, 307/587-3980, www.elephantheadlodge.com, is a no-frills dude ranch with a gracious main lodge built in 1910. Guests stay in 13 modernized cabins, all with private baths and most with decks. Because of its proximity to the park, Elephant Head makes a good base for exploring Yellowstone. Peak-season lodging-only rates are $110 d per day. The largest cabin—it's actually more like a luxury apartment—sleeps eight people comfortably and has a full kitchen; $170. All-inclusive packages with lodging, meals, and horseback rides are $250 for two people per day. Elephant Head's restaurant is open for breakfast and dinner and is locally famous for steaks, pork chops, and other carnivorous fare. It's a frequent destination for Cody folks looking for an evening out. Horseback rides are also available for both guests and the general public. The ranch is open mid-May through September.

Absaroka Mountain Lodge

Find old-time hospitality and adventure at Absaroka Mountain Lodge, 307/587-3963, www.absarokamtlodge.com, 38 miles west of Cody (12 miles east of Yellowstone). Guests stay in comfortable log cabins with private baths and dine in the historic main lodge, built in 1910. Nightly rates start at $76–108 for one bed, up to $145–155 for a two-bedroom cabin that sleeps eight. Their package plan includes lodging, three meals a day, and four hours per day of horseback rides for $135 per person per day. Open May–Sept. Trail rides and meals are also available to folks who aren't staying here.

Blackwater Creek Ranch

Thirty-five miles west of Cody (15 miles east of Yellowstone), Blackwater Creek Ranch, 307/587-5201 or 888/243-1607, www.blackwatercreekranch.com, is a fine place to relax amid the natural beauty of the area. Featured attractions include horseback rides, trout fishing, hiking, games, barbecues, and plenty of kid activities. The gracious log cabins contain fireplaces, and meals are served in the modern Old West–style lodge. Also here are an outdoor pool, a large hot tub, and a game room with billiards and table tennis. All-inclusive one-week stays cost $2,400 for two people, and the ranch is open May–September.

UXU Ranch

A classic Western dude ranch, UXU Ranch, 307/587-2143 or 800/373-9027, www.uxuranch.com, is 33 miles west of Cody (17 miles east of Yellowstone). It offers horseback riding, hiking, fly-fishing, mountain biking, and day trips to Yellowstone and Cody. Guests stay in comfortable cabins containing private baths and porches; some also have fireplaces or gas stoves. After a day of trail riding, you can relax in the big hot tub or visit with new friends in the main lodge. Special children's activities and nature talks are available, and the gourmet meals are memorable. All-inclusive six-night stays cost $2,750 for two people, or four people can stay in the luxurious Hollister cabin (featured in *Architectural Digest*) for $6,100. The ranch is open June–September.

Bill Cody Ranch

Located halfway between Cody and Yellowstone (25 miles in either direction), Bill Cody Ranch, 307/587-6271 or 800/615-2934, www.billcodyranch.com, has graceful log cabins, a comfortable lodge, horseback rides, creekside cookouts, and trout fishing. All-inclusive stays are $270 for two people per night; lodging-only rates are $115 d. Looking for more room and privacy? The guest ranch is open May–September. They also rent out a comfortable fully furnished home with space for 10 guests at $365 per day; three-night minimum stay for the house. Meals, chuck wagon cookouts, and horseback rides are also offered to those not staying at Bill Cody Ranch.

Rimrock Dude Ranch

Twenty-five miles west of Cody (25 miles east of Yellowstone), Rimrock Dude Ranch, 307/587-3970, www.rimrockranch.com, is a classic place with creekside log cabins, horseback riding, back-country pack trips, a large swimming pool, river rafting, hearty family-style meals, and grand mountain country. Pack trips into the mountains are a special favorite. In the winter, this is a popular destination for snowmobilers; the ranch rents snowmobiles and leads tours into Yellowstone. Summertime weekly rates are $2,700 for two people, all-inclusive. Rimrock is open May to mid-September and December–March.

LOWER WAPITI VALLEY ACCOMMODATIONS

The places listed are east of the midpoint between Yellowstone and Cody, in the broad and open portion of Wapiti Valley; those listed under Upper North Fork Accommodations are west of the midpoint, in the more secluded and wooded canyon country.

Built in 1922, **Trail Shop Inn & Cafe,** 307/587-3741, www.trailshopinn.com, 23 miles west of Cody (27 miles east of Yellowstone), sits off the road and along the North Fork Shoshone River. Rustic cabins with private baths are $80 s or d. Open May–Sept.

Green Creek Inn and RV Park, 307/587-5004 or 877/587-5004, www.greencreekinn.com, 22 miles west of Cody (28 miles east of Yellowstone), has roadside motel rooms for $55–65 d; add $5 per person for additional guests. RV sites (no tents) are $17, but they lack showers or a restroom! Open mid-Apr. to mid-Nov.

Stay in modern log cabins at **DNR Ranch at Rand Creek,** 307/527-7176 or 888/412-7335, www.dnrranch.com, 19 miles west of Cody (31 miles east of Yellowstone). Small cabins cost $95 for up to four guests; the largest can sleep eight

for $163. All-inclusive stays are also available; a full week is $2,000–3,000 for two people, including horseback rides, lodging, and breakfast and dinner daily. Built in 1905, DNR Ranch's main lodge is the oldest building in the area. The ranch is open May–December. Trail rides are also offered to folks who are not staying here.

Rocking D River Ranch, 17 miles west of Cody (33 miles east of Yellowstone), 307/587-8329 www.rockingd-riverranch.com, has off-the-road lodging in a loft cabin, bunkhouse, sheepwagon, or tepee. Meals are available upon request. **Wapiti Lodge & Steak House,** 18 miles west of Cody (32 miles east of Yellowstone), 307/587-6659, is "downtown" Wapiti, with a bar, restaurant, and post office in the same building. The restaurant is closed Mondays and Tuesdays but open all year. Breakfast is served until 3 P.M.

At **Yellowstone Valley Inn,** 307/587-3961 or 877/587-3961, www.yellowstonevalleyinn.com, 18 miles west of Cody (32 miles east of Yellowstone), small cabins are $69 d, motel rooms cost $79–125 d, tent spaces are $15, and RV sites with full hookups run $25. The inn sits right on the North Fork Shoshone River and has a restaurant, lounge, and laundromat. Open May–Nov.

Streamside Inn, 307/587-8242 or 800/285-1282, www.wtp.net/streamside, is 15 miles west of Cody (35 miles east of Yellowstone) near the east end of Buffalo Bill Reservoir. Modern motel rooms go for $70 s or $74 d, including a continental breakfast. Kitchenettes are $10 extra. Campers can pitch a tent for $15, and RV hookups cost $25. Guests have access to the large outdoor pool and horseback rides are offered. The inn is open May–October.

Red Pole Ranch, 307/587-5929 or 800/326-5929, www.redpoleranch.com, 11 miles west of Cody (39 miles east of Yellowstone), has eight updated log cabins starting for $75 d, up to $125 for one that sleeps six and has a full kitchen. Open May–Sept.

BUFFALO BILL STATE PARK

Six miles west of Cody on U.S. Hwy. 14/16/20, **Buffalo Bill Reservoir** is a popular place for local boaters and fishermen. Buffalo Bill State

Park, 307/587-9227, http://wyoparks.state.wy.us, encompasses the reservoir and includes two campgrounds ($12 for nonresidents or $6 for Wyoming residents; open May–Sept.) on the north shore. Day use of the park is $4 for non-resident vehicles or $2 for those with Wyoming plates. **Cody Country Outdoors** operates a general store near the main entrance to the park and has groceries, bait and tackle, skiff rentals, and guided charters; 307/527-7999.

Atop the dam, the impressive **Buffalo Bill Dam visitor center,** 307/527-6076, www.bbdvc.org, has historical displays and jaw-dropping views into the canyon, which plummets 350 feet below you. The center is open daily 8 A.M.–8 P.M. May–Sept.; closed the rest of the year. Even if it's closed, stop for the view over the dam.

Fishing is good for rainbow, cutthroat, brown, and Mackinaw trout in Buffalo Bill Reservoir. The lake also offers some of the finest windsurfing conditions anywhere, with nearly constant 30 mph winds; *Outside* magazine once rated it among the country's 10 best spots. The water's cold: You'll need a wetsuit until mid-June.

History

In 1899, Buffalo Bill Cody acquired the rights to build canals and irrigate some 60,000 acres of land near the new town of Cody. With passage of the Reclamation Act of 1902, the project was taken over by the Reclamation Service and an enormous concrete-arch dam was added to provide water. The 328-foot-high dam was begun in 1904 and required five years to finish. It cost nearly $1 million and when finally completed was the tallest dam in the world. Seven men died along the way, including a chief engineer, and the first two contractors were forced into bankruptcy as a result of bad weather, floods, engineering difficulties, and labor strife. A lack of sand and crushed gravel forced them to manufacture it from granite, and 200-pound boulders were hand-placed into the concrete to save having to crush more gravel.

Originally named Shoshone Dam, the impoundment was renamed in honor of Buffalo Bill in 1946. A hydroelectric plant and a 25-foot addition to the top were completed in 1993, bringing the total dam height to 353 feet and increasing water storage by 50 percent. The dam irrigates more than 93,000 downstream acres through the Shoshone Reclamation Project, making it one of the only Wyoming irrigation schemes that actually benefits the state's farmers to a large extent.

Cody

The city of Cody (pop. 8,800) marks the transition point between the forested mountains of northwest Wyoming and the sage-covered plains of Bighorn Basin. It's a favorite stopping place for Yellowstone tourists. The park is just 54 miles due west of downtown, and other magnificent country spreads in all directions—the Beartooth Mountains and Sunlight Basin to the north, the Absaroka Range and Wapiti Valley to the west and south. Established as an agricultural and tourism center, Cody retains both roles today, although tourism seems to be gaining in importance with each passing year. The town is one of the few places in Wyoming that continued to prosper throughout the 1990s; only Jackson Hole exceeds Cody as a tourism center. Not surprisingly, both are gateways to the national parks that dominate northwest Wyoming. Cody is also home to several midsize companies, including oil, mining, and logging operations. One of the biggest employers (after the hospital, the school district, and Wal-Mart) makes—I kid you not—ear tags for livestock.

Cody has several attractions, including the justly famous Buffalo Bill Historical Center, along with Trail Town and other local sights. The Shoshone River flows right through town, providing the opportunity for scenic float trips. Lots of events crowd the summer calendar, from nightly rodeos and shoot-outs to parades and powwows; biggest of all is the annual Cody

Stampede in July. The town also takes pride in a long list of artists that includes Charles Cary Rumsey and Harry Jackson. Famed abstract expressionist Jackson Pollock was born here but achieved his reputation in New York and never returned to his birthplace.

HISTORY

Just west of Cody—past the Wal-Mart, RV parks, fireworks stands, and gas stations—are the Absaroka Mountains, named for the Native Americans who first lived here. They called themselves the Absaroka, or "Children of the Large Beaked Bird." Whites interpreted this as crow, and the natives have been called Crow Indians ever since. Explorer John Colter passed through this region in 1808 while recruiting Indians to supply beaver furs. When Colter returned to the semblance of civilization called Fort Manual Lisa, everyone laughed at his tales of a spectacular geothermal area along the "Stinkingwater River." Soon everyone was calling it "Colter's Hell." But the geysers were real, and they still steam along the Shoshone (formerly the Stinkingwater) just west of present-day Cody. Other mountain men came later, followed by miners who found copper and sulfur in Sunlight Basin. The first real settler in the area was a Prussian, Otto Franc,

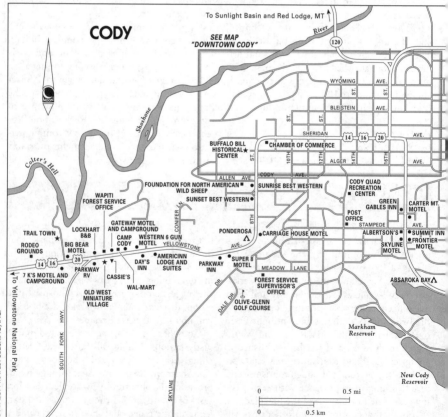

who developed a large cattle spread at the famous Pitchfork Ranch. (Franc is said to have helped finance the Wyoming Stock Growers during the Johnson County War. He was later murdered, and some blamed men affiliated with the homesteaders.)

In 1895, William F. "Buffalo Bill" Cody and two partners began plans for the Shoshone Land and Irrigation Company, with headquarters along the Shoshone River just west of the present city of Cody. Cody had spent much time in the Bighorn Basin, guiding parties of wealthy sportsmen, and was convinced that a combination of tourism and irrigated farming could transform this desert land. Officially

founded in 1896, the name Cody was a natural choice for this new settlement. At the urging of Buffalo Bill, the Chicago, Burlington, & Quincy Railroad arrived in 1901, bringing in thousands of tourists who continued west up Shoshone Canyon to Yellowstone by stagecoach. Tourism is still a cornerstone of Cody's economy, fueled both by its status as an entry point into the park, and also because of the world famous Buffalo Bill Historical Center. Oil was first discovered near Cody in 1904, and Park County remains an important oil producer. Other local businesses include a wallboard manufacturing plant, a lumber mill, and a producer of ranch products.

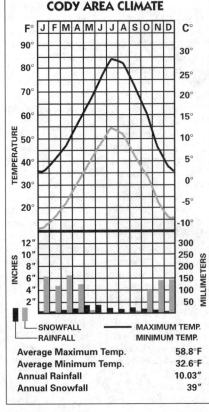

CODY AREA CLIMATE

SNOWFALL	MAXIMUM TEMP.
RAINFALL	MINIMUM TEMP.

Average Maximum Temp.	58.8°F
Average Minimum Temp.	32.6°F
Annual Rainfall	10.03"
Annual Snowfall	39"

BUFFALO BILL CODY

For many people today, the name "Buffalo Bill" brings to mind a man who helped slaughter the vast herds of wild bison that once filled the West. But William F. Cody cannot be so easily pigeonholed, for here was one of the most remarkable men of his or any other era—a man who almost single-handedly established the aura of the "Wild West." More than 800 books—many of them the dime-store novels that thrilled generations of youngsters—have been written about Cody. In many of these, the truth was stretched far beyond any semblance of reality, but the real life of William Cody contains so many adventures and plot twists that it seems hard to believe one person could have done so much.

Young Cody

Born to an Iowa farm family in 1846, William Cody started life as had many others of his era. His parents moved to Kansas when he was six, but his abolitionist father, Isaac Cody, soon became embroiled in arguments with the many slaveholders. While defending his views at a public meeting, Isaac Cody was stabbed in the back and fled for his life. When a mob learned of his father's whereabouts, the eight-year-old Will Cody rode on his first venture through enemy lines, galloping 35 miles to warn of the impending attack. Three years later, when Isaac Cody died of complications from the stabbing, 11-year-old Will Cody became the family's breadwinner. There were four other children to feed. Will quickly joined the company of Alexander Majors, running dispatches between army supply wagons and giving his $40 monthly wages to his mother. In Cody's autobiography he claimed to have killed his first Indian on this trip, an action that gave him the then-enviable title "youngest Indian slayer of the plains."

On his first long wagon trek west, the army supply wagons were attacked by Mormon zealots who took all the weapons and horses, forcing Cody to walk much of the thousand miles back to his Kansas home. It was apparently on this walk that Cody met Wild Bill Hickok. At Wyoming's Fort Laramie, young Will sat in awe as famed scouts Jim Bridger and Kit Carson reminisced about their adventures. The experience was a turning point in Cody's life; he resolved to one day become a scout. Cody's next job offered excellent training: he became a rider for the Pony Express. At just 15 years of age he already was one of the finest riders in the West and a crack shot with a rifle. On one of his Pony Express rides, Cody covered a total of 320 miles in just 21 hours and 40 minutes—the longest Pony Express ride ever. The Civil War had begun, and at age 18 Cody joined the Seventh Kansas Regiment, serving as a scout and spy for the Union Army.

After the Civil War, Will Cody tried his hand at the hotel business and then briefly joined Gen. George Custer as a scout before returning to Kansas to do a little land speculating along the route of the newly built railroad. Cody and a partner bought land and laid out a town that they named Rome. For a short while it boomed. One day a man appeared in Rome, offering to take over the town while leaving Cody with only a small portion of the place he had founded. Thinking it was only intimidation from a shady operator, Cody laughed at the man, not knowing that he was president of the railroad's townsite company. The railroad quickly chose another townsite, and three days later all the inhabitants of Rome moved east to the new site, taking their buildings with them. Cody was left with a worthless patch of land.

Buffalo Hunter and Scout

In 1867, Cody found work hunting buffalo to supply fresh meat for the railroad construction crews, a job that soon made him famous as "Buffalo Bill" and paid a hefty $500 per month. With 75 million bison spread from northern Canada to Mexico, and herds so vast that they took many days to pass one point, it seemed impossible that they could ever be killed off. Cody was one of the best hunters in the West; in just eight months, he slaughtered 4,280 buffalo, often saving transportation by driving the herd toward the camp and dropping them within sight of the workers. Cody's name lives on in the jingle: "Buffalo Bill, Buffalo Bill; never missed and never will; always aims and shoots to kill; and the company pays his buffalo bill . . ."

After this stint, Cody finally got the job he wanted—chief scout for the U.S. Army in the West, a job packed with excitement and danger. Conflicts with Indians had reached a fever pitch as more and more whites moved into the last Indian strongholds. Cody worked as scout for Gen. Philip Sheridan, providing information on the Indians' movements, leading troops in pursuit of the warriors, and joining in the battles, including one in which he supposedly killed Chief Tall Bull. His men considered Buffalo Bill good luck because he managed to keep them out of ambushes.

During the Indian campaigns, the writer/preacher/scoundrel Ned Buntline began writing of Cody's exploits for various New York papers, giving Buffalo Bill his first taste of national acclaim. Soon Buntline had cranked out several romantic novels loosely based on Cody's adventures. America had a new national hero. European and Eastern gentry began asking Cody to guide them on buffalo hunts. On the trips, Cody referred to them as "dudes" and to his camps as "dude ranches"—perhaps the first time anyone had used the terms for such hunters. One of Wyoming's most unusual businesses had begun. Cody's incredible knowledge of the land and hunting impressed the men, but they were stunned to also discover in him a natural showman. In 1872, the Grand Duke Alexis of Russia came to the United States and was guided by Cody on a hunt that made national headlines and brought even more fame to the 26-year-old. On a trip to New York in 1872, Cody met Buntline again and watched a wildly distorted theater production called *Buffalo Bill*. Amazingly, Cody adjusted quickly to the new surroundings. Dressed in the finest silk clothes but with his long scout's hair under a Western hat, Cody suddenly entered the world of high society.

In a short while, Cody was on the stage himself, performing with Ned Buntline and fellow scout Texas Jack in a play called *Scouts of the Plains*. Although meant to be serious, the acting of all three proved so atrocious that the play had audiences rolling in the aisles with laughter. A New York reviewer called the play "so wonderfully bad it was almost good. The whole performance was so far aside of human experience, so wonderful in its daring feebleness, that no ordinary intellect is capable of comprehending it." Audiences packed the theaters for weeks on end. But Cody was suddenly called back west, for the Sioux were again on the warpath.

Shortly after Cody had returned to guide Gen. Eugene Carr's forces, they learned of the massacre of Custer's men at the Battle of the Little Big Horn. In revenge, Carr's men set out to pursue Indians along the border between Nebraska and Wyoming. Under Cody's guidance, they surprised a group of warriors at War Bonnet Creek. Cody shot the chief, Yellow Hand, and immediately scalped him, raising the scalp above his head with the cry "first scalp for Custer!" (Cody later claimed that he scalped the chief because he was wearing an American flag as a loincloth and had a lock of yellow hair from a white woman's scalp pinned to his clothing.) The Sioux immediately fled. If Cody had been famous before, this event propelled him to even more acclaim. It became the grist for countless dime-store novels and was embellished in so many ways over the years that the true story will never be known.

The Wild West Show

Buffalo Bill's days in the real Wild West were over, and he returned to staging shows, eventually starting his famed Wild West extravaganza. This was unlike anything ever done before—an outdoor circus that seemed to transport all who watched to the frontier. One newspaper remarked that Cody had "out-Barnumed Barnum." There were buffalo stampedes, cowboy bronc riding, Indian camps, a Deadwood stage and outlaws, crack shooting by Annie Oakley, and, of course, Buffalo Bill. At its peak in the late 1890s, the show made Cody more than a million dollars in profit each year.

Amazingly, Sitting Bull and Buffalo Bill became good friends. Cody, who had earlier bragged of his many Indian killings, changed his attitude,

continued on next page

BUFFALO BILL CODY (cont'd)

eventually saying, "In nine cases out of 10 when there is trouble between white men and Indians, it will be found that the white man is responsible." Cody's other attitudes also continued to evolve. He criticized the buffalo hunters of the 1870s and 1880s for their reckless slaughter, and he later became an ardent supporter of game preserves and limitations on hunting seasons.

The Wild West Show became one of the most popular events anywhere in America and Europe, attracting crowds of up to 40,000 people. Queen Victoria was a special fan (although rumors of an affair are probably false). At the peak of his fame around the turn of the 20th century, Buffalo Bill was arguably the world's best-known man. Cody, however, continued to drink heavily. One day, an obviously drunken Buffalo Bill insisted that his cowboys ride Monarch, a massive and dangerous bison in the entourage. When they refused in front of thousands of spectators, Cody himself climbed on top and was immediately thrown to the ground. He spent the next two weeks in a hospital. For the next decade the show continued to tour but gradually lost its novelty as other forms of entertainment, especially movies, came along. Cody used his money to buy the 40,000-acre TE Ranch in northwestern Wyoming near Yellowstone National Park. For him the Bighorn Basin was paradise. The town that he helped establish here was named Cody in his honor, and he backed the massive Shoshone irrigation project.

A Sad Farewell

Unfortunately, Buffalo Bill seemed to have no comprehension of how to save his wealth. He was a notoriously soft touch and would give money to almost anyone who asked. As his fortune slipped away and his show became more dated, Cody was finally forced to join up with H. H. Tammen, the crooked owner of the *Denver Post*. Tammen used the aging Cody's fame to attract people to his own circus. He forced Cody's Wild West Show into bankruptcy in 1913, sold

off all of the incredible collection of historical artifacts that had been amassed over the years, and left workers to find their own way home. Buffalo Bill was heartbroken but, still trusting Tammen (or in desperation), agreed to join his circus almost as a sideshow act.

Three years later, Cody died while visiting his sister in Denver and was buried on Lookout Mountain near Denver. Cody had wanted to be buried on Cedar Mountain above the town of Cody, but even this wish was denied by Tammen, who apparently paid Cody's widow Louisa $10,000 for the privilege of choosing the burial site (and to use the funeral parade to the burial site as an advertisement for his circus troop). When rumors came that folks from Wyoming intended to dig up Cody's body and take it back to its rightful burial place, Tammen had tons of concrete dumped on top of the grave. Louisa Cody went on to outlive not only her husband but also all four of her children. She ended up caring for her four grandchildren.

Despite the unhappy ending to Buffalo Bill's life, there are few individuals who lived such a diverse and adventure-filled life and who could count so many people as their friends, from the lowliest beggar to the richest king. Cody's life spanned one of the most remarkable eras in American history, and his impact on American culture is still felt today, not just in the image of the West that he created, which lives on in hundreds of Western movies, but also in the Boy Scouts (an organization inspired partly by his exploits), in the city of Cody, and even in the dude ranches that dot Wyoming.

Late in life, Cody was asked how he wanted to be remembered. He replied: "I don't want to die and have people say 'Oh, there goes another old showman.' When I die I want the people of Wyoming who are living on the land that has been made fertile by my work and expenditure to remember me. I would like people to say, 'This is the man who opened up Wyoming to the best of civilization.'"

BUFFALO BILL HISTORICAL CENTER

Each year, more than 220,000 people visit Cody's main attraction, the Buffalo Bill Historical Center (BBHC). The center actually houses five separate museums covering Buffalo Bill, the Plains Indians, Western art, firearms, and natural history, plus a research library, the boyhood home of Buffalo Bill, and two sculpture gardens. This is the largest and most impressive museum in Wyoming and the finest Western museum in the world. Nowhere else in America is such a major museum located in a town with so few people. The late author James Michener once labeled the BBHC "the Smithsonian of the West," and his term is even truer today with the addition of a natural-history wing in 2002. The museum's collection focuses—not surprisingly—on the Western frontier and includes thousands of artifacts and works of art, culture, and natural history spread throughout more than 300,000 square feet of space.

History

The original Buffalo Bill Museum opened in 1927 in what is now the chamber of commerce log cabin. Opening in 1959, the Whitney Gallery of Western Art formed a nucleus for the current museum location; later additions included the Buffalo Bill Museum, the Plains Indian Museum, and the Cody Firearms Museum. A new natural-history museum is under development and should open early in the 21st century.

Practicalities

Buffalo Bill Historical Center, 307/587-4771 or 800/227-8483, www.bbhc.org, is open year-round. In the busy summer season from June through mid-September, it's open daily 7 A.M.–8 P.M. At other times, hours are reduced: daily 8 A.M.–5 P.M. mid-September through October; daily 10 A.M.–5 P.M. in April; and daily 8 A.M.–8 P.M. in May. From November through March the museum is open Tuesday–Sunday 10 A.M.–3 P.M. Closed Thanksgiving, Christmas, and New Year's Day.

Admission costs $15 adults, $13 seniors, $6 students 18 and older, and $4 ages 6–17. Children under six get in free. The admission is good for two days, and it may well take you two days to explore this massive collection! Tours are generally offered only for school groups and VIPs, but the Historical Center often has summertime demonstrations, and the helpful docents can provide additional info.

On the Museum Grounds

Before heading inside, stop to view Buffalo Bill's **boyhood home,** a tiny yellow building built in 1841 by Isaac Cody. The house stood in LeClarie, Iowa, for almost a century. In 1933 it was sawed in half, loaded on two railcars, and hauled to Cody to be reassembled and refurbished. The house is on your left as you face the museum. Flanking the museum on the opposite side is *The Scout,* a dramatic, larger-than-life statue of larger-than-life Buffalo Bill. This huge bronze piece was created by New York sculptor Gertrude Vanderbilt Whitney and was unveiled in 1924. Her family later donated 40 acres of surrounding land to the Buffalo Bill Museum. Directly in front of the historical center are three colorfully painted **tepees,** a treat for kids. Once you enter the museum, ask for directions to the **Visitor's Lounge,** where a 10-minute orientation video provides a good introduction. Just inside the entrance on the left is a magnificent feathered cape made in 1839 by a Mesquakie woman from the Great Lakes area; don't miss it.

Buffalo Bill Museum

The Buffalo Bill Museum is a real joy. In it, the life of Buffalo Bill Cody is briefly sketched with all sorts of memorabilia from his Wild West Show, including the famous Deadwood Stage, silver-laden saddles, enormous posters, furniture, guns, wagons, and clothing. Be sure to look for "Lucretia Borgia," the Springfield rifle that helped William Cody gain his nickname. Also here are some of the gifts given to Buffalo Bill by European heads of state—including a fur carriage robe from Czar Alexander II—and by Wild Bill Hickok and Sitting Bull. Original film footage from the Wild West Show runs continuously, offering a fascinating and sometimes unintentionally comical glimpse into the past. Amazingly choreographed marching soldiers, fake Indian battles, sign-language conversations, and bucking broncos make it easy to see how the Wild West Show helped inspire Western movies.

Whitney Gallery of Western Art

The Whitney Gallery contains a stunning collection of masterworks by such Western artists and sculptors as Charles Russell, Frederic Remington, Carl Bodmer, George Catlin, Thomas Moran, Albert Bierstadt, Alfred Jacob Miller, Edgar Paxson, N. C. Wyeth, and others. The studios of Frederic Remington and W. H. D. Koerner have been re-created, and Gertrude Vanderbilt Whitney's *The Scout* is visible from a large window on the north end. The collections of both "cowboy artist" Charles Russell and Frederic Remington—best known for his paintings of battles during the Indian wars—are the most complete here; the museum has more than a hundred of each man's paintings. Next to the Whitney Gallery is the **Joseph Henry Sharp Garden,** where you'll find his "Absarokee Hut" filled with the painter's paraphernalia.

The **Kriendler Gallery of Contemporary Western Art** is upstairs from the entrance to the Whitney Gallery and contains a diverse collection of pieces, including several with a delightfully whimsical twist. Well worth the detour.

Plains Indian Museum

The largest exhibition space in the historical center encloses the Plains Indian Museum, with items from the Sioux, Cheyenne, Blackfeet, Crow, Arapaho, Shoshone, and Gros Ventre tribes. At first it may seem incongruous that a museum featuring the man once called the "youngest Indian slayer of the plains" should include so much about the culture of Indians, but Cody's later maturity forced him to the realization that Indians had been severely mistreated and that their culture was of great value. His Wild West Shows re-created some semblance of that lost society, if only for show. Some of the more important items here were given to Buffalo Bill by various Indian performers over the years, and the collection of artifacts is now one of the finest in America.

On exhibit are an extraordinary painted buffalo robe from 1890 that depicts the Battle of Little Big Horn, elaborately decorated baby carriers, ghost-dance dresses, beaded arrow quivers, dance shields (including a Gros Ventre shield from 1700), leather garments, war bonnets, ceremonial pipes, and even a Pawnee grizzly claw necklace. One of the more unusual items is Lone Dog's Winter Count, with figures representing a 71-year sequence of events affecting the Sioux; it was created in 1877. The Hitatsa earth lodge is another highlight. One easy-to-miss area is the special exhibitions gallery downstairs and to the left of the Crow tepee village display. The exhibits change but are always well worth viewing. On the other side of the tepees is a room containing computers and additional displays.

Walking through this remarkable collection always leaves me with mixed emotions. I'm impressed at the beauty of the items and their

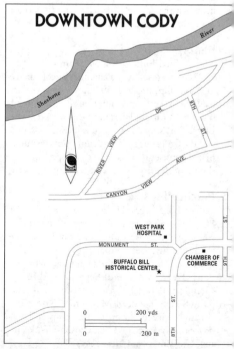

DOWNTOWN CODY

BIGHORN BASIN

historical and cultural significance, but saddened by the way all museums—of necessity—remove things from their environment and create a visually enticing setting, but one that is devoid of the living, breathing people who created these objects. If only we could step back into the past to see how life really was, dirt and all.

Draper Museum of Natural History

This newest addition to the BBHC opened in 2002 to rave reviews. The $17-million facility covers 55,000 square feet, with state-of-the-art exhibits on the Greater Yellowstone Ecosystem and the integral role of humans. Guests begin at a pair of cabins, one of which serves as a naturalist's field station. The other serves as a classroom (of sorts), with a seismograph and computer stations to learn about glaciers, volcanoes, and other natural forces. The main section of the Draper descends along a spiral-

ing path through a giant rotunda, with exhibits describing alpine areas, forests, meadows, and lowland plains ecosystems in the Yellowstone landscape. It's like taking a virtual safari through the area. Multidisciplinary exhibits invite interaction, with lots of kid-friendly audio and video stations, a walk-in beaver lodge, a wolf den, a prairie dog colony, and much more. The winding path ends at a colorful tile map of the Yellowstone ecosystem and an exhibition of children's art.

Cody Firearms Museum

The Cody Firearms Museum houses one of the most comprehensive collections of American firearms in the world, including everything from 16th-century matchlocks to self-loading semiautomatic pistols. This is one museum where the men outnumber the women. Start your visit by viewing "Lock, Stock, & Barrel," a 10-minute video that describes the history of

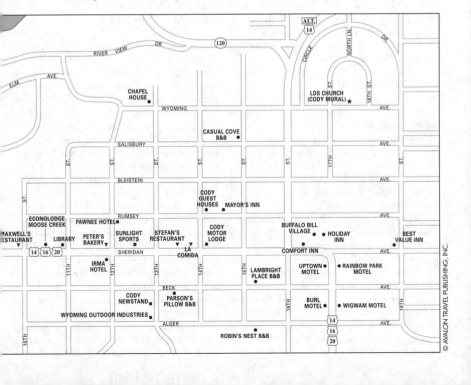

guns and how they work; it's interesting even for those of us who consider the proliferation of guns a national menace. In fact, the entire firearms collection is remarkably informative and well worth taking time to view.

The museum now contains more than 5,000 weapons, but these aren't just rows of guns in glass cases. Some of the more unusual items include a 10-shot repeating flintlock rifle made for the New York Militia around 1825 and a 17th-century windlass crossbow. There are all sorts of displays to explore, including a colonial gun shop, a Western stage station, an early-1900s firearms factory, and a truly extraordinary collection of embellished arms. One of the most lavish is an intricately carved flintlock sporting carbine presented by Empress Elizabeth I of Russia to King Louis XV of France. The Boone and Crockett Club's collection of trophy animal heads is here, including an elephant-sized moose housed in a re-created hunting lodge. Take the elevator to the basement for even more gun displays. All told, this museum houses more implements of destruction and mayhem than you're likely to see at an NRA convention.

Additional Exhibits

Downstairs from the Buffalo Bill Museum is a spacious gallery used for special exhibitions (always worth a look), along with the **Harold McCracken Research Library,** open Monday–Friday 8 A.M.–noon and 1–5 P.M. May–October. The library houses 250,000 historical photos and 15,000 books, including more than 300 volumes about Buffalo Bill—mostly dime novels and comic books.

Other spaces to view include the **Photography Gallery** near the entrance to the Draper, with changing exhibits, and **Ranch and Range,** a collection of wonderful photos taken by Charles Beldon on the Pitchfork Ranch in the 1930s.

Other facilities at the Buffalo Bill Historical Center include an outstanding **gift shop and bookstore,** plus a café for light meals. Head to the sculpture garden for a lunchtime buffalo burger or Polish dog at the **Western cookout** beneath the aspen trees.

Activities and Events

During summer you'll find a wide range of demonstrations every day, including wool-spinning demonstrations, historical talks, cowboy singing, storytelling, and various lectures. Get a brochure at the front desk for today's activities. The **Larom Summer Institute in Western American Studies** is an in-depth two-week history course with two sessions offered each June. Contact the museum for details.

The BBHC plays host to many annual events, including Cowboy Songs and Range Ballads in April, the Plains Indian Powwow in mid-June, and the Old West Show & Auction, also in June. See Events section for details on these and other museum activities.

OTHER SIGHTS

Trail Town

Point your horses toward the mountains and head 'em two miles west of Cody to a unique collection of historic buildings at Trail Town, 307/587-5302. The site is open daily 8 A.M.–8 P.M. mid-May through September only; $5 entrance (free for kids under 13). Trail Town is the creation of Bob Edgar, the man who discovered Mummy Cave—one of the most important archaeological finds in the West—in 1957. Edgar purchased the old Arland and Corbett trading post, and then began dragging in other historic Wyoming cabins. Some were transported whole, others were disassembled and then put back together at Trail Town. Currently the site holds 26 buildings dating from 1879 to 1901, plus 100 wagons.

For those who love history, Trail Town is an incredible treasure trove without the fancy gift shops and commercial junk that tag along with most such endeavors. This is the real thing, low-key and genuine. Probably the most famous building here is an 1883 cabin from the Hole-in-the-Wall country that Butch Cassidy and the Sundance Kid used as a rendezvous spot. Also at Trail Town is the oldest saloon (another hangout of the gang) from this part of Wyoming, complete with bullet holes in the door, and a cabin where Jim White—one of the most fa-

© DON PITCHER

Trail Town, Cody

mous buffalo hunters—was murdered in 1879. The log home of Crow Indian scout Curley stands along main street, too. (Curley was the only one of General Custer's command who escaped alive from the Battle of the Little Big Horn.) Be sure to step inside **Museum of the Old West,** a more recent log cabin filled with artifacts that include a black hearse, rifles found at Indian battlefield sites, arrowheads, beaded necklaces, a cradleboard, and items from the fur traders. Look above the display cases for what may be the most significant discovery, a dugout canoe that was found buried along the Yellowstone River in Montana. It might have belonged to a trapper but is remarkably similar to the ones used by Lewis and Clark. They buried canoes while heading west, planning to dig them up on their return trip. The wood dates to that era; could this be one they left behind?

The bodies of buffalo hunter Jim White and several other historic figures have been reinterred in a small graveyard at Trail Town. One of the most interesting of these is Belle Drewry, a pros-

titute known as "The Woman in Blue." After bouncing around several 19th-century mining towns, she ended up in the lawless and now-abandoned town of Arland, located northwest of Meeteetse. One night in 1897 she shot a cowboy to death during a dance. The following night his outlaw friends took retribution by murdering her. Belle was buried in the blue dress that she always wore. Also buried in the cemetery is **John "Liver Eating" Johnston,** the mountain man portrayed by Robert Redford in the movie *Jeremiah Johnston.* Those who have seen the film will be surprised to learn that Johnston died in 1900 at the Old Soldiers' Home in Los Angeles! Friends sent him there by train from Montana when his health deteriorated, but he only spent a month in California before his death at the age of 76. After the movie came out, schoolchildren in Los Angeles helped promote moving Johnston's body closer to his mountain home. Nearly 2,000 people showed up for the reburial in 1974, including Robert Redford. A memorial to explorers John Colter and Jim Bridger also stands near the graveyard. The historic buildings, artifacts, and graves at Trail Town provide a fine counterpoint to the glitzier Buffalo Bill Historical Center.

Irma Hotel

Pick up a copy of the *Cody Historic Walking Tour* brochure ($2) at the visitors center for an informative introduction to local buildings and their history. One of the most engaging stories is about the Irma Hotel, named for Buffalo Bill Cody's daughter. It was built in 1902 to house tourists arriving by train and was one of three way stations to Yellowstone that Cody built. The luxurious saloon has a French-made cherrywood back bar given to Buffalo Bill by Queen Victoria. The queen spent $100,000 to have it built—no doubt helping to fuel rumors of a romance between her and Buffalo Bill. Many famous people have gathered at the bar over the years.

The **Cody Gunslingers** perform in front of the Irma Monday–Friday June–September. Cody was established long after the era of gunfights in the streets, so this isn't particularly authentic, but it does attract a crowd each evening. The gunfight officially starts at 6 P.M., but the first 15 minutes or so are typically wasted on ads for local businesses. You know you're in America when the advertising even delays a gunfight! Call 307/587-4221 for details on the gunslingers.

Harry Jackson Art Museum

Cody's most famous living artist, Harry Jackson, has a large gallery at 602 Blackburn Avenue. It doesn't look like much outside, but inside you'll discover an amazing diversity of works, covering the palette from abstract expressionist paintings, dark World War II pieces, collages, and cubist studies to his more recent paintings and sculptures (many of which contain distinctively painted surfaces). His other sculptures include the monumental *Sacajawea* at the Buffalo Bill Historical Center and *Horseman* in Beverly Hills. Jackson's pieces have been exhibited throughout the United States and in Italy, where his works are cast. Now something of a living legend, Jackson divides his time between Cody and Italy. All bronzes (but not his paintings) displayed here are for sale, but they're only for serious art patrons

willing to spend thousands of dollars—a 10-foot painted Sacagawea goes for $400,000. The gallery is typically open Monday–Friday 8 A.M.–5 P.M., but call 307/587-5508 for the latest, or visit them virtually at www.harryjackson.com. Entrance costs $4.

Art Galleries

The **Buffalo Bill Historical Center** (described previously) houses an excellent gift shop with art prints, Indian jewelry, and reproductions of bronze sculptures. Next to the chamber of commerce office at 836 Sheridan Avenue is the **Cody Country Art League,** 307/587-3597, www.codyart.vcn.com, displaying paintings, sculptures, photos, and crafts for sale. They also offer workshops and juried art shows.

Simpson Gallagher Gallery, 1161 Sheridan Ave., 307/587-4022, www.sggfineart.com, is one of the best in Cody, with works that go well beyond the standard Western clichés. Just down the street is **Wyoming Artisans,** 307/527-7000, a cooperative where everything is made in Wyoming, including paintings, pottery, lamps, jewelry, and carvings. Of less interest but possibly worth a peek are two shops with predictable artworks: **Big Horn Gallery,** 1167 Sheridan Ave., 307/587-6762, www.bighorngalleries.com, and **Kilian Gallery,** 1361 Sheridan Ave., 307/527-5380.

Old West Miniature Village

Cody has an abundance of offbeat attractions, from talking sheep to sanctified ceilings. The most unusual—and actually worth a visit—is **Old West Miniature Village and Museum** (a.k.a. Tecumseh's Trading Post), 142 W. Yellowstone Ave., 307/587-5362, www.imt.net/~rodeo/mini.html. Owner Jerry Fick has spent decades creating an enormous diorama that offers a truncated version of Wyoming and Montana history. The term "kitsch" quickly enters your head when you step inside, but you've got to appreciate the effort that went into creating thousands of hand-carved figures and an array of miniature villages. Of considerably more interest is his collection of artifacts that includes a knife from the Battle of Little Bighorn, old-time cowboy garb, the bow and arrows that belonged to Geronimo, and many Plains

Indian artifacts. Entrance is $3, and the collection is open daily 8 A.M.–8 P.M. May–Sept.; call for winter hours.

ACCOMMODATIONS

The tourist town of Cody is jam-packed with places to stay, but be ready to pay more than anyplace in Wyoming except Jackson Hole. Budget accommodations are nonexistent during the summer, although rates plummet with the first cold nights of fall. The town doesn't have a hostel, but one is definitely needed! Most of the year, finding lodging in Cody is not a problem as long as you check in before 4 P.M., but during July and August you should reserve a week ahead—and longer for the Cody Stampede in early July.

Cody Area Central Reservations, 307/587-0200 or 888/468-6996, www.wyvacation.com, makes reservations for many local motels, mountain lodges, and B&Bs at no additional charge. It's a good one-stop place to plan your trip to the Cody and Jackson Hole area. In addition to these places, you will find many dude ranches and lodges in the mountain country around Cody; these are described previously in the Wapiti Valley/North Fork, Sunlight Basin, and South Fork Area sections.

Under $50

Cody's least expensive place to stay is also its oldest: the **Pawnee Hotel,** 1032 12th St., 307/587-2239. Built in 1900, the hotel contains 22 refurbished rooms, including four with clawfoot bathtubs. Rates start at $28 s or $34 d with a shared bath down the hall. Rooms with private baths are $32–38s or $42–48 d, and a four-person suite is $48. The owner is very accommodating.

$50–100

Stay in attractive log cabins from the 1920s at **Carriage House Motel,** 1816 8th St., 307/587-2572 or 800/531-2572. The cabins are small and don't have phones, but they have been lovingly remodeled. Rates are $50'60 for one bed, $70 for two beds, or $90 for a two-room suite that sleeps five. Open May–Oct.

Frontier Motel, 1801 Mountain View Dr., 307/527-7119 or 800/707-4940, is a good bargain place with small rooms and dated—but clean—furnishings. Rates start at $54 s or $56 d, or $84 for two queen beds. Kitchenette units (no dishes) are $84 d. Across the road is **Skyline Motel,** 1919 17th St., 307/587-4201 or 800/843-8809, which also has older furnishings, but the rooms are large and there's a big heated outdoor pool, plus a fenced play area for children. Rates are $50 s, $60 d, or $68–76 for four.

Rainbow Park Motel, 1136 17th St., 307/587-6251 or 800/710-6930, is an older motel with clean, well-kept rooms for $54 s or $67 d; kitchenettes cost $5 extra.

Uptown Motel, 1562 Sheridan Ave., 307/587-4245, is a 10-unit motel with well-maintained rooms; $59 for one queen bed or $69 for two. Half the rooms contain microwaves and fridges.

Gateway Motel and RV Park, 203 Yellowstone, 307/587-2561, has basic motel rooms (some with kitchenettes) for $60–70 d. Rustic cabins (built in 1946) are $60–70 d. No phones are provided in the rooms or cabins, but guests can use the computer in the lobby to check their email. Gateway is open May–September.

Buffalo Bill Cody's historic **Irma Hotel,** 1192 Sheridan Ave., 307/587-4221 or 800/745-4762, www.irmahotel.com, has a great downtown location and all the ambience you could want. It's the real thing—a classic Old West hotel. The eight suites in the original building ($93 s or $100 d) provide updated rooms, or you can stay in the far less noteworthy motel rooms in the annex for $67 s or $74 d. Be sure to ask about the ghost (of Buffalo Bill?) that supposedly haunts the rooms.

Carter Mountain Motel sits atop the hill near Albertson's at 1701 Central Ave., 307/587-4295, www.kswope.vcn.com, and features nicely maintained rooms. Standard units (some with fridges) are $69–79 s or d. Suites with full kitchens are $95–149; the largest can sleep nine. A very good moderately priced option is **Summit Inn,** 1714 Stampede Ave., 307/587-4040 or 800/587-9008, with 17 modern rooms—all with two queen beds—for $79 s or d. Open May–Sept.

The appropriately named **Burl Inn,** 1213

17th St., 307/587-2084 or 800/388-2084, features a unique decor that includes hand-crafted burled wood beds and lamps, along with velvet paintings. The rooms are large and clean: $85 s or $90 d for standard rooms, or $105 d for the honeymoon suite with a king bed and jetted tub. Closed Nov.–Jan. **Cody Motor Lodge,** 1455 Sheridan Ave., 307/527-6291 or 800/340-2639, features large rooms for $89–92 s or d, and two suites (one has a kitchen) for $135 d or $150 for five people.

$100 and Up

Green Gables Inn, 1636 Central Ave., 307/587-6886 or 800/707-4940, is an attractive new two-story motel on the south side of Cody. Standard rooms are $100 s or d, and suites run $125 for up to six guests. A continental breakfast is served each morning. Open May–Oct.

EconoLodge Moose Creek, 1015 Sheridan Ave., 307/587-2221 or 800/424-6423, www.econolodge.com, has newly refurbished rooms just a couple of blocks from the Buffalo Bill Historical Center. Smaller rooms with one queen bed are $118 s or d, and large rooms with two beds cost $128 for four guests. Amenities include an indoor pool and continental breakfast.

Buffalo Bill Village Resort consists of three separate operations that total nearly 350 rooms: Holiday Inn, Comfort Inn, and Buffalo Bill Village Resort. All three are located in the heart of Cody at 1701 Sheridan Avenue and share the same phone numbers and website: 307/587-5555 or 800/527-5544, www.blairhotels.com/bbv. Guests at all three facilities can use the outdoor heated pool and small fitness center at the Holiday Inn and are welcome to join the free wine and champagne reception each evening. **Holiday Inn at Buffalo Bill Village Resort,** includes 189 attractively decorated rooms for $129–159 s or d. Priority club members get nicer rooms at no extra charge, and you can sign up when you register. **Comfort Inn at Buffalo Bill Village Resort** charges $129–149 s or d, including a light breakfast. The most distinctive of this Cody lodging triumvirate is **Buffalo Bill Village Resort,** which consists of 83 cozy log cabins. These cabins were built in the 1920s to house workers and their families for nearby Buffalo Bill Dam. The cabins were later moved here and have since been updated to include phones, TVs, private baths, and air-conditioning. Small cabins have a queen or king bed for $109. Family cabins ($139–159) have two bedrooms with three or four double beds. The cabins are open May to mid-October.

One of the nicest chain motels in town, **Kelly Inn,** 307/527-5505 or 800/635-3559, www.kellyinns.com, is one mile east of Cody at 2513 Greybull Highway. The spacious standard rooms are $92 s or $110 d, six-person family rooms with fridges and microwaves go for $145, and rooms with hot tubs cost $145 d. Also here are a sauna and hot tub. A light breakfast is available in the lobby. You'll find fine motel accommodations at **Best Western Sunset,** 1601 8th St., 307/587-4265 or 800/624-2727, www.bestwestern.com/sunsetmotorinn, where the rooms are $109'129 s or d. Amenities include indoor and outdoor pools, a hot tub, playground, and fitness facility.

AmericInn Lodge and Suites, 508 Yellowstone Ave., 307/587-7716 or 800/634-3444, www.americinn.com, is one of the newest places to stay in Cody and offers some of the nicest rooms. All are large, with standard rooms (king or two queen beds) for $139 d, and luxurious suites (some with jetted tubs and fireplaces) for $160–210. Other amenities include an indoor pool, hot tub, and sauna, plus a light breakfast.

Guesthouses

Families may want to stay in one of 20 nicely furnished homes, cottages, apartments, and lodges managed by **Cody Guest Houses,** 307/587-6000 or 800/587-6560, www.codyguesthouses.com. Prices start at $99 d for a small cottage, up to $350 for a luxurious three-bedroom lodge in Wapiti Valley.

Cosy Cody Cottages, 307/587-9253, www.cosycodycottages.com, has two cottages located at 1403 and 1405 Rumsey Avenue. Rates are $100 d ($110 for four guests), and both places contain private baths, full kitchens, and laundry facilities.

Bed-and-Breakfasts

Several historic buildings are now part of the Cody B&B scene, offering a taste of the genteel past. **Parson's Pillow B&B,** 1202 14th St., 307/587-2382 or 800/377-2348, www.cruising-america.com/parsonspillow, is probably one of the most interesting and enjoys a good central location. Completed in 1902, the building served for many years as a Methodist-Episcopal Church. Today it's a cozy and well-maintained B&B with antique furnishings, five guest rooms, private baths, and full breakfasts; $85–95 s or d. Kids older than age five are accepted and will appreciate the room with bunk beds.

Built in 1924, **Lambright Place B&B,** 1501 Beck Ave., 307/527-5310 or 800/241-5310, www.lambrightplace.com, was originally a farmhouse. Three rooms in the large main house are available for $90–95 d, and a separate cottage/bunkhouse with a Western theme sleeps five for $140. All rooms have private baths, and the breakfasts are memorable. Kids are welcome, and the bunkhouse works well for families.

Also recommended is **Robin's Nest B&B,** 1508 Alger Ave., 307/527-7208 or 866/723-7797, www.robinsnestcody.com. On a quiet street just a few blocks from the heart of town, this 1928 brick and frame home features a relaxing and shady backyard, a large living room, and three guest rooms with private baths; $100 d. Most unique is the treehouse suite, situated on an upstairs porch. A full breakfast is served each morning, and well-behaved kids are accepted.

For lodging in a classic Cody home, stay at **The Mayor's Inn,** 1413 Rumsey Ave., 307/587-0887 or 888/217-3001, www.mayorsinn.com, built in 1909 by Frank Houx, the town's first mayor. In 1997 it was moved to the present site and restored to its original opulence. The four guest rooms ($95–205 d) include private baths with jetted tubs, down comforters, terrycloth robes, and heated floors. The nicest room has a king bed and jetted tub. A full breakfast is served each morning; no young children allowed. Also available is a separate cottage with full kitchen for $80 (no breakfast). In addition to lodging, Mayor's Inn also serves gourmet dinners Friday–Sunday evenings with a limited menu. Reservations are required.

Casual Cove B&B, 1431 Salisbury, 307/587-3622 or 866/559-7444, www.casualcove.com, is a renovated 1908 home with three guest rooms, all with private baths. Room rates are $60–70 s or d, including a full breakfast. No kids under age six are permitted.

Lockhart B&B Inn, 109 Yellowstone, 307/587-6074 or 800/377-7255, www.codyvacationproperties.com, has seven guest rooms with private baths and a country decor. Rates are $95–100 d, including a full breakfast and access to a treat-filled refrigerator. Kids are welcome, and the B&B is open May to mid-November. The home once belonged to the writer Caroline Lockhart; see the Special Topic "Caroline Lockhart" for more about her life.

Cody Guest Houses maintains three delightful B&Bs in the Cody area, all with a full breakfast. These include Victorian House B&B, Angel's Keep B&B, and Heart 2 Heart Bed, Barn and Breakfast. For details on any of these, call 307/587-6000 or 800/587-6560, or find more on the web at www.codyguesthouses.com. **Victorian House B&B** is a beautiful three-bedroom home with private baths and an indoor hot tub. Rates are $135–185 d for individual rooms, or $450 for the entire six-person house. **Angel's Keep B&B** is housed within a restored 1930s church and has two rooms for $95–105 d. Located on a ranch seven miles north Cody, **Heart 2 Heart Bed, Barn and Breakfast** has two bedrooms with a shared bath for $85 d.

CAMPING

The closest public campground ($12 for nonresidents, or $6 for Wyoming residents) is 11 miles west in Buffalo Bill State Park. Find many more campgrounds ($5–10) in Shoshone National Forest; the nearest is 28 miles west of Cody in the upper North Fork.

Private Campgrounds

You'll find eight private RV park/campgrounds in Cody. Rates range widely: $20–30 for RVs, or $10–18 for tents. The two best ones are **Ponderosa Campground,** 1815 8th St., 307/587-9203, open mid-Apr. to mid-Oct.; and **7 K's**

RV Park, 232 W. Yellowstone Ave., 307/587-5890, open May–Sept. Both of these have shade trees, and Ponderosa also has tepees ($21) and basic cabins ($34). **Cody KOA,** two miles east on U.S. Hwy. 14/16/20, 307/587-2369 or 800/562-8507, www.koa.com, opened in 1964 as the first franchised KOA. Rates are $24–30 for tents and $30–39 for RVs. Open May–Sept., with an outdoor pool, free pancake breakfast, and rodeo shuttle, and simple cabins for $44–56 d. **Camp Cody,** 415 W. Yellowstone Ave., 307/587-9730 or 888/231-2267, has RV hookups for $18 and tent spaces for $12.50. It's open year-round and includes an outdoor pool.

Other park-it spots (around $10–12 for tents or $15–20 for RVs) include **Gateway Motel and RV Park,** 203 W. Yellowstone Ave., 307/587-2561; **Rivers View RV Park,** 109 W. Yellowstone Ave., 307/587-6074 or 800/377-7255, www.codyvacationproperties.com; **Parkway RV Campground** 132 W. Yellowstone Ave., 307/527-5927 or 800/484-2365, ext. 3881; and **Absaroka Bay RV Park,** U.S. Hwy. 14/16/20 South, 307/527-7440 or 800/557-7440. You can also park RVs at several of the Wapiti Valley lodges (described previously), including **Green Creek Inn and RV Park** and **Yellowstone Valley Inn.** Noncampers can take showers for $5 at Gateway Campground, 7 K's RV Park, or Ponderosa Campground.

FOOD

Because Cody is a tourist town, it's no surprise to find many fine places to eat, covering the spectrum from buffalo burgers to Chinese won tons. Of course, Cody also has all of the Wyoming standards—Taco John's, Subway, Quizno's, McDonald's, Taco Bell, and more.

Breakfast and Lunch

Hang out with the farmers over breakfast or lunch at **Our Place,** 148 W. Yellowstone, 307/527-4420. The coffee is still just 25 cents. **Cody Coffee Company & Eatery,** 1702 Sheridan Ave., 307/527-7879, has espresso, pastries, soups, and deli sandwiches.

Peter's Bakery, 1191 Sheridan Ave., 307/527-5040, bakes breads, cookies, bagels, and turnovers. It's a great place for sub sandwiches, soups, burgers, and more. You won't want to go back to Subway after this; the bread they use is made from scratch, not pulled from the freezer. On weekday evenings, they also have mix-and-match pasta dishes.

Dinner

Proud Cut Saloon, 1227 Sheridan Ave., 307/587-7343, is a fine old-time Wyoming bar and restaurant offering unusual sandwiches at lunchtime and outstanding steak and prime rib for dinner. It's the real thing, with a rustic Old West decor. **Irma Hotel,** 1192 Sheridan Ave., 307/587-4221, www.irmahotel.com, is a long-time favorite of locals for lunch and dinner, but the food is nothing special. Drop by in the morning for their big breakfast buffet.

Bubba's Bar-B-Que, 512 Yellowstone Ave., 307/587-7427, is one of a small chain of Bubba's, with the original in Jackson. It has the best salad bar in town, big breakfasts, and inexpensive ribs, steak, or chicken for dinner. In existence since 1922, **Cassie's Supper Club,** 214 Yellowstone Ave., 307/527-5500, www.cassies.com, is famous locally for its steaks, prime rib, and shrimp. The Wednesday lunchtime Mexican specials attract a crowd.

Eclectic

The ever-popular **Maxwell's Fine Food & Spirits,** 937 Sheridan Ave., 307/527-7749, dishes up homemade lunches that include sandwiches, pasta, and salads. It's a bright and friendly setting, with a patio for sunny days, and a small bakery/coffeeshop. The dinner menu features pasta, seafood, chicken, beef, and vegetarian dishes. Closed Sunday.

Stefan's Restaurant, 1367 Sheridan Ave., 307/587-8511, is an enjoyable place with a diverse menu available three meals a day. Dinner entrées are unconventional takes on such favorites as steaks, baby back ribs, Kung Pao chicken, and shrimp scampi. The atmosphere is a bit upscale but not stuffy. Be sure to save room for the luscious desserts.

Also of note is **The Mayor's Inn,** 1413 Rumsey Ave., 307/587-0887 or 888/217-3001, www.mayorsinn.com, where gourmet dinners are served Friday–Sunday evenings in a quaint Victorian setting. The limited menu changes every week; reservations required.

International

In the heart of town, **La Comida,** 1385 Sheridan Ave., 307/587-9556, serves excellent Mexican food for reasonable prices. Take in the local scene from the outside patio. On the west side of town, **Zapata's,** 1362 W. Yellowstone Ave., 307/527-7181, offers New Mexican–style meals and good margaritas.

For decent Chinese food—including a lunch buffet and family-style dinners—visit **Hong Kong Restaurant,** 1201 17th St., 307/587-6420. **Dragon Wall Buffet,** 225 Yellowstone Ave., 307/587-8899, has all-you-can-eat buffets for both lunch ($6.50) and dinner ($9.50).

Groceries and Specialty Foods

Cody's grocers include an **Albertson's,** on the south side of Cody at 1825 17th St., 307/527-7007, and a big **Wal-Mart SuperCenter,** on the west end at 321 Yellowstone Ave., 307/527-4673. For natural foods and Wyoming-made gifts, head to **Whole Foods Trading Co.,** 1239 Rumsey, 307/587-3213. **Wyoming Buffalo Company,** 1280 Sheridan Ave., 307/587-8708 or 800/453-0636, specializes in buffalo jerky, salami, sausage, and fresh meat, with a variety of gift packages. Stop in for a free sample.

EVENTS AND ENTERTAINMENT

Summer is a busy time in Cody, with special events nearly every weekend. Cody calls itself "Rodeo Capital of the World," and it packs the calendar with nightly summertime rodeos, plus the famous Cody Stampede. The rodeo grounds are one mile west of town on U.S. Hwy. 14/16/20.

Cody Nite Rodeo

After nearly 60 years of operation, the Cody Nite Rodeo is still one of the best in a state filled with rodeos. Shows begin at 8:30 P.M. nightly June–August and always attract a crowd. The best performances take place Friday and Saturday nights,

when you'll see events sanctioned by the Professional Rodeo Cowboys Association (PRCA). A crowd favorite is the calf scramble, starring kids from the stands. Tickets cost $12 adults and $6 children; free for kids under six. For top-of-the-action seats, be sure to get there early and follow the signs to the "buzzards roost" section ($2 extra). Get rodeo details at 307/587-5155 or 800/207-0744, www.codystampederodeo.org.

Cody Stampede

Independence Day sets the stage for Cody's main event, the Cody Stampede, held July 1–4. Established in 1922, it attracts thousands of visitors from all over the nation. Parade fans are treated to one each morning (including a kiddie parade), with dozens of marching bands, mountain men, vintage autos, floats, cowboys, and tons of free candy. Special PRCA rodeo performances, a street dance, art shows, running events, fireworks, and a carnival complete the schedule. Get details at 307/587-5155 or 800/207-0744, www.codystampederodeo.org.

More Events

At 6 P.M. each summer evening, the **Cody Gunslingers** perform downtown at the Irma Hotel. The mock gunfights are Western-style entertainment. They're worth a look if you haven't seen one before, but still corny and quite out of character for settled-down Cody.

Cowboy Songs and Range Ballads is a unique Western musical festival held the second weekend of April at the Buffalo Bill Historical Center. You'll hear true cowboy music (not country-and-western), along with poetry and stories from cowboys, ranchers, musicians, and folklorists. Get details at 307/587-4771, www.bbhc.org/events.

Held in the Robbie Powwow Garden in front of the Buffalo Bill Historical Center in late June, the **Plains Indian Powwow** attracts several hundred participants from all over the Rockies and Canada vying for $10,000 in prize money. It includes daylong singing and dancing in tribal regalia and various dance competitions. Visitors can purchase Indian arts and crafts and taste Indian tacos and fry bread. Contact the BBHC for specifics: 307/587-4771, www.bbhc.org/events.

The **Old West Show & Auction** in mid-June offers a chance for collectors to purchase quality old cowboy gear. It's considered the finest such event in the nation and attracts a wealthy crowd. Get details at 307/587-9014, www.codyoldwest.com. The **Yellowstone Jazz Festival** in mid-July brings both regional and national jazz groups; details at www.yellowstonejazz.com.

The **Buffalo Bill Art Show & Sale** in mid-September is the largest art event of the year, with exhibitions, a symposium, receptions, and an auction; 307/587-5002 or 888/598-8119, www.buffalobillartshow.com.

Music and Entertainment

The downtown City Park band shell is the place to be for Friday evening **Concerts in the Park** in July and August. These free musical performances—in a variety of genres—start at 6 P.M. **Cassie's,** 214 Yellowstone Ave., 307/527-5500, www.cassies.com, has Wednesday night country swing dance lessons, along with country-and-western and mellow rock tunes nightly throughout the summer. Hang around the bar long enough and you can join in that old Cassie's favorite, barroom brawling.

Park Drive In, on the east end of Big Horn Dr., 307/587-2712, is one of the few drive-in theaters left in Wyoming. Open Thurs.–Sun. only. For the indoor version, head to **Cody Theatre,** 1171 Sheridan Ave., 307/587-2712, or the fourplex version: **Big Horn Cinemas,** 2525 Big Horn Ave., 307/587-8009.

RECREATION

River Rafting

One of the most popular summertime activities in Cody is floating the class I and II Shoshone River. Beware, however, that even with these mild conditions, you should plan on getting soaked in the rapids. Expect to pay around $22 adults ($20 kids) for a six-mile run that lasts 90 minutes, or $30 adults ($28 kids) for a 13-mile (three-hour) float. For details, contact **Wyoming River Trips,** 233 Yellowstone Hwy., 307/587-6661 or 800/586-6661, www.wyomingrivertrips.com; **River Runners,**

1491 Sheridan Ave., 307/527-7238 or 800/535-7238, www.imt.net/~rodeo/rrunners.html; or **Red Canyon River Trips,** 1374 Sheridan Ave., 307/587-6988 or 800/293-0148, www.imt.net/~rodeo/raft.html.

If you want to try rafting or kayaking on your own, you'll find several miles of technical class IV water with some class V drops below the dam and above DeMaris Springs. Above the dam are stretches of class I and II water with good access from the main highway. Ask locally for flow conditions before heading out because snowmelt and dam releases can dramatically affect water levels. The rafting companies offer half-day whitewater trips down the North Fork above the reservoir for $55 per person including lunch. These trips only run late May–July, when the water level is high.

Most rafters put in three miles west of Cody off Demaris Street. Just upstream from the put-in point is DeMaris Springs, a part of **"Colter's Hell"** that is on private property and not open to the public. The area was once far more active, with hot springs bubbling out of the river and sulfurous smoke rising all around. People actually died from the poisonous gas. Today the geothermal activity has lessened, but the air still smells of sulfur and small hot springs color the cliff faces. Miners worked over nearby hillsides in search of sulfur; the diggings are still apparent. It's also pretty obvious why they first called this the Stinkingwater River.

Horse and Wagon Rides

Horseback rides are available from **Cedar Mountain Trail Rides,** 307/527-4966, located one mile west of the rodeo grounds; and **Buffalo Bill's Trail Rides,** at the Cody KOA one mile east of the airport, 307/587-2369 or 800/562-8507, www.koa.com. Hour-long trail rides are $20. Many of the lodges in Wapiti Valley (described previously) also offer horseback rides. Get a complete listing of Cody-area outfitters and guides from the chamber of commerce, and a list of permitted outfitters from local Forest Service offices.

Each August, horse enthusiasts join in a week-long trip called **High Country Trail Ride.** Most folks bring their own horse, but rentals are also available. The route takes participants through

Sunlight Basin, with overnight camping, a support staff, veterinarians, catered meals, and entertainment beneath the circus tent. Call 307/527-7468 for details.

More Recreation

The newly built **Cody Quad** is an impressive recreation center on the south side of town at 1402 Heart Mountain St., 307/587-0400. It houses a large indoor pool, hot tub, wading pool, basketball and racquetball courts, an indoor track, and exercise machines. Nonresident rec center passes are $10 adults, $5 kids. Next door is the **Victor J. Riley Arena and Community Events Center,** 307/587-1400, which serves as a summertime convention center and winter ice rink.

Wheel Fun Rentals, 1390 Sheridan Ave., 307/587-4779, www.wheelfunrentals.com, rents a variety of offbeat peddle-powered vehicles, including fringe-topped surreys. I can't imagine pedaling around in these contraptions—at least not without a mask—but tourists seem to love them. Wheel Fun also rents mountain bikes and rollerblades. **Cody Bike Tours,** 307/587-9520, www.codybiketours.com, guides backroads cycling trips in the area.

The 18-hole **Olive Glenn Golf and Country Club,** 802 Meadow Lane, 307/587-5308, is a PGA championship course with a complete golf shop and upscale restaurant. Families enjoy playing **miniature golf** at the downtown city park, 307/587-3685. It's open summers only.

Outdoor Gear

For quality backcountry equipment, especially if you travel by horse, be sure to drop by **Wyoming Outdoor Industries,** 1231 13th St., 307/527-6449 or 800/725-6853. You won't find Gore-Tex jogging bras here, just tough equipment for backcountry use (especially horsepacking), including folding woodstoves, pack saddles, bear-resistant panniers, and wall tents. They also have a mail-order catalog.

Sunlight Sports, 1251 Sheridan Ave., 307/587-9517, is the largest outdoors shop in town, with tents, climbing equipment, clothes, topographic maps, and more, all housed within a classic building with hardwood floors and a tin ceiling. Sunlight Sports also rents cross-country and downhill skis, snowboards, and snowshoes during the winter and is the place to get details on ice climbing in the South Fork area.

North Fork Anglers, 1438 Sheridan Ave., 307/527-7274, www.northforkanglers.com, has anything you might need for fly-fishing, including a full-service retail shop, professional fishing guides, and fly-tying clinics. **Sierra Trading Post,** 1402 8th St., 307/578-5802, has an outlet store in the large log building across from the Buffalo Bill Historical Center.

SHOPPING

As you might expect from a tourist town, Cody has more than its share of shops dealing in clunky jewelry, crass T-shirts, and fake Indian trinkets. Fortunately, it's also home to several places with a bit more class.

Cody Rodeo Company, 1291 Sheridan Ave., 307/587-5913, www.codyrodeocompany.com, has a big selection of cowboy hats and also sells Western wear, rodeo memorabilia, and decorative items in a playful setting. Get fancy Western duds at **Custom Cowboy Shop,** 1286 Sheridan Ave., 307/527-7300. **Corral West Ranchwear,** 1625 Stampede Ave., 307/587-4493, www.corralwest.com, has inexpensive Western wear.

Traditions West Antique Mall, 1131 Sheridan Ave., 307/587-7434, and **Old West Antique Mall,** 1215 Sheridan Ave., 307/587-9014, are good places to look for Western antiques.

New books are available from **Cody Newsstand,** 1121 13th St., 307/587-2843, and **The Thistle,** 1243 Rumsey, 307/587-6635. Cody Newsstand also has one of the best magazine selections in Bighorn Basin. **Wyoming Well Book Exchange and Oilfield Supply,** 1902 E. Sheridan Ave., 307/587-4249, has the oddest combination in town: bodice-buster novels and oil-drilling equipment!

INFORMATION AND SERVICES

Get local information from the **Cody Country Chamber of Commerce,** 836 Sheridan Ave.,

307/587-2297 or 800/393-2639, www.cody-chamber.org. Hours are Monday–Saturday 8 A.M.–6 P.M. and Sunday 10 A.M.–3 P.M. Memorial Day to Labor Day, and Monday–Friday 8 A.M.–5 P.M. the rest of the year. This log building housed the original Buffalo Bill Museum from 1927 to 1969 and was built as a replica of Cody's TE Ranch. It's on the National Register of Historic Places. A regional tourism organization, **Park County Travel Council,** is also based here, providing publications (call 800/393-2639) and web information (www.yellowstone.org) to travelers heading through Cody, Powell, Meeteetse, and Wapiti Valley. Another good source for Cody information is **Cody Wyoming Net,** www.codywyomingnet.com.

The **BLM's Cody Field Office** is at 1002 Blackburn Ave., 307/578-5900, www.wy.blm.gov. The Forest Service has two local offices: the **Shoshone National Forest Supervisor's Office,** 808 Meadow Lane, 307/527-6241, www.fs.fed.us/r2/shoshone, and the smaller **Wapiti Ranger District Office,** 203 W. Yellowstone, 307/527-6921.

The **Park County Library,** 1057 Sheridan Ave., 307/587-6204, has regional titles and computers for Internet access.

Cody's **West Park Hospital,** 707 Sheridan Ave., 307/527-7501 or 800/654-9447, www.westparkhospital.org, is the largest in Bighorn Basin and one of the finest in the state. The hospital's **Urgent Care Clinic,** 702 Yellowstone Ave., 307/587-7207, is open daily and evenings. No appointment needed.

Get fast cash at **ATMs** scattered throughout Cody, including one inside the Buffalo Bill Historical Center and another in the Wal-Mart SuperCenter.

Wash clothes at **Eastgate Laundry,** next to Albertson's at 1813 17th St., 307/587-5355; and **Quick Coin-Op Laundromat,** 930 12th St., 307/587-6519.

TRANSPORTATION

Yellowstone Regional Airport (www.flyra.com) is just east of town on U.S. Hwy. 14/16/20. **Sky-West/Delta,** 307/587-9740 or 800/221-1212, www.delta.com, has daily flights to Salt Lake City, while **Great Lakes Aviation,** 307/432-7000 or 800/554-5111, www.greatlakesav.com, has daily service to Denver and Rock Springs. **Spirit Mountain Aviation,** 307/587-6732, offers scenic flights and charter service.

Phidippides Shuttle Service, 307/527-6789 or 866/527-6789, www.phidpdes.com, provides shuttle vans to the airport in Billings, Montana.

Rent cars at the airport from Budget, Hertz, or Thrifty. See the "Rental Car Contacts" Special Topic in the On the Road chapter.

Buses from **Powder River Transportation/Coach USA,** 307/682-0960 or 800/442-3682, stop at Kelly Inn, 2513 Greybull Highway, providing service north to Billings, Montana, east to Rapid City, South Dakota, and south to Denver. They stop in most Bighorn Basin towns, and serve much of central and eastern Wyoming.

TOURS

The **Cody Trolley,** 307/527-7043, www.codytrolleytours.com, takes you on an informative hour-long tour of town (and up to Buffalo Bill Dam) for $11. These tours are offered several times a day in summer.

During summer, daily tours of Yellowstone National Park—$60 adults, $54 seniors, and $30 kids—are available through **Powder River Tours/Coach USA,** 307/527-3677 or 800/442-3682. These tours cover either the southern park loop or the northern portion, and two-day tours that include the whole shebang are $110 adults, $99 seniors, and $55 kids. You can stay overnight in Yellowstone and return on a later bus for no extra charge (on a space-available basis) or transfer to Gray Line buses to reach Jackson (307/733-4325 or 800/443-6133, www.jacksonholealltrans.com) or West Yellowstone (406/646-9374 or 800/523-3102, www.graylineyellowstone.com).

For a more personalized trip, call **Grub Steak Expeditions,** 307/527-6316 or 800/527-6316, www.grubsteaktours.com. It leads 12-hour auto tours of the park, along with visits to Sunlight Basin, Wapiti Valley, and the South Fork. One-day tours cost $300 for two people, plus $100 for each additional guest. These tours are popular with families looking for a unique perspective on the park, and some are led by the co-owner, a retired Yellowstone park ranger. **Yellowstone Expedition Services,** 307/587-5452 or 888/808-7990, www.yellowstoneparktours.com, also offers customized auto tours into Yellowstone with a maximum of six people per group.

Wildlife biologist Sean Sheehan leads **Wyoming Nature Tours,** 307/527-6306, www.wyomingnaturetours.com, with natural-history trips throughout the Big Horn Basin, including to Bighorn Canyon.

Cody Vicinity

See earlier in this chapter for Wapiti Valley, Buffalo Bill Reservoir, Sunlight Basin, and the wonderful mountain country west of Cody.

HEART MOUNTAIN

Halfway between Cody and Powell is Heart Mountain, so named because its twin summits faintly resemble the traditional valentine. The mountain is visible for many miles in all directions. Geologists scratch their heads over this seemingly upside-down mountain. The Heart Mountain detachment fault stretches for more than a hundred miles, cutting southwest from near Cooke City, Montana. To the east are enormous blocks of land that have slid onto the top of more recent deposits, reversing the normal situation in which older rocks lie beneath more recent ones. Scientists know that these limestone and dolomite blocks moved around 45 to 50 million years ago, but none have been able to adequately explain how entire mountains, including Heart, could have slid for dozens of miles.

The Nature Conservancy's **Heart Mountain Preserve,** 307/587-1655, www.tncwyoming.org, encompasses the north and east slopes of the mountain, along with part of the surrounding plains. The region supports a surprising diversity of plants, including several rare species.

Heart Mountain Relocation Center

For Americans of Japanese ancestry, Heart Mountain might as well have been called Broken Heart Mountain. After the Japanese attack on Pearl Harbor in 1941, Japanese-Americans found their

© DON PITCHER

Heart Mountain

patriotism under increasing suspicion, and the following spring President Roosevelt signed an executive order establishing the War Relocation Authority to move them away from the coasts. The authority built 10 remote "relocation centers" to imprison anyone of Japanese ancestry; one such center went up just east of Heart Mountain and housed 10,767 Japanese-Americans (two-thirds of them born in America). The camp became Wyoming's third-largest settlement. It took just 62 days to complete the 468 barracks, 40 laundry-toilet buildings, Buddhist and Christian churches, a high school, fire station, recreation hall, power station, mess hall, hospital, sewage plant, administrative offices, and numerous other structures. (No environmental impact reports on this baby!) Barbed wire surrounded the perimeter, and military police staffed nine guard towers with high-beam searchlights and machine guns.

Camp Life

Most of the Japanese-Americans took the forced relocation with remarkable aplomb, realizing the futility of any escape attempt. It almost seemed the patriotic thing to do; "shikata-ga-nai" ("I guess it cannot be helped") became the accepted phrase. Although life in the camp maintained a sense of normalcy—some kids came to enjoy their peaceful high-school years and the picnics in Yellowstone—the camp was far from idyllic. Three or four people were jammed into each room, furniture was minimal, people had to share communal bathhouses, and the winter winds blew through the uninsulated tar paper buildings. Local folks resented the Japanese-Americans but appreciated the cheap farm labor that they provided while Wyoming's sons were off fighting the Germans and Japanese.

After the War

With the war's end in 1945, the camp was closed and the internees were given $25 and a one-way bus ticket home (or rather, to what remained; many found their homes ransacked or sold to others). Over the next four years the 740 acres of land was opened to homesteading, and the barracks were sold at two for $1. Most of the buildings ended up as temporary homes for the new

settlers. None of the Japanese-American internees remained in the area, and most of the survivors have little desire to even visit what seemed such a desolate, godforsaken place. They would rather try to forget. See Gretel Ehrlich's *Heart Mountain* for a fictional treatment of life inside the camp.

The Camp Today

Today the only reminders of the Heart Mountain Relocation Center are three buildings, the largest of which is the old hospital heating plant with its tall brick chimney. Several plaques also mark the camp's site, one noting the more than 600 men who left Heart Mountain facility to join the U.S. Army in Europe. Twenty-one internees and a camp teacher died while fighting in Europe.

The site is 11 miles east of Cody on U.S. Hwy. 14A. Barley fields now surround the former camp, while Heart Mountain stands guard over the western flank. Efforts are underway to preserve the remaining buildings and to someday open a visitors center and museum. The nonprofit **Heart Mountain Wyoming Foundation** works to preserve the memory of this painful era; get details at 307/754-2272 www.heartmountain.org.

HEADING EAST FROM HEART MOUNTAIN

The historic **Eagles Nest Stage Station** stands east of the relocation camp as you continue toward Powell. The log cabins and barns were built a century ago by the Lanchbury family, which homesteaded here. Their ranch served as a stage station midway between Meeteetse (then the largest town in Bighorn Basin) and Red Lodge, Montana. Today a fifth generation of Lanchburys lives in the restored buildings of historic Eagles Nest. If you're looking for trivia, stop in the tiny settlement of **Ralston** to see the railroad bridge over a highway bridge, atop a creek. This odd collection made it into *Ripley's Believe It or Not!* The town is home to **Mule Days,** in mid-June, a chance to learn about the ornery critters and to enjoy the unique mule rodeo.

Meeteetse

Along the western edge of Bighorn Basin is a charming little ranching center called Meeteetse (pop. 350). The name is a Shoshone Indian word meaning "Meeting Place of the Chiefs." The Absaroka Mountains rise gently to the south and west, and the Greybull River flows right through town, cottonwood trees on either side. To the north, the highway crosses a rolling land of sage and greasewood, while to the south are rugged badlands. Meeteetse has wooden sidewalks and hitching rails, occasional cattle drives right down Main Street, and an interesting museum.

HISTORY

One of the oldest towns in Bighorn Basin, Meeteetse was first settled in the late 1870s by homesteaders and wealthy European cattle barons. By 1890 it was the largest community in the basin. Several original buildings are still standing, including the impressively large **Meeteetse Mercantile,** built in 1899 but now closed. A few doors away is the **Cowboy Bar,** with more than a century of rough-and-tumble history. The saloon opened in 1893, and it still has the original rosewood and cherry wood back bar. Historical artifacts and local brands fill the walls. More than a few guns have gone off here over the years; at last count the bar contained 56 bullet holes and a shotgun blast! Many well-known people have spent time in this bar, including Buffalo Bill Cody, Tom Horn, Butch Cassidy, and Amelia Earhart.

The last wild black-footed ferrets were discovered just a dozen miles to the west at the famed Pitchfork Ranch. They were captured in 1987 after an outbreak of canine distemper threatened to kill all of the remaining wild ferrets. A bronze ferret statue guards tiny but picturesque Riverside Park in town, but it may be many decades (if ever) before living ferrets return.

SIGHTS AND INFORMATION

The **Beldon and Meeteetse Museum,** 307/868-2423, is open Monday–Saturday 10 A.M.–4 P.M. from Memorial Day to September, and Monday, Tuesday, Thursday, and Friday 10 A.M.–4 P.M. the rest of the year. Inside are artifacts from the famous Pitchfork Ranch, including the collection of Charles Beldon's classic cowboy photographs from the 1930s. Also here is one of the largest grizzlies ever taken in the Lower 48 (it's eight feet tall), items from early settlers of the area, plus early photos from the mining town of Kirwin. They also have the (stuffed) ferret that was dragged in by a dog in 1981.

The building also houses the Meeteetse Visitor Information Center, 307/868-2454, www.meeteetsewy.com, with brochures on the area. It's open Thursday–Monday 10 A.M.–5 P.M. in summer, and Wednesday–Saturday 10 A.M.–5 P.M. the rest of the year.

Down the street is the historic **Bank Museum,** now restored to the way it looked in 1901, with banking artifacts, the original safe, and Meetetse photos.

ACCOMMODATIONS

Oasis Motel and RV Park, 1702 State St., 307/868-2551 or 888/868-5270, www.oasismotelwyoming.com, has motel rooms for $35 s or d; cabins with kitchenettes for $45 s or d; campsites for $11; and RV spots for $16. Ask about their chuck wagon diners. **Vision Quest Motel,** 2207 State St., 307/868-2512 or 866/478-2987, www.vqmotel.com, charges $42–45 s or d, or $59–69 d for suites. Most rooms contain kitchenettes. RV parking costs $13. Both Oasis and Vision Quest are open year-round.

Broken Spoke B&B, 1947 State St., 307/868-2362, www.meeteetsewy.com, isn't a traditional B&B, but it does have two simple rooms (no TVs) over the café of the same name for just $30 s, $40 d, or $50 for four. Guests are served a full breakfast downstairs.

FOOD AND NIGHTLIFE

Elkhorn Bar & Grill has the best local burgers and is a meeting spot for local folks, especially on weekend evenings, when country bands sometimes play. Other times you can try your hand at pool or darts. **Outlaw Parlor Cafe** at the Cowboy Bar also has good pizzas and steaks, along with old photos from early-day Meeteetse. Be sure to ask the bartender at the Cowboy for the "true" origins of the word Meeteetse. Meals can also be found at **Lucille's Cafe,** 307/868-9909, and **Broken Spoke Cafe,** 307/868-2362.

OTHER PRACTICALITIES

Get local information from the town museums. An indoor **swimming pool** is at the high school.

Visit Meeteetse over **Labor Day weekend** for a small-town parade, street games, a country rodeo, barbecue, arts and crafts, live music, and dancing. Great fun, and its been going on for more than 90 years.

MEETEETSE AREA
Wood River Valley

Southwest of Meeteetse, beautiful Wood River Valley is an enjoyable drive or bike ride at any time of the year. It's a great place to watch for moose and elk in the bottomlands, along with a variety of smaller animals. Two free Forest Service **campgrounds** (open June–Nov.) are available near the end of the road. From here you can hike into the **Washakie Wilderness** along any of several different trails; see Shoshone National Forest earlier in this chapter for details.

Wood River Valley Ski Touring Park (free) is 22 miles southwest of town on Wood River Road. The Meeteetse Recreation District runs the park and provides ski rentals in town. The cross-country ski area includes 25 km of groomed trails, wonderful mountain scenery, a warming

hut, and a custom-made tent with a woodstove for overnight stays. For more info, call 307/868-2603. **Wood River Lodge,** 307/868-9211 or 800/228-9211, www.wood-river.com, has year-round accommodations just two miles away and also runs pack trips into the backcountry.

Kirwin

The abandoned mining town of Kirwin is accessible from the Brown Creek Campground at the end of Wood River Road. You'll need a 4WD (or at least a high-clearance vehicle) to continue the 11 miles past the campground to Kirwin, at an elevation of 9,200 feet. Mountain bikers in good shape will also enjoy this challenging road. The road is typically accessible late June to early October.

Gold was discovered in the Kirwin area in 1885, and within a few years more than 200 miners were living in this remote high-elevation site. A 1907 avalanche killed three people and proved the last straw for miners who had been struggling for years with little or no profit. Most of them abandoned their cabins and claims with what they could carry on their backs, never to return. Now within Shoshone National Forest, the old mining town is a fascinating place to explore, with the decaying remains of a hotel and cabins, along with rusting farm and mining machinery. On the drive into Kirwin you pass what remains of Double D Dude Ranch, established in 1931. Famed aviatrix **Amelia Earhart** was having a summer cabin built near here shortly before her 1934 disappearance during an around-the-world flight. The cabin was never finished, and only a few rotting logs remain. A monument to Amelia Earhart stands in Meeteetse, and the flight jacket she wore when she became the first woman to cross the Atlantic alone is in the Buffalo Bill Historical Center.

More Nearby Sights

Another historic place—**Palatte Ranch**—is at the end of Pitchfork Road, a gravel road paralleling the Greybull River. The road ends 30 miles west of Meeteetse at Jack Creek Campground (free). A seven-mile hike from the campground takes you to **Anderson Lodge,** an archetypal log home that was restored by the Forest Service.

Palatte Ranch was once owned by A. A. Anderson, first superintendent of the Yellowstone Park Timberland Reserve (now Shoshone National Forest). Check with the Forest Service office in Cody for more information on this area.

Northwest of Meeteetse is an important archaeological site, the **Great Arrow,** a 58-foot-long arrow made from rocks and placed atop a long hogback ridge. Of unknown age, the arrow points toward the Medicine Wheel in the Big Horn Mountains 70 miles to the northeast. The Great Arrow is on private land and not accessible to the public. (See Big Horn Mountains in the Powder River Country chapter for more on Medicine Wheel.) The turnoff to impressive **Legend Rock Petroglyph Site** is 32 miles southeast of Meeteetse along State Hwy. 120. For details, see Thermopolis later in this chapter.

Powell

One of the most pleasant settlements in Bighorn Basin, Powell (pop. 5,300) is a clean and prosperous farming, oil, and college town halfway between Cody and Lovell. Declared an All-America City in 1994, it sits at the center of a rich farming region where sugar beets, dry beans, and malting barley (grown for Coors and Anheuser-Busch) are raised. Because these crops are harvested at different times of the year, many farmers grow all three. Tall bean elevators border the railroad tracks on the south edge of town, and a dozen miles to the north is the giant Elk Basin oil field. First discovered in 1915, it had 150 wells pumping more than 4,200 barrels a day within five years. The field has proven a major factor in the growth of the northern Bighorn Basin, although production is declining as the supply is exhausted.

HISTORY

Powell was named for Maj. John Wesley Powell (1834–1902), the famed one-armed explorer of the Colorado River and an early director of the U.S. Geological Survey. His 1889 report on the agricultural potential of Western desert lands had asserted the value of irrigation in "reclaiming" these areas and proposed a system of dams and canals funded by the government. One of the earliest of these was the mammoth Shoshone Project, involving Buffalo Bill Dam and a series of canals to feed water to the fields along the Shoshone River. Powell is right at the center of all this irrigation, and homesteaders flocked here in the first two decades of the 20th century. The town sprang up at a campsite used by workers on the Shoshone Project.

With the arrival of the Chicago, Burlington and Quincy Railroad (now Burlington Northern), Powell became an agricultural shipping point.

Earl Durand

Folks still talk about "Tarzan of the Tetons," a local kid gone bad. Earl Durand was a crack shot and a mountain man of sorts. He had once traveled by horse and foot to Mexico and bragged that he could survive on practically anything, even raw bobcat meat. Durand hated being cooped up inside buildings, so when he was arrested for poaching in 1939, he escaped the Cody jail. Five people died in the shooting rampage that followed, and the murders attracted intense national attention. The climax came when Durand robbed a Powell bank and suddenly found himself surrounded. A 17-year-old kid shot— but didn't kill—Durand as he came out of the bank with a screen of hostages. Sensing the futility of the situation, Durand went back inside and committed suicide. Powell's Homesteader Museum has lots of old newspaper clippings on this sad story, and the incident inspired *The Legend of Earl Durand,* a minor 1974 movie starring Slim Pickens, Peter Haskell, and Martin Sheen.

SIGHTS

The **Homesteader Museum,** on the corner of 1st and Clark Streets, 307/754-9481, is open Friday–Saturday 10 A.M.–5 P.M. May–September, and Tuesday–Friday 1–4 P.M. the rest of the year. The museum captures the hardscrabble life of early-1900s homesteaders in the northern Bighorn

BIGHORN BASIN

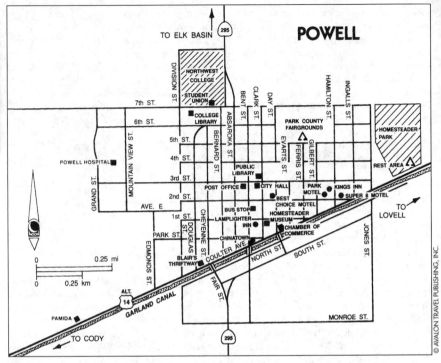

POWELL

TO ELK BASIN

295

DIVISION ST.

NORTHWEST COLLEGE

STUDENT UNION

7th ST.

6th ST.

COLLEGE LIBRARY

5th ST.

4th ST.

POWELL HOSPITAL

3rd ST.

PUBLIC LIBRARY

POST OFFICE

CITY HALL

2nd ST.

AVE. E

1st ST.

BUS STOP

LAMPLIGHTER INN

BEST CHOICE MOTEL

HOMESTEADER MUSEUM

PARK ST.

CHINATOWN

CHAMBER OF COMMERCE

BLAIR'S THRIFTWAY

COULTER AVE.

NORTH ST.

SOUTH ST.

MOUNTAIN VIEW ST.

GRAND ST.

BERNARD ST.

ABSAROKA ST.

BENT ST.

CLARK ST.

DAY ST.

EVARTS ST.

FERRIS ST.

GILBERT ST.

HAMILTON ST.

INGALLS ST.

PARK COUNTY FAIRGROUNDS

HOMESTEADER PARK

REST AREA

PARK MOTEL

KINGS INN

SUPER 8 MOTEL

TO LOVELL

CHEYENNE ST.

DOUGLAS ST.

EDMONDS ST.

JONES ST.

0   0.25 mi

0   0.25 km

ALT. 14

GARLAND CANAL

FAIR ST.

295

PAMIDA

TO CODY

MONROE ST.

© AVALON TRAVEL PUBLISHING, INC.

Basin. You'll find interesting old photographs, a beautiful collection of dryhead agate, some Indian artifacts, a century-old porcelain doll, and a German grandfather clock, chairs, and bench covered with carved bears. There's more junk to check out, but take the time to watch the videotape detailing the history of the nearby Heart Mountain Relocation Center. An adjacent building is filled with horse-drawn machines and old tractors, while outside are a caboose and various pieces of old farm equipment. Museum entrance is free.

The chamber of commerce offers individualized **agricultural tours** of the farms and ranches around Powell, providing a good way to learn about irrigation systems, dairy farms, feed lots, sheep and cattle breeding, irrigation, and crop production. These reasonably priced trips include transportation, a guide, and lunch; the cost depends on the trip length and group size. Call 307/754-3483 or 800/325-4278 for reservations.

Founded in 1946, **Northwest College** is one

of the state's top junior colleges, with nearly 2,000 students. The 124-acre campus is quite attractive, with modern brick buildings and fluorescent green lawns (at least in the summer). Two-thirds of the students live on campus, but the school does offer evening classes in the surrounding towns. Northwest is a cultural and social center for Powell and the surrounding area, bringing a variety of theater productions and entertainment, plus art exhibits at the **Northwest Gallery** (open Mon.–Fri. 9 A.M.–4:30 P.M. Sept.–May). Learn more at 307/754-6111 or 800/442-2946, www.northwestcollege.org.

ACCOMMODATIONS

Although it is just 24 miles from Cody, travelers will find distinctly less-expensive accommodations in Powell. **Best Choice Motel,** 337 E. 2nd St., 307/754-2243 or 800/308-8447, has rooms for $42 s or d, some with microwaves and fridges.

Lamplighter Inn, 234 1st St., 307/754-2226, has standard rooms for $49–69 s or d. **Park Motel,** 737 E. 2nd St., 307/754-2233 or 800/506-7378, offers comfortable rooms for $52–59 s or $62–69 d; half of them contain fridges and microwaves.

Super 8 Motel, 845 E. Coulter, 307/754-7231 or 800/800-8000, www.super8.com, has motel rooms for $63–69 s or $73–79 d. Nicest in town is **King's Inn,** 777 E. 2nd St., 307/754-5117 800/441-7778, where rooms cost $69–77 s or d, including use of a seasonal heated outdoor pool.

CAMPING

Park County Fairgrounds, 307/754-5421, has RV sites ($15) and shower facilities. Open Apr.–Sept. RVers park for free (no hookups) at the highway rest area in the 57-acre **Homesteader Park** on the east end of town. You can also pitch a tent on the grass here, but the sprinklers come on at night. Open all year.

FOOD

Start your day with an espresso from **Parlor News Coffeehouse,** 135 E. 2nd St., 307/754-0717m www.parlornews.com. It's a cozy spot to relax; stop by for ice cream on a warm summer afternoon. Meet the locals for breakfast at **Skyline Family Dining,** 141 E. Coulter, 307/754-2772, where you'll also find a mean chicken-fried steak for dinner, a decent salad bar, and breakfast buffets on Saturday and Sunday mornings.

Two places have tasty south-of-the-border fare in Powell: **Pepe's Mexican Restaurant,** 333 E. 2nd, 307/754-4665, and **El Tapatio,** 112 N. Bent, 307/754-8085.

Powell Drug, 140 N. Bent, 307/754-2031, has an old-fashioned soda fountain where the root beer floats and malts still attract kids. **Hansel & Gretel's,** 113 S. Bent, 307/754-2191, serves spaghetti, soups, sandwiches, and delicious homemade pies.

The **Lamplighter Inn,** at the corner of 1st and Clark, 307/754-2226, is the fanciest place in town, with sandwiches, burgers, and daily specials for lunch, along with prime rib, steaks, chicken, and seafood for dinner.

Get pizzas from **Pizza on the Run,** 215 E. 1st, 307/754-5720, or **Pizza Hut,** 855 E. Coulter Ave., 307/754-9588. The latter has a popular lunchtime buffet. **Chinatown Restaurant,** 151 E. Coulter, 307/754-7924, has Chinese food to eat in or take out, and a buffet lunches and dinners Tuesday–Friday.

For sweets, head to **Powell Bakery,** 242 N. Bent St., 307/754-2971, or **Linda's Sandwich and Ice Cream Shoppe,** 121 N. Bent St., 307/754-9553.

Pick up groceries at **Blair's Market,** 311 W. Coulter Ave., 307/754-3122, or **Food Basket IGA,** 421 E. 1st, 307/754-3602. Blair's contains a good deli and bakery.

ENTERTAINMENT

Time Out Lounge has occasional country-and-western bands and sports on the TVs the rest of the time. Good bar food, too, including Rocky Mountain oysters. **La Vina's,** 238 S. Douglas, 307/754-4713, occasionally has live music.

For movies, drop by **Vali Cinema,** 204 N. Bent St., 307/754-4211, or, for the outdoor version (a rare treat these days), **Vali Drive-In Theatre,** 1070 Rd. 9, 307/754-5133.

EVENTS

The popular **Foxtrotter Horse Show and Sale** takes place on Father's Day weekend in June. The last full week of July brings the **Park County Fair,** with parades, pig mud wrestling, 4-H shows, a demolition derby, tractor pulls, a horse pull, dancing, headline acts, and a carnival; 307/754-5421. The second weekend of September brings the grandiosely named **All America Quilt Show** to downtown Powell. If you happen to be in the area on the first weekend of December, stop by for **Country Christmas,** a three-day festivity with activities and craft exhibits as well as a torchlight parade and a parade with lighted floats.

RECREATION

Homesteader Park has several modern recreation facilities, including a kids'll-love-it green frog slide at the wading pool. In winter, there is a free ice arena here with skate rentals and a warming hut. The public **swimming pool** is in the high school. The 18-hole **Powell Golf Club** is five miles east of Powell, 307/754-3039 or 800/325-4278. **Classic Lanes,** 162 N. Clark, 307/754-2422, is the local bowling alley.

SHOPPING

Basin & Range Book Co., 109 N. Bent, 307/754-4504, is a pleasant little bookshop in the center of town with both new and used titles. **Powell Office Supply** also sells books, along with topographic maps, as does the **Northwest College Bookstore,** 307/754-6308. Also check out **The Merc,** 227 N. Bent, 307/754-5888, a unique clothing store that is co-owned by many locals; they sold 800 shares to start the store in 2002.

Get camping and hiking supplies at **War Surplus,** 130 N. Bent, 307/754-2694; there always seems to be a surplus of wars, so you might as well buy a couple while you're in town.

INFORMATION AND SERVICES

The **Powell Valley Chamber of Commerce,** 111 S. Day, 307/754-3494 or 800/325-4278, www.powellchamber.org, is open Monday–Friday 8 A.M.–5 P.M. year-round. Pick up their walking-tour map for historical tidbits on downtown Powell.

Relax with a book at the modern **Powell Public Library,** 217 E. 3rd, 307/754-2261, or the **John Hinkley Memorial Library** on the Northwest College campus, 307/754-6207. (No, it isn't named for the man who shot President Reagan.)

Powder River Transportation/Coach USA, 307/682-0960 or 800/442-3682, has daily bus service from Powell to other towns in Bighorn Basin, along with Billings, Montana. They can also take you throughout central and eastern Wyoming and all the way to Denver or Rapid City. Buses stop at Best Choice Motel, 337 E. 2nd Street.

EAST TO LOVELL

A tangle of roads wanders through the country between Lovell and Powell, tying together a cluster of agriculture and oil settlements established by Mormon emigrants. **Cowley** (pop. 560) has several impressive old sandstone buildings, plus **Cowtown Cafe** serving good food, homemade pies, and enormous cinnamon rolls. Ask for directions to ancient Indian petroglyphs north of town in Blue Wash. The local event is **Pioneer Day** in late July.

Byron (pop. 560) has quite a few old log buildings and is surrounded by dairy farms. Check out the "roadkill" burger (with three patties) at **Half Fast Diner,** 307/548-7249.

Just two miles south of the Montana border on U.S. Hwy. 310, **Frannie** (pop. 200) straddles the line between Park and Big Horn Counties. Residents say it's "The Biggest Little Town in Wyoming because it takes two counties to hold the people." Stop by **Frannie Tack Shop,** 307/548-2344 or 800/552-8836, to see the saddles or get repairs on canvas or leather items. The local ice cream shop is also popular.

Deaver has a population of 180 folks but no attractions of note, unless you count the gazebo in the town park. The dot of a place called **Garland** (pop. 100) is home to a boxy old schoolhouse (now occupied by a Church of God) that was built in the early 1900s.

Just east of Lovell, the pungent odors of sulfur and oil hang in the air, and the dry badlands are punctuated by oil pumpjacks in the large Byron Oil Field, discovered in 1918. The other business here is farming. Much of this desert land is now under irrigation, and the lush green farmlands are filled with sugar beets, beans, malting barley, alfalfa, and corn. A sign along U.S. Hwy. 14A notes the **Sidon Canal,** built in 1900 by Mormon settlers of the Bighorn Basin. The 37-mile-long canal was entirely self-financed with land donated by the government and transports water from the Shoshone River to 20,000 acres of farmland. Mormons claim that Prayer Rock, a large impediment to the canal's construction, was miraculously split as a result of their supplications.

Lovell

The sleepy little burg of Lovell (pop. 2,300; pronounced "LOVE-ul") calls itself the "City of Roses," a title that comes from Dr. William Horsley, who lived here from 1924 until his death in 1971. Horsley loved roses and in the course of a lifetime of cultivating them became one of the nation's foremost authorities. The "Rose Doctor's" enthusiasm rubbed off on others, and today gardens around town are packed with roses. Oil fields surround Lovell, and a Georgia Pacific wallboard plant and two bentonite plants are substantial local employers, but farming is king. The Western Sugar factory stands on the edge of town, providing jobs for workers and a market for local farmers who contract with the plant to grow sugar beets. In late fall, huge mounds of straw-covered beets pile up beside the factory, and the rancid/sweet odor of cooking beets fills the air. Stray beets, spilled from overloaded farm trucks, lie along the highway for miles.

Downtown Lovell seems to specialize in empty storefronts, and the settlement doesn't offer much for tourists, unless they're in search of an almost ghost town. It's one of the few towns in Wyoming without a museum and is known for an insular attitude toward outsiders, but the surrounding country includes fascinating Bighorn Canyon National Recreation Area and the majestic Big Horn Mountains. A state-run fish-rearing station at Tillett Springs, 17 miles north of Lovell, raises cutthroat and rainbow trout.

Like most towns in the northern Bighorn Basin, Lovell is dominated by Mormons. An enormous brick Latter-day Saints church fills an entire block along the main drag and is often mistaken for an imposing office building. Lovell has wide, clean streets crowded with summertime flower boxes.

HISTORY

The town of Lovell has its roots in the enormous ML Ranch, founded in 1880 by Anthony L. Mason and Henry Clay Lovell (see ML Ranch in the Sights section for more on the ranch). In 1900, Mormon settlers moved to the remote Bighorn Basin (partly to escape prosecution for polygamy) and working on the Burlington Railroad and developing irrigation projects. The area boomed with the discovery of natural gas and the opening of various factories. A few years later, German emigrants provided labor for the farm fields and then settled down to acquire their own land. Yellowtail Dam on the Bighorn River was built in 1965, and the surrounding land became a national recreation area the following year.

Lovell is said to have the lowest crime rate in Wyoming, but nowhere in the tourist brochures does the city mention the history of two of its most prominent doctors. A few years before his 1971 death, Dr. William Horsley, the famed "Rose Doctor," was forced to resign from the local hospital following a series of homosexual incidents with boys. (You *definitely* won't read this in the glowing stories about Horsley's life in the local press.) But another respected physician, Dr. John Story, gained considerably more notoriety for his actions. Story arrived in 1958 to practice general medicine, joined the local Baptist church, and became a strong conservative community leader. Unfortunately, over the next 25 years he also raped or molested dozens (some say hundreds) of women and girls in his office. A combination of strict Mormon upbringing, sexual ignorance, shame, and fear prevented the victims from talking, and the few who did speak up were called liars. Finally, in 1983, the charges began to surface. The trial turned Lovell inside out. Despite intense pressure from local and state politicians (then-Governor Herschler called the victims' testimony "hogwash"), Story was convicted in April 1985 on several rape charges and is currently serving a 20-year sentence in the Wyoming State Penitentiary. Jack Olson's harrowing book, *Doc,* describes this sorry chapter in recent Wyoming history.

MOTELS

Stay at one of four places in Lovell. Cheapest is **Cattleman Motel,** off the main drag at 470 Montana Ave., 307/548-2296, where the rooms run $29 s or $36–44 d. Microwaves and fridges are available on request. **Western Motel,** 180 W. Main St., 307/548-2781, rents newly refurbished rooms for $34–44 s or d, and has kitchenettes.

Horseshoe Bend Motel, 375 E. Main St., 307/548-2221 or 800/548-2850, has comfortable rooms (some with microwaves and fridges) for $44–54 s or d, including access to an outdoor pool. **Super 8 Motel,** 595 E. Main St., 307/548-2725 or 800/800-8000, www.super8.com, charges $50 s or $54 d.

GUEST RANCHES

A 45,000-acre cattle ranch, the **TX Ranch,** 406/484-2583, www.txranch.com, offers a unique chance to take part in the cowboy life. It isn't a dude ranch, and visitors end up joining in during spring or fall cattle drives, branding calves and doing roundups. You'll be riding 6–10 hours per day here, and you'll stay in wall tents at the cow camps. No electricity, phones, TVs, fax machines, or other modern conveniences to interfere with a real Old West adventure. The ranch is primarily in Montana, but some of the operation is in Wyoming. All-inclusive weekly rates are $1,800 for two people. There's a seven-day minimum stay, for a maximum of 18 guests. Open mid-Apr. through Oct.

The **Schively Ranch,** 307/548-6688, consists of two ranches that cover 40,000 acres on the eastern side of the Pryor Mountains and just across the border inside Montana. Guests can take part in a 50-mile cattle drive each spring or fall, or help in a variety of ranch chores at other times. It's a great way to learn about the real West. One-week rates are $1,800 for two people all-inclusive or $2,200 for two people during the cattle drives, with a maximum of 16 guests. Lodging is in rustic cabins with a central bathhouse. The guest ranch is open mid-April to mid-November.

CAMPING

The best campsites in the Lovell area lie within nearby Bighorn Canyon National Recreation Area ($5; see Bighorn Canyon National Recreation Area section of this chapter); closest is Horseshoe Bend Campground, 14 miles from Lovell. In town, camp for free (including showers) at **Lovell Camper Park** on Quebec Avenue north of Main Street. It's a quiet place surrounded by cottonwoods. RVers can pay to stay behind the Super 8 Motel at **Camp Big Horn RV Park,** 595 E. Main St., 307/548-2725. The price is $10 for tents, $15 for RVs; open year-round.

FOOD

Lange's Kitchen, 483 Shoshone Ave., 307/548-7121, is popular for breakfast and lunch; they offer a Sunday breakfast buffet and Friday night prime rib special. For pizzas, run over to **Pizza on the Run,** 5th St. at Shoshone Ave., 307/548-2206. The nicest local eatery is **Big Horn Restaurant,** next to the Super 8 at 605 E. Main St., 307/548-6811. This is where folks go for a dinner out or to enjoy a leisurely breakfast. Prime rib is the featured attraction on Friday and Saturday nights.

Queen Bee Honey Candy, 262 Main St., 307/548-2543, www.qbee.cc, harvests their own honey to create a variety of delicious and unique candies. These are sold at their shop or by mail order. Drop by to see them at work or for a sample.

Get groceries and deli food at **Red Apple Supermarket,** 9 E. Main St., 307/548-9907, which also houses a War Memorial.

RECREATION AND EVENTS

You'll find an Olympic-size indoor **swimming pool** and other recreation facilities on the southwest end of town; 307/548-6466. **Foster Gulch Golf Course,** 307/548-2445, is a nine-hole course in the same area.

The big annual event in Lovell is **Mustang Days,** held the last full week in June. Activities include a parade, fireworks, barbecue, a follies show, rodeo, demolition derby, and crowning of the Rose Queen.

INFORMATION AND SERVICES

For local info, visit the **Lovell Information Center** 287 E. Main, 307/548-7552, www.lovell chamber.com. Hours are Monday–Friday 8:30 A.M.–12:15 P.M. and 1–5 P.M. from Memorial Day to Labor Day and Monday–Friday 8:30 A.M.–12:15 P.M. the rest of the year. The Bighorn National Forest's **Paintrock Ranger District Office,** 604 E. Main, 307/548-6541, www.fs.fed.us/r2/bighorn, has information on the Medicine Wheel and Bighorn National Forest.

The town **library** is at 3rd St. and Oregon Ave., 307/548-7228, and the **post office** is at 167 W. 3rd, 307/548-7605. Find an **ATM** at First National Bank & Trust of Powell, 284 E. Main Street. Wash clothes at **Mustang Laundry,** 340 E. Montana Avenue. **North Big Horn Hospital,** 115 Lane 12, 307/548-2271, has physicians on staff.

Powder River Transportation/Coach USA, 307/682-0960 or 800/442-3682, has daily bus service from Lovell to other Bighorn Basin towns as well as Billings, Montana, and to points throughout northern and eastern Wyoming.

Bighorn Canyon National Recreation Area

Just east of Lovell is one of America's lesser-known but most stunning sights, Bighorn Canyon. Over the eons, the Bighorn River has slowly carved out a 2,200-foot-deep chasm through the desert country. Since 1967, when water backed up behind the 525-foot-tall Yellowtail Dam, the canyon has lain under a deep blanket of water—water that provides 250,000 kilowatts of electricity for the western United States and irrigates thousands of acres of Montana farmland. The dam itself is—as the raven flies—more than 20 miles north of the Wyoming–Montana border, but its impact reaches 70 river miles upstream, creating Bighorn Lake.

The Setting

The 120,000-acre Bighorn Canyon National Recreation Area is managed by the National Park Service. A $5 per-vehicle day-use fee is charged, and it's good for 24 hours from the time of purchase. An annual Bighorn Canyon pass is $30, or pay $50 for a National Park Pass that provides access to all Park Service areas. The fee (or pass) covers camping, boat launching, hiking, and other activities in the recreation area.

Separate facilities on both ends of the recreation area are linked by a circuitous 180-mile route that takes you through Billings, Montana. (A shorter route includes 18 miles of gravel road.) Because of the distances, most road-bound visitors come to either the Montana side or the Wyoming side but not both. Boaters can traverse the entire reach of the canyon.

Attractions accessible only from Montana include a visitors center at the dam, 406/666-2412, a short nature trail, and the site of two Bozeman Trail features: Fort C. F. Smith and the Hayfield Fight (both on private land). For details on sights north of the Wyoming border,

Devil Canyon is part of Bighorn Canyon National Recreation Area.

© DON PITCHER

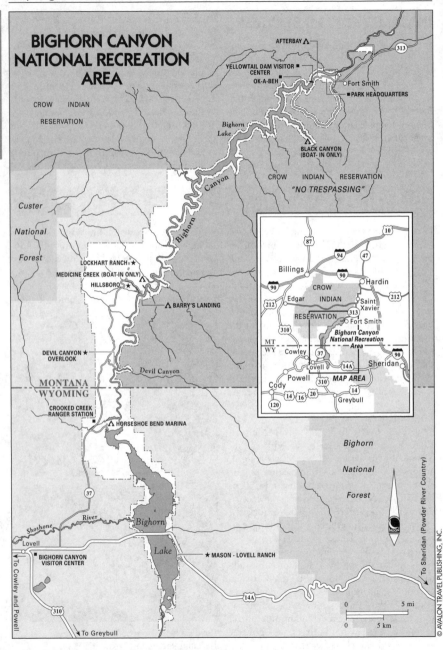

BIGHORN CANYON
NATIONAL RECREATION
AREA

CROW   INDIAN

RESERVATION

*Bighorn
Lake*

BLACK CANYON
(BOAT- IN ONLY)

CROW   INDIAN   RESERVATION

"NO TRESPASSING"

AFTERBAY

YELLOWTAIL DAM VISITOR
CENTER
OK-A-BEH
Fort Smith
PARK HEADQUARTERS

313

Bighorn

Canyon

Custer

National

Forest

LOCKHART RANCH
MEDICINE CREEK (BOAT-IN ONLY)
HILLSBORO

BARRY'S LANDING

DEVIL CANYON
OVERLOOK

Devil Canyon

MONTANA
WYOMING

CROOKED CREEK
RANGER STATION

HORSESHOE BEND MARINA

Billings   87   10
94   47
90   Hardin
90   CROW   212
212   Edgar   INDIAN
Saint
Xavier
313
RESERVATION   Fort Smith
310   *Bighorn Canyon*
National Recreation
MT   *Area*
WY   Cowley
37
90
Powell   Lovell   14A   Sheridan
310   **MAP AREA**
Cody   14
120   14 16 20   14
Greybull

Bighorn

National

Forest

37

Shoshone   *River*   *Bighorn*

Lovell

BIGHORN CANYON
VISITOR CENTER   *Lake*   MASON - LOVELL RANCH

To Cowley and Powell

310

To Greybull

14A

To Sheridan (Powder River Country)

MOON

0   5 mi

0   5 km

© AVALON TRAVEL PUBLISHING, INC.

see *Moon Handbooks Montana,* by W. C. McRae and Judy Jewell (www.moon.com).

From the Wyoming side, things are considerably more interesting, even though some of the sights actually lie across the Montana border. A paved road extends 27 miles along the western side of the recreation area, with a rough dirt road continuing 15 more miles to the Crow Indian Reservation. Along the way are a couple of campgrounds, the historic Bad Pass Trail, two old ranches, magnificent Bighorn Canyon, and a good chance to see bighorn sheep and wild horses. The road cuts through impressive red and gray badlands carpeted by juniper, sagebrush, and mountain mahogany.

SIGHTS

Devil Canyon Area

The pièce de résistance of Bighorn Canyon National Recreation Area is **Devil Canyon Overlook,** where Devil Canyon joins Bighorn Canyon. From the overlook, the earth drops suddenly away. More than a thousand feet below, motorboats look like miniature toys in a bathtub. A real treat in the canyon is the chance

to see **bighorn sheep** up close; more than 100 of these majestic animals live in the national recreation area. Although the more impressive rams tend to hang out in remote parts of the Pryor Mountains in the summer, you can spot ewes and lambs along the road between the state line and Layout Creek. The rams are more likely to be seen during the November–December rutting season, but some will probably be visible until late May.

Precipitous Bighorn Canyon was known as **Bad Pass** by the Indians. The trail they used to reach the buffalo herds followed the canyon rim for many miles and was marked by rock cairns. Some of these cairns are still visible between Devil Canyon Overlook and Barry's Landing, as are some of the caves where they wintered near the canyon bottoms.

Before it was dammed, the river offered a torrent of rushing rapids and falls, with jagged rocks waiting to punch holes in any boat and a canyon so deep that the sun only reached the bottom for a few hours each day. In 1825, the famed mountain man and guide Jim Bridger decided to take a wooden raft down the canyon to see if it could provide a way to ship furs

More than 100 bighorn sheep live in the national recreation area.

back east. It was a feat that was not matched for many decades, when a motorboat finally ran the wild currents.

Hillsboro

The ghost settlement of Hillsboro is about one mile above Barry's Landing and is accessible only by foot. Established around the turn of the 20th century by a self-proclaimed physician, Grosverner William Barry, the site was originally promoted as a gold-mining center. When that didn't pan out (they didn't get enough gold to pay for the operation of a dredge), he turned to dude ranching and promoted his ranch as a place where guests could cruise through Bighorn Canyon in motorboats or ride his English Hackney horses. The dude ranch flourished until the 1930s, but the collection of antique furniture and paintings was destroyed by a fire in the winter of 1947–1948. Still standing are the old post office and various cabins.

ML Ranch

The great ML Ranch was founded in 1883 by Anthony L. Mason and Henry Clay Lovell. Lovell trailed herds of cattle up from Kansas to this newly opened country, building his main headquarters along the Bighorn River just east of the community that was later named for him. The vast unfenced ranch became known as the "Big Outfit" and employed hundreds of cowhands. Grazed by 25,000 cattle, it stretched from Thermopolis all the way to the Crow Reservation in Montana, 90 miles away.

Most of the buildings from the old ML Ranch are now gone, but you can still visit the restored bunkhouse, the blacksmith shop, and two cabins. Most interesting is the bunkhouse—actually three cabins connected by dogtrots (covered breezeways). The end cabins acted as sleeping quarters, the middle one as a cook shack and mess hall. Get here by heading east from Lovell across the bridge over Bighorn Lake. A sign points out the ranch.

Lockhart Ranch

The Lockhart Ranch was where writer Caroline Lockhart lived off and on from 1926 until 1955. Located north of the Barry's Landing area, it's accessible via a two-mile dirt road. The road is fine for cars but not advised for large RVs. A quarter-mile path leads down to the ranch, where you'll find more than a dozen log buildings set among the cottonwoods and box elder trees along Davis Creek (a.k.a. Medicine Creek). It's a fascinating and bucolic place to explore.

Other Sights

Adjacent to the Bighorn Canyon National Recreation Area is the 19,424-acre **Yellowtail Wildlife Habitat Management Unit,** a popular place for hunters and birdwatchers. Many dirt roads and trails crisscross the area, and wildlife of all types abounds. During fall migration, the wetlands here are jammed with up to 10,000 ducks. The Park Service and Wyoming Game and Fish departments cooperatively manage the land, and maps of Yellowtail roads and trails are available at the Bighorn Canyon Visitor Center.

Caves create a latticework under portions of the recreation area. On the east side of Bighorn Lake is **Bighorn Caverns.** Access is limited to experienced spelunkers and requires 4WD vehicles; get the gate key and directions at the Bighorn Canyon Visitor Center. Not far away is **Horsethief Cave.** Although closed to the public, **Natural Trap Cave** is of paleontological value. Thirty-five miles northeast of Lovell, a 12- by 15-foot opening drops into the 80-foot-deep cavern. Over the centuries many animals—from prehistoric horses to rabbits—have fallen in here.

PRACTICALITIES

Camping

There are three campgrounds in the southern half of Bighorn Canyon and two in the north half. No extra charge to camp; it's included in your $5 entrance fee. Folks in RVs park at **Horseshoe Bend,** which has water, toilets, picnic tables, a playground, and shelters to ward off the wind and sun. The rocky surface and windy conditions make this a challenging place for anyone in a tent. The drive in to Horseshoe Bend passes lovely red sandstone badlands. Campfire programs are generally

CAROLINE LOCKHART

The West overflows with famous men, but women sometimes get unjustly shunted aside in the accolades. One of the most interesting was Caroline Lockhart (1871–1962), a woman who began her career as an actress but turned quickly to journalism as a writer for a Boston newspaper. Using the pen name "Suzette," she became one of the country's first female newspaper reporters. The job led her into all sorts of adventures, from entering a circus cage with a lion that had killed his trainer the previous day to testing the Boston Fire Department's new fire nets by jumping out of a fourth-story hotel window. When she heard of a "Home for Intemperate Women" where the women were being severely mistreated, Caroline decided to investigate by posing as a derelict. She got her story all right, but it took considerable convincing from her editor to get her out. "Release!" shouted the matron running the house. "We can't! She's not cured yet." One of Lockhart's most lasting impacts was the creation of Mother's Day. Although Anna Jarvis came up with the concept, Caroline Lockhart made it a reality by tirelessly promoting the idea in the newspapers.

In 1904, Lockhart took a bold step. After an interview with Buffalo Bill Cody in the town named for him, she decided to move to Wyoming. She purchased the local newspaper, the *Cody Enterprise,* and quickly made a name for herself as a crusader against prohibition and "game hogs" (hunters who killed everything in sight). She also founded the Cody Stampede, the big annual event in Bighorn Basin. Lockhart authored seven novels, including *The Lady Doc,* a book that managed to ruffle local feathers with its too-close-to-the-truth descriptions of real-life Cody people. Despite this controversy, her witty, humorous, and insightful writing gained a national reputation.

In 1925, she sold the *Cody Enterprise* and acquired a ranch that eventually included 7,000 acres of land along the Bighorn River north of Lovell, dividing her time between her Cody home (now the Lockhart Bed and Breakfast) and her ranch. She died at the age of 92. Today her old ranch lies within Bighorn Canyon National Recreation Area.

offered at Horseshoe Bend amphitheater on Saturday evenings in the summer.

Barry's Landing Campground has fewer sites but is a much nicer place to stay. Bring your own water. RVers can park overnight above the boat ramp. Firewood is usually available at both Horseshoe Bend and Barry's Landing. In addition, you can pitch a tent at **Medicine Creek Campground,** although you'll need to hike in along a two-mile dirt road or float in by boat.

Backcountry camping is available throughout the southern end of the recreation area; check at the visitors center for current restrictions and access information. Also be sure to avoid trespassing on the nearby Crow Indian Reservation.

Hiking

Although there are only a few trails in Bighorn Canyon, the open badlands country makes hiking relatively easy. Some trails lead to spectacular canyon rim overviews. Best times are in the fall or in February and March, when temperatures are milder and you're less likely to meet a rattler. Prairie rattlesnakes and black widow spiders are both common in this desert country, so be aware, especially when exploring old buildings. Ask at the visitors center for their little handout detailing 10 local places to hike in Bighorn Canyon. In addition to the trails listed, you can also hike the mile-long dirt path to the ghost town of Hillsboro, described earlier.

Crooked Creek Nature Trail, a short half-mile path with self-guiding brochures, takes off from the Horseshoe Bend campground. The appropriately named **State Line Trail** is an easy one-mile hike that starts just north of the Montana state line. Rock cairns mark the path along through juniper forests to the canyon rim for dramatic vistas. **Sullivan's Knob Trail** is another delightful one-mile hike that leads to the canyon rim. The rock-cairn-marked route starts one mile north of the Devil Canyon Overlook and cuts along the base of a geological feature called Sullivan's Knob. **Upper Layout Creek**

Trail is another interesting two-mile (each way) path. It starts five miles north of the turnoff for Devil Canyon Overlook and follows an old road along the creek before entering Layout Creek Canyon. The route isn't well marked once you get off the road, but you just follow the creek uphill.

On the Water

Most visitors come to Bighorn Canyon to play on the water. You'll see lots of people tooling around in powerful boats, towing water-skiers, trolling for fish, or windsurfing. Fishing is the biggest attraction; walleye, rainbow, and brown trout, yellow perch, ling, crappie, and catfish are commonly caught. Because the lake straddles the state line, you'll need a fishing license for whichever state you are in. If you fish both sides of the border, you'll need to purchase licenses for both Wyoming and Montana. Launch ramps are at Barry's Landing and Horseshoe Bend, plus Ok-A-Beh Marina at the north end of the lake. Swimmers hang out at the Horseshoe Bend beach, the only place with a lifeguard; check with the visitors center to see when they're on duty.

Horseshoe Bend Marina, 307/548-7230, rents inner tubes, canoes, fishing boats, paddle boats, and pontoon boats, and sells boat gas, food, and beer. The café sells burgers and snacks. Open mid-May to Labor Day.

Droughts are fairly common in Wyoming, and when they occur lake levels may be too low for boating or other water activities. In 2002—the third consecutive year of a severe drought—the Horseshoe Bend boat ramp and marina were closed and the water was at a record low level. But as locals like to say, it is always a fluid situation (ha, ha), so call the National Recreation Area for the latest.

Ok-A-Beh Marina, 406/665-2349, on the Montana side, has limited fishing supplies, plus food, boat gas, and boat rentals. Hours are Monday–Friday 10 A.M.–7 P.M. and Saturday–Sunday 8 A.M.–8 P.M. Memorial Day to Labor Day.

Information

For a good orientation to the area, stop by **Bighorn Canyon Visitor Center,** 307/548-2251, just east of Lovell along U.S. Hwy. 14A. It's open daily 8 A.M.–6 P.M. Memorial Day to Labor Day, and daily 8:30 A.M.–5 P.M. the rest of the year (closed Thanksgiving, Christmas, and New Year's Day). The solar-heated center is an attraction in itself; 70 percent of its heat comes directly from the sun. Inside are a three-dimensional relief map of the canyon, displays on local animals, books and topo maps for sale, and movies on Bighorn Canyon, Pryor Mountain Wild Horse Range, and Medicine Wheel. Check the notice board for other talks or hikes in the recreation area, including the weekend **campfire programs** at Horseshoe Bend Campground (summer only). Be sure to pick up a copy of *Canyon Echoes,* the free visitor guide with current information. A ranger station is located at Crooked Creek, just south of the Horseshoe Bend junction. The **Ewing-Snell Historical Site** at Layout Creek contains a restored one-room schoolhouse.

PRYOR MOUNTAIN WILD HORSE RANGE

Pryor Mountain Wild Horse Range covers 46,000 acres on the western side of Bighorn Canyon. Established in 1968 as the nation's first wild horse range, it is managed by the Bureau of Land Management. (Two other wild horse ranges now exist, in Nevada and Colorado, and there are another 3,000 wild horses in the Red Desert of southwestern Wyoming.) Pryor Mountain's desert country supports three subherds, and periodic roundups keep the population near the carrying capacity of 120 horses. Most horses remain out of sight in remote box canyons, but you're likely to see some relatively tame ones along the road between Horseshoe Bend and Layout Creek Ranger Station.

Most "wild horses" of the West are of mixed origin. Some are primarily domestic horses that were released into the wild by local ranchers, whereas others can trace at least some of the bloodlines to Spanish mustangs brought to the New World in the 16th century. Studies of wild horses found that the mustangs at Pryor Mountain are the most strongly Spanish of any feral horse herd in America, although there is some intermixing from more recent breeds. This Spanish influence is exhibited in the distinctive colors that include dun, blue roan, grulla, and sabino. Many have dark manes and tails. Other common characteristics are dark leg stripes and a dark line running down the back.

Before protection of the wild horses, many were rounded up for use on ranches or for the pet food industry. After 1971, when it became illegal to harass or kill wild horses, their numbers began to grow rapidly. Each year's colt crop increases the herd by 20 percent, placing increasing demands on a limited forage supply. Today, the BLM controls numbers through its adopt-a-horse program, removing 40–50 horses every few years from Pryor Mountain and offering them to the public. For details on acquiring a wild horse, call the BLM at 406/896-5013, or visit them online at www.wildhorseandburro.blm.gov.

The **Pryor Mountain Wild Mustang Center** is expected to open in 2004 on land adjacent to the Park Service's Bighorn Canyon Visitor Center, and several of the wild horses are in the pasture here. For additional info, call 307/548-9453.

Greybull

For travelers en route to Yellowstone, the crossroads town of Greybull (pop. 1,800) is a splotch of irrigated green surrounded by desert country. Greybull lies near the junction of Shell Creek and the Bighorn River and at the intersection of U.S. Hwys. 14 and 16/20. As such, it is both an agricultural center and a commercial center. Most of the town lies along the western shore of the river behind a long levee; barren rocky bluffs line the opposite bank. There are bentonite processing plants just north of town, oil pumpjacks farther afield, and irrigated farms along the river. Tip: If you're heading west to Cody and Yellowstone, fill up here because gas prices get more expensive as you approach the mountains.

HISTORY

The land around Greybull was first settled in the 1880s by stockmen, with several hundred Mormon homesteaders moving in a decade later to dig irrigation ditches and establish the minuscule farming settlements of **Burlington** (pop. 250) and **Otto** along the Greybull River. Nearby **Emblem** was established by 600 German farmers in the late 1890s. A diversion of the Greybull River was begun in 1895, the first reclamation project under the Carey Act. Originally called Germania, the name was changed to Emblem (a reference to the American flag) during the anti-German hysteria of World War I.

The origins of the name Greybull are unclear, although the town was named for the nearby Greybull River. Some say that it was named for a huge albino buffalo that once roamed this country. A more likely explanation is that the river was named after a Crow Indian medicine man named Chief Grey Bull who spent considerable time in the area.

The town is primarily a creation of the Burlington Railroad in 1909–1910, but much of its growth has been fueled by oil and gas developments in the surrounding country. Completion of U.S. Hwy. 14 across the Big Horn Mountains in the 1930s brought tourists and led to Greybull's development as a way station for folks heading east to the Black Hills or west to Yellowstone. Beginning in 1934, scientists excavated a dozen complete skeletons of dinosaurs near Greybull, and in 1991 Swiss paleontologists excavated one of the largest *allosauruses* ever found. The railroad is still a major employer in Greybull, as are two bentonite plants, along with Hawkins and Powers Aviation.

SIGHTS
Greybull Museum

The local museum is in the same building as the library (325 Greybull Ave., 307/765-2444). It's open Monday–Friday 10 A.M.–8 P.M. and Saturday 10 A.M.–6 P.M. June–September, Monday–Friday 1–5 P.M. in the spring and fall, and

Monday, Wednesday, and Friday 1–4 P.M. in the winter. No charge. Inside are agate collections and polished petrified wood pieces, a fine fossil collection that includes one of the largest fossil ammonites ever found, fossil turtles, and dinosaur bones. Also here are various Indian arrowheads and other historical artifacts, including a New England church made from royal icing!

Aerial Firefighting Museum

South Big Horn County Airport, atop a hill just north of town, is the home of Hawkins & Powers Aviation, a major source of planes used to drop fire retardant on forest fires throughout the West. During the summer fire season it's often a center of intense activity, with nine air tankers and seven helicopters based here. Included are four of the five PB4Y-2s still flying. During World War II, PB4Ys played an important role in routing the Japanese from the South Pacific. Hawkins & Powers planes have appeared in several movies, including a C-119 used in the Steven Spielberg firefighting film *Always.* The company experienced disastrous losses in 2002 when two of their air tankers—a PB4Y-2 and a C-130—crashed while fighting fires. Five crewmembers perished in the crashes.

Fourteen retired firefighting aircraft are included in a display across from the rest area just west of the airport. It's called the **Museum of Flight and Aerial Firefighting,** 307/765-4322, www.tctwest.net/~flight. Take a look through the fence at any time, or pay to walk around for a close-up view; $3.50 adults, $2 kids, and free for children under age six. Open daily 8 A.M.–6 P.M. in summer, and Mon.–Fri. 8 A.M.–5 P.M. the rest of the year.

Other Attractions

Five miles northeast of Greybull is **Devil's Kitchen,** a fascinating arroyo filled with brilliantly colored badlands and many fossils. Get a map from the chamber of commerce and follow it closely; the last turnoff is easy to miss.

Sheep Mountain, a 15-mile-long hogback of eroded land just north of Greybull, is a favorite of geologists, who marvel at this fossil-packed anticline. Photographers love the vivid reds, browns, and yellows of this desert landscape. A bit farther afield is the Red Gulch Dinosaur Tracksite; see Shell Valley for details on this important discovery.

fire-fighting air-retardant tankers at Hawkins & Powers Aviation, Greybull

A couple of **Indian petroglyphs** are one-half mile north of town and just east on a dirt road. Look for the bluff across from the bentonite plant, where you'll see a bison with an arrow in it and a couple of human figures, along with more recent graffiti and gunshots courtesy of the jerks.

Find an attractive flower garden in the shape of the Wyoming state flag at the west end of Greybull Avenue. Folks traveling with children should make a detour to the **city park** with its extensive play area, plus picnic tables and grills, a jogging path, restrooms, and a lonely chimney from the first house built in Greybull.

Possibly worth a visit is Morency and Sons Taxidermy, A.K.A. the **Greybull Wildlife Museum,** 420 Greybull Ave., 307/7675-2002, with a small collection of stuffed critters.

SHOPPING

Probst Western Store, 547 Greybull Ave., 307/765-2171 or 888/765-2171, www.probstwestern.com, has a great selection of cowboy hats, boots, and Western clothes, plus gifts and jewelry. They've been in business since 1945. A few doors up the street at 532 Greybull Ave., **Big Horn Quilts,** 307/765-2304 or 877/586-9150, is a surprisingly complete and bustling quilt shop with 6,000 bolts of fabric. The walls are lined with intricate quilts from local artisans, and quilting bees take place every Thursday. Big Horn Quilts has a loyal international following through its website, www.bighornquilts.com, and features quilt and doll shows and contests in February and August.

If you are into chainsaw carving, drop by the appropriately named **Bearly Art Chainsaw Carvings,** 307/765-2368, www.tctwest.com/~bearlyart, located one mile south of town on Hwy. 20.

ACCOMMODATIONS

Sage Motel, 1135 N. 6th St., 307/765-4443, has older rooms for $35 one bed or $45 for two beds. Most rooms contain small fridges. **Antler Motel,** 1116 N. 6th St., 307/765-4404, is a quiet place with rooms for $35 s or $40–45 d.

Three rooms contain kitchenettes, and there's a mini-golf course on the grounds.

Three Chief Motel, 625 N. 6th St., 307/765-4626, has recently remodeled rooms for $40 s or $40–50 d; open Apr.–Oct. All rooms are non-smoking and include fridges and HBO.

K-Bar Motel, 300 Greybull Ave., 307/765-4426, charges $42 s or $47–56 d for well-maintained rooms, some with small fridges. Two-room suites are $65 for four people. The friendly owner will be glad to provide tips on local sights. Comfortable **Greybull Motel,** 300 N. 6th St., 307/765-2628, charges $52 for one bed or $68 for rooms with two beds, microwaves, and fridges. The grounds are nicely maintained, with flowers and shade trees.

Yellowstone Motel, 247 Greybull Ave., 307/765-4456, offers renovated rooms for $52–62 s or $62–72 d, including an outdoor pool. On the north end of town and next to a 24-hour restaurant of the same name, **Wheels Motel,** 1324 N. 6th St., 307/765-2105, is one of the better local motels. Rates are $52–62 s or $62–72 d; some rooms contain fridges and recliners.

Located west of Greybull near the town of Burlington, **Wayfaring Traveler Ranch,** 307/762-3536, www.tctwest.net/~wtr, is a working llama ranch that offers a secluded guest house, guided llama treks to nearby Table Mountain, and llama rentals. It's a quiet getaway with more than 30 llamas. The guesthouse has a kitchenette and bath. Up to four guests can stay for $70; $15 per person for additional guests. Kids are welcome.

CAMPING

Green Oasis RV Park, 540 N. 12th Ave., 307/765-2856 or 888/765-2856, www.greenoasiscampground.com, has tent sites for $15; RV sites for $25. Showers for noncampers cost $5. Open mid-Apr. to mid-Oct.

Greybull KOA, 333 N. 2nd Ave., 307/765-2555 or 800/562-7508, www.koa.com, charges $20 for tent sites, $25–29 for RVs. Showers cost $5 for noncampers. Open mid-Apr. to mid-Oct., with trees and an outdoor pool. It also has basic cabins for $35 d.

FOOD

For family dining three meals a day, it's hard to fault **Buffalo Rose Restaurant,** 601 N. 6th St., 307/765-4781. Prices are reasonable, the setting is kid-friendly, and the food is good. There are daily specials and prime rib every Friday night. Step back in time to the **Sugar Shack,** 509 Greybull Ave., 307/765-9650, a 1950s soda fountain and gift shop with banana splits, sundaes, and ice cream sodas, plus locally made items.

Uptown Cafe, 536 Greybull Ave., 307/765-2152, is right downtown next to the stoplight and has the best biscuits and gravy in town, plus daily specials and homemade soups and pies. **Lisa's Fine Food & Spirits,** 200 Greybull Ave., 307/765-4765, www.lisasfinefoods.com, serves all the standard meat-and-potato fixes, along with spicy Southwest fare such as fajitas and tequila chipolte barbecue-grilled pork loin. It fills with locals most evenings.

Open 24 hours a day, **Wheels Inn Restaurant,** 1336 N. 6th St., 307/765-2456, serves standard American fare and has a Sunday breakfast buffet and daily salad bar. Check out their dinosaur mural. **CC's Pizza,** 427 Greybull Ave., 307/765-4510, is the local pizza joint. Also in Greybull (on N. 6th St.) are a Subway and an A&W drive-in for quick eats.

Ron's Food Farm, 909 N. 6th St., 307/765-2890, is the local grocery store; it has a deli with hot lunch specials daily and a drive-up espresso stand in the parking lot. Traveling seniors are welcome at the **Greybull Senior Center,** 307/765-4488, during lunch on weekdays; it's located next to the city park.

ENTERTAINMENT AND EVENTS

For live music, try **Smokehouse Saloon** 562 Greybull Ave., 307/765-2232, or **Silver Spur,** 445 Greybull Ave., 307/765-2300. The Smokehouse has a 19th-century cherry wood back bar, plus pool tables, darts, and pub grub. It's a favorite of bikers.

Greybull's big annual event is **Days of '49** (1949 that is), held the second weekend in June; there's a top-notch rodeo, a parade, barbecue in the park, dancing, tug-of-war contests, and demolition derby. A **Mountain Man Rendezvous** is held that same weekend, with traders, black powder shoots, and tomahawk and knife throwing.

The **National Chainsaw Carving Competition** comes to Greybull in early July, with plenty of chainsaw action, a barbecue, and an auction.

RECREATION

A marvelous 1920s log building houses the **Greybull Roller Rink,** 527 S. 1st Ave., 307/765-2761. Swim and take showers at the **pool** across from the high school on N. 6th St.; 307/765-9575. There's also a great kids' playground at the **city park** at 3rd Ave. South and S. 2nd Street. Five miles south of Greybull, **Midway Golf Club,** 307/568-9575, is a nine-hole course open to the public.

INFORMATION AND SERVICES

The **Greybull Chamber of Commerce** is downtown at 521 Greybull Ave., 307/765-2100 or 877/765-2100, www.greybull.com. They're open mornings and evenings in summer, with local artwork on display.

The **Greybull Public Library** is at 325 Greybull Ave., 307/765-2551, and has a computer for Internet access. Find the local **post office** at 401 Greybull Ave., 307/765-4771, and **ATMs** at 1st Interstate Bank, 601 Greybull Ave., and inside Ron's Food Farm at 909 N. 6th St. and the Overland Express Mart, 500 N. 6th Street. Wash clothes at **Coin-Op Laundromat,** across the street from the A&W on N. 6th Street.

Powder River Transportation/Coach USA, 307/682-0960 or 800/442-3682, has daily bus service from Greybull to other towns in Bighorn Basin, along with Billings, Montana. They can also take you throughout central and eastern Wyoming and all the way to Denver or Rapid City. Buses stop in front of the chamber of commerce office on Greybull Avenue; get tickets inside.

Greybull Vicinity

BASIN

South of Greybull, the highway parallels the Bighorn River. Sharp bluffs rise along the eastern side of the river, and cottonwoods and willows crowd the banks. As you head away from the broad river valley, the endless hills are covered with dry grass, sage, and greasewood. It's a plain-Jane, arid landscape. Eight miles away lies the struggling town of Basin (pop. 1,200), puttering along on its status as Big Horn County seat and the presence of a big state retirement center. The shady town park has a nice kids' playground.

Established in 1896, the town has always been an agricultural center, with both farming and ranching in the surrounding land. In 1897, a bitter custody battle for the county seat split voters between Basin City, as it was then known, and the older town of Otto. Basin City won by 38 votes.

State Hwy. 789 heads south from Basin to dinky **Manderson** (pop. 100), where **Hiway Cafe,** 307/568-2384, has a Sunday buffet and salad bar. South of here the road splits and continues on both sides of Bighorn River to Worland. The main road (on the east side of the river) plays tag with the irrigation ditch much of the way, passing eroded desert bluffs to the east and flat farm country closer to the river. A thin strip of trees runs right down the middle; in fall they look like skeletons against the skyline. Lots of barley, sugar beet, and hayfields can be seen here.

Accommodations and Camping

The **Lilac Motel,** 710 W. C St., 307/568-3355, has a quiet location and costs just $35 s or $44 d. All rooms include microwaves and fridges. Free **camping** is available next to the boat ramp along the Big Horn River. Park RVs ($20) at **Rose Garden RV Park,** 307/568-2943, on the south end of town. They also have a few tent spaces for $12; open mid-Apr. through Oct.

Other Practicalities

Start your day with a fine breakfast (served anytime) at **Tom's Cafe,** 602 S. 4th St., 307/568-

2246. Lunch and dinner include such Wyoming favorites as chicken-fried steak, burgers, sandwiches, and a chicken basket with fries and coleslaw. Get fast food at **Overland Express,** 155 N. 4th St. 307/568-2722. **Wheeler's IGA Market,** 114 S. 4th St., 307/568-2325, has groceries and an **ATM.**

For books, stop by **Big Horn County Library,** 103 W. C St., 307/568-2388. Wash clothes at the laundromat on D and 4th Streets. There's an outdoor **swimming pool** at the high school.

Stockman's Bar, 105 S. 4th St., 307/568-9942, has live country music a couple of times a month. In early August, Basin hosts the **Big Horn County Fair,** with livestock judging, a rodeo, barbecue, and more small-town fun; details at 307/568-2968, www.tctwest.net/~bhfair.

Powder River Transportation/Coach USA, 307/682-0960 or 800/442-3682, has daily bus service from Basin to other towns in Bighorn Basin, along with Billings, Montana. They can also take you throughout central and eastern Wyoming and all the way to Denver or Rapid City.

SHELL VALLEY

Shell Valley is farming and ranching country, its lush irrigated hayfields contrasting sharply with the arid landscape to the west. The tiny town called Shell has a country store/bar and several places to stay. Several old log-and-stone buildings are in Shell, including the Community Church, built in 1903. Also from that same era is a distinctive **old stone school** several miles west of Shell; it served as a one-room school until the 1950s.

Head two miles east of Shell for **Dirty Annie's,** 307/765-2304, with burgers and ice cream, and **Wagonwheel Restaurant and Lounge,** 307/765-2561, with a dinner menu of prime rib, seafood, and steaks. Summer visitors will enjoy their outdoor patio.

One mile east of Shell is **Art Shelter Studio Gallery,** where Earl Miller and Karyne Dunbar (and other artists) display their unusual pieces in a converted barn. Call 307/765-9605 to make sure they're in when you visit.

Red Gulch and Dinosaur Tracks

The Bureau of Land Management's **Red Gulch Scenic Byway** is a 32-mile dirt road through remote and striking country. The northern access point starts on the south side of U.S. Hwy. 14 four miles west of Shell (10 miles east of Greybull) and is well-marked. The first 10 miles of the byway are the most interesting, with spectacular red badlands of the Chugwater Formation on both sides of the road. The road gets slick and muddy when wet, so don't venture out after a day of rain. If it hasn't rained in awhile the road is usually passable in a two-wheel-drive vehicle. This is some of the most remote country in Wyoming; even ranches are few and far between. No phones, gas, or other services are available until Hyattville, 32 miles from your starting point. The area is rich in Indian history; tepee rings and pictographs are scattered over the countryside.

Approximately five miles south of the turnoff from U.S. Hwy. 14 is a parking area (with picnic tables, restrooms, and a wooden walkway) for **Red Gulch Dinosaur Tracksite.** In 1997, geologist Erik Kvale was looking over this area when a relative asked him if dinosaur tracks might be found in this formation. "No," he responded. But when he looked at the rocks at his feet, he corrected himself, "but here is one right in front of me." Dr. Kvale's discovery attracted national attention, and the site has become a major attraction for both paleontologists and anyone interested in dinosaurs. Hundreds of three-toed tracks crisscross more than 40 acres. The tracks were apparently made when theropods (meat-eating dinosaurs) walked in mud along a lakeshore. Most are 2–10 inches in length, fairly shallow, and easiest to see in the low-angled light of morning or dusk. Volunteer guides are at the site 6–8 P.M. Wednesday–Saturday in the summer.

The discovery of these tracks has changed the way paleontologists view the geologic history of Bighorn Basin. Previously it was believed that this entire area had been underwater during the middle Jurassic period (165 million years ago),

but these tracks are from land-dwelling dinosaurs. For more information on the tracks and Red Gulch, contact the BLM's Worland Field Office at 307/347-5100, or see the informative website, accessed through www.wy.blm.gov. The Geo-Sciences website (www.geo-sciences.com) has additional information on the area.

Geo-Science Adventures, 307/765-2259 or 866/765-2259, www.geo-sciences.com, conducts informative tours of both the Red Gulch dinosaur tracksite and a second tracksite on the nearby Flitner Ranch. Half-day tours are $20 per person; all day costs $75 per person and includes hands-on explorations of local geology and palentology. Tours are offered from mid-April to mid-September.

Accommodations

Trapper's Rest Guest Cabin, 307/765-9239 or 877/765-5233, has two comfortably furnished two-bedroom cabins with bath; one has a kitchenette. The cabins are three miles southeast of Shell in a peaceful and quiet setting with a tree-lined trout stream nearby. They rent for $50 s or d, and can sleep up to five. A cook-tent is nearby, complete with a well-supplied kitchen. Archaeologists working a nearby dig occupy one of the cabins in the summer and provide occasional evening programs. You might also catch a stargazing or wildflower talk here. Trapper's Rest is open June–October and kids are welcome. Camping is available.

At the foot of the Big Horns, **The Hideout at Flitner Ranch** is a fifth-generation working cattle ranch in operation since 1906. Popular with European tourists, the ranch has an incredible 250,000 acres of leased or deeded land, so you'll find plenty of country to explore. Guests stay in modern log cabins with all the amenities, including private baths, phones, televisions, and a hot tub. Activities center on horseback riding and fly-fishing, and there's an indoor riding arena. All-inclusive six-night rates are $3,800 for two people in the peak season, or you can just rent a cabin and find your own fun for $175 d per night. The ranch provides space for a maximum of 24 guests. Contact them at 307/765-2080 or 800/354-8637, www.thehideout.com. Open late March–Oct.

Bear Creek Ranch, 307/765-9319 or 888/770-8769, www.bilbrey.net, has a variety of options on their 57,000-acre ranch, including six-night ranch vacations for $1,000 per person, all-inclusive. This is a good place to live the cowboy life of working cattle, branding calves, and other activities. Trail rides and camping are also available.

Kedesh Guest Ranch, four miles east of Shell along U.S. Hwy. 14, 307/765-2791 or 800/845-3320, www.kedesh.com, offers log cabin accommodations in grand mountain country. Ranch activities include horseback riding, fishing, and whitewater rafting, but guests can also join organized trips to Cody or to explore petroglyphs and dinosaur digs. The hot tub awaits after a long day. All-inclusive weekly rates are $2,300 for two people, and the ranch books a maximum of 20 guests at a time. A three-night minimum is required; open June–Sept.

Wagonwheel Restaurant and Lounge, 307/765-2561, has a pair of simple roadside cabins (no TV or phones) two miles east of Shell; $30 d.

Park RVs ($20) or pitch tents ($15) in Shell at **Shell Campground,** 307/765-9924, www.shell-campground.com; open May–Oct. Sites are shaded, and showers cost $3 for those not camping here.

HYATTVILLE AREA

Twenty-one miles east of Manderson on State Hwy. 31 is the tiny ranching center of Hyattville. Built in 1905, **Paintrock Grill,** has meals and alcohol downstairs and old-fashioned rooms over the bar. Meals are also available at **Hyattville Cafe,** 307/469-2242. **Paintrock Adventures,** 307/469-2274, leads fishing trips and trail rides. Check out the **Hyattville Old-Timers Picnic** on the last weekend of July at nearby Medicine Lodge State Park. Bring a salad or dessert and join in the fun.

Medicine Lodge State Park

One of Wyoming's most famous archaeological sites, Medicine Lodge State Park is well worth the detour. Get here by heading north from Hyattville and turning right onto Cold Springs Road. After four miles, turn left again at the "Medicine Lodge" sign and follow the dirt road 1.5 miles to the park (the road gets slippery when it rains).

The main attraction at Medicine Lodge is a 750-foot-long low cliff that served as a backdrop to 10,000 years of Indian settlements. The cliff is covered with dozens of petroglyphs and pictographs. A small log **visitors center,** 307/469-2234, http://wyoparks.state.wy.us—built almost a century ago as a cowboy bunkhouse—is open Monday–Friday 8 A.M.–5 P.M. and Saturday–Sunday 9 A.M.–8 P.M. May to Labor Day. Inside are displays on the area's incredibly rich archaeological history. Beginning in 1969, researchers uncovered some 60 cultural levels and thousands of artifacts and bones here. It's considered one of the most significant archaeological sites in the West.

A delightful creekside **campground** ($12 for nonresidents or $6 for Wyoming residents) is just a short distance from the petroglyphs and has restrooms, water, and good fishing for brown trout in the creek. Wheelchair fishing access is also provided. Ask at the visitors center to pick fruit from the old apple trees next to the cabin.

A three-quarter-mile **nature trail** begins near the visitors center, or you can hike up the trail/4WD road along Dry Medicine Lodge Creek. This route passes a natural arch approximately three miles up and goes through a BLM wilderness study area. It's a great place for mountain-biking or a peaceful evening walk.

Staying on Cold Springs Road—instead of turning off to Medicine Lodge State Park—takes you 15 miles to Paint Rocks Lakes, a jumping-off point for Cloud Peak Wilderness (described under Big Horn Mountains in the Powder River Country chapter).

Trapper Canyon

North of Hyattville, another interesting place awaits folks willing to do a lot of adventuring. **Trapper Canyon,** located on public land, has colorful walls rising 1,200 feet above Trapper Creek. No trails, and tough access requires serious 4WD vehicles; check with the BLM office in Worland for details.

Worland

The prosperous community of Worland (pop. 5,300) depends on a mixture of agriculture (primarily malt barley and sugar beets), sheep and cattle ranching, oil production, and manufacturing. Sheep glean plowed fields near town, and the Holly Sugar Company's plant on the southwest edge of Worland provides economic stability, keeping more than 20,000 acres in beets. Also important is a major aluminum can factory that produces three million cans per day, and a Pepsi bottling plant that fills many of these. The town has a pleasant Midwestern feel, with nightly baseball games throughout the summer, tree-bordered streets and simple homes in the center, and suburban ranch-style homes spreading across the surrounding countryside. The slow Bighorn River twists its way along the edge of Worland, but just a few miles farther west is desert country with dry rocky buttes, sagebrush, and sheep.

HISTORY

Worland is named for Charlie "Dad" Worland, one of the first homesteaders in this part of the Bighorn Basin and the manager of a stage station and saloon built along the old Bridger Trail in 1900. It wasn't much to look at—a cave dug into the riverbank, with log walls out front. His bar quickly acquired the nickname "The Hole-in-the-Wall." A cigar box just behind the bar served as the local bank, and anyone needing money could borrow it and leave behind an IOU. Other folks settled around Dad Worland, and A. G. Rupp added a general store nearby, also built into the side of the riverbank to save precious timber. Ray Pendergraft in *Washakie: A Wyoming County History,* relates the following story about early Worland:

> Once a compactly-built man rode into the settlement, refreshed himself at Worland's saloon, then went on to Rupps for some supplies. On one wall of the store was a poster, complete with a picture. It read, "$5,000 Reward, Dead or Alive Robert Leroy Parker, alias Butch Cassidy." The

> visitor examined it. "It's not a very good likeness," he told Rupp. Rupp examined the poster, looked at the man, and readily agreed. "You don't want it up there do you, Mr. Rupp?" the man politely asked. "No, I don't," replied Mr. Rupp. "I'll take it down for you," the man said, did so and went on about his selection of supplies.

Originally located on the western side of the Bighorn River, Worland moved to the other side after the Chicago, Burlington, and Quincy Railroad announced plans to build along the east bank. The nucleus of Worland, 10 buildings, was slid across the river on the ice during the winter of 1905–1906. The following year, construction was finished on the 54-mile-long Big Horn irrigation canal, opening some 30,000 acres to agriculture. It had been begun almost 20 years earlier. A new sugar beet processing plant in 1917 attracted more farmers and workers from the Midwest and many Germans and Ukrainians. The discovery of oil in the Hidden Dome field in that same year brought boom times as speculators flooded the area. Oil and agriculture, especially sugar beets, have remained important ever since, although oil production has declined as the fields have been pumped out.

SIGHTS

Housed in an old Mormon church, the **Washakie Museum and Cultural Center,** 1115 Obie Sue Ave., 307/347-4102, www.trib.com /~wmuseum, is open Monday–Saturday 9 A.M.–5 P.M. in summer, and Tuesday–Saturday 10 A.M.–5 P.M. the rest of the year. A donation is requested. Inside are Indian artifacts from cave sites near Ten Sleep, a re-creation of the A. G. Rupp Store, old photos, cowboy and ranch equipment, and a fine geology and fossil collection. The museum's highlight is a Sheepeater Indian lodge constructed in the 1860s from 130 poles. It was moved here from its original location near Soapy Peak. Also here are mammoth bones from the 11,000-year-old Colby Site, three miles east of Worland. This was one of the largest and oldest known mammoth kills in North America. Kids will enjoy the Family Discovery Center, with art activities and other hands-on fun. Across the street is a pleasant **city park** with picnic tables, shade trees, and a playground.

Next to the County Court House, at the corner of Big Horn Ave. and 10th St., is a fountain fed by a 4,330-foot-deep **artesian well** 23 miles north of Worland. The well flows at an impressive 14,000 gallons per minute and with sufficient pressure to push water all the way to Worland. The fountain is a good place to fill water jugs for your desert travels. Also on the courthouse grounds is a grotesque 15-foot-tall **Indian statue** carved out of wood by Peter Toth

and placed here in 1980. **Pioneer Square,** just across the road, has unusual metal sculptures depicting pioneer settlers.

Head two miles north on State Hwy. 433 to **Duck Swamp,** with picnic tables, a paved interpretive trail, and an overlook. A sign describes the Bridger Trail that passed through here.

West of Worland in the Painted Desert, you'll find some of the most interesting badlands country in Wyoming. Of particular note are the **Gooseberry Badlands** (A.K.A. 15-Mile Badlands) on Bureau of Land Management (BLM) property near Squaw Teats and right along State Hwy. 431. The BLM has developed a 1.5-mile nature trail through the colorful hoodoo formations here; pick up a descriptive handout from their office in Worland. There's plenty of eroded country to explore, including arches and a variety

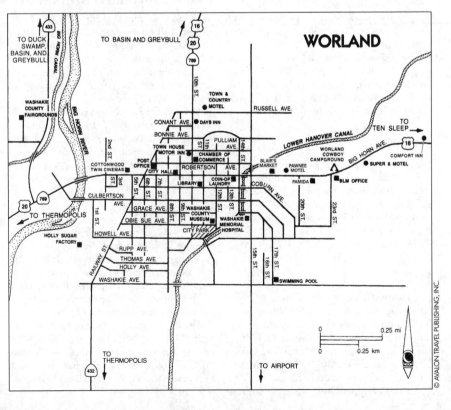

of bizarrely carved shapes, and the bones of a prehistoric horse, *Eohippus,* have been found in the area. Get details from the BLM in Worland, 307/347-5100, www.wy.blm.gov/wfo/index.htm.

ACCOMMODATIONS

The cheapest and most basic Greybull places are **Town House Motor Inn,** 119 N. 10th St., 307/347-2426, where rooms cost $36–42 s or $45–48 d; and **Econo Inn (also called Town & Country Motel),** 1021 Russell St., 307/347-3249, where rooms are $38 s or $42 d. Both of these motels have some rooms with fridges and microwaves.

Super 8 Motel, 2500 Big Horn, 307/347-9236 or 800/800-8000, www.super8.com, charges $50–60 s or $61–70 d. One of the nicest places in town is **Days Inn,** 500 N. 10th St., 307/347-4251 or 800/329-7466, www.daysinn.com, with rooms for $42–62 s or $48–78 d, including a continental breakfast.

Worland's newest motel is **Comfort Inn,** 100 N. Rd. 11, 307/347-9898 or 800/228-5150, www.comfortinn.com. Rates are $75–85 d; suites for $135 d. Amenities include an indoor pool, hot tub, and continental breakfast.

CAMPING

No public campgrounds are near Worland (although you can pitch a tent on nearby BLM lands), but the private **Worland Cowboy Campground,** 2311 Big Horn Ave., 307/347-2329, www.worlandcowboycampground.com, has shady tent sites for $16, RV spaces for $22. Showers for noncampers cost $5. Open May–Oct.

FOOD

Maggie's Cafe, 541 Big Horn Ave., 307/347-3354, has reasonable meals, including homemade soups and breads. The most expensive dinner is $7! Get good breakfasts and lunchtime sandwiches (homemade bread) at **The Office,** 1515 Big Horn Ave., 307/347-8171; drop by on Friday night for the prime rib special.

Antone's Supper Club, three miles east of town on U.S. Hwy. 16, 307/347-9924, has enormous hamburgers and hand-cut steaks in a friendly setting. **Season's Supper Club,** 1620 Big Horn Ave., 307/347-9261, is the fanciest place in town and grills the best steaks around.

Ranchito Mexican Food, 544 Big Horn Ave., 307/347-8501, serves authentic south-of-the-border fare, and **China Garden,** 616 Big Horn Ave., 307/347-6168, brings you a touch of Asia. **Pizza Hut,** 1927 Big Horn Ave., 307/347-2434, and **Pizza on the Run,** 1214 Big Horn Ave., 307/347-2453, are the local pizza joints.

A good selection of groceries can be found at **Jon's IGA Food Basket,** 221 N. 10th St., 307/347-3628, or **Blair's Market,** 1801 Big Horn Ave., 307/347-8500. Both have in-store delis.

EVENTS AND ENTERTAINMENT

Worland's big annual event is the **Washakie County Fair** on the first week of August. It includes a parade, country music, and other country-fair fun. In early September, the **Harvest Fest and Car Show** has hot-air balloons, classic cars, food booths, arts and crafts, contests, and even a sugar-beet-carving contest.

Two places have live bands most weekends: **The Office Lounge,** 1515 Big Horn Ave., 307/347-8171, and **Antone's Supper Club,** three miles east of town on U.S. Hwy. 16, 307/347-9924. **Cottonwood Twin Cinemas,** 401 Robertson, 307/347-8414, is the local movie palace.

RECREATION

During summer, many people float and fish the **Bighorn River** north from Worland. The river is gentle in many stretches, but get detailed information and a map of access sites from the BLM office before putting in. Upstream from Worland to Thermopolis, the river has many hazards, and this stretch is not recommended for novices.

There's a community **swimming pool** at the high school, 1706 Washakie Ave., 307/347-4113, and an 18-hole **Municipal Golf Course,** 307/347-2695, next to the airport. Roll black balls toward white pins at **Hurricane Lanes,** 612 S. 12th, 307/347-4044.

INFORMATION AND SERVICES

The **Worland Area Chamber of Commerce** office, 307/347-3226, www.worlandchamber.com, sits in front of the county courthouse at 120 N. 10th Street and stays open Monday–Friday 8 A.M.–noon and 1–5 P.M.

The **Washakie County Library,** 1019 Coburn Ave., 307/347-2231, has Internet access. Drop by the **BLM's Worland Field Office** at 101 S. 23rd Street, 307/347-5100, www.wy.blm.gov/wfo /index.htm, for information on scenic back roads and nearby places to hike or mountain-bike. The building also houses Bighorn National Forest's **Worland Information Office,** 307/347-5105, www.fs.fed.us/r2/bighorn.

Wash clothes at **Coin-Op Laundry,** 1401 Big Horn Avenue. You'll find **ATMs** at the Conoco Station at 944 Big Horn Ave. and at Key Bank, 120 N. 7th Street. For medical emergencies, head to **Washakie Medical Clinic,** 400 S. 15th St., 307/347-3221.

TRANSPORTATION

The Worland Airport is two miles south of town and is served by **Great Lakes Aviation,** 307/432-7000 or 800/554-5111, www.greatlakesav.com, with daily service to Denver and Riverton. Rent cars from **Big Horn Chevrolet,** 545 N. 10th Ave., 307/347-4229, or **Worland Ford,** 500 Big Horn Ave., 307/347-4236.

Powder River Transportation/Coach USA, 307/682-0960 or 800/442-3682, has daily bus service from Worland to other towns in Bighorn Basin, along with Billings, Montana. They can also take you throughout central and eastern Wyoming and all the way to Denver or Rapid City. Buses stop at the Sinclair Station on S. 10th St. and Big Horn Avenue.

Ten Sleep

Ten Sleep (pop. 300) has one of the most picturesque settings in all of Wyoming. The drive in from Worland offers a traipse across dry desert badlands crowded with oil pumpjacks and then up into rolling grass and sagebrush country with the tree-covered Big Horn Mountains marking the distant horizon. Great views can be seen from atop the long hills before the road descends sharply into a lush green valley cut through by Nowood and Tensleep Creeks. Because of its mountain valley location, the town of Ten Sleep offers an escape from the oppressive summer heat of Bighorn Basin. This verdant valley is one of the few places in Wyoming where apple, peach, and pear trees grow. Rustic log buildings fill this tiny ranching and tourism center. Take away the cars and the asphalt and it's easy to imagine Ten Sleep as the location for some Hollywood film about the Green Valley.

The name Ten Sleep comes from the Sioux Indians who frequently stopped in this valley during their travels between a permanent camp along the Clarks Fork River in Montana and another one along the Platte River. Halfway between the two was Ten Sleeps, so named because they measured distances in the number of nights it took to get to a place. The town of Ten Sleep was established as a trading center for the Scottish and Irish sheepmen who came here in the 1890s.

SIGHTS

The main sights in Ten Sleep are the comfortable, slow-paced town itself and its pretty setting. **Pioneer Museum** behind the Flagstaff Cafe has local artifacts and is open daily 9 A.M.–4 P.M. in the summer. An old sheriff wagon sits on main street ready to haul off the bad guys. Ask at the museum for directions to the Indian pictographs on the Walt Patch Ranch. Lions Club Park has an artesian well that is a favorite place to fill jugs with cold water.

Drop into the **Ten Sleep Saloon,** 307/366-9208, or the **Big Horn Bar,** 307/366-9222, for a cold one with local ranchers and cowboys. Ten Sleep Saloon has a bar inlaid with 5,052 pennies (oldest is from 1906) and 233 nickels;

the bartender claims that they started out with inlaid silver dollars, but this is all they had left after the taxes!

NEARBY SIGHTS

Just west of Ten Sleep is the turnoff to **Castle Gardens,** a scenic area of wind-carved sandstone badlands in all sizes and shapes. It's an eight-mile drive via a dirt road that may become impassable when wet. Castle Gardens has two free campsites, picnic tables, and an outhouse. A few miles south of Castle Gardens are the **Honeycombs,** where the landscape is pockmarked with holes. Not far away, **Big Cedar Ridge** contains an abundance of fossilized leaves and flowers on BLM land. You can dig in existing pits, but don't start new holes.

Another great drive connects Ten Sleep with tiny Lysite, approximately 60 miles to the south. The first 21 miles are paved to a spot on the map called Big Trails. South of here, the road turns to gravel and takes you along lazy Nowood River through dramatic canyons and past grand old ranches. As you approach Lysite the landscape turns desertlike, with cactus mixing with sage and sand. It's a classic Wyoming drive and passable in two-wheel-drive vehicles.

The **Salt Lick Trail** is an enjoyable short hike (1.25 miles) into an open forest of ponderosa pine and juniper, with fine views across Bighorn Basin. The trailhead is 5.5 miles east of Ten Sleep.

TENSLEEP CANYON

Six miles east of town, U.S. Hwy. 16 passes the entrance to the 8,500-acre **Tensleep Preserve,** managed by The Nature Conservancy, 307/366-2671, www.tncwyoming.org. The preserve follows a 12-mile stretch of Canyon Creek and is a great place for day hikes and to watch for peregrine falcons and Cooper's hawks. Workshops and conservation projects take place here throughout the summer, with lodging in cozy wall tents and delicious meals in the newly built lodge. The preserve is open to visitors from late May to mid-October.

Shortly beyond the turnoff to the Tensleep Preserve, the highway climbs up spectacular Tensleep Canyon toward 9,666-foot Powder River Pass in the Big Horn Mountains. **Wigwam Fish Rearing Station,** run by the Wyoming Game and Fish Department, is five miles east of town. Another six miles up is the turnoff to the old log buildings that house **Ten Sleep Fish**

the sleepy town of Ten Sleep

© DON PITCHER

THE TEN SLEEP RAID

Cattlemen have always viewed sheep with disdain, regarding them as despoilers of the range, "locusts with hooves" or "range maggots." Cattle reached Wyoming's grazing lands first, and when sheep began to arrive in large numbers around the turn of the 20th century, the cattle owners fought back with intimidation and violence. In many places, the cattlemen declared a "dead line," and any sheep or sheepherder that came into that area risked being killed. (One such line existed in Jackson Hole; even today the county has just 300 sheep as opposed to 12,000 cattle.) Despite these threats, sheep ranching was simply too lucrative to pass up; by 1889, Bighorn Basin was overrun with more than 387,000 sheep—and boasted fewer than 22,000 cattle.

Perhaps 10,000 sheep throughout the state were killed by cattlemen; some flocks were driven over cliffs, others were dynamited or attacked by dogs, and thousands more died from gunshots. Many of Wyoming's sheepherders were viciously attacked, and at least 16 were murdered. The most notorious of all these incidents took place along Spring Creek near Ten Sleep in 1909. Joe Emge, a hotheaded cattleman turned sheepman, announced plans to trail his sheep across the dead line set up in the Nowater Creek area. One April night just after the sheep had reached the grazing grounds, at least half a dozen masked men burst into the camp and murdered Emge, his partner, and a herder. The killers set the wagons afire and shot many sheep before disappearing into the night, leaving a grisly scene to be discovered the next morning.

The investigation pointed directly at a local cattleman, and after testifying before a grand jury one of the suspected raiders was found dead. Officials judged it a suicide, but many suspected that the cattleman had been waylaid by others seeking to silence anyone who might tell the truth. Eventually, two men broke the silence and fingered five others, including several prominent ranchers. All five were convicted and spent from three years to life in prison for the murders. Like the Johnson County War two decades earlier, this incident helped turn many people against the cattlemen. Sheep continued to grow in importance for a while—Wyoming became the largest wool producer in the country—but overgrazing, the severe winter of 1911–1912, and the removal of a wool tariff the next year led to a long decline. Even today, though, Wyoming is America's second-largest producer of wool.

Hatchery. Both of these operations are open daily for tours. (See the Powder River Country chapter for sights east of here as U.S. Hwy. 16 climbs over the majestic Big Horns.)

ACCOMMODATIONS AND CAMPING

Log Cabin Motel, 307/366-2320, www.tensleep-wyoming.com/logcabin, has comfortable rooms (some with microwaves and fridges) for $42–54 s or d, and kitchen units for $45–57. Park RVs or pitch a tent for $15. If you're camping elsewhere, take showers at the laundromat here for $3. The nicest local place to stay is **Valley Motel,** 307/366-2321, where rooms cost $35 s or $44–48 d. It also has a kitchenette; $54 for four people.

Pitch your tent in town at **Ten Broek RV Park,** 307/366-2250, for $13 ($19 for RVs);

open Apr.–Oct. The closest public camping is eight miles east of Ten Sleep inside Bighorn National Forest at **Tensleep Creek Campground.** Only five sites are available ($9; open mid-May through Oct.) at this peaceful riverside spot surrounded by tall cottonwoods. You can also stay at a dozen other Forest Service campgrounds farther east for $7–10.

FOOD

Flagstaff Cafe, 307/366-2745, has great breakfasts, burgers, and steaks. Housed in a building that dates from 1914, **Mountain Man Cafe,** 307/366-2660, still has the original tin ceiling. American meals include a salad bar and homemade pies; closed winters.

A classic country store, **Ten Sleep Mercantile,** 307/366-2224, sells groceries and supplies.

A lot of fruit grows in the country around town; ask here to see who might have it for sale.

EVENTS

Come to Ten Sleep on the **Fourth of July** for a popular rodeo, parade, outdoor dances, and a kids' sheep ride. The **Ten Sleep Celebration** (second weekend in July) brings a junior rodeo, an ice cream social, races, and family events of all types. The **Nowood Stock Music Fest** (get it?) takes place in early August, with a variety of jazz, blues, country, and rock bands.

Thermopolis

The town of Thermopolis (pop. 3,200) lies on the southern edge of the Bighorn Basin surrounded by the Owl Creek Mountains. It's one of two Wyoming towns established because of a hot springs; the other is Saratoga. Thermopolis comes from the words *thermae* (Latin for "hot springs") and *polis* (Greek for "city"). It is a fitting title because the world's largest hot springs are the centerpiece of Thermopolis. Hot Springs State Park is right in town, encompassing both a wonderful public bathhouse and several commercial endeavors. The economy of Thermopolis was for a long while dependent on oil and ranching, but tourism has become increasingly important.

Thermopolis came into existence with the 1896 purchase of Big Springs from the Shoshone and Arapahoes. Streets were laid out wide enough for a 16-mule team to turn around in the middle of the block—something still obvious today, although you don't often see mule teams on the streets. Because of their medicinal value, the hot springs attracted many people, and the town became a health center, particularly for those suffering from arthritis and polio. There wasn't much timber around here, so the first lodging place, the Sage Brush Hotel, was made from a wooden frame laced with sagebrush and covered with a thatched roof of more sage.

HOT SPRINGS STATE PARK
History

Shoshone legend tells of a young warrior and his lover who were standing in the Wind River Canyon when an eagle feather—earned in battles with the enemy—blew out of his hair and wafted down the canyon. They raced after it and found it floating in an enormous hot spring with steam gushing from its mouth. The springs were a gift from the Great Spirit.

Originally a part of the Wind River Reservation, Big Springs and 10 square miles of surrounding land were sold to the U.S. government in 1896 for the bargain-basement price of $60,000. The treaty was signed by Shoshone Chief Washakie and Arapaho Chief Sharp Nose. In it, Washakie stipulated that some of the water must remain free to all people and that a campground be set aside for Indians: "I, Washakie, chief of Shoshones, freely give to the great white father these waters, belov'd by my people; that all may receive that great blessing of bodily health in the bathing." Thus was established Wyoming's first state park.

Today the park is the third most popular attraction in Wyoming; only Yellowstone and Grand Teton National Parks bring in more visitors. The park includes a variety of facilities: a state-run bathhouse, two commercial establishments, a senior center, a rehabilitation center, and even a small herd of **buffalo.** Adjacent is the Holiday Inn spa facility. Park headquarters is the A-frame structure at the corner of Park St. and U.S. Hwy. 789. Just behind here is an impressive travertine cone created when workers put in a vent pipe.

Big Springs

Big Springs flows at a rate of approximately 2,575 gallons per minute at 135°F and is considered the largest hot springs in the world. The springs are at the base of a small butte; just in case there might be some confusion, someone has placed white rocks along the hillside spelling out "World's Largest Mineral Hot Spring." Several cooling

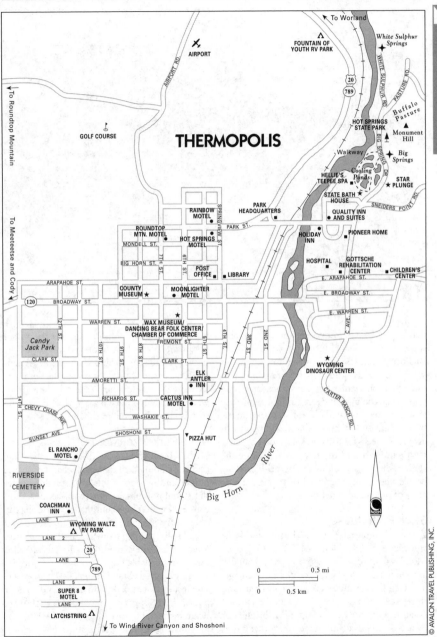

THERMOPOLIS

To Worland

White Sulphur Springs

FOUNTAIN OF YOUTH RV PARK

AIRPORT

AIRPORT RD.

WHITE SULPHUR RD.

PASTURE RD.

Buffalo Pasture

GOLF COURSE

HOT SPRINGS STATE PARK

Monument Hill

Walkway

Big Springs

BIG SPRING DR.

To Roundtop Mountain

Cooling Ponds

HELLIE'S TEEPEE SPA

STAR PLUNGE

STATE BATH HOUSE

SNEIDERS POINT RD.

RAINBOW MOTEL

PARK HEADQUARTERS

SPRINGVIEW ST.

PARK ST.

QUALITY INN AND SUITES

PIONEER HOME

ROUNDTOP MTN. MOTEL

HOT SPRINGS MOTEL

HOLIDAY INN

MONDELL ST.

7TH ST.

6TH ST.

BIG HORN ST.

HOSPITAL

GOTTSCHE REHABILITATION CENTER

CHILDREN'S CENTER

POST OFFICE

LIBRARY

E. ARAPAHOE ST.

To Meeteetse and Cody

ARAPAHOE ST.

COUNTY MUSEUM

MOONLIGHTER MOTEL

E. BROADWAY ST.

(120) BROADWAY ST.

12TH ST.

E. WARREN ST.

WARREN ST.

WAX MUSEUM/ DANCING BEAR FOLK CENTER/ CHAMBER OF COMMERCE

4TH ST.

3RD ST.

2ND ST.

C AVE.

Candy Jack Park

10TH ST.

9TH ST.

8TH ST.

5TH ST.

FREMONT ST.

CLARK ST.

CLARK ST.

AMORETTI ST.

ELK ANTLER INN

WYOMING DINOSAUR CENTER

RICHARDS ST.

CACTUS INN MOTEL

14TH ST.

CHEVY CHASE AVE.

WASHAKIE ST.

SHOSHONI ST.

SUNSET AVE.

PIZZA HUT

CARTER RANCH RD.

EL RANCHO MOTEL

River

RIVERSIDE CEMETERY

COACHMAN INN

LANE 1

Big Horn

WYOMING WALTZ RV PARK

LANE 2

(20)

LANE 3

(789)

LANE 5

SUPER 8 MOTEL

LANE 7

LATCHSTRING

To Wind River Canyon and Shoshoni

0   0.5 mi

0   0.5 km

MOON

© AVALON TRAVEL PUBLISHING, INC.

Hot Springs State Park

ponds spread out in front of the springs, dropping water over terraces of lime and gypsum to the Bighorn River. (Because of the hot water, this stretch of the Bighorn River remains open throughout the winter, attracting ducks and other birds.) The cooling ponds are colorful, with algae and minerals (particularly calcium carbonate, bicarbonate, sulfate, and sodium) adding splashes of reds, greens, browns, and yellows. A concrete path winds around the terraces and along the river, leading to a scenic **swinging bridge.** Many people who drink the mineral-rich water claim an array of medicinal benefits.

State Bath House

For an incredibly relaxing soak, be sure to visit the very nice State Bath House, 307/864-3765, open Monday–Saturday 8 A.M.–5:30 P.M. and Sunday and holidays noon–5:30 P.M. No entry charge. The facilities are always exceptionally clean, and there are lockers to store your clothes. Rent towels and swimsuits here if you didn't bring your own. Soak in private tubs inside the locker rooms (where you can temper the 104°F mineral water

with cooler water), or head to the central indoor pool or a seasonal outdoor soaking pool. The pools are fully handicapped accessible. Attendants make sure folks don't stay in the hot water for more than 20 minutes because the heat can be weakening. This is not a place to clean up, and no soap is allowed—even in the showers.

More Park Attractions

Hellie's Teepee Spa, 307/864-9250, in the white domed building next to the state bathhouse, has indoor and outdoor pools, two spiraling water slides, four hot tubs, a steam room, a sauna, mineral spa, weight room, and snack bar. Adults pay $8, seniors $5, and kids $4; free for kids under four. Hellie's is open daily 9 A.M.–9 P.M. all year. Massages, including an in-the-water version called *watsu*, are available.

Even bigger is **Star Plunge,** 307/864-3771, also inside the state park, with indoor and outdoor pools, three slippery water slides, a high dive, steam room, vapor cave, three hot tubs, and tanning booths ($5 extra). The 500-foot-long outdoor slide is one of the longest in the nation.

Admission to Star Plunge costs $8 adults, $5 seniors, and $3 kids under five. Towels, swimsuits, and inner tubes can also be rented. It's open daily 9 A.M.–9 P.M. year-round. (The state's largest outdoor mineral swimming pool, at Fountain of Youth RV Park, is described under Camping.)

Also on the grounds of the state park are **Gottsche Rehabilitation Center** (www.gottsche-rehab.com), an outpatient treatment facility established in 1959 to make use of the medicinal properties of the hot springs; **Big Horn Basin Children's Center** for children with severe disabilities; and a **Wyoming Pioneer Home** for the elderly. A small **museum** in the basement of the Pioneer Home features arrowheads, baskets, and other Indian artifacts, as well as antiques from nearby ranches. A statue commemorating Chief Washakie's "gift of the smoking waters" stands in front of the home. Washakie would be proud of all the good his gift has done.

In addition to facilities associated with the hot springs, the park includes shady picnic tables and playgrounds. A rough trail cuts to the top of **Monument Hill** right behind Big Springs. The northeast portion of Hot Springs State Park includes a pasture where a herd of 20 or so **buffalo** roam. A loop road through the pasture gives you a chance to drive by them. They are fed daily at 8:30 A.M.

OTHER SIGHTS

Hot Springs Historical Museum

The Hot Springs Historical Museum, 700 Broadway, 307/864-5183, www.trib.com/~history, calls itself "one of the best small museums in the country" and lives up to this billing with an impressive collection of ranching and cowboy gear, historical photos, wagons, Indian artifacts, and much more. The museum is open Monday–Saturday 8 A.M.–5 P.M. and Sunday noon–4 P.M. Memorial Day through Labor Day, and Monday–Saturday 9 A.M.–4 P.M. the

rest of the year. Entrance costs $4 adults, $2 seniors and youths. Kids under five get in free.

The museum sprawls throughout two floors of the main building and across the street to include an agriculture building, an old schoolhouse, a petroleum building, and a caboose. The main museum houses various displays of frontier life: a newspaper shop, dentist's office (complete with frightening tools), blacksmith shop, and general store. The cherry wood bar from the Hole-in-the-Wall Saloon is particularly popular; here members of the famous outlaw gang tipped their glasses with sympathetic locals.

The Indian artifact collection downstairs is impressive, not just because of the thousands of arrowheads but also because it includes an elk hide painted by Shoshone Chief Washakie. Outside, the 1920 Middleton Schoolhouse comes complete with old desks; check out the amusing letters from present-day schoolchildren. Kids of all ages love traipsing through the old Burlington Northern caboose and trying to figure out how the agriculture building's amazing 1926 Case threshing machine worked. The petroleum building houses exhibits on drilling for and refining oil, including old gusher photos and a gigantic power unit once used to pump oil before the arrival of electric pumps.

> *Wyoming Dinosaur Center, housed in a warehouse-type building on the eastern edge of Thermopolis, displays more than a dozen full-size skeletons and casts from dinosaurs found not only nearby but also in Russia, Germany, and China.*

Wyoming Dinosaur Center

In 1992, three Germans formed a prospecting company to search for fossils in the Bighorn Basin. With the help of an American fossil expert they located a promising site just out of Thermopolis and the following year discovered a sauropod (a plant-eating dinosaur from the Jurassic Period). Realizing that many more dinosaurs lay below the surface, the leader, Dr. Burkhard Pohl (a Frankfurt veterinarian), purchased the 7,000-acre Warm Springs Ranch and began digging, later unearthing the most complete skeleton of a brachiosaur ever found, along with many more species. The discoveries led to the creation of the Wyoming Dinosaur Center, housed in a warehouse-type metal building on the eastern edge of town. The facility displays more than a dozen full-size skeletons and casts from dinosaurs found not only nearby but also in Russia, Germany, and China. These include a 19-foot skeleton of a *Camarasaurus* from the site, a *Triceratops horridus* from southeast Wyoming, and a cast of Tyrannosaurus rex, plus dinosaur eggs, and marine reptiles.

Although this is a for-profit venture with a gift shop selling educational dinosaur toys, it's not just a gee-whiz exhibit to wow the kids; the emphasis is heavily on science. Excellent displays reveal the evolution of life on the planet. Visitors can watch workers prepare specimens in the lab or take a tour of the Warm Springs Ranch dig sites two miles away, where excavations continue every summer. There's no chance of running out of specimens; the deposit contains an estimated 100,000 bones. The informative, hour-long tours include a bus ride from the Dinosaur Center and details about the local geology and digging techniques. One of the sites contains a feeding ground with tracks. Tours are offered hourly throughout the day and cost $10 adults, $7 kids and seniors, and free for children under four. Entrance to the Dinosaur Center is $6 adults, $3.50 kids and seniors, and free for children under four. A better option is a combination tour and museum entrance; $12 adults, $8 seniors and kids, free for children under four. Special Kids' Digs take place several times each summer and include classes, geology lessons, and fossil digging. The museum is open daily 8 A.M.–6 P.M. mid-May to mid-September, and daily 10 A.M.–5 P.M. the rest of the year. Get more information at 307/864-2997 or 800/455-3466, www.wyodino.org.

Wax History and Teddy Bears

Thermopolis seems to attract an unusual mix of attractions, the strangest conglomeration being the **Old West Wax Museum and Dancing Bear Folk Center,** 119 S. 6th, 307/864-9396, www.westwaxmuseum.com. The 500 teddy bears hang out downstairs, and some are arranged in "historical" settings—including teddy bears on the Titanic. Also here is a textile studio with quilts and looms, plus classes and demonstrations. Upstairs is a wax museum that resided in Jackson for 30 years, with various Old West figures such as Butch Cassidy, Chief Washakie, Jim Bridger, Big Nose George, and General Custer. This odd combination of wax figures and stuffed bears is open daily 10 A.M.–4 P.M. year-round. Entrance for both costs $4.50 adults, or $3 seniors and kids; free for children under four. The museum also houses the chamber of commerce office.

A couple of other downtown sights are worth a look, including the big statue of a **cowboy and horse** on Broadway, and the **swastikas** embedded in the bricks at 509 Broadway. The latter are actually Indian symbols from a pre-Nazi era.

Legend Rock Petroglyph Site

One of the finest sites for Indian rock art in Wyoming lies in the foothills of the Owl Creek Mountains. Get there by driving 21 miles northwest from Thermopolis on State Hwy. 120. Turn left at the *second* Hamilton Dome turnoff (marked with a High Island Ranch sign) and after 5.5 miles, turn right onto the gravel Cottonwood Creek Road. Continue two miles, and just past the second cattle guard take the road on your left. Follow it a short distance to a parking area in front of a green gate marked "Legend Rock." The petroglyphs are a half-mile walk down from here. (If you want to drive down the hill, borrow the key for the gate from the Hot Springs State Park office in Thermopolis, 307/864-2176.) The total distance from State Hwy. 120 to the petroglyph site is eight miles.

Hundreds of petroglyphs covering several time periods and styles have been found on the nearby sandstone cliffs. There are deer, bison, elk, and various human figures, but most unusual is a rabbit, the only one known in Wyoming rock art. The rabbit is similar to ones on Mimbres ceramic items from A.D. 1000; the Mimbres are from New Mexico. The rock art at Legend Rock may have been associated with shamanism and ritual healing, and some sections have been dated to 2,000 years old. Please do your part to protect this sacred site by not touching the petroglyphs. Owl Creek flows not far away, and oil pumpjacks dot the nearby hills (Hamilton Dome is one of the most important oil fields in Bighorn Basin).

West of Legend Rock is **Anchor Dam,** a major engineering blunder. Shortly after the dam was completed in 1960, a 300-foot-wide sinkhole developed in the porous limestone underlying the reservoir. The hole was filled with dirt and rock, but it collapsed again. The second time the repair held, but new sinkholes appear each year. After decades of this—and millions of dollars down the proverbial sinkhole—the reservoir still only fills halfway in the best years.

Ghost Towns

Ghost town aficionados shouldn't miss the old coal-mining settlement of **Gebo,** where you'll find eight stone buildings, a fascinating graveyard, and various other structures. The town was established in 1906 and abandoned in the 1950s. Get to Gebo by driving 10 miles north of Thermopolis on U.S. 20 and turning west onto Sand Draw Road. The remains are approximately four miles in. A mile or so south of Gebo is another ghost town, **Crosby,** with additional mine ruins. The Hot Springs Historical Museum has historical photos from the mines.

ACCOMMODATIONS

Because of the popularity of Thermopolis during the summer, it's a good idea to reserve ahead (or check in early) to be assured of a place.

Under $50

Hot Springs Motel, 401 Park St., 307/864-2303, wins the prize for cheapest rooms in town: $30 s or $37–43 d, including some with kitchenettes. No phones are provided in the rooms, and you may want to check them out before staying here. **Cactus Inn,** U.S. Hwy. 20 South, 307/864-3155 or 877/621-7811, www.cactusinn.com, charges $45–50 s or d for standard rooms, and $74 for a two-room suite that sleeps four. All rooms have fridges and microwaves. Kitchenettes are available.

Elk Antler Inn, 501 S. 6th, 307/864-2325 or 800/320-4028, has nicely remodeled rooms with log furnishings; $46 for one bed, or $56 for two beds. All rooms contain fridges and microwaves. **Coachman Motel,** 112 U.S. Hwy. 20 South, 307/864-3141 or 888/864-3854, www.coachmanmotel.com, also has remodeled rooms, some with small fridges, for $43 s or $53 d. **El Rancho Motel,** 924 Shoshoni Rd., 307/864-2341 or 800/283-2777, charges $45 for one bed or $55 for two beds.

$50 and Up

Rainbow Motel, 408 Park St., 307/864-2129 or 800/554-8815, www.thermop.com, has a wide range of remodeled rooms with custom log furnishings. Standard rooms (some with fridges and microwaves) are $59 s or d, kitchenettes are $79 d, and six-person suites and family rooms (some with kitchenettes) run $100.

Roundtop Mountain Motel, 412 N. 6th, 307/864-3126 or 800/584-9126, www.roundtopmotel.com, charges $65–69 s or d for motel rooms, or $69 s or d for nicely remodeled log cabins with full kitchenettes. Recommended.

Moonlighter Motel (Budget Host), 600 Broadway, 307/864-2321 or 800/283-4678, www.budgethost.com, has rooms for $55–69 s or d, including access to the heated outdoor pool.

The modern **Super 8 Motel** on the southern edge of town at Lane 5, Hwy. 20 South, 307/864-5515 or 800/800-8000, www.super8.com, is a good midrange choice, with an indoor pool and hot tub, plus a light breakfast. Most rooms go for $90 d, but they also have a couple of family rooms with bunk beds, microwaves, and fridges for $99. Prices on weekdays are $10 less. Suites and handicapped-accessible rooms are also available.

Plaza Hotel/Quality Inn & Suites, 307/864-2939 or 888/919-9009, www.wyomingvacations.com, is a beautifully restored historic brick building within Hot Springs State Park. Bright and spacious rooms feature custom-made lodgepole furniture. Rates are $89–99 s or d (lower on weekdays), including a continental breakfast. Suites—all with fridges and microwaves and some with fireplaces—cost $129 for up to four guests. The courtyard contains a small swimming pool and hot mineral spa.

A longtime favorite within Hot Springs State

Park, **Holiday Inn of the Waters,** 307/864-3131 or 800/465-4329, www.hollidayinnthermopolis.com, is popular with the 65-and-older set. Facilities include an outdoor pool, racquetball courts, an exercise room, mineral spa, soaking tubs, a steam room, massage, and more. Most of these amenities cost extra. Summertime room rates are $79–119 s or d, but the rest of the year the hotel offers reasonable two-night packages ($140–160 d) that include a complimentary prime rib dinner and bottle of champagne.

Ranches

The 130,000-acre **High Island Ranch & Cattle Co.,** 307/867-2374 (summer) or 307/864-5389 (winter), www.highislandranch.com, is a working ranch with a gorgeously remote setting at Hamilton Dome north of Thermopolis. Guests can take part in cattle drives four times a year. Especially popular are the authentic 1800s cattle drives (no vehicles used). No hot tubs here: This is the real thing, with guests staying in canvas tents along the trail (bring your sleeping bag) and rustic cabins or bunkhouses at the ranch. Visits are by the week only and cost $1,300 to $1,600 per person, all-inclusive. There's room for a maximum of 25 guests, and ranch activities take place late May to mid-September.

CAMPING

The closest public camping is 17 miles south in Wind River Canyon (see Wind River Canyon section of this chapter). **Fountain of Youth RV Park,** two miles north of Thermopolis on U.S. Hwy. 20, 307/864-3265, www.trib.com/~foyrvpk, boasts Wyoming's largest mineral swimming pool, fed by what was intended to be an oil well. In 1918, C. F. Cross began drilling, but instead of hitting oil he struck hot mineral water, blowing the pipe casing out of the ground. Eventually a small travertine cone formed around the old casing. The "Sacajawea" well still flows at a rate of 1.3 million gallons per day. Not surprisingly, this is a popular place with the "snowbird" RV crowd. The Labor Day breakfast in the pool is a favorite event. Open mid-March through September, it costs $21 for RVs—same rate for tent spaces.

Wyoming Waltz RV Park, 720 Shoshoni Hwy. 20 South, 307/864-2778, has tent spaces and RV hookups for $18. Showers for noncampers cost $3. Open May–Sept. **Eagle RV Park,** on the south edge of town, 307/864-5262 or 888/865-5707, www.eaglervpark.com, charges $13 for tents, $19 for RVs. Basic cabins cost $29, and showers for noncampers are $6. Open year-round.

Country Campin', 307/864-2416 or 800/609-2244, www.trib.com/~camp, lives up to its name with a country location five miles northeast of Thermopolis along the Bighorn River. Tent spaces are $15, and RV hookups cost $20. Tepee rentals may be available, and kids will love the petting zoo. Open mid-Apr. through Sept.

FOOD

Some of the best meals in Thermopolis can be found at **Pumpernick's,** 512 Broadway, 307/864-5151. The diverse menu encompasses teriyaki chicken, steaks, seafood, prime rib on weekends, and homemade pies. Dinner entrées run $9–17. Pumpernick's outside patio is a pleasant place for summer dining.

Manhattan Restaurant, 526 Broadway, 307/864-2501, is another of the town's best, with homemade ravioli, steaks, marinated southwest chicken, and nightly specials. Closed Mondays.

For quick eats, stop by the little seasonal trailer on the corner of Water and S. 6th streets, **Henry Lee's Smoked Ribs & BBQ.** Also popular is **Dairyland,** an old-fashioned burger and shake stand at 510 Park St., 307/864-2757. The mini-golf place is right next door.

Las Fuentes Mexican Restaurant, 530 Arapahoe, 307/864-2695, has decent fajitas, chimichangas, burritos, and margaritas, plus outdoor dining in the summer.

The Safari Club, at the Holiday Inn within Hot Springs State Park, 307/864-3131, has reasonably priced buffet breakfasts and a diverse dinner menu that includes blackened prime rib, Alaskan king crab, and buffalo burgers. The walls are lined with dozens of big-game trophy mounts and pictures of great white hunters standing over their deceased quarry. Owner Jim Mills killed most of the animals hanging around here, creating what might be called a low-maintenance zoo. It's either appealing or appalling, depending on your perspective. Bands sometimes play in the adjacent bar, where you can join the locals watching a game on the big-screen TV or at the pool table.

Get groceries from **Consumers' Thriftway,** 600 S. 6th, 307/864-3112, or **Don's IGA,** 225 S. 4th, 307/864-5576. Don's also houses a small deli and bakery. Espresso and books are available at **The Storyteller,** 528 Broadway, 307/864-3272. Thermopolis has several fast-food places, including Pizza Hut, McDonald's, Taco John's, Taco Bell, Blimpie's, and Subway.

EVENTS AND ENTERTAINMENT

Held the first weekend in August at Hot Springs State Park, the **Gift of the Waters Pageant** commemorates the transfer of Big Springs to the federal government in 1896. The pageant has been presented every summer since 1950, with a cast that includes both local residents and Shoshone from the Wind River Indian Reservation in full regalia. A tepee camp is set up near the hot springs for the festivities. Other events during Gift of the Waters include Indian dancing, a parade, and an arts-and-crafts fair. **Hot Springs County Fair** starts on the Pageant weekend and goes through the following weekend, with all the standard agricultural and ranching exhibits.

The **Thermopolis Night Rodeo** takes place on Wednesday and Thursday nights, with bull riding only on Friday nights in the summer. Call 307/864-5638 for details about this authentic small-town event (or to enter as a rider if you're loony enough).

Catch the latest flicks at **The Ritz,** 309 Arapahoe, 307/864-3118.

HORSEBACK RIDES

LZ Ranch guides one- to four-hour horseback rides in impressive country six miles northwest of town; call 307/921-1100 for an appointment. **HorseWorks Wyoming,** 307/867-2367 or 877/807-2367, www.horseworkswyoming.com, leads five-day trail rides and cattle drives into

the mountains around Grass Creek, 40 miles northwest of Thermopolis.

A unique way to discover the Old West is the **Outlaw Trail Ride** in late July and early August. This weeklong, 100-mile trip follows the "Outlaw Trail" from the Hole-in-the-Wall country of Butch Cassidy and the Sundance Kid to Thermopolis. This isn't for dudes—you'll need to bring your own horse (although they can also be rented from HorseWorks Wyoming), bedroll, and gear—but excellent meals are provided. A trail ride fee covers catered meals, horse feed, nightly entertainment, and more. Get additional information on this authentic not-for-profit adventure at 307/864-2287 or 888/362-7433, www.trib.com/~outlaw.

OTHER RECREATION

Most of the recreation in Thermopolis takes place around the hot springs pools, but there are other things to do as well. **Roundtop Mountain,** the distinctive butte that dominates the area, is an enjoyable but fairly steep hike. Take 7th St. to Airport Hill and turn at the first left. After the cemetery, turn right on a gravel road that takes you to the trailhead.

The nine-hole **Legion Golf Course,** 307/864-5294, is on Airport Hill north of town. Miniature golfers may prefer **Sweet Spot Mini Golf,** 510 Park Street. The local bowling alley is also the A&W stand; find **A&W Bowling Center** at 942 Shoshoni, 307/864-3887.

INFORMATION AND SERVICES

The **Thermopolis Chamber of Commerce,** 307/864-3192 or 800/786-6772, www.thermopolis.com, has its office in the Old West Wax Museum building at 119 S. 6th Street. While you're here, pick up their historic Thermopolis walking-tour brochure to learn more about the town's building. Hours are Monday–Friday 8 A.M.–5 P.M., but the brochure racks are available whenever the Wax Museum is open.

Hot Springs County Library is at 344 Arapahoe St., 307/864-3104. Wash your clothes at **Wishy Washy Laundromat,** 630 Shoshoni; open

24 hours a day in the summer. Get cash from **ATMs** at Don's IGA on 4th and Warren or the Texaco station on the south end of town.

Wild Bunch Gallery, 426 S. 6th St., 307/864-2208 or 800/637-5340, sells prints and local pieces. Of more interest is **Domhoff Pottery,** 307/864-3710, located on a bluff overlooking the river north of town.

For medical emergencies 24 hours a day, head to **Hot Springs County Memorial Hospital,** 150 E. Arapahoe, 307/864-3121.

Powder River Transportation/Coach USA, 307/682-0960 or 800/442-3682, has daily bus service from Thermopolis to other towns in Bighorn Basin. They can also take you throughout central and eastern Wyoming and all the way to Denver, Billings, or Rapid City. Buses stop at the Texaco station.

Wind River Canyon

South of Thermopolis, the highway cuts across lush irrigated farm fields. Turn around and you'll see the steep slopes of Roundtop Mountain dominating the vistas. The highway bridges the Bighorn River and then, four miles south of town, abruptly enters magnificent Wind River Canyon. At this point the river's name changes just as abruptly. Lewis and Clark had named the Bighorn River, Crow Indians the Wind River. Early explorers somehow concluded that they were two separate waterways and in the confusion Wind River Canyon became the "Wedding of the Waters." Above this point the river is called the Wind, below it the Big Horn. A bit confusing.

FLOATING AND FISHING

Many people float the Bighorn River, putting in at the Wedding of the Waters and taking out in Thermopolis. It's an enjoyable and leisurely drift with nice scenery and excellent fishing for rainbow trout (average size 15 inches). A special permit is required to fish in the canyon above Wedding of the Waters because it is part of the Wind River Indian Reservation. **Canyon Sporting Goods,** 903 Shoshoni in Thermopolis, 307/864-2815, sells permits, along with fishing, boating, and camping gear.

Wind River Canyon Whitewater, 307/864-9343 or 800/246-9343, www.windrivercanyon-raft.com, leads exciting raft trips through the canyon during summer, with the biggest water generally in June and July. Trips range from a quick 1.5-hour drenching ($35 per person) to five-hour trips that take you through the entire canyon and include lunch ($75 per person). In addition, this Indian-owned company offers guided fishing. See the chamber of commerce in Thermopolis for a listing of other fishing outfitters.

GEOLOGIC HISTORY LESSON

The drive through Wind River Canyon is one of the most dramatic in Wyoming; U.S. Hwy. 20

Wind River Canyon

clings to the eastern bank of the river, and canyon walls rise up to 2,500 feet overhead. Tracks of the Burlington Northern Railroad (built in 1913) parallel the river on the other side, threading in and out through several tunnels. This place is a geologist's dream, slicing through rocks that grow progressively older as you continue south, with the oldest dating back to the Precambrian era, 2.7 billion years ago. A succession of roadside signs notes the various rock formations, and the Thermopolis Chamber of Commerce can provide you with a descriptive log of the canyon's complex geology.

At the upper end of the canyon, the road quickly climbs past Boysen Dam and into the open country of Boysen State Park (see the Wind River Mountains Country chapter). Within the canyon you'll find two attractive **campgrounds,** Upper and Lower Wind River State Park ($12 for nonresidents or $6 for Wyoming residents). The river flows right alongside, and there are many big old cottonwoods, but highway noise may keep you awake at night. Free tours of **Boysen Powerplant** have been offered in the past, but security concerns may prevent them. Call 307/864-3772 for the current situation.

Powder River Country

Powder River country is the most historically interesting part of a state overflowing with history. For the Indians who made this area their home, the basin was paradise, a place of massive bison herds and abundant forage for horses. Because of this richness, the area became a confrontation point between various Indian tribes and later between Indians and invading whites along the Bozeman Trail. Still later, the clashes were among the whites: cattlemen versus homesteaders, outlaws against lawmen. Today the clashes have faded into memory, but the rich country remains. Coal, coalbed methane gas, cattle, and sheep rule.

The Powder River Basin stretches from the crest of the Big Horn Mountains to the Black Hills and then south to Casper. The three largest settlements—Gillette, Sheridan, and Buffalo—dominate the region's economy. Sheridan and Buffalo provide gateways to the magnificent Big Horn Mountains, a recreation paradise capped by barren alpine peaks. Rolling grassland predominates across the Powder River Basin, accented by steep-sided buttes

in the town of Spotted Horse

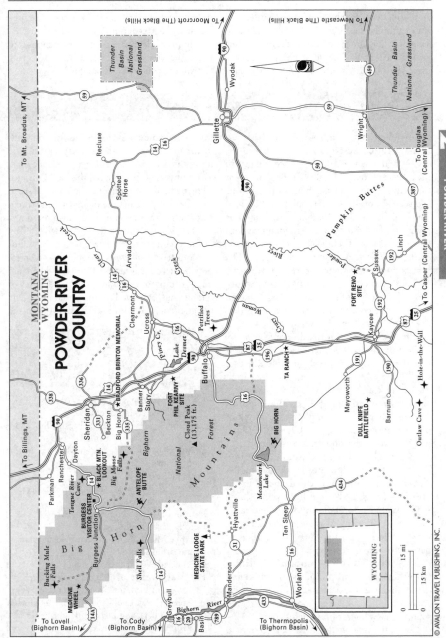

POWDER RIVER
COUNTRY

MONTANA
WYOMING

To Mt. Broadus, MT

To Billings, MT

© AVALON TRAVEL PUBLISHING, INC.

To Newcastle (The Black Hills)

To Moorcroft (The Black Hills)

Thunder
Basin
National
Grassland

Wyodak

Gillette

Recluse

Spotted
Horse

Arvada

Clearmont

Ucross

Piney Cr.

Lake
DeSmet

Petrified
Trees

Wright

To Douglas
(Central Wyoming)

Pumpkin Buttes

Linch

Sussex

FORT RENO
SITE

To Casper (Central Wyoming)

Kaycee

Hole-in-the-Wall

Powder
River

Woman
Creek

Thunder
Basin
National Grassland

Crazy
Woman

BRADFORD BRINTON MEMORIAL

Sheridan

Beckton

Big Horn

Banner

Story

FORT
PHIL KEARNY
SITE

Cloud Peak
(13,175 ft.)

Bighorn

National

Forest

Mountains

BIG
HORN

TA RANCH

Mayoworth

Barnum

DULL KNIFE
BATTLEFIELD

Outlaw Cave

Buffalo

Ranchester

Dayton

Parkman

Tongue River
Cave

BLACK MTN.
LOOKOUT

Big Moose
Falls

ANTELOPE
BUTTE

BURGESS
VISITOR CENTER

Burgess Junction

Big Horn

Bucking Mule
Falls

Shell Falls

MEDICINE
WHEEL

To Lovell
(Bighorn Basin)

Greybull

To Cody
(Bighorn Basin)

Basin

Bighorn
River

Manderson

MEDICINE
LODGE
STATE PARK

Hyattville

Meadowlark
Lake

Ten Sleep

Worland

To Thermopolis
(Bighorn Basin)

WYOMING

0   15 mi
0   15 km

POWDER RIVER

and lush riversides. The land is grazed extensively by cattle and sheep, although alfalfa and wheat are grown in many places. Coal, oil, and methane gas resources are vital to the economy of the area, especially around Gillette, making this the most important energy region in Wyoming. Despite the many large coal mines, the land remains relatively untouched. Nearly everyone chooses to live in the cities and smaller settlements, leaving enormous open expanses of land.

Big Horn Mountains

Sandwiched between two broad basins—Bighorn to the west and Powder River to the east—are the majestic Big Horn Mountains. To the early explorers, this 70-mile-long range was the Shining Mountains, a name inspired by its snowcapped peaks, some topping 13,000 feet. The Indians called it "Ahsahta," meaning "The Big Horns," after the Rocky Mountain bighorn sheep found here. Eventually, whites applied the name to all sorts of places in the region. The mountain country here is carpeted primarily with lodgepole pine, with Engelmann spruce and subalpine fir at higher elevations. Although much of the country here is not as rugged as the mountains on the western border of Wyoming, the Big Horns do contain many rocky peaks above 9,000 feet, with 13,175-foot Cloud Peak crowning the skyline. Hundreds of small lakes reflect this dramatic scenery within the Cloud Peak Wilderness.

Nearly the entire range lies within **Bighorn National Forest,** a 1.1-million-acre chunk of public land set aside by Pres. Grover Cleveland in 1897. Forest headquarters is in Sheridan at 2013 Eastside 2nd Street, (just east of the I-90 Welcome Center/Rest Stop), 307/674-2604, www.fs.fed.us/r2/bighorn, with district offices in Lovell, 307/548-6514, and Buffalo, 307/684-1100, and an information office in Worland, 307/347-5105. Any of these offices can provide detailed forest maps ($6) and listings of permitted local outfitters.

The **Big Horn Mountain Coalition** (www.bighorns.com) promotes recreation and development in the area and has links to local chambers of commerce. Another useful web source is www.bighornmountains.com.

This is multiple-use country, with recreation, grazing, and timber production the primary attractions. Commercial logging has gone on within the forest for almost a century, and old tie flumes are still visible near Dayton. At one time, vast numbers of sheep grazed the Big Horns, totaling perhaps half a million. Thousands of sheep and cattle still graze in these mountains, and sheepherder camps are common in the high meadows.

Most visitors simply drive through the Big Horns on one of the three scenic highways, but the country is well worth stopping to savor, especially if you're a fan of waterfalls. There are many campgrounds, more than 850 miles of hiking trails, and good fishing for rainbow, cutthroat, brook, and brown trout. Come winter, the

POWDER RIVER COUNTRY SIGHTSEEING HIGHLIGHTS

Big Horn Mountains, including Medicine Wheel and Cloud Peak Wilderness

Trail End State Historic Site, Sheridan Inn, and King's Saddlery in Sheridan

Bradford Brinton Memorial Museum near Big Horn

Fort Phil Kearny

Jim Gatchell Memorial Museum and Occidental Hotel in Buffalo

Hole-in-the-Wall Country near Kaycee

Paleo Park south of Newcastle

Rockpile Museum and Einstein's Adventurarium in Gillette

Gillette and Wright area coal mines

Popular events: College National Finals Rodeo in Gillette (June), Sheridan Wyo Rodeo (July), Don King Days in Big Horn (September), and Deke Latham Memorial PRCA Rodeo in Kaycee (September)

mountains become a popular destination for cross-country skiers, snowboarders, downhill skiers, and snowmobilers. More than 350 miles of groomed trails help make the Big Horns one of the top 10 snowmobiling destinations in America. Several mountain lodges rent the beasts.

There's quite a bit of wildlife to see here, too. Bighorn sheep have been reintroduced to the area and may be seen on the west slope of the mountains. No grizzlies roam here, but quite a few black bears live in the mountains, especially on the northeastern slopes. Also look for mule and white-tailed deer, elk, and moose. (The moose are not native; they were transplanted from Jackson Hole beginning in 1948.)

CRUISIN' THROUGH

Three paved highways cut across the Big Horn Mountains, providing popular connections between Yellowstone and the Black Hills. U.S. Hwys. 14 and 16 are both kept plowed through the winter, while U.S. Hwy. 14A generally closes November through May. All three have Scenic Byway status, something that becomes more obvious with each mile you travel.

Highway 16

U.S. Hwy. 16 climbs across the southern end of the range from Ten Sleep to Buffalo and is the easiest way across the Big Horns. More than a dozen Forest Service campgrounds line the route. This was the original "Black and Yellow Trail," first proposed in 1912 as a link between Chicago, the Black Hills, and Yellowstone. The first caravan of automobiles made it over the old sheepwagon track the following year, reaching Yellowstone after 18 hard days on the road. By the 1920s, the highway was marked by poles with alternating black and yellow bands. For many years, this was the main route to Yellowstone.

East from Ten Sleep, U.S. Hwy. 16 parallels cottonwood-lined Tensleep Creek, climbing past spectacular red and yellow cliffs. A cross and marker commemorate Gilbert Leigh, an Irish nobleman who fell to his death while hunting here in 1884 (he was caught in an October snowstorm and, unable to see his way, slipped over the cliff). Eventually the switchbacks take you up to **Meadowlark Lake,** a popular winter destination for both cross-country skiers and snowmobilers. The dirt road to **High Park Lookout Tower** is two miles east of here. Look for flower-bedecked **St. Christopher's Chapel of the Big Horns** as this side road climbs to the fire tower (not in use). Great views are seen from the top. East of here, the road winds over Powder River Pass, providing breathtaking views into Cloud Peak Wilderness.

Highway 14

Open all year, U.S. Hwy. 14 offers an equally impressive passage over the Big Horns between Greybull and Dayton. Above the dot of a town called Shell the road passes a remarkably phallic rocky butte, then catches Shell Creek and winds with it through the deep red rocks of dramatic **Shell Canyon,** past Shell Falls and the Antelope Butte Ski Area, before topping out at Granite Pass. (The name "Shell" appears repeatedly throughout the local topography thanks to the fossil invertebrate shells commonly found in the rocks.) At 120-foot-high **Shell Falls,** approximately eight miles east of Shell on U.S. Hwy. 14, you'll find a visitors center with books and maps. It's open daily mid-May to mid-September. Nearby are several short walking trails with interpretive signs. Keep your eyes open for water ouzels, the water-loving gray birds that often nest beneath waterfalls. After joining U.S. Hwy. 14A at **Burgess Junction,** the road continues to Twin Buttes, Sibley Lake, and the amusing jumble of rocks called Fallen City, before zigzagging sharply down to Tongue River Canyon and the town of Dayton. A Forest Service **visitors center,** located 1.5 miles east of Burgess Junction near Twin Buttes, is open daily 8 A.M.–5:30 P.M. from mid-May through September and puts on occasional educational programs.

Highway 14A

U.S. Hwy. 14A (officially this is Alternate U.S. Hwy. 14) is generally cleared of snow by Memorial Day, remaining open until mid-October. Engineers like this road, modeled after similar routes in the Alps. At the time it was built, it was said to be the most expensive stretch of road in America. Locals claim the "A" in "U.S. Hwy. 14A" stands for adventure, and with three different runaway truck ramps and 10 percent grades on some stretches, it's easy to see why. The climb to the top is *very* long and steep, but the views make the tough climb worthwhile. U.S. Hwy. 14A rises over the Big Horns from Lovell to Burgess Junction, where it meets U.S. Hwy. 14. Along the way you're treated to miles of open sage-and-grass country with timbered islands on Bald and Little Bald Mountains, spectacular Bucking Mule Falls, and the famous Medicine Wheel. Watch for moose and deer in the meadows near Burgess Junction.

An enjoyable side loop is **Burgess Road** (Forest Rd. 15). The gravel road starts at Burgess Junction and continues approximately 20 miles to a junction with U.S. Hwy. 14A near Bald Mountain. This side loop provides fine opportunities to view deer and elk, and it provides a grand vista from Burgess Rd. Overlook.

CAMPING

With 34 different Forest Service campgrounds ($8–13) in the area, you should have no trouble finding places to commune with nature. Most are above 5,000 feet in elevation, making for welcome escapes from summertime heat. During weekends in July and August, campgrounds along the main roads are frequently filled (get there before 2 P.M.), but harder-to-reach campgrounds usually have space. Reservations ($9 fee) are available for 10 popular campgrounds at 518/885-3639 or 877/444-6777, www.reserveusa.com. Forest Service offices in Sheridan, Buffalo, and Lovell can all provide details on dates, cost, and access to these camping places, or find the same information on the web at www.fs.fed.us/r2/bighorn. In addition to the official campgrounds, you can camp anywhere in Bighorn National Forest for free, as long as you are one-half mile off the main highways.

The BLM's delightful **Five Springs Campground** ($7; open year-round) is two miles off U.S. Hwy. 14A, on the western border of the national forest. The road is steep and narrow, so

no RVs more than 25 feet should travel this route. Scenic **Five Springs Falls** is nearby.

ACCOMMODATIONS AND FOOD

Scattered throughout the Big Horns are seven mountain lodges and a guest ranch, most of which have bars and restaurants. Several of these are open year-round, providing a good base for snowmobiling and skiing adventures. Note that phone service can be spotty in the mountains, and you may not always be able to get through to the resorts.

Lodges Along U.S. Highway 14

You'll find year-round accommodations at **Bear Lodge Resort,** located at Burgess Junction (8,300 feet in elevation), 307/752-2444, www.bearlodgeresort.com. Modern motel rooms are $79 s or d; $99 for the hot tub suite. Rustic cabins cost $30 (one of these sleeps nine people), but you'll need to bring your own linen and take showers in the lodge. The cabins are only available mid-May to mid-November. Guests will enjoy an indoor swimming pool and fitness center, plus the indoor and outdoor hot tubs. Pitch a tent for $8, or park RVs for $13–18. If you're staying elsewhere, take a shower for $2. The lounge is a great place to shoot a game of pool or tip a brew, and it occasionally has live music. Also here are a full-service restaurant, gas pumps, and a gift shop with a few groceries and supplies. Winter snowmobile rentals are available.

Arrowhead Lodge, 307/655-2388, four miles east of Burgess Junction on U.S. Hwy. 14, has a large and modern motel, but it may or may not be in business when you visit.

Snowshoe Lodge, 307/899-8995 or 800/354-8637, www.thesnowshoelodge.com, is seven miles out a dirt road that turns off near Antelope Butte Ski Area (south of Burgess Junction on U.S. Hwy. 14). Because of its mountain location, the lodge is particularly popular with snowmobilers and skiers in the winter. It's also a favorite spot for summertime weddings and family reunions. One room is available in the main lodge, along with three delightful and modern log cabins with kitchenettes and private baths. Lodging—plus a delicious homecooked dinner and breakfast—costs $85 s or $170 d; folks come back just for the meals. Other amenities include an outdoor hot tub, sauna, lounge, and double-deck porches facing the mountains. The lodge is only accessible by snowmobile or skis in the winter; they pick you up at Burgess Junction. Winter is the busy season here, and you'll need to book a year ahead for weekends in February and March.

Spend a delightful week in the Big Horn Mountains at historic **Ranger Creek Guest Ranch,** 307/751-7787 or 888/817-7787, www.rangercreekranch.net. The lodge is 16 miles east of Shell on Forest Service land near Antelope Butte Ski Area. Guests (maximum 30 people) stay in rustic log cabins around a central bathhouse and enjoy horseback rides, trout fishing, children's programs, day trips to Cody, evening barbecues, and nature talks. The ranch is open year-round, with fall hunting trips and winter snowmobiling. A hot tub is available to soak those tired bones at day's end. All-inclusive six-night rates are $2,000 for two people.

Located near the crest of the mountains and one mile west of Burgess Junction, **Bighorn Mountain Lodge,** 307/751-7599, www.bighorn-mountainlodge.com, is a large place with modern facilities that include a café, bar, lodging, gift shop, and gas. The cozy duplex cabins are $60–65 d (plus $5 for each additional guest); winter rates are $80–85 d. Two-bedroom kitchenette units sleep four for $185, and all have private baths. RV parking is $20 with full hookups, and tent sites cost $9. If you aren't staying here, showers are $2. Snowmobile rentals are available.

Lodges Along U.S. Highway 16

Deer Haven Lodge, 18 miles east of Ten Sleep on U.S. Hwy. 16, 307/366-2424 or 888/244-4676, www.thebighorn.com, charges $45 d for small cabins, or $59 for larger four-person cabins. All are plain-Jane basic units with woodstoves and a separate bathhouse; bring your own towels. The lodge also has older motel rooms that sleep four for $69. A lounge is on the premises.

The owners of Deer Haven Lodge also run **Meadowlark Lake Resort,** 22 miles east of Ten Sleep (42 miles west of Buffalo) along U.S. Hwy. 16, 307/366-2424 or 888/244-4676, www.thebighorn.com, where a variety of accommodation options are available. Rustic cabins with a central bathhouse are $50 for one bed up to $104 for four beds. Motel rooms with private baths are $75–89 d, and comfortable cottages with kitchenettes cost $94 d for one-bedroom units, or $119 for units that can sleep six. The resort also rents rowboats, canoes, and paddle boats for the lake, as well as mountain bikes to explore surrounding country. It has a restaurant serving three meals a day, plus a lounge and gift shop; open year-round.

The Pines Lodge, 14 miles west of Buffalo on U.S. Hwy. 16, 307/351-1010 or 307/684-5204, www.pines-lodge.com, has a variety of cabins. Rates start at $38 d for a rustic cabin with separate bathhouse. Duplex cabins that share a bath are $52 d. Larger cabins have private baths and kitchens, and some contain fireplaces or wood stoves. These run $60–105, with the biggest one sleeping eight. RV hookups are $20, and tent spaces cost $15. Kids can throw in a line at the private fishing pond. The cabins and camping spaces are open May–October, and the restaurant and lounge are also open winter weekends.

South Fork Mountain Lodge, 16 miles west of Buffalo on U.S. Hwy. 16, 307/267-2609, www.southfork-lodge.com, has simple cabins with a shared bathhouse for $99 d, and a six-person cabin with private bath for $150. Also here is a restaurant and small bar, along with horseback rides and drop-camp trips. The lodge is open May–November and on weekends only December–March; closed in Apr.

The Forest Service's historic **Muddy Guard Station** was constructed by the Civilian Conservation Corps in the 1930s and is now available for the public. The log building has propane lights and a woodstove but no running water or electricity. It sleeps up to six and rents for $40 per day. Located 25 miles west of Buffalo on U.S. Hwy. 16, this unique cabin is open year-round; call 307/684-1100 for reservations.

WINTER SPORTS

Cross-Country Skiing

The Big Horns provide some of the finest snow in Wyoming, with groomed cross-country ski trails at several locations. **Sibley Lake** has 15 miles of trails and a warming hut off U.S. Hwy. 14; **Willow Park** has 23 miles of trails near Meadowlark Lake; and **Pole Creek** has 13 miles of trails and a warming hut off U.S. Hwy. 16. Trail descriptions are available from local Forest Service offices. The rest of the forest makes for outstanding skiing most of the winter, but you'll need to break your own trail.

Downhill Skiing and Snowboarding

Big Horn Ski Resort, 307/366-2424 or 888/244-4676, www.thebighorn.com, is next to Meadowlark Lake Resort along U.S. Hwy. 16 (22 miles east of Ten Sleep and 42 miles west of Buffalo). This small area has an 800-foot vertical rise, with a double and a triple chairlift, lights on all runs, and extensive snowboard facilities that include three half-pipes and a terrain park. Snowmaking equipment lengthens the ski season, and ice skating is also available. The resort opens around Thanksgiving and closes in April. Lifts operate daily throughout winter, and full-day lift tickets cost $23 adults, $19 students, or $12 kids. Get food, drinks, and rentals at the modern base lodge. Ski and snowboard lessons are offered, and you can also rent snowmobiles.

Antelope Butte Ski Area, 307/655-9530, www.skiantelopebutte.com, is a small family ski area 60 miles west of Sheridan and 35 miles east of Greybull on U.S. Hwy. 16. It has two chairlifts and a platter lift, with a vertical rise of 1,000 feet from a base elevation of 8,400 feet. The lift lines are short, and the terrain is challenging. Antelope Butte is open Wednesday–Sunday and holidays 9:30 A.M.–4 P.M. mid-December through March. Lift tickets cost $25 adults, $20 ages 13–18, $15 ages 7–12, and free for young-uns. Rent skis and snowboards, or take lessons from the ski school. The lodge serves light meals.

Snowmobiling

Snowmobilers will find 300 miles of groomed trails throughout the national forest; get a route map from chamber of commerce offices or the Forest Service. Rent snowmobiles at **Big Horn Ski Resort,** 307/366-2424 or 888/244-4676, www.thebighorn.com; **Bighorn Mountain Lodge,** 307/751-7599, www.bighornmountainlodge.com; or **Bear Lodge Resort,** 307/752-2444, www.bearlodgeresort.com.

HIKES AND SIGHTS

You'll find plenty to see and do in the Big Horns, including Medicine Wheel and the Cloud Peak Wilderness (see Cloud Peak Wilderness section in this chapter). Stop by the Forest Service office in Sheridan, Buffalo, or Lovell for descriptions of other hiking trails.

Sheep Mountain Area Trails

Several trails take off from Sheep Mountain Road on U.S. Hwy. 14A approximately 30 miles east of Lovell and three miles east of the turnoff to Medicine Wheel. **Littlehorn Trail** parallels the Little Bighorn River for 18 miles. Along the way you'll see 1,600-foot canyon faces and water fountaining off the limestone cliffs of Leaky Point. The trailhead is two miles up Sheep Mountain Road (Forest Rd. 14). One-half mile farther up the road is the trailhead for **Porcupine Falls,** a 200-foot-tall cascade accessible via a very steep half-mile path. Along the way the trail passes a 1930s-era gold mine. Much of the area here was burned in a 1988 forest fire.

One of the not-to-be-missed places in the Big Horns is spectacular **Bucking Mule Falls,** a 600-foot cascade dropping into Devil Canyon. The trailhead for Bucking Mule Falls lies 11 miles off U.S. Hwy. 14A via Sheep Mountain Road and Devil Canyon Road, and the waterfall is a three-mile round-trip hike. You can also do an 11-mile hike by following the trail to the falls and then continuing south to Porcupine Campground.

More Hikes and Caves

Black Mountain Lookout, west of Dayton on U.S. Hwy. 14, offers surprisingly dramatic vistas from the top of a 9,300-foot peak. This old Forest Service fire lookout is open to the public and sits at the end of a one-mile trail. Get there by turning south on Forest Rd. 16 when it leaves U.S. Hwy. 14 two miles west of the Fallen City area and follow it four miles to the trailhead.

The trailhead for **Tongue River Canyon** is 3.5 miles southwest of Dayton to the end of Tongue Canyon Road. This trail climbs up the canyon for a total of 11.5 miles, offering glimpses of the old McShane brothers' tie flume—built in 1894 and stretching for 26 miles—the fast-flowing blue-ribbon fishing stream (cutthroat, rainbow, brook, and German brown trout), and canyon walls reaching 1,000 feet into the air. Ambitious hikers may want to continue all the way to Burgess Junction. Locals float down parts of the river during the spring, when water levels are high.

Tongue River Cave is near the Tongue River Canyon trailhead and stays open all year. With more than one mile of passages, it's one of Wyoming's most popular caves but has been considerably vandalized with broken formations, trash, and graffiti. Because of its size, inexperienced spelunkers can become lost, so ask locally for someone willing to act as a guide. More than 100 other caves honeycomb this country; see the Forest Service for locations and precautions.

Another trail worth exploring if you want an out-of-the-way adventure is the **Little Bighorn River Canyon Trail** starting west of Ranchester along the Wyoming–Montana border. Contact the Forest Service in Sheridan for directions and details on this multiday trek.

An enjoyable waterfall is **Big Goose Falls.** Follow Forest Rd. 26 (it starts approximately five miles south of Burgess Junction on U.S. Hwy. 14) to Big Goose Ranger Station, then continue on via Forest Rd. 296 to the end. The falls are about five miles below the ranger station along the East Fork of Big Goose Creek. They include plunge pools and water-sculpted rocks.

Crazy Woman Canyon

One of the most fascinating drives in the Big Horns slices through Crazy Woman Canyon. Several stories exist for the origin of the canyon's name. One claims it's named for an Indian squaw who went insane while living alone in her tepee here. Another version says it came from a white settler who was pushed to insanity when Indians murdered and scalped her husband. Soldiers from Fort Laramie reportedly found her wandering the area. Either way, it wasn't exactly a soothing name for migrants on the old Bozeman Trail! The canyon cut by cascading Crazy Woman Creek is a stunning one with steep cliffs on both sides. A rough gravel road (high-clearance vehicles are recommended; this isn't for trailers or RVs) heads down from U.S. Hwy. 16 and continues all the way to the mouth of the canyon and then out to State Hwy. 196. The drive is actually more interesting (and easier on your brakes) if you do it from Buffalo westward, but be ready for a long and difficult trip in either direction.

MEDICINE WHEEL

High atop a windswept mountain plateau sits one of the best-known and least-understood archaeological sites in America, the Medicine Wheel. Measuring 80 feet across, this uneven "wagon wheel" of stones seems ready to roll over the nearby slopes. Twenty-eight rock spokes radiate out from a central hub, with six smaller rock cairns scattered around the rim. A variety of lesser-known rock structures surround the Medicine Wheel on nearby slopes, including an arrow that supposedly points southwest to another "wheel" near Meeteetse 70 miles away, a large rectangle of stones, and more than 50 tepee rings. An ancient cairn-marked travois trail continues northwest from Medicine Wheel over the Big Horn Mountains.

Origins

Medicine Wheel's origins are shrouded in the depths of time. White prospectors from the nearby gold-mining camp of Bald Mountain City (now entirely gone) discovered the Medicine Wheel around 1885. Carbon-14 dating of wood fragments found in one of the cairns yielded the date A.D. 1760, and scientists now believe the wheel was constructed some time between A.D. 1200 and 1700.

Prevailing theories about the purpose behind the Medicine Wheel fall into two schools: it was either an astronomical observatory or a site for sacred ceremonies. One of the most interesting theories was suggested by astronomer John Eddy in a 1977

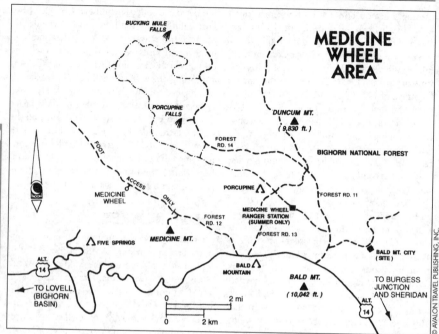

National Geographic article. He noted that the 28 spokes are equal to the number of days in the lunar month and that two of the cairns served as horizon markers for sunrise and sunset, with the other four cairns marking the rising of three of the brightest stars. These could have signaled the summer solstice. Interestingly, similar alignments occur on a stone wheel in Saskatchewan, Canada.

Other scientists counter that the Indians would have little reason to care exactly when summer solstice occurred—since they were not farmers— and that the rocks probably served some religious function. These researchers point out the striking similarities between the wheel and medicine lodges used during Cheyenne and Sioux sundance ceremonies: both have 28 spokes. The first published report (1885) described the Medicine Wheel as consisting of a central hub with spokes leading to stone huts: "It is said that these smaller huts were, during religious ceremonies, occupied by medicine men of different tribes, while the larger hut in the center was supposed to be the abode of Manitour." Various later reports attrib-

uted it to the Crow, Sheepeater, Arapaho, and Cheyenne tribes. University of Montana anthropologist Gregory Campbell considers the wheel a source of religious power to Native Americans and notes that it is a place where "powerful events come to the fore" for those who search for strength.

Regardless of its origins or earliest uses, the Medicine Wheel *was* used in historical times— and is still used today—as a place for prayer, meditation, renewal, and vision quests. Chief Joseph of the Nez Perce fasted here, and Shoshone Chief Washakie was said to have gained his "medicine" here. Because of the Medicine Wheel's location and the importance of ceremony in Native American life, it certainly remains a sacred site, whether or not it served any astronomical function.

Visiting Medicine Wheel

The signed gravel road into the Medicine Wheel parking area turns off U.S. Hwy. 14A approximately 27 miles east of Lovell. You'll need to walk the last 1.5 miles to the site, although exceptions are made for people with disabilities and the elderly. Be sure to carry water with you, and take your time; at 9,800 feet in elevation you may get winded easily. The road passes an FAA radar dome on nearby Medicine Mountain; it's used to monitor air traffic in a three-state area and is a disturbing structure to find near such a significant Native American site. Medicine Wheel is open to the public all the time (except during Native American ceremonies), and interpreters provide guided tours at the wheel daily 8 A.M.–6 P.M. July–September. The road to Medicine Wheel is usually covered with snow from mid-October to mid-July. For more information, call the Forest Service office in Lovell, 307/548-6541.

A wire fence surrounding the wheel is frequently festooned with strips of cloth, feathers, bells, herbs, flowers, sacred bundles, and other offerings left behind by Indians who come here on personal vision quests and other ceremonies. Such articles are particularly evident following solstices and equinoxes. Respect the importance of this religious site by not disturbing these items.

It is obvious why this mountain was chosen for the Medicine Wheel. The surrounding open country has scattered pine, juniper, and spruce, and the ridge drops off a 150-foot precipice just 50 feet away. From its 9,956-foot elevation, a vast panorama stretches to include the Bighorn Basin, the Wind River, the Absaroka Range, and the Pryor Mountains. Medicine Wheel is also a good place to look for hawks wheeling through the sky, especially red-tailed hawks and kestrels.

CLOUD PEAK WILDERNESS

Although maintained as a primitive area since 1932, the 189,000-acre Cloud Peak Wilderness did not receive official wilderness status until 1984. It's named for 13,175-foot **Cloud Peak,** a rocky mountain visible for 100 miles in all directions. At one time this entire range was glaciated, and reminders abound in the sharpened peaks, broad U-shaped valleys, and multitude of lakes in glacial tarns. There are even a few small patches of glacial ice. The Big Horns still get plenty of snow, leaving many hiking trails in the high country blocked until July. One oddly named mountain in the wilderness is **Bomber Mountain,** just south of Cloud Peak. An Air Force B-17 bomber crashed here in 1943, killing all 10 men on board. It was not found for two years. For the sad but fascinating story, see *The Bomber Mountain Crash: A Wyoming Mystery* by R. Scott Madsen (Buffalo, WY: Mountain Man Publishing).

POWDER RIVER

© DON PITCHER

Medicine Wheel

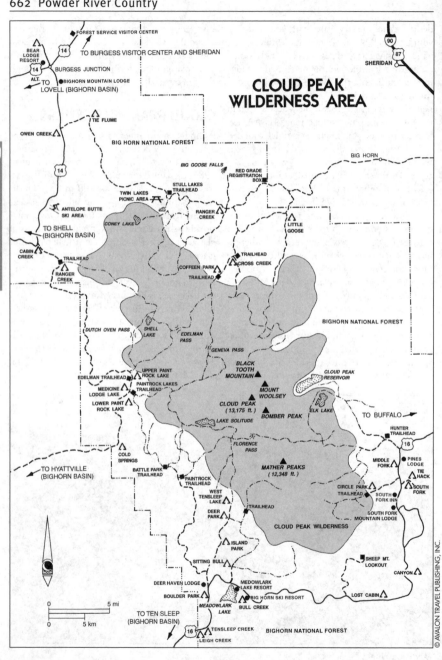

© AVALON TRAVEL PUBLISHING, INC.

With more than 140 miles of trails and thousands of acres more above timberline, hiking and horsepacking opportunities abound throughout Cloud Peak. Bears are not usually a problem in the Cloud Peak Wilderness. Backcountry users must fill out registration cards, available at the trailheads or local Forest Service offices. Be sure to camp at least 100 feet from water sources and trails and hang all food out of reach of black bears. Use existing campsites whenever possible to lessen your impact. No campfires are permitted above 9,200 feet. The Forest Service produces a free map/guide to the wilderness area, which lists additional precautions.

For complete trail and historical information on the wilderness, get *Hiking Wyoming's Cloud Peak Wilderness* by Erik Molvar (Helena, MT: Falcon Press). Be sure to purchase topographic maps before heading out. Local bookstores and Forest Service offices sell a waterproof Trails Illustrated/National Geographic **wilderness map** for $10. It's worth getting. Check with the Forest Service office in Sheridan, Buffalo, or Lovell for a list of permitted outfitters and wilderness regulations. Always practice "no trace" camping; if you don't know what this means, pick up a handout from any of the Forest Service offices.

Access into Cloud Peak Wilderness is via several entry roads along U.S. Hwy. 16 on the southern border—most of the use comes from this side—and from the north (U.S. Hwy. 14) at Cross Creek and Ranger Creek Campgrounds and near Twin Lakes Picnic Ground. Other entrance points surround Cloud Peak, but many require long hikes up 4WD roads to get to the wilderness boundary.

Trails

The **Stull Lakes-Coney Lake Trail** is one of the shortest hikes into the lake country of Cloud Peak. It climbs three miles from the trailhead (located one-quarter mile west of the Twin Lakes picnic area), passes Stull Lake, and ends in the alpine country surrounding Coney Lake. Watch for elk and deer in late summer.

An excellent 21-mile loop hike begins at **Paintrock Lakes Trailhead** on the west side of the wilderness. This route traverses a wide vari-

ety of country, from dense timber to rocky mountain passes and small glaciers. The path climbs to a trail junction 1.5 miles west of Cliff Lake. From here, turn left and follow the trail to Geneva Pass (10,300 feet). The trail drops down to Lake Geneva and then follows East Fork Creek to the junction with the Edelman Trail. This path leads over Edelman Pass, around Emerald Lake, and then back down to the Edelman Trailhead, just 1.5 miles by road from your starting point. You'll find all sorts of other hikes and side trips in this area.

Another loop trip takes you to **Lake Solitude.** Begin at the Battle Park Trailhead approximately 15 miles north of Meadowlark Lake. Take the road to Tyrell Ranger Station and turn left after one mile, continuing up the rough gravel road to the trailhead. The trail climbs up Paint Rock Creek past Grace Lake and Lake Solitude to Mistymoon Lake. Beyond this you can either return on the same route or follow the trail down a steep valley to the waterlily-filled Lily Lake. Continue downhill to the Paintrock Trailhead on Forest Rd. 17, and turn right (northwest), following the road one mile back to your starting point. The loop is approximately 17 miles round-trip.

The easiest—and probably busiest—route to the top of **Cloud Peak** takes off from West Tensleep Trailhead on Forest Rd. 27. Plan on a strenuous 10 hours for the 11-mile climb up and back. This is not a developed trail and will require considerable rock hopping, but the spectacularly desolate scenery makes it worthwhile. Be prepared for sudden weather changes, and carry an ice axe into August. For detailed route instructions up Cloud Peak, get a topographic map and a copy of Erik Molvar's trail guide.

The **Elk Lake Loop** (19 miles round-trip) begins at Hunter Trailhead on the southeast side of the wilderness and involves lots of climbing. Follow the old jeep trail to Soldier Park, a scenic grassy meadow. Turn north at the trail junction and follow the path to Elk Lake. Along the way are some outstanding views across the alpine terrain to Cloud Peak. Turn left at Elk Lake, head up over a pass, and then south to North Clear Creek Trail. Follow it downhill to Soldier Park and back to the trailhead.

Sheridan

The attractive and vibrant small city of Sheridan (pop. 16,000) has plenty to see, several fine restaurants and art galleries, great country in the nearby Big Horn Mountains, and a genuine sense of history. At just 3,745 feet above sea level, it claims the lowest elevation of any Wyoming town, making for hot summer days. It's only 25 miles from Sheridan to the Montana border via I-90.

The country around Sheridan was settled by a broad mixture of Europeans—everyone from British lords to Polish coal miners. Their heritage carries on in such events as an annual polka festival and weekly polo matches at Big Horn Equestrian Center, the oldest polo club in the nation. Locals brag that Sheridan has a wealth of things to do and a surprising cultural richness without the crowds of Yellowstone and Jackson Hole. The town is, however, losing some of the hard-edged cowboy feel from the past and gaining more Westernwear boutiques, gift shops, galleries, antique stores, and eateries all the time.

HISTORY

Sheridan, like other towns in the Powder River Basin, was built on coal, cattle, farming, and the railroad. In 1882, John D. Loucks took a liking to the country here and decided to establish a town, drawing up a plat on a piece of brown wrapping paper. He named the new place for his commanding officer during the Civil War, Gen. Philip Sheridan, and immediately set about getting others to come. For several years Sheridan competed with nearby Big Horn City for the county seat, a title that ensured survival. Finally, in 1885, Sheridan promoters offered cowboys at the fall roundup free lots in the town. When most accepted, Sheridan finally had enough folks to incorporate. Almost overnight (literally, in some cases), businesses in Big Horn City moved to Sheridan, sometimes bringing their buildings along with them.

When the Burlington and Missouri Railroad reached Sheridan in 1892, the town suddenly changed. Now ranchers could get their cattle to market more easily and visitors could stay in the sumptuous Sheridan Inn. Farming became more profitable as investors built large grain mills and a sugar-processing plant. The first underground coal mines opened in 1883, but the Burlington Railroad didn't begin using the coal in its engines until 1903. For the next several decades these "black diamonds" were mainstays of the local economy. Sheridan soon had 1,500 people, wooden sidewalks, 30 saloons, six churches, and two opera houses. Small mining towns—Dietz, Acme, Kooi, Model, Riverside, and Carneyville—opened in the surrounding countryside, inhabited by thousands of European emigrants; newspapers often featured ads in both Polish and English. Electric

DOWNTOWN SHERIDAN

5TH ST.
SILVER SPUR CAFE
SHERIDAN INN
★ HISTORIC TRAIN DEPOT
4TH ST.
3RD ST.
HISTORIC STREET CAR ★
0   200 yds
0   200 m
SHERIDAN CENTER MOTOR INN
GOULD
2ND ST.
1ST ST.
Goose Creek
BROOKS ST.
MAIN ST.
DOW ST.
THE CHOCOLATE TREE
BROADWAY
MANDEL ST.
LIBRARY ■
BIG HORN MTN. SPORTS
SANFORD'S
ALGER ST.
SHERIDAN STATIONERY ■
CITY HALL
GRINNELL AVE.
MOON
KING'S SADDLERY ■
MINT BAR
PAOLO'S PIZZERIA/ RISTORANTE VEZUVIO
SCOTT ST.
SMITH ST.
THURMOND ST.
JAVA MOON
THE BOOK SHOP
BROOKS ST.
BRUNDAGE ST.
OLIVER'S/BRUNDAGE ST. GOURMET
AUNTIE M'S B&B ●
POST OFFICE ■
LOUCKS ST.
CAMEO ROSE B&B ●

© AVALON TRAVEL PUBLISHING, INC.

SHERIDAN

POWDER RIVER

© AVALON TRAVEL PUBLISHING, INC.

POWDER RIVER

COALBED METHANE

The Powder River Basin is in the midst of the largest mineral boom in Wyoming history as gas producers rush to drill and develop coalbed methane wells throughout the region. The scale of development is staggering: within the next two decades some 50,000–120,000 wells will be drilled here in the pursuit of natural gas.

First, the Good News

Incredible deposits of coal underlie this part of Wyoming, and methane gas is found within these beds. It's a relatively easy process to extract the gas: just drill a 400- to 1,500-foot well, drop in a submersible pump to remove the water, and pipe out the gas. (Okay, it is really considerably more complex than that, but the overall operation is straightforward.) Estimates of coalbed methane reserves in the Powder River Basin are 6–40 trillion cubic feet of gas, and producers say they can supply at least a billion cubic feet of methane daily, or enough for four million households. In addition to all the jobs this development is bringing to the area, local landowners have benefited from royalty payments that help ranchers survive in a tough cattle market.

The Downside

Unfortunately, the impacts from coalbed methane developments may last much longer than the 5–15 years until the gas is gone from a given well. Each well requires electricity, a gas line, and a water pipe, plus roads to get to the site and various related developments such as noisy compressor stations to transport the gas to market. The result is a spiderweb of dirt roads leading to the wellheads, and when you multiply this by the thousands of planned wells, the impacts are enormous. Not to mention all those pickups and semis kicking up dust clouds.

Another serious issue is over water. Gas drillers discovered that pumping water from underground aquifers allowed the methane trapped in the coal to escape, particularly in the first two years of production at a site. Millions of gallons of water are being pumped from gas wells in the Powder River Basin and poured into reservoirs and streams. This affects not just the amount of groundwater in the aquifer but also the surface because the water contains salts that accumulate over time, causing irreversible soil damage in some places.

Environmental groups are very concerned over the cumulative impacts from coalbed methane gas development on the region but are fighting an uphill battle because there is so much money involved: $1 billion has already been invested in the Powder River Basin. For the industry version of coalbed methane development, head to the **Powder River Coalbed Methane Information Council's** website, www.cbmwyo.org. For an environmental take on the issue, visit the **Powder River Basin Resource Council's** website, www.powderriverbasin.org.

---

streetcars were added in 1911, with frequent interurban service to the surrounding coal mines.

World War II brought prosperity as local mines operated at full tilt and new technology allowed construction of the first open-pit mine. After the war, however, trains shifted to diesel and homes began burning less-polluting natural gas, so that by 1953 the last of the old coal towns had died. With increasing demand for western coal in the 1970s, Sheridan's population boomed again. Sheridan's economy now depends on a mixture of mining, the railroad, ranching, government jobs, and tourism. Many locals cross into Montana for jobs at the Decker and Spring Creek coal mines, while others work at the local

veterans' hospital or the Burlington Northern switching yard. Coalbed methane gas production has become an increasingly important part of the economy, and you'll see compressor stations and gleaming pipelines throughout the area.

SIGHTS

Trail End State Historic Site

On spacious grounds overlooking Sheridan, Trail End Historic Center is the city's best-known attraction. This was the home of John B. Kendrick, a wealthy rancher and a powerful Democratic politician. Born in Texas in 1857, Kendrick was raised as an orphan. He became a ranch hand by

© DON PILCHER

POWDER RIVER

Trail End State Historic Site, Sheridan

age 15 and, after trailing cattle north to Wyoming, fell in love with the country and took a job as a ranch foreman. At age 34, he married 17-year-old Eula Wulfgen, and they lived on a ranch in southeastern Montana for the next 18 years.

Over the years Kendrick acquired more than 200,000 acres of land in Wyoming and Montana, grazing tens of thousands of his cattle. He personally financed local homesteaders, friends, former employees, and relatives. Politics beckoned once Kendrick was firmly established as a rancher and businessman, and he served first as governor, then as a U.S. senator until his death in 1933. One paper called him "the craftiest politician the state has ever produced." Kendrick helped expose the Teapot Dome Scandal and gained funding for the massive Kendrick Project, a series of dams and irrigation canals on the North Platte River.

Shortly before entering politics, Kendrick selected the site for his end-of-the-trail mansion high atop a hill overlooking Sheridan. Begun in 1908, Trail End took five years to complete and served primarily as a summer

home because politics kept Kendrick away the rest of the year. The mansion is in the Flemish Revival style, with curvilinear gables on the third-floor windows, a red-tile roof, hardwood floors, mahogany walls, and exposed-beam ceilings. Many of the sumptuous original furnishings (including a 25-foot-long Kurdistan rug) are still inside. Look for photos of several of Kendrick's ranches upstairs.

The house cost $165,000 in an era when typical homes went for less than $1,000. Its 18 rooms include a third-floor ballroom with a loft where musicians could play without interfering with the dancers below. The built-in central vacuum system still works. Heating Trail End sometimes required up to one ton of coal each day. Out back is a sod-roofed **log cabin** that was moved onto the grounds. Built in 1878, this historic structure served as Sheridan's first post office, and later it was used as a school, store, law office, and bank.

Find Trail End at 400 Clarendon Ave., 307/674-4589, www.trailend.org. It is open daily 9 A.M.–6 P.M. June–August, and daily 1–4 P.M. April, May, and September to mid-December. They're closed mid-December through February. Entrance costs $2 for nonresidents or $1 for Wyoming residents.

Sheridan Inn

Built in 1893, Sheridan Inn was considered by many to be the premier hotel between Chicago and San Francisco. Visitors included Presidents Theodore Roosevelt, Taft, and Hoover, along with such celebrities as Will Rogers and Ernest Hemingway. Architect Thomas Kimball modeled the inn after a Scottish hunting lodge, with dormer windows on all 62 rooms; *Ripley's Believe it or Not!* labeled it "The House of 69 Gables," a name that has stuck through the years. Inside, carpenters added hand-hewn ponderosa pine beams, three large cobblestone fireplaces, the Buffalo Bill Bar (imported from England), elegant oak furnishings, and the first electric lights in Sheridan. Col. William F. (Buffalo Bill) Cody was later a co-owner of the hotel and used the veranda to audition performers for his Wild West Show. It was operated as a hotel until 1965 and later as a restaurant and bar.

On the corner of 5th and Broadway, the inn is a registered National Historic Landmark. Tall, century-old cottonwoods guard the front, and the huge porch wraps around the sides. Try to see if you can find all 69 gables. Step inside to explore this gracious place or enjoy a pleasant lunch or dinner. The gift shop sells an interesting booklet about Kate Arnold, who lived here for 65 years and whose ashes are buried in an upstairs wall. Her ghost still shows up periodically to make sure the inn is well managed. Tours are available in summer for $5 ($3 seniors, free for kids under 12), but two days' advance notification is required. A self-guided tour brochure costs $2, and the basement houses a few historical items.

A local nonprofit group is restoring the Sheridan to its original status as a classy lodging, eating, and drinking establishment, but the project will probably not be completed until 2007, when the upstairs rooms will be restored. Call 307/674-5440 for details.

King's Saddlery

Well worth a stop is King's Saddlery, 184 N. Main St., 307/672-2702 or 800/443-8919, a Sheridan-area fixture since the 1940s. When you step inside the doors, the smell of leather is almost overwhelming. The long, narrow shop has handmade saddles, leatherwork, ropes, spurs, chaps, belt buckles, cowboy hats, and various other tack for horses and their riders. Be sure to check out the many miles of ropes filling racks in the back room. Many top rodeo cowboys come in to purchase their lariats, and King's sells 40,000 high-quality ropes a year.

The free **King's Western Museum** in the back is jammed with 500 gorgeous saddles and other cowboy tools of the trade. It's one of the finest collections of cowboy memorabilia anywhere. Featured attractions include a Hope saddle (the earliest Western saddle), one owned by Gene Autrey, and the saddle used the only time the famous bronc Steamboat was ever ridden. Also here is an impressive display of Indian artifacts, including a beaded pottery vase and bridles made a century ago. Lots of trivia too: John Wayne's pants from *Red River,* Gary Cooper's cowboy hat, and even a unicorn cow. Leather craftsman Jim Jackson is in the back most days, carving new saddles. King's Saddlery is fittingly named: both Queen Elizabeth and the king of Saudi Arabia have visited, and Presidents Clinton and Reagan were both given King's leather belts. King's Saddlery is open Monday–Saturday 8 A.M.–5 P.M. The store also has a mail-order catalog.

Fort Mackenzie

Built in 1902, Fort Mackenzie never really served much of a military function. Pushed through Congress by Wyoming's powerful senator Francis E. Warren, the fort was ostensibly built as a base to put down Indian uprising on nearby reservations, but the last major Indian battles had occurred 20 years earlier. It was named for Gen. Ranald S. Mackenzie, a veteran of the Civil War and various Indian battles. Over the decades, the size of the fort shrank from 6,280 to 342 acres, and the last troops departed during World War I. In 1922, it became a 339-bed hospital for mentally ill vets. You're welcome to walk around the grounds and admire the old brick buildings, but check in at the administration building first. Signs describe the various buildings.

Sheridan County Library

Sheridan's excellent library at 320 N. Brooks, 307/674-8585, encloses a small collection of Indian artifacts and items from early settlers. The Wyoming Room has an extensive collection of old books, maps, and paintings, including a mural of the Wagon Box Fight; upstairs you'll find more historical exhibits and current artwork and a model of the Medicine Wheel. On the library walls are 11 paintings by Bill Gollings (1878–1932), a self-taught, but accomplished, cowboy artist.

Other Sights

A historical marker on the corner of W. Dow and Alger commemorates **General Crook's campsite.** In 1876 the general camped here at the junction of Big and Little Goose Creeks with 1,325 men and 1,900 pack animals after being forced to a stalemate by Sioux and Crow war-

riors on the Rosebud River. The fight took place just eight days before Custer would die at nearby Little Big Horn.

Directly across from the Sheridan Inn is the old red Sheridan **train depot,** built in 1892 and now housing a bar. Nearby is a huge Chicago, Burlington, and Quincy Railroad **locomotive.** Downtown on 3rd and Gould Streets is a Sheridan **streetcar** from the early 1900s. History and architecture buffs should pick up a copy of the guide to Sheridan's **Main Street Historic District** at the visitors center. One of the buildings included—the **Mint Bar,** 151 N. Main St., 307/674-9696—offers a genuine taste of the West. Cartoonist Linda Barry's description of the Mint says it all: "Stuffed animal heads galore. Taxidermied fish galore. Burlwood carpentry galore."

Across the road from the state rest area/information center on 5th Street, the **Wyoming Game & Fish Department Visitor Center** contains several professionally produced and informative wildlife and fish displays. Although small, this collection is well worth a visit. Hours

are Monday–Friday 8 A.M.–5 P.M. year-round; call 307/672-2790 for details.

In summer you can hop on the **Sheridan Trolley,** 307/672-2485 or 800/453-3650, at the state information center for a ride through town. It runs all day Monday–Saturday, and costs $1.

ACCOMMODATIONS

The Chamber of Commerce's website, www.sheridanwyoming.org, has an overview and web links to local lodging, including B&Bs, and campgrounds. Most of Sheridan's motels lie along Coffeen Avenue and Main Street. During the off-season—through early May—you're likely to find lower prices, less than $30 per night at the budget motels.

Under $50

Parkway Motel, 2112 Coffeen Ave., 307/674-7259, is an okay low-priced choice: $36 s or $38–40 d. Kitchenettes are available. **Stage Stop Motel,** 2167 N. Main St., 307/672-3459, is a small place with basic rooms for $40 s or $43 d, and updated ones containing log furniture for $3 more. All of these rooms have microwaves and fridges.

The units aren't new, but they're clean and well-maintained at **Aspen Inn,** 1744 N. Main St., 307/672-9064. Rates are $34 s or $40–50 d. The same owners run the adjacent **Sundown Motel,** 1704 N. Main St., 307/672-2439, where remodeled rooms are available for $50–60 s or d. A small heated outdoor pool is on the premises at Sundown Motel.

Super Saver Inn, 1789 N. Main St., 307/672-0471, has reasonable rates ($40 for one bed or $50 for two), but you may want to check out the rooms first. **Alamo Motel,** 1326 N. Main St., 307/672-2455 or 866/631-6195, is a decent budget place, with rooms for $40 s or $43–50 d. Also worth a look is **Holiday Lodge,** 625 Coffeen Ave., 307/672-2407, with remodeled rooms for $48–68 s or d.

$50 and Up

Bramble Motel & RV Park, 2366 N. Main St., 307/674-4902, has motel rooms for $53 s or $56–63 d. A few kitchenettes are available. Find

spacious and clean motel rooms for $45–55 s or $60–65 d at **Guest House Motel,** 2007 N. Main St., 307/674-7496 or 800/226-9405.

Trails End Motel, 2125 N. Main St., 307/672-2477 or 800/445-4921, has a mix of old and new rooms for $56–64 s or d. Family units are $76 for six people, and log cabins cost $52–66 d. An indoor pool is on the premises. Stay at **Apple Tree Inn,** 1552 Coffeen Ave., 307/672-2428 or 800/670-2428, for $65 s or $75 d, where amenities include a hot tub, sauna, and playground. Some rooms also have microwaves and small refrigerators.

Super 8 Motel, 2435 N. Main St., 307/672-9725 or 800/800-8000, www.super8.com, charges $60–90 s or d, including a continental breakfast. **Evergreen Inn,** 580 E. 5th St., 307/672-9757 or 800/771-4761, is a nice place with an outdoor hot tub and fridges and microwaves. Rates are $66 s or $76 d.

Occupying a historic flour mill, the **Mill Inn,** 2161 Coffeen Ave., 307/672-6401 or 888/357-6455, www.sheridanmillinn.com, lends a new meaning to the term "hitting the sack." Rates are $60–90 s or $75–105 d, and amenities include an exercise facility, an Old West lobby, and a light breakfast. One of the best local places to stay is **Comfort Inn,** 1450 E. Brundage Lane, 307/672-5098 or 800/228-5150, www.comfortinn.com, where rooms cost $75–85 s or d, including a continental breakfast and access to the hot tub.

At **Days Inn,** 1104 E. Brundage Lane, 307/672-2888 or 800/329-7466, www.daysinn.com, amenities include an indoor pool, hot tub, and light breakfast. Rates are $75–135 s or d. **Holiday Inn,** 1809 Sugarland Dr., 307/672-8931 or 800/465-4329, www.holiday-inn.com, is the largest and most elaborate place to stay in Sheridan. The hotel features an atrium with a waterfall and two restaurants, plus a small indoor pool, sauna, hot tub, exercise room, and racquetball court. Rates are $79–109 s or d.

Best Western Sheridan Center Motor Inn, 609 N. Main St., 307/674-7421 or 877/437-4326, www.bestwestern.com/sheridancenter, is one of the better places in town, with indoor and outdoor pools, a hot tub, and courtesy van. Rates are $90 s or $100 d.

Bed-and-Breakfasts

Built in 1888, **Auntie M's B&B,** 323 W. Loucks St., 307/674-7035, is a quaint Victorian place with a small porch and antique furnishings. The two-room suite is $120 for up to four, and a room is available for $85 d. Both of these have private baths, and guests are served a full breakfast.

Right across the street is another building from the same era, **Cameo Rose B&B,** 306 W. Loucks St., 307/673-0500, www.alphamarketingsystems.com. The large corner house has a wraparound porch and three Victorian-style guest rooms, all with private baths and entrances. Rooms are $70 s or $85 d, including a full breakfast.

Constructed in 1887, **Edee's B&B,** 549 S. Main St., 307/672-6136, is another historic in-town home with three rooms (private or shared bath) for $70 s or d, including a full breakfast. In addition to these places, several excellent bed-and-breakfasts are out in the country south of Sheridan; see Big Horn.

Dude Ranches

The Sheridan area is home to a pair of classic dude ranches. The first in the region was run by the Hilman family, who took in their first paying dudes in 1889. It operated until the 1930s. Famous **Eaton's Ranch,** 18 miles west of Sheridan, 307/655-9285 or 800/210-1049, www.eatonsranch.com, is one of the oldest, largest, and best-known dude ranches in America. The three Eaton brothers—Howard, Alden, and Willis—began ranching in North Dakota in 1879 but soon found themselves overwhelmed by visiting friends from the east. Eventually one offered to pay, and thus was born the first dude ranch. Initially these "dudes" (a term that both Buffalo Bill and Howard Eaton took credit for using first in this context) stayed wherever they could find space, eating the cowboy's grub and joining in on chores. In 1904, the brothers bought a ranch along Wyoming's Wolf Creek that would eventually grow to 7,000 acres. Fourth- and fifth-generation members of the Eaton family still run the ranch. The ranch is a big one, accommodating up to 125 guests in modernized cabins. Many families return year after year to the Eaton's. The emphasis—not surprisingly—is on horseback rides;

this is one of the few dude ranches where experienced riders can head out on their own (with permission from the ranch). Other facilities include an outdoor pool, trout fishing, and a nearby nine-hole golf course. The ranch is open June–September with a one-week minimum stay in midsummer. Weekly all-inclusive rates are $2,300 for two people.

High in the Big Horn Mountains 30 miles southwest of Sheridan, **Spear-O-Wigwam Dude Ranch** has been in operation since 1923. This classic dude ranch—Ernest Hemingway wrote *A Farewell to Arms* while staying here—has comfy log cabins, a large lodge with a stone fireplace, a hot tub, pool tables, and horseback rides or overnight trips into the nearby Cloud Peak Wilderness. A fishing guide is available to teach fly-fishing. There's a three-night minimum stay, and all-inclusive rates are $350 for two people per night, or $2,300 for two people per week. The ranch plays host to a maximum of just 30 guests and is open mid-June to mid-September. For reservations or more information, call toll-free at 888/818-3833, or call direct at 307/674-4496 in summer or 307/655-3217 in winter. Find them on the web at www.spear-o-wigwam.com.

CAMPING

Many campgrounds ($8–13) operate within nearby Bighorn National Forest; they're described in the Big Horn Mountains section. **Bighorn Mountain KOA,** 63 Decker Rd., 307/674-8766 or 800/562-7621, www.koa.com, has quiet tent sites for $19 and RV sites for $27. Noncampers may shower for $5 (before 4 P.M. only). Basic cabins are $39 d. It's open May to early October and has a pool, hot tub, and mini-golf.

Bramble Motel & RV Park, 2366 N. Main St., 307/674-4902, has a handful of year-round RV sites for $21; no tents. **Peter D's RV Park,** 110 S. Joe St., 307/673-0597, is the newest local RV park, with such amenities as cable TV and Internet hookups. They're open seasonally. In addition to the official RV parks, many folks hitch up their wagons in the old-time country setting of the Wal-Mart parking lot. No charge, and a delightful ambience to boot.

FOOD

Sheridan has a broad choice of eateries, including a remarkable number of notable restaurants. You'll find cowboy breakfasts, gourmet lunches, brewpub favorites, and an Italian bistro all within a few blocks of each other.

Breakfast and Lunch

Sheridan Palace Cafe, 138 N. Main St., 307/672-2391, is an old-time downtown establishment that opens at 6 A.M. for the breakfast early birds.

Java Moon, 176 N. Main St., 307/673-5991, is a fun hangout place with a couple of streetside tables out front and a piano inside. Check out the daily lunch specials, including various panini sandwiches with soup for $5. They also serve espresso, teas, smoothies, juices, freshly baked breads, salads, ice cream, and even sushi.

Another place that gets crowded for lunch is **The Chocolate Tree,** 423 N. Main St., 307/672-6160, where the menu includes gourmet sandwiches, burgers, shrimp scampi, salads, daily specials, and decadent chocolates. It's also open for breakfast and dinner.

Burgers and Pizza

The best local burgers can be found—surprisingly enough—at **Dairy Queen,** 544 N. Main St., 307/674-9379. **Golden Steer Restaurant,** 2071 N. Main St., 307/674-9334, is a family dining place with good steaks. Fill up on barbecued buffalo, chicken, and ribs during the summer evening chuck wagon cookouts at **Bighorn Mountain KOA,** 63 Decker Rd., 307/674-8766 or 800/562-7621.

Little Big Men Pizza, 1424 Coffeen Ave., 307/672-9877, has reasonable pizza, burger, and salad meal deals, including all-you-can-eat lunch and dinner smorgasbords.

Fine Dining

Sheridan's finest lunches and dinners are found at the spacious and surprisingly chic **Oliver's Bar & Grill,** 55 N. Main St., 307/672-2838. Diners can watch the chefs at work in the open kitchen while sampling the delectable appetizers, sipping a fine wine from the extensive list, or enjoying a dinner with such treats as spice-rubbed beef tenderloin, baked stuffed fresh pasta, or seared elk chop. Get here early for lunch to avoid the lines, and make reservations for dinner. Dinner entrées are $9–26. Highly recommended. The restaurant is run by Matt Wallop, son of former U.S. Senator Malcolm Wallop. **Brandage St. Gourmet** adjoins Oliver's and sells freshly baked breads, along with gourmet cheeses and wines.

On the corner of 5th and Broadway, the historic **Sheridan Inn** (described in Sights) serves three meals a day Tuesday–Saturday in summer; lunch and dinner only Thursday–Saturday in winter. The front porch makes a delightful seasonal dining spot. The restaurant's reputation has suffered recently, but things may have improved by the time you visit. Call 307/674-5440 for reservations.

International

For authentic Italian meals, don't miss **Ristorante Vezuvio,** downtown at 123 N. Main St., 307/672-3853. Chef Paolo Formisano moved here from Italy and cranks out delicious pizzas and salads in an attractive bistro setting.

Get reasonably authentic Chinese cookery at **Golden China Restaurant** in the T&C Shopping Center at Brundage and Coffeen, 307/674-7181. **Dragon Wall Restaurant,** 425 N. Brooks, 307/673-6888, has a big Chinese buffet for lunch or dinner, including a not-so-Chinese salad and dessert bar. **Kim's Family Restaurant,** 2004 N. Main St., 307/672-0357, is one of the only Korean restaurants in Wyoming.

Pablo's Restaurant & Cantina, 1274 N. Main St., 307/672-0737, serves reasonably priced Mexican food and has a full bar. **Los Agaves,** 922 Coffeen Ave., 307/674-0900, is also of note.

Pubs and Brewpubs

Sanford's Grub, Pub & Brewery, 1 E. Alger St., 307/674-1722, is a popular pub with garage-sale flotsam and jetsam dangling from the ceiling, TVs in all directions, and rock tunes blasting over the speakers. The bar claims one of the largest beer selections in Wyoming with more than 125 brews, including 37 on draught. Several of these are made in the brewpub on the premises. The diverse menu makes this a popular (and noisy) place to hang out with friends. It's part of a small chain of pubs—others are in Cheyenne, Gillette, and Casper, along with Rapid City and Spearfish, South Dakota.

Pony Bar & Grill, 3 S. Gould St., 307/674-7000, combines a sports bar with tasty burgers, quesadillas, buffalo wings, and other bar favorites. It's also popular with the business lunch crowd and is a Friday evening hangout.

Groceries
Sheridan has several large grocers, including Albertson's, Safeway, Wal-Mart SuperCenter, Warehouse Market, and Carl's North Food Center, but your best bet is **Carl's Corner IGA,** on the south side of town at 2254 Coffeen Ave., 307/674-7945.

ENTERTAINMENT
During summer, **WYO Theater,** 42 N. Main St., 307/672-9084, www.wyotheater.com, has live plays and musical events. A highlight is their **Shakespeare in the Park** production in late July at Kendrick Park. **Carriage House Theater** at Trail End, 307/672-9886, www.trailend.org, presents plays October–May and sometimes has children's theater in the summer. Drop by the Kendrick Park band shell for free Tuesday night **concerts in the park** all summer. Music ranges from polka to jazz.

Enjoy live rock-and-roll on weekends at **Little Big Men Pizza,** 1424 Coffeen Ave., 307/672-9877, or watch sports on its big-screen TV. Check **Scooter's,** at the Holiday Inn, 1809 Sugarland Dr., 307/672-8931, and **Sutton's Tavern,** 1402 N. Main St., 307/672-5213, for DJ tunes on weekends. Pool, snooker, and darts are featured attractions at the **Bruce's Caboose Bar,** in the old depot across from the Sheridan Inn. For all-around fun and drinking with your friends, it's hard to beat the classic **Mint Bar,** 151 N. Main St., 307/674-9696.

Watch movies inside **Centennial Theatres,** 36 E. Alger St., 307/672-5797, or visit one of Wyoming's few surviving drive-ins: **Skyline Drive In,** 1739 E. Brundage Lane, 307/674-4532.

EVENTS
Cowboyography, www.cowboyography.com, is a fun mid-February cowboy poetry and music festival at the Sheridan Inn. Early July attracts chefs and chili connoisseurs to Sheridan for the **Wyoming Chili Cook-off.** The six-day **Sheridan Wyo Rodeo,** 307/672-2485 or 800/453-3650 www.sheridanwyorodeo.com, comes around the second week of July, bringing with it not just professional rodeo cowboys at the "world's largest one go-round rodeo" but also a parade down Main Street, a pancake breakfast, carnival, country-and-western bands, and street dances.

The third weekend of July is the **Prairie Rose Arts Festival,** held at the historic Sheridan Inn. This juried event attracts a wide range of artists, woodworkers, potters, and jewelers. See Big Horn for other popular local events: the **Fourth of July** fireworks show, **Red, White, and Bluegrass Festival** in early July, **Canyon Ranch Indian Paintbrush Festival** in mid-August, and **Don King Days** over Labor Day weekend.

In early August, visit the **Sheridan County Fair,** www.sherfair.org, followed by the **Sheridan County Rodeo** later in the month. The rodeo even includes stick-horse races for those under age four! **Big Horn Mountain Polka Days** is a fun Labor Day weekend event that attracts hundreds of polka enthusiasts to the Holiday Inn Convention Center. Oom-pa-pa!

RECREATION
Kendrick City Park has a small game preserve where bison and elk are visible, plus a great playground for kids. Swim at the summer-only **outdoor swimming pool** in the park, and feel like a kid again on the 90-foot-long water slide. Details at 307/674-9434, www.city-sheridan-wy.com. The **YMCA,** 417 N. Jefferson, 307/674-7488, has two swimming pools, plus racquetball and tennis courts and a fitness center.

Golfers will want to try out two 18-hole courses: **Kendrick Golf Course,** three miles west of town, 307/674-8148, and the acclaimed **Powder Horn Golf Club,** in Big

Horn, six miles south of Sheridan, 307/672-5323, www.thepowderhorn.com.

Nelson Outfitters, 307/672-6996, www.hunt wyoming.com, has horseback rides from its base nine miles west of Sheridan.

Big Horn Mountain Sports, 334 N. Main St., 307/672-6866, www.bighornmountain-sports.com, has a big choice of outdoor gear and topographic maps. Much of this gear can also be rented, including cross-country skis, snowboards, snowshoes, tents, sleeping bags, backpacks, inline skates, fly rods, and float tubes. The staff teaches classes in skiing, kayaking, fly-tying, fly-fishing, and rock climbing. **Back Country Bikes,** 307/672-2453, inside Big Horn Mountain Sports, rents mountain bikes and has helpful maps of nearby cycling trails.

Fly Shop of the Big Horns, 227 N. Main St., 307/672-5866 or 800/253-5866, www.troutangler.com, has Orvis gear, classes in fly-casting and fly-tying, and guided fishing trips on the Big Horn and Platte Rivers. Rent float tubes and fins here.

SHOPPING

You'll find a fine selection of Wyoming titles at **The Book Shop,** 117 N. Main St., 307/672-6505, and **Sheridan Stationery,** 206 N. Main St., 307/672-8080 or 888/266-5730. The Book Shop also has occasional poetry readings and other literary events.

Western Gear

Custom Cowboy Shop, 350 N. Main St., 307/672-7733, has quality boots, hats, saddles, and tack. Also be sure to visit **King's Saddlery,** 184 N. Main St., 307/672-2702 or 800/443-8919, described under Sights. **Little Willow Traders,** 166 N. Main St., 307/672-0200, is a fun shop with distinctive gift items, furnishings, and knick-knacks.

Bits and Spurs, 655 Riverside, 307/672-8459 or 800/672-8459, www.tombalding.com, is a unique shop where you'll find surprisingly beautiful bits and spurs welded by Tom Balding. In addition to his craftsmanship, the shop also sells cowboy music, leather goods, art, and jewelry.

Galleries

Several Sheridan art galleries provide enjoyable browsing, including **Bozeman Trail Gallery,** next to King's Saddlery at 190 N. Main St., 307/672-3928, and **Bucking Buffalo Supply Co.,** 317 N. Main St., 307/674-4999. The last of these is a fun place packed with quality Western wear, home furnishings, and Indian-made items. **Wyoming Expressions,** 250 N. Main St., 307/673-9698, www.bighornmtncreations.com, sells rustic Wyoming-made furniture.

INFORMATION AND SERVICES

The **Sheridan Visitor Center/State Information Center,** 307/672-2485 or 800/453-3650, www.sheridanwyoming.org, is in the rest area at the 5th St. exit off I-90. Inside are various historical displays, a 3-D map, and a panoramic view of the Big Horns from the windows. The center is open daily 8 A.M.–7 P.M. mid-May to mid-October, and Monday–Friday 8 A.M.–5 P.M. the rest of the year. The **Bighorn National Forest Supervisor's Office** is at 1969 S. Sheridan Ave., 307/674-2600, www.fs.fed.us/r2/bighorn.

The **Sheridan County Library,** 335 W. Alger St., 307/674-8585, www.sheridanwyolibrary.org, houses computers where you can check email or surf the web. Check out the Wyoming Room, with a variety of Indian artifacts, including vests, moccasins, pipes, and weapons.

With 1,500 students, **Sheridan College,** 307/674-6446, www.sheridan.edu, is one of the largest two-year schools in the state. Founded in 1948, it offers degrees in both academic and technical fields.

Wash clothes at **Econ-O-Wash Laundry,** 19 E. 5th St., 307/672-7899, **Super Saver Laundromat,** 1789 N. Main St., 307/672-0471, or **Sugarland Laundromat,** in Sugarland Village, 307/672-5736.

Memorial Hospital of Sheridan County, 1401 W. 5th St., 307/672-1000, www.sheridanhospital.org, has a 24-hour emergency room.

TRANSPORTATION

By Air

Sheridan airport is just southwest of town. **Great Lakes Aviation,** 307/432-7000 or 800/554-5111, www.greatlakesav.com, has daily flights between Sheridan and Denver. Based in Sheridan, **Bighorn Airways,** 307/672-3421, www.bighornairways.com, has charter flights throughout the region. They're the largest air charter service in Wyoming.

By Car and Bus

Rent cars at the airport from Avis or Enter-prise. See the "Rental Car Contacts" Special Topic in the On the Road chapter. Get them in town from **Truck Corral Auto Rental,** 1320 Coffeen Ave., 307/672-7955.

Powder River Transportation/Coach USA, 307/674-6188 or 800/442-3682, has daily bus service to Billings, Montana, and most towns in central and eastern Wyoming. Buses stop next to Evergreen Inn at 580 E. 5th Street.

The **Sheridan Trolley,** 307/672-2485 or 800/453-3650, leaves the information center Monday–Saturday in the summer, with tours of town; $1.

Northwest of Sheridan

RANCHESTER

Fifteen miles north of Sheridan, the little village of Ranchester (pop. 700) has a couple of interesting historical sites. **Connor Battlefield State Historic Site** is right in Ranchester's city park. It's a very pleasant place with picnic tables, year-round camping ($9 for nonresidents, $4 for Wyoming residents), and tall cottonwood trees along the Tongue River (so named because of a tonguelike rock along a tributary). Good fishing for brown trout can be found here. A cable footbridge leads across the river.

Despite its bucolic setting, the park has a gruesome history representing one of the worst atrocities in the Powder River Basin. The massacre took place in 1865, during a time of hit-and-run battles throughout the plains set off by mass killing of the Cheyenne at Sand Creek in Colorado and continued in dozens of Indian attacks on settlers and emigrants. Red Cloud had just struck against Platte Bridge Station (see Casper in the Central Wyoming chapter) a few weeks before, killing 28 men, and the army was eager to avenge that raid as well as attacks along the Bozeman Trail.

General Patrick E. Connor—a proponent of the shoot-first, ask-questions-later school of military diplomacy—attacked Indian villages throughout the West, killing 200 Shoshone in an 1863 Utah attack and then rampaging through Nevada and Idaho. Connor's 1865 expedition to the Powder River included nearly a thousand soldiers and 179 Pawnee and Winnebago scouts. Most of the effort was a failure as Indians kept ahead of the ponderous military wagons, but on August 29 Connor's men came upon Chief Bear's Arapaho village along the Tongue River. Connor ordered his men, "You will not receive overtures of peace or submission from the Indians, but will attack and kill every male Indian over 12 years of age." In a pell-mell rush, Connor's men slaughtered 63 men, women, and children, destroyed 250 lodges along with much of their winter supplies, and captured more than 1,100 ponies. Eight troopers died. No one ever determined whether the Arapaho they encountered were the same ones who had been attacking along the Bozeman Trail. The expedition ended when the government realized it was costing more than $1 million per month for transportation alone. A chastened Connor stashed his supplies at Fort Connor (later renamed Fort Reno) and returned to Fort Laramie.

Four miles west of here on U.S. Hwy. 14, another monument marks the **Sawyer Fight.** Here, two days after Connor attacked the Arapaho along the Tongue River, Arapahoes retaliated against a 100-man roadbuilding expedition led by Col. James Sawyer. Three of his men were killed and the rest were pinned down for nearly two weeks before finally being rescued by Connor's troops.

BILL NYE ON RUSTLING

Three years ago a guileless tenderfoot came into Wyoming, leading a single Texas steer and carrying a branding iron; now he is the opulent possessor of six hundred head of fine cattle—the ostensible progeny of that one steer. . . . A poor boy can in a few years, with an ordinary Texas steer and a branding iron, get together a band of cattle that would surprise those who figure simply on the ordinary rate of increase. Men soon learn that it is possible and even frequent for a cow wearing a "Z" brand to be the fond and loving mother of a calf wearing the "X" brand, and vice versa. Sometimes a calf will develop a brand that has never been in the family before.

Accommodations

Stay at the clean and friendly **Ranchester Western Motel,** 307/655-2212 or www.ranchester-motel.com, for $55–60 s or $60–65 d. There's an outdoor pool, and most rooms have microwaves and small fridges. **Lazy R RV Park & Campground,** 307/655-9284 or 888/655-9284, has year-round RV sites for $17, and a couple of tent sites for $15.

Built in 1899 by cattle baron Samuel H. Hardin, the **Historic Old Stone House B&B,** 135 Wolf Creek Rd., 307/655-9239, www.wyomingbnb-ranchrec.com/osh.html, caps a hilltop south of Ranchester. The stone house—hence the name—has guest rooms and suites in the main house and an adjacent carriage house; $88–120 d. All of these rooms have private baths and are furnished with arts-and-crafts pieces, including some antiques. A full breakfast and evening wine are served. Kids are welcome.

Other Practicalities

Kelly's Kitchen, 307/655-9016, has ice cream and fast food. Get groceries at **Buckhorn Gro-**

ceries, 307/655-9766, and cash from the **ATM** at Ranchester State Bank. The local mini-mall has a laundromat. Children will enjoy the kid-designed **wooden playground** of forts and slides at the elementary school.

Ranchester Days in June features a horse-shoe tournament, horse-drawn parade, arts-and-crafts booths, and street dance.

DAYTON

The village of Dayton (pop. 670) contains the little log-cabin studio of watercolorist **Hans Kleiber** (1887–1966). The studio is now used as a combination museum and visitors center, with iffy hours. Kleiber was known as "Artist of the Big Horns," and his works are internationally collected today. Inside are his press, art books, and several etchings. Call 307/655-2216 for details. Dayton's old **bell tower,** built in 1910 to warn of fires, is now in the city park.

Accommodations and Food

Foothills Campground and Motel, 307/655-2547, has cabins for $25–40 s or d, along with kitchenettes that cost $30–40 for up to four people. Camp along the river here for $13, or park RVs for $19. Noncampers can shower for $2. Both campground and cabins are open May–October only. Meals, including a weekend breakfast buffet, are available at **The Branding Iron Restaurant,** 307/655-2334.

Built in 1904, **Whitehorse B&B,** 306 Main St., 307/655-0245, www.whitehorsebedandbreakfast.com, is a comfortable inn with three large rooms and private baths. A full breakfast is served, and children are welcome. Rates are $75–99 d.

Four Pines B&B, 114 Dayton East Rd., 307/655-3764 or 866/366-2607, www.fourpines.com, houses two guest rooms in a quiet setting. Rates are $60–75, with private or shared bath. The back deck is a fine place for breakfast each morning, kids are welcome, and the owners have a pasture for horses.

Other Practicalities

Dayton Days, held the last weekend in July,

has the usual country favorites, including a parade, food and craft booths, a firefighters' water fight, Indian dancing, and a street dance. Anglers will find blue-ribbon trout fishing along the Tongue River. Dayton also has an outdoor **swimming pool** next to the Kleiber cabin; open June–Aug. The nine-hole **Horseshoe Moun-** **tain Golf Course,** 307/655-9525, is west of town at the foot of the mountains and includes some unique hazards: horse-hoof-sized potholes from the thoroughbred ranch here.

Summerhouse Books, 307/655-2367, sells both new and used books. An **ATM** is inside the Sinclair station.

East of Sheridan

POWDER RIVER

Some of the prettiest plains country in Wyoming lies along U.S. Hwy. 14, a quiet and scenic road that curls through miles of ranchland and winter wheat. The road heads southeast from Sheridan, gradually narrowing as it climbs through rugged hills and down a long green valley filled with fine ranches and modern homes.

UCROSS

At the crossroads called Ucross, a huge red barn ("Big Red") dominates the view. The 22,000-acre Ucross Ranch is headquarters for the nonprofit Ucross Foundation, 307/737-2291, www.ucrossfoundation.org, which operates an important retreat for writers, painters, poets, composers, sculptors, playwrights, photographers, and other artists. Each year some 60 selected artists enjoy a two- to eight-week residency program that includes individual workspaces, a printmaking studio, a gallery, and comfortable living accommodations. It's all to give time for artists to focus on ideas, theories, and works. Author E. Annie Proulx wrote both *Postcards* and *The Shipping News* while staying here; the latter won her a Pulitzer Prize in 1992. Drop in for a tour of the immaculate buildings or to check out gallery exhibitions.

The **Big Red Art Gallery** at Ucross is open Monday–Friday 9 A.M.–4 P.M. all year, plus Saturday–Sunday 11 A.M.–3 P.M. in summer. Big Red was headquarters for the enormous Pratt and Ferris Cattle Co., a spread that extended 35 miles along Clear Creek. At one time, more than 35,000 calves were branded each fall, and the huge barn could hold 30 teams of horses. The "U Cross" was their brand. If you're in the area around the **Fourth of July,** stick around for food, games, live bluegrass music, and a spectacular fireworks display.

Ucross is also home to **The Ranch at Ucross,** 307/737-2281 or 800/447-0194, www.blairhotels.com/rau, a luxurious guest ranch that fills with Tauck Tour buses during summer. The ranch typically has a few rooms available for other travelers, but don't expect to have the place to yourself. Guests stay in condo-type rooms or modern cabins for $159 s or d, including a full breakfast in the restaurant and access to the outdoor pool and tennis court. Horseback rides cost $20 per hour. The Ranch at Ucross is open May–October only.

CLEARMONT AND LEITER AREA

The 20 miles east from Ucross are some of the most distinctive in Wyoming. The road parallels cottonwood-bordered Clear Creek, winding its way down the grassy hillsides. The Big Horn Mountains form a dramatic Western backdrop, and large ranches dot the countryside with stone buildings and spreading old trees. It's easy to see why the Sioux fought so hard to keep this country out of white hands!

The largest settlement between Gillette and Sheridan, **Clearmont** is a pleasant place with a bit more than 100 folks and tall deciduous trees lining the handful of streets, a combination library/community center, and a pretty little town park with an old concrete jail. Get mediocre meals or a beer at **Red Arrow Cafe & Bar,** 307/758-4455. RV hookups are $12. Stop by the small **Pay & Save Groceries** to find food, crafts, and homemade quilts. The last of these is actually part of a web and mail-order quilt business called

Best Kept Secret, 307/758-4456 or 877/758-4456, www.thebestkeptsecret.com.

East from Clearmont is minuscule **Leiter,** with Joe's Motel, a bar, and the **Leiterville Country Club,** 307/758-4343, locally famous for their steaks.

The highway crosses the Powder River at the little settlement called **Arvada** and then heads east to Spotted Horse. **Powder River Experience,** 307/758-4381 or 888/736-2402, www.buffalowyoming.com/prexp, offers ranch vacations on a 24,000-acre spread three miles south of Arvada. Guests ride horseback and join in short cattle drives or other ranch activities. You can stay by the night or the week in the two comfortable guesthouses with shared or private baths; meals and lodging included. The ranch is open year-round and accepts a maximum of 15 guests at a time. Rates vary widely depending on the length of stay and activities included.

SPOTTED HORSE

At Spotted Horse—named for a minor Cheyenne chief—the combination country store/gas station/saloon/café is worth a stop, if only to hang out with locals in the bar. Hard times show in the faces of local ranchers. The bar has a jukebox, a few fast-food items on the menu, and cold beer. Its walls are carpeted with an amusing collection of old junk, historic photos, and cheesecake biker shots.

The 1811 overland expedition of the Astorians passed through the Spotted Horse area. During the 1930s, tourists en route to Yellowstone posed on a stuffed bucking bronc in the back paddock, but once I-90 was completed, business plummeted and the local economy suffered a long decline.

Southeast from Spotted Horse, the highway curves toward the coal mines of Gillette and

past an ever-increasing number of coalbed methane gas developments. The red scoria rock of the highway points through summer-green grass. (Also called clinker, this rock was created when coal burned underground, baking adjacent shale and sandstone to a bright red. Similar red roads exist all over Powder River Basin.) Old windmills pump water for cattle and sheep. From atop the hills a landscape of fences, phone lines, plowed fields, bales of hay, and horses spreads out in all directions. The sun darts between cotton ball clouds as a lone cyclist pumps up the road, swerving around the smashed jackrabbits and passed by pickup trucks with gun racks and drivers with tipped-back cowboy hats. This is the true West, not the region cutesified for tourists. Red-sided buttes rise above the rolling plains. The new ranch houses—trailer homes—stand next to aging farmsteads and collapsed log cabins; imported pickups sit in the driveways and satellite dishes guard the front yards. If you like grass and sky, brilliant starry nights, antelope, haystacks, and oil wells, you'll love this place. Stop for a while and listen to the silence broken only by the meadowlarks and the wind. God's country.

South of Sheridan

Although I-90 cuts south of Sheridan toward Buffalo, U.S. Hwy. 87 offers a much more interesting route, taking you through rolling ranch country and past cottonwood-lined draws. Along the way are the little settlements of Big Horn and Story and the historically rich country around old Fort Phil Kearny and the Bozeman Trail. The area's beauty has long attracted wealthy corporate executives and politicians, who come here to relax as gentlemen ranchers in ostentatious homes.

BIG HORN

Tiny Big Horn was founded in 1879 by O. P. Hanna (local Indians called him "Big Spit" because of his tobacco chewing), a ceaseless promoter who sent glowing accounts of "Big Horn City" to various newspapers. A reporter decided to investigate and found that the town consisted primarily of a few outlaws, including "Big Nose" George Parrott and Jesse James' outlaw brother, Frank. A few homesteaders and settlers did take the bait, however: by 1884 Big Horn City had a hotel, three stores, two blacksmith shops, three saloons, a newspaper, a school, a church, and even a college of sorts.

Sights

Over the years, most of Big Horn's businesses moved to Sheridan, but still here is **Big Horn Mercantile,** built in 1882 and considered the oldest business in northern Wyoming. In addition to the basics, the market now also serves espresso, tasty sandwiches, and pizza by the slice or pie. Take a look inside for the photo of Queen Elizabeth, who visited this historically British area in 1984. From the same era is **Bozeman Trail Inn,** 307/672-9288, where you'll find one of the oldest bars in Wyoming. A very good restaurant here is open daily.

A historic 1881 blacksmith shop houses the **Bozeman Trail Museum.** Open Sat.–Sun. 11 A.M.–6 P.M. mid-May to Labor Day, and on many weekday evenings; ask at Big Horn Mercantile for access when they're closed. The mu-seum displays various local memorabilia, historical photos, and a small gift shop. The ceiling is "branded" with local cattle brands. No admission charge. The town park next door makes a pleasant picnic spot.

The **State Bird Farm,** 307/674-7701, six miles south of town on Bird Farm Rd., raises 13,000 pheasants each year. These birds are released around Wyoming shortly before the fall hunting season, just in time to get shot as "wild game." The farm also has show birds, including more than a dozen species of pheasants, along with peacocks, turkey, chukkar, and guinea hens. Come here in early May to see the cute pheasant chicks.

For a panoramic view of the surrounding country, follow State Hwy. 335 west from Big Horn. The road turns to gravel after three miles and then continues into the Big Horn Mountains as **Red Grade Road** (Forest Rd. 26). The route's a bit rough and too steep for RVs, but it provides outstanding vistas after just a couple of miles. The road eventually connects with U.S. Hwy. 14, but bring along a Forest Service map.

Polo

Certainly the last thing one might expect to find in Big Horn is a polo field, but the English tradition lives on at **Big Horn Equestrian Center** south of town on Bird Farm Road, 307/674-8687, www.bighornpoloclub.com. Tournament polo games are held on Sundays mid-May to early September, with practice games on Wednesdays and Fridays. The caliber of play varies, but you may see topnotch visiting players from South America.

Polo games began on the **Polo Ranch,** www.poloranch.com, a couple miles west of Big Horn, before moving to the present equestrian center in the 1980s. The Polo Ranch is hard to miss, with an enormous white barn and immaculate white picket fences. It positively reeks of money. The current owner is Joe Schuchert, an executive with American Standard, the toilet-fixture company, and a financial backer to right-wing Christian radio stations around Wyoming. The ranch was formerly

Spear Ranch B&B, Bighorn

owned by ex-U.S. senator Malcolm Wallop, the grandson of Sir Oliver H. Wallop, seventh earl of Portsmouth (who served in the Wyoming Legislature before returning to England to sit in the House of Lords). Oliver Wallop and the two Moncrieffe brothers bought Western horses for the British Army during the Boer War, shipping 20,000 of them overseas. To test the ponies, the British purchasing officer would ride them the length of a polo field. Malcolm Moncrieffe trained a team on this field and later competed with them in England. Thus began what is believed to be the oldest polo club in America.

Accommodations

At **Bozeman Trail B&B,** 307/672-2381 or 877/672-2381, a graceful blue barn (built in 1919) has been transformed into a country bed-and-breakfast. Owners Toby and Marie Johnson welcome guests, providing four rooms and three baths, a tasty full breakfast, and a relaxing hot tub on their 30-acre farm. Sheep, longhorn cattle, and a horse graze in the adjacent pasture. Toby Johnson is a hunting guide, so animal heads fill the interior of the B&B.

Room rates are $85 d; the loft is perfect for families and friends ($115 for four people).

Two miles southwest of Big Horn, **Spear Ranch B&B,** 170 Brinton Rd., 307/673-0079, www.spearranch.com, is an extraordinary 140-acre estate with luxuriant lawns, flower gardens, a white picket fence out front, and a shady deck in the back overlooking Little Goose Creek. Built in 1920, the mansion was lavishly remodeled in the 1990s. Open the door to find hardwood floors, antique furnishings, and a grandfather clock and grand piano in the sitting room. The five guest rooms (shared or private baths) range from a small bachelor's quarters ($70 s) to a spacious room with a mahogany bed, creek views, and gas fireplace ($90 d). Two rooms can be joined to create a suite for $150. Also on the grounds is a private carriage house ($125) containing two bedrooms, a kitchen, and living room, and the cozy caretaker's cottage ($150). The latter sits on the banks of a small pond, sleeps six comfortably, and has a three-night minimum stay. Both of these cottages are not available in July. A gourmet breakfast is included, and children will love the big jungle gym and sandbox, along with the dogs, cats, horses, chickens, and rabbits. This is lodging at its most elegant and the perfect spot for weddings and retreats.

In the cool pine forests seven miles west of Big Horn, **Spahn's Big Horn Mountain Bed & Breakfast,** 307/674-8150, www.bighorn-wyoming.com, is another of the nicest B&Bs in Wyoming. The beautiful three-story log home was built by Ron Spahn, a former geologist and lawyer who runs the place with his wife Bobbie, a retired nurse. Enjoy a full breakfast on the porch, where the view extends all the way to Montana, a hundred miles across Powder River Basin. It's a great place to watch distant lightning storms. Guests stay in three rooms inside the main house or in one of two cabins just a short walk away. The cabins are perfect for families or honeymooners. Rates are $100–140 d. Plan on spending several days here; there's lots to do nearby, and the country is grand.

Located on a 3,000-acre ranch owned by the Wallop family, **Canyon Ranch Lodge,** 307/672-22976, www.canyonranchbighorn.com, is a stylish building that rents for $135 per person with a three-night minimum. The price includes three meals a day, and a variety of guided fishing packages are available. You can also stay by the week at a cozy and remote cabin: $1,575 for up to six guests.

In addition to a championship 18-hole course, **Powder Horn Golf Course,** 307/674-9545 or 800/329-0598, www.thepowderhorn.com, has furnished homes for rent next to the greens, including a three-bedroom home for $300. Also available are rooms in a refurbished 1940s home; $70, including a continental breakfast.

Events

The **Fourth of July** fireworks show at Big Horn Equestrian Center is the biggest in the Sheridan area. On the weekend closest to Independence Day, the **Red, White, and Bluegrass Festival** brings a day of live music at the Equestrian Center; www.redwhiteandbluegrass.com. The big annual event in Big Horn is **Don King Days** over Labor Day weekend, with steer roping and bronc riding at the equestrian center; 800/453-3650. **Canyon Ranch Indian Paintbrush Festival** in late August is a popular musical event held at the Wallop Ranch in Big Horn; 307/673-9035.

BRADFORD BRINTON MEMORIAL MUSEUM

In 1892, two Scottish brothers, William and Malcolm Moncrieffe, built a spacious two-story ranch house along Little Goose Creek. It became headquarters for their Quarter Circle A Ranch. A businessman and lover of the West, Bradford Brinton purchased the ranch in 1923 and enlarged the home to 20 rooms, filled it with elegant furniture, and lined the walls with his art collection. Bradford's sister Helen owned the house after his death in 1936, and upon her passing in 1960 the building became a museum honoring her brother. The museum, 307/672-3173, www.bradfordbrintonmemorial.com, is open daily 9:30 A.M.–5 P.M. from May 15 to early September (closed the rest of the year), with guided tours of the home and a creekside cabin. A donation is requested.

Step inside to taste the genteel life and to view works by some of the West's best-known artists, many of whom were friends of Bradford Brinton. The collection includes more than 600 pieces by such artists as John James Audubon, Hans Kleiber, Charles M. Russell, Frederic Remington, and Will Gollings. Also here are impressive Indian handicrafts, a Jefferson peace medal originally given to an Indian chief, books, and historic documents. A small gallery in the museum sells high-quality gifts. The log lodge of Bradford Brinton sits along Little Goose Creek and is filled with big game trophies. Horses are still raised on the 600-acre ranch, and the rural setting is most enjoyable: mountains rise on two sides and big old cottonwoods border the drive. Get to the Quarter Circle A by heading five miles west on State Hwy. 335 from the junction with U.S. Hwy. 87. Signs point the way.

STORY

The town of Story (pop. 900) is surprisingly different from nearby Sheridan and Buffalo. The road into Story winds more than 1,000 feet above

POWDER RIVER

the valley floor to the pine-covered slopes of the Big Horns. Locals and visitors come up to escape the hot summer air, to enjoy the restaurants, and to look for deer, elk, moose, and wild turkeys. Story is the site of "Piney Island," a stand of timber used to build nearby Fort Phil Kearny in 1866. The town was named for Nelson Story, the first man to trail cattle north across the Powder River Basin. **Story Fish Hatchery,** established in 1907, raises trout for Wyoming lakes and streams. The visitors center has interpretive exhibits and is open daily 8 A.M.–5 P.M. from mid-April to mid-September; 307/683-2234. **Piney Creek Pottery,** 307/683-2181, sells ceramics and other artwork.

Accommodations

Several places provide relaxing lodging in the Story area. Set on five wooded acres, **Piney Creek Inn B&B,** 307/683-2911, www.pineycreekinn.com, is a quiet place with a variety of accommodations, all with private baths. The rambling log house contains a guest room ($95 d) and two-bedroom suite ($130 for four people). Two cabins are also available. The larger one ($150 d or $175 for four) has two bedrooms, a kitchen, and spiral staircase, while the newer cabin ($150 d) is a favorite of honeymooners and contains a fireplace, kitchenette, and jetted bathtub. A hearty full breakfast is included, and guests will enjoy the hot tub off the main lodge and the large porch out front. Children are welcome. The friendly owners at Piney Creek also set up tours of the area, trail rides, and a variety of ranch activities.

Wagon Box Inn, 307/683-2444 or 800/308-2444, www.wilderwest.com/story/wagonbox, has cozy cabins starting for $55 d, up to a secluded six-person cabin with kitchen for $95. Also available are shared-bath bunkhouse accommodations for $30 s or d. All guests can use the sauna and hot tub. Reserve a month ahead for midsummer visits here.

Story Pines Inn, 307/683-2120 or 800/596-6297, www.storypinesinn.com, is a small motel with modern accommodations for $65 s or d, including access to a hot tub and picnic area. The town laundromat is also here.

Occupying a 1,000-acre spread south of Story, **Rafter Y Ranch,** 307/683-2258, has space for just 20 guests in comfortable log cabins with fireplaces, porches, and private baths. It's a fine place to ride horses or just relax in the foothills of the Big Horns. No minimum stay, but most guests stay at least four days. Open July–Aug.

Food

Wagon Box Inn, 307/683-2444 or 800/308-2444, www.wilderwest.com/story/wagonbox, serves some of the best lunches and dinners in the area, with the house specialty—prime rib—plus steaks, pasta, chicken, seafood, and a substantial wine list. On weekend nights, folks come here for live music. There's also a large patio.

Piney Creek General Store, 307/683-2400, is an old-fashioned country store with crowded aisles and a surprisingly good selection. A tiny café (Waldorf A' Story) here serves three wonderful meals a day, including homemade soups, creative sandwiches, and other treats. A few tables are inside, with more outside on the deck. There are nightly specials, including Saturday night ribs. Well worth a stop!

Lodore Supper Club and Lounge, 307/683-2355 or 877/763-6737, opened in 1919 and remains a popular dinner destination, with good steaks and all-you-can-eat prime rib and seafood. There's an outside deck, and the bar—it's called Jumpin' Jax Niteclub—has Karaoke on Wednesday nights and DJ music Thursday–Saturday nights.

Tunnel Inn, 307/683-2296, is an attractive log building with gourmet steaks, fish, and more.

The Bloody Bozeman

The discovery of gold in Montana during the 1860s triggered an avalanche of miners and businessmen. The fastest route to the Virginia City goldfields headed northwest from Bridger's Ferry (near present-day Douglas) through the Powder River Basin, and then west across Montana. One of the pioneers who scouted and constantly promoted the "Montana Road" was John M. Bozeman (as in Bozeman, Montana). Before being killed by Indians on the Yellowstone River in 1867, he led several groups up the Bozeman Trail, as the route became known. Hundreds of others would die along Bozeman's route to the goldfields. Guide Jim Bridger knew that the Sioux would never stand for whites in their Powder River country—a place they had recently wrested from the Crows, the Shoshone, and the Arapahoes. Instead, he recommended a different route that would cut west of the Big Horn Mountains. Unfortunately, Bridger's advice went unheeded, and as attacks on emigrant wagon trains increased in 1864, so did pressure to protect them from the Sioux. Appeals to Washington brought military assistance in the form of forts filled with soldiers and cavalry. Parallels between the events that followed and America's experience in Vietnam—from the guerrilla warfare to the hurried exit of U.S. troops at the end of the conflict—are disconcerting.

RED CLOUD'S WAR

The first salvo by the army came in General Connor's savage wanderings through the Powder River in 1865 (see Ranchester). The following year, while treaty negotiations were being held at Fort Laramie, Col. Henry B. Carrington and a battalion of infantry marched in, heading for the Bozeman Trail, where they planned to construct new forts. Red Cloud, a fiery military leader of the Oglala Sioux, grew more and more angry, shouting,

Great Father sends us presents and wants new road, but White Chief goes with soldier, to steal road before Indian says yes or no. . . . White man lies and steals. My lodges were many, but now they are few. The white man wants all. The white man must fight, and the Indian will die where his fathers died.

The treaty was signed by older chiefs and the "Laramie Loafers," who hung around the fort, but not by Red Cloud. He and his warriors stormed out, arriving at Powder River ahead of Colonel Carrington.

Carrington was a strange man to direct this massive undertaking. A political appointee with no battlefield experience—let alone experience with guerrilla warfare—he approached the task of building forts and protecting travelers along the Bozeman Trail with a take-no-chances attitude that rankled his trigger-happy men. The troupe left Nebraska with a 30-piece brass band, carriages, and comfortable furnishings, earning the name "Carrington's Overland Circus."

Once finally in the Powder River country, Carrington split his men into three groups, stationing some at Fort Reno near present-day Buffalo (begun the previous year by General Connor) and sending others to build Fort C. F. Smith in Montana. These way stations were to provide military escorts for travelers and havens from Indian attacks. Instead, they came under attack, and Carrington's men nearly became prisoners inside them.

FORT PHIL KEARNY

In the heart of the Powder River country along Little Piney Creek, Carrington found good water, grass so thick that horses could barely walk through it, and timber close at hand. It seemed the perfect site for a fort. His guide, the famed Jim Bridger, pushed instead for a site farther north, away from the center of Sioux country.

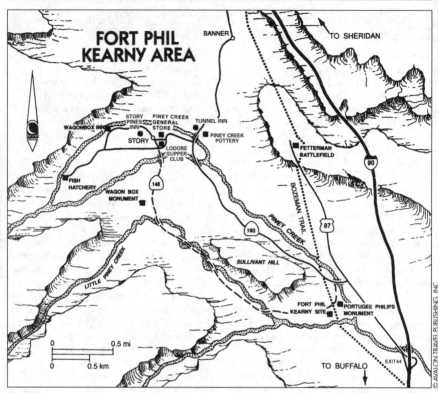

To Bridger, these "damn paper collar soldiers" seemed bound and determined to get killed.

Construction on the fort began on Friday, July 13th, 1866. The new garrison—named Fort Phil Kearny for a Civil War general—measured 600 by 800 feet and was entirely enclosed by a heavy log stockade. Big enough for 1,000 men, it never housed anything close to that many. Both Indian attackers and white defenders came to view this as the West's most-hated fort. From the first day, Carrington was harassed by the Sioux; by mid-December, more than 50 raids on the troops and civilians had left 17 military men and 58 civilians dead. Many of the horses and mules were stolen in the raids, and more than 700 cattle were lost when the Indians created a stampede by driving a herd of buffalo into them. With winter setting in, food and ammunition shortages made conditions worse, and even the nightly band concerts could not maintain morale. Jim Bridger revealed something of even greater concern after one of his scouting trips:

> *Crow chiefs report that it took a half a day's ride to go through the villages of the war parties on Tongue River. The Sioux chiefs said they would not touch the new fort on Powder River [Fort Reno] but would destroy the two new forts, in their hunting grounds, meaning Phil Kearny and C. F. Smith.*

FETTERMAN FIGHT

Again and again, the Sioux tempted soldiers into traps, drawing them away with attacks on the vital wood wagons (more than 4,000 logs were used in the stockade) and workers cutting hay, or by stealing horses and then attacking the pursuers. Carrington's caution caused dissension in the ranks, and when a new company of cavalry arrived, led by Capt. William J. Fetterman, the dissension edged on open revolt. Fetterman, like Gen. George A. Custer, had achieved fame for his bravery during the Civil War and, like Custer, would meet an early death. Fetterman viewed the Sioux with reckless disdain, claiming, "I can take 80 men and go to Tongue River through all the Sioux forces." Jim Bridger responded to this boast by telling him, "Your men who fought down South are crazy! They don't know anything about fighting Indians."

On the morning of December 21, 1866, Indians attacked a wood train, and a force of cavalry and infantrymen under Captain Fetterman was sent out. Disobeying orders from Colonel Carrington, Fetterman responded to taunts by Sioux decoys (including young Crazy Horse) by following them into an ambush. Perhaps 2,000 warriors of Red Cloud, High Back Bone, Red Leaf, and Little Wolf suddenly appeared in the tall grass. Within a half hour, all 81 soldiers had been killed. Until Custer's last stand a decade later, this event was the worst annihilation of any American force. Carrington had lost his most experienced fighters. Perhaps 30 Sioux died in the raid. Troops sent out to investigate what had happened found the frozen bodies horribly mutilated. They buried the men in a mass grave.

Portugee Phillips' Ride

After the Fetterman Fight, just 119 soldiers remained to guard against several thousand Sioux. Fearing further attacks, Carrington put the fort on full alert and sent messengers to Fort Laramie in a desperate bid for help. John "Portugee" Phillips made the 236-mile ride in four nights of hard riding, struggling through subzero temperatures and blinding blizzards and traveling at night to avoid Indian attacks. In a scene straight out of a Hollywood movie, Phillips staggered into a gala Christmas-night ball with the stunning news. His exhausted horse collapsed and died from pneumonia two weeks later. Because of bad weather, help did not reach Fort Phil Kearny for another two weeks, but the feared Indian attacks

never came. Colonel Carrington was reassigned to Fort McPherson in Nebraska—accidentally shooting himself in the foot on the way out—and it took many years to clear his name of the Fetterman disaster.

WAGON BOX FIGHT

Fearful of another attack, soldiers removed running gear from the woodcutter's wagons (used to haul logs for the fort), creating a makeshift fortress from the wagon boxes. They filled these boxes with ammunition and supplies in case of attack, and waited. The attack came on August 2, 1867, when Red Cloud's 3,000 warriors suddenly surrounded 32 woodchoppers and soldiers led by Capt. James Powell. This time the tables were turned. Unbeknown to Red Cloud, the soldiers were armed with new Springfield rifles that could fire up to 20 rounds per minute. Expecting the soldiers to take time to reload, Red Cloud sent waves of men, only to meet withering gunfire each time. Finally, after six hours of this devastation, soldiers from Fort Phil Kearny arrived with their howitzer and sent the Sioux fleeing. Four soldiers died in the Wagon Box Fight, while estimates of Indian casualties range from six to more than a thousand—Sioux warriors removed their dead after a battle, making it impossible to know how many had been killed.

THE FIGHTING ENDS

By late 1867, public sentiment had turned against the army's invasion of Sioux country, and the Bozeman Trail had become an anachronism, with miners heading to Montana via steamboat up the Missouri River. Besides, the Union Pacific Railroad was well on its way across Wyoming, and the diversion was no longer needed. (Some historians believe this was the primary reason for the forts being built in the first place.) In 1868, the three Bozeman Trail forts were all abandoned. As the soldiers left Fort Phil Kearny, they turned back to see smoke on the horizon. The Sioux were burning it to the ground. Thus ended, at least temporarily, one of the most senseless conflicts in American history. Red Cloud finally returned to Fort Laramie to sign the treaty, having (he thought) forced the government to leave Powder River to the Sioux. Actually the treaty was ambiguous and contradictory, giving them rights to hunt buffalo on the Powder River but saying they would have to live on reservations in Dakota Territory. Six years later, the country would again boil over when another gold rush—this time in the Black Hills—brought General Custer north to fight the Sioux.

EXPLORING THE BOZEMAN TRAIL

The site of **Fort Phil Kearny** is now a National Historic Landmark and is managed by the Wyoming Department of Parks and Cultural Resources. The fort is 17 miles north of Buffalo and 21 miles south of Sheridan off I-90 (take exit 44). Day use at the fort costs $2 for nonresident adults, $1 for Wyoming residents; free for youths under 18. The fort is long gone—it was, after all, burned to the ground by the Indians—but a reconstruction project completed in 2000 includes two corner walls of the stockade and blockhouses on the original site. Also here is a CCC cabin from the 1930s that replicates a noncommissioned officer's room. Signs note former building locations, the cemetery, and the Bozeman Trail.

A fine small **museum** is open daily 8 A.M.–6 P.M. from mid-May through September, and Wednesday–Sunday noon–4 P.M.

October to mid-May. Inside, find an excellent model of the fort, videos about the Bozeman Trail and Fort Phil Kearny, and displays on Indian life. Get more information on the fort at 307/684-7629 or 307/684-7687, www.phil kearny.vcn.com. Another excellent website, www.bozemantrail.org, is maintained by the Frontier Heritage Alliance.

The third weekend of June brings **Bozeman Trail Days** to Fort Phil Kearny, with archaeological tours of the fort and nearby battlegrounds, a living-history encampment, gold panning, and more.

OTHER BOZEMAN TRAIL SIGHTS

Ruts from the Bozeman Trail are still visible along much of its path, and the battle sites are all marked with monuments of various sorts. Portugee Phillips's ride is noted by a pyramid-shaped memorial not far from Fort Phil Kearny. Get to the site of the **Wagon Box Fight** by heading one mile south from Story (good road) or driving northwest from Fort Phil Kearny on a narrow, winding gravel road.

The **Fetterman Fight** is marked by a stone obelisk atop the hill where the final stand was made. Informative plaques provide a full description of events leading up to the battle and its consequences, and a one-mile interpretive trail crosses the battlefield. Access is only from the south; the north section of the road is blocked by a landslide.

Buffalo

At the base of the Big Horn Mountains, Buffalo (pop. 3,900) is one of those delightful small towns that seem to define rural America. Tourists and locals relax on summer mornings along Clear Creek, while dogs sit in the back of pickup trucks parked on Main Street. Despite the fact that Buffalo's Main Street curves along an old bison trail, the town got its name from Buffalo, New York—the name was picked out of a hat.

Buffalo—the Johnson County seat—is primarily a government, ranching, and tourism center for the area, with coalbed methane becoming an increasingly important source of jobs (and of royalty income for local ranchers). The county constitutes the heart of sheep ranching in Wyoming, and some of these flocks are still tended by Basque shepherds. Longtime residents of Basque heritage are now pillars of the local community.

HISTORY

During Gen. George Crook's 1876 campaign against the Sioux, he had Capt. Edwin Pollock build a supply center along the Powder River. Originally called Cantonment Reno, it was later renamed **Fort McKinney,** after Lt. John A. McKinney, who had been killed in the Dull Knife Battle. In 1878, Fort McKinney was moved 40 miles north to where the Bozeman Trail crossed Clear Creek. Gradually the new fort took shape, not as one of the stockade-walled structures generally thought of, but rather as a collection of barracks, mess halls, and two-story houses with board-and-batten exteriors. Soldiers marched from here to South Dakota's Pine Ridge Reservation to put down the Ghost Dance uprising in 1890. More than 150 Sioux and 25 soldiers died at Wounded Knee, the last major battle between Indians and whites in North America.

The establishment of Fort McKinney created an immediate market for all sorts of businesses. Carpenters, blacksmiths, farmers, loggers, merchants, bartenders, and prostitutes arrived and quickly established the town of Buffalo two

miles downstream. By 1883, a Cheyenne newspaper noted a dozen saloons and no churches. "Houses of dissipation" seemed more numerous than any other establishment. Much of the barley harvested locally went to supply two breweries. Buffalo had become the largest town in the northern part of Wyoming. This boom suddenly ended in 1894, when the army declared Fort McKinney excess property and abandoned it. The buildings became the Wyoming Soldiers' and Sailors' Home in 1903 and now house the Veterans' Home of Wyoming. It is still one of the county's largest employers.

After World War II, oil and gas exploration and development of the region's vast coal deposits turned Buffalo into an energy center. Today the coal resources of Johnson County remain essentially undeveloped, but substantial amounts of oil and gas are produced. Downtown Buffalo has undergone a facelift in recent years as new tourist-oriented businesses move in selling gifts, artwork, antiques, espresso, fly-fishing gear, upscale kids' clothing, and health food.

SIGHTS

Jim Gatchell Memorial Museum

The Powder River Basin's rich history comes to life in this impressive collection, one of the finest small museums in the American West. The focus is on life in the 19th century, when a rugged mix of Indians, soldiers, miners, homesteaders, wealthy cattlemen, and outlaws brought turmoil to this land. Historic artifacts were gathered by druggist Theodore James Gatchell form the core of a collection of some 15,000 articles. The museum now fills two downtown buildings, along with an attached carriage house.

Displayed in the carriage house are several historic wagons, including the de rigueur sheepherder's wagon and chuck wagon. The front (annex) building contains historic photos, a model of Fort Phil Kearny, two videos about Bomber Mountain, and traveling exhibits. Inside the main building are two floors; downstairs is the standard

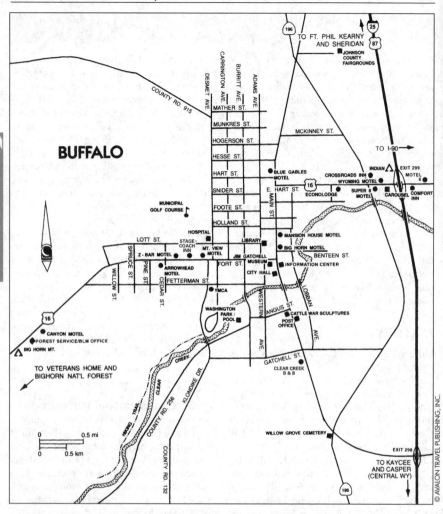

BUFFALO

TO FT. PHIL KEARNY AND SHERIDAN

JOHNSON COUNTY FAIRGROUNDS

TO I-90 →

INDIAN

EXIT 299

CARRINGTON AVE.
BURRITT AVE.
ADAMS AVE.
DESMET AVE.

COUNTY RD. 915

MATHER ST.
MUNKRES ST.
HOGERSON ST.
HESSE ST.
HART ST.
SNIDER ST.
FOOTE ST.
HOLLAND ST.

McKINNEY ST.

BLUE GABLES MOTEL

CROSSROADS INN
WYOMING MOTEL

MOTEL 6

E. HART ST.
ECONOLODGE
SUPER 8 MOTEL
CAROUSEL
COMFORT INN

MUNICIPAL GOLF COURSE

LOTT ST.

HOSPITAL
STAGE-COACH INN
MT. VIEW MOTEL

LIBRARY
MANSION HOUSE MOTEL
BIG HORN MOTEL
BENTEEN ST.

Z - BAR MOTEL
SPRUCE ST.
PINE ST.
CEDAR ST.

ARROWHEAD MOTEL
FETTERMAN ST.

FORT ST.

JIM GATCHELL MUSEUM
CITY HALL
INFORMATION CENTER

YMCA

WILLOW ST.

WASHINGTON PARK / POOL

WESTERN AVE.
ANGUS ST.
LOBBAN AVE.

CATTLE WAR SCULPTURES
POST OFFICE

16

CANYON MOTEL
FOREST SERVICE/BLM OFFICE
BIG HORN MT.

TO VETERANS HOME AND BIGHORN NAT'L FOREST

CLEAR CREEK

PIKING TRAIL

COUNTY RD. 256

KLONDIKE DR.

COUNTY RD. 132

GATCHELL ST.
CLEAR CREEK B & B

WILLOW GROVE CEMETERY

EXIT 298

TO KAYCEE AND CASPER (CENTRAL WY)

0   0.5 mi
0   0.5 km

© AVALON TRAVEL PUBLISHING, INC.

collection of old homestead and pioneer artifacts, along with walk-through re-creations of the past. Upstairs is a treasure trove of unusual items, including one of the largest collections of Indian artifacts in Wyoming. Featured are detailed dioramas and displays of items found at the sites of various local battles, including the Wagon Box Fight, the Johnson County War, and the Fetterman Fight. Most touching is the flattened horn of bugler Adolph Metzger, one of the last to die at the

Fetterman Fight. The note here says his body was the only one the Indians did not mutilate after the massacre but instead covered it with a buffalo robe out of respect for his valor. Other stories say that after trying to fight off the warriors with his hands and bugle, he was taken captive and tortured to death at the Sioux camp.

Scattered around the room are other surprises: an extensive photographic exhibit on the Powder River, a pair of Cheyenne medicine rattles used in the Dance of Victory after Custer's defeat at Little Big Horn, an arrowhead that belonged to Red Cloud, a cartridge belt made by mountain man Jim Bridger, along with hired gunman Tom Horn's spurs and a bridle he braided while awaiting execution. Ask the folks at the museum to point out a rifle probably used by the cavalry at Little Big Horn and a shell from Custer's handgun. Look around and you'll find even more surprises at this impressive small museum.

The Jim Gatchell Museum is downtown on the corner of Main and Fort streets, 307/684-9331, www.jimgatchell.com; $4 adults, $2 ages 6–16, free for younger kids. A gift shop sells historical books, old Wyoming license plates, and other items. The museum is open daily 8 A.M.–7 P.M. from Memorial Day to Labor Day (closed Fourth of July) and has reduced hours in the spring and fall. It's closed January–March, but you can call for an appointment or ask across the street at the chamber of commerce.

Occidental Hotel

Completed in 1910, the Occidental Hotel at 10 N. Main Street was the place where Owen Wister's Virginian "got his man." Over the years many famous people walked through these doors, including Teddy Roosevelt, Herbert Hoover, Calvin Coolidge, Buffalo Bill Cody, Butch Cassidy, and Calamity Jane. In later years it was a residential hotel before closing in 1985. The owners of Zoobooks (a children's series) bought the dilapidated building in the late 1990s and proceeded to lovingly return the structure to its glory days. Many of the original fixtures and other items were returned, including the billiard table, stained glass, tin ceilings, light fixtures, piano, and back bar. Today the Occidental is operated as a combination museum, hotel, restaurant, and saloon. Brochures provide self-guided tours, and dozens of historical photos line the walls. The museum portion is open Monday–Saturday 9 A.M.–8 P.M. June to mid-September, and Tuesday–Saturday 10 A.M.–4 P.M. the rest of the year. Get details at 307/684-0451, www.occidentalwyoming.com.

Several other interesting structures line Main Street; pick up a walking-tour brochure of Buffalo's other historic buildings from the chamber of commerce.

Petrified Forest

One of the more unusual local sights is a petrified forest on BLM land seven miles south of Buffalo. Take the Red Hills exit from I-90 and follow the road another seven miles to Dry Creek Petrified Forest. An easy three-quarter-mile trail loops through the hot sagebrush country, and markers along the way describe the geological history. Some 60 million years ago, this was a swampy plain dominated by towering metasequoia trees. You can still count the growth rings on the petrified stumps, some of which are more than four feet in diameter and 60 million years old.

Other Sights

Two bronze sculptures occupy a small park across the street from First National Bank on S. Main Street. Created by local sculptor D. Michael Thomas, they represent combatants in the Johnson County War of 1892. The Johnson County War helped dissuade the Chicago, Burlington, and Quincy Railroad from coming through Buffalo, and for many years Buffalo remained America's largest inland city without a railway. Eventually a spur line was built, connecting Buffalo to Clearmont. Locals called it BC&BM (Buffalo-Clearmont and Back, Maybe) but even it was abandoned in 1946 because of competition from trucking companies. Wyoming Railroad's **Engine 105** now rusts in the city park.

Children (and those who never really grew up) will love the antique **Carousel Park,** 307/684-7033, www.bozemancrossing.com, on the east end of town behind Col. Bozeman's Restaurant. This is the only carousel in Wyoming and is open daily Memorial Day to Labor Day for just $1.50 per ride. It includes a dozen custom-carved Wyoming bucking horses. Also here is a 1936 Ferris wheel and a mini-golf course.

Willow Grove Cemetery, on the south end of town, is an interesting place to explore. Here you will find the graves of rustlers Nate Champion

THE JOHNSON COUNTY WAR

Wyoming's history is a story of constant conflict—between emigrants and Indians, Chinese and white miners, big ranchers and homesteaders, sheepherders and cattlemen. The Powder River has seen more than its share of confrontations; one of the most notorious was the so-called Johnson County War of 1892, the setting for the 1980 box-office megaflop *Heaven's Gate*.

Barons and Grangers

The first white settlers in the Powder River Basin were the "cattle barons," men who owned enormous herds of cattle but who generally resided on the land only part of the year. During the 1880s, more and more homesteaders ("grangers") began to settle here, fencing their spreads and gradually forcing the large cow outfits onto less and less land. The barons tried to force homesteaders off the land, and several Johnson County grangers were found face-down in gullies, shot in the back. Homesteaders retaliated by appropriating cattle that wandered onto their land—and outlaws made off with other stock.

As rustling increased along the Powder River, the big ranchers found little sympathy in nearby Buffalo, the largest town north of the Platte River. Local juries, either sympathetic with or

intimidated by cattle rustlers, failed to convict men who were caught, and even the Buffalo sheriff, "Red" Angus, was accused of being in cahoots with rustlers. The cattle barons feared for their lives. The small ranchers and homesteaders in Buffalo were soon openly at odds with the absentee cattle barons based in the largest town south of the Platte—Cheyenne.

The Invasion

In 1892, the small Johnson County ranchers organized their own roundup, an action that proved too much for the powerful Wyoming Stock Growers Association. In a secret meeting, the association proposed a military coup d'état. On April 6, two days after the association's annual meeting in Cheyenne, a train headed for Douglas with 25 hired Texas gunmen (mostly ex-sheriffs and ex-U.S. marshals) and an equal number of Wyoming men. With them they carried a hit list of 70 suspected rustlers. Cutting the telegraph lines to keep advance word from reaching folks in Johnson County, and traveling in darkened railway cars, the "Invaders" headed north, stopping the train near Casper and continuing on horseback.

They first came to the KC Ranch—actually just a couple of cabins—and discovered two of the most

and Nick Ray, Sheriff "Red" Angus, homesteader John Tisdale, and others involved in the Johnson County War. The chamber of commerce has a little map of the gravesites.

Injured or aged veterans live on the grounds of the **Wyoming Veterans' Home** (old Fort McKinney), two miles west of Buffalo on U.S. Hwy. 16. Of the original fort, only an old cavalry stable and the post hospital building are still standing. Check in at the office (307/684-5511) before sightseeing.

ACCOMMODATIONS

You'll discover plenty of comfortable, exceptionally clean, and friendly motels to choose from in Buffalo, but it's a good idea to reserve well ahead for the midsummer, when tourists flood the area. Motel prices may rise precipi-

tously during the peak summer season, and you may have to pay $80 or more per night.

Under $50

Canyon Motel, 997 Fort St., 307/684-2957 or 800/231-0742, has some of the least expensive local rooms: $30–48 s or $45–60 d, with kitchenettes and two-bedroom units with full kitchens available. **Arrowhead Motel,** 749 Fort St., 307/684-9453, has rooms for $32–45 s or $45–60 d; kitchenettes are $5 extra.

Stagecoach Inn, 733 Fort St., 307/684-0713, has four motel rooms next to the restaurant of the same name. Rates are $35–40 s or d, and one room ($55 for up to four people) has a full kitchen. **Z-Bar Motel,** 626 Fort St., 307/684-5535 or 888/313-1227, www.zbar-motel.com, features very nice log cabins for

notorious rustlers, Nate Champion and Nick Ray, holed up inside. In the daylong shoot-out that followed, Ray died quickly, but Champion managed to hold off the Invaders until dusk, when they finally torched the cabin and shot him as he ran for safety. A bloodstained diary found on Champion described his last hours. It ended: "Shooting again. I think they will fire the house this time. It's not night yet. The house is all fired. Goodbye, boys, if I never see you again. Nathan D. Champion."

After this initial success, the Invaders headed on to the friendly TA Ranch, 30 miles north, to rest up for their planned siege of Buffalo. But word got out, and the Invaders suddenly found themselves under attack by a mob of 200 well-armed grangers and rustlers led by Sheriff Red Angus (who was on the hit list). In the shoot-out that followed, two Texans died. The tables had been turned, and the desperate Invaders faced almost certain annihilation. Meanwhile, word had gotten out to acting governor Amos W. Barber (a supporter of the Invaders), who cabled President Harrison for help. Troops from nearby Fort McKinney arrived before the townsfolk could attack with their tanklike wagon and dynamite bombs. Newspapers around the nation castigated the cattle barons for their ef-

frontery; the *Laramie Sentinel* noted, "of all the fool things the stock association ever did this takes the cake."

Justice Denied

The events that followed made a mockery of the legal system. After being rescued by army troops, the Invaders were taken to Cheyenne to stand trial. Not surprisingly, two trappers who had happened on the raid at the KC Ranch mysteriously disappeared until the trial was over, leaving no witnesses for the prosecution. Everyone pleaded not guilty, but when the judge discovered that Johnson County was unable to pay for the prisoners' room and board, he ordered them all released on their own recognizance. After being paid by the cattle barons, the hired Texas gunmen immediately skipped town, never to be seen again. The Wyoming men involved in the raid were released when Johnson County had no more money to prosecute. Many of Wyoming's most prominent citizens, including Governor Barber and Senators Carey and Warren, would later be implicated as supporters of the raid. Johnson County would take years to settle down after the battles of 1892, and for a while the big cattlemen lived in fear for their lives.

$45 s or $49–54 d, with fridges in all; cabins with kitchenettes are $6 extra.

$50 and Up

Guests at **Historic Mansion House Inn,** 313 N. Main St., 307/684-2218 or 888/455-9202, www.mansionhouseinn.com, can stay in either a century-old home or newer motel units (some with fridges). Rates are $45 s or $65–70 d, including an indoor hot tub and continental breakfast. **Big Horn Motel,** 209 N. Main St., 307/684-7822 or 800/936-7822, has nicely maintained rooms and suites for $48–62 s or $54–76 d.

It's hard not to use the word cute for the clean and well-maintained log cabins at **Blue Gables Motel,** on the north side of town at 662 N. Main St., 307/684-2574 or 800/684-2574, www.blue-gables.com. Rates are $50 s or $60 d, and some

cabins contain fridges and microwaves. No phones are provided in the rooms, but the motel does have a heated outdoor pool. Also on the premises is a comfortable two-bedroom home with full kitchen, and space for eight folks at $150.

You'll also find cozy modern cabins at the clean and friendly **Mountain View Motel and Campground,** 585 Fort St., 307/684-2881, www.buffalowyoming/mtnview. Cabins go for $45–59 s or d. Buffalo's newest place to stay is **Motel 6,** 100 Flat Iron Dr., 307/684-7000 or 800/466-8356, www.motel6.com, where rooms are a surprisingly steep $70 s or $76 d.

Wyoming Motel, U.S. Hwy. 16 at I-25, 307/684-5505 or 800/666-5505, www.buffalowyoming.com/wyomotel, is a comfortable and modern place with a heated outdoor pool (with slides) and an indoor hot tub. Rates are

$71 for one queen bed, or $87 for two beds; some rooms have fridges and microwaves. An eight-person family unit with kitchen is $97. **Super 8 Motel,** U.S. Hwy. 16 at I-25, 307/684-2531 or 800/800-8000, www.bozemancrossing.com, has standard rooms for $74–85 s or d, plus an abundance of attractions for kids that include a carousel, mini golf, and ferris wheel.

Comfort Inn, 65 U.S. Hwy. 16 East, 307/684-9564 or 800/228-5150, www.comfortinn.com, charges $95–125 s or d; amenities include an indoor hot tub and continental breakfast. The renovated **Best Western Crossroads Inn,** 75 North Bypass, 307/684-2256 or 800/528-1234, www.bestwestern.com/crossroadsinn, charges $94 s or $114 d and features an unheated outdoor pool and gazebo-enclosed hot tub. Some rooms contain fridges and microwaves.

Buffalo's most historic lodging option is the **Occidental Hotel,** 10 N. Main St., 307/684-0451, www.occidentalwyoming.com. See Sights for details on this famous spot. The old rooms have been combined to create seven comfortable Victorian-style suites, the largest of which has three rooms and a king bed for $165 d. Other suites are $100–155 d. Downstairs is a classy bar and restaurant.

Other Options

For homey and historic lodging, stay at **Clear Creek B&B,** 330 S. Main St., 307/684-2317 or 888/865-6789, www.clearcreekbb.com, an attractive 1883 home with a wraparound porch and stone fireplace. Four guest rooms are available: two share a bath and cost $65, and the other two have private baths and run $85 d. A filling breakfast is included, and kids older than 10 are welcome.

Dry Creek Guest House, 307/684-7433, is a spacious and modern log cabin ($100 d) two miles east of town. There's a fine view of the Big Horn Mountains from the deck, and the interior contains a kitchen and private bath.

Dude Ranches

Thirteen miles west of Buffalo on Hwy. 16, **Paradise Guest Ranch,** 307/684-7876, www.paradiseranch.com, is a long-time dude ranch with luxurious log cabins, an outdoor pool, and an indoor hot tub. In addition to the main attraction—horseback riding—the ranch has fly-fishing instruction and trips, chuck wagon cookouts and special children's camp-outs, along with adults-only weeks in September. All-inclusive weekly summertime rates are $3,350 for two people. The guest ranch is open late May–September.

Another popular dude ranch is **Klondike Guest Ranch,** 307/684-2390 or 800/362-2982, www.klondikeranch.com, 15 miles southwest of Buffalo along Crazy Woman Creek. Horseback riding and fishing keep folks busy, or you can join in the ranch work and help move cattle. Guests stay in log cabins with private baths and eat in the main lodge. There's also a hot tub for end-of-the-day relaxing. All-inclusive weekly rates are $2,350 for two people.

One of the oldest dude ranches in America, **HF Bar Ranch,** 307/684-2487, www.hfbar.com, has 25 comfortably restored cabins—mostly from the 1920s and '30s—on a historic 9,000-acre ranch 15 miles northwest of Buffalo. Guests get two horseback rides per day, access to the outdoor pool, plus all three meals. The ranch also offers a strong kid's program, guided fly-fishing, exercise and yoga classes, sporting clays, weekly swing dancing, and pack trips (extra fee). All-inclusive rates are $370 for two people per day; no minimum stay, but most guests stay at least a week. There's space for 110 guests at this big and well-known ranch. The dude ranch is open June–September.

Gardner's Muddy Creek Angus is a 3,900-acre cattle and horse ranch at the base of the Big Horn Mountains west of Buffalo. Two cabins rent for $75–100 per night, with the larger one sleeping six. There's a three-night minimum stay, and horseback rides are available for an extra charge. Contact the ranch at 307/684-7797 or 800/584-5281, www.gardnersmuddycreekangus.com.

CAMPING

There's camping ($6) at **Lake DeSmet,** eight miles north of Buffalo, but the sites can get steaming hot in midsummer. It is mostly for the RV crowd but has no water or hookups. Other nearby public campgrounds ($7–10) are in Bighorn National Forest approximately 15 miles west of Buffalo on U.S. Hwy. 16.

Big Horn Mountains Campground, two miles west on U.S. Hwy. 16, 307/684-2307, www.buffalocamping.com, has an outdoor heated pool and tent spaces for $15, RV sites for $19. Showers for noncampers cost $3; open year-round (except Dec.). **Mountain View Motel and Campground,** 585 Fort St., 307/684-2881, www.buffalowyoming/mtnview, has RV campsites for $18 and tent sites for $15. Open all year. **Blue Gables Motel,** 662 N. Main St., 307/684-2574 or 800/684-2574, www.bluegables.com, has a couple of tent spaces in a fenced-off area for $15, including access to their outdoor pool.

The friendly folks at **Indian Campground,** 660 E. Hart St. (off U.S. Hwy. 16 east of town), 307/684-9601, www.indiancampground.com, charge $15 for tents or $23 for RVs in shady spots. Simple camping cabins are $31. Showers for noncampers run $5. It's open early April–October.

Farther out on U.S. Hwy. 16 is **Deer Park Campground,** 307/684-5722 or 800/222-9960, www.deerparkrv.com, where sites cost $16 for tents or $23–27 for RVs. They have an outdoor heated pool and hot tub, plus a pleasant creekside trail. Nightly ice-cream socials are a summertime favorite. Open May–Sept.

Also along U.S. Hwy. 16 east of town, the **Buffalo KOA,** 307/684-5423 or 800/562-5403, www.koa.com, has tent sites for $17–23, RV spaces for $22–36, teepees for $26, and basic "kamping kabins" for $44–50 d. Open mid-April to mid-October, it boasts an outdoor heated pool, a hot tub, and pancake breakfasts. **Big Horn Travel Plaza,** 207 S. Bypass Rd., 307/684-5246, has a handful of RV sites for $19.

FOOD

Despite its small size, Buffalo has several pleasant eateries.

Breakfast and Lunch

DeerField Boutique & Espresso Bar Cafe, 7 N. Main St., 307/684-2778, is a delightful spot for homemade soups, salads, sandwiches, espresso, and desserts. The decor is bright and playful, with a patio on the side for sunny days. The café sits at the back of DeerField, a boutique filled with women's clothing, trinkets, and cards.

Artworks Too and Cowgirl Coffee Cafe, 86 S. Main St., 307/684-1299, mixes art on the walls with espresso, bagels, and sinful sweets. The back deck has tables facing the mountains, and espresso drinkers can surf the web for free. Cloud Peak.net, downstairs, has computer rentals by the hour.

Tom's Main Street Diner, 41 N. Main St., 307/684-7444, is a very good place for breakfast and lunch. Several of the chains-including McDonald's, Hardee's, Pizza Hut, Subway, and Taco John's—are out E. Hart St., but a better choice is **The Breadboard,** 107 E. Hart St., 307/684-2318, with decent subs on homemade bread, plus soups and spicy chili for lunch. Another good place for fast food, including excellent hickory-smoked fried chicken and ribs, is **Dash Inn,** 620 E. Hart, 307/684-7930. Downtown, **Seney's Rexall Drug,** 38 S. Main St., 307/684-7182, has an old-fashioned soda fountain offering thick shakes and malts.

Dinner

The **Occidental Hotel,** 10 N. Main St., 307/684-0451, www.occidentalwyoming.com, serves a steak and seafood menu, with dinners year-round. In summer, they expand to lunches and set up creekside tables on the deck. The classic saloon here is one of the few nonsmoking bars in the state. **Winchester Steak House,** 117 Hwy. 16 E., 307/684-8636, has a similar menu and a casual setting. Nightly specials, too.

A favorite of families and retirees, **Col. Bozeman's,** 675 E. Hart, 307/684-5555, serves buffalo steaks, burgers, and Mexican dishes. When folks are looking for an enjoyable evening away from town, they drive to Pines Lodge or South Fork Mountain Lodge (see Lodges Along U.S. Highway 16 in the Big Horn Mountains section).

Crossroads Inn (I-25 at Bypass Rd.) is home to both **La Corcevia,** 307/684-2256, with American and Italian specials, along with the popular **Hoot N' Owl Pub.**

POWDER RIVER

Groceries

Get groceries from two markets on the west end of town: **Rocky Mountain Fresh Food IGA,** 440 Fort St., 307/684-2239, and **DJ's Thriftway,** 895 Fort St., 307/684-2518.

ENTERTAINMENT

Buffalo has three places to go for live country-and-western tunes on weekends: **Hoot N' Owl Pub** at the Best Western Crossroads Inn, 75 North Bypass, 307/684-2256; **The White Buffalo,** U.S. Hwy. 16 E, 307/684-0101; and the **Century Club,** 14 S. Main St., 307/684-2821. Roll balls down the lanes at **Buffalo Bowl,** 90 S. Cedar St., 307/684-2613.

EVENTS

Powder River Ranch Rodeo in June features a unique rodeo in which teams rather than individuals compete. Come to Buffalo in late June for a **Horseshoe Tournament.** The Jim Gatchell Museum's **Living History Day** in July includes mountain men, horse-drawn wagons, quilting, saddlemaking, Basque dancing, old-time cooking, and more.

All Girls Rodeos take place throughout the summer at the county fairgrounds. Every Wednesday night mid-June through August, the **Lions Club Rodeo,** has events at the fairgrounds; call 307/684-5649.

End the summer with a Labor Day weekend country-and-western music **Invitational Jam Session** at the fairgrounds. Buffalo's biggest annual event is the **Johnson County Fair and Rodeo,** held in early August; call 307/684-7357 for details. A **Christmas Parade** comes to town the first Saturday of December.

RECREATION

The free **outdoor swimming pool** in Washington Park is one of the largest in the Rocky Mountains, stretching 120 meters by 80 meters. It has swimming lanes, two diving boards, a slide, and a wading pool for tots. Open daily 11 A.M.–6 P.M. during summer, this is a great place to play on a hot day. Inside the modern **YMCA,** 101 Klondike Dr., 307/684-9558, you'll find a pool, hot tub, and weight room, along with racquetball and handball courts.

Buffalo's popular **Clear Creek Trail System** makes for a delightful afternoon stroll or bike ride. It follows the creek for 11 miles and is paved to the edge of town, reaching all the way to the foot of the Big Horn Mountains.

Rent bikes from **Indian Campground,** on U.S. Hwy. 16 east of town, 307/684-9601. Three miles out of town, **Triple Three Ranch,** 307/684-2832, www.triplethreeranch.com, offers horseback rides. Trail rides are also available from Pines Lodge and South Fork Mountain Lodge (see Lodges Along U.S. Highway 16 in the Big Horn Mountains section).

The 18-hole **Buffalo Golf Course,** on the northwest edge of town, 307/684-5266, is one of the finest in Wyoming. One hole features a 90-foot vertical drop over 140 yards.

Buffalo has two good fishing shops: **Just Gone Fishing,** 777 Fort St., 307/684-2755, and **The Sports Lure,** 66 S. Main St., 307/684-7682 or 800/684-7682, www.sportslure.com. The latter also sells (and rents) hiking, skiing, mountain-biking, and backpacking gear. See Lake DeSmet for other fishing options.

SHOPPING

Get books on Wyoming from **The Office,** 33 N. Main St., 307/684-2215 or 800/359-0209, or from the Jim Gatchell Museum gift shop.

Several local art galleries sell standard Western art prints, but much more distinctive is **Margo's Pottery,** 1 N. Main St., 307/684-9406, where you'll find all sorts of playful earthenware from nationally known potters. Also sold here are blown glass pieces, jewelry, and other works. The shop opens into the adjacent Deerfield Boutique and Espresso Bar Cafe. Also worth a visit are **Amish Furnishings,** 76 S. Main St., 307/684-2594, with beautiful furniture from Pennsylvania; and **Powder River Traders,** 17 N. Main St., 307/684-7337, for pelts, coats, and other furry items sure to make trapping opponent's blood boil.

INFORMATION AND SERVICES

The **Buffalo Chamber of Commerce** office, 55 N. Main St., 307/684-5544 or 800/227-5122, www.buffalowyo.com, is open Monday–Friday 8 A.M.–6 P.M. and Saturday–Sunday 10 A.M.–4 P.M. June–August, and Monday–Friday 8 A.M.–5 P.M. the rest of the year.

The **Johnson County Public Library** is at the intersection of Adams and Lott Sts., 307/684-5546 or 800/661-7071, and has Internet access. Rent computer time at **CloudPeak.net,** 86 S. Main St., 307/684-2225.

Get information on Bighorn National Forest from the **Powder River Ranger District,** 1425 Fort St., 307/684-1100, www.fs.fed.us/r2/bighorn. The BLM's **Buffalo Resource Field Office,** is in the same building and has the same phone number, www.wy.blm.gov.

Wash clothes at **Tanner's Coin Laundry,** 334 N. Main St., 307/684-2205, and at **Squeeky Kleen,** 631 E. Hart, 307/684-9666.

TRANSPORTATION

Powder River Transportation/Coach USA, 307/682-0960 or 800/442-3682, connects Buffalo with the rest of northern and eastern Wyoming, with additional service to Billings, Denver, and Rapid City. Buses stop at Just Gone Fishing, 777 Fort Street.

Rent cars from **Northside Car Sales** (Avis), north of Buffalo, 307/684-5136 or 800/831-2847, www.avis.com. The airport in Buffalo does not have scheduled service, so it came as quite a surprise one day in 1979 when a Western Airlines 737 carrying 94 passengers landed in Buffalo instead of Sheridan. Mistakes were made.

Buffalo Vicinity

LAKE DeSMET

Eight miles north of Buffalo is Lake DeSmet, a deep natural lake surrounded by open range country. A stone **monument** to the Belgian Jesuit missionary Father Pierre Jean DeSmet (1801–1873) stands along the western shore. DeSmet was one of the few 19th-century men who maintained lifelong friendships with both Indians and whites. The Plains Indians called him "Blackrobe" and trusted him with various peacemaking roles at Fort Laramie. But the Indians viewed the lake named for DeSmet with suspicion, as did early settlers, who told of "Smetty the sea monster" who emerged at night from the seemingly bottomless body of water. When first found by DeSmet in 1851, it was a salt lake—the second-largest in the West (after Great Salt Lake)—but dams and dikes have increased its size and decreased its salinity.

Today Lake DeSmet is a popular place for local boaters and windsurfers. Try your luck at catching one of the mermaids, but you're more likely to pull in a big rainbow trout. Also here

are brown trout, crappie, yellow perch, and rock bass. **Lake DeSmet Fishing Derby** is held each Memorial Day weekend and awards more than $55,000 in prizes and cash; call 307/684-2755. Just north of the lake is a bed of coal that, in some places, is more than 200 feet thick—second in thickness only to one in Manchuria. No wonder Chevron-Texaco owns most of the land around Lake DeSmet!

Practicalities

You'll find **camping** ($6) at the Lake DeSmet recreation area along the water. The area has volleyball nets, picnic tables, and outhouses but no shade or drinking water. **Lake Stop Resort,** 307/684-9051, www.lonewolfoutfitters.com, rents fishing boats, ski boats, and jet skis. Also here are modern cabins with bath for $49–69), along with RV hookups ($19), a heated outdoor pool, café, grocery store, and bait shop, plus skiff and personal watercraft rentals.

Angler's West, 307/684-5857 or 877/996-2626, www.anglers-west.com, guides boating and fishing trips to Lake DeSmet.

KAYCEE

The town of Kaycee (pop. 250) is named for the nearby KC Ranch and serves as a bentonite, oil, and ranching center. Drive the side roads in spring or fall and you're likely to find yourself behind huge flocks of sheep being herded into or out of the Big Horn Mountains.

Frewen Castle

When the Powder River country was opened to white settlers in the late 1870s, it quickly attracted ranchers and farmers of all types, from homesteaders trying to prove up their 160 acres to wealthy international investors. Two of the most interesting were the English brothers Moreton and Richard Frewen, relatives of Sir Winston Churchill. Coming originally to hunt buffalo, the two saw the lush Powder River area and decided to invest in cattle. Near present-day Kaycee, they erected an elaborate two-story log house, filled it with furniture and fixtures from England, and even added an incredible luxury—a telephone. Frewen Castle, as it was soon called, became the center of an enormous spread with at least 60,000 cattle.

Their kingdom attracted English hunting parties and became something of an unofficial dude ranch. (To keep their ladies in the proper spirit, the Frewens set up relay stations to bring hothouse flowers from Denver on galloping horses.) The Frewens' Powder River Cattle Company, Ltd., attracted investments from the British royal family and various lords before reality struck. The cattle did not do as well as expected, competition from surrounding ranchers and rustlers cut into profits, and the disastrous winter of 1886–1887 forced the company to the brink of bankruptcy. The Frewens and many other "cattle barons" never really recovered. Today almost nothing remains of Frewen Castle.

Sights

Kaycee's free **Hoofprints of the Past Museum,** 307/738-2381, is open Monday–Saturday 9 A.M.–5 P.M. and Sunday 1–5 P.M. Memorial Day to October, and Monday–Saturday 2–5 P.M. and Sunday 1–5 P.M. from Labor Day to October. It's closed November to Memorial Day. Inside is a nice collection of items from early settlers, outlaws, and the cattle wars. Look for the wooden potato planter. The museum offers historical tours of the region on the third Saturday of June.

Just south of Kaycee, a marker describes the killing of rustlers Nate Champion and Nick Ray in the Johnson County War of 1892. The old **KC Ranch house,** where the two were killed by the Invaders, stood here. See Accommodations for the TA Ranch, where the Invaders holed up after raiding the KC Ranch.

Ten miles east of Kaycee on State Hwy. 192 is a marker noting the first buildings in northern Wyoming, constructed in 1834 by Portuguese trapper Antonio Montero. The log stockade and trading post (known as the **Portuguese Houses**) were abandoned around 1839, and nothing remains on the site. The site of old **Fort Reno** (1865–1868) is in the same general vicinity; ask in Kaycee for directions. A monument marks the place, and various remains are still present from this little-known fort.

Fans of country music will know that singer Chris LeDoux (www.chrisledoux.com) has a sheep ranch in the vicinity of Kaycee. LeDoux was a rodeo cowboy for many years, winning the 1976 PRCA world championship in bareback riding. He used his musical abilities to pay for his rodeo travels, and today he sings cowboy songs with a measure of authenticity lacking in other musicians. He still plays the rodeo circuit with his band, but he's also gained a national following.

Accommodations

Two older places have basic rooms in "downtown" Kaycee, both without phones: **Cassidy Inn Motel,** 307/738-2250, for $33 s or $40 d; and **Siesta Motel,** 307/738-2291, for $25 s or $31 d. The newest place to stay is just west of town at the **Kaycee Motel,** 307/738-2213, next to the Sinclair station. The seven-unit motel runs $40 s or d, or $50 for up to four people, but they're often booked. The station also contains an ATM and showers ($6). Just across the road is **Powder River RV Park,** 307/738-2233, offering RV sites with hookups for $15, and simple cab-

ranch signs near Kaycee

ins for $28. They have a second location on the south end of Kaycee. You'll find **free camping** at the Kaycee town park.

Ranches

Famous **TA Ranch,** 307/684-5833 or 800/368-7398, www.taranch.com, is approximately 30 miles north of Kaycee along State Hwy. 87. Bullet holes are still visible in many of the wonderful old ranch buildings, which are being preserved for posterity. Still a working cattle ranch covering 8,200 acres, the TA takes in guests April–October and has a capacity of 24 people. The ranch specializes in horseback rides, cattle drives, and fly-fishing, but also offers tours to the Hole-in-the-Wall area and other historic sites. All-inclusive weekly rates are $2,200 for two people.

Willow Creek Ranch at Hole-in-the-Wall, 307/738-2294, www.willowcreekranch.com, is 35 miles southwest of Kaycee and offers one of the most authentic ranch experiences in Wyoming. The ranch covers 57,000 beautiful and remote acres in the Red Wall country made famous by the Hole-in-the-Wall gang. Guests take part in ranch activities, including branding and cattle drives. Photography, birdwatching,

fishing, and hunting are other popular activities, along with the all-time favorite, kicking back and relaxing. Established in 1882, this working cattle and sheep ranch has space for a maximum of 12 guests, who stay in the renovated 1890 bunkhouse. In addition, two private cabins eight miles away offer the ultimate in solitude. The ranch is a great place to explore, with lots of outlaw history, plus Indian petroglyphs and tepee rings. All-inclusive nightly rates are $235 per person per day, and they suggest that you stay at least two nights because of the remote location; you'll certainly want to spend more time here. Open May to mid-Oct.

Greenhorn Ranch B&B, 307/738-2548, is a furnished homestead house 21 miles west of Kaycee out Barnum Road. Located on a working cattle ranch near the Red Wall, the house enjoys a grand setting. The home contains three bedrooms, a full bathroom, large kitchen, laundry room, screened sunroom, and living room with a piano and woodstove. Breakfast is included; call for rates.

Other Practicalities

Kaycee has two bars and three restaurants serving all-American meals. You won't go wrong at

POWDER RIVER

THE WILD BUNCH

Glorified in the 1969 Oscar-winning film *Butch Cassidy and the Sundance Kid,* the Wild Bunch is one of the most famous of all Western outlaw gangs. The Wild Bunch consisted of a constantly changing membership held together by two friends, Robert Parker ("Butch Cassidy") and Harry Longabaugh (the "Sundance Kid"). In 1884, Parker, then a teenager, met up with a local ranch hand and part-time cattle rustler named Mike Cassidy. Rebelling against a strict Mormon upbringing, Parker picked up a few of the master's tricks before getting caught by the law and told to move on. But when he left Utah for Colorado and Wyoming, he took with him his mentor's name, Cassidy. (The "Butch" apparently came later, when he worked in several Rock Springs butcher shops.) Linking up with other outlaws, Cassidy held up the San Miguel Valley Bank of Telluride and then drifted back to horse stealing in Wyoming. Several years later, those horses landed him in the Wyoming State Prison in Laramie. Cassidy was pardoned by the governor after 18 months, reportedly after agreeing not to pursue that line of work in Wyoming anymore. Other places, however, were fair game.

The Gang

If anything, prison made Cassidy more determined than ever to outwit the lawmen. Joining up with Longabaugh (who picked up his Sundance Kid sobriquet while serving time in the Sundance, Wyoming, jail for horse thievery) and Harvey Logan, alias Kid Curry (a deadly and fearless Montana fugitive), Cassidy assembled a rogues' gallery of rustlers, drifters, killers, and wanted men soon known as the Wild Bunch. They operated from remote hidden canyons in the West, especially Brown's Park in western Colorado, Bighorn Canyon in Montana, Wyoming's Wind River Valley, and the famous Hole-in-the-Wall southwest of Buffalo, Wyoming—places where entire herds of stolen cattle could be hidden and where the finest horses could be trained for quick getaways.

The Wild Bunch achieved a measure of respect from local ranchers who bought horses and cattle at low prices and found ready workers when the outlaws needed to rest up awhile. For many, Cassidy seemed a modern-day Robin Hood, taking from the rich railroads, banks, mines, and cattle barons while leaving the small folks alone. To this day, locals in Kaycee, Wyoming, still talk fondly of the affable Butch Cassidy.

The gang's activities reached a peak in the late 1890s, with bank robberies in Utah, South Dakota, and Idaho (the latter to pay for a lawyer to clear a gang member on a murder charge). Cassidy—breaking his promise to Wyoming's governor—also led a train robbery in Wilcox, Wyoming, which netted $50,000, but only after he'd blown up the safe with 10 pounds of dynamite, sending money and banknotes in all directions. Within hours, a sheriff's posse was in hot pursuit, and in a gun battle near Casper the sheriff was killed. Somehow, the Wild Bunch managed to slip through the posse's lines for a clean getaway.

In 1900, they struck another Union Pacific train near Tipton, Wyoming (just east of Rock Springs). Amazingly, the same express messenger was present for both robberies; the first time he had refused

---

Invasion Bar Restaurant, 307/738-2211. **Kaycee Country Market** is a delightful old-fashioned place for supplies.

Events in Kaycee include the **Sheepherders Rodeo and Dog Trials** on the first weekend after the Fourth of July, and the popular **Deke Latham Memorial PRCA Rodeo** on the second weekend of September. Kaycee is the smallest town in America with its own PRCA rodeo, and visitors will be impressed; the rodeo is one of Wyoming's best.

HOLE-IN-THE-WALL COUNTRY
Outlaw Heaven

The remote country used by the Wild Bunch and other outlaws lies some 30 miles west of Kaycee. Get here by following State Hwy. 190 for 16 miles to where the pavement ends. At the road junction—maps call this Barnum, but there is no town here—a side road leads to Blue Creek Ranch (private), land once homesteaded by Butch Cassidy and the Sundance Kid. Surrounding you are gorgeous red-walled

to open the railcar door and was literally blown out with explosives. The second time the conductor persuaded him to open the door. Perhaps he knew that the safe held only $54; the train carrying $100,000 worth of gold had passed just a few hours before. Then the Wild Bunch was off to Winnemucca, Nevada, where a bank holdup netted them a cool $32,000. After a fling at Fanny Porter's Sporting House in San Antonio, the gang members bought some new hats at a Fort Worth haberdasher and, dressed as dudes, posed for the famous group portrait later used by Pinkerton detectives. Cassidy and two other gang members tried their hands once more at train robbery in 1901, taking at least $40,000 from a dynamited safe in Montana. The law was closing in, however. Of the gang members who stayed behind, all but one died a violent death. For Butch Cassidy and the Sundance Kid, the future lay in South America.

Gringos

In 1901, Butch and Sundance headed for Argentina. Accompanying them on the journey was Etta Place—a strikingly beautiful woman whom Sundance apparently met in Fanny Porter's Sporting House. (Butch later called her "a fine housekeeper, but a whore at heart.") There they settled with their ill-gotten wealth to a quiet life of ranching, traveling occasionally to Buenos Aires, where they stayed in the finest hotels and dressed in formal clothes befitting their new role as bourgeois American settlers. But even in South America, Pinkerton detectives managed to pick up their trail, and, sensing this, the three decided to try their skills in virgin territory. They robbed three banks in Argentina and a train in Bolivia before Etta Place came down with acute appendicitis. A hurried trip took the trio back to the States, but in Denver, where the operation was performed, the Sundance Kid got in trouble for shooting up his hotel room while drunk. Rather than face the law, he fled to New York, where he and Cassidy again boarded a steamer bound for Argentina. Etta remained behind.

The two outlaws now worked part-time at a Peruvian gold mine, using the work as a cover for their periodic forays into banks, trains, and stores in search of money. For many years, most believed that Butch Cassidy and the Sundance Kid died in a blaze of gunfire at a remote village on the Bolivian–Argentine border in 1909. Today, however, it appears that Cassidy escaped (and perhaps the Kid as well), using his reported death as a convenient opportunity to change his ways. According to Larry Pointer's *In Search of Butch Cassidy,* Cassidy later fought with Pancho Villa in the Mexican Revolution, met Wyatt Earp in Alaska, and settled down to running a Spokane machine shop, living under the name of William T. Phillips until his death from cancer in 1937. Several Wyoming residents, old friends of the famous outlaw, met him in Lander and Riverton on several occasions before his death. Cassidy reportedly spent considerable time in a fruitless effort to recover buried loot that he had stashed near Mary's Lake in the Wind River Mountains. Today, the Butch and Sundance legends refuse to die. Stop by the towns of Rock Springs, Lander, Laramie, Worland, Dubois, Baggs, or Kaycee, and you'll be regaled with more tales of their exploits.

canyons rising above the Middle Fork of the Powder River. Its waters provide a fine place to fish for rainbow, brook, and brown trout.

Turning right (north) leads you to the **Dull Knife Battlefield,** named for an 1876 incident. General Crook's soldiers surprised Dull Knife's band of Northern Cheyenne in this remote valley. The attack killed at least 40 Cheyenne and ended what whites viewed as a campaign of terror and which the Indians viewed as retaliation for the invasion of their last stronghold.

To reach other area sites, turn left (south) on the graded gravel road that parallels the river. Follow the road five miles, past the Bar C Ranch, and bear right at the signed 4WD side road for Outlaw Cave. Beyond the intersection, the road is really only passable in high-clearance vehicles, so you may want to walk the last two miles to the cave. The road crosses a three-quarter-mile-long stretch of prehistoric **rock cairns** and then tops a knoll where you'll find **Outlaw Cave Campground** (free but no water). Stop here for impressive views of the Hole-in-the-Wall area.

From the campground, a steep half-mile path drops 660 feet down to **Outlaw Cave,** actually two small caves used as hideouts by the Wild Bunch and other outlaws. One of the caves is little more than a depression in the rocks, but the other is room-sized. Take your fishing pole down to try for trout.

On the opposite side of the road from the campground and up another one-third mile is **Indian Rock Art Cave.** The cave (actually just a rock overhang) contains distinctive but faint Indian rock art, including a large warrior figure, bear claws, and shield designs. A major buffalo jump site (where Indians hunted buffalo by driving them over a cliff) is nearby, along with many tepee rings. The BLM office in Buffalo (307/684-1100, www.wy.blm.gov) can provide more detailed access information for the Outlaw Caves/Hole-in-the-Wall country.

Hole-in-the-Wall

The wealthy Frewen brothers who ranched here in the 19th century named this country after London's Hole-in-the-Wall Tavern. The "Hole" lies at the end of a steep "V" in the red cliffs bordering Buffalo Creek. It was accessible via a trail that cuts up the talus slope and into a narrow, funnel-shaped opening. The setting was perfect for rustling and as a hideout from the law, especially for gunmen such as Jesse James, the Logan brothers, and George "Flat Nose" Currie. Some 30–40 bandits hung out here in six log cabins, including the most fa-

mous inhabitants, the Wild Bunch of Butch Cassidy and the Sundance Kid. The cabins have collapsed over the years, and today a few chunks of foundation are the only remaining evidence of the 19th-century rustlers who were based here. The cliff was easy to defend and offered a vantage point where sentries could warn of approaching lawmen.

Hole-in-the-Wall is on public (BLM) land, but much of the surrounding land belongs to ranchers who guard their privacy closely. In addition, the unmaintained roads can turn into a quagmire when it rains and a rutted mess when the mud dries out. High-clearance vehicles are required. After more than a century, horses are still the most dependable way to reach Hole-in-the-Wall! The BLM has signed the route into Hole-in-the-Wall, and a 1.5-mile primitive trail crosses public land to the site. For access information, check with the BLM in Buffalo, 307/684-1100, www.wy.blm.gov. One of the best ways to see this area is by staying at the historic Willow Creek Ranch (described previously), where the owners will take guests in on horseback.

Both **Western Encounters,** 307/332-5434 or 800/572-1230, www.horseriders.com, and **Historic Trails West,** 307/266-4868 or 800/327-4052, www.historictrailswest.com, offer horseback trips across various parts of Wyoming, including the "Outlaw Trail" through Hole-in-the-Wall. These typically last a week and include horses, meals, equipment, and tents. In addition, the Kaycee Museum offers a **historical tour** to Hole-in-the-Wall in mid-June; call 307/738-2381 for details.

Gillette

Campbell County proclaims itself the "Energy Capital of the United States," a title gained by producing more coal and oil than any other county in Wyoming. Although oil production is in decline, coal mining continues to increase every year, and local mines shovel up an eighth of the total U.S. production of coal. In addition, the Powder River Basin has the focus of extensive coalbed methane gas development in recent years. At the center of all this is Gillette (pop. 22,000), Wyoming's fourth-largest city.

Gillette is a base for tours of nearby coal mines and coalbed methane gas projects, but it isn't otherwise known as a tourist destination. It does, however, provide a good base for exploring the wide-open spaces of northeastern Wyoming.

HISTORY

When you drive into Gillette, the sense of history permeating much of Wyoming quickly gives way to the raucous present. History is decidedly not Gillette's strong suit, even though the town is more than a century old. When you drive into Gillette, the sense of history permeating much of Wyoming quickly gives way to the raucous present. His-
When the Burlington and Missouri route to Sheridan was being planned, it was originally set to go south of the present location, but astute surveyor Edward Gillette discovered a route farther north that saved construction of 30 bridges. Initially, the new company-platted town was to be called "Donkey Town" for its proximity to Donkey Creek, but instead it was named for Gillette. (Edward Gillette later served a term in Washington as a congressman from Wyoming; however, he preferred to live in the more scenic town of Sheridan than in his namesake.) The railroad reached Gillette in 1891, and the town was incorporated the following year. It became a shipping point for local ranchers and homesteaders and grew slowly over the ensuing decades.

Gillette's oil boom began in the fall of 1967, when a drilling company hit an oil gusher that ignited an enormous fire; Firefighter Red Adair was called in to extinguish the flames. John Wayne's Hellfighters *was based on these events.*

The Present

Since the late 1960s, Gillette has ridden an enormous growth rocket, powered first by oil, then by coal, and most recently by coalbed methane. Gillette's oil boom began in the fall of 1967, when a drilling company hit an oil gusher that ignited an enormous fire. Firefighter Red Adair was called in to extinguish the flames, attracting worldwide attention. Hollywood soon followed—John Wayne's *Hellfighters* was based on these events. Other oil companies flooded the area with exploratory rigs, and almost overnight Gillette grew from a sleepy cow town into a major energy center. A frantic scramble for the almighty dollar ensued, with real-estate values quadrupling between 1966 and 1970.

Unlike the rest of Wyoming, where the oil boom of the '70s was quickly followed by the bust of the '80s and '90s, Gillette caught the coal wave just as the oil tide was heading back out to sea. With enormous reserves of low-sulfur coal throughout the surrounding countryside, Campbell County quickly became a major player on the energy scene and is now one of the most prosperous counties in Wyoming. The city's population continues to grow as coal mining, coalbed methane gas production, and the Wyodak power plant expand. Today Gillette is a prosperous version of the American dream: shopping malls, spreading suburbia, used-car lots, and fast-food joints, especially on the south end of town. Author Wallace Stegner's description of a California town could fit just as well here: "But mostly it is Main Street, Anywhere, a set used over and over in a hundred B movies, a stroboscopic image pulsing to reassure us by subliminal tricks that though we are nowhere, we are at home."

POWDER RIVER

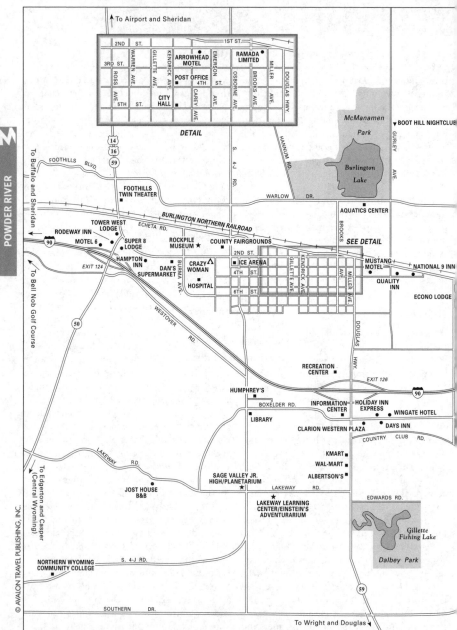

POWDER RIVER

To Airport and Sheridan

DETAIL

2ND ST.
3RD ST.
WARREN AVE.
GILLETTE AVE.
KENDRICK AVE.
ROSS AVE.
CAREY AVE.
5TH ST.
CITY HALL
POST OFFICE 4TH
ARROWHEAD MOTEL
EMERSON ST.
OSBORNE AVE.
RAMADA LIMITED
BROOKS AVE.
MILLER AVE.
DOUGLAS HWY.
1ST ST.

McManamen Park
BOOT HILL NIGHTCLUB
Burlington Lake
GURLEY AVE.

To Buffalo and Sheridan
FOOTHILLS BLVD.
14 16 59
FOOTHILLS TWIN THEATER
S. 4-J RD.
HANNUM RD.
WARLOW DR.
AQUATICS CENTER
BURLINGTON NORTHERN RAILROAD
ECHETA RD.
SEE DETAIL

90
EXIT 124
To Bell Nob Golf Course
RODEWAY INN
MOTEL 6
TOWER WEST LODGE
SUPER 8 LODGE
HAMPTON INN
DAN'S SUPERMARKET
ROCKPILE MUSEUM
BURMA AVE.
CRAZY WOMAN
HOSPITAL
ICE ARENA
2ND ST.
4TH ST.
6TH ST.
COUNTY FAIRGROUNDS
GILLETTE AVE.
KENDRICK AVE.
MILLER AVE.
BROOKS
MUSTANG MOTEL
QUALITY INN
NATIONAL 9 INN
ECONO LODGE

50
WESTOVER RD.
DOUGLAS HWY.
RECREATION CENTER
EXIT 126
90

HUMPHREY'S
BOXELDER RD.
LIBRARY
INFORMATION CENTER
HOLIDAY INN EXPRESS
WINGATE HOTEL
CLARION WESTERN PLAZA
DAYS INN
COUNTRY CLUB RD.

LAKEWAY RD.
KMART
WAL-MART
ALBERTSON'S
EDWARDS RD.

To Edgerton and Casper (Central Wyoming)
JOST HOUSE B&B
SAGE VALLEY JR. HIGH/PLANETARIUM
LAKEWAY RD.
LAKEWAY LEARNING CENTER/EINSTEIN'S ADVENTURARIUM
Gillette Fishing Lake
Dalbey Park

© AVALON TRAVEL PUBLISHING, INC.

NORTHERN WYOMING COMMUNITY COLLEGE
S. 4-J RD.
SOUTHERN DR.
59
To Wright and Douglas

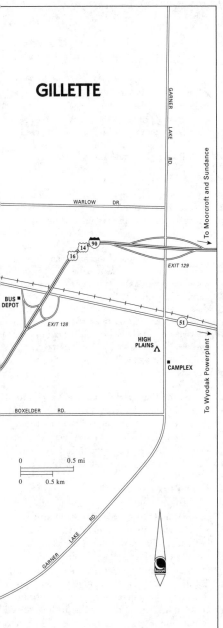

SIGHTS

History and Art

Gillette's fine **Rockpile Museum,** on U.S. Hwy. 14/16, 307/682-5723, www.gillett-tewyoming.com/rockpile, is open Monday–Saturday 9 A.M.–8 P.M. and Sunday 12:30–6:30 P.M. June–August, and Monday–Saturday 9 A.M.–5 P.M. the rest of the year. No charge. Out front is a minor local landmark for which the museum was named, along with a Burlington Northern caboose. This museum contains sheep wagons, a horse-drawn hearse—originally from Montana, its first eight customers died from gunshots—a blacksmith shop, an impressive arrowhead collection, and dozens of elaborate spurs and old rifles. A big board contains a directory of several hundred brands. Be sure to check out the floating rocks from Lake DeSmet. Out front is a tiny one-room schoolhouse that could have served double duty as a doghouse. The metal building next door houses some strange sandstone rocks.

The **Campbell County Public Library,** 2101 4-J Rd., 307/682-3223, www.ccpls.org, is one of the best in the state. Besides a large collection of books about Wyoming, it houses a remarkable collection of art, including paintings by Hans Kleiber, Gene Kloss, and Conrad Schwiering. Out front are life-size bronze statues of cowboys and horses.

Coal Mine Tours

During summer, free one-hour tours of Eagle Butte Coal Mine are offered through the Gillette Information Center. These take place on weekdays at 9 and 11 A.M. June–August. For reservations, call 307/686-0040 or 800/544-6136. The Black Thunder Mine also leads free tours; call 307/464-2201 for reservations.

Five miles east of Gillette on I-90 is the **Wyodak Mine,** where tours are available; call 307/682-3410. In existence since 1922, the mine feeds the adjacent Wyodak Power Plants, which also offers tours; 307/687-4280. If tours aren't an option, you may want to peer into the **Eagle Butte Mine** from an overlook five

POWDER RIVER

STRIP MINING

Wyoming's Powder River Basin has not always been the relatively arid place that it is today. Some 55 million years ago the region was covered by freshwater lakes, creeks, and enormous peat swamps. These swamps were buried in sediments over the eons, and compression and heat combined to form thick coal beds.

Coal mining has been an important part of the Campbell County economy for many years. The first mines were underground, but once the technology developed to remove the overlying soil, strip mining became feasible. Today, 10 Campbell County surface mines (the industry's preferred term) are scattered along an enormous coal seam five miles wide, more than 70 miles long, and 70–180 feet thick—enough to last hundreds of years. Together, the mines produce more than one-quarter of the nation's coal, and if Campbell County were a nation it would rank fourth in the world in coal reserves, behind the United States, Russia, and China! Most of the mines are owned by giant multinational corporations including Peabody Energy, Kennecott Energy, RAG Coal West, and Arch Coal.

Coal production in these mines has risen rapidly in recent years and now tops a staggering 370 million tons annually. The North Antelope/Rochelle Complex (near Wright) is the largest mine in America, producing more than 70 million tons of coal per year, followed by the nearby Black Thunder Mine that produces almost as much annually. Other giants are the Cordero Rojo Complex, Jacobs Ranch, Caballo, and Antelope coal mines, all of which produce more than 20 million tons. The Wyodak Mine is the oldest in the Powder River Basin—it opened in 1922—and feeds one of the world's largest air-cooled power plants (also on the site).

Digging the Coal
Powder River Basin mines are heavily mechanized and highly efficient operations with relatively few employees; despite massive increases in production, the number of employees continues to drop. Mining coal here is a relatively simple process, made easier through the use of machinery and blasting equipment that are something beyond gargantuan; all the vehicles seem to be on steroids. Imagine a truck that carries 240 tons of coal—2.5 railroad coal cars' worth—and is powered by a 2,200-horsepower engine. They cost around $1.6 million each. Try changing a flat on it—the tire stands 11 feet tall and weighs four tons! (And a new one sells for $20,000; and coal sells for less than $5 per *ton*.)

---

miles north of Gillette on U.S. Hwy. 14/16. It's open during daylight hours, except when blasting is taking place.

Science Experiments
Kids of all ages will have a blast (pun intended) at **Einstein's Adventurarium,** housed in the Lakeway Learning Center at 525 W. Lakeway Rd., 307/686-3821, www.ccsd.k12.wy.us/adventuarium. The best science museum/kids' center in Wyoming, it is packed with an array of ingenious science exhibits that make learning fun. You can play in the bubble room, learn about light and sound, or meet a parrot, chinchilla, lizard, and ferret. The science center is open Monday–Friday 9–11:30 A.M. and 1–3 P.M. in the school year, but it's only open for groups or by reservation in summer.

Just up the road is another enjoyable family venue: the **Planetarium** at Sage Valley Junior High, 1000 W. Lakeway Road. This sophisticated star chamber is one of the finest in any school district in America and includes a laser light system. Special programs are given every Monday evening; call 307/682-2225 for details.

Cam-Plex
This large and modern multievents center east of town on Garner Lake Road contains an art gallery with changing exhibits, as well as a beautiful 960-seat theater for concerts. Out front of Cam-Plex is an odd collection of items from the past and present. You'll discover early-1900s log cabins and an old locomotive just a few feet from a drilling rig and an enormous coal-hauling dump truck. Kids are guaranteed to have fun in the gargantuan tires. Also here is **Cam-Plex Park** with a shady picnic area, play-

Even this behemoth is dwarfed by the dragline used at the Black Thunder Coal Mine. Its 300-foot boom pulls in a 170-cubic-yard bucket (a typical dump truck holds 12 cubic yards). Powered by electricity, the 3,600-ton machine waddles along like a duck, dragging its power line behind. Blasting loosens the overburden, which is then stripped away and dumped into waiting trucks. (Topsoil is stored for use in later reclamation.) Below this overburden lies the deep black coal seam that must be drilled and blasted. Electric shovels scoop up the loosened coal and dump it into the trucks for delivery to crushing and storage facilities.

The entire scale of the operation comes into focus by watching as 1.5-mile-long, 110-car trains move constantly through the loading facility, loading a car every minute. Workers can fill up to a dozen trains in a day—more than 150,000 tons.

Environmental Impacts

The strip mining of coal has always been a controversial subject, with environmentalists concerned over the impacts from burning coal in an era of acid rain (97 percent of Wyoming coal is burned for electricity), global warming, and escalating atmospheric carbon dioxide. They also question whether reclamation will really work on Wyoming's arid lands, although reclamation does appear to be working. The other impacts from mining are equally important: access roads divide up antelope and deer habitat, subdivisions for the workers spread out over the countryside (take a look at Gillette for a worst-case scenario), and wells draw down the water table. Mining companies, however, point with pride to herds of antelope grazing near the coal mines and believe that the land can be restored after the coal is gone. Besides, the low-sulfur coal found here is some of the cleanest-burning coal in America.

A visit to the coal mines is an eye-opening odyssey into the Super Bowl of strip mining. No matter what you think about strip mining, a tour of the mines is well worth taking, if only to see the enormous equipment and ponder what burning all this coal will do to the global environment. For tour information, contact the Gillette Visitors Center at 307/686-0040 or 800/544-6136, www.visitgillette.net. The Black Thunder Mine also leads tours, but reservations are advised; call 307/464-2201. Learn more about coal mining at the Wyoming Mining Association's website, www.wma-minelife.com.

POWDER RIVER

grounds, ornamental gardens, and hiking paths. Friday evening melodramas are a summertime treat; get details at 307/682-0552, www.cam-plex.com.

ACCOMMODATIONS

Gillette is dominated by the chain motels, including three new ones that opened in 2002. Rates tend to plummet in winter, but they escalate during the Sturgis Motorcycle Rally Week in early August, when everything fills up.

Under $50

Arrowhead Motel, 202 Emerson Ave., 307/686-0909, is one of the few surviving Gillette motels that isn't part of a national chain. Rates are $39 s or $43. Two older economy places—with rooms mostly rented by the week—are **Circle L Motel,** 410 E. 2nd St, 307/682-9375, and **Mustang Motel,** 922 E. 3rd St., 307/682-4784 or 877/543-1141.

$50–100

Get dependable economy accommodations from **Motel 6,** 2105 Rodgers Dr., 307/686-8600 or 800/440-6000, www.motel6.com, where the rooms go for $50 s or $56 d, including access to an indoor hot tub. **Budget Inn Express,** 2011 Rodgers Dr., 307/686-1989 or 800/709-6123, is another corporate-style place with such amenities as an indoor pool, sauna, hot tub, and a light breakfast. Rates are $50 s or $61 d.

National 9 Inn, 1020 E. U.S. Hwy. 14/16, 307/682-5111 or 800/524-9999, charges $53 s or $59 d and has an outdoor pool. Some rooms have fridges and microwaves.

Stay at **Super 8 Motel,** 208 S. Decker Ct., 307/682-8078 or 800/800-8000, www.super8 .com, for $50–80 s or d, including a continental breakfast. **Ramada Limited,** 608 E. 2nd St., 307/682-9341 or 888/298-2054, www.ramada.com, has an outdoor heated pool and hot tub, along with in-room fridges, microwaves, and a light breakfast. This is an older motel, with rooms for $53 s or $63 d.

Econo Lodge, 409 Butler Spaeth Rd., 307/682-4757 or 800/553-2666, www.econolodge.com, has rooms for $57–62 s or $63–68 d, including a continental breakfast. **Quality Inn,** 1002 E. 2nd St., 307/682-2616 or 800/228-5151, www.qualityinn.com, charges $60–65 s or $70–75 d, including a light breakfast.

One of Gillette's nicest places is the **Best Western Tower West Lodge,** 109 N. U.S. Hwy. 14/16, 307/686-2210 or 800/762-7375, www.bestwestern.com/towerwestlodge. The rooms here go for $70–80 s or $75–85 d; amenities include an indoor pool, hot tub, weight room, and business center. **Days Inn,** 910 E. Boxelder Rd., 307/682-3999 or 800/329-7466, www.daysinn.com, charges $72–90 s or $77–100 d, including a continental breakfast.

$100 and Up

Clarion Western Plaza, 2009 S. Douglas Hwy., 307/686-3000 or 800/686-3368, www.clarion.com, offers standard rooms for $99 s or d, and luxurious business suites for $120–150 s or d. Amenities include a large indoor pool, atrium, sauna, business center (with Internet access), fitness room, and a recreation area (pool table, ping pong, and games).

A trio of corporate hotels close to I-90 opened in Gillette in 2002. All offer the same upscale, but cookie-cutter facilities that are especially popular with business travelers and families: large rooms with work tables and queen or king beds, an indoor pool, exercise room, hot tub, business center, and light breakfast. **Holiday Inn Express,** 1908 Cliff Davis Dr., 307/686-9576 or 866/690-9800, www.holiday-inn.com, charges $79–89 s or d for standard rooms, or $99–139 s or d for suites. **Hampton Inn,** 211 Decker Court, 307/686-2000 or 800/426-7866, www.hampton-inn.com, charges $99–129 s. At **Wingate Hotel,** 1801 Cliff Davis Dr., 307/685-2700 or 800/228-1000, www.wingateinngillette.com, rooms cost $99 s or d, and $119–129 d for suites (some with hot tubs).

Bed-and-Breakfast

Gillette's only B&B, **Jost House Inn,** 2708 Ridgecrest Dr., 307/687-1240 or 877/685-2707, is a modern home with two big guest rooms containing Victorian-style furnishings. Both contain king beds, and one has a sitting room and private bath. The expansive yard, gardens, and columned front porch add to the appeal. A big full breakfast is served each morning, and children older than three are welcome. Rates are $69–79 d.

CAMPING

Campers and RVers will enjoy **Crazy Woman Campground,** 1001 W. 2nd St., 307/682-3665 or 800/392-1951; open year-round. It's a pleasant place with genuine shade trees, a rarity in Wyoming's private campgrounds. Also here are a hot tub, an outdoor pool, and bike rentals. Rates are a stiff $21–23 for RVs or $16 for tents. The rather bleak **High Plains Campground,** Garner Lake Rd., 307/687-7339, has additional RV sites next to Cam-Plex on the east side of town. Open year-round.

FOOD

The Gillette restaurant scene tends toward middle-brow fare, but several places are a vast improvement over the rows of fast-food joints that border the main drags.

Breakfast

A cozy little eatery in the heart of downtown, **Lula Belle Cafe,** 101 N. Gillette Ave., 307/682-9798, is best known for its tasty and filling breakfasts. Another place for breakfasts—served all day—is **Packard's Grill,** 408 S. Douglas Hwy., 307/686-5149, a nonsmoking restaurant. Daily lunch specials (including soup served in bread bowls) and inexpensive all-American dinner choices make this a popular family place.

Get cappuccinos, lattes, light breakfasts, earthy lunches, and sweet treats at **Coffee Friends,** 320 S. Gillette Ave., 307/686-6119. **Polar Bear Frozen Yogurt,** 307/682-3155, is next to McDonald's at 900 Camel Dr., but the menu is substantially different, with deli sandwiches, fruit smoothies, frozen yogurt, and espresso. Check your email on their computer.

Lunch and Dinner

Humphrey's Bar & Grill, 408 W. Juniper Lane, 307/682-0100, www.humphard.com, is a favorite lunch place for the business crowd, with a diverse pub grub menu and Wednesday night ribs. Humphrey's has more than 50 beers on tap. The feeling is a bit formulaic: walls crowded with sporting photos and memorabilia and TVs tuned to all-sports channels.

The big salad bar/dessert bar at **Golden Corral,** 2700 S. Douglas Hwy., 307/682-9130, makes for a bargain meal. **Bailey's Bar & Grill,** 301 S. Gillette Ave., 307/686-7667, is a fine place for such homemade lunch and dinner specialties as chicken-fried steak, burgers, and Mexican fare. Great finger food, too.

The award-winning **Prime Rib Restaurant,** 1205 S. Douglas Hwy., 307/682-2944, is a very good place for prime rib, and it also has a diverse menu of steak, pasta, chicken, and seafood. The wine and champagne list is extensive.

Gillette's new culinary standout, **The Chophouse Restaurant,** 307/682-6805, is housed in a historic downtown brick building at 113 S. Gillette Avenue. It's a classy spot with white linen, a nice choice of wines, and gourmet dining. Most dinner entrées cost $15–25, and featured items include slow-roasted prime rib of beef, steaks, barbecued ribs, Alaskan halibut, and more. They're also open for lunch, with salads, sandwiches, fish & chips, and other lighter fare.

International

Gillette is blessed with an excellent—and authentic—Chinese eatery: **Hong Kong Restaurant,** 1612 W. 2nd St., 307/682-5829. Also of note is **China Buffet,** 2701 S. Douglas Hwy., 307/682-7868, with popular lunch and dinner buffets, including that famous Chinese delicacy: chocolate brownies with icing. Get pizza and pasta at **Ole's Pizza Parlor,** 114 N. U.S. Hwy. 14/16, 307/682-8484. For Mexican food and great margaritas, try **Las Margaritas,** 2107 S. Douglas Hwy., 307/682-6545. Also of note is **Casa del Rey,** 409 S. Douglas Hwy., 307/682-4738.

Groceries and Bakeries

Get groceries from Albertson's, Buttery, or the new Wal-Mart SuperCenter. **Breanna's Bakery,** downtown at 208 S. Gillette Ave., 307/686-0570, has doughnuts, sweets, pastries, sandwiches, and freshly baked breads. Stop by **Main Bagel,** 2610 S. Douglas, 307/687-1616, for fresh bagels and bagel sandwiches.

ENTERTAINMENT

Head to Gillette City Park on Thursday nights at 7 P.M. during June and July for the free **Concerts in the Park** series. Music ranges from bluegrass to classical. The **Powder River Symphony Orchestra,** 307/686-5767, www.prs.vcn.com, performs at Cam-Plex in March, May, October, and December. You'll find community drama at its corniest during the **melodrama shows** held at Cam-Plex on Friday evenings June–August. Get details at 307/686-3025, www.cam-plex.com.

Top 40 and oldies bands play most nights at **Partners Saloon** inside the Tower West Lodge at 109 N. U.S. Hwy. 14/16, 307/686-2210. **Kicks Lounge** in the Holiday Inn at 2009 S. Douglas Hwy., 307/686-3000, is the place to go for rock and pop tunes six nights a week. **Prime Rib Restaurant,** 1205 S. Douglas Hwy., 307/682-2944, also has occasional live entertainment, as does **Jake's Tavern,** 5201 S. Douglas Hwy., 307/686-3781. **Mingles,** 2209 S. Douglas Hwy., 307/686-1222, has a half-dozen pool tables and a big-screen TV. **Good Times Lounge,** 2701 S. Douglas Hwy., 307/682-0808, has live country-and-western music some nights.

For movies, head to **Foothills Twin Theatre,** 650 N. U.S. Hwy. 14/16, 307/682-6766, or **Sky-Hi Theatres,** on S. Douglas Hwy., 307/682-7628.

EVENTS

All summer long you'll find racing on Saturday nights at **Thunder Basin Stock Car Track** on Garner Lake Road. Gillette's **Fourth of July** celebration is the biggest in northeastern Wyoming. In addition to an impressive fireworks show, you'll find a pancake breakfast, a parade, mud volleyball, firehose water fights, and even a Ping-Pong drop (a Ping-Pong drop?).

Gillette is home to the **College National Finals Rodeo**, 800/442-2256, www.cnfr.com, in mid-June during 2004 and 2005. This event attracts 350 of the best young cowboys and cowgirls from all over the nation with a full range of events.

The **Wyoming Celtic Festival and Highland Games**, www.wyomingcelticfestival.org, 307/682-5785 or 877/688-6201, takes place in early July. **Campbell County Fair**, 307/687-0200, www.campbellcountyfair.com, in early August includes livestock judging, arts-and-crafts exhibits, concerts, and other old-time favorites.

Cam-Plex, a large and modern multievents center east of town on Garner Lake Road, frequently has concerts, livestock shows, rodeos, RV rallies, conventions, and other events. During summer, rodeos take place almost every weekend, the biggest being the **PRCA Rodeo** in late July and early August. In late November and early December, Gillette plays host to a series of **Christmas crafts fairs**—call the visitors center at 307/686-0040 or 800/544-6136 for details.

RECREATION

Gillette has some of the finest recreation facilities in Wyoming, a reflection of the prosperous local economy. **Campbell County Recreation Center**, 1000 S. Douglas Hwy., 307/682-5470, www.ccprd.com, houses an indoor pool with a diving well, the 383-foot Thunder Run Water Slide (summers only), weight rooms, racquetball and squash courts, a gym, and a sauna. Enjoy fabulous *free* summertime swimming at the **Gillette Water Park**, 307/682-1962. Located outdoors at Gillette and 10th, the park has a main pool with geysers and waterfalls, a wading pool with a slide for kids, a deep diving pool, and a sand play area. There's also an indoor **Aquatic Center** in town for competitive swimming events; 307/686-3757.

Bird-watchers should head to **McManamen Park** on W. Warlow Dr., where viewing blinds let you look for ducks and other birds.

Campbell County's modern **ice arena**, 121 S. 4-J Rd., 307/687-1555, is open mid-October to mid-March. Roller skaters will enjoy **Razor City Skateland**, 885 Hannum Rd., 307/682-3529, and bowlers can roll their own at **Camelanes Bowling Center**, 1005 W. 2nd St., 307/682-4811, or **Frontier Lanes**, 5700 S. Douglas Hwy., 307/687-0261. Golfers hobnob at **Bell Nob Golf Links**, 1316 Overdale Dr., 307/686-7069, or **Gillette Golf Club**, 1800 Country Club Rd., 307/686-4774.

SHOPPING

Gillette has many of the national discount stores on South Douglas Hwy., including a **Wal-Mart SuperCenter**, 307/686-5166, and a **Kmart**, 307/682-3212.

Local Color is a fine arts co-op gallery with watercolor, glass art, raku pottery, fabric art, photography, and more at 101 W. Lakeway Rd., 307/686-0508. Get books at **Hastings**, 2601 S. Douglas Hwy., 307/682-6417, www.gohastings.com.

INFORMATION AND SERVICES

The **Gillette Visitors Center**, 307/686-0040 or 800/544-6136, www.visitgillette.net, is at 1810 S. Douglas Hwy. (next to the Flying J Truckstop at exit 126), and is open daily 8 A.M.–6 P.M. Memorial Day to Labor Day, and Monday–Friday 8 A.M.–5 P.M. the rest of the year. Get additional online information at www.gillettewyoming.net.

Gillette is home to the state's fastest-growing junior college (more than 900 students), the **Gillette Campus** of Northern Wyoming Community College. Located on W. 4-J Rd., 307/686-0254, www.gc.cc.wy.us, the campus offers a range of classes and degree programs from business to mining and is building a new campus that opens in 2004.

The **Campbell County Memorial Hospital,** 501 S. Burma Ave., 307/682-8811, www.ccmh.net, has 24-hour emergency care.

TRANSPORTATION

By Air

The Gillette airport is five miles north of town. **Great Lakes Aviation,** 307/432-7000 or 800/554-5111, www.greatlakesav.com, has daily flights between Gillette and Denver. **Big Sky Airlines,** 406/247-3910 or 800/237-7788, www.bigskyair.com, has daily service between Billings and Gillette.

By Car and Taxi

Be sure to fill up with gas in Gillette because prices are usually higher in Buffalo and Sheridan. Rent cars from **A & A Auto & RV Rental,** 307/686-8250; or **U-Save Auto Rental,** 307/682-2815 or 800/272-8728, www.usave.net. National chains include Avis, Enterprise, and Hertz. Avis and Hertz have cars at the airport. See the Special Topic "Rental Car Contacts" in the On the Road chapter.

The two local taxi companies are **American Couriers,** 307/686-0905, and **City Cab,** 307/685-1000.

By Bus

Powder River Transportation/Coach USA, 1700 E. U.S. Hwy. 14/16, 307/682-0960 or 800/442-3682, has daily bus service throughout northern and eastern Wyoming. (Look for the big Petrolane propane tank to find this easy-to-miss bus station.)

South from Gillette

Two roads point south from Gillette; more remote State Hwy. 50 is a distinctive red highway built from scoria. The alternative route, State Hwy. 59, takes you into the heart of the mixed-grass prairie, with oil pumpjacks, windmills, enormous bales of hay, and thousands of cattle and sheep. Tumbleweeds are plastered against the barbed-wire fences, and abandoned farm equipment rusts on hilltops. The Belle Ayr mine stands on the eastern horizon a dozen miles south of town, with flat-topped mesas and nipple-shaped buttes adding a little spice to the scenery. Far to the west, the Big Horn Mountains rise from the plains. Be sure to pause for a look at the grasses; blue grama is especially pretty when seen up close.

DURHAM BUFFALO RANCH

Approximately 30 miles south of Gillette is Durham Buffalo Ranch, home of the largest private buffalo herd in existence. The Flocchini family owns a 55,000-acre spread here and is dedicated to returning the land to its original state, when bison and other native animals dominated the prairie landscape. Watch for some of the 4,000 head of buffalo along the highway. Herds more than 1,000 times this size once roamed across the land, and this is a rare opportunity to see bison today in a relatively natural setting. Call 307/939-1271 or 800/444-5687 for tour information (groups only).

WRIGHT

Wright sits right in the center of America's largest low-sulfur coal deposit. Established in 1976, the town quickly grew to some 1,200 residents. Modern schools, a small shopping mall, and six churches popped up, along with trailer courts and suburban split-level homes on curving streets. Funded partly by Arco, Wright was built to house workers for nearby coal mines. It's a pretty weird place. Imagine an enclave of middle-class America plunked down in a setting straight out of *High Plains Drifter*.

Sights

On the east end of town off State Hwy. 387, the small **Wright Centennial Museum,** 307/464-1222, houses homestead-era items. Out front is a 70-ton truck that was retired from hauling coal when it was replaced with much larger versions. The museum is open Monday–Friday 10 A.M.–5 P.M. and Saturday 10 A.M.–3 P.M. from mid-May to mid-October. No charge.

Gargantuan coal strip mines surround Wright; all of them use Paul Bunyan–scale equipment and skeleton crews of employees to mine coal selling for less than $5 per ton. Much of this is public land belonging to Thunder Basin National Grassland, meaning enormous revenues for the federal government and severance taxes for the state of Wyoming. The coal trains seem to never end. Stop on the railroad overpass near the dot of a settlement called **Bill** and you'll see a hundred cars of coal pass by every couple of minutes, with empty trains waiting on the sidings. Most of this coal is on its way to electric-generating plants in Texas and the Midwest. (Bill got its name from four early settlers, all of whom had the same first name.)

Practicalities

The **Latigo Hills Mall** is Wright's focal point and includes a grocery store, café, bar, pizza shop, hardware store/gift shop, library, bank (with ATM), post office, bowling alley (Rolling Thunder Lanes), dentist, laundromat, and hair salon. There's even a massage therapist.

Wright Area Chamber of Commerce, 307/464-1312, www.wrightareachamber.com, is also in the mall and is open Monday–Friday 8 A.M.–noon and 1–5 P.M. Get buffalo burgers at **Reno Junction Cafe,** 307/939-1298, at the junction of State Hwys. 387 and 59. The town also has a fine **recreation center,** 307/464-0198, with an indoor pool, racquet-

> ## CROW COUNTRY IS JUST RIGHT
>
> *The Crow country is a good country; the Great Spirit has put it in exactly the right place. It is good for horses—and what is a country without horses? On the Columbia, the people are poor and dirty; they paddle about in canoes and eat fish. On the Missouri the water is muddy and bad. To the north of the Crow country it is too cold, and to the south it is too hot. The Crow country is just right. The water is clear and sweet. There are plenty of buffalo, elk, deer, antelope, and mountain sheep. It is the best wintering place in the world and has plenty of game. Is it any wonder that the Crows have fought long and hard to defend this country, which we love so much?*
>
> —Crow Chief Arapooish, describing Powder River Basin

ball courts, a weight room, and a gym. There's a nine-hole golf course nearby, **Haycreek Golf Club,** 307/464-0747.

Stay at **National 9 Inn,** 307/464-1510 or 800/524-9999, where rooms go for $60–70 s or $65–75 d; kitchenettes are available. Park RVs ($19) or pitch a tent ($10) at **Sagebluff RV Park,** one mile west of town on State Hwy. 387, 307/464-1305; open all year.

The annual event here is **Wright Days,** held in late August, with games, a barbecue, and races.

The Black Hills

In Wyoming's Northeast corner, the Black Hills of South Dakota roll across an arbitrary line, bringing a quiet beauty that differs greatly from other parts of the state. Here, the Belle Fourche River (pronounced "bell-FOOSH," French for "Beautiful Fork") cuts northeast past rich pastures before taking a sudden right angle to the southeast as it heads to the Missouri River. Tiny towns nestle in the forested hills, and cattle graze on the riverbanks. Nearby, one of the most stunning of all sights—Devils Tower—seems almost alive in its abrupt rise from the pastoral landscape. South of the Black Hills in Weston County, the hill country quickly opens into the mixed-grass prairie of the plains. This out-of-the-way part of Wyoming is truly a special place. It's no wonder that the Sioux considered the Black Hills the home of the Great Spirit.

Only 13,000 people live in Crook and Weston counties, scattered on rural ranches or in the small settlements of Sundance and Hulett in the midst of Wyoming's Black Hills, along with Newcastle, Moorcroft, and Upton along the southern edge. Cattle grazing, bentonite mining, oil wells, logging, and tourism provide the jobs.

THE LAND

The Black Hills stretch in a long ellipse, 125 miles north to south and 65 miles across, rising 3,000–4,000 feet above the surrounding plains. South Dakota's

Devils Tower National Monument

THE BLACK HILLS

MONTANA
WYOMING

Alzada

Colony

212

112

WYOMING
SOUTH DAKOTA

To Belle Fourche, SD

To Belle Fourche, SD

212

New Haven

112

Belle

Fourche

River

Black Hills
National
Forest

Lowest Elevation in Wyoming
(3,125 ft.)

Thunder

Basin

National

Grassland

Missouri   Buttes

Hulett

24

Alva

24

Aladdin

34

BEAR
LODGE

Oshoto

DEVILS TOWER
NATIONAL
MONUMENT

COOK
LAKE

Beulah

90

24

Bear   Lodge   Mountains

111

14

Black Hills
National
Forest

WARREN PEAK
OVERLOOK

Grand Canyon

Black Hills
National
Forest

To Deadwood, SD

To Spearfish, SD

14

REUTER

Sundance

KEYHOLE
STATE
PARK

Keyhole Reservoir

90

116

To Gillette (Powder River Country)

MOON

113

90

Moorcroft

Pine   Ridge

Moskee

585

Buckhorn

85

To Deadwood, SD

16

116

Inyan Kara
Mountain
(6,368 ft.)

Upton

116

Four Corners

WYOMING
SOUTH DAKOTA

Thunder

Basin

National

Grassland

16

Osage

85

WYOMING

85   16

Newcastle

To Jewel Cave and
Mt. Rushmore, SD

To Lusk (Southeast Wyoming)

THE BLACK HILLS

0   10 mi

0   10 km

WYOMING

© AVALON TRAVEL PUBLISHING, INC

BLACK HILLS SIGHTSEEING HIGHLIGHTS

Anna Miller Museum in Newcastle
Crook County Museum in Sundance
Black Hills National Forest north of Sundance
Aladdin Store
Devils Tower National Monument
Popular events: Spring Fling Rodeo in Newcastle (May), Weston County Fair in Newcastle (August), Crook County Fair and Rodeo in Sundance (August), Sturgis Bike Rally (August)

Harney Peak, at 7,242 feet, is the tallest mountain in the Black Hills; in fact, it's the tallest peak between the South Dakota–Wyoming line and the Atlantic Ocean. The most famous attraction in this part of Wyoming is Devils Tower, but the Black Hills north of Sundance are captivating, especially in the spring and fall. Most visitors who come to northeast Wyoming do so as part of a trip that includes Yellowstone and various South Dakota sights: Mt. Rushmore, Deadwood, the Crazy Horse Memorial, and Jewel Cave.

From a distance, the dusky green carpet of ponderosa pine darkens the hills—hence the Sioux name *Paha Sapa,* meaning "Hills that are Black." The Black Hills are a blend of rocky hills crowded with pine and aspen forests, open meadows, and valleys lined with bur oak. This is one of the few places you're likely to see native oak trees in Wyoming.

White-tailed deer are abundant throughout the Black Hills, and herds of elk are found southeast of Sundance. Merriam's turkeys are a common sight all through this country. Introduced from New Mexico in 1948, they are now the most widespread game-bird species in northeast Wyoming.

Newcastle

Newcastle (pop. 3,000) sits at the junction of several major roads and serves as a gateway to the Black Hills. Like much of northeast Wyoming, the town's economy is a mixture of energy, ranching, and logging. Every half hour, day and night, traffic backs up on the railroad tracks across Main Street to wait as a hundred soot-black coal cars rumble past bound for Midwestern power plants. A Newcastle refinery produces jet fuel for South Dakota's giant Ellsworth Air Force Base, and a natural-gas processing plant sits 25 miles south of town in the midst of the Finn-Shurley fields. Large ranches encompass the town, dotted with oil pumpjacks, windmills, and Herefords.

HISTORY

The first white settlement of the Newcastle area came in 1875, when Professor Walter P. Jenney and Lt. Col. R. I. Dodge led 432 soldiers and an army of mining engineers, scientists, and mapmakers to a base camp along Beaver Creek. They built the Jenney Stockade, which became a stage station and distribution point along the Cheyenne-Deadwood Trail. Many of the West's most famous characters stopped by en route to Deadwood, including Wild Bill Hickok, Calamity Jane, and Wyatt Earp.

Tubb Town

In 1888, the Chicago, Burlington, and Quincy Railroad announced plans to construct tracks across northeast Wyoming and into Montana. Speculators established Tubb Town, a ramshackle collection of saloons, hotels, and "sporting houses" along the proposed railroad route. All visitors were required to pay a toll (of sorts) on entrance: "set 'em up for the bunch." The party didn't last long—when the Burlington Railroad decided instead to build a town a few miles west at present-day Newcastle, Tubb Town faded into history. At Whoopup Canyon (so named because the spring floods came "a-whoopin' through"), a railroad worker attempted to pry the cap off a 25-pound can of black powder. After struggling without success, he decided to try a more forceful

THE BLACK HILLS

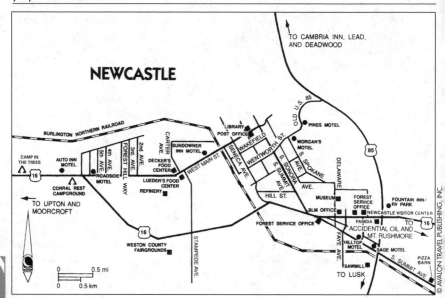

approach—using a pickax to punch a hole in the lid. His co-workers found little left to bury.

The Cambria Mines

Coal was discovered in Cambria Canyon in the 1880s, and the coal-mining town of Cambria popped up almost overnight. It became a model community, with a water system, modern homes, three churches, electric lights, and some of the safest underground mines in the nation. Alcohol was banned, along with bawdy entertainment. At its peak, more than 1,500 people lived in Cambria, but when the coal ran out in 1928, the mines were forced to close.

The discovery of coal at Cambria led the Burlington Railroad to establish a townsite as near the mouth of Cambria Canyon as possible, with a spur to the four mines. The town was called Newcastle, after the English coal port of Newcastle-upon-Tyne. At first, the wide-open frontier sensibility of Newcastle contrasted sharply with that of quiet, sedate Cambria. When the new mayor, Frank Mondell (who had established the Cambria mines), decided to get rid of 20 of Newcastle's undesirables, a local hotel owner—fearing that he would lose most of his business—shot the mayor. Mondell (who later served for 26 years as Wyoming's lone congressional representative) carried the bullet in his spine the rest of his life.

After the Cambria mines closed, the town of Newcastle faded, but with the discovery of huge oil deposits nearby in the 1950s it boomed again. By the mid-1950s more than 25,000 people crowded the surrounding countryside. A bust soon followed, only to lead to a similar cycle in the 1970s. Now Newcastle perks along on an economy of equal parts oil, coal, logging, and ranching. Folks from Nebraska or Kansas would feel right at home among the quiet streets, staid older homes, pickup trucks, and freight trains.

SIGHTS

Anna Miller Museum

The Newcastle museum at Delaware Street and U.S. Hwy. 16, 307/746-4188, is open Monday–Friday 9 A.M.–5 P.M. all year; donation requested. It's housed in the old National Guard Cavalry Barn, a stone structure built in the 1930s by the Work Projects Administration. Inside is the typical collection of local paraphernalia: items from the Cambria mines, a horse-drawn hearse, a noose (not, however, the one vigilantes used to hang murderer Diamond Slim Clifton from the Newcastle railroad trestle), dinosaur bones, and a scale model of the giant KB&C ranch. Be sure to try a couple of cranks on the old noisemaker—it was used to disrupt newlyweds on their first night. Anna Miller, for whom the museum was named, was a local school superintendent whose husband, Sheriff Billy Miller, was the last white man to die in a battle with the Indians in 1903.

Outside the museum you'll find a furnished one-room schoolhouse built in 1890, a homesteader cabin, and the **Jenney Stockade cabin** (built in 1875), the oldest building in the Black Hills. Ask at the museum for directions to the Cheyenne-Deadwood Trail ruts.

Accidental Oil Company

Certainly the most amusing sight around Newcastle is the kitschy Accidental Oil Company. In 1966 (around the time Jed Clampett of television's *Beverly Hillbillies* was "shootin' at some food, and up from the ground came a bubbling crude—oil, that is, black gold, Texas tea . . ."), Newcastle rancher Al Smith decided to dig a hole to see how far down it was to oil. Using a pick and shovel, and later dynamite, he reached it at 21 feet. The "world's only hand-dug oil well" is now a small tourist trap along U.S. Hwy. 16 four miles east of Newcastle. Outside are steam-powered oil rigs and antique pumps. An old oil-storage tank encloses a rather nice gift shop, and you can walk down to view the oil-bearing rock under black light (which makes the seeping oil visible). It's more interesting than it sounds. Accidental Oil, 307/746-2042, www.trib.com/~debran, is open daily 9 A.M.–6 P.M. June–August; they're closed the rest of the year, although the gift shop remains open. Thirty-minute tours of the well, including a discussion of petroleum geology, cost $5 adults, $3 kids, or $15 families. Pure Americana.

Paleo Park

Located on the 9,000-acre Zerbst Ranch, Paleo Park, 307/334-2270, www.paleopark.com, is just about as remote as you can get—32 miles southwest of Newcastle, then 24 miles out a gravel road. The country consists of open grassland with to-the-

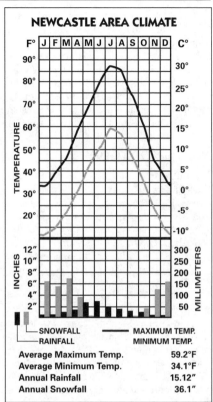

NEWCASTLE AREA CLIMATE

SNOWFALL — MAXIMUM TEMP.
RAINFALL — MINIMUM TEMP.

Average Maximum Temp.	59.2°F
Average Minimum Temp.	34.1°F
Annual Rainfall	15.12"
Annual Snowfall	36.1"

horizon vistas and quietude almost lost elsewhere in America. The ranch lies near the center of the famous Lance Creek fossil area, where the late Leonard Zerbst discovered one of the most complete specimens of Triceratops in 1998. Named Kelsey Ann, this giant horned dinosaur roamed the land 65 million years ago, and the mounted skeleton now resides with the Children's Museum of Indianapolis. Other finds here have included an amazing tracksite with the tracks of dinosaurs and birds together, the skull of a **pachycephalosaur**, a mummified duckbill dinosaur now at the American Museum of Natural History in New York, and even a Tyrannosaurus rex with skin impressions, something never seen before. Several internationally known paleontologists, including Dr. Paul Sereno from the University of Chicago, use the ranch as a base for summertime digs.

THE BLACK HILLS

Paleo Park is owned by Arlene Zerbst, who leads two-hour tours ($20 per person, or $26 with lunch) that include the chance to see additional dinosaur bones in situ, check out a microsite filled with thousands of bone fragments and teeth (including a *T. rex*), plus a visit to the dinosaur tracksite. Call a day ahead for tour reservations and to make sure the road is passable. Open Memorial Day to Labor Day.

ACCOMMODATIONS
Motels

You'll find a good variety of lodging options in Newcastle. During Sturgis Rally Week (the first week of August; www.sturgis.com) rates at many local motels rise sharply, and the rooms are often booked up almost a year in advance.

Two places provide older rooms for economy prices. **Hilltop Motel,** 1121 S. Summit, 307/746-4494, www.trib.com/~hilltop, charges $35 s or $39–44 d. All rooms have microwaves and fridges. **Sage Motel,** 1227 S. Summit, 307/746-2724 or 877/746-2724, www.sagemotel.vcn.com, may be a better bet, with comfortable and cozy rooms for $36–40 s or $50–58 d.

On the west end of town, **Auto Inn Motel,** 2503 W. Main, 307/746-2734 or 877/228-8646, www.autoinnmotel-campground.com, has remodeled rooms for $42 s or $48–52 d. All have fridges and microwaves, and a continental breakfast is served.

Two attractive, clean, and friendly motels—Morgan's and Pines—have quiet, out-of-the-way locations just a few blocks off the main drag. Open April–November, **Morgan's Motel,** 205 S. Spokane, 307/746-2715, charges $38 s or d. Just up the hill is **Pines Motel,** 248 E. Wentworth, 307/746-4334 or 800/946-4334, www.trib.com/~mcarthr, where rooms with fridges cost $45 s or $50 d. Kitchenette units sleep up to four for $66–70, and a two-bedroom unit with full kitchen runs $80 for up to six. A hot tub is on the grounds.

On the east end of town, **Fountain Inn,** 307/746-4426 or 800/882-8858, www.trib.com/~barbarv, is the largest Newcastle motel and the only one with an outdoor pool. Rates here are $63 s or $68–74 d. **Roadside Motel,** 1605 W. Main St., 307/746-9640, also has reasonably priced rooms, some with kitchenettes.

Other Options

Set amid majestic Black Hills country eight miles north of Newcastle, the **Flying V Cambria Inn,** 307/746-2096, www.trib.com/~flyingv, offers country accommodations in a historic stone building. Built in the 1920s, the inn has a good restaurant and 10 guest rooms with a mix of antique and modern furnishings. Room rates are $49 s or $69 d, including a full breakfast. Some rooms have shared baths. The Cambria is open June–December.

In the Black Hills 17 miles northeast of Newcastle, **EVA—Great Spirit Ranch B&B,** 307/746-2537, www.wyomingbnb-ranchrec.com/EVA.html, is a spacious modern log home on 1,000 acres of ranch land. Owner Irene Spillane cooks up big country breakfasts and will fill you with details on the area's rich human and natural history. The three guest rooms have shared or private baths and cost $74 s or d. Kids are welcome. This is a delightful place to relax in a remote and peaceful setting.

Tours of remote **Paleo Park** are described under Sights. The ranch also has overnight lodging in a bunkhouse dorm built for paleontology researchers and groups. Lodging and three big meals is $100 per person per night, but the dorm is generally filled with students in July. Camping under the stars is another option. Paleo Park is open Memorial Day to Labor Day.

CAMPING AND CABINS

You can pitch a tent for free anywhere on nearby public lands within both Thunder Basin National Grassland and Black Hills National Forest. For access to the latter, head nine miles east on U.S. Hwy. 16 and then turn north up Forest Rd. 117 (just a few hundred feet before the South Dakota border). **Beaver Creek Campground** ($8; open all year) is right on the Wyoming–South Dakota border 23 miles northeast of Newcastle near the place called Mallo. The Park Service's **Jewel Cave National Mon-**

ument, 605/673-2288, has camping inside South Dakota, 25 miles east of Newcastle.

For something completely different, stay at the Forest Service's **Summit Ridge Lookout** on the South Dakota–Wyoming border northeast of Newcastle. You don't actually stay in the fire tower itself because it's still in use, but in the log cabin at the base. Rates are $35 per day, with space for four people; call 307/746-2782 for reservations.

Flying V Cambria Inn, eight miles north of Newcastle, 307/746-2096, www.trib.com/~flyingv, has seasonal RV parking for $15.

Back in Newcastle, **RimRock RV & Camp,** 2206 W. Main, 307/746-2007, has tent sites for $10 and RV sites for $17; open mid-Apr. to mid-Nov. Showers for noncampers cost $3, and the RV park has an indoor pool and convenience store.

Crystal Park Campground in front of Fountain Inn, 3 Seminoe Ave., 307/746-4426 or 800/882-8858, www.trib.com/~barbarv, is open April–October, with tent sites for $10, and RV spaces for $18. Showers for noncampers are $3. The fishing pond out front is stocked with trout and bass.

Auto Inn Motel, 2503 W. Main, 307/746-2734 or 877/228-8646, www.autoinnmotel-campground.com, has year-round sites for RVs ($18–22) and tents ($15).

FOOD

For filling breakfasts, a good salad bar, American dinners, and homemade pies, head to **Old Mill Inn,** 500 W. Main, 307/746-4608. The building itself is worth a look; they don't build places like this anymore. Completed in 1905, the mill produced Toomey's Flapjack Flour and Toomey's Biscuit Mix until going out of business in 1965. It was later transformed into a restaurant.

Historic **Flying V Cambria Inn,** eight miles north of town on U.S. Hwy. 85, 307/746-2096, offers delicious prime rib, steaks, seafood, and Italian meals. Big portions and great food in a nostalgic setting; open June–Dec. only.

The Hop, 1114 W. Main, 307/746-2585, is popular for burgers, hot dogs, fries, and shakes. Get it to go to avoid the chain-smokers. For fast food and sit-down meals in a friendly diner set-

ting, head to **Hi-16 Drive In,** 2951 W. Main, 307/746-4055. Newcastle's other in-a-rush dining choices include Subway, Taco John's, and Pizza Hut (the lunch and Tuesday night buffets here are good deals).

The best meal deals (and entertainment) in the area are across the South Dakota line. Deadwood's gambling casinos serve a big variety of food, including inexpensive steak dinners. This is where Newcastle folks go for an evening out. Two recommended Deadwood restaurants are Biff Malibu's and Kitty's Chinatown. The meals may be reasonable, but be forewarned that lodging in Deadwood is on the pricey side.

Get groceries in Newcastle at **Decker's Food Center,** 709 W. Main, 307/746-2779, or **Woody's Food Center,** 622 W. Main, 307/746-3511. Decker's has a good bakery and deli.

ENTERTAINMENT

The **Dogie** (as in "Git along, little dogie"), 111 W. Main St., 307/746-2187, is the local movie house. The bar at **Old Mill Inn,** 500 W. Main, 307/746-4608, has more than 100 beers, including many microbrews. Newcastle's live music scene is almost nonexistent; to party, locals head 50 miles away to happenin' Deadwood, South Dakota.

EVENTS

The biggest local event isn't in Newcastle. It's South Dakota's **Sturgis Bike Rally** (www.sturgis.com), which takes place the second week of August. Not a good time to come through town on a Honda motorcycle! During the Rally, locals pull out the stops with a **Pig Roast** at the Fountain Inn and **Bag Lady Days** at the Flying V.

Several events actually take place in Newcastle, including the **Spring Fling Rodeo** in late May. This unique professional event is the largest female rodeo in Wyoming. You're likely to find other rodeos going on at the fairgrounds most summer weekends. Also in May are **Living History Days,** when visitors will learn about the lives of pioneers.

The annual **Perino Horse Sale** in June brings

people from all over the nation and is a great opportunity to see these beautiful animals. Also popular is **Western Heritage Days** in August, featuring a parade, carnival, watermelon feed, street dance, and other events. Newcastle's main local event is the **Weston County Fair**, held the first week of August.

INFORMATION AND SERVICES

Just west of the intersection of U.S. Hwys. 16 and 85, the **Newcastle Visitor Center**, 307/746-2739 or 800/835-0157, http://newcastle.1wyo.net, is open Monday–Friday 9 A.M.–5 P.M. all year, plus Saturday 9 A.M.–1 P.M. and Sunday noon–4 P.M. May–September. While here, be sure to pick up *Beaver Creek: A Trip Through Time,* a booklet describing a loop tour of sites in the area; it's filled with fascinating descriptions of historical events.

The **BLM's Newcastle Field Office** is at 1101 Washington, 307/746-6600, www.wy.blm.gov, and the Black Hills National Forest's **Hell Canyon Ranger District** is at 1225 Washington Blvd., 307/746-2783, www.fs.fed.us/r2/blackhills. Nearly all of the land they manage is across the border in South Dakota.

Check your email at the **Weston County Library**, 23 W. Main, 307/746-2206, www-wsl.state.wy.us/weston, or swim a few laps at the new **Kozisek Aquatic Center**, 15 Stampede, 307/746-2713. Play a round of golf at the nine-hole **Newcastle Country Club**, 2302 W. Main, 307/746-2639.

Weston County Health Services, 1124 Washington St., 307/746-4491, has 24-hour emergency care.

Newcastle does not have bus or plane service. Both local banks have **ATMs,** and others can be found in the Pamida store and at Coffee Cup Fuel Stop.

Newcastle Vicinity

North of Newcastle, U.S. Hwy. 85 climbs quickly into the pine-covered Black Hills, providing wide vistas over the town and across the open plains to the south. Eight miles north of Newcastle is **Flying V Cambria Inn,** constructed in 1928 as a resort for and memorial to the Cambria miners. It was completed just a few months before the mines closed down for good. Now listed on the National Register of Historic Places, the inn is open for meals and lodging, 307/746-2096. The ghost town of Cambria slowly crumbles on private land nearby.

Another nine miles north is **Red Butte,** a steep-sided sandstone peak rising right along the road like a miniature Devils Tower. A local landmark, it was said to have been used by both Indians and early whites as a lookout. Not far away is the site of the 1878 Canyon Springs robbery on the old Cheyenne-Deadwood Stage Route. A passenger and an outlaw died in the shoot-out, and at least $20,000 (some accounts claim up to $140,000) in gold was taken and buried nearby. Many years later, a local farmer digging potatoes near Red Butte apparently found some of the loot. Packing up his family, he split town without a word.

FOUR CORNERS AREA

North of Red Butte, the land begins to open up into an undulating grassy terrain with rich red-black soil. Just a couple more miles up the road is a country inn and post office at **Four Corners.** The owners also run the adjacent **Four Corners Country Inn,** 307/746-4776 or 800/890-4776, www.trib.com/~hjohnsn, with nicely furnished rooms (shared or private baths) for $25 s or $35 d. Get a full breakfast for another $5 per person. RV sites with hookups are $20; no tents. Open year-round.

Mallo Road (gravel) heads east from Four Corners into South Dakota, offering a colorful fall drive as the aspens turn a brilliant yellow. The Forest Service's **Beaver Creek Campground** ($8; open all year) is six miles east of Four Corners and right across the state line inside South Dakota. Just one mile inside Wyoming is spacious **Mallo Camp & Motel,** 307/746-4094,

Black Hills north of Newcastle

where modern motel rooms are $40–45 d, including access to two large communal kitchens. Mallo Resort is a popular snowmobile destination in winter, with many trails on nearby Black Hills National Forest land.

HEADING SOUTH

South of Newcastle, U.S. Hwy. 85 is an arrow aimed at the horizon, pointing across the almost-flat landscape of grass, wind, and antelope. A few bottomland trees line the creeks, and the Cheyenne River etches a narrow line through the land, which is nearly dry in the late-summer heat. This is the heart of the great mixed-grass prairie that borders eastern Wyoming and reaches into adjacent Nebraska and south into Colorado.

UPTON AREA

On the edge of Upton (pop. 870), a sign makes no bones about where you are: the "Best Town on Earth!" Who am I to argue? Like its neighbors—Osage and Newcastle—Upton lies right along the edge of the Black Hills, with ponderosa pines topping the ridge to the north (ap-propriately named Pine Ridge) and open-range country spreading to the south. The Chicago, Burlington, and Quincy Railroad established a depot here in 1892, and railroad tracks now form Upton's southern border. Beyond this point, State Hwy. 116 climbs over gentle grassy hills through the heart of Thunder Basin National Grassland. It's a high-plains landscape filled with windmills and scattered ranches and grazed by sheep, cattle, antelope, and mule deer. The sky completely dominates the landscape, sending giant white thunderheads over the plains. Upton's limited economy depends on local ranchers, oil pumping, and coal mining in nearby Campbell County.

Upton's tiny **Red Onion Museum,** 307/468-2672, houses pioneer items and local memorabilia, including the featured attraction: a two-headed Hereford calf born on a local ranch. The museum is open Monday–Friday 9 A.M.–noon and 1–5 P.M. On the east end of Upton is **Old Town,** an interesting cluster of eight reconstructed cabins (one built from bales of straw) near the original townsite. Find out more about Upton on the web at www.trib.com/~uptonwy.

Osage

Halfway between Newcastle and Upton, tiny Osage (pop. 200) has a bar but not much else to show for having once been the center of the oil industry in northeast Wyoming. In 1920, a huge gusher turned the surrounding country into a madhouse of oil prospectors and transformed Osage into a tent city of 1,500 people. When the boom inevitably turned to bust, only a core of folks remained in what is now a railroad way station. The only surviving business is a bar.

Upton Practicalities

Stay at the basic **Upton Motel,** 307/468-9282, for $35 s or $40 d; or the much nicer **Weston Inn Motel,** 307/468-2401, for $38 s or $48 d.

If you don't mind in-town, no-shade camping in a parking lot, the **C Mart Conoco,** 307/468-2551, has $10 electrical hookups for RVs. In a pinch you could put up a tent for $3 (no showers).

The Drug Store, 307/468-2770, claims the "best malts in Wyoming." Drop by to see for yourself. Get groceries at **Joe's Food Center,** 307/468-2372. You can hang out (or check your email) at the branch **library** on Pine and 4th Sts., 307/468-2324.

Upton Fun Days, held the third weekend of July, is the main event. Activities include a pancake breakfast, parade, street dance, kids games and kids rodeo, tractor pull, and free barbecue. **Cedar Pines Country Club** is a public nine-hole course three miles north of town on State 116.

Moorcroft and Vicinity

Moorcroft (pop. 800) is a nondescript ranching and oil field town perched within a few miles of popular Keyhole Reservoir. It isn't particularly attractive, but it will do as a stop on the way to somewhere else. Because the famed Texas Trail passed through it, Moorcroft became an important cattle town. Up until the end of World War II, it served as the largest cattle shipping point along the entire Chicago, Burlington, and Quincy Railroad. The local historical stopping place is **Helen Robinson Zimmerschied Western-Texas Trail Museum,** at 200 S. Bighorn, 307/756-9300. Open Mon.–Fri. noon–4 P.M. summers only; no charge. The name is almost bigger than the museum's collection of local items.

ACCOMMODATIONS AND CAMPING

Lodging is available at tiny **Wyoming Motel and Camping Park,** 111 W. Converse, 307/756-3452, for $38–44 s or d, $20 for RVs. **Cozy Motel,** 219 W. Converse, 307/756-3486, is another good place with rooms for $39 s or $42–44 d. **Rangeland Court Motel and RV Park,** 108 N. Yellowstone Ave., 307/756-3760, is a modern and spotless 10-unit place with

rooms (some with microwaves and fridges) for $45 s or d. RV hookups cost $15.

The town's largest place to stay is **Moorcroft Motel,** 214 Yellowstone Ave., 307/756-3411, with rooms for $68, including fridges and microwaves.

OTHER PRACTICALITIES

Get meals at **Donna's Diner,** 203 W. Converse, 307/756-3422, and groceries from **Diehl's Super Market** on N. Bighorn Ave., 307/756-3491. For quick sandwiches, drop by the **Subway** on the east end of Moorcroft.

The main summertime event is **Moorcroft Jubilee Days** on the second Saturday in July, featuring a parade, games, barbecue, street dance, and bed races.

No local visitors center; drop by **Town Hall,** 104 N. Big Horn, 307/756-3526, for more about the moors and mores of Moorcroft. Moorcroft's **library** is at 105 E. Converse, 307/756-3232. Wash clothes at the **Laundry Basket Laundromat** on the west side of town.

Powder River Transportation/Coach USA, 307/682-0960 or 800/442-3682, has daily bus service from Moorcroft to Billings, Rapid City, Denver, and much of northern and eastern Wyoming.

KEYHOLE STATE PARK

Keyhole State Park, 307/756-3596, http://wyo parks.state.wy.us, surrounds Keyhole Reservoir, a 14,720-acre warm-water lake that backs up water from the Belle Fourche River. (The name comes from the "keyhole" brand, used by a local ranch.) The dam was built in 1952 by the Bureau of Reclamation and supplies irrigation water for South Dakota farmers. Most of the visitors are locals, but it's an okay place to camp. Pine trees crowd hills to the east, while grass and sage grow around the reservoir's western shore. Anglers angle for the biggest walleye and northern pike in the state, bird watchers watch for Merriam's turkeys and white pelicans, and snowmobilers 'bile around in winter.

Practicalities

Day use of the park is $4 for nonresident vehicles, $2 for Wyoming vehicles. **Camping** costs $12 for nonresidents, or $6 for Wyoming residents, at eight different state campgrounds along the lake's east and south shores. Nicest are Pats Point and Pronghorn Campgrounds.

Get to Keyhole State Park from I-90 by taking the Pine Ridge exit and continuing eight miles north. You'll find a swimming beach here, and the little settlement of **Pine Haven** (pop. 220; http://pinehaven.1wyo.net) contains **Keyhole Marina,** 307/756-9529, with supplies and boat rentals, a café, and RV hookups. Get supplies, booze, and grub from **Pine Haven Bar & Grill,** 307/756-9707. **Keyhole Golf Club,** 307/756-3775, has a nine-hole golf course. Every **Fourth of July,** the town of Pine Haven launches a grand display of fireworks over Keyhole Reservoir.

Sundance

The quiet hamlet of Sundance (pop. 1,200) nestles at the foot of Sundance Mountain. The mountain—"Temple of the Sioux"—rises a thousand feet above town and was an important sacred spot to the various tribes who claimed this land. Sundances were performed at its base each year. Sundance got its start in 1879, when rancher Albert Hoge set up a trading post here. The town grew slowly until the 1950s, when Sundance Air Base arrived. Since its closing, the town of Sundance has settled into middle age, with the old standbys of ranching and logging its economic mainstays, although tourism is increasingly important.

SIGHTS

Crook County Museum

The local museum, 307/283-3666, is housed in the basement of the Crook County Courthouse on Cleveland Street. Hours are Monday–Friday 8 A.M.–8 P.M. June–August, and Monday–Friday 8 A.M.–5 P.M. the rest of the year. Inside you'll find the usual collection of local paraphernalia, such as arrowheads, wooden wheelchairs, bison skulls, a Civil War battle

flag, and cowboy gear, plus more interesting displays on the Vore buffalo jump site, a 1910 Studebaker buggy, along with dioramas of an Indian buffalo trap and of Custer's 1874 camp at Inyan Kara Creek. The real attractions are the mementos from Harry Longabaugh's visit to the town. Better known as the "Sundance Kid," Longabaugh spent 18 months in Sundance's Crook County Jail for horse stealing before being pardoned by the governor in 1889. The museum has his indictment and wanted poster, along with the criminal bar docket signed by Longabaugh during his trial and furnishings from the original courthouse. A replica (built in 1983) of the jail that once housed the Sundance Kid stands beside the old stone high school.

Around Sundance

Access to 5,829-foot **Sundance Mountain** is via a dirt road that heads east from State Hwy. 116 about one-half mile south of town. An enjoyable trail leads to the top, gaining 800 feet in elevation along the way. From the summit, you're treated with views of the nearby Black Hills and,

THE BLACK HILLS

SUNDANCES

The most spectacular religious ceremony of the Plains Indians was the sundance. An annual event, it frequently attracted hundreds or even thousands of tribal onlookers, serving not simply as an important religious service but also as a social and political rally. Native American legends say that it originated centuries ago when a hunter was approached by a buffalo that suddenly spoke to him, offering a cure for sickness. Much later, an eagle came to another young man in a dream, prescribing the complete ceremony. The name is something of a misnomer because the dance was not a worship of the sun but a highly involved ceremony representing the creation of life and the triumph of good over evil. The specifics varied somewhat among the tribes. A common Native American term for it is "Thirsting Dance," referring to the long periods of dancing without water.

The sundance was always held in late spring or early summer and led by a young man who spent considerable time learning the complex ceremonial steps from a priest. If he passed the test, the pledger gained immense status in the village as a fearless leader. The festivities lasted up to two weeks, with the main ceremony an intense four-day event. Central to the sundance were an eagle representation (air), a buffalo head (earth), and a pole connecting the two to signify the sacred Tree of Life. The ceremony took place in a lodge, generally built around a central pole that forked at the top. After the sacred cottonwood tree had been selected by a scouting party, warriors attacked the tree in a furious charge. If it withstood this symbolic assault, the tree was cut down by a respected tribal woman and carried to the sun-dance site, where it was carefully erected. A bundle of brush (to represent an eagle or thunderbird nest) and a buffalo-skull altar were placed in the fork of the pole. Twelve other poles (the number varied with different tribes) were erected around the central one, with cross beams to the center. (Missionaries would later claim that the 12 poles around the central one were ritualistic representations of Jesus and the 12 apostles.) Brush was then laced around the outside to provide partial shade.

Supplicants spent four days without food or water, dancing, praying, blowing on eagle-bone whistles, and staring at the buffalo head, the sun, or a sacred doll as they waited for a vision of power. In most tribes, the sundance also involved self-mutilation. Assistants commonly cut small pieces of skin from the candidates' arms and shoulders as a blood sacrifice to the Great Spirit. (According to several accounts, before the battle at Little Big Horn, Sitting Bull sacrificed 100 pieces of flesh in a sun-dance ceremony, after which a vision told him of the coming destruction of General Custer and his men.) Torture commonly went even further, as assistants cut slices into the back or chest of the dancers and slid bone skewers into the muscle. Thongs would be attached between the skewers and the central pole, while other skewers held heavy buffalo skulls to be dragged behind. Candidates would lean back until the ropes were taut, jerking as they danced. Eventually the skin and muscle ripped loose and the dancers collapsed on the ground. In some tribes, the dancers were actually lifted off the ground by these tethers.

Whites found the sundance's torture difficult to understand and thought even less of such sexual aspects of the ceremony as the parading of a giant phallus. When the Indians were forced onto reservations, the sundance was outlawed, although some tribes continued to practice it secretly. Finally, in the late 1920s, the government relented, and a more sedate version of the dance was resurrected. The traditional blood sacrifice still exists among some tribes but not in Wyoming. Today, the sundance is performed in separate ceremonies by both the Shoshone and the Arapahoes on the Wind River Reservation. Visitors may watch but cannot take photos or videos.

The sundance is now performed primarily as a thanksgiving ceremony, to cure disease, and to pray for the coming year. After several days of preparation, the main ceremony lasts for four days. Without food or water, the dancers move into a trance state that brings visions and power. One authority describes dancers seeing the buffalo head shaking and steam coming out of its nostrils as the power is imparted. On the fourth day, a bucket of water is passed around to signal the end of the sundance, and that evening more dancing and feasting complete the ceremony.

on clear days, even the Big Horn Mountains 180 miles west. Call landowner Cecil Cundy at 307/283-2193 for permission to hike this trail.

Three miles west of the small settlement of **Beulah** (on the South Dakota border, 18 miles east of Sundance) is the **Vore Buffalo Jump,** where Indians drove thousands of bison into a pit between A.D. 1500–1800. The 200-foot-deep sinkhole is visible from I-90 and is marked by a small sign. Scientists believe 20,000 bison may have been killed here over the centuries.

The drive south from Beulah to Buckhorn provides a good taste of the Black Hills canyon country. Follow Sand Creek Road south from the freeway at Beulah, and you can drive for about 30 miles through canyons, the deserted mining town of Moskee, and on to Buckhorn along U.S. Hwy. 85. In the spring and fall a 4WD may be needed for the muddy conditions, and the route is closed in winter. The Sand Hill Country Club and state fish hatchery at Ranch A are favorites of deer, especially in fall and early winter, when hundreds of deer are visible from the road. There's no hunting here, so you're likely to see several trophy-sized animals.

Eleven miles south of Sundance on State Hwy. 116 is **Inyan Kara Mountain** (an Indian name meaning "Stone-Made Peak"), a 6,368-foot summit that dominates the surrounding country. In 1874, Gen. George A. Custer led a large scientific expedition through this region en route to the Black Hills. Among others, Custer climbed the mountain, carving "G. Custer '74" on a rock near the summit. The inscribed rock is still here, but call landowner Marshall Nussbaum at 307/283-2851 for permission to cross his land on the way up the mountain.

ACCOMMODATIONS

Visitors will find five places to stay in the Sundance area. Be sure to book a room up to one year ahead if you plan to visit during the Sturgis Rally Week the first week of August. (Some local motels jack the rates up 50 percent for this event.)

Find very nice accommodations at **Best Value Inn Bear Lodge,** 218 Cleveland, 307/283-1611 or 888/315-2378, which has rooms for $58–64 s or d. Some rooms have microwaves and fridges. **Arrowhead Motel** (Budget Host), right next door, 307/283-3307 or 800/456-6016, www.budgethost.com, has comfortable rooms for $55–60 s or d.

Deane's Pine View Motel, 117 N. 8th St., 307/283-2262, has cabins for $50 s or d and five-person units with kitchenettes for $75. Open Apr.–Nov. **Sundance Mountain Inn,** 26 Hwy. 585, 307/283-3737 or 888/347-2794, www.sundancewyoming.com/sundancemountaininn, offers renovated rooms for $59–89 s or $69–99 d. Amenities include an indoor pool and hot tub. Open mid-May through Nov.

The town's fanciest lodging is the **Best Western Inn at Sundance,** on the east edge of town at 121 S. 6th, 307/283-2800 or 800/238-0965, www.bestwestern.com/sundance. Rates are $60–80 s or 65–85 d, including a light breakfast and access to an indoor pool and hot tub.

Sundance Mt. Hideaway, 42 Sundance Mt. Rd., 307/283-3766 or 877/838-0063, www.sundancemountainhideaway.com, rents out two modern log cabins with private baths, kitchenettes, and covered porches. These are a good deal: $75 d with a filling homemade breakfast.

CAMPING

You can reserve a spot at the Forest Service's fine **Reuter Campground** ($9; open year-round), just four miles northwest of Sundance, by calling 518/885-3639 or 877/444-6777 ($9 fee). Make reservations on the web at www.reserveusa.com. Other public campgrounds in the Black Hills are described throughout this chapter. The private **Mountain View Campground,** 307/283-2270 or 800/792-8439, 1.5 miles east of town, has tent sites for $18, RV spaces for $24. An outdoor pool is on site, and they even have cable TV. Open Apr.–Oct.

FOOD

Higbee's Cafe, 101 N. 3rd, 307/283-2165, is open Monday–Friday only, cranking out dependably good American breakfasts and lunches. For three meals a day with daily specials, head to **Log Cabin Cafe,** 1620 Cleveland, 307/283-3393. **Aro Family Restaurant,** 307 Cleveland, 307/283-2000, has homemade soups and Friday-night prime rib; it's probably the best place in town.

Country Cottage, downtown on Cleveland, 307/283-2450, has frozen yogurt cones and a Subway shop for quick lunches. Get groceries from **Decker's Food Center,** 106 N. 7th, 307/283-3155.

RECREATION AND EVENTS

Swim in the large **outdoor pool** at the grade school, 307/283-2133; open June–Sept. Golfers will enjoy the nine-hole **Sundance Country Club,** 307/283-1191, on the east end of town.

The main event in Sundance is the **Sturgis Rally** during the first week of August (www.sturgis.com). Thousands of motorcyclists pass through or stay in Sundance, and the town sometimes puts on special biker events.

If you're around during late July and early August, don't miss the **Crook County Fair and Rodeo,** featuring sheep dog trials, various agricultural shows, pig wrestling, a parade, live music, and rodeo action.

INFORMATION AND SERVICES

The small **Sundance Information Center,** in the rest area at exit 189 off I-90, 307/283-2440, is open daily 7 A.M.–7 P.M. from April–September, then daily 8 A.M.–5 P.M. until mid-October; it's closed the rest of the year. You can also request brochures from the **Sundance Chamber of Commerce,** 307/283-1000, www.sundancewyoming.com.

The Forest Service's **Bearlodge Ranger District** is one mile east of town, 307/283-1361, www.fs.fed.us/r2/blackhills. The **post office** is at 2nd and Main Sts., 307/283-3939, and the **Crook County Library** is at 414 Main St., 307/283-1006. Get fast cash from **ATMs** inside the Texaco and Conoco gas stations.

Powder River Transportation/Coach USA, 307/682-0960 or 800/442-3682, has daily service to other parts of eastern and northern Wyoming, plus eastward runs to Spearfish, Sturgis, and Rapid City, South Dakota. They also can take you all the way to Billings or Denver.

Black Hills National Forest

Black Hills National Forest lies primarily within South Dakota but reaches across the state line near Sundance. Pres. Grover Cleveland established it in 1897 after a series of large forest fires focused attention on the need to protect the timber resource. The Forest Service's first commercial timber sale was held within the Black Hills, and the area is still a supplier for a Hulett lumber mill. Nearby, South Dakota's Black Hills contain a wide range of justifiably famous sites, including historic Deadwood—now a gambler's mecca—Jewel and Wind Caves, Mt. Rushmore, Crazy Horse Memorial, and an enormous bison herd inside Custer State Park. Black Hills National Forest offices inside Wyoming can be found at Sundance, 307/283-1361, and Newcastle, 307/746-2782. Stop by for a forest map and information on camping and local sights, or find them on the web at www.fs.fed.us/r2/blackhills.

SCENIC DRIVES

Many gravel roads wind up through the forested hills, and fall colors are brilliant along the aspen-lined stretches of the road just south of Cook Lake. A considerable amount of logging goes on within the ponderosa pine forests here, but it is selective logging, not clearcutting, and hence not as visible. Be sure to stop at **Warren Peak Lookout** eight miles north of Sundance. The road is paved to this point, and you can climb the tower for a magnificent vista and a chance to visit folks at one of the few active fire lookouts remaining in Wyoming. Another interesting drive heads

JUST A-RIDIN'

When my earthly trail is ended
And my final bacon curled
And the last great roundup's finished
At the Home Ranch of the world
I don't want no harps nor halos,
Robes nor other dressed up things—
Let me ride the starry ranges
On a pinto hawse with wings!

Just a-ridin', a-ridin'—
Nothing I'd like half so well
As a-roundin' up the sinners
That have wandered out of hell,
And a-ridin'

—Charles Badger Clark, Jr.

through the **Grand Canyon** area southeast of Sundance along Forest Road 863.

HIKING

Dozens of miles of hiking, biking, horseback riding, and cross-country ski trails twist through the hills just north of Sundance. For details,

pick up a "Sundance and Carson Draw Trails" map from the Forest Service office in Sundance or Newcastle. Good starting points for day hikes are the Cook Lake, Reuter, and Sundance Campgrounds mentioned as follows.

CAMPING

Four campgrounds lie within the Wyoming portion of the national forest. **Sundance Campground** ($14; open May–Nov.) has campsites and horse corrals just three miles north of Sundance. **Reuter Campground** ($9; open all year) is five miles northwest of Sundance, and **Cook Lake Campground** ($10; open year-round) is 16 miles north of Sundance on a tiny forest pond. You can make advance reservations for all three of these sites ($9 fee) by calling 518/885-3639 or 877/444-6777, or make reservations on the web at www.reserveusa.com. Free camping is also available at small **Bearlodge Campground** (open all year), seven miles west of Aladdin on State Hwy. 24. In addition, free dispersed camping is allowed on Forest Service land throughout the Black Hills. Over on the South Dakota side of the line, you'll find more than two-dozen additional Forest Service campgrounds.

THE BLACK HILLS

The Northern Black Hills

ALADDIN AND VICINITY

Aladdin (pop. 10) was established in the 1870s to supply coal for gold smelters in Lead and Deadwood, South Dakota. During Prohibition, these mines housed moonshine stills. At 3,740 feet, it's the lowest settlement in Wyoming. Don't blink or you'll miss it, but if you do blink, turn around and stop for a visit. Aladdin is dominated by the fluorescent red **Aladdin Store,** 307/896-2226, built in 1896 and operating continuously ever since. Out front is a "liar's bench" for local storytellers; inside is a potbelly stove and an ancient post office with the original boxes. It's worth a visit for a taste of unspoiled Americana. A small antique shop is upstairs with interesting col-

lectibles from the area, and RVs can park in the old rodeo grounds across the street.

Next to the store is **Aladdin Hard Buck Cafe,** 307/896-2100, with all-American grub. A basic motel is also here; call the general store for details. More surprising is the homeopathic doctor's office; he's regarded as one of the best in the region. Across the street is a shady town park.

Just south of Aladdin is **The Bunkhouse,** 307/283-3542, a modern place with three bedrooms and a bathroom for $50 d. The owners live nearby and come over to make a filling breakfast each morning. Only one couple or family can stay here at a time, so you get the entire place to yourself.

Ten miles northeast of Aladdin is the **lowest point in Wyoming.** From here, the Belle Fourche

River drops only another 3,125 feet on its several-thousand-mile descent to the sea via the Missouri and Mississippi Rivers. Just east of Aladdin is the **Tipple Mine Historical Site,** with restored coal-loading chutes and other facilities. Approximately two miles east of Aladdin is a historical marker noting the still-visible tracks left by the party of 110 wagons, 2,000 animals, and 1,000 men led by Gen. George A. Custer in the summer of 1874. Despite the Treaty of 1868 that reaffirmed this as Sioux Indian land, Custer's geologists, scouts, miners, and engineers had come to explore the Black Hills and investigate the rumors of gold. Gold was indeed found by Custer's miners, and when word got out, the rush was on. Custer's own rush to judgment at Montana's Little Big Horn had also begun. He and all 268 of his men would die there just two years later.

On the other side of Aladdin, State Hwy. 24 follows Beaver Creek past 150-foot-tall sandstone cliffs, ridge-top pines, and valley-bottom oaks. Old farmsteads appear, surrounded by fields filled with huge pyramid-like hay piles. The dot of a place called **Alva** (pop. 50) has a few old homes in the midst of the Bear Lodge Mountains but nothing in the way of services. West of Alva the road climbs up into rolling grassy hills with trees in the draws and cattle grazing along the Belle Fourche River.

HULETT

The tiny logging and ranching town of Hulett (pop. 400) lies right along the Belle Fourche and is just 10 miles north of Devils Tower National Monument. Two lumber mills saw up timber from the adjacent Black Hills National Forest. The side of **Hulett National Bank** has burned-in brands from local cattle ranchers. A couple of miles west of Hulett you'll see bison grazing at a private ranch while magnificent Devils Tower looms on the horizon.

Sights

Rogues Gallery, 307/467-5869, www.devilstowermuseum.com, sells antiques, Indian artifacts, and the paintings of local artists Bob Coronato and Tom Waugh. There's a little museum in the back with Indian artifacts. Open summers only.

Food and Accommodations

For food in Hulett, try **Ponderosa Cafe** or **Pizza Plus.** The town also has a country grocery store, a bank, a hardware store, and a medical clinic. Get espresso at **Hulett Motel,** 307/467-5220, where standard rooms are $55 s or d, and suites cost $65 d. Open May–Nov. **Pioneer Motel,** 307/467-5656, has rooms for $50 s or d. Most contain fridges, and kitchenettes are also available. Park RVs at **S-A RV Camp,** a not-so-glorified parking lot that's open May–November.

Ten miles southeast of Hulett, **Diamond L Guest Ranch,** 307/467-5236 or 800/851-5909, www.diamondlranch.com, houses a dozen or so guests at a time. The main activity is horseback riding, but you can also join in the chores and pretend to be a real ranch hand or just soak in the hot tub. There's a three-night minimum stay in the summer, but most guests book by the week. All-inclusive weekly rates are $2,100 for two people. Open May–Sept.

Tumbling T Guest Ranch, 307/467-5625, www.tumblingt.com, is an 8,000-acre ranch just four miles from Devils Tower. The ranch accommodates up to 38 guests in a newly built lodge and bunkhouse, and meals are a culinary treat. It's open all year, with horseback riding and fly-fishing the primary activities in summer, followed by hunting in the fall and cross-country skiing all winter. Lodging is available on a nightly basis for $30 s or $60 d, including a full breakfast, or on an all-inclusive weekly rate of $1,400 for two people.

7 W Ranch, 307/878-4493, www.7wranch .com, serves up ranch vacations based in their modern home on a 20,000-acre spread near Hulett. There's space for up to nine guests, with horseback rides, cattle drives, wagon rides, and fishing on the agenda. Rates are $350 per day for two people, with a three-day minimum. Open year-round.

Entertainment and Events

For entertainment, most evenings you'll find

folks at the horseshoe pit next to the hardware store, or you can head to **Rodeo Saloon** or **Ponderosa Bar** for a beer.

Hulett Rodeo takes place on the second weekend of June each year and is a great local event. Actually, the biggest local event isn't actually in Hulett but in nearby Sturgis, South Dakota. Sturgis Rally Week (first week of August; www.sturgis.com) attracts thousands of motorcyclists to the Black Hills, filling every hotel and bar for a hundred miles in all directions. Hulett's **Ham and Jam**—a hog roast on Wednesday of Rally Week—is a huge local draw, with live music at the bars and throngs of bikers filling the streets, and a mechanical bull to test your manhood.

Other Practicalities

Get Hulett information on the web at www.hulett.org. Hulett's **library** is in the high school. Golfers will appreciate **Devils Tower Country Club**, 307/467-5773 or 877/467-5773, www.devilstowergolf.com, which has a publicly accessible 18-hole course. Mini-golfers can putter around at **Rendezvous Ridge Mini-Golf**, 307/467-5912.

OSHOTO

West and then south from Hulett is the tiny town of Oshoto (a Native American word meaning "Bad Weather"), accessible only via gravel roads. No services are available; all that's here is a post office. The **Brislawn Cayuse Ranch,** 307/467-5394, near Oshoto is one of the few places in America that has pure-blooded Spanish Mustangs—tough, small horses that were the pride of the Wild West. These are not the wild horses of the West, but true descendants of those brought by the Spanish. Bob Brislawn ("Mr. Mustang") started working to save the mustangs in 1925 and founded the Spanish Mustang Registry (www.spanishmustang.org) in 1957. He died in 1979, but his son Emmett carries on the tradition at the ranch.

ALZADA AND COLONY

North from Hulett, State Hwy. 112 heads to the Montana border settlement of Alzada, cutting across land not unlike the foothills of California's Sierra Nevada. Cottonwoods and oaks fill the draws, and grassy meadows alternate with tree-topped hills. This land is very scenic, with an abundance of white-tailed deer all the way. The road doesn't really go anywhere that most tourists are heading; therefore, it is perfect for cyclists and anyone with an explorer's streak. From Alzada, U.S. Hwy. 212 cuts southeast across Wyoming and to the South Dakota town of Belle Fourche. Along the way it passes a couple of bentonite mines in the grass-and-sage country around the nothing settlement called Colony. Antelope and cattle abound. Talk about confusion: Since there's no post office in Colony, Wyoming, locals have South Dakota addresses on a Montana delivery route!

Devils Tower National Monument

In the 1977 film *Close Encounters of the Third Kind,* Devils Tower was used as the contact point for aliens and humans. It was an appropriate choice. Rising 1,267 feet above the surrounding plain, this otherworldly apparition seems an appropriate metaphor for the mystery of life and our attempts to understand the universe. The flat-topped column of rock seems to push out of the earth like an enormous sawed-off stump from Paul Bunyan's forest. From a distance, Devils Tower looks as if some giant beast had scratched it, with parallel gouges running up the sides. Up closer, the gouges turn into enormous columns of rock molded into hexagonal columns (some have four, five, or seven sides). In the setting sun, Devils Tower glows a golden red long after the surrounding hills no longer reflect the sun's rays, and as night comes on, the stars and moon outline its bold shape against the horizon.

Ponderosa pine and burr oak forests surround Devils Tower, and the winding Belle Fourche River flows less than one mile away. A large colony of **black-tailed prairie dogs** prospers along the river just inside the park, with hundreds of the little critters running around, much to the delight of tourists. You're also likely to see white-tailed deer feeding in the meadows. On top, Devils Tower is a fairly flat oval approximately 300 feet by 180 feet.

GEOLOGY

Geologists still dispute the precise way that Devils Tower formed, but they agree that the process began approximately 65 million years ago when a mass of molten magma was forced up through the overlying sedimentary rocks. As the igneous material cooled and contracted, vertical fractures formed in the magma, creating long columnar joints—the "scratches" up the side of Devils Tower today. (Some of these columns are as big as 14 feet in diameter!) Eventually, precipitation and gravity eroded away the softer sedimentary rock and the Belle Fourche River carried it away, leaving behind the harder core of Devils Tower. Surround-

ing the 1,000-foot-wide base of the Tower is a mass of talus from fallen pieces of columns, but erosion of this very hard igneous rock is very slow. The four prominent peaks of the **Missouri Buttes,** four miles northwest of Devils Tower, were formed in a similar manner. At 500 to 800 feet in height, they are not as dramatic and lie outside the national monument's boundaries.

HISTORY

Devils Tower is known to Native Americans by a variety of names, most commonly Bear Lodge, Tree Lodge, or Bear's Tepee. Fur trappers and early explorers certainly knew of the existence of Bear Lodge, but no note of it was made until 1857, when an exploration party led by Lt. G. K. Warren saw the rock from a distance. In 1875, Col. Richard I. Dodge finally led a U.S. Geological Survey party to the formation. Dodge somehow came up with the name Devils Tower, claiming that the Native Americans called it "Bad God's Tower." Despite protests that "Bear Lodge" had long been the aboriginal name, the label Devils Tower stuck. Indians in the area regard the name Devils Tower an affront because they consider this rock a sacred place.

Establishing the Monument

After the Indians had been driven from their traditional homeland in the 1870s, northeast Wyoming was opened to settlement by whites. Most lands were available to the homesteaders, but the General Land Office prevented developers from gaining this freak of geology. Wyoming already had America's first national park in Yellowstone, and support soon grew to make the Tower a second one. After years of effort, Pres. Theodore Roosevelt proclaimed Devils Tower the country's first national monument in 1906. Unfortunately, the final monument was only 1,153 acres in size and excludes the Missouri Buttes.

The First Climb

In the early years of Devils Tower National Monument, the area served as a popular spot for picnics and camping, especially on the Fourth of July, when Independence Day celebrations attracted settlers from the entire region. The most famous of all these events came in 1893. Handbills announced that the "unclimbable" summit would be scaled and "On July 4th, 1893, Old Glory will be flung to the breeze from the top of the Tower, 800 feet from the ground by Wm. Rogers." The stunt was well planned. Several days before, two local ranchers, William Rogers and Willard Ripley, drove wooden pegs into a long crack that led to the top and tied the pegs together with strips of wood to make a ladder. They hauled a 12-foot flagpole to the top and returned on July 4 to scale the ladder in front of 800 people. Once on top (it took an hour to climb), Rogers unfurled a flag but a gust of wind blew it off. Wives of the promoters tore it up and sold the pieces as souvenirs (stripes cost 25 cents, stars 50). The climb was a smashing success.

On July 4, 1895, Mrs. Rogers became the first woman to climb the ladder to the top of Devils Tower, and many other adventurous folks followed over the next several decades. The ladder was last climbed in 1927, but pieces of it are still visible today along the southeast side of the Tower. An iron stairway to the top, proposed by Wyoming's Congressman Mondell as a tourist attraction, was never built.

Developing the Tower

For many years, Devils Tower remained undeveloped, and a bridge across the Belle Fourche River to the site was not built until 1928. During the Depression, the CCC constructed a log visitors center, new roads, trails, picnic areas, and a campground. Visitation increased as access became easier and more families acquired automobiles. One of the strangest events came in 1941, when George Hopkins—one of the top skydivers in the world—parachuted out of a plane to the top of Devils Tower as a publicity stunt. He had planned to descend on a 1,000-foot rope, but the rope landed on the side of the Devils Tower, leaving him stranded on top. Newspapers all over the country headlined his plight. Food and blankets were dropped to him, and for the next six days he spent a lonely vigil on top waiting to be rescued. Finally, Jack Durrance, a mountain climber who had scaled Devils Tower three years before, arrived to lead seven other

Devils Tower National Monument

© DON PITCHER

THE BLACK HILLS

climbers to the top and help Hopkins down. Many years later, in 1976, *Close Encounters of the Third Kind* was filmed here. Several hundred locals appeared in the crowd scenes. When the movie was released the following year, tourism here suddenly hit the stars.

CLIMBING DEVILS TOWER

Although Devils Tower was first climbed in 1893 on a wooden ladder, the first ascent using modern rock-climbing techniques was not until 1937. Led by Fritz Wiessner, three New York City climbers made it to the top in a little less than five hours. Over the years, as climbing technology has improved and as more people have been attracted to the sport, Devils Tower has become one of the favorite climbing spots in the nation. During summer you're bound to meet several dozen climbers heading for the base of Devils Tower each morning. More than 50,000 people have reached the top, and the figure grows by 2,000 each year.

Climbing has not been without controversy. Some Indian leaders have called climbing the rock a sacrilege and demanded that it be closed, while climbers have trumpeted it as one of the premier crack-climbing areas in the nation. The Park Service came up with a compromise plan that includes a voluntary climbing closure for the month of June. Additional regulations were put into place emphasizing clean climbing techniques and restricting access to falcon nesting areas during the breeding season. Be sure to contact the monument for specifics and safety information before you climb.

For information on the various routes (at least 220 have been climbed), pick up one of the technical guidebooks in the visitors center: *Devils Tower National Monument—A Climber's Guide* by Steve Gardiner and Dick Guilmette (Devils Tower Natural History Association) or the more technical *Free Climbs of Devils Tower* by Dingus McGee and The Last Pioneer Woman (I somehow suspect that these are pseudonyms). Displays in the visitors center and at a kiosk out front describe climbing routes and techniques. Climbing demonstrations are given here daily during July and August. If you're planning to climb Devils Tower, be sure to register at the visitors center.

Climbing Guides

Those who want to climb Devils Tower but lack the skills or equipment can choose from several permitted guide companies. Even rank beginners can summit the Tower if they are in good condition but will need a day of climbing instruction ($125 or so), plus a second day to do the actual climb for a total of around $250–300. You can choose either private instruction or groups of up to four students per guide (cheaper, of course).

You won't go wrong with Frank Sanders of **Above All Guiding/Devils Tower Lodge,** www.devilstowerclimbing.com, who has been climbing here since 1972. Other recommended guides include **Black Hills Rock & Ice Climbing Guides,** in Spearfish, South Dakota, 605/722-0081, www.rockandiceguides.com; **Jackson Hole Mountain Guides** in Jackson, 307/733-4979 or 800/239-7642, www.jhmg.com; **Exum Mountain Guides,** 307/733-2297, www.exumguides.com; **National Outdoors Leadership School (NOLS)** in Lander, 307/332-4784,

---

KIOWA DEVILS TOWER LEGEND

The place we call Devils Tower was known to the Kiowa Indians as T'sou'a'e, meaning "Aloft on a Rock." Many tales are told about the origins of this mystical place, but the best known is that of the Kiowa.

Once upon a time, the people camped along a stream that had many bears. Seven sisters and their brother were playing nearby when the boy suddenly turned into a ferocious bear and began chasing the girls. In desperation, the girls climbed on a small rock and prayed, "Rock, take pity on us—rock, save us!" The rock started to grow, pushing them higher and higher as the bear clawed at the sides, trying to get them. Eventually the seven girls were pushed upward into the sky, forming the points of the Big Dipper. The gouges from the bear remain today on the sides of Devils Tower.

www.nols.edu; and **Sylvan Rocks Climbing School and Guide Service** in Hill City, South Dakota, 605/574-2425, www.sylvanrocks.com. You might also want to contact Andy Petefish of **Above Ouray Ice & Tower Rock Climbing School,** 307/756-9470 or 888/345-9061, www.towerguides.com.

HIKING TRAILS

Four different trails loop through this small national monument, providing fine views of Devils Tower and the surrounding country. Most popular is the 1.3-mile **Tower Trail,** which circles the Tower. It's an easy paved path with periodic openings offering impressive views of the summit, along with side paths to see the nearby Missouri Buttes and the Belle Fourche River. Be sure to look through the peep sight to find the old wooden ladder that once went all the way to the top of Devils Tower.

   Red Beds/South Side Trail is a three-mile dirt path that also takes off near the visitors center but makes a longer, less-crowded loop around Devils Tower. Along the way you get nice views of the Belle Fourche River and the Red Beds—iron-stained bluffs near the river. A 30-minute side loop, the 1.5-mile **Valley View Trail,** takes you to the prairie dog town and the Belle Fourche River.

   You'll catch the finest views of Devils Tower from the **Joyner Ridge Trail,** a 1.5-mile path. Views from this hilltop trail are unforgettable, especially at sunrise and sunset. It's a delightful secret escape from crowds elsewhere.

ACCESS AND INFORMATION

For general park information, call the **Devils Tower National Monument office** at 307/467-5283, or visit them on the Internet at www.nps.gov/deto. The monument is 33 miles northeast of Moorcroft. Access is from State Hwy. 24, seven miles north of its junction with U.S. Hwy. 14. Entrance costs $8 for vehicles, $3 for hikers or cyclists, and the passes are good for seven days. Annual passes to the monument cost $20, or you can purchase a National Park Pass ($50), which lets you into all national parks

black-tailed prairie dog

and monuments. Seniors get in free with a Golden Age Pass (for a one-time fee of $10). The monument is open year-round 24 hours a day, although most of the more than 400,000 annual visitors arrive during summer.

   Beyond the entrance station, it is approximately three miles along a paved road to the base of Devils Tower, where you'll find a pleasant old log **visitors center,** 307/467-5283, and a parking lot that overflows on sunny summer days with rock climbers, day-hikers, and gawkers. The visitors center is open daily 8 A.M.–8 P.M. from Memorial Day to Labor Day, and daily 9 A.M.–4 P.M. from mid-March to Memorial Day and from Labor Day to mid-November (but these hours could change). Inside the visitors center, you can look at ecological displays and photos showing the dozens of climbing routes, and buy books on local lore. The center is closed from mid-November to mid-March, but you can get information on winter weekdays from park headquarters.

   Campfire programs are held several times a week during the summer at the campground amphitheater, with the standard Park Service

THE BLACK HILLS

fare of talks, tunes, and transparencies. Ranger walks and talks take place throughout summer; ask at the visitors center for upcoming events.

CAMPING, FOOD, AND ACCOMMODATIONS

The Park Service maintains a fine **campground** ($12; open May–Oct.) one-half mile inside the entrance. In midsummer, get a space at the campground in the morning to be sure of having a spot. There's an eight-person limit at the campsites. Unfortunately, the Park Service is planning to close the campground, although this probably won't happen until 2008 or later.

Just outside the monument are two private campgrounds. At **Devils Tower KOA,** 307/467-5395 or 800/562-5785, www.koa.com, sites cost $16 for tents, $20 for RVs, and $40 d for simple cabins. The KOA has a heated outdoor pool and is open mid-May to late September. Horseback and hayrides are available here, and if you haven't seen it before, you can watch *Close Encounters* on the TV. Most folks stock up on food in nearby towns, but the café here serves meals, ice cream, and espresso, and a general store sells limited supplies and gifts.

Devils Tower Trading Post, 307/467-5295, www.devilstowertradingpost.com, is directly across the road from the KOA and stocks a few food items, gifts, and trinkets, and has a fast-food eatery. During the Sturgis Rally, they fly an enormous American flag.

Just up the road from the entrance is the other nearby private campground: **Fort Devils Tower RV Park,** 307/467-5655. Rates are $16 for tents or $20 for RVs. It's open mid-April through October, with a saloon and restaurant for meals.

Andy Petefish of **Tower Guides,** 307/756-9470 or 888/345-9061, www.towerguides.com, has cozy rental cabins ($35 with private or shared bath) and campsites ($10) next to his office 3.5 miles south of Devils Tower on U.S. Hwy. 24.

THE MORAL OF THE STORY

If the reader thinks he is done, now, and that this book has no moral to it, he is in error. The moral of it is this: If you are of any account, stay at home and make your way by faithful diligence; but if you are "no account," go away from home, and then you will have to work, whether you want to or not. Thus you become a blessing to your friends by ceasing to be a nuisance to them—if the people you go among suffer by the operation.

—Mark Twain in *Roughing It*

Owned by climbing guide Frank Sanders, **Devils Tower Lodge,** 307/467-5267 or 888/314-5267, www.devilstowerlodge.com, is an attractive home hidden away on 21 acres near the base of Devils Tower. Four guest rooms are available, all with private baths and access to the hot tub and large indoor gym. Rates are $105–155 d, including breakfast and a full dinner. Also available is a comfortable three-bedroom, two-bath home three miles from the Tower. This one has stunning views of Devils Tower, with space for 12. It rents for $125 d, plus $10 per person for additional guests, and has a full kitchen. In addition to accommodations, Devils Tower Lodge also offers several climbing packages for everyone from beginners to experienced climbers, including a five-day seminar for climbers who want to kick their abilities to a higher level.

A **post office,** 307/467-5937, stands just outside the park entrance gate. Each Fourth of July folks come from miles around to watch a big **fireworks** show put on by the KOA near Devils Tower.

Resources

Suggested Reading

Note: Several of the following books are now out of print. You can find many of them in Wyoming libraries, or check the web for special orders or rare book auctions. Websites like www.amazon.com, www.barnesandnoble.com, and others will also search used bookstores for out-of-print titles.

Description and Travel

Anderson, Susan. *Living in Wyoming: Settling for More.* New York: Fodor's Travel Publications, www.fodors.com, 1990. A witty and insightful book about the people of Wyoming. Outstanding photos by Zbigniew Bzdak.

Burt, Nathaniel. *Wyoming.* New York: Fodor's Travel Publications, www.fodors.com, 2002. Provides a tour of Wyoming and its historical attractions. Photography by Don Pitcher.

Cook, Jeannie (ed.). *Buffalo Bill's Town in the Rockies: A Pictorial History of Cody, Wyoming.* Cody, WY: Park County Historical Society, 1996. A photographic visit to Cody's interesting past.

Ehrlich, Gretel. *A Match to the Heart.* New York: Pantheon Books, www.randomhouse.com, 1994. The harrowing story of the author's long recovery after being struck by lightning while working on the Wyoming range.

Ehrlich, Gretel. *The Solace of Open Spaces.* New York: Viking Penguin, www.penguinputnam.com, 1985. A stunningly beautiful collection of observations and stories about ranch life in Wyoming from one of America's finest writers.

Kilgore, Gene. *Gene Kilgore's Ranch Vacations.* Emeryville, CA: Avalon Travel Publishing, www.travelmatters.com, 2001. The definitive guide to dude and guest ranches in Wyoming and the rest of North America. Includes detailed, up-to-date descriptions of the best places to be a city-slicker cowboy.

Lewis, Dan. *8,000 Miles of Dirt: A Backroad Travel Guide to Wyoming.* Casper, WY: Hawks Book Co., 1992. Describes dozens of the state's most enjoyable back roads in a folksy but not always informative manner. (Example: The chapter on the Outlaw Cave drive doesn't bother to mention the cave's most famous inhabitant, Butch Cassidy!)

McClure, Michael. *Camping Wyoming.* Atlantic City, WY: WigRaf Publishing, www.campwyo.com, 1999. An amazingly detailed guide to virtually every possible Wyoming camping spot.

Munn, Debra D. *Ghosts on the Range: Eerie True Tales of Wyoming.* Boulder, CO: Pruett Publishing, www.pruettpublishing.com, 1991. A popular book filled with ghost stories from across the state.

Parent, Laurence. *Scenic Driving Wyoming.* Guilford, CT: Globe Pequot Press (Falcon), www.falconbooks.com, 1997. The best and most complete guide to scenic roads in Wyoming.

Pitcher, Don. *Moon Handbooks Yellowstone & Grand Teton.* Emeryville, CA: Avalon Travel Publishing, www.moon.com, 2003. The companion guide to this one, with in-depth coverage for Wyoming's most-visited corner.

Roberts, Steven L., David L. Roberts, and Phil Roberts. *Wyoming Almanac.* Laramie, WY: Skyline West Press, 2001. Packed with almost 500 pages of Wyoming trivia, including such things as the average market price for Wyoming low-sulfur coal and the number of cabooses now used for other purposes. Hard to plow through it all (no index), but there are some real gems buried in this avalanche of facts.

Urbanek, Mae. *Wyoming Place Names.* Missoula, MT: Mountain Press Publishing, www.mountainpress.com, 1988. An excellent sourcebook for the names of everything from Abiathar Peak to the town of Zenith.

Williamson, Chilton, Jr. *Roughnecking It.* New York: Simon and Schuster, www.simonsays.com, 1982. A funny, insightful, and disturbing portrait of Wyoming during the oil-boom years of the early 1980s. Gonzo journalism at its best. Out of print.

Work Projects Administration. *Wyoming: A Guide to its History, Highways, and People.* Lincoln, NE: University of Nebraska Press, www.unp.udl.edu, 1981. Reprint of a depression-era guide to Wyoming originally printed in 1940, this classic guide still makes fascinating reading. Out of print.

Geology and Geography

Blackstone, D. L., Jr. *Traveler's Guide to the Geology of Wyoming.* Laramie, WY: Geological Survey of Wyoming, www.wsgsweb.uwyo.edu, 1988. An excellent overview of Wyoming's geological history and how to see it in today's landscapes.

Largeson, David R., and Darwin R. Spearing. *Roadside Geology of Wyoming.* Missoula, MT: Mountain Press Publishing, www.mountainpress.com, 1988. Wyoming is perhaps the most geologically interesting of all the states. This is an invaluable road guide for anyone wanting to know more about geology without resorting to dense textbooks.

McPhee, John. *Basin and Range.* New York: Farrar, Straus & Giroux, www.fsgbooks.com, 1980. The book details how the landscape of Wyoming was created. Only this Pulitzer Prize–winning author could turn the complex story of plate tectonics into such an easy-to-read volume.

McPhee, John. *Rising from the Plains.* New York: The Noonday Press, 1986. A delightful intertwining of the story of Wyoming's complex geology and the life of its preeminent geologist, David Love.

Robinson, Charles. *Geology of Devils Tower.* Devils Tower, WY: Devils Tower Natural History Association, 1995. The definitive geologic story of this famous national monument.

Fiction

Ehrlich, Gretel. *Heart Mountain.* New York: Viking Penguin, www.penguinputnam.com, 1988. A touching novel about life in the Heart Mountain Relocation Camp near Cody, the forced home for hundreds of Japanese-Americans during World War II.

Nye, Bill. *Bill Nye's Western Humor.* Lincoln, NE: University of Nebraska Press, www.unp.unl.edu, 1968. A collection of delightfully wry essays by one of America's best-known 19th-century humorists. Out of print.

Proulx, Annie. *Close Range: Wyoming Stories.* New York: Scribner, www.simonsays.com, 1999. Pulitzer Prize–winning novelist Annie Proulx now lives in Wyoming, and this book takes on the characters in her home state. Wyomingites may take umbrage at her unflattering portrayals, but take these stories for what they are—fiction. A good read.

Wister, Owen. *The Virginian.* Originally published in 1902 and now available from various publishers. The classic Western novel that established the cowboy hero and the lure of Wyoming.

Biography

Alter, Cecil J. *Jim Bridger.* Norman, OK: University of Oklahoma Press, www.oupress.com, 1979. The incredible story of the most famous of all mountain men.

Anonymous. *The Sweet Smell of Sagebrush: A Prisoner's Diary 1903–1912.* Rawlins, WY: Friends of the Old Penitentiary, 1990. This wonderful small volume contains the writings of an "anonymous" criminal (John Kirby), who served four terms in the Rawlins penitentiary for horse stealing and other crimes. It not only provides descriptions of his many escapades outside the law but also opens a window on the criminal mind.

Killoren, John J. *Come Blackrobe, DeSmet and the Indian Tragedy.* Norman, OK: University of Oklahoma Press, www.oupress.com, 1995. The story of Jesuit missionary Pierre Jean DeSmet, who spent his life in a futile attempt to protect the Plains Indians from the Manifest Destiny of American culture.

Olsen, Jack. *Doc: The Rape of the Town of Lovell.* New York: Dell, www.randomhouse.com, 1990. The true but hard-to-believe story of a respected physician who raped dozens of women in this small, religious town.

Pointer, Larry. *In Search of Butch Cassidy.* Norman, OK: University of Oklahoma Press, www.oupress.com, 1989. A thoroughly researched book that seems to show that Butch Cassidy's death in South America was a ruse and that he died much later in Seattle.

Rosa, Joseph G., and Robin May. *Buffalo Bill and His Wild West.* Lawrence, KS: University Press of Kansas, www.kansaspress.ku.edu, 1989. One of the newer books on Buffalo Bill, with a somewhat revisionist take on his life and times. Rich in detail on Cody's Wild West show.

Russell, Don. *The Lives and Legends of Buffalo Bill.* Norman, OK: University of Oklahoma Press, www.oupress.com, 1979. The most complete biography on the life of Buffalo Bill Cody.

Woods, L. Milton. *Moreton Frewen's Western Adventures.* Boulder, CO: Roberts Rinehart, www.roberts-rinehart.com, 1986. The strange tale of a wealthy British adventurer who made and lost his (and other folks') fortunes in Wyoming. Out of print.

Outdoor Recreation

Additional recreation titles are listed under the headings for Jackson Hole and Grand Teton National Park and Yellowstone National Park. Several years back, Falcon Books suddenly produced an incredible array of outdoor recreation titles, covering virtually every possible niche in the Rockies. At last count, they had 34 books on Wyoming alone! Falcon is now owned by Globe Pequot Press, and they are in turn owned by Morris Communications. I'm sure there's a lesson here somewhere about overreaching, but readers are the beneficiaries, with detailed coverage for some rather obscure topics. I'm still waiting for Falcon to do a guide for left-handed birdwatchers in the Beartooth Mountains. A few of the Falcon titles are listed as follows; find the rest at www.falconbooks.com.

Birkby, Jeff. *Touring Montana and Wyoming Hot Springs.* Guilford, CT: Globe Pequot Press (Falcon), www.falconbooks.com, 1999.

Fanselow, Julie. *Traveling the Oregon Trail.* Guilford, CT: Globe Pequot Press (Falcon), www.falconbooks.com, 2001.

Graham, Kenneth L. *Camping Wyoming and the Black Hills.* Guilford, CT: Globe Pequot Press (Falcon), www.falconbooks.com, 2001.

Graham, Kenneth Lee. *Fishing Wyoming.* Guilford, CT: Globe Pequot Press (Falcon), www.falconbooks.com, 1998. A 300-page tome that goes far beyond the standard coverage of Yellowstone and Jackson Hole.

Guillmette, Richard, Renée Carrier, and Steve Gardiner. *Devils Tower National Monument: A Climber's Guide.* Devils Tower, WY: Devils Tower Natural History Association, 1995. A detailed guide to one of the most varied and enjoyable rock faces in Wyoming.

Herrero, Stephen. *Bear Attacks: Their Causes and Avoidance.* Guilford, CT: The Lyons Press, www.lyonspress.com, 2002. An authoritative volume on the lives of bears and staying safe in their country.

Hunger, Bill. *Hiking Wyoming.* Guilford, CT: Globe Pequot Press (Falcon), www.falconbooks.com, 2003. A fine, detailed book that describes 75 different hikes in all parts of the state.

Kelsey, Joe. *Climbing and Hiking in the Wind River Mountains.* Guilford, CT: Globe Pequot Press (Falcon), www.falconbooks.com, 1996. Accurate information on most of the hiking trails and descriptions of hundreds of technical climbs.

Lewis, Dan. *The Floater's Guide to Wyoming Rivers.* Douglas, WY: Wyoming Naturalist, 1991. Filled with details on 27 Wyoming rivers and 1,700 miles of river trips.

Mitchell, Finis. *Wind River Trails.* Salt Lake City, UT: University of Utah Press, www.upress.utah.edu, 1999. A folksy, inexpensive guide by a man who hiked this country for 80 years.

Molvar, Erik. *Hiking Wyoming's Cloud Peak Wilderness.* Guilford, CT: Globe Pequot Press (Falcon), www.falconbooks.com, 1999. A complete guide to the Big Horn's dramatic wilderness country.

Phillips, Wayne. *Central Rocky Mountain Wildflowers: Including the Greater Yellowstone Ecosystem.* Guilford, CT: Globe Pequot Press (Falcon), www.falconbooks.com, 1999.

Retallic, Ken. *Flyfisher's Guide to Wyoming.* Gallatin Gateway, MT: Wilderness Adventures Press, 1998. An excellent guide; particularly helpful for anglers headed to Yellowstone.

Schneider, Bill. *Bear Aware: Hiking and Camping in Bear Country.* Guilford, CT: Globe Pequot/Falcon, www.faloconbooks.com, 2001. A handy pocket-size book that is easy to read and up to date.

Travsky, Amber. *Mountain Biking Wyoming.* Guilford, CT: Globe Pequot Press (Falcon), www.falconbooks.com, 1999.

Woods, Rebecca. *Walking the Winds: A Hiking & Fishing Guide to Wyoming's Wind River Range.* Alpenbooks, www.alpenbooks.com, 1994. A useful guide to hiking trails in the Winds.

History

Baber, D. F. *The Longest Rope.* Caldwell, ID: The Caxton Printers, www.caxtonprinters.com, 1953. The fascinating story of the Johnson County War as told by William Walker, the only surviving "rustler" witness of the siege at KC Ranch. Out of print.

Bille, Ed. *Early Days at Salt Creek and Teapot Dome.* Casper, WY: Mountain States Lithographing Co., www.mtstlitho.com, 1978. The story of oil boom times in Wyoming's most famous oil fields. Many fine old photos. Out of print.

Brown, Larry K. *The Hog Ranches of Wyoming: Liquor, Lust, and Lies Under Sagebrush Skies.* Glendo, WY: High Plains Press, 1995. A playful book about the saloon/dance hall/brothels that sprang up around Wyoming's frontier forts.

Bryans, Bill. *Deer Creek: Frontiers Crossroad in Pre-Territorial Wyoming.* Casper, WY: Mountain States Lithographing Co., www.mtstlitho.com, 1990. A surprisingly engaging history of the Glenrock area, an important way station on the Oregon/Mormon/California Trail.

Burt, Struthers. *Powder River: Let 'er Buck.* New York: Rinehart, www.roberts-rinehart.com, 1938. A classic book on this famous part of Wyoming by one of the finest writers to come out of the state. Out of print.

Carlisle, Bill. *Lone Bandit. An Autobiography.* Pasadena, CA: Trails End Publishing Co., 1946. The story of the last of the old Wyoming outlaws, the "gentleman train robber" who later opened a popular Laramie motel. Out of print.

Coffman, Lloyd W. *Blazing a Wagon Trail to Oregon.* Springfield, OR: Echo Books, 1993. The experience and drama—much told in the participants' own words—of the "great migration," with details on Fort Bridger, Fort Laramie, Independence Rock, and other Wyoming stopping places.

Combs, Barry B. *Westward to Promontory: Building the Union Pacific Across the Plains and Mountains.* New York: Crown Publishers, 1986. How the West was really won. Includes a wonderful collection of historic photos by Andrew J. Russell. Out of print.

DeVoto, Bernard. *Across the Wide Missouri.* New York: Houghton Mifflin Co., www.hmco.com, 1990. Reissue of a 1947 book on the Rocky Mountain fur trade and how it shaped American culture. A classic.

Edgar, Bob, and Jack Turnell. *Brand of a Legend.* Greybull, WY: Wolverine Gallery, 1978. The story of the Pitchfork, one of Wyoming's most famous ranches. Includes many of Charles Belden's wonderful old photographs. Out of print.

Gowans, Fred R. *Rocky Mountain Rendezvous: A History of the Fur Trade Rendezvous 1825–1840.* Layton, UT: Gibbs Smith Publisher, 1989. Describes each of the rendezvous in detail.

Gowans, Fred R., and Eugene E. Campbell. *Fort Bridger, Island in the Wilderness.* Provo, UT: Brigham Young University Press, www.byu.edu, 1975. An excellent book about the first way station specifically built to serve emigrants on the Oregon Trail. Out of print.

Hafen, Leroy Reuben, and Ann W. Hafen. *Handcarts to Zion.* Lincoln, NE: University of Nebraska Press, www.unp.unl.edu, 1992. The true story of the Mormon handcart pioneers, told in a very readable manner.

Haines, Aubrey L. *Historic Sites Along the Oregon Trail.* St. Louis, MO: The Patrice Press, www.patricepress.com, 1994. Details many of the interesting places on this historic route.

Haines, Aubrey L. (ed.). *Journal of a Trapper: Osborne Russell.* Lincoln, NE: University of Nebraska Press, www.unp.unl.edu, 1965 (reprinted from the 19th-century original volume). The fascinating first-person account of a fur trapper from 1834–1843. A classic and surprisingly well-written book.

Hanna, Oliver Perry. *An Old-Timer's Story of the Old Wild West.* Casper, WY: Endeavor Books, 1984. Fascinating tales from the founder of Big Horn, Wyoming.

Hedgpeth, Don. *Spurs Were A-Jinglin'.* Cody, WY: Northland Press, 1975. Brief text follows the excellent photos by Charles J. Belden of cowboys and ranching in the early parts of the 20th century. Out of print.

Suggested Reading

Homsher, Lola M. (ed.). *South Pass, 1868: James Chisholm's Journal of the Wyoming Gold Rush.* Lincoln, NE: University of Nebraska Press, www.unp.unl.edu, 1960. Tales of life in the gold-mining town of South Pass shortly after the first wave of boomers had left. Very interesting.

Junge, Mark. *Wyoming: A Pictorial History.* Virginia Beach, VA: The Donning Co. Publishers, www.donning.com, 1989. A gorgeous coffee-table book filled with historic black-and-white photos from throughout Wyoming. Out of print.

Kahin, Sharon, and Laurie Rufe. *In the Shadows of the Rockies: A Photographic History of the Pioneer Experience in Wyoming's Bighorn Basin.* Powell, WY: Northwest Community College, www.nwc.cc.wy.us, 1983. Outstanding photos and interesting historical quotes on the Bighorn Basin. Out of print.

Larson, T. A. *History of Wyoming.* Lincoln, NE: University of Nebraska Press, www.unp.unl.edu, 1990. The definitive tome (663 pages worth) on Wyoming's history, with an emphasis on politics and development rather than on outlaws and Indian wars.

Lavender, David. *Fort Laramie and the Changing Frontier.* Washington, DC: Government Printing Office, http://bookstore.gpo.gov, 1984. An interesting little book filled with the history of the people who made Fort Laramie a primary center of trade and war in the West. Excellent illustrations, too.

Lindmier, Tom, and Steve Mount. *I See by Your Outfit: Historic Cowboy Gear of the Northern Plains.* Glendo, WY: High Plains Press, 1996. An authoritative guide to what *real* cowboys wore. Filled with interesting historical photos.

Marcy, Randolph B. *The Prairie Traveler.* New York: Perigee Books, www.penguinput-nam.com, 1859, reprinted in 1994. A telling portrait of life on the frontier as told by a U.S. Army captain. It was considered the essential handbook for travelers.

Mercer, Asa Shinn. *Banditti of the Plains* or *The Cattlemen's Invasion of Wyoming in 1892: The Crowning Infamy of the Ages.* Norman, OK: University of Oklahoma Press, www.oupress.com, 1976. A reprint of a classic book about the Johnson County War.

Morgan, Dale (ed.). *Overland in 1846: Diaries and Letters of the California-Oregon Trail.* Lincoln, NE: University of Nebraska Press, www.unp.unl.edu, 1994. A two-volume collection of diaries offering many fascinating insights into the lives of the emigrants.

Mothershead, Harmon Ross. *The Swan Land and Cattle Company, Ltd.* Norman, OK: University of Oklahoma Press, www.oupress.com, 1971. The story of the most famous of all Wyoming ranches, the million-acre spread begun by Alexander Swan in 1883. Out of print.

Munkres, Robert L. *Saleratus and Sagebrush: The Oregon Trail Through Wyoming.* Cheyenne, WY: Wyoming State Archives and Historical Department, 1974. This interesting small book offers eyewitness accounts from many travelers along the Oregon Trail. Out of print.

Murray, Robert A. *The Bozeman Trail: Highway of History.* Boulder, CO: Pruett Publishing Company, www.pruettpublishing.com, 1988. An attractively illustrated history of the West's most violent trail.

Osgood, Ernest Staples. *The Day of the Cattleman.* Chicago, IL: University of Chicago Press, www.press.uchicago.edu, 1929. An authoritative history of the 50 years when cowboys and cattle barons ruled Wyoming and Montana. Out of print.

Parkman, Francis. *The Oregon Trail.* New York: Viking Penguin, www.penguinputnam.com, 1886. A classic first-person account of the great westward migration. Reprinted in 1989.

Pinkerton, Joan Tregs. *Knights of the Broadax.* Caldwell, ID: The Caxton Printers, www.caxtonprinters.com, 1981. An account of the life of tie hacks in the upper Wind River country.

Rhode, Robert B. *Booms & Busts on Bitter Creek: A History of Rock Springs, Wyoming.* Boulder, CO: Pruett Publishing Co., www.pruettpublishing.com, 1999. A fine history of one of Wyoming's most turbulent cities.

Sandoval, Judith Hancock. *Historic Ranches of Wyoming.* Casper, WY: Mountain States Lithographing, www.mtstlitho.com, 1986. Details nearly one hundred of the state's classic old ranches. Out of print.

Spring, Agnes Wright. *The Cheyenne and Black Hills Stage and Express Routes.* Lincoln, NE: University of Nebraska Press, www.unp.unl.edu, 1948. Tales from the early days of eastern Wyoming. Out of print.

Stamm, Henry E., IV. *People of the Wind River: The Eastern Shoshones 1825–1900.* Norman, OK: University of Oklahoma Press, www.oupress.com, 1999. The definitive source for the history of the Shoshones.

Thybony, Scott, Robert G. Rosenberg, and Elizabeth Mullett Rosenberg. *The Medicine Bows: Wyoming's Mountain Country.* Caldwell, ID: The Caxton Printers, www.caxtonprinters.com, 1985. An outstanding historical account of the Indians, explorers, miners, and tie hacks who called this scenic part of Wyoming home. Out of print.

Twain, Mark. *Roughing It.* New York: New American Library, www.penguinputnam.com, 1994. First published in 1872, this is one of the classics of American literature. Samuel Clemens' witty descriptions of the Old West seem ageless.

Native Americans

Clark, Ella E., and Margot Edmonds. *Sacagawea of the Lewis and Clark Expedition.* Berkeley, CA: University of California Press, www.ucpress.edu, 1984. A fascinating investigation into the true stories behind one of the best-known women in American history. Bursts a few bubbles.

Flynn, Janet. *Tribal Government: Wind River Reservation.* Lander, WY: Mortimore Publishing, 1998. A good introduction to tribal government on the reservation, with a brief history of the tribes.

Frison, George C. *Prehistoric Hunters of the High Plains.* New York: Academic Press, www.academicpress.com, 1991. The authoritative source on the earliest inhabitants of Wyoming.

Hendry, Mary Helen. *Indian Rock Art in Wyoming.* Lincoln, NE: Augstams Printing, 1983. Detailed descriptions of rock-art sites in the state. The author's listed ages for the rock art are probably too recent, and she intentionally omits locations.

Lowie, Robert. *Indians of the Plains.* Lincoln, NE: University of Nebraska Press, www.unp.unl.edu, 1982. Famed anthropologist Robert Lowie presents a detailed picture of life on the plains before the arrival of whites.

Nadeau, Remi. *Fort Laramie and the Sioux Indians.* New York: Crest Publishers, 1997. A thorough historical account of the impact of Fort Laramie on the high-plains Indians.

Trenholm, Virginia Cole. *The Arapahoes, Our People.* Norman, OK: University of Oklahoma Press, www.oupress.com, 1986. The story of this important Wyoming tribe from prehistory to the tribe's forced relocation to the Wind River Reservation.

Trenholm, Virginia Cole, and Maurine Carley. *The Shoshonis: Sentinels of the Rockies.* Norman, OK: University of Oklahoma Press, www.oupress.com, 1964. The history of Chief Washakie and the Shoshone tribe.

Urbanek, Mae. *Chief Washakie.* Boulder, CO: Johnson Publishing Co., 1971. The fascinating story of the chief who led the Shoshone people for 60 years while always remaining a friend of whites. Out of print.

Utley, Robert M. *The Indian Frontier of the American West 1846–1890.* Albuquerque, NM: University of New Mexico Press, www.unmpress.com, 1984. An evenhanded portrayal of a half-century of conflict between Indians and whites.

Natural History

Note: See also following sections on Jackson Hole and Grand Teton National Park, and Yellowstone National Park.

Baxter, George T., and Michael D. Stone. *Amphibians and Reptiles of Wyoming.* Cheyenne, WY: Wyoming Game and Fish Department, http://gf.state.wy.us, 1985. Everything you wanted to know about the state's snakes, frogs, toads, salamanders, and other cold-blooded critters.

Clark, Tim W., and Mark R. Stromberg. *Mammals in Wyoming.* Lawrence, KS: University Press of Kansas, www.kansaspress.ku.edu, 1987. The definitive guide to 117 native or naturalized Wyoming mammals: their identification, distribution, biology, and ecology.

Crowe, Douglas M. *Furbearers of Wyoming.* Cheyenne, WY: Wyoming Department of Game and Fish, http://gf.state.wy.us, 1986. A small book describing the state's fur-coated critters, with distribution maps.

Dorn, Robert D. *Manual of the Vascular Plants of Wyoming.* Cheyenne, WY: Mountain West Publishing Company, 1988. The authoritative key to Wyoming plants; a dense book with few illustrations. For botanists. Out of print.

Galvin, James. *The Meadow.* New York: Henry Holt and Co., www.henryholt.com, 1993. A hauntingly beautiful book about a meadow on the Wyoming border near Tie Siding, and a century of the people who have lived there.

Knight, Dennis H. *Mountains and Plains: the Ecology of Wyoming Landscapes.* New Haven, CT: Yale University Press, www.yale.edu/yup, 1994. The definitive textbook on the ecology of Wyoming. Thorough and well written, but the $50 price may scare you away.

Petersen, David. *Among the Elk.* Flagstaff, AZ: Northland Publishing, www.northland-pub.com, 1988. The story of wapiti, with outstanding photos by Alan D. Carey. Out of print.

Jackson Hole and Grand Teton National Park

Note: Several natural history and geology books encompass both Yellowstone and Grand Teton National Parks. See the following section on Yellowstone National Park for additional titles with overlapping coverage.

Geology

Good, John M., and Kenneth L. Pierce. *Interpreting the Landscape: Recent and Ongoing Geology of Grand Teton and Yellowstone National Parks.* Moose, WY: Grand Teton Natural History Association, www.grandtetonpark.org, 1996. This attractive book has the latest geologic research on the parks and presents it in an understandable format with excellent illustrations.

Love, J. D., and John C. Reed, Jr. *Creation of the Teton Landscape: the Geologic Story of Grand Teton National Park.* Moose, WY: Grand Teton Natural History Association, www.grandtetonpark.org, 1995. A small but authoritatively detailed guide to the geology of Jackson Hole and the Tetons.

History

Betts, Robert B. *Along the Ramparts of the Tetons: the Saga of Jackson Hole, Wyoming.* Boulder, CO: University Press of Colorado, www.upcolorado.com, 1978. A substantial, detailed, and beautifully written book about the history of Jackson Hole.

Burt, Nathaniel. *Jackson Hole Journal.* Norman, OK: University of Oklahoma Press, www.oupress.com, 1983. Tales of growing up as a dude in Jackson Hole. Contains some very amusing stories.

Huidekoper, Virginia. *The Early Days in Jackson Hole.* Boulder, CO: University Press of Colorado, www.upcolorado.com, 1978. Filled with more than 100 photos from old-time Jackson Hole. Out of print.

Righter, Robert W. *Crucible for Conservation: The Creation of Grand Teton National Park.* Boulder, CO: University Press of Colorado, www.upcolorado.com, 1982. The story of how the Tetons were spared through a half-century battle.

Thompson, Edith M., and William Leigh Thompson. *Beaver Dick: The Honor and the Heartbreak.* Laramie, WY: Jelm Mountain Press, 1982. A touching historical biography of Beaver Dick Leigh, one of the first white men to settle in Jackson Hole. Out of print.

Natural History

Carrighar, Sally. *One Day at Teton Marsh.* Lincoln, NE: University of Nebraska Press, www.unp.unl.edu, 1979. A classic natural history of life in a Jackson Hole marsh. Made into a movie by Walt Disney. Out of print.

Clark, Tim W. *Ecology of Jackson Hole, Wyoming: A Primer.* Salt Lake City, UT: Paragon Press, www.paragon-press.com, 1981. An excellent scientific introduction to ecological interrelationships within Jackson Hole. Out of print.

Murie, Margaret, and Olaus Murie. *Wapiti Wilderness.* Boulder, CO: University Press of Colorado, www.upcolorado.com, 1986. The lives of two of America's most-loved conservationists in Jackson Hole and their work with elk.

Shaw, Richard J. *Plants of Grand Teton and Yellowstone National Parks.* Salt Lake City, UT: Wheelwright Press, 1981. Photos and descriptions of the most commonly found plants in the parks.

Travsky, Amber. *Mountain Biking Jackson Hole.* Guilford, CT: Globe Pequot Press (Falcon), www.falconbooks.com, 2001. Thirty-one rides in Jackson Hole, Grand Teton National Park, and surrounding areas.

Recreation

Carter, Tom. *Day Hiking Grand Teton National Park.* Garland, TX: Dayhiking Press, 1993. A pocket-size guide to 15 day-treks in the park.

Dufy, Katy, and Darwin Wile. *Teton Trails.* Moose, WY: Grand Teton Natural History Association, www.grandtetonpark.org, 1995. A useful guide to more than 200 miles of trails in the park.

Jackson, Reynold G. *A Climber's Guide to the Teton Range.* Seattle, WA: Mountaineers Books, www.mountaineerbooks.org, 1996. The definitive (415 pages!) climbing guide for the Tetons.

Prax, Brian, and Mark Schultheis. *The Book: Guide to Mountain Biking in the Jackson Hole Area.* Jackson, WY: Prax Photography and

Productions, 2001. This spiral-bound book is the most complete guide to local cycling options and includes coverage on Teton Valley.

Rossiter, Richard. *Teton Classics: 50 Selected Climbs in Grand Teton National Park.* Guilford, CT: Globe Pequot Press (Falcon), www.falconbooks.com, 1994. A small and nicely illustrated guide to 50 climbing routes in the Tetons.

Stone, Robert. *Day Hikes in Grand Teton National Park and Jackson Hole.* Guilford, CT: Globe Pequot Press (Falcon), www.falconbooks.com, 2000.

Viola, Bob, and Thomas Turiano. *Jackson Hole Ski Guide.* Guilford, CT: Globe Pequot Press (Falcon), www.falconbooks.com, 1998.

Watters, Ron. *Winter Tales and Trails: Skiing, Snowshoeing and Snowboarding in Idaho, the Grand Tetons and Yellowstone National Park.* Pocatello, ID: Great Rift Press, 1997. A book that combines lucid writing on the area's rich history with guides to winter trails. More than 350 pages of details from an expert in the field.

Woods, Rebecca. *Jackson Hole Hikes.* Jackson, WY: White Willow Publishing, 1999. An excellent guide that includes trails in Grand Teton National Park and surrounding national forest areas. Easy to use and informative.

Yellowstone National Park

Note: Several natural history and geology books encompass both Yellowstone and Grand Teton National Parks. See previous sections on Jackson Hole and Grand Teton National Park for additional titles with overlapping coverage.

Geology

Bryan, Scott. T. *The Geysers of Yellowstone.* Boulder, CO: University Press of Colorado, www.upcolorado.com, 1995. The definitive guide to more than 400 geysers and other geothermal features in Yellowstone.

Fritz, William J. *Roadside Geology of the Yellowstone Country.* Missoula, MT: Mountain Press Publishing Co., www.mountain-press.com, 1986. All of the park roads are covered in this easy-to-follow Yellowstone geology primer.

Schreier, Carl. *Yellowstone's Geysers, Hot Springs and Fumaroles.* Moose, WY: Homestead Publishing, 1987. An attractive small book filled with color photos and brief descriptions.

History

Bartlett, Richard A. *Yellowstone: A Wilderness Besieged.* Tucson, AZ: University of Arizona Press, www.uapress.arizona.edu, 1989. The history of Yellowstone and the fight to prevent its destruction by railroad magnates, concessioners, and others.

Haines, Aubrey L. *The Yellowstone Story: A History of Our First National Park.* Boulder, CO: University Press of Colorado, www.upcolorado.com, 1996. A definitive two-volume history of the park. Volume one (history up to the park's establishment) is the most interesting.

Janetski, Joel C. *Indians of Yellowstone Park.* Salt Lake City, UT: University of Utah Press, www.upress.utah.edu, 1987. A general overview of the earliest settlers in Yellowstone and later conflicts with incoming whites.

Milstein, Michael. *Yellowstone Album: 125 Years of America's Best Idea.* Billings, MT: The Billings Gazette, www.billingsgazette.com, 1996. A delightful book filled with historical photographs, along with photos of postcards, souvenirs, and other tourist artifacts.

Schreier, Carl (ed.). *Yellowstone: Selected Photographs 1870–1960.* Moose, WY: Homestead Publishing, 1989. An outstanding collection of historical photographs from the park.

Natural History

Craighead, Frank J. *Track of the Grizzly.* San Francisco, CA: Sierra Club Books, www.sierraclub.org, 1982. The life of grizzlies in Yellowstone, by one of the most famous bear researchers.

Krakell, Dean, II. *Downriver: A Yellowstone Journey.* San Francisco, CA: Sierra Club Books, www.sierraclub.org, 1987. An extraordinarily moving journey down the magnificent Yellowstone River.

McEneaney, Terry. *Birds of Yellowstone.* Boulder, CO: Roberts Rinehart, www.roberts-rinehart.com, 1988. A guide to Yellowstone birds and where to find them.

Schullery, Paul (ed.). *Yellowstone Bear Tales.* Boulder, CO: Roberts Rinehart Publishers, www.roberts-rinehart.com, 1991. First-person stories of bear encounters from a range of travelers—including President Theodore Roosevelt—between 1880 and 1950.

Schullery, Paul. *Searching for Yellowstone.* New York: Houghton Mifflin Co., www.hmco.com, 1997. An eloquently written book by a longtime park ranger whose knowledge of the park goes far beyond the hype. Must-reading for anyone who cares about Yellowstone.

Scott, Douglas M., and Suvi A. Scott. *Wildlife of Yellowstone and Grand Teton National Parks.* Salt Lake City, UT: Wheelwright Press, 1990. A brief descriptive guide to Yellowstone and Grand Teton critters.

Shaw, Richard J. *Wildflowers of Yellowstone and Grand Teton National Parks.* Salt Lake City, UT: Wheelwright Press, 1992. Color photos and short descriptions of more than 100 wildflowers in the Greater Yellowstone Ecosystem.

Recreation

Bach, Orville E., Jr. *Hiking the Yellowstone Backcountry.* San Francisco, CA: Sierra Club Books, www.sierraclub.org, 1998. A pocket-size guide to hiking, canoeing, biking, and skiing in the park.

Charlton, Robert E. *Yellowstone Fishing Guide.* Ketchum, ID: Lost River Press, 1995. A detailed guide to fishing in the park. Leaves no trickle unfished.

Henry, Jeff. *Yellowstone Winter Guide.* Boulder, CO: Roberts Rinehart Publishers, www.roberts-rinehart.com, 1998. A detailed guide to visiting Yellowstone in the winter; especially good for cross-country skiers.

Lilly, Bud, and Paul Schullery. *Bud Lilly's Guide to Fly Fishing the New West.* Portland, OR: Frank Amato Publications, 2000. The authoritative fishing source from the father of Western trout fishing.

Marschall, Mark C. *Yellowstone Trails: A Hiking Guide.* Yellowstone National Park, WY: The Yellowstone Association, www.yellowstoneassociation.org, 1999. An excellent, up-to-date, and detailed guidebook to the park's 1,000 miles of hiking trails.

Parks, Richard. *Fishing Yellowstone.* Guilford, CT: Globe Pequot Press (Falcon), www.falconbooks.com, 1998. One of several authoritative guides, this one provides details on fly- and lure fishing, along with descriptions of more than 100 sites.

Schneider, Bill. *Hiking Yellowstone National Park.* Guilford, CT: Globe Pequot Press (Falcon), www.falconbooks.com, 1997. Clear maps and helpful trail profiles make this the most useful book for anyone heading out on Yellowstone hiking routes. Contains descriptions of more than 100 trails.

Stone, Robert. *Day Hikes in Yellowstone National Park and Jackson Hole.* Guilford, CT: Globe Pequot Press (Falcon), www.falconbooks.com, 2000.

Varley, John D., and Paul D. Schullery. *Yellowstone Fishes: Ecology, History, and Angling in the Park*. Mechanicsburg, PA: Stackpole Books, 1998, www.stackpolebooks.com. The comprehensive guide to the fish of Yellowstone, written by two authorities in the field.

Internet Resources

State of Wyoming
www.state.wy.us

This is the state's official home on the web and a good spot to learn more about history, events, state government, and a range of other subjects.

Wyoming Division of Tourism and State Marketing
www.wyomingtourism.org

The state's tourism site has everything you'd expect in the way of an interactive visitors center and much more.

Wyoming Department of Transportation
www.wyoroad.info

This website has updated road conditions, webcams, and details on road construction projects.

Wyoming Cultural Guide
www.wyomingculturalguide.org

This website contains descriptions of museums, theaters, galleries, art studios, and cultural events.

Wyoming Public Radio
http://uwadmnweb.uwyo.edu/wpr

A good starting place for information on public radio around Wyoming.

Wyoming State Trails Program
http://wyotrails.state.wy.us/trails

Check out this website for details on hiking, biking, cross-country skiing, snowmobile trails, Volksmarch, and other trails around the Wyoming.

Department of State Parks and Cultural Resources
http://wyoparks.state.wy.us

This site contains details on 26 state parks, historic sites, recreation areas, and archaeological sites scattered across Wyoming.

Wyoming Homestay & Outdoor Adventures
www.wyomingbnb-ranchrec.com

Better known as WHOA, this organization maintains links to several dozen bed-and-breakfasts, dude ranches, guest cabins, and other distinctive lodging options.

Wyoming Press Association
www.wyopress.org

This website has a complete listing of newspapers in the state, including weblinks.

Wyoming State Library
www-wsl.state.wy.us

This site has information and links to the state's public libraries.

Wyoming Game and Fish Department
http://gf.state.wy.us

Head to this website for details on fishing licenses and seasons, along with current issues affecting fish. You can even download application forms.

Wyoming Fishing Network
www.wyomingfishing.net

An exceptionally useful online source for Wyoming anglers.

National Park Service
www.nps.gov

Wyoming contains two national parks (Grand Teton National Park, www.nps.gov/grte, and Yellowstone National Park, www.nps.gov/yell), two national monuments (Devils Tower National Monument, www.nps.gov/deto, and Fossil Butte National Monument, www.nps.gov/fobu), plus Bighorn Canyon National Recreation Area, www.nps.gov/bica, and

Fort Laramie National Historic Site, www.nps.gov/fola. All of these are managed by the National Park Service.

U.S. Fish & Wildlife Service
www.fws.gov
The F&WS has four refuges in Wyoming. The two largest have their own websites: the National Elk Refuge in Jackson, http://nationalelkrefuge.fws.gov, and Seedskadee National Wildlife Refuge northwest of Green River, http://seedskadee.fws.gov.

Bureau of Land Management
www.wy.blm.gov
Wyoming's largest landholder—it manages 18 million acres in the state—is the BLM. Their website has details on recreation opportunities and much more.

U.S. Forest Service
www.fs.fed.us
This federal agency manages land within eight national forests in Wyoming, mostly located in the mountainous regions. They are Bighorn National Forest, www.fs.fed.us/r2/bighorn, Black Hills National Forest, www.fs.fed.us/r2/blackhills, Bridger-Teton National Forest, www.fs.fed.us/btnf, Ashley National Forest (Flaming Gorge National Recreation Area) www.fs.fed.us/r4/ashley, Medicine Bow-Routt National Forest, www.fs.fed.us/r2/mbr, Shoshone National Forest, www.fs.fed.us/r2/shoshone, Caribou-Targhee National Forest, www.fs.fed.us/r4/caribou, and Wasatch-Cache National Forest, www.fs.fed.us/wcnf.

Wyoming Outfitters and Guides Association
www.wyoga.org
Interested in a backcountry pack trip? Visit this website to find outfitters for the area you plan to visit.

Dude Ranchers' Association
www.duderanch.org
This national organization's helpful homepage has links to the websites of 30 different Wyoming guest ranches.

Centers for Disease Control
www.cdc.gov
This is the best web source for information on diseases such as West Nile virus, Hantavirus, and other diseases found in Wyoming.

Great Lakes Aviation
www.greatlakesav.com
This company is the primary air carrier into several Wyoming towns.

Index

A

Abbey, Edward: 505
Abiathar Peak: 527
Absaroka-Beartooth Wilderness: 578, 587
accommodations: general discussion 50–53;
    Cheyenne 86–89; Cody 605–607; Jackson
    Hole 390–403; Yellowstone National Park
    545–546, 550–554, 563–564, 571–573,
    576–577; *see also* bed-and-breakfasts; guest
    ranches; historic lodgings; *specific place*
Adair, Red: 701
Adams, Ansel: 387, 467
Adobe Town: 176
aerial trams: *see* chairlifts/aerial trams
Afton: 231–234
agriculture: general discussion 36; Bighorn Basin
    579–580; Farson 358; Flywheelers Antique
    Engine and Tractor Show 301; irrigation
    280–281, 456–457, 593, 620; Lovell 620,
    621; Powell 618; Shell Valley 633; Sheridan
    664; tours/guides 618; Worland 636; *see also*
    cattle ranching; sheepherding/sheep ranching;
    specific place
airlines: 69
air travel: general discussion 67–68; Casper 275;
    Cheyenne 97; Cody 612; Evanston 221;
    Gillette 709; Jackson Hole 438–439; Lander
    311; Laramie 146; Riverton 300; Rock
    Springs 198; Saratoga 169; Sheridan 675;
    tours/guides 450; Yellowstone National Park
    569–570
Aladdin: 725–726
Alaska Basin: 445, 472
Albany: 157
Albin: 100
Albright, Horace: 457, 505
Alcova Dam/Reservoir: 283–284
alfalfa: 620
Alpine: 237–239
Alsop, Tom: 26
Alta: 451–452
Alum Creek: 531
Alva: 726
Alzada: 727
Ames, Oliver and Oakes: 148

Amphitheater Lake: 472
Anchor Dam: 647
Anderson, A. A.: 580, 617
antelope: *see* pronghorn antelope
Applegate Wagon Train: 19
Apres Vous Mountain: 428
Arapahoe (town): 321
Arapaho tribe: Arapaho Community Powwow
    319; Arapaho Cultural Museum 323; Big
    Springs 642; Ethete Powwow 55, 321; Fletch-
    er, Mary and Lizzie 155, 321; history
    317–318; Northern Arapaho Powwow 321;
    Powder River Massacre/Sawyer Fight 675;
    Vedauwoo 148; *see also* Wind River Indian
    Reservation
Arapooish (Crow chief): 710
archaeological sites/museums/exhibits: Castle
    Gardens 291; Great Arrow 617; Hell's Half
    Acre 289–290; Hell Gap 109; High Plains Ar-
    chaeology Museum and Field Lab 99; Medi-
    cine Lodge State Park 635; Medicine Wheel
    659–661; Mummy Cave 590, 602; Pine
    Bluffs 98–99; Saratoga Museum 165; Spanish
    Diggings 109; Vore Buffalo Jump 723; Win-
    dows of the Past Interpretive Center 98–99;
    see also paleontological sites/museums; petro-
    glyphs
Archie Neal Park: 226
Arlington: 154–155
Arnold, Kate: 668
artesian wells: 637
art festivals/museums/shows: Albright Visitor
    Center 523–524; All America Quilt Show
    619; American Heritage Center 136–137;
    Arts and Crafts Festival 273; Arts for the Parks
    National Art Competition 415; Bradford
    Brinton Memorial Museum 681; Buffalo Bill
    Art Show & Sale 610; Campbell County Pub-
    lic Library 703; Central Wyoming College
    Arts Center 300; Cheyenne Frontier Days
    Western Art Show and Sale 93; Colter Bay In-
    dian Arts Museum 465; Community Fine Arts
    Center 194; Douglas Invitational Art Show
    249; Harry Jackson Art Museum 604; Jackson
    Hole Fall Arts Festival 56, 415; Kriendler

Gallery of Contemporary Western Art 600; Mountain Artists' Rendezvous Art Fair 415; National Art Show 332; National Chainsaw Carving Competition 632; National Museum of Wildlife Art 383–385; Nicolaysen Art Museum 266; Platte Valley Festival of the Arts 168–169; Prairie Rose Arts Festival 673; University of Wyoming Art Museum 136; Whitney Gallery of Western Art 600; see also galleries; specific artist; place

Artist Point: 530

Arvada: 678

Ashley, J. M.: 25

Ashley, William H.: 369

Aspen Valley: 173–174

Astorians: 18, 263, 368, 678

Atlantic City: 354–356

ATMs: see specific place

Auburn: 237

auto races/shows: Casper 273; Douglas International Raceway 249; Harvest Fest and Car Show 638; Rock Springs 197; Thunder Basin Stock Car Track 708; Yellowstone Rod Run 567

auto tours: 612–613

Avalanche Peak: 533, 534

avalanches: 431, 568, 616

Averell, James: 283

Ayres Natural Bridge Park: 252

B

Back Basin: 519

backcountry treks: general discussion 43–45; Bighorn Canyon 627; Cloud Peak Wilderness 663; ethics/etiquette 44; Grand Teton National Park 470–472; licenses/permits/regulations/fees 341, 345, 535, 663; National Outdoor Leadership School 305–306; safety 45–46, 338, 471, 548, 587; Yellowstone National Park 534–541; see also hiking/backpacking; specific place

badlands: Devil's Kitchen 630; Dubois 328; Gooseberry Badlands 637–638; Grand Teton National Park 469; Hell's Half Acre 289–290; Red Gulch Scenic Byway 634; Shoshoni 301; Wind River Indian Reservation 325

Badlands Interpretive Trail: 328

Bad Pass: 625

Baggs: 176

Bairoil: 185

Baldwin Creek Rock Climbing Area: 310

ballooning: see hot air ballooning

banking: 65–66; currency exchange 436, 559; see also specific place

Bannock tribe: 340, 378, 525, 584

Barber, Amos W.: 691

bareback bronc riding: 60

bark beetles: 503

barley: 579, 618, 620, 636

BED-AND-BREAKFASTS

general discussion: 52

Afton: 233

Albany: 157

Alcova Dam/Reservoir: 283–284

Atlantic City: 355

Big Horn 680–681

Buffalo: 692

Casper: 269

Centennial: 158

Cheyenne: 88–89

Cody: 607

Dayton: 676

Douglas: 247

Dubois: 329–330

Encampment/Riverside: 171–172

Etna: 237

Evanston: 218

Gillette: 706

Jackson Hole: 395–397, 449, 452

Lander: 307

Newcastle: 716

Pinedale: 361

Ranchester: 676

Riverton: 298

Saratoga: 167

Sheridan: 671

Snowy Range: 162

Story: 682

Thayne: 236

West Yellowstone: 572

Wheatland: 105

Wind River Indian Reservation: 325

see also historic lodgings; specific place

barrel racing: 61
Barronette Peak: 527
Barry, Linda: 669
bars: *see specific place*
baseball: 274
Basin: 633
battles/raids/massacres: Chinese Massacre 193; Connor Battle 675; Custard's Wagon Train Fight 264; Dull Knife Battle 687, 699; Fetterman Fight 684–685, 686, 688; Grattan Massacre 113; Johnson County War 29, 245, 689, 690–691; Little Big Horn, Battle of 17, 597; Mormon War 205; Nez Perce War 498; Red Cloud's War 263–264, 683–686; Sand Creek Massacre 16, 23; Sawyer Fight 675; Ten Sleep Raid 29, 641; Wagon Box Fight 685, 686; Wounded Knee Massacre 17
beans: 618, 620
Bear River State Park: 217
bears: Big Horn Mountains 655; Grand Teton National Park 471; Grizzly and Wolf Discovery Center 562; Hidden Corral Basin 444; North Absaroka Wilderness 583; safety 46–49, 337, 341, 441–442, 471, 492, 581–583; Yellowstone National Park 491–492, 531, 538, 540; *see also specific place*
Bears Ears Trail: 346
Beartooth High Lakes Trail: 587
Beartooth Lake: 587
Beartooth Loop National Recreational Trail: 587
Beartooth Mountains: 586–587
Beartooth Pass: 587
beaver fever: 45
Beaver Ponds Trail: 524
beavers: 274, 377–378, 464
Bechler River: 496, 540
Bedford: 237
beer/breweries: Brewfest 273; Evanston 219; Green River 202; Jackson Hole 410, 447; Laramie 143; Pinedale 363; Saratoga 168; Sheridan 672–673; West Yellowstone 566; Wyoming Brewer's Festival 94; Wyoming Microbrewery Competition 169
Beery, Wallace: 458
Beldon, Charles: 602, 615
Bessemer Bend: 279
Beulah: 723
Big Bear Canyon: 256
Big Cedar Ridge: 640
Big Hollow: 156–157

BICYCLING/MOUNTAIN BIKING

general discussion: 69–70
Badlands Classic Mountain Bike Race: 332
Casper: 273
Cody: 611
Flaming Gorge National Recreation Area: 208
Grand Targhee Ski Resort: 426
Grand Teton National Park: 469, 476
Great Divide Mountain Bike Route: 365
High Uintas Classic Stage Race: 219
Jackson Hole: 421–422, 450
Pole-Pedal-Paddle Race: 414
Riverton: 300
Snider Basin: 235
Snowy Range: 162
tours/guides: 422, 543, 611
Wolverine Ridge XC Race: 219
Worland: 639
WYDAHO Mountain Bike Race: 427, 450
Yellowstone National Park: 533, 543, 567, 574
see also specific place

Big Horn: 679–681
Bighorn Basin: 579–651; Bighorn Canyon National Recreation Area 623–629; Cody 592–613; Greybull 629–635; Heart Mountain 613–614; highlights 580; Lovell 621–623; Meeteetse 615–617; Powell 617–620; Shoshone National Forest 580–587; Ten Sleep 639–642; Thermopolis 642–650; Wapiti Valley 588–593; Wind River Canyon 650–651; Worland 636–639
Bighorn Canyon National Recreation Area: 623–629
Big Horn Mountain Coalition: 654
Big Horn Mountains: 654–663
Bighorn National Forest: 654
Bighorn Peak: 517–518
Bighorn River: 638
bighorn sheep: Bighorn Canyon 625; Big Horn Mountains 655; Laramie Mountains 256; National Bighorn Sheep Center 327–328; North Absaroka Wilderness 583; Seminoe Reservoir 281; Sinks Canyon 313; Whiskey Basin Wildlife Habitat 326; Wind River Mountains

337; Yellowstone National Park 492–493

Big Piney: 371

Big Robber (Crow chief): 325

Big Sandy trails: 343–344

Bill (settlement): 710

Bird, Edwin R.: 263

birds/birdwatching: Ayres Natural Bridge Park 252; Downar Bird Farm 121; Edness Kimball Wilkins State Park 267; Grand Teton National Park 475–476; Hot Springs State Park 644; Kaycee 697; Keyhole State Park 721; Medicine Wheel 661; North Absaroka Wilderness 583; Pathfinder National Wildlife Refuge 282; Platte Valley Festival of Birds 168; Saratoga 165; Seedskadee National Wildlife Refuge 205; Shell Falls 655; State Bird Farm 679; Tensleep Preserve 640; Thunder Basin National Grassland 253; Upton-Osage Area 254; Yellowstone National Park 490–491, 531; see also specific bird; place

Biscuit Basin: 512–513

bison: general discussion 11–14; Bear River State Park 217; brucellosis 494; Durham Buffalo Ranch 709; Grand Teton National Park 456, 466, 468; Hot Springs State Park 642, 645; Silver Sage Bison Ranch 125; slaughter of 596–597; Yellowstone National Park 489, 493–494, 526, 545; see also specific place

Black Canyon of the Yellowstone: 538

black-footed ferret: 104–105, 152, 153, 251, 615

Black Hills: general discussion 711; Aladdin 725–726; Devil's Tower National Monument 728–732; highlights 713; Hulett 726–727; land 711–713; Moorcroft 720–721; Newcastle 713–720; Sundance 721–724

Black Kettle (chief): 16

Black Mountain Lookout: 256, 658–659

Black Sand Basin: 512

Blacktail Butte: 467, 474

black-tailed prairie dog: see prairie dogs

Blacktail Plateau Drive: 525

Blacktail Pond: 525

black widow spiders: 627

Blain, Mary: 576

Blaine, James G.: 499

Bliss Pass Trail: 539

Boars Tusk: 190

boating/marinas: Alcova Reservoir 283; Bighorn Canyon 628; Boysen State Park 302; Buffalo Bill State Park 592–593; Flaming Gorge 208;

Grand Teton National Park 463, 475; Kemmerer 226; Keyhole State Park 721; Lake DeSmet 695; Pathfinder Reservoir 282; Pinedale 365; Seminoe Reservoir 281; Yellowstone National Park 533, 542

Bomber Basin Trail: 345

Bomber Mountain: 661

Bondurant: 372

Bonneville (captain): 285, 289

bookstores: see specific place

Boone, Daniel: 11

Bosler: 149

Bothwell, A. J.: 283

Boulder: 366–367

Boulder Lake: 365

Bourke, John G.: 113

bowling: see specific place

Boxelder Canyon: 259

Boyd, William: 136

Boysen Power Plant: 651

Boysen State Park: 302

Bozeman, John M.: 683

Bozeman Trail: 16, 23, 683–686

Bradley Lake: 461

branding: 28

Bridge Bay: 533

Bridger, Jim: 23, 211, 212–213, 499, 596, 625–626, 683–685

Bridger-Teton National Forest: 441–444

Bridger Valley: 210–214

Bridger Wilderness: 341–344

Bright, William: 350

Brimmer Point Overlook: 110

Brink of the Lower/Upper Falls: 530

Brinton, Bradford: 681

Brookover, David: 388

Brooks Lake: 335

brucellosis: 494

Buffalo: 687–695

Buffalo Bill: 597; see also Cody, Buffalo Bill

Buffalo Bill Reservoir/Dam: 592–593

Buffalo Bill State Park: 592–593

Bull Lake: 325

bull riding: 60

Bunsen Peak: 520–521

Buntline, Ned: 597

Bureau of Land Management: 31, 64; see also specific place

Burgess Junction: 655

Burlington: 629

Burlington and Missouri Railroad: 664
Burlington Railroad: 629
Burns, Isabelle: 222–223
Burt, Nathaniel: 458
Burt, Struthers: 26, 28, 457
bus service: general discussion 70–71; Basin 633; Buffalo 695; Casper 275; Cheyenne 97; Cody 612; Douglas 249; Evanston 221; Gillette 709; Grand Teton National Park 477, 481–482; Greybull 632; Jackson Hole 427, 428, 430, 439–440; Laramie 146; Lovell 623; Lyman 210; Powell 620; Rawlins 183; Riverton 300; Rock Springs 198; Sheridan 675; Shoshoni 301; Sundance 724; Torrington 121; tours 440, 481–482, 557; Wheatland 106; Worland 639; Yellowstone National Park 570; *see also specific place*
Byron: 620

C
Cabin Creek Trail: 239
Cadwell, William H.: 165
Calamity Jane: 84, 212, 352–353
Calcite Springs: 527
calf roping: 59
calf scramble: 61
Campbell, Gregory: 660
Campbell, John A.: 25, 77
campgrounds/RV parks: general discussion 54; Afton 233; Alpine 238; Arlington 154–155; Atlantic City 356; Bairoil 185; Basin 633; bears 48–49; Bighorn Canyon 626–627; Big Horn Mountains 656; Big Piney 371; Black Hills National Forest 725; Boulder 366; Bridger Wilderness 342, 343; Buffalo 692–693; Casper 269–270; Casper Mountain 276–277; Cheyenne 89; Cody 607–608; Cokeville 229; Daniel 367; Dayton 676; Devil's Tower 732; Douglas 247; Dubois 330–331; Encampment 172; Evanston 218; Farson 357; Flaming Gorge 209; Fort Laramie 117; Four Corners 718; Gillette 706; Glenrock 259; Grand Teton National Park 468, 477–478; Green River 201–202; Green River Lakes 340; Greybull 631; Greys River Loop Road 235; Guernsey 108; Hole-in-the-Wall 699–700; Horse Creek 333; Hulett 726; Jackson Hole 403–405, 447, 449; Jedediah Smith Wilderness 445; Jeffrey City 313; Kemmerer 225; Lamont 185; Lander 308; Laramie 142; Laramie Mountains 256;

Lovell 622; Lusk 125; Lyman 210; Meeteetse 616; Newcastle 716–717; Pine Bluffs 100; Pinedale 362–363, 365; Popo Agie Wilderness 346; Powell 619; Ranchester 676; Rawlins 182; Riverton 298–299; Rock Springs 196; Saratoga 168; Seedskadee National Wildlife Refuge 205; Sheridan 671; Sierra Madre 174; Sinks Canyon 314; Snake River Canyon 239; Snowy Range 161; Sundance 723; Sunlight Basin 585, 586; Ten Sleep 641; Thayne 236; Thermopolis 648; Togwotee Pass 335, 336; Torrington 120; Wapiti Valley 590; Wheatland 105; Wind River Canyon 651; Wind River Indian Reservation 326; Worland 638; Wright 710; Yellowstone National Park 529, 540, 549–550, 564–565, 573, 577; *see also specific place*
Camp Guernsey: 31
Cam-Plex Park: 704–705
Camp Monaco: 588
Camp Pilot Butte: 194
Campylobacter jejuni: 45
Canary, Martha Jane: *see* Calamity Jane
Candlish, James: 30
canoeing/kayaking: Grand Teton National Park 475; Gray Reef Reservoir 283; Green River 365; Greys River 235; Platte River Trust Whitewater Park 274; Pole-Pedal-Paddle Race 414; Salt River Canoe Race 236–237; Seedskadee National Wildlife Refuge 205; Yellowstone National Park 542; *see also specific place*
Canyon Rim Trail: 207
Canyon Village: 529, 551
Carey, Joseph M.: 25
Carey Act: 104, 280, 579
Caribou-Targhee National Forest: 444–445
Carlin, William: 150
Carousel Park: 689
Carpenter, Robert E.: 501
Carr, Eugene: 597
Carriage House Theater: 673
Carrington, Henry B.: 27, 683–685
Carson, Kit: 370, 596
car travel: general discussion 68; auto tours 612–613; Grand Teton National Park 459–470; rental cars 68; road closures 506, 545; speed traps 505; Yellowstone National Park 504, 505–534, 545; *see also specific place*
Cascade Canyon: 463
Cascade Canyon-Paintbrush Canyon Loop Trail: 471

Casper: 260–275; accommodations 268–270; climate 260; economy 264–265; entertainment/events 271–273; food/restaurants 270–271; history 263–265; information/services 275; shopping 274–275; sights 265–268; sports/recreation 273–274; transportation 275

Casper Mountain: 276–279

Casper Planetarium: 268

Casper Rockies: 274

Castle Gardens: 291, 302, 640

Castle Rock: 201

Caswell, Rip: 388

Cathedral Group: 463

cattle barons: general discussion 28–29, 77–79; Cattle Baron's Row 84; Cheyenne Club 85; Frewen Castle 696; Johnson County War 690–691; Wyoming Hereford Association 85

cattle ranching: general discussion 26–29; branding 28; Central Wyoming Livestock Exchange 259; lingo 34–35; Moorcroft 720; Pinedale 360; range etiquette 44–45; Riverton Livestock Auction 297; rustling 28–29, 675; Swan Land and Cattle Company 101; Ten Sleep Raid 641; Thunder Basin National Grassland 253; Torrington Livestock Market 119; Worland 636; *see also* cattle barons; outlaws/rustlers; rodeos; *specific place*

caves/caverns: Bighorn Caverns 626; Horsethief Cave 626; Indian Rock Art Cave 700; Mummy Cave 590, 602; Natural Trap Cave 626; Outlaw Cave 700; Tongue River Cave 659

cell phones: 69, 471, 560

Celtic festivals: 708

cemeteries/graveyards: Cumberland 221; Douglas Park Cemetery 246; Gebo 647; Independence Rock 285; Mammoth Hot Springs 524; Mt. Moriah Cemetery 353; Rock in the Glen 258–259; Sacagawea Graveyard 324; St. Joseph's Cemetery 180; St. Stephens Mission 321; Washakie Graveyard 324; Willow Grove Cemetery 689–690

Centennial: 157–158

Centennial Complex: 136

Central Pacific Railroad: 24

Central Wyoming: general discussion 240; Ayres Natural Bridge Park 252; Casper 260–279; Castle Gardens 291; Douglas 243–249; Fort Fetterman 250–251; Glenrock 257–260; Hell's Half Acre 289–290; highlights 242; Lake Dis-

trict 280–284; land 240–242; Laramie Mountains 254–257; Lost Cabin 290–291; Oregon Trail landmarks 284–287; Powder River 289; Salt Creek Oil Field 287–289; Thunder Basin National Grassland 253–254

chainsaw art: 632

chairlifts/aerial trams: 422, 426, 428, 658

charcoal kilns: 211–212

cheese factories: 236

Cheyenne: accommodations 86–89; climate 75; economy 75; entertainment 91–93; food/restaurants 89–91; history 75–79; information/services 96; shopping 95–96; sights 79–85; sports/recreation 94–95; transportation 97

Cheyenne Depot: 79

Cheyenne Greenway: 95

Cheyenne Opera House: 77

children's museums/activities: Cam-Plex Park 704; Carousel Park 689; Cody Stampede 55, 609; Einstein's Adventurarium 704; Gillette Water Park 708; Jackson Hole 436–437; Junior Ranger Program 558; junior rodeos 125, 236; Kid's Club at Targhee 426; Lander Children's Museum 305; Targhee Institute 426; Washakie Museum and Cultural Center 636–637; Wyoming Children's Museum & Nature Center 140; Wyoming Dinosaur Center 258, 645–646; Wyoming State Museum 81; Yellowstone National Park 558–559; *see also specific place*

chili cookoffs: Aniel Daniel Chili Cookoff 367; Bull Riders Rodeo and Saratoga Chili Cookoff 169; Chugwater Chili Cook-Off 56, 101; Evanston Chili Cook-Off 220; Wyoming Chili Cook-Off 673

Chinese immigrants: 193, 216–217, 219

Chinese Spring: 510

chinooks: 5

Chisholm, James: 16, 24, 75, 336, 349–350

Chittenden, Hiram: 501

Chivington, John M.: 16

Chorley, Kenneth: 457

Christmas celebrations: *see specific place*

chuck wagon cookouts: 412–413, 420, 544, 555, 672

Chugwater: 101–102

Church Buttes: 204

churches/missions/temples: Afton Tabernacle 232; Chapel of the Sacred Heart 463; Chapel of the Transfiguration 461; Christ Episcopal Church 245; Church of Our Father's House 323; Esterbrook log church 255; First United Methodist Church 84; Oregon Trail Baptist Church 357; Presbyterian Church 171; St. Andrews Episcopal Church 355; St. Christopher's Chapel of the Big Horns 655; St. Mark's Episcopal Church 84; St. Mary's Catholic Cathedral 84; St. Michael's Mission 322–323; St. Stephens Mission 321; Saints Cyril and Methodius Catholic Church 194; Shoshone Episcopal Mission 324

Cirque of the Towers: 347
Cistern Spring: 519
Clark, Charles Badger: 725
Clay Butte: 587
Clear Creek Trail: 342; System 694
Clearmont: 677–678
Cleveland, Grover: 654, 724
climate: general discussion 4–7; Casper 260; Cheyenne 75; Cody 595; Jackson Hole 380, 428; Laramie 131–133; Newcastle 715; Riverton 297; Rock Springs 192; Yellowstone National Park 508, 544

CLIMBING

Baldwin Creek Rock Climbing Area: 310
Boars Tusk: 190
Devil's Tower National Monument: 730–731
Disappointment Peak: 477
Electric Peak: 539
Fitzpatrick Wilderness: 345
Fremont Canyon: 283
Fremont Peak: 342–343
Gannett Peak: 345
Grand Targhee Ski Resort: 426
Grand Teton National Park: 467, 472–474
International Climbers' Festival: 310–311
Jackson Hole: 423
Laramie: 145
schools: 473–474
Sinks Canyon: 313
tours/guides: 730–731
Vedauwoo: 148
Water Fall Ice Roundup: 586
Wild Iris Climbing Area: 310
see also specific place

Cloud Peak: 661, 663
Cloud Peak Wilderness: 661–663
Clyman, James: 284
coalbed methane: 666, 701
coal mining: general discussion 31; Black Thunder Coal Mine 253; Cambria Mines 714; Gillette 701, 703–704; Point of Rocks 189; Rock Springs 192–193; Sheridan 664–666; strip mining 704–705, 710; Tipple Mine Historical Site 726; tours/guides 703–704; Wright 710
Cody: 592–613; general discussion 593–594; accommodations 605–607; camping 607–608; climate 595; entertainment/events 609–610; food/restaurants 608–609; history 594–598; information/services 611–612; shopping 611; sights 599–605; sports/recreation 610–611; transportation 612
Cody, Buffalo Bill: general discussion 5, 12, 22–23, 279, 596–598; American Heritage Center 136–137; boyhood home 599; Buffalo Bill Dam 593; Buffalo Bill Historical Center 599–602; Buffalo Bill Museum 599–600; and Calamity Jane 353; Cody, founding of 595; Pahaska Tepee 588–589; Sheridan Inn 668; Shoshone National Forest 581; Wild West Show 597–598
Cody, Louisa: 598
Cokeville: 229
Colby Site: 636–637
colleges/schools/universities: Casper College 267; Central Wyoming College 300; Eastern Wyoming College 120; Exum Mountain Guides 473–474; Jackson Hole Mountain Guides 473; Laramie County Community College 96; Larom Summer Institute in Western American Studies 602; National Outdoor Leadership School 305–306; Northern Wyoming Community College 708–709; Northwest College 618; Sheridan College 674; Targhee Institute 426; Teton Science School 468; Trial Lawyers College 328; University of Wyoming 134–137; University of Wyoming College of Agricultural Research and Extension Center 120; Western Wyoming Community College 194–195, 258; Yellowstone Association Institute 490, 526, 557, 559
Collins, Caspar: 263–264
Colony: 727
Colter, John: 17, 376–377, 446, 498, 594
Colter's Hell: 610

Index

CONSERVATION/WILDERNESS AREAS

Absaroka-Beartooth Wilderness: 578, 587
Bridger Wilderness: 341–344
Cloud Peak Wilderness: 661–663
Encampment River Wilderness: 174–175
Fitzpatrick Wilderness: 344–345
Gros Ventre Wilderness: 443–444
Heart Mountain Preserve: 613
High Uintas Wilderness: 207, 221
Huston Park Wilderness: 174
Hutton Lake National Wildlife Refuge: 140
Jedediah Smith Wilderness: 444–445
National Bighorn Sheep Center: 327–328
National Elk Refuge: 385–387
North Absaroka Wilderness: 583
Pathfinder National Wildlife Refuge: 282
Platte River Wilderness: 158
Popo Agie Wilderness: 346–347
Pryor Mountain Wild Horse Range: 628–629

Savage Run Wilderness: 158
Scott's Bottom Nature Area: 201
Seedskadee National Wildlife Refuge: 205
Sheep Creek Geological Area: 207
Spence/Moriarity Habitat Management Area: 328
Sunlight Basin: 584–586
Sweetwater River Project: 312
Sybille Wildlife Research and Conservation Education Unit: 104–105, 153
Tensleep Preserve: 640
Teton Wilderness: 441–443
Thunder Basin National Grassland: 253–254
Washakie Wilderness: 583–584, 616
Whiskey Basin Wildlife Habitat: 326
Winegar Hole Wilderness: 444
Yellowtail Wildlife Habitat Management Area: 626

Colter Bay Village: 458, 464–465
colt race: 61
Como Bluff: 149–150, 258
condo rentals: *see specific place*
Conger, Patrick H.: 500–501
Connor Battlefield State Historic Site: 675
Continental Divide: 4; National Scenic Trail 43; Snowmobile Trail 39–42, 354, 365–366, 435, 476–477
Cooke, Jay: 499
Cooke City (Mont.): 575–578
Cook-Folsom-Peterson Expedition: 499, 515
coots: 205
Cope, E. D.: 150
Corbet's Couloir: 428
Coulter Creek Trail: 440–441
Covey, S. M.: 203
cowboy poetry: Carbon County Gathering of Cowboy Poets 182–183; Cowboyography 673; Cowboy Poet & Music Festival 197; Cowboy Poetry Roundup 300
Cowley: 620
coyotes: 227, 253, 337, 494–495
Craig Pass: 508
Crandall, Marvin: 584
Crazy Horse (chief): 17
Crazy Woman Canyon: 659

credit cards: 65–66
Credit Mobilier of America: 148
Crook, George: 669, 687
Crooked Creek Nature Trail: 627
cross-country skiing: general discussion 39; Big Horn Mountains 658; Casper Mountain 278; Deadhorse Ski Trail 220; Dubois 332; Flaming Gorge 208; Jackson Hole 430–432; Laramie Mountains 257; Lily Lake Touring Area 220; North Fork Nordic Trails 589; Pole-Pedal-Paddle Race 414; Rendezvous Marathon Ski Race 567; safety 548; Sierra Madre 175; Skyline Drive Nordic Touring Trails 365; Snowy Range Ski and Recreation Area 163; South Pass Cross-Country Ski Trails 354; Star Valley 234; tours/guides 432; Wood River Valley Ski Touring Park 616; Yellowstone National Park 547–548, 568; *see also specific place*
Crowheart Butte: 325
Crow tribe: 325, 594, 710
Cub Creek: 441
Curley (Crow scout): 603
currency exchange: 436, 559
Curt Gowdy State Park: 97–98
Custer, George A.: 17, 596, 723, 726
cutter races: 56, 234, 236

D

Daniel: 367

Dave Johnson Power Plant: 259

Dawes, Henry M.: 499

Dayton: 676–677

Dead Indian Pass/Trail: 585

Deadman's Bar: 467

Death Canyon: Loop Trail 471–472; Patrol Cabin 470

Deaver: 620

deer: general discussion 10; Big Horn Mountains 655, 656; Flaming Gorge 207; Fossil Butte 227; Greys River Loop Road 234; Laramie Mountains 254; North Platte River 274; Seedskadee National Wildlife Refuge 205; Story 682; Thunder Basin National Grassland 253; Wind River Mountains 337; Yellowstone National Park 495, 526; *see also specific place*

Deer Creek Trail: 584

DeLacy Creek Trail: 508

Delano, Columbus: 13

Dellenbaugh, Frederick: 198

DeSmet, Pierre Jean: 15–16, 285, 367–370, 695

Devil Canyon: 625–626

Devil's Gate: 285–286

Devil's Kitchen: 630

Devil's Tower National Monument: 728–732

dinosaurs: 258; *see also* paleontological sites/ museums

Disappointment Peak: 472

Dixon: 175–176

Dodge, Grenville M.: 13, 23–24, 75, 133, 147–148, 176

Dodge, Richard I.: 713, 728

Dog Creek Trail: 239

Dogshead Trail: 507

dogsledding: Gallatin National Forest 568; Granite Hot Springs 373; International Pedigree Stage Stop Sled Dog Race 56, 414; Jackson Hole 426, 434; Togwotee Pass 332, 336; tours/guides 336, 373, 426; *see also specific place*

Doheny, Edward: 289

Donner Party: 19

Dougherty, T.: 584

Douglas: 243–249

Dowd Mountain-Hideout Canyon Trail: 207

Downey, Stephen W.: 134

Dragon's Mouth: 531

drag races: *see* auto races/shows

Drewry, Belle: 603

Driggs (Idaho): 448–451; Town Park 450

Druid Peak wolf pack: 497, 526–527

Dubois: 326–333

ducks: 165, 205, 274, 464, 466, 531, 644

Duck Swamp: 637

Dude Ranchers' Association: 53

dude ranches: 52–53; *see also* guest ranches

DuFran, Dora: 353

Dull Knife Battlefield: 699

Dunraven Pass: 493, 528

Durrance, Jack: 729–730

E

Eagle Bronze Foundry: 305

Eagle Butte Mine: 703–704

eagles: 253, 274, 281, 491, 583

Earhart, Amelia: 616

earthquakes: 454, 512, 561, 563

Earthquake Visitor Center: 563

East Yellowstone Valley: *see* Wapiti Valley

economy: general discussion 31–36; energy boom and bust 31, 245, 257, 264–265, 664–666; *see also specific industry; place*

Eddy, John: 659–660

Eden: 357

Edgar, Bob: 602

Edgerton: 288

Edison, Thomas A.: 173

Edness Kimball Wilkins State Park: 267–268

Ehrlich, Gretel: 2, 6, 50

ehrlichiosis: 67

Electric Peak: 538

Elephant Back Mountain Trail: 533

elk: general discussion 10–11; Bear River State Park 217; Big Horn Mountains 655, 656; brucellosis 494; Elk Feedground 237–238; Flaming Gorge 207; Laramie Mountains 254; National Elk Refuge 385–387; North Absaroka Wilderness 583; Seminoe Reservoir 281; Story 682; Thunder Basin National Grassland 253; Wapiti Valley 590; Wind River Mountains 337; Yellowstone National Park 495–496, 521, 526, 545; *see also specific place*

elk antlers: arches 231–232, 383; auctions 56, 414

Elk Feedground: 237–238

Elk Fork Trail: 583

Elkhart Park: 342–343

Elk Lake Loop: 663

Elk Mountain: 155

Elk Park: 518

Emblem: 629
Emerson, Willis George: 170
Emge, Joe: 641
Emigrant's Washtub: 108
Emigrant Hill: 108
Emma Matilda Lake: 464
Encampment: 169–172
endangered species: black-footed ferret 104–105, 152, 153, 615; Heart Mountain Preserve 613; Kendall dace 340; prairie dogs 251
energy industry: 30, 31; *see also* coal mining; oil/gas industry; *specific place*; uranium deposits
entertainment: *see specific place*
environmental groups: Buffalo Field Campaign 494; Draper Museum of Natural History 601; Greater Yellowstone Coalition 560; Jackson Hole Conservation Alliance 379; Jackson Hole Land Trust 379; Nature Conservancy 306; Red Canyon Ranch Preserve 347; Sierra Club 492; Wildlife Education Center 305; Wyoming Outdoor Council 306; Yellowstone Grizzly Foundation 492
environmental issues: coalbed methane 666; fire management 502–504; Greater Yellowstone ecosystem 489; Jackson Hole overdevelopment 379; nonnative diseases/introductions 541–542; snowmobile use 485, 545; strip mining 704–705; wildlife management 485, 491–492, 494; *see also* conservation/wilderness areas; endangered species; *specific place*

Esterbrook: 254–255
etiquette: 44–45
Etna: 237
Evanston: 215–221
events: general discussion 55–56; Alpine Mountain Days 239; Cheyenne Cowboy Symposium and Celebration 94; Chinese New Year 219; Cowboy State Games 56, 272; Fort D. A. Russell Days 94; Fort Fetterman Days 249, 251; Gold Rush Days 354; Grand Teton Summer Festival 427; Loggers and Lager 144; Midsummer's Eve 279; Mounted Shooting Sports 125; Platte Valley Cribbage Tournament 111; Shakespeare in the Park 673; Wyoming Celtic Festival and Highland Games 708; *see also specific interest; type of event*
Everts, Truman: 499
Expedition Island: 201
expeditions: 499–500

F
falcons: 640
Fall, Albert B.: 289
Falls River: 496
Farney, Henry: 136
Farson: 357–358
fauna: *see* wildlife
fees: *see* licenses/permits/regulations/fees
ferries: Fort Caspar 265; Menor's Ferry 461; Mormon ferry 263

FAIRS/CARNIVALS

Albany County Fair: 144
Campbell County Fair: 708
Carbon County Fair and Rodeo: 183
Central Wyoming Fair and Rodeo: 56, 273
Cody Stampede: 55, 609
Crook County Fair and Rodeo: 724
Fremont County Fair and Rodeo: 299–300
Goshen County Fair: 121
Green River Winter Carnival: 364
Hot Springs County Fair: 649
Johnson County Fair and Rodeo: 694
Laramie County Fair: 94
Lincoln County Fair: 233
Mini Fair and Rodeo: 100
Niobrara County Fair: 125

Park County Fair: 619
Platte County Fair and Rodeo: 106
Platte County Summer Festival: 106
Sheepherder Fair: 289
Sheridan County Fair: 673
Sierra Madre Winter Carnival: 172
Sublette County Fair: 371
Sweetwater County Fair: 197
Teton County Fair: 415, 450
Uinta County Fair: 220
Weston County Fair: 718
Wild West Winter Carnival: 299
Wyoming State Fair: 248–249
Wyoming State Winter Fair: 310

Ferris, Angus: 511
Fetterman, William J.: 685
film festivals: 567
Firehole Canyon: 207
Firehole Lake: 515
Firehole River: 541
Firehole River Basin: 493
fires: Gillette 701; Grand Teton National Park 461, 463, 465; management 502–504; Museum of Flight and Aerial Firefighting 630; Wapiti Valley 589; Yellowstone National Park 502–504, 517, 520, 520–521, 576
fishing: general discussion 38–39; Absaroka-Beartooth Wilderness 578; Beartooth Mountains 587; Bighorn Canyon 628; Boysen State Park 302; Buffalo 694; Buffalo Bill State Park 592–593; Dayton 677; Dubois 332; Flaming Gorge Fishing Derby 208; Fontenelle Reservoir 229; Glendo Marina Walleye Tournament 111; Governor's Cup Walleye Tournament 302; Grand Teton National Park 475; Greys River 234; Ice Fishing Derby 226; Jackson Hole 418–419; Kaycee 697; Keyhole State Park 721; Lake DeSmet Fishing Derby 695; Lake Viva-Naughton 226; licenses/regulations 39, 315, 541, 542, 628; North Laramie River 256; North Platte River 166, 274; Open Water Fishing Derby 226; Pathfinder Reservoir 282; Pinedale 365; Saratoga Lake Ice Fishing Derby 168; Seedskadee National Wildlife Refuge 205; Seminoe Reservoir 281; tours/guides 419, 542, 567, 578, 611, 650; Wind River Canyon 650; Wind River Indian Reservation 315; Yellowstone National Park 517, 526, 531, 539, 541–542, 567; see also hatcheries; specific place
Fishing Bridge: 532–533
Fishing Cone: 507
Fitzpatrick, Thomas: 15, 113, 344–345
Fitzpatrick Wilderness: 344–345
Flagg Canyon Trail: 465
Flaming Gorge Dam: 206–207
Fletcher, Mary and Lizzie: 155, 321
flies: 583
flightseeing: Jackson Hole 450; Lander 311
floating/tubing: 208, 274; see also rafting
flora: see vegetation
Fontenelle Reservoir: 228
food/restaurants: general discussion 54–55; Jackson Hole 404–411; see also chili cookoffs;

chuck wagon cookouts; specific place
football: 144, 274
Forces of the Northern Range Self-Guiding Trail: 525
Ford, Gerald R.: 297
forests: Bighorn National Forest 654; Black Hills National Forest 724–725; Bridger-Teton National Forest 441–444; Caribou-Targhee National Forest 444–445; fire management 502–504; Gallatin National Forest 568; Shoshone National Forest 580–587
Forsling, Neal and Jim: 278
Fort Bonneville: 367
Fort Bridger: 19
Fort Bridger: (town), 214
Fort D. A. Russell: 75, 79
Fort Halleck: 155
Fort Laramie: 15–16, 18–19
Fort Mackenzie: 668–669
Fort McKinney: 687
Fort Sanders: 133, 140
Fort Stambaugh: 354
Fort Supply: 213
Fort Wise Treaty: 15–16
Fort Yellowstone: 501, 524
fossils: see paleontological sites/museums
foundries: 305
Fountain Flat: 515–517
Fountain Paint Pot: 515
Four Corners: 718–719
Fourth of July celebrations: see specific place
4WD touring: Bighorn Caverns 626; Crazy Woman Canyon 659; Gros Ventre River Valley 469; Hole-in-the-Wall 699; Kirwin 616; Laramie Mountains 256; Sierra Madre 173; Trapper Canyon 635
Franc, Otto: 594–595
Frannie: 620
Fraughton, Edward: 80
Freedom: 237
Freeman, Legh: 24, 25
Frémont, John C.: 222, 282, 285, 343
Fremont Canyon: 283
Fremont Lake: 365
Fremont Peak: 342–343
French Creek: 160
Friend Park Trail: 256
Frink, Margaret A.: 348
frontier museums/exhibits: Anna Miller Museum 714–715; Bozeman Trail Museum 679; Crook

GEYSERS

general discussion: 486–487
Beehive Geyser: 511
Big Whiligig Geyser: 519
Castle Geyser: 512
Clepsydra Geyser: 515
Cliff Geyser: 512
Constant Geyser: 519
Daisy Geyser: 512
Echinus Geyser: 519
Excelsior Geyser: 514–515
Fountain Geyser: 515
Geyser Hill: 511
Giantess Geyser: 511
Giant Geyser: 512
Grand Geyser: 512
Great Fountain Geyser: 515
Grotto Geyser: 512
Imperial Geyser: 514
Lion Geyser Group: 511
Lone Star Geyser: 508
Lower Geyser Basin: 515–516
Midway Geyser Basin: 514–515
Monument Geyser Basin: 518
Morning Geyser: 515

Norris Geyser Basin: 518–519
Old Faithful: 510–511
Pink Cone Geyser: 515
Porkchop Geyser: 519
Radiator Geyser: 512
Riverside Geyser: 512
Rustic Geyser: 539
safety: 510, 544
Sawmill Geyser: 512
Shoshone Geyser Basin: 539
Shoshone River: 594
Solitary Geyser: 511
Sponge Geyser: 511
Spray Geyser: 514
Steady Geyser: 515
Steamboat Geyser: 519
Sylvan Springs Geyser Basin: 518
Tardy Geyser: 512
Turban Geyser: 512
Upper Geyser Basin: 508–514
vandalism: 488, 512
West Thumb Geyser Basin: 507
White Dome Geyser: 515
see also hot springs

County Museum 721; Dubois Museum Day 332; Fort Phil Kearny 686; Fossil Country Frontier Museum 223; Frontier Days Old West Museum 81–82; Frontier Festival 272–273; Helen Robinson Zimmerschied Western-Texas Trail Museum 720; Homesteader Museum 617–618; Homesteaders Museum 118–119; Hoofprints of the Past Museum 696; Hot Springs Historical Museum 645; Jackson Hole Historical Museum 385; Jim Gatchell Memorial Museum 687–689; King's Western Museum 668; Living History Days 694, 717; Museum of the American West 305; Museum of the Mountain Man 360; Museum of the Old West 603; National Historic Trails Interpretive Center 265–266; Nelson Museum of the West 82; Old West Show & Auction 610; Pioneer Museum 232, 245; Platte Bridge Encampment 273; Red Onion Museum 719; Rockpile Museum 703; Wright Centennial Museum 709–710; *see also specific place*

Frost, Lane: 58
frostbite: 45–46
Frying Pan Spring: 520
fumaroles: 488, 515

G
Gallatin National Forest: 568
Gallatin River: 496, 541, 567
galleries: Casper 267; Cheyenne 96; Cody 602, 604; Cooke City 576; Dubois 332; Gardiner 574; Hulett 726; Jackson Hole 387–388; Laramie 140; Pinedale 366; Powell 618; Saratoga 169; Shell Valley 633–634; Sheridan 674; Thermopolis 650; Ucross 677; Wind River Indian Reservation 324; *see also specific place*
Gannett Peak: 345
gardens: Botanic Gardens 82–83; Joseph Henry Sharp Garden 600; Range Herbarium 137; Rocky Mountain Herbarium 137; Williams Botany Conservatory 137
Gardiner (Mont.): 571–575

GHOST TOWNS

general discussion: 41
Battle: 173
Cambria: 718
Carbon: 154
Copperton: 173
Crosby: 647
Cumberland: 221
Dillon: 170, 173
Gebo: 647
Hillsboro: 626
Jay Em: 122
Jeffrey City: 312–313
Kirwin: 616
Lewiston: 355
Old Jelm: 160
Piedmont: 211–212
Rambler: 173
Rudefeha: 170, 173
Sunrise: 109
Superior: 190

GRAND TETON NATIONAL PARK

accommodations: 466, 473, 477–479
backcountry sports: 470–474
bicycling/mountain biking: 469, 476
boating: 475
climbing: 467, 472–474
fires: 461, 463, 465
flora: 466, 467
food and drink: 479–480
geology: 454–455, 468–469
highlights: 454
hiking/backpacking: 459–470, 474
history: 456–458
information/services: 480–481
licenses/permits/regulations/fees: 470–471, 473, 480
snowmobiling: 465
thunderstorms: 463, 470, 471
tours/guides: 440, 481–482
transportation: 477, 481–482
water sports/recreation: 474–475, 476
wildlife: 456, 464, 466, 467, 468, 475–476
winter sports/recreation: 476–477
see also Jackson Hole; *specific place*

Gardiner, Steve: 1
Gardner River Canyon: 493
Garland: 620
gas: *see* oil/gas industry
Gascho, Noel R.: 29
Gas Hills: 302
geese: 165, 274, 282, 466, 531
geography: *see* land
Gertrude Krampert Theater: 272
ghosts: 203, 668, 695
Giardia lamblia: 45
Gibbon Meadows: 518
Gillette: 701–709
Gillette, Edward: 701
glaciers: 454–455, 463, 467, 486
Glacier Trail: 345
Glendo: 110–111; State Park 110
Glenrock: 257–260
Golden Gate: 520
Golden Rule Stores: 224
gold mining: discovery 170; history 16, 19; Snowy Range 133; South Pass 348, 349–350, 355; *see also* ghost towns
golf: Afton 234; Big Horn 681; Buffalo 694; Casper 274; Cheyenne 95; Cody 611; Dayton 677; Douglas 248; Dubois 332; Evanston 220; Glenrock 259; Grand Targhee Ski Resort 426; Greybull 632; Guernsey 108; Hulett 727; Jackson Hole 423–424; Keyhole State Park 721; Lander 310; Laramie 145; Lovell 622; Lusk 125; Newcastle 718; Pinedale 364; Powell 620; Rawlins 183; Riverton 300; Rock Springs 197; Sheridan 673–674; Sinclair 185; Sundance 724; Thermopolis 649; Torrington 121; Upton 720; Wheatland 106; Worland 638; Wright 710; *see also specific place*
Gooseberry Badlands: 637–638
Goosewing Ranger Station: 443
government: 36–37
Gowdy, Curt: 97
Grand Canyon of the Yellowstone: 528–531
Grand Prismatic Spring: 514–515
Grand Targhee Ski Resort: 424–427
Grand Teton (peak): 463, 472–473
Grand Teton Lodge: 458

Grand Teton National Park Foundation: 481
Grand Teton Natural History Association: 481
Grandview: 530
Granger: 204
Grant, Ulysses S.: 13, 24, 500
Grant Village: 507, 551
Grasshopper Glacier: 578
Grassroots Trail: 120
Grassy Lake Road: 466, 540
Gray Reef Reservoir: 283
Grayrocks Reservoir: 105, 116
"Great American Desert": 2, 11
Great Divide Basin: 189
Great Divide Mountain Bike Route: 365
Greater Yellowstone ecosystem: 489, 601
Green Mountain Park: 313
Green River: 198–203
Green River Greenbelt: 201
Green River Lakes: 338–340, 360; trails 342
Greeves, R. V.: 324
Greybull: 629–632
Grinnell, Joseph Bird: 501
Grizzly Lake Trail: 469
Gros Ventre Geological Trail: 469
Gros Ventre River Valley: 469–470
Gros Ventre slide: 468–469
Gros Ventre Wilderness: 443–444
Guernsey: 107–111
Guernsey State Park: 109–110

Guinard, Louis: 263
Gull Point Drive: 533
gunfights: Cheyenne Gunslingers 85, 91–92;
    Cody Gunslingers 604, 609; Jackson Town
    Square shootout: 383
gyms: see specific place

H
Haggerty, Ed: 170
Haines, Aubrey L.: 485, 497
Half Moon Lake: 365
handgun factories: 237
handicap access: Chief Washakie Plunge 324;
    Grand Teton National Park 480; Lee McCune
    Braille Trail 277; Medicine Lodge State Park
    635; Medicine Wheel 660–661; Popo Agie
    Falls Trail 314; Yellowstone National Park 550
hang-gliding: 274
Hanna: 152–154
hantavirus: 66–67
Hardin, Samuel H.: 676
Harrison, Benjamin: 25, 580
Hartville: 108–109
hatcheries: Auburn Fish Hatchery 237; Dan
    Speas Fish Hatchery 279; Jackson National
    Fish Hatchery 386; Saratoga National Fish
    Hatchery 165; Ten Sleep Fish Hatchery
    640–641; Wigwam Fish Rearing Station 640
hawks: 274, 640

GUEST RANCHES

Arvada: 678
Boulder: 367
Buffalo: 692
Cheyenne: 86
Chugwater: 102
Curt Gowdy State Park: 98
Daniel: 367
Douglas: 247
Dubois: 330, 335–336
Elk Mountain: 155
Grand Teton National Park: 466
Hulett: 726
Jackson Hole: 400–402, 447, 457
Kaycee: 697
LaGrange: 100
Lander: 308

Laramie: 141
Lovell: 622
Pinedale: 362
Popo Agie Wilderness: 346
Rock River: 149
Saratoga: 167–168
Savery: 175
Shell Valley: 635
Sheridan: 671
Snowy Range: 158, 162
South Fork: 586
Story: 682
Sunlight Basin: 585–586
Thermopolis: 648
Ucross: 677
Wapiti Valley: 590–592

Hawk Springs: 122; State Recreation Area 121–122

Hayden, Ferdinand V.: 252, 259, 499

Hayden Expedition: 464, 472–473, 499–500

Hayden Valley: 492, 493, 496, 531, 557

Headquarters Trail: 147

health and safety: general discussion 66–67; altitude 661; avalanches 431, 568; backcountry 45–46, 338, 471, 548; bears 46–49, 337, 341, 441, 442, 492, 581–583; bicycling/mountain biking 543; black widows 627; climbing 343; cross-country skiing 548; essentials 587; geysers/hot springs 510, 544; highway 68, 140, 239, 438; insects 337, 583; lightning 6, 254, 338, 587; radiation 466; rattlesnakes 9–10, 207, 254, 627; winter travel 69; Yellowstone National Park 490; see also specific place

Heart Lake: 507, 539–540

Heart Mountain: Preserve 613; Relocation Center 613–614

Heart Mountain Wyoming Foundation: 614

Hedrick Pond: 467

Hell's Half Acre: 289–290

Hellroaring Creek: 538

Hemingway, Ernest: 671

Henderson, A. Bart: 530

Hennes, Joanne: 388

Hermitage Point: 464–465

herons: 205

Hickok, Wild Bill: 84, 353, 596

Hidden Corral Basin: 444

highland games: 708

highlights: general discussion 40–41; Bighorn Basin 580; Black Hills 713; Central Wyoming 242; Grand Teton National Park 454; Jackson Hole 376; Medicine Bow Country 130; Powder River Country 654; Southeast Wyoming 74; Southwest Wyoming 188; Wind River Mountains 294; Yellowstone National Park 484

Highline Trail: 342, 343, 443

High Park Lookout Tower: 655

hiking/backpacking: Beartooth Mountains 587; Bighorn Canyon 627–628; Big Horn Mountains 658–659; Black Hills National Forest 725; Bridger-Teton National Forest 441; Bridger Wilderness 342–344; Buffalo 694; Cloud Peak Wilderness 663; Devil's Tower 731; Fitzpatrick Wilderness 345; Flaming Gorge 207; Fossil Butte 227; Grand Teton National Park 459–470, 474; Greys River Loop

Road 235; Gros Ventre Wilderness 443–444; Jackson Hole 420–421; Jedediah Smith Wilderness 444–445; Laramie Mountains 256–257; North Absaroka Wilderness 583; Pinedale 338–340, 360; Popo Agie Wilderness 346–347; Riverton 300; Shoshone National Forest 581; Snake River Canyon 239; Snowy Range 159–160, 162; Sunlight Basin 585; Tensleep Preserve 640; Teton Wilderness 442–443; Thermopolis 649; tours/guides 421; Washakie Wilderness 583–584; Wood River Valley 616; Worland 639; Yellowstone National Park 507–513, 514–534; see also backcountry treks; specific place; trail

Hill, Nancy: 228

historic lodgings: general discussion 51; Absaroka Mountain Lodge 591; Auntie M's B&B 671; Big Sandy Lodge 343; Bow River Ranger Station 161; Bozeman Trail B&B 680; Brooklyn Lodge B&B 162; Brooks Lake Lodge 402–403; Casual Cove B&B 607; Centennial Trust B&B 158; Crossed Sabres Ranch 590; Eaton's Ranch 671; Edee's B&B 671; Elephant Head Lodge 591; Elk Mountain Hotel 155; Evy Williams Guard Station 174; Far Out West B&B 167; The Hideout at Flitner Ranch 634; Historic Old Stone House B&B 676; Hood House B&B 167; Huff House Inn 396; Hynds Lodge 97; Jackson Lake Lodge 464; Jakey's Fork Homestead 329; Keystone Ranger Station 161; Lake Yellowstone Hotel 533, 551–552; Little Brooklyn Lake Guard Station 161; Lockhart B&B Inn 607; Madison Hotel 563; Mammoth Hot Springs Hotel 524, 552; The Mayor's Inn 607; Medicine Bow Lodge & Guest Ranch 162; Miner's Delight B&B 355; Mountain View Historic Hotel 158; Occidental Hotel 689; Old Depot B&B 171; Old Faithful Inn 513–514, 553–554; Painted Porch 396; Parson's Pillow B&B 607; Plains Hotel 87; Rainsford Inn 88; Roosevelt Lodge 527, 554; Spear-O-Wigwam Dude Ranch 671; Spear Ranch B&B 680–681; Spruce Mountain Fire Lookout Tower 161; TA Ranch 697; Triangle X Ranch 467; Virginian Hotel 151; Whitehorse B&B 676; Willow Creek Ranch at Hole-in-the-Wall 697; Wolf Hotel 165, 166; Yellowstone Inn B&B 572; Yellowstone Suites B&B 572

historic sites/structures: Anderson Lodge

616–617; Atlantic City Mercantile 354–355; Bank Club Bar 176; Bank Museum 615; Beeman-Cashin Implement Depot 216; Big Horn Mercantile 679; Boulder Store 366; Bozeman Trail Inn 679; Carissa Mine 355; The Castle 110; College Inn Bar 248; Connor Battlefield State Historic Site 675; Cooke City General Store 576; Cooper Mansion 136; Cowboy Bar 615; Cowfish 309; Cunningham Cabin 466–467; Daniel schoolhouse 367; Dayton bell tower 676; Depot Square 216; Dull Knife Battlefield 699; Duncan Mine 355; Eagle's Store 562; Eagles Nest Stage Station 614; East Entrance Ranger Station 534; Evanston Depot 216; Farson Mercantile 357; Ferris Mansion 181; Flying V Cambria Inn 718; Fort Bridger 212–214; Fort Caspar 265; Fort Fetterman 250–251; Fort Fred Steele 183–184; Fort Laramie National Historic Site 115–116; Fort Phil Kearny 686; Fort Yellowstone 524; Frontier Prison 178–180; Gaddis-Matthews House 176; Garden Spot Pavilion 155; Goose Egg Ranch 279; Governor's Mansion 80–81; Gratrix Cabin 355; Gros Ventre Lodge 340; Ivinson Mansion 139–140; Jenney Stockade cabin 715; Joss House 216–217; King's Saddlery 668; Lake Lodge 533; Lake Ranger Station 533; Lander Bar 309; Lincoln County Courthouse 223; Lockhart Ranch 626; Lusk 124; McAuley Store 355; Meeteetse Mercantile 615; Miners Bar 108–109; Mint Bar 669; ML Ranch 626; Mormon Handcart Visitors Center 286–287; Mormon Row 467–468; Morris cabin 351; Museum of the Yellowstone 561–562; Nagle-Warren Mansion 84, 88; Northeast Entrance Station 527; Odd Fellows Hall 245; Okie Mansion 290–291; Old Bedlam 115–116; Old Main 137; Overland Stage station 189; Pahaska Tepee 588–589; Palatte Ranch 616–617; Penney House 223; Plains Complex 245–246; Platte County Court House 104; Quarter Circle 5 Ranch 370; Rock Springs Historical Museum 193–194; Rosie's Cabin 466; Sheridan Inn 668; Sheridan Main Street Historic District 669; Slovenski Dom 194; Smith Sherlock Co. Store 351; South Pass State Historic Site 350–351; Spud Drive-In 448; State Capitol 80; Sunlight Ranger Station 585; Sweetwater County Jail 351; Sweetwater Mines 348; Swett Ranch

207; Tipple Mine Historical Site 726; Trail End State Historic Site 666–668; Trail Town 602–604; Union Pacific Railroad Depot 83–84; Upton Old Town 719; Wapiti Ranger Station 589; Whipple House 84; White House 324; Wyoming Hereford Ranch 85; Wyoming Territorial Park 137–139; *see also* churches/missions/temples; ghost towns; historic lodgings

history: general discussion 14–30; Arapaho 317–318; Atlantic City 354; Ayres Natural Bridge Park 252; bison slaughter 12–13, 289, 596–597; Bozeman Trail 683–686; Buffalo 687; Buffalo Bill Historical Center 599; Casper 263–265; cattle ranching 26–29; Cheyenne 75–79; Cheyenne Frontier Days 92–93; Cody 594–598; Como Bluff 149–150; Cooke City/Silver Gate 575–576; Devil's Tower 728–730; Douglas 243–245; Dubois 327; Encampment 170; energy industry 30; Evanston 215–216; Fort Bridger 212–213; Fort Fetterman 250; Fort Laramie National Historic Site 111–114; Gillette 701; Grand Teton National Park 456–458; Green River 198–200; Greybull 629; Hot Springs State Park 642; Jackson Hole 376–380; Lander 304–305; Laramie 133–134; Medicine Bow 130, 151; Meeteetse 615; National Elk Refuge 385–386; Native Americans 14–17; Oregon Trail 17–21, 112, 284–287; Overland Trail 23; Pinedale 358–360; Pony Express 20–23; Powell 617; railroads 23–24; Rawlins 176–178; Riverton 295–297; Rock Springs 192–193; rodeo 57; Salt Creek Oil Field 287–288; Saratoga 163–165; sheepherding 29–30; Sheridan 664–666; Shoshone 315–317; Shoshone National Forest 580; South Pass 348–350; Southwest Wyoming 188; Star Valley 230–231; statehood 24–26; Teapot Dome 288–289; Teton Valley: 446; Torrington 117–118; trappers/explorers 17; West Yellowstone 561; Wheatland 102–104; women's suffrage 25–26, 134, 350, 379; Worland 636; Yellowstone National Park 497–505; *see also* battles/raids/massacres; Native Americans; outlaws/rustlers; *specific person; specific place*

Hoback Canyon: 372

Hogadon Ski Area: 277–278

Holdsworth, Henry: 388

Hole-in-the-Wall: 698–700
Holladay, Ben: 23
Homesteader Park: 619–620
Honeycombs: 640
The Hoodoos: 521
Hopkins, George: 729–730
horseback riding/trail rides: general discussion 42–44; Absaroka-Beartooth Wilderness 578; Casper 273; Cheyenne 94–95; Encampment 172; Grand Targhee Ski Resort 426; Grand Teton National Park 476; High Country Trail Rides 610–611; Hole-in-the-Wall 700; Jackson Hole 419–420; Lander 310; Laramie 145; licenses/permits/regulations/fees 346; Oregon Trail 354; Outlaw Trail Ride 42, 649, 700; Pinedale 364; Popo Agie Wilderness 346; Shoshone National Forest 581; Teton Wilderness 442; tours/guides 172, 354, 420, 442, 592, 700; Wapiti Valley 592; Yellowstone National Park 529, 538, 543–544, 567; see also specific place
Horse Creek: 333
horse racing: 219
Horseshoe Bend: 626–627
horse shows/sales: Cheyenne: 94; Cutting Horse Contest 175–176; Foxtrotter Horse Show and Sale 619; Perino Horse Sale 717–718
Horsley, William: 621
hostels: 52, 563, 586
hot air ballooning: Grand Teton Summer Festival 450; Hot Air Balloon Rally 299; Jackson Hole 423; Teton Valley 450
Hot Lake: 515
hot springs: general discussion 488; Alcova Hot Springs 283; Angel Terrace 523; Artist Paint Pots 518; Beauty Pool 512; Big Springs 642–644; Black Dragons Cauldron 531; Canary Spring 523; Chico Hot Springs 544; Chief Washakie Plunge 324; Chocolate Pots 518; Chromatic Pool 512; Churning Cauldron 531; Columbia Pool 539; Crested Pool 512; Doublet Pool 511; Emerald Pool 512; Emerald Spring 519; Gottsche Rehabilitation Center 645; Granite Hot Springs 372–373, 423; Handkerchief Pool 512; Hobo Pool 165; Hot Springs State Park 642–645; Huckleberry Hot Springs 466; Kendall Warm Springs 340; Mammoth Hot Springs 521–524; Morning Glory Pool 512; New Blue Spring 523; Palate Spring 523; Potts Hot Springs Basin 533;

Rainbow Pool 512; safety 510, 544; Saratoga 163–165; Silex Spring 515; State Bath House 644; Sulphur Cauldron 531; see also geysers
Hot Springs State Park: 642–645
Hudson: 302–303
Hulett: 726–727
hunting: general discussion 38–39; Kaycee 697; licenses 39; One-Shot Antelope Hunt 311; One-Shot Evans-Dahl Memorial Museum 305; Union Pass 340; see also specific place
Hyattville: 635
hypothermia: 45

I

ICBM missiles: 79, 102
Icebox Canyon: 527
ice fishing: 97, 283
ice skating: 433
Ice Slough: 312
Independence Rock: 284–285
Indian Bathtubs: 171
information/services: general discussion 61–65; Afton 234; Buffalo 695; Casper 275; Cheyenne 96; Cody 611–612; Devil's Tower 731–732; Douglas 249; Evanston 220; Fort Laramie 117; Green River 203; Jackson Hole 385, 435–438 451; Kemmerer 226; Lander 311; Lovell 623; Pinedale 366; Powell 620; Rawlins 183; Riverton 300; Rock Springs 198; Saratoga 169; Sheridan 674; Snowy Range 158; Sundance 724; Torrington 121; trails 43; Wheatland 106; Wind River Mountains Country 295; Worland 639; Yellowstone National Park 506, 538, 546, 569, 574–575, 578; see also specific place
in-line skating: 450
Inspiration Point: 463, 529–530
Internet access: 61; see also libraries; specific place
Inyan Kara Mountain: 723
iron-ore mining: 354
irrigation: 280–281, 456–457, 579, 593, 620
Irwin, C. B.: 245
Island Lake: 587

J

jackalopes: 244
Jackson, Harry: 594, 604
Jackson (town): 380–387
Jackson, William H.: 500, 523–524
Jackson Hole: general discussion 374–376;

accommodations 390–403; Bridger-Teton National Forest 441–444; Caribou-Targhee National Forest 444–445; climate 380, 428; Community Pathways 421; entertainment 411–413; environmental issues 379; events 413–415; food/restaurants 404–411; highlights 376; history 376–380; information/services 385, 435–438, 451; Jackson (town) 380–387; Mountain Resort 427–429; Nordic Center 430; Playhouse 412; residence in 437–438; shopping 387–389, 450–451; sights 383–387; summer recreation 415–424; Teton Valley 446–452; transportation 427, 428, 430, 438–441; winter recreation 424–435; Grand Teton National Park

Jackson Lake/Dam: 456–457, 463–464, 466

jade: 305, 313

Japanese-American relocation camps: 613–614

JCPenney: 224

Jedediah Smith Wilderness: 444–445

Jenney, Walter P.: 713

Jenny Lake: 461–463

Johnston, John ("Liver Eating"): 603

Jones, Daniel W.: 286

Joseph (Nez Perce chief): 498, 584, 660

Joy, Fred: 388

Joy, Louis: 457

Joyner Ridge Trail: 731

K

Kaycee: 696–698

Kelly Warm Spring: 468

Kemmerer: 221–226

Kendall: 340

Kendall dace: 340

Kendrick, John B.: 25, 666–667

Kendrick City Park: 673

Kennaday Peak Lookout: 160

Keyhole State Park: 721

Killpecker Dunes: 190

Kiowa tribe: 730

kites: 274

Kitty Creek Trail: 583

Kleiber, Hans: 676

Kortes Dam: 281

Kvale, Erik: 634

L

La Barge: 228

La Bonte Canyon Trail: 256

Labor Day celebrations: see specific place

Lacey, John W.: 84

LaGrange: 100

Lajeunesse, Basil: 343

Lake Alice: 229

Lake Butte Overlook: 534

Lake DeSmet: 695

Lake Marie: 160

Lakeshore Trail: 465

Lake Solitude: 663

Lakes Trail: 162

Lake Village: 551–552

Lake Viva-Naughton: 226

Lamar River: 496

Lamar Valley: 492, 493, 525–526, 545

Lambert, Mel: 58

Lamont: 185

Lance Creek: 126–127

land: general discussion 3–4; Black Hills 711–713; Central Wyoming 240–242; Devil's Tower 728; Grand Teton National Park 454–455; Wind River Canyon 650–651; Wind River Mountains Country 292–295; Yellowstone National Park 486–489, 523, 528–529; see also specific place

Lander: 303–312; City Park 308; Cutoff 230–231, 358, 371–372

landslides: 468–469

Lane County: 119

Langford, Nathaniel P.: 472–473, 499, 500

language/lingo: 34–35

Lapham, Hiram C.: 440, 446

Laramie: accommodations 141–142; climate 131–133; entertainment/events 143–144; food/restaurants 142–143; history 133–134; information/services 146; shopping 145; sights 134–140; sports/recreation 144–145; transportation 146

Laramie Mountains: 254–257

Laramie Peak Trail: 256

Laramie Plains: 156–157

Laramie River: Greenbelt 145; Interpretive Trail 139

laundromats: see specific place

lawmen: Angus, Red 690, 691; National U.S. Marshals Museum 138–139; Wyoming Peace Officers Museum 180; see also specific person

LeDoux, Chris: 696

Leek, Stephen N.: 386

Lee McCune Braille Trail: 277

The Legend of Rawhide: 55, 125–126
LeHardy Rapids: 531
Leigh, Richard ("Beaver Dick"): 464–465
Leigh Lake: 463
Leiter: 678
Lewis and Clark Expedition: 322, 376–377
Lewis Channel Trail: 507
Lewis Lake: 506–507
Lewis Park: 105
Lewis River: 496; Canyon 506
Libby Flats: 160
Liberty Cap: 523
libraries: general discussion 96; Albany County
    Library 146; Big Horn County Library 633;
    Campbell County Public Library 703; Carbon
    County Public Library 183; Casper College li-
    brary 267; Crook County Library 724; Dubois
    Library 333; Encampment Library 172; Glen-
    rock Library 259; Greybull Public Library 632;
    Guernsey 108; Harold McCracken Research
    Library 602; Hot Springs County Library 649;
    John Hinkley Memorial Library 620; Johnson
    County Public Library 695; Lincoln County
    Library 226; Lovell 623; Natrona County Li-
    brary 275; Niobrara County Library 125; Park
    County Library 612; Pine Bluffs 100; Platte
    County Library 106; Powell Public Library
    620; Riverton Public Library 300; Rock
    Springs 198; Saratoga 169; Sheridan County
    Library 669, 674; Star Valley Branch Library
    234; Sublette County Library 366; Sweetwater
    County Library 203; Teton County Library
    436; Torrington 121; Uinta County Library
    220; University of Wyoming libraries 146;
    Washakie County Library 639; Weston Coun-
    ty Library 718; White Mountain Library 198;
    William Robertson Coe Library 146
license plates: 2
licenses/permits/regulations/fees: backcountry
    341, 345, 470–471, 514, 663; Bighorn
    Canyon 617, 628; boating 418, 475; climbing
    473; Devil's Tower 731; hunting/fishing 39,
    208, 475, 541, 542, 628; mountain biking
    421; rafting 418; snowmobiling 548; Wind
    River Indian Reservation 315, 325, 337; Yel-
    lowstone National Park 548
lightning: 6, 254, 338
Lightning Protection Institute: 6
Lincoln, Abraham: 79, 147
Lingle: 122

Lions Club Park: 226
Lisa, Manuel: 377
Little America: 203–204
Little Bighorn River Canyon Trail: 659
Little Firehole Meadows: 513
Little Hole National Recreation Trail: 207
Littlehorn Trail: 658
Little Snake River Valley: 175–176
Little Theater Players: 92
living history: *see* frontier museums/exhibits;
    mountain men/rendezvous
llama trips: 44, 420, 440, 538
Lockhart, Caroline: 627
lodgepole pines: 502–504
logging: 489
Lonesome Lake: 347
Lookout Point: 530
Loop Road: 313–314
Lost Cabin: 290–291
Lost Lake Trail: 162, 527
Loucks, John D.: 664
Lovell: 621–623
Lower Saddle: 473
Lusk: 123–127
Lyman: 210
Lyme disease: 67
Lysite: 290

M
Madison Junction: 517, 518
Madison River: 541
Mainstage Theater: 412
Majors, Alexander: 21, 22–23
mammoth bones: 636–637
Mammoth Hot Springs: 521–524, 552
Manderson: 633
Mangelsen, Tom: 388
Manifest Destiny: 17
Manila (Utah): 209
Manning, William: 378
Mansface Rock: 201
Manville: 109
maps: car travel 68; geology 137
Marbleton: 371
marinas: *see* boating/marinas
marmots: 337
Marsh, Othniel Charles: 149–150
Martin, Edward: 286
Martin's Cove: 286–287
Mather, Stephen: 505

Maverick Bill: 28
McAuley, Eliza Ann: 19
Meadowlark Lake: 655
medical services: Afton 234; Casper 275; Cody 612; Douglas 249; Gillette 709; Grand Teton National Park 480; Green River 203; Jackson Hole 436; Lander 311; Lovell 622; Newcastle 718; Riverton 300; Rock Springs 198; Saratoga 169; Sheridan 674; Teton Valley 451; Thermopolis 645, 650; West Yellowstone 569; Wheatland 106; Worland 639; Yellowstone National Park 546, 558
Medicine Bow: 150–152
Medicine Bow Country: general discussion 128–130; economy 130; Encampment/Riverside 169–172; highlights 130; history 130; Laramie 131–146; Medicine Bow 149–155; Medicine Bow Mountains 156–163; Pole Mountain 147–148; Rawlins 176–183; Saratoga 163–169; Sierra Madre 173–176; Vedauwoo 148
Medicine Bow Mountains: 156–163
Medicine Bow Peak: 160; Trail 162
Medicine Lodge State Park: 635
Medicine Wheel: 659–661
Meeteetse: 615–617
Menor's Ferry: 461
Merriam's turkeys: 713, 721
Metzger, Adolph: 688
Michener, James: 599
Middle Fork Trail: 346
Midwest: 288
Miller, Alfred Jacob: 136
Miller, Grace: 379
miniatures: Miniature Show and Sale 385; Old West Miniature Village and Museum 604–605
mining: *see specific type of mining*
Miracle Mile: 281
Mirror Lake: 160
Missouri Buttes: 728
Mitchell, Finis: 338
Moe, Tommy: 429
Mokler, Alfred: 29
Molesworth, Thomas: 589
Moncrieffe, William and Malcolm: 680, 681
Mondell, Frank W.: 231, 714
Moneta: 290
Monument Hill: 645
monuments: 1840 rendezvous site: 367–370;

Firefighters' Memorial 589; Parting of the Ways 348–349; Sawyer Fight 675; Willie Handcart Company 355–356
Moonlight, Thomas: 113–114
moonshine: 222
Moorcroft: 720–721
Moore, Asa: 133
moose: Big Horn Mountains 655; Bridger Wilderness 342; Grand Teton National Park 464, 466, 470; Greys River Loop Road 234; North Absaroka Wilderness 583; Seedskadee National Wildlife Refuge 205; Story 682; Wind River Mountains 337; Yellowstone National Park 496; *see also specific place*
Moose: 459
Moose Meadows: 445
Moose-Wilson Road: 470
Moran, Thomas: 387, 500, 523, 530
Moran Junction: 466
Morgan, John T.: 26
Mormon heritage/settlements: Blacktail Butte/Mormon Row 467–468; Casper 263, 265; Church Buttes 204; emigration 19–20; Freedom 237; Grattan Massacre 113; handcart disasters 286–287, 355–356; Heritage Days 450; Lovell 621; Lyman 210; Mormon ferry 263; Mormon Handcart Visitors Center 286–287; Mormon Pioneer Days 210; Mormon Pioneer Trail 204; Mormon War 205; Star Valley 230–231; Teton Valley 446; Willie Handcart Company monument 355–356; Young, Brigham 204, 213, 263; *see also specific place*
Morris, Esther Hobart: 80, 350, 351
mosquitoes: 535, 583
Mother Featherlegs: 123
moths: 335, 491–492
motorcycle events: Ham and Jam 727; Sturgis Bike Rally 249, 717, 724
Mt. Haynes: 517
Mt. Jackson: 517
Mt. Moran: 466
Mt. Owen: 463
Mt. Sheridan: 533; Trail 539
Mt. Washburn: 493, 528, 556–557
mountain biking: *see* bicycling/mountain biking
mountaineering: *see* climbing
mountain goats: 585
Mountain Home: 161
Mountain View: 210

MOUNTAIN MEN/RENDEZVOUS

general discussion: 55–56, 368–370
Bear River Rendezvous: 220
Burnt Hole Mountain Man Rendezvous: 567
1840 rendezvous site: 367–370
Esterbrook Rendezvous: 255
Fort Bridger Rendezvous: 56, 214
Green River Rendezvous: 364
Hams Fork Rendezous: 204
Henrys Fork Mountain-Man Rendezvous: 206
Mountain Man Rendezvous: 299, 632
Mountain View: 210
Museum of the Mountain Man: 360
Popo Agie Rendezvous: 310
Riverton Rendezvous: 299
Sierra Madre Mountain Man Rendezvous: 172
U.S. Marshals Day & Posse Rendezvous: 144
see also specific person; place

movie locations/props/inspirations: *Always* 630; *The Big Trail* 466; *Butch Cassidy and the Sundance Kid* 698; *Close Encounters of the Third Kind* 728, 730; *Dances With Wolves* 245; *Heaven's Gate* 690; *Hellfighters* 279, 701; *Jeremiah Johnston* 603; *Leaving Normal* 190; *The Legend of Earl Durand* 617; Marlboro ads 585; *Prison* 179; *Red River* 668; *Shane* 468; *Spencer's Mountain* 467; *Starship Trooper* 290; *War Paint* 315
Muddy Gap: 185
mud pots: 488
Mud Volcano Area: 531
Mueller, Ellen: 353
Muench, David: 388
Mule Creek Junction: 127
mule deer: *see* deer
mule rodeos: 614
mummies: 590
Murie, Olaus and Mardie: 386
museums: general discussion 65; Anthropology Museum 137; Bank Museum 615; CallAir Museum 232; Carbon County Museum 180; Chugwater Museum 101–102; Cody Firearms Museum 601–602; Crimson Dawn Museum 278–279; Draper Museum of Natural History

601; Dubois Museum 328; Entomology Museum 137; Fort Fetterman 250; Glenrock Historical Museum 258; Grand Encampment Museum 170–171; Guernsey State Park Museum 110; Hanna Basin Museum 154; Jackson Hole Historical Center 385; Laramie Peak Museum 104; Little Snake River Museum 175; Medicine Bow Museum 151–152; Museum of the National Park Ranger 520; Museum of the Yellowstone 561–562; Nici Self Museum 157; Norris Museum 519; Old West Wax Museum and Dancing Bear Folk Center 646; One-Shot Evans-Dahl Memorial Museum 305; Parco/Sinclair Museum 184; Pathfinder Interpretive Center 282; Riverton Museum 297; Rock River Museum 149, 258; Rock Springs Historical Museum 193–194; Salt Creek Museum 288; Sweetwater County Historical Museum 200–201; Tate Geological Museum 267; Teton Valley Museum 448; Texas Trail Museum 99–100; Trona Mining Museum 210; Uinta County Museum 216; Warbirds Museum 448; Warren ICBM & Heritage Museum 83; Werner Wildlife Museum 267; Windows of the Past Interpretive Center 98–99; Wyoming Geological Museum 137, 258; Wyoming State Museum 81; Wyoming Veteran's Memorial Museum 268; *see also* archaeological sites/museums/exhibits; art festivals/museums/shows; children's museums/activities; frontier museums/exhibits; paleontological sites/museums; *specific place*
music festivals: Beartrap Summer Festival 273; Big Horn Mountain Polka Days 673; Canyon Ranch Indian Paintbrush Festival 673, 681; Cowboyography 673; Cowboy Poet & Music Festival 197; Cowboy Songs and Range Ballads 609; Grand Teton Music Festival 56, 412, 414; Greater Yellowstone Music Camp 332; High Plains Old-Time Music Show 249; Hoedown on the Smiths Fork 210; Invitational Jam Session 694; Lander Jazz Festival 311; Laramie Peak Bluegrass Festival 249; Music in the Hole 414; Nowood Stock Music Fest 642; Oyster Ridge Music Festival 226; Pinedale Blues Festival 364; Red, White, and Bluegrass Festival 673, 681; Targhee Bluegrass Festival 427, 450; Wyoming State Championship Old-Time Fiddle Contest 301; Yellowstone Jazz Festival 610; *see also* performing arts;

specific place; symphonies/bands
muskrats: 274
mustangs/wild horses: Brislawn Cayuse Ranch 727; Cheyenne Frontier Days 61; Jeffrey City 313; Mustang Days 622; Pryor Mountain Wild Horse Range 628–629; Rock Springs 195

N

Nagle, Erasmus: 84
Names Hill: 228
National Elk Refuge: 385–387
National Historic Trails Center: 21
National Park Mountain: 518
National Park Service: 31, 64, 504–505, 561
national parks/monuments/historic sites:
    Bighorn Canyon National Recreation Area 623–629; Devil's Tower National Monument 728–732; Fort Laramie National Historic Site 115–116; Fort Phil Kearny 686; Fossil Butte National Monument 227, 258; Thunder Basin National Grassland 253–254; *see also* forests; Grand Teton National Park; *specific place*; Yellowstone National Park
Native Americans: general discussion 14–17; arts/crafts 324; Ayres Natural Bridge 252; bison 12–13; Colter Bay Indian Arts Museum 465; Dead Indian Pass 585; Devil's Tower National Monument 728; Great Arrow 617; Indian Bathtubs 171; life on reservation 318–319; Medicine Wheel 659–661; Native American Cultural Programs 310; Obsidian Cliff 520; Treaty Day Celebration 319; Vore Buffalo Jump 723; Wind River Indian Reservation 315–326; *see also* archaeological sites/museums/exhibits; battles/raids/massacres; petroglyphs; powwows; *specific place*; tribe
Natrona County Parks: 278
Natural Bridge: 533
Natural Corrals: 190
Naval Petroleum Reserve: 31
Newcastle: 713–718
Newell, Robert: 370
New Fork Lake/Trail: 340, 342
newspapers: 65, 96, 275, 436, 480, 627
New Zealand mud snails: 542
Nez Percé tribe: 498, 584, 660
nightlife: *see specific place*
Noble, Maude: 461
Norris, Philetus W.: 500

Norris Junction: 519–521
North Absaroka Wilderness: 583
North Crandall Trail: 583
Northern Pacific Railroad: 499–504
northern pike: 721
North Fork Trail: 346
North Gap Lake Trail: 162
North Gate Canyon: 166
North Laramie River Trail: 256
North Platte Valley: 163–172
North Rim Trail: 529–530
Nye, Edgar ("Bill"): 4, 26, 135, 675

O

Observation Point Loop Trail: 511
Obsidian Cliff: 520
Ocean Lake: 325
Odd Fellows Park: 165
offbeat attractions: general discussion 40; chicken-poop poker 111; largest bronze bust in U.S., 147; largest Virgin Mary statue in U.S., 99; monuments to prize bulls 85; mule rodeo 614; oldest consecutive tournament in U.S. 111; Two Ocean Creek 441–442; world's largest elk antler arch 231–232; world's largest hot spring 642–644; world's largest jade bar 151; "world's oldest building" 150; world's only hand-dug oil well 715
oil/gas industry: general discussion 31; Accidental Oil Company 715; Buffalo 687; Casper 264; Cody 595; Douglas 245; Gillette 701; Newcastle 714–715; Osage 720; Salt Creek Oil Field 287–289; Thunder Basin National Grassland 253; Yellow Creek Oil Field 216
Ojo Caliente: 517
Okie, John B.: 290
Old Faithful: 510–511
Opal: 228
Oregon Buttes: 348
Oregon Trail: history 17–21, 112; Kemmerer 228–229; landmarks 284–287; origins 15–16; tours/guides 354; trail ruts 107–108, 116, 245, 268, 313
organized tours: auto tours 612–613; bicycling/mountain biking 422, 543, 611; bison ranch 125; bus tours 440, 481–482 557; climbing 345, 730–731; coal mines 703–704; cowboy adventures 371; cross-country skiing 432, 548; dinosaur tracksites 634; dogsledding 336, 373, 426; farms/ranches 618;

OUTLAWS/RUSTLERS

Burris, Dutch Charlie: 179
Carlisle, William: 179–180
Cassidy, Butch: 42, 138, 149, 176, 189, 206, 212, 304, 602, 636, 700
Champion, Nate: 245, 689–690, 691, 696
Clifton, Diamond Slim: 715
Durand, Earl: 617
Harrington, Ed: 440, 446
Hole-in-the-Wall: 698–700
Horn, Tom: 28–29, 84, 85, 178–179, 245
Hudson, William Stanley: 180
James, Frank: 179
Middleton, Doc: 246
Packer, Alferd: 250
Parrot, Big Nose George: 179, 180
Pike, George W.: 246
Ray, Nick: 690, 691, 696
Sundance Kid: 698–699
Wild Bunch: 42, 698–699, 700
Young, Big Steve: 133

fishing 335, 365, 542, 567, 578, 611, 650; Flaming Gorge Dam 206–207; flightseeing 450; Grand Teton National Park 440, 481–482; hiking/backpacking 421; historic sites 533; horseback riding/trail rides 172, 346, 354, 420, 442, 578, 592, 700; National Elk Refuge 386; natural history 613; photography 556–557; rafting 416–418, 474, 567, 574, 585, 610, 650; snowcoach tours 546–547, 568; snowmobiling 366, 435, 592; snowshoeing 426, 433, 548; van tours 440–441, 482; wildlife 328, 426, 440, 468, 482, 490, 556–557; Yellowstone National Park 440, 533, 556–557, 570, 612–613; *see also specific place*
Osage: 254, 720
Osborne, John E.: 180
Oshoto: 727
osprey: 206, 342, 366, 491
Otto: 629
Our Lady of Peace Shrine: 99
outfitters: Absaroka-Beartooth Wilderness 578; Alpine 239; Brooks Lake 336; Casper 274; Flaming Gorge 208; Green River 202–203; Jackson Hole 420, 434, 450–451; Pinedale

365, 366; Saratoga 166; Savery 175; Sheridan 674; Teton Wilderness 440; *see also specific place*
Overland Trail: 23, 157
Overthrust Belt: 216
Owen, William: 472–473
Oxbow Bend: 466

P

Pahaska-Sunlight Trail: 583
Paintbrush Canyon: 471
Painter: 586
Paintrock Lakes Trail: 663
paleontological sites/museums: Como Bluff 149–150; Glendo Historical Museum 110; Glenrock Paleontological Museum 257–258; Gooseberry Badlands 637–638; Greybull Museum 258, 629–630; Kemmerer 223–225; Lance Creek 127; Paleo Park 124, 127, 258, 715–716; Rawlins Uplift 181; Red Gulch Dinosaur Tracksite 258, 634; Rock River Museum 149; tours/guides 634; University of Wyoming Geological Museum 137; Wamsutter 189; Washakie Museum and Cultural Center 636–637; Wyoming Dinosaur Center 258, 645–646
Palisades Reservoir: 237
paragliding: 422
parks: *see specific park*; *place*; state parks
Pathfinder Dam/Reservoir: 281–283
Pathfinder National Wildlife Refuge: 282
Pavillion: 325
Pebble Creek Trail: 539
Pelican Creek Nature Trail: 534
pelicans: 282, 464, 491, 531, 533, 721
Pelican Valley: 493
Pendergraft, Ray: 636
Penney, James Cash: 223, 224
performing arts: general discussion 65; Auburn 237; Casper 272; Cheyenne 92; Cody 610; Gillette 704–705, 707; Jackson Hole 412, 447; Laramie 139, 144; Riverton 299; Sheridan 673; Silver Gate 578; West Yellowstone 566; *see also* music festivals; *specific place*
Periodic Spring: 232
permits: *see* licenses/permits/regulations/fees
petrified forests/wood: 512, 515–516, 525, 583, 689
petroglyphs: Castle Gardens 291; Flaming Gorge 207; Indian Rock Art Cave 700; Kaycee 697; Legend Rock Petroglyph Site 617, 646–647;

Medicine Lodge State Park 635; Red Gulch Scenic Byway 634; Saratoga 165; Sheep Mountain 631; Whiskey Basin 326; White Mountain Petroglyphs 190; *see also* archaeological sites/museums/exhibits
Phelps Lake Overlook: 470
Phillips, John ("Portugee"): 685
Photographer's Point: 342, 360
photography: Adams, Ansel 387, 467; Beldon and Meeteetse Museum 615; Beldon, Charles 602, 615; galleries 602; tours/guides 556–557
Pierre's Hole: 446
Pierre's Playhouse: 447
pikas: 337
Pilot Butte: 195
Pinchot, Gifford: 580
Pine Bluffs: 98–100
Pinedale: 358–366
Pinnacle Buttes: 335
Pioneer Square: 637
Plains Indians: bison 12–13; Lake DeSmet 695; Museum 600–601; Powwow 55 609; sundances 722; University of Wyoming Anthropology Museum 137
planetariums: 268, 704
Platte River: Parkway 268; Trail 162
Platte River Trust Whitewater Park 274
Playmill Theater: 566
Pohl, Burkhard: 645
Point of Rocks: 189
Polecat Creek Loop Trail: 465
Pole Mountain: 147–148
Polish immigrants: 664–666
polka: 673
Pollock, Jackson: 594

polo: Big Horn Equestrian Center 679; Polo Ranch 679–680
polygamy: 231
ponderosa pine: 713
Pony Express: 20–23, 596
Popo Agie Falls Trail: 314
Popo Agie River: 313–314
Popo Agie Wilderness: 346–347
Porcelain Basin: 519
Porcupine Trail: 342
post offices: 66; *see also specific place*
The Potholes: 463
Powder River: 289
Powder River Basin: 666; Resource Council 666
Powder River Coalbed Methane Information Council: 666
Powder River Country: general discussion 652–654; Big Horn Mountains 654–663; Bozeman Trail 683–686; Buffalo 687–700; Gillette 701–710; highlights 654; Sheridan 664–682
Powell: 617–620
Powell, John Wesley: 200, 201, 205, 617
prairie dogs: 152, 227, 251, 268, 728
Predock, Antoine: 136
Prexy's Pasture: 136
prisons: 138
pronghorn antelope: general discussion 10; Gas Hills 302; Grand Teton National Park 468; Laramie Mountains 254; North Platte River 274; One-Shot Antelope Hunt 311; Seedskadee National Wildlife Refuge 205; Thunder Basin National Grassland 253; Yellowstone National Park 496; *see also specific place*
Proulx, E. Annie: 677
Pryor Mountain Wild Horse Range: 628–629

QR
quilts: 619, 631
radio: 65
rafting: Bighorn River 638; Clarks Fork 585; Fremont Canyon 283; Gallatin River 567; Grand Teton National Park 474; Jackson Hole 415–418; North Gate Canyon 166; Seedskadee National Wildlife Refuge 205; Shoshone River 610; Snake River Canyon 239; tours/guides 474, 567, 574, 585, 610, 650; Wind River Canyon 650; Yellowstone River 574; *see also specific place*
railroads: 23–24; Big Boy locomotive 84;

POWWOWS

general discussion: 55, 320
Arapaho Community Powwow: 319
Eastern Shoshone Indian Days Powwow and Rodeo: 55, 319–321
Ethete Powwow: 55, 321
Lander Valley Powwow: 310
Northern Arapaho Powwow: 321
Plains Indian Powwow: 55, 609
Shoshoni Tribal Fair: 321
Wyoming Indian High School Powwow: 321

Douglas Railroad Interpretive Center 245;
French Merci train 84; Oregon Short Line
railroad car 562; Quincy Railroad locomotive
669; Rawlins steam locomotive 181; Sheridan
train depot 669; tie hacks 327; Tubb Town
713–714; Union Pacific Railroad Depot
83–84; Yellowstone National Park 499–504
Ralston: 614
Ranchester: 675–676
rattlesnakes: 9–10, 207, 254, 627
Rawhide Buttes: 126
Rawlins: 176–185
Rawlins Uplift: 181
Reclamation Act of 1902: 280–281, 593
Red Beds/South Side Trail: 731
Red Butte: 718
Red Canyon Overlook: 207
Red Canyon Ranch Preserve: 347
Red Cloud (Sioux chief): 263–264, 683–686

Red Desert: 188–190
Red Gulch Dinosaur Tracksite: 258, 634
Red Lodge (Mont.): 587
Red Mask Mine: 160
Red Rock Point: 530
redwood water tower: 124
Reed, William: 150
reenactments: *see* frontier museums/exhibits;
mountain men/rendezvous
Register Cliff: 108
regulations: *see* licenses/permits/regulations/fees
Reliance tipple: 195
Rendezvous Mountain: 428
Rendezvous Mountain-Death Canyon Loop
Trail: 472
Rendezvous Trail: 568
rental cars: *see specific place*
reservations/reservation services: 435–436, 550,
605

RODEOS

general discussion: 57–61
Afton: 233
All Girls Rodeos: 125, 694
Big Piney Chuckwagon Days: 371
Bull Riders Rodeo and Saratoga Chili Cookoff:
169
Carbon County Fair and Rodeo: 183
Central Wyoming Fair and Rodeo: 56, 273
Cheyenne Frontier Days: 55, 57, 60, 61, 86,
92–94
Cody Nite Rodeo: 609
College National Finals Rodeo: 273, 708
Cowboy Days: 220
Crook County Fair and Rodeo: 724
Days of '49: 632
Deer Creek Days: 259
Don King Days: 673, 681
Eastern Shoshone Indian Days Powwow and
Rodeo: 55, 319–321
Evanston Rodeo Series: 219
Flaming Gorge Days: 202
Fremont County Fair and Rodeo: 299–300
Gardiner Ranch Rodeo: 574
Hulett Rodeo: 727
Jackson Hole Rodeo: 412
Johnson County Fair and Rodeo: 694

Lander Pioneer Days: 57, 310
Lions Club Rodeo: 694
Little Buckaroo Rodeo: 371
Little Snake River Valley Rodeo: 175
Mini Fair and Rodeo: 100
Mule Days: 614
Outlaw Saloon Summer Rodeo Series: 100
Overland Stage Stampede Rodeo: 202
Pine Bluffs Trail Days: 100
Platte County Fair and Rodeo: 106
Powder River Ranch Rodeo: 694
PRCA rodeos: 249, 708
Red Desert Roundup: 197
Senior Pro Rodeo: 125, 249
Sheridan County Rodeo: 673
Sheridan Wyo Rodeo: 673
Spring Fling Rodeo: 717
Ten Sleep Celebration: 642
Thayne Junior Rodeo: 236
Thermopolis Night Rodeo: 649
Wild West Yellowstone Rodeo: 567
Woodchopper's Jamboree and Rodeo: 172
Wyoming High School Rodeo Finals: 249
Wyoming Junior Rodeo: 125
see also specific place

restaurants: *see* food/restaurants; *specific place*
Ribbon Lake Trail: 531
Richard, John: 263
ring-necked pheasants: 121, 679
Ripley's Believe It or Not: 614, 668
Ripley, Willard: 729
Riverside: 169–172
Riverside Park: 247, 248
Riverside Trail: 568
Riverton: 295–300
Roaring Fork Trail: 342
Roaring Mountain: 520
Robertson: 212
Robertson, Mary S.: 58
Rochelle Hills: 254
rock cairns: 699
rock climbing: *see* climbing
rock collecting: 301, 313, 328
Rock Creek Stage Station: 155
Rockefeller, John D.: 457–458, 464; Memorial Highway 465
Rock in the Glen: 258
Rock Lake: 105
Rock River: 149
Rock Springs: 191–198
Rocky Mountain spotted fever: 67
Rocky Point: 229
rodeo clowns: 60–61
Rogers, William: 729
Roosevelt, Theodore: 84, 458, 527, 580, 729
Roosevelt Arch: 571
roses: 621
Ross, Nellie Tayloe: 26
Roundtop Mountain: 649
Rumsey, Charles Cary: 594
Rupp, A. G.: 636
Russell, David A.: 79
Russell, Osborne: 312, 369, 377, 441–442, 499, 514, 525
Russell, William H.: 21, 22
Russin, Robert I.: 147, 267
RV parks: *see* campgrounds/RV parks
Ryan Park: 162

S
Sacagawea: 322–323
saddle bronc riding: 60
sagebrush: 9
sage grouse: 227, 268, 281
sailboarding: 274, 283

saloons: 75
Salt Creek Oil Field: 287–289
sandhill cranes: 205, 253
Saratoga: 163–169
Savage Run Trail: 162–163
Savery: 175
Schnell, Fred: 58
schools: *see* colleges/schools/universities
Schullery, Paul: 485
Schwabacher Landing: 467
Schwiering, Conrad: 266, 387
Scouts of the Plains: 597
Seminoe Dam/Reservoir: 281
Seminoe State Park: 281
Sepulcher Mountain Trail: 524
Seven Mile Hole Trail: 530
Shadow Lake Trail: 343
Shadow Mountain: 468
Sheep Bridge Trail: 346–347
Sheepeater Cliff: 520
Sheepeater tribe: 328, 492, 497–498, 520
sheepherder's wagon: 30
sheepherding/sheep ranching: 29–30, 207, 341, 636, 641, 687
Sheep Lake Trail: 162
Sheep Mountain: 630–631
Shell Canyon: 655
Shell Valley: 633–635
Shephard, Matthew: 134
Sheridan: 664–675
Sheridan, Philip: 12, 16, 17, 501, 597, 664
Sherman, John: 16
Sherman, William T.: 498
Shirley Basin: 152
shopping: Afton 234; Buffalo 694; Casper 274–275; Cheyenne 95–96; Cody 611; Dubois 332; Evanston 220; Jackson Hole 387–389, 450–451; Lander 311; Pinedale 366; Riverton 300; Rock Springs 197; Saratoga 169; Yellowstone National Park 569, 574; *see also specific place*
Shoshone Lake: 507, 539
Shoshone National Forest: 580–587
Shoshone Point: 508
Shoshone River: 586, 594
Shoshone tribe: Big Springs 642; Chief Washakie 16, 17, 55, 213, 316, 317, 325, 645, 660; Eastern Shoshone Indian Days Powwow and Rodeo 55, 319–321; Gift of the Waters Pageant 55, 648; history 315–317; Periodic

Index

SCENIC DRIVES

general discussion: 2, 41
Beartooth Highway: 586–587
Big Horn Mountains: 655–656
Big Horn/Red Wall Byway: 289
Black Hills National Forest: 724–725
Bosler/Wheatland: 149
Buffalo Valley Road: 466
Burgess Road: 656
Chief Joseph Scenic Highway: 584
Chugwater/Cheyenne (Hwy. 211): 102
Crazy Woman Canyon: 659
Dubois scenic overlook: 328
Farson/Boulder: 358
Granite Hot Springs: 372–373
Grassy Lake Road: 466
Greys River Loop Road: 234–236
Hoback Junction/Jackson Hole (Hwy. 189/191): 372

Mirror Lake/Wyoming 150: 221
Palmer Canyon Road: 104
Red Grade Road: 679
Red Gulch Scenic Byway: 634
Rochelle Hills: 254
Rockefeller, John D., Memorial Parkway: 465
Shadow Mountain: 468
Sinks Canyon Loop Road: 313–314
Skyline Drive: 360
Snider Basin: 235
Snowy Range (Hwy. 230): 159–161
South Fork Road: 586
Ucross: 677
Union Pass: 333–334
West Yellowstone (Hwy. 191): 517
Wind River Canyon: 650–651
see also specific place

Spring 232; Sacagawea 322–323; Shoshone Episcopal Mission 324; Shoshone Tribal Cultural Center 324; Shoshoni Tribal Fair 321; *see also* Wind River Indian Reservation
Shoshoni: 301
Shoulders, Jim: 58
shuttle services: Cody 612; Jackson Hole 439, 440; Lander 311–312; Pinedale 366; Riverton 300; Saratoga 169; Yellowstone National Park 548; *see also specific place*
Sidon Canal: 620
Sierra Madre: 173–176
Signal Mountain: 463
Silver Gate (Mont.): 575–578
Simpson, Milward: 457–458
Simpson Hollow: 205
Sinclair: 184–185
Sinclair, Harry: 84, 289
Sinks Canyon State Park: 313–314
sinter: 488
Sioux tribe: Fort Fetterman 250; Grattan Massacre 113; Red Cloud's War 263–264, 683–686; Sundance Mountain 721; treaties 114
Sitting Bull (Sioux chief): 17
skiing/snowboarding: general discussion 39; Big Horn Mountains 658; Cowboy Ski Challenge 413–414; Grand Teton National Park 476;

Hogadon Ski Area 277–278; Jackson Hole 424–430; Nordic Fest 427; Pole-Pedal-Paddle Race 414; safety 431; Sierra Madre Winter Carnival 172; Sleeping Giant Ski Area 589; Snowshoe Hollow Ski Area 234; Snowy Range Ski and Recreation Area 163; Twin Lakes Ski Area 587; *see also* cross-country skiing; *specific place*
sky: 2
Skyline Drive: 360; Nordic Touring Trails 365
Sky Rim Trail: 518
sleigh rides: 386, 426, 433–434
Slough Creek: 541; Trail 526
Smith Lake Trail: 346
Snake River Canyon: 239
Snake River cutthroat: 418
Snake River Overlook: 467
Snider Basin: 235
snowcoach tours: 546–547, 568
Snow King Resort: 429–430
snowmobiling: general discussion 39–42; Big Horn Mountains 658; Continental Divide Snowmobile Trail 354, 365–366, 476–477; Cooke City 578; Dubois 332; Evanston 220; Flaming Gorge 209; Grand Teton National Park 465, 476–477; Jackson Hole 435; Laramie Mountains 257; Sierra Madre 175; Snowy Range 163; Star Valley 234; Wapiti

Valley 592; World Snowmobile Expo 567; Yellowstone National Park 489, 545, 548–549, 568–569; *see also specific place*

Snowshoe Hollow Ski Area: 234

snowshoeing: 426, 433, 476, 547–548

Snowy Range: 158–163

Soda Butte: 527

Soda Fork Meadow: 441

Soleil, Thomas De Beau: 286

South Buffalo Fork River: 441

Southeast Wyoming: general discussion 72–74; Cheyenne 74–97; Fort Laramie National Historic Site 111–117; Guernsey 107–111; highlights 74; Lusk 123–127; Pine Bluffs 98–100; Torrington 117–122; Wheatland 102–106

South Fork: 586; Trail 584

South Pass: 347–349; City 349–354; Cross-Country Ski Trails 354

South Rim Trail: 530–531

Southwest Wyoming: general discussion 186; Bridger Valley 210–214; Evanston 215–221; Flaming Gorge National Recreation Area 205–209; Fossil Butte National Monument 227; Green River 198–205; highlights 188; history 188; Kemmerer 221–226; Red Desert 188–190; Rock Springs 191–198; Star Valley 230–239

Spalding, Eliza: 367

Specimen Ridge: 493, 526

Spence, Gerry: 328

Spence/Moriarity Habitat Management Area: 328

Split Rock: 287

sports/recreation: general discussion 38–50; *see also specific place*; *sport*

Sportsman Lake Trail: 538

Spotted Horse: 678

Spread Creek: 467

Spring Creek Ranch Nordic Center: 432

spring water: 232

Square Top Mountain: 341

Squirrel Meadows: 466

stagecoaches: general discussion 23; Cheyenne and Black Hills Stage 81; Eagles Nest Stage Station 614; Fort Hat Creek Stage Station 126; Granger Stage Station 204; Horseshoe Creek Stage Station 110; Overland Stage Station 189; rides 543–544; Robber's Roost Stage Station 127; Stagecoach Museum 123–124

Stage III Community Theater: 272

Standing Bear (Sioux chief): 14

Star Valley: 230–239; Historical Theater 237

statehood: 24–26

State Line Trail: 627

state parks/historic sites/recreation areas: general discussion 64–65; Bear River State Park 217; Boysen State Park 302; Buffalo Bill State Park 592–593; Connor Battlefield State Historic Site 675; Curt Gowdy State Park 97–98; Edness Kimball Wilkins State Park 267–268; Glendo State Park 110; Guernsey State Park 109–110; Hawk Springs State Recreation Area 121–122; Hot Springs State Park 642–645; Keyhole State Park 721; Medicine Lodge State Park 635; Seminoe State Park 281; Sinks Canyon State Park 313–314; South Pass State Historic Site 350–351; Trail End State Historic Site 666–668

state symbols: 36–37

Steamboat Point: 534

steer roping: 59–60

steer wrestling: 58–59

Stegner, Wallace: 701

Stevenson Island: 533

Stiegler, Pepi: 429

stock car racing: *see* auto races/shows

Storm Point Trail: 534

Story: 681–682

Story John: 621

Story, Nelson: 27

Story, Worth: 79

Street, William D.: 11–12

String Lake: 463

Stuart, Robert: 348

Stull Lakes-Coney Lake Trail: 663

Sublette, William: 19, 111, 285

Sublette Cutoff: 228, 358

sugar beets: 579, 618, 620, 636

Sugarloaf Recreation Area: 159–160

Sullivan's Knob Trail: 627

Sundance: 721–724

Sundance Mountain: 721–723

sundances: 722

Sunlight Basin: 584–586

Sunlight Gorge: 585

Sunset Lake: 512

Sunset Ridge Trail: 257

Swain, Louisa Gardner ("Grandma"): 134

Swan, Alexander: 77–79, 85, 101

Swan, Thomas: 85, 101

Swan Lake-Heron Pond Trail: 465

Swartz, Ed: 1
swastikas: 646
Sweetwater River Project: 312
swimming: *see specific place*
Sylvan Lake: 534
Sylvan Pass: 534
sylvatic plague: 152, 153, 251
symphonies/bands: Casper Municipal Band 272;
    Casper Troopers Drum and Bugle Corps 272;
    Cheyenne Symphony Orchestra 92; Powder
    River Symphony Orchestra 707; University of
    Wyoming Symphony Orchestra 144

T

Taggart Lake: 461
Tammen, H. H.: 598
Tayo Creek Trail: 346
Teapot Dome: 288–289; Scandal 667
teddy bears: 646
Teewinot: 463
Ten Sleep: 639–642
Tensleep Canyon: 640–641
Tensleep Preserve: 640
Ten Sleep Raid: 29, 641
tepee rings: 634, 697
Teton Crest Trail: 470
Tetonia (Idaho): 451
Teton Pines Cross-Country Ski Center: 430
Teton Valley (Idaho): 446–452
Teton Village: 429
Texas Jack (scout): 597
Texas Trail: 99
Thatcher, Agnes Lake: 84
Thatcher, Bryce: 473
Thayne: 236–237
Thermopolis: 642–650
Thermus aquaticus: 488
The Thorofare: 540–541
Thunder Basin National Grassland: 253–254
thunderstorms: 6, 254, 338, 470, 471, 587
ticks: 67, 535
Titcomb Basin: 342
Togwotee Pass: 335–336
Tollgate Rock: 201
Tongue River Canyon: 659
Tonnar, John: 467
tornados: 442
tourism: 36
Tower Junction: 525
Tower Ranger Station: 525

Tower Trail: 731
Town Square: 383
trails: information/services 43; *see also specific trail*
transportation: general discussion 67–71; *see also
    specific mode of transportation; place*
Trapper Canyon: 635
trappers: 17, 368–370, 498–499; *see also moun-
    tain men/rendezvous; specific person*
travertine: 488
Tri-State Corner Marker: 99
trivia: 62–63
trolleys/trolley tours: 79, 670
trona mining: 36, 200, 210
trout: Bighorn Canyon 628; Flaming Gorge
    208; Greys River 234; Lake DeSmet 695;
    Laramie Mountains 254; nonnative
    diseases/introductions 541–542; North
    Laramie River 256; North Platte River 165;
    Pathfinder Reservoir 282; Sinks Canyon 314;
    Tongue River 677; Wind River Mountains
    337; Yellowstone National Park 517, 531,
    541–542; *see also specific place*
Trout Lake: 527
True, Allen T.: 80
trumpeter swans: 464, 467, 490–491, 531
Tubb Town: 713–714
tubing: 434
Turpin Meadow: 441, 466
Twain, Mark: 312, 349, 732
Two Ocean Creek: 441–442
Two Ocean Lake: 464

U

Ucross: 677
Uncle Tom's Trail: 530
undulant fever: 494
Union Pacific Railroad: 23–24, 198, 201, 561, 685
Union Pass: 333–334, 340
United States Fish & Wildlife Service: 64
United States Forest Service: 64
universities: *see colleges/schools/universities*
Upper Layout Creek Trail: 627–628
Upton: 254, 719–720
uranium deposits: 253, 295, 302, 312–313
Urbanek, Mae: 17
Ute Mountain Fire Tower: 207

V

Valley View Trail: 731
van tours: 440–441, 482

Vásquez, Louis: 212–213
Vedauwoo: 148
vegetation: general discussion 7, 8; Basin 633;
    Big Horn Mountains 654; Black Hills 713;
    Heart Mountain Preserve 613; lodgepole
    forests 502–504; Shoshone National Forest
    580; Thunder Basin National Grassland 719;
    Wapiti Valley 588; Yellowstone National Park
    539; *see also specific place*
Verendrye, François and Louis-Joseph: 17
Veteran: 121
Vieux Pierre (Iroquois trapper): 446
Virginia Cascades Road: 520
visitors centers: 61; *see also specific place*
volcanism: 485–486
Voyager II (spacecraft): 387

W
Waddell, William Bradford: 21
wagon rides/trains/treks: Casper 273; Grand
    Teton National Park 476; history 17–21; Jack-
    son Hole 420; Lander 310; Laramie 145; Ore-
    gon Trail 354; tours/guides 42–43; *see also
    specific place*
Wahb Springs: 527
walking tours: Buffalo 689; Casper 268; Cody
    604; Encampment 171; Green River 201;
    Jackson Hole 385, 421; Laramie 140; Rawlins
    181; *see also specific place*
walleye: 111, 282, 302, 628, 721
Wallop, Oliver H.: 680
Wamsutter: 189
wapiti: *see* elk
Wapiti: 590
Wapiti Valley: 588–593
Ware, Florence E.: 140
warming huts: 546
Warren, Francis E.: 25, 79, 84, 134, 668; Air
    Force Base 31, 83
Warren Peak Overlook: 724
Washakie (Shoshone chief): 16, 17, 55, 213,
    316, 317, 325, 645, 660
Washakie Trail: 343–344
Washakie Wilderness: 583–584, 616
Washburn Expedition: 499
water ouzels: 655
water skiing: 281
Watson, Ella ("Cattle Kate"): 283
wax museums: 646
Western gear: *see specific place*

WATERFALLS

Big Goose Falls: 659
Brooks Creek Falls: 335
Bucking Mule Falls: 658
Fairy Falls: 514
Firehole Falls/Cascades: 517
Gibbon Falls: 518
Granite Falls: 372–373
Hidden Falls: 463
Kepler Cascades: 508
Knowles Falls: 538
Lewis Falls: 506
Lower Falls: 529, 530
Moose Falls: 506
Mystic Falls: 513
Osprey Falls: 521
Porcupine Falls: 658
Rustic Falls: 520
Shell Falls: 655
Silver Cord Cascade: 530
South Fork Falls: 441
Tower Fall: 527–528
Undine Falls: 525
Upper Falls: 529, 530
Virginia Cascades: 520
Water Fall Ice Roundup: 586
Wraith Falls: 525

West Nile virus: 66
West Thumb: 507–508
West Yellowstone (Mont.): 561–570
Wheatland: 102–106; Reservoir 105
Whetstone Creek: 440–441
Whipple, Ithamar C.: 84
whirling disease: 542
Whiskey Basin Wildlife Habitat: 326
Whiskey Gap: 185
Whiskey Mountain Trail: 345
White, Jim: 13, 602–603
White Bird (Nez Perce chief): 498
White Mountain: 190
white-tailed deer: *see* deer
whitewater rafting: *see* rafting
Whitman, Marcus: 19
Whitman, Narcissa: 367
Whitney, Gertrude Vanderbilt: 599
Wiessner, Fritz: 730

Wiggins Fork Trail: 584
Wilcox, Jim: 388
wild horses: *see* mustangs/wild horses
Wild Iris Climbing Area: 310
wildlife: general discussion 7–14; Big Horn
  Mountains 655, 656; Black Hills 713; Grand
  Teton National Park 456, 464, 466, 467, 468;
  Greybull Wildlife Museum 631; Grizzly and
  Wolf Discovery Center 562; National Muse-
  um of Wildlife Art 383–385; Story 682;
  Thunder Basin National Grassland 719;
  tours/guides 328, 426, 440, 468, 482, 490,
  556–557; Wind River Mountains 337; Yel-
  lowstone National Park 490–497, 526, 531;
  see also conservation/wilderness areas; *specific
  animal; place*
wild turkeys: 253, 254, 682
Willie, James G.: 286, 355–356
Willow Flats: 464
Willow Lake: 365
Willow Park: 496, 520
Wilson, Nick: 378
windmills: 154, 719
Wind River Canyon: 650–651

Wind River Indian Reservation: 315–326; Arapaho (tribe) 317–318; Arapahoe (town) 321;
  Crowheart Butte 325; dancers 320; Ethete
  322–323; Fort Washakie 323–325; life on
  reservation 318–319; oil revenue 319; Pavillion 325; powwows 319–321; public access
  315, 337; St. Stephens Mission 321; Shoshone
  315–317; Whiskey Basin Wildlife Habitat 326
Wind River Lake: 335
Wind River Mountains: 336–347; Bridger
  Wilderness 341–344; Fitzpatrick Wilderness
  344–345; Green River Lakes 338–340; highlights 294; information/services 295; land
  292–295; Popo Agie Wilderness 346–347;
  wildlife 337
windsurfing: 695
wind turbines: 152
Windy Mountain Trail: 585
Winegar Hole Wilderness: 444
Wister, Owen: 151–152, 250, 279, 440, 444,
  459, 689
wolves: 456, 496–497, 526–527, 545, 562
women's suffrage: 25–26, 134, 350, 379
Woodchopper's Jamboree: 56

YELLOWSTONE NATIONAL PARK

general discussion: 483–485
accommodations: 545–546, 550–554,
  563–564, 571–573, 576–577
backcountry treks: 534–541
camping: 529, 549–550, 564–565, 573, 577
climate: 508, 544
controversies: 485, 491, 494, 496–497,
  502–504, 545
Cooke City/Silver Gate: 575–578
ecosystem: 489
employment in: 560–561
entertainment/events: 566–567, 574, 578
fires: 502–504, 517, 520, 520–521, 576
fishing: 517, 526, 531, 539, 541–542, 567
flora: 489, 531, 539
food and drink: 554–555, 565–566, 573,
  577–578
Gardiner: 571–575
geology: 486–489, 523, 528–529
Grand Canyon of the Yellowstone: 528–531
highlights: 484

hiking/backpacking: 507–513, 514–534
history: 497–505
information/services: 506, 538, 546, 558–560,
  569, 574–575, 578
licenses/permits/regulations/fees: 504, 505,
  506, 514, 515–516, 520, 535, 541, 556
loop tour: 505–534
Mammoth Hot Springs: 521–524, 552
museums: 519, 520, 561–562
safety: 490, 540, 543
shopping: 569
summer recreation: 541–544, 567, 574, 578
tours/guides: 556–557, 570, 612–613
transportation: 556–557, 569–570
West Yellowstone: 561–570
wildlife: 490–497, 526, 531, 534
winter recreation: 544–549, 568–569, 578
Yellowstone Lake: 532–533
see also geysers; hot springs; *specific place; trail;*
  waterfalls

Index

Wood River Valley: 616
wool production: 641
Worland: 636–639
World War II POW camp: 244
Worthen Reservoir: 346
Wright: 709–710
Wyodak Mine: 703
Wyoming Brand Book: 28
Wyoming Cavalry: 274
Wyoming Fishing Network: 39
Wyoming Game and Fish Department: 9, 39, 85
Wyoming Heritage Trail: 300
Wyoming Homestay & Outdoor Adventures
 (WHOA): 52–53
Wyoming Outfitters and Guides Association:
 39, 44
Wyoming Peak: 235
Wyoming Public Radio: 65
Wyoming Range National Recreational Trail: 235
Wyoming State Board of Outfitters and
 Professional Guides: 44
Wyoming State Trails Program: 43
Wyoming Stock Growers Association: 28
WYO Theater 673

XYZ
yellow-bellied marmots: 337
Yellow Hand (Sioux chief): 597
Yellowstone Film Festival: 567
Yellowstone hotspot: 486
Yellowstone Lake: 496, 507–508, 532–533, 541;
 Overlook 508
Yellowstone Park Foundation: 558
Yellowstone River: 528–531, 538, 541, 574;
 Picnic Area 526
Yellowtail Wildlife Habitat Management Area:
 626
Young, Brigham: 213, 263
yurts: 468
Zerbst, Leonard: 715

Acknowledgments

Now in its fifth incarnation, this version of *Moon Handbooks Wyoming* has diverged somewhat from its sister, *Moon Handbooks Yellowstone & Grand Teton*. It would be impossible to thank all of the people who helped me update this book, but several individuals particularly deserve my heartfelt gratitude.

A special thank you goes to the following chamber of commerce and visitor center folks who opened doors to their hometowns or reviewed my manuscript for problems: Lee Anne Ackerman in Cody, Sue C. Anderson in Greybull, Ruth Benson in Gillette, Marlyn Black in Casper, Suzzane Blair in Saratoga, Donna Boyd in Riverton, Jackie Bredthauer in Lusk, Barbara Byrne in Sundance, P. J. Crow in Laramie, Toddi Darlington in Thermopolis, Jo Ann B. Davis in Laramie, Sharon Earhart in Powell, Nadine Gross in Buffalo, Kathy L. Gundersen in Lander, Suzy Hahn in Cooke City, Chris Hansen in Jackson, Mark Madia in Evanston, Jeanne Miyoshi in Driggs, Jon Mobeck in Jackson, Jesse O'Connor in Jackson, Carole Perkins in Sheridan, Janet Redfield in Douglas, Darren Rudloff in Cheyenne, Nancy Rumney in Newcastle, Kate Sherrod in Saratoga, Dawn Svalberg in Pinedale, Mike Yauck in Worland, and Claudia Wade in Cody. Without their help this revision would have been nearly impossible.

The following hard-working government employees provided a similar service for their areas of expertise: Paul Blackman from Medicine Bow-Routt National Forest, Jude Carino from the BLM in Casper, Linda Coates-Markle from Pryor Mountain Wild Horse Range, Christine Czazasty from Devils Tower National Monument, Marcia Fagnant from Fossil Butte National Monument, Steve Fullmer from Fort Laramie National Historical Site, Megan Lyons Bogle from Caribou-Targhee National Forest, Linda Meriglino from Bridger-Teton National Forest, Karen Peterson from Black Hills National Forest, Brent Spencer from Flaming Gorge National Recreation Area, Jim Staebler from Bighorn Canyon National Recreation Area, Joel Strong from Bighorn National Forest, and Gordon K. Warren from Shoshone National Forest.

I also wish to thank Rick Hoeninghausen of Xanterra Parks & Resorts, Judith Blair of Blair Hotels in Cody, Debbie Disney of Holiday Inn Cheyenne, Dixie Winters of Holiday Inn Laramie, Bill and B. J. Farr of Far Out West B&B in Saratoga, and the staff of the Wort Hotel in Jackson for their generous assistance. And a tip of the hat to alert readers Michael and Pat Anthony for their comments. This book was shepherded through the production process by my editor, Amy Scott. Thanks to her and the rest of the gang at Avalon Travel Publishing for getting this book into your hands.

I offer a very special thanks to my wife, Karen Shemet, and our children, Aziza and Rio, for keeping me grounded while I researched and wrote this book.

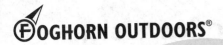

U.S.~Metric Conversion

1 inch	=	2.54 centimeters (cm)
1 foot	=	.304 meters (m)
1 yard	=	0.914 meters
1 mile	=	1.6093 kilometers (km)
1 km	=	.6214 miles
1 fathom	=	1.8288 m
1 chain	=	20.1168 m
1 furlong	=	201.168 m
1 acre	=	.4047 hectares
1 sq km	=	100 hectares
1 sq mile	=	2.59 square km
1 ounce	=	28.35 grams
1 pound	=	.4536 kilograms
1 short ton	=	.90718 metric ton
1 short ton	=	2000 pounds
1 long ton	=	1.016 metric tons
1 long ton	=	2240 pounds
1 metric ton	=	1000 kilograms
1 quart	=	.94635 liters
·1 US gallon	=	3.7854 liters
1 Imperial gallon	=	4.5459 liters
1 nautical mile	=	1.852 km

To compute celsius temperatures, subtract 32 from Fahrenheit and divide by 1.8. To go the other way, multiply celsius by 1.8 and add 32.

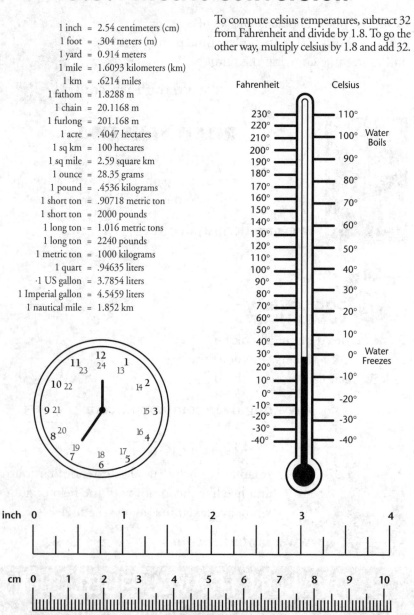